C000172576

ISBN 978-0-332-75114-6
PIBN 11239295

FB &c Ltd, Dalton House, 60 Windsor Avenue, London, SW19 2RR.
Company number 08720141. Registered in England and Wales.

For support please visit www.forgottenbooks.com

A TREATISE

ON THE

LIMITATION OF ACTIONS

AT LAW AND IN EQUITY

By H. G. WOOD

Author of "The Law of Nuisances," "Master and Servant," "Fire Insurance," "Landlord and Tenant," "Law of Railroads," Etc.

THIRD EDITION

By JOHN M. GOULD, Ph. D.

Author of "Waters," Joint Author of "Gould and Tucker's Notes on the U. S. Statutes," Editor of Kent's Commentaries (14th Ed.), Etc.

FOURTH EDITION

REVISED AND ENLARGED

By DEWITT C. MOORE, of the New York Bar

Author of "Carriers," and "Fraudulent Conveyances."

IN TWO VOLUMES

VOL. II.

ALBANY, N. Y.

MATTHEW BENDER & COMPANY,

INCORPORATED.

1916.

WM. BOYD PRINTING CO.
ALBANY, N. Y.

TABLE OF CONTENTS.

VOLUME II.

CHAPTER XVI.

Miscellaneous Causes of Action.

CHAPTER XVII.

SPECIALTIES.

CHAPTER XVIII.

TORTS QUASI E CONTRACTU.

CHAPTER XIX.

EXECUTORS AND ADMINISTRATORS.

CHAPTER XX.

TRUSTS AND TRUSTEES.

CHAPTER XXI.

MORTGAGOR AND MORTGAGEE.

CHAPTER XXII.

DISABILITIES IN PERSONAL ACTIONS.

CHAPTER XXIII.

PENDENCY OF LEGAL PROCEEDINGS, INJUNCTION, OR STAY.

CHAPTER XXIV.

ADVERSE POSSESSION AND REAL ACTIONS.

CHAPTER XXV.

DOWER.

CHAPTER XXVI.

FRAUD, IGNORANCE, MISTAKE, AND CONCEALMENT OF CAUSE OF ACTION.

CHAPTER XXVII.

MUTUAL ACCOUNTS, ACCOUNTS IN GENERAL, ETC.

CHAPTER XXVIII.

SET-OFF, RECOUPMENT, AND DEFENSES IN GENERAL.

CHAPTER XXIX.

CO-CONTRACTORS, ETC.

CHAPTER XXX.

JUDICIAL PROCESS.

CHAPTER XXXI.

Commencement of Action or Other Proceeding.

Appendix.

STATUTES
OF
THE LIMITATION OF ACTIONS.
VOLUME II.

CHAPTER XVI.

Miscellaneous Causes of Action.

§ 141. Contracts, express or implied.

Upon contracts of all classes, whether written or verbal, the statute begins to run from the time when a right of action accrues.[1] Thus, where goods or property of any description are sold, and no time is fixed for payment, the law implies a promise to pay when the purchase is made; and the plaintiff cannot, by showing a custom on his part to give one year's credit, prevent the running of

1. Baxter v. Gay, 14 Conn. 119; Tisdale v. Mitchell, 12 Tex. 68, 15 Tex. 480; Jones v. Lewis, 11 id. 359; Sprague v. Sprague's Estate, 30 Vt. 483; Rabsuhl v. Lack, 35 Mo. 316; Justices, etc. v. Orr, 12 Ga. 137; Clark v. Jenkins, 3 Rich. (S. C.) Eq. 318; Hayes v. Goodwins (4 Metc.) 80; Guignard v. Parr, 4 Rich. Law (S. C.) 184; Sims v. Goudelock, 6 id. 100; Payne v. Gardiner, 29 N. Y. 146; Hikes v. Crawford, 67 Ky. (4 Bush) 19; Pittsburgh, etc., R. Co. v. Plummer, 37 Pa. 413; Taggart v. Western, etc., R. R. Co., 24 Md. 563, 89 Am. Dec. 760; Davies v. Cram, 6 N. Y. Super. Ct. (4 Sandf.) 355; Daniel v. Whitfield, 44 N. C. (Bush. L.) 294; Berry v. Doremus, 30 N. J. Law 399; Waul v. Kirkman, 25 Miss. 609; Payne v. Slate, 39 Barb. (N. Y.) 634; Turner v. Martin, 27 N. Y. Super. Ct. (4 Robt.) 661; Peck v. New York, etc., U. S. Mail S. S. Co., 18 N. Y. Super. Ct. (5 Bosw.), 226; Murray v. Coster, 20 Johns. (N. Y.) 576, 11 Am. Dec. 333. In Catholic Bishop of Chicago v. Bauer, 62 Ill. 188, where plans of a church were completed more than five years before suit brought, but the architect furnishing them continued to superintend the work until within five years of bringing the suit, when he was discharged, it was held that the statute did not begin to run until the architect was discharged, and that a suit brought within five years of that time was in season to save the debt from the statute. In Clark v. Lake Shore & M. S. Ry. Co., 94 N. Y. 217, it was held that the code exemption from the operation of the statute limiting the time for the commencement of actions, a case where a person was entitled to commence an action when the code took effect, and declaring that in such a case, "the provisions of law applicable thereto immediately before this act takes effect, continue to be so applicable, notwithstanding the repeal thereof," does not refer simply to statutory provisions, but within the meaning of said exception a rule or doctrine established by judicial decision is a "provision of law" equally with one enacted by the legislature; and that, where the plaintiff was entitled to, and had commenced his action before the code went into effect, that the provision of the code, making the statute of limitations of the place of residence of a non-resident defendant available as a defense in certain cases, did not apply; but that the case was governed by the rule in force when the code went into effect, *i. e.*, that the statute of limitations of a foreign State constituted no defense in an action brought here.

the statute from the day of sale.[2] Where the terms of a contract are express, and the time of payment is agreed upon, of course the statute begins to run from that time, unless the time has been extended by the agreement of the parties; and when a contract has been made, and the time of payment has been fixed, and more property is delivered than was to be delivered under the contract, or more or extra work is done, and no contract is made as to the time of payment for the extra goods, or extra work, the statute begins to run as soon as the goods are delivered or the extra work is completed. Thus, when a contract was entered into to build a ship at an agreed price, and afterwards the ship was built larger, but without any further agreement as to the time of payment for the extra labor, it was held that the statute began to run as soon as the work was completed.[3] Where a term of credit is agreed upon, of course, the statute does not begin to run until the time of credit has expired,[4] and in this class of contracts little or no difficulty in determining the time when the statute begins to run exists. The only difficulty arises with that class of contracts where the time for payment is not

2. Brent & Co. v. Cook, 51 Ky. (12 B. Mon.) 267. In Hursh v. North, 40 Pa. 241, evidence of a custom of the plaintiff to give a credit of six months was held not admissible for the purpose of proving that the price was not to be paid when the goods were sold, but on a certain date thereafter, so as to avoid the statute by showing that the bill was not due until within the statutory period. In Roberts v. Ely, 113 N. Y. 128, 20 N. E. 606, where the plaintiff brought an action, in 1881, to recover a specific portion of certain insurance money collected by E., the defendant's testator, in 1872, of which portion the plaintiff claimed he was the equitable owner, it was held that the alleged cause of action was a liability implied by law, which arose when the money was received by E., that it was not barred by the six years' statute then in force, and that money in the hands of one person, to which another is equitably entitled, may be recovered by the latter in a common-law action for money had and received, subject to the restriction that the mode of trial and the relief which can be given in a legal action is adapted to the exigencies of the case, and is capable of adjustment in such an action, without prejudice to the interest of other parties.

3. Peck v. New York, etc., U. S. Mail S. S. Co., 18 N. Y. Super. Ct. (5 Bosw.) 226.

4. Tisdale v. Mitchell, 12 Tex. 68; Bush v. Bush, 9 Penn. St. 260.

fixed, but is left to legal inference. In a contract for services, if the work is done under a continuous contract, and no time for payment is fixed, a right of action does not accrue until the work is completed;[5] but although the work is continuous, yet if it is done under distinct contracts, a right of action accrues under each contract, and the statute begins to run from the time when it is completed.[6]

The statute begins to run upon a claim for the taking of usurious interest from the time when such interest is paid.[7] And each payment of usury furnishes a distinct cause of action against which the statute immediately commences to run.[8]

In Louisiana, it is held that the statute does not run against a debt secured by a pledge as long as the creditor has possession of the pledge. The detention of it being treated as a constant recognition of the debt, a renunciation of prescription which prevents the statute from beginning to run.[9]

§ 142. Deposits, certificates of deposits, etc.

In England a general deposit in a bank is treated as a loan, and the statute begins to run *instanter;*[10] but in this country it has been

5. Eliot v. Lawton, 89 Mass. (7 Allen) 274, 83 Am. Dec. 683. In Little v. Smiley, 9 Ind. 116, where in an action for work done for the plaintiff's intestate no time for payment was specified, and no time of service was agreed on, it was held that the statute did not begin to run as to any of the work until the work was fully completed, although it extended through a series of years. But in Davis v. Gorton, 16 N. Y. 255, 69 Am. Dec. 694, where a person entered into the defendant's employment at a fixed salary, but for no definite time, and no time for payment was agreed on, it was held to be a general hiring from year to year, the pay for each year's service becoming due at the end thereof, so that the statute began to run on each year's wages from the end of each year. McLaughlin v. Maund, 55 Ga. 689; Pursell v. Fry, 19 Hun (N. Y.) 595, 58 How. Prac. 317.

6. Davis v. Gorton, *supra.*. See Decker v. Decker, 108 N. Y. 128, 15 N. E. 307.

7. Rahway National Bank v. Carpenter, 52 N. J. Law 165, 19 Atl. 181.

8. Albany v. Abbott, 61 N. H. 157; Barker v. Strafford Co. Savings Bank, 61 N. H. 147.

9. Citizens' Bank v. Hyams, 42 La. Ann. 729, 7 So. 700.

10. Pott v. Clegg, 16 M. & W. 321. In Wright v. Paine, 62 Ala. 340, 34 Am. Rep. 24, where money was deposited with an individual under a

held that an action cannot be maintained for such a deposit without an actual demand; [11] and from these cases it follows that, as a right of action does not accrue until there has been a demand, the statute of limitations does not begin to run until a demand or something equivalent thereto has been made. If a special deposit is made, payable at a specific time, or upon notice of a certain duration, of course the statute does not begin to run until the time has expired or the notice been given and expired. Thus, in Massachusetts,[12] it was held that where a balance was struck monthly on a savings-bank book of a depositor the statute began to run from the time the balance was struck. Where money or property is deposited with a bank or individual to be paid or returned upon demand, it is not payable or returnable, so that an action will lie therefor, until a demand has first been made therefor, consequently the statute does not begin to run until after demand; [13] so where money is deposited with an individual who is to pay interest entered thereon, with an agreement that it is not to be withdrawn except by draft at thirty days after sight, the statute does not begin to run, nor does the presumption of payment arise until a draft therefor has been presented and dishonored.[14]

Where money is deposited with one man for the use of another, it is held that a cause of action accrues to the person for whose use it was deposited, from the time of deposit, unless a time within which it is to be paid is fixed upon; [15] but this would seem

writing by which the depositary acknowledges the receipt of a certain number of dollars in gold, "on deposit to be paid" to the depositor "on demand," it was held that, in the absence of any evidence of extrinsic facts to aid its construction, it would be treated as a loan rather than a bailment, and, therefore, became due and payable, and the statute began to run thereon from its date.

11. Johnson v. Farmers' Bank, 1 Harr. (Del.) 117; Watson v. Phoenix Bank, 49 Mass. (8 Metc.) 217, 41 Am. Dec. 500; Downes v. Phoenix Bank, 6 Hill (N. Y.) 297.

12. Union Bank v. Knapp, 20 Mass. (3 Pick.) 96, 15 Am. Dec. 181.

13. Finkbone' Appeal, 86 Pa. 368. See *infra*, n. 17.

14. Sullivan v. Fosdick, 10 Hun (N. Y.) 173; Payne v. Gardiner, 29 N. Y. 146.

15. Buckner v. Patterson, 16 Ky. (Litt. Sel. Cas.) 234.

to depend upon the nature of the contract to be implied from the circumstances of the case. If the money was left with the third person at the request of the person for whom it was intended, the rule stated above would doubtless be correct; but, if not, the period from which the statute would run would seem to be, according to the cases, from the time when a demand was made for the money, unless the circumstances are such as to raise an implied promise on the part of the depositary to seek the beneficiary and pay him the money at all events.[16] Where a certificate of deposit is issued its terms may be decisive of the period when the statute attaches thereto; the statute is often held not to begin to run thereon until a demand had been made for the money,[17] and usually such a certificate is not dishonored until

16. Hutchins v. Gilman, 9 N. H. 359.

17. National Bank of Fort Edward v. Washington Co. Nat. Bank, 5 Hun (N. Y.) 605. See Smiley v. Fry, 100 N. Y. 262, 3 N. E. 186.

Certificates of deposit, in the usual form, are now generally held negotiable; they are, in effect, promissory notes, and are governed, with certain exceptions, by the same rules as those instruments. Klauber v. Biggerstaff, 47 Wis. 551, 3 N. W. 357, 32 Am. Rep. 773; Curran v. Witter, 68 Wis. 6, 31 N. W. 705, 60 Am. Rep. 827; Citizens' Nat. Bank v. Brown, 45 Ohio St. 39, 11 N. E. 799, 4 Am. St. Rep. 526; Mereness v. First Nat. Bank, 112 Iowa 11, 51 L. R. A. 410, 84 Am. St. Rep. 318, 83 N. W. 711; Tobin v. McKinney, 14 S. D. 52, 84 N. W. 228, 91 Am. St. Rep. 688, aff'd 15 S. D. 257, 88 N. W. 572, 91 Am. St. Rep. 694; O'Neill v. Bradford, 1 Pinney (Wis.) 390, 42 Am. Dec. 575, and note; 14 Harvard L. Rev. 468. In Iowa and other States, a deposit of money in a bank in the usual course of business amounts to a loan to the bank, which becomes the depositor's debtor therefor, and not his bailee. Lowry v. Polk County, 51 Iowa 50, 49 N. W. 1049, 33 Am. Rep. 114; Mereness v. First Nat. Bank, *supra;* 3 Am. & Eng. Encl. of Law, p. 826. And the depositor's death does not interrupt the running of the statute of limitations on a demand certificate given for such a deposit. Mereness v. First Nat. Bank, *supra.* On the other hand, the transaction is viewed in New York and certain other States not only as creating a debt, but also as being a real deposit and a bailment rather than a loan, making a demand necessary before the holder of the certificate is entitled to a return of the money deposited. Smiley v. Fry, 100 N. Y. 262, 3 N. E. 186; Shute v. Pacific Nat. Bank, 136 Mass. 487; Hunt, Appellant, 141 Mass. 515, 6 N. E. 554; Bellows Falls Bank v. Rutland County Bank, 40 Vt. 377; McGough v. Jamison, 107 Pa. 336; see *supra,* § 118, note 13.

presented.[18] But, where money is deposited in a bank from time to time, subject to check at sight, the relation between the parties is not that of trustee and *cestui que trust,* but of debtor and creditor. When received, in the absence of any express stipulation to the contrary, the money at once becomes the property of the bank, and the bank becomes the debtor of the depositor, under an implied contract to discharge the indebtedness by honoring the checks drawn thereon by the depositor,[19] and also to

As to municipal orders, whether negotiable or not, the general rule is that actions will not lie thereon till they have been presented to the proper officer for payment. See Blaisdell v. School District, 72 Vt. 63, 47 Atl. 173; Pekin v. Reynolds 31 Ill. 529, 83 Am. Dec. 244.

18. Howell v. Adams, 68 N. Y. 314; Payne v. Gardiner, 29 N. Y. 146; Farmers' & Merchants' Bank v. Butchers' & Drovers' Bank, 14 N. Y. 623. Such also is the rule in Indiana. Brown v. McElroy, 52 Ind. 404. But in Meador v. Dollar Savings Bank, 56 Ga. 605, it was held that a certificate of deposit payable to the order of the depositor, but containing no other indication of the time of payment than was to be derived from the words, "with interest at the rate of seven per cent. on call and ten per cent." per annum is payable on demand, and therefore due immediately. So also in Illinois. Brahm v. Adkins, 77 Ill. 263; Adams v. Orange Co. Bank, 17 Wend. (N. Y.) 514; Girard Bank v. Bank of Penn Township, 39 Pa. 92, 80 Am. Dec. 507; Brummagin v. Tallant, 29 Cal. 503, 89 Am. Dec. 61. And a certificate of deposit payable "on return of this certificate" is payable on demand. Tripp v. Curtenius, 36 Mich. 494, 24 Am. Rep. 610. The demand need not be made by the depositor in person. Bank of Kentucky v. Wister, 27 U. S. (2 Pet.) 318, 7 L. Ed. 437. A demand is not necessary after the bank has rendered an account claiming it as paid. Bank of Missouri v. Benoist, 10 Mo. 519. And consequently the statute would run from the time when by its acts the bank had rendered a demand unnecessary (probably), or when it has given the depositor notice that his claim will not be paid. Farmers' & Mechanics' Bank v. Planters' Bank, 10 Gill. & J. (Md.) 422.

19. National Bank of the Republic v. Millard, 77 U. S. (10 Wall.) 152, 19 L. Ed. 897; Buchanan Farm Oil Co. v. Woodman, 1 Hun (N. Y.) 639; Dawson v. Real Estate Bank, 5 Ark. 283; Foster v. Essex Bank, 17 Mass. 479, 9 Am. Dec. 168; Coffin v. Anderson, 4 Blackf. (Ind.) 395; Bank of Kentucky v. Wister, 27 U. S. (2 Pet.) 318, 7 L. Ed. 437; Albany Commercial Bank v. Hughes, 17 Wend. (N. Y.) 94; Keene v. Collier, 58 Ky. (1 Metc.) 415; Corbit v. Bank of Smyrna, 2 Harr. (Del.) 235, 30 Am. Dec. 635; Matter of Franklin Bank, 1 Paige (N. Y.) Ch. 249, 19 Am. Dec. 413; Graves v. Dudley, 20 N. Y. 76; Marsh v. Oneida Central Bank, 34 Barb. (N. Y.) 298; Lund v. Seamen's Savings

repay on the demand of the depositor any balance which may be due at the time of demand.[20] This rule does not apply where the thing deposited is a commodity such as "Confederate notes," and the agreement was that the collection should be made in like notes;[21] nor does it apply to lands or other securities or packages of money deposited with it under a special contract that the same shall be returned.[22] But, while the bank becomes a debtor to the extent of the deposit it is not liable to pay interest thereon in the absence of any contract to that effect.[23] Where money is paid into court, and is placed in the custody of the clerk or other officer designated by law to have the custody of it, the statute does not begin to run against the party mutually entitled thereto until a demand has been made for the money.[24] And the same

Bank, 37 Barb. (N. Y.) 129, 23 How. Prac. 258; Wray v. Tuskegee Ins. Co., 34 Ala. 58; Bank of Northern Liberties v. Jones, 42 Pa. 536; Downes v. Phenix Bank, 6 Hill (N. Y.) 297; Chapman v. White, 6 N. Y. 412, 57 Am. Dec. 464; Ellis v. Linck, 3 Ohio St. 66. It is held that a bank, having without objection received the bills of other banks, without diminution or discount, notwithstanding that at the time of the deposit, or subsequently thereto, they were worth less than par, is liable to pay the par value therefor. Marine Bank of Chicago v. Chandler, 27 Ill. 525, 81 Am. Dec. 249. Bank of Kentucky v. Wister, *supra*, is a strong case upon this point.

20. Boyden v. Bank of Cape Fear, 65 N. C. 13. And this rule is applied between banks where one be comes a depositary for another. Phelan v. Iron Mountain Bank, 16 Bankr. Reg. (U. S.) 308, 4 Dill. (U. S.) 88.

21. Planters' Bank v. Union Bank, 83 U. S. (16 Wall.) 483, 21 L. Ed. 473; Ruffin v. Orange Co. Com'rs, 69 N. C. 498; Lilly v. Cumberland Co. Com'rs, id. 300.

22. Hale v. Rawallie, 8 Ken. 136; Smith v. First National Bank, 99 Mass. 605, 97 Am. Dec. 59; Lancaster Co. Nat. Bank v. Smith, 62 Pa. 47; Maury v. Coyle, 34 Md. 235.

23. Parkersburg Nat. Bank v. Als, 5 W. Va. 50.

24. In Lynch v. Jennings, 43 Ind. 276, an action was brought for the specific performance of a contract to convey certáin lands. In his complaint A. alleged a tender and refusal of the purchase-money, and brought it into court, and it remained in the hands of the clerk. After years of litigation a final decree was entered in A.'s favor. The executors of B. then demanded the money of the administrators of the clerk, who had died, and on their refusal to pay brought an action for its recovery. The court held that the statute did not begin to run in such cases until a demand upon the defendants for the money.

rule has been applied where money has been paid to a commissioner in equity.[25]

§ 142a. Money received by one for use of another.

Where money is received by one to and for the use of another, under such circumstances that it is the duty of the former to pay it over, an action for money had and received may be brought to recover it without a demand, and the statute of limitations begins to run from the day of the receipt of the money. A mortgagee who has received moneys, the proceeds of sale of the mortgaged property, is not trustee of an express trust; if in any sense a trustee, it is simply an implied trust, and, as to the liability growing out of such a trust, the ordinary rules of limitation apply.[26]

25. Heriot v. McCauley, Riley (S. C.) Ch. 19. In Viets v. Union Nat. Bank of Troy, 101 N. Y. 563, 5 N. E. 457, 54 Am. Rep. 743, it was held that while a check drawn by a depositor against a general bank account does not operate as an assignment of so much of the account, it authorizes the payee, or one to whom he has indorsed and delivered it, to make a demand, and a refusal of the bank to pay on presentation gives the drawer a right of action, in case he has funds in bank to meet the check and the refusal was without his authority; and that the implied contract between a bank and its depositors is that it will pay the deposits when and in such sums as are demanded, the depositor having the election to make the whole payable at one time by demanding the whole, or in instalments by demanding portions; and whenever demand is made by presentation of a genuine check in the hands of a person entitled to receive the amount thereof, for a portion of the amount on deposit, and payment is refused, a cause of action immediately arises, and the statute begins to run as against the instalment so made due and payable.

26. Mills v. Mills, 115 N. Y. 80, 21 N. E. 714. In this case T., the plaintiff's intestate, deeded certain lands to the defendant, and assigned to him a mortgage as security for indebtedness, with the understanding that the latter might sell the lands, collect the mortgage, and reimburse himself, by agreeing to re-convey on payment of the debt and expenses and all subsequent loans. During the life of T., who died in 1871, defendant sold all the lands and received the proceeds, except one item, which was received in 1872. In an action brought in 1881, for an accounting and payment over of any surplus, held, that the proceeds of the lands which came to defendant's hands after he had been fully reimbursed, were received by him to and for the use of T.; it was his duty at once

§ 143. Money Misappropriated.

When money is paid to a person for a special purpose, and is by him applied to another, the statute begins to run from the date of such misappropriation. Thus, where a county treasurer, instead of applying taxes assessed on the property of a railroad corporation, in a town, to the payment or redemption of bonds of the town, issued in aid of the construction of the road of such corporation, as required by the act of 1869, as amended in 1871, applied them in payment of county and State taxes, with, and as part of, other moneys, raised by the town for those purposes, it was held that an action. as for money had and received, was maintainable on behalf of the town against the county to recover the money so misappropriated; that the liability included as well the portion of the funds applied in payment of the State taxes as that applied for other county purposes; also, that the action was properly brought by the supervisor of the town in his name as its representative. The cause of action in such case arises when the misappropriation is made,[27] and the statute then begins to run against it. While every duty imposed upon a public officer is in the nature of a trust, persons injured by a violation of the duty for which they may maintain an action of law, must pursue that remedy within the period of limitation of legal actions; and the fact that the supervisors of the town for the period of fourteen years were apprised from year to year, while sitting as members of the board of supervisors of the county, of the misappropriation, and made no objection thereto, did not estop the town from claiming a repayment of the money.

to pay them over, and upon his failure to do so, he was liable without demand; the action was barred; that, by the six years' limitation, even though an accounting was required, as whatever might be the form of the action the legal rule of limitations applied; and that, as there was no unlawful interference by him with the estate of the intestate after his death, the defendant could not be held as executor *de son tort*.

27. Strough v. Jefferson County

A town cannot be estopped by the neglect of its supervisors to assert a claim against the county, the grounds of which are equally known to all the members of the board of supervisors. A county treasurer in the payment of State taxes to the State comptroller acts as agent for the county, and pays on its behalf.[28]

§ 143a. Forged or invalid instruments.

Where a bank pays a draft or check drawn upon it, payable to the order of A., to an indorsee thereof, and it subsequently transpires that the indorsement thereon was forged, the statute does not run against its claim for indemnity against the indorsee until it has been notified by the drawer of his intention to insist on the defect of title and cancel the credit given it on the draft. Thus,[29] where the United States Treasurer in 1867, made a draft on the First National Bank of B. payable to the order of O., the indorsement of O. was forged, and the check was sent by a third party to the M. bank for collection. The M. bank indorsed it and sent it to the drawee, by which it was paid and sent to the United States Treasury, where it was credited to the drawee. In 1877 the United States sued the drawee for the amount of the draft upon the ground that the indorsement was forged; of which suit the M. bank was notified, and employed counsel in defending the suit. Judgment was rendered against the drawee. In an action by the drawee commenced against the M. bank, after it had paid the judgment to the United States, the M. bank set up the statute of limitations. The court held that the action was not barred, as the statute did not begin to run at the time of the payment of the draft, nor until the United States elected

Supervisors, 119 N. Y. 212, 23 N. E. 552, 50 Hun 54, 3 N. Y. Supp. 110.

28. Ibid; Bridges v. Sullivan County Supervisors, 92 N. Y. 570, distinguished, so far as it relates to the liability of the county for the portion of the fund applied in payment of State taxes.

29. Merchants' Nat. Bank v. First Nat. Bank, 3 Fed. 66, 4 Hughes 9.

to insist on the defect of title and cancel the credit given to the drawee on the draft.[30]

§ 144. Money had and received.

Where an action is brought for money had and received by the defendant to his use, the statute only begins to run from the time when it was received by him. Thus,[31] when a municipal corporation, acting through its officers in the execution of a power conferred upon it to collect a tax assessed upon a particular citizen, enforces its collection out of the property of another, in nowise liable therefor, and appropriates the proceeds of collection to its own use, with full knowledge of the illegality of the proceedings, it becomes liable to the owner for the spoliation of his property. In an action to recover of the defendant the money received into its treasury through proceedings taken to collect a tax assessed upon the stockholders of a bank, doing business within its corporate limits, it appeared that the property levied upon and sold by the defendant was not the property of the stockholders, but of the bank. By the defendant's charter, its mayor is its executive head and clothed with the duty and power of supervision of it and its officers in all departments. Its treasurer and tax receiver are intrusted with the duty and power of collecting taxes and keeping

30. The court relied upon Cowper v. Godmond, 9 Bing. 748. In that case the question was, whether a plea of the statute of limitations was a bar to an action for money had and received to recover the consideration money of a void annuity, when the annuity was granted more than six years before the action was brought, but was treated by the grantor as an existing annuity within that time. "That question," said the court, "depends upon another: At what time did the cause of action arise? The cause of action comprises two steps: the first is the original advance of the money by the grantee; the second is the grantor's election to avail him self of the defect in the memorial of the annuity. The cause of action was not complete until the last step was taken." See Ripley v. Withee, 27 Tex. 14, where it was held that an action for damages arising from the sale of a forged land-warrant did not accrue until the certificate had been prescribed to the court of claims and rejected by it.

31. Teall v. City of Syracuse, 120 N. Y. 184, 24 N. E. 450.

the moneys for the defendant. The collector was directed, when he received the warrant from the treasurer and tax receiver, to go to the bank and levy upon everything in the bank, to make the levy and sale of its property, and the mayor was so informed, and the treasurer received the tax from the collector, knowing that it was obtained by such levy and sale. It was held that the plaintiff was entitled to recover; that the proceedings of the defendant's officers in collecting the tax were unlawful; and that knowledge thereof was justly imputable to the defendant; and that the defendant's knowledge of the illegal levy and sale relieved the plaintiff from demanding the money before bringing this action, and that the action, being for money had and received, the statute of limitation did not begin to run until the defendant had received the money.

§ 144a. Implied warranty.

Where property is sold under such circumstances that the law will imply a warranty, the statute begins to run from the date of the warranty. Thus, where the payee of a negotiable note indorses the same the law raises an implied warranty that the note was given for a valuable consideration, and upon this warranty an action for its breach accrues and the statute begins to run at once.[32] In the case of contract for the mutual exchange of lands which contains nothing from which it can be inferred that one conveyance was to precede the other, the law implies that the conveyances are to be made concurrently, and that the mutual covenants of the parties are dependent, and that the statute does not begin to run thereon against the vendor until he has performed by giving a deed, nor against the purchaser until he has made a tender of the price.[33] Where a party transfers a note, knowing it to be affected by usury, to one who is ignorant of the fact, he instantly becomes liable to the purchaser for the deceit; but the statute only begins

32. Blethen v. Lovering, 58 Me. 437.

33. Brennan v. Ford, 46 Cal. 7.

to run from the time the fraud was discovered.[34] Upon an implied warranty of title to chattels sold, it has been held that the statute does not begin to run until the vendee has been disturbed in his title.[35]

§ 145. Sureties, indorsers, etc.

Where a surety is compelled to pay a debt, the statute begins to run against his claim from the day of such payment, and not from the date of the original obligation,[36] and this is also the rule as to

34. Persons v. Jones, 12 Ga. 371, 58 Am. Dec. 476.

35. Gross v. Kierski, 41 Cal. 111.

A warranty of goods sold, if not fulfilled, is usually to be treated as broken when the goods are delivered, and in the absence of fraud, an action for such breach must be brought within the statute time for suing on contracts. Bogardus v. Wellington, 27 Ontario App. 530.

36. Hammond v. Myers, 30 Tex. 375, 94 Am. Dec. 322; Burton v. Rutherford, 49 Mo. 255; Reeves v. Pulliam, 66 Tenn. (7 Bax.) 119; Thayer v. Daniels, 110 Mass. 345; Barnsback v. Reiner, 8 Minn. 59; Walker v. Lathrop, 6 Iowa, 516; Thompson v. Stevens, 2 N. & M. (S. C.) 493; Scott v. Nichols, 27 Miss. 94, 61 Am. Dec. 503. In Wesley Church v. Moore, 10 Pa. 273, it was held that where the property of a surety was sold on an execution to pay the debt, the statute began to run from the date of the sale. Ponder v. Carter, 34 N. C. (12 Ired. L.) 242; Hale v. Andrus, 6 Cow. (N. Y.) 225; Garrett's Adm'rs v. Garrett, 27 Ala. 687; Preslar v. Stallsworth, 37 id. 402; Walker v. Lathrop, 6 Iowa (6 Clarke) 516; Bennett v. Cook, 45 N. Y. 368; Scott v. Nichols, 27 Miss. 94, 61 Am. Dec. 503. The law implies a promise on the part of the principal to reimburse the surety and the action is upon this implied promise. Ward v. Henry, 5 Conn. 596, 13 Am. Dec. 119; Powell v. Smith, 8 Johns. (N. Y.) 249; Hassinger v. Solms, 5 Serg. & R. (Pa.) 8; Gibbs v. Bryant, 18 Mass. (1 Pick.) 118; Bunce v. Bunce, Kirby (Conn.) 137; Hulett v. Soullard, 26 Vt. 295; Smith v. Sayward, 5 Me. 504; Lonsdale v. Cox, 23 Ky. (7 T. B. Mon.) 405; Appleton v. Bescom, 44 Mass. (3 Met.) 169; Holmes v. Weed, 19 Barb. (N. Y.) 128. It is not necessary that he should pay in money; it is sufficient if he pays in land or personal property. Bonney v. Seely, 2 Wend. (N. Y.) 481; Randall v. Rich, 11 Mass. 494; Ainslee v. Wilson, 7 Cow. (N. Y.) 662, 17 Am. Dec. 532. But the implied promise is only to indemnify the surety; consequently it secures a discharge of the debt for less than its amount. He can recover no more than he paid; and, if he paid the debt in depreciated currency at par, he can only recover the amount which it was worth at the time of payment. Owings v. Owings, 26 Ky. (3 J. J. Mar.) (Ky.)

contribution against a co-surety.[37] No action, however, can be

590; Hall's Adm'r v. Creswell, 12 G. & J. (Md.) 36; Jordan v. Adams, 7 Ark. 348; Crozer's Trustees v. Gray, 27 Ky. (4 J. J. Mar.) 514. So he may sue at once if he has taken up the original note, and given his own in lieu of it which has been accepted in payment. Downer v. Baxter, 30 Vt. 467; Elwood v. Deifendorf, 5 Barb. (N. Y.) 398. But in Indiana it is held that he can maintain no action until he has actually paid a note given in lieu of the original note, Pitzer v. Harmon, 8 Blackf. (Ind.) 112, 44 Am. Dec. 738; Romine v. Romine, 59 Ind. 346; even though it was secured by mortgage, Bennett v. Buchanan, 3 Ind. 47. A demand is not necessary. The statute attaches at once upon payment. Odlin v. Greenleaf, 3 N. H. 270; Sikes v. Quick, 52 N. C. (7 Jones L.) 19.

In Stone v. Hammell, 83 Cal. 547, 23 Pac. 703, 8 L. R. A. 425, 17 Am. St. Rep. 272, McFarland, J., in a well-considered opinion, says: "The general rule is, undoubtedly, that a surety can recover of the principal only the amount or value which the surety has actually paid. If he has paid in depreciated bank notes taken at par, he can recover only the actual value of the bank notes so paid and received. If he has paid in property, he can recover only the value of the property. If he has compromised, he can recover only what the compromise cost him. The rule is that he shall not be allowed to "speculate out of the principal." Brandt, Sur., § 182, and cases there cited; Estate of Hill, 67 Cal. 243.

Perhaps a preponderance of authority, to the point, is that if a surety, by giving his negotiable promissory note, satisfies the claim of the creditor, and extinguishes the debt of the principal to the creditor, he may recover from the principal the amount of the debt without showing that he has paid his promissory note.

But the authorities are not uniform upon the subject. In Indiana, North Carolina, and some other States, it is held that the surety cannot recover of the principal until he has paid the money, and that the giving of a note is not sufficient. Brisendine v. Martin, 23 N. C. (1 Ired. L.) 286; Nowland v. Martin, id. 307; Romaine v. Romaine, 59 Ind. 346.

Many of the cases hold that, if the surety discharges the debt by a negotiable note, he may maintain an action against the principal, while, if he does so by means of a bond, or any non-negotiable instrument, he cannot, upon the theory that a negotiable note is analogous to money—a distinction which is founded upon no apparent good reason. Boulware v. Robinson, 8 Tex. 327, 58 Am. Dec. 117; Peters v. Barnhill, 1 Hill (S. C.) 234.

37. Singleton v. Townsend, 45 Mo. 379; Wood v. Leland, 1 Met. (Miss.) 387; Peters v. Barnhill, 1 Hill (S. C.) 234; Maxey v. Carter, 18 Tenn. (10 Yerg.) 521; Lowndes v. Pinckney, 1 Rich. (S. C.) Eq. 155; Sherwood v. Dunbar, 6 Cal. 53; Knotts v. Butler, 10 Rich. (S. C.) Eq. 143. An action for contribution arises at once upon the payment of the whole

maintained until the surety has actually paid the debt. The fact that a judgment has been rendered against him, and that he has been committed to jail upon an execution thereon, does not entitle him to an action against the principal for money paid, etc.[38] Where money is paid by one person for another, and no time is fixed for payment, the statute attaches from the date of its payment.[39] The statute begins to run against the right of sureties to

debt by one surety against his co-sureties for the proportion of the debt each should pay. Whitman v. Gaddy, 46 Ky. (7 B. Mon.) 591; Paulin v. Kaighn, 29 N. J. Law 480; Labeaume v. Sweeney, 17 Mo. 153; Samuel v. Zachary, 26 N. C. (4 Ired. L.) 377; Stallworth v. Preslar, 34 Ala. 505, and 37 id. 402; Chaffee v. Jones, 36 Mass. (19 Pick.) 260; Lee v. Forman, 60 Ky. (3 Met.) 114; Pinkston v. Taliaferro, 9 Ala. 547; M'Donald v. Magruder, 28 U. S. (3 Pet.) 470, 7 L. Ed. 744; Fletcher v. Jackson, 23 Vt. 581, 56 Am. Dec. 98; Foster v. Johnson, 5 Vt. 64; Stout v. Vause, 1 Rob. (Va.) 169; Cage v. Foster, 13 Tenn. (5 Yerg.) 261, 26 Am. Dec. 265. And he is not first bound to pursue the principal. Caldwell v. Roberts, 31 Ky. (1 Dana) 355.

The rule is founded on the reason that if the surety, by giving his own obligation, discharges the original debt of the principal, the latter is as much benefited as if he had discharged it by actually paying the money. Its weakness lies in the possibility of the surety recovering the whole amount of the principal, and never paying his own note, thus violating the cardinal rule that the surety shall not speculate out of the principal. But, if we assume the rule to be as first above stated, it is not so clearly commendable as to deserve pushing further than adjudicated cases have already carried it; and in all cases to which our attention has been called the rule has been enforced against the principal in favor only of the surety who has extinguished the debt to the original creditor. Chipman v. Morrill, 20 Cal. 136.

The liability of the surety must first be settled; and the claim for contribution is not affected by the fact that the statute has already run as between the principal creditor and the co-surety. Wolmershausen v. Gullick (1893), 2 Ch. 514. See Robinson v. Harkin (1896), 2 Ch. 415; Martin v. Frantz, 127 Pa. 389, 18 Atl. 20, 14 Am. St. Rep. 359; Fullerton v. Bailey, 17 Utah 85, 53 Pac. 1020. In Texas a right of subrogation as to securities held by another arises upon an implied contract and is within the two years' statute of limitation, which statute will never be superseded in equity in favor of one seeking subrogation to such a lien. Darrow v. Summerhill, 93 Texas 92, 105, 53 S. W. 680, 77 Am. St. Rep. 833. See Tate v. Winfree, 99 Va. 255, 37 S. E. 956.

38. Rodman v. Hedden, 10 Wend. (N. Y.) 498.

39. Bowman v. Wright, 70 Ky. (7 Bush) 375.

be subrogated to the payee's right to securities, etc., from the time of payment of the debt by them.[40] So strict is this rule and so rigidly is it adhered to that, even when a surety procures an extension of time from the holder, and gives collateral security, and ultimately pays the debt, it is held that the statute does not begin to run against him until he has actually paid the debt.[41] The rule may be said to be that so long as any liability on the maker's part upon the original debt remains the surety has no right of action against him, and consequently the statute does not begin to run against him; but, although the surety may not have paid the debt in money, yet if he has in any manner assumed the debt, so that the maker's liability upon it is at end, from that time the statute begins to run against the surety.[42] If the note or obligation is payable by installments, the statute begins to run against the surety from the time when each installment was paid by him.[43] But if the note is not so payable, and the surety in fact pays the note by installments, the statute does not begin to run from the date of each payment, but from the date of the last payment made by him, in liquidation of the note.[44] When two persons execute to each other written instruments in the form of deeds, which are defective as conveyances for the want of attestation or acknowledgment, each instrument being the consideration of the other, and possession is given and taken by each, the statute at once commences to run, and, after the lapse of the statutory period, perfect a title which will maintain or defeat an action of ejectment.[45]

Where a mortgage is given by the maker of a note to a person

40. Bennett v. Clark, 45 N. Y. 268. The right of subrogation, when merely incidental to the relief sought in an action, does not affect the relation of the note or other cause of action to the statute of limitations. Campbell v. Campbell, 133 Cal. 33, 65 Pac. 134.

41. Norton v. Hall, 41 Vt. 471.

42. Hitt v. Sharer, 34 Ill. 9.

43. Bullock v. Campbell, 9 G. & J. (Md.) 182.

44. Barnsback v. Reiner, 8 Minn. 59.

45. Hall v. Caperton, 87 Ala. 285, 6 So. 388.

who becomes surety thereon, conditioned that if the maker pays the note and saves the surety harmless from all demands upon it the conveyance should be void, the statute does not begin to run against the mortgagee until he has actually paid the note or some part of it, and the note is discharged.[46] The same rule prevails as to indorsers. The statute begins to run against them from the time when they actually paid the debt, and not from the time when they become liable to pay it.[47] But, unless the surety or indorser pays the note within the time limited by statute, he cannot, by a payment made by him afterwards, make the maker liable to him therefor, especially in those States where by statute payment or acknowledgment by one co-maker, etc., does not take the debt out of the statute as to the others.[48] Where one sued as indorser sets up in defense that the transfer was made to the plaintiff to deprive him of the defense of want of consideration, the indorser's cause of action against the last indorser arises

46. M'Lean v. Ragsdale, 31 Miss. 701.

In Schoener v. Lissauer, 107 N. Y. 111, 13 N. E. 741, it was held that the provision of the Code, applying a six years' limitation to actions "to procure a judgment other than for a sum of money on the ground of fraud, in a case," formerly "cognizable by the Court of Chancery," does not apply to an action by the owner of the fee to remove a cloud upon title to land, by the cancellation of a mortgage thereon, to which the owner has a good defense.

The right to bring such an action is never barred by the statute of limitations. Ibid.; Solinger v. Earl, 82 N. Y. 393, 60 How. Prac. 116, and Haynes v. Rudd, 102 N. Y. 372, 7 N. E. 287, 55 Am. Rep. 815.

47. Pope v. Bowman, 27 Miss. 194.

A surety has no actionable claim against his co-sureties for contribution until he is damnified by the fact, and it is actually ascertained that he has paid more than his due proportion of liability. *Ex parte* Snowdon, 17 Ch. D. 44; Gardner v. Brooke (1897), 2 I. R. 6. When bonds are pledged as collateral by a mortgagor, who in the same instrument agrees to pay any difference between the net proceeds of the bonds and the amount due, this is not a new and independent obligation postponing the statute until realization on the securities, but the statute runs from the date fixed for repayment of the loan. *In re* McHenry (1894), 3 Ch. 290.

48. In Williams v. Durst, 25 Tex. 667, 78 Am. Dec. 548, it was held that where an accommodation indorser pays a note before the statute runs upon it, but does not bring suit until after the statute has run on

from the date of judgment.[49] If a surety or indorser pays a note before it becomes due, his right of action does not accrue until the note by its terms becomes due;[50] as a surety cannot change the legal relations of the maker to the note by any action of his before it becomes payable, nor by forestalling its payment can he acquire any rights against the maker which the holder of the note did not possess.

The rule that a right of action accrues to the surety from the time he pays the money, and not from the time when the original debt becomes payable, is subject to the exception, that he must have paid the original debt before the statute had run thereon; as otherwise, especially in those States where by statute payment by one joint contractor or promisor does not remove the statutory bar as to the other, a recovery could not be had by him if the original debt was then barred as to the principal debtor.[51] When the principal debtor, by reason of the running of the statute, has been released from any legal liability to pay the debt, a surety who has been compelled to pay it, because, by reason of some statutory exception, the statute has not run as to him, cannot recover of the principal debtor.[52] Instances may arise where the surety has no redress; as, where he becomes surety upon a note for an infant, not given for necessaries. In such a case, if the infant escapes upon a plea of infancy, and judgment is rendered against the surety, he has no right of re-

the note, he cannot recover of the maker; because he acquires no greater rights than the holder of the note possessed.

49. Price v. Emerson, 16 La. An. 95.

50. Tillotson v. Rose, 52 Mass. (11 Metc.) 299.

51. The law will not raise a promise on the part of the principal to reimburse the surety where the surety was under no legal obligation to pay. Kimble v. Cummins, 60 Ky. (3 Met.) 327. This rule was adopted in Cocke v. Hoffman, 73 Tenn. (5 Lea) 105, 40 Am. Rep. 23, and a surety who paid the debt after it was barred as to the sureties was held not entitled to recover of a co-surety. See also Campbell v. Brown, 86 N. C. 376, 41 Am. Rep. 464.

52. Stone v. Hemmell, 83 Cal. 547, 23 Pac. 703, 8 L. R. A. 425, 17 Am. St. Rep. 272.

dress from the infant, but stands to the note and judgment in the relation of principal.[53] But where a note is given by an infant for necessaries, with a surety, and the surety pays the debt, he has an immediate right of action against the infant thereon, and the statute runs from that time.[54] Where there are two or more sureties, and each pays a moiety of the debt, each has a separate and distinct cause of action against him therefor; consequently, in such a case, the statute begins to run against the claim of each from the time when each paid his share.[55] The remedy of a surety is the same whether he was surety upon a simple contract or a specialty debt.[56] His remedy is by *indebitatus assumpsit* for money, and not for money had and received.[57]

At the common law, a payment made by the principal debtor upon a note before the bar of the statute has become complete, keeps the debt alive both as to himself and the surety; but where the payment is made after the completion of the bar of the statute, it revives the debt only as to the party making the payment.[58]

So long as demands secured by a mortgage are not barred by

53. Short v. Bryant, 40 Ky. (10 B. Mon.) 10.

54. Conn. v. Coburn, 7 N. H. 368, 26 Am. Dec. 746.

55. Peabody v. Chapman, 20 N. H. 418.

56. Cunningham v. Smith, 1 Harp. (S. C.) Eq. 90; United States v. Preston, 4 Wash. (U. S. C. C.) 446. But *contra*, see Shultz v. Carter, Speers (S. C.) Eq. 533, where it was held that the surety could, upon payment of a specialty debt, set it up as a specialty.

57. Ward v. Henry, 5 Conn. 595, 13 Am. Dec. 119; Powell v. Smith, 8 Johns. (N. Y.) 249.

58. Cross v. Allen, 141 U. S. 528, 12 Sup. Ct. 67, 35 L. Ed. 843, where the court said: "Under the Civil Code of Oregon, the period of limitation for promissory notes is six years; and it is argued that, as the notes in this controversy were not sued on until more than six years from the date when they respectively became due, an action on them would not lie, notwithstanding the fact that the maker made payments of interest upon them from time to time.

"At common law, a payment made upon a note by the principal debtor before the completion of the bar of the statute served to keep the debt alive, both as to himself and the surety. Whitcomb v. Whiting, 2 Dougl. 652; Burleigh v. Stott, 8 Barn. & C. 36; Wyatt v. Hodson, 8 Bing. 309; Mainzinger v. Mohr, 41 Mich. 685, 3 N. W. 183.

the statute, there can be no laches in prosecuting a suit upon the mortgage to enforce them. Lamar, J., says:[59] "The question of laches and staleness of claim virtually falls with that of the defense of the statute of limitations. So long as the demands secured were not barred by the statute of limitations there could be no laches in prosecuting a suit upon the mortgage to enforce

"That is the rule in many of the States of this Union—in all, in fact, where it has not been changed by statute. National Bank of Delavan v. Cotton, 53 Wis. 31, 9 N. W. 926; Quimby v. Putnam, 28 Me. 419. At common law, and in those States where the common-law rule prevails, a distinction is made between those cases in which a part payment is made by one of several promisors of a note before the statute of limitations has attached, and those in which the payment is made after the completion of the bar of the statute; it being held in the former that the debt or demand is kept alive as to all, and in the latter, that it is revived only as to the party making the payment. Atkins v. Tredgold, 2 Barn. & C. 23; Sigourney v. Drury, 31 Mass. (14 Pick.) 391; Ellicott v. Nichols, 7 Gill. (Md.) 85, 48 Am. Dec. 546, and cases cited. The reason of this distinction lies in the principle that, by withdrawing from a joint debtor the protection of the statute, he is subjected to a new liability not created by the original contract of indebtedness. There is no statute of Oregon, so far as we have been able to discover, changing the common-law rule of liability with reference to sureties. Consequently, under the admitted facts of this case, it must be held that the statute of limitations of the State never operated as a bar to the enforcement of the original demands against both the principal and the surety.

"Nor do we think the death of the surety before either of the demands matured makes any difference, in principle, where, as in this case, the liability is not of a personal nature, but is an incumbrance upon the surety's property. We are aware that there is authority holding that payment of interest by the principal debtor, after the death of the surety, but before the statute of limitations has run against the note, will not prevent the surety's executors from pleading the statute. Lane v. Doty, 4 Barb. (N. Y.) 530; Smith v. Townsend, 9 Rich. (S. C.) L. 44; Byles, Bills, § 353; 2 Parsons, Notes & Bills, 659, and note *t*. But we know of no authority extending this rule to the representatives of a deceased surety whose liability was not personal but upon mortgaged property. On the contrary the cases of Miner v. Graham, and Bank of Albion v. Burns, *supra*, seem to recognize the doctrine which we are inclined to accept. We conclude, therefore, that the contract of suretyship in this case was not terminated by the death of the surety before the maturity of the indebtedness."

59. Cross v. Allen, 141 U. S. 528, 537, 12 Sup. Ct. 67, 35 L. Ed. 843.

those demands. The mortgage is virtually a security for the debt, and an incident of it.[60] And it is immaterial that the failure to sue upon the demands may have resulted injuriously to the surety, so long as there was no variation in the original contract of suretyship, either as respects a new consideration or a definite extension of time; since it is a familiar principle of law that the mere omission of forebearance to sue the principal without the request of the surety will not discharge the surety."[61]

§ 146. Contract of indemnity, guaranties, etc.

Contracts of indemnity are so largely dependent upon the particular stipulation that the guarantor has made that no general rule can be given as to when his liability attaches against those for whom he has assumed that position that will be applicable in all cases, except that the statute begins to run when the promisee has taken all the requisite steps to charge him with liability, and his liability under his contract to pay the debt is full and complete,[62] and the promisee cannot prolong this period of liability by any unreasonable delay in taking these requisite steps.[63] A guaranty has aptly been termed a contract to indemnify another upon a contingency, and is in the nature of a claim for unliquidated damages.[64] They are either absolute or contingent,[65] and the distinction between them in this respect is of vital importance in

60. Ewell v. Daggs, 108 U. S. 143, 2 Sup. Ct. 408, 27 L. Ed. 682.

61. In England section 8 of the 37 and 38 Vict., c. 57, relates not only to suits to enforce mortgage securities against the land, but also to suits to enforce covenants personally against those bound thereby, such, *e. g.*, as a surety who joins in a joint and several covenant for payment of the mortgage debt. Sutton v. Sutton, 22 Ch. D. 511; Allison v. Frisby, 43 id. 106.

62. See Colvin v. Buckle, 8 M. & W. 680.

63. In Eddowes v. Neil, 4 U. S. (4 Dall.) 133, 1 L. Ed. 772, a delay of nineteen years fully accounted for was held not of itself sufficient to discharge the guarantor.

64. Sampson v. Burton, 2 B. & B. 89.

65. Rudy v. Wolf, 16 Serg. & R. (Pa.) 79; Woods v. Sherman, 71 Pa. 100; Moakley v. Riggs, 19 Johns. (N. Y.) 69, 10 Am. Dec. 196; Sylvester v. Downer, 18 Vt. 32; Allison v. Waldham, 24 Ill. 132.

determining the time when the statute begins to run in favor of the guarantor. Thus, an absolute guaranty is one by the terms of which the guarantor undertakes that another person shall perform by the time fixed in the contract, and upon which he becomes liable to pay the debt or damages at maturity upon the other's failure; as, "I guarantee the payment of this note at maturity."[66] Such a guaranty is absolute, and a right of action accrues against the guarantor immediately upon the maturity of the note, without taking any steps against the maker of the note.[67] So where on the sale of goods it was agreed that they should be paid for on delivery, and the defendant signed a guaranty as follows: "On the part of A. and B. I hold myself responsible with them on the above contract," it was held that his undertaking bound him to a direct performance of the contract, and was in effect that he or his principals would pay for the goods on delivery.[68] Where the guaranty is absolute, the guarantor is not entitled to demand or notice; but his liability to suit arises and is fixed at the same moment that an action accrues against the principal debtor, or, if a later period is in terms fixed upon, upon the arrival of the time named therein,[69] and the guarantor may be

66. Koch v. Melhorn, 25 Pa. 89, 64 Am. Dec. 685; Cochran v. Dawson, 1 Miles (Penn.) 276.

67. Roberts v. Riddle, 79 Pa. 468; Reigart v. White, 52 Pa. 438; Anderson v. Washabaugh, 43 Pa. 115. See Williams v. Granger, 4 Day (Conn.) 444.

Where a person contracts to indemnify a person and save him harmless from certain claims, the statute does not begin to run until the person to whom the indemnity is given has paid the debt. Hall v. Thayer, 53 Mass. (12 Met.) 130. And such also is the rule where money is paid for another at his request. Perkins v. Littlefield, 87 Mass. (5 Allen) 370.

68. King v. Studebaker, 15 Ind. 45; Cross v. Ballard, 46 Vt. 415; Campbell v. Baker, 46 Pa. 243; Kramph v. Hatz, 52 Pa. 525. A writing in the words "I will guarantee the payment to you of $625 in treasury warrants to be paid on or before the 20th August on and for account of J. W." was held an original and absolute promise. Matthews v. Chrisman, 20 Miss. 595, 51 Am. Dec. 124.

69. Smith v. Ide, 3 Vt. 301; Dickerson v. Derrickson, 39 Ill. 574; Bowman v. Curd, 55 Ky. (2 Bush) 565; Young v. Brown, 3 Sneed (Tenn.) 89; Lane v. Levillian, 4 Ark. 76; Ege v. Barnitz, 8 Pa. 304; Breed v. Hillhouse, 7 Conn. 523; Douglass v. Howland, 24 Wend. (N. Y.) 35; Noyes v. Nichols, 28 Vt. 160; Sibley v. Stuhl,

sued thereon without any previous suit against the principal debtor.[70] Contingent guaranties are those in which the guarantor does not assume an absolute liability, but binds himself to perform in case the debtor fails to do so. Thus, where a person guarantees that a note "is collectible," he does not bind himself absolutely to pay the note but only to do so in the event that the maker proves insolvent.[71] In other words, a contingent guaranty is one which only becomes absolute when the creditor, by due and unsuccessful diligence to obtain satisfaction from the principal, fails to do so, or by circumstances that excuse diligence.[72] A guaranty "against loss" on a note, bond, or mortgage, is a contingent one, putting the creditor on his diligence; [73] so also a guaranty that a note "is good," [74] or to pay in case the holder "fails to recover the money on said note," [75] are all contingent guaranties; and, indeed, so are all that impose upon the person to whom they are given the duty of first exhausting his remedies against the principal.[76] The distinction, then, to be observed is, that in the case of a contingent guaranty a right of action does not accrue against the guarantor immediately upon the failure of the principal to perform, but it imposes upon the creditor the duty of ex-

15 N. J. Law 332; Bank of South Carolina v. Hammond, 1 Rich. (S. C.) 281; Bebee v. Dudley, 26 N. H. 249, 59 Am. Dec. 341; McDougal v. Calef, 34 N. H. 534; Simons v. Steele, 36 N. H. 73; Cox v. Brown, 51 N. C. (6 Jones L.) 100.

70. Bank of New York v. Livingston, 2 Johns. (N. Y.) Cas. 409; Morris v. Wadsworth, 17 Wend. (N. Y.) 103; Huntress v. Patton, 20 Me. 28; Koch v. Melhorn, 25 Pa. 89, 64 Am. Dec. 685; Roberts v. Riddle, 79 Pa. 468; Cochran v. Dawson, 1 Miles (Pa.) 276; Smeidel v. Lewellyn, 3 Phila. (Pa.) 70; Douglass v. Reynolds, 32 U. S. (7 Pet.) 113, 8 L. Ed. 626; Brown v. Curtis, 2 N. Y. 225.

71. M'Doal v. Yomans, 8 Watts (Pa.) 361.

72. Gilbert v. Henck, 30 Pa. 205; Woods v. Sherman, 71 Pa. 100; Hoffman v. Bechtel, 52 Pa. 190.

73. Griffith v. Robertson, 15 Hun (N. Y.) 344; McMurray v. Noyes, 72 N. Y. 523, 28 Am. Rep. 180.

74. Cooke v. Nathan, 16 Barb. (N. Y.) 342.

75. Jones v. Ashford, 79 N. C. 172.

76. Cumpston v. McNair, 1 Wend. (N. Y.) 457; Pollock v. Hoag, 4 E. D. Sm. (N. Y. C. P.) 473; Vanderkemp v. Shelton, 11 Paige (N. Y.) 28; Newell v. Fowler, 23 Barb. (N. Y.) 628.

hausting his remedy against the principal before he resorts to the guarantor, or showing satisfactorily that the affairs of the principal were in such a condition that any pursuit of him would have proved fruitless.[77] Consequently, in the case of a contingency guaranty, as the statute begins to run when the right of action against the guarantor becomes complete, it follows that it only attaches in his favor when the necessary steps to fix his liability have been taken and are fully completed.

§ 147. Money paid for another.

Where money is paid for another under such circumstances that the law will imply a promise to repay it, and no time is fixed for its repayment, the right of action accrues at once; but if payment is made in liquidation of a note or contract not matured, the right of action does not accrue until the debt has matured, and if anything remain to be done to effectuate the payment, a right of action does not accrue until that is done. Thus, where an administratrix brought an action to recover money paid in liquidation, one of two notes secured by mortgage, it was held that the statute began to run from the date of the discharge of the mortgage, and not from the time when the payment was made.[78]

§ 148. Action under enabling acts.

Where a statute gives a party the right to sue on an existing claim where such right did not exist before, and is silent as to the time when the statute shall begin to run thereon, it attaches and begins to run from the day the act took effect, unless suit might have been brought in the name of another—as the assignor of a lease—in which case it begins to run from the time the claim first accrued.[79]

77. Dyer v. Gibson, 16 Wis. 557; Parker v. Culvertson, Wall. Jr. (U. S.) 149; Benton v. Fletcher, 31 Vt. 418; Wheeler v. Lewis, 11 Vt. 265; Dana v. Conant, 30 Vt. 246; Sandford v. Allen, 55 Mass. (1 Cush.) 473; McClurg v. Fryer, 15 Pa. 293; Cody v. Sheldon, 38 Barb. (N. Y.) 103; Stark v. Fuller, 42 Pa. 320; Thomas v. Woods, 4 Cow. (N. Y.) 173.

78. Luce v. McLoon, 58 Me. 321.

79. Cross v. United States, 4 Ct. of Cl. (U. S.) 271.

§ 149. Actions against stockholders of corporations.

Where, by statute, the stockholders of a corporation are made liable for the debts of the corporation, their liability commences when the liability of the corporation commences, and ends at the same time that liability on the part of the corporation ends.[80]

80. See Seattle Nat. Bank v. Pratt, 103 Fed. 62, aff'd 111 Fed. 841, 49 C. C. A. 662; Santa Rosa Nat. Bank v. Barnett, 125 Cal. 407, 58 Pac. 85; Ryland v. Commercial & Sav. Bank, 127 Cal. 525, 59 Pac. 989; First Nat. Bank v. King, 60 Kansas, 733, 57 Pac. 952; Chase v. Horton Bank, 9 Kan. App. 186, 40 Central L. J. 210, 59 Pac. 39; Thompson v. Reno Savings Bank, 19 Nev. 103, 7 Pac. 68, 3 Am. St. Rep. 797, 827, 872, n. The liability of a shareholder in a national bank is often held to be contractual; in which case the statute of limitations does not commence to run against the enforcement of his entire liability or of any particular portion of it until the comptroller of the currency has called the entire liability or the particular part of it in issue. Glenn v. Liggett, 135 U. S. 533, 10 Sup. Ct. 867, 34 L. Ed. 262; Aldrich v. Campbell, 97 Fed. 663, 669, 38 C. C. A. 347; Deweese v. Smith, 106 Fed. 438, 441, 45 C. C. A. 408, 66 L. R. A. 971, aff'd 187 U. S. 637, 23 Sup. Ct. 845, 47 L. Ed. 344. As the national bank act fixes no limit of time for collecting such an assessment, the limitation is that of the statutes of the State where the action is brought. Aldrich v. Skinner, 98 Fed. 375.

Where, as in Massachusetts, it is held that a foreign statute, like that of Kansas, making stockholders in one of its own corporations liable by assessment to judgment creditors of the corporation, such liability is transitory, and may be enforced in any State where personal service can be made upon the stockholder; if the statute of limitations of the judgment State, like that of Kansas, provides that if a person is out of the State when a cause of action against him accrues, the period limited for the commencement of the action does not begin to run until he comes into the State, which provision is in Kansas held to apply to non-residents, and there is no statutory requirement that the above right of action must be enforced within a specified period of time, such right of action is not barred by the foreign statute of limitations. Broadway Nat. Bank v. Baker, 176 Mass. 294, 57 N. E. 603. See Stebbins v. Scott, 172 Mass. 356, 52 N. E. 535; Whitman v. Oxford Nat. Bank, 176 U. S. 559, 20 Sup. Ct. 477, 44 L. Ed. 587; Hancock Nat. Bank v. Farnum, U. S. 640, 20 Sup. Ct. 506, 44 L. Ed. 619; Marshall v. Sherman, 148 N. Y. 9.

Where an insolvent corporation is in the hands of a receiver, limitation begins to run in favor of a stockholder as to unpaid assessments on his stock, from the time when the court orders the assessment to be made. Glenn v. Marbury, 145 U. S. 499, 12 Sup. Ct. 914, 36 L. Ed. 790. See Hobbs v. Nat. Bank of Commerce, 96 Fed. 396, 37 C. C. A. 513; Hunt v. Ward, 99 Cal. 612, 34 Pac. 335, 37 Am. St. Rep. 87; Partridge v. Butler,

But, if the statute provides that no action shall be commenced against them until after judgment and execution unsatisfied against the corporation, their liability does not begin, nor the statute begin to run in their favor, until the return of the execution aforesaid. But if, notwithstanding such provision, the statute also provides that they may be jointly sued with the corporation, the statute begins to run in their favor at the same time that it begins to run

113 Cal. 326, 45 Pac. 678, 28 Am. L. Rev. 906; 29 id. 109, 435, 777; 6 Ry. & Corp. L. J. 83.

As to a stockholder's claim to a certificate of stock even if the coropration can ever rely on lapse of time in such a case, the statute certainly will not begin to run in its favor until the stockholder is notified by some unequivocal act that his right to the stock is disputed. Commonwealth v. Springfield, M. & H. Turnpike Co., 73 Ky. (10 Bush) 254; Owingsville, etc., Road Co. v. Bondurant, 21 Ky. Law Rep. 1219, 107 Ky. 505, 54 S. W. 718. The right of a member of a voluntary corporation, such as a building and loan association, on his withdrawal therefrom, to require payment of his demand, does not accrue until a sufficient fund is accumulated by the association to meet such demand, and until then the statute of limitations does not begin to run against it. Andrews v. Roanoke Building Ass'n, 98 Va. 445, 36 S. E. 531, 49 L. R. A. 659.

81. Conklin v. Furman, 8 Abb. (N. Y.) Pr. n. s. 161, 57 Barb. 484, aff'd 48 N. Y. 527; Baker v. Atlas Bank, 50 Mass. (9 Metc.) 182. No privity exists between the stockholders and a creditor of the corporation. The stockholder can only be reached by the creditor through the corporation; and if the debt due from the stockholder is barred as against the corporation, the creditor cannot enforce its payment in equity. Bassett v. St. Albans Hotel Co., 47 Vt. 313; Terry v. Anderson, 95 U. S. 628, 24 L. Ed. 365; Manufacturing Co. v. Bank, 6 Rich. Eq. (S. C.) 234; Cherry v. Lamar, 58 Ga. 541. And the running of the statute between the corporation and the stockholder is not suspended by the recovery of a judgment against the corporation, or by any note or written obligation of the corporation given by the officers after it has gone into liquidation. Stilphen v. Ware, 45 Cal. 110. After a corporation has gone into voluntary liquidation, it is to all intents and purposes in the same condition as a dissolved partnership, and cannot create any new debt against a corporation. White v. Knox, 111 U. S. 784; Parker v. Macomber, 35 Mass. (18 Pick.) 505. It cannot renew or extend any stock liability by any contract made with the creditor. Where a bill in equity is brought by a creditor against a corporation in behalf of all the creditors, no creditor is entitled to recover who does not come forward to present his claim. Richmond v. Irons, 121 U. S. 27, 7 Sup. Ct. 788, 30 L. Ed. 864. See Trinity Church v. Vanderbilt, 98 N. Y. 170,

in favor of the corporation.[81] The statute begins to run upon sub-

as to barring taxes and water-rates imposed each year.

In Brinckerhoff v. Bostwick, 99 N. Y. 185, 1 N. E. 663, reversing 39 Hun, 352 it was held that the provision of the Code, limiting to three years the time for bringing an action against a director or stockholder of a moneyed corporation "to recover a penalty or forfeiture imposed, or to enforce a liability created by law," does not apply to an equitable action against the director of such a corporation to require an accounting and to recover damages for their neglect and inattention to the duties of their trusts whereby they suffered corporate funds to be lost and wasted. Such an action is simply the enforcement of a common-law liability, while the words of the provision, "a liability created by law," have reference only to a liability created by statute. The limitation applicable to such an action is ten years. Where a national bank had become insolvent, and one of its directors had been appointed receiver, an action was brought against him and the other directors for neglect of their duties, by one of the stockholders on behalf of himself and the other stockholders. Held, that as to other stockholders who became parties to the action upon their petition, the statute of limitations began to run from the time of the commencement of the action, not from the time of filing their petitions; that for the purposes of the statute of limitations the action must be treated as if all the stockholders were original plaintiffs. The original plaintiff could, at any time before other stockholders were made parties, and before judgment, have settled his individual claim, and executed a release thereof and discontinued the action, but upon prosecution to judgment it was for the benefit of all the stockholders and he ceases to have control over it. If stockholders do not come in, the suit having been commenced for their benefit, their rights are not barred by any lapse of time after the commencement. Cunningham v. Pell, 6 Paige (N. Y.), 655, was distinguished.

The stockholders of a corporation are not personally liable for the debts of a corporation against which the statute had run before its charter expired. Van Hook v. Whitlock, 3 Paige (N. Y.) 409.

In Hollingshead v. Woodward, 107 N. Y. 96, 13 N. E. 621, under the provision of the general manufacturing act, declaring, "that no suit shall be brought against any stockholder" of a company organized under said act, "who shall cease to be a stockholder, * * * unless the same shall be commenced within two years from the time he shall have ceased to be a stockholder," whenever a stockholder shall be divested of his interest in or control over the affairs of the corporation, by actual dissolution thereof by formal judgment, or by a surrender of its corporate rights, privileges, and franchises, the time begins to run, and at the end of two years therefrom the stockholder is no longer liable for any debt of the corporation.

In Jagger Iron Co. v. Walker, 76 N. Y. 521 (followed in City Nat. Bank v. Phelps, 86 N. Y. 484, 491), it was held that, under a statute by which

scriptions to stock of a corporation from the time when each call is made for an installment of the amount subscribed for.[82]

§ 150. Stock subscriptions.

Where no time is fixed for payment by the terms of a subscription for the stock of a corporation, but the same is left subject to call, the statute begins to run from the date of each call for an installment thereof by the proper authority.[83] In a Pennsylvania case,[84] by the terms of the subscription the money therefor was payable " in such manner, at such times, and in such proportions as shall be determined by the president and managers," and it was held that the statute did not begin to run thereon until after such determination and a demand made in pursuance thereof. But if the statute fixes the time within which payment shall be made, or if the time of payment is fixed in the subscription contract, the statute begins to run from the time therein designated for payment, as at that time, and not before, an action will lie for its recovery. If no time is designated either by statute or in the subscription itself, it would probably be treated as due upon demand, and the statute would begin to run from the date of subscription, upon the ground that where no time for payment is designated, it is treated as a debt due on demand, and the statute attaches from its date.[85] Where such notes are made payable upon a certain number of days' notice, a right of action does not accrue until the expira-

suit cannot be brought against the stockholders of manufacturing corporations after one year from the time when the debt became due, such debt is due at the maturity of the first of several notes, although there had been renewals. See 25 Am. L. Rev. 307, criticising and reviewing this decision. See Brunswick Terminal Co. v. Baltimore Nat. Bank, 99 Fed. 635, 40 C. C. A. 22, 48 L. R. A. 625; Seattle Nat. Bank v. Pratt, 103 Fed. 62; Sedgwick v. Sanborn, 63 Kan. 884, 65 Pac. 661.

82. Western R. Co. v. Avery, 64 N. C. 491; Kincaid v. Dwinelle, 59 N. Y. 548, distinguished and limited.

83. Western R. R. Co. v. Avery, 64 N. C. 491; Pittsburg & Connellsville R. Co. v. Plummer, 37 Pa. 413.

See Johnson v. Bank of Lake, 125 Cal. 6, 57 Pac. 664, 73 Am. St. Rep. 17; Crofoot v. Thatcher, 19 Utah, 212, 57 Pac. 171, 75 Am. St. Rep. 725.

84. Sinkler v. Turnpike Co., 3 P. & W. (Pa.) 149.

85. Grubb v. Vicksburg & B. R. Co., 50 Ala. 398; Phoenix Warehousing Co. v. Badger, 67 N. Y. 294.

tion of such notice duly given.[86] If, by the charter or law under which the corporation is founded, the subscriptions do not become due until called for by resolution of the board of directors, the statute does not begin to run until such call has been regularly made.[87] If the subscription fixes the time of payment, no demand is necessary, and the subscription becomes payable upon the arrival of the time named therein;[88] and such also is the rule when the time of payment has been fixed by a by-law of the company.[89] Thus, where by the terms of the subscription shares of stock were to be paid for by installments of ten per cent. every sixty days after the work was put in contract, it was held the subscriber was not entitled to notice of the time of the contract, and that bringing a suit upon the subscription was a sufficient demand.[90] In other words, in such cases the subscriber is bound to inquire for himelf and ascertain whether his subscription becomes due at the time specified or not. Generally, unless notice of an assessment or call is required by the charter or subscription, it is not an indispensable requisite to a right to bring an action; and, where it is not, the right of action doubtless dates from the date of the call.[91]

86. Cole v. Joliet Opera House Co., 79 Ill. 96.

87. Bouton v. Dry Dock, etc., Stage Co., 4 E. D. Sm. (N. Y.) 420; Ross v. Lafayette, etc., R. R. Co., 6 Ind. 297. See Williams v. Taylor, 120 N. Y. 244, 24 N. E. 288; Lake Ontario, etc., R. Co. v. Mason, 16 N. Y. 451; Howland v. Edmonds, 24 N. Y. 307, 23 How. Prac. 152; Tuckerman v. Brown, 33 N. Y. 297, 88 Am. Dec. 386, distinguished.

88. New Albany & S. R. Co. v. Pickens, 5 Ind. 247.

89. Schenectady, etc., Plank Road Co. v. Thatcher, 11 N. Y. 102; Winter v. Muscogee R. Co., 11 Ga. 438.

90. Breedlove v. Martinsville, etc., R. Co., 12 Ind. 114.

91. Eppes v. Mississippi, etc., R. Co., 35 Ala. 33. In Glenn v. Liggett, 135 U. S. 533, 10 Sup. Ct. 867, 34 L. Ed. 262, it was held that a stockholder is bound by a decree against the corporation, such as making an assessment in the enforcement of a corporate duty, although as an individual he was not a party to the action, the corporation being treated as his agent; and this is so although the corporation has ceased the prosecution of the objects for which it was organized. It being held, that for the collection of the debts, the enforcement of liabilities, and the payment of its creditors, its corporate powers still remain unimpaired. Upon the insolvency of a corporation, the obligation of the stockholder to pay enough of the amount unpaid on his

§ 151. Money payable by installments.

We have already seen[92] that where money is payable by installments, the statute begins to run upon each installment from the time when it becomes due.[93] But we have also seen that this rule does not apply to interest payable annually; but that in such a case, although an action lies for the interest as it matures, yet the statute does not begin to run thereon until some part of the principal becomes due.[94] In Pennsylvania [95] it was held that where there was a parol guaranty of the sufficiency of a mortgage given to secure a bond payable by installments, the statute does not begin to run until six years after the last installment becomes due.[96] So where subscriptions to the stock of a turnpike company by a statute were made payable at such times and in such proportions "as shall be determined by the president and managers," it was held that the statute did not begin to run on any part thereof until after such determination, and a demand made in pursuance thereof.[97]

stock to pay its debts does not become complete until a call or demand for payment, and the statute does not begin to run until such call or demand is made; and he cannot set up the statute as a bar to an action to collect his subscription for the payment of creditors because the company did not discharge its corporate duty in respect to its creditors earlier.

92. *Supra*, § 126 *et seq.*

93 Bush v. Stowell, 71 Pa. 208, 10 Am. Rep. 694; Baltimore & H. G. Turnpike Co. v. Barnes, 6 Har. & J. (Md.) 57; Burnham v. Brown, 23 Me. 400. In Robertson v. Pickerell, 77 N. C. 202, where the plaintiff made a contract with the defendant to do certain work, which was to be measured and paid for monthly, it was held that the statute began to run at the end of each month.

94. Grafton Bank v. Doe, 19 Vt. 463, 47 Am. Dec. 697; Ferry v. Ferry, 56 Mass .(2 Cush.) 92; Henderson v. Hamilton, 1 N. Y. Super. Ct. (1 Hall) 350.

95. Overton v. Tracey, 14 Serg. & R. (Pa.) 311.

96. See also to the same effect Jones v. Trimble, 3 Rawle (Pa.) 381; Poe v. Foster, 4 W. & S. (Pa.) 351. In Gonsoulin v. Adams, 28 La. Ann. 598, where the purchase-money for lands sold at sheriff's sale was payable by instalments, it was held that the statute began to run in favor of the purchaser from the time the first instalment became due, and that the right of the vendor to bring an action to set aside the sale became complete upon the first default, and presumption ran against it from that time, and not from the date of the last instalment.

97. Sinkler v. Turnpike Co., 3 P.

§ 152. Over-payments—Money paid by mistake.

Where money is paid by one to another by mistake, the statute begins to run from the time of payment and not from the time the mistake was discovered.[98] Thus, where under a mistake as to their liability the plaintiffs paid upon the return of a bill of exchange drawn in Kentucky and payable in New Orleans, which was protested, ten per cent. as damages, where under the laws of Kentucky no damages were collectible, it was held that the statute began to run, upon the right to recover it back, from the time the money was paid, and not from the time when they ascertained what their rights were in the premises.[99] But where the parties are in the habit of striking balances at stated periods, it is held that the statute begins to run from the striking of such balance. In an action by a bank to recover of a depositor an amount of money overpaid to him through mistake, it was held that the statute began to run from the date of the monthly balance struck in the depositor's bankbook, and not from the time the money was paid.[1] And where an administrator paid a debt under the erroneous belief that the estate was solvent, it was held that the statute did not begin to run against his claim to recover it back from the time the money was paid, but from the time of the insolvency of the estate as ascertained by a decree of insolvency and order of distribution.[2] But where an executor voluntarily paid over money to a legatee, and ten years after-

& W. (Pa.) 149. In order to prevent the operation of the statute, because of a contingency, the contingency must be one named in the contract itself; and the fact that a demand depends upon the contingency of the rectification of a mistake in the contract by a court of equity, does not prevent the operation of the statute. Jones' Ex'rs v. Lightfoot, 10 Ala. 17.

98. Clarke v. Dutcher, 9 Cow. (N. Y.) 674.

99. Bank of United States v. Daniel, 37 U. S. (12 Pet.) 32, 9 L. Ed. 980; Shelburne v. Robinson, 8 Ill. 597.

1. Union Bank v. Knapp, 20 Mass. (3 Pick.) 96, 15 Am. Dec. 181. In Johnson v. Rutherford, 10 Pa. 455, where money was overpaid on a contract for work, it was held that the statute did not begin to run until the payment of the balance on final settlement.

2. Walker v. Bradley, 20 Mass. (3 Pick.) 261.

wards claimed that he had paid too much and brought an action to recover it back, it was held that the action was barred.[3] And also, where an administrator found a mortgage-deed among the testator's papers, and assigned it, and it turned out to be a forgery, it was held that the statute began to run from the date of the assignment.[4]

§ 153. Failure of consideration.

Where money has been paid upon a consideration that ultimately fails, the statute does not begin to run until such event; as, until that time, no right of action accrues to recover back the money paid.[5] Thus, if money is paid upon a contract for the sale of land, which the vendor refuses to or is unable to convey the statute does not begin to run against the vendor for the money paid until the vendor has refused or become unable to convey the land, at which time the consideration fails, and a right of action to recover it back arises;[6] and it has been held in some of the cases that the same rule obtains where personal property to which the vendor had no title is sold.[7] But in Kentucky it has been held that an implied warranty of title is broken at once if the vendor has no title, and that the statute begins to run from the date of the contract;[8] and such seems to be the doctrine generally held,[9] espec-

3. Shelburne v. Robinson, 8 Ill. 597. See also Gamble v. Hicks, 27 Miss. 781; Johnson v. Rutherford, 10 Pa. 455.

4. Bree v. Holbech, 2 Doug. 654.

5. Richards v. Allen, 17 Me. 296. Where a debtor conveys lands to his creditor as collateral security for a debt, under an agreement that it shall be reconveyed on payment of the debt, the statute does not begin to run upon the creditor's agreement to reconvey until an offer of settlement has been made. Hall v. Felton, 105 Mass. 516. See Eames v. Savage, 14 Mass. 425, as to the time when the statute begins to run for the consideration paid upon a parol contract for the sale of lands. Hilton v. Duncan, 41 Tenn. (1 Coldw.) 313.

6. Taylor v. Rowland, 26 Tex. 293; Harris v. Harris, 70 Pa. 170; Evans v. See, 23 Pa. 88; Bowles v. Woodson, 6 Gratt. (Va.) 78; Stewart v. Keith, 12 Pa. 238. See Baxter v. Gay, 14 Conn. 119.

7. Caplinger v. Vaden, 24 Tenn. (5 Humph.) 629; Gross v. Kierski, 41 Cal. 111.

8. Chancellor v. Wiggins, 43 Ky. (4 B. Mon.) 201, 39 Am. Dec. 49.

ially relative to breaches of warranties as to the quality of property sold.[10] Where, however, lands are purchased and conveyed by a warranty-deed that is invalid because of the guarantor's failure to comply with certain statutory requirements, the grantee instantly has a right of action to recover it back, and the statute begins to run from that time. Thus, where a person purchased land of a guardian, and the guardian having failed to comply with certain statutory provisions the deed was a nullity, in an action by the grantee to recover back the consideration-money it was held that the statute began to run from the day the money was paid, and not from the time that the defect in the conveyance was ascertained;[11] and the same doctrine was held in Alabama in a case where a person went into possession under a void deed.[12] Where under a parol or even a written contract for the sale of lands, no time is fixed for a conveyance, the statute does not begin to run against the purchaser, as to the money paid, until he has demanded a deed or the other party has died,[13] the rule being that the statute does not begin to run against a person who has paid money under a voidable contract until some act has been done by the other party, or by the person paying the money, evincing an intention to rescind the contract.[14]

9. Richards v. Allen, *supra*.

10. Baucum v. Streater, 50 N. C. (5 Jones L.) 70.

11. Furlong v. Stone, 12 R. I. 437. See Bishop v. Little, 3 Me. 405.

12. Molton v. Henderson, 62 Ala. 426. In this case it was held that where the legal title to land resides in trustees or the survivors of them and such lands are sold under void proceedings by a guardian of the *cestui que trust*, and the purchaser goes into possession, the statute of limitations begins to run from the date of such sale and possession under it, and is not suspended by the death of the trustee after such possession accrued. Miller v. Sullivan, 4 Dillon (U. S.) 340. See also Edge, 62 Ga. 289, where an administrator and another person bought land of the estate, and the administrator settled with the distributees therefor; in an action by him against his co-purchaser for his share of the purchase-money, it was held that the statute began to run from the date of the sale, and not from the ratification by the distributees.

13. Eames v. Savage, *supra*.

14. Collins v. Thayer, 74 Ill. 138.

§ 154. Sheriff, action against, for breach of duty.

The statute does not begin to run against a sheriff for moneys collected on an execution until a demand has been made upon him therefor, or until he has made a proper return of the execution as required by law,[15] or, if no return has been made, until the lapse of the time within which, by law, the return is required to be made. But in Georgia it has been held that the statute begins to run from the time the money was received.[16] But this doctrine can hardly be regarded as well founded, because the sheriff has the whole period fixed by law within which to make his return, and until that time has elapsed the creditor has no means of knowing whether the sheriff intends to pay over to him the money collected or not, nor, until the return-day has passed, can he maintain an action against him either for not collecting, or for refusing to pay over the money when collected. In Louisiana it is held that the statute does not begin to run in such cases until the judgment creditor has demanded the money.[17] For money collected by a sheriff on foreclosure proceedings, the statute does not begin to run until the sale is perfected by delivery of the deed.[18] For not returning an execution on time, the statute begins to run the moment the time for returning expires,

15. Governor v. Stonum, 11 Ala. 679; State v. Minor, 44 Mo. 373. Where an officer receives from an execution debtor a note in satisfaction thereof, payable to himself, the statute does not begin to run against the judgment creditor's right to recover of him the proceeds of such note, until the creditor has made a demand upon the officer therefor, especially where the note remained uncollected until a short time before demand. Childs v. Jordan, 106 Mass. 321, and the same rule prevails as to money collected on an execution by an officer. Weston v. Ames, 51 Mass. (10 Metc.) 244. An officer who sells an equity of redemption upon execution, and holds the surplus, upon a second attachment, which has since failed, is not liable to the judgment debtor for such surplus until he has received notice of the dissolution of the second attachment; consequently the statute does not begin to run in his favor until such notice is given. King v. Rice, 66 Mass. (12 Cush.) 161.

16. Thompson v. Central Bank, 9 Ga. 413; Edwards v. Ingraham, 31 Miss. 272.

17. Fuqua v. Young, 14 La. Ann. 216.

18. Van Nest v. Lott, 16 Abb. Pr. (N. Y.) 130.

without demand or notice.[19] The cause of action against a sheriff for damages occasioned by his unauthorized release of property attached on mesne process does not arise from the date of the release but from the date of the judgment, and the statute begins to run from that time.[20] In an action against a sheriff for an escape, the statute begins to run from the time of the escape.[21] For making an insufficient return on mesne process, by reason of which the plaintiff lost the benefit of the attachment, the statute begins to run from the time the writ was returned to the proper officer, and not from the time when the damage therefrom accrued; [22] and this is also the rule where he attaches insufficient property on the original writ, when he was directed to, and might have attached sufficient.[23] But for taking insufficient bail it is held that the statute does not begin to run until a return of *non est inventus* has been made on the execution. The distinction being that the persons becoming bail only guarantee that the debtor shall be forthcoming to respond to the execution, and do not become liable to pay the debt except upon failure in that

19. Peck v. Hurlburt, 46 Barb. (N. Y.) 559.

20. Lesen v. Neal, 53 Mo. 412.

21. Rosborough v. Albright, 4 Rich. (S. C.) 39; West v. Rice, 50 Mass. (9 Metc.) 564; French v. O'Neal, 2 H. & M. (Md.) 401; Crockram v. Welby, 2 Mod. 212.

22. Miller v. Adams, 16 Mass. 456; Cæsar v. Bradford, 13 Mass. 169. In Bank of Hartford County v. Waterman, 26 Conn. 324, it was held, in a case where an officer made a false return, that the statute did not begin to run until the plaintiff had sustained actual damage therefrom. But see Ellsworth, J., dissenting. In Newell v. Whigham, 102 N. Y. 20, 6 N. E. 673, held that a sheriff's return to a writ of possession is not conclusive as to the execution of the writ; and that, as against a mortgagee of a leasehold interest, who is not in possession of the demised premises, to set the six months' statute of limitations running, and to cut off his right to redeem, the execution of a writ of possession, issued in an action of ejectment brought by the landlord because of non-payment of rent, must be an open, visible, and notorious change of possession; a mere nominal and secret execution of the writ is not sufficient. See Witbeck v. Van Rennsselaer, 64 N. Y. 27, distinguished.

23. Betts v. Norris, 21 Me. 314, 38 Am. Dec. 264 (denied in a Connecticut case, Bank of Hartford County v. Waterman, 26 Conn. 324); Garlin v. Strickland, 27 Me. 443.

respect, consequently no right of action exists in favor of the creditor until it is ascertained that the debtor is not forthcoming upon the execution;[24] and the same rule prevails in actions for taking insufficient receiptors for property attached or sureties in replevin suits.[25] For a failure by a sheriff to return goods attached on mesne process to the debtor, after the plaintiff in such process has been defeated, the statute does not begin to run until the attachment is dissolved by the act of the plaintiff therein or by operation of law.[26]

§ 155. Fraudulent representations in sales of property.

In an action to recover damages for fraudulent representations made in the sale of lands, in regard to incumbrances, the cause of action arises at once upon the completion of the sale by a conveyance of the land.[27] In such cases, the fact that the grantee did not discover the fraud until six years after the conveyance is of no consequence, as it is the misrepresentation and not the resulting

24. West v. Rice, 50 Mass. (9 Metc.) 564; Cæsar v. Bradford, 13 Mass. 169; Mather v. Green, 17 Mass. 60. An action against a sheriff for making insufficient bail accrues from the time of the return of *non est inventus* on the execution against the principal, and the statute runs from that time. Ibid.; Rice v. Hosmer, 12 Mass. 127. And an action against him for an insufficient return on an original writ begins to run from the time when the writ was returned. Miller v. Adams, 16 Mass. 456.

25. Harriman v. Wilkins, 20 Me. 93.

26. Bailey v. Hall, 16 Me. 408.

As to the bonds of public officers, such as sheriffs or auditors, the rule appears to be now settled that an action will not lie against the sureties on such a bond after the cause of action, as against the principal, has become barred. Paige v. Carroll, 61 Cal. 211; Sonoma County v. Hall, 129 Cal. 659, 62 Pac. 213; 132 Cal. 589, 62 Pac. 257, 65 Pac. 12, 459; State v. Conway, 18 Ohio 234, Ryus v. Gruble, 31 Kansas, 767, 3 Pac. 518; Davis v. Clark, 58 Kansas, 454, 49 Pac. 665; Spokane County v. Prescott, 19 Wash. 418, 53 Pac. 661, 67 Am. St. Rep. 733.

27. Northrop v. Hill, 57 N. Y. 351, 15 Am. Rep. 501, aff'g 61 Barb. (N. Y.) 136. In Owen v. Western Savings Fund, 97 Pa. 47, 39 Am. Rep. 794, it was held that the statute begins to run against a recorder of deeds for a false certificate of search from the time when the search was given, and not from the time when damage was sustained.

damage which constitutes the ground of action; and, as the fraud might have been discovered by an examination of the proper records, the fault is the grantee's if he has failed to use that diligence which common prudence suggests in ascertaining the truth.[28]

There is also a wide distinction between a case where the action is predicated upon the fraud of a party in the sale of property, or where he has fraudulently thrown a person off his guard, and prevented such an investigation as would have revealed the truth, and one which is predicated upon a breach of contract of warranty, however false the warranty may be. In the former case the statute would not begin to run until the fraud was, or reasonably could have been, discovered; while in the latter case the statute begins to run at once, although there was no means by which the vendee could have ascertained the falsity of the warranty.[29]

§ 156. When leave of court to sue is necessary—Effect of, on commencement of limitation.

When an action cannot be brought until leave to sue is granted by a court, especially when this preliminary is imposed by statute, the statute of limitations does not begin to run upon the cause of

28. In Binney's Appeal, 116 Pa. 169, 9 Atl. 186, the statute was held to run from the erroneous entry of satisfaction on the record of a mortgage, though the plaintiff's loss did not occur until more than six years later. If a person, in good faith, guarantees a signature which is in fact a forgery, the guarantor's implied promise is broken when it is made; the right of action accrues immediately, and the statute runs from the date of the guaranty. Lehigh Coal & Nav. Co. v. Blakeslee, 189 Pa. 13, 41 Atl. 992, 69 Am. St. Rep. 788. Upon an illegal resolution of directors of a corporation, authorizing a payment of its money to the president, the statute begins to run in their favor from the date of such resolution, and not from the date of the payment of the money. Link v. McLeod, 194 Pa. 566, 45 Atl. 340.

29. See Allen v. Ladd, 6 Lans. (N. Y.) 222; Battley v. Fulkner, 3 B. & Ald. 288; Troup v. Smith, 20 Johns. (N. Y.) 33; Leonard v. Pitney, 5 Wend. (N. Y.) 30; Argall v. Bryant, 3 N. Y. Super. Ct. (1 Sandf.) 98; Allen v. Mille, 17 Wend. (N. Y.) 202.

action until such leave has been granted;[30] although if a party has slept upon his rights unreasonably, and has neglected to make application to the court for leave to sue for such a period of time that his demand may fairly be regarded as stale, it would seem to furnish ample ground for a refusal by the court of the necessary leave to use its process to enforce the claim. It would be exceedingly unreasonable to hold that the statute runs upon a claim when the party has no power to maintain a suit thereon, and although formerly perhaps a contrary rule would have been held, yet, according to the tendency of the courts at the present time, there can be no question that the Minnesota case expresses the true rule.

§ 157. Orders of court.

The statute ordinarily begins to run against an order of a court from the time when it is made, but when such order partakes of the nature of an interlocutory decree, the statute does not begin to run against it until the proceedings are at an end. Especially is this the case in relation to orders of probate courts made during the progress of administration, upon which it is held that the statute does not begin to run until the time of final settlement.[31]

§ 158. Property obtained by fraud.

When property is obtained by fraud, so that a present right of action arises either for the tort or for the value of the property under an implied contract, the statute begins to run from the time when the fraud was, or by the exercise of reasonable diligence might have been, discovered; and even though the statute may have run against the tort, yet an action upon the implied contract may be maintained, unless the statute has also run upon it. Thus, where the maker of an overdue note induced the payee to surrender it to him without payment, by fraud, it was held equivalent to obtaining so much money, and that the creditor might waive the tort and maintain an action for money had and received, and that

30. Wood v. Myrick, 16 Minn. 494.

31. Tindal v. McMillan, 33 Tex. 484.

the statute did not begin to run until the fraud was actually discovered, or the lapse of a reasonable time within which the plaintiff should have discovered it.[32]

§ 159. Promise to marry.

A promise to marry, especially where the parties thereto, through a period of several years, do not act to indicate an intention or purpose not to fulfil it, is treated as a continuous promise, and the statute does not begin to run thereon until there is a breach thereof, either by one of the parties having put it out of his or her power to perform it by marrying another person, or by notice of a purpose not to perform it, or an absolute refusal to perform it.[33] That is, the party setting up the statute as a defense to an action upon such a contract must, in order to avail himself of its protection, show that the contract was broken by him in such a manner that a present right of action against him thereon has existed for the whole period requisite to establish the statutory bar.[34]

§ 160. Contracts void under statute of frauds—Actions for money paid under.

Where money has been paid under a contract that is void under the statute of frauds, because not in writing, the statute does not begin to run upon an action to recover it back from the time when it was paid, but rather from the time when the other party has done some decisive act evincing an intention to rescind the contract.[35] Until that time, no right of action exists; and, as the statute does not attach until a full, complete, and present right of ac-

32. Penobscot R. R. Co. v. Mavo, 67 Me. 470, 24 Am. Rep. 45. See also Outhouse v. Outhouse, 13 Hun (N. Y.) 130.

Embezzlement, by one member of a firm of attorneys, of money collected for a client does not establish fraud committed by his innocent copartner because of the partnership relation; the latter is liable only for money had and received, and the statute of limitations applicable to that form of action is the only one that applies to him. Gibson v. Henley, 131 Cal. 6, 63 Pac. 61.

33. Blackburn v. Mann, 85 Ill. 222.

34. Id.

35. Collins v. Thayer, 74 Ill. 138.

tion exists, it follows, of course, that the statute does not begin to run until such right arises, by a refusal of the party to perform the contract under which the money was paid.[36]

§ 161. Against heirs, when tenancy by curtesy or dower exists.

The statute does not begin to run against the heirs of a married woman whose husband survives her, and is entitled to an estate in her lands as tenant by curtesy, until his estate is terminated therein;[37] and the same rule prevails where there is a tenancy by dower in a husband's lands, the rule being that the statute does not begin to run against a person entitled to an estate in remainder until he or she has a right of possession.[38]

§ 162. Actions against sureties on administrator's bonds.

Ordinarily the statute will not begin to run in favor of the sureties on an administrator's bond, by a distributee of the estate, until his administration is closed; but as his death, before the estate is settled, determines his trust, the statute begins to run against the distributees in favor of the sureties, from the date of his death.[39] In Maryland, under the statute of 1798 the statute of limitations begins to run on a guardian's bond from the time it was passed.[40]

36. Cairo F. R. Co. v. Parks, 32 Ark. 131.

37. Dyer v. Brannock, 66 Mo. 391, 27 Am. Rep. 359.

38. Bailey v. Woodbury, 50 Vt. 166.

39. Harrison v. Heflin, 54 Ala. 552; Biddle v. Wendell, 37 Mich. 452.

40. State v. Miller, 3 Gill (Md.) 335.

In Massachusetts when a cause of action for the breach of an administrator's bond arises from his failure to account within one year, and is barred by the statute of limitations, his neglect to render an account, when cited so to do by the Probate Court, is an independent breach which is not barred by the lapse of twenty years from the date of the bond. Prescott v. Read, 62 Mass. (8 Cush.) 365; Fuller v. Cushman, 170 Mass. 286, 49 N. E. 631. In Minnesota, it has recently been held, overruling two earlier decisions in that State, that, as to suit upon such a bond, the statute runs from the final decree of distribution, the obtaining leave of court to sue being treated as not a part of the cause of action. Ganser v. Ganser, 83 Minn. 199, 85 Am. St. Rep. 461, 86 N. W. 18.

§ 163. Actions against guardians, by wards.

An action by a ward against a guardian for a settlement does not accrue until the relation is terminated;[41] but if a female ward marries, before she becomes of age, with an adult husband capable of suing to enforce her rights, the relation ceases, and the statute begins to run from the date of the marriage.[42] A right of action does not accrue to a guardian to recover of his ward for expenses incurred, until the termination of the guardianship; and the rule is not changed, or his rights in this respect affected, by the circumstances that the ward removes to another state before he becomes of age.[43] When a guardian is removed from his trust and, subsequently thereto, sales made by him are set aside, and he is compelled to refund the money received therefrom, the statute begins to run from the time the sales are set aside and the money refunded, and not from the time of settling his guardianship account.[44]

41. Alston v. Alston, 34 Ala. 15; Caplinger v. Stokes, 19 Tenn. (Meigs.) 175. In Louisiana, the action of a minor against his tutor, respecting the acts of his tutorship, is prescribed by four years from the time he becomes of age, and the tacit mortgage given him by law against the property of the tutor is extinguished at the same time. Aillot v. Aubert, 20 La. Ann. 509. If a person, without legal authority to do so, assumes to act as guardian for another, and as such receives money belonging to the ward, the statute begins to run against him at once, unless there is some existing disability. Johnson v. Smith's Adm'r, 27 Mo. 591.

See State v. Parsons, 147 Ind. 579, 47 N. E. 17, 62 Am. St. Rep. 430; Potter v. Douglas, 83 Iowa 190, 48 S. W. 1004; Hale v. Ellison (Tenn.) 59 S. W. 673; Slaughter v. Slaughter, 7 Houst. (Del.) 482, 32 Atl. 857. In Tinker v. Rodwell, 69 L. T. 591, it was held that, when a father enters into possession of realty as natural guardian for his infant son, the latter's coming of age does not alter such possession, and, if nothing else has occurred to change its character, the statute of limitations does not begin to run in favor of a person claiming against the son, until the father's death.

42. Finnell v. O'Neal, 76 Ky. (13 Bush.) 176.

43. Taylor v. Kilgore, 33 Ala. 214.

44. Shearman v. Akins, 21 Mass. (4 Pick.) 283. In State v. Henderson, 54 Md. 332, it was held that the statute begins to run upon a guardian's bond immediately upon the ward becoming of age. "From the moment the ward is emancipated from the authority of his guardian, by reaching the age prescribed by law, his cause of action is complete, and the

§ 164. Assessments, taxes, etc.

Where an assessment or tax is laid, and by ordinance or statute a certain time is fixed within which it may be paid, the person against whom it is laid has the whole of such period within which to pay it, and the statute does not begin to run thereon until such time has expired. Thus, where an assessment was imposed by an ordinance which provided that, unless paid within twenty days, the debtor should be subjected to penalty and interest, it was held that the statute began to run from the expiration of the twenty days;[45] and the same rule applies in the case of taxes. If the statute or the note under which it was raised specifies a certain time within which it shall be paid, the taxpayer has the whole of that period to pay it in, and the statute does not begin to run until such period has elapsed.

§ 165. Agreement to pay incumbrances.

When the grantee of land assumes and agrees to pay certain incumbrances on the land, and no time is fixed within which he shall

statute of limitations begins to run." Dorsey, J., in Green v. Johnson, 3 G. & J. (Md.) 387. See also Munroe v. Phillips, 65 Ga. 390. In State v. Henderson, *supra*, Irving, J., in remarking upon the provision of the Code providing that "on the ward's arrival at age" the guardian shall pass his account and pay over the moneys in his hand, says, "So long as he (the guardian) delayed, it was not a new breach, but a continuing default and a continuing breach." Alvey, J., dissented, and insisted that the statute did not begin to run until the balance due had been ascertained by a settlement of his accounts in the Orphan's Court; citing Thurston v. Blackiston, 36 Md. 501; Byrd v. State, 44 id. 492; Griffith v. Parks, 32 id. 1, 8; Sanders v. Coward, 15 M. & M. 48.

45. Reynolds v. Green, 27 Ohio St. 416. See White v. City of Brooklyn, 122 N. Y. 53, 25 N. E. 243, aff'd 139 N. Y. 651, 35 N. E. 207; Reid v. Albany County Sup'rs, 128 N. Y. 364, 28 N. E. 367; *In re* Rosenbaum, 119 N. Y. 24, 23 N. E. 172; *In re* Duffy, 133 N. Y. 512, 31 N. E. 517. In People *ex rel.* Edison, etc., Co. v. Wemple, 133 N. Y. 617, 30 N. E. 1002, 4 Silvernail 260, it was held that there is no limitation as to the time in which a corporation may apply to the comptroller for a revision of a tax levied upon it, under the provision of the act providing for the taxation of certain corporations as amended in 1889, which authorizes that officer to revise and readjust tax accounts against corporations theretofore settled.

pay them, he is treated as contracting to pay them as they mature; and in such a case, where the incumbrances at the time the deed is delivered have not matured, the statute would not begin to run upon his contract until such incumbrances became due; but if they are due at the time the contract is made, the statute begins to run in his favor from the time when he accepted the deed.[46] Where, however, the grantor is to pay the incumbrances, the statute does not begin to run against the grantee's right to recover back his purchase-money, etc., until he has been evicted in consequence of the nonpayment of the incumbrances by the grantor.[47]

§ 166. General provisions.

In many of the statutes, after specifically providing for certain classes of actions, there is a general provision, by which it is provided that all causes of action not limited by any previous sections of the statute shall be brought within a certain period. Thus, in Maine,[48] it is provided that "all personal actions on any contract, not limited by the foregoing sections, or any other law of the State, shall be brought within twenty years after the accruing of the cause of action;" and a similar provision exists in Massachusetts,[49] Michigan,[50] and Wisconsin.[51] In Ohio,[52] it is provided that all other actions not enumerated in the statute shall be brought within four years after such right of action accrued. This clause is sweeping, and embraces every species of action, whether upon a contract, bond, deed or other obligation, or for any act, wrong or injury not specially provided for. In Oregon, an equally sweeping clause exists, which limits non-enumerated causes of action to ten years;[53] so also in Nevada[54] and Nebraska,[55] the limitation being four years.

§ 167. For advances upon property.

Where money is advanced upon property in store, the property

46. Schmucker v. Sibert, 18 Kan. 104, 26 Am. Rep. 765.
47. Taylor v. Barnes, 69 N. Y. 430.
48. Appendix, Maine.
49. Appendix, Massachusetts.
50. Appendix, Michigan.
51. Appendix, Wisconsin.
52. Sec. 1, subd. 6.
53. Appendix, Oregon.
54. Appendix, Nevada.
55. Appendix, Nebraska.

is treated as the primary fund for the repayment of the advances; and, as an action for the money can only be brought when the consignee can no longer look to the property for reimbursement, it follows as a matter of course that the running of the statute dates from the same period.[56]

§ 168. Usurious interest.

Where a contract is usurious, and the usurious interest is paid in advance at the time when the contract is made, the statute begins to run against the person paying it, and against the State, where it is made an indictable offense at once, and does not rest in abeyance until the debt is paid;[57] but the rule as to an action to recover back the money would be otherwise where the usurious interest is not paid until the debt matures. In no event can a right of action accrue until the interest is paid.[58]

§ 169. Between tenants in common of property.

Where property belonging to two persons is sold by one of them, the statute does not begin to run from the time of sale, but from the time when the pay therefor is received. Thus, in an action by one tenant in common against his co-tenant for the proceeds of trees sold by him, it was held that the statute began to run from the time of payment, not of sale; and that if a note was taken upon which the purchaser from time to time made payments, the statute begins to run from the date of each payment.[59]

56. Grimes v. Hagood, 27 Tex. 693.

57. Commonwealth v. Frost, 5 Mass. 53Ɩ.

58. As to usurious transactions with national banks, § 5198 of the U. S. Rev. Stats. distinguishes between the interest which a negotiable instrument carries with it, and which has been agreed to be paid thereon, and interest already paid. If an obligee actually pays usurious interest as such, the usurious transaction occurs then, and not before, and he must sue within two years thereafter. Brown v. Marion Nat. Bank, 169 U. S. 416, 18 Sup. Ct. 390, 42 L. Ed. 801; National Bank of Daingerfield v. Ragland, 181 U. S. 45, 21 Sup. Ct. 536, 45 L. Ed. 738.

59. Miller v. Miller, 24 Mass. (7 Pick.) 133, 19 Am. Dec. 264.

§ 170. When the law gives a lien for property sold.

In the case of a sale of property consisting of several parcels, under a special contract, where the law gives a lien therefor, as in the case of a sale of goods to a vessel, the lien attaches on the day of the delivery of the first parcel, but the statute does not begin until the day after the delivery of the last parcel.[60] Of course, if a term of credit is agreed upon, the statute does not attach until the credit has fully expired.

§ 171. Co-purchasers, co-sureties, etc.

Where one of two or more persons who have become jointly liable under a contract or obligation, whether partners or not, pays the whole or a portion of the debt, the statute attaches from the time of each payment by him;[61] but this rule is, of course, subject to the exception, that, if the payment is made before the debt becomes due, the statute will not apply until its maturity. It has been held that, even where the liability of one joint maker of a note is barred by the statute, but has been kept on foot as against the other by partial payments made by him, he may nevertheless recover of the other a moiety of the amounts so paid by him, unless the statute has also run against such payments;[62] and this doctrine is well grounded in principle and sustained by authority,[63] the rule being that the statute only begins to run from the date of each payment.[64]

60. The Mary Blane v. Beebler, 12 Mo. 477.

61. Campbell v. Calhoun, 1 Penn. 140.

62. Peaslee v. Breed, 18 N. H. 489, 34 Am. Dec. 178.

63. Bullock v. Campbell, 9 Gill (Md.) 182; Brown v. Agnew, 6 W. & S. (Penn.) 235; Sherwood v. Dunbar, 6 Cal. 53; Lomax v. Pendleton, 3 Call (Va.) 538; Buck v. Spofford, 40 Me. 328; Regis v. Hebert, 16 La. Ann. 224.

64. Bullock v. Campbell, 9 Gill. (Md.) 182.

See Gross v. Davis, 87 Tenn. 226, 11 S. W. 92, 10 Am. St. Rep. 635, 647, n.; Leeds Lumber Co. v. Haworth, 98 Iowa 463, 67 N. W. 383, 60 Am. St. Rep. 199, n. When the statute has run against one of two parties entitled to a joint action, it is a bar to such joint action. Shipp v. Miller, 15 U. S. (2 Wheat.) 316, 324, 4 L. Ed. 248; Davis v. Coblens, 174 U. S. 719, 725, 19 Sup. Ct. 832, 43 L.

Ed. 1147; Dickey v. Armstrong, 8 Ky. (1 A. K. Marsh.) 39. It is usually held that one joint debtor cannot revive a debt barred by the statute of limitations, as against his co-debtors, without their consent. State Loan & Trust Co. v. Cochran, 130 Cal. 245, 62 Pac. 466, 600; McKenney v. Bowie, 94 Me. 397; Connecticut Trust, etc., Co. v. Wead, 67 N. Y. Supp. 466, 33 Misc. 374, judg. modified 69 N. Y. Supp. 518, 58 App. Div. 493; modified 172 N. Y. 497, 65 N. E. 261, 92 Am. St. Rep. 756. See 32 Am. L. Rev. 846; Maddox v. Duncan, 143 Mo. 613, 45 S. W. 688, 41 L. R. A. 581, 65 Am. St. Rep. 678 and n. A payment by one of several persons who are severally or jointly and severally liable for a debt does not prevent the statute running in favor of the others. *In re* Wolmershausen, 62 L. T. 541. But a payment of interest by one of several joint obligors in a bond, or of different co-makers of a note, before the statute of limitations attaches, takes the case out of the statute as to the others. Craig v. Callaway County Court, 12 Mo. 94; Bennett v. McCanse, 65 Mo. 194. See Bergman v. Bly, 66 Fed. 40, 13 C. C. A. 319; Woonsocket Inst. for Sav. v. Ballou, 16 R. I. 351, 16 Atl. 144, 1 L. R. A. 555.

CHAPTER XVII.

SPECIALTIES.

§ 172. Sealed instruments.

In all those States where sealed instruments, or "specialties," as they are technically called, are expressly brought within the statute,[1] the statute begins to run from the time when a cause of action arises thereon, and the bar is complete at the expiration of the statutory period, while in those States where this class of instruments are not provided for, the common-law presumption of payment attaches from the time when a cause of action arises, and becomes complete as a presumptive bar at the expiration of twenty years from that time;[2] and the mere lapse of twenty years without any demand, of itself raises a presumption of payment.[3] The state-

1. See *supra*, §§ 31, 37, for instances in which such statutes have been adopted in different States.

2. Bass v. Bass, 25 Mass. (8 Pick.) 187; Jackson, Ex. dem. Sackett v. Sackett & Raymond, 7 Wend. (N. Y.) 94; Oswald v. Leigh, 1 T. R. 271.

3. Wanmaker v. Van Buskirk, 1 N. J. Eq. 685, 23 Am. Dec. 748; Mease v. Stevens, 1 N. J. Law 443; Evans

ment of the law by Buller, J., in the case last cited, is generally adopted in this country; and mere lapse of time less than twenty years does not afford any ground for a presumption of payment

v. Huffman, 5 N. J. Eq. 354; Moore v. Smith, 81 Pa. 182; Henderson v. Lewis, 9 S. & R. (Pa.) 379, 11 Am. Dec. 733. But in Vermont, where, by statute, the prescriptive period is fifteen years, such a presumption is raised from the lapse of that period. Whitney v. French, 25 Vt. 663.

In Oswald v. Leigh, *supra*, Buller, J., said: "it is manifest that this doctrine of twenty years' presumption was first taken up by Lord Hale, who only thought it a circumstance from which a jury might presume payment. In this he was followed by Lord Holt, who held, that if a bond be of twenty years' standing, and no demand proved thereon, or good cause of so long forebearance shown on *solvit ad diem*, he should intend it paid. 6 Mod. 22. This doctrine was afterwards adopted by Lord Raymond in the case of Constable v. Somerset, Hil. 1 Geo. II., at Guildhall.

"This opinion seems to fortify the idea which I took up at the trial, in answer to a dictum which was then cited (1 Burr. 424), that the question of presumption of payment within a less time than tewnty years had been left to a jury, which was that it must have been left to them upon some evidence; and in such case the slightest evidence is sufficient. In one of the Winchelsea cases (4 Burr. 1963), Lord Mansfield expressly said that if a bond had lain dormant for twenty years, it shall be presumed to be paid. The court, however, inclining to believe the real truth of the case was with the defendant, desired that he would make an affiadvit; which being read upon a subsequent day, and not proving satisfactory, they discharged the rule. And Lord Mansfield, C. J., said that there was a distinction between length of time as a bar, and where it was only evidence of it; the former was positive, the latter only presumptive; and he believed that in the case of a bond no positive time had been expressly laid down by the court; that it might be eighteen or nineteen years."

In this country it is generally held that no period short of twenty years will raise a presumption of payment of a bond, Clark v. Bogardus, 2 Edw. (N. Y.) Ch. 387; or of a mortgage, Grafton Bank v. Doe, 19 Vt. 463, 47 Am. Dec. 697; Heyer v. Pruyn, 7 Paige (N. Y.) Ch. 465, 34 Am. Dec. 355; Ingraham v. Baldwin, 9 N. Y. 45; or of a covenant of any kind, Stockton's Adm'r v. Johnson, 45 Ky. (6 B. Mon.) 408. Eighteen years and a half has been held not sufficient as to a bond. Boltz v. Bullman, 1 Yeates (Pa.) 584; Lesley v. Nones, 7 Serg. & R. (Pa.) 410; Hughes v. Hughes, 54 Pa. 240. Such a presumption may, in connection with other circumstances, be raised by the lapse of a less period, Moore v. Smith, 81 Pa. 182; Henderson v. Lewis, 9 Serg. & R. (Pa.) 379, 11 Am. Dec. 733, but to have that effect it must be aided by persuasive circumstances, Hughes v. Hughes, *supra*.

Courts of equity act in analogy to the statute of limitations; and if, in a suit for the foreclosure of a mort-

or satisfaction of a specialty, whether it be a bond,[4] mortgage,[5]

gage, the lapse of time be such that the orator could not maintain a suit at law for the recovery of the mortgaged premises, a court of equity would presume payment and satisfaction of the mortgage debt. This period is fixed, by statute, in Vermont, at fifteen years. Martin v. Bowker, 19 Vt. 526. See also McDonald v. Sims, 3 Ga. (3 Kelly) 383; Field v. Wilson, 45 Ky. (6 B. Mon.) 479. But the payment of interest upon the debt, by the defendant, or of any portion of the principal, or any other act recognizing the existence of the mortgage, and that it was unsatisfied and obligatory upon him, would be sufficient to repel the presumption of payment, and take the case out of the operation of the statute. Martin v. Bowker, 19 Vt. 526.

Presumptions under the statute of limitations do not always have the same force and effect. Thus, under the Mass. Pub. Stats., c. 197, § 23, providing that "every judgment and decree of a court of record of the United States, or of this or any other State, shall be presumed to be paid and satisfied at the expiration of twenty years after the judgment or decree was rendered," the evidence need not be as strong as that required to take a case out of the general statute of limitations, but any legal evidence tending to show that the judgment has not been satisfied is competent, and if it convinces that such is the case, it is sufficient to rebut the presumption, even though it would be of no avail against the general statute of limitations. Walker v. Robinson, 136 Mass. 280; Day v. Crosby, 173 Mass. 433, 53 N. E. 880.

4. Diamond v. Tobias, 12 Pa. 312; Brubaker's Adm'r v. Taylor, 76 Pa. 83; Moore v. Smith, 81 Pa. 182; Miller v. Smith's Ex'rs, 16 Wend. (N. Y.) 425. That this presumption does not avail in less than twenty years as to any specialty, see Heyer v. Pruyn, 7 Paige (N. Y.) 465, 34 Am. Dec. 355, and this was held as to bonds. Clark v. Bogardus, 2 Edw. (N. Y.) Ch. 387. A lapse of eighteen years and a half was held not sufficient to raise a presumption that a bond was void. Boltz v. Bullman, 1 Yeates (Pa.) 584; Hughes v. Hughes, 54 Pa. 240; Dehart v. Gard, Add. (Pa.) 344; M'Carty v. Gordon, 4 Whart. (Pa.) 321; Lesley v. Nones, 7 Serg. & R. (Pa.) 410; nor will the lapse of any time, short of twenty years, *per se* raise such a presumption. Henderson v. Lewis, 9 Serg. & R. (Pa.) 379. Twelve years was held insufficient. Kinna v. Smith, 3 N. J. Eq. 14; Rogers v. Burns, 27 Pa. 525. And this includes all species of bonds, official or otherwise, where the statute provides no special period of limitation, Backestoss v. Commonwealth, 8 Watts. (Pa.) 286; Diemer v. Sechrist, 1 Pa. 419; or recognizances, Ankeny v. Penrose, 18 Pa. 100; Darlington's Appropriation, 13 Pa. 430; Allen v. Sawyer, 2 P. & W. (Pa.) 325; Galbraith v. Galbraith, 6 Watts (Pa.) 112.

5. Flagg v. Ruden, 1 Bradf. (N. Y. Surr.) 192; Bander v. Snyder, 5 Barb. N. Y.) 63; Reynolds v. Green, 10 Mich. 355; Howland v. Shurtleff, 42 Mass. (2 Metc.) 26, 35 Am. Dec. 384; Martin v. Bowker, 19 Vt. 526; Hoffman v. Harrington, 33 Mich. 392; Inches v. Leonard, 12 Mass. 379; Don-

judgment,[6] legacy,[7] notes under seal,[8] or any instrument in the nature of a specialty,[9] as recognizance, rent reserved in deeds,[10] or arrears of ground-rent, taxes on leased lands;[11] and that the consideration named in a deed as received has been paid.[12] In Pennsylvania where the parties had made a parol partition of lands, with an agreement for an owelty of partition after the lapse of twenty years, it was held that payment of the same would be presumed; and it may be stated as a general proposition that this

ald v. Sims, 3 Ga. (3 Kelly) 383; Cheever v. Perley, 93 Mass. (11 Allen) 584; Bacon v. McIntire, 49 Mass. (8 Metc.) 87; Hughes v. Edwards, 22 U. S. (9 Wheat.) 498, 6 L. Ed. 142; Peck v. Mallams, 10 N. Y. 509, Seld. Notes, 199; Wilkinson v. Flowers, 37 Miss. 579, 75 Am. Dec. 78; Newcomb v. St. Peter's Church, 2 Sandf. (N. Y.) Ch. 636; Collins v. Torry, 7 Johns. (N. Y.) 278, 5 Am. Dec. 273; Field v. Wilson, 45 Ky. (6 B. Mon.) 479; Jackson *ex dem.* People v. Wood, 12 Johns. (N. Y.) 242, 7 Am. Dec. 315; Giles v. Baremore, 5 Johns. (N. Y.) Ch. 545, 552; Cleveland Ins. Co. v. Reed, 65 U. S. (24 How.) 284, 16 L. Ed. 686; Downs v. Sooy, 28 N. J. Eq. 55; Green v. Fricker, 7 W. & S. (Pa.) 171; or any lien, Brock v. Savage, 31 Pa. 410. See Chap. XVIII., Mortgages.

6. Miller v. Smith's Ex'rs, *supra;* Cope v. Humphreys, 14 Serg. & R. (Pa.) 15; Summerville v. Holiday, 1 Watts (Pa.) 507; Denny v. Eddy, 39 Mass. (22 Pick.) 533. But the presumption does not attach until the judgment is complete; that is, until the amount is fixed, both debts and costs. Wills v. Gibson, 7 Pa. 154.

7. Foulk v. Brown, 2 Watts (Pa.) 209; Strohm's Appeal, 23 Pa. 351; Kingman v. Kingman, 121 Mass. 249.

8. Rickert v. Geistwite, 1 Pittsb. (Pa.) 153.

9. Galbraith v. Galbraith, 6 Watts (Pa.) 112; Ankeny v. Penrose, 18 Pa. 190; Allen v. Sawyer, 2 P. & W. (Pa.) 325.

10. McGuesney v. Hiester, 33 Pa. 435; St. Mary's Church v. Miles, 1 Whart. (Pa.) 229; or rent reserved by deed, Bailey v. Jackson, 16 Johns. (N. Y.) 210, 8 Am. Dec. 309; Lyon v. Odell, 65 N. Y. 28.

11. McLaughlin v. Kain, 45 Pa. 113; Woodburn v. Farmers', etc., Bank, 5 W. & S. (Pa.) 447. Municipal assessments are presumed to have been paid by lapse of twenty years. *Ex parte* Serrill, 9 Hun (N. Y.) 283; Fisher v. New York, 6 id. 64; *Ex parte* Striker, 71 N. Y. 603. Such assessments are treated as in the nature of judgments, City of New York v. Colgate, 12 N. Y. 140. But in New York this species of assessments is confirmed by the courts, and for that reason properly partake of the nature of judgments; but when they are not required to be so affirmed, they cannot in any sense be said to have any of the attributes of a judgment.

12. Pryor v. Wood, 31 Pa. 142.

presumption attaches to every species of specialty claim.[13] But it must be borne in mind that, unless the instrument or obligation creates a present right of action, the presumption, like the statute, only attaches from the time when the right of action accrued. But being a common-law presumption, even though it is also made so by statute, it may be set up by a defendant, whether he is a resident of the State in which the action is brought or not; [14] the distinction being, that where the statutory presumption is relied upon it should be pleaded, while the common-law presumption is a mere matter of evidence, and may be urged at the trial without having been pleaded. There is still another distinction between a presumption raised by the law and one that is prescribed by the statute; and that is, that the latter is absolute, unless made otherwise in terms, while the former is dependent upon a variety of circumstances which (as we have seen) may entirely destroy its force. In New York [15] the presumption may be repelled by proof of payment of some part, or by a written acknowledgment. In North Carolina,[16] the presumption is reduced to ten years, except as to mortgages, which is thirteen years, subject to the same rules as exist at common law. In Arkansas [17] similar provisions exist, except that payment of part, or a written acknowledgment, is necessary to remove the presumption; so also in Missouri,[18] except that the period is twenty years. In England, by Stat. 3 & 4 Wm. IV., c. 42, specialties are brought within the statute, and are barred in ten years.

§ 173. Covenants—Quiet enjoyment, etc.

There is often a question as to covenants of a more or less continuous nature, such as covenants for title and quiet enjoyment, as to how far in those States where the statute embraces specialties they are within the statute. In an English case,[19] arising under the

13. Higgs v. Stimmel, 3 P. & W. (Pa.) 115.

14. Sanderson v. Olmsted, 1 Chand. (Wis.) 190; 1 Pin. (Wis.) 224.

15. See Appendix.

16. See Appendix.

17. See Appendix.

18. See Appendix.

19. Spear v. Green, L. R. 9 Ex. 99.

statute 3 & 4 Wm. IV., Kelly, C. B.,[20] said: "There is a distinction between the covenant for title and the covenant for quiet enjoyment. The covenant for title is broken by the existence of an adverse title in another, as in this case, by a lease, its mere existence rendering the land of less value.[21] The covenant for quiet enjoyment is broken only when the covenantee is disturbed, as in this case by the entry into the mine and the taking the fragments of coal in 1848.[22] The deed of purchase having conveyed

20. Id. 116. The judgment of the majority of the court in the case was different from that of the Chief Baron but principally upon different grounds. The facts of the case sufficiently appear from the judgment. Banning on Limitations, 177-187.

21. If the grantor was not seised, the covenant of seisin is immediately broken. Greenby v. Wilcocks, 2 Johns. (N. Y.) 1, 3 Am. Dec. 379; Bingham v. Weiderwax, 1 N. Y. 509; Hamilton v. Wilson, 4 Johns. (N. Y.) 72, 4 Am. Dec. 253; Grannis v. Clark, 8 Cow. (N. Y.) 36; M'Carty v. Leggett, 3 Hill (N. Y.) 134; Scantlin v. Allison, 12 Kan. 85; Coleman v. Lyman, 42 Ind. 289; Dale v. Shively, 8 Kan. 276; Salmon v. Vallejo, 41 Cal. 481. But it was held in Scott v. Twiss, 4 Neb. 133, that if the grantor was in exclusive possession under claim of title, the covenant of seisin is not broken until the purchaser or those claiming under him are evicted by title paramount. To constitute a breach, the person claiming title must have had a valid right thereto. Jerald v. Elly, 51 Iowa 321, 1 N. W. 639.

The covenants of waranty and of quiet enjoyment being prospective, an actual ouster or evidence is necessary to constitute a breach of them as ground for an action; but the covenants of seisin, of a right to convey, and of freedom from incumbrances are personal and unassignable covenants, which are broken as soon as the deed is made, if they are not true; and as a cause of action accrues at once, limitation then begins to run. Howard v. Maitland, 11 Q. B. D. 695; Carr v. Dooley, 119 Mass. 294; Linton v. Allen, 154 Mass. 432, 28 N. E. 780; Montgomery v. Reed, 69 Me. 510; Jewett v. Fisher, 9 Kan. App. 630, 58 Pac. 1023; Loring v. Groomer, 142 Mo. 1, 43 S. W. 647.

In New York, the covenant of quiet enjoyment is not broken until there is an eviction, actual or constructive, from the premises conveyed, or some part thereof; but when there is an outstanding title to an easement in the premises conveyed, materially interfering with the possession and use of some portion thereof, the covenant is broken although there is not a technical physical ouster. Shriver v. Smith, 100 N. Y. 471, 477, 3 N. E. 675, 53 Am. Rep. 224. See 4 Kent's Com. (14th ed.) 471.

22. As illustrative of the time when the statute begins to run for breaches of a covenant for quiet enjoyment, it may not be amiss to give instances of acts which constitute a breach. Breaches of this covenant may occur either by a molestation arising from a suit at law or in equity relating to

to Jameson, and afterwards to the plaintiff, the mines under the

the title or possession, or by any act by which the lessee is disturbed in the possession of the premises. Of the first kind is a recovery by ejectment by a person having a lawful title, or any other suit by which the peaceable occupation of the premises is prevented. Thus, a covenant in a lease that the lessee should quietly enjoy the estate discharged from taxes is broken by a suit for them, although commenced after the expiration of the term. Laming v. Laming, Cro. Eliz. 316. But where the breach assigned was, "that the defendant had exhibited a bill in chancery against him for ploughing meadow, and obtained an injunction, which had been dissolved with costs," it was held on demurrer to be no breach of covenant; for the covenant was for quiet enjoyment, and this was a suit for waste. Morgan v. Hunt, 2 Vent. 215. But a suit in equity that involves the title and estate operates as a breach. Coulston v. Carr, Cro. Eliz. 847; Lanning v. Lovering, id. 916; Morgan v. Hunt, 2 Vent. 213; Dowdenay v. Oland, Cro. Eliz. 768; Ashton v. Martyn, 2 Keb. 268. So does a recovery in ejectment. Coble v. Wellborn, 13 N. C. (2 Dev. L.) 388; Mitchell v. Warner, 5 Conn. 497, 522. But *contra*, and holding that it does not constitute a breach, see Kerr v. Shaw, 13 Johns. (N. Y.) 236. Or in trespass where the title is involved. Coble v. Wellborn, *supra*, But *contra*, see Webb v. Alexander, 7 Wend. (N. Y.) 281. But the language of the covenant must be looked to, and it may be such that a mere judgment in an action involving the title will not operate as a breach. Thus if the covenant is that "the lessee shall enjoy the premises without lawful eviction" (Anonymous, 3 Leon, 71, pl. 100), it has been held that a bill in equity involving the title, brought against the lessor alone, does not operate as a breach. See also Selby v. Chute, 1 Rol. Ab. 430, pl. 15. The covenant may be either general or qualified; but in either case it runs with the land. Campbell v. Lewis, 8 Taunt. 715; Noke v. Awder, Cro. Eliz. 373. Even though the language of the covenants is that, "subject to the payment of the rent and the performance of the covenants," the lessee shall quietly enjoy, yet such words do not constitute a condition precedent, and a recovery may be had by the lessee for a breach of the covenant, although he has not paid the rent or performed his covenants. Dawson v. Dyer, 5 B. & Ad. 584; Allen v. Babbington, 1 Sid. 280; Hayes v. Bickerstaff, 2 Mod. 34; Anonymous, 2 Show. 202; Wakeman v. Waker, 1 Vent. 294. Any description of annoyance to the occupation of the premises which prevents the lessee from enjoying his property in so ample a manner as he is entitled to do by the terms of the lease, amounts to a breach of the covenant for quiet enjoyment of the second sort. Thus, if a man covenants that he will not interrupt the covenantee in the enjoyment of premises, the erection of a gate which intercepts them is a breach of the covenant, although he had a right to erect it. Andrews v. Paradise, 8 Mod. 318. A mere demand of rent by a person having a superior title does not amount to a breach, nor does any act of the lessor that merely amounts to a trespass. There

land, as well as the surface, the covenant of the defendant was that

must be either an actual or constructive eviction. Cowan v. Silliman, 15 N. C. (4 Dev. L.) 46; City of New York v. Mabie, 13 N. Y. 151, 64 Am. Dec. 538; Vatel v. Herner, 1 Hilt. (N. Y. C. P.) 149; Lounsbery v. Snyder, 31 N. Y. 514. Nor does an unlawful act of another disturbing the tenant's possession amount to a breach. There must be a rightful interruption by a paramount title. Rantin v. Robertson, 2 Strobh. (S. C.) 366. But there may be an eviction and a consequent breach without a judgment. Coble v. Wellborn, 13 N. C. (2 Dev. L.) 388; Stewart v. Drake, 9 N. J. Law 139; Grist v. Hodges, 14 N. C. (3 Dev. L.) 198. Such a covenant may be said to be broken whenever there has been an involuntary loss of possession by the hostile assertion of an irresistible title, whether with or without judgment, or whether an actual dispossession has transpired or not. It is enough if the title is paramount, and is asserted so that the tenant must either quit possession or yield to it. McGary v. Hastings, 39 Cal. 360, 2 Am. Rep. 456. So if, after a demise of mines containing the usual covenant for quiet enjoyment, the lessor digs a quarry over the mines, and makes holes, through which water percolates and escapes into the mines, although he had a legal right to work the quarry, his doing so in such a manner amounts to a breach of the covenant for quiet enjoyment of the mines. Shaw v. Stenton, 2 H. & N. 858. An action on the covenant for quiet enjoyment may be maintained for the disturbance of a way of necessity, Morris v. Edgington, 3 Taunt. 24; or of a way by grant from the covenantor, Pomfret v. Ricroft, 1 Saund. 322. It must be remembered, however, that the act done must be in the assertion of title, and not a mere tortious act for which an action of trespass might be maintained. Sedden v. Senate, 13 East 72.

A covenant for quiet enjoyment does not oblige the lessor to rebuild or repair in case the buildings are destroyed or injured by fire, tempest, or otherwise, as there is no implied obligation upon a landlord to keep the premises tenantable. Brown v. Quilter, Ambler 620. The covenant only extends to lawful interuptions, whether the word "lawful" is used in the covenant or not. Foster v. Pierson, 4 T. R. 617; Dudley v. Folliot, 3 id. 584; Major v. Grigg, 2 Mod. 213. And an allegation of a breach that does not show an interruption by title is bad. Rantin v. Robertson, 2 Strobh. (S. C.) 366; City of New York v. Mabie, 13 N. Y. 151, 64 Amer. Dec. 538; Perry v. Edwards, 1 Strange 400; Nicholas v. Pullin, 1 Lev. 83; Holmes v. Seller, 3 id. 305; Bailey v. Hughes, W. Jo. 242; Hamond v. Dod, Cro. Car. 5; Anonymous, Lofft, 460; Chanudflower v. Prestley, Yelv. 30. General covenants for quiet enjoyment are not broken by a tortious eviction, but by an eviction by title only. Hayes v. Bickerstaff, Vaughan, 118; Hunt v. Allen, Winch. 25; Tisdale v. Essex, Hob. 35. And, in an action for a breach of such a covenant, the plaintiff's declaration must set up an eviction by title paramount. Walton v. Hele, 2 Saund. 177; Lanning v. Lovering, Cro. Eliz. 916; Nokes' Case, 4 Coke 80 *b;* Bloxam v. Walker, Freem. 124; Fos-

he had good title to the mines. That covenant, I think, was broken

ter v. Mapes, Cro. Eliz. 212; Brocking v. Cham, Cro. Jac. 425; Hamond v. Dod, Cro. Car. 5; Cowper v. Pollard, W. Jo. 197.

But a disturbance of the lessee by the lessor himself is not regarded with the same lenity as an eviction by a stranger; it being clear that the lessor exposes himself to an action on his covenant, although he enters wrongfully, notwithstanding the covenant provides against lawful evictions only. Corus v. ——, Cro. Eliz. 544; Andrew's Case, id. 214; Penning v. Plat, Cro. Jac. 383; Pemberton v. Platt, 1 Rol. 267; Cave v. Brookesby, W. Jo. 360; Crosse v. Young, 2 Show. 425; Lloyd v. Tomkies, 1 T. R. 671. And see Seaman v. Browning, 1 Leon. 157. For, in such a case, the court will not consider the word "lawful;" nor drive the plaintiff to his action of trespass, when by the general implied covenant in law the lessor has engaged not to avoid his own deed, either by a rightful or tortious entry. Crosse v. Young, *supra;* Lloyd v. Tompkies, *supra.* Indeed, it would hardly be consistent with reason to allow the lessor to defeat the tenancy by pleading his own wrong.

So, if a lessor covenants for quiet enjoyment against himself and his executors, the lessee, on eviction by the executor, need not show that the executor entered by title, any more than in the case of the lessor himself. Forte v. Vine, 2 Rol. 21; Ratcliff v. ——, 1 Bl. & Gold. 80.

To support an action against the lessor, it is not necessary that he should have a title to enter; it is sufficient if he enters under a claim of one. Lloyd v. Tomkies, 1 T. R. 671. And in the case just cited, where a vendor prevented a purchaser from enjoying a new appurtenance to the house sold, by locking it up against the purchaser's will, the court held that this was such an assertion of right as to render the lessor liable to an action. The covenant goes to the possession, and not to the title, and is not broken by a failure of the lessor's title merely. Parker v. Dunn, 47 N. C. (2 Jones L.) 203; Waldron v. M'Carty, 3 Johns. (N. Y.) 471; Howard v. Doolittle, 10 N. Y. Super. Ct. (3 Duer.) 464; Whitbeck v. Cook, 15 Johns. (N. Y.) 483, 545, 8 Am. Dec. 272; Boothby v. Hathaway, 20 Me. 251; Webb v. Alexander, 7 Wend. (N. Y.) 281; Krotz v. Carpenter, 5 Johns. (N. Y.) 120; Van Slyck v. Kimball, 8 id. 198; Grist v. Hodges, 14 N. C. (3 Dev. L.) 198; Coble v. Wellburn, 13 N. C. (2 Dev.) 388. And it has been held that a mere recovery in ejectment does not have that effect. Kerr v. Shaw, 13 Johns. (N. Y.) 236. Or in trespass as a person claiming title to the land. Webb v. Alexander, *supra.* But the better rule would seem to be that recovery against the lessor in any action either at law or in equity involving his title or estate, and affecting his immediate right of possession, operates as a breach of the ordinary covenant for quiet enjoyment. Martin v. Martin, 12 N. C. (1 Dev. L.) 413; 2 Platt on Leases, 289, and cases cited. But in order to constitute a breach there must be a union of acts of disturbance and title, and a disturbance by a mere intruder does not create a breach. Hoppes v. Cheek, 21 Ark. 585; Rantin v. Robertson, 2 Strobh.

as soon as it was made, by reason of his having before become party

(S. C.) 366. And the eviction and disturbance must be under rights or a title existing at the time when the lease was made, and not under rights subsequently acquired. Ellis v. Welch, 6 Mass. 246, 4 Am. Dec. 122. The rule is, as expressed in Knapp v. Town of Marlboro, 34 Vt. 235, that, to sustain an action for the breach of a covenant for quiet enjoyment, it is necessary for the plaintiff to prove that he was evicted by a person who had a lawful and paramount title, existing before or at the time when the covenant was entered into, as the covenant relates only to the acts of those claiming title and to rights existing at the time it was entered into. See also Grist v. Hodges, 14 N. C. (3 Dev. L.) 198. A mere demand of possession by a person having title does not operate as a breach of this covenant. Cowan v. Silliman, 15 N. C. (4 Dev. L.) 46. Nor does an eviction from a part of the premises under a statute, or municipal authority. Frost v. Earnest, 4 Whart. (Pa.) 86.

An accidental trespass on the premises in hunting, Seddon v. Senate, 13 East 72, or an entry for the purpose of beating the lessee, would not have that effect. Penn v. Glover, Cro. Eliz. 421. If the lessor covenants for quiet enjoyment against the acts of a person particularly specified, a disturbance by that person will amount to a breach, whether it is a rightful or tortious disturbance. Foster v. Mapes, Cro. Eliz. 212; Tisdale v. Essex, Hob. 35; Hill v. Browne, Freem. 142; Perry v. Edwards, 1 Stra. 400; Nash v. Palmer, 5 M. &. S. 374; Fowle v. Welsh, 1 B. & C. 29. But see Hayes v. Bickerstaff, Vaugh. 118. Where one covenanted for quiet enjoyment without interruption by any person "having or claiming, or pretending to have or claim," any right of common, and a breach was assigned, alleging an interruption by one J. B., who claimed common, etc., it was held that the plaintiff need not show any title in J. B., for the covenant expressly extended not only to those who had right, but to those who claimed or pretended to a right; and, therefore, whether the claim were rightful or groundless, the covenantor was liable. Southgate v. Chaplin, 10 Mod. 383; Perry v. Edwards, Stra. 400.

If a general covenant for quiet enjoyment contains an exception of particular persons, the exception will be construed strictly, so as not to include any others than those expressly named. Woodroff v. Greenwood, Cro. Eliz. 518. A covenant for the quiet enjoyment of certain premises demised, excepting from the demise to one E. K. a certain close, parcel thereof, does not amount to a covenant for quiet enjoyment against an interruption by E. K. as to the lands actually comprised in the lease. Ibid; Rashleigh v. Williams, 2 Vent. 61.

In assigning a breach of a covenant for quiet enjoyment, where the interruption is the act of a third party, against whom the covenant has not specifically provided, it is not sufficient to allege that having lawful right and title he entered, without alleging also that he had such lawful title before or at the time of the date of the lease to the plaintiff; for possibly he might have derived title

to a lease of the mines, which lease was then in force.[23] It was a

from the plaintiff himself. Kirby v. Hanksaker, Cro. Jac. 315; Wooten v. Hele, 2 Saund. 177; Proctor v. Newton, 1 Vent. 184; Norman v. Foster, 1 Mod. 101; Forte v. Vine, 2 Rol. 21; Skinner v. Kilbys, 1 Show. 70; Anon., 2 Vent. 46; Rashleigh v. Williams, 2 Vent. 61; Buckley v. Williams, 3 Lev. 325; Jordan v. Twells, Cartemp. Hard. 171; Foster v. Pierson, 4 T. R. 617; Hodgson v. East India Co., 8 T. R. 278; Campbell v. Lewis, 3 B. & Ald. 392. And see Noble v. King, 1 H. Bl. 34; Brookes v. Humphreys, 5 Bing. N. C. 55; Fraser v. Skey, 2 Chit. 646. It is not necessary, however, for the declaration to show what title he had. A different rule would impose insuperable difficulties on the plaintiff, a knowledge of the title being only to be acquired by inspection of the deeds, to which he could not have access. Proctor v. Newton, *supra;* Foster v. Pierson, *supra;* Hodgson v. East India Co., *supra.* But where the interruption is by the lessor himself, Corus v. ——, Cro. Eliz. 544, or by a person against whose acts the covenant has specially provided, it is sufficient to allege an entry by him, without stating under what title or pretense, or whether by right or wrong, Foster v. Mapes, *supra.* Some particular act, however, by which the plaintiff is interrupted must be shown, otherwise the breach will not be well assigned. Anon., Com. 228. In an action on a covenant that the lessor is seised in fee, a breach may be assigned in terms as general as the covenant, viz., that he was not seised in fee, without showing that another was so seised, nor why the defendant was not so seised. Muscot v. Ballet, Cro. Jac. 369; Glinister v. Audley, T. Raym. 14; Glimston v. Audly, 1 Keb. 58. So, on a covenant that the lessor has good right to demise, the lessee may assign as a breach that he had not good right, without showing in whom the right was vested. Bradshaw's Case, 9 Coke 60 *b;* Salman v. Bradshaw, Cro. Jac. 304; Lancashire v. Glover, 2 Show. 460.

In an action on a covenant for quiet enjoyment, an allegation, as a breach, that the plaintiff (lessee) entered and was evicted by the defendant (lessor), is not supported by proof that he made a demand of possession and was refused, an explusion, which is a putting out, not having taken place; for a party who comes to claim, but has never entered, cannot be expelled. The breach is not for expelling, but for not letting in. Hawkes v. Orton, 5 Ad. & El. 367; Warn v. Bickford, 9 Price 43. The ordinary covenant, by the lessor, for quiet enjoyment as against any person claiming by, from, or under him, is broken by an eviction of the tenant by the lessor's widow entitled under a conveyance taken by the lessor to the use of himself and his wife. Butler v. Swinnerton, Cro. Jac. 657. Also, by an eviction by a person claiming under a prior appointment by the covenantor and another person. Calvert v. Sebright, 15 Beav. 156. But a distress for arrears of land-tax due from the lessor at the time of the demise will not operate as a breach. Stanley v. Hayes, 3 Q. B. 105. The lessee of a house and garden, forming part of a large area of building ground, is not entitled under this covenant to restrain the lessor or persons claim-

covenant running with the land, and a continuing covenant, and

ing under him from building on the adjoining land so as to obstruct the free access of light and air to the garden. Potts v. Smith, L. R. 6 Eq. 311. When contained in a lease of the exclusive right of shooting and sporting over a farm, this covenant does not hinder the tenant of the farm from using the land in the ordinary way, or from destroying furze and underwood in the reasonable use of the land as a farm; and the lessor will not be liable for wrongful acts committed by such tenant contrary to the reservation of his landlord. Jeffryes v. Evans, 19 C. B. N. S. 246. See Newton v. Wilmot, 8 M. & W. 711. Under a covenant in the form above mentioned contained in a lease of a stream of water excepting so much as should be sufficient for the supply of persons with whom the lessor should have already contracted, diversions occasioned by contracts made previously to the demise will not constitute breaches. Blackford v. Plymouth, 3 Bing. N. C. 691. Where the covenant provides that the lessee shall quietly hold and enjoy the premises for and during the said term, the last words must be taken to refer to the term which the lessor assumed to grant by the lease, and not to the term which he had actually had power to grant. Evans v. Vaughan, 4 B. & C. 261, 268.

A general covenant for quiet enjoyment extends only to the acts of persons claiming under a lawful title. Dudley v. Folliott, 3 T. R. 584. For the law will never adjudge that a lessor covenants against the wrongful acts of strangers, except his covenant is express to that purpose. Wotton v. Hele, 2 Wms. Saund. 178, note (8). The construction, however, is different where an individual is named; for there the covenantor is presumed to know the person against whose acts he is content to covenant, and may therefore reasonably be expected to stipulate against any disturbance from him, whether by lawful title or otherwise. Lord Ellenborough, C. J., in Nash v. Palmer, 5 M. & S. 387; Fowle v. Welsh, 1 B. & C. 29.

Under a general covenant for quiet enjoyment contained in the lease of a coal mine the working of iron-stone lying between the surface and the demised coal in such a manner as to interrupt the lessee in his occupation of the mine, will constitute a breach. Shaw v. Stenton, 2 H. & N. 858.

Under a covenant by the lessor, in an underlease, that the lessee shall hold the premises without any lawful eviction, etc., by the lessor, or any persons whomsoever claiming by, from, under or in trust for her, or by or through her acts, means, right, etc., an eviction of the underlessee by the original lessor for a forfeiture incurred by the use of the premises as a shop, contrary to a covenant in the original lease, of which the underlessee had not been informed, is not an eviction by means of the lessor within the meaning of the covenant. Spencer v. Marriott, 1 B. & C. 457. See Woodhouse v. Jenkins, 9 Bing. 431. Under a covenant that the tenant, paying the rent and performing the covenants, shall quietly enjoy, the payment of rent is not a condition precedent to the performance of the covenant for quiet enjoyment. Daw-

a breach of it by means of the lease was a continuing breach,[24] and although the plaintiff might have sued upon it upon his becoming possessed, and might have recovered the damages he had sustained (if any) by reason of the breach, he was not bound to do so; and I am of the opinion that he continued entitled to sue for any damage afterwards sustained whenever any such should have resulted from the breach; and, finally, that if the statute of limitations apply at all to covenants for title, the time of limitation does not necessarily begin to run from the making of the covenant,

son v. Dyer, 5 B. & Ad. 584. A clause in a deed, whereby the lessor "for himself, his heirs and assigns, the premises unto the lessee, his executors, administrators, and assigns, under the rent, covenants, etc., before expressed, against all persons whatsoever lawfully claiming the same, shall and will, during the term, warrant and defend," operates as an express covenant for quiet enjoyment during the whole term granted by the lease. Williams v. Burrell, 1 C. B. 402.

23. Covenants of this character are broken by the existence of any incumbrance upon the land the instant the deed or lease is delivered. Seitzinger v. Weaver, 1 Rawle (Pa.) 377; Knepper v. Kurtz, 58 Pa. 480; Bingham v. Weiderwax, 1 N. Y. 509; Stewart v. Drake, 21 N. J. Law 139; Hamilton v. Wilson, 4 Johns. (N. Y.) 72, 4 Am. Dec. 253; M'Carty v. Leggett, 3 Hill (N. Y.) 134; Mott v. Palmer, 1 N. Y. 564; Chapman v. Holmes, 10 N. J. Law 20; Garrison v. Sandford, 22 id. 261. But if a covenant of seisin is qualified by subsequent covenants in the deeds, as if the grantor covenants generally that he is well seised, etc., and warrants the premises to the grantee, etc., "against all claims and demands except the lord of the soil," both covenants must be construed together, and the last qualifies the first, so that the title of the lord of the soil does not operate as a breach of the first covenant. Cole v. Hawes, 2 Johns. Cas. (N. Y.) 203.

24. But it is generally held that a general covenant of title in a deed does not run with the lands, because being broken by the delivery of the deed or lease in which it is contained, it is *instanter* converted into a chose in action, which is not assignable. Blydenburgh v. Cotheal, 8 N. Y. Super. Ct. (1 Duer.) 176; Harsha v. Reid, 45 N. Y. 415; Mirick v. Bashford, 38 Barb. (N. Y.) 191; Carter v. Denman, 23 N. J. Law 260; Lot v. Thomas, 2 id. 260. But such a covenant in a lease stands upon a different footing. In Maine by statute, and in Missouri, Dickson and Gautt v. Desire's Adm'r, 23 Mo. 151, 66 Am. Dec. 661; Indiana, Martin v. Baker, 5 Blackf. (Ind.) 232; and in Ohio, Devore v. Sunderland, 17 Ohio 52, 49 Am. Dec. 442, such covenants are treated as continuous, fully sustaining the doctrine of Kingdom v. Nottle, 1 M. & S. 355, and 4 id. 53.

or of a lease which is a breach of the covenant, and that it is no bar as long as the lease continues, and any damage nominal or substantial is or may be sustained.[25] I do not understand it to be questioned that the conveyances passed the mines as well as the land to the plaintiff, nor that a covenant for title runs with the land, nor therefore that the plaintiff is entitled to the benefit of this covenant, nor that it was broken by the making of the lease. And I am of opinion that he is entitled to sue upon it now, upon the ground that the existence of the lease, until it expired in 1865, was an incumbrance upon the land, and rendered it of less value than if it had not existed; and, further, that it made the entry of the lessees lawful and so enabled them to take the fire-clay from the mine; and, although they themselves and not the defendant are liable to the plaintiff for the value of the fire-clay taken, it is a damage to the plaintiff that he is put to his action against them, and may incur extra costs in such action which he could not have been exposed to but for the right of entry conferred upon them by the defendant.[26] I am also of opinion that the entry into the mine, and the taking the fragments of coal in 1848 by virtue of the lease, which was within the twenty years, was a breach of the covenant for quiet enjoyment.

"The case of Kingdon v. Nottle,[27] upon a covenant for title, and

25. It would be an exceedingly arsh rule that would compel a tenant, who is in the quiet enjoyment of remises, under a lease for a long erm, to bring an action within twenty ears, or any shorter term, for a reach of such a covenant, where his lamages would be only nominal, and hus preclude himself from any remdy, if by an actual eviction, at a ater period, he sustained heavy damges; and the courts appear to be nclined latterly, to hold that this a continuous covenant, and runs ith the land. See Martin v. Baker, *upra;* Devore v. Sunderland, *supra;* Dickson & Gautt v. Desire's Adm'r, *supra;* Bennett v. Waller, 23 Ill. 97.

26. A covenant against incumbrances is continuous, but only nominal damage can be recovered for its breach until the covenantee has been actually damnified thereby. Reading v. Gary, 37 N. Y. Super. Ct. (5 J. & S.) 79; Standard v. Eldridge, 16 Johns. (N. Y.) 254; De Forest v. Leete, 16 id. 122; Hall v. Dean, 13 id. 105; Funk v. Voneida, 11 S. & R. (Pa.) 109; Cathcart v. Bowman, 5 Pa. 317.

27. 1 M. & S. 355, 4 id. 53. See also Backhouse v. Bonomi, 9 H. L.

King v. Jones,[28] upon a covenant for further assurance, are authorities to show that these covenants are continuing covenants and the breaches of them continuing breaches, and that a right of action accrues *toties quoties* when and as often as damage actually arises from the breach of either covenant.[29]

"It is true when these cases were decided there was no statute of limitations expressly taking away the right to sue upon a covenant after a certain number of years from the breach. But the language of the statute is that no action shall be brought but within twenty years after the action has accrued; and we have only to consider the real nature of the covenant for title, and of the various kinds of breaches of it, which may be committed, to see that the statute of limitations is wholly inapplicable to such breaches, except where the right of action is upon an eviction of the whole property conveyed, so that there is no land with which the covenant may run and nothing left upon which the covenant can operate.[30] In such a case the statute may apply, and from such an eviction the time may begin to run."

C. 503; E. B. & E. 654. See also Bennett v. Waller, 23 Ill. 97.

28. 5 Taunt. 418; 4 M. & S. 188.

29. Where the grantor or lessor was in possession at the time the instrument was delivered, and the grantee or lessee enters in pursuance of the deed or lease, the covenant for title runs with the land, and the grantor or lessor is answerable thereon to the assignee of the grantee or lessee. Slater v. Rawson, 47 Mass. (6 Metc.) 439. The same rule is adopted as to a covenant against incumbrances where it existed at the time of the conveyance and continued at the time of the assignment, so as to continually enlarge the damages, and the assignee is entitled to sue for damages subsequent to the assignment. Sprague v. Baker, 17 Mass. 589. But where the grantor or lessor is not in possession, the covenant is broken at once, and does not run with the land. Bartholomew v. Candee, 31 Mass. (14 Pick.) 167. A covenant for further assurance runs with the land. Bennett v. Waller, 23 Ill. 97.

30. The covenant being continuous, each breach constitutes a separate cause of action, and, if within the statute, it should apply only to breaches occurring more than the statutory period before action brought; but the great majority of cases in this country hold that the covenant of seisin does not run with the land; that it is *in praesenti*, and, being broken, if at all, when the deed is delivered, the claim for damages thereby becomes personal in its nature to the grantee, and is not transferred by a coveyance to a subsequent grantee. But in Iowa, where deeds

Previously to this statute, as before stated, a specialty debt was presumed to have been paid at the end of twenty years. And it seems that even in England, if the statute, through some defect in pleading, cannot be taken advantage of, yet the fact of payment may still be presumed.[31]

have been reduced to forms of great simplicity, the English doctrine, as stated in the text, has been fully adopted. A contrary rule operates oppressively in all cases where the land has been conveyed either to the grantee or subsequent purchaser, and legislative intervention may be needed to correct the evils resulting from the doctrine so generally adopted here. The purchaser, if evicted, should receive the indemnity of the covenant; being the first and only sufferer in every instance, except where he has not paid for the land, and for the grantee under the deed, who has sold and received his pay for the land, to recover damages under this covenant, is unjust. If there is a covenant of warranty in the first grantor's deed, then he is liable over to his grantee under this covenant; but if there is no such covenant, then a party who has no interest can recover damages where he has sustained none. Schofield v. Iowa Homestead Co., 32 Iowa 317, 7 Am. Rep. 197. In such a case the rule of damages being usually the consideration money and interest (Vail's Adm'r v. Junction R. Co., 13 Ohio Dec. 728, 1 Cinc. (Ohio) 317), a party can profit at the expense of others by a rule of law that is both unwise and unjust. Richard v. Bent, 59 Ill. 38, 14 Am. Rep. 1. In Indiana, Massachusetts, South Carolina, Ohio, and Missouri, the courts have applied the doctrine stated in the text. Martin v. Baker, 5 Blackf. (Ind.) 282; Devore v. Sunderland, 17 Ohio 52; Dickson & Gautt v. Desire's Adm'r, 23 Mo. 151; M'Crady's Ex'rs v. Brisbane, 1 Nott & McCord (S. C.) 104, 9 Am. Dec. 676.

31. Best on Presumptions, 188. The rule as to mortgages is, that, where the mortgagee has never entered under the mortgage, and there has been no payment of interest, nor demand thereof, nor any admission of the mortgagee as a subsisting lien, within twenty years, the mortgage is presumed satisfied. Dunham v. Minard, 4 Paige (N. Y.) 441; Blethen v. Dwinal, 35 Me. 556; Chick v. Rollins, 44 Me. 104; Boyd & Hance v. Harris, 2 Md. Ch. 210; Cheever v. Perley, 93 Mass. (11 Allen) 584; Wanmaker v. Van Buskirk, 1 N. J. Eq. 685; Evans v. Huffman, 5 id. 354; Collins v. Torry, 7 Johns. (N. Y.) 278, 5 Am. Dec. 273; Jackson v. Hudson, 3 id. 375; Giles v. Baremore, 5 Johns. (N. Y.) Ch. 545. See also Jackson v. Pratt, 10 Johns. (N. Y.) 381; Jackson v. Delancey, 11 id. 365; Belmont v. O'Brien, 12 N. Y. 394. The same rule applies to all sealed instruments for the payment of money. A mortgage, if satisfied in equity, may be presumed satisfied at law, ordered to be canceled. Kellogg v. Wood, 4 Paige (N. Y.) 578.

§ 174. Covenants of warranty, against incumbrances, etc.

Covenants running with the land are such as relate to and concern the land, and pass with it where there is a privity of estate. Of this class are covenants of warranty, which are in effect the same as those for quiet enjoyment, and extend to the possession as well as the title, so that any disturbance of the free and uninterrupted use of the premises under a superior right, even without an actual expulsion therefrom, is in law an eviction and a breach of the covenant.[32] There can be no breach of this covenant until there is an actual eviction either from the whole or some part of the premises,[33] and the eviction must be stated in the declaration.[34] Consequently neither the statute, the common law, nor statutory presumption attaches to actions upon this covenant until the grantee or lessee is evicted from some part of the premises. But covenants against incumbrances are said to be broken as soon as the deed is delivered, if the grantor or his predecessors in the title had previously mortgaged or incumbered the same,[35] and, although the mortgage is not due, nominal damages are recoverable;[36] but, according to the English doctrine and some American cases, the grantee may wait until the mortgage becomes due, and neither the statute nor the presumption from lapse of time will attach to the covenant for actual damages until that time.[37] But little difficulty will be experienced in determining when the stat-

32. Rea v. Minkler, 5 Lans. (N. Y.) 196; Withy v. Mumford, 5 Cow. (N. Y.) 137; Suydam v. Jones, 10 Wend. (N. Y.) 180.

33. Cowdrey v. Coit, 44 N. Y. 382, 4 Am. Rep. 690; Kent v. Welch, 7 Johns. (N. Y.) 258; Knepper v. Kurtz, 58 Pa. 480; Patton v. McFarlane, 3 P. & W. (Pa.) 419; Flowers v. Foreman, 64 U. S. (23 How.) 132, 16 L. Ed. 405.

34. Clarke v. M'Anulty, 3 Serg. & R. (Pa.) 364; Paul v. Witman, 3 W. & S. (Pa.) 407; West v. Stewart, 7 Pa. 122.

35. Cathcart v. Bowman, 5 Pa. 317.

36. Funk v. Voneida, 11 S. & R. (Pa.) 109.

37. This rule is fully adopted in Richard v. Bent, 59 Ill. 38, 14 Am. Rep. 1. The justice and reason of this doctrine are incontrovertible; but in a great majority of the States a contrary doctrine is held, and the statute attaches to this covenant as soon as the deed is delivered. Chapman v. Kimball, 7 Neb. 399.

ute begins to run upon or the presumption attaches to a covenant, because in all cases it begins to run from the time of a breach thereof; and it is only necessary to ascertain at what time an action could first have been maintained thereon, to determine the period from which the running of the statute began.

Enough has already been stated to show the distinction between continuous covenants and those which are exhausted by a single breach; and this distinction is important and should not be lost sight of.

§ 175. Bonds.

Upon bonds, the statute, in those States where this class of obligations is within it, does not begin to run until there is a breach of condition; and if there are several distinct conditions, it only begins to run upon each condition from the time each was broken;[38] and the same rule prevails as to sureties and principals therein.[39] Upon an indemnity bond the statute does not begin to run until the party to whom it was given has been damnified; and it is doubtful whether the mere fact that a judgment has been obtained against him is sufficient to put the statute in motion. The fact that he has become liable to pay, without payment in fact, is not believed to be sufficient.[40] In an English case,[41] where the plaintiff's declaration was framed upon a bond not setting out a condition, and the defendant pleaded that the cause of action did not accrue within twenty years, and issue was joined thereon, and it appeared at the trial that the bond had been executed more than twenty years before the action was brought, but that it was a *post-obit* bond for the payment of a sum of money after the death of a person who was proved to have died within twenty years, it was held that the

38. Salisbury v. Black's Adm'r, 6 H. & J. (Md.) 293, 14 Am. Dec. 279. See McKim v. Glover, 161 Mass, 418, 37 N. E. 443.

39. Thurston v. Blackiston, 36 Md. 501.

40. Illies v. Fitzgerald, 11 Tex. 417, In Hall's Adm'r v. Creswell, 12 G. & J. (Md.) 36, it was held that the right of action accrued from the time of payment, and consequently that the statute then began to run.

41. Sanders v. Coward, 15 M. & W. 56.

statute did not begin to run until the death of such person, and consequently that the action was seasonably brought. Where acts are, by the terms of a bond, to be done successively in a series of years, a new cause of action arises from each omission to do the act at the proper time; and, if the plaintiff can show any breach within the statutory period, he is entitled to recover for that.[42] If a bond is given, conditioned for the faithful discharge of the duties of a certain office, the statute begins to run in favor of the surety thereon from the time of an actual breach. Thus, where an action was brought upon a bond given by a commissioner to sell real estate, an action accrues against the surety after the lapse of a reasonable time within which the commissioner neglects to pay over the money, and from that time the statute begins to run in the surety's favor.[43]

If no time is fixed within which the condition of a bond is to be performed, but it is left contingent upon the happening of a certain event, the statute does not attach thereto until such event transpires.[44]

Where, however, no time for performance is specified, and performance is not dependent upon any contingency, a right of action begins to run within a reasonable time. Thus, where a bond was conditioned to pay an outstanding mortgage on land bought by the mortgagee, and no time within which payment should be made was fixed in the bond, it was held that a right of action accrued and that the statute began to run at the end of a reasonable time after the mortgagee would be obliged to receive the money.[45] But in such a case it seems that the right of the mortgagor to pay and of the mortgagee to sue for the money arose at once, and there seems to be no reason why the rights of

42. Blair v. Ormond, 20 L. J. Q. B. 452; Amott v. Holden, 22 id. 19. In Keefer v. Zimmerman, 22 Md. 274, it was held no defense to an action for the breach of a covenant that there has been a previous breach upon which the statute has run.

43. Owen v. State, 25 Ind. 107.

44. Sweet v. Irish, 36 Barb. (N. Y.) 467.

45. Gennings v. Norton, 35 Me. 308.

either party should be subjected to any such uncertainty as the rule last stated entails upon them; and in a case where a mortgage was executed, and fixed no time for redemption, it was held that the right to redeem attached at once, and the statute began to run from the execution of the mortgage.[46] Where a covenant fixed no time for payment, but provided for a reference to arbitration in case of any disagreement as to the amount to be paid, it was held that the statute attached to the demand from the date of the covenant, and that the statute of limitations did not begin to run until after the demand made by the obligee's executors after the devisee's death. But if a specific time for performance is named, then the statute attaches at that time.[47] In Maine,[48] where a question arose in an action upon a jail-bond, whether, where there were two distinct breaches of the bond, the statute began to run upon the first breach, so as to bar an action upon the second; the court held that it did, because the amount recoverable upon the first breach would have been the same as for both. But in an action upon a bond where the liability is continuous, and arises for each breach, as upon a bond given to a sheriff by his deputy, conditioned for the faithful performance of his duties as such, the statute only runs from the date of each breach, and a recovery may be had as to breaches not barred, although the statute has run as to others.[49]

In the case of bonds conditioned for the conveyance of real estate, or title bonds as they are called, the statute does not begin to run against a suit by the obligee for a specific performance until a demand for a deed and a refusal by the obligor or some other decisive act of the obligor indicating an intention to claim the land or repudiate the sale;[50] but the statute attaches from the date of the first demand, and a new right cannot be acquired by a new demand.

46. Tucker v. White, 22 N. C. (2 D. & B. Eq.) 289.

47. Wilson v. Wilson, 1 McMull. (S. C.) Eq. 329. And see Smith v. Fiske, 31 Me. 512.

48. Browne v. Houdlette, 10 Me. 399.

49. Austin v. Moore, 48 Mass. (7 Metc.) 116.

50. Yeary v. Cummins, 28 Tex. 91.

§ 176. Effect of acknowledgment of payment on specialties.

In those States where no provision is made by statute relative to specialties, the effect of acknowledgment is thus expressed by Mr. Banning in his work on Limitations:[51] "The principle on which the courts acted previously to the statute we are now considering was this:[52] there was then no statute which prevented a bond creditor coming and claiming his debt at any time; but the courts of law, and the courts of equity following them, held the doctrine of presumption, that after a certain lapse of time payment must be presumed, and when an action was brought on a bond or other specialty, what the courts of law did with respect to a defense founded on a lapse of time was, that after twenty years the judge would direct the jury to presume payment.[53] Of course that presumption, like any other, was capable of being rebutted by evidence, and the court held that evidence of an acknowledgment would be sufficient to rebut the presumption.[54]

51. Page 185. See Blair v. Ormond, 17 Q. B. 423.

52. See Moodie v. Bannister, 4 Drew. 432. See Hart v. Nash, 2 C. M. & R. 337, and Hooper v. Stephens, 4 Ad. & El. 71; Worthington v. Grimsditch, 7 Q. B. 479; Callander v. Howard, 10 C. B. 655; Bealy v. Greenslade, 2 C. 740; and the note in 1 Smith's Lead. Cas. 321, on Whitcomb v. Whiting, 2 Dougl. 652; Lucas v. Jones, 5 Q. B. 949; Gillingham v. Waskett, 13 Price 434; Sanders v. Coward, 15 M. & W. 48, 56; Tuckey v. Hawkins, 4 C. B. 655; Beady v. Greenslade, 2 C. & J. 61; Hollis v. Palmer, 2 Bing. New Cas. 713, and Savile v. Jackson, 13 Price 715.

53. In Jackson v. Pierce, 10 Johns. (N. Y.) 414, where a mortgage had lain dormant from April, 1774, to March, 1802, it was held that, after deducting the period of the American Revolution, the lapse of time was sufficient to afford the presumption of payment. The presumption becomes absolute after the lapse of the period fixed by statute for prescription in analogous cases. If there is no entry or payment of interest, and being a presumption of law, it is in itself conclusive, unless encountered by distinct proof. Whitney v. French, 25 Vt. 663. In Ware's Adm'rs v. Bennett, 18 Tex. 794, a neglect to foreclose a mortgage for four years after it falls due was held not conclusive ground for assuming, in favor of purchasers of the mortgagor's interest, that the mortgage had been paid. See also Appleton v. Edson, 8 Vt. 239.

54. But this presumption is effectually repelled by a payment of interest within the statutory period before action brought, Hughes v. Blackwell, 69 N. C. (6 Jones Eq.) 73; and the admissions of a mortgagor that the mortgage debt is due are evidence

In fact, it was impossible for a debtor against whom an action was brought to ask the court to pronounce that the debt has been paid, when he had himself acknowledged the existence of the debt. It appears, therefore, to be a correct statement that, in the case of a specialty debt, the court could receive in evidence any acknowledgment of the alleged debtor in any shape, even when that acknowledgment was made to a third person, and that it was not necessary that such acknowledgment should amount to a new cause of action."[55]

Where specialties are brought within the statute, and no provision is made for keeping them on foot by an acknowledgment, an acknowledgment can have no effect in suspending the operation of the statute, because the action thereon is not founded upon a promise, but upon an obligation of a higher nature, and in order to keep it on foot the recognition of its validity and continuance must be of as high a character as the instrument creating

to rebut the presumption of payment, especially where it does not appear that the true tenant had an interest before the admissions were made. Frear v. Drinker, 8 Pa. 520.

The presumption of payment, so far as mortgages are concerned, does not apply so long as the possession of the mortgaged premises is in the mortgagee. Crooker v. Jewell, 31 Me. 306.

55. In New Hampshire, in Howard v. Hildreth, 18 N. H. 105, it was held that when a mortgagor has retained possession of mortgaged premises for more than twenty years after the execution of the mortgage, but has acknowledged the debt and paid interest upon it within twenty years there is no presumption that the debt is discharged; and the same has also been held in South Carolina. Wright v. Eaves, 10 Rich. (S. C.) Eq. 582. But in Gould v. White, 26 N. H. 178, it was held that unexplained possession of the mortgaged premises for more than twenty years, may be left to the jury in connection with proof of partial payments and other evidence, as tending to show that the mortgage debt was fully paid. A presumption of payment is not like an actual payment which satisfies the debt as to all the debtors; it operates as a payment only in favor of the party entitled to the benefit of the presumption; and, in case of the lapse of over twenty years from the time when a bond secured by mortgage becomes due, the presumption of payment of the mortgage will not, as to the purchaser and those claiming under him, be repelled by proof of a payment made by the mortgagor after he had conveyed the prmeises to another person. New York L. Ins. & Trust Co. v. Covert, 29 Barb. (N. Y.) 435.

the obligation. Payments, however, as will be seen, may have this effect.[56]

§ 176a(1). Sealed instruments in general—Limitations applicable.

A contract under seal is not governed, in New York, by the six-years statute of limitations.[57] The right to enforce specific performance of a contract under seal acted on by the parties up to within less than twenty years of the commencement of the suit for specific performance is not barred by limitations, in North Carolina.[58] As a general rule, sealed instruments within the limitation statute include all sealed contracts regardless of their nature, and an action on a sealed contract, executed in 1898, to make monthly payments for rent due, is controlled by Wisconsin St. 1898 § 4220, permitting actions on sealed instruments within twenty years after the action accrues.[59] In Virginia, the three-year statute of limitations is inapplicable to an obligation evidenced by a writing under seal.[60] In South Dakota, the distinction between sealed and unsealed instruments is abolished, by statute, except with respect to the period of limitation.[61]

§ 176a(2). What constitutes instrument under seal in general.

A recital in an unsealed instrument that it is under seal makes

56. See Chap. XVIII., Mortgages.

57. City of New York v. Third Ave. R. Co., 87 N. Y. Supp. 584, 42 Misc. Rep. 599, aff'd 101 N. Y. Supp. 1116, 115 App. Div. 899.

An action under Code Civ. Proc., § 1843, to charge an heir at law with liability arising out of a sealed instrument of his ancestor in title, is not, because statutory, limited to six years by § 382, but, founded on the original obligation of the ancestor, is not barred by a less time than would have barred the ancestor. City Equity Co. v. Bodine, 126 N. Y. Supp. 439.

58. Parrott v. Atlantic & N. C. R. Co., 165 N. C. 295, 81 S. E. 348.

59. Mariner v. Wiens, 137 Wis. 637, 119 N. W. 340.

Under St. 1913, §§ 4220, 4221, an agreement under seal by a surety is not barred until twenty years if the cause of action arose in the State or ten years if it arose without the State. John A. Tolman & Co. v. Smith, 159 Wis. 361, 150 N. W. 419.

60. Lurty's Curator v. Lurty, 107 Va. 466, 59 S. E. 404.

61. Gibson v. Allen, 19 S. D. 617, 124 N. W. 275, under Rev. Civ. Code S. D., §§ 58, 1243.

the instrument a sealed one for the purpose of the statute of limitations.[62] The mere attaching of a seal after the signature does not raise the presumptoin that a note is a sealed instrument, unless there be a recognition of the seal in the body of the instrument by some such phrase as "Witness my hand and seal" or "Signed and sealed;" and, in the absence of such circumstances, the seal is regarded merely as surplusage, and the character of the note is not changed.[63] A mortgage reciting, "In witness whereof, the said parties of the first part have hereunto set their hands and seals," and in which the word "seal" follows the name of each mortgagor, is a "sealed instrument" within South Dakota Code Civ. Proc., § 58, permitting an action on such an instrument any time within twenty years.[64] An instrument in the form of a bond, reciting that it was sealed, is not within the Wisconsin six-year statute, but is a sealed instrument, though without scroll or flourish after the names of the signers.[65] Rhode Island Gen. Laws 1896, c. 234, § 4, allowing twenty years for bringing an action on a specialty, and not chapter 288, § 8, allowing one year for bringing suits founded on any penal statute, is the statute of limitations applicable to an action authorized by chap. 180, § 22, to enforce the individual liabil-

62. Slade v. Bennett, 133 App. Div. 666, 118 N. Y. Supp. 278.

63. *In re* Pirie, 198 N. Y. 209, 91 N. E. 587, judg. modified on rehearing 198 N. Y. 209, 91 N. E. 1144, aff'g order 117 N. Y. Supp. 753.

64. Green v. Frick, 25 S. D. 342, 126 N. W. 579.

The words "Witness——hand and seal," at the conclusion of an instrument, followed by the signature of the maker, with the word "Seal" in bracketts annexed to the signature, are equivalent to "Witness my hand and seal," or "Signed and sealed," and the instrument is an instrument under seal, within Georgia Civ. Code 1895, § 3765, limiting the time for an action on an instrument under seal but providing that no instrument shall be considered under seal unless so recited in its body. Anderson v. Peteet, 6 Ga. App. 69, 64 S. E. 284.

65. Oconto County v. MacAllister, 155 Wis. 286, 143 N. W. 702; Oconto County v. Lindgren, 155 Wis. 303, 143 N. W. 707.

Where a guaranty, not sealed, of the performance of a contract, was indorsed on the back of the contract, the guarantor did not thereby adopt the seal to the contract, so as to make his contract of guaranty a contract under seal, and subject to the twenty-year limitation prescribed by Wis. Rev. St. 1898, § 4220. Spenser v. Holman, 113 Wis. 340, 89 N. W. 132.

ity of stockholders for the debts of the corporation in case of non-performance of statutory duties, since the action, though of a penal character, is not an action to enforce a penalty, within the meaning of the words "penal statute," as used in chapter 288.[66]

§ 176a(3). Mortgages.

In New York, where a life tenant paid a mortgage on the property for the protection of her life estate and became subrogated to the rights of the mortgagor, she had twenty years from the time of the final payment in which to foreclose the bond and mortgage, which were under seal.[67] In Arkansas, where a note and mortgage, both under seal, were executed after the act of 1889, the period of limitation is five years.[68] In South Carolina, a mortgage invalid as a legal mortgage through insufficient attestation, but enforceable as an equitable mortgage, is governed by Code Civ. Proc. 1902, § 111, limiting the time to suits on sealed instruments, other than notes or bonds to pay money only to twenty years, and not by the six-year statute.[69] An action to foreclose a mortgage on land in the state is a local proceeding, which cannot be maintained in the courts of any other state, and consequently accrues in the state, although both plaintiff and defendant reside in another state, and the debt secured by the mortgage is made payable there; and such action is not within the Wisconsin statute, limiting to ten years actions upon sealed instruments, accruing without the state.[70]

66. Kilton v. Providence Tool Co., 22 R. I. 605, 48 Atl. 1039.

67. Bonhoff v. Wiehorst, 57 Misc. Rep. 456, 108 N. Y. Supp. 437.

68. Simpson v. Brown-Desnoyers Shoe Co., 70 Ark. 598, 70 S. W. 305.

But where a mortgage executed in 1884 was under seal and contained an express covenant to pay the debt, the period of limitation for foreclosure was ten years from the accrual of the right of action. Livingston v. New England Mortgage Security Co., 77 Ark. 379, 91 S. W. 752. See also Hance v. Holiman, 69 Ark. 57, 60 S. W. 730; New England Mortgage Security Co. v. Reding, 65 Ark. 489, 47 S. W. 132.

69. Stelts v. Martin, 90 S. C. 14, 72 S. E. 550. See also Jennings v. Peay, 51 S. C. 327, 28 S. E. 949, under Code Proc. 1870, § 113, which made the same limitation.

70. Wells v. Scanlan, 124 Wis. 229, 102 N. W. 571, under Wis. Rev. St. 1898, § 4221, subd. 2.

§ 176a(4). Sealed note or indorsement thereon.

While a negotiable note need not be under seal, if the parties attach a seal thereto, it becomes a contract under seal, within Massachusetts Rev. Laws, c. 202, § 1, providing that actions on contracts under seal are limited to twenty years next after the cause of action accrued.[71] Where the owner of a judgment note under seal is wrongfully deprived of the possession thereof by the maker, and subsequently at a date more than six years from the act of dispossession but within twenty years from the date of the note, the executor of the owner brings suit to recover the amount due on the note, he may show the unlawful dispossession and the amount due and his recovery cannot be defeated by a plea that the suit was not instituted until after six years from the date of the dispossession.[72] A note signed by two parties as makers, the signature of each being followed by the letters " L. S.," and which had the words " Given under the hand and seal of " each party in the body of the note, contained a sufficient recital that it was under seal to make it a sealed instrument, within Georgia Civ. Code, § 3765, authorizing action thereon within twenty years.[73] An instrument stating that a corporation has caused its corporate seal to be affixed and " this promissory note is to be signed by its president," signed " The P. Co., by F., President," with the corporate seal attached, is the bond of such company, but is not necessarily a sealed instrument

71. Clarke v. Pierce, 215 Mass. 552, 102 N. E. 1094.

72. Smith v. Smith, 35 Pa. Super. Ct. 323.

73. Barnes v. Walker, 115 Ga. 108, 41 S. E. 243.

Though the contract of the maker of a note was under seal, the contract of one who wrote his name on the back of such note merely for the purpose of guarantying its payment, but whose signature was not necessary to its negotiation, was not, by reason thereof, under seal; and hence an action against him was barred after the expiration of the period for bringing action on simple contracts. Ridley v. Hightower, 112 Ga. 476, 37 S. E. 733. The statutory bar applicable to the indorsement of a sealed note by the payee thereof is twenty years, though no seal follows the signature of the payee. Baldwin Fertilizer Co. v. Carmichael, 116 Ga. 762, 42 S. E. 1002.

as to the stockholders, who signed their names on the back before delivery, to give credit thereto.[74]

§ 176a(5). Coupons.

In Pennsylvania, a suit on bond coupons is governed by the statute of limitations applicable to sealed instruments, and not that applicable to simple contract debts; [75] and, in New York, interest coupons of bonds therein described are not outlawed until the bonds are, though they are detached from the bonds.[76]

§ 176a(6). Covenants in conveyance

An action for breach of covenants of a deed is within the Colorado statute, prescribing a three years' limitation from date of accrual of cause of action for all personal actions, on any contract, not otherwise limited.[77] In Georgia, when a grantee accepts a deed and becomes bound by the covenants therein, and the instrument is under seal, the period of limitation applicable to a suit brought for a breach of the covenants is twenty years.[78] In New York, where a grantee of land accepted a covenant obligating her to pay a sum of money to a third person, such a covenant is barred only by the twenty-year statute of limitations.[79] Where a railroad mortgage executed to a trustee contained no express covenant on the part of the trustee, one cannot be implied, unless clearly growing out of the language or the obvious intent of the parties; and a suit by the bondholders secured, against the trustee, for its failure to properly protect their interests, is one for a breach of duty implied by law, and not for a breach of covenant, for the purposes of determining the statute of limitations applicable to such suit.[80] In

74. Somers v. Floria Pebble Phosphate Co., 50 Fla. 275, 39 So. 61.

75. Prescott v. Williamsport & N. B. R. Co., 159 Fed. 244 (U. S. C. C., Pa.).

76. Kelly v. Forty-Second St., etc., Ry. Co., 55 N. Y. Supp. 1096, 37 App. Div. 500.

77. Hayden v. Patterson, 39 Colo. 15, 88 Pac. 437, under Mills' Ann. St. Colo., § 2905.

78. Kytle v. Kytle, 128 Ga. 387, 57 S. E. 748.

79. Anguish v. Blair, 160 App. Div. 52, 145 N. Y. Supp. 392.

80. Frishmuth v. Farmers' Loan &

Missouri, where a grantee accepts a deed to himself, reciting that he assumes and agrees to pay the mortgage debt on the land, he becomes bound as a covenantor to discharge the mortgage, and the ten-year, and not the five-year, statute of limitations is applicable.[81] A covenant against incumbrances is, in effect, that the premises are free from incumbrances at the time of the conveyance and, if any incumbrances exist, the covenant is broken, and a cause of action accrues which will be barred by limitation, under Nebraska Code Civ. Proc., § 10, barring actions on specialties in five years.[82] In North Carolina, an action in contract for the breach of covenants of seisin and warranty in a deed, and not in tort for fraud is governed by Code, § 158, limiting the right to commence such an action to ten years after its accrual.[83]

§ 176a(7). Bonds in general.

In Kentucky, an action on a bond taken by a court commissioner to secure the payment of the purchase money for lands of a decedent, together with an action to enforce a purchase-money lien reserved upon the land, is barred after the lapse of more than fifteen years from the maturity of the bond.[84] In Massachusetts,

Trust Co., 107 Fed. 169, 46 C. C. A. 222 (U. S. C. C. A., N. Y.).

Where there was no positive covenant by the trustee to carry out the provisions of a mortgage executed by a railroad to a trust company as trustee for certain bondholders, an action against it for failure to so comply is not an action on the mortgage within the twenty years statute of limitations relating to actions on sealed instruments. Rhinelander v. Farmers' Loan & Trust Co., 172 N. Y. 519, 65 N. E. 499, aff'g judgs. 58 App. Div. 473, 69 N. Y. Supp. 437; 58 App. Div. 619, 69 N. Y. Supp. 1144.

81. Smith v. Davis, 90 Mo. App. 533.

82. Bellamy v. Chambers, 50 Neb. 146, 69 N. W. 770.

83. Shankle v. Ingram, 133 N. C. 254, 45 S. E. 578, and § 155 (9), limiting the right to commence an action for fraud to three years after the discovery of the fraud, does not apply.

84. French v. Bowling, 27 Ky. Law Rep. 639, 85 S. W. 1182, under Ky. St. 1903, § 2514, requiring actions on bonds to be commenced within fifteen years.

See Pilcher v. McCowan, 8 Ky. Law Rep. (abstract) 786, an action on a replevin bond is barred after fifteen years.

where an action against executors on a bond executed by their testator was supported by a previous demand, and was brought within twenty years from the execution of the bond, it was not barred by the general statute of limitations.[85] Under the Nebraska Code Civ. Proc., § 14, providing that an action on an official bond or undertaking of any officers, or on the bond or undertaking in attachment or in any case whatever required by statute, can be brought only in ten years, an action on an appeal bond is not barred until after ten years.[86] In Mississippi, where a trust fund was created for the payment of levee bonds, as the right to sue for trust funds is controlled by the ten-year statute of limitations, the holders of such bonds were barred from seeking to enforce them after ten years.[87] Where a bond was not sued on for twelve years after it became due, and no evidence was introduced to take the case out of the statute of limitations, a plea of the statute of limitations was good, and will defeat a recovery on the bond.[88] In Washington, an action on a public contractor's bond is barred when brought more than three years after the debt was contracted.[89]

§ 176a(8). Official bonds.

A state law prohibiting actions on testamentary bonds more than six years from their date does not affect a suit by a receiver of an insolvent national bank against executors and legatees of a deceased stockholder to enforce statutory liability.[90] Although a city treasurer was guilty of a breach of his official bond in failing to pay over interest derived from municipal funds, an action therefor by

85. Herbert v. Squire, 186 Mass. 189, 71 N. E. 534.

As to actions on bail bonds, see Lane v. Smith, 19 Mass. (2 Pickle) 281; Fitch v. Burr, 1 Root (Conn.) 365.

86. Crum v. Johnson, 3 Neb. (Unof.) 826, 92 N. W. 1054.

87. Woodruff v. State, 77 Miss. 68, 25 So. 483.

88. Galbreath v. City of Knoxville, 105 Tenn. 453, 59 S. W. 178.

89. Kepl v. Fidelity & Deposit Co. of Maryland, 81 Wash. 135, 142 Pac. 489, under Rem. & Bal. Code, § 1159. See also Johnson Service Co. v. Aetna Indemnity Co., 46 Wash. 434, 90 Pac. 590, under Pierce's Code, § 6121 (Ballinger's Ann. Codes & St., § 5925).

90. Rankin v. Miller, 207 Fed. 602 (U. S. D. C.).

he city was not founded upon the contract as evidenced by the bond, and Montana Rev. Codes, § 6445, did not apply.[91] An action against a principal in an administrator's bond is barred under Kentucky St., § 2514, after fifteen years from the accrual of the cause of action, except in case of trusts within section 2543.[92] An action on the official bond of a county judge is barred in ten years after the cause of action accrued, in Nebraska.[93] In Penn-

91. City of Butte v. Goodwin, 47 Mont. 155, 134 Pac. 670.

An action on a bond of a county treasurer, whose duties are defined by Rev. Codes, § 2986, is on a "liability created by statute," which is barred in two years by § 6449, subd. 1, and not on a " liability on an instrument in writing," barred in eight years by § 6445. Gallatin County v. United States Fidelity & Guaranty Co., 50 Mont. 55, 144 Pac. 1085.

In Wisconsin, a county's right of action on defaults by its treasurer, occurring in 1897 and 1899, in view of St. 1878, § 4976, is governed in both cases by Laws 1893, c. 268 (St. 1898, § 984), if it had notice of the default, or, if not, by Rev. St. 1878, § 4220, fixing a twenty-year limitation as to the default occurring prior to the Revision of 1898, which exempted such actions from the purview of § 4220. Oconto County v. MacAllister, 155 Wis. 286, 143 N. W. 702; Oconoto County v. Lindgren, 155 Wis. 303, 143 N. W. 707.

92. Baugh's Adm'x v. Baugh's Adm'r, 159 Ky. 320, 167 S. W. 124; Hargis v. Sewell's Adm'r, 87 Ky. 63, 9 Ky. Law Rep. 920, 7 S. W. 557, the limitation of fifteen years applies to the obligor and that of five years to his surety.

Ky. St., § 2514, allows fifteen years within which to commence an action on the official bond of a sheriff. Section 2515 allows five years within which to commence an action for torts. An action against a sheriff on his bond for his official misconduct in attaching property under process against a third person is barred in fifteen years; the misconduct not being a tort, within § 2515. Hill v. Ragland, 114 Ky. 209, 24 Ky. Law Rep. 1053, 70 S. W. 634. A surety on a sheriff's official bond is discharged, by Ky. St., § 2551, from liability thereon for the sheriff's official misconduct, when seven years have elapsed without suit thereon. Id. The seven-year limitation statute releases the sureties on a special commissioner's bond executed in the course of a judicial proceeding. Isaacs v. Murphy, 1 Ky. Law Rep. (abstract) 409.

An action on the official bond of a county judge is not barred until the lapse of fifteen years. Commonwealth v. Tilton, 111 Ky. 341, 23 Ky. Law Rep. 753, 63 S. W. 602.. The fifteen-years statute applies to an action by a creditor for an accounting by an assignee. Richardson v. Whitaker, 103 Ky. 425, 20 Ky. Law Rep. 121, 45 S. W. 774.

93. Chicago, B. & Q. R. Co. v. Philpott, 56 Neb. 212, 76 N. W. 550.

sylvania, where a county treasurer has received money belonging to a city as the proceeds of liquor licenses, the fact that the money was not received by the treasurer within six years of the commencement of the suit is not a defense in an action on his official bond, since the obligation to pay is secured by a sealed instrument.[94]

§ 176b(1). Covenants and conditions in general—Accrual of right of action.

Where a lease for three years provided for a percentage of the lessee's gross sales as rent, the amount to be determined weekly, the lessee turning all moneys over to the lessor, who agreed to pay the salaries of lessee's employes and return the balance after deducting rent and payments, there were facts sufficient to support an action of covenant under a claim against the lessor, as affecting the running of limitations.[95] While a cause of action on a covenant accrues on the occurrence of any breach thereof, the statute of limitations is not set in motion where such a breach is merely formal, so as to prevent recovery of substantial damages subsequently resulting, but the statute begins to run as to those damages from the time they occur.[96] A warranty as to the kind and quality

94. Lehigh County v. Gossler, 24 Pa. Super. Ct. 406.

As to limitation of action on official bonds, see also:

Ala.—Rasco v. Jegerson, 142 Ala. 705, 38 So. 245, constable's bond.

Ga.—Griffin v. Collins, 122 Ga. 102, 49 S. E. 827, guardian's bond.

S. D.—Connor v. Corson, 13 S. D. 550, 83 N. W. 588, sheriff's bond.

Va.—Jennings v. Taylor, 102 Va. 191, 45 S. E. 913, county treasurer's bond.

95. *In re* O'Gorman Co., 195 Fed. 650 (U. S. D. C.).

Where a lease dated July 15, 1889, for fifteen years, stipulated for the payment of rent subject to the right of the landlord to re-enter in case of default, and for the erection by the tenant of a building, and the purchase thereof by the landlord at the expiration of the lease for two-thirds of its then appraised value, and the landlord took possession of the premises in June, 1898, for non-payment of rent, an action on the covenant to pay for the building, construed as requiring payment on the landlord taking possession, was barred when brought more than six years after the landlord took possession. Toellner v. McGinnis, 55 Wash. 430, 104 Pac. 641.

96. State *ex rel.* Patterson v. Tittman, 134 Mo. 162, 35 S. W. 579.

of goods sold, if breached at all, is generally breached when made, and limitations run from the date of the sale; but where a warranty of goods sold relates to a future event by which it will be ascertained whether the warranty will be breached or not, the warranty is not breached until the happening of the future event.[97]

§ 176b(2). Covenants in sale or conveyance.

Where a covenant of seisin and warranty is broken at the time the deed is delivered limitations begin to run against an action on the covenant from the delivery of the deed.[98] In Missouri, where any estate passes by a deed containing covenants of seisin, or the grantee takes actual possession, the estate or possession carries the covenants, and makes them run with the land, and the covenants are substantially breached only when the grantee is deprived of the estate conveyed, or when he has been ousted from actual possession by the holder of the paramount title, and limitations run only from that time.[99] In Iowa, where a grantee takes possession of land under a deed with covenants of seisin and general warranty, though there may be a technical breach of the covenant of seisin if the grantor has no title, no substantial damage accrues until the

97. Ingalls v. Angell, 76 Wash. 692, 137 Pac. 309.

98. Shankle v. Ingram, 133 N. C. 254, 45 S. E. 578; Pigeon River Lumber & Iron Co. v. Mims (Tenn.), 48 S. W. 385.

99. Falk v. Organ, 160 Mo. App. 218, 141 S. W. 1.

A covenant of seisin implied from the use of the statutory words "grant, bargain and sell" in a deed, like a covenant of warranty, is a covenant of indemnity running with the land, so that an action for breach thereof so far as the recovery of substantial damages is concerned only accrues from the date of eviction because of a paramount title. Leet v. Gratz, 124 Mo. App. 394, 101 S. W. 696; Pineland Mfg. Co. v. Guardian Trust Co., 139 Mo. App. 209, 122 S. W. 1133. Limitations do not begin to run on a covenant of seisin until the covenantee suffers actual loss. Jones v. Hazeltine, 124 Mo. App. 674, 102 S. W. 40.

Covenant of seisin is breached at the date of the deed, and the statute then commences to run; the covenantor having then no estate, title, or possession, but merely a tax deed, void because based on a judgment against one dead at time of its rendition. Frank v. Organ, 167 Mo. App. 493, 151 S. W. 504.

grantee is evicted, and the statute of limitations does not begin to run until such eviction; but if no possession or right passes under the conveyance, the covenants are broken at once, the right of action immediately accrues and is barred if not prosecuted within the statutory period.[1] In Minnesota, the statute of limitations does not begin to run against an action for breach of a covenant of seisin from the delivery of the deed, but from the time the covenantee is compelled to yield to a superior outstanding title.[2] The same rule is maintained in Kentucky,[3] North Carolina,[4] Oregon,[5] and Texas.[6] In Kansas, the covenants of seisin and of the right to convey, and that the land is free from incumbrances, are broken as soon as the deed is executed, if the title be bad, and a cause of action accrues at once.[7] In Massachusetts and Nebraska, if incumbrances exist at the time of the conveyance, the covenant against incumbrances is broken, and a cause of action accrues.[8] In New

1. Sturgis v. Slocum, 140 Iowa 25, 116 N. W. 128; Foshay v. Shafer, 116 Iowa 302, 89 N. W. 1106.

Although a technical right of action for breach of warranty against incumbrances arises at the time of the execution of the deed on which nominal damages might be recovered, the right to substantial damages does not arise until the incumbrances have been enforced against the land; and hence limitations against an action for breach of covenant commences to run from the latter date. Tukey v. Reinholdt (Iowa), 130 N. W. 727; McClure v. Dee, 115 Iowa 546, 88 N. W. 1093, 91 Am. St. Rep. 181.

2. Brooks v. Mohl, 104 Minn. 404, 116 N. W. 931.

3. Chenault v. Thomas, 119 Ky. 130, 26 Ky. Law Rep. 1029, 83 S. W. 109.

4. Wiggins v. Pender, 132 N. C 628, 44 S. E. 362, 61 L. R. A. 772.

5. Northern Pac. R. Co. v. Montgomery, 86 Fed. 251, 30 C. C. A. 17 (U. S. C. C. A., Or.).

6. Hays v. Talley (Tex. Civ. App.), 161 S. W. 429; Coleman v. Luetcke (Tex. Civ. App.), 164 S. W. 1117; Sievert v. Underwood (Tex. Civ. App.), 124 S. W. 721; Huff v. Reilly, 26 Tex. Civ. App. 101, 64 S. W. 387; Herr v. Rodriguez (Tex. Civ. App.), 50 S. W. 487; Seibert v. Bergman, 91 Tex. 411, 44 S. W. 63, 872.

7. Jewett v. Fisher, 9 Kan. App. 630, 58 Pac. 1023.

In an action by the grantee on a covenant against taxes, limitations commence to run from the time he paid the taxes, and not from the time it was assessed. Greer v. McCarter, 5 Kan. 17.

8. Kramer v. Carter, 136 Mass. 504; Bellamy v. Chambers, 50 Neb. 146, 69 N. W. 770. See also Watson v. Heyn, 62 Neb. 191, 86 N. W. 1064, as to limitation against action on covenant of warranty. Where a minor

York, the assertion and exercise of an easement created by a lane partly on each of two adjoining lots by one adjoining owner is a sufficient eviction to entitle the other to sue for a breach of a covenant against incumbrances, and hence to start the running of limitations against an action for such breach.[9] In West Virginia, if land conveyed by general warranty is in adverse possession under paramount title at the execution of a deed, the grantee's eviction dates, and the statute of limitations against an action for breach of warranty runs, from that date.[10]

§ 176b(3). Bond or contract of suretyship in general.

Limitations do not begin to run against a cause of action on an administrator's bond until there is a final judgment in probate court which is violated by the administrator.[11] Where an administrator was removed for failure to file a new report and pay into court the money in his hands, limitations did not begin to run against a suit on his bond until he was removed for failure to comply with the order.[12] Where the judgment approving an administrator's final report including a fraudulent credit was set aside, and he was ordered to account therefor, his refusal to do so was a breach of his bond, and limitations began to run from the date of his refusal to comply with the order.[13] Since no action accrues

conveys realty and subsequently disaffirms the deed, covenants in deeds granted by persons holding under conveyance from such minor were not broken until the disaffirmance, and hence limitations did not begin to run against the action of covenant until that time. Pritchett v. Redick, 62 Neb. 296, 86 N. W. 1091.

9. Ladue v. Cooper, 32 Misc. Rep. 544, 67 N. Y. Supp. 319.

10. Ilsley v. Wilson, 42 W. Va. 757, 26 S. E. 551.

In Wisconsin, limitations begin to run against an action for breach of warranty from the date of recording a tax deed, the statute giving the grantee therein constructive possession of the land and amounting to an eviction. Bray v. Fletcher, 132 Mich. 272, 9 Detroit Leg. N. 610, 93 N. W. 624.

In Arkansas, a cause of action for breach of warranty of title accrues at the time of the conveyance, and not when the contract to convey is made. Crawford County Bank v. Baker, 95 Ark. 438, 130 S. W. 556.

11. Hall v. Cole, 71 Ark. 601, 76 S. W. 1076.

12. Craven v. State, 50 Ind. App. 30, 97 N. E. 1021.

13. Tucker v. Stewart, 147 Iowa 294, 126 N. W. 183.

against the sureties on an administrator's bond until there has been some breach of the conditions thereof, the statute of limitations does not begin to run until such breach has occurred.[14] In Kentucky, an administrator and his surety may be sued by the heir for a settlement and distribution at any time after nine months after administration; and limitation runs from the time when he might first be sued.[15] In Missouri, a right of action accrues to the distributees on the bond for the failure of an executor to account and distribute the assets, when their right to those assets have become fixed by law, and limitation begins to run when the right of action accrues.[16] In Nebraska, limitations do not

As to an attachment bond, see Valley Bank of Clarinda v. Shenandoah Nat. Bank, 109 Iowa 43, 79 N. W. 391.

14. Carr v. Catlin, 13 Kan. 393.

An action to recover damages on an attachment bond should be commenced within five years from the final determination of the court that the order was wrongfully obtained. Baker v. Skinner, 63 Kan. 83, 64 Pac. 981; Cook v. Smith, 67 Kan. 53, 72 Pac. 524.

As to limitation on action on bond of a contractor for the erection of a public building, see Hull v. Massachusetts Bonding & Ins. Co., 86 Kan. 342, 120 Pac. 544.

15. Donnelly v. Pepper, 11 Ky. Law Rep. (abstract) 365.

The seven-year limitation is a bar to an action against a surety, without regard to the obligee's knowledge of the suretyship. Weller v. Ralston, 28 Ky. Law Rep. 572, 89 S. W. 698; Jefferson's Adm'r v. Jefferson, 4 Ky. Law Rep. (abstract) 723; Nunn v. Pedigo, 6 Ky. Law Rep. (abstract) 743.

As to other actions against sureties barred in seven years, see: Dohn v. Bronger, 20 Ky. Law Rep. 823, 47 S. W. 619; Deposit Bank of Midway's Assignee v. Hearne, 20 Ky. Law Rep. 1019, 104 Ky. 819, 48 S. W. 160; Dugan v. Champion Coal & Towboat Co., 105 Ky. 821, 20 Ky. Law Rep. 1641, 49 S. W. 958; Ryan v. Caldwell, 106 Ky. 543, 20 Ky. Law Rep. 2030, 50 S. W. 966; Howard v. Lawrence, 23 Ky. Law Rep. 680, 63 S. W. 589. No cause of action could arise on a receiver's bond until he had settled his accounts and made his report and until the court determined to whom the money was to be paid, and hence limitations would only run from such time. United States Fidelity & Guaranty Co. v. Shields, 157 Ky. 371, 163 S. W. 203.

16. State *ex rel.* Fagan v. Grisby, 92 Mo. 419, 5 S. W. 39.

The statute of limitations does not run in favor of an administrator on his bond until ten years after his final settlement. Nelson v. Barnett, 123 Mo. 564, 27 S. W. 520. As to limitation to an action on a sheriff's bond, see State, to the Use of Blacker v. O'Neill, 114 Mo App. 611, 90 S. W. 410; State, to the Use of Lindsay (Mo. App.), 90 S. W. 413.

begin to run against an action on a bond of an administrator for failure to pay over the money found due the estate on his final accounting until the decree directing payment is entered.[17] In New York, where an administrator was directed, on a judicial settlement, to retain funds in his hands till further order of the court, and on a subsequent settlement he was discharged on the payment of the balance due, limitations run against an action to recover such balance from him and his bondsmen from the date of the last order.[18] In North Carolina, limitations do not run upon a cause of action against the surety for a wrongful attachment until the judgment in the suit is rendered for the defendant.[19] In Texas, limitations begin to run against a bond given by an employe conditioned on his accounting for all moneys received by him when the contract of employment is terminated.[20]

§ 176b(4). Guardian's bond.

In Arkansas, where a guardianship is closed, and the probate court adjusts the accounts, a cause of action to recover the amount due from the guardian against the guardian's sureties accrues at once, if there is some person capable of suing therefor.[21] In Indiana, limitations run against an action on a guardian's bond from the time of the breach.[22] In Iowa, when the ward becomes of age, the statute of limitations begins to run against a cause of action on the bond for failure to account, whether or not demand for an

17. Mortenson v. Bergthold, 64 Neb. 208, 89 N. W. 742.

As to limitations on other actions for breach of bonds, see: Northern Assur. Co. v. Borgelt, 67 Neb. 282, 93 N. W. 226; Newell v. Clark, 73 N. H. 289, 61 Atl. 555; Jordan v. Meyer, 90 Tex. 544, 39 S. W. 1081; Cookus v. Peyton's Ex'r, 1 Grat. (Va.) 431; Sharpe's Ex'r v. Rockwood, 78 Va. 24; McCormick's Ex'rs v. Wright's Ex'rs, 79 Va. 524.

18. Betts v. Avery, 46 App. Div. 342, 61 N. Y. Supp. 525.

19. Smith v. American Bonding Co., 160 N. C. 574, 76 S. E. 481, under Revisal N. C. 1905, § 763.

20. Wharton v. Fidelity Mut. Life Ins. Co. of Philadelphia (Tex. Civ. App.), 156 S. W. 539.

21. Wallace v. Swepston, 74 Ark. 520, 86 S. W. 398, 109 Am. St. Rep. 94. See also State v. Buck, 63 Ark. 218, 37 S. W. 881.

22. State v. Parsons, 147 Ind. 579, 47 N. E. 17, 62 Am. St. Rep. 430, action is barred after three years from the final settlement.

accounting be made, and whether or not the guardian be ordered to account by the court.[23] In Kentucky, where no suit was brought against sureties on a guardian's bond for his defalcation until more than five years had elapsed after the ward became of age, the sureties were discharged from liability.[24] In Maryland, limitations in favor of a guardian's bondsman do not begin to run until the guardian fails to turn over the ward's estate on his becoming of age, where such failure is the only breach of the bond.[25] In Minnesota, the allowance of a guardian's account and the establishment of a claim against him arising out of his guardianship do not set in motion the limitations prescribed in Gen. St. 1894, § 5927, providing that no action shall be maintained unless commenced within one year from the time the claim is allowed or established in favor of legatee or heir of the surety on his bond.[26]

23. Ackerman v. Hilpert, 108 Iowa 247, 79 N. W. 90.

24. Bybee's Ex'r v. Poynter, 117 Ky. 109, 25 Ky. Law Rep. 1251, 77 S. W. 698.

See Blake v. Wolfe, 105 Ky. 380, 20 Ky. Law Rep. 1212, 49 S. W. 19; Brooks v. Troutman, 104 Ky. 392, 20 Ky. Law Rep. 640, 47 S. W. 271, rehearing denied 104 Ky. 392, 47 S. W. 877.

25. State v. Reilly, 89 Md. 162, 43 Atl. 58.

26. Holden v. Turrell, 86 Minn. 214, 90 N. W. 395.

CHAPTER XVIII.

Torts Quasi e Contractu.

§ 177. Time runs from date of tort.

In the case of torts arising *quasi e contractu,* the statute usually commences to run from the date of the tort, not from the occurrence of actual damage.[1] And ignorance of the facts on the part of the plaintiff will make no exception to the rule, though he discovers his injury too late to have a remedy.[2] This will be the case too, even

1. See Winters v. De Turk, 133 Pa. 359, 19 Atl. 354, 7 L. R. A. 658, and note.

2. See 34 Am. L. Reg. (N. S.) 461; Alabama & Vicksburg Ry. Co. v. Jones, 73 Miss. 110, 19 So. 105, 55 Am. St. Rep. 488, 515, n.

where the defendant has betrayed the plaintiff into permitting the time to elapse in fruitless inquiries and negotiations.[3]

There may be cases where the injured party may bring trespass or trover, or may waive both, and bring assumpsit for the proceeds of the property when it has been converted into money, and in the last case the tortfeasor cannot allege his own wrong so as to bring time back to the day of the tort.[4] And where a party has his election between trover and assumpsit, the fact that one remedy is barred will not defeat the other if the statute has not run upon that.[5] Thus, where the maker of a note which was outlawed asked the holder to see it, and upon its being shown, destroyed it, it was held that trover lay for the note, and that the measure of damages was the face of the note with interest. notwithstanding the fact that the statute might have been successfully interposed against an action upon the note itself.[6] The ground upon which this ruling rests is, that it cannot be presumed that, in an action upon a note or other obligation, so unlawfully destroyed by the maker, he would, although entitled to do so, have set up the statute to defeat it.[7]

§ 178. Consequential injury.

Although, as has been seen, time commences usually to run in defendant's favor from the time of his wrongdoing, and not from the time of the occurrence to the plaintiff of any consequential damage, yet in order to produce this result it is necessary that the wrongdoing should be such that nominal damages may be immediately recovered. Every breach of duty does not create an individual right of action; and the distinction drawn by moralists be-

3. East India Co. v. Paul, 7 Moo. P. C. 85. See as to directors of insolvent bank, Hinsdale v. Larned, 16 Mass. 65.

4. Lamb v. Clark, 22 Mass. (5 Pick.) 193. But there must be an actual conversion. Jones v. Hoar, id. 285. See Lamine v. Dorrell, 2 Ld. Raym. 1216; Hitchin v. Campbell, 2 W. Bl. 827; Hambly v. Trott, Comp. 371.

5. Ivey v. Owens, 28 Ala. 641.

6. Outhouse v. Outhouse, 13 Hun (N. Y.) 130.

7. Ibid.; Booth v. Powers, 56 N. Y. 22.

tween duties of perfect and imperfect obligation may be observed in duties arising from the law. Thus a breach of public duty may not inflict any direct immediate wrong on an individual; but neither his right to a remedy nor his liability to be precluded by time from its prosecution, will commence till he has suffered some actual inconvenience.[8] But it is otherwise where there is a private relation between the parties, where the wrongdoing of one at once creates a right of action in the other; and it may be stated as an invariable rule that when the injury, however slight, is complete at the time of the act, the statutory period then commences, but, when the act is not legally injurious until certain consequences occur, the time commences to run from the consequential damage, whether the party injured is ignorant of the circumstance from which the injury results or not.[9] In a case where

8. Hurst v. Parker, 1 B. & Ald. 92; Tanner v. Smart, 6 B. & C. 603.

9. In Bank of Hartford Co. v. Waterman, 26 Conn. 324, where an officer who had undertaken to attach real estate on mesne process made return that he had attached a certain piece of land belonging to the defendant, and had left with the town clerk, as in such cases he was required by the statute to do, a true and attested copy of the writ and of his return thereon, but in fact he had left a copy of the writ and his return in the town clerk's office, describing another and different piece of the defendant's land from that described in his return on the original writ, Storrs, J., said: "Ignorance of his rights, on the part of the person against whom the statute has begun to run will not suspend its operation. He may discover his rights too late to take advantage of the appropriate remedy. Such is one of the occasional hardships necessarily incident to a law arbitrarily making legal remedies contingent on mere lapse of time. Brown v. Howard, 2 B. & B. 73; Sims v. Britton, 5 Exch. 802; Short v. McCarthy, 3 B. & Ald. 626; Blair v. Bromley, 5 Hare 542; Battley v. Faulkner, 3 B. & Ald. 288. When the injury, however slight, is complete at the time of the act, the statute period commences, Wordsworth v. Harley, 1 B. & Ald. 391; but when the act is not legally injurious until certain consequences occur, the statute begins to run from the consequential injury, Roberts v. Read, 16 East 215. In Gillon v. Boddington, 1 Car. & P. 541, it is agreed that the language of the English statute was even somewhat strained to make its construction comport with 'this very just principle, the limitation by that enactment taking date from the 'fact committed,' and the court extending the meaning of this term so as to make consequential damage an essential part of the fact referred to.

"It only remains, therefore, to de-

the plaintiff had been damaged by the cutting away of certain pillars of coal which supported the surface, and which ultimately injured in consequence, it was considered that time commenced to run against the plaintiff on the occurrence of the damage, and not from the date of the removal of the pillars.[10] So where

termine whether a neglect to serve mesne process, or a false return of such process, is actionable in itself, or whether it becomes so only when a real injury follows from it. No distinction can be drawn between a neglect to serve and a false return in deciding the point presented. Lord Denman, in Wyne v. Birch, 4 Q. B. 566. See Planck v. Anderson, 5 T. R. 37; Barker v. Green, 2 Bing. 317; Brown v. Jarvis, 1 M. & W. 708; Williams v. Moyston, 4 M. & W. 145. If we suppose a direct relation between the plaintiff and the officer—a legal reciprocity of right and duty between them, and concede that damages are to be presumed where the former is invaded or the latter violated, it is clear that neither of these incidents occurs until something more than a neglect to attach or an incorrect return is imputable to the officer. The doctrine to which our course of reasoning has brought us is not novel as a general proposition. Lord Tenterden, in Lewis v. Morland, 2 B. & Ald. 64, previous to the decision of Barker v. Green, *supra*, used this language: 'Supposing the sheriff to be guilty of a breach of duty in letting the party out of custody, it does not thence follow that any action can be maintained against him for such breach of duty.' The opinion of Lord Denman, in the case of Randell v. Wheble, 10 Ad. & El. 719, contains this passage: 'We agree with the case of Brown v. Jarvis, that it is the duty of the sheriff to arrest the party on the first opportunity that he can; but we also agree with the court in that case, that some actual damage must be shown in order to make the negligence of the sheriff in that respect a cause of action.' In a later case, the same judge says: 'When the clear right of a party is invaded in consequence of another's breach of duty, he must be entitled to an action against that party for some amount.' Clifton v. Hooper, 6 Ald. & El. 468." The court held that the statute of limitations took date from the time of the consequential injury, and not from the misfeasance or nonfeasance of the officer, and gave judgment for the plaintiff. See also Roberts v. Read, 16 East 215, and Gillon v. Boddington, 1 C. & P. 541; and see Whitehouse v. Fellowes, 10 C. B. N. S. 765; and Denys v. Shuckburgh, 4 Y. & C. 42.

10. Bonomi v. Backhouse, 5 Jur. 9 H. L. Cas. 503.

A cause of action does not arise for so mining coal as to cause, years afterwards, a subsidence of the soil above, until such subsidence occurs, whether it happens by fits and starts, or goes on gradually and continuously. See Darnley Main Colliery Co. v. Mitchell, 11 A. C. 127; Crumbie v. Wallsend Local Board (1891), 1 Q. B. 503. See Hall v. Norfolk (1900), 2 Ch. 493; Lewey v. H. C. Fricke Coke Co., 166 Pa. 536, 31 Atl. 261, 28 L.

the trustees of a turnpike company negligently made and continued in their road improper catchpits for water, so that on some occasions the water flowed over and injured the plaintiff's land, it was held that the continuance of the catchpits afforded a new cause of action every time such damage was caused, and that the statute only ran on each cause of action from the time it arose.[11]

In an action for maliciously opposing the discharge of an insolvent debtor, time was considered to run from the date of the opposition, and not from the cessation of imprisonment.[12] But in an action for false imprisonment the statute does not begin to run until the imprisonment ends.[13] But in an action for malicious prosecution or arrest, the statute begins to run as soon as the process is served or the arrest is made.[14]

An important distinction exists between actions arising from

R. A. 283, 45 Am. St. Rep. 684; Scranton Gas & Water Co. v. Lackawanna Iron & Coal Co., 167 Pa. 136, 31 Atl. 484; 9 Harvard L. Rev. 147. See *infra*, § 275, n. (*a*)

11. Whitehouse v. Fellows, 10 C. B. N. S. 765.

12. See Nicklin v. Williams, 10 Ex. 259; Violett v. Sympson, 8 El. & Bl. 344.

13. Dusenbury v. Keiley, 8 Daly (N. Y.) 537. In Eggington v. Lichfield, 1 Jur. N. S. 908, the plaintiff was imprisoned upon an illegal warrant, and upon an application to court an order was made for his discharge. Previously to the making of the order another warrant had been given to the jailer by the parties who obtained the first warrant, and the jailer detained the plaintiff upon this warrant after the granting of the order. The last was subsequently adjudged illegal. Held, that the imprisonment under the first warrant was terminated by the order, and that the statute of limitations began to run from that period.

14. Pratt v. Page, 18 Wis. 337. In Nicklin v. Williams, *supra*, Parke, B., referring to the above cases as to consequential damage, said: "It remains to consider some cases cited and much relied on, showing that the limitation of actions under particular statutes directed to be brought within a certain time 'from the fact committed,' dated from the period when consequential damage was occasioned, and therefore it was said that the damage was the cause of action. These statutes mean no doubt the limitation to run from the act, that is the cause of action. But on examining these cases they do not appear to be for injuries to rights, which this is, but solely for consequential damages, where the original act itself was no wrong and only became so by reason of those damages."

torts and upon assumpsit, in that the right to the former cannot be revived by acknowledgment.[15]

§ 179. Negligence.

In actions from injuries resulting from the negligence or unskilfulness of another, the statute attaches and begins to run from the time when the injury was first inflicted, and not from the time when the full extent of the damages sustained has been ascertained.[16] The gist of the action is the negligence or breach

15. Galligher v. Holingsworth, 3 H. & M. (Md.) 122; Goodwyn v. Goodwyn, 16 Ga. 114.

16. Crawford v. Gaulden, 33 Ga. 173; Wilcox v. Plummer, 29 U. S. (4 Pet.) 172, 7 L. Ed. 821; The Governor v. Gordon, 15 Ala. 72; Bank of Utica v. Childs, 6 Cow. (N. Y.) 238; Morgan v. Plumb, 9 Wend. (N. Y.) 287; Mardis v. Shackleford, 4 Ala. 493; Brown v. Howard, 2 B. & B. 73; Thurston v. Blackiston, 36 Md. 501. In Bank of Utica v. Childs, 6 Cow. (N. Y.) 238, a notary neglected to charge a prior indorser by giving the requisite notice of non-payment, etc., and the bank was compelled to pay damages. The action in favor of the bank not having been commenced until more than six years after the negligent act was done, was held barred by the statute, because its right of action against the notary accrued immediately on the omission, and was not dependent upon the payment of damages by it. In Wilcox v. Plummer, *supra,* where a note was placed in the hands of an attorney for collection, and he neglected to join an indorser in the action, and subsequently he sued the indorser, but, because of a mistake in the process, it finally failed, and the statute having then run as against the indorser, and by reason thereof his liability upon the note ceased, the question being whether the cause of action arose against the attorney when the mistake was made, or from the time when the damage was finally developed, the court held that it arose and became complete when the mistake was made, and as, dating from that period, the statute had run in his favor, he had judgment in his favor in the action.

In Dickinson v. Mayor, etc., 92 N. Y. 584, where the plaintiff's complaint alleged that the defendant "improperly, carelessly, negligently, and unlawfully suffered ice and snow to be and remain upon the crosswalks," at the intersection of two streets in the city of New York; that in consequence thereof the plaintiff, while passing over said crosswalk, was thrown to the ground and injured, and plaintiff asked to recover the damages sustained, it was held that the action was "to recover damages for a personal injury resulting from negligence" within the meaning of the provision of the Code, limiting the time for the commencement of such action to three years; citing Irvine v. Wood, 51 N. Y. 228; Clifford v. Dam, 81 N. Y. 56; Sexton v. Zett,

of duty, and not the consequent injury resulting therefrom.[17] But where a person or corporation is primarily liable for the negligence or misfeasance or malfeasance of another, the statute does not begin to run upon the remedy of such person or corporation against the person guilty of such negligence or breach of duty until the liability of such person or corporation has been finally fixed and ascertained; [18] because in the latter case, the gist of the action is the damage, while in the former it is the negligence or breach of duty. In actions for negligence, the jury are not restricted to damages accrued up to the time of action brought, but may include all which have accrued up to the time when the verdict is rendered, as well as such as are likely to result in the future.[19] There seems generally to be no distinction as to the time when the statute applies between actions for misfeasance or malfeasance and any ordinary action on the case.[20]

44 N. Y. 430; Creed v. Hartmann, 29 N. Y. 591; Congreve v. Smith, 18 N. Y. 79; Fisher v. Mayor, etc., 67 N. Y. 76.

In Watson v. Forty-second Street F. R. R. Co., 93 N. Y. 522, where the plaintiff was injured by reason of the defendant's negligence in April, 1877, and she commenced this action to recover damages in January, 1880, it was held that the statute of limitations was not a bar, as the case was governed by the three years' limitation prescribed by the Code, not by the one year's rule previously existing; that the case was not within the exception in the provision of the Code, making the rule of limitations therein prescribed the only one thereafter applicable to civil actions, except where a person was entitled, when the Code took effect, to commence an action, and did so within two years thereafter. See Acker v. Acker, 81 N. Y. 143.

17. Thurston v. Blackiston, *supra;* Gustin v. Jefferson County, 15 Iowa 158; Northrop v. Hill, 57 N. Y. 351, 15 Am. Rep. 501, aff'g 61 Barb. (N. Y.) 136; Lathrop v. Snellbaker, 6 Ohio N. S. 276; Argall v. Kelso, 1 Sandf. (N. Y.) 98; Ellis v. Kelso, 57 Ky. (18 B. Mon.) 296; Sinclair v. Bank, 2 Strobh. (S. C.) 344; Cook v. Rives, 13 S. & M. (Miss.) 328; Battley v. Faulkner, 3 B. & Ald. 288; Howell v. Young, 5 B. & C. 259.

18. Veazie v. Penobscot R. Co., 49 Me. 126.

19. Wilcox v. Plummer, *supra.*

20. Baker v. Atlas Bank, 50 Mass. (9 Metc.) 182; Hinsdale v. Larned, 16 Mass. 65; Mather v. Green, 17 Mass. 60; Fisher v. Pond, 1 Hill (N. Y.) 672.

See Robinson v. Moore, 76 Miss. 89, 23 So. 631; Moores v. Winter, 67 Ark. 189, 53 S. W. 1057; Ott v. Great Northern Ry. Co., 70 Minn. 50, 72 N. W. 833. A general provision of stat-

But in actions of this class a question may arise as to the exact time when the default arose, and, as a right of action does not exist until default, this question is material. Questions of this character most frequently arise in actions against public officers.[21] Where a statute provides that, unless a claim for damages done by reason of the negligence or wrongful act of a person or corporation, is made within a certain time, as, within thirty days, three months, etc., if a claim is made within that time, the action is not barred, if brought before the statute of limitations has run upon the class of actions to which it belongs.[22]

§ 180. Nuisances.

The rule in reference to acts amounting to a nuisance is, that every continuance is a new nuisance for which a fresh action will lie, so that, although an action for the damage from the original nuisance may be barred, damages are recoverable for the six years preceding the bringing of the action, provided such a period of time has not elapsed that the person maintaining it has acquired a presumptive right to do so.[23] Thus,[24] in an action

ute limiting actions on contracts not expressly mentioned, depends upon the nature of the action, and not upon its form. Hence it does not apply to trespass on the case in assumpsit for negligence causing personal injuries; and generally, in that form of action, when the cause of action is injury to the person, the limitation in assumpsit is the same as if the action were *ex delicto* in form. See Anderson v. Hygeia Hotel Co., 92 Va. 687, 24 S. E. 269; Brimingham v. Chesapeake & Ohio Ry. Co., 98 Va. 548, 2 Va. Sup. Ct. Rep. 465, 37 S. E. 17.

As to the effect of the statute in relation to negligence in the examination of titles to land, see Brown v. Sims, 22 Ind. App. 317, 53 N. E. 779, 72 Am. St. Rep. 308, 319, n.; *infra*, § 289 note 3. In actions for personal injuries resulting in death, limitation begins to run at the time of the death and not of the injury. Louisville, Evansville & St. Louis R. Co. v. Clarke, 152 U. S. 230, 14 Sup. Ct. 579, 38 L. Ed. 422; Nestelle v. Northern Pac. R. Co., 56 Fed. 261; Hanna v. Jeffersonville R. Co., 32 Ind. 113. See Epperson v. Hostetter, 95 Ind. 583.

21. *Supra*, § 154.

22. East Tenn. R. Co. v. Bayliss, 74 Ala. 150. Such actions belong to the class called at the common law "actions on the case." Newton v. N. Y. & N. E. R. Co., 56 Conn. 21.

23. Staple v. Spring, 10 Mass. 72; Holmes v. Wilson, 10 Ad. & El. 503;

brought to recover damages for injuries sustained by reason of the erection of a dam, which set back the water of a stream and overflowed the plaintiff's land, it was held that while the plaintiff was barred from recovering damages arising from the erection of the dam, he might recover for its continuance. The same rule was adopted in an English case,[25] where the defendants, as trustees of a turnpike-road, who had erected buttresses to support it, on the plaintiff's land, were held liable for its continuance there, although they had already been sued, and responded in damages for its erection.[26] But while this is the rule as to nuisances of a transient rather than of a permanent character, yet, when the original nuisance is of a permanent character so that the damage inflicted thereby is of a permanent character, and goes to the entire destruction of the estate affected thereby, or will be likely to continue for an indefinite period, and during its existence deprive the landowner of any beneficial use of that portion of his estate, a recovery not only may but must be had for the entire damage in one action, as the damage is deemed to be original;[27] and as the entire damage accrues from the time the nuisance is created, and only one recovery can be had, the statute of limitations begins to run from the time of its erection against the owner of the estate or estates affected thereby.[28]

Bowyer v. Cook, 5 De G. & S. 236; McConnell v. Kibbe, 29 Ill. 483. See Silsby Manuf. Co. v. State of New York, 104 N. Y. 562, 11 N. E. 264.

24. Staple v. Spring, *supra.*

25. Holmes v. Wilson, 10 Ad. & El. 503.

26. McConnell v. Kibbe, 29 Ill. 483. In Bowyer v. Clarke, 4 C. B. 236, the defendant placed stumps and stakes in a ditch on the plaintiff's land, and the plaintiff, having recovered against him for placing the stumps and stakes there, brought a second action for continuing them there, and it was held that he could recover, as the continuance of the original nuisance amounted to a new nuisance each day it was continued.

27. Troy v. Cheshire R. R. Co., 23 N. H. 101; Anon., 4 Dall. (U. S.) 147. See also Kansas R. R. Co. v. Mihlman, 17 Kan. 224.

28. In Powers v. Council Bluffs, 45 Iowa, 652 (See Wood on Nuisances, 889), the plaintiff was the owner of certain lots in Council Bluffs. In 1859, the lots were crossed by a meandering stream called Indian Creek. In order to remove the stream from one of the streets of the city, the city deter-

§ 181. Action must be brought before prescriptive right has been acquired.

While, as we have stated, each continuance of a nuisance is treated as a new nuisance, and furnishes a new ground of action which affords a good ground of recovery, although the statute

mined to and did cut a ditch along the side of the street and across the end of the plaintiff's lots. The stream was turned into the ditch. This was done in 1859 and 1860. The ditch was extended to a county ditch, but was not cut as deep as the county ditch, into three feet; in consequence of which, owing to the nature of the soil, a cavity was created at the point where the city ditch fell into the county ditch, which cut back up the stream. It reached the plaintiff's lots in 1866, when he began to sustain damages from the action of the water. Prior to the commencement of the action against the city for damages, the ditch had become fifty feet wide and twelve feet deep; and to arrest the action of the water and confine it within its proper channel the plaintiff built a wall, which accomplished the desired result. The statute of limitations being pleaded, the court below directed the jury to find a verdict for the defendant, which was sustained upon appeal. Without questioning the general doctrine announced by the court, that, when the damage is complete by the original act creating the nuisance, the statute begins to run from that time; yet, in the particular case under the facts stated, we cannot assent to the ruling of the court, that the plaintiff's remedy was full and complete where damage first intervened from the defendant's acts. According to the statement of the court, the damages resulted from day to day by the widening of the ditch, until, from a ditch of a few feet in width, it extended to a width of fifty feet, and might, except for the act of the plaintiff by the erection of the wall, have extended indefinitely. To say that the plaintiff was bound to know from the first injury to the estate that this result, in the very nature of things, would ensue, is neither logical nor natural; and it is not within the reason of the case of Troy v. Cheshire R. R. Co., *supra*, upon which the court relied. In that case the damage was complete when the act creating the nuisance was completed; but in the Iowa case the damage was progressing from day to day, and could not have been foreseen.

A. is the owner of a house, and B. is the owner of a mine under it, and, in working the mine, B. leaves insufficient support to the house. The house was not damaged until some time after the workings have ceased. Held, that A. could bring an action at any time within six years after the mischief happened, and was not bound to bring it within six years after the work was done which originally led to the mischief. Backhouse v. Bonomi, 9 H. L. Cas. 503, 1 El. B. & E. 622.

The defendants were the trustees

may have run upon former injuries from the same nuisance, yet this proposition only holds good when the action is brought

of a turnpike road, and the plaintiff alleged that they so negligently made and maintained certain catchpits for carrying off the water from the road that large quantities of water ran into his land and collieries, whereby he was greatly damaged. The plaintiff first complained in July, 1859, and the defendants made some alterations; he was again damaged, and complained in December of the same year, and eventually brought this action. On behalf of the defendants, it was contended that the action was not brought in time, inasmuch as it was not brought within three months after the act complained of was committed, as enacted by sec. 147 of the Turnpike Road Act, 3 Geo. IV., c. 126. Held, that the action was in time, as no cause of action arose to the plaintiff so long as the works of the defendants caused him no damage, and that the cause of action first accrued when the plaintiff received actual damage. Whitehouse v. Fellowes, 9 C. B. N. S. 901; Same v. Same, 10 id. 765. See Plumer v. Harper, 3 N. H. 38; Hamer v. Knowles, 6 H. & N. 454. In Polly v. McCall, 37 Ala. 20, an action was brought for injuries resulting to the plaintiff's land from the diversion of the water of a brook by means of a ditch and levee, which when first constructed did not injure the plaintiff's land, except at times of great floods. Subsequently, the ditch became filled with sand, and the plaintiff's land was injured by the overflow of water from it. The court held that, as no action could accrue to the plaintiff until his lands were injured from the maintenance of the ditch, the defendant could acquire no title by presumption except from that period.

We think that is the Iowa case the court failed to make a proper distinction between a wrongful act amounting to a nuisance which of itself creates a complete and permanent injury, and a nuisance, which is permanent, but the injury from which is not only continuous but also constantly increasing. In the former case, there can be no doubt but that the statute would run from the completion of the thing creating the nuisance; but in the latter case successive actions would lie until the nuisance is abated. See Whitehouse v. Fellowes, *supra*. In Colrick v. Swinburne, 105 N. Y. 503, 12 N. E. 427, it was held that the diversion by the owner of land on which is a spring, of the water of the spring from its natural channel, whereby an owner below is deprived of the use of the water on his premises, is a legal injury for which the party injured is entitled to compensation in damages. Whether the use made by the owner of the spring is a reasonable exercise of his right, is a question of fact for a jury. Where the injury complained of was the diversion of the waters of a spring from the plaintiff's tannery, it was held that the diminished rental value during the period of diversion was the proper measure of damages.

The general rule is that no private right can be acquired by lapse of time to maintain a public nuisance

before the person erecting or maintaining the nuisance has acquired a prescriptive right to do so, by the lapse of such a period as bars an entry upon lands adversely held by another,[29] that being the period universally adopted in this country for the ac-

or to interfere with the established rights of the government or of the public; but this rule is subject to some exceptions, especially as to rights in the seashore, in fisheries, and in great ponds. See West Roxbury v. Stoddard, 89 Mass. (7 Allen), 158; Hittinger v. Eames, 121 Mass. 539; Atty.-Gen. v. Revere Copper Co., 152 Mass. 444, 25 N. E. 605, 9 L. R. A. 510; Kellogg v. Thompson, 66 N. Y. 88; Kelley v. New York, 27 N. Y. 164; Dyer v. Curtis, 72 Me. 181; Cedar Lake Hotel Co. v. Cedar Lake Hydraulic Co., 79 Wis. 297, 48 N. W. 371; State v. Holman, 104 N. C. 861, 10 S. E. 758; Olive v. State, 86 Ala. 88, 5 So. 653, 4 L. R. A. 33; Williams v. Harter, 121 Cal. 47, 53 Pac. 405.

In cases of continuing nuisances or trespasses, usually their continuance, if accompanied by fresh damage to the plaintiff, constitutes a fresh cause of action. See Whitehouse v. Fellowes, 10 C. B. N. S. 705, 781; Lamb v. Walker, 3 Q. B. D. 389; Peden v. Chicago, etc., Ry. Co., 78 Iowa, 131, 42 N. W. 625, 4 L. R. A. 401; Hempsted v. Cargill, 46 Minn. 118, 48 N. W. 558; Murray v. Scribner, 74 Wis. 602, 43 N. W. 549; Smith v. Sedalia, 152 Mo. 283, 53 S. W. 907, 48 L. R. A. 711; Doran v. Seattle, 24 Wash. 182, 64 Pac. 230, 54 L. R. A. 532, 85 Am. St. Rep. 948. So in actions for flowing land, limitation begins only when actual damage is sustained therefrom, and not when the defendant's dam or other cause of the injury is erected; and the fact that the first flowage is already barred does not defeat a suit for such continuance of the wrong as occurs within the time limited by the statute. Burleigh v. Lumbert, 34 Me. 322; Vickery v. Providence, 17 R. I. 651; Stanchfield v. Newton, 142 Mass. 110, 7 N. E. 703; Miller v. Keokuk, etc., Ry. Co., 63 Iowa 680, 16 N. W. 567; St. Louis, etc., Ry. Co. v. Biggs (52 Ark. 240), 12 S. W. 331, 6 L. R. A. 804, 20 Am. St. Rep. 174, and n.; Daneri v. Southern Cal. Ry. Co., 122 Cal. 507, 55 Pac. 243; Hocutt v. Wilmington & W. R. Co., 124 N. C. 214, 32 S. E. 681; Miller v. Hayden, 91 Ky. 215, 15 S. W. 243, 667, 12 Ky. Law Rep. 805; Alabama Gt. So. R. Co. v. Shahan, 116 Ala. 302, 22 So. 509; Chattanooga v. Dowling, 101 Tenn. 342, 47 S. W. 700; Eastman v. St. Anthony Falls Water Power Co., 12 Minn. 137.

In North Carolina it is held that the unlawful diversion of water from a stream, though not strictly an easement, is so nearly in the nature of an easement as to require a continuous and adverse use for twenty years in order to raise the presumption of a grant, and that such diversion is not a "continuing trespass" under the statute requiring actions therefor to be brought within three years. Geer v. Durham Water Co., 127 N. C. 349, 37 S. E. 474.

29. Wood on Nuisances, 717 *et seq.*

quisition of prescriptive rights.[30] It has been doubted, in at least one case,[31] whether a prescriptive right could be acquired to maintain a nuisance that merely polluted the atmosphere with offensive smells, or smoke and noxious or destructive vapors; but, regardless of this case, it may be said that according to the authorities such a right can be acquired.[32] The burden of establishing the right by user is upon him who asserts it; and, applying the rules applicable to the acquisition of such rights there are very few cases in which it can be clearly established.[33]

§ 182. What requisite to establish prescriptive right.

The fact that a noxious trade has been exercised for twenty years in a particular locality does not by any means establish a prescriptive right to exercise it there. It is, however, evidence from which, in connection with other proof, the right may be established. But, in order to establish the right as against any party complaining, the burden is imposed upon the defendant,

30. Marr v. Gilliam, 41 Tenn. (1 Cold.) 488; Sibley v. Ellis, 77 Mass. (11 Gray) 417.

31. Campbell v. Seaman, 2 T. & C. (N. Y.) 231, aff'd 63 N. Y. 568, 20 Am. Rep. 567.

32. Duncan v. Earl of Moray, 15 F. C. (Scotch) 302. See Dana v. Valentine, 46 Mass., 5 Met. 8. When a party's right of property is invaded he may maintain an action for an invasion of his right, without proof of actual damage. Grant v. Lyman, 45 Mass. (4 Met.) 470, 477; Atkins v. Bordman, 2 id. 457; Bolivar Manuf. Co. v. Neponset Manuf. Co., 33 Mass. (16 Pick,) 247. In Charity v. Riddle, 14 F. C. (Scotch) 302, the defendants had erected or carried on in the suburbs of Glasgow for more than twenty years an establishment for the manufacture of glue, which emitted nauseous and offensive stenches. Upon a hearing upon a petition for an interdict to prevent the defendant from enlarging his works, the court held that, by an unmolested, uninterrupted exercise of his trade there for more than twenty years, the defendant had acquired a prescriptive right, as against the plaintiff, to continue it, but that he could not increase the nuisance by increasing the capacity of his works, and prohibited him from enlarging them. Colville v. Middleton, 19 F. C. (Scotch) 339; Miller v. Marshall, 5 Mur. (Scotch) 32; Tipping v. St. Helen Smelting Co., 11 H. L. Cas. 643; Biss v. Hall, 6 Scott, 500; Elliotson v. Feetham, 2 Bing. N. C. 134; Roberts v. Clark, 18 L. T. N. S. 48; Flight v. Thomas, 10 Ad. & El. 590.

33. Bradley's Fish Co. v. Dudley, 37 Conn. 136.

who sets up the right as a defense, of proving that for the period of twenty years he has sent over the premises in question from his works an atmosphere equally as polluted and offensive as that complained of.[34] Proof that he has polluted the air is not enough: he must show that for the requisite period he has sent over the land an atmosphere so impure and polluted as to operate as an actual invasion of the rights of those owning the premises affected thereby, and in such a manner that the owner of the premises might have maintained an action therefor.[35] Less than that

34. Flight v. Thomas, 10 Ad. & El. 590.

35. Roberts v. Clarke, 18 L. T. N. S. 49; Luther v. Winnissimmet Co., 63 Mass. (9 Cush.) 171. It is not enough to show that a noxious trade has been exercised in a particular locality for twenty years, and a plea setting up a prescriptive right in that way would be bad, and a verdict for the defendant upon such a plea would be set aside. In Flight v. Thomas, 10 Ad. & El. 590, where the plaintiff brought an action against the defendant for sending offensive smells over his premises, Lord Denman, C. J., said: "There is no claim of an easement, unless you make it appear that the offensive smell has been used for twenty years to go over to the plaintiff's land. The plea may be completely proved without proving that the nuisance ever has passed beyond the limits of the defendant's own land." Littledale, J., said: "The plea only shows that the defendant has enjoyed as of right, and without interruption for twenty years, the benefit of something that occasioned a smell in his own land." The judgment was reversed and judgment rendered for the plaintiff *non obstante veredicto.* The right being only to the extent of the use, and it being incumbent upon the defendant to establish the right by proving a use as extensive as that complained of, Ballard v. Dyson, 1 Taunt. 179; Richardson v. Pond, 81 Mass. (15 Gray) 387; Atwater v. Bodfish, 77 Mass. (11 Gray) 150; and in addition thereto, to prove that for the requisite period the noxious smells have passed over the plaintiff's premises, to such an extent as to be a nusiance, and actionable as such, Flight v. Thomas, 10 Ad. & El. 590; and the presumption being that he who does an act upon his own premises confines all its ill effects there, the difficulty of establishing a prescriptive right in such a case is obvious, Flight v. Thomas, *supra.* The burden assumed by the plaintiff in such cases is, of showing that during the whole prescriptive period the user has been unlawful, Monks v. Butler, 1 Roll. 83; Powell v. Millbank, 2 H. Bl. 851; Branch v. Doane, 17 Conn. 402; Casper v. Smith, 9 S. & R. (Pa.) 33; Cooper v. Barber, 3 Taunt. 99; Polly v. McCall, 37 Ala. 20; Murgatroyd v. Robinson, 7 El. & B. 391. The rule is that "a prescription is entire and cannot be split" by either the party setting it up or the party opposing it. In Rogers v. Allen, 1 Camp. 308, the

is insufficient. He must also show that his user at the time when the action is brought is not substantially in excess of that which he has exercised during the period requisite to acquire the right.[36] The right is restricted to and measured by the use.[37] For

plaintiff brought an action of trespass against the defendant for breaking and entering a several fishery. The plaintiff alleged in his declaration a prescriptive right of fishing over four places in a navigable river. Upon trial, he failed to prove a right in but three; and the court held that when an action is brought to recover for an injury to a prescriptive right, the prescription must be proved as laid, and that if the right is only shown to exist in three of the places named in the declaration, the variance is fatal, and no recovery can be had even though it is also shown that the trespasses were committed in one of the three places over which the right existed. The party does not fail because he shows the right to be more ample than he has laid it, Johnson v. Thoroughgood, Hob. 64; Bushwood v. Bond, Cro. Eliz. 722; but he must prove it to exist to the full extent claimed. Rotheram v. Green, Noy 67; Congers v. Jackson, Clay. 19; Corbett's Case, 7 Coke 5; Hickman v. Thorny, Freem. 211; Kingsmill v. Bull, 9 East 185; Morewood v. Jones, 4 T. R. 157. The effect of this rule is this: where a person sets up a prescriptive right to do an act with which he is charged in an action on the case, as for the pollution of the atmosphere over the plaintiff's premises, by carrying on a particular trade, he is bound to set up a right to do all that he is charged with doing, in the declaration that forms the basis of an action for damages. He cannot defend by setting up a prescriptive right to do less; and if he sets up a prescriptive right to do all that he is charged with doing, his plea fails if he does not show a right as extensive as the one exercised by and charged against him in the declaration. Therefore he does not sustain his plea by proof of a right to pollute the air, unless he also shows that he had a right to pollute it to the extent and with the results charged and proved against him. This was held as early as Rotheram v. Green, Noy 67, and has not been materially varied since. The soundness of the doctrine is apparent, and is well sustained by authority. Tapling v. Jones, 11 H. L. Cas. 290; Weld v. Hornby, 7 East 195; Bailey v. Appleyard, 3 Nev. & P. 172; Welcome v. Upton, 6 M. & W. 536.

36. Weld v. Hornby, 7 East 195; Topling v. Jones, 11 H. L. Cas. 265; Goldsmith v. Tunbridge Wells Imp. Co., L. R. 1 Eq. 352; Baxendale v. Murray, L. R. 2 Ch. 790; Ball v. Ray, 8 id. 467; Crossly v. Lightowler, L. R. 3 Eq. 279; Stein v. Burden, 24 Ala. 130.

37. Ballard v. Dyson, 1 Taunt. 279; Jackson v. Stacey, 1 Holt 455; Cowling v. Higginson, 4 M. & W. 245; Peardon v. Underhill, 16 Q. B. 123; Davies v. Williams, id. 547; Bower v. Hill, 2 Bing. N. C. 339; De Rutzen v. Lloyd, 5 Ad. & El. 456; Allan v. Gomme, 11 id. 759; Higham v. Rabett,

all excess of user an action lies. The enjoyment of a limited right cannot lawfully be enlarged, and any excess of use over that covered by the actual user under which the right was gained will be actionable.[38]

In order to establish a right by prescription, the acts by which it is sought to establish it must operate as an invasion of the particular right which it is sought to quiet, to such an extent that during the whole period of use the party whose estate is sought to be charged with the servitude could have maintained an action therefor. The rule is, that a prescription can only operate against one who is capable of making a grant. Therefore, if the estate was in the possession of a tenant for life,[39] or for a term,[40] or if the owner of the fee was a minor,[41] a married woman,[42] or an insane person,[43] no right can be acquired during the term, or while the disability exists. In order to acquire the right, the person owning the estate affected thereby must be in a condition to resist it. But where the adverse use has begun before the owner of the servient estate lets it, the letting of the estate does not prevent the acquisition of the right. He having been in a posi-

5 Bing. N. C. 622; Henning v. Barnett, 8 Exch. 187; Brooks v. Curtis, 4 Lans. (N. Y. S. C.) 283; Wright v. Moore, 39 Ala. 593; Atwater v. Bodfish, 77 Mass. (11 Gray) 150; Rexford v. Marquis, 7 Lans. (N. Y.) 257; Simpson v. Coe, 4 N. H. 301; Horner v. Stillwell, 35 N. J. L. 307; Noyes v. Morrill, 108 Mass. 396; Stiles v. Hooker, 7 Cow. (N. Y.) 266; Burrell v. Scott, 9 id. 279; Dyer v. Dupey, 5 Whart. (Pa.) 584; Rogers v. Allen, 1 Camp. 309; Martin v. Goble, id. 320; Bealey v. Shaw, 6 East 208.

38. Chandler v. Thompson, 3 Camp. 80; Weld v. Hornby, 7 East 195; Tapling v. Jones, 11 H. L. Cas. 290; Staight v. Burn, L. R. 5 Ch. 163.

39. McGregor v. Wait, 76 Mass. (10 Gray) 72; Barker v. Richardson, 4 B. & Ald. 579; Wood v. Veal, 5 B. & Ald. 454; Harper v. Charlesworth, 4 B. & C. 574.

40. Wood v. Veal, *supra*. In Bright v. Walker, 1 C. M. & R. 211, it was held that the user must be such as to give a right against all persons having estates in the lands affected thereby. See Winship v. Hudspeth, 10 Exch. 5, Alderson, B.

41. Watkins v. Peck, 13 N. H. 360; Mebane v. Patrick, 46 N. C. (1 Jones) 26.

42. McGregor v. Waite, *supra*.

43. Edson v. Munsell, 92 Mass. (10 Allen) 557.

tion to resist the adverse use, cannot, by voluntarily putting himself in a position where he cannot resist it, prevent the perfection of the right while the estate is in possession of the tenant.[44] Neither does the fact that the premises are in the possession of a tenant prevent the perfection of the right, if the injury is of such a character, and is known to the landlord, that he could maintain an action for an injury to the reversion.[45]

It is only as against such rights as operate an injury to the reversion, so that an action can be maintained by the reversioner therefor, that a prescriptive right can be acquired while the premises are in the possession of a tenant; and then, in order to acquire the right, the user must be open, and of such a character that the reversioner may fairly be presumed to have knowledge of it, or actual knowledge must be shown. Indeed, the user must be such that it can fairly be said to be with the acquiescence of the reversioner, and an acquiescence by the tenant does not bind him.[46] The user must also be shown to have been peaceable and uninterrupted, so that it can be said to have been acquiesced in by the owner of the estate affected by it.[47] The prescription begins to run from the time when a legal right is actually invaded by the nuisance, so that the law will imply damage therefrom, and must continue for the period requisite under the statute for acquiring a title to land by adverse enjoyment.[48]

44. Mebane v. Patrick, *supra;* Cross v. Lewis, 2 B. & C. 686; Tracy v. Atherton, 36 Vt. 503; Tyler v. Wilkinson, 4 Mason (U. S.) 402.

45. Wallace v. Fletcher, 30 N. H. 434; Shadwell v. Hutchinson, 4 C. & P. 333; Tucker v. Newman, 11 Ad. & El. 40.

46. Bradbury v. Grinsell, 2 Wm. Saunders 516.

47. Bealey v. Shaw, *supra;* Stillman v. White Rock Co., 3 W. & M. (U. S.) 549; Nichols v. Aylor, 7 Leigh (Va.) 546; Smith v. Miller, 77 Mass. (11 Gray) 145; Tracy v. Atherton, 36 Vt. 514; Powell v. Bagg, 74 Mass. (8 Gray) 441; Bailey v. Appleyard, 3 N. & P. 157.

48. Pollard v. Barnes, 56 Mass. (2 Cush.) 191; Parks v. Mitchell, 11 Exch. 788. But as to what is such a continuous user as will perfect the right, is a question to be determined from the circumstances of each particular case, and is to be determined with reference to the nature and character of the right claimed. It is not to be understood that the right

§ 183. Trover.

The statute begins to run in an action of trover from the time of conversion.[49] Thus, in the Pennsylvania case cited in the last note, an action of trover was brought for a United States certifi-

must be exercised continuously, in the strict sense of the word, without cessation or interruption, but that it is to be exercised as continuously and uninterruptedly as the nature of the right claimed requires, in order to satisfy a jury that the right claimed is commensurate with the user. Thus, in order to acquire a right across another's land, it is not essential that the person asserting the right should have passed over the way every day in the year, or even every month in the year. It is sufficient if he has used the way as his convenience and necessity required, and that his user be such as to leave no room to doubt his intention to maintain his use of the way as of right. Pollard v. Barnes, 56 Mass. (2 Cush.) 191; Bodfish v. Bodfish, 105 Mass. 317; Lowe v. Carpenter, 6 Exch. 630; Parks v. Mitchell, 11 Exch. 788, Hogg v. Gill, 1 McMullan (S. C.) 329; Nash v. Peden, 1 Speers (S. C.) 17. But he must not suffer unreasonable periods to elapse between his acts of user. Thus it has been held that where a party claiming a right of way over another's land to get the hay from an adjoining lot once each year, the exercise of this right once a year, as of right, will sustain a prescriptive right for such a use. Carr v. Foster, 3 Q. B. 581. But such a user would not confer a right of way for any purpose and at any time that the party might see fit to exercise it. The continuity must not be broken, and whether or not it has been depends upon the nature of the easement claimed, and non-user in reference thereto. In Coke's Litt. 1136, the doctrine as borrowed from Bracton is laid down as follows: "The possession must be long, continuous, and peaceable. Long, that is, during the time required by law; continuous, that is, uninterrupted by any lawful impediment; and peaceable, because if it be contentious, and the opposition be on good grounds, the party will be in the same condition as at the beginning of his enjoyment. There must be long use, without force, without secrecy, as of right, and without interruption." Here all the requisite elements to acquire a prescriptive right are concisely stated; and whether or not they exist in a given case is a question of fact to be determined by the jury, in view of the right claimed, the manner in which it has been used, and the purpose of its use. The burden of establishing the existence of all these elements, and consequently of establishing the right, is always upon him who asserts it. Pollard v. Barnes, 56 Mass. (2 Cush.) 191; Watt v. Trapp, 2 Rich. (S. C.) 136; Gerenger v. Summers, 24 N. C. (2 Ired.) 229; Winnipiseogee Lake Co. v. Young, 40 N. H. 420, 436.

49. Horsefield v. Cost, Add. (Pa.) 152; Outhouse v. Outhouse, 13 Hun (N. Y.) 130; Montague v. Sandwich, 7 Mod. 99; Fishwick v. Sewall, 4 H.

cate levied upon and sold on an execution, and it was held that the statute began to run from the date of sale. But, if there had been a demand upon the officer for the certificate before the sale, the statute would have run from the time of demand and refusal, because a refusal to deliver up property which the defendant has

& J. (Md.) 393. In this view it becomes important to ascertain what amounts to a conversion; and it may be said that any illegal act of dominion over the property of another which amounts to the assertion of a title therein, and in defiance of the real owner's title, is a conversion, Beckley v. Howard, 2 Brev. (S. C.) 94; Webber v. Davis, 44 Me. 147; whether the person knew of the plaintiff's title thereto or not, Harris v. Saunders, 2 Strobh. Eq. (S. C.) 370; and even though a person does not claim title in the goods, yet if he exercises dominion over them, as if he threatens to sue the owner if he enters upon his premises to take them away, he is chargeable with their conversion, Hare v. Pearson, 26 N. C. (4 Ired.) 76. Where the original taking is wrongful, a right of action accrues immediately without a demand, and of course the statute begins to run from that time, Farrington v. Payne, 15 Johns. (N. Y.) 431; Woodbury v. Long, 25 Mass. (8 Pick.) 543; Davis v. Duncan, 1 McCord (S. C.) 213; nor is a demand necessary where there has been an actual conversion, Durell v. Mosher, 8 Johns. (N. Y.) 445; Tompkins v. Haile, 3 Wend. (N. Y.) 406; Hines v. McKinney, 3 Mo. 382; Jewett v. Partridge, 12 Me. 243. But when goods are rightfully obtained, and there has been no actual conversion, a demand is necessary before an action can be brought, and in such a case the statute begins to run from the time of demand. Montague v. Sandwich, *supra;* Thorogood v. Robinson, 6 Q. B. 722; Baldwin v. Cole, 6 Mod. 212.

Trover and replevin were early held to be included in the words "actions on the case" in § 3 of the statute of James. Swayn v. Stevens, Cro. Car. 245; 2 Wm. Saund. 395. In this country limitation begins to run as to trover from the time of the conversion, and, in the absence of proof as to the date, it is presumed to have occurred when the property was taken into possession. Parker v. Harden, 121 N. C. 57, 28 S. E. 20. See as to trover under the statute, Struthers v. Peckham, 22 R. I. 8, 45 Atl. 742; Hawkins v. State Loan & Trust Co., 79 Fed. 50; Hine v. Commercial Bank, 119 Mich. 448, 78 N. W. 471; Britt v. Pitts, 111 Ala. 401, 20 So. 484; Morris v. Lowe 97 Tenn. 243, 36 S. W. 1098; Thompson v. Whitaker Iron Co., 41 W. Va. 574, 23 S. E. 795; Mutual L. Ins. Co. v. Garland, 23 (Tex. Civ. App.) 380, 56 S. W. 551; People v. Kendall, 14 Colo. App. 175, 59 Pac. 409; Fry v. Clow, 3 N. Y. Supp. 393, 50 Hun 574, 20 N. Y. St. Rep. 847; Bowman v. Huffman, 47 N. Y. St. Rep. 487, 20 N. Y. Supp. 415, 22 Civ. Proc. 371.

Amendment of the complaint in an action for conversion, by adding a charge of trespass, does not cause the statute of limitations to run to the

no right to keep on demand amounts to a conversion of itself.[50] Where an actual conversion is shown to have been made, although not known to the owner, the statute runs from the date of the conversion, unless the defendant has fraudulently concealed the fact,

date of the amendment, if it states the same cause of action, since the allegation of trespass may be treated as surplusage. Woodham v. Cline, 130 Cal. 497, 62 Pac. 822.

The statute applies only to a wrongful act done by the defendant himself; if one person is guilty of a conversion, and afterwards another person is guilty of a conversion of the same thing, the application of the statute to the first of them in no way affects the other. Miller v. Dell (1891), 1 Q. B. 468, 471.

50. Read v. Markle, 3 Johns. (N. Y.) 523; Montague v. Smith, *supra*. In Compton v. Chandless, 4 Esp. 18, Lord Kenyon said, as to the plea of the statute of limitations, that the inclination of his mind was that the plea was insufficient. That in the case of an action for trover, if the goods are left with another the statute of limitations does not begin to run from the time of delivery; but from the time of demand and refusal. According to Lord Holt, the very assuming to one's self the property and right of disposing of another man's goods is a conversion of them. "And certainly," observes Lord Ellenborough, "a man is guilty of a conversion who takes my property by assignment from another, who has no authority to dispose of it; for what is that but assisting that other in carrying his wrongful act into effect?" M'Combie v. Davies, 6 East 540. And if such person acts as agent for another who subsequently, although without knowledge that the sale was illegal, adopts it, the latter will also be liable. Hilbery v. Hatton, 33 Law J. Exch. 190; Fowler v. Hollins, L. R. 7 Q. B. 616.

When the chattels of the plaintiff have been wrongfully taken possession of by the defendant, but have come into his hands in a lawful manner, he cannot be made responsible for a conversion of them until they have been demanded of him by the owner or the person entitled to the possession of them, and he has refused to deliver them up. Whenever, therefore, the goods of one man have lawfully come into the hands of another, the owner, or person entitled to the possession of them, should go himself, or send some one with a proper authority to demand and receive them; and if the holder of the goods then refuses to deliver them up, or permit them to be removed, there will be evidence of a conversion. Thorogood v. Robinson, 6 Q. B. 772; for "whoever," observes Holt, C. J., "takes upon himself to detain another man's goods from him without cause, takes upon himself the right of disposing of them," and is guilty of a conversion. Baldwin v. Cole, 6 Mod. 212. The demand and refusal do not in themselves constitute the conversion. They are evidence of a conversion at some previous period. Wilton v. Girdlestone, 5 B. & Ald. 847.

or been guilty of fraud to prevent the owner from obtaining knowledge of it within the statutory period.[51] So where the original taking is unlawful, as no demand is necessary, or proof of actual conversion, a right of action accrues from the time of the taking.[52] The question as to how far the title to personal property is affected by its retention by a person until the statute has barred an action for its recovery is one of considerable importance; and it may be said that, within the jurisdiction where the statute has run upon the claim, there seems to be no question but that the effect of the statute is to transfer the legal title to the person in possession, so that he may maintain an action even against the former owner for any interference therewith.[53] Thus, where a tenant erects buildings upon leased premises and permits them to remain there for more than six years after his time has expired, the statute of limitations bars all claim for their recovery by him, and transfers the title thereto to the owner of the land.[54] But, in order to defeat the title of the true owner to the property, the possession must be adverse, the same rule obtaining in this respect as obtains relative to lands;[55] but the possession must be

51. Granger v. George, 5 B. & C. 149; Johnson v. White, 21 Miss. 584; Smith v. Newby, 13 Mo. 159; Short v. McCarthy, 3 B. & C. 626; Melville v. Brown, 15 Mass. 82; Ward v. Dulaney, 23 Miss. 410; Clarke v. Marriott, 9 Gill (Md.) 331; Brown v. Howard, 2 B. & B. 73; Jordan v. Thornton, 7 Ga. 517; Dench v. Walker, 14 Mass. 500; Ashmead v. Kellogg, 23 Conn. 70. That a fraudulent concealment of the fact of conversion will defeat the operation of the statute, except from the time when the facts were or ought to have been discovered, has been held in South Carolina and Mississippi, and doubtless would be held in all the States where fraud is regarded as sufficient to suspend the operation of the statute in any case. Fears v. Sykes, 35 Miss. 633; Clarke v. Reeder, 1 Speers (S. C.) 398; Simons v. Fox, 12 Rich. (S. C.) L. 392.

52. Davis v. Duncan, 1 McCord (S. C.) 213; Woodbury v. Long, 25 Mass. (8 Pick.) 543.

53. Mercein v. Burton, 17 Tex. 206; Winburn v. Cochran, 9 Tex. 123 Cockfield v. Hudson, 1 Brev. (S. C.) 311; McArthur v. Carrie, 32 Ala. 75; Howell v. Hair, 15 Ala. 194; Bohannon v. Chapman, 17 Ala. 696; Ewell v. Tedwell, 20 Ark. 136; Vandever v. Vandever, 60 Ky. (3 Met.) 137; Clark v. Slaughter, 34 Miss. 65; Divine v. Bullock, 60 Ky. (3 Met.) 418.

54. Preston v. Briggs, 16 Vt. 124.

55. Baker v. Chase, 55 N. H. 61.

continuous in the person seeking to avail himself thereof, and he cannot tack it to the possession of another, and thus acquire title under the statute.[56] If the property is held as bailee under a contract, or in recognition of the owner's title, the statute does not run against the owner until the person so holding it has done some decisive act evincing a determination to deny the owner's title. Thus, where bonds were pledged to a person as security for a loan, and held by him for several years, it was held that the statute did not begin to run against the owner until he had repaid the loan and demanded the bonds; and then, upon the refusal or neglect of the pledgee to return them, the statute began to run, and not before.[57] In such a case, the owner has his choice of remedies, either in trover for the conversion or in assumpsit for the value, of the property, upon the implied contract to return the property on payment of the loan; consequently, although an action of trover may be barred, a remedy may still remain upon the implied contract.[58]

§ 184. Trespass, Assault, etc.

In an action for seizing personal property under an execution against a stranger, the statute begins to run from the date of seizure, and the fact that a claim to the property is interposed and litigated in the same case will not suspend the operation of the statute,[59] and in all cases of trespass, either to the person or property,

56. Beadle v. Hunter, 3 Strobh. (S. C.) 31; Hobbs v. Ballard, 37 Tenn. (5 Sneed) 395; Moffatt v. Buchanan, 30 Tenn. (11 Humph.) 369; Wells v. Ragland, 31 Tenn. (1 Swan) 501.

57. Roberts v. Berdell, 61 Barb. (N. Y.) 37, 52 N. Y. 644; Jones v. Jones, 18 Ala. 248.

If the defendant has in good faith, and without notice of the plaintiff's rights, received in pledge the latter's goods from his bailee, and has afterwards sold them, limitation commences to run when the defendant acquired possession, and not from the time of his subsequent sale of the goods. Harpending v. Meyer, 55 Cal. 555; Kinkead v. Holmes & B. F. Co., 64 Pac. 157, 24 Wash. 216. See Hennessey v. Stempel, 52 La. Ann. 449, 26 So. 1004.

58. Kirkman v. Philips, 54 Tenn. (7 Heisk.) 222.

59. Baker v. Boozer, 58 Ga. 195.

the statute runs from the time it was committed,[60] and not from the time when the full extent of the injury was ascertained. This is also the rule as to trespass *quare clausum fregit* for mesne profits.[61] In equity as well as at law, in the absence of any special circumstances to the contrary, a trespasser in possession of the estate of another must account for the mesne profits for the whole time he has been in possession, so far as the account is not barred by any express statute. But such circumstances are readily assumed; and where the defendants have been in justifiable ignorance of plaintiff's title, the account will usually be taken only from the date of the filing of the bill.[62] In an adverse suit in the nature of an ejectment bill, the account is directed only from the filing of the bill; but in a suit against a person in a fiduciary character the account is taken either from the original period, or if the court thinks fit, on account of the plaintiff's laches, for the six years only previous to the filing of the bill.[63] But this is so only in cases where there is " no fraud, no suppression, no infamy." [64]

§ 185. Criminal conversation.

An action for *crim. con.* is treated as an action on the case rather than in the nature of trespass, as the injury is consequential rather than direct, and consequently the life of the remedy depends upon the statutory period provided for actions on the case.[65] Of course the statute begins to run from the time when the offence was committed.[66]

60. Kerns v .Schoonmaker, 4 Ohio 331.

61. Hill v. Myers, 46 Pa. 15; Lynch v. Cox, 23 Pa. 265.

62. Dormer v. Fortescue, 3 Atk. 124; Pettiward v. Prescott, 7 Ves. 541; Bowes v. East London Waterworks, 3 Madd. 375-383; Atty-Gen. v. Exeter, 2 Russ. 45; Clarke v. Yonge, 5 Beav. 523.

63. Per Wood, V. C., in Thomas v. Thomas, 2 K. & J. 79.

64. Hicks v. Sallitt, 3 De G. M. & G. 782.

65. Cook v. Sayer, 2 Wils. 85; Sanborn v. Neilson, 5 N. H. 314; Macfadzen v. Olivant, 6 East 387.

66. Tidd's Practice, 5.

In Illinois, where a wife can sue for enticing away her husband, her cause of action is not " for an injury to the person," limited to two years, but is one not specially provided for, and so within the five years' limita-

§ 186. Seduction.

In an action for seduction, the statute begins to run from the date of the seduction; but in an action by a parent for the loss of service resulting from such seduction, the statute does not begin to run until the birth of the child and the mother's recovery therefrom,[67] or in other words, until the loss of service has accrued.

§ 187. Failure to perform duty imposed by statute.

Where the statute imposes a duty, and specifies a time within which it shall be performed, and gives to certain parties a remedy if it is not performed, the statute begins to run immediately upon the failure to perform within the time specified. Thus, where the statute requires the officers of a corporation to file an annual report in a certain office, on or before a certain day, and provides certain remedies upon a failure to make such report, the statute begins to run immediately upon a failure to perform by the day named.[68] In all such cases, the decisive question is, When did the plaintiff's right of action first accrue? and from that date the statute runs.

§ 187a. Torts in general—Limitations applicable.

The Alabama statute, limiting actions for any injury to the person or rights of another, not arising from contract and not otherwise specially enumerated, to one year, applies to an action for injuries to a lower riparian proprietor for pollution of a water course.[69] An action against a carrier for wrongful ejection of a

tion. Bassett v. Bassett, 20 Ill. App. 543, 548.

67. Wilhoit v. Hancock, 68 Ky. (5 Bush) 567.

68. Duckworth v. Roach, 8 Daily (N. Y.) 159.

The modern action provided by statute for indemnity, from the officers of a corporation who make false reports, is for indemnity only for the fraud, and is not an action for a penalty given by statute. American Credit Indemnity Co. v. Ellis, 156 Ind. 212, 59 N. E. 679. See Louisville & N. R. Co. v. Pittman, 21 Ky. Law Rep. 1037, 53 S. W. 1040.

69. Tutwiler Coal, Coke & Iron Co. v. Nichols, 145 Ala. 666, 39 So. 762, 146 Ala. 364, 119 Am. St. Rep. 34.

passenger by trainmen is not within Kirby's Dig. Ark., § 5065(1), providing that actions for criminal conversation, assault and battery, and false imprisonment shall be commenced within one year after accrual of cause of action, but is within section 5064, prescribing a three years' limitation for all actions founded on any contract or liability, expressed or implied, not in writing.[70] An action for conversion is governed by Cal. Code Civ. Proc., § 338, subd. 3, requiring an action for taking, detaining, or injuring any goods or chattels to be brought within three years.[71] In Georgia, an action by a father to recover damages for the seduction of his daughter is barred by the statute of limitations, unless brought within two years from the time the right of action accrued.[72] The Kansas tort statute of limitations has no application to an action on *quasi* contract to recover money paid by mistake.[73] The right of action by a city, sued for injuries in collision with an obstruction in the street, against one responsible for the obstruction, is subject to Ky. St., § 2515, requiring actions for injuries not arising on contract to be commenced within five years.[74] The one-year prescription under La. Civ. Code, art. 3536, for damages from offenses and *quasi* offenses, applies to damages from the in-

70. St. Louis, etc., Ry. Co. v. Mynott, 83 Ark. 6, 102 S. W. 380.

See, as to application of Arkansas statute of limitations to other actions, Cockrill v. Cooper, 86 Fed. 7, 29 C. C. A. 529, rev'g Cockrill v. Butler, 78 Fed. 679; Emrich v. Little Rock Traction & Electric Co., 71 Ark. 71, 70 S. W. 1035.

71. Allsopp v. Joshua Hendy Mach. Works, 5 Cal. App. 228, 90 Pac. 39; Lowe v. Ozmun, 137 Cal. 257, 70 Pac. 87.

72. Hutcherson v. Durden, 113 Ga. 987, 54 L. R. A. 811, 39 S. E. 495.

73. Kansas City v. R. J. & W. M. Boyd Const. Co., 86 Kan. 213, 120 Pac. 347.

An employe's action for injuries from the master's failure to comply with the Factory Act Laws 1903, c. 356, Gen. St. 1909, §§ 4676, 4683), is not barred by Code Civ. Proc., § 17, subd. 4 (Gen. St. 1909, § 5610), providing that an action upon a statute for a penalty or forfeiture shall be barred within one year, but is an action for injury to the rights of another not arising on contract, which carries a two-years' limitation. Slater v. Atchison, etc., Ry. Co., 91 Kan. 226, 137 Pac. 943.

74. City of Louisville v. O'Donaghue, 157 Ky. 243, 162 S. W. 1110.

An action against a railroad for damages for depreciation in the value

fringement of some right personal to the individual, or the violation of some duty imposed by law.[75] An action for fraud, being an action of tort, is barred by Mass. Rev. Laws 1902, c. 202, §§ 2, 10, after six years, and no better standing can be acquired by bringing a suit in equity.[76] In Missouri, the five-year statute of limitations is applicable to an action by the receiver of a bank against the directors for negligence in managing the bank.[77] In New Jersey, an action for alienating a wife's affections, for enticing her away, and for criminal conversation is an action on the case and barred only after six years.[78] In an action for nuisance, a defense that the cause of action did not accrue within three years is insufficient, under N. Y. Code Civ. Proc., § 382, subd. 3.[79] In Oregon, an action by plaintiff for interfering with his rights,

of the use of plaintiff's residence, as well as for personal inconvenience by reason of unwholesome odors from a stagnant pool maintained by the road along its right of way, must be brought within five years. Cumberland R. Co. v. Bays, 153 Ky. 159, 154 S. W. 929.

75. Sims v. New Orleans Ry. & Light Co., 134 La. 897, 64 So. 823.

For actions barred by the prescription of one year, see: J. A. Bel Lumber Co. v. Stout, 134 La. 987, 64 So. 881, action for recovery of logs, or for damages; Thomas v. Whittington, 127 La. 551, 53 So. 860, action for fraud of a notary public in causing one to sign a deed; Goodwin v. Bodcaw Lumber Co., 109 La. 1050, 34 So. 74; Levert v. Sharpe, 52 La. Ann. 599, a claim for punitive damages for trespass; Dobbins v. Lyons, Man. Unrep. Cas. 215.

For actions not barred by the prescription of one year, see: Gordon v. Stanley, 108 La. 182, 32 So. 531, action for breach of official bond; Vaudry v. New Orleans Cotton Exchange, 2 McGloin 154; Fairex v. New Orleans City R. Co., 36 La. Ann. 60, action to recover from a corporation dividends wrongfully paid; Loeb v. Decuir, Man. Unrep. Cas. 402, action to enforce a lease; Illinois Cent. R. Co. v. S. Segari & Co., 205 Fed. 998.

The plea of three years' prescription applies only to cases arising from contract, but the plea of one year prescription is the proper one to be applied in actions for torts. Standard Chemical Co. v. Illinois Cent. R. Co., 130 La. 148, 57 So. 782.

76. Marvel v. Cobb, 200 Mass. 293, 86 N. E. 360.

77. Stone v. Rottman, 183 Mo. 552, 82 S. W. 76.

78. Crane v. Ketcham, 83 N. J. 327, 84 Atl. 1052, and is not an action for "injury to the person," barred after two years under Statute of Limitations, § 3, as amended in 1896 (3 Comp. St. 1910, p. 3164).

79. McClusky v. Wile, 70 Misc. Rep. 135, 128 N. Y. Supp. 190, judg. rev'd 129 N. Y. Supp. 455.

under an agreement made with defendant to settle and establish the respective rights of the parties to the water and ditches therein mentioned, in that defendant entered upon the ditch upon his own land and diverted water so that it failed to reach the lands of the plaintiff, but did not enter upon the plaintiff's land, is an action on the case, and is barred in two years.[80] An action against a judgment creditor for directing the levy and sale under execution of exempt personal property is within Utah Comp. Laws 1907, § 2877, providing that an action for taking personalty must be commenced within three years.[81] An action by the creditor of a corporation against the purchaser of its assets based on the conversion of the property is barred by the Texas two-year statute of limitations.[82] Where a city misappropriated moneys belonging to a special fund, a mandamus brought by the holder of a warrant drawn on such fund to compel its payment is barred in three years under the Washington statute of limitations.[83]

§ 187b. Injuries to the person.

The Connecticut Revision of 1902 (Gen. St. 1902, § 1119), which provides that no action against a municipal or other corporation for injury to the person shall be brought but within one year from the date of the injury, applies to actions against any corporation, public or private, for an injury to the person.[84] Whether an ac-

Where an action for the conversion of bonds was brought within six years after their conversion, and within two years and seven months after plaintiff's discovery of the conversion, the six-year limitation was not a defense. MacDonnell v. Buffalo Loan, Trust & Safe Deposit Co., 193 N. Y. 92, 85 N. E. 801, aff'g judg. Medina Gas & Electric Light Co. v. Buffalo Loan, Trust & Safe Deposit Co., 119 App. Div. 245, 104 N. Y. Supp. 625.

80. Dalton v. Kelsey, 58 Or. 244, 114 Pac. 464, under Or. L. O. L., § 8, and is not an action on the contract or for trespass, which are barred in six years by L. O. L., § 6, subd. 1.

81. Snow v. West, 35 Utah 206, 99 Pac. 674.

82. Clevenger v. Galloway & Garrison (Tex. Civ. App.), 104 S. W. 914.

83. Quaker City Nat. Bank v. City of Tacoma, 27 Wash. 259, 67 Pac. 710, under Ballinger's Ann. Code & St. Wash., § 4800, subd. 2.

84. Fitzgerald v. Scovil Mfg. Co. 77 Conn. 528, 60 Atl. 132.

tion against a carrier for a personal injury is in form *ex contractu* or *ex delicto,* it is governed by Cal. Code Civ. Proc., § 340, subd. 3, relating to limitation on actions for personal injuries.[85] An action by a husband for damages for loss of the services of his wife occasioned by her personal injuries is barred by the two-year limitation fixed by Burns' Ann. St., Ind. 1908, § 295.[86] In Georgia, an action for injuries to the person must be brought within two years after the cause of action accrues.[87] In Illinois, an action over by an employer against an amploye on a judgment for damages for injuries caused by the employe's negligence need not be brought within two years, the time limited for bringing actions for personal injuries.[88] The one-year limitation prescribed in Ky. St., § 2516, and not that in section 2515, applies to an action by a widow, under section 4, to recover damages for the wanton shooting of her husband.[89] In New Jersey, the two-year limitation applies to actions for personal injuries caused outside the state.[90] In Florida, an action against a physician for damages

An action to recover for injuries caused by negligence is barred when not brought within one year by Gen. St. 1902, § 1119, as amended by Laws 1893, c. 149. Sharkey v. Skilton, 83 Conn. 503, 77 Atl. 950.

85. Basler v. Sacramento Electric, Gas & Ry. Co., 166 Cal. 33, 134 Pac. 993.

86. Mullen v. Town of New Castle, 180 Ind. 386, 103 N. E. 1.

87. Brown v. Emerson Brick Co., 15 Ga. App. 332, 83 S. E. 160, under Civ. Code Ga. 1910, § 4497.

88. Sherman House Hotel Co. v. Butler Street Foundry & Iron Co., 168 Ill. App. 549.

The right of action given by the mines and miners act to the widow, etc., of a person killed through the willful violation of such act, is governed by the general law in regard to the limitation of actions. Donk Bros. Coal & Coke Co. v. Sapp, 133 Ill. App. 92.

89. Irwin v. Smith, 150 Ky. 147, 150 S. W. 22.

The damages for failure to deliver a telegram, or delay in delivering it, are not "injuries to the person," within the meaning of Ky. St. 1903, § 2515, prescribing limitations of one year in actions against corporations for injuries to the person. Western Union Telegraph Co. v. Witt, 33 Ky. Law Rep. 685, 110 S. W. 889.

90. Mooney v. Camden Iron Works, 83 N. J. Sup. 32, 83 Atl. 770, supplement of March 24, 1896, to the statute of limitations (P. L. p. 119).

This applies only to actions for personal injuries, and hence not to an action to recover for injury to a vessel caused by a negligent collision.

ɔr negligent treatment causing injury is a cause of action upon n obligation or liability not founded upon an instrument in writ- ıg, and is barred in three years.[91] The limitation prescribed by tatute in Kansas in actions for trespass to person is one year.[92] n Louisiana, actions for damages for personal injuries resulting rom offenses or *quasi* offenses are prescribed by one year.[93] In Iebraska, a civil action for assault and battery with circum- tances of aggravation must be begun within one year.[94] In Michi- an, an action for seduction is an action for personal injuries, arred in three years.[95] The complaint against a street surface ailroad for personal injury from a hole in the part of a street hich, by Raiload Law (Consol. Laws, c. 49), § 178, it is required ɔ keep in a good and safe condition, alleging the injury was due ɔ defendant "suffering" said hole to be and remain, states a ause of action for negligence, within the three-year limitation rescribed by N. Y. Code Civ. Proc., § 383; though, if the railroad reated the hole, it would be liable for the injury as the creator of nuisance, and the six-year limitation of section 382 would apply.[96] ın action against a city for injuries to an employe is governed by he six-year limitation prescribed by Minn. Rev. Laws 1905, § 076, subd. 5, and not by the two-year limitations prescribed by ection 4078, subd. 1.[97] In Maryland, an action for personal in-

ailey v. Kiernan, 75 N. J. Law, 275, 7 Atl. 1027.

91. Palmer v. Jackson, 62 Fla. 249, 7 So. 240, under Fla. Gen. St. 1906, 1725, subd. 5.

92. Smith v. Cline, 3 Kan. 506, un- er Code of 1858.

93. Warner v. New Orleans & C. . Co., 104 La. 536, 29 So. 226.

A street car passenger's action for ıjuries while she was attempting to light is barred by prescription under iv. Code, art. 3536, when not brought ithin one year. Sims v. New Or- ans Ry. & Light Co., 134 La. 897, 64 o. 823.

94. Borchert v. Bash, 97 Neb. 593, 150 N. W. 830, under Neb. Civ. Code, § 13.

95. May v. Wilson, 17 Detroit Leg. N. 1023, 128 N. W. 1084, under Pub. Acts 1899, No. 155, a "personal" wrong or injury being an invasion of personal right and pertaining to the person.

96. Hayes v. Brooklyn Heights R. Co., 200 N. Y. 183, 93 N. E. 469, rev'g judg. 134 App. Div. 912, 118 N. Y. Supp. 810.

97. Quackenbush v. Village of Slay- ton, 120 Minn. 373, 139 N. W. 716.

Section 5138, Gen. St. 1894, subsec.

juries resulting from negligence merely is not within the one-year statute of limitation.[98] In Ohio, an action for injuries resulting from malpractice must be brought within one year.[99] In an action for malicious prosecution, the six-year limitation under the Pennsylvania Act of 1713 (1 Smith's Laws, p. 76), which provides that actions on the case other than for slander shall be commenced within six years, governs.[1] In Rhode Island, whatever the form, actions for personal injuries, whether by breach of contract or duty, such as malpractice, or by force, must be brought within two years.[2]

1, as amended by Laws 1895, c. 30, providing that the following actions may be brought within two years: "Libel, slander, assault, battery, false imprisonment, or other tort resulting in personal injury,"—includes an action for malicious prosecution. Bryant v. American Surety Co., 69 Minn. 30, 71 N. W. 826.

"Personal injury" actions, the result of negligence, are not within Gen. St. 1878, c. 66, § 8, subd. 1, making two years the limit for the action for battery, nor are they within the rule of *ejusdem generis*, as applied to an action for battery. Ott v. Great Northern Ry. Co., 70 Minn. 50, 72 N. W. 833.

98. Baltimore City Passenger Ry. Co. v. Tanner, 90 Md. 315, 45 Atl. 188, under Md. Code Pub. Gen. Laws, art. 57, § 1, prescribing a one-year limitation for actions "of assault, battery, and wounding, or any of them."

99. Tucker v. Gillette, 12 O. C. D. 401, 22 Ohio Cir. Ct R. 664, under Rev. St., § 4983, prescribing limitations of one year for an action of libel, slander, and malpractice. See also Shuman v. Drayton, 8 O. C. D. 12, 14 Ohio Cir. Ct. R. 328.

1. Boyd v. Snyder, 207 Pa. 330, 56 Atl. 924, Act June 24, 1895 (P. L. 236), applying only to injuries to the person not resulting in death, and not to a suit for malicious prosecution. And see Rodenbaugh v. Philadelphia Traction Co., 190 Pa. 358, 42 Atl. 953, 24 Wkly. Notes Cas. 105.

2. Griffin v. Woodhead, 30 R. I. 204, 74 Atl. 417, the period allowed by Court and Practice Act 1905, § 248; such actions being excepted from §§ 249 and 250, relating to actions of trespass, case, and debt on contract.

As to actions for personal injuries in other jurisdictions, see:

Tenn.—Blackwell v. Memphis St. Ry. Co., 124 Tenn. 516, 137 S. W. 486, one year limitation prescribed by Code 1858, § 2772 (Shannan's Code, § 4469).

Tex.—Texas Cent. R. Co. v. Hawkins (Tex. Civ. App.), 163 S. W. 132, two-year limitation; Kelly v. Western Union Tel. Co., 17 Tex. Civ. App. 344, 43 S. W. 532, one year in action for injuries resulting from non-delivery of a telegram.

Va.—Birmingham v. Chesapeake & O. Ry. Co., 98 Va. 548, 37 S. E. 17, 2 Va. Sup. Ct. Rep. 465, one year, in

§ 187c. Injuries to property.

In Alabama, an action by a riparian proprietor for pollution of a water course is within the statute of limitations of one year.[3] In Arkansas, the three years limitations applies to an action for injury to land by the obstruction by a railroad right of way embankment of the surface water so as to divert it upon the land.[4] In Connecticut, an action by a tenant against his landlord for damages to a stock of merchandise from the collapse and fall of the leased building because of defendant's alleged negligence is an action "for an injury to personal property."[5] In California, a discharge of sewage so as to render impassable the street in front of premises of others, and so as to wash away the soil of such premises, is not a trespass, subject to the limitation of three years.[6] In Colorado, an action for the wrongful conversion of money is not

action for trespass on the case in assumpsit to recover damages for personal injuries resulting from negligence, as the limitation is determined by the object of the action, and not by its form.

W. Va.—Curry v. Town of Mannington, 23 W. Va. 14, one year; Kuhn v. Brownfield, 34 W. Va. 252, 12 S. E. 519, 11 L. R. A. 700, one year, in action for malpractice.

Wis.—Donner v. Graap, 134 Wis. 523, 115 N. W. 125, one year, under St. 1898, § 4222, subd. 5, in an action to recover for injuries sustained by being accidentally struck with a beer glass.

3. Tutwiler Coal, Coke & Iron Co. v. Nichols, 145 Ala. 666, 39 So. 762, 146 Ala. 364, 119 Am. St. Rep. 34; Parsons v. Tennessee Coal, Iron & R. Co., 186 Ala. 84, 64 So. 591. See Western Ry. of Alabama v. Hart, 160 Ala. 599, 49 So. 371, as to action against a carrier as a warehouseman.

4. Kelly v. Kansas City Southern Ry. Co., 92 Ark. 465, 123 S. W. 664, under Kirby's Dig., § 5064.

5. Miner, Read & Garrette v. McNamara, 82 Conn. 578, 74 Atl. 933, within Gen. St. 1902, § 1119, as amended by Laws 1903, p. 114, c. 149, barring such action in one year.

An action by a riparian owner against a city for pollution of a water course by the discharge of sewage is within the six-year limitation for actions founded on a tort unaccompanied by force. Platt Bros. & Co. v. City of Waterbury, 80 Conn. 179, 67 Atl. 508.

6. Crim v. City & County of San Francisco, 152 Cal. 279, 92 Pac. 640, under Code Civ. Proc., § 338, subd. 2.

An action for conversion is within Code Civ. Proc., § 338. Lowe v. Ozmun, 137 Cal. 257, 70 Pac. 87. An action by the owner of a lot to abate an obstruction of the street opposite his lot is not barred by § 318, Code Civ. Proc. within five years. McLean v. Llewellyn Iron Works, 2 Cal. App.

one for relief against fraud, to be commenced within three years, but may be commenced within six years.[7] An action to recover damages to land which was washed away by reason of structures built in a river by defendant is one for a "trespass."[8] In Georgia, a suit to recover damages to realty must be brought within four years.[9] In Illinois, the five-year period applies as to real property damaged, but not actually taken by a company having the right of eminent domain.[10] In Iowa, where a landowner, claiming the right to repel surface water coming from an adjacent tract, erects a barrier on the partition line and maintains the same with the knowledge, or express or implied consent, of the owner of the adjacent tract for ten years, the right of the latter to an injunction against the maintenance of the obstruction is barred.[11] An action for trespass through the permanent obstruction of the channel of a stream so as to divert its natural flow against the opposite bank, and thereby destroy a portion of plaintiff's land, is barred by the Kansas two-year statute of limitations.[12] In Kentucky, an action for the wrongful diversion of a natural stream across lands is barred by a period of five years.[13] In Louisiana, a claim for dam-

346, 83 Pac. 1082, rehearing denied 2 Cal. App. 346, 83 Pac. 1085. See also Scrivner v. Woodward, 139 Cal. 314, 73 Pac. 863, as to action for conversion of bonds.

7. Colorado Fuel & Iron Co. v. Chappell, 12 Colo. App. 385, 55 Pac. 606.

8. Cartwright v. Southern Pac. Co., 206 Fed. 234 (U. S. D. C.).

9. Adams v. Macon, D. & S. R. Co., 141 Ga. 701, 81 S. E. 1110, under Civ. Code 1910, § 4495. See also Taylor v. James, 109 Ga. 327, 34 S. E. 674; Burns v. Horkan, 126 Ga. 161, 54 S. E. 946; Crawford v. Crawford, 134 Ga. 114, 67 S. E. 673.

10. Bell v. Mattoon Waterworks & Reservoir Co., 163 Ill. App. 615.

11. Thiessen v. Claussen, 135 Iowa 187, 112 N. W. 545.

12. Taylor v. Newman, 91 Kan. 864, 139 Pac. 369.

An action for wrongfully recording an instrument conveying lands is within the two-year limitation. Hatfield v. Malin, 6 Ka. App. 855, 50 Pac. 108. Where the complaint alleges the conversion of personalty in 1902, the action therefor in 1910 is barred, though there is a prayer for an accounting. Blackwell v. Blackwell, 88 Kan. 495, 129 Pac. 173.

13. Chicago, etc., R. Co. v. Hoover, 147 Ky. 33, 143 S. W. 770; Moore v. Lawrence County, 143 Ky. 448, 136 S. W. 1031; King v. Board of Council of City of Danville, 32 Ky. Law Rep.

ages for unauthorized establishment of a right of way by a railroad company is barred by the ten-year statute of limitations.[14] In North Carolina, the unlawful diversion of water in a stream is not a trespass on realty, within Code, § 155, as amended by Laws 1895, c. 165, requiring actions for a continuing trespass to be brought within three years, but is an action for permanent damages within the five-year statute.[15] In Missouri, the injury for polluting a stream by the construction of a sewer entering into the stream is permanent, and an action therefor is barred in ten years.[16] In Ohio, an action against a street railway company for injury to a city pavement, requiring repairs by the paving contractor under its contract with the city, is barred in four years.[17] The New Jersey statute of limitations of six years does not apply to recovery of

1188, 107 S. W. 1189. See, as to other limitations, Richardson v. Louisville & N. R. Co., 33 Ky. Law Rep. 916, 111 S. W. 343, rehearing denied 112 S. W. 582; City of Louisville v. Seibert, 21 Ky. Law Rep. 328, 51 S. W. 310.

14. Brewer v. Yazoo & M. V. R. Co., 128 La. 544, 54 So. 987; McCutchen v. Texas & P. Ry. Co., 118 La. 436, 42 So. 42.

Action for damages for alleged taking of right of way in street is an action *ex delicto*, barred by prescription of one year. Standard Chemical Co. v. Illinois Cent. R. Co., 130 La. 148, 57 So. 782. One year also bars an action by a co-owner of lands against the owner in possession for damages for cutting timber. Davis v. Ruddock Orleans Cypress Co., 132 La. 985, 62 So. 114. See also Gilmore v. Schenck, 115 La. 386, 39 So. 40; Shields v. Whitlock & Brown, 110 La. 714, 34 So. 747.

15. Owenby v. Louisville & N. R. Co., 165 N. C. 641, 81 S. E. 997; Geer v. Durham Water Co., 127 N. C. 349, 37 S. E. 474; Roberts v. Baldwin, 151 N. C. 407, 66 S. E. 346.

16. Luckey v. City of Brookfield, 167 Mo. App. 161, 151 S. W. 201.

An action for the building of solid railway embankments causing a permanent backing up of surface water is barred in sixteen years. Gorman v. Chicago, B. & Q. R. Co., 166 Mo. App. 320, 148 S. W. 1009.

17. Barber Asphalt Paving Co. v. Northern Ohio Traction & Light Co., 202 Fed. 817, 121 C. C. A. 125, under Gen. Code Ohio, § 11224, barring torts.

If an action is on "a liability created by st tute other than a forfeiture or penalty," for which Gen. Code Ohio, § 11222, provides a six-year limitation, it is controlled by such section. Hocking Valley R. Co. v. New York Coal Co., 217 Fed. 727. See City of Norwalk v. Blatz, 29 Ohio Cir. Ct. R. 306, action for flooding of land, four years.

award in condemnation proceedings or interest thereon.[18] In Texas, in trespass to try title to land wrongfully appropriated by a railroad company for its right of way, action is barred by the two-years statute.[19] An unlawful change in the grade of a street is not a taking of the property of an adjoining owner or a continuing nuisance, and a right of action to recover for damages thereby occasioned accrues at completion of the change and is barred within six years by New York Code Civ. Proc., §§ 381, 382.[20] In Tennessee, an action in assumpsit for the value of standing timber wrongfully cut and removed is barred in six years.[21] An action of trespass, in Idaho, is limited to three years.[22] In Pennsylvania, the reversioner under a 999-year lease can recover for coal unlawfully mined and converted only as to coal taken

18. Watson v. Jersey City, 84 N. J. 422, 86 Atl. 402.

19. Southern Kansas Ry. Co. of Texas v. Vance (Tex. Civ. App.), 155 S. W. 696. See also Chicago, etc., Ry. Co. v. Johnson (Tex. Civ. App.), 156 S. W. 253. An action against a carrier for nondelivery of goods without sufficient excuse, or for injuries to freight, is barred in two years. Missouri, K. & T. Ry. Co. v. Harris (Tex. Civ. App.), 138 S. W. 1085; R. W. Williamson & Co. v. Texas & P. By. Co. (Tex. Civ. App.), 138 S. W. 807. An action for cutting timber on land belonging to intervenors is barred in two years. Kirby v. Hayden (Tex. Civ. App.), 99 S. W. 746. Likewise an action for damages to property caused by the construction of an embankment and switch track. Houston & T. C. R. Co. v. Barr (Tex. Civ. App.), 99 S. W. 437. See Davies v. Texas Cent. R. Co. (Tex. Civ. App.), 133 S. W. 295, as to what acts the word "trespass" includes. An action for conversion must be brought within two years. Texarkana Water Co. v. Kizer (Tex. Civ. App.), 63 S. W. 913; Galveston, etc., Ry. Co. v. Clemons, 19 Tex. Civ. App. 452, 47 S. W. 731.

In West Virginia, the period of limitation for unlawful conversion of personal property, or its proceeds, is five years. Thompson v. Whitaker Iron Co., 41 W. Va. 574, 23 S. E. 795.

20. Kehres v. City of New York, 147 N. Y. Supp. 825.

Action to compel the removal of structures in a street appurtenant to abutting property, which were unlawful and constituted an interference with relator's easement as lessee of adjoining property, is barred in twenty years. People v. Ahearn, 124 App. Div. 840, 109 N. Y. Supp. 249.

21. Whitaker v. Poston, 120 Tenn. 207, 110 S. W. 1019.

22. Hill v. Empire State-Idaho Mining & Developing Co., 158 Fed. 881 (U. S. C. C., Idaho).

within six years before bringing the action.[23] In Oklahoma, an action for wrongfully killing cattle must be brought within two years.[24] In Maine, the right of action for trespass is barred in six years.[25] An action to recover damages for unauthorized registry of land in Porto Rico is barred in one year.[26] "Trespass on real property," as used in the Washington Code, does not apply to an action involving mere consequential injuries resulting from the raising of a street grade.[27]

23. Trustees of Proprietors of Kingston v. Lehigh Valley Coal Co., 241 Pa. 469, 88 Atl. 763, unless the injury was not discovered until within the six-year period.

An action against the city for damages from the giving of an erroneous street grade is barred in six years. Moore v. City of Lancaster, (Pa.) 58 Atl. 890.

24. Missouri, K. & T. Ry. Co. v. Wilcox (Okl.), 121 Pac. 656, under Comp. Laws 1909, § 5550, subd. 3.

25. Rollins v. Blackden, 112 Me. 459, 92 Atl. 521.

26. People of Porto Rico v. Emmanual, 35 Sup. Ct. 33, under Porto Rico Civil Code 1902, § 1869.

27. Denney v. City of Everett, 46 Wash. 342, 89 Pac. 934, under Ballinger's Ann. Codes & St., § 4800, subd. 1.

Action for taking or injuring property without compensation.

Ark.—Memphis & L. R. R. Co. v. Organ, 67 Ark. 84, 55 S. W. 952.

Cal.—Robinson v. Southern California Ry. Co., 129 Cal. 8, 61 Pac. 947.

Ill.—Dickson v. Epling, 170 Ill. 329, 48 N. E. 1001, rev'g judg. 61 Ill. App. 78.

Ind.—Southern Indiana Ry. Co. v. Brown, 30 Ind. App. 684, 66 N. E. 915.

Ky.—Rowlstone v. Chesapeake & O. Ry. Co., 21 Ky. Law Rep. 1507, 54 S. W. 2; Trustees Common School Dist. No. 14 v. Nashville, etc., R. Co., 22 Ky. Law Rep. 243, 56 S. W. 990; Ferguson v. Civington, etc., Bridge Co., 108 Ky. 662, 24 Ky. Law Rep. 1183, 1233, 71 S. W. 6; Klosterman v. Chesapeake & O. Ry. Co., 114 Ky. 426, 24 Ky. Law Rep. 1183, 1233, 71 S. W. 6.

N. C.—Cherry v. Lake Drummond Canal & Water Co., 140 N. C. 422, 53 S. E. 138, 111 Am. St. Rep. 850.

Ohio.—Fries v. Wheeling & L. E. Ry. Co., 56 Ohio St. 135, 46 N. E. 516.

S. D.—Johnson v. Hawthorne Ditch Co., 32 S. D. 499, 143 N. W. 959; Faulk v. Missouri River & N. W. Ry. Co., 28 S. D. 1, 132 N. W. 233.

Tex.—Galveston & W. Ry. Co. v. Kinkead (Tex. Civ. App.), 60 S. W. 468; Tietze v. International & G. N. R. Co., 35 Tex. Civ. App. 136, 80 S. W. 124.

Overflowing land.

Cal.—Hicks v. Drew, 117 Cal. 305, 49 Pac. 189.

Ky.—Leezer v. City of Louisville, 7 Ky. Law Rep. (abstract) 829.

N. C.—Ridley v. Seaboard & R. R. Co., 124 N. C. 34, 32 S. E. 325.

§ 187d(1). Torts in general—Accrual of right of action.

A right of action for tort accrues immediately upon the infliction of the injury.[28] Where an injury is complete at the time of the act causing it, limitations run from that time.[29] For the purpose of computing the running of limitations on an action to restrain the maintenance and operation of an elevated railroad in front of premises, the cause of action accrued when the road was completed and operations begun.[30] The statute of limitations begins to run as against a cause of action sounding in tort of which fraud is the basis as soon as the fraud and consequent injury have occurred, and not when the fraud is discovered, unless there has been a fraudulent concealment of the cause of action.[31] The cause of action by the

28. Brown v. Emerson Brick Co., 15 Ga. App. 332, 83 S. E. 160; Raleigh & G. R. Co. v. Western & A. R. Co., 6 Ga. App. 616, 65 S. E. 586. Where the commission of a wrong is attended immediately by resulting damage, the date at which the damage commenced is the point of the running of the prescription. Griffin v. Drainage Com. of New Orleans, 110 La. 840, 34 So. 799.

29. Lyman v. Holmes (Vt.), 92 Atl. 829.

An action for damages for abuse of legal process may be maintained before the action in which such process is used is terminated, and therefore the statute begins to run from the time the acts complained of were committed. Montague v. Cummings, 119 Ga. 139, 45 S. E. 979.

30. Goggin v. Manhattan Ry. Co., 104 N. Y. Supp. 548, 54 Misc. Rep. 472.

Where a railroad erected a water tank on its right of way, and such erection and use amounted to a nuisance to the occupant of a neighboring dwelling, limitations did not begin to run against an action by him for damages until the tank was built and operated. Texas & Pac. Ry. Co. v. Edrington, 100 Tex. 496, 101 S. W. 441, 9 L. R. A. (N. S.) 988.

31. Nelson v. Petterson, 131 Ill. App. 443, judg. aff'd 229 Ill. 240, 82 N. E. 229.

Where defendants fraudulently represented to plaintiff the value of certain shares of stock which they put up to secure the discount of notes, under an agreement that, "if said notes are not paid when due, then, in that event," the collateral might be sold, a cause of action for the fraud accrued so as to set limitations running at the time of the discount of the notes and the acceptance of the stock in reliance on such representation. First Nat. Bank v. Steel, 146 Mich. 308, 13 Detroit Leg. N. 762, 109 N. W. 423.

Limitations run against a cause of action for deceit by which stock subscription was induced from the date of the subscription, though part of the price was not paid until later. Ball v. Gerard, 160 App. Div. 619,

creditor of a corporation against the purchaser of its assets based on the conversion of the property arises on the day of the purchase, and limitations run from that date, though corporate property remains in the hands of a stockholder.[32]

§ 187d(2). Negligence.

In actions for injuries resulting from the negligence of another, the statute begins to run from the time the injury was inflicted, and not from the time when the full extent of the damages sustained has been ascertained.[33] In an action for injuries claimed to be caused

146 N. Y. Supp. 81. See also Reusens v. Gerard, 160 App. Div. 625, 146 N. Y. Supp. 86.

The right of minority stockholders of a corporation to compel defendant controlling it, to satisfy a judgment obtained against it, based on the fraudulent division by defendant of the surplus earnings of the corporation, accrues when the corporation is compelled to pay the judgment, and not when the wrongful division of the earnings was made; a juncture of wrong and damage giving rise to a cause of action. Dodd v. Pittsburg, etc., R. Co., 32 Ky. Law Rep. 605, 106 S. W. 787.

Where a purchaser, in buying stock of a national bank, relied on false statements as to the condition of the bank, which was in fact insolvent, and soon went into the hands of the receiver, and under the national banking law the receiver made an assessment on the stock, and obtained a judgment against the purchaser for the amount thereof, the purchaser's right of action for the amount of the assessment against those liable for the false statements did not accrue until payment of the judgment. Houston v. Thornton, 122 N. C. 365, 29 S. E. 827, 65 Am. St. Rep. 699.

Where the cashier of plaintiff bank embezzled its money by means of drafts either drawn to the order of or indorsed to defendant to cover losses in speculative transactions, the statute of limitations did not begin to run against the bank's right to recover the money from defendant until the drafts were collected. St. Charles Sav. Bank v. Orthwein Inv. Co., 160 Mo. App. 369, 140 S. W. 921.

32. Clevenger v. Galloway & Garrison (Tex. Civ. App.), 104 S. W. 914.

The rule that one who has taken part in the conversion of timber may be held as a joint wrongdoer with any one who thereafter does anything in pursuance of such conversion does not prevent the statute of limitations from running in favor of one who took such part without any knowledge that any wrong was intended, and did not participate in subsequent acts of conversion. Knisely v. Stein, 52 Mich. 380, 18 N. W. 115.

33. Calumet Electric St. Ry. Co. v. Mabie, 66 Ill. App. 235.

Expenditures made on account of

by the negligence of a city in respect to a waterway damages for injuries done six years before the suit was begun cannot be recovered.[34] Where the directors of an insolvent national bank by their negligent and wrongful acts caused the stockholders to lose their stock and subjected them to the payment of assessments which were levied upon them as stockholders, the right of action of the stockholders against the directors for damages sustained accrued at the time of the commission of the wrongful acts, and not at the time at which the assessments were levied or paid, or the damages actually sustained.[35]

§ 187d(3). Negligence in performance of professional services.

A cause of action against an abstracter of titles for giving a wrong certificate of title accrues at the date of the delivery, and not at the time the negligence is discovered or consequential damages arise.[36] Where it is claimed that an attorney was negligent in passing upon the title to certain real estate, an action against him is barred in five years from the date of such negligence and not from the date of a decision of the Supreme Court holding that the client had no title.[37] Where a physician and surgeon operates on a patient for what he pronounces to be appendicitis, and neglects or carelessly forgets to remove a sponge which he has placed in the abdominal cavity, and closes the incision with the sponge remaining therein, and this condition continues during his entire professional relation to the case, and is present when he abandons the same, limitations do not commence to run against the right to

injuries received as the result of the negligence of another does not prevent the statute of limitations from commencing to run from the time of the original injury. Birmingham v. Chesapeake & O. Ry. Co. 98 Va. 548, 2 Va. Sup. Ct. Rep. 465, 37 S. E. 17.

34. Prime v. City of Yonkers, 131 App. Div. 110, 115 N. Y. Supp. 305, judg. aff'd 199 N. Y. 542, 93 N. E. 1129.

35. Brinckeroff v. Bostwick, 34 Hun 352, judg. rev'd 99 N. Y. 185, 1 N. E. 663.

36. Provident Loan Trust Co. v. Walcott, 5 Kan. App. 473, 47 Pac. 8; Walker v. Bowman, 27 Okl. 172, 111 Pac. 319, rev'g judg. 105 Pac. 649.

37. Maloney v. Graham, 171 Ill. App. 409.

sue on account of such want of skill and attention until the case has been so abandoned or the professional relation otherwise terminated.[38] This decision is based on the theory that the injury to the patient and the negligence of the physician were continuous, and that the statute does not run against an action therefor until the relationship is ended. To the contrary it has been held that a cause of action against a physician for malpractice in setting a broken arm, based on the improper setting of the bones and on the negligent omission to discover that fact, accrues when the negligent acts were committed by the physician, without reference to the time of his discharge.[39]

§ 187d(4). Injuries to person.

A cause of action under the Employers' Liability Act of April 22, 1908, and supplements thereto, for the death of an employe of a railroad company engaged in interstate commerce, accrues on the death of the employe.[40] The cause of action for alienation of affections arises from the enticement of the spouse away, and where the spouse does not return, but remains with the enticer, and there is no new enticement, the cause of action is barred by limitations after six years from the enticement.[41] A father's cause

38. Gillette v. Tucker, 67 Ohio St. 106, 65 N. E. 865, 93 Am. St. Rep. 639 (by divided court). See also Tucker v. Gillette, 12 O. C. D. 401, 22 Ohio Cir. Ct. R. 664.

Under Ohio Rev. St. § 4983, in an action for malpractice it is the breach of dutv that gives rise to the action and causes it to accrue, and not knowledge of the fact evidenced by resulting injury. Fronce v. Nichols, 22 Ohio Cir. Ct. Rep. 539, 12 O. C. D. 472.

39. Lotten v. O'Brien, 146 Wis. 258, 131 N. W. 361.

40. Bixler v. Pennsylvania R. Co., 201 Fed. 553 (U. S. D. C.). A cause of action against a railroad company for injuries to a servant, brought by the servant's administrator, accrued on the infliction of the injury. Louisville & N. R. Co. v. Simrall's Adm'r, 31 Ky. Law Rep. 1269, 104 S. W. 1011, 32 Ky. Law Rep. 240, 104 S. W. 1199.

41. Hall v. Smith, 80 Misc. Rep. 85, 140 N. Y. Supp. 796.

A husband's cause of action for the alienation of his wife's affections accrues at the time when he discovers her in the act of adultery; and an action therefor against her paramour, brought more than six years after such discovery, is barred by the

of action for the seduction of his daughter arises when the act of seduction is complete, and not when he discovers that his daughter has been seduced.[42] Seduction is a continous act, and, so long as the illicit relations are kept up by continuous acts, promises, or artifices of the man, the statute of limitations will not run against an action by the woman for damages.[43] Limitations begin to run against an action for personal injury from the date of the injury, when the right of action accrues.[44] Limitations begin to run against an action for false imprisonment when the alleged false imprisonment ends; [45] and against an action for malicious prosecution when the prosecution is ended or abandoned.[46] The

statute of limitations (Pub. St. c. 197, § 1, cl. 4). Sanborn v. Gale, 162 Mass. 412, 38 N. E. 710, 26 L. R. A. 864.

A complaint for alienating a wife's affections, stating that four years before, defendant began to poison the wife's mind, does not show that it is barred by the two-years' limitation, when it appears that the wife did not leave her husband, and declare she would no longer live with him, until two weeks before suit commenced. Bockman v. Ritter, 21 Ind. App. 250, 52 N. E. 100. The cause of action accrued at the time of the separation. Farneman v. Farneman, 46 Ind. App. 453, 90 N. E. 775, rehearing denied 91 N. E. 968.

42. Davis v. Boyett, 120 Ga. 649, 48 S. E. 185, 66 L. R. A. 258, 102 Am. St. Rep. 118. An action by a father to recover damages for the seduction of his daughter is barred by limitations, unless brought within two years from the time the right of action accrued. Hutcherson v. Durden, 113 Ga. 987, 39 S. E. 495, 54 L. R. A. 811.

Since successive acts of seduction constitute but one wrong, plaintiff's action for seduction was not barred by the two-years' statutory limit, where it was brought within two years of the final act of sexual intercourse, though the first act of seduction had occurred more than four years before the bringing of the action. Gunder v. Tibbitts, 153 Ind. 591, 55 N. E. 762.

43. Ferguson v. Moore, 98 Tenn. 342, 39 S. W. 341.

Ala.—Wiliams v. Alabama Great Southern R. Co., 158 Ala. 396, 48 So. 485.

44. *Ind.*—Indianapolis St. Ry. Co. v. Fearnaught, 40 Ind. App. 333, 82 N. E. 102.

Okl.—Waugh v. Guthrie Gas, etc., Co., 37 Okl. 239, 131 Pac. 174.

45. *U. S.*—Alexander v. Thompson, 195 Fed. 31 (C. C. A., Mich.).

Ga.—Gordon v. West, 129 Ga. 532, 59 S. E. 232, 13 L. R. A. (N. S.) 549.

46. *Ill.* — McElroy v. Catholic Press Co., 254 Ill. 290, 98 N. E. 527.

La.—Carnes v. Atkins Bros. Co., 123 La. 26, 48 So. 572. See King v. Erskins, 116 La. 480, 40 So. 844.

right of action for damages from the sale of intoxicating liquors to plaintiff's husband was not barred when brought within four years after defendant had ceased to supply the husband with intoxicating liquor, causing him to become an habitual drunkard.[47]

§ 187d(5). Injuries to property in general.

The statute commences to run against an action for injury to land from negligence in maintaining a ditch at the time the injury occurs, whatever the time of the negligence.[48] An action for damages, caused by the negligent construction of a building attached to a party wall, accrues at the time of the infliction of the damages.[49] Where defendant railroad company constructed a rail-

Tex.—Von Koehring v. Witte, 15 Tex. Civ. App. 646, 40 S. W. 63.

But see Ma-ka-ta-wah-qua-twa v. Rehok, 111 Fed. 12 (U. S. C. C., Iowa), wherein it was held that in an action for malicious prosecution limitation ran from the date of the arrest. See also Virtue v. Creamery Package Mfg. Co., 123 Minn. 17, 142 N. W. 930, 1136.

47.—Colman v. Loeper, 94 Neb. 270, 143 N. W. 295.

See also, as to actions for injuries to the person:

D. C.—Jackson v. Emmons, 19 App. D. C. 250.

Ga.—Cooper v. P. P. Most Nursery Co., 10 Ga. App. 351, 73 S. E. 414.

La.—D'Echaux v. D'Echaux, 133 La. 123, 62 So. 597, action for slander.

Tex.—Texas Cent. R. Co. v. Hawkins (Civ. App.), 162 S. W. 132.

48. City of Huntsville v. Ewing, 116 Ala. 576, 22 So. 984; Sloss-Sheffield Steel & Iron Co. v. Sampson, 158 Ala. 590, 48 So. 493.

Though defendant was a party to the wrongful conversion of a sawmill, if the owner afterwards engaged him for hire to keep possession of the sawmill, the owner's possession was thereby restored, so that its subsequent conversion by defendant was a new conversion, as to which limitations did not begin to run until it was committed. Plummer v. Hardison, 6 Ala. App. 525, 60 So. 502.

49. Evans v. Pettus, 112 Ark. 572, 166 S. W. 955.

Where a railroad company constructed an embankment along the side of a ditch, which was obstructed by the falling of dirt from the embankment, limitations run from the time of the obstruction. Chicago, R. I. & P. Ry. Co. v. McCutchen, 80 Ark. 235, 96 S. W. 1054. As against the mortgagee's action for conversion of mortgaged chattels by a subsequent transferee, limitation begins to run from the date of purchase, the transferee being in possession of and using the chattels. Ozark Land Co. v. Lane-Bodley Co,. 64 Ark. 301, 42 S. W. 281.

road on plaintiff's land without commencing condemnation proceedings, the injury was of a permanent nature, the entire cause of action for damages accruing therefor when the trespass was committed.[50] A suit against an abutting owner for injuries caused by stepping into a hole in the top of a catch-basin unlawfully placed in a highway, commenced four years after the catch-basin was constructed, but within two years from the time of injury, was not barred by limitations.[51] Whenever a nuisance is of a permanent character and its construction and continuance is necessarily injurious, the damage is original and may be at once fully compensated; and in such case limitation begins to run against an action for relief from the construction of the nuisance.[52] An action against a railroad company for damages alleged to have been caused by the operation of the road is barred in five years, under the rule that an action by an adjoining property owner to recover damages in such cases for injuries to his property by reason of prudent operation of the railroad is barred in five years after the operation of the railroad was begun.[53] An action by an abut-

50. Williams v. Southern Pac. R. Co., 150 Cal. 624, 89 Pac. 599. See also Cobb v. Wrightsville & T. R. Co., 129 Ga. 377, 58 S. E. 862.

But where defendants constructed ditches on their own land to carry away surface water, no right of action accrued to plaintiff, an adjoining owner, until actual injury. Meigs v. Pinkham, 159 Cal. 104, 112 Pac. 883. Where a railroad is a nuisance, it is a permanent one, and an action for damages therefor will be barred, unless brought within the statutory period. Southern Ry. Co. v. McMenamin, 113 Va. 121, 73 S. E. 980.

51. Georgia Railway & Electric Co. v. Tompkins, 138 Ga. 596, 75 S. E. 664.

See Adams v. Macon, D. & S. R. Co., 141 Ga. 701, 81 S. E. 1110, as to an action for trespass against a railroad for appropriating land for right of way.

52. Cubbins v. Mississippi River Commission, 204 Fed. 299 (U. S. D. C.).

An action for a permanent nuisance is barred by failure to bring an action within the period of limitation after its existence and discovery. Gorman v. Chicago, B. & Q. R. Co., 166 Mo. App. 320, 148 S. W. 1009.

53. Kilcoyn v. Chicago, etc., R. Co., 141 Ky. 237, 132 S. W. 438. See also Louisville Ry. Co. v. Wiggington, 156 Ky. 400, 161 S. W. 209.

Where a sewer was adequate at the time of its original construction, but became inadequate, owing to the connection of other sewers with it, a

ting owner for damages for the negligent construction of a street improvement by municipal authorities accrues at the time the work is negligently done and the abutting property is thereby sensibly impaired.[54] Where a nuisance is of a permanent character, inflicting damages of a permanent nature, a cause of action therefor accrues at the time of the creation of the nuisance, and limitations begin to run from that time.[55] A cause of action against a carrier for the conversion of goods delivered to it for shipment, but which were never delivered to the consignee, accrues, so that limitations begin to run, at the time of the delivery of the goods to the carrier.[56] An action against a railroad com-

cause of action for injuries arising after such connection accrued at the time the injury was inflicted, and not at the time the sewer was originally constructed. City of Louisville v. Kramer's Adm'x, 151 Ky. 117, 151 S. W. 379, judg. rev'd on rehearing 151 Ky. 577, 152 S. W. 544. And see Cumberland R. Co. v. Bays, 153 Ky. 159, 154 S. W. 929, action for nuisance; City of Louisville v. Coleburne, 108 Ky. 420, 22 Ky. Law Rep. 34, action by life tenant to recover damages for injury to the use or rental value of the property.

54. Earnhardt v. Board of Com'rs of Town of Lexington, 157 N. C. 234, 72 S. E. 864; Smith v. City of Seattle, 18 Wash. 484, 51 Pac. 1057, 63 Am. St. Rep. 910. See Campbell v. Raleigh & C. R. Co., 159 N. C. 586, 75 S. E. 1105, as to action for damages to land caused by a railroad embankment.

55. Uvalde Electric Light Co. v. Parsons (Tex. Civ. App.), 138 S. W. 163; Parsons v. Missouri, K. & T. Ry. Co. of Texas (Tex. Civ. App.), 137 S. W. 475.

Where defendant's lessor laid its track in the street in front of plaintiff's residence, but plaintiff was not damaged until the track was leased by defendant, limitations did not begin to run until the beginning of the damage. Houston Belt & Terminal Ry. Co. v. Ashe (Tex. Civ. App.), 158 S. W. 205. And see Trinity & B. V. Ry. Co. v. Jobe (Tex. Civ. App.), 126 S. W. 32; International & G. N. R. Co. v. Doeppenschmidt (Tex. Civ. App.), 120 S. W. 928.

An action for damages, in that a railroad by failure to construct openings in its fence and a crossing over its roadbed entirely cut off a field and deprived the owner of its use, accrues when the fence is built, so as to start the statute of limitations running. Sutherland v. Galveston, etc., Ry. Co. (Tex. Civ. App.), 108 S. W. 969.

56. Hooks v. Gulf, etc., Ry. Co. (Tex. Civ. App.), 97 S. W. 516.

A cause of action in favor of a chattel mortgagee for conversion of the property accrued when the property was applied to claims other than the mortgage in repudiation of the mortgage unless he was excusably ignorant of the cause of action.

pany for the value of land wrongfully appropriated by it for *quasi* public purposes would accrue when the land was wrongfully appropriated.[57] Where an elevated railroad was completed January 15, 1880, though not opened to the public until March 1, 1880, it was in operation from the former date, so that an action first brought by the plaintiff or his predecessors on February 28, 1900, to restrain its operation and maintenance, was barred by the statutory period of twenty years.[58] When the cause of injury to realty is not permanent, the statute of limitations does not begin to run until the injury is suffered.[59] The placing by railroad companies upon streets of permanent structures that prevent the public use

Beaumont Rice Mills v. Port Arthur Rice Milling Co. (Tex. Civ. App.), 141 S. W. 349, Judg. rev'd Port Arthur Rice Milling Co. v. Beaumont Rice Mills, 105 Tex. 514, 143 S. W. 926. Where a buyer in a conditional contract did not consent to the seller's assumption of control over the goods, and renting them to third persons before the maturity of any installment of the price, the cause of action for the seller's conversion accrued at that time. Roberon v. Withers (Tex Civ. App.), 152 S. W. 1160. An action against shippers of grain for conversion by reason of the appropriation of the proceeds of grain delivered to them for shipment, the money to be held until rent was satisfied, accrued at the time of the appropriation of the money. Hopper v. Hays, 82 Mo. App. 494. See also Nashville, etc., Ry. v. Dale & N. Milling Co., 68 Kan. 108, 74 Pac. 596.

57. Rivard v. Missouri Pac. Ry. Co., 157 Mo. 135, 165 S. W. 763.

58. Rothmann v. Interborough Rapid Transit Co., 155 App. Div. 192, 139 N. Y. Supp. 1031, rev'g judg. 121 N. Y. Supp. 200, 66 Misc. Rep. 378.

59. Waugh v. Guthrie Gas, Light, etc., Co., 37 Okl. 239, 131 Pac. 174.

Limitations do not begin to run in favor of an electric light company trimming trees of owners of property abutting on the street until it trims the trees. Slabaugh v. Omaha Electric Light & Power Co., 87 Neb. 805, 128 N. W. 505. Where crops are destroyed by the negligence of a railway company in permitting a waterway to become obstructed, the cause of action accrues when the crops are destroyed. Gray v. Chicago, etc., R. Co., 90 Neb. 795, 134 N. W. 961. Limitations begin to run against an action for damages to property growing out of the erection of a standpipe from the erection and completion of such pipe. Doyle v. City of Sycamore, 81 Ill. App. 589, aff'd 193 Ill. 501, 61 N. E. 1117.

See also, as to injuries to property in general:

Ariz. — Henshaw v. Salt River Canal Co., 9 Ariz. 418, 84 Pac. 908, action for wrongful appropriation of water rights.

Ind.—Pickett v. Toledo, etc., R. Co., 131 Ind. 562, 31 N. E. 200, action for

of such streets is a public nuisance, in favor of which limitations do not run; especially if such structures when so placed were claimed by such railroads to be subservient to the public use to which the premises had been dedicated as a street, and pursuant to a lawful agreement with such city to that end.[60]

§ 187d(6). Continuing injury in general.

The fact that damages for a portion of the acts complained of

tortious entry upon lands. Seigmund v. Tyner, 52 Ind. App. 581, 101 N. E. 20.

La.—Louisiana Stave Co. v. South Arkansas Lumber Co., 135 La. 232, 65 So. 226; Jones v. Texas & P. Ry. Co., 125 La. 542, 51 So. 582, action for damages for death of a mule struck by a train.

Mich.—Jenks v. Hart Cedar & Lumber Co., 143 Mich. 449, 13 Detroit Leg. N. 44, 106 N. W. 1119, 114 Am. St. Rep. 673.

Minn.—Preston v. Cloquet Tie & Post Co., 114 Minn. 398, 131 N. W. 474, an action for the conversion of timber.

Ohio.—Duff v. United States Gypsum Co., 189 Fed. 234 (C. C., Ohio), action for injury to a gypsum mine from water percolating from an adjoining mine accrued at the date of the flooding.

N. J.—Rector, etc., of Church of Holy Communion v. Paterson Extension R. Co., 66 N. J. Law, 218, 49 Atl. 1030, 55 L. R. A. 81.

Iowa.—Valentine v. Widman, 156 Iowa, 172, 135 N. W. 599, action for damage to land by extension of drains accrued at time of extension; Soderburg v. Chicago, etc., R. Co. (Iowa), 149 N. W. 82, action for continuing nuisance from soot and smoke of a railroad may be maintained at any time.

Or.—Bergman v. Inman, Poulsen & Co., 43 Or. 456, 72 Pac. 1086, 99 Am. St. Rep. 771, 73 Pac. 341.

Pa.—Noonan v. Pardee, 200 Pa. 474, 50 Atl. 255, 55 L. R. A. 410, 86 Am. St. Rep. 722, action for the caving in of the surface from failure of the operator of a coal mine to leave proper support accrues when the coal is removed without leaving proper support. Patterson v. Williams, 52 Pa. Super. Ct. 299, action for conversion of a horse.

Tex.—City of Houston v. Parr (Civ App.), 47 S. W. 393, action for damages for construction of a ditch by a city; Kruegel v. Trinity Cemetery Co. (Civ. App.), 63 S. W. 652, action for burial of corpses of person not connected with him on plaintiff's lot.

W. Va.—Day v. Louisville Coal & Coke Co., 60 W. Va. 27, 53 S. E. 776, 10 L. R. A. (N. S.) 167.

Wis.—Grunert v. Brown, 119 Wis. 126, 95 N. W. 959, action for conversion of timber accrued at the time of the original trespass.

60. Cleveland & P. Ry. Co. v. City of Cleveland, 33 Ohio Cir. Ct. R. 482.

are barred by the statute of limitations does not preclude complainant from recovering damages for acts done within the time limited, where it appears that the nuisance was a continuing one.[61] Altough a suit for the creation of a nuisance may be barred by the statute of limitations, yet if the nuisance be of a continuing character, which can and should be abated, suit may be brought for damages arising from its maintenance.[62] Where a permanent structure legally authorized, such as a railroad embankment, is built and there is no improper or negligent construction, all damages, past, present and future are sustained when the structure is erected and its operation begun, and the statute of limitations begins to run on the completion of the structure. In case of negligent or improper construction, the injured party may, at his election, either treat the structure as permanent and sue for all damages, or he may treat it as temporary and transient and sue and recover for each recurring injury.[63] When a nuisance continues, and creates

61. Whaley v. Wilson, 112 Ala. 627, 20 So. 922. Where the obstruction of a water course was of a continuing character and caused damages at each heavy rainfall, plaintiff was entitled to recover all damages sustained within one year before the commencement of his action, regardless of when the obstruction was placed there. Black v. Hankins, 6 Ala. App. 525, 60 So. 502.

62. Gabbett v. City of Atlanta, 137 Ga. 180, 73 S. E. 372; City Council of Augusta v. Marks, 124 Ga. 365, 52 S. E. 539; Southern Ry. Co. v. Morris, 119 Ga. 234, 46 S. E. 85. If a structure is not necessarily and of itself a permanent and continuing nuisance, but only becomes such in consequence of some supervening cause, which produces special injury at different periods, a separate action lies for each injury thus occasioned, and the statute of limitations begins to run against such cause of action only from the time of its accrual. City Council of Augusta v. Lombard, 101 Ga. 724, 28 S. E. 994.

63. Horner v. Baltimore, etc., R. Co., 165 Ill. App. 370.

Where action is for damages to real estate from extension of railroad and operation of the extension, length of time the other part has been constructed does not affect the question of limitation. Illinois Cent. R. Co. v. Turner, 194 Ill. 575, 62 N. E. 798, aff'g judg. 97 Ill. App. 219. See also Calumet & C. Canal & Dock Co. v. Morawetz, 195 Ill. 398, 63 N. E. 165. Where an injury to property is caused by the construction of a railway for proper railway uses, the statutes of limitations begin to run from the date of the existence of the causes which produced the injury. Illinois Cent. R. Co. v. Ferrell, 108 Ill. App. 659.

a fresh injury daily, there may be a right of action, although the original right of action has been lost by lapse of time.[64] For injury to an abutting property owner for the failure of a railroad company to place in proper repair a street on which it has built its railroad, successive actions may be maintained until the injury has been abated by placing the street in a proper condition, and the fact that the actions for the earlier injuries are barred by limitations will not affect the bringing of actions for later injuries.[65] A continuing nuisance arising from the operation of a railroad in an improper manner is not barred until the statutory period has run from the last repetition.[66] In the case of a continuous injury or trespass without fresh violence, and of constantly accruing damages, the statute of limitations can cut off only back of six years from suit brought.[67] Where a nuisance is a continuing one, the party complaining thereof cannot recover on the original cause of action after the expiration of the statutory period, but may for its continuance for any time within such period.[68] Limitations do

64. Peck v. Michigan City, 149 Ind. 670, 49 N. E. 800. And see May v. George, 53 Ind. App. 259, 101 N. E. 393.

65. Stein v. Chesapeake & O. Ry. Co., 132 Ky. 322, 116 S. W. 733. Where a sewer becomes increasingly inadequate by the increasing demands on its capacity, due to the growth of the city, each recurrence of injury attributable to the changed condition is a separate cause of action, and limitations do not begin to run until the accrual of such a cause of action. City of Louisville v. Leezer, 143 Ky. 244, 136 S. W. 223.

66. Willson v. New York Cent. & H. R. R. Co., 146 N. Y. Supp. 208.

67. Wheeler v. Town of St. Johnsbury, 87 Vt. 46, 87 Atl. 349.

68. Cohen v. Bellenot (Va.), 32 S. E. 455.

Continuous trespass.—See Graf v. City of St. Louis, 8 Mo. App. 562, memorandum.

"Continuing trespass," within the statute of limitations, refers to trespass by structures of a permanent nature, and not to separate and distinct acts of wrongfully cutting timber. Sample v. Roper Lumber Co., 150 N. C. 161, 63 S. E. 731.

For continuing injury in general. see also

Conn.—Knapp & Cowles Mfg. Co., New York, etc., R. Co., 76 Conn. 311, 56 Atl. 512, 100 Am. St. Rep. 994.

Fla.—Savannah, etc., Ry. Co. v. Davis, 25 Fla. 917, 7 So. 29.

Colo.—Wright v. Ulrich, 40 Colo. 437, 91 Pac. 43, the nuisance caused by the operation of a slaughter house is a continuing one against which limitations do not commence to run at the inception thereof.

not begin to run, because of a nuisance, from the time of the erection of an electric plant, but only from the time its operation constitutes a nuisance and causes an injury to plaintiff's health.[69]

§ 187d(7). Injuries to property by flowage, diversion or obstruction of waters.

A cause of action resulting from the negligent construction of a railway embankment, which arrested and held upon lands the flood waters of a natural stream, accrues at the date of the injury, and not of the construction of the improvement.[70] When a perman-

Ga.—Monroe v. McCranie & Vickers, 117 Ga. 890, 45 S. E. 246.

Iowa.—Pettit v. Incorporated Town of Grand Junction, Greene County, 119 Iowa, 352, 93 N. W. 381; J. K. & W. H. Gilcrest Co. v. City of Des Moines, 128 Iowa, 49, 102 N. W. 831, the custom of a railroad company of causing trains to stand at the intersection of certain streets constitutes a continuing nuisance.

Ky.—Illinois Cent. R. Co. v. Hodge, 21 Ky. Law Rep. 1479, 55 S. W. 688; Klosterman v. Chesapeake O. Ry. Co., 22 Ky. Law Rep. 192, 56 S. W. 820.

La.—Egan v. Hotel Grunewald Co., 134 La. 740, 64 So. 698; Barrow v. Gaillardanne, 122 La. 558, 47 So. 891, the prescription of one year is not pleadable in bar of a demand for an injunction against a present continuing nuisance; Drews v. Williams, 50 La. Ann. 579, 23 So. 897; Griffin v. Drainage Commission of New Orleans, 110 La. 840, 34 So. 799.

Mich.—Hoffman v. Flint & P. M. R. Co., 114 Mich. 316, 72 N. W. 167, 4 Detroit Leg. N. 790; Phelps v. City of Detroit, 120 Mich. 447, 79 N. W. 640, 6 Detroit Leg. N. 199.

Mo.—De Geofroy v. Merchants' Bridge Terminal Ry. Co., 179 Mo. 698, 79 S. W. 386, 64 L. R. A. 959, 101 Am. St. Rep. 524.

N. C.—Hodges v. Western Union Tel. Co., 133 N. C. 225, 45 S. E. 572.

Tex.—Missouri, K. & T. Ry. Co. v. Harris (Tex. Civ. App.), 138 S. W. 1085, continuous shipment of freight; City of Houston v. Merkel (Civ. App.), 153 S. W. 385; Brown v. Texas Cent. R. Co., 42 Tex. Civ. App. 392, 94 S. W. 134.

Va.—Virginia Ry. & Power Co. v. Ferebee, 115 Va. 289, 78 S. E. 556.

Wash.—Doran v. City of Seattle, 24 Wash. 182, 64 Pac. 230, 54 L. R. A. 532, 85 Am. St. Rep. 948; Sterrett v. Northport Mining & Smelting Co., 30 Wash. 164, 70 Pac. 266.

W. Va.—Pickens v. Coal River Boom & Timber Co., 58 W. Va. 11, 50 S. E. 872.

69. Parsons v. Uvalde Electric Light Co. (Tex.), 163 S. W. 1, rev'g judg. Uvalde Electric Light Co. v. Parsons (Civ. App.), 138 S. W. 163.

70. *Ark.*—St. Louis, etc., Ry. Co. v. Stephens, 72 Ark. 127, 78 S. W. 766.

Ind.—New York, etc., R. Co. v.

ent structure causes an overflow and resulting damage to another, limitations run against his claim from the time the obstruction is completed, if the nature and extent of the damage can be reasonably ascertain; if not, there may bc as many successive recoveries as there are successive injuries developed.[71] Limitations against an action for flooding plaintiff's land from waters of a stream does not begin to run from the time defendant filled in low land beside the stream, causing the overflow, but only from the time when, during high water, it was actually overflowed.[72] The right of action

Hamlet Hay Co., 149 Ind. 344, 47 N. E. 1060; Kelly v. Pittsburgh, etc., Ry. Co., 28 Ind. App. 457, 63 N. E. 233, 91 Am. St. Rep. 134.

Neb.—Chicago, B. & Q. R. Co. v. Emmert, 53 Neb. 237, 73 N. W. 540, 68 Am. St. Rep. 602; Chicago, R. I. & P. Co. v. Andreesen, 62 Neb. 456, 87 N. W. 167; Missouri Pac. Ry. Co. v. Hemingway, 63 Neb. 610, 88 N. W. 673; Chicago, B. & Q. R. Co. v. Mitchell, 74 Neb. 563, 104 N. W. 1144.

S. C.—Lawton v. Seaboard Air Line Ry., 75 S. C. 82, 55 S. E. 128. See also St. Louis, etc., Ry. Co. v. Hoshall, 82 Ark. 387, 102 S. W. 207; St Louis, etc., Ry. Co. v. Russell (Ark.), 171 S. W. 891; St. Louis Southwestern Ry. Co. v. Morris, 76 Ark. 542, 89 S. W. 846; McClure v. City of Broken Bow, 81 Neb. 384, 115 N. W. 1081; Reed v. Chicago, B. & Q. R. Co., 86 Neb. 54, 124 N. W. 917; Christensen v. Omaha Ice & Cold Storage Co., 92 Neb. 245, 138 N. W. 141, 41 L. R. A. (N. S.) 1221; Atchison, etc., Ry, Co. v. Eldridge, 41 Okl. 463, 139 Pac. 254; Texas & P. Ry. Co. v. Ford (Tex. Civ. App.) 117 S. W. 201; Gulf, etc., Ry. Co. v. Caldwell (Tex. Civ. App.), 102 S. W. 461; St. Louis Southwestern Ry. Co. of Texas v. Beck (Tex. Civ. App.), 80 S. W. 538.

71. Chicago, R. I. & P. Ry. Co. v. Humphreys, 107 Ark. 330, 155 S. W. 127. See also Board of Directors of St. Francis Levee Dist. v. Barton, 92 Ark. 406; Kelly v. Kansas City Southern Ry. Co., 92 Ark. 465, 123 S. W. 664; Turner v. Overton, 86 Ark. 406, 111 S. W. 270; Perry v. Chicago, etc., Ry. Co. (Tex. Civ. App.), 162 S. W. 1185; Bigham Bros. v. Port Arthur Canal & Dock Co. (Tex. Civ. App.), 126 S. W. 324; Adilene Light & Water Co. v. Clack (Tex. Civ. App.), 124 S. W. 201; International & G. N. R. Co. v. Kyle (Tex. Civ. App.), 101 S. W. 272.

72. Sloss-Sheffield Steel & Iron Co. v. Mitchell, 167 Ala. 226, 52 So. 69. See also Sloss-Sheffield Steel & Iron Co. v. Dorman, 159 Ala. 321, 49 So. 242; McCalla v. Louisville & N. R. Co., 163 Ala. 107, 50 So. 971. The statute of limitations will not begin to run, in an action for injuries to the soil by mining operations, causing a failure of support, until some actual damage has been done. West Pratt Coal Co. v. Dorman, 161 Ala. 389, 49 So. 849.

against a city for injury from the flooding of property by the negligent construction of a sewer accrues when the property is flooded, and limitation runs only from that date.[73] Limitations barring an action for damages caused by an overflow resulting from the digging of a ditch begin to run from the date of the injury, and not from that of the digging of the ditch.[74] Where the grantee of a right of way for a flume across an irrigation ditch under a grant providing that the crossing should be made so as not to impede the flow of the water constructed the flume so as to obstruct such flow, the right of action for the obstruction accrued when the flume was built, and limitations then began.[75] A cause of action for flooding land by the erection of a dam accrues when the land is flooded, and not when the dam is erected.[76] Where defendants construct an embankment so defectively that it causes plaintiff's land to be overflowed, each overflow causing damages creates a new cause of action, and the statute of limitations runs from the date of the injury, and not from the time the embankment was improperly constructed.[77] A tile drain, taking water

73. Kansas City v. King, 65 Kan. 64, 68 Pac. 1093; City of Louisville v. Norris, 111 Ky. 903, 23 Ky. Law Rep. 1195, 64 S. W. 958, 98 Am. St. Rep. 437.

See Massengale v. City of Atlanta, 113 Ga. 966, 39 S. E. 578; City of Houston v. Houston, etc., R. Co., 26 Tex. Civ. App. 228, 63 S. W. 1056.

74. Fremont, etc., R. Co. v. Harlin, 50 Neb. 698, 70 N. W. 263, 36 L. R. A. 417, 61 Am. St. Rep. 578; Hocutt v. Wilmington & W. R. Co., 124 N. C. 214, 32 S. E. 681; St. Louis Southwestern Ry. Co. of Texas v. Clayton (Tex. Civ. App.), 118 S. W. 248; Simon v. Nance (Tex. Civ. App.), 100 S. W. 1038.

75. Centerville & Kingsburg Irr. Ditch Co. v. Sanger Lumber Co., 140 Cal. 385, 73 Pac. 1079.

The injuries to land from water seeping from a properly constructed irrigation ditch which is intended to be permanent constitutes a single cause of action, and as affected by the statute of limitations accrues at the beginning of the injury. Middelkamp v. Bessemer Irrigating Ditch Co., 46 Colo. 102, 103 Pac. 280; Barnum v. Bessemer Irrigating Ditch Co., 46 Colo. 125, 103 Pac. 287.

76. Greeley Irr. Co. v. Von Trotha, 48 Colo. 12, 108 Pac. 985; Irvine v. City of Oelwein (Iowa), 160 N. W. 674.

77. Fincher v. Baltimore, etc., R. Co., 179 Ill. App. 622. See also Jones v. Sanitary Dist. of Chicago, 252 Ill. 591, 97 N. E. 210.

onto the land of another, is not a permanent nuisance, so that all the damages accrue when it is first put in; but recovery may be had for the damages suffered therefrom during the five years preceding action.[78] Limitations commence to run against an action against a city for damages for flooding of land owing to the negligence of the city in the paving and guttering of a street at the time of the flooding, and not at the time of the improvement causing the same.[79] Where the flooding of a bathing beach was caused by the raising during each season of a bear trap upon the top of a lawfully constructed dam, the injury is a recurring one, and the statute of limitations as to each injury runs from the time of that flooding.[80] Where injury to real property results from the construction of a permanent structure, the cause of action accrues on the completion of the structure;[81] but where the waters of a stream

78. Jones v. Stover, 131 Iowa 119, 108 N. W. 112, 6 L. R. A. (N. S.) 154.

The fact that a system of sewers, by means of which sewage was discharged into a stream, was of permanent construction, did not render the nuisance occasioned by such discharge a permanent one. Vogt v. City of Grinnell, 123 Iowa 332, 98 N. W. 782. See also Geneser v. Healy 124 Iowa, 310, 100 N. W. 66.

79. City of Kansas City v. Frohwerk, 10 Kan. App. 116, 62 Pac. 252.

Under Civ. Code, § 18, subd. 3, an action against a city for injuries by the change of the channel of a stream by a permanent improvement must be brought within two years after such change. Parker v. City of Atchison, 58 Kan. 29, 48 Pac. 631. An owner's right of action for permanent damages from the pollution of a stream by operation of a sewer system and oil refinery is barred in two years after the sewer system and refinery are in operation. McDaniel v. City of Cherryvale, 91 Kan. 40, 136 Pac. 899.

80. Deffenbaugh v. Washington Water Power Co., 24 Idaho, 514, 135 Pac. 247. See also Hill v. Empire State-Idaho Mining & Developing Co., 158 Fed. 881 (U. S. C. C., Idaho). Dikes built by a railroad company along the bank of a river to prevent the current from washing away its roadbed are permanent structures, and damages for injuries to adjoining land by the deflection of the current of the river, both present and prospective, are recoverable in a single action, the right to bring which accrued at once when the dikes were completed and the injury commenced. Gulf, etc., Ry. Co. v. Moseley, 161 Fed. 72 (C. C. A., Ind. T.).

81. King v. Board of Council of City of Danville, 32 Ky. Law Rep. 1188, 107 S. W. 1189. See also Madisonville, H. & E. R. Co. v. Graham, 147 Ky. 604, 144 S. W. 737; Hay v.

were diverted by means of a culvert, and thereafter the culvert filled up, throwing the water over and injuring plaintiff's lands, limitations run against an action for the injury from the occurrence thereof, and not from the time of the diversion.[82] An action for damages sustained within six years by the wrongful continuance of a dam is not barred by the statute of limitations, although the dam was erected without right more than six years before the date of the writ.[83] Where a drain is obstructed, and a destructive flood results, limitations then begin to run against the right of action for the obstruction.[84] The right of action for the negligent construction of a levee, in that it was built as a solid bank of earth across an outlet of a lake, instead of having a flood gate for drainage purposes, whereby water which would have drained off was caused to overflow lands, does not accrue when the levee is built, but when the overflowing actually occurs.[85] Damages from ponding or diverting water on land accruing within three years before

City of Lexington, 144 Ky. 665, 24 Ky. Law Rep. 1495, 71 S. W. 867; Tietze v. International & G. N. R. Co., 35 Tex. Civ. App. 136, 80 S. W. 124; Cape v. Thompson, 21 Tex. Civ. App. 681, 53 S. W. 368.

82. Illinois Cent. R. Co. v. Taylor, 28 Ky. Law Rep. 139, 89 S. W. 121.

See also Illinois Cent. R. Co. v. Haynes (Ky.), 122 S. W. 210; Ireland v. Bowman & Crockrell, 130 Ky. 153, 114 S. W. 338, rehearing 113 S. W. 56, denied; Town of Central Covington v. Beiser, 122 Ky. 715, 29 Ky. Law Rep. 261, 92 S. W. 973; Crabtree Coal Min. Co. v. Hamby's Adm'r, 28 Ky. Law Rep. 687, 90 S. W. 226; Finley v. City of Williamsburgh, 24 Ky. Law Rep. 1336; Louisville & N. R. Co. v. Cornelius, 111 Ky. 752, 23 Ky. Law Rep. 1069, 64 S. W. 732.

A cause of action against a county for injury resulting from casting more than the natural flow of water upon plaintiff's land accrues when the injury becomes reasonably apparent. Moore v. Lawrence County, 143 Ky. 448, 136 S. W. 1031; Chesapeake & O. Ry. Co. v. Robbins, 154 Ky. 387, 581, 157 S. W. 903.

83. Prentiss v. Wood, 132 Mass. 486. And see Stanchfield v. City of Newton, 142 Mass. 110, 7 N. E. 703.

84. Erwin v. Erie R. Co., 98 App. Div. 402, 90 N. Y. Supp. 315, aff'd 186 N. Y. 550, 79 N. E. 1104.

85. Barnett v. St. Francis Levee Dist., 125 Mo. App. 61, 102 S. W. 583.

See also Kellogg v. City of Kirksville, 149 Mo. App. 1, 129 S. W. 57; Powers v. St. Louis, etc., Ry. Co., 158 Mo. 87, 57 S. W. 1090, 71 Mo. App. 570.

action brought may be recovered, although the injury arose at a more remote period; the injury being regarded as a renewing trespass.[86] Filling certain streets in such a manner as to cause established drains to become worthless, and to cause water to set back on adjacent property, constitutes a continuing nuisance, upon which suit may be brought from time to time, and in which the a boom causes deposit of sand in a stream injuring the capacity statute of limitations may be pleaded.[87] Where the operation of of a mill, limitations begin to run, not from the construction of the boom, but when the damage occurs.[88]

§ 187d(8). Wrongful seizure of property.

The statute begins to run against an action for wrongful attachment from the time of attachment, or at latest from the time the property was sold in the attachment suit; and not from the time of final judgment in said suit against the plaintiff therein, though the owner intervened therein, and though, after the owner's intervention, he was made a defendant in the suit.[89]

86. Duval v. Atlantic Coast Line R. Co., 161 N. C. 448, 77 S. E. 311.

And see Barcliff v. Norfolk Southern R. Co., 168 N. C. 268, 84 S. E. 290; Savage v. Norfolk Southern R. Co., 168 N. C. 241, 84 S. E. 292; Pickett v. Atlantic Coast Line R. Co., 153 N. C. 148, 69 S. E. 8; Harrell v. Norfolk & C. R. Co., 122 N. C. 822, 29 S. E. 56; Ridley v. Seaboard & R. R. Co., 124 N. C. 34, 32 S. E. 325.

87. City of Toledo v. Lewis, 17 Ohio Cir. Ct. R. 588, 9 O. C. D. 451.

And see Detwiler v. City of Toledo, 13 Ohio Cir. Ct. R. 579, 6 O. C. D. 300.

88. Pickens v. Coal River Boom & Timber Co., 66 W. Va. 10, 65 S. E. 865. See also Eells v. Chesapeake & O. Ry. Co., 49 W. Va. 65, 38 S. E. 479, 87 Am. St. Rep. 787; Skipwith v. Albemarle Soapstone Co., 185 Fed. 15, 107 C. C. A. 119 (Va.); Brisky v. Leavenworth Logging, Boom & Water Co., 68 Wash. 386, 123 Pac. 519.

89. Smyth v. Peters Shoe Co., 111 Iowa 388, 82 N. W. 898.

Where, during a dispute between a landlord and tenant as to the right of possession under an oil lease, the landlord told the lessee to remove his personal property from the premises, and thereafter the landlord, having secured a judgment in attachment, took possession of the personal property, limitations did not begin to run against an action by the lessee for conversion of the property at the time of the notice to remove the same. Sattler v. Opperman, 14 Pa. Super. Ct. 42.

CHAPTER XIX.

EXECUTORS AND ADMINISTRATORS.

§ 188. Executor may pay barred debts or not, in his discretion.

When the remedy for a debt is barred by lapse of time, an executor or administrator is nevertheless not obliged to take advantage of the statute, but may at his discretion satisfy the debt.[1]

1. *In re* Huger, 100 Fed. 805; Woods v. Irwin, 141 Pa. 278. In New Jersey, the rule that a personal representative may waive the statute of limitations applies both as to personalty and also as to realty when the latter is sold under a decree for sale which does not direct that the land be sold free from the lien of debts due to creditors. First Nat. Bank v. Thompson, 61 N. J. Eq. 188, 48 Atl. 333, 339.

In England an executor cannot, however, lawfully pay a barred debt of the testator after it is judicially declared that it is not recoverable because barred by the statute, and probably also if such payment is against the testator's declared wish; if he does so, he is guilty of a *devas-*

"No executor," said Lord Hardwicke, "is compellable either in law or equity to take advantage of the statute of limitations against a claim otherwise well founded."[2] In fact, it has been treated as almost a duty in some cases for an executor to satisfy in that way, in his representative character, the conscience of

tavit, and a creditor who receives such payment with notice or knowledge, may be required to repay it to the estate. Midgley v. Midgley (1893), 3 Ch. 282. When an executor refuses to set up the bar of the statute, a residuary legatee may, it seems, raise this objection. *In re* Wenham (1892), 3 Ch. 59.

In New York it is held that an acknowledgment of a debt by an executor does not, in the absence of an express promise to pay, take the case out of the statute. Schutz v. Morette, 146 N. Y. 137, 40 N. E. 780; Yates v. Wing, 59 N. Y. Supp. 78, 42 App. Div. 356. Also that an executor can neither by him promise nor acknowledgment, oral or written, revive a debt against the estate of his testator which is already barred by the statute. Butler v. Johnson, 111 N. Y. 204, 18 N. E. 643; Adams v. Fassett, 149 N. Y. 61, 66, 43 N. E. 408.

See also, Schouler on Wills, Executors and Administrators, Vol. 2, § 1389, and cases there cited, as to disregarding the bar of limitations imposed by general and special statutes.

2. Norton v. Frecker, 1 Atk. 524; Fairfax v. Fairfax, 2 Cranch (U. S. C. C.) 25; Walter v. Radcliffe, 2 Desau. (S. C.) 577; Jacson, J., in Scott v. Hancock, 13 Mass. 162; Woods v. Elliott, 49 Miss. 168; Ritter's Appeal, 23 Pa. 95; Biddle v. Moore, 3 Pa. 178; McFarland's Estate, 4 Pa. 149; Fritz v. Thomas, 1 Whart. (Pa.) 66; Hodgdon v. White, 11 N. H. 208; Pollard v. Scears, 28 Ala. 484; Amoskeag Mfg. Co. v. Barnes, 48 N. H. 25; Emerson v. Thompson, 16 Mass. 431; Tunstall v. Pollard, 11 Leigh (Va.) 1; Kennedy's Appeal, 4 Pa. 149; Smith's Estate, 1 Ashm. (Pa.) 352; Steel v. Steel, 12 Pa. 67; Miller v. Dorsey, 9 Md. 317; Batson v. Murrell, 29 Tenn. (10 Humph.) 301; Semmes v. Magruder, 10 Md. 242; Thayer v. Hollis, 44 Mass. (3 Met.) 369; Chambers v. Fennemore, 4 Harr. (Del.) 368; Payne v. Pusey, 71 Ky. (8 Bush.) 564; Barnwall v. Smith, 58 N. C. (5 Jones Eq.) 168. While an administrator may pay a debt barred by the statute, he cannot pay a debt that accrued under a contract void under the statute of frauds; and if he does so, he is chargeable with *devastavit*. Baker v. Fuller, 69 Me. 152. The reason is that in the one case a legal liability at some time existed on the part of the deceased to pay the debt, while in the other case no such liability ever existed, and the executor has no power to render a void contract made by his testator valid. Under the statute in Florida, in a suit against an administrator or executor on an open account, the court should expunge therefrom every item due five years before the death of a testator or intestate. Patterson v. Cobb, 4 Fla. 481.

his testator.[3] And Lord Hatherley, in overruling a case,[4] remarks as follows: "It certainly cannot be considered to be law at the present day, that executors paying a debt against the recovery of which the statute of limitations might be pleaded as a legal bar, render themselves liable to those who are interested in the testator's property."[5]

3. Williamson v. Naylor, 3 Y. & C., 211 note (*a*); Stanhlschmidt v. Lett, 1 Sm. & G. 415; Byrd v. Wells, 40 Miss. 711. Parker, C. J., in Hodgdon v. White, 11 N. H. 208; Scott v. Hancock, 13 Mass. 162. In Mississippi, Byrd v. Wells, *supra;* Trotter v. Trotter, 40 Miss. 704. In Patterson v. Cobb, 4 Fla. 481, it is held that he cannot pay debts that were barred anterior to the granting of administration, but that he may pay those which became barred after he has qualified. Byrd v. Wells, *supra*. In Kennedy's Appeal, 4 Pa. 149, the court held that an executor may pay a just debt, though barred by the statute, and that such payment is valid as against the distributees.

4. McCulloch v. Dawes, 9 D. & Ry. 40.

5. Hill v. Walker, 4 K. & J. 166. The rule is that an executor may, in the exercise of his discretion, pay a debt barred by the statute, although the personal estate of the testator is insufficient, and that the effect of such payment by him is to throw the burden thereof upon devisees of real estate, upon which the other debts are in consequence thrown. Lowis v. Rumney, L. R. 4 Eq. 451, where Lord Romilly, M. R., remaks: "I think it is much to be regretted that the statute did not destroy the debt, instead of merely taking away the remedy for it. The result is that questions constantly arise, and amongst others, whether an executor may not pay a debt barred by lapse of time. I am of opinion that in the exercise of his discretion he may do so, and that it does not make the slightest difference whether the personal estate is sufficient or insufficient. If it be insufficient, the statute gives the creditor a remedy against the real estate, but that does not interfere with the discretion of the executor."

An executor may, therefore, at his discretion, pay debts due to others, the remedy for which is barred by lapse of time. Norton v. Frecker, 1 Atk. 533; *Ex parte* Dewdney, 15 Ves. 498; Williamson v. Naylor, 3 Y. & C. 211, note (a); Williams on Executors (6th ed.), 1664. He may also retain assets of the testator sufficient to pay such debts when due to himself. Stahlschmidt v. Lett, 1 Sm. & G. 415; Coates v. Coates, 33 Beav. 249; Courtenay v. Williams, 3 Hare 539. This is so even when the debts were barred in the lifetime of the testator. Hill v. Walker, 4 K. & G. 166. And his right to payment is not affected by payment of the testator's effects into court. In Woodyard v. Polsley, 14 W. Va. 211, it was held that when, in a creditor's suit in equity against an administrator and the heirs, the court takes into its own hands the administra-

He may pay a debt due to himself upon which the statute has run with the same propriety that he may pay one so barred, due to any other person; and neither the heirs or other distributees of the estate have any remedy against him therefor.[6] It has

tion of the assets by referring the cause to a commissioner to take an account of the debts of the intestate, the statute ceases to run against the creditor, not a formal party to the bill, the bill not being in form a creditor's bill, from the date of such decree in the case; and that, if in such a case the statute has not been specially pleaded nor relied on before the commissioner, and he failed to recognize the statute, and therefore indorsed no exception upon the report, the appellate court will consider the limitation as out of the case, although the report upon its face shows that some of the claims allowed by the commissioner were barred by the statute. Where the testator in his will expressly directs the executor to disregard the statute, there can be no question as to his right to pay all just debts without reference to whether they are barred or not, even though the statute requires him to plead the statute of limitations. Campbell v. Shoatwell, 51 Tex. 27.

6. Payne v. Pusey, 71 Ky. (8 Bush) 564. It was also held in this case, and such is the general rule, that, if he is unable to realize his debt out of the personal estate, and seeks to make the heirs liable therefor, the heirs may set up any defense to the claim which the intestate could have set up including the statute of limitations. When he goes into a court of equity, the administator stands like any other creditor for the purpose of making his debt out of the heirs, as he has no right or title in that part of the estate any more than any other creditor of the estate. In Massachusetts, in Scott v. Hancock, 13 Mass. 762, where the period had expired within which an administrator was, under the statute, liable to a suit, no action having been brought against him, the court refused a license to him to sell the real estate to pay debts; and generally, if all the debts are barred by the statute applicable to administrators, a license to sell will be denied. Wellman v. Lawrence, 15 Mass. 326; *Ex parte* Allen, 15 Mass. 58. If granted, it is void, as by permitting the statutory period to elapse without bringing their action, they lose all lien upon the real estate for the payment of their debt. Heath v. Wells, 22 Mass. (5 Pick.) 140; Thompson v. Brown, 16 Mass. 172. And the levy of an execution under a judgment obtained in an action brought after the statutory period has elapsed, is void as against the heirs or devisees. Thayer v. Hollis, 44 Mass. (3 Met.) 369. But this is not the rule in New York. Thus, in Butler v. Johnson, 111 N. Y. 204, 18 N. E. 643, reversing 44 Hun 206, it was held that although a creditor was not bound, as the law stood in 1872, to institute proceedings to compel the sale of real estate to pay debts until after an executor or administrator had rendered an account, such omis-

been held that if the surplus of the personal estate, after payment of the debts and legacies, is bequeathed to a residuary legatee, and several creditors, although barred by the statute of limitations, commence actions therefor against the executor, a court of equity will not, on his refusal to plead the statute, compel him to plead it in favor of the residuary legatee;[7] nor can a residuary legatee set up the statute, if the executor refuses to do so, in an action by a creditor to recover his debt.[8] But this rule is subject to the exception that, when it is sought to charge the real estate of the deceased with the payment of debts due from the estate, either the heir, or a devisee, residuary legatee, or any person interested therein, may interpose the statute.[9] In Arkansas[10] and

sion did not stop the running of the statute as against the debt. An executor or administrator is bound to set up the bar of the statute of limitations, and has no authority to allow a claim so barred, and as against an estate, a debt barred by the statute is to be regarded as no debt.

7. Castleton v. Fanshaw, Prec. Chan. See also *Ex parte* Dewdney, 15 Ves. 498. A contrary rule prevails in France under the rule of Napoleon, § 2225: "*Les creanciers ou toute autre personne ayant interet a ce que prescription soit acquise peuvent l' opposer encore que le debiteur ou le proprietaire y renonce;*" and this rule certainly is more reasonable than that generally adopted by our courts.

8. Briggs v. Wilson, 5 De G. M. & G. 12; Fuller v. Redman, 26 Beav. 614; Alston v. Trollope, L. R. 2 Eq. 205. But under the common practice and decree in England by administration suit, where the bill has been filed and the decree obtained by a residuary legatee, if a creditor applies to prove a debt barred by lapse of time, the executor refused to plead the statute, and the plaintiff insisted upon doing so, it is competent for the plaintiff or any other person interested in the fund to take advantage of the statute before the master, notwithstanding the refusal of the executor to interpose it. Shewen v. Vanderhorst, 1 Russ. & My. 347; Phillips v. Beal, 32 Beav. 26; Moodie v. Bannister, 4 Drew. 432; Fuller v. Redman, 26 Beav. 614. In New York it is held that, in taking an account in the master's office, any party in interest may interpose the statute in bar of any claim presented.' Partridge v. Mitchell, 3 Edw. (N. Y.) Ch. 180. In Warren v. Poff, 4 Bradf. (N. Y.) 260, it was held that heirs and devisees might interpose the statute when it is sought to charge the real estate with the payment of debts of the estate.

9. Partridge v. Mitchell, *supra;* Warren v. Paff, 4 Bradf. (N. Y. Surr.) 260; Bond v. Smith, 2 Ala. 660.

in Florida[11] it is held to be the duty of the administrator or executor of an estate to plead the statute where the debt or claim was barred during the lifetime of the intestate, or even where it is so stale as to raise the presumption of payment from lapse of time.[12]

But while it is generally held that an executor is not, unless otherwise provided by statute, obliged to plead the general statute of limitations, yet he is in all cases bound to set up, in opposition to a claim, a statute which limits the time within which a claim may be presented for payment, or within which an action shall be commenced against him in his official capacity to enforce a claim.[13] But while the executor at law must interpose this

10. Rector v. Conway, 20 Ark. 79; Rogers v. Wilson, 13 Ark. 507.

11. Patterson v. Cobb, 4 Fla. 481.

12. See also Briggs v. Wilson, 5 De G. M. & G. 12; Beeching v. Morphew, 8 Hare, 129; Hunter v. Baxter, 3 Giff. 214, for instances when a legatee, heir, etc., may interpose the statute.

In re Kendrick, 107 N. Y. 104, 13 N. E. 762, it was held that the provision of the Code declaring that "the term of eighteen months after the death of a person within this State, against whom a cause of action exists, is not a part of the time limited for the commencement of an action against his executor or administrator," does not apply to the provision declaring that a judgment shall be conclusively presumed to be paid after twenty years from the time the party recovering it was entitled to a mandate to enforce it, except as against one, who, within the twenty years has made a payment or acknowledged an indebtedness thereon, and there is no provision contained in the Code which, under any circumstances, extends the time within which an acknowledgment or payment must be made in order to rebut the otherwise conclusive presumption of payment after the lapse of twenty years; and that, upon the settlement of an administrator's accounts, creditors whose claims are not barred by the statute of limitations, are entitled to object to those which are, when the assets are insufficient to pay both.

13. Schouler on Wills, Executors and Administrators, Vol. 2, §§ 1390, citing Wood on Limitations, §§ 1388-1390; Sugar River Bank v. Fairbanks, 49 N. H. 140; Scott v. Hancock, 13 Mass. 162; Wiggins v. Lovering, 9 Mo. 259; Hodgdon v. White, 11 N. H. 208; Hall v. Woodman, 49 id. 295; Walker v. Cheever, 39 id. 420; Amoskeag M'f'g. Co. v. Barnes, 48 id. 25; Heath v. Wells, 22 Mass. (5 Pick.) 140; Lamson v. Schutt, 86 Mass. (4 Allen) 359; Waltham Bank v. Wright, 90 Mass. (8 Allen) 122; Emerson v. Thompson, 16 Mass. 432. In most of the States, provision is made that claims against an estate shall be presented within a certain

statutory defense, it was held in the case first cited in the preceding note that where the presentation of a claim against an insolvent estate within the time limited is prevented by the fraud-

time after the death of the creditor, or the appointment of an executor or administrator, or be forever barred; and these statutes must be strictly complied with. Ticknor v. Harris, 14 N. H. 272; Badger v. Kelly, 10 Ala. 944; Pickett v. Ford, 5 Miss. (4 How.) 246; French v. Davis, 38 Miss. 218; Thrash v. Sumwalt, 5 Mo. 13; Walker v. Cheever, 39 N. H. 420; Whitmore v. Foose, 1 Den. (N. Y.) 159; Scovil v. Scovil, 45 Barb. (N. Y.) 517; Barsalou v. Wright, 4 Bradf. (N. Y.) 164; Williams v. Chaffin, 13 N. C. (2 Dev. L.) 333; Goodman v. Smith, 15 N. C. (4 Dev. L.) 450; Hubbard v. Marsh, 29 N. C. (7 Ired. L.) 204; Harter v. Taggart, 14 Ohio St. 122; Estate of Smith, 1 Ashm. (Pa.) 352; Demmy's Appeal, 43 Pa. 155; Atwood v. R. I. Agricultural Bank, 2 R. I. 191; New England Bank v. Newport, etc., Co., 6 R. I. 154; Hooper v. Bryant, 11 Tenn. (3 Yerg.) 1; Kelly v. Hooper, id. 395; Crawbaugh v. Hart, id. 431; Hawkins v. Walker, 12 Tenn. (4 Yerg.) 188; Foster v. Maxey, 14 Tenn. (6 Yerg.) 224; Trott v. West, 17 Tenn. (9 Yerg.) 433; 19 Tenn. (1 Meigs) 163; State Bank v. Vance, 17 Tenn. (9 Yerg.) 471; Greenway v. Hunter, 19 Tenn. (1 Meigs.) 74; Rogers v. Winton, 21 Tenn. (2 Humph.) 178; F. & M. Bank v. Leath, 11 id. 515; State v. Crutcher, 2 Swan 504; Allen v. Farrington, 34 Tenn. (2 Sneed) 526; Maynard v. May, 42 Tenn. (2 Coldw.) 44; Hall v. McCormick, 7 Tex. 269; Perry v. Munger, id. 589; Crosby v. McWillie, 11 id. 94; Cobb v. Norwood, id. 556; Coles v. Portis, 18 id. 155; Jennings v. Browder, 24 id. 192; Peyton v. Carr, 1 Rand. (Va.) 436; Mann v. Flinn, 10 Leigh (Va.) 93; Ready v. Thompson, 4 S. & P. (Ala.) 52; Jones v. Pharr, 3 Ala. 283; Starke v. Keenan, 5 id. 590; King v. Mosely, id. 610; Cawthorne v. Weisinger, 6 id. 714; State Bank v. Gibson, id. 814; Badger v. Kelfy, 10 id. 944. See McHenry v. Wells, 28 id. 451; McDougald v. Dawson, 30 id. 553; Bank of Montgomery v. Plannett, 37 id. 222; Walker v. Byers, 14 Ark. 246; State Bank v. Walker, id. 234; Biscoe v. Sandefur, id. 568; Bennett v. Dawson, 15 id. 412; Hill v. State, 23 id. 604; Danglada v. De la Guerra, 10 Cal. 386; Fanning v. Coit, Kirby (Conn.) 423; Rowan v. Kirkpatrick, 14 Ill. 1; Ryan v. Jones, 15 id. 1; Stillman v. Young, 16 id. 318; Peacock v. Haven, 22 id, 23; Wingate v. Pool, 25 id. 118; Mason v. Tiffany, 45 Id. 392; Beard v. Presbyterian Church, 15 Ind. 490; Preston v. Day, 19 Iowa, 127; Goodrich v. Conrad, 24 id. 254; McPhetres v. Halley, 32 Me. 72; Pettengill v. Patterson, 39 id. 498; Thurston v. Lowder, 47 id. 72; Rawlings v. Adams, 7 Md. 26; Bemis v. Bemis, 79 Mass. (13 Gray) 559. Unless the statute gives the court power to excuse delay, no remedy exists where the party has neglected to present his claim, whatever may have been the reason for delay. Sanford v. Wicks, 3 Ala. 369; Bigger v. Hutchings, 2 Stew. (Ala.) 445. These statutes, however, do not apply to

ulent concealment of the claim by the decease, a court of equity may decree satisfaction thereof out of the surplus, if any, in the hands of heirs and distributees, if the bill praying for such relief is filed promptly after the discovery of the claim.[14] But a general request by the executor to the creditors of the estate for delay, from time to time, or his assurance to them that the debt is good, will not, unless otherwise provided in the statute, save the operation of the statute limiting the presentation or enforcement of claims; and if he pays such claims after they are barred

strictly equitable claims, as mortgages, Bradley v. Norris, 3 Vt. 369; Austin v. Jackson, 10 id. 267; Locke v. Palmer, 26 Ala. 312; McMurray v. Hopper, 43 Pa. 468; Allen v. Moer, 16 Iowa, 307; Fisher v. Mossman, 11 Ohio St. 42; Menard v. Marks, 2 Ill. 25; or to compel the application of trust funds, Pope v. Boyd, 22 Ark. 535; Stark v. Hunton, 3 N. J. Eq. 300; or to claims which originate after the period named, Griswold v. Bingham, 6 Conn. 258; Hawley v. Botsford, 27 id. 80; Chambers v. Smith, 23 Mo. 174; or to a claim for the recovery of specific property, Andrews v. Huckabee, 30 Ala. 143; Sims v. Canfield, 2 id. 555; or where administration is suspended because the administrator fails to qualify, Morgan v. Dodge, 44 N. H. 255; Abercrombie v. Sheldon, 90 Mass. (8 Allen) 532; nor to a claim in the Orphan's Court, Yingling v. Hesson, 16 Md. 112; Glenn v. Hebb. 17 id. 260. Nor do these statutes attach until a claim is due; therefore, where the statute provides that all claims must be presented or sued within one year after they accrue, and a claim does not become due until two years after an administrator is appointed, the creditor has a year after the claim becomes due in which the present it. Neil v. Cunningham, 2 Port. (Ala.) 171.

14. See Sugar River Bank v. Fairbanks, 49 N. H. 140. *In re* Haxtun, 102 N. Y. 157, 6 N. E. 111, reversing 33 Hun, 364, it was held that the fact that a claim against the estate of a deceased person has been presented to and rejected by the executor or administrator, does not deprive the surrogate of jurisdiction to determine the validity of the claim in proceedings instituted under the Code, upon petition of the creditor to sell the real estate of the deceased. The surrogate may, in such a proceeding, determine the validity of all claims upon the estate which are not already liens upon the real property, as well that of the petitioning creditor as of other creditors.

The six months' limitation within which an action must be brought against an executor or administrator upon a claim rejected by him does not apply to a claim presented and rejected before the amendment of the statute of 1882 (Chap. 399, Laws of 1882), where no notice to creditors was ever published by the executor or administrator.

under such statute, he is guilty of devastavit.[15] If the executor neglects to plead the statute limiting the time within which claims may be presented or sued, the judgment will not be binding upon the estate, and an execution issuing thereon, levied upon the real estate of the deceased, is void as to all persons except the executor or administrator who permitted it to issue;[16] and money paid by him in satisfaction of such a judgment will not be allowed to him in his final account.[17] Thus, the executor or administrator is absolutely bound to take advantage of the statutes referred to specially intended for the quieting of claims against estates, although he is invested with an unqualified discretion as to whether he will or not interpose the bar of the general statute of limitations; and while he may obtain a license to sell real estate to pay debts barred by the general statute,[18] unless it appears that they are so stale as to raise a presumption of payment,[19] yet a license will not be granted to sell real estate, when no claims have been presented against the estate, or sued within the time prescribed by law, because in that case there are no debts to be paid,[20] and a license, if granted, would be void, upon the ground that the order is issued by the court without any actual jurisdiction over the subject-matter to which it relates, because there are no debts, and, therefore, there is no authority on the

15. Langham v. Baker, 64 Tenn. (5 Baxter) 701. But it seems that a request made by an administrator to creditors of the estate, to forbear until he can collect money enough to pay, is a special request, sufficiently definite to suspend the operation of the general statute of limitations. McKizzack v. Smith, 33 Tenn. (1 Sneed) 470.

16. Thayer v. Hollis, 44 Mass. (3 Metc.) 369; Amoskeag Mfg. Co. v. Barnes, 48 N. H. 25.

17. Stillman v. Young, 16 Ill. 318; Hodgdon v. White, 11 N. H. 208.

18. Hodgdon v. White, 11 N. H. 208.

19. Scott v. Hancock, 13 Mass. 162; Mooers v. White, 6 Johns. (N. Y.) Ch. 360; Hodgdon v. White, *supra*.

20. Tarbell v. Parker, 106 Mass. 347; Hall v. Woodman, 49 N. H. 304; Lamson v. Schutt, 86 Mass. (4 Allen) 359; Ferguson v. Scott, 49 Miss. 500; Robinson v. Hodge, 117 Mass. 222; Nowell v. Nowell, 8 Me. 220.

part of the court under the statute to issue the order.[21] These special statutes of limitation do not apply to an offset set up by a person who is sued by an administrator to recover a debt due from him to the estate.[22]

§ 189. Effect of statute when creditor is executor or administrator; when debtor is executor, etc.

The question of the statute does not arise where a legatee is also an executor of the testator, so that the same hand gives and receives.[23] Thus, where such a condition existed, Lord Hatherley, V. C., said:[24] "Having the whole of the testator's assets in his hands, he could not sue himself, the legacy was, therefore, either at home, that is to say, it would have been satisfied if there had been assets, or it was kept alive, because in ordinary circumstances a bill might have been filed to keep it alive; but this gentleman (the administrator) could not have taken so absurd a step as to file a bill against himself for the purpose of making himself pay his own legacy." This reasoning does not in terms, but in effect would seem to, apply to a case where the executor is an ordinary creditor of his testator, and, as such is the rule where the debtor is administrator to the creditor, it would seem to hold good in the

21. Tarbell v. Parker, *supra;* Hudson v. Hulbert, 32 Mass. (15 Pick.) 425; Thayer v. Hollis, *supra;* Lamson v. Schutt, *supra;* Heath v. Wells, 22 Mass. (5 Pick) 140.

22. Thus, where an administrator sued a bank for money deposited by his testator, and for dividends on stock of the bank owned by him, and the bank set up an offset thereto, to which the administrator objected on the ground that the claim was not presented to the probate court for allowance within the time prescribed by statute, and consequently was barred, the court held that the objection was not well grounded, because the statute only contemplated cases where the creditor in the first instance brought his claim against the estate, and had no application to suits by the administrator against a creditor, where the demand of the latter was set up as a counterclaim, and that in such a case the only statute that could be set up against the counterclaim or set-off was the general statute of limitations. Lay v. Mechanics' Bank, 61 Mo. 72.

23. Binns v. Nichols, L. R. 2 Eq. 256; Prior v. Horniblow, 2 Y. & C. Exch. 200; Adams v. Barry, 2 Coll. 285.

24. Binns v. Nichols, *supra.*

converse case.[25] Notwithstanding the almost universal rule, that when time has once commenced to run in these cases no alteration of circumstances in the way of any disability on the part of plaintiff or defendant will prevent it continuing to run, yet in cases where the debtor takes out administration to the creditor, time will not run in the debtor's favor, even though it has commenced to run previously to his administration. It appears that where administration of the goods of a creditor is given to a debtor, this, being done by act of law, *is not an extinction of the debt, but a suspension of the remedy.*[26] And where a debtor was appointed one of several executors of his creditor's will, but did not prove his debt until it was already barred by lapse of time, yet it was held that the debt was revived by his subsequently proving the will, inasmuch as that proof related back to the testator's death, and he was ordered to account for the sum owing with interest.[27] Yet *an executor or administrator will have no right, under any circumstances, to pay a debt or charge which has absolutely become extinguished by statute.*[28]

25. In Maryland, the statute of limitations of 1815, which is still in force also in the District of Columbia, does not apply to a claim by an executor against his estate, as he cannot sue himself at law. Glover v. Patten, 165 U. S. 394, 405, 17 Sup. St. 411, 41 L. Ed. 760.

26. Seagram v. Knight, L. R. 2 Ch. 628; Needham's Case, 8 Coke, 135 *a;* Wankford v. Wankford, 1 Salk. 299.

27. Ingle v. Richards (No. 2), 28 Beav. 366.

In Hooper v. Hooper, 125 N. Y. 400, 26 N. E. 457, 12 L. R. A. 237, 53 Hun, 394, it was held that by the phrase "foreign executor," the mere non-residence of the individual holding the office is not referred to, but the foreign origin of the representative character; that is, the sole product of the foreign law, and depending upon it for existence, cannot pass beyond the jurisdiction of its origin; but that where ancillary letters testamentary have been issued to a foreign executor, as prescribed by the Code, he thereby acquires an official and representative character as executor here, and so may sue or be sued in his representative character in this State; and that an action may be brought here against an ancillary executor, as such, by a non-resident, at least when the cause of action arose in this State.

28. Lewis v. Rumney, L. R. 4 Eq. 451.

§ 190. Acknowledgment by an executor.

In England [29] and in some of the States in this country [30] it is held that an acknowledgment of an executor takes a debt due from the estate out of the statute. But generally in this country the rule is that an acknowledgment by an executor does not remove the statute bar after it has once attached to the debt, although it may be sufficient to suspend the operation of the statute if made before the bar is complete;[31] and this doctrine is certainly consistent

29. Browning v. Paris, 5 M. & W. 117; Taft v. Stephenson, 1 De G. M. G. 28, 41; Briggs v. Wilson, 5 id. 12; Fordham v. Wallis, 10 Hare, 217.

30. Semmes v. Magruder, 10 Md. 242; Northcut's Adm'r v. Wilkinson, 51 Ky. (12 B. Mon.) 408; Walker v. Cruikshank, 23 La. An. 252; Hall v. Darrington, 9 Ala. 502; Griffin v. The Justices, 17 Ga. 96; Tazewell's Ex'r v. Whittle's Adm'r, 13 Gratt. (Va.) 329; Quynn v. Carroll, 10 Md. 197; Brewster v. Brewster, 52 N. H. 52; Hodgdon v. White, 11 id. 211; Townes v. Ferguson, 20 Ala. 147; Farmers' & Mechanics' Bank v. Leath, 30 Tenn. (11 Humph.) 615; Buswell v. Roby, 3 N. H. 467; McWhorter v. Johnson, 29 Tenn. (10 Humph.) 209; Dayo v. Jones, 19 Wend. (N. Y.) 491; Buchanan v. Buchanan, 4 Strobh. (S. C.) 63; Chambers v. Fennemore's Adm'r, 4 Harr. (Del.) 368; Shreve v. Joyce, 36 N. J. L. 44, 13 Am. Rep. 417; McCann v. Sloan, 25 Md. 575; Head v. Mannin, 28 Ky. (5 J. J. Mar.) 255; Hard v. Lee, 2 Monr. (Ky.) 131; Johnson v. Beardslee, 15 Johns. (N. Y.) 3; Emerson v. Thompson, 16 Mass. 429.

31. Schouler on Wills, Executors and Administrators, Vol. 2, §§ 1389, and cases cited; Forney v. Benedict, 5 Pa. 225; Sanders v. Robertson, 23 Miss. 389; Moore v. Hardison, 10 Tex. 467; Haselden v. Whitesides, 2 Strobh. (S. C.) 353; Miller v. Dorsey, 9 Md. 317; Clark v. Maguire's Adm'x, 35 Pa. 259; Heath v. Grenell, 61 Barb. (N. Y.) 190; Riser v. Snoddy, 7 Ind. 442; Moore v. Hillebrant, 14 Tex. 312, 65 Am. Dec. 118; Peck v. Botsford, 7 Conn. 172, 18 Am. Dec. 92; Crandall v. Gallup, 12 id. 365; Thompson v. Peter, 25 U. S. (12 Wheat.) 565, 6 L. Ed. 730; Richmond, Petitioner, 2 Pick. (Mass.) 567; Manson v. Felton, 13 id. 206; Foster v. Starkey, 12 Cush. (Mass.) 324; McLaren v. McMartin, 36 N. Y. 88; Huntington v. Bobbitt's Heirs, 46 Miss. 528; Seig v. Acord, 21 Gratt. (Va.) 365, 8 Am. Rep. 605. In Fritz v. Thomas, 1 Whart. (Pa.) 66, 29 Am. Dec. 39, Gibson, J., laid down the doctrine as stated in the text, and said: "The concession that the plaintiff's claim is just, and the promise to see what could be done for him, would doubtless be sufficient to maintain an action, if the consideration were the defendant's own debt. But can any acknowledgment by an executor or administrator preclude him from pleading the statute of limitations to a count on the original

with the present theory of acknowledgment, as upon principle,

cause of action? In Jones v. Moore, 5 Binn. (Pa.) 573, and subsequently in Bailey v. Bailey, 14 S. & R. (Pa.) 195, and Scull v. Wallace, 15 id. 231, it was doubtless taken for granted that a recovery may be had against a plea of the statute, on proof of an acknowledgment by the personal representative. But it is to be remarked that the point has not been adjudged, and that no recovery has in fact been had; and the inquiry is consequently not clogged by the authority of a precedent." * * * Why should we not finish what was so well begun in Jones v. Moore, by making the law of the subject consistent in all its parts, and giving to the statute entire effect, both in substance and in form? To do so would involve no violation of that case as a precedent, for, as I have said, the point was not adjudged; and the step remaining to be taken in the progress of departure from the doctrine of revival is no greater than what was taken there. Indeed, there is no course open to us but to follow the principle out, or abandon it altogether; for, to be consistent, we must either return to the doctrine of revival without qualification, or maintain that an action on his own promise lies not against an executor or administrator in his official character. And for saying it does not, we have the authority of Thompson v. Peter, 25 U. S. (12 Wheat.) 565, 6 L. Ed. 730, and Peck v. Botsford, 7 Conn. 178, in both of which the point was directly ruled."

In a subsequent case in that State it was held that an executor's promise to pay a debt of the testator will not take it out of the statute, and the court rely upon Fritz v. Thomas, *supra*, to support the ground that, as the old promise was not revived, but superseded by the new one, the consideration of a moral obligation would be wanting to make the executor personally liable. Reynolds v. Hamilton, 7 Watts (Pa.) 420. An admission by one co-executor of a debt due from his testator is nowhere receivable as evidence in a suit for the debt, against another co-executor, to establish the origin of the demand, so as to make the other personally liable; though otherwise to take it out of the statute, if the original demand against the testator is *aliunde* established. Hammond v. Huntley, 4 Cow. (N. Y.) 493; Deyo v. Jones, 19 Wend. (N. Y.) 491. In Williams on Executors, 1889 (7th ed.), it is said: "Where, in assumpsit by an executor, in which all the promises were laid to be made to the testator in his lifetime, the defendant pleaded that he did not promise within six years next before the obtaining of the original writ of the plaintiff, and the plaintiff replied that the original was sued on such a day, and that within six years before the day of obtaining thereof, that is to say, on such a day, letters testamentary were granted to him, by which the plaintiff's action accrued to him within six years; this replication was held bad; because the time of limitation must be computed from the time when the action first accrued to the testator, and not from the time of proving the will; for that

a new promise by an executor is invalid because it lacks even a

gave no new cause of action, and therefore the time of proving the will is perfectly immaterial. Hickman v. Walker, Willes, 27; note to Hodsden v. Harridge, 2 Saund. 64; Hapgood v. Southgate, 21 Vt. 584; Warren v. Paff, 4 Bradf. Surr. (N. Y.) 260; Conant v. Hitt, 12 Vt. 285; Boyce v. Foote, 19 Wis. 199.

"But where to an action by an administrator for money had and received to his use by the defendant, who had received the interstate's money after his death, six years and upwards before the commencement of the action, but within six years after letters of administration granted to the plaintiff the defendant pleaded the statute of limitations, and the plaintiff replied the special matter above mentioned; it was held, upon demurrer, that the statute was no bar, because this was not a cause of action in the intestate, the money having been received after his death, and the plaintiff's title commenced by taking out letters of administration, before which time no cause of action accrued to him. Cary v. Stephenson, 2 Salk. 421. [See Stanford's Case, cited Cro. Jac. 61; Hansford v. Elliott, 9 Leigh (Va.) 792. In Dunning v. Ocean Bank, 6 Lans. (N. Y.) 296, the court say: 'If there was no person or party in being at the time the money in question came to the possession of the defendant, who could lawfully demand and receive the same, and in whom a right for the recovery thereof vested, or since, * * * the action is not barred. This is well settled, until there is some one entitled to demand and take, there is no obligation to pay, and no promise can be implied. The statute does not begin to operate until then.' Davis v. Gare, 6 N. Y. 124; Bucklin v. Ford, 5 Barb. (N. Y.) 395; Vaughn v. Mohawk Ins. Co., 13 Wend. (N. Y.) 267; Richards v. Richards, 2 B. & Ald. 447; Piggott v. Rush, 4 Ad. & El. 912; Witt v. Elmore, 2 Bailey (S. C.) 595; Fergusson v. Fyffe, 8 Cl. & F. 121; Johnston v. Humphrys, 12 S. & R. (Pa.) 395; Geiger v. Brown, 4 McCord (S. C.) 418; Fishwick v. Sewall, 4 H. & J. (Md.) 393; Jones v. Brodie, 3 Mon. (Ky.) 354; Grubb v. Clayton, 2 Hayw. (N. C.) 378.] So where an action was brought by an administrator against the acceptors of bills of exchange payable to the intestate, and accepted after his death, but before the grant of letters of administration, it was held that the statute ran only from the grant of the letters. Murray v. East India Company, 5 B. & Ald. 204; Pratt v. Swaine, 8 B. & C. 285; s. c. 1 M. & Ry. 351; Perry v. Jenkins, 1 My. and Cr. 18. [In many of the States, express provision is now made by statute as to the time when the statute shall attach to a claim in favor of a deceased creditor, and in some instances the statute is saved where it had run only thirty or a certain other specified number of days before the creditor's death.]

"It must be observed that where, in assumpsit by an executor, on a contract made with his testator, all the promises in the declaration were laid to be made to the testator, and the defendant pleaded the statute of

moral consideration to support it. But, while an acknowledgment

limitations, the plaintiff could not in his replication set forth a promise made to himself within six years, without being guilty of a departure, any more than he could in such case give evidence of a promise made to himself within six years upon an issue joined on the plea of the statute of limitations. Hickman v. Walker, Willes, 29; Dean v. Crane, 6 Mod. 309; Executors of the Duke of Marlborough v. Widmore, 2 Stra. 890; 2 Saund. 63 *l*. However, in Heylin v. Hastings, Carth. 471, it is said to have been admitted that a promise made to an executor is sufficient to prove the issue of assumpsit to the testator within six years; because the promise does not give any new cause of action, but only revives the old cause, and is of no other use but to prevent the bar by the statute of limitations. But this seems not to be well founded; and it has since been determined, that evidence of an acknowledgment by the defendant within six years of an old existing debt, of above six years' standing, due to the plaintiff's intestate, but which acknowledgment was made after the intestate's death, will not support a count by the administrator, laying the promise to be made to his intestate. Sarell v. Wine, 3 East, 409; s. p. Ward v. Hunter, 6 Taunt. 210; s. p. by Bayley, J., in Short v. M'Carthy, 3 B. & Ald. 626. [This rule has been adopted in Pennsylvania, Jones v. Moore, 5 Binn. (Pa.) 573; but not in New Hampshire, Buswell v. Roby, 3 N. H. 467; nor Massachusetts, Baxter v. Penniman, 8 Mass. 134.] Therefore, where it was necessary to rely on an acknowledgment, made since the death of the testator, to bar the statute, counts were required in the declaration laying promises to the plaintiff as executor. As to what is sufficient evidence of an account stated with the plaintiff as executor, see Purdon v. Purdon, 10 M. & W. 562.

"Accordingly, if an executor brought an action on a bill or note, and intended to rely on an acknowledgment or promise made to himself in order to bar the statute, he had to state in his declaration the making of the bill or note, and must then have proceeded to aver that, after the death of his testator or intestate, the defendant promised him (the plaintiff) as executor or administrator to pay him. And where the declaration was so framed, such promises might have been denied by a plea of *non assumpsit*. For the mere production and proof of the note would not prove the promise as made to the executors, as it would if the promise were laid as made to the testator. The right of action indeed is transferred to the executor, but no promise is implied by law to pay him; otherwise the statute of limitations would run from the death of the payee, and not from the time of the note becoming due. In order, therefore, to support the action, there must be an express promise to the executor, that is to say, an express promise as contradistinguished from a promise contained in the note itself, or anything implied out of it; and the cause of action is the existence of the note, with the express

by an executor will not take a debt against the estate out of the

promise to the executor to pay the amount of it; whereas the rule is confined to cases where the action is only on the note. Timmis v. Platt, 2 M. & W. 720; Gilbert v. Platt, 5 Dowl. 748; Rolleston v. Dixon, 2 Dowl. & L. 892. The effect of the plea of *non assumpsit* is in such a case to admit that the bill or note was signed by the defendant, but to deny that he made any promise to the executor.

"In Clark v. Hooper, 10 Bing. 840, 4 M. & Sc. 353, payment of interest on a promissory note to an administrator who had omitted to take out administration in the diocese in which the note was a *bonum notabile*, was held a sufficient acknowledgment of the debt to bar the statute.

Upon this decision, see Stamford, S. & B. Banking Co. v. Smith, [1892] 1 Q. B. 765, *supra*, § 103, n.

"If an executor sues in assumpsit, within a year after the death of his testator, the six years not being elapsed before, though they expire within that period, yet it is held to be sufficient to take the case out of the statute. Tidd, 28 (9th ed.), citing Cawer v. James, Bull, N. P. 150. But see s. c. reported in Willes, 255 *nomine* Karver v. James. But the contrary was held in Penny v. Brice, 18 C. B. N. S. 393.

"Where a party brings an action before the expiration of six years, and dies before judgment, the six years being then expired, it has been held that his executor or administrator may, within the equity of the fourth section of the statute of limitations (21 Jac. I., c. 16), bring a new action, Matthews v. Phillips, 2 Salk. 425; Kinsey v. Heyward, 1 Lutw. 260; provided he does it recently, or within a reasonable time. No precise time is fixed as to what shall be deemed a reasonable time; but it should seem that the statute is the best guide upon the subject, and as that provides that a new action, in the cases enumerated in it, must be commenced within a year so an executor ought also to bring a new action within that period. 2 Saund. 64, note to Hodsden v. Harridge. [In many of the States of this country express provision is made to save the statute to a party who has brought his action in season, but which has failed by reason of some technical or other ground other than the voluntary act of the party, and the period within which a fresh action may be brought is generally fixed. See Appendix.) In Kinsey v. Heyward, 1 Ld. Raym. 434, a year is said to be a reasonable time, and the Court of King's Bench appears to be of this opinion in Wilcox v. Huggins, 2 Str. 907, Fitzg. 170, 289, where it is said that the most that had ever been allowed was a year, and that within the equity of the proviso in the statute, which gives the plaintiff a year to commence a new action, where the judgment is arrested or reversed; and that they would not go a moment further, for it would let in all the inconveniences which the statute was made to avoid. Indeed, if the executor had been retarded by suits about the will or administra-

statute, an acknowledgment made to him by a debtor to the

tion, and had shown that in pleading it would have been otherwise, because the neglect would then have been accounted for. And Lee, J., said: 'I think what is or is not a recent prosecution in a case of this nature is to be determined by the discretion of the court from the circumstances of the case; but, generally, the year in the statute is a good direction.' However, in Lethbridge v. Chapman, 15 Vin. Abr. 103, *in margine*, the action was allowed to be brought within fourteen months after the testator's death, though no reason was assigned for it. Upon the whole, therefore, it was deemed prudent for the executor to bring a new action as soon as he possibly could after the death of his testator, and at all events not to delay it beyond a year. 2 Saund. 64 *b*, note. But in Curlewis v. Mornington, 7 E. & B. 283, it was expressly held that the executor was not bound to the year, if under the circumstances he can fairly be said to have used due diligence.

"Again, if an executor brought assumpsit, but died before judgment and the six years run, his executor might, notwithstanding, bring a fresh action, so as he brought it in a reasonable time, which is to be decided at the discretion of the justices upon the circumstances of the case. Bull, N. P. 150 *a*.

"The principle of these cases, according to the judgment of Lord Chief Justice Treby, in the case of Kinsey v. Heyward, is, that when once the proviso in the statute of limitations is complied with by the commencement of an action within due time, the party is out of the purview of the act, and set at liberty out of the restraint of the said statute. But the true ground of these decisions appears to be that they proceed upon the equity of the fourth section of the statute, and that the courts have extended that section to the case of an executor whose testator has died pending an action brought by him; which, though not within the words of it, was evidently within the mischief. 2 Ad. & El. 403, 404. In Adam v. The Inhabitants of the City of Bristol, 2 Ad. & El. 389, the premises of A., a termor, having been burnt by a riotous assembly, A. complied with all the requisites of the statute 7 & 8 Geo. IV., c. 31, and commenced an action against the inhabitants of the city and county within three months from the offense. Before verdict or judgment, and after the expiration of the three months, A. died. His executrix commenced an action against the inhabitants on the seventh day from A.'s death. And the Court of King's Bench held that, supposing an executrix entitled to sue in any such case (as to which the court gave no opinion), the action, having been commenced more than three months from the offense, was too late under the provision of section 3 of the statute, and that there was no analogy between this case and the above decisions on the general statute of limitations. But the same equitable construction that has been applied to the fourth section of the statute of James has been followed

estate will remove the bar as to such debt;[32] and it has even been held that payments made by a debtor to the estate, to a person who had not then been, but was subsequently appointed administrator, was sufficient to revive the debt and remove the statute bar.[33] In any event, if an acknowledgment of an executor or administrator is relied on to take a debt out of the statute, it must be shown to have been made by him in his representative capacity.[34] The declaration should contain a count upon a promise by the executor or administrator as such,[35] although in New Hampshire this is held to be unnecessary.[36] In accordance with this rule it has been held by the English courts that, if an action is brought against an executor or administrator on a bill or note given by the testator or intestate, and the declaration alleges a promise by the defendant to pay the bill or note, such promise may be denied by a plea of *non assumpsit,* notwithstanding the rule abolishing the plea of *non assumpsit* to a declaration on a bill or note.[37] However, it is said to have been held [38] that if the

as to the limitation of actions on bonds, etc., imposed by the Stat. 3 & 4 Wm. IV., c. 42, § 3; Sturgis v. Darrell, 4 H. & N. 622; 6 id. 120.

"Where the right of action accrued to the testator during his residence abroad, and he died abroad, never having returned after the accrual thereof, the statute is no bar to an action by his executors, although it accrued more than six years before action was brought; at all events if it is brought within six years after his death. Townsend v. Deacon, 3 Exch. 706. See also Forbes v. Smith, 11 Exch. 161." Hammon v Huntley, 4 Cow. (N. Y.) 493; Cayuga Bank v. Bennett, 5 Hill (N. Y.) 236; Forsyth v. Ganson, 5 Wend. (N. Y.) 558; Oakes v. Mitchell, 15 Me. 360; M'Intire v. Morris, 14 Wend. (N. Y.) 90; Patterson v. Cobb, 4 Fla. 481; Moore v. Porcher, Bailey (S. C.) Eq. 195; Reigne v. Desportes, Dudley (S. C.) 118; M'Teer v. Ferguson, Riley (S. C) 159; Pearce v. Zimmerman, Harp. (S. C.) 305; Henderson v. Ilsley, 19 Miss. 9; Fisher v. Duncan, 1 H. & M. (Va.) 563; Oakes v. Mitchell, 15 Me. 360; Banker v. Athearn, 35 id. 364.

32. Martin v. Williams, 17 Johns. (N. Y.) 330; Townsend v. Ingersoll, 12 Abb. Pr. (N. Y.) N. S. 354; Jones v. Moore, 5 Binn. (Pa.) 573.

33. Townsend v. Ingersoll, *supra.*

34. Scholey v. Walton, 12 M. & W. 510.

35. Browning v. Paris, 5 M. & W. 117.

36. Buswell v. Roby, 3 N. H. 467.

37. Rolleston v. Dixon, 2 Dowl. & L. 892.

38. Poile v. ——, Exor. Sitt. after Tr. T. 1823, *coram* Abbott, C. J., 2

declaration charges the executor, on a promise made by his testator, and the defendant pleads the statute of limitations, to which the plaintiff replies, that the testator did promise within six years; proof on the part of the plaintiff, that the executor promised within six years, and that the testator's death was within this period, will support the count in the declaration; for that the executor's promise shows a liability to pay, existing before the time of the testator's death, and the law will imply a promise by the testator to pay what he was liable to pay.

The mere existence of a debt owing by the testator or intestate is not evidence of a promise to pay by the executor or administrator, as executor or administrator.[39] Hence, as against an executor or administrator, an acknowledgment merely by him of the debt's existence is not sufficient to take the case out of the statute; there must be an express promise.[40] In an action of assumpsit against several executors, who pleaded the general issue and the statute of limitations, Abbott, C. J., held, that neither an acknowledgment of the debt by all the executors, nor an express promise by one of them, took the case out of the statute; there ought to have been an express promise by all.[41] In New Jersey it has been held that a sole executor has the power, by a new promise, to remove the bar of the statute, and that all of several, or one of two, executors or administrators may bind the estate by a new promise without making the representatives personally liable.[42]

Phil. Ev. 531, 6th ed. But this case is omitted in the seventh edition.

39. Atkins v. Tregold, 2 B. & C. 23, by Abbott, C. J.

40. Tullock v. Dunn, Ry. & M. 416.

41. Scholey v. Walton, 12 M. & W. 510.

By the weight of English authority an acknowledgment or promise by one of several executors did not bind the others before Lord Tenterden's Act; but, under that statute, he thereby binds the testator's estate, and the creditor may recover judgment against him thereon in an action against all the executors, while § 2 enables the creditor to sue such executor alone. In re Macdonald, [1897] 2 Ch. 181; Astbury v. Astbury, [1898] 2 Ch. 111. As to payment of interest by one of several mortgagees, see Bailie v. Irwin, [1897] 2 I. R. 614.

42. Shreve v. Joyce, 36 N. J. L. 44.

§ 191. What acknowledgment by an executor is sufficient.

It was formerly held in England [43] that an acknowledgment or promise by an executor, in order to be operative to remove the statute bar, must be express, or at least of a more definite character than one which would be sufficient to bind the original debtor if it had been made by him. But under the present theory as to acknowledgments it would undoubtedly be held in England, as well as in the States where the English doctrine as to the effect of an acknowledgment made by an executor prevails, that an acknowledgment which would be binding on the original debtor, would also be sufficient if made by his executor.[44]

§ 192. Where executor is also devisee in trust.

It has been held in England that, where an executor acts in a double capacity, as where he is both executor and trustee of real estate, and in that capacity makes a payment which amounts to an acknowledgment of a debt in his character of executor, it does not revive a debt against the realty as in such a case no principle of marshaling exists;[45] and such is doubtless the rule in all those States where the acknowledgment of an executor is regarded as sufficient to revive a debt, except where real estate and personal property are put upon the same footing in the hands of an executor.

§ 193. Where statute has run against debt before testator's death.

Where the statute has run against a debt due the estate, before the death of the testator although upon the very day of his death, it will be barred, although the executor brings an action within a reasonable time after his death,[46] unless it is saved by the express provisions of the statute, as is the case in several of the States.[47]

43. Tullock v. Dunn, Ry. & Moo. 416.

44. Banning on Limitations, 228; Briggs v. Wilson, 5 De G. M. & G. 12.

45. Fordham v. Wallis, 10 Hare, 217.

46. Penny v. Brice, 18 C. B. N. S. 393.

47. The general rule, sometimes

§ 194. When statute has begun to run during the life of testator.

Except in those States where the statute otherwise provides, when the statute has begun to run upon a claim during the life of a creditor it is not suspended by his death, although no personal representative has been appointed;[48] but, when the statute has not begun to run during his life, it will not begin to run against his estate until an executor or administrator has been duly appointed and qualified, upon the principle that the statute cannot begin to run until there is a person in existence capable of suing or being sued upon the claim.[49]

regulated by State statutes, as in Nevada (§ 2898), and Montana (§ 156), now is that an executor or administrator cannot revive claims against his testator or intestate which were barred before the latter's death. Stiles v. Laurel Folk Oil & Coal Co., 47 W. Va. 838, 35 S. E. 986; Bambrick v. Bambrick, 157 Mo. 423, 58 S. W. 8; Jones v. Powning, 25 Nev. 399, 60 Pac. 833; In re Mouillerat's Estate, 14 Mont. 245, 36 Pac. 185; Schlicker v. Hemenway, 110 Cal. 579, 52 Am. St. Rep. 116, n., 42 Pac. 1063.

See Schouler on Wills, Executors and Administrators, Vol. 2, §§ 1390a, and cases there cited.

48. Nicks v. Martindale, Harp. (S. C.) 135; Abbott v. McElroy, 18 Miss. 100; Davis v. Garr, 6 N. Y. 124; Burnett v. Bryan, 6 N. J. L. 377; Hull v. Deatly, 70 Ky. (7 Bush) 687; Baker v. Brown, 18 Ill. 91; Byrd v. Byrd, 28 Miss. 144; Tynan v. Walker, 35 Cal. 634; Brown v. Merrick, 16 Ark. 612; Dekay v. Darrah, 14 N. J. L. 288; Jackson v. Hitt, 12 Vt. 285; Stewart v. Spedden, 5 Md. 433; Hayman v. Keally, 3 Cranch C. C. 325. In Young v. Mackall, 4 Md. 362, a right of action accrued on one of two bonds in 1834, and on the other in 1835 and the obligee died in 1837, in which year his executor filed a bill against the obligor, which suit abated by the death of the complainant in 1841. The obligor died in 1846. An administrator *de bonis non* on the obligee's estate was appointed in October, 1849, and the claim on the bond was filed the same month. It was held that as the Maryland statute (running twelve years on bonds) had begun to run in the lifetime of the obligee, none of the facts above stated stopped its operation. If a suit is abated and not revived, it takes no time out of the statute. Boatwright v. Boatwright, L. R. 17 Eq. 71; Rhodes v. Smethurst, 4 M. & W. 42.

49. Jolliffe v. Pitt, 2 Vern. 694; Burdick v. Garrick, L. R. 5 Ch. 233; Webster v. Webster, 10 Ves. 93. The statute is suspended until the appointment of an administrator. Briggs v. Thomas, 32 Vt. 176; Toby v. Allen, 3 Kan. 399; Etter v. Finn, 12 Ark. 632; McKenzie v. Hill, 51 Mo. 303; Hull v. Deatly, *supra;* Nelson v. Herkell, 30 Kan. 456; Whitney v. State, 52 Miss. 732.

Thus, where property was acquired after the death of the intestate, it has been held that the statute does not commence to run against an action of trover therefor until administration is granted;[50] and where the statute gives a remedy to the executor or administrator of an estate of a person killed by the negligence of another, and also provides that the action shall be brought within one year from the time when the right of action accrued, the action is not treated as having accrued until the appointment of an administrator;[51] but the rule would be otherwise if the statute provided that an action therefor should be brought within one year from the time of such intestate's death, because in that case the statute attaches immediately, and the bar becomes complete at the end of a full year from that time. There is also another element that enters into cases of this character, and that is, that the statute gives the right to sue, and no such right exists independent thereof, it only exists in the manner and for the period provided by the statute; and, strictly speaking, the provision as to the period within which action must be brought is a condition imposed upon the right, rather than a limitation, and unless the statute is complied with, the right is defeated, and can never be revived either by an acknowledgment or promise.[52] The

50. Johnson v. Wren, 3 Stew. (Ala.) 172; Clark v. Hardiman, 2 Leigh (Va.) 347; Bucklin v. Ford, 5 Barb. (N. Y.) 393.

51. Andrews v. Hartford, etc., R. Co., 34 Conn. 57; Sherman v. Western, etc., Co., 24 Iowa, 515.

52. In Andrews v. Hartford, etc., R. Co., *supra*, an action was brought against the defendant to recover under a statute of the State, for injuries inflicted by the negligence of the defendant, upon the plaintiff's intestate, of which he subsequently died. The statute provided a remedy in such cases, but limited the right of action to one year after the cause of action arose. The injury was inflicted Dec. 29, 1864, and death ensued a few days afterwards. The action was not commenced until June 14, 1866, considerably more than one year after the plaintiff's intestate died, but within one year after letters of administration were taken out upon his estate. The defendants insisted that, as the action was not commenced within one year after the intestate's death, the remedy was lost. The court held that the remedy was not lost, because the cause of action did not arise until an executor or administrator was appointed upon the estate. "The

rule is well settled, that where a cause of action does not accrue until after the death of the creditor or claimant the statute does not begin to run until administration is granted;[53] but if it accrues before his death, the running of the statute is not suspended,[54] unless express provision to that effect is made in the statute. In the case of an infant, or indeed any person under a statutory disability at the time of their death, the statute does not begin to run until administration is granted.[55] The circum-

cause of action," said Butler, J., "would have been perfect on the happening of the death, and would have been barred at the end of one year from the happening of the event, if an ordinary case, or there had been an executor. But it is a rule of law, recognized by the court (Hobart v. Connecticut Turnpike Co., 15 Conn. 145), that a cause of action accruing to an administrator after the death of the intestate is not complete, and does not arise and exist so that the statute can begin to run upon it until an administrator is appointed who can bring suit. And the legislature seem to have had that rule in view when they enacted the statute; for they did not say that the action should be barred unless commenced within one year from the death, or the happening of the events for which it is given, but 'unless commenced within one year after the cause of action shall have arisen.' Inasmuch, then, as under a well-settled rule no cause of action can arise and exist in favor of an administrator until he comes into existence as such and this suit was brought within one year after the plaintiff received his appointment, it was not barred." In Sherman v. Western, etc., R. R. Co., *supra*, the same rule was adopted in a case arising under a similar statute, where the plaintiff's intestate was thrown from a boat and capsized by reason of the negligence of the employees of the defendant stage company, whose passenger she was, and after struggling ten minutes, more or less, to save her life, was drowned. See also Wood v. Ford, 29 Miss. 57, where a similar rule was applied.

53. Hobart v. Connecticut Turnpike Co., *supra;* Beauchamp v. Mudd, 5 Ky. (2 Bibb.) 537; Abbott v. Mc. Elroy, 18 Miss. 100; Fishwick v. Sewell, 4 H. & J. (Md.) 393.

In general, limitation does not begin to run if there is no administration on a decedent's estate when the cause of action accrues. See Bullard's Estate, 116 Cal. 355, 48 Pac. 219. In Kansas, it is held that the statute begins to run against a decedent's estate after the lapse of a reasonable time, though there is no administration. Kulp v. Kulp, 51 Kan. 341, 32 Pac. 1118, 21 L. R. A. 550; Black v. Elliott, 63 Kan. 211, 65 Pac. 215, 88 Am. St. Rep. 239.

54. Nicks v. Martindale, Harp. (S. C.) 135; Burnet v. Bryan, 6 N. J. L. 377; Davis v. Garr, 6 N. Y. 124; Goodhue v. Barnwell, Rice (S. C.) Ch. 198.

55. Goodhue v. Barnwell, *supra*. In re Tilden, 98 N. Y. 434, it was

stance that an executor is named in the will does not change the rule, as the statute does not attach until he has been duly qualified to act as such by proof of the will;[56] and it seems that when

held that when there have been several accountings of executors, and it appears that each subsequent accounting was based upon the result as found upon the preceding one, that the validity of each previous accounting was unchallenged by any objection upon the one next succeeding, and that the last accounting was based upon a citation duly issued and served upon the parties interested, and upon proceedings regularly conducted, it is binding and conclusive upon all the parties as to the validity of the prior decrees.

56. Forrest v. Douglas, 4 Bing. 704; Garland v. Milling, 6 Ga. 310; Ellison v. Allen, 8 Fla. 206; Hobart v. Conn. Turnpike Co., 15 Conn. 145. The view adopted in the text, that where a statute gives a right, and provides a period within which it shall be enforced, the clause relating to the time of its enforcement is a condition rather than a limitation, is sustained in Pittsburgh, etc., R. Co. v. Hine, 25 Ohio St. 629, and in Boyd v. Clark, 8 Fed. 849, where Brown, D. J., said: "The *lex loci contractus* governs the rights of parties, but the *lex fori* determines the remedy. The principle has been applied in a large number of cases arising upon contracts; but in Dennick v. Central R. Co. of N. J., 103 U. S. 11, 26 L. Ed. 439, it was applied to a statute of this description, where the administrator brought his action in another State. An almost unbroken series of adjudications has also established that the time within which an action may be brought relates generally to the remedy, and must be determined by the law of the forum. Hence, it would follow that if this statute contained no limitation of time within which an action must be brought, and the time had been left to depend upon the general statutes of limitations in the Province of Ontario, it is clear that we should have disregarded such statute, and permitted the plaintiff to bring this action at any time before actions of this description would be barred by the statutes of this State.

"An exception to this general rule, however, is suggested in Story's Conflict of Laws, sec. 582, of cases where the statutes of limitation or prescription of a particular country do not only extinguish the right of action, but the claim of title itself, *ipso facto*, and declare it a nullity after the lapse of the prescribed period; and the parties are within the jurisdiction during the whole of that period, so that it has actually and fully operated upon the case.

"The cases of Shelby v. Guy, 24 U. S. (11 Wheat.) 361, 6 L. Ed. 495; Goodman v. Munks, 8 Port. (Ala.) 84 (overruled by Jones v. Jones, 18 Ala. 248); Brown v. Brown, 5 Ala. 508; and Fears v. Sykes, 35 Miss. 633, do in fact lend support to this distinction; the general tenor of these cases being to the effect that where the statute of one State declares that the possession of personal property for a certain period vests an absolute title, such prescription

an executor accepts the trust under the will the statute begins to run from the time of acceptance, and not from the time of giving public notice thereof.[57] But it has been held in North Carolina that as the executor's right to the personal property of his testator commences at the death of the testator, the statute begins to run against him from that time.[58] But such is not the rule gen-

will be enforced in every other State to which the property may be removed or wherein the question may arise.

"In the Pittsburgh, etc., R. Co. v. Hine, 25 Ohio St. 629, it was held that under an act requiring compensation for causing death by wrongful act, neglect, or default, which gave a right of action, provided such action should be commenced within two years after the death of such deceased person, the proviso was a condition qualifying the right of action, and not a mere limitation on the remedy. It was further held that the plaintiff's right must be determined as the act originally stood, and was therefore subject to the restrictions contained in the proviso, and the action, not having been brought within the two years, could not be sustained. The case differs from the one under consideration only in the fact that the limitation was contained in a proviso to the section directing in whose name the action should be brought.

"In Eastwood v. Kennedy, 44 Md. 563, it was held that where a statute of the United States for the District of Columbia gave a claim for the recovery of usurious interest, provided suit to recover the same be brought within one year after the payment of such interest, it would not be competent for a party to recover in Maryland after the lapse of a year, and that the courts of that State were bound to respect and apply the limitations contained in the act. The cases of Baker v. Stonebraker, 36 Mo. 338, 349, and Huber v. Stiener, 2 Bing. N. C. 202, are somewhat analogous, but throw little additional light upon the question.

"We are compelled then to deal with it to a certain extent as an original question. The true rule I conceive to be this: that where a statute gives a right of action unknown to the common law, and either in a proviso to the section conferring the right or in a separate section limits the time within which an action shall be brought, such limitation is operative in any other jurisdiction in which action may be brought."

57. Sewall v. Valentine, 23 Mass. (6 Pick.) 276.

58. Arnold v. Arnold, 35 N. C. (13 Ired.) 174. The statute is a good defense where time has once begun to run in favor of a debtor to an estate in the lifetime of the intestate, the absence of a personal representative in such a case not being sufficient to make an exception to the almost universal rule that when time has once commenced to run it will never cease. Rhodes v. Smethurst, 4 M. & W. 42; Freake v. Cranefeldt, 3 Myl. & Cr. 499; 2 Wms. Saund. 63 k; Sturgis v. Darell, 4 H. & N. 622. This rule,

erally adopted.[59] The appointment of an administrator in one State does not put the statute in motion either for or against the estate in another State; but, as to all property or claims existing in such other jurisdiction, the statute remains suspended until proof of the will, or the appointment of an administrator there.[60]

however, as we shall see, is not absolutely without exception. And where an action abated by the death of a defendant debtor, it was allowed to be continued a reasonable time, though the statutory period had elapsed in the interval. Curlewis v. Mornington, 7 El. & Bl. 283. In England, the rule of the North Carolina case is adopted where the creditor has not died intestate, but has appointed an executor, and that executor simply neglects to prove the will. There does not then exist any saving until proof. The reason of this distinction is that while an administrator derives his title wholly from the Court of Probate, and has no title to the property of the deceased till the grant of letters of administration is made out, an executor has a title immediately by virtue of the will. Woolley v. Clark, 5 B. & Ald. 744. If, however, such executor eventually renounces probate, inasmuch as such renunciation relates back to the death of the testator, it seems doubtful how far the testator's estate could be held to have been represented at all, or time to have commenced to run against it. In fact, it may be argued that though, when an executor delays to prove a testator's will, time runs against him from the testator's death, yet that if he eventually fails to prove at all, and an administrator is appointed, time does not run against the latter until his appointment. But upon this point there is no direct authority.

59. Garland v. Milling, *supra;* Forrest v. Douglas, *supra.*

60. Lee v. Gause, 24 N. C. (2 Ired. L.) 440. In Hobart v. Conn. Turnpike Co., *supra,* the testatrix died in New York owning stock in the defendant company, upon which certain dividends had been declared. The court held that the statute did not begin to run until administration had been granted in Connecticut, and that the proving of the will and qualification of the executor in New York did not affect the question, saying: "When did the statute begin to run against this claim? Was it when the dividends accrued, or when administration was granted on her estate? And this precise question was decided in the case of Murray v. East India Co., 5 B. & Ald. 204, in which Abbott, C. J., giving the unanimous opinion of the Court of King's Bench, after referring to the authorities, and coming to the conclusion that they sustained the claim of the plaintiff that the statute did not begin to run until the granting of administration, says: 'Now, independently of authority, we think it cannot be said that a cause of action exists unless there be also a person in existence capable of suing.'" See also Perry v. Jenkins, 1 Myl. & Cr. 118; Cary v. Stephenson, 2 Salk. 421; Burdick v. Garrick, L. R. 5 Ch. 241.

§ 195. Executors de son tort.

An important exception to the rule previously stated exists where the defendant has taken possession of the property of the deceased debtor as executor *de son tort,* and subsequently obtains letters of administration. In such case time begins to run in favor of the estate from the time when the defendant became such executor *de son tort,* because such an executor can be sued either at law or in equity as soon as he assumes to act as such,[61] and his previous acts

61. In Webster v. Webster, 10 Ves. 93, the plea of the statute was allowed by an executor whose testator died in 1788, but of whose will no probate had been taken out until 1802, and within six years of the filing of the bill, inasmuch as the defendant, the executor, had possessed himself of the testator's personal estate, and therefore might have been sued as executor *de son tort* previously to 1802.

In Boatwright v. Boatwright, L. R. 17 Eq. 71, the case of Webster v. Webster was quoted as an authority, and as applicable to a case where the executor *de son tort* and the person who subsequently proved the will of a deceased debtor were different persons. This case was mainly decided on the ground that the cause of action had already accrued in the testator's lifetime.

There is conflict of opinion as to how far an executor *de son tort* may be sued alone, without the appointment of a legal personal representative to his testator. In Rayner v. Koehler, L. R. 14 Eq. 262, a bill was thus sustained against an executrix *de son tort.* In Cary v. Hills, L. R. 15 Eq. 79, Lord Romilly, M. R., declined to follow Rayner v. Koehler, and in Roswell v. Morris, Sir G. Jessel, M. R., did the same. L. R. 17 Eq. 20. And see Penny v. Watts, 2 Ph. 149; Beardmore v. Gregory, 2 H. & M. 491; Coote v. Whittington, L. R. 16 Eq. 534. See also *In re* Lovett, 3 Ch. D. 198, and held that the law of the court was that a suit for administration is defective when the legal personal representative was not before it. This may possibly diminish the authority of cases where a plaintiff has been denied a fresh right on the appointment of a legal personal representative of his debtor, on the ground that he could have proceeded in the absence of such legal personal representative to recover his debt against the executor *de son tort;* a course which, in equity at all events, will be no longer open to him. In Boatwright v. Boatwright, *supra,* the Master of the Rolls remarked: "I think it must be held, when the point comes to be decided, that if the remedy against the personal estate is barred, and the remedy against the real estate has been kept alive by reason of payment, that the court will find some means of making the real estate liable, although the creditor cannot make the legal representative a party to the suit." Banning on Limitations, 231-233.

are legalized by his taking out letters of administration.[62] But it seems that an express promise to pay a debt due from the estate, made by an executor *de son tort*, is not binding so as to suspend or remove the statute bar, although he is subsequently appointed administrator;[63] for, although a person who undertakes to discharge and settle accounts of the estate of a deceased person before he is appointed administrator will, after his appointment as such, be responsible for his acts, upon the ground that his appointment retroacts to the time of the intestate's death,[64] yet this rule is not carried to such an extent that the estate can be prejudiced by his acts. Such executors are liable only to the extent of the assets which come into their hands;[65] and while he is liable as executor, and may use proper means to protect the assets in his hands, yet he possesses none of the rights or powers which an executor derives on account of his office.[66] They are liable to account to distributees or legatees like other executors, and cannot rely on the statute of limitations to protect them from such liability.[67] An executor *de son tort* of an executor *de son tort* represents the first testator, so that, where property was held in trust by him, the statute of limitations does not begin to run in his favor until the relationship is ended.[68]

§ 196. Statutory provisions relative to suits in favor of decedents' estates.

In Maine, provision is made that, in case of the death of a party entitled to bring an action before or within thirty days after

62. Manger v. Ryan, 19 Mo. 196; Priest v. Watkins, 2 Hill (N. Y.) 225; Shillabaer v. Wyman, 15 Mass. 322; Rattoon v. Overacker, 8 Johns. (N. Y.) 126; Alvord v. Marsh, 94 Mass. (12 Allen) 603.

63. Haselden v. Whitesides, 2 Strobh. (S. C.) L. 353.

64. Alvord v. Marsh, *supra*.

65. Cook v. Sanders, 15 Rich. (S. C.) 63; Hill v. Henderson, 21 Miss. 688; Mitchell v. Lunt, 4 Mass. 654.

66. M'Intire v. Carson, 9 N. C. (2 Hawks) 544; Meigan v. M'Donough, 10 Watts (Pa.) 287.

67. Hansford v. Elliott, 9 Leigh (Va.) 79.

68. Dawson v. Callaway, 18 Ga. 573.

the statute has run, and the cause of action survives, an action may be commenced therefor against the executor or administrator within two years after his appointment, and not afterwards;[69] and practically the same provision exists in Vermont, Massachusetts, and Michigan.[70] In Rhode Island,[71] where a person entitled to bring an action dies before the statute has run or within sixty days thereafter, and the cause of action survives, an action may be brought by his executor or administrator within one year after the granting of letters testamentary or administration. In New York,[72] where a person entitled to bring an action dies before the statute has run upon the claim, an action may be commenced by his representatives any time within the statutory period, or within one year after the death of such person; and practically the same provision exists in the States of Mississippi, Missouri, Connecticut, South Carolina, Illinois, Arkansas, Colorado, California, Oregon, Florida, Iowa, Kentucky, Nevada, Dakota, Idaho, New Mexico, and Minnesota, except that in the latter State six months between the death of the party and granting administration and six months thereafter are not to be included in computing the statutory period.[73] In New Jersey,[74] six months from the time of death is given where the statute has not already run, in all actions of trespass, trover, replevin, debt on simple contract, for arrearages of rent, on a parol demise, account, upon the case, except for slander, and

69. Appendix, Maine.

70. See Appendix.

71. Appendix, Rhode Island.

72. Appendix, New York.

In Harrington v. Keteltas, 92 N. Y. 40, it was held that an executor, having notice that there is a debt due the estate, is bound to active diligence for its collection; he may not wait for a request from the distributees. In case the debt is lost through his negligence, he becomes liable as for a devastavit. And if the case is one of such doubt, that an indemnity is proper, he must at least ask for it; and at any rate he takes the risk of showing that the debt was not lost through his negligence. The statute of limitations does not begin to run in favor of an executor, as against a claim for damages occasioned by his negligence in collecting a debt due the estate from the time of the probate of the will, but at best only from the time of the loss.

73. Appendix, Minnesota.

74. Appendix, New Jersey.

such actions as concern the trade of merchandise between merchants, their factors, agents, and servants. This provision embraces, also, all actions upon sealed instruments, sheriffs' and constables' bonds, and judgments. In Tennessee and Arizona the same period, under the same circumstances, is allowed in reference to all claims. In Indiana,[75] eighteen months after the expiration of the time is given in all cases where the person in whose favor a claim existed dies before the statute has run. In Texas,[76] twelve months after the expiration of the statutory period are given, in all cases where the claimant dies before the statute runs, unless an executor or administrator is sooner appointed; but in the latter case, twelve months from the date of such appointment constitutes the limit. In Montana,[77] if the plaintiff in an action dies, and judgment in his favor is subsequently reversed, his heirs or representatives may commence a new action within one year after such reversal. In Georgia, a period not exceeding five years after the death of a party is given within which an action may be brought, if the statute has not already run at the time of his death; and practically the same provision exists in Virginia and West Virginia.[78] In Wisconsin, the fact that there is no person to sue does not extend the time to more than double the period otherwise prescribed by law. In North Carolina,[79] the time during which any contest is pending relative to the probate of a will or the granting of administration is excluded, unless an administration is sooner appointed, and even in the latter case such time is excluded, unless by law a claimant is required to sue him within a shorter period. Except in these States, no statutory provision exists relative to actions in favor of deceased claimants, and the common-law rule prevails.

§ 197. When parties in interest may set up the statute.

While, as previously stated, an executor or administrator is not

75. Appendix, Indiana.

76. Appendix, Texas.

77. Appendix, Montana.

78. Appendix, Wisconsin.

79. Appendix, North Carolina.

bound to set up the statute, and cannot be compelled to do so, and no person can set it up without his assent, yet, after a decree has been obtained, any person interested, who takes advantage of the decree, may set up the statute whether the executor assents thereto or not.[80] Before a decree is made the statute applies, and the plaintiff will be barred on lapse of the appropriate length of time after administration.[81] There is a question as to how far an executor or administrator is liable as for a devastavit if he allows time to run in favor of a debtor, and against the estate he represents; and it may be said to be probable, that where such a case results from undue delay on the part of the executor or administrator, he is liable;[82] but this point, and the question which may arise as to how far an executor or administrator is at liberty to revive debts barred by acknowledgment or part payment, and also what is the position as to the right to contribution of a co-executor who has acknowledged and thus revived a debt against his co-executors and the estate, if judgment is recovered against him singly, does not appear to be settled by the authorities.[83]

§ 198. Right of executor to set off debt barred.

An executor may retain out of a legacy a debt due from the legatee to the estate, although the statute has run upon it, and an administrator may set off such a debt against the debtor's share, upon the ground that one of the next of kin of an intestate can

80. Briggs v. Wilson, 5 DeG. M. & G. 12; Fuller v. Redman, 26 Beav. 614.

81. Higgins v. Shaw, 2 Dr. & War. 356; Alsop v. Bell, 24 Beav. 451, 464; Hollingshead's Case, 1 P. Wms. 742, 744; Hayward v. Kinsey, 12 Mod. 573; East v. East, 5 Hare, 348.

82. Hayward v. Kinsey, *supra;* Williams, Executors (8th ed.), p. 1805.

83. In Peaslee v. Breed, 10 N. H. 489, 34 Am. Rep. 178, it was held that the joint maker of a note who has kept the debt against himself revived by partial payments may, on the payment of the note, obtain contribution from the other maker, notwithstanding that the payee's claim against the latter was barred.

take no share of the estate until he has discharged his obligations to it in full.[84]

§ 199. Rule in equity as to claims against decedent's estate.

The rule seems to be the same in equity as at law, that, where time has once begun to run against a debt in the testator's lifetime, it does not cease to run between the date of his death and the appointment of an executor or administrator.[85] But in cases of fraud and mistake, courts of equity hold that the statute runs from the discovery, because the laches of the plaintiff commences from that date.[86] An executor cannot protect himself by the statute from payment of a debt due from himself to his testator by deferring proof of the will. In such cases the probate will be considered to have relation to the testator's death, and the debt will be treated as assets in the executor's hands at that time.[87] The testator may revive a debt barred by the statute,

84. Courtenay v. Williams, 3 Hare, 539; *In re* Cordwell's Estate, L. R. 20 Eq. 644.

85. Freake v. Cranefeldt, 3 My. & Cr. 499.

86. Brooksbank v. Smith, 2 Y. & C. 58. See Schouler on Wills, Executors and Administrators, Vol. 2, § 1390a.

Where an administratrix sold real estate to pay debts, and afterwards, before confirmation, purchased it from those who bid at the sale, the heirs were held barred, by an unexplained delay of seven years, from cancelling her purchase, she having meanwhile made permanent improvements on the land, and paid the debts with the proceeds of the sale. Gibson v. Herriott, 55 Ark. 85, 17 S. W. 589, 29 Am. St. Rep. 17.

The Rhode Island Pub. States., c. 205, § 9, limiting the time for suing executors and administrators to three years, does not apply to citing them to appear and defend a suit begun against the decedent in his lifetime. Sprague v. Greene, 20 R. I. 153, 157, 37 Atl. 699.

87. Ingle v. Richards, 28 Beav. 366. In Scott v. Jones, 1 Russ. & My. 255, it was held in equity that a notice published by an executor in a newspaper that he will pay all debts justly due from his testator, will prevent a debt from being barred by the statute; but this doctrine is entirely inconsistent with the rule laid down in Tanner v. Smart, 6 B. & C. 603, and is not believed to be tenable; but it was also held that a notice published by an executor requesting all persons having claims against the estate to hand them in before they are submitted to a person before whom persons claiming to be purchasers are to be examined relative to the validity

by the provisions of his will; but in such case it is only revived

of their claims, will not remove the statute bar.

Under 22 & 23 Vict., c. 35, § 29, the mere notice and making of a claim against the estate by a creditor in answer to the executor's notice does not keep his claim alive so as to prevent the statute of limitations from running. *In re* Stephens, 43 Ch. D. 39, 44. See Bambrick v. Bambrick, 157 Mo. 423, 58 S. W. 8; Barclay v. Blackinton, 127 Cal. 189, 59 Pac. 834; Ulster County Sav. Inst. v. Young, 161 N. Y. 23, 55 N. E. 483.

When the Probate Court allows a will and an appeal is taken, the two years allowed by statute for creditors to sue the executor begin to run from the day when the probate decree is affirmed on appeal. Smith v. Smith, 175 Mass. 483, 56 N. E. 594. The running of the time is not stopped in favor of a creditor who did not know of his debtor's death. Beekman v. Richardson, 150 Mo. 430, 51 S. W. 689. The allowance by the Probate Court of a claim against the testator's estate amounts to a judgment, if not appealed from, and the statute of limitations does not apply thereto. McCord v. Knowlton, 79 Minn. 299, 82 N. W. 589. *In re* Corrington, 124 Ill. 363, 16 N. E. 252. An executor's or administrator's annual or partial account is only a judgment *de bene esse.* In Illinois, the allowance of a claim by the County Court is not conclusive against the heir excepting to the administrator's final report, when such allowance is subject to impeachment for fraud or collusion in a court of equity. Ibid; Schlink v. Maxton, 153 Ill. 447, 38 N. E. 1063; Bliss v. Seaman, 165 Ill. 422, 46 N. E. 279; Marshall v. Coleman, 187 Ill. 556, 58 N. E. 628. By the voluntary filing of their account and having, on their application, a citation issued to all persons interested executors waive the statute of limitations, and admit their liability to account as existing, and, although they are only technically trustees of the testator's property, yet, as against the beneficiaries under his will, the statute of limitations cannot be availed of so long as such trust relation exists. *In re* Lyth, 67 N. Y. Supp. 579, 32 Misc. Rep. 608.

As to laches as affecting creditors and those interested in the distribution of a decedent's estate, see Harris v. Starkey, 176 Mass. 445, 57 N. E. 698, 79 Am. St. Rep. 322; Maldaner v. Beurhaus, 108 Wis. 25, 84 N. W. 25; Roth v. Holland, 56 Ark. 633, 20 S. W. 521, 35 Am. St. Rep. 126; Kipping v. Demint, 184 Ill. 165, 56 N. E. 330, 75 Am. St. Rep. 164.

Under the Mass. Pub. Stats., c. 136, § 11, requiring an executor or administrator to account for new assets received more than two years after his giving bond, and allowing a creditor to sue, as against the same, within two years, and one year after he has notice thereof, not everything omitted from the inventory by any cause, such as accident, is new assets, although the omission has not affected the other party's conduct. The section must be given a serious meaning and clearly does not include all tangible property first received by the representative after two years,

to the extent and in the manner stated in the will.[88] Generally speaking, the statute does not run against a trust,[89] and executors

though not included in the inventory. Gould v. Camp, 157 Mass. 358, 32 N. E. 225; Quincy v. Quincy, 167 Mass. 536, 46 N. E. 108. As to failure of the action for defect of form under § 12 of the above chapter, see Taft v. Stow, 174 Mass. 171, 54 N. E. 506. Section 13 of the same chapter, authorizing the retention of assets to satisfy claims not accruing within the two years, probably relates only to the retention of personal assets. Clark v. Holbrook, 146 Mass. 366, 16 N. E. 410; Forbes v. Harrington, 171 Mass. 386, 50 N. E. 641.

If the estate is solvent and consists wholly of land, and the heirs, to avoid the loss resulting from a forced sale, authorize the executor to agree with a creditor that, if he delays enforcing his demand, the executor will pay him as fast as the land can be advantageously sold, and this is assented to by the creditor, and is to his advantage, there being no other interested persons excluded from the arrangement, it is not culpable neglect for the creditor thus to suffer the time to expire within which an action may be brought against the executor. Knight v. Cunningham, 160 Mass. 580, 36 N. E. 466; Ewing v. King, 169 Mass. 97, 47 N. E. 597. See Morey v. American Loan & Trust Co., 149 Mass. 253, 21 N. E. 384.

In Warner v. Morse, 149 Mass. 400, 21 N. E. 960, the statute of limitations was held not a bar to a bill to establish an equitable lien in real estate partly paid for with the funds of a decedent's estate.

88. In Williamson v. Naylor, 3 Y. & C. 208, where the testator provided that one-fifth of his estate should be divided among certain of his creditors named in a schedule to his will, it was held that the direction so given prevented the operation of the statute, and that, as a specific fund was appropriated for that purpose, if the fund proved insufficient to pay the debts in full, the creditors must take ratably. See also Rose v. Gould, 15 Beav. 189. In Barton v. Tattersall, 1 Russ. & My. 237 (see also Ward v. Painter, 5 Myl. & Cr. 298), it was held that, where a deceased person before his death had taken the benefit of the insolvent acts, the rights of creditors scheduled under the insolvency were not affected by the statute, on the ground that the liability arose in respect of a lien created by those acts, rather than by virtue of any promise to be implied from the scheduling of the debts.

In Sirdefield v. Price, 2 Y. & J. 73, on a bill by a creditor against an executor for payment of a demand and an account of the testator's estate, the court, entertaining some doubt as to the validity of the debt, retained the bill for one year, with liberty to the plaintiff to bring his action; and the statute having taken effect between the filing of the bill and the decree, the court restrained the defendant from insisting on the statute.

89. Wren v. Gayden, 1 How. (Miss.) 365; Lafferty v. Turley, 35 Tenn. (3 Sneed) 157; Bailey v. Shannonhouse, 16 N. C. (1 Dev. Eq.) 416; Hollis's Case, 2 Vent. 345;

and administrators are treated as express trustees, in whose favor the statute does not run to bar the claims of legatees or distributees of the estate.[90] Therefore, a charge created by will upon the real estate for the payment of the testator's debts prevents the running of the statute upon such debts as were not barred in his lifetime,[91] but it does not revive a debt which was barred at the time of his decease;[92] nor does a charge upon the personal estate prevent the running of the statute, because, as the law vests the personal property in the executor or administrator for the payment of the decedent's debts, the will creates no special trust for that purpose.[93] But if a charge is created upon both the real and personal estate for the payment of debts, as if the testator directs that his debts shall be paid out of his real and personal estate, and also provides that, if his personal estate shall be insufficient to pay his debts, then his executors may enter into the receipt of the rents of his freehold until the same are wholly paid, it has been held that, even though the personal estate is sufficient to pay the debts in full, yet a trust is created by the will for the payment of the debts, so as to prevent the statute from running upon them.[94]

Legacies, unless expressly so provided therein, are not barred by the statute;[95] but a presumption that the legacy is paid arises

Woodhouse v. Woodhouse, L. R. 8 Eq. 514; Wedderburn v. Wedderburn, 2 Keen, 722; Obee v. Bishop, 1 De G. F. & J. 137; Brittlebank v. Goodwin, L R. 5 Eq. 545.

90. Lafferty v. Turley, *supra;* Picot v. Bates, 39 Mo. 292; Knight v. Brawner, 14 Md. 1; Amos v. Campbell, 9 Fla. 187; Smith v. Smith, 7 Md. 55.

91. Pettingill v. Pettingill, 60 Me. 423.

92. Burke v. Jones, 2 V. & B. 275; Hargreaves v. Mitchell, 6 Madd. 326; Hughes v. Wynne, 1 T. & R. 307.

93. Evans v. Tweedy, 1 Beav. 55; Scott v. Jones, 4 Cl. & F. 382; Freake v. Cranefeldt, 3 Myl. & Cr. 499.

94. Crallan v. Oulton, 3 Beav. 1; Moore v. Petchell, 22 Beav. 172.

95. Sparhawk v. Buell, 9 Vt. 41; Thompson v. M'Gaw, 2 Watts (Pa.) 161; Cartwright v. Cartwright, 7 Tenn. (4 Hayw.) 134; Perkins v. Cartmell, 4 Harr. (Del.) 270; Irby v. M'Crae, 4 Desaus. (S. C.) 422; Doebler v. Snavely, 5 Watts (Pa.) 225; Souzer v. De Meyer, 2 Paige (N. Y.) 574; Norris's Appeal, 71 Pa. 106; Kent v. Dunham, 106 Mass. 586; Wood v. Ricker, 1 Paige (N.

from permitting the assets to be distributed without claiming the legacy, and is a good ground of defense by way of answer.[96] But this presumption, like all other presumptions relating to payment, is liable to be rebutted by proof that payment has not in fact been made. Courts of equity are never active in extending relief to stale demands, except upon very special grounds. Although the statutes generally do not bind those courts by express terms, so as to enable a defendant to plead them in bar to a suit for a legacy, yet, for the sake of convenience, they have adopted their provisions by analogy, in many instances in which fraud makes no ingredient. Upon this principle it has been determined that a legacy not demanded for forty years should be considered as *prima facie* satisfied; but this presumption is not so absolute as to support a demurrer to a bill for such a legacy; for the point of satisfaction is an inference, only arising from the length of time which has elapsed from the period the legacy became payable, and which may be repelled by clear, strong, and relevant evidence. If, then, the merits of the question were allowed to be decided in a summary way upon a demurrer, the legatee would be precluded from the opportunity of producing such testimony.[97]

Y.) 616; Smith v. Kensington, 42 Barb. (N. Y.) 75; Brooks v. Lynde, 89 Mass. (7 Allen) 64; McCartee v. Camel, 1 Barb. (N. Y.) Ch. 455; Anon., 2 Freem. 22, pl. 20; Parker v. Ash, 1 Vern. 257. But now in England, under Stat. 3 & 4 Wm. IV., c. 27, legacies are barred in twenty years.

96. Higgins v. Crawford, 2 Ves. Jr. 572; Andrews v. Sparhawk, 30 Mass. (13 Pick.) 393; Kingman v. Kingman, 121 Mass. 249; Skinner v. Skinner, 24 Ky. (1 J. J. Marsh.) 594; Carr v. Chapman, 5 Leigh (Va.) 164; Sager v. Warley, Rice (S. C.) Ch. 26; Hayes v. Goode, 7 Leigh (Va.) 452; Pickering v. Stamford, 2 Ves. Jr. 582; Grenfell v. Girdlestone, 2 Y. & C. 662; Prior v. Horniblow, id. 200; Jones v. Tuberville, 2 Ves. Jr. 11; Baldwin v. Peach, 1 Y. & C. 453; Brown v. Claxton, 3 Sim. 225; Campbell v. Graham, 1 Russ. & Myl. 453.

97. See Jones v. Turberville, 2 Ves. Jr. 11; Pickering v. Stamford, id. 272. In Montressor v. Williams, MSS. 1823, March, 3, April 16, and May 7, which came before Sir John Leach, V. C., upon exceptions to the Master's report, one Duval, a lessee under a lease from the Portland family for ninety-nine years from 1765, by his will dated December, 1789, proved 3d May, 1794, charged his general estate with legacies, subject to which the lease passed to his

In England, under the statute of 3 & 4 Wm. IV., it is held that, when an executor is called to account for moneys which were bequeathed to him upon certain trusts, and which have been severed by the executor from the testator's personal estate, and the interest of which has been for a time applied upon the trusts

son as executor and residuary legatee. Duval, the son, in 1808, granted an underlease, which after various mesne assignments, came to Wigan, who obtained a further term of fourteen years from Duval, and then assigned the under lease to the defendant, who contracted with General Montresor, the plaintiff, for the sale of the leasehold premises and the furniture. Among other objections to the title referred to the Master, it was insisted that the lease being charged with the legacies, demands in respect of these might be made upon the purchaser. Releases were subsequently procured. When the cause came on upon the exceptions to the Master's report, his Honor said: "These releases are unneccessary. The vendor has no right to them. Even without them, I should have held that, where an executor, twenty years after the death of the testator, sells a leasehold charged by the will with legacies, and no demand has during all that time been made upon it, there was evidence that the charges had been paid." In Campbell v. Graham, 1 Russ. & Myl. 453, 2 Cl. & Fin. 429, Lord Brougham, C., observed: "A party buying a legacy of £500 for £25, after seven and twenty years have elapsed, and then allowing four years more to pass before filing his bill, making altogether a laches of more than thirty years, in my apprehension has himself to blame, if he finds, when he comes into this court, that his remedy is gone. 4 Barr. 1962; Oswald v. Leigh, 1 T. R. 270; Fladong v. Winter, 19 Ves. 196; Wynne v. Waring, cited in previous case; Hercy v. Dinwoody, 4 Bro. C. C. 257; Smith v. Clay, 3 id. 639, n.; Jones v. Turberville, and Pickering v. Stamford, *supra*. Upon the principle of some of these cases, therefore, and upon the authority of others, admitting nevertheless that no one has gone so far as to say that mere lapse of time can be pleaded as a bar, and stating also that I can find no case in which the precise period of seven and twenty years has been held sufficient to shut the doors of a court of equity against such a demand as too stale to be enforced—upon the reasoning and principle of some of these cases, and the actual decision in others, I am disposed to hold that the plaintiff has come too late, and that the doors of this court ought not now to be thrown open to him, inasmuch as, to use Lord Camden's expression, the court cannot be called into activity to aid a demand, be it for a legacy or for a debt, unless with good faith and with good conscience a reasonable degree of diligence shall have been used." Presumptions of payment of legacies will not be made from mere lapse of time, where payment by the executor would be out of the ordinary course. Lee v. Brown, 4 Ves. 362; Prior v. Horniblow, 2 Y. & C. 200.

of the will, so that the fund has ceased to bear the character of a legacy, and has assumed that of a trust fund, the action to compel an account is treated as a suit for a breach of trust, and not as a suit for a legacy, and consequently is not within the statute,[98] as it is held that that statute does not apply to cases of express trust.[99]

§ 199a. Death of person entitled to sue.

The death of the creditor, after an action has accrued to him, does not interrupt the running of the statute of limitations.[1] Where limitations begin to run against the ancestor of a posthumous child, the ancestor's death does not interrupt the statute,

98. Estate of Brown, 8 Phila. (Pa.) 197; Marshfield v. Cheever, 3 Dane Abr. 503; Sawyer v. Smith, 5 id. 405; Pedrick v. Saunderson, 5 id. 403; Bass v. Bass, 25 Mass. (8 Pick.) 187; Denny v. Eddy, 39 Mass. (22 Pick.) 533; Ravenscroft v. Frisby, 1 Coll. 16; Phillip v. Munnings, 2 Myl. & Cr. 309. In re Powers, 124 N. Y. 361, 26 N. E. 940, it was held that to render a provision in a will effectual to furnish a greater security than that given by law for the payment of debts in due course of administration, by charging them upon the real estate of the testator, the purpose must quite clearly appear; a mere direction to pay debts out of the property will not suffice. See In re McComb, 117 N. Y. 378, 22 N. E. 1070.

99. Watson v. Saul, 1 Giff. 188; King v. Dennison, 1 V. & B. 260; Dix v. Bufford, 19 Beav. 409; Butler v. Carter, L. R. 5 Eq. 276; Edmunds v. Waugh, L. R. 1 Eq. 418; Dinsdale v. Dudding, 1 Y. & C. 265; Brougham v. Poulett, 19 Beav. 119; Commissioners v. Wybrants, 2 Jones & L. 182; Jacquet v. Jacquet, 27 Beav. 332; Playfair v. Cooper, 17 id. 187; Mason v. Broadbent, 33 id. 296; Tyson v. Jackson, 30 id. 384; Hodgson v. Bibby, 32 id. 221; Dickinson v. Teasdale, 31 id. 511; Round v. Bell, 30 id. 121; Davenport v. Stafford, 14 id. 319; Downes v. Bullock, 25 id. 54; Smith v. Acton, 26 id. 210; Proud v. Proud, 32 id. 234; Gough v. Bult, 16 Sim. 323; Francis v. Grover, 5 Hare, 39; Roch v. Callen, 6 id. 531; Lewis v. Duncombe, 29 Beav. 175; Hunter v. Nockolds, 1 Mac. & G. 640, 683; Snow v. Booth, 2 K. & J. 132; Cox v. Dolman, 2 De G. M. & G. 592; Burrowes v. Gore, 6 H. L. Cas. 907; Young v. Waterpark, 13 Sim. 199.

1. *Ala.*—Johnson v. Wren, 3 Stew. 172; Daniel v. Day, 51 Ala. 431.

Ky.—Beauchamp v. Mudd, 5 Ky. (2 Bibb.) 537.

Md.—Stewart v. Spedden, 5 Md. 433.

Ohio.—Granger's Adm'r v. Granger, 6 Ohio (6 Ham.) 35.

Vt.—Conant v. Hitt, 12 Vt. 285.

menced to run against a cause of action during the life of the holder thereof, continue to run after his death, in the absence of anything to the contrary in the statute.[9] In Maryland, the death of one holding the legal title to property, but out of possession, does not stop the running of limitations as against his interest therein.[10] In Massachusetts, it is held that, where a guardian is discharged by the death of his ward, it cannot be said that, at the time of such discharge, the person entitled to bring an action on the guardian's bond is out of the state. The statute, relating to such cases, contemplates the absence from the commonwealth of some person who is entitled to bring the action, or to have the action brought for his benefit, and who subsequently returns into the state.[11] In Michigan, where plaintiff's suit, which

Nat. Bank, 112 Iowa 11, 83 N. W. 711, 51 L. R. A. 410, 84 Am. St. Rep. 318.

The disability of an insane person is terminated by death, and a proceeding to vacate a judgment fraudulently obtained against such person must be commenced within a year thereafter, under the express provisions of Code, § 4094. Wood v. Wood, 136 Iowa 128, 113 N. W. 492, 12 L. R. A. (N. S.) 891.

An action by the heir of a minor to redeem from a tax sale must be commenced within one year after the death of the minor. Gibbs v. Sawyer, 48 Iowa, 443.

9. Boughner v. Sharp, 144 Ky. 320, 138 S. W. 375; Baker's Adm'r v. Baker's Adm'r, 52 Ky. (13 B. Mon.) 406; Hull v. Deatly's Adm'r, 70 Ky. (7 Bush) 687; Doty v. Jameson, 29 Ky. Law Rep. 507, 93 S. W. 638.

Ky. St. § 2526 (Russell's St. § 192), providing, if a person entitled to bring an action dies before expiration of time for its commencement, and the cause survives, the action may be brought by his representative after the expiration of that time, if commenced within a year after his qualification, does not extend the time for action because of delay of the administrator in qualifying; he having qualified more than a year before expiration of the time in which deceased could have sued. Halcomb v. Cornett, 146 Ky. 339, 142 S. W. 686.

In applying the five-year statute of limitations to a suit brought by an administrator to recover the value of decedent's support, for which her son-in-law was obligated, the period when there was no administrator should be deducted. Bryson's Adm'r v. Briggs, 32 Ky. Law Rep. 159, 104 S. W. 982.

10. Baumeister v. Silver, 98 Md. 418, 56 Atl. 825.

11. McKim v. Mann, 141 Mass. 507, 6 N. E. 740.

In Montana, even if the cause of action on a guardian's bond does not accrue until accounting by the guardian, the administrator of the de-

though plaintiff was yet unborn.[2] In Arkansas, the statute of limitations will not run on a note belonging to the estate of the intestate, who left no liabilities, while there was no administrator of the estate and the heirs were not all of age;[3] and if the statute begins to run against an infant during his life, it will continue as against his representative.[4] In California, where a cause of action does not accrue until after the death of the party who would have been entitled to sue, the running of the statute of limitations is not interrupted because there happens to be no administrator entitled to sue, since the persons beneficially interested have the full period of limitation in which to obtain administration and bring action.[5] The death of the creditor, after an action has accrued to him, does not affect the running of the statute of limitations, in Illinois, where the debt had more than one year to run at the time of the death of the creditor.[6] In Indiana, a claim against a decedent's estate which accrued during the decedent's lifetime is barred by limitations, where no administrator is appointed until after the time fixed by the statute has elapsed.[7] In Iowa, the statute of limitations is not tolled by the death of a person after the statute has commenced to run against a cause of action in his favor.[8] In Kentucky, limitations, having com-

2. Oliver v. Williams, 163 Ala. 376, 50 So. 937.

3. Chisholm v. Crye, 83 Ark. 495, 104 S. W. 167.

4. Bozeman v. Browning, 31 Ark. 364.

Where a widow, on the death of her minor child, is in possession of his land under claim of title, the statute of limitations begins to run against the minor's heirs from the date of his death. Sanson v. Harrell, 55 Ark. 572, 18 S. W. 1047.

5. Cortelyou v. Imperial Land Co., 166 Cal. 14, 134 Pac. 981.

The want of an administration upon an estate does not suspend the statute of limitations upon a mortgage in favor of such estate. Sanford v. Bergin, 156 Cal. 43, 103 Pac. 333.

6. Pinkney v. Pinkney, 61 Ill. App. 525, notwithstanding Ill. Rev. St. c. 83, § 19.

7. Hildebrand v. Kinney (Ind. App.), 83 N. E. 379, under Ind. Rev. St. 1881, § 298 (Burns' Ann. St. 1901, § 299).

8. Ackerman v. Hilpert, 108 Iowa, 247, 79 N. W. 90.

The running of limitations against a certificate of deposit was not interrupted by the death of the holder of the certificate. Mereness v. First

was within the ten-year statute of limitations, would not have been barred until more than two years after the grant of letters testamentary or of administration on decedent's estate, the statute granting such time to sue did not apply and so did not "extend" the time within which to sue thereon.[12] In Missouri, where a person entitled to sue dies before the expiration of the time limited for the commencement of the suit, and the cause of action survives to his representatives, the right of action given by the statute is expressly limited to one year from the date of the death of the decedent, and cannot be brought within a year from the date of the appointment of an administrator.[13] In New Jersey, one holding an overdue obligation may not prevent the running of limitations after his death, by providing in his will that his executor shall not institute any proceeding to enforce the obligation or take any steps to collect the same during the lifetime of a person named, or during any other period, measured in any way.[14] In New York, limitations on decedent's right to recover land, having commenced to run before his death, are not interrupted by his death, nor by

ceased ward is not for that reason under "disability" between the ward's death and such accounting, within Prob. Prac. Act, § 404, requiring action against the sureties on a guardian's bond to be commenced within three years from the discharge of the guardian, unless at the time of the discharge the person entitled to bring the action is under "legal disability" to sue. Berkin v Marsh, 18 Mont. 152, 44 Pac. 528, 56 Am. St. Rep. 565.

12. Morse v. Hayes, 150 Mich. 597, 114 N. W. 397, 14 Detroit Leg. N. 785, 13 L. R. A. (N. S.) 1200.

13. Smith v. Settle, 128 Mo. App. 397, 107 S. W. 430.

Mo. Rev. St. 1899, § 4267 (Ann. St. 1906, p. 2342), providing that if a married woman, entitled to sue to recover real estate, shall die, her heirs may sue within three years after her death, does not bar an action by heirs where the deed attacked, on its face, in the light of the record title, conveyed nothing, and cast no cloud on the mother's title while she lived, because not recorded until after her death, and she was without knowledge of it. Starr v. Bartz, 219 Mo. 47, 117 S. W 1125; Starr v. Kisner, 219 Mo. 64, 117 S. W. 1129.

14. Swinley v. Force, 78 N. J. Eq. 52, 78 Atl. 249.

Where a ward attaining her majority in 1883, died in 1885, before the guardian had rendered an account; the guardian died in 1905; in 1906 an administrator of the deceased ward was appointed, and sued, in the same year, the represen-

the infancy of some of his heirs.[15] In Oklahoma, a person cannot prevent the operation of the statute of limitations by delay in taking action incumbent upon him.[16] In Ohio, if a cause of action which has been pleaded as a set-off occurred in the lifetime of plaintiff's intestate, the running of the statute was not interrupted by his death, in the absence of an express exception in the statute declaring that it should have that effect.[17] In Pennsylvania, the running of the statute of limitations on a note is not stayed by the death of the holder.[18] In South Carolina, where a trust has been repudiated to the knowledge of the beneficiary, and the statute of limitations has thus been set in operation against him, the running of the statute is not suspended by the death of the beneficiary, although his administrator has no knowledge of the trust.[19] In Texas, where three years have elapsed with no application for administration of an estate, decedent's widow may maintain an action on a judgment which was their community property, and was rendered seven years before his death, and thus save it from the bar of limitations.[20] In Washington, where limitations begin to run before the death of the party having the right of action, they are not arrested by his death, unless expressly provided for

tative of the deceased guardian for an accounting, the suit was not barred by limitations, though the cause of action accrued on the ward's death, since limitations did not begin to run until the appointment of her representative. Stevenson v. Markley, 73 N. J. Eq. 731, 70 Atl. 1102, aff'g 72 N. J. Eq. 686, 66 Atl. 185.

15. Lewine v. Gerardo, 112 N. Y. Supp. 192, 60 Misc. Rep. 261.

Where plaintiff's testator's right of action was barred by limitations prior to his death, his death did not create a new right of possession in his devisees. Baker v. Duff, 120 N. Y. Supp. 184, 136 App. Div. 13.

See Conway v. City of New York, 124 N. Y. Supp. 660, 139 App. Div. 446, as to action against a city for negligent death, brought by an administrator of the deceased.

The statute of limitations having commenced to run is suspended by death only in the cases, and to the extent expressly provided by the same or some other statute. Beach v. Reynolds, 64 Barb. (N. Y.) 506.

16. Glazier v. Heneybuss, 19 Okl. 316, 91 Pac. 872.

17. Irwin v. Garrettson, 1 Cin. R. (Ohio) 533.

18. Appeal of Amole's Adm'rs, 115 Pa. 356, 8 Atl. 614.

19. Boyd v. Munro, 32 S. C. 249, 10 S. E. 963.

20. Walker v. Abercrombie, 61 Tex. 69.

in the statute.[21] In West Virginia, when an action has accrued to a party capable of suing against a party who may be sued, the statute of limitations begins to run, unless this be prevented by the case coming within some exception of the statute; and, after it has begun to run, its running is not suspended because of the subsequent death of either of the parties, or because of the lapse of time before either has a personal representative.[22] In Wisconsin, the statute which provides that, if a person entitled to bring an action die before the expiration of the time limited for the commencement thereof, and the cause of action survive, action may be commenced by his representative after the expiration of that time, and within a year from his death, is limited to cases where the death of the person occurs during the last year of his right to commence the action.[23] In Kansas, as against heirs of a grantor of unsound mind, who so continues until his death, limitations do not begin to run until such death. [24]

§ 199b. Accrual of cause of action before issuance of letters testamentary or of administration.

In Alabama, under Code 1907, § 4854, providing that the time between death and the grant of administration, not exceeding six months, is excepted from the time limited for the commencement of an action by the administrator, the statute, even though it has begun to run against decedent, is suspended for a period of not less than fifteen days and until letters are granted, within the limit of six months.[25] In Arkansas, the statute of limitations does not begin to run against a claim accruing to an estate after one's death until there is a personal representative competent to sue.[26] In

21. McAuliff v. Parker, 10 Wash. 141, 38 Pac. 744.

22. Handy v. Smith, 30 W. Va. 195, 3 S. E. 604.

23. Palmer v. O'Rourke, 130 Wis. 507, 110 N. W. 389.

24. Jenkins v. Jenkins, 94 Kan. 263, 146 Pac. 414.

25. Larue v. C. G. Kershaw Contracting Co., 177 Ala. 441, 59 So. 155.

26. Sorrels v. Trantham, 48 Ark. 386, 4 S. W. 281; Word v. West, 38 Ark. 243; Worthington's Adm'r v. De Bardlekin, 33 Ark. 651.

Delaware, where a cause of action does not arise until after a person's death, the act of limitations does not begin to run until there are parties capable of suing and being sued.[27] In the District of Columbia, limitation does not begin to run against a claim in favor of a decedent's estate until after the granting of letters of administration.[28] In Florida, on the abandonment of a suit by the death of a plaintiff, limitations will not run until administration on his estate has been taken, or in the absence of a person who is capable of suing.[29] In Georgia, where, in an action against an administrator, the oldest item in the account sued on was of a date less than five years before the bringing of the suit, and the creditor was prohibited from bringing an action against the administrator until after twelve months from his appointment, the statute was tolled for that period and no item of the account was barred by the statute of limitations.[30] In Indiana, limitation does not begin to run against claims arising after death, until administration is had; a creditor's right to take letters, under the statute, being merely a right, and not a duty.[31] In Kansas, where a person who was to render services under an entire contract died before the completion of the contract, the statute of limitations did not begin to run against an action to recover compensation for the services rendered until administration of the deceased's estate.[32] Under the Kentucky statute, providing if a person entitled to bring an action dies before expiration of the time limited for its commencement it may be brought by his personal representative after expiration of that time, if commenced within a year after his qualification, he, not qualifying before the cause of action

27. Conwell's Adm'r v. Morris Adm'r, 5 Har. (Del.) 299.

28. Tucker v. Nebeker, 2 App. D. C. 326.

29. Coe v. Finlayson, 41 Fla. 169, 26 So. 704.

30. Hinkle v. James Smith & Son, 127 Ga. 437, 56 S. E. 464. And see Taylor v. Jacoway, 54 Ga. 500; Garland v. Milling, 6 Ga. 310.

31. Hildebrand v. Kinney, 172 Ind. 447, 87 N. E. 832, rev'g (Ind. App.), 83 N. E. 379; Burns' Ann. St. 1908, §§ 2742, subd. 3, 2744. See also Douglass v. McOarer, 80 Ind. 91.

32. Carney v. Havens, 23 Kan. 82. See Green v. Goeble, 7 Kan. 297.

is barred, may not bring the action.[33] In Connecticut, in an action by an administrator for money converted after intestate's death, but before the administrator had been appointed, where the money was converted more than six years before the action was commenced, but the administrator was appointed less than a year before the commencement thereof, the cause of action did not accrue, so that limitations ran against it, until the administrator was appointed, and hence the action was not barred by the statute.[34] In Louisiana, where one claimed to be sole heir to an estate, but a will was afterwards found, on the probate of such will, his cause of action as creditor of the estate accrued, and the statute of limitations then began to run.[35] In Massachusetts, where within six years after the dissolution of a partnership one of the partners died, and within two years after the granting of letters of administration on his estate, but more than six years after the partnership was dissolved, his administrators brought a bill in equity against the other partners to compel them to account, the case was not barred by the statute of limitations.[36]

In Michigan, the running of limitations, prescribed by the statute providing that actions for personal injuries must be brought within three years from the occurrence on which the claim for liability is founded, is not suspended by the death of the person injured until the appointment of an administrator, notwithstanding Comp. Laws, § 9737, providing that, where any person entitled to bring an action shall die and the cause of action survives, the action may be commenced by the administrator at any time within two years after granting of letters of administration; the former

33. Boughner v. Sharp, 144 Ky. 320, 138 S. W. 375, under Ky. St. § 2526 (Russell's St. § 192); Louisville & N. R. Co. v. Brantley's Adm'r, 106 Ky. 849, 21 Ky. Law Rep. 473, 51 S. W. 585; Wilson's Adm'r v. Illinois Cent. R. Co., 29 Ky. Law Rep. 148, 92 S. W. 572; Pitchford v. Gatewood's Adm'r, 10 Ky. Law Rep. 112.

34. Root v. Lathrop, 81 Conn. 169, 70 Atl. 614.

35. Succession of Dubreuil, 25 La. Ann. 370.

36. Chandler v. Chandler, 21 Mass. (4 Pick.) 78, under St. 1793, c. 75, § 3. See Gen. St. c. 155, § 10.

statute not making an exception in favor of causes of action which survive.[37] In Minnesota, Gen. St. 1894, § 5149, providing that the time which elapses between the death of a person and the granting of letters testamentary or of administration on his estate, not exceeding six months, and the period of six months after the granting of such letters, are not to be deemed any part of the time limited for the commencement of actions by executors and administrators, prescribes the general rule, and section 5148, providing that, if a person entitled to bring an action dies before the expiration of the time limited for the commencement thereof, and the cause of action survives, an action may be commenced by his personal representatives after the expiration of that time, and within one year from his death, applies only to special cases, where the person entitled to bring the action dies within the last year of the term of limitation.[38] In Mississippi, although a right of action has accrued, the statute of limitations will not commence to run until, by appointment of an administrator or otherwise, some party is in being who has power to sue.[39] In Missouri, limitations do not begin to run against a cause of action accruing after the death of a person, in favor of his administrator, until the granting of letters of administration.[40] In New Hampshire, notwithstanding the statute provides that suits against an executor

37. Colling v. McGregor, 144 Mich. 651, 108 N. W. 87, 13 Detroit Leg. N. 310. As to action to recover moneys charged on land, see Field v. Loveridge, 114 Mich. 220, 72 N. W. 160, 4 Detroit Leg. N. 515.

38. Wood v. Bragg, 75 Minn. 527, 78 N. W. 93.

39. Metcalf v. Grover, 55 Miss. 145. See also Stauffer v. British & American Mortgage Co., 77 Miss. 127, 25 So. 299; Boswell v. Thigpen, 75 Miss. 308, 22 So. 823; Wood v. Ford, 29 Miss. (7 Cushm.) 57; Byrd v. Byrd, 28 Miss. (6 Cushm.) 57.

40. Greisel v. Jones, 123 Mo. App. 45, 99 S. W. 769; Ryan v. Ford, 151 Mo. App. 689, 132 S. W. 610; White v. Blankenbeckler, 115 Mo. App. 722, 92 S. W. 503.

While, on the death of a debtor, limitations do not run against the creditor during the time administration is delayed, yet, where the creditor is the decedent, limitations on a matured obligation continue to run, as his heirs cannot prolong the period of limitations in their own favor by delaying to take out letters of administration. Stanton v. Gibbins, 103 Mo. App. 264, 77 S. W. 95.

must be begun within three years after the appointment, such action may be brought after that time by the administrator of a person who at the time of her death had the right of such action, if brought " within two years after the original grant of administration " as provided by statute.[41] In New York, a claim against an insurance company for a loss occurring after the death of the insured, not being a cause of action which accrued to him, is not affected by Code Civ. Proc., § 402, extending the time within which an action may be brought after the death of the person in whose favor the claim exists.[42] In North Carolina, where a right of action survives in favor of an intestate, the action must be brought within a year after his death, without reference to the time of administration, but where a right of action survives against an intestate, the running of the statute of limitations is suspended between the time of his death and the appointment of his administrator.[43] In Pennsylvania, where a beneficiary of a wagering life insurance policy collects the money due on the policy, limitations do not begin to run against the right of the legal representative of the assured to sue for the money until administration is granted.[44] In Ohio, where a right of action survived in favor of an intestate, the statute of limitations continued to run, though the intestate died shortly after the action accrued, and no administrator was

41. Perkins v. Perkins, 68 N. H. 264, 38 Atl. 1049.

42. Matthews v. American Cent. Ins. Co., 41 N. Y. Supp. 304, 9 App. Div. 339, 75 N. Y. St. Rep. 716, judg. modified 154 N. Y. 449, 48 N. E. 751, 39 L. R. A. 433, 61 Am. St. Rep. 627.

The running of limitations against the claim of a deceased creditor to the surplus arising from a sale of mortgaged land is not suspended while the surplus remains undistributed, though the sale occurred within four years from the issuance of letters of administration. *In re* Knapp, 54 N. Y. Supp. 927, 25 Misc. Rep. 133, 2 Gibbons, 581, 28 N. Y. Civ. Proc. R. 220.

The fact that there is no legal representative of a deceased creditor entitled to sue the demand does not prevent the operation of the statute of limitations. Partridge v. Mitchell, 3 Edw. Ch. (N. Y.) 180.

43. Coppersmith v. Wilson, 107 N. C. 31, 12 S. E. 77; Dunlap v. Hendley, 92 N. C. 115. See also Matthews v. Peterson, 152 N. C. 168, 67 S. E. 340.

44. Riner v. Riner, 166 Pa. 617, 31 Atl. 347, 45 Am. St. Rep. 693. See Marsteller v. Marsteller, 93 Pa. 350.

appointed.[45] In South Carolina, the statute of limitations does not begin to run against the creditors of an estate, or against representatives of an intestate, until administration is granted.[46] In Texas, limitations do not run against an action for an injury done to an estate of a decedent after his death, and before the qualification of his legal representatives, until the expiration of one year from his death.[47] In Virginia, the statute of limitations does not begin to run against a claim asserted for a decedent's estate until a qualification of an executor or administrator of the estate.[48] In South Dakota, the statute of limitations does not begin to run against the claim of a decedent's estate, a right of action upon which did not accrue until the appointment of an administrator, until such appointment.[49] In West Virginia, as to a demand which accrues to a decedent's estate after his death, limitation is counted from the time his personal representative qualifies, if within five years of his death; but, if there is no personal representative within five years, then the period is counted from the last day of the five years after his death.[50] In Wisconsin, where defendant converted certain personal property belonging to decedent after her death and before the appointment of an administrator, an

45. Tobias v. Richardson, 26 Ohio Cir. Ct. R. 81.

46. King v. Aughtry, 3 Stroh. Eq. (S. C.) 149; Harvin v. Riggs, Rich. Eq. Cas. (S. C.) 287.

47. William J. Lemp Brewing Co. v. La Rose, 20 Tex. Civ. App. 575, 50 S. W. 460. The same rule applies to an action to recover lands. Carter v. Hussey, (Tex. Civ. App.) 46 S. W. 270; Hasseldenz v. Dofflemyer, (Tex. Civ. App.) 45 S. W. 830. But it does not apply where the decedent transferred a note in blank, and the transferee has authority to sue, though the decedent had an interest in it. Davis v. Dixon, 61 Tex. 446.

48. Hansford v. Elliott, 9 Leigh (Va.) 79; Lyon's Adm'r v. Magagnos' Adm'r, 7 Grat. (Va.) 377; Smith's Adm'r v. Charlton's Adm'r, 7 Grat. (Va.) 425.

In computing time under the statute of limitations, a period of one year from the qualification of the personal representatives of a person for whose benefit an action is brought in the name of another cannot be excluded, since such person is not a party of record. Fadely's Adm'r v. Williams' Adm'r, 96 Va. 397, 31 S. E. 515.

49. McPherson v. Swift, 22 S. D. 165, 116 N. W. 76.

50. Crawford's Adm'r v. Turner's Adm'r, 67 W. Va. 564, 68 S. E. 179, under Code 1906, c. 104, § 17.

action could be commenced within double the period otherwise perscribed by law and not be barred.[51]

§ 199c(1). Death of person liable in general.

Where a contract provides that performance shall take place upon the happening of a certain contingency or condition, the statute of limitations begins to run when the event occurs and the condition is complied with, and the death of the party making the promise, before the contingency happens, does not set the statute in motion in favor of his estate.[52] The running of limitations against a cause of action for breach of a marriage promise is not suspended by the death of the promisor.[53] Where a cause of action has accrued, and the statute of limitations has commenced to run, it is not suspended by the death of the debtor except by special statutory enactment.[54] Where limitations started against a judgment in the lifetime of a judgment creditor, the operation of the statute was not suspended by his death.[55] The

51. Palmer v. O'Rourke, 130 Wis. 507, 110 N. W. 389. See also Stehn v. Hayssen, 124 Wis. 583, 102 N. W. 1074; Wis. Rev. St. 1898, § 4251.

52. Waterman v. Kirk's Estate, 139 Ill. App. 451.

53. *In re* Oldfield's Estate, 158 Iowa, 98, 138 N. W. 846.

The running of the five years' limitations, under Code, § 3447, against an action to recover a loan of money, was not tolled by the death of the borrower. Widner v. Wilcox, 131 Iowa, 223, 108 N. W. 238.

54. Johnson v. Equitable Life Assur. Society of United States. 137 Ky. 437, 125 S. W. 1074.

An action against a personal representative on a cause of action against the decedent is never barred until the expiration of at least one year after his appointment, and an action against the heir is never barred until at least two years after the decedent's death, and in neither case is the action ever barred at any time within which it might have been brought against the decedent. Pilcher v. McCowan, 8 Ky. Law Rep. (abstract) 786. Where an administrator qualifies November 28, 1864, and his surety dies January 23, 1871, under Rev. St., c. 97, § 13, limitation runs in favor of an heir of the surety, against whom an action was brought October 15, 1872, by heirs of the administrator's intestate. Murrell's Adm'r v. McAllister, 79 Ky. 311; Marshall v. Sanford, 9 Ky. Law Rep. 855.

55. Brooks v. Preston, 106 Md. 693, 68 Atl. 294, and his administrator could not revive it by *scire facias* issued about 13 years after the recov-

four-year period of limitations, fixed by the Nebraska statute on actions to set aside fraudulent conveyances, is not tolled by the death of the fraudulent grantor.[56] Where a trustee dies and leaves all his property to his widow and executrix, who die without accounting for the fund, and her property goes to the hands of her executors, an action against them brought by the beneficiary within seven years and six months from the time the trustee without authority paid the fund to another is not barred under New York Code Civ. Proc., § 382, authorizing such an action within six years, and section 403, suspending the running of limitations for eighteen months after the death of the trustee.[57] Where a cause of action accrues for or against a party, the West Virginia statute of limitations does not stop because of his death or until he has a personal representative.[58] The running of the Washington statute of limitations for foreclosing a mortgage is not suspended by the death of the mortgagor unknown to the mortgagee.[59]

§ 199c(2). Effect of administration of estate of decedent or want thereof.

In Arkansas, where a maker of a note secured by mortgage dies before the five-year limitations have run against the note, limitations cease to run and are succeeded by the two-year statute of nonclaim, which runs from the granting of letters of administra-

ery of the judgment, though more than eight years elapsed between the death of the judgment creditor and the appointment of the administrator.

56. Lesieur v. Simon, 73 Neb. 645, 103 N. W. 302.

57. Judg. and order 34 Misc. Rep. 661, 70 N. Y. Supp. 592, aff'd. Hopper v. Brown, 67 App. Div. 620, 74 N. Y. Supp. 1132, aff'd 173 N. Y. 613, 66 N. E. 1110.

58. Rowan v. Chenoweth, 49 W. Va. 287, 38 S. E. 544, 87 Am. St. Rep. 796.

59. Fuhrman v. Power, 43 Wash. 533, 86 Pac. 940.

As to the effect on limitations of the death of the person liable in other jurisdictions. See

Ind.—Harris v. Rice, 66 Ind. 267; Emerick v. Chesrown, 90 Ind. 47.

Ind. T.—Murray v. Houghton, 2 Ind. T. 504, 52 S. W. 48.

N. C.—Alexander v. Alexander's Ex'rs, 4 N. C. 28.

Va.—Templeman's Adm'r v. Pugh, 102 Va. 441, 46 S. E. 474.

tion, and the note and mortgage are in force for two years after that date.[60] A cause of action against a mortgagor having arisen after her death, and when no administration on her estate existed, limitations, in California, did not begin to run until letters of administration were issued.[61] In Georgia, limitations as to debts of a decedent are suspended between the time of his death and the appointment of an administrator, if such period does not exceed five years.[62] The Illinois limitation law applies to a suit to foreclose a mortgage to secure a note given by deceased, though the personal representative is not a necessary party thereto, where action could have been brought against him on the note.[63] If there was liability, either express or implied, to pay a claim for money paid a physician for services to decedent, or for an invalid chair for his use, the obligation arose before death, and the statute which began to run when the obligation arose, was not suspended by

60. McGill v. Hughes, 84 Ark. 238, 105 S. W. 255; Montgomery v. Gantt, 100 Ark. 629, 140 S. W. 260. See also Ross v. Frick Co., 73 Ark. 45, 83 S. W. 343; Salinger v. Black, 68 Ark. 449, 60 S. W. 229; Whipple v. Johnson, 66 Ark. 204, 49 S. W. 827.

61. Hibernia Savings & Loan Society v. Farnham, 153 Cal. 578, 96 Pac. 9; *In re* Bullard's Estate, 116 Cal. 355, 48 Pac. 219; Heeser v. Taylor, 1 Cal. App. 619, 82 Pac. 977. Code Civ. Proc., § 353, only interrupts the running of the statute as against the representatives of the deceased mortgagor. California Title Ins. & Trust Co. v. Muller, 3 Cal. App. 54, 84 Pac. 453; Casey v. Gibbons, 136 Cal. 368, 68 Pac. 1032. As to the effect of administration or want thereof on other limitations. See Vandall v. Teague, 142 Cal. 471, 76 Pac. 35.

62. Hawes v. Glover, 126 Ga. 305, 55 S. E. 62, since the passage of Acts 1882-83, p. 104 (Civ. Code, 1895, § 3782). The appointment of a temporary administrator does not constitute "representation" on the estate of a decedent, within Civ. Code 1910, § 4376, so as to cause limitations to run against the estate on such appointment. Baumgartner v. McKinnon, 137 Ga. 165, 73 S. E. 518.

Where a partner dies, and a partnership is dissolved thereby, limitations run in favor of his estate, after the expiration of 12 months from the grant of administration thereon, as to all demands of the surviving partner out of the partnership transactions. Willis v. Sutton, 116 Ga. 283, 42 S. E. 526.

63. Wellman v. Miner, 179 Ill. 326, 53 N. E. 609, rev'g judg. 73 Ill. App. 448; Roberts v. Tunnell, 165 Ill. 631, 46 N. E. 713, aff'g judg. 65 Ill. App. 191, under Limitation Law, § 19 (2 Starr & C. Ann. St. 2nd ed. p. 2639).

his death, nor by the failure to appoint an administrator, in the absence of statute.[64] A cause of action for the foreclosure of a mortgage does not accrue on the death of the mortgagor and the allowance by the probate court of the note secured by the mortgage, as a demand against the estate, without regard to the maturity of the mortgage debt, and it does not set limitations running against such action.[65] In the absence of administration on the estate of an owner of land who died in 1863, his debts would not be barred by the general statute of limitations, which does not run under such circumstances.[66] A note given by testatrix was not barred by special limitations where the executor never gave notice of his appointment as required by the Maine statute.[67] New York Code Civ. Proc., § 1843, authorizes suit against heirs on a debt of a decedent. Section 1844 declares that no such action shall be instituted till three years after letters granted, and section 406 that time during which an action is prohibited shall not be counted as a part of the time limited. Testator made a payment on his note to plaintiff October 21, 1898, and died May 31, 1899. Letters were issued July 10, 1899, and action brought against the heirs under section 1843, on January 17, 1908. It was held that the nine years within which plaintiff could have sued dated from the payment on the note, and not from death, and hence action was barred.[68]

64. Hildebrand v. Kinney, 172 Ind. 447, 87 N. E. 832, rev'g judg. (Ind. App.), 83 N. E. 379. As to action for seduction against the administrator of the seducer. See Gimbel v. Smidth, 7 Ind. 627.

65. Linn v. Ziegler, 68 Kan. 528, 75 Pac. 489.

66. Austin v. Shipman, 160 Mo. App. 206, 141 S. W. 425. Limitations do not run in favor of an estate during the time there is no administration. Little v. Reid, 75 Mo. App. 266.

67. McGuire v. Murray, 107 Me. 108, 77 Atl. 692.

68. Hill v. Moore, 131 App. Div. 365, 115 N. Y. Supp. 289, order aff'd 198 N. Y. 633, 92 N. E. 1086. Code Civ. Proc. § 1844 is a statutory prohibition against the commencement of an action, within section 406. *Id.* See also De Crano v. Moore, 50 App. Div. 361, 64 N. Y. Supp. 3.

Where an administrator dies, the right of his successor to compel an accounting by his personal representative, as authorized by Code Civ. Proc. § 2606, is not barred by limitations until after ten years from the appointment of the new administra-

§ 199c(3). Death of person jointly liable.

Under California Code Civ. Proc., § 337, providing that an action on any contract founded on an instrument in writing executed in the state must be brought within five years, the bar of the statute as to a mortgagor is not affected merely by the death of a co-mortgagor before the note given with the mortgage is barred. *In re* Lesser's Estate, 119 App. Div. 507, 104 N. Y. Supp. 213.

As to the effect of administration of the estate of a decedent or want thereof on the application of statutes of limitations in different jurisdictions, reference may be made to the following authorities:

U. S.—Updike v. Mace, 194 Fed. 1001 (D. C.); Alice E. Mining Co. v. Blanden, 136 Fed. 252 (C. C., Iowa); Platt v. Hungerford, 116 Fed. 771 (C. C., N. Y.); Fidelity Ins., etc., Co. v. Mechanics' Sav. Bank, 97 Fed. 297, 38 C. C. A. 193, 56 L. R. A. 228 (C. C. A., Pa.).

Colo.—McGovney v. Gwillim, 16 Colo. App. 284, 65 Pac. 346.

Idaho.—Miller v. Lewiston Nat. Bank, 18 Idaho, 124, 108 Pac. 901.

Iowa.—German v. Heath, 139 Iowa, 52, 116 N. W. 1051; Malone v. Averill, 166 Iowa 78, 147 N. W. 135.

Ky.—Walker's Adm'r v. Turley, 28 Ky. Law Rep. 809, 90 S. W. 576; Southern Contract Co's Assignee v. Newhouse, 23 Ky. Law Rep. 2141, 119 Ky. 704, 66 S. W. 730; Farris v. Hoskins, 23 Ky. Law Rep. 596, 63 S. W. 577; Mason's Adm'x v. Mason, 3 Ky. Law Rep. (abstract) 397; Jones v. Mitchell's Adm'r, 9 Ky. Law Rep. (abstract) 858.

Md.—Eirley v. Eirley, 102 Md. 452, 62 Atl. 962.

Mass.—Corliss Steam Engine Co. v. Schumacher, 109 Mass. 416.

Mich.—Murphy v. Cady, 145 Mich. 33, 13 Detroit Leg. N. 412, 108 N. W. 493; Steuard v. Sellman's Estate, 175 Mich. 700, 141 N. W. 878.

Miss.—Klaus v. Moore, 77 Miss. 701, 27 So. 612.

Mont.—Whiteside v. Catching, 19 Mont. 394, 48 Pac. 747.

Nev.—Schwart v. Stock, 26 Nev. 155, 65 Pac. 357.

N. C.—Matthews v. Peterson, 150 N. C. 132, 63 S. E. 721; Lowder v. Hathcock, 150 N. C. 438, 64 S. E. 194; Winslow v. Benton, 130 N. C. 58, 40 S. E. 840; Phifer v. Ford, 130 N. C. 208, 41 S. E. 280; Copeland v. Collins, 122 N. C. 619, 30 S. E. 315; Person v. Montgomery, 120 N. C. 111, 26 S. E. 645.

N. D.—Colonial & United States Mortg. Co. v. Flemington, 14 N. D. 181, 103 N. W. 929, 116 Am. St. Rep. 670.

Ohio.—Hoiles v. Riddle, 26 Ohio Cir. Ct. R. 363; *In re* Ward's Estate, 21 Ohio Cir. Ct. R. 753, 12 O. C. D. 44; Hoiles v. Riddle, 74 Ohio St. 173, 78 N. E. 219, 113 Am. St. Rep. 936.

Or.—*In re* Morgan's Estate, 46 Or. 233, 77 Pac. 608.

R. I.—Petition of Johnson, 15 R. I. 438, 8 Atl. 248.

Tenn.—Stidham v. McCarver, (Ch. App.) 57 S. W. 212; Webb v. Branner, 58 Tenn. (11 Heisk.) 305.

Tex.—First Nat. Bank of New Boston v. Daniel, (Civ. App.) 172 S. W.

red.[69] Under Kentucky St., § 2552, where a surety on a note was dead at the time a judgment was rendered thereon, limitations were suspended during the time such surety had no personal representative and six months additional.[70] Where a surety on a note paid a judgment thereon, the subsequent death of his cosurety suspended the running of limitations as to the time in which the surety must sue for contribution, until letters of administration were issued.[71] Though remedy against the principal, on a note of a principal and surety, is barred by limitations, yet, it not being barred against the estate of the surety because of the suspension of the statute by reason of his death, the claim may be proved against the estate.[72] Since creditors of a firm are not entitled to sue the surviving parties pending administration of the firm assets in the probate court on the death of a partner, limitations do not run against the creditors' claims pending such settlement.[73] If a suit be brought on a joint and several note against a debtor and the administrators of a co-debtor, as under the N. Y. Code it may be, the latter are to

747; Herbert v. Herbert, (Civ. App.) 59 S. W. 594; Morgan v. Baker, (Civ. App.) 40 S. W. 27; Hanrick v. Gurley, 93 Tex. 458, 54 S. W. 347, judg. modified 93 Tex. 458, 55 S. W. 119, 56 S. W. 330; Groesbeck v. Crow, 91 Tex. 74, 40 S. W. 1028, rev'g judg. Crow v. Groesbeck, (Civ. App.) 39 S. W. 1003.

Wash.—Frew v. Clark, 34 Wash. 561, 76 Pac. 85; Gleason v. Hawkins, 32 Wash. 464, 73 Pac. 533.

W. Va.—Western Lunatic Asylum v. Miller, 29 W. Va. 326, 1. S. E. 740, 6 Am. St. Rep. 644.

Wis.—Boyd v. Mutual Fire Ass'n, 116 Wis. 155, 90 N. W. 1086, 61 L. R. A. 918, 96 Am. St. Rep. 948, modified 94 S. W. 171.

69. Hibernia Savings & Loan Soc. v. Boland, 145 Cal. 626, 79 Pac. 365.

70. Apperson v. Farmers' Nat. Bank, 7 Ky. Law Rep. 153; Apperson's Ex'r v. Farmers' Nat. Bank, 6 Ky. Law Rep. 743. See also Davis' Adm'r v. Auxier, 19 Ky. Law Rep. 719, 41 S. W. 767; Farmer v. Edwards, 9 Ky. Law Rep. (abstract) 816; Pusey v. Smith's Adm'r, 12 Ky. Law Rep. (abstract) 604.

71. Hinshaw v. Warren's Estate, 167 Mo. App. 365, 151 S. W. 497.

72. Charbonneau v. Bouvet, 98 Tex. 167, 82 S. W. 460.

See also, as to suspension of limitation as to a guarantor or surety on a note when the principal obligor is dead, Acers v. Acers, 22 Tex. Civ. App. 584, 56 S. W. 196.

73. Brigham-Hopkins Co. v. Gross, 30 Wash. 277, 70 Pac. 480, under Ballinger's Ann. Codes & St. §§ 6188, 6190.

be regarded, if the statute of limitations is pleaded, as if they had been sued separately, and the eighteen months are to be added.[74]

§ 199c(4). Death after commencement of action.

California Code Civ. Proc., § 581, as amended in 1889, requiring that no action shall be further prosecuted unless summons shall have been issued within one year and served within three years from bringing suit, includes an action in which defendant dies within the year.[75] Where an action on a note was commenced within the time limited, but defendant died and while the first action was pending, no non-suit having been suffered or judgment arrested or reversed, and after the expiration of the time limited plaintiff brought an action in the probate court, such action was barred.[76]

74. Parker v. Jackson, 16 Barb. (N. Y.) 33. See, as to suspension of limitations against the estate of a deceased co-owner of property purchased at a joint venture, Freschsi v. Bellesheim, 14 N. Y. St. Rep. 610.

See, as to suspension of limitations on death of person jointly liable in other jurisdictions:

Ala.—Goldsmith v. Eichold, 94 Ala. 116, 10 So. 80, 33 Am. St. Rep. 97.

N. C.—Buie v. Buie, 24 N. C. 87.

Tenn.—Nashville Bank v. Campbell, 15 Tenn. (7 Yerg.) 353.

75. Davis v. Hart, 123 Cal. 384, 55 Pac. 1060.

76. Hill v. Pipkins, 72 Ark. 549, 81 S. W. 1216, under Sand. & H. Dig. Ark. § 4841.

As to the rule in other jurisdictions, see:

Conn.—Bassett v. McKenna, 52 Conn. 437.

Md.—Parker's Ex'rs v. Fassit's Ex'rs, 1 Har. & J. 337.

N. Y.—Jackson v. Horton, 3 Caines, 197.

S. C.—Allen v. Roundtree, 1 Speers, 80.

Va.—Brown's Ex'rs v. Putney, 1 Wash. 302.

CHAPTER XX.

TRUSTS AND TRUSTEES.

SECTION 200. General rule.
201. Express trusts.
202. Assignees in bankruptcy, insolvency, etc.
202. *Cestui que trust* in possession.
204. Guardians.
205. Executors as trustees.
206. Executor or administrator of a trustee.
207. Power to sell property.
208. Effect on *cestui que trust* when trustee is barred. Sale of trust estate.
209. Factors and agents.
210. Partners.
211. Acknowledgment by one partner.
212. How trustee may put statute in operation in his favor.
213. Exceptions to the rule relative to express trusts.
214. Stale trusts not favored in equity.
215. Constructive or resulting trusts.
216. Mistake of trustee in possession.
217. Funds of societies vested in trustees.
218. The liability of trustee for breach of trust creates trust debt.
219. Vendor and vendee of land.
220. Purchaser of property for benefit of another.
220a (1). Existenee of trust. In general.
220a (2). When relation exists in general.
220a (3). Possession of property.
220a (4). Express or continuing trust.
220a (5). What constitutes express or continuing trust.
220a (6). Resulting or implied trust.
220a (7). What constitutes resulting or implied trust.
220a (8). Constructive trust.
220a (9). What constitutes constructive trust.
220a (10). Rights of parties claiming under trustee.
220a (11). Termination of trust.
220b (1). Repudiation or violation of trust. In general.
220b (2). Necessity for disclaimer or repudiation.
220b (3). What constitutes repudiation or violation of trust.
220b (4). Notice of repudiation.

§ 200. General rule.

It is well settled that a subsisting, recognized, and acknowledged trust, as between the trustee and *cestui que trust,* is not within the operation of the statute of limitations.[1] But this rule must be

1. Bridgman v. Gill, 24 Beav. 302; Attorney-General v. Fishmongers' Co., 5 My. & Cr. 16; Wedderburn v. Wedderburn, 4 id. 41; Coate's Estate, 2 Pars. Sel. Cas. (Pa.) 258; Maury v. Mason, 8 Port. (Ala.) 211; Shibla v. Ely, 6 N. J. Eq. 181; Lyon v. Marclay, 1 Watts (Pa.) 271; Bertine v. Varian, 1 Edw. (N. Y.) Ch. 343; Redwood v. Reddick, 4 Munf. (Va.) 222; Evarts v. Nason, 11 Vt. 122; Lexington v. Lindsey, 9 Ky. (2 A. K. Mar.) 443; Chaplin v. Givens, 1 Rice (S. C.) Ch. 132; Pinson v. Ivey, 9 Tenn. (1 Yerg.) 296; Pinkerton v. Walker, 6 Tenn. (3 Hayw.) 221; Kutz's Appeal, 40 Pa. 90; West v. Sloan, 56 N. E. (3 Jones Eq.) 102; Willard v. Willard, 56 Penn. St. 119; Byrant v. Puckett, 6 Tenn. (3 Hayw.) 252; Jones v. Person, 9 N. C. (2 Hawks) 269; State v. McGowen, 37 N. C. (2 Ired. Eq.) 9; Armstrong v. Campbell, 11 Tenn. (3 Yerg.) 201; Cook v. Williams, 2 N. J. Eq. 209; Pugh v. Bell, 1 J. J. Mar. (Ky.) 399; Oliver v. Piatt, 41 U. S. (3 How.) 333, 11 L. Ed. 622; Thomas v. Floyd, 13 Ky. (3 Litt.) 177; Prevost v. Gratz, 19 U. S. (6 Wheat.) 481, 5 L. Ed. 311; Haynie v. Hall, 24 Tenn. (5 Humph.) 290; Boone v. Chiles, 35 U. S. (10 Pet.) 177, 9 L. Ed. 388; Simms v. Smith, 11 Ga. 195; Decouche v. Savetier, 3 Johns. (N. Y.) Ch. 190; Wilmerding v. Russ, 33 Conn. 67; Platt v. Oliver, 2 McLean (U. S. C. C.) 267; Coster v. Murray, 5 Johns. (N. Y.) Ch. 522; Wood v. Wood, 3 Ala. 756. The statute cannot be pleaded to a remedy given by the legislature to enforce a trust. Bethune v. Dougherty, 30 Ga. 770.

It is equaly true that fraud as trust is not within the statute. Kane v. Bloodgood, 7 Johns. (N. Y.) Ch. 90, 122; Hunter v. Spotswood, 1 Wash. (Va.) 145.

A purchaser for a valuable consideration, if affected with notice, becomes a trustee for the true owner, and will not be protected by the statute. Wamburzee v. Kennedy, 4 Desau. (S. C.) 474; Thayer v. Cramer, 1 McCord Ch. (S. Car.) 395, 398. As a rule, the statute does not operate in cases of fraud and of trusts; but as soon as the fraud is discovered it commences to run. Wamburzee v. Kennedy, 4 Desau. (S. C.) 474; Payne v. Hathaway, 3 Vt. 212; Sweat v. Arrington, 2 Hayw. (N. C.) 129. The statute does not reach to matters of direct trust, as between trustee and *cestui que trust,* Coster v. Murray, 5 Johns. (N. Y.) Ch. 531; Turner v. Debell, 2 Marsh. (Ky.) 384; nor to parties standing in the relation of principal and agent, or factor, Murray v. Coster, *supra.* The statute cannot, either in a court of law or equity, protect a trustee against the demands of his *cestui que trust,* Thomas v. White, 13 Ky. (3 Litt.) 177; Lexington v. Lindsay, 9 Ky. (2 A. K. Marsh.) 445; or of persons claiming under him. Redwood

understood as applying only to those technical and continuing

v. Riddick, 4 Munf. (Va.) 222. So long as the trust subsists, the *cestui que trust*, cannot be barred. The *cestui que trust*, can only be barred by excluding the estate of the trustee. Cholmondeley v. Clinton, 2 Meriv. 360. Prevost v. Gratz, 19 U. S. (6 Wheat.) 497, 5 L. Ed. 311; Hemenway v. Gates, 22 Mass. (5 Pick.) 321.

A legacy of trust is not within the statute, but after a length of time payment will be presumed; yet such presumption may be rebutted by facts convincing to a jury. Durdon v. Gaskill, 2 Yeates (Pa.) 268. In Van Rhyn v. Vincent, 1 McCord (S. C.) Ch. 310, the rule was held to apply only to technical equitable trusts, and not to constructive trusts of which a court of law as well as a court of equity have jurisdiction.

If a *bona fide* purchaser without notice, who is a trustee by implication, is to be affected by an equity, that equity must be pursued within a reasonable time. Shaver v. Radley, 4 Johns. (N. Y.) Ch. 310; Thompson v. Blair, 7 N. C. (3 Murph.) 583.

A trustee cannot avail himself of the statute without plain, strong, and unequivocal proof of his renunciation of the trust. Boteler v. Allington, 3 Atk. 453, 459. The possession of the *cestui que trust* is not adverse to the title of the trustee, nor is the possession of the trustee adverse to his *cestuis*. Smith v. King, 16 East, 283; Keene v. Deardon, 8 id. 248; Smith v. Wheeler, 1 Vent. 128.

A *cestui que trust* is "tenant at will" to the trustee, and the possession of the *cestui que trust* is "the very possession in consideration of law of the trutee." Earl of Pomfret v. Lord Windsor, 2 Ves. 472; Lethieullier v. Tracy, 3 Atk. 728; Dighton v. Greenvil, 2 Ventr. 329. No conveyance by the *cestui que trust* can work a forfeiture of the legal estate of the trustee; it has been held that a fine or other alienation by *cestui que trust* for life does not work a forfeiture of his life estate. Sanders on Uses, 201; Lethieullier v. Tracy, 3 Atk. 729. The rule that trust and fraud are not within the statute of limitations is subject to this modification, that if the trust is constituted by the act of the parties, the possession of the trustee is the possession of the *cestui que trust*, and no length of such possession will bar; but if a trust is constituted by the fraud of one of the parties, or arises from a decree of a court of equity, or the like, the possession of the trustee becomes adverse, and the statute will run from the time the fraud is discovered. Thompson v. Blair, 7 N. C. (3 Murph.) 583; Van Rhyn v. Vincent, 1 McCord (S. C.) Ch. 310.

An executor entering on lands of the estate of his testator, and occupying them, is to be considered as holding them in trust for the heirs or devisees, unless he proves that he held adversely with notice to the heirs or devisees; in which case the proof lies on him to establish the claim at law, on an issue directed. Ramsay v. Deas, 2 Desau. (S. C.) 233. The statute is not allowed to run in favor of a man who was employed to act as agent, but purchased for himself. He is considered as a trustee, and his employer shall be entitled to the bene-

trusts which are alone cognizable in a court of equity;[2] and trusts

fit of the purchase. Hutchinson v. Hutchinson, 4 Desau. (S. C.) 77. See Bell v. Levers, 3 Yeates (Pa.) 26. In Starr v. Starr, 2 Ohio, 321, the court said: "That this trust was not formerly declared or expressed between parties is no reason why it cannot exist. The law is not to be evaded by contrivances of this nature. A trust tacitly created is more difficult to reach than one that is expressed; but where it is ascertained the consequence is attached to it." The general rule is, that after a sale of land, and before a conveyance of the legal title, the vendor is the trustee of the vendee, and the statute will have no operation. But where the vendor disavows the trust, and after having delivered possession to the vendee makes a lease to a third person in opposition to the title of the vendee, and the lessee enters and holds possession, the jury may presume a disseisin; and if the vendee suffers twenty-one years to elapse without prosecuting his claim, it will be barred by the act of limitations. Pipher v. Lodge, 4 S. & R. (Pa.) 310. But to prevent length of time from barring a claim, on the ground that the possession of the defendant was fiduciary, such possession must have been fiduciary as to the plaintiff or those under whom he claims; its being fiduciary as to any other person is not sufficient. Spotswood v. Dandridge, 4 Hen. & M. (Va.) 139.

2. Hayward v. Gunn, 82 Ill. 385; Partridge v. Wells, 30 N. J. Eq. 176; Prewett v. Buckingham, 28 Miss. 92; Tinnen v. Mebane, 10 Tex. 246; Paff v. Kinney, 1 Bradf. (N. Y. Surr.) 1; Cooke v. McGinnis, 8 Tenn. (M. & Y.) 361; Carter v. Bennett, 6 Fla. 214; Presley v. Davis, 7 Rich. (S. C.) Eq. 105; Maury v. Mason, 8 Port. (Ala.) 211; Zacharias v. Zacharias, 23 Pa. 452; Fox v. Cash, 11 Pa. 207; Heckert's Appeal, 24 Pa. 482; Kane v. Bloodgood, 7 Johns. (N. Y.) Ch. 90; Sayles v. Tibbitts, 5 R. I. 79; Thomas v. Brinsfield, 7 Ga. 154; Finney v. Cochran, 1 W. & S. (Pa.) 112; Raymond v. Simonson, 4 Blackf. (Ind.) 77; White v. White, 1 Md. Ch. 53; Johnson v. Smith's Adm'r, 27 Mo. 591; Lexington, etc., R. Co. v. Pridges, 46 Ky. (7 B. Mon.) 556; McDonald v. Sims, 3 Ga. 383. The principle that the statute will not protect trustees applies only to express or technical trusts. Farnam v. Brooks, 26 Mass. (9 Pick.) 212; Hayman v. Keally, 3 Cranch C. C. 325; Bank v. Beverly, 42 U. S. 134; Pugh v. Bell, 24 Ky. (1 J. J. Mar.) 398; Harris v. King, 16 Ark. 122. In Kutz's Appeal, 40 Pa. St. 90, it was held that where money is held in trust, and therefore not recoverable at law but only in equity, the statute will not run. In Coster v. Murray, 5 Johns. (N. R.) Ch. 522, where the defendant received goods consigned to him on his own account and the account of the plaintiff, who paid one-third of the price, and was to receive one-third of the proceeds; and the defendant, having sold the goods, refused to account to the plaintiff for his share, and set up the statute to bar the claim, this was held not a dealing between merchant and merchant, within the exception in the statute, but the defendant was held to be the factor of the plaintiff, and his liability a trust within the stat-

which arise from an implication of law, or constructive trusts, are not within the rule, but are subject to the operation of the statute,[3]

ute. See also White v. Leavitt, 20 Tex. 703. In Hutchinson v. Hutchinson, 4 Desau. (S. C.) 77, where an agent for the purchase of land took a title in his own name for the benefit of the principal, it was held that the statute did not run against the principal's claim to the land. In Van Rhyn v. Vincent, 4 McCord (S. C.) 310, A. sent abroad goods by B., who having died, the goods were disposed of by an agent, and the proceeds were transmitted to C., who, it seems, had no previous connection with A., and it was held that C. was not trustee for A., so as to relieve A.'s demand against him from the statute of limitations. But in McDonald v. May, 1 Rich. Eq. (S. C.) 91, where a person purchased land at a sheriff's sale under an agreement to hold the property for the benefit of the debtor, it was held that a technical trust was thereby created upon which the statute did not run. But it seems that a purchase under such an agreement, the debtor to remain in possession and refund the money at an indefinite time, does not create a continuing trust which bars the statute. Hughes v. Hughes, Cheves (S. C.) 33.

Where a sale of an infant's property was made by a master under a decree by which he was directed to sell, and apply the interest, and as much as might be necessary of the principal, of the proceeds, to the support of the infant, it was held that he was a trustee, and that the statute did not run against a suit, by the infant, for an account, until he had denied his liability. Houseal v. Gibbes, Bailey (S. C.) Ch. 482. So where a person gave to his children, by deed, property, real and personal, to be enjoyed by them after his death, himself retaining a life estate, it was held that he was a trustee for the children, and could not set up the statute of limitations against them, in consequence of his possession. Dawson v. Dawson, Rice (S. C.) Cr. 243.

In Armstrong v. Campbell, 11 Tenn. (3 Yerg.) 201, A. being the owner of land warrants, he and B. entered into an agreement and covenants with each other, by which B. was to find the land, and was authorized to sell and convey the same, and to receive to his own use one-third of the purchase money, or other consideration received for the same, and he covenanted to pay, deliver, and transfer the other two-thirds to A., and it was held that this transaction constituted B. a trustee in relation to the interest of A. by express contract, and that, though there were concurrent remedies upon the contract at law and in equity, it was not within the statute. In Lafferty v. Turley, 35 Tenn. (3 Sneed) 157, it was held that where there is a concurrent remedy at law the equitable bar from lapse of time is generally applied by analogy to the statute of limitations, but where, as in cases of express trust, the matter is alone cognizable in equity, the bar may be applied according to the merits of the case.

3. Edwards v. University, 21 N. C.

unless there has been a fraudulent concealment of the cause of

(1 D. & B. Eq.) 325; Walker v. Walker, 16 S. & R. (Pa.) 379; Buehan v. James, Speers (S. C.) Ch. 375. "By the whole current of modern authorities," says Hinman, C. J., in Wilmerding v. Russ, 33 Conn. 77, "implied trusts are within the statute, and the statute begins to run from the time the wrong was committed, by which the person becomes chargeable as trustee by implication." Kane v. Bloodgood, *supra;* Robinson v. Hook, 4 Mass. (U. S.) 152. In Swindersine v. Miscally, Bailey (S. C.) Ch. 304, this rule was applied where an administrator became a purchaser at his own sale as administrator, for a fair price, and afterwards mortgaged the property to secure his private debts. The court held that the mortgagee, being a trustee by implication only, might avail himself of the statute. So in Haynie v. Hall, 24 Tenn. (5 Humph.) 290, where a father received a legacy for his minor child, it was held that by operation of law he became a trustee in respect thereto, and might avail of the statute. In Baubien v. Baubien, 64 U. S. (23 How.) 190, 16 L. Ed. 484, the court says, "In cases of an implied trust to be raised by evidence, equity obeys the statute." McDowell v. Goldsmith, 6 Md. 319; Lloyd v. Currin, 22 Ten. (3 Humph) 462; Murdock v. Hughes, 15 Miss. 219; Armstrong v. Campbell, 11 Tenn. (3 Yerg.) 201; Harlow v. Dehon, 111 Mass. 195; Manion v. Titsworth, 57 Ky. (18 B. Mon.) 582; Haynie v. Hall, 24 Tenn. (5 Humph.) 290; Sheppards v. Turpin, 3 Gratt. (Va.) 373; Cuyler v. Bradt, 2 Cai. Cas. (N. Y.) 326. The time generally fixed for enforcement of trust claims has been twenty years, but in some cases a shorter period is sufficient, and in others a longer one will not protect the trustee. In Phillips v. Holman, 26 Tex. 276, it was held that a contract wherein P. assigned and transferred to H. certain stock certificates, in trust to be disposed of according to H.'s best judgment, P. to receive thereupon the original cost and half the profits realized, with no stated time for performance and account, did not create that kind of "technical and continuing" trust which cannot be affected by the statute of limitations, and it devolved on H. to perform the obligation and account within a reasonable time. Lapse of time does not bar express trusts; especially where the trustee and those claiming under him have not asserted an adverse claim above two years, although the *cestui que trust* has neglected to claim the benefit of the trust for nearly forty years before. Pinson v. Ivey, 9 Tenn. (1 Yerg.) 296. In Alabama it is held that the lapse of twenty years without any acknowledgment of the existence of the trust will constitute a presumptive bar to a proceeding of a legatee or distributee for a settlement of the estate; but that time is to be computed from the time when a settlement could first have been compelled, and not from the date of the trust, and that the running of the statute in favor of the sureties of an executor or administrator does not bring him within the statute, as there is no statutory limitation to a

action,[4] and the statute is as complete a bar in equity as at law. Courts of equity have always refused to assist a person who has slept upon his rights and shows no excuse for his laches in asserting them, and this is so, independent of any statute of limitations. Laches and neglect always have been discountenanced in equity.[5] When the bill shows upon its face that the plaintiff, by reason of lapse of time and of his own laches, is not entitled to relief, the objection may be taken by demurrer.[6] Therefore a trust, in

trust. Greenlees v. Greenlees, 62 Ala. 336. But where there is a violation of the terms of a trust, a right of action accrues at once, and the statute begins to run thereon from that time. Wilson v. Greene, 49 Iowa 251.

4. Speidel v. Henrici, 120 U. S. 377, 7 Sup. Ct. 610, 30 L. Ed. 718. In Loring v. Palmer, 118 U. S. 321, 6 Sup. Ct. 1073, 30 L. Ed. 211, it was held that laches could not be set up to defeat an equitable action where the delay was induced by the fraud on the part of the person setting it up.

5. Smith v. Clay, 3 Bro. Ch. 640; Piatt v. Vattier, 34 U. S. (9 Pet.) 405, 9 L. Ed. 173; McKnight v. Taylor, 42 U. S. (1 How.) 161, 11 L. Ed. 86; Bowman v. Wathen, 42 U. S. (1 How.) 189, 11 L. Ed. 97; Wagner v. Baird, 48 U. S. (7 How.) 234, 12 L. Ed. 681; Badger v. Badger, 69 U. S. (2 Wall.) 87, 17 L. Ed. 836; Marsh v. Whitmore, 88 U. S. (21 Wall.) 178, 22 L. Ed. 482; Sullivan v. Portland & K. R. Co., 94 U. S. 806, 24 L. Ed. 324; Godden v. Kimmell, 99 U. S. 201, 25 L. Ed. 431. In Hume v. Beale's Ex'x, 84 U. S. (17 Wall.) 336, 348, 21 L. Ed. 602, the court, in dismissing, because of an unexplained delay in suing, a bill by *cestui que trust* against a trustee under a deed, observed that it was not important to determine whether he was the trustee of a mere dry, legal estate, or whether his duties and responsibilities extended further. See also Bright v. Legerton, 29 Beav. 60, and 2 De Gex, F. & J. 606.

6. Maxwell v. Kennedy, 49 U. S. (8 How.) 210, 12 L. Ed. 1051; National Bank v. Carpenter, 101 U. S. 567, 25 L. Ed. 815; Lansdale v. Smith, 106 U. S. 391, 1 Sup. Ct. 350, 27 L. Ed. 219.

The established rule now is, in the Federal courts and in Massachusetts and other States, that the defense of laches appearing on the face of the bill, may be taken by demurrer, but it need not be so taken, as the court will notice it, though not pleaded at all. Taylor v. Holmes, 127 U. S. 489, 8 Sup. Ct. 1192, 32, L. Ed. 179; Norris v. Haggin, 136 U. S. 386, 10 Sup. Ct. 942, 34 L. Ed. 424; Lant v. Manley, 71 Fed. 7, 16; Dawkins v. Penrylın, 4 A. C. 51; Noyes v. Crawley, 10 Ch. D. 31; Rolfe v. Gregory, 31 L. J. Ch. 710; French v. Dickey, 3 Tenn. Ch. 302; Bell v. Johnson, 111 Ill. 374; *supra*, § 7; Fogg v. Price, 145 Mass. 513, 14 N. E. 471; Snow v. Boston Blank Book Manuf. Co., 153 Mass. 456, 26

order to be exempt from the operation of the statute, must be direct or express, and of a nature not cognizable at law, but solely in equity.[7] If this limitation was not imposed, and the statute was not permitted to operate where an implied trust exists, the exceptions would so be endless, as, in fact, every case of deposit or bailment in a certain sense creates a trust, and the instances in which an implied trust may be raised are almost innumerable; and there is much wisdom in the rule that restricts the saving operation of the statute to those express and continuing trusts which are not cognizable at law, and where the plaintiff has no legal title, the estate being vested in the trustee.[8] Strictly speak-

N. E. 1116. In the last of these cases it was held that the withdrawal or waiver of a demurrer in equity, which assigned laches as one ground thereof, did not waive this defense.

7. Clay v. Clay, 70 Ky. (7 Bush) 95; Hayward v. Gunn, *supra;* Mcclane v. Shepherd, 21 N. J. Eq. 76; Partridge v. Wall, *supra.* In Harlow v. Dehon, 111 Mass. 195, an instrument under seal, signed by P. and W., reciting that P. has received from the executors of the estate of W's father $2,000, and covenanting that until P. invests the sum as a special trust fund he will pay interest thereon to W.; and when the sum is so invested, pay W. the income thereof, and, on the death of W., pay over the same, or the proceeds thereof, to W.'s administrator; and, in case of P.'s death before W., P.'s executors are to execute the same trust — was construed to constitute at most only a constructive trust, and to be barred by the lapse of six years from the appointment of W.'s administrator. Galvin's Estate, Myrick's Prob. (Cal.) 82. In Maine, under the statute, it has been held that a bill against heirs for a specific performance of a contract to convey land does not apply to a trust evidenced in writing. Frost v. Frost, 63 Me. 399. In McGuire v. Linneus, 74 Me. 344, it was held that where a town holds money belonging to an individual, the statute does not begin to run against the *cestui que trust* until it has announced its intention to hold it adversely. In Hamer v. Sidway, 124 N. Y. 538, 27 N. E. 256, 12 L. R. A. 463, 21 Am. St. Rep. 693, where S. died in 1887 without having paid any portion of the sum agreed upon, it was held that, under an agreement made in 1875, the relation of the parties thereafter was not that of debtor and creditor, but of trustee and *cestui que trust;* and that, therefore, the claim was not barred. See Mallory v. Gillett, 21 N. Y. 412; Belknap v. Bender, 75 N. Y. 466, 31 Am. Rep. 476; Berry v. Brown, 107 N. Y. 659, 14 N. E. 289; Beaumont v. Reeve, Shirley's L. C. 6; Porterfield v. Butler, 47 Miss. 165; Duvoll v. Wilson, 9 Barb. 487; Robinson v. Jewett, 116 N. Y. 40, 22 N. E. 224.

8. Lockey v. Lockey, Prec. Ch. 518; Lawly v. Lawly, 9 Mod. 32; Cholmondeley v. Clinton, 2 Jac. & W. 171;

ing, in their technical sense, trusts are known only in equity, and

Blount v. Robeson, 56 N. C. (3 Jones Eq.) 14; Tucker v. Tucker, 1 McCord (S. C.) Ch. 176; Burham v. James, 1 Speers (S. C.) Eq. 375; Farnam v. Brooks, 26 Mass. (9 Pick.) 212; Finney v. Cocrran, 1 W. & S. (Pa.) 118; Johnston v. Humphrys, 14 S. & R. (Pa.) 394; Walker v. Walker, 16 id. 379; Culbert v. Fleming, 5 Leg. & Ins. Rep. 19; Fox v. Lyon 33 Pa. 474; Clark v. Trindle, 52 id. 492; Best v. Campbell, 62 id. 476; Mussey v. Mussey, 2 Hill (S. C.) Eq. 496; McDowell v. Goldsmith, 6 Md. 319; Sayles v. Tibbitts, 5 R. I. 79; Marsh v. Oliver, 1 N. J. Eq. 209; Martin v. Decatur Branch Bank, 31 Ala. 115.

Suit by a *cestui que trust* against his trustee, when the trust is express and cognizable only in equity, are usually not within the statute of limitations as applied in equity, since the trustee's possession is ordinarily the possession of the *cestui;* and as their attitude towards each other is not hostile or antagonistic, there is no cause of action to be barred. Dyer v. Waters, 46 N. J. Eq. 484, 19 Atl. 129; Ryder v. Loomis, 161 Mass. 161, 36 N. E. 836; Low v. Low, 173 Mass. 580, 54 N. E. 257; Cone v. Dunham, 8 L. R. A. 647, and note. But when the trustee of an express trust has assumed a hostile attitude against the *cestui* by denying his right or disavowing the trust, or has committed a breach of trust causing loss to the estate, which has come to the *cestui's* knowledge, and has refused to make it good, the *cestui* has, by the weight of authority, a present cause of action as to which the statute of limitations will run, although numerous authorities hold that the statute does not run in equity, even against such a breach of an express trust. See Soar v. Ashwell, [1893] 2 Q. B. 390; Lindsley v. Dodd, 53 N. J. Eq. 69; Treadwell v. Treadwell, 176 Mass. 554. When, however, the trust arises merely by implication of law, laches may bar relief, as where beneficiaries delayed for thirteen years after knowledge of the trustee's misappropriation of the trust funds to take action against those who had received the funds, they were held to be deprived, by their laches, of the right to follow the trust funds. McLaflin v. Jones, 155 Ill. 539, 40 N. E. 330. See Gillette v. Wiley, 126 Ill. 310, 19 N. E. 287, 9 Am. St. Rep. 587; Le Gendre v. Byrnes, 44 N. J. Eq. 372, 14 Atl. 621; Kennedy v. Winn, 80 Ala. 165; Day v. Brenton, 102 Iowa 482, 63 Am. St. Rep. 460, 475, note, 71 N. W. 538.

A *cestui que trust* who appeals for relief to a court of equity must specifically set forth in his bill what were the impediments to an earlier prosecution of his claim; how he came to be so long ignorant of his rights, the means used by the respondent to fraudulently keep him in ignorance, and how and when he first came to a knowledge of the matters alleged in the bill. Badger v. Badger, 69 U. S. (2 Wall.) 87, 95, 17 L. Ed. 836; Hardt v. Heidweyer, 152 U. S. 547, 559, 14 Sup. Ct. 671, 38 L. Ed. 548; Teall v. Slaven, 14 Sawyer (U. S.) 364. In Ames v. Brooks, 143 Mass. 344, 9 N. E. 737, the beneficiary's delay in enforcing a trustee's personal liability was held not to affect his right to receive the trust fund when collected by the trustee.

fall within its peculiar and exclusive jurisdiction; and this class of trusts, so long as they continue, as between trustee and *cestui que trust* cannot be reached by the statute of limitations.[9] This doctrine rests upon the case of Cholmondeley v. Clinton, before

9. Story, J., in Baker v. Whiting, 3 Sum. (U. S. C. C.) 486; Kane v. Bloodgood, *supra;* Partridge v. Wells, 30 N. J. Eq. 176; Greenwood v. Greenwood, 5 Md. 334; Lowe v. Watkins, 40 Cal. 547; Bourne v. Hall, 10 R. I. 144; Baylor v. Digarnette, 13 Gratt. (Va.) 152; Hostetter v. Hollinger, 117 Pa. 606; Collard v. Tuttle, 4 Vt. 491; People v. Oran, 121 Ill. 650; Buckingham v. Ludlam, 37 N. J. Eq. 144; McClane v. Shepherd, 21 id. 76. No lapse of time bars a direct trust until it is repudiated, because until that time no right of action accrues to the *cestui que trust.* Robinson v. Robinson, 5 Lans (N. Y.) 165; Bigelow v. Catlin, 50 Vt. 410. In Rushing v. Rushing, 42 N. J. Eq. 594, it was held that the statute did not apply where the *cestui* is the wife of the trustee. In Comstock's App., 55 Conn. 214, the court held that money received by the husband from his wife's separate estate was received by him as statutory trustee, and therefore that the statute did not run in his favor.

While the trustee, who has never repudiated his trust, is in possession of the trust estate the statute does not run. Gilbert v. Sleeper, 71 Cal. 290; Humphrey v. Clearfield Co. Nat. Bank, 113 Pa. 417. In Price v. Mulford, 107 N. Y. 303, 14 N. E. 298, *reversing* 36 Hun, 247, it was held that where one receiving money in his own right is afterwards by evidence or construction changed into a trustee, he may plead the statute of limitations as a bar in an action to recover the money.

In Hovenden v. Annesley, 2 Sch. & Lef. 607, Lord Redesdale thus states the reason for this rule: "If a trustee is in possession, and does not execute his trust, the possession of the trustee is the possession of the *cestui que trust;* and if the only circumstance is that he does not perform his trust, his possession operates nothing as a bar, because his possession is according to his title." This doctrine is in obedience to the rule that equity will give effect to the statute of limitations in all cases where there is a concurrent jurisdiction at law and in equity. Roosevelt v. Mark, 6 Johns. (N. Y.) Ch. 266; Mann v. Fairchild, 2 Keyes (N. Y.) 106; Prevost v. Gratz, 19 U. S. (6 Wheat.) 481, 5 L. Ed. 311; Union Pac. Railroad Co. v. Durant, 95 U. S. 576, 24 L. Ed. 391; Lewis v. Hawkins, 23 Wall. (U. S.) 119; Atty.-Gen. v. Purmont, 5 Paige (N. Y.) Ch. 620; Clark v. Ford, 3 Keyes (N. Y.) 170; Stafford v. Bryan, 1 Paige (N. Y.) Ch. 239; Spoor v. Wells, 3 Barb. (N. Y.) Ch. 199; Lindsay v. Hyatt, 4 Edw. (N. Y.) Ch. 97; Frost v. Frost, id. 733.

A solicitor to a trust, into whose hands the trustees have permitted the trust funds to come, is in position of an express trustee as to such funds; or, if regarded as a stranger to the trust, having received the money under a breach of trust in which he concurred, his trust is still

cited, and has been universally adopted in the courts of this country, as well as in England, ever since.

The reason why express trusts are treated as not being within the statute of limitations is because the possession of the trustee is presumed to be the possession of the *cestui que trust.*[10]

But to this rule there is this qualification, and that is, that when the trustee openly disavows the trust, and clearly and unequivocally sets up a right and interest adverse to the *cestui que trust,* and which is made known to the latter, the statute begins to run in his favor.[11]

express, as he has assumed to act and has acted as a trustee. Soar v. Ashwell, [1893] 2 Q. B. 390. See Heynes v. Dixon, [1900] 2 Ch. 561; *In re* Lands Allotment Co., [1894] 1 Ch. 616. A cause of action for negligence and concealment in advising a client to invest on a mortgage dates, as to limitation, from the time of the negligent act, and the duty to disclose does not continue from day to day. Wood v. Jones, 61 L. T. 551.

10. Union Pac. R. R. Co. v. Durant, 95 U. S. 576, 24 L. Ed. 391; Prevost v. Gratz, 19 U. S. (6 Wheat) 481, 5 L. Ed. 311; Speidel v. Henrici, 120 U. S. 377, 7 Sup. Ct. 610, 30 L. Ed. 718.

11. Philippi v. Philippi, 115 U. S. 151, 5 Sup. Ct. 1181, 29 L. Ed. 336; Willison v. Watkins, 28 U. S. (3 Pet.) 43, 7 L. Ed. 596; Bacon v. Rives, 106 U. S. 99, 1 Sup. Ct. 3, 27 L. Ed. 69; Oliver v. Piatt, 44 U. S. (3 How.) 333, 11 L. Ed. 622; Kane v. Bloodgood, 7 John. Ch. (N. Y.) 90; Robinson v. Hook, 4 Mason (U. S.) 139; Boone v. Chiles, 35 U. S. (10 Pet.) 177, 9 L. Ed. 388; Seymour v. Freer, 75 U. S. (8 Wall.) 202, 19 L. Ed. 306. In Speidel v. Henrici, 120 U. S. 377, 7 Sup. Ct. 610, 30 L. Ed. 718, Mr. Justice Gray says: "As a general rule, doubtless, length of time is no bar to a trust clearly established, and express trusts are not within the statute of limitations, because the possession of the trustee is presumed to be the possession of his *cestui que trust.* Prevost v. Gratz, 19 U. S. (6 Wheat.) 481, 5 L. Ed. 311; Lewis v. Hawkins, 90 U. S. (23 Wall.) 119; 23 L. Ed. 113; Union Pac. R. R. Co. v. Durant, 95 U. S. 576, 24 L. Ed. 391. But this rule is in accordance with the reason on which it is founded, and, as has been clearly pointed out by Chancellor Kent and Mr. Justice Story, subject to this qualification: that time begins to run against a trust as soon as it is openly disavowed by the trustee, insisting upon an adverse right and interest which is clearly and unequivocally made known to the *cestui que trust* as when, for instance such transactions take place between the trustee and the *cestui que trust* as would in case of tenants in common amount to an ouster of one of them by the other." Kane v. Bloodgood, 7. Johns. Ch. 90; Robinson v. Hook, 4 Mason (U. S.), 139, 152; Baker v. Whiting, 3 Sumn. (U.

§ 201. Express trusts.

An express trust must be actually expressed in terms by deed, will, or some writing, or in some manner so as to vest the legal estate in the trustee. In an English case,[12] Lord Westbury said that "to create an express trust two things must combine,—there must be a trustee with an express trust, and an estate or interest vested in the trustee." To create an express trust in lands, under the statute of frauds, it must be created, *or evidenced* in writing;[13] and if it is not created in writing, it must be proved by a writing under the hands of the party to be charged.[14] In Vermont, it is

S.) 475, 486; Oliver v. Piatt, 44 U. S. (3 How.) 333, 11 L. Ed. 622.

See *In re* Davis, [1891] 3 Ch. 9; *In re* Barker, [1892] 2 Ch. 491; Riddle v. Whitehill, 135 U. S. 621, 10 Sup. Ct., 924, 34 L. Ed. 283; Alsop v. Riker, 155 U. S. 448, 460, 15 Sup. Ct. 162, 39 L. Ed. 218; Gildersleeve v. New Mexico Mining Co., 161 U. S. 573, 16 Sup. Ct. 663, 40 L. Ed. 812; Whitney v. Fox, 166 U. S. 637, 17 Sup. Ct. 713, 41 L. Ed. 1145, *supra*, § 58, note 1.

The statute of limitations does not begin to run in favor of a trustee against the *cestui que trust* until the former has repudiated the trust, and knowledge of the repudiation has come home to the latter. Childs v. Jordan, 106 Mass. 321; Jones v. Mc. Dermott, 114 Mass. 400; Davis v. Coburn, 128 Mass. 377; French v. Merrill, 132 Mass. 528; Dickinson v. Leominster Savings Bank, 152 Mass. 49, 25 N. E. 12, 2 Perry on Trusts (5th ed.), §§ 863, 865, and notes. As the statute of limitations does not extinguish a debt, so it does not affect a trust created for its payment, so long as the trust subsists. Campbell v. Maple, 105 Pa. 304, 307; Townsend v. Tyndale, 165 Mass. 293, 43 N. E. 107, 52 Am. St. Rep. 513. But a trustee's claim, known to the beneficiary, that he has fully accounted for and turned over the trust property that was in his possession, must be attended to, as limitation against a claim upon the trustee to account commences to run from the time of such knowledge. Wolf v. Wolf, 97 Iowa, 279, 66 N. W. 170, in which case the plaintiff placed his property with another for payment of his debts. See Jones v. Home Savings Bank, 118 Mich. 155, 76 N. W. 322, 74 Am. St. Rep. 377.

A savings bank so far holds a trust relation to its depositors that when it sets up the fact of a demand and notice in its own defense, and not the want thereof, six years before action brought, it must show a denial or repudiation of liability on its part. Dickinson v. Leominster Savings Bank, *supra*. See Campbell v. Whoriskey, 170 Mass. 63, 48 N. E. 1070.

12. Dickinson v. Teasdale, 1 De G. & J. Sm. 52. See *In re* Frazer, 92 N. Y. 239.

13. Hovey v. Holcomb, 11 Ill. 660; Eldridge v. See Yup Co., 17 Cal. 44.

14. Unitarian Society v. Woodbury, 14 Me. 281; Brown v. Brown, 1

held that an express trust, except in lands, may be created without writing;[15] and generally it may be said that trusts in personal property may be created and proved by parol,[16] and so, also, a mere resulting or constructive trust may be established by parol,[17] as the statute of frauds has no application to it,[18] even though it relates to real estate; and where land is purchased in the name of one person, and the consideration is paid by another, the person in whose name the deed is taken holds the land in trust for the person who furnished the money, and the trust may be established by parol;[19] but not where the person taking the conveyance

Strobh. (S. C.) Eq. 363; Maccabbin v. Cromwell, 7 G. & J. (Md.) 157; Hertle v. McDonald, 2 Md. Ch. 128; Rutledge v. Smith, 1 McCord (S. C.) Ch. 119; Wright v. King, Harr. (Mich.) Ch. 12; Riggs v. Swan, 59 N. C. (6 Jones Eq.) 118; Steere v. Steere, 5 Johns. (N. Y.) Ch. 1; James v. Fulcrod, 5 Tex. 512; Peaslee v. Barney, 1 D. Chip. (Vt.) 331; Lane v. Ewing, 31 Miss. 73.

15. Porter v. Bank of Rutland, 19 Vt. 410.

16. Kirkpatrick v. Davidson, 2 Ga. 297; Saunders v. Harris, 38 Tenn. (1 Head) 185; Gordon v. Gordon, 10 Ga. 534; Kimball v. Morton, 5 N. J. Eq. 26; Hooper v. Holmes, 11 id. 122; Higgenbottom v. Peyton, 3 Rich. (S. C.) Eq. 398; Day v. Roth, 18 N. Y. 448.

17. Hovey v. Holcomb, 11 Ill. 660; Enos v. Hunter, 9 id. 211; Farringer v. Ramsay, 4 Md. Ch. 33; Slaymaker v. St. John, 5 Watts (Pa.) 27; Kelly v. Mills, 41 Mo. 267; Farrington v. Barr, 36 N. H. 86; Cloud v. Ivie, 28 Mo. 578.

18. Peabody v. Tarbell, 56 Mass. (2 Cush.) 226; Leakey v. Gunter, 25 Tex. 400; Dean v. Dean, 6 Conn. 285; Caple v. McCollum, 27 Ala. 461; McGuire v. Ramsey, 9 Ark. 518; Hauff v. Howard, 56 S. C. (3 Jones Eq.) 440; Jackson v. Matsdorf, 11 Johns. (N. Y.) 91.

19. Barron v. Barron, 24 Vt. 375; Osborne v. Endicott, 6 Cal. 149; Bayles v. Baxter, 22 id. 575; Millard v. Hathaway, 27 id. 119; Smith v. Strahan, 16 Tex. 314; Neill v. Keith, 5 id. 23; Lang v. Steiger, 8 id. 460; Strimpfler v. Roberts, 18 Pa. 283; Lynch v. Cox, 23 id. 265; Lyford v. Thurston, 16 N. H. 399; Bruce v. Roney, 18 Ill. 67; Smith v. Sackett, 10 id. 534; Page v. Page, 8 N. H. 187; Johnson v. Dougherty, 18 N. J. Eq. 406; Williams v. Hollingsworth, 1 Strobh. (S. C.) Eq. 103; Thomas v. Walker, 25 Tenn. (6 Humph.) 93; Taliaferro v. Taliaferro, 6 Ala. 404; Dorsey v. Clarke, 4 H. & J. (Md.) 551; Claussen v. La Franz, 2 Iowa, 437; Murdock v. Hughes, 15 Miss. 219; Paul v. Chouteau, 14 Mo. 580; Hollis v. Hayes, 1 Md. Ch. 479; Bank v. Carrington, 7 Leigh (Va.) 566; Creed v. Lancaster Bank, 1 Ohio St. 1; Ragan v. Walker, 1 Wis. 527; Pinney v. Fellows, 15 Vt. 525.

also furnishes the money to pay for the same,[20] nor where a person conveys land to another absolutely, under an agreement that he shall reconvey upon request.[21] "A trust," says the court in Massachusetts,[22] "must result, if at all, at the instant the deed passes," and this is the general rule.[23] Where it is attempted to avoid the bar of the statute on the ground that the possession of the defendant is fiduciary it must be shown that it is fiduciary in respect to the plaintiff, or those under whom he claims; it is not sufficient that it is fiduciary as to a third person.[24]

§ 202. Assignees in bankruptcy, insolvency, etc.

It is held that an assignee in bankruptcy, after the property of the bankrupt is vested in him, becomes a trustee for the creditors, and from that time the statute ceases to run against them.[25] The

20. Dorsey v. Clarke, 4 H. & J. (Md.) 551; Fawke v. Slaughter, 10 Ky. (3 A. K. Mar.) 56. In sample v. Coulson, 9 W. & S. (Pa.) 62, held that a trust in lands cannot be established by the proof of parol declarations made by the purchasers of land at or after the sale. Gee v. Gee, 32 Miss. 190; Francestown v. Deering, 41 N. H. 438; Pinnock v. Clough, 16 Vt. 500; Alexander v. Tams, 13 Ill. 221; Cutter v. Tuttle, 19 N. J. Eq. 549: Barnet v. Dougherty, 32 Pa. 371; Barnard v. Jewett, 97 Mass. 87; Steere v. Steere, 5 Johns. (N. Y.) Ch. 1; Bernard v. Bougard, Harr. (Mich.) 130; Forsyth v. Clark, 3 Wend. (N. Y.) 637; Mahorner v. Harrison, 21 Miss. 53; Rogers v. Murray, 3 Paige (N. Y.) Ch. 390; Perry v. McHenry, 13 Ill. 227; Botsford v. Burr, 2 Johns. (N. Y.) Ch. 205; Foster v. Trustees, 3 Ala. 302. If several persons furnish each a part of the purchase money, a trust arises in favor of each in proportion to the amount of the consideration furnished by him. Tebbetts v. Tilton, 31 N. H. 273; Baumgartner v. Guessfeld, 38 Mo. 36; Pinney v. Fellows, 15 Vt. 525; Chadwick v. Felt, 35 Pa. 305; Buck v. Swazey, 35 Me. 41; Shoemaker v. Smith, 30 Tenn. (11 Humph.) 81. But it is held that the part payment must be a definite part of the purchase money, as one-half, one-third, or the like. Sayre v. Townsend, 15 Wend. (N. Y.) 647.

21. Dean v. Dean, 6 Conn. 285; Titcomb v. Morrill, 92 Mass. (10 Allen) 15.

22. Gould v. Lynde, 114 Mass. 366.

23. Midmer v. Midmer, 26 N. J. Eq. 299; Sale v. McLean, 29 Ark. 612; Payne v. Patterson, 77 Pa. 124.

24. Spotswood v. Dandridge, 4 H. & M. (Va.) 139.

25. *Ex parte* Ross, 2 Glyn & Jam. 46, where, upon appeal, the Lord Chancellor said: "The effect of the commission is clearly to vest the property in the assignees for the

same rule also applies to insolvent debtors who avail themselves of insolvency statutes, or who are forced into insolvency by their creditors, and the statute is suspended from the time when notice of the proceedings is given in the manner provided by law.[26] So, too, this rule applies when an insolvent debtor makes an assignment under the statute for the benefit of his creditors, and it is held in such cases that the statute ceases to run from the date of the assignment.[27] The discharge of a debtor under insolvent laws does not suspend the running of the statute in his favor.[28]

benefit of creditors, and therefore they are in effect trustees; and it is an admitted rule that unless debts are already barred by the statute of limitations when the trust is created, it is not afterwards affected by lapse of time." See *In re* Eldridge, 12 Nat. Br. No. 12, 1875.

26. Minot v. Thacher, 48 Mass. (7 Met.) 348. In all cases of concurrent jurisdiction, where a party has a legal and equitable remedy in regard to the same subject-matter, courts of equity obey the law, and give to the statute the same effect and operation in the one court as in the other. Dugan v. Gittings, 3 Gill (Md.) 138; Hertle v. Schwartze, 3 Md. 366; Kane v. Bloodgood, 7 Johns. (N. Y.) Ch. 90; *In re* Leiman, 32 Md. 225, 3 Am. Rep. 132. By the insolvent laws of Maryland property vested in the trustee is no longer within the reach of process by the creditors, and the insolvent, being discharged from the payment of his debts, is no longer liable to suit, and the trustee being answerable only for a breach of trust, no proceedings can be instituted against him until the ratification of the audit, because, until then, and notice thereof, he is not guilty of a breach of trust. See Wiliams v. Williams, 3 Md. 163; Buckey v. Culler, 18 id. 418; *Ex parte* Ross, 2 Glyn & Jam. 46; Minot v. Thayer, 48 Mass. (7 Met.) 348. In Strike's Case, 1 Bland (Va.) 57, where the proceeding was to set aside certain fraudulent conveyances, and for a sale of the property for the benefit of creditors, and although in the disposition of some of the questions which arose, the Chancellor likened it to a case of insolvency, the distinct question in regard to the statute of limitations raised by these appeals did not arise, and cannot be said to have been directly passed upon. This question was decided in Strike v. McDonald & Son, 2 H. & G. (Md.) 191.

27. Willard v. Clark, 48 Mass. (7 Met.) 435. In Heckert's Appeal, 24 Pa. 482, the court held that an assignment for the benefit of creditors is a trust exclusively cognizable in equity and that the trustee could not interpose the statute of limitations to the claim of a creditor.

28. Shoenberger v. Adams, 4 Watts (Pa.) 430; Gest v. Heiskill, 5 Rawle (Pa.) 134; West v. Creditors, 1 La. An. 365.

§ 203. Cestui que trust in possession.

Where a *cestui que trust* under an express trust is in possession of the trust estate, he is held to occupy the relation of tenant at will to the trustee,[29] and consequently no lapse of time will give him a title as against the trustee.[30] But this rule only holds as between the trustee and *cestui que trust,* and does not apply where an assignee of the *cestui que trust,* or other person claiming under him, is in possession, as such persons are not precluded by the fact that the property is subject to a trust from availing themselves of the benefit of the statute;[31] nor does it apply to a constructive trustee in possession, as a purchaser holding under an agreement to purchase. This latter doctrine was affirmed in a case before the United States Supreme Court,[32] and the court say: "Equity makes the vendor without deed a trustee for the vendee for the conveyance of the title; the vendee is a trustee for the payment of the purchase money, and the performance of the terms of the purchase. But the vendee is in no sense the trustee of the vendor as to the possession of the property sold. The vendee claims and holds it of his own right, for his own benefit, subject to no right of the vendor, save the terms which the contract expresses; his possession is therefore adverse as to the property, but friendly as to the performance of the conditions of the purchase." [33] The vendor of lands under an executory contract, having performed, holds the lands in trust for the vendee, and continues to do so until he manifests an intention to hold them as his own;[34] and

29. Freeman v. Barnes, 1 Vent. 86.

30. Reade v. Reade, 8 T. R. 118; Keen v. Deardon, 8 East, 248; Pomfret v. Windsor, 2 Ves. 272; Smith v. King, 16 East 283; Garrard v. Tuck, 8 C. B. 231; Burrell v. Egremont, 7 Beav. 205; Jacobs v. Phillips, 10 Q. B. 130.

31. Melling v. Leake, 16 C. B. 652; Stanway v. Rock, 4 M. & G. 30.

32. Blight's Lessee v. Rochester, 20 U. S. (7 Wheat.) 535, 5 L. Ed. 516; Stanway v. Rock, *supra.*

33. In Garrard v. Tuck, 8 C. B. 231, under the Statute 3 & 4 Wm. IV., it it said: "The object of the statute is to settle the rights of persons adversely litigating, not to deal with cases of trustee and *cestui que trust,* where there is but one simple interest, viz., that of the person beneficially interested."

34. Hemming v. Zimmerschitte, 4

the same rule prevails as to one who enters into possession under a contract to purchase [35] until after the purchase money is due, and from that period the statute begins to run in his favor.[36] If a portion of trust funds, the income of which is to be paid to a married woman for her life, and after her death to her husband for his life, with remainder over of the principal fund, is lent to the husband upon his note, payable with interest semi-annually, and it is agreed by all the parties that the trustee shall not collect the interest, in order to avoid the trouble of receiving the same from the husband and paying it over to the wife, and in pursuance of this agreement the trustee omits for more than six years to collect the interest, the note is not thereby barred by the statute of limitations; but the trustee may set off the same in equity, after the wife's death, against a claim of the husband for the income.[37]

§ 204. Guardians.

While the relation of guardian and ward subsists, the guardian stands in the relation of trustee to the ward, and the statute is not applicable to his account;[38] and even after the relation is terminated, it has been held that the statute will not bar a guardian's claim against his ward if the delay is sufficiently explained;[39] but there would seem to be no good ground for such a doctrine, and the better rule seems to be that the statute begins to run from the termination of the guardianship,[40] ex-

Tex. 159. The rule is that after a sale of real estate, and before a conveyance, the vendor is trustee of the legal title for the vendee; and the vendor's possession, while it can be reasonably supposed to be in accordance with the trust, will be construed to be that of the vendee, and the statute of limitations will not operate. Graham v. Nelson, 24 Tenn. (5 Humph.) 605.

35. Richardson v. Broughton, 2 N. & M. (S. C.) 417; Richards v. M'Kie, 1 Harp. (S. C.) Ch. 184.

36. Ray v. Goodman, 33 Tenn. (1 Sneed) 586.

37. Upham v. Wyman, 89 Mass. (7 Allen) 499.

38. Kimball v. Ives, 17 Vt. 430; Mathes v. Bennett, 21 N. H. 204.

39. Kimball v. Ives, *supra*.

40. Taylor v. Kilgore, 33 Ala. 214.

cept in cases where the cause of action arises from matters occurring after the guardianship has ceased.[41]

§ 205. Executors as trustees.

Executors are technically trustees of the property of their testator, and consequently cannot, as against the beneficiaries under the will, set up the statute of limitations to bar their claims, so long as the relation exists.[42]

A legacy may be so held as to be a trust and where the executor has become a trustee of a legacy for the legatee the ordinary rules that exist between trustee and *cestui que trust* apply and the legatee will not be barred by any lapse of time.[43] This happens more readily in the case where the executor is also expressly a trustee than where he is simply executor. Where an executor upon trust, who has therefore the double character of executor and trustee, has set apart and appropriated a sum to satisfy a certain legacy, he is considered to have changed the character of executor for that of trustee,[44] as much as if he had been trustee only, and a different person as executor had transferred to him the money. In a case before cited,[45] an executor upon trust had assented to a specific legacy, and it was held that the legacy

41. Shearman v. Akins, 21 Mass. (4 Pick.) 283.

42. Norris's Appeal, 71 Pa. 106; Arden v. Arden, 1 Johns. (N. Y.) Ch. 313; Decouche v. Savetier, 3 id. 190; Dillebaugh's Estate, 4 Watts (Pa.) 177; Ward v. Reeder, 2 H. & M. (Md.) 145; Dundon v. Gaskill, 2 Yeates (Pa.) 271.

Length of time and neglect on the part of the *cestui que trust* furnish a rebuttable presumption that an executor or administrator has paid over to and distributed among those entitled to them the funds and property in his hands. Fuller v. Cushman, 170 Mass. 286, 49 N. E. 631. This does not depend upon the statute of limitations, but upon the rule that, independently of that statute equity will not assist a person who has slept upon his rights, and has acquiesced for a great length of time. St. Paul's Church v. Atty.-Gen., 164 Mass. 188, 200, 41 N. E. 231; see *supra*, §§ 58-60, and notes.

43. Phillipo v. Munnings, 2 Myl. & Cr. 309.

44. Byrchall v. Bradford, 6 Madd. 13, 235; Dix v. Burford, 19 Beav. 409; Brougham v. Poulett, 19 Beav. 133.

45. Dix v. Burford, *supra*.

became thereby clothed with a trust. An executor in trust becomes a trustee of a residue as soon as it is ascertained,[46] and he may be a trustee either by virtue of the wording of the will, or by implication arising from his acts. In the latter case, if the legacy is bequeathed simply, yet the executor may make himself a trustee by implication, by appointing assets for a particular legacy, although, as a fact, in most of the cases the executor had been made a trustee by the terms of the will.

The reason why an executor should not be permitted to set up the statute to bar a legacy is because his retention of the money is consistent with the capacity in which he holds it, and indicates no intention on his part to claim it as his own.[47] But if an executor should give notice to a legatee that unless a legacy was claimed within a certain period he would not pay it, after the lapse of that period the statute would undoubtedly run in his favor, because from that time he is treated as having disavowed his trust,[48] as such notice would be equivalent to a notice that from that time he should hold the funds adversely.[49] Long delay in making a demand for a legacy, when the party entitled knows of his rights thereto, raises a presumption, either that it has been paid to him, or that he intended to relinquish his claim to it.[50]

46. Willmott v Jenkins, 1 Beav. 401; *Ex Parte* Dover, 5 Sim. 500; Davenport v. Stafford, 14 Beav. 319, 331; Dinsdale v. Dudding, 1 Y. & C. Ch. 265; Freeman v. Dowding, 2 Jur. N. S. 1014; Downes v. Bullock, 25 Beav. 54; Bullock v. Downes, 9 H. L. C. 1. In Tyson v. Jackson, 30 Beav. 384, Romilly, M. R., said: "It is clear, when an executor retains the money for payment of the legacy, that he becomes, as in the case of Phillipo v. Munnings, a trustee of the particular fund or sum of money retained distinctly from his character of executor. It is as distinct as if the testator had directed his executor to pay the legacy over to A. B. in trust for the legatee, and it had actually been paid over. A. B. would then be a trustee for the legatee. So, too, the executor, when he has retained that sum of money, is in exactly the same situation." See *Ex parte* Dover, 5 Sim. 500.

47. Kane v. Bloodgood, *supra*. ...

48. Robson v. Jones, 27 Ga. 266.

49. Robson v. Jones, *supra;* Lewis v. Castleman, 27 Tex. 407; Coleman v. Davis, 2 Strobh. (S. C.) 334.

50. Thompson v. M'Gaw, 2 Watts (Pa) 161; Higgins v. Crawford, 2 Ves. Jr. 572; Parker v. Ash, 1 Vern. 256. Thus, where a hill to recover a

But each case depends upon its peculiar circumstances;[51] and where a party is ignorant of his rights, an account will be allowed after a very considerable time has elapsed.[52] An executor does not cease to be a trustee upon a settlement of his accounts in the proper court, but he still holds the assets remaining in his hands for the purposes of the will, and not adversely to it,[53] unless at the time of the settlement of his accounts, and afterwards, he denied that it was due, in which case the statute begins to run from the date of the settlement;[54] and in some cases such denial may be presumed.[55] A bequest of personal property to an executor "in trust" to pay debts does not in any respect change his relation to the creditors, or in any manner change the operation of the statute, because in law executors are regarded as trustees for the creditors of his testator, and there is nothing added to his legal liability from the mere circumstance of the testator having declared in express terms that the estate shall be subject to the payment of his debts.[56] But where the testator creates a trust for the payment of certain creditors, naming them, the rule would doubtless be otherwise.[57] But a bequest of real estate in trust to pay debts stands upon a different footing, because it imposes upon the devisee a duty in excess of his legal liability, unless the

legacy to a married woman was filed thirty-one years after the death of the testator, twenty-four years after the settlement of the estate, and seventeen years after the death of the executor, and no cause for the delay was shown, the bill was dismissed on the ground of a presumption that the demand had been paid, arising from the lapse of time. Peacock v. Newbold, 4 N. J. Eq. 61.

51. Dean v. Dean, 9 N. J. Eq. 425; Pickering v. Stafford, 2 Ves. Jr. 584.

52. Pickering v. Stafford, 2 Ves. Jr. 584; Jones v. Tuberville, 4 Bro. C. C. 115.

53. Thompson v. M'Gaw, 2 Watts (Pa.) 161.

54. App v. Dreisbach, 2 Rawle (Pa.) 287; Doebler v. Snavely, 5 Watts (Pa.) 225.

55. Webster v. Webster, 10 Ves. 93; State v. Blackwell, 20 Mo. 97; Fisher v. Tucker, 1 McCord (S. C.) 176.

56. Scott v. Jones, 4 Cl. & F. 382; Proud v. Proud, 32 Beav. 234; Oughterloney v. Powis, Amb. 231; Anon., 1 Salk. 154; Blakeway v. Strafford, 2 P. & W. 373; Andrews v. Brown, Prec. Ch. 385; Burke v. Jones, 2 V. & B. 275.

57. Williamson v. Naylor, 2 Y. & C. 208, 210, note.

statute of a State makes both the real and personal estate assets in the hands of an executor or administrator for the payment of the debts of the testator, and such a devise will suspend the operation of the statute as to all debts not barred at the time of the testator's decease.[58] As we have already seen, in order to create an express trust, there must be an estate or interest vested in the trustee, therefore a mere power in gross to sell the realty, conferred upon the executor by the terms of the will, does not constitute him a trustee, even though it is for the purpose of paying the testator's debts.[59] But an executor under such a provision in the will may by his conduct, which operates to put creditors and claimants off their guard relative to the collection of their claims, suspend the operation of the statute thereon.

The fact that a testator in his will directs that all his just debts shall be paid, does not create a trust for the payment of his debts which will prevent the statute of limitations from applying to a demand against the estate.[60] But the rule is otherwise where the debts are scheduled, and the schedule is referred to and made a part of the will.[61]

§ 206. Executor or administrator of a trustee.

The executor or administrator of a person who was trustee for

58. Burke v. Jones, 2 V. & B. 275; Scott v. Jones, Cl. & F. 282. But not such as are barred, but when clear and explicit and not merely implied, it suspends the statute on debts which are due at the death of the testator. Agnew v. Fetterman, 4 Pa. 56.

59. Dickinson v. Teasdale, 14 De G. J. S. 52. Thus, where an executor to whom the testator had given full power to sell, dispose of, lease, or mortgage any or all of his real estate, for the payment of his debts and legacies, and for the distribution of the balance among the devisees named in the will, by his acts held himself out to the devisees as engaged in winding up the estate, and discharging claims prior to theirs, it was held that while he was doing this, or professing to do it, the statute of limitations could not run against those who had no rights against him until those prior claims were paid. Carroll v. Carroll, 11 Barb. (N. Y.) 293. See Jacquet v. Jacquet, 27 Beav. 332.

60. Bloodgood v. Bruen, 4 Sandf. (N. Y.) 427; Parker v. Carter, 8 Tex. 318.

61. Williamson v. Naylor, 2 Y. & C. 210, note.

another cannot set up the statute to defeat the claim of the *cestui que trust* for the settlement of the trust.[62] Trust property held by the decedent, which was kept separate from his own property, is not assets in the hands of his executor; and if the trust funds were invested by the decedent in personal securities, and kept distinct from his own estate, and they pass into the hands of his executor with the express trust on their face, they are in equity, to all intents and purposes, the property of the *cestui que trust*, and equity will compel their specific delivery; but if, instead of subsisting in the hands of the executor, as executor, it has become a mere money transaction, although it originated in a trust, it assumes the character of a debt, and the *cestui que trust* becomes a creditor, and liable to be barred as such.[63]

§ 207. Power to sell property.

A simple power conferred by one person upon another to sell property does not create an express trust which suspends the operation of the statute as to the avails of the sale, because the legal estate still remains in the person conferring the authority;[64] but it has been held that a power of attorney given by A. to B., placing the whole property of A. at the disposal of B., with full authority to collect all claims and make sale of all property, real or personal, and out of the interest of the proceeds to pay for the maintenance of A., with a provision that B. shall account whenever desired, is a direct trust, which lapse of time or the statute of limitations will not bar.[65] So where it is the duty of a trustee to give a *cestui que trust* notice of the sale of trust property, the statute will not begin to run until such notice is given.[66]

62. Johnson v. Overman, 55 N. C. (2 Jones Eq.) 182.

See *supra*, § 199, note. When trust duties are imposed on an executor, and final administration by payment to legatees is deferred, the right to a final accounting accrues only at the time fixed for final distribution. *In re* Post's Estate, 64 N. Y. Supp. 369, 374, 30 Misc. Rep. 551.

63. Trecothick v. Austin, 4 Mason (U. S. C. C.) 16.

64. Dickinson v. Teasdale, *supra*.

65. Cook v. Williams, 2 N. J. Eq. 209.

66. Fox v. Cash, 11 Pa. 207.

§ 208. Effect on cestui que trust when trustee is barred—Sale of trust estate.

When the legal title of property is vested in a trustee who can sue for it, and fails to do so within the statutory period, an infant *cestui* who has only an equitable interest will also be barred;[67] but the rule is otherwise when the legal title is vested in the infant, or cast upon him by operation of law.[68] The rule only applies in cases where the trustee might have brought an action, but neglected to do so. If he has estopped himself from suing by a sale of the property, thus uniting with the purchaser in a breach of his trust, the wrong is to the beneficiaries, not to him, and, while he cannot sue, the beneficiaries, if under any disability, are not affected by the statute.[69] And if the *cestui que trust*

67. Wingfield v. Virgin, 51 Ga. 139; Brady v. Walters, 55 id. 25; Molton v. Henderson, 62 Ala. 426; Williams v. Otey, 27 Tenn. (8 Humph.) 563; Woodbridge v. Planters' Bank, 33 Tenn. (1 Sneed) 297; Pendergrast v. Foley, 8 Ga. 1; Goss v. Singleton, 39 Tenn. (2 Head) 67.

In Willson v. Louisville Trust Co., 102 Ky. 522, 44 S. W. 12, 19 Ky. Law Rep. 1590, this rule was held also to apply in the case of a constructive trustee who became so by buying trust property from the actual trustee, knowing that the latter was committing a breach of trust. See 12 Harvard L. Rev. 132.

68. Wingfield v. Virgin, *supra*.

69. Parker v. Hall, 39 Tenn. (2 Head) 641; Evertson v. Tappen, 5 Johns. (N. Y.) Ch. 497; Fish v. Wilson, 15 Tex. 430; Jones v. Goodwin, 10 Rich. (S. C.) Eq. 226. Where trustees, by authority of an act of assembly, sold and conveyed land, reserving in the deed a ground rent, to be paid to the proprietor of the land, when he should be ascertained, and the proprietor of the land afterwards filed a bill against the purchaser to recover the ground rents, the statute of limitations was held to be no bar to the recovery. Mulliday v. Machir, 4 Gratt. (Va.) 1.

Where a sale of infants' property was made by a master, under a decree by which he was directed to sell, and apply the interest, and as much as might be necessary of the principal, of the proceeds, to the support of the infants, it was held that he was a trustee, and that the statute did not run against a suit, by the infants, for an account, until he had denied his liability. Houseal v. Gibbes, Bailey (S. C.) Ch. 482.

A person giving to his children, by deed, property, real and personal, to be enjoyed by them after his death, himself retaining a life estate, is a trustee for the children, and cannot set up the statute of limitations against them in consequence of his possession. Dawson v. Dawson, Rice (S. C.) Ch. 243.

A purchase at a sheriff's sale, un-

was ignorant of the sale, and the purchaser knew of the trust, the *cestui que trust* will not be barred. If one having notice of the trust purchases of the husband and trustee a negro held in trust for the wife, he will not acquire a title under the statute of limitations by a continued possession of the negro for the statutory period, the wife being ignorant of the sale.[70] The rule is that a person who purchases of a trustee the whole or part of the trust property, *bona fide,* and without notice or knowledge of the trust, will acquire a good title as against the *cestui que trust;*[71] but a person who purchases trust property with notice of the trust holds the title as trustee, and stands in the place of his grantor, and is chargeable with the trust.[72]

§ 209. Factors and agents.

A common and very important fiduciary relation is that of an agent or factor to his principal. If a person acts as a general agent for another, and there is a current account, the rule is said to be that the statute does not begin to run until the expiration of the agency;[73] but in Connecticut [74] a doctrine antagonistic to this was

der an agreement to hold the property for the benefit of the debtor, constitutes a technical trust not within the statute of limitations. McDonald v. May, 1 Rich. (S. C.) Ch. 91. But the purchase of one's land at a sheriff's sale, with an agreement that he shall remain in possession and refund the money at an indefinite period, does not create a "continuing trust" to bar the statute. Hughes v. Hughes, Cheves (S. C.) 33. If a sheriff and a judgment creditor hold money in trust to pay over to other creditors who have appealed from that judgment, they cannot avail themselves of the bar of the statute. Gay v. Edwards, 30 Miss. 218.

Where an agent for the purchase of land took a title in his own name for the benefit of the principal, it was held that the statute did not run against the principal's claim to the land. Hutchinson v. Hutchinson, 4 Desaus. (S. C.) 77.

70. Jones v. Goodwin, *supra.*

71. Wyse v. Dandridge, 35 Miss. 672; Henderson v. Dodd, 1 Bailey (S. C.) Eq. 138; Prevo v. Walters, 5 Ill. 35; Hudnal v. Wilder, 4 McCord (S. C.) 294; Christmas v. Mitchell, 38 N. C. (3 Ired. Eq.) 535; Bracken v. Miller, 4 W. & S. (Pa.) 102.

72. Stewart v. Chadwick, 8 Iowa, 463; Pinson v. Ivey, 9 Tenn. (1 Yerg.) 296; Jones v. Shattuck, 41 Ala. 262; Murray v. Ballou, 1 Johns. (N. Y.) Ch. 566; Webster v. French, 11 Ill. 254.

73. Hopkins v. Hopkins, 4 Strobh.

adopted as to an agent for the collection of rents, the sale of lands, etc., and given full authority and control in that respect over the plaintiff's land, and the recovery in that case was restricted to such items as had accrued within six years next preceding the bringing of the action. It is held that, where the agency is special, the statute attaches upon the consummation of each transaction or the accrual of each item.[75] Where an agent receives money for his principal, it is generally held that the statute does not attach until a demand has been made upon him therefor by the principal.[76] But this question depends largely upon the contract between the agent and his principal relative to accounting. If a person is constituted an agent for the collection of rents, the sale of property, etc., and agrees to receive the money and account for the same, he is treated as agreeing to account immediately upon the receipt of the money and without demand;[77] but if money is deposited with him to be invested, and he agrees to account therefor on demand, a right of action does not accrue against him until a demand has been made upon him for an account, and consequently, whether the money has been loaned by him, or converted to his own use in violation of his trust, the statute does not attach until demand has been made.[78] As be-

(S. C.) Eq. 207, 53 Am. Dec. 663. See Parris v. Cobb, 5 Rich. (S. C.) Eq. 450; Estes v. Stokes, 2 id. 133. This principle is well illustrated in a New York case, Davy v. Field, 1 Abb. (N. Y.) App. Dec. 490, in which it was held that, where a sheriff collects money for several creditors upon successive attachments against a single debtor, the fund will be treated as entire, and the statute does not begin to run against any creditor from the time when his claim was collected, but from the time when the whole is called.

An agent who stands in a fiduciary relation to his principal cannot set up the statute of limitations to bar a suit by the latter for an account. Burdick v. Garrick, L. R. 5 Ch. 233; *In re* Bell, 34 Ch. D. 462; Dooby v. Watson, 39 Ch. D. 178.

74. Appeal of Hart, 32 Conn. 520.

75. Hopkins v. Hopkins, *supra*.

76. Taylor v. Spears, 8 Ark. 429; Hyman v. Gray, 49 N. C. (4 Jones L.) 155; Gardner v. Peyton, 5 Cranch C. C. (U. S.) 560; Lever v. Lever, 1 Hill (S. C.) Eq. 62; Merle v. Andrews, 4 Tex. 200; Judah v. Dyott, 3 Blackf. (Ind.) 324, 25 Am. Dec. 112.

77. Appeal of Hart, *supra*.

78. Baker v. Joseph, 16 Cal. 173; S. P. Sadowsky v. M'Farland, 33 Ky.

tween a factor and consignor of goods, sent to the former to be sold, in the absence of any special contract relative to an accounting for the same, he is treated as contracting to account therefor on demand, consequently the statute does not run against the consignor until demand for an accounting is made by him,[79] or an account is rendered by the factor to the consignor, in which case the statute begins to run from the time of the rendition of the account,[80] or directions from the consignor to remit the proceeds.[81]

§ 210. Partners.

The statute does not run between partners so long as the partnership continues, and each partner is in the exercise of his right, nor necessarily after its dissolution, where there are debts due to or from it.[82] There is no definite rule of law that the statute begins to run immediately upon the dissolution of the partnership, and the question as to whether it does or not must depend upon the peculiar circumstances of each case.[83] But unless there is some covenant or agreement, express or implied, fixing a period for accounting beyond the time of dissolution, or circumstances that

(3 Dana) 204. For a more extended review of the rules and authorities bearing upon this question, see *supra*, Chap. XI.

79. Baird v. Walker, 12 Barb. (N. Y.) 298; Topham v. Braddick, 1 Taunt. 571; Green v. Johnson, 3 Gill. & J. (Md.) 389; Collins v. Benning, 12 Mod. 444; Hyman v. Gray, 49 N. C. (4 Jones L.) 155; Kane v. Cook, 8 Cal. 449.

80. Murray v. Coster, 20 Johns. (N. Y.) 576, 11 Am. Dec. 333; Farmers' & Mechanics' Bank v. Planters' Bank, 10 Gill. & J. (Md.) 422; Clark v. Moody, 17 Mass. 145. It is a factor's duty to account in a reasonable time, without demand. Eaton v. Walton, 32 N. H. 352; Lyle v. Murray, 6 N. Y. Super. Ct. (4 Sandf.) 590.

81. Ferris v. Paris, 10 Johns. (N. Y.) 285; Burns v. Pillsbury, 17 N. H. 66; Halden v. Crafts, 4 E. D. Sm. (N. Y.) 490, 2 Abb. Pr. 301; Cooley v. Betts, 24 Wend. (N. Y.) 203.

82. McNair v. Ragaland, 16 N. C. (1 Dev. Eq.) 533; Hammond v. Hammond, 20 Ga. 556. In Atwater v. Fowler, 1 Edw. (N. Y.) Ch. 417, it was held that where two persons are partners in certain stocks, which are left by one in the hands of the other for sale, the statute does not begin to run until the stocks are finally disposed of. Miller v. Miller, L. R. 8 Eq. 499; Foster v. Hodgson, 19 Ves. 183; Millington v. Holland, W. R. Nov. 22, 1869; Robinson v. Alexander, 2 Cl. & F. 717.

83. Massey v. Tingle, 29 Mo. 437.

render an accounting impossible, the statute begins to run from the time when the partnership is in fact dissolved.[84] If at the date of dissolution there are debts due to or from the firm, the partnership liability continues until such matters are liquidated, or until they are barred by the statute; and, if one of the partners is appointed to liquidate the affairs of the firm, he may bind the late firm by a note given for money borrowed by him to pay the firm debts;[85] and if no one of the partners is clothed with special authority to liquidate the affairs of the firm, any one of the partners may bind the others by notes given in satisfaction of a debt of the firm;[86] but none of the partners have authority to bind the others by any promise to pay a debt of the firm which is barred by the statute;[87] and except where provision is otherwise made by statute, one partner may bind another by a promise to pay a debt upon which the statute has not run.[88] Upon the death of a partner, the firm is *ipso facto* dissolved, and the statute begins to run for and against his personal representatives at once.[89] There is one serious difficulty in the application of this doctrine, and that is, where, after the lapse of six years, valuable partnership assets come into the hands of the surviving partner, in which the estate of the deceased partner ought to participate.[90]

84. Taylor v. Morrison, 37 Ky. (7 Dana) 241; Massey v. Tingle, *supra;* Hammond v. Hammond, *supra.*

85. McCowin v. Cubbison, 72 Pa. 358; Davis's Estate, 5 Whart. Pa. 530; Robinson v. Taylor, 4 Pa. 242.

86. Ward v. Tyler, 52 Pa. 393.

87. Bush v. Stowell, 71 Pa. 208; Levy v. Cadet, 17 S. & R. (Pa.) 126; Reppert v. Colvin, 48 Pa. 248.

88. McCoon v. Galbraith, 29 Pa. 293.

89. Weisman v. Smith, 59 N. C. (6 Jones Eq.) 124. In Knox v. Gye, L. R. 5 H. L. 674, it was held that a court of equity will not decree an account between a surviving partner and a deceased partner's estate after the lapse of six years, whether the surviving partner be plaintiff or defendant, and that the *punctum temporis* from which time commences to run is the date at which the partnership estate is vested in the surviving partner. See Lackey v. Lackey, Prec. in Ch. 518. Lord Hatherley dissented in Knox v. Gye. In Tatam v. Williams, 3 Hare, 347, Wigram, V. C., said: "In this court there is direct and very high authority for the proposition that a court of equity will not, after six years' acquiescence, * * * decree an account between a surviving partner and the estate of a deceased partner."

90. This difficulty was anticipated

Where partnership affairs are unsettled at the time the firm is dissolved, and by a written agreement one of the partners is designated to keep and dispose of the firm assets at such prices and upon such terms as he can, a continuing trust is thereby created, and the statute does not begin to run in favor of the

in Knox v. Gye, by Lord Colonsay, who said: "I do not say that if a sum is unexpectedly recovered after the lapse of six years, the executor of the deceased partner, though he has lost the right to sue for an account of the partnership concerns, may not in another kind of suit demand a share of the particular fund so recovered." And Lord Chelmsford said: "There may be a difficulty in determining what is the right of an executor of a deceased partner when he has allowed the statute of limitations to run against his claim to an account, and a debt has been received by the surviving partner after the six years has elapsed. But this is a difficulty occasioned by his own laches, and I see no reason why, if he thinks that his interest in the sum received has not been absorbed by its application to pay debts due from the partnership, he should not have a right to sue for his share in this sum (a very different thing from a suit for an account of all the partnership transactions), the surviving partner being at liberty to defend himself by alleging and proving that the whole sum received has been applied, or was applicable, to the payment of partnership liabilities."

It may be remarked, however, that according to the dictum of Lord Westbury, in the same case, the representative of a deceased partner has no specific interest in or claim upon any part of the partnership estate, so that it seems doubtful how far he would be able, as suggested by Lord Colonsay, to sue for the share of any newly acquired asset as *prima facie* due to him, and in that way, in fact, obtain an account from the defendant by throwing the onus of proof (which would, in fact, require an account of the partnership transactions) upon the defendant, to show that the whole or part of such plaintiff's *prima facie* share was applicable to satisfy partnership liabilities. So, too, it is difficult to see how laches could be imputed on the part of the representatives of a deceased partner, at all events in respect of unexpected assets which fall in after the lapse of six years, in respect that he has not kept alive his right to have an account by filing a bill, or even, as suggested by Lord Hatherley, by filing continuous bills at sexennial intervals. It was contended that a surviving partner was a trustee of the partnership assets, and as such not within the statute; but this contention was overruled, Lord Westbury expressing a clear opinion that there was no fiduciary relation between a surviving partner and the representatives of one deceased, and that the former was not a trustee in the strict and full sense of the term, the term being so used only by a convenient but deceptive metaphor, and the rights of the parties being strictly legal rights.

liquidating partner so long as he acts under the trust or admits its continuance.[91]

§ 211. Acknowledgment by one partner.

As long as a partnership continues, each partner is an agent for the purpose of making an acknowledgment under the statute of limitations.[92]

Under the old theory of acknowledgment, an acknowledgment made by a liquidating partner after a dissolution of partnership might revive a debt;[93] but under the new theory, and since the essential changes in these statutes both in this country and England, such agency will terminate at dissolution, and after a partnership is dissolved one of the late firm cannot by his act or admission involve his copartner in any new legal liability.[94] It is possible, however, that it might be otherwise if the admission consisted of a part payment out of assets belonging to the late firm.[95]

A right of action to sue for the settlement of partnership affairs does not, as a matter of law, accrue at the time of the dissolution of the firm, but depends on circumstances.[96]

91. Causler v. Wharton, 62 Ala. 358.

92. Watson v. Woodman, L. R. 20 Eq. 730.

A part payment of a firm debt by one partner, without his copartner's knowledge or authority, takes the debt out of the statute of limitations. Buxton v. Edwards, 134 Mass. 567; Harding v. Butler, 156 Mass. 34, 30 N. E. 168. See Tucker v. Tucker (1894), 3 Ch. 429.

93. Wood v. Braddick, 1 Taunt. 104; Pritchard v. Draper, 1 R. & My. 191.

94. Watson v. Woodman, L. R. 20 Eq. 721; Thompson v. Waithman, 3 Drew 628; Bristow v. Miller, 11 Ir. L. R. 461; Kilgour v. Finlyson, 1 H. Bl. 155.

See Kerper v. Wood, 40 Ohio St. 613, 29 N. E. 501, 15 L. R. A. 656, and note.

95. Watson v. Woodman, L. R. 20 Eq. 721.

96. When the right of action accrues, so as to set the statute of limitations in motion, depends upon circumstances, and cannot be held as matter of law to arise at the date of the dissolution, or to be carried back by relation to that date. Todd v. Rafferty, 30 N. J. Eq. 254; Partridge v. Wells, id. 176; Prentice v. Elliott, 72 Ga. 154; Hammond v. Hammond, 20 Ga. 556; Massey v.

When the partnership affairs are being wound up without antagonism between the parties, and assets are being realized and debts paid, the statute does not begin to run. Where the dissolution is effected by the debt or assignment of one partner, the surviving or solvent partners hold the partnership property for the purpose of closing up its affairs. And where there is an agreement that one partner shall close up the business of the firm and settle its affairs, which have been under his management, a trust has been created and the statute does not begin to run against the right to account, so long as such partner acts under the trust until he repudiates it himself.[97]

If a partner dies during the partnership, it seems that the maxim *contra non volentem agere non currit lex* prevails, and that time will not run against his estate, and in favor of the surviving

Tingle, 29 Mo. 437; McClung v. Capehart, 24 Minn. 17; Hendy v. March, 75 Cal. 566; Foster v. Rison, 17 Gratt. 321; Boggs v. Johnson, 26 W. Va. 821; Atwater v. Fowler, 1 Edw. Ch. 423, 6 N. Y. Ch. (L. ed.) 195. In Causler v. Wharton, 62 Ala. 358, the court held that where one partner, by a written agreement with the other, left the partnership assets with him to dispose of, whenever he could do so at a fair price, a continuing trust was thereby created, and the bar of the statute of limitations would not begin to run against the right to an account of the partnership dealings, so long as the party to whom the assets were delivered acted under the trust or admitted that it was still continuing.

In Adams v. Taylor, 14 Ark. 62, it was held that "the relation between co-partners does not create such a trust as will exempt a bill for a mere account and settlement from the operation of the statute of limitations, or the analogous bar by lapse of time, or staleness of the demand." McGuire v. Ramsey, 9 Ark. 519. See Chouteau v. Barlow, 110 U. S. 238, 3 Sup. Ct. 620, 28 L. Ed. 132.

Suits between partners to obtain an account and settlement of the partnership affairs are subject to the statute of limitations, which begins to run at the date of the dissolution, in the absence of any express contract, or of conduct of the parties working an extension of the time for bringing suit. Currier v. Studley, 159 Mass. 17, 33 N. E. 709; Noyes v. Crawley, 10 Ch. D. 31, 39; Allen & Sons v. Woonsocket Co., 11 R. I. 288, 295; Richardson v. Gregory, 126 Ill. 166, 18 N. E. 777; Campbell v. Clark, 101 Fed. 972; Gray v. Kerr, 46 Ohio St. 652, 23 N. E. 136; Gilmore v. Ham, 142 N. Y. 1, 36 N. E. 826, 40 Am. St. Rep. 554; *supra*, § 24.

97. Riddle v. Whitehill, 135 U. S. 621, 10 Sup. Ct. 924, 34 L. Ed. 283.

partner, till there is administration to the estate of the dead partner, unless there have been disputes so as to give a cause of action before the death of the dead partner.[98]

§ 212. How trustee may put statute in operation in his favor.

It is, as previously stated, a well-established rule in regard to direct, technical trusts, that, so long as the trust subsists, the rights of the *cestui que trust* will not be barred by the possession of the trustee, however long continued, as the possession of the trustee is treated as the possession of the *cestui que trust,* and although he does not execute his trust, his mere possession and inactivity as to the trust, of themselves, afford no *indicia* of an adverse claim by him.[99] But if the trustee denies the trust, and assumes absolute ownership of the trust property in such a manner that the *cestui que trust* has actual or constructive notice of the repudiation of the trust by the trustee, the statute attaches and begins to run from that time against the *cestui que trust,*[1]

98. Spann v. Fox, 1 Ga. Dec. 1; Gardner v. Cummings, 1 Ga. Dec. Part I.; Banning on Limitations, 204-208.

99. Redwood v. Riddick, 4 Munf. (Va.) 222; Howard v. Aiken, 3 McCord (S. C.) 467; North v. Barnum, 12 Vt. 205; Overstreet v. Bates, 24 Ky. (1 J. J. Marsh.) 370; Thompson v. Blair, 7 N. C. (3 Murph.) 583; Wamburzee v. Kennedy, 4 Desau. (S. C.) Eq. 474; Armstrong v. Campbell, 11 Tenn. (3 Yerg.) 201; Martin v. Jackson, 27 Pa. 504; Jones v. Persons, 9 N. C. (2 Hawks) 269; Goodhue v. Barnwell, 1 Rice (S. C.) Eq. 198; Bowman v. Wathen, 2 McLean (U. S. C. C.) 376; Alexander v. M'Murry, 8 Watts (Pa.) 504; Hovenden v. Annesley, 2 Sch. & Lef. 633; Hemenway v. Gates, 22 Mass. (5 Pick.) 321; Steel v. Henry, 9 Watts (Pa.) 523; Fishwick v. Sewell, 4 H. & J. (Md.) 393; Lawson v. Blodgett, 20 Ark. 195; Young v. Mackall, 3 Md. Ch. 395; McDonald v. Sims, 3 Ga. 383.

1. When the trustee openly disavows his trust, the statute begins to run. Thomas v. Merry, 113 Ind. 83; Reynolds v. Sumner, 126 Ill. 58; Ward v. Harvey, 111 Ind. 471; Reizenstein v. Marquardt, 75 Iowa 294; Gilbert v. Sleeper, 71 Cal. 290; Roach v. Caraffa, 85 Cal. 436; Hill v. McDonald, 58 Hun (N. Y.) 322; Hamilton v. Pritchard, 107 N. C. 128; Marshall's Est. 138 Pa. 285; State v. Shires, 39 Mo. App. 560; Bacon v. Rives, 106 U. S. 99, 1 Sup. Ct. 3, 27 L. Ed. 69; Ord v. De La Guerre, 54 Cal. 298; Governor v. Woodworth, 63 Ill. 254; Hayward v. Gunn, 82 Ill. 385; Grant v. Burr, 54

unless the latter is at the time under some one of the statutory disabilities, or is under undue influence proceeding from the trustee.[2] Such denial of the trust, and assertion of an adversary claim in himself, is an abandonment of the fiduciary character

Cal. 298; Belknap v. Gleason, 11 Conn. 160; Hickox v. Elliott, 22 Fed. 13; Hartley v. Head, 71 Ga. 95; *Re* McKinley, 15 Fed. 912; McGuire v. Linneus, 74 Me. 344; Robertson v. Dunn, 87 N. C. 191; Hastie v. Aiken, 67 Ala. 313; Bonner v. Young, 68 Ala. 35; Zuck v. Culp, 59 Cal. 142; Lakin v. Sierra Buttes Gold Mine Co., 25 Fed. 337; Bostwick v. Dickson, 65 Wis. 593; Fox v. Tay, 89 Cal. 339; Smith v. Glover, 44 Minn. 260; Butler v. Hyland, 89 Cal. 575; Byars v. Thompson, 80 Tex. 468; Hill v. McDonald, 58 Hun (N. Y.) 322; Hinton v. Pritchard, 107 N. C. 128; Wilson v. Brookshire, 126 Ind. 497; Conger v. Lee, 75 Tex. 114; Wren v. Hollowell, 52 Ark. 76; Dyer v. Waters, 19 Atl. (N. J. Eq.) 129; *Re* Camp, 50 Hun (N. Y.) 388; Murphy v. Murphy, 80 Iowa 740; Hall v. Ditto, 11 Ky. Law Rep. 667; Charter Oak L. Ins. Co. v. Gisborne, 5 Utah 319; Chadwick v. Chadwick, 59 Mich. 87; Robson v. Jones, 27 Ga. 266. Where an act is done by the trustee purporting to be an execution of the trust, he is from that time regarded as standing at arm's length from the *cestui que trust*, who is then put to the assertion of his claim at the hazard of being barred by the statute. Thus, where an infant executed a receipt as a discharge in full of a legacy to which he was entitled in right of his wife, and four years after filed a bill against the executors for the recovery of her legacy, it was held that he was barred. Coleman v. Davis, 2 Strobh. (S. C.) Eq. 334; Moore v. Porcher, 1 Bailey (S. C.) Ch. 195; Britton v. Lewis, 8 Rich. (S. C.) Eq. 271; Gisborne v. Charter Oak L. Ins. Co., 142 U. S. 326, 12 Sup. Ct. 277, 35 L. Ed. 1029; Miles v. Thorne, 38 Cal. 335; Seymour v. Freer, 75 U. S. (8 Wall.) 202, 19 L. Ed. 306; Bacon v. Rives, 106 U. S. 99, 1 Sup. Ct. 3, 27 L. Ed. 69; Henry v. Confidence Gold and Silver M. Co., 1 Nev. 619. In Lammer v. Stoddard, 103 N. Y. 672, 9 N. E. 328, the court said: "Edward Lammer was not the actual trustee of this fund, and he never acknowledged a trust as to the money loaned him. He could, at most, have been declared a trustee *ex maleficio*, or by implication or construction of law, and in such a case the statute begins to run from the time the wrong was committed, by which the party became chargeable as trustee by implication." Wilmerding v. Russ, 33 Conn. 67; Ashurst's Appeal, 60 Pa. 290; McClane v. Shepherd, 21 N. J. Eq. 76; Decouche v. Savetier, 3 Johns. Ch. 190, 216; Kane v. Bloodgood, 7 id. 90; Ward v. Smith, 3 Sandf. Ch. 592; Higgins v. Higgins, 14 Abb. N. C. 13; Clarke v. Boorman, 75 U. S. (18 Wall.) 493, 21 L. Ed. 904; Perry on Trusts, § 865.

2. Keaton v. McGwier, 24 Ga. 217; Wheeler v. Piper, 56 N. C. (3 Jones Eq.) 249; Welborn v. Rogers, 24 Ga. 558.

in which he has stood to the property, and from that time the claim of the *cestui que trust* is subject to the operation of the statute.[3] But in order to put the statute in motion, it must appear that the *cestui que trust* had, or ought to have had, knowledge of the trustee's denial, repudiation, or adverse claim, and that the trustee has been guilty of no fraud in that regard.[4]

§ 213 Exceptions to the rule relative to express trusts.

The rule that a direct and technical trust is not within the operation of the statute is subject to two exceptions: first, that no open denial or repudiation of the trust is brought home to the knowledge of the *cestui que trust,* which requires him to act as upon an asserted adverse title; and, second, that no circumstances

3. Murdock v. Hughes, 15 Miss. 219; Kane v. Bloodgood, *supra;* Smith v. Ricords, 52 Mo. 581; Farnam v. Brooks, 26 Mass. (9 Pick.) 212; White v. Leavitt, 20 Tex. 703; Andrews v. Smithwick, 20 id. 111; Lucas v. Daniels, 34 Ala. 188; Boone v. Chiles, 35 U. S. (10 Pet.) 177, 9 L. Ed. 388; Pipher v. Lodge, 4 S. & R. (Pa.) 310; Robson v. Jones, 27 266; Willison v. Watkins, 28 U. S. (3 Pet.) 52, 7 L. Ed. 596; Cunningham v. McKindley, 22 Ind. 149; Green v. Johnson, 3 G. & J. (Md.) 89; Starke v. Starke, 3 Rich. (S. C.) 438; Sollee v. Croft, 7 Rich. Eq. (S. C.) 34; Perkins v. Cartmell, 4 Harr. (Del.) 270; Sheldon v. Sheldon, 3 Wis. 699; Tinnen v. Mebane, 10 Tex. 246.

4. Keaton v. Greenwood, 8 Ga. 97; Fox v. Cash, 11 Pa. 207; Roberts v. Berdell, 61 Barb. (N. Y.) 37, 52 N. Y. 531; Moffatt v. Buchanan, 30 Tenn. (11 Humph.) 369; Grumbles v. Grumbles, 17 Tex. 472; Houseal v. Gibbs, Bailey (S. C.) Eq. 482; Robinson v. Hook, 4 Mason (U. S.) 152.

When the trust is repudiated by clear and unequivocal words and acts of the trustee, who claims to hold the trust property as his own, and such repudiation and claim are brought to the notice of the beneficiary in such a manner that he is called upon to assert his equitable rights, the statute of limitations will begin to run from the time such repudiation and claim came to the knowledge of the beneficiary. Turner v. Smith, 11 Tex. 620; Williams v. First Presbyterian Society, 1 Ohio St. 478; Oliver v. Piatt, 44 U. S. (3 How.) 333, 11 L. Ed. 622; Badger v. Badger, 69 U. S. (2 Wall.) 87, 17 L. Ed. 863; Provost v. Gratz, 19 U. S. (6 Wheat.) 481, 5 L. Ed. 311; Merriam v. Hassam, 96 Mass. (14 Allen) 516; Atty.-Gen. v. Federal St. Meeting-House, 69 Mass. (3 Gray) 1; Kane v. Bloodgood, 7 Johns. Ch. (N. Y.) 90; Wedderburn v. Wedderburn, 4 Myl. & Cr. 41; Bright v. Legerton, 2 De G. F. & J. 606.

exist to raise a presumption from lapse of time that the trust has been extinguished.[5] There is, as we have seen in a former chapter,[6] a defence peculiar to courts of equity founded on lapse of time and the staleness of the claim, where no statute of limitations applies to it. In such cases, courts of equity often act upon their own inherent doctrine of discouraging antiquated claims, for the peace of society, by refusing to interfere where there has been gross laches in prosecuting the right, or acquiescence in the assertion of an adverse right.[7]

5. Story, J., in Baker v. Whiting, 3 Sumner (U. S.) 466; Edmands v. University, 21 N. C. (1 D. & B. Eq.) 325.

It is true, as a general rule, that when the relation of trustee and *cestui que trust* is uniformly admitted to exist, and there is no assertion of adverse claim or ownership by the trustee, lapse of time can constitute no bar to relief. But when the trust relation is repudiated, and time and long acquiescence have obscured the nature and character of the trust, or the acts of the parties or other circumstances give rise to presumptions unfavorable to its continuance, in all such cases a court of equity will refuse relief on the gound of lapse of time, and its inability to do complete justice. Nettles v. Nettles, 57 Ala. 539; Philippi v. Philippi, 61 Ala. 41; Lansdale v. Smith, 106 U. S. 391, 1 Sup. Ct. 350, 27 L. Ed. 219; Goodwyn v. Baldwin, 59 Ala. 127; Maury v. Mason, 8 Port. (Ala.) 211; Philippi v. Philippi, 115 U. S. 157, 5 Sup. Ct. 1181, 29 L. Ed. 336. If twenty years are allowed to elapse from the time from which proceedings could have been instituted for the settlement of a trust without the commencement of such proceedings, and there has been no recognition or admission within that period of the trust as continuing and undischarged, a presumption of settlement arises which operates as a positive bar. McCarty v. McCarty, 74 Ala. 546; Greenlees v. Greenlees, 62 id. 330; Harrison v. Heflin, 54 id. 552; Rhodes v. Turner, 21 id. 210; Blackwell v. Blackwell, 33 id. 57; Worley v. High, 40 id. 171; Ragland v. Morton, 41 id. 344; and this may be said to be the settled law of equity jurisprudence. Cholmondeley v. Clinton, 2 Jac. & Walk. 1,138. Hovenden v. Annesley, 2 Sch. & Lef. 607; Elmendorf v. Taylor, 23 U. S. (10 Wheat.) 152, 6 L. Ed. 289; Wagner v. Baird, 48 U. S. (7 How.) 233, 12 L. Ed. 681; Bowman v. Wathen, 42 U. S. (1 How.) 189, 11 L. Ed. 97; Kane v. Bloodgood, 7 Johns. Ch. (N. Y.) 90.

6. "Equitable actions," Chap. VI.

7. Wagner v. Baird, *supra;* Kennedy v. Bank of Georgia, 49 U. S. (8 How.) 586, 12 L. Ed. 1209; Stearns v. Page, 48 U. S. (7 How.) 819, 12 L. Ed. 928; Piatt v. Vattier, 34 U. S. (9 Pet.) 405, 9 L. Ed. 173; Fenson v. Sanger, 5 N. Y. Leg. Obs. 43. "A court of equity," says Lord Camden, "which is never active in

§ 214. Stale trusts not favored in equity.

Courts of equity do not apply the statute to matters peculiarly and exclusively within their own jurisdiction, and for this reason no lapse of time will preclude a court of equity from investigating transactions and accounts between parties standing in the relative situation of trustee and *cestui que trust,* where the transactions between them are not closed, and the delay of the claim is attributable to the trustee not having given that information to his *cestui que trust* to which he was entitled, and accounted with him in such manner as he ought to have done,[8] or where the circum-

relief against conscience or public convenience, has always refused its aid to stale demands, where the party has slept upon his rights. Nothing can call forth this court into activity but good conscience, good faith, and reasonable diligence. Where these are wanting, the court is passive and does nothing. Laches and neglect are always discountenanced, and therefore from the beginning of this jurisdiction there was always a limitation to suits. But as the court has no legislative authority, it could not properly define the time of bar by positive rule; it was governed by circumstances. But as often as Parliament had limited the time of action and remedies to a certain period in legal proceedings, the Court of Chancery adopted that rule, and applied it to similar cases in equity; for when the legislature had fixed the time at law, it would have been preposterous for equity, which by its own proper authority always maintained a limitation to countenance laches beyond the period that the law has been confined to by Parliament, and therefore in all cases where the legal right has been barred by Parliament, the equitable right to the same thing has been concluded by the same bar." Smith v. Clay, 3 Bro. C. C. 640, note. In Mellish's Estate, 1 Pars. (Pa.) 482, the court refused to compel a trustee to account after an unexplained delay of thirty years.

8. Wedderburn v. Wedderburn, 2 Keen 749; Sheldon v. Weldman, 1 Ch. Cas. 26; Phillipo v. Munnings, 2 Myl. & Cr. 315; Hollis's Case, 2 Vent. 345; Smith v. Pocock, 23 L. J. Ch. 596. Ignorance of one's rights, at law, does not prevent the operation of the statute of limitations. Campbell v. Long, 20 Iowa 382; Bossard v. White, 9 Rich. (S. C.) Eq. 483; Martin v. Bank, 31 Ala. 115; Davis v. Cotton, 55 N. C. (2 Jones Eq.) 430; Abell v. Harris, 11 G. & J. (Md.) 367. This is so even though the action is founded on a breach of trust. Cole v. McGlathry, 9 Me. 131. But in equity it would operate as an excuse for delay, especially if the trustee had failed to inform the *cestui que trust* of the facts. Pugh v. Bell, 24 Ky. (1 J. J. Marsh.) 399; Halsey v. Tate, 52 Pa. 311.

stances are such as to operate as a reasonable excuse for the delay;[9] and where fraud is imputed and proved, the length of time during which the fraud has been concealed and practiced is rather an aggravation of the offence than a circumstance to execute delay.[10] In a Pennsylvania case,[11] where after a delay of seventy years, upon a bill brought for an accounting for certain stocks which had been sold in trust for a person who was then dead, who knew the facts, but never set up any claim under the trust, the court refused to interfere.[12] Equity will decline to interfere to relieve against a trustee after a long lapse of time and the character of the trust has become obscure, or the acts of the parties or other circumstances raise a presumption against it.[13] So, also, equity will refuse to interfere where there has been a clear breach of trust, and the *cestui que trust* has for a long time acquiesced in the misconduct of the trustee, with full knowledge of the breach.[14]

§ 215. Constructive or resulting trusts.

The rule relative to express trusts has no application to that

9. Prevost v. Gratz, 19 U. S. (6 Wheat.) 481, 5 L. Ed. 311.

10. Bank of the United States v. Beverley, 42 U. S. (1 How.) 134, 11 L. Ed. 75; Michoud v. Girod, 45 U. S. (4 How.) 503, 11 L. Ed. 1076.

11. Halsey v. Tate, 52 Pa. 311.

12. See Robertson v. Maclin, 6 Tenn. (3 Hayw.) 76, where great delay in seeking relief under a trust was held to have great weight against the application. Lapse of time without any claim or admission of an existing trust, coupled with circumstances tending to show that the trust has been executed, raises a presumption of its execution, and, in the case of a guardian, may authorize the court to require a less specific statement of the items of the account, and raise a presumption of payment to and for the ward to the amount. Gregg v. Gregg, 15 N. H. 190. Lapse of time does not operate as a bar of express trusts, especially where the trustee and those claiming under him have not asserted an adverse claim for more than two years, and the rights of the *cestui que trust* will not be barred though he has neglected to claim the benefit of the trust for nearly forty years before. In order that lapse of time shall operate to raise a presumptive bar, the trustee must have so conducted with reference to the estate, as to lead to the conclusion that he claimed and regarded it as his own. If he holds it in recognition of the trust, no length of time will bar the *cestui*. Pinson v. Ivey, 9 Tenn. (1 Yerg.) 296.

13. Taylor v. Blair, 14 Mo. 437; Whedbee v. Whedbee, 58 N. C. (5 Jones Eq.) 392.

14. Broadhurst v. Balgany, 1 Y. & C. 28.

species of trusts which arise from implication or operation of law, and consequently are the ground of an action at law.[15] One who is not actually a trustee, but upon whom that character is forced by a court of equity, only for the purpose of a remedy, may avail himself of the statute.[16] Within what time a constructive trust will be barred must depend on the circumstances of each case. There are few cases where a constructive trust can be enforced against a

15. Wisner v. Barnet, 4 Wash. (U. S. C. C.) 631; Hayman v. Keally, 3 Cranch (U. S. C. C.) 325; Boone v. Chiles, 35 U. S. (10 Pet.) 177, 9 L. Ed. 388; Lexington v. Ohio R. R. Co., 46 Ky. (7 B. Mon.) 556; Walker v. Walker, 16 S. & R. (Pa.) 379; Smith v. Calloway, 7 Blackf. (Ind.) 86; Singleton v. Moore, Rice (S. C.) Eq. 110; Ramsay v. Deas, 2 Desaus. (S. C.) 233; Mussey v. Mussey, 2 Hill (S. C.) Ch. 496; Spotswood v. Dandridge, 4 H. & M. (Va.) 139; Stephen v. Yandle, 3 N. C. (3 Hayw.) 231; Talbot v. Todd, 35 Ky. (5 Dana) 199; Cook v. Williams, 2 N. J. Eq. 209; Rush v. Barr, 1 Watts (Pa.) 110; Paige v. Hughes, 41 Ky. (2 B. Mon.) 138; Kane v. Bloodgood, 7 Johns. Ch. (N. Y.); Sheppards v. Turpin, 3 Gratt. (Va.) 373; Wagstaff v. Smith, 39 N. C. (4 Ired. Eq.) 1; Green v. Johnson, 3 G. & J. (Md.) 387; Hawley v. Cramer, 4 Cow. (N. Y.) 717; Wylly v. Collins, 9 Ga. 223; Ball v. Lawson, 4 W. & S. (Pa.) 557; Finney v. Cochran, 1 id. 112; Johnson v. Smith's Adm'r, 27 Mo. 591; Alston v. Alston, 84 Ala. 15; Buchan v. Janes, 1 Speers (S. C.) Eq. 375.

16. Elmendorf v. Taylor, 23 U. S. (10 Wheat.) 152, 6 L. Ed. 289. Thus, where a bill in chancery was filed by persons residing in Canada, claiming title to property in Detroit, which had been in the possession of the defendants and those claiming under them since 1793, without, as far as appeared, any right being set up by the complainants, or by those claiming under them, to the title or the possession of the premises, until the filing of the bill, or any claim to the rents or profits, or to an account as tenants in common, or for partition, or to be admitted to the enjoyment of any rights as co-heirs, it was held that the case rested upon the enforcement of an implied trust and that a court of equity must follow the courts of law in applying the statute of limitations. Beaubien v. Beaubien, 64 U. S. (23 How.) 190, 16 L. Ed. 484.

One who is merely a constructive trustee may avail of the statute, though he has not repudiated the trust. In California, such a trustee does not become an express trustee until he signs some writing amounting to a declaration of trust, his oral recognition of the beneficiary's rights being not sufficient for this purpose. Hecht v. Slaney, 72 Cal. 363, 14 Pac. 88; Nougues v. Newlands, 118 Cal. 102, 50 Pac. 386; Stillwater & St. Paul R. Co. v. Stillwater, 66 Minn. 176, 68 N. W. 836; 2 Story Eq. Jur. (13th Ed.), § 1520a; Potter v. Douglass, 83 Iowa 190, 48 N. W. 1004; *supra*, § 58, notes.

person who has held peaceable possession for twenty years, claiming in his own right, but whose acts have made him a trustee by implication.[17] And the same rule prevails where a person is converted into a trustee on the ground of fraud,[18] and the statute begins to run from the discovery of the fraud.[19]

§ 216. Mistake of trustee in possession.

We have already seen that the possession of the trustee is treated as the possession of the *cestui que trust,* consequently a mistake by a trustee in the possession of land, who treats a wrong person as equitably entitled will not affect the rights of the real claimant;[20] but when the trust is merely implied, the rule is otherwise. Thus, if a person receives money or goods from a person believing that they belonged to him, when in fact they belonged to a stranger, an implied trust is raised, and the stranger is entitled to sue at once, and he is barred by the statute unless suit is brought in time.[21]

§ 217. Funds of societies vested in trustees.

Where the funds of an association in the nature of a benefit society were vested in trustees, it was held that neither the association nor the trustee were trustees for the purposes of the statute; and a claim to a pension due to the widow of a member of such a society was held barred as to the chief part thereof after the lapse of more than twenty years; in the particular case, the claim being to a sum of money payable *de anno in annum,* the plaintiff was allowed so much thereof as had become due within six years before filing the bill, with interest from the filing of the bill.[22] Persons, however, appointed trustees of the assets of a certain benefit society, called the Rational Society, which was insolvent, were consid-

17. Michoud v. Girod, 45 U. S. (4 How.) 503, 11 L. Ed. 1076.

18. Wheeler v. Piper, 56 N. C. (3 Jones Eq.) 249.

19. Moore v. Greene, 60 U. S. (19 How.) 69, 15 L. Ed. 533.

20. Lester v. Pickford, 34 Beav. 576.

21. Buchan v. James, 1 Speers (S. C.) Eq. 375.

22. Edwards v. Warden, 9 Ch. 495.

ered to be trustees for the creditors within the statute. There is no fiduciary relation between a mutual assurance society or its trustees and a policy-holder or grantee of an annuity.[23]

§ 218. The liability of trustee for breach of trust creates trust debt.

The liability of a trustee for a breach of trust creates only a simple debt, except when the trust is created by specialty. But when the trust is created by specialty, it is a trust debt to which neither the trustee nor his executor can plead the statute.[24] In several Irish cases,[25] it has been held that, while the statute will not run in favor of the trustee in his lifetime, it will run in favor of his executor; but according to the doctrine of the English case [26] cited, the trustee and his executor are put upon the same footing as regards the statute in cases of breach of trust, and this is in accordance with the dicta of several previous cases.[27]

§ 219. Vendor and vendee of land.

Upon the execution of a contract to convey, the vendee in equity becomes the owner of the land, subject, however, to have his title defeated if he fails to perform his agreement. But upon full perform-

23. Pare v. Clegg, 29 Beav. 589; Banning on Lim. 198.

24. Brettlebank v. Goodwin, L. R. 5 Eq. 545.

25. Dunne v. Doran, 13 Ir. Eq. Rep. 545; Adair v. Shaw, 1 Sch. & Lef. 243; Brinton v. Hutchinson, 3 Ir. Ch. Rep. 361.

26. Brettlebank v. Goodwin, *supra*.

27. Baker v. Martin, 5 Sim. 380; Obee v. Bishop, 1 D. F. & J. 137; Story v. Gape, 2 Jur. N. S. 706.

When the English Trustee Act, 1888, was passed, no existing statute of limitations applied to an action against a trustee, founded on a breach of trust, to recover money; that act limited the time for such an action to six years from the time when the loss occasioned by the breach of trust occurred. See *In re* Swain (1891), 3 Ch. 233. See also on that Act, Thorne v. Heard (1895), A. C. 495; Leahy v. De Moleyns (1896), 1 I. R. 206.

It is not negligence or laches on the part of the *cestui que trust* to allow all the instruments of title, including title deeds and negotiable certificates of stock, to remain in the trustee's custody. Carritt v. Real and Personal Advance Co., 42 Ch. D. 263, 270.

ance by him, equity treats him as absolute owner of an indefeasible estate, and the vendor is a naked trustee, having no estate and charged with the simple duty to convey to the vendee upon demand, and the statute does not begin to run upon his rights to a specific performance of the contract by a conveyance of the land by the vendor, until the vendor has given him notice of his intention not to convey, or done some other unequivocal act indicating that he claims and holds the land adversely.[28] Equity regards the vendee as owner upon the principle that it regards that as done which ought to be done, and will compel the conveyance of the legal title to him, because at law his equitable title is not recognized, and so long as the vendee is in possession under his contract, the statute cannot run upon his right to a conveyance.[29]

The trust which arises upon the sale of land, where the purchase money has been paid, is a resulting trust. It is excepted out of the statute of frauds, and in cases which admit of doubt, parol evidence is admissible to rebut the presumption that a trust was intended, as in the case where lands are purchased in the name of one, and the purchase money paid by another. Although from the circumstances a trust would be implied, it may be shown that it was intended as a loan or an advance. Like express trusts, these trusts arise from a confidence reposed in the trustee, and are in accordance with the intention of the parties. In this respect they differ widely from those constructive trusts which are established by evidence and forced upon the conscience of the trustee against his will, and generally to prevent the consummation of a fraud. In the latter case the relation of the parties is hostile from the beginning, and the possession of the trustee adverse; and there being no actual confidence reposed in the trustee, there can be no pretense that, according to the intent and contract of the parties, the relation was to be a continuous

28. Love v. Watkins, 40 Cal. 547, 6 Am. Rep. 624.

29. Temple, J., in Bodley v. Ferguson, 30 Cal. 511; Morrison v. Wilson, 13 id. 498; Richardson v. Kuhn, 6 Watts (Pa.) 299; Martin v. Willink, 7 S. & R. (Pa.) 297.

one. As to the former, the relation being friendly, and a real confidence reposed in the trustee, which may be intended as a continuous one, so long as the relation is recognized and acted upon by the parties, the same reason that induced courts of equity to recognize the trust at all would compel them to recognize its continued existence. The purpose of the trust may have been that the trustee should continue to hold the title, and the same confidence that led to the trust in the beginning would prevent the beneficiary from compelling a conveyance of the legal estate to him. The only respect in which this trust differs from an express trust is as to the mode in which it is established or proven. That is, there it no declaration or agreement by which the terms are stated upon which the trustee is to hold the trust property. When established, they are recognized and enforced precisely as express trusts are enforced; the only difference being that perhaps a different presumption might arise from the possession of the trustee. The trust, though implied from the evidence, is in reality an express trust, and will be treated as such by the court. That is, implied trusts are considered as really the expression of the donor or grantor as those which are denominated express trusts; the difference is only in the form of language by which the trust is expressed. They derive their authority from the will of the donor, grantor, etc., as gathered from his actions or expressions.[30]

30. Tiffany & Bullard on Trusts, 19. In Bartlett v. Judd, 23 Barb. (N. Y.) 263, aff'd 21 N. Y. 200, 78 Am. Dec. 131, which was an action to reform a deed, the vendee having been in possession, and more than ten years having elapsed, the court held that he was not barred, notwithstanding the provision of the statute that "bills for relief shall be filed within ten years after the cause of action accrued, and not after." It was held that when the equitable owner of land is in possession, and is afterwards evicted by the owner of the legal title, his cause of action to establish his equitable right does not arise until after eviction. See also Varick v. Edwards, 11 Paige (N. Y.) 290. In Harris v. King, 16 Ark. 122, the court even held that if the vendor, having received the full purchase money, executes a bond to convey, and then remains in possession, he will be presumed to hold as trustee or agent, and the statute does not

The conveyance from the trustee to the *cestui que trust* in such cases is but the execution of the trust; the right to obtain the legal title is but an incident to the estate of the *cestui que trust.* So long, therefore, as the estate exists, so long will the right to acquire the legal title subsist. It is like the right of a tenant in common to compel a partition, and is not a cause of action which accrues in the sense of the statute of limitations, and which may be lost by the lapse of time. The trustee and *cestui que trust* have the same title, and do not hold adversely so long as the rights of neither are denied. If A. purchases land with his own money, but, for proper reasons, the deed is taken in the name of B. with his consent, and A. goes into possession and continues to use the property as his own, this would be an implied trust; but no one would think the statute of limitations would deprive A. of his estate for a failure to obtain the legal title within four years. He is guilty of no laches in asserting his rights. His possession is the most effective assertion of them.

In Texas, this question has been considerably discussed, and the decisions are in accordance with this view. The trust created is held to be a continuing trust; that the vendee is clothed with the equitable title, and the statute does not run against his right

run in his favor against the vendee. This is held upon the doctrine of trusts, it being held that an equitable title to real estate can be lost only in the same manner as a legal title, by adverse possession. The same was held in Scarlett v. Hunter, 56 N. C. (3 Jones Eq.) 84. See also Boone v. Chiles, 35 U. S. (10 Pet.) 177, 9 L. Ed. 388; Ahl v. Johnson, 61 U. S. (20 How.) 511, 15 L. Ed. 1005; Barlow v. Whitelock, 4 Munf. (Va.) 180; Crofton v. Ormsby, 2 Sch. & Lef. 583, 603; Burke v. Length, 3 J. & L. 193; Longworth v. Taylor, 1 McLean (U. S. C. C.) 395; Miller v. Bear, 3 Paige (N. Y.) Ch. 466; Waters v. Travis, 9 Johns. (N. Y.) 450; New Barbadoes Toll Bridge Co. v. Vreeland, 4 N. J. Eq. 157. In Coulson v. Walton, 34 U. S. (9 Pet.) 62, 9 L. Ed. 51, a special performance was decreed forty-four years after an action might have been brought for that purpose by the vendee. It was held that the statute would be good in all cases in equity by analogy, when at law it would have been held good under similar circumstances; that a legal title could only be barred by adverse possession, and, therefore, an equitable title could only be barred in the same way.

to enforce a specific performance, so long as he remains in possession with the acquiescence of the vendor.[31]

§ 220. Purchaser of property for benefit of another.

It is a well-settled rule that where one person purchases lands or other property for another, and the purchase money is paid by the beneficiary or out of his funds, although the title is taken in the name of the person making the purchase, a trust results, and the purchaser holds the land or other property in trust for the person whose money paid for the same, whether the trust was created by writing, or vests merely in parol.[32] If a part only of the purchase money is paid by the person claiming the benefit of the trust, the resulting trust is limited to the amount so paid, even though he subsequently pays the balance, or offers to pay it,[33] unless a note or other obligation is given for the balance;[34] and if the consideration is paid by two or more persons jointly, a trust results in favor of each, to the extent of the consideration furnished by each.[35] The rule is well settled that the trust must result at the time of the execution of the deed, and cannot be raised by matters subsequent thereto,[36] and it is under this latter rule that the trust is restricted to the amount of the purchase money actually furnished by the person claiming the benefit of the purchase at the time of or before the execution of the conveyance, as the trust must result at the very instant the deed is executed, or it cannot result at all.[37]

31. Hemming v. Zimmerschitte, 4 Tex. 159; Mitchell v. Sheppard, 13 Tex. 484; Holman v. Criswell, 15 Tex. 394; Vardeman v. Lawson, 17 Tex. 10; Newson v. Davis, 20 Tex. 419.

32. Havens v. Bliss, 26 N. J. Eq. 363; Cutler v. Tuttle, 19 N. J. Eq. 549; Stratton v. Dialogue, 16 N. J. Eq. 70.

33. Baldwin v. Campbell, 8 N. J. Eq. 891.

34. Depeyster v. Gould, 3 N. J. Eq. 474; Baldwin v. Campbell, *supra*.

35. Cutler v. Tuttle, *supra*.

36. Tunnard v. Littell, 23 N. J. Eq. 264.

37. Davis v. Wetherell, 93 Mass. (11 Allen) 19; Barnard v. Jewett, 97 Mass. 87.

§ 220a(1). Existence of trust—In general.

To exempt a trust from the bar of the statute of limitations, it must be (1) a direct trust; (2) it must be of the kind belonging exclusively to the jurisdiction of a court of equity; and (3) the question must arise between the trustee and the *cestui que trust.*[38] So long as the duties of a trustee remain undischarged, he cannot avail himself of the statute of limitations as a defense.[39] Where one received money under a parol trust, and never repudiated the trust, limitations did not run against the *cestui que trust.*[40] Limitations apply to an action to compel conveyance of land which defendant executor held in trust.[41] A participant in a breach of trust cannot invoke the defense of limitations.[42] Where a trustee with-

38. Wilson v. Equitable Trust Co., 98 Ill. App. 81, judg. rev'd Equitable Trust Co. v. Wilson, 200 Ill. 23, 65 N. E. 430; Larwill v. Burke, 19 Ohio Cir. Ct. R. 449, 513, 10 O. C. D. 605.

39. Wilson v. Equitable Trust Co., *supra,* judg. rev'd Equitable Trust Co. v. Wilson, *supra.*

Where a trust company, as receiver, obtains possession of a fund in the capacity of a trustee, the statute of limitations does not apply; and such relation is not changed merely because the fund has been paid over to it in a different capacity. Id.

40. Stanley's Estate v. Pence, 160 Ind. 636, 66 N. E. 51, 67 N. E. 441.

Where, by agreement between them, defendant took possession of the funds of plaintiff and invested them as he saw fit, and he loaned a sum on worthless security, limitations did not begin to run against an action against defendant for the sum negligently loaned, and lost, until the termination of the trust relation. Hitchcock v. Cosper, 164 Ind. 633, 69 N. E. 1029, judg. rev'd 164 Ind. 633, 73 N. E. 264.

41. McQuerry v. Gilliland, 89 Ky. 434, 11 Ky. Law Rep. 656, 12 S. W. 1037, 7 L. R. A. 454.

Where testatrix directed a sale of her real estate to discharge an indebtedness her son owed her daughter-in-law, and provided for a division of the surplus, the administrator of testatrix had no right to hold the property as trustee, but the daughter-in-law or her administratrix could sue for it; and an action therefor was barred by the 15-year statute of limitations (Ky. St. § 2514). Baugh's Adm'x v. Baugh's Adm'r, 159 Ky. 320, 167 S. W. 124.

Limitation begins to run against the claim of the beneficiary against his trustee from the time when the beneficiaries could have brought suit against the trustee for the fund sought to be charged to him. Mercer v. Glass's Ex'r, 15 Ky. Law Rep. 710, 25 S. W. 114.

42. Duckett v. National Mechanics' Bank, 86 Md. 400, 38 Atl. 983, 39 L. R. A. 84, 63 Am. St. Rep. 513.

out power of sale sold trust property and applied the proceeds to his own use, and the purchaser knew of the character of the trust and dealt with the trustee in an attempt to acquire the property freed from the trust he perpetrated a legal fraud on the beneficiaries, who might sue him to impress the property in his hands with a trust, though the trustee was barred by limitations.[43] Even though a loan under promise of a lien should constitute a trust, the debt can be recovered at law, and the fact that the lender is entitled to equitable relief does not extend the statute.[44] Where a trustee diverts the proceeds of property to the purchase of land, taking title in his own name, the beneficiaries may pursue the land, unaffected by the bar of the statute of limitations.[45] Where a person taking title to land, part of the price of which had been paid by another, recognizes his rights, limitations do not run against the person paying such portion of the price.[46] An action against a county to enforce the trust imposed on it by Texas Const., art. 7, § 6, is not barred by limitations, though the county wrongfully diverted the proceeds, but did not repudiate the trust.[47] The act of limitations does not run between trustee and *cestui que trust.* This is generally true as to express trusts.[48] The trusts against which

43. Elliott v. Landis Mach. Co., 236 Mo. 546, 139 S. W. 356.

44. Ray v. Ray, 24 Misc. Rep. 155, 53 N. Y. Supp. 300.

45. Kaphan v. Toney (Tenn. Ch. App.) 58 S. W. 909.

46. Miller v. Saxton, 75 S. C. 237, 55 S. E. 310.

47. Comanche County v. Burks (Tex. Civ. App.), 166 S. W. 470.

Where plaintiff claimed that money sued for was left on deposit with defendant's decedent, to be used in a business conducted by her, while defendant claimed that the money was contributed by plaintiff to the business, and that she was a partner, limitations could not be successfully pleaded in either event. Altgelt v. Elmendorf (Tex. Civ. App.), 86 S. W. 41.

A complaint in an action to recover an interest inherited by plaintiff in realty on the theory that a certain instrument created a trust, though in form a release, is not primarily a suit to set aside the instrument, so as to be barred by limitations if not brought within the statutory time. Williams v. Emberson, 22 Tex. Civ. App. 522, 55 S. W. 595.

48. Redford v. Clarke, 100 Va. 115, 4 Va. Sup. Ct. Rep. 36, 40 S. E. 630. See also Pendleton v. Whiting, Wythe (Va.) 38 (Orig. Ed. 94); Lamar's Ex'r v. Hale, 79 Va. 147; Rowe v. Bentley, 29 Grat. (Va.) 76.

the statute of limitations does not run are those technical and continuing trusts not cognizable at law, and falling within the proper, peculiar, and exclusive jurisdiction of equity; but such other trusts as may be ground of action at law are subject to the operation of the statute.[49] Limitations run in favor of a trustee unless the trust is an express one, and is a technical and continuing one, such as falls within the peculiar jurisdiction of equity.[50]

§ 220a(2). When relation exists in general.

The statute of limitations will not run against the liability of a city under its agreement, upon voluntarily purchasing with drainage warrants a plant for perfecting its drainage system, to facilitate the collection of assessments, and not to divert such collections from payment of the warrants until it repudiates the trust, although judgments are substituted for the warrants against its own property.[51] A city cannot plead limitations against a suit to require it to account for taxes collected in behalf of its school board, as it holds such taxes in trust, and cannot acquire rights therein by prescription.[52] The fund for the payment of outstanding liabilities pro-

49. Rowan v. Chenoweth, 49 W. Va. 287, 38 S. E. 544, 87 Am. St. Rep. 796.

Express trusts, cognizable only in equity, are alone free from limitation created by laches or statute. All other trusts, whether legal or equitable, are either subject to the statute of limitations or liable to be barred by laches. Woods v. Stephenson, 43 W. Va. 149, 27 S. E. 309. The statute of limitations cannot be pleaded by a trustee against his *cestui que trust* claiming a settlement of the trust accounts; the possession of the trustee being the possession of the *cestui que trust.* Weinrich v. Wolf, 24 W. Va. 299.

50. Merton v. O'Brien, 117 Wis. 437, 94 N. W. 340.

51. Warner v. City of New Orleans, 81 Fed. 645, 26 C. C. A. 508, decree modified, City of New Orleans v. Warner, 175 U. S. 120, 20 Sup. Ct. 44, 44 L. Ed. 96. See also Warner v. City of New Orleans, 87 Fed. 829, 31 C. C. A. 238.

52. City of New Orleans v. Fisher, 91 Fed. 574, 34 C. C. A. 15, modified 180 U. S. 185, 21 Sup. Ct. 347, 45 L. Ed. 485.

The 10-year statute of limitations is no bar to a suit by judgment creditors of a city school board, whose claims are payable out of the school taxes, to require the city to account for the amount of such taxes collected and held in trust by it for the payment of the expenses of the public schools, where the bill was filed within ten years after the judgments were rendered. Id.

vided by U. S. Rev. St., § 306, is a trust fund, and the statutes of limitation cannot be set up against a claimant who has been credited under such appropriation.[53] An action by the state for proceeds of a school section (No. 16) loaned is not subject to the statute of limitations, the United States having granted to the State section No. 16 in every township, "for the use of the inhabitants of such township for the use of schools," whereby the state assumed a trust for the purpose of discharging a governmental duty, and such action being to enforce the trust.[54] The fact that an attorney who had collected money promised, in writing, to pay over the same to the client after he had paid certain fees chargeable against the fund, did not render him a trustee to pay himself a fee, and pay other fees chargeable against the fund, and pay the balance to the client, so as to relieve the client's cause of action from the bar of the statute of limitations.[55] The relation between a stockholder and the corporation is not such that unpaid subscriptions in the subscriber's hands are a trust fund, so as to prevent limitations running against a suit by a creditor of the corporation against the stockholder.[56] Directors of a national bank, while implied trustees, are not technical trustees, and hence directors who had ceased to be such, prior to the failure of the bank, were entitled to plead

53. Wardwell v. United States, 32 Ct. Cl. (U. S.) 30, aff'd United States v. Wardwell, 172 U. S. 48, 19 Sup. Ct. 86, 43 L. Ed. 360.

Money deposited in the land office for the purpose of purchasing land is held in trust for that use, and the transaction may remain open until finally acted on by the secretary of the interior; and the statute of limitations does not begin to run until the final action of the department. Nelson v. United States, 35 Ct. Cl. (U. S.) 47.

54. State v. Burk, 63 Ark. 56, 37 S. W. 406.

See also Miller & Lux v. Batz, 142 Cal. 447, 76 Pac. 42, holding that moneys arising from the sale of swamp lands are held by the state in trust for the purchasers, so that limitations do not begin to run against an action to recover part of it till the trust is repudiated.

55. Schofield v. Woolley, 98 Ga. 548, 25 S. E. 769, 58 Am. St. Rep. 315.

56. Parmelee v. Price, 208 Ill. 544, 70 N. E. 725, aff'g judg. 105 Ill. App. 271.

limitations as a defense to a suit by a receiver of the bank, to recover losses sustained by their malfeasance or gross negligence.[57] The refusal of an administrator to render an account when thereto cited constitutes an independent breach of his bond, which is not barred by limitations, even if it occurred more than twenty years after the date of his bond.[58] The relation between a principal and an agent who has ceased doing business for his principal, and whose duty it is merely to collect and remit the money due his principal on outstanding mortgages, is not such a trust relation as suspends the running of limitations.[59] An agreement to assign an interest in certain patent rights, and a payment of a portion of the purchase money, does not constitute the promisor a trustee for the promisee under an executed trust, so as to prevent the running of the statute of limitations, but the contract is an executory one for conveyance, and is to be governed by the rules for specific performance.[60] Where a stranger to a trust has assumed to act and has acted as trustee, and by his officious acts has rendered himself liable as a trustee *de son tort,* he is estopped from setting up by way of limitation that his acts were in hostility to the trusts.[61] A claim

57. Emerson v. Gaither, 103 Md. 564, 64 Atl. 26, 8 L. R. A. (N. S.) 738.

58. Fuller v. Cushman, 170 Mass. 286, 49 N. E. 631.

An administrator is a trustee, and cannot set up the statute of limitations in bar to the next of kin or persons entitled to the distribution of the assets. Rubey v. Barnett, 12 Mo. 3, 49 Am. Dec. 112.

59. Jewell v. Jewell's Estate, 139 Mich. 578, 12 Detroit Leg. N. 10, 102 N. W. 1059.

Where an agent acting for the owners, though infants, collects rents for them, limitations do not run against the trust. Carroll v. Montgomery, 128 N. C. 278, 38 S. E. 874.

60. Harrigan v. Smith, (N. J. Ch.) 40 Atl. 13, rev'd 57 N. J. Eq. 635, 42 Atl. 579.

61. Hart v. Goadby, 72 Misc. Rep. 232, 129 N. Y. Supp. 892.

The term "fiduciary capacity" in N. Y. Code Civ. Proc. § 410, limiting the time to sue for the receipt or detention of property by one acting in a fiduciary capacity, defines a relation based on personal confidence reposed by one person in another, and does not apply to an action against a corporation wrongfully transferring corporate stock on a forged power of attorney. Glover v. National Bank of Commorce of New York, 156 App. Div. 247, 141 N. Y. Supp. 409.

Where the assignment of an insurance policy on the life of the husband for the benefit of his wife was abso-

of a wife against the estate of her husband in bankruptcy for a fund which he held in trust for her was not barred by limitations, nor by her laches; where up to within three years he had been in prosperous financial circumstances, and there had been nothing to awaken her suspicions that her money was in danger, or that there was any breach of trust.[62] Where a party complied with the conditions of a bond for a deed to certain land, so that he was entitled to a conveyance, but none was made, and neither he nor any one claiming under him had possession of the land, the vendors cannot be treated as trustees of the legal title for the vendee in order that the statute of limitations might not run against the right of the vendee to recover the land until notice of the breach of the relation.[63] Where an heir appoints an agent to collect his share of the estate and turn it over to him, there is no trust, and limitations commence to run against his claim for the share collected from the date of collection, whether demand is made or not.[64] Money deposited by one person with another to be paid to a third, and not paid, does not create a trust cognizable only in equity, not subject to limitations, but is only a legal demand, and subject to the statute.[65] As to when the trust relation exists between parties generally, see other cases cited in the note below.[66]

lutely void, because the written consent of the husband to such assignment was not obtained, her right to contest the validity of such assignment cannot be barred by the statute of limitations. Dannhauser v. Wallenstein, 52 App. Div. 312, 65 N. Y. Supp. 219, rev'g judg. 60 N. Y. Supp. 50, 28 Misc. Rep. 690, order rev'd 169 N. Y. 199, 62 N. E. 160.

62. *In re* Carpenter, 179 Fed. 743 (U. S. D. C., S. C.).

63. Edwards v. Beck, 57 Wash. 80, 106 Pac. 492.

64. Hasher's Adm'x v. Hasher's Adm'r, 96 Va. 584, 32 S. E. 41.

65. Burbridge v. Sadler, 46 W. Va. 39, 32 S. E. 1028.

A deputy sheriff is agent of the sheriff, and the statute of limitations applies between them as between agent and principal. Rowan v. Chenoweth, 49 W. Va. 287, 38 S. E. 544, 87 Am. St. Rep. 796.

66. *Ark.*—Leigh v. Evans, 64 Ark. 26, 41 S. W. 427.

Ga.—Cannon v. Lynch, 112 Ga. 660, 37 S. E. 858.

Ind.—Sheaf v. Dodge, 161 Ind. 270, 68 N. E. 292.

Md.—Constable v. Camp, 87 Md. 173, 39 Atl. 807.

Mass.—Pierce v. Perry, 189 Mass. 332, 75 N. E. 734, 109 Am. St. Rep. 637.

Mich.—O'Toole v. Hurley, 115

§ 220a(3). Possession of property.

Limitations do not begin to run against the enforcement of a resulting trust so long as the beneficiary was in possession and there was no adverse holding or repudiation of the trust by the trustee.[67] The statute of limitations does not run against a *cestui que trust* in possession.[68] A beneficiary cannot claim to hold adversely under his own trustee.[69] An executor holding property of his decedent under a trust which he has acknowledged cannot avail himself of the statute of limitations in defense to a bill in equity to compel him to account for such porperty.[70] One in possession of land as trustee cannot claim adversely to the title under which he enters without first surrendering the possession.[71] To defeat an open and unquestioned possession of lands for fifty years, on the ground that the party in possession held as trustee of an express trust, it must clearly appear that the possession was taken while the trust was subsisting.[72] The statute begins to run against the recovery of funds held in trust at the time the funds were due the beneficiary.[73]

§ 220a(4). Express or continuing trust.

The statute of limitations has no application to a case involving

Mich. 517, 4 Detroit Leg. N. 965, 73 N. W. 805.

Tenn.— Cullen v. Coal Creek Min. & Mfg. Co., (Tenn. Ch. App.) 42 S. W. 693.

Tex.— Morris v. Unknown Heirs of Hamilton, (Tex. Civ. App.) 95 S. W. 66.

Va.— Lesslie's Ex'r v. Brown's Ex'rs, 1 Pat. & H. 216.

67. Lufkin v. Jakeman, 188 Mass. 528, 74 N. E. 933.

68. Norton v. McDevit, 122 N. C. 755, 30 S. E. 24.

69. Newton v. McLean, 41 Barb. (N. Y.) 285.

Where an admission is made to the trustee of personal property, by the beneficiary, that he holds the property subject to the trusts for which the deed has been given, this shows that the beneficiary's possession was not adverse, and so prevents the statutory bar, although the acknowledgment would not revive the debt secured by the deed. Sullivan v. Hadley, 16 Ark. 129.

70. Colbert v. Daniel, 32 Ala. 314.

71. O'Halloran v. Fitzgerald, 71 Ill. 53.

72. Starkey v. Fox, 52 N. J. Eq. (7 Dick.) 758, 29 Atl. 211.

73. Merrill v. Town of Monticello, 66 Fed. 165.

a direct trust between the *cestui que trust* and the trustee, cognizable only in a court of equity.[74] Express or direct and continuing trusts are not within the statute of limitations.[75] An administration of an estate, while a trust, is not a continuing express trust against which limitations do not run under the Kentucky statute.[76] As between the beneficiaries of an express trust and the trustee, who has never denied his relation to the trust, or that moneys were due thereunder, the statute of limitations has no application.[77]

74. McGillis v. Hogan, 85 Ill. App. 194, aff'd 190 Ill. 176, 60 N. E. 91.

The defense of limitations is never available against an express and continuing trust as between trustees and *cestui que trust*. Morton v. Harrison, 111 Md. 536, 75 Atl. 337.

75. Parks v. Satterthwaithe, 132 Ind. 411, 32 N. E. 82; Jones v. Henderson, 149 Ind. 458, 49 N. E. 443.

76. Prewitt v. Morgan's Heirs (Ky.), 119 S. W. 174, under Ky. St. 1909, § 2543 (Russell's St. § 209), providing that the chapter (limitation of actions) shall not apply to a continuing and subsisting trust. The statute does not apply in behalf of the trustee under an express enforceable parol trust respecting land. Smith v. Smith (Ky.), 121 S. W. 1002. An action to surcharge the settlement of an executrix's account is not within the statute, which includes only such continuing trusts as entitle the trustee to hold the estate independent of the *cestui que trust*. Wren's Ex'r v. Wren's Ex'x, 31 Ky. Law Rep. 1096, 104 S. W. 737.

A vendee going into possession of land under an executory contract for the purchase of it, and continuing therein until sued for the balance due on the purchase price, is not entitled to the benefit of the statute. Bargo v. Bargo, 27 Ky. Law Rep. 680, 86 S. W. 525.

Where a husband received the proceeds of his wife's property under an agreement that he would hold it in trust for her, and during a period of 30 years recognized the existence of the obligation, limitations did not run against the wife's right to enforce the trust, nor did this right become stale. Bohannon v. Bohannon's Adm'x, 29 Ky. Law. Rep. 143, 92 S. W. 597. Express trusts being created by the direct, intentional, and declaratory acts of the party, as to such trusts the statutes of limitations do not apply. Rogers v Reid, 14 Ky. Law. Rep. (abstract) 811.

77. Merritt v. Merritt, 32 App. Div. 442, 53 N. Y. Supp. 127, judg. aff'd 161 N. Y. 634, 57 N. E. 1117.

Where a will created testator's executors trustees for the purpose of carrying on testator's business and accumulating the income and profits thereof for a certain period, beneficiaries of the trust were not barred by limitations from contending that, in so far as the will attempted to create an accumulation of income after the beneficiaries arrived at majority, it was void, so long as such testamentary trustees still continued

In the case of an express trust the statute of limitations commences to run in favor of the trustee only on his open repudiation of the trust.[78] The purpose of the statute of limitations in providing that the limitations shall not apply to continuing and subsisting trusts is that the possession and ownership, or either, of the trustee, is the possession and ownership of the *cestui que trust;* but when this relation is severed, and the parties so understand it, then the possession and ownership of the trustee will no longer be the possession and ownership of the *cestui que trust,* and, from such time of the denial of the trust, the statute will run against the *cestui que trust* as against any other person.[79] The rule that limitations do not run against an express trust does not apply to an

the management of the business, and held the proceeds of the estate for distribution. Thorn v. DeBreteuil, 86 App. Div. 405, 83 N. Y. Supp. 849, modified 179 N. Y. 64, 71 N. E. 470.

The duty of a trustee to account for a fund being a continuing duty, the statute of limitations cannot be invoked by the trustee in an action for an accounting, where the trustee has never publicly renounced the trust. *In re* Jones' Estate, 30 Misc. Rep. 354, 63 N. Y. Supp. 726, judg. aff'd 51 App. Div. 420, 64 N. Y. Supp. 667.

78. Townsend v. Crowner, 125 N. Y. Supp. 329, judg. aff'd 145 App. Div. 906, 129 N. Y. Supp. 1148.

Where an executor is engaged in the discharge of his duties as such, and is maintaining a proceeding to recover money claimed by him to belong to the estate of the testator, that he may distribute it under the will, the right of a legatee to require the executor to account is not barred by limitations, though 12 years and 9 months have elapsed since the issuance of letters testamentary. *In re* Anderson, 122 App. Div. 453, 106 N. Y. Supp. 818.

79. Larwill v. Burke, 19 Ohio Cir. Ct. R. 449, 513, 10 O. C. D. 605, the only continuing and subsisting trust that may not be barred by the statute of limitations is one where the *cestui que trust* has no cause of action that he can bring until such time as the trust is terminated by lapse of time.

Where property was held in trust, and the trust was continued, the statute of limitations was not applicable. Moore v. Idlor, 26 Ohio Cir. Ct. R. 502. Continuing and subsisting trusts, which arise only by appointment or contract, are without the statute of limitations, as there is no time at which the cause of action accrues and can only be satisfied by performance. Jones v. Jones, 18 Ohio Cir. Ct. R. 260, 10 O. C. D. 71. In excepting continuing and subsisting trusts from the operation of the statute of limitations, the legislature was merely recognizing and saving a prevailing rule. Id.

action to foreclose a deed of trust or for the appointment of a substituted trustee thereunder.[80] The statute of limitations can never run as between the *cestui que trust* and the trustee, and while in general this rule holds good only as between the *cestui que trust* and the trustee, and not between the *cestui que trust* and the trustee on one side and strangers on the other, yet the statute does not run between a *cestui que trust* and a trustee *ex maleficio*.[81] Where a trustee under a will procured no release from a beneficiary, and there was no direct or presumptive evidence to justify the conclusion that the acts of the trustee, though in the interest of the beneficiary, were performed by him and accepted by the beneficiary in discharge of the trust, the trust must be deemed to have continued, since against an express and subsisting trust the statute of limitations affords no bar.[82] The functions and duties of partners are largely those of trustees and agents, and there must be some action taken against a partner, as a demand for an acounting, in order to terminate the fiduciary relation, to start limitations running, so that, where a partner receives the firm assets to pay firm debts,

80. Rowe v. Mulvane, 25 Colo. App. 502, 139 Pac. 1041.

So far as the statute of limitations is concerned, it is not material whether a suit is brought to enforce an express or resulting trust. Dennison v. Barney, 49 Colo. 442, 113 Pac. 519.

81. Canada v. Daniel, 175 Mo. App. 55, 157 S. W. 1032.

Heirs of church trustees, suing in their individual right, and not as representatives of the church or its members, cannot defeat limitations by asserting that the statute, as between *cestui que trust* and trustee, does not run in favor of either, as against the other, in an express trust. Dudley v. Clark, 255 Mo. 570, 164 S. W. 608.

82. Jones v. Haines, 79 N. J. Eq. 110, 80 Atl. 943.

The statute of limitations is not applicable to an equitable interest in a fund held in trust by a building association for distribution among the holders of shares in a matured series. Campbell v. Perth Amboy Mut. Loan, etc., Ass'n, 76 N. J. Eq. 347, 74 Atl. 144.

The six-years' statute of limitations will not be enforced in a court of equity as a bar to an accounting, if the complaint asserts and sucoessfully proves that moneys were collected under an express trust created by him and accepted by the defendant, where the latter has never claimed any ownership in the moneys collected. Carrard v. Niles (N. J. Eq.), 45 Atl. 266.

he acts as trustee for the copartner, and limitations do not run in his favor until the fiduciary relation has ceased.[83] That the reversioner under a 999-year lease is a trustee will not toll the statute of limitations as to injuries from the unlawful mining of coal by assigns of a tenant, where the controversy is between *cestuis que trustent,* and the trustees on one side, and strangers on the other.[84] The rule that limitations do not run against the trustee of an express trust applies only in equitable actions between the trustee and the *cestuis que trustent.*[85] The statement of an account between a trustee and a *cestui que trust* did not start the running of limitations against the trustee's duty to account, nor in the absence of a demand that he pay over the balance, so long as there was an agreement that the trust should continue.[86] As between trustee and *cestui que trust,* in the case of an express trust the statute of limitations has no application, and no length of time is a bar.[87]

83. Baker v. Brown, 151 N. C. 12, 65 S. E. 520.

The trust reposed in the guardian of a lunatic terminates upon the lunatic's death, and limitations then begin to run against the right of the lunatic's distributees to call for an accounting. Lowder v. Hatchcock, 150 N. C. 438, 64 S. E. 194.

84. Trustees of Proprietors of Kingston v. Lehigh Valley Coal Co., 241 Pa. 469, 88 Atl. 763.

Where a person acts as trustee for others of a fund raised by the sale of property, the statute of limitations has no application in an action for an accounting where it appears that several years were spent by attorneys in endeavoring to secure a settlement without suit. Horine v. Mengel, 30 Pa. Super. Ct. 67.

85. State v. City and County of Milwaukee, 152 Wis. 228, 138 N. W. 1006.

A statute of limitations does not run in favor of a guardian, as against a ward, while the guardianship relation continues. Duffy v. McHale, 35 R. I. 16, 85 Atl. 36.

Limitations are not available to the personal representative of a deceased administrator and the sureties on his official bond in a suit for an accounting. Elizalde v. Murphy, 163 Cal. 681, 126 Pac. 978.

An administrator cannot plead limitations as regards his individual debt to the estate. Long v. Long, 118 Md. 198, 84 Atl. 375.

86. Watson v. Dodson, (Tex. Civ. App.) 143 S. W. 329.

Executors sued by a legatee for an accounting and to recover plaintiff's distributive share cannot invoke the statute of limitations. Farrell v. Cogley, (Tex. Civ. App.) 146 S. W. 315. See also, as to an express or continuing trust, Honea v. Arledge, (Tex. Civ. App.) 120 S. W. 508.

87. Hatt v. Green, 180 Mich. 383, 147 N. W. 593.

Where a brother managed the entire business affairs of his sister, the period which would bar the right to an accounting could not have its inception prior to the last act done in recognition of the trust.[88] An express trust never having been fully performed, it is still a subsisting and continuing trust, against which limitations do not run.[89]

§ 220a(5). What constitutes express or continuing trust.

Where money appropriated by Congress is not paid to the beneficiary, but is covered into the treasury, and carried to the credit of the party for whose benefit the appropriation was made, it may be regarded as an express trust, subject to the qualification that the statute of limitations will begin to run as soon as the trust is openly

As to money received by a county treasurer in good faith as commissions he is not a trustee of an express trust, and may defeat an action to recover it by plea of the three-year statute of limitations. Board of Sup'rs of Hanover County v. Vaughan (Va.), 83 S. E. 1056.

The statute of limitations begins to run against a claim for money bequeathed in trust to a town, on the ground that the trust is void, as soon as the money is paid to the town. Smith v. Inhabitants of Town of Norton, 214 Mass. 593, 102 N. E. 270.

88. Snodgrass v. Snodgrass, 185 Ala. 155, 64 So. 594.

One assuming the management of the property of an imbecile, and performing continuous active duties in controlling the property and supporting the imbecile, cannot claim that an action for an accounting is barred by the lapse of 20 years from the time the management of the property first began. Snodgrass v. Snodgrass, 176 Ala. 276, 58 So. 199.

Where a ward after majority, and after final decree of settlement of the guardianship, continued to reside in the family of the guardian, her uncle, and he continued to act for her, the three years' limitation provided by Ala. Code 1907, § 3178, would not defeat a suit by her to set aside the decree for fraud. Manegold v. Beaven (Ala.), 66 So. 448.

Where the executor of an estate agreed with a legatee to pay her the legacy in installments of $10 each, in an action by the legatee for the balance of the legacy which the executor through mistake failed to pay to her, the defense that the claim was barred by limitations was without merit, since limitations did not commence to run until after demand and refusal to pay. Glennon v. Harris, 149 Ala. 236, 42 So. 1003.

89. Felkner v. Dooly, 27 Utah, 350, 75 Pac. 854, judg. modified on rehearing, 28 Utah, 236, 78 Pac. 365. As to an express or continuing trust under the Montana statute, see Goodell v. Sanford, 31 Mont. 163, 77 Pac. 522.

disavowed by the trustee.[90] Where land is sold under bond for title to be made upon payment of the purchase-money notes, the vendee becomes the trustee of the purchase money for the vendor, and in view of this express trust the statute of limitations will not begin to run on the purchase-money notes until there is a termination of the trust relation.[91] Where money was sent to decedent in trust for children, and decedent acknowledged the trust, and declared his intention to perform it, the trust was a continuing one, and limitations never began to run, the trustee having never disavowed.[92] Where plaintiff made her brother her agent to sell property, and to collect the purchase money, and keep it at interest for her, a continuing trust was created, and limitations did not run against plaintiff's claim.[93] Where an express trust, created by an assignment for the benefit of creditors, is still subsisting and unexecuted, limitations are not a bar to a creditor's claim which was not barred at the time of the assignment.[94] An assignee for the

90. Russell v. United States, 37 Ct. Cl. (U. S.) 113, under Rev. St. § 306 (U. S. Comp. St. 1901, p. 181).

91. Williams v. Young, 71 Ark. 164, 71 S. W. 669.

92. Cowan v. Henika, 19 Ind. App. 40, 48 N. E. 809.

93. Caldwell's Adm'r v. Hampton, 21 Ky. Law Rep. 793, 53 S. W. 14.

Where all the parties interested in the estate of a decedent, including the administrator, placed the funds of the estate in the hands of certain persons in trust to pay the debts of the decedent, an express trust for the benefit of creditors was created, and therefore the plea of the statute of limitations is not available against the creditors, who, when they had properly proved their demands, became the beneficiaries under the trust. Feighey v. Feighey's Adm'r, 12 Ky. Law Rep. (abstract) 557.

The obligor, by executing a note payable to the sureties, in a guardian's bond for the use of the ward, did not thereby create such a "continuing or subsisting trust" as prevented the statute of limitations from running in his favor. Campbell v. Colvin, 4 Ky. Law Rep. (abstract) 365.

94. Davis v. Boyden, 123 N. C. 283, 31 S. E. 492.

Where land was conveyed to a redemptioner in 1886, and he agreed to reconvey to the owner on payment of the purchase money, and the heirs of the owner remained in possession until 1896, as the redemptioner held the land under an express trust the statute of limitations was not applicable, especially in view of such possession. Owens v. Williams, 130 N. C. 165, 41 S. E. 93.

enefit of creditors is a trustee, and cannot plead the statute of imitations against the creditors.[95] A trustee of an implied trust, xecuting a trust deed providing that the land shall take the course rescribed by the trust, thereby so recognizes the trust that limitaions will not run in his favor against the *cestui que trust,* though he trust deed is not his conveyance, because his name is not in the ody of it.[96] If plaintiff gave money to another person on his promse to put it at interest for plaintiff and return it when wanted, if his created a trust, it was not a technical, continuing, or subisting trust against which limitations would not run.[97] Under the Visconsin statute, providing that express trusts may be created for he beneficial interests of any person when such trust is fully exressed and clearly defined on the face of the instrument creating ;, the officers and directors of a mutual insurance company, the ature of whose trust was necessarily stated in the articles of inorporation, were the trustees of an express trust, and the statute f limitations does not run in their favor against the creditors of

95. *In re* Passmore's Estate, 194 a. 632, 45 Atl. 417.

Where a testator directed that all s debts be paid as soon after his cease as possible, and that all his operty be sold, and converted into oney, and granted his executors five ars in which to make sale of his estate as aforesaid," there was no press trust to sell for payment of bts, and hence such provision in e will did not prevent limitations om running against testator's bts during such five years. Hempll v. Pry, 183 Pa. 593, 41 W. N. C. 7, 38 Atl. 1020.

Even if such provision created an press trust to sell for payment of bts, it did not affect the operation the statute, where the power to l was not exercised within the five ars limited by the will. Id.

96. Barnett v. Houston, 18 Tex. Civ. App. 134, 44 S. W. 689.

97. Pollard v. Allen, (Tex. Civ. App.) 171 S. W. 530.

A mere admission in the nature of an estoppel, of the receipt of money for the benefit of another, while sufficient to establish liability, does not establish a continuing trust, or transform a former constructive trust into a continuing one, so as to postpone the running of limitations until knowledge of repudiation by the trustee is brought home to the *cestui que trust,* unless that admission is kept alive by others of like character, or by conduct recognizing a duty to perform the obligation assumed. Bridgens v. West, 35 Tex. Civ. App. 277, 80 S. W. 417.

the corporation.[98] Other instances where parties have been held by the courts either to be or not to be trustees of an express or continuing trust may be found in the cases cited in the note below.[99]

§ 220a(6). Resulting or implied trust.

A suit against a trustee for a breach of implied duties, and which is not brought to recover property or funds in his hands, is subject to the bar of limitations.[1] When a trust is imposed by law, as in the case of a resulting trust, the statute of limitations begins to run in favor of the holder of the legal title against the equitable owner at the time of the conveyance, if there is no recognition of the rights of the *cestui que trust;* but, if the latter's rights are

98. Boyd v. Mutual Fire Ass'n, 116 Wis. 155, 90 N. W. 1086, 61 L. R. A. 918, 96 Am. St. Rep. 948, modified on rehearing 94 N. W. 171, 98 Am. St. Rep. 948, under Rev. St. Wis. 1898, § 2081, subd. 5.

But they are not trustees of a technical and continuing trust, cognizable only in equity, so as to be precluded from pleading limitations when sued by a receiver for acts of malfeasance and misfeasance for which they were amenable to an action at law at any time, either by the corporation or its stockholders, or, on insolvency, its creditors, the statute (section 4206) making no exception as against trustees of any kind. Id.

99. *Cal.* — Nichols v. Board of Police Pension Fund Com'rs of City and County of San Francisco, 1 Cal. App. 494, 82 Pac. 557.

Ga.— McCray v. Harrison, 136 Ga. 404, 71 S. E. 789, where an executor was appointed in January, 1900, and in a suit against him a decree was rendered in October, 1901, adjudging that one of the legatees was entitled to one-fifth of the proceeds of certain land, the executor did not, after such decree, sustain a fiduciary relation to the legatee, and the rule as to the limitation of action in cases of subsisting trusts is not applicable.

Iowa.— Smith v. Smith, 132 Iowa 700, 109 N. W. 194, where a husband purchased land with his wife's money, taking title in his name, limitations did not run against the trust until repudiation of it by the trustee.

N. Y.—*In re* Smith's Estate, 66 App. Div. 340, 72 N. Y. Supp. 1062, order aff'd 179 N. Y. 563, 71 N. E. 1140.

Ohio.— Irwin v. Lloyd, 20 Ohio Cir. Ct. R. 339, 110 C. D. 212.

Tex.— Laguerenne v. Farrar, 25 Tex. Civ. App. 404, 61 S. W. 953; Vernor v. D. Sullivan & Co., (Tex. Civ. App.) 126 S. W. 641.

Wis.— Gibson v. Gibson, 108 Wis. 102, 84 N. W. 22; Merton v. O'Brien, 117 Wis. 437, 94 N. W. 340.

1. Frishmuth v. Farmers' Loan & Trust Co., 95 Fed. 5.

recognized, the statute begins to run from the time when the holder of the legal title asserts an adverse right.[2] The statute of limitations will not begin to run against the enforcement of a resulting trust until the beneficiary learns of the existence of the trust.[3] The statute of limitations begins to run against an action to establish or enforce a trust on the discovery of the facts constituting the trust.[4] In implied trusts, the statute of limitations begins to run as soon as the facts are brought to the knowledge of the *cestui que trust,* so that he can take steps to enforce the trust.[5] Limitations do not commence to run in favor of trustees of a savings bank for their wrongful acts until discovery of the wrong.[6] Limitations run against actions to enforce an implied trust to pay money on demand.[7] Limitations run between a trustee and the *cestui que trust* in an implied trust.[8] Limitations begin to run against an implied trust from the time the wrong was committed by which the person becomes chargeable as trustee by implication.[9] Where a testator bequeathed a portion of his property, which was in the form of

2. Haney v. Legg, 129 Ala. 619, 30 So. 34, 87 Am. St. Rep. 81. And see Brackin v. Newman, 121 Ala. 311, 26 So. 3.

3. Cliff v. Cliff, 23 Colo. App. 183, 128 Pac. 860.

The statute of limitations operates as a bar of the right of the *cestui que trust* to maintain an action to enforce an ordinary trust imposed by law. Parks v. Satterthwaite, 132 Ind. 411, 32 N. E. 82.

4. Shelby County v. Bragg, 135 Mo. 291, 36 S. W. 600; Smith v. Ricords, 52 Mo. 581; Ricords v. Watkins, 56 Mo. 553.

5. Freeland v. Williamson, 220 Mo. 217, 119 S. W. 560; Smith v. Ricords, *supra*; Ricords v. Watkins, *supra*. See also Hudson v. Cahoon, 193 Mo. 547, 91 S. W. 72; Prewitt v. Prewitt, 188 Mo. 675, 87 S. W. 1000.

A purchaser from a trustee with knowledge of the trust held to be a trustee *ex maleficio* in whose favor limitations did not run as against the *cestui que trust*, and hence upon her death the remainder-men could recover possession from those claiming under such purchaser. Case v. Goodman, 250 Mo. 112, 156 S. W. 698.

6. Greenfield Savings Bank v. Abercrombie, 211 Mass. 252, 97 N. E. 897.

7. Dunn v. Dunn, 137 N. C. 533, 50 S. E. 212.

8. Redford v. Clarke, 4 Va. Sup. Ct. Rep. 36, 100 Va. 115, 40 S. E. 630.

9. Beecher v. Foster, 51 W. Va. 605, 42 S. E. 647.

money, to his sister, but gave a small legacy to his brother and father; a few days thereafter he had the money drawn from the bank and given to him, and he then gave it to his sister and told her to keep it all, limitations in favor of the sister commenced to run against an action by the public administrator to enforce a trust on such money at the time when she received it.[10]

§ 220a(7). What constitutes resulting or implied trust.

The directors of a national bank are not trustees of an express trust, with respect to the property or funds of the bank, but of an implied or resulting trust created by the operation of the law upon their official relation to the bank; and the statute of limitations and the doctrine of laches may be invoked in their defense, when sued for a breach of such trust.[11] Where there is no express trust created in personal property, and no subsequent declaration of trust, the purchase of real estate with the personalty does not create an express resulting trust which will prevent the running of limitations until the trust is repudiated.[12] If plaintiff's share of the money collected by defendants, her coheirs, on a judgment obtained by them was a trust fund, the trust was an implied one to which the exception of the statute of limitations does not apply.[13] Where a wife is before death the owner of a homestead which de-

10. Barker v. Hurley, 132 Cal. 21, 63 Pac. 1071.

11. Cooper v. Hill, 94 Fed. 582, 36 C. C. A. 402.

12. Barker v. Hurley, 132 Cal. 21, 63 Pac. 1071.

Where a vendee of land, in possession thereof, has performed his part of the contract of sale, the statute of limitations will not commence to run against his right of action for specific performance of the contract as long as he remains in possession of the land; the vendor, during such period, being the equitable trustee of the legal title for the vendee. Fleishman v. Woods, 135 Cal. 256, 67 Pac. 276.

Where defendants furnished money to enable plaintiff's husband to buy land, taking title in their own name, and he afterwards paid them the amount advanced, they held as trustees, and limitations did not run against the right to compel them to execute a conveyance of the land until demand made therefor. White v. Costigan, 138 Cal. 564, 72 Pac. 178.

13. Clarke v. Seay, 21 Ky. Law Rep. 394, 51 S. W. 589.

Whenever a trustee or other person in a fiduciary capacity, acting

scended to her children, and the father after her death, collects the rents of the homestead, the father was not a trustee of the children in collecting the rent so as to suspend limitations.[14] The fraud or collucion of the purchaser at the sale under a deed of trust of property of a corporation with the president of the corporation in preventing a redemption by the corporation does not raise a trust in favor of the corporation; but the stockholders must redeem, on refusal of the corporation, within two years of the sale, or within a year after knowledge of the fraud.[15] Where a husband fraudulently appropriated property belonging to his wife, an implied, and not a direct, trust arises, to which the statute of limitations applies.[16] Where a trust is created by the purchase of land with the money of one person and its conveyance to another, it is created by implication of law, and the statute of limitations may begin to run before the trust is broken.[17] Where the owner of a mortgage purchases the land at mortgage sale, and agrees with the person liable on the bond that, if the mortgage sale is not set aside, he will sell the land at private sale, accounting to such person for any surplus over the amount of the debt, it is a promise to hold title to land for the benefit of another, which cannot be enforced after five years, unless in writing, under the Pennsylvania statute.[18] Where

apparently within the scope of his powers, purchases property with trust funds and takes title thereto in his own name without any declaration of trust, a trust arises in favor of the beneficiary which belongs to that class of trusts known as constructive trusts, and as to such trusts limitation applies. Rogers v. Reid, 14 Ky. Law Rep. (abstract) 811.

14. Carroll v. Carroll, 92 Ark. 625, 121 S. W. 947, limitations do not affect the rights of the *cestui que trust* so long as the trust relation continues.

15. McLester v. Woodlawn Cemetery, 165 Ala. 213, 51 So. 793.

Breach of promise, made by one buying notes secured by deed of trust on the property of a corporation to the stockholder thereof of whom he bought them, that he would defer for a year exercise of the power of sale under the deed, does not render the sale void, so as to make him, on purchasing at the sale, a trustee for the corporation, so as to suspend running of limitations against a suit to redeem. Id.

16. Reed v. Painter, 145 Mo. 341, 46 S. W. 1089.

17. Norton v. McDevit, 122 N. C. 755, 30 S. E. 24.

18. Mellerio v. Freeman, 211 Pa.

land bought with community funds was by mistake conveyed to the wife as a part of her separate property, a suit by the husband after the wife's death to correct the mistake was to enforce a resulting trust, within the statute of limitations.[19]

§ 220a(8). Constructive trust.

The statute of limitations begins to run against the right of an heir to enforce a constructive trust growing out of a trust existing in favor of his ancestor at the same time that it begins to run against the ancestor.[20] A suit to enforce a constructive trust to land is not stale and barred by limitations, where both parties continue to live on the premises together.[21] In cases of constructive or implied trusts the statute of limitations will not bar a suit where there is fraud.[22] The statute of limitations commences to run in favor of the trustee of an involuntary or constructive trust as soon as the trust relation is created.[23] The statute of limitations runs against the right to assert a constructive trust.[24] Limitations do not begin to run where a guardian of a ward purchases property for him, and has title taken in the name of a third person, until the ward has knowledge that the deed was taken in the name of another.[25] The provision of the Kentucky statute of limitations that it shall not apply " in the case of a continuing and subsisting trust " applies only to trusts of an exclusively equitable character,

202, 60 Atl. 735; Freeman v. Lafferty, 207 Pa. 32, 56 Atl. 230, under Act April 22, 1856, § 6 (P. L. 533). And see Frost v. Bush, 195 Pa. 544, 46 Atl. 80.

19. Strickland v. Baugh, (Tex. Civ. App.) 169 S. W. 181.

20. Lide v. Park, 135 Ala. 131, 33 So. 175, 93 Am. St. Rep. 17.

The right to enforce a constructive trust is barred in two years, unless there are special circumstances justifying greater delay. Id.

21. Ackley v. Croucher, 203 Ill. 530, 68 N. E. 86.

22. Parks v. Satterthwaite, 132 Ind. 411, 32 N. E. 82.

23. Earle v. Bryant, 12 Cal. App. 553, 107 Pac. 1018.

24. Markley v. Camden Safe Deposit & Trust Co., 74 N. J. Eq. 279, 69 Atl. 1100.

25. Manahan v. Holmes, 58 Misc. Rep. 86, 110 N. Y. Supp. 300. See, as to a trust created in shares of corporate stock, Putnam v. Lincoln Safe Deposit Co., 49 Misc. Rep. 578, 100 N. Y. Supp. 101, modified 118 App. Div. 468, 104 N. Y. Supp. 4.

where the trustee has the right to hold the estate and the *cestui que trust* has no right to sue for it, and therefore constructive trusts are not excluded from the operation of the statute.[26] Under the Iowa statute, an action to enforce a constructive trust is barred because not brought within five years after the discovery of the fraud relied on.[27]

§ 220a(9). What constitutes constructive trust.

The statute of limitations does not commence to run against the claim of a husband that money in the possession of his wife was community property until the death of the wife, as the possession of community property by the wife is the possession of the husband.[28] A stockholder, receiving in good faith dividends declared

26. Stubbins' Adm'r v. Briggs, 24 Ky. Law Rep. 230, 68 S. W. 392.

A trustee of a fund paid over by mistake a portion of the body of the estate to the *cestui que trust* and on resigning was sued by his successor for the amount so paid. The *cestui que trust* claimed the money as her own, and the trustee more than 10 years after suit was brought, in which judgment went against him, sued the *cestui que trust* to recover the amount paid. Ky. St. §§ 2515, 2519 (Russell's St. §§ 224, 229), barred in 5 and 10 years' actions for mistake and fraud. It was held that, though the statute did not apply to matters relating to express trust, it applied to the particular transaction, since at most the *cestui que trust* was only a constructive trustee of the amount paid by mistake, and there was no express trust, as the trustee had resigned 10 years before the action. Blakley v. Hanberry, 137 Ky. 283, 125 S. W. 703.

Constructive trusts are subject to the statute of limitations, and do not come within the excepted class of Ohio Rev. St. § 4974, exempting "continuing and subsisting trusts" from the operation of the chapter relating to time of commencing actions. Ward v. Ward, 12 O. C. D. 59. For other instances of the application of statutes of limitation to constructive trusts, see: Boyd's Ex'r v. Laurel County, 140 Ky. 430, 131 S. W. 171; Commonwealth v. Folz, 23 Pa. Super. Ct. 558.

27. Burch v. Nicholson, 157 Iowa, 502, 137 N. W. 1066, under Iowa Code § 3447, par. 6, and section 3448.

28. Fennell v. Drinkhouse, 131 Cal. 447, 63 Pac. 734, 82 Am. St. Rep. 361.

Where a husband, on the death of his wife, converted assets which had been their community property, and bought land therewith in his own name, and afterwards held exclusive use and possession of it, and refused to allow the heirs to share his use and occupation, his title is one of constructive trust, and limitation as

by the officers of a corporation, without knowledge that they were paid out of the capital instead of the profits, holds them under a constructive trust, and an action by a receiver for their recovery to make assets to pay debts is barred in six years.[29] Where a husband obtained money belonging to his wife without her consent in writing, and she elected to treat him as an implied or constructive trustee, such trust was not such as to suspend the statute of limitations which ran from its creation.[30] Where one, by reason of his position or superior knowledge, overreaches another so as to deprive him of his right to money, equity has exclusive jurisdiction in granting relief on the ground of a constructive trust, so that the right to relief will not be barred by the statute of limitations.[31] Where a complaint alleged that defendants, as agents for plaintiff's husband, sold land belonging to him, and converted a part of the consideration to their own use; that after the conversion plaintiff's husband consented to a retention of such sum on condition that defendants used the same when necessary in the payment of a certain debt; and that defendants at no time assumed any position inconsistent with their being joint trustees of the fund, the cause of action was based on a constructive trust, not an express trust, and hence was subject to limitations.[32] The trustee of an express trust cannot, by wrongfully conveying the property to himself, render the trust a constructive one.[33]

to such land would run against the heirs from the date of the land purchase in the husband's individual name. Clifton v. Armstrong, (Tex. Civ. App.) 54 S. W. 611.

29. Mills v. Hendershot, 70 N. J. Eq. 258, 62 Atl. 542.

30. Smith v. Settle, 128 Mo. App. 379, 107 S. W. 430.

31. Taber v. Zehner, 47 Ind. App. 165, 93 N. E. 1035, limitations do not run against a claim based upon a trust.

32. Buttles v. DeBaun, 116 Wis. 323, 93 N. W. 5.

33. Canadian & American Mortgage & Trust Co. v. Edinburgh-American Land-Mortgage Co., 16 Tex. Civ. App. 520, 42 S. W. 864.

As to what constitutes constructive trust, see also:

Cal.— Broder v. Conklin, 121 Cal. 282, 53 Pac. 699.

Ky.— Commonwealth v. Clark, 119 Ky. 85, 26 Ky. Law Rep. 993, 83 S. W. 100, 9 L. R. A. (N. S.) 750.

Ohio.—Ward v. Ward, 12 O. C. D. 59.

Tex.— Lawson v. Lawson, 30 Tex. Civ. App. 43, 69 S. W. 246; Gridgens

§ 220a(10). Rights of parties claiming under trustee.

A purchaser of trust property cannot avail himself of the benefit of the statute of limitations to defeat an action by the *cestui que trust* to enforce the trust.[34] Where a deed to a husband as trustee for the wife provided by mistake or fraud that, if she should die without issue, the husband should become the owner of the property conveyed free of the trust, the heirs of the husband cannot plead the statute of limitations in bar of an action to correct the deed, as they, having taken with notice of the trust, also became trustees.[35] If a trustee of land in a constructive trust sells the land as his own to a *bona fide* purchaser having no knowledge of the facts, who goes into immediate possession, the possession of the purchaser is adverse to the beneficiary.[36] While the statute quieting possession does not ordinarily run in favor of a trustee against the beneficiary, it will run against the latter in favor of a purchaser of the trust estate.[37]

§ 220a(11). Termination of trust.

Where persons had acted for many years as agents for decedent in the management of her property, and no settlement or adjustment had been made or demanded, but decedent had unqualifiedly recognized her liability for the services and given assurance that they would be paid for, the statute of limitations did not begin to run against the claim until decedent's death, when the agency expired.[38] Where the trustees under a will have in their hands undivided income of the trust funds, an agreement entered into between the beneficiaries determining

v. West, 35 Tex. Civ. App. 277, 80 S. W. 417.

34. Milner v. Hyland, 77 Ind. 458.

A person does not hold adverse possession of land, when he took a voluntary conveyance from one who he knew to be trustee, and repeatedly recognized the right of the beneficiary, and signed and acknowledged a deed of conveyance in pursuance of the trust so cast upon him. Moore v. Worley, 24 Ind. 81.

35. Schwartz v. Castlen, 22 Ky. Law Rep. 1063, 59 S. W. 743.

36. McMasters v. Mills, 30 Tex. 591.

37. *In re* Post, 13 R. I. 495.

38. McGrew's Ex'r. v. Congleton, 31 Ky. Law Rep. 609, 102 S. W. 1185.

See also, as to when trust termi-

their respective rights to such income, and declaring it to be their property in certain proportions, does not remove such income fund from the trust so as to make such trustees simple debtors, and start limitations running against a claim therefor.[39] Under a trust terminating on the creator's death, with provision for distribution of the residue then remaining among his daughters, right of action by one of the daughters against the trustee and his estate for an accounting accrued at such death; no fraud of the trustee appearing.[40] Where a bond and mortgage are assigned in trust, the trustee to raise funds for the mortgagee and account to him for the proceeds, and such accounting is had, the trust relation is at an end, and limitations begin to run in favor of the trustee from such accounting.[41] The trust relation between a grantor and grantee created by a conveyance of real estate to be sold by the latter, and the proceeds, after the payment of certain debts, to be paid to the grantor, is not terminated by the sale of such land by the grantee, and the relation of creditor and debtor substituted therefor, and limitations do not commence to run against the grantee for conversion of the surplus at the time of such sale and payment of debts.[42]

nated: Richardson v. Whitaker, 103 Ky. 425, 20 Ky. Law Rep. 121, 45 S. W. 774; Jolly v. Miller, 30 Ky. Law Rep. 341, 98 S. W. 326; Hendrick v. Miller, 30 Ky. Law. Rep. 330, 98 S. W. 330.

39. Pearson v. Treadwell, 179 Mass. 462, 61 N. E. 44.

40. Olmstead v. Dodd, 144 App. Div. 809, 129 N. Y. 519.

The heirs of a wife sued the heirs of a husband to enforce a trust as to the property of the wife, on the ground of a parol agreement between them that the wife's property should go to her heirs. The wife's administrator turned over her property to the husband, and the suit was not commenced until after his death, 13 years later. It was held that the right of action was barred both by the 6-year and the 10-year statute of limitations; the cause of action having accrued at once, upon his receipt of the property and failure to turn it over to the wife's heirs. Townsend v. Crowner, 125 N. Y. Supp. 329, judg. aff'd 145 App. Div. 906, 129 N. Y. Supp. 1148. See also, as to when trust terminated: *In re* Sack, 70 App. Div. 401, 75 N. Y. Supp. 120; *In re* Farmers' Loan & Trust Co., 47 App. Div. 448, 62 N. Y. Supp. 359.

41. Hayes v. Walker, 70 S. C. 41, 48 S. E. 989.

42. Irwin v. Holbrook, 26 Wash. 89, 66 Pac. 116.

§ 220b(1). Repudiation or violation of trust—In general.

The liability of a mortgage trustee to bondholders for loss resulting from his neglect to record the mortgage whereby a subsequent mortgage obtains priority, accrues on the date the latter mortgage is recorded.[43] When a trustee denies the trust to the *cestui que trust,* and claims the trust property by a title independent of the trust and adversely to the claim of the beneficiary, the statute of limitations will run in favor of such trustee.[44] A sale by a trustee for his own interest is a repudiation of the trust, and limitations begin to run against the *cestui que trust* from the date of the sale; hence, if the bank was a trustee holding title for the benefit of remaindermen when the stock was sold, there was a renunciation of the trust, in which the bank joined, and a cause of action arose at once in favor of the remaindermen.[45] Since no action accrues against an administrator in his individual capacity until there has been some violation of his trust, the statute of limitations does not begin to run until the date of such violation.[46] A grantee for life by conveying in fee repudiated his trust, so as to make limitation begin to run upon the taking of possession by

As to terminaton of trust, see also:

Ala.—Lide v. Park, 135 Ala. 131, 33 So. 175, 93 Am. St. Rep. 17.

La.—O'Neill v. Lienicke, 49 La. Ann. 3, 21 So. 113.

N. C.—Dunn v. Dunn, 137 N. C. 533, 50 S. E. 212.

Ohio.—Larwill v. Burke, 19 Ohio Cir. Ct. R. 449, 10 O. C. D. 605.

Tenn.—Lucas v. Malone, 106 Tenn. 380, 61 S. W. 82.

43. Miles v. Vivian, 79 Fed. 848, 25 C. C. A. 208 (C. C. A., N. Y.).

44. Larwill v. Burke, 19 Ohio Cir. Ct. R. 449, 513, 10 O. C. D. 605.

Where a trust is of a nature of continuing and subsisting trust, and, under the articles of the law creating it, there is given a legal action for the violation of the trust, then the statute of limitations will run from the time that such legal action might have been brought. *Id.*

45. Yeager v. Bank of Kentucky, 32 Ky. Law Rep. 547, 106 S. W. 806.

46. Carr v. Catlin, 13 Kan. 393.

Where an administrator purchases or acquires title to property of an estate, and afterwards, with the knowledge of the heirs, notoriously asserts title in himself and claims adversely to the estate, he may avail himself of the statute of limitations against the heirs, and in the same manner against the distributees, from the date of final settlement and order of distribution. Tapley v. McPike, 50 Mo. 589.

the grantee of the life tenant.[47] Where a grandfather sent a sum of money to his son to be held in trust for his grandson and paid to him on his attaining his majority, and such sum was accepted in trust for the benefit of such grandson, the statute of limitations did not run against such trust unless the son openly and expressly disavowed and repudiated the trust, and such repudiation was brought to the knowledge of the grandson, and after receiving such personal knowledge he failed to use diligence in prosecuting his claim.[48]

§ 220b(2). Necessity for disclaimer or repudiation.

Limitation does not begin to run in favor of a trustee under an express trust until a termination or repudiation thereof.[49] Limitations do not run against an express trust, until there has been a repudiation thereof by the trustee, with notice thereof to the *cestui que trust.*[50] Limitations do not begin to run in favor of a trustee, as against the beneficiary, until the trustee repudiates the trust,

47. Horan v. O'Connell, (Tex. Civ. App.) 144 S. W. 1048.

48. Dawes v. Dawes, 116 Ill. App. 36.

As to repudiation or violation of trust in general, see:

U. S.—Patterson v. Hewitt, 11 N. M. 1, 66 Pac. 552, 55 L. R. A. 658, aff'd 195 U. S. 309, 25 Sup. Ct. 35, 49 L. Ed. 214; Nash v. Ingalls, 79 Fed. 510, aff'd 101 Fed. 645, 41 C. C. A. 545 (C. C. A., Ohio.).

Ill.— Maher v. Aldrich, 205 Ill. 242, 68 N. E. 810.

Kan.— Main v. Payne, 17 Kan. 608, followed, Kennedy v. Kennedy, 25 Kan. 151.

Ky.—Stillwell v. Leavy, 84 Ky. 379, 8 Ky. Law Rep. 321, 1 S. W. 590.

N. Y.—Greenley v. Shelmidine, 83 App. Div. 559, 82 N. Y. Supp. 176.

Utah.— Felkner v. Dooly, 27 Utah, 350, 75 Pac. 854, modified on rehearing 28 Utah, 236, 78 Pac. 365.

49. *Ind.*— Parks v. Satterthwaite, 132 Ind. 411, 32 N. E. 82.

Mass.— Andrews v. Tuttle-Smith Co., 191 Mass. 461, 78 N. E. 99.

Miss.— Stanton v. Helm, 87 Miss. 287, 39 So. 457.

Tex.—Barnett v. Houston, 18 Tex. Civ. App. 134, 44 S. W. 689.

Wis.— Boyd v. Mutual Fire Ass'n, 116 Wis. 155, 90 N. W. 1086, 61 L. R. A. 918, 96 Am. St. Rep. 948, modified on rehearing 94 N. W. 171, 98 Am. St. Rep. 948.

In the case of an express trust the statute of limitations commences to run in favor of the trustee only on his open repudiation of the trust. Townsend v. Crowner, 125 N. Y. Supp. 329, judg. aff'd 145 App. Div. 906, 129 N. Y. Supp. 1148.

50. *Mich.*— Frank v. Morley's Es-

and the beneficiary has notice thereof.[51] The statute does not commence to run in favor of a trustee of land, as against the beneficiary, until a renunciation of the trust.[52] A denial or repudiation of an implied or resulting trust is not necessary to cause limitation to run in favor of the trustee, but it commences at the time of the creation of the trust.[53] Limitations do not begin to run against the enforcement of an express trust until there is a repudiation of the trust by the trustee or some act by him amounting to a violation of the trust.[54] No disaffirmance of an involuntary or constructive trust is necessary to set the statute of limitations in motion.[55] The statute of limitations begins to run against the enforcement of a trust against the trustee only upon the open disavowal of the trust.[56] Since limitations do not run against a trust

tate, 106 Mich. 635, 64 N. W. 577; Shepherd v. Shepherd's Estate, 108 Mich. 82, 65 N. W. 580; Thorne v. Foley, 137 Mich. 649, 11 Detroit Leg. N. 438, 100 N. W. 905.

Tex.— Bateman v. Ward, (Civ. App.) 93 S. W. 508.

W. Va.— Jones v. Lemon, 26 W. Va. 629.

51. *Idaho.*— Nasholds v. McDonell, 6 Idaho, 377, 55 Pac. 894.

Ind.— Daugherty v. Wheeler, 125 Ind. 421, 25 N. E. 542.

N. Y.— Hutton v. Smith, 74 App. Div. 284, 77 N. Y. Supp. 523, aff'd 175 N. Y. 375, 67 N. E. 633.

Tex.—Barnett v. Barnett, (Civ. App.) 80 S. W. 537.

52. *Ind.*—Warner v. Warner, 132 Ind. 213, 31 N. E. 466.

Kan.— Kansas City Inv. Co. v. Fulton, 4 Kan. App. 115, 46 Pac. 188.

53. *Cal.*— Barker v. Hurley, 132 Cal. 21, 63 Pac. 1071.

Ind.—Jackson v. Landers, 134 Ind. 529, 34 N. E. 323.

54. Title Ins. & Trust Co. v. Ingersoll, 158 Cal. 474, 111 Pac. 360.

Where defendant received plaintiff's goods to be sold by defendant as plaintiff's agent and accounted for, defendant was a trustee of an express trust, and hence limitations did not run against defendant's obligation to account until after defendant had repudiated its agency. Allsopp v. Joshua Hendy Mach. Works, 5 Cal. App. 228, 90 Pac. 39.

Where the pleadings and the evidence established a continuous trust, limitations did not commence to run until demand and a refusal to account for the property delivered pursuant to the trust. Dillon v. Cross, 5 Cal. App. 766, 91 Pac. 439.

55. Earle v. Bryant, 12 Cal. App. 553, 107 Pac. 1018.

So long as a trustee in a resulting trust under section 853 does not repudiate the same, limitations do not run against an action by the *cestui que trust* to have himself declared the owner. Faylor v. Faylor, 136 Cal. 92, 68 Pac. 482.

56. Scott v. Dilley, 53 Ind. App. 100, 101 N. E. 313.

until repudiation of it by the trustee, limitations do not run against the right to enforce a trust obligation of a purchaser of premises on a mortgage foreclosure, to refund to the mortgagor what she had invested in the premises, until he repudiated the trust; for until that time he was charged as trustee, with the general duty of making repayment as a condition to holding his title as against the mortgagor.[57] After a trust is repudiated the statute of limitations may be invoked by way of defense.[58] The statute of limitations would not run in favor of a liquidating partner against the creditors and other members of the firm to bar an action for fraudulent misconduct in dealing with the firm assets until there was an offer to account as liquidating partner or an open repudiation of his trusteeship.[59] Where defendants held property acquired through legal proceedings by way of equitable mortgage, or transaction amounting to the same thing, in trust for plaintiff, on being paid what should appear to be due by him, the statute of limitations did not begin to run until the defendants repudiated the trust.[60] Where a trust results by implication of law, a recognition by the trustee of the rights of the equitable owner tolls the running of limitations

To start the statute running against an action for money held by one as trustee, there must be a clear and unequivocal repudiation of the trust. Lewis v. Hershey, 45 Ind. App. 104, 90 N. E. 332.

The statute does not run in favor of one collecting money under a foreclosure, where the mortgage provided that all money derived from the foreclosure should be held by him as trustee for the bondholder, so long as he asserts no claim hostile to the bondholder. Jones v. Henderson, 149 Ind. 458, 49 N. E. 443.

57. Carr v. Craig, 138 Iowa, 526, 116 N. W. 720.

See also, as to necessity for repudiation of trust: Newis v. Topfer, 121 Iowa 433, 96 N. W. 905; Widner v. Wilcox, 131 Iowa 223, 108 N. W. 238.

58. Babcock v. Farwell, 146 Ill. App. 307, judg. aff'd 245 Ill. 14, 91 N. E. 683.

59. Breyfogle v. Bowman, 157 Ky. 62, 162 S. W. 787.

A mutual life insurance company holds the equitable value of a policy in trust for the policy holder, and the latter's cause of action on the policy is not barred by the statute of limitations until after a demand for an accounting and a refusal to comply with the demand. Southern Mut. Life Ins. Co. v. Hodge, 13 Ky. Law Rep. 42.

60. Potter v. Kimball, 186 Mass. 120, 71 N. E. 308.

until the holder of the title disavows the trust.[61] As between the trustee of an express trust and the *cestui que trust,* limitations do not run until repudiation by the trustee and knowledge thereof by the *cestui.*[62] Limitations do not run in favor of an executor against one otherwise entitled to an accounting until the executor has by some act openly repudiated his trust.[63] The statute of limitations does not begin to run in favor of the trustee and against the beneficiary in personal property until the trustee does some act in open hostility to the trust, indicating a purpose to repudiate his obligation and assert an individual right to the property constituting the *corpus* of the estate[64] The six years' limitation prescribed by

61. Hunnicut v. Oren, 84 Kan. 460, 114 Pac. 1059.

Limitations ordinarily do not commence to run against a trustee until he repudiates the trust or denies his liability, and it should appear that the beneficiary had, or ought to have had, knowledge of such repudiation or denial. Cooley v. Gilliam, 80 Kan. 278, 102 Pac. 1091.

62. Watson v. Payne, 143 Mo. App. 721, 128 S. W. 238.

Limitations did not begin to run against enforcing a parol trust in favor of trustee's mother, intended to be continued until her death, until repudiation of the trust by the trustee or his death. Murry v. King, 153 Mo. App. 710, 135 S. W. 107.

Where a trustee permitted land held in trust to be sold for taxes and bid in for himself to cure a defect in title, the statute of limitations did not begin to run, as against the beneficiary, until the trustee repudiated the trust by selling the land to an innocent purchaser. Bender v. Zimmerman, 80 Mo. App. 138.

63. *In re* Anderson, 122 App. Div. 453, 106 N. Y. Supp. 818; *In re* Wood's Estate, 70 Misc. Rep. 467, 128 N. Y. Supp. 1102; *In re* Meyer's Estate, 181 N. Y. 562, 74 N. E. 1120, aff'g order 98 App. Div. 7, 90 N. Y. Supp. 185. See also *In re* Asheim's Estate, 111 App. Div. 176, 97 N. Y. Supp. 607, aff'd 185 N. Y. 609, 78 N. E. 1099; *In re* Jones' Estate, 30 Misc. Rep. 354, 63 N. Y. Supp. 726, judg. aff'd 51 App. Div. 420, 64 N. Y. Supp. 667; *In re* Lyth, 32 Misc. Rep. 608, 67 N. Y. Supp. 579; Mount v. Mount, 35 Misc. Rep. 62, 71 N. Y. Supp. 199, judg. rev'd 68 App. Div. 144, 74 N. Y. Supp. 148.

64. Devoe v. Lutz, 133 App. Div. 356, 117 N. Y. Supp. 339.

The rule that the limitation of actions against a trustee for an accounting does not begin to run until the trustee repudiates the trust does not apply to an action for an accounting against a trustee *in invitum* or a constructive trustee, since the law will not presume that the trustee is not acting adversely to his trust. Hart v. Goadby, 72 Misc. Rep. 232, 129 N. Y. Supp. 892.

Property being purchased for joint account of two, and title taken by one

the Minnesota statute, for actions to enforce a trust, does not begin to run against the suit by a monastic brotherhood to enforce its ownership under the constitution of the order in the gains of a member until the latter's death, where there has been no repudiation of the trust.[65] Where the vendee has repeatedly offered to pay the price and to receive a conveyance and stands able and willing to do so, the vendor holds the legal title in trust for the vendee; and limitations do not begin to run against specific performance until the vendor repudiated such trust, as by refusal to convey or recognize the contract.[66] Limitation begins to run in favor of a trustee *ex maleficio* of a constructive trust from the time of the discovery of the fraud, but does not begin to run in favor of the trustee of a resulting trust until he by some act clearly repudiates his trust.[67] The statute never runs against the enforcement of an express trust until by some declaration or act of the trustee an end is put to the relation of trustee and *cestui que trust.*[68] The statute of limitations does not run against an action on a bond as community administrator for failure to turn over assets until there is a repudiation of the trust or adverse holding under such circumstances as to be notice to the *cestui que trust.*[69] Where a

advancing the price under agreement that the other would pay his share in three years, but he did not, and afterwards died without repudiating liability or request of performance, limitations could not be interposed by heirs in a suit two years after repudiation. Barney v. Hoyt, 150 App. Div. 361, 135 N. Y. Supp. 126. See also, as to the necessity for disclaimer or repudiation of trust relation: Seitz v. Seitz, 59 App. Div. 150, 69 N. Y. Supp. 170; Barnes v. Courtright, 37 Misc. Rep. 60, 74 N. Y. Supp. 203.

65. Order of St. Benedict of New Jersey v. Steinhauser, 234 U. S. 640, 34 Sup. Ct. 932.

66. Wright v. Brooks, 47 Mont. 99, 130 Pac. 968.

67. Hanson v. Hanson, 78 Neb. 584, 111 N. W. 368.

68. Greenleaf v. Land & Lumber Co., 146 N. C. 505, 60 S. E. 424; Ruckman v. Cox, 63 W. Va. 74, 59 S. E. 760.

If the equity consists of a right on the part of the plaintiff to call upon the court to declare the holder of the legal title a trustee for any of the causes recognized by courts of equity, the statute runs from the time the right or cause of action accrues. Greenleaf v. Land & Lumber Co., *supra.*

69. Wingo v. Rudder (Tex. Civ. App.), 120 S. W. 1073.

locative interest in land was held in trust, and possession was taken under such equitable title, limitations did not begin to run until the trust was repudiated.[70] Where plaintiff deeded property to her son upon his representation that title would remain in her and lived on the property until he claimed it as his own, limitations did not run against an action to cancel the deeds until defendant disclaimed the trust.[71] In a suit for the enforcement of an express trust, limitations do not begin to run until repudiation or adverse possession by the trustee and knowledge thereof by the beneficiary.[72] A beneficiary of an express trust is not barred by limita-

70. Logan v. Robertson (Tex. Civ. App.), 83 S. W. 395.

If a person held title to land in trust for a county, his possession would not be adverse, so as to start the statute of limitations, until there was a repudiation of the trust. Bell county v. Felts (Tex. Civ. App.), 122 S. W. 269.

A suit to cancel a deed of land in trust for specific purposes is not barred by the four-year statute of limitations, though applicable to the case, where the evidence did not show a repudiation of the trust four years before the institution of the suit. Smith v. Olivarri (Tex. Civ. App.), 127 S. W. 235.

Limitations, laches, or stale demand cannot be urged against the enforcement of a resulting trust until the trust has been repudiated. Pearce v. Dyess (Tex. Civ. App.), 101 S. W. 549.

A corporation cannot plead limitation against its beneficiaries' demand until repudiation of the trust by it. Yeaman v. Galveston City Co. (Tex. Civ. App.), 167 S. W. 710, 173 S. W. 489. See also, as to necessity for disclaimer or repudiation of the trust: Yeary v. Crenshaw, 30 Tex. Civ. App. 399, 70 S. W. 579; Oaks v. West (Tex. Civ. App.), 64 S. W. 1033; Canadian & American Mortgage & Trust Co. v. Edinburgh-American Land-Mortgage Co., 16 Tex. Civ. App. 520, 41 S. W. 140; Scott v. Farmers' & Merchants' Nat. Bank (Tex. Civ. App.), 66 S. W. 485, 67 S. W. 343, rev'd 97 Tex. 31, 75 S. W. 7, 104 Am. St. Rep. 835.

71. Garvey v. Garvey, 52 Wash. 516, 101 Pac. 45.

Where land was devised by a testator to trustees absolutely, and there was no repudiation of the trust nor demand made upon the trustees for the land which the latter sold and conveyed, the statute of limitations does not begin to run against an action by one claiming to be the owner by descent from the testator to recover the same from the grantee until the date of the conveyance to him. Korsstrom v. Barnes, 156 Fed. 280 (U. S. C. C., Wash.).

72. Weltner v. Thurmond, 17 Wyo. 268, 98 Pac. 590, aff'd 17 Wyo. 268, 99 Pac. 1128.

tions from compelling the trustee to account, unless there has been an unequivocal repudiation of the trust.[73]

§ 220b(3). What constitutes repudiation or violation of trust.

Where money appropriated by Congress is not paid to a beneficiary, but is covered into the treasury under the statute, and carried to the credit of the party for whose benefit the appropriation was made, an act repealing the appropriation must be regarded as a disavowal of the trust, and it must be held that the statute of limitations began to run at the date of the repealing act.[74] Where the issuance of stock certificates was deferred pending the formation of a pool, the issuance of the certificates to one not authorized, who sold them to another company, which was followed by two more unauthorized transfers, constituted a repudiation of the trust by the corporation sufficient to start the running of the statute of limitations, when brought to the knowledge of the owner of the stock.[75] Where heirs of an alleged trustee claimed ownership of the trust property, such claim was a renunciation of any trust, and limitations began to run against an action to enforce it from such time.[76] Where the grantee under deeds operating as mortgages conveys the land to a third person, such act is a disavowal of any trust resulting in the grantor's favor after payment of the

73. *In re* McClear's Will, 147 Wis. 60, 132 N. W. 539.

74. Russell v. United States, 37 Ct. Cl. (U. S.) 113.

75. Cortelyou v. Imperial Land Co., 166 Cal. 14, 134 Pac. 981.

Where an executor claimed land under a patent issued to the heirs of testator, the statute of limitations ran from the date the executor notified an heir in Pennsylvania of all the facts respecting the patent. Andreson Co. v. Regenold, 166 Cal. 44, 134 Pac. 999.

Where plaintiffs and defendant contributed equally for the purchase of real property and the title to the same was taken in the name of the defendant, plaintiffs could not sue to establish a resulting trust until adverse claim by defendant, and the statute of limitations would begin to run only from that time. Pavlovich v. Pavlovich, 22 Cal. App. 500, 135 Pac. 303. See also, as to what constitutes repudiation or violation of trust: Castro v. Adams, 153 Cal. 382, 95 Pac. 1027; Norton v. Bassett, 154 Cal. 411, 97 Pac. 894; Bowes v. Cannon, 50 Colo. 262, 116 Pac. 336.

76. Benson v. Dempster, 183 Ill. 297, 55 N. E. 651.

debt secured, and starts the statute of limitations running in the grantee's behalf against the grantor's suit for an accounting and to recover the lands.[77] Even if a bank is trustee of funds out of which a check certified by it is payable, its refusal of payment when demanded is a repudiation of the trust, and limitation runs from that time.[78] Where plaintiff conveyed land to defendant under an agreement to reconvey on demand, the fact that defendant sold part of the land and accounted to plaintiff for the proceeds did not constitute such a repudiation of the agreement as to the remaining land as would start limitations against the plaintiff's right to recover the value of the latter on defendant's refusal to reconvey on demand.[79] The acts of a trustee in selling a half interest in the trust estate with the full knowledge of the *cestui que trust* and his subsequent delivery of possession to the vendee without protest or objection, and in destroying a letter containing a recognition of the trust in the presence of the *cestui que trust* and his wife, were sufficient to indicate the repudiation of the trust by

77. Adams v. Holden, 111 Iowa 54, 82 N. W. 468.

A trustee *ex maleficio* of land repudiates his trust, so as to initiate limitations, by selling the land. Blackledge v. Blackledge (Iowa), 91 N. W. 818.

The failure to institute within the statutory period an action to enforce a trust in real estate based on the misconduct of the trustee in conveying the land to another is not excused by the fact that the beneficiaries supposed that the grantee, who was unmarried, would not live long, and that the property would revert to them as his heirs. Burch v. Nicholson, 157 Iowa 502, 137 N. W. 1066.

Where a husband who purchased land with his wife's money did not deny the existence of the resulting purchase-money trust, but impliedly admitted it, he cannot rely on limitations to prevent its enforcement. Johnson v. Foust, 158 Iowa 195, 139 N. W. 451.

Enforcement of resulting trust in favor of a wife held not barred by limitations, where the husband had never repudiated or questioned his wife's rights. *In re* Mahin's Estate, 161 Iowa 459, 143 N. W. 420.

78. Blades v. Grant County Deposit Bank, 101 Ky. 163, 19 Ky. Law Rep. 340, 40 S. W. 246.

Limitations against an action by a Grand Lodge against a bank for the amount of an overdraft by the defaulting treasurer of the lodge do not begin to run in favor of the bank until the beneficiary discovered the breach of trust. Washbon v. Linscott State Bank, 87 Kan. 668, 125 Pac. 17.

79. Cromwell v. Norton, 193 Mass. 291, 79 N. E. 433.

the trustee and to set limitations in motion against the enforcement of the trust.[80] Where a trustee permits land, which by express agreement he holds for his *cestui que trust,* to be sold for taxes and bid in for himself, such act will not start the statute of limitations to run in favor of the trustee as against the *cestui que trust.*[81] Where a person receives the money of another and holds it in trust for his principal, the statute of limitations does not begin to run in favor of the person receiving the money until he assumes an attitude hostile to his principal's right, and indicates that his disposition of the money is no longer responsive to his principal's will.[82] That a trustee mingled the trust funds with her own in the purchase of property, and took title in her own name, does not justify a presumption that she thereby intended to repudiate the trust so as to set the statute of limitations running.[83] While the

80. Stanton v. Helm, 87 Miss. 287, 39 So. 457.

In 1879 S. purchased land with his wife's money, and in 1880 it was conveyed by a deed in which the wife joined, and the proceeds reinvested with her consent in a lot, and in 1882 the wife became of age, and died in 1884. It was held that a bill filed in July, 1900, by the wife's heirs to establish a resulting trust in the lot, was barred by the 10-year statute of limitations, which began to run from the time the wife reached her majority. Cox v. Menzing (Miss.), 30 So. 41.

81. Bender v. Zimmerman, 80 Mo. App. 138.

82. Morrison v. Blake, 33 Pa. Super. Ct. 290, 298.

Where a will of testator, who died in 1892, made certain provisions for his widow, and the executors, under the widow's construction of the will, made payments to her between 1892 and 1898, and the payments were not questioned by the residuary legatee until after the widow's death in 1906, the widow having received the money under a claim of right and not as a trust fund, the relation between her and the residuary legatee was that of debtor and creditor, and the residuary legatee could not reclaim the payments from the widow's administrator, the claim being barred by limitation. *In re* Skeel's Estate, 228 Pa. 407, 77 Atl. 635.

83. Hutton v. Smith, 74 App. Div. 284, 77 N. Y. Supp. 523, aff'd 175 N. Y. 375, 67 N. E. 633.

Though a testamentary trustee characterizes his payments to the beneficiary as gifts, this is not such a disavowal of the relationship as will set in operation the statute of limitations. *In re* McCormick, 27 Misc. Rep. 416, 59 N. Y. Supp. 374.

Where one negotiating a sale of land took the purchase-money bond and mortgage in his own name, and assigned them, and the assignee fore-

statute of limitations is not available to the husband, who has qualified and taken possession of the community property, as against his children, so long as the trust relation continues, yet there is a repudiation of the trust, so that the statute commences to run against them, where there are unsuccessful negotiations for a compromise, and he retains possession of the estate adversely to them.[84] A sale of land claimed by the son of the grantor to be impressed with a trust in his favor is a repudiation of the trust, setting in operation the statute of limitations in favor of the grantee.[85] If one occupying a position of trust makes false representations to

closed, in a suit by the owner to have the property declared impressed with a trust, whether the trust was an express one or one *ex maleficio*, limitations commenced to run when the mortgage was foreclosed by the assignee, under Code Civ. Proc., § 388. Talmadge v. Russell, 74 App. Div. 7, 76 N. Y. Supp. 854.

In an action by a remainderman against the personal representatives of a trustee, and beneficiary for an accounting and to enforce a liability against the estate of the beneficiary as a trustee, where it appeared that certain securities had stood in the name of the beneficiary, and were indorsed and sold by her, checks to her order being given in payment, and it does not appear how she disposed of the money, she, not having been a party to the decree adjudicating a trust, is presumed to hold the fund as trustee; so that the statute of limitations did not commence to run in her favor until her death, when the remaindermen became entitled to the possession of the estate. Putnam v. Lincoln Safe Deposit Co., 100 N. Y. Supp. 101, 49 Misc. Rep. 578, modified 118 App. Div. 468, 104 N. Y. Supp. 4.

84. Koppelmann v. Koppelmann (Tex. Civ. App.), 59 S. W. 827.

Where parents, holding property in trust as common family property of all the children, conveyed it to a son, and deed was duly acknowledged, delivered, and recorded, and the son entered into possession and dealt with the property as his own, a suit by the other children to set aside the deed, brought over nine years after the execution and recording of the deed, and the taking of possession by the son, was barred by limitations. Ryman v. Petruka (Tex. Civ. App.), 166 S. W. 711.

85. Phillips v. Sherman (Tex. Civ. App.), 39 S. W. 187.

The wrongful sale of the trust property by the trustee does not set limitations running against the beneficiaries, where the trustee, after the sale, recognizes the continuance of the trust. Mixon v. Miles (Tex. Civ. App.), 46 S. W. 105.

Where plaintiffs' father without their consent used money belonging to them to buy land for himself, such act was a repudiation of the trust, and limitations then commenced to run, unless they were ignorant of

the beneficiary, who relies thereon to his injury, he does an actionable wrong, and the limitations run from the commission of such wrong.[86] Where a county upon collection of a city's taxes retained an amount, as commission, in excess of that allowed by statute, but the retention was public and open under a claim of right in good faith, and known to the city, limitations ran against each amount so retained by the county from the date of each settlement with the city, and back of six years the statute of limitations was a bar to recovery of the excess retained.[87]

§ 220b(4). Notice of repudiation.

The statute of limitations will not run against a positive voluntary trust resting in parol, until repudiation of the trust by the trustee and knowledge of the repudiation by the beneficiaries.[88] The

their rights. Oakes v. West (Tex. Civ. App.), 64 S. W. 1033

Where a *cestui que trust* abandoned and dismissed a suit to enforce the trust because of circumstances leading him to believe that his title was not in fact repudiated by the trustee, and that the suit was not necessary, limitations did not run against the *cestui*. Snouffer v. Heisig (Tex. Civ. App.), 130 S. W. 912.

86. Ott v. Hood, 152 Wis. 97, 139 N. W. 762.

87. City of Centerville v. Turner County, 25 S. D. 300, 126 N. W. 605, aff'g judg. 23 S. D. 405, 122 N. W. 350; City of Parker v. Turner County, 26 S. D. 85, 127 N. W. 532.

A mere change in the course of studies, contrary to the condition on which a Protestant Mission was transferred by the American Board of Commissioners for Foreign Missions to the Hawaiian government, viz., that the government should continue the same as an institution for the cultivation of sound literature and solid science, and should teach no religious tenet or doctrine contrary to those theretofore inculcated by the mission, as set forth in a confession of faith, the institution, in case of breach of such condition, to revert to the mission with an alternative, at the election of the government, to pay a stipulated sum, does not instantly operate to make the grantor of the property a claimant for money against whom the statute of limitations immediately begins to run. Lowrey v. Territory of Hawaii, 215 U. S. 554, 30 Sup. Ct. 209, 54 L. Ed. 325.

88. Taylor v. Morris, 163 Cal. 717, 127 Pac. 66.

Where defendant in a suit to quiet title set up by cross claim that plaintiff's title as trustee was derived from defendant by fraud and undue influence, and it appeared that a conveyance had been made on an understanding that the property would be

statute of limitations applicable to an action for repudiation of a resulting trust commences to run at the time notice of the repudiation is brought to the beneficiary.[89] A cause of action to enforce a resulting trust accrues when the trust is repudiated by the trustee, and plaintiff has knowledge thereof.[90] Limitations do not begin to run against trover by a bailor against the bailee until the bailor has knowledge of facts putting him on notice of the bailee's repudiation of the bailment.[91] Though limitations do not run against the right of the *cestui que trust* to recover the trust property from the trustee in a direct and continuing trust, yet when the trustee openly repudiates the trust and unequivocally sets up a right adverse to the *cestui que trust,* to the latter's knowledge, the statute begins to run.[92] A transferee of trust property becomes trustee by construction of law, and the statute of limitations ordinarily begins to run from the time of transfer, or as soon as the *cestui que trust* has knowledge.[93] Where an express trust is re-

managed by plaintiff, and defendant taken care of by her, limitations did not run against the cause of action set up in the cross complaint until a time when it had been brought to the notice of defendant that plaintiff asserted title in herself. Odell v. Moss, 130 Cal. 352, 62 Pac. 555.

89. Bradley Bros. v. Bradley, 20 Cal. App. 1, 127 Pac. 1044.

The statute of limitations operates against an express trust only from the time the trustee assumes a position of hostility to the trust. MacMullan v. Kelly, 19 Cal. App. 700, 127 Pac. 819, aff'g judg. 124 Pac. 93.

90. Dennison v. Barney, 49 Colo. 442, 113 Pac. 519.

A corporation being a trustee for its stockholders, before lapse of time begins to run by limitation or laches against the stockholder's right to an accounting for dividends on stock, the company must have repudiated the relation and claimed the stock adversely, and brought the repudiation and claim to the knowledge of the stockholder. Mountain Waterworks Const. Co. v. Holme, 49 Colo. 412, 113 Pac. 501. See also, as to notice of repudiation of trust: Ballard v. Golob, 34 Colo. 417, 83 Pac. 376; French v. Woodruff, 25 Colo. 339, 54 Pac. 1015.

91. Plummer v. Hardison, 6 Ala. App. 525, 60 So. 502.

92. Hitchcock v. Cosper, 164 Ind. 633, 73 N. E. 264, rev'g judg. (Ind. App.), 69 N. E. 1029.

93. Blackett v. Ziegler, 147 Iowa 167, 125 N. W. 874.

The statute of limitations does not begin to run in favor of one holding land in trust, as against the beneficiary, until the former has clearly notified the latter that he claims the land adversely. Zunkel v. Colson, 109 Iowa 695, 81 N. W. 175.

pudiated, limitations begin to run from the time the beneficiary has notice thereof.[94] Whenever a trustee, whether the trust be created by power of attorney or by appointment as guardian, executor, or administrator, repudiates the trust and asserts title to the subject of the trust, the statute of limitations begins to run when a knowledge of the repudiation is brought home to the *cestui que trust.*[95] Where there is an express trust limitations will not bar equitable relief, so long as the trustee has not repuidated the trust to the knowledge of the beneficiary.[96] Limitations run against an action for the recovery of trust funds on the performance of the trust, or when the trustee repudiates the trust, and the beneficiary is notified.[97] Limitations do not begin to run against a con-

94. Olympia Min. & Mill. Co. v. Kerns, 24 Idaho 481, 135 Pac. 255.

The statute of limitations does not run against an action by the *cestui que trust* after becoming of age until she has notice that the trustee denies her right to the property. Goodman v. Smith, 94 Neb. 227, 142 N. W. 521.

Limitations run in favor of a trustee only after he repudiates the trust and asserts an adverse claim to the knowledge of the *cestui,* and while the latter is *sui juris* and not under undue influence. Caro v. Wollenberg, 68 Or. 420, 136 Pac. 866.

95. Jolly v. Miller, 30 Ky. Law Rep. 341, 98 S. W. 326; Hendrick v. Miller, 30 Ky. Law Rep. 330, 98 S. W. 330. See also, as to notice of repudiation: Williams v. Williams' Ex'r, 25 Ky. Law Rep. 836, 76 S. W. 413, judg. modified 25 Ky. Law Rep. 1085, 77 S. W. 184; Teeter v. Anderson, 7 Ky. Law Rep. (abstract) 600, 8 Ky. Law Rep. 108.

96. Allen v. Stewart, 214 Mass. 109, 100 N. E. 1092.

The statute of limitations does not begin to run in favor of a defendant alleged to hold in trust property paid for by plaintiff, until defendant's repudiation of the trust has been brought to plaintiff's knowledge. Martin v. Barnes, 214 Mass. 29, 100 N. E. 1023.

97. Johnston v. Johnston, 107 Minn. 109, 119 N. W. 652. See also, *In re* Welles' Estate, 79 Minn. 53, 81 N. W. 549.

A cause of action accrues and limitations begin to run, under Miss. Rev. Code 1892, § 2763, in case of a trust, either express or implied, not cognizable by the courts of common law, where by express declaration or act adverse to the recognition and existence of the trust relation the *cestuis que trust* are actually advised of the repudiation of the trust by the trustee. Stanton v. Helm, 87 Miss. 287, 39 So. 457.

Where complainant and L. purchased a part of a mining claim, and the deed to the interest of both was taken in L.'s name, the five-year statute of limitations prescribed by Mont. Code Civ. Proc., § 518, began to run against an action by complainant to

structive trust arising from a disavowal or assertion of an adverse right by the trustee in possession of the trust property until the *cestui que trust* has learned, or from the circumstances should have learned, of such disavowal or assertion.[98] Where the *cestui que trust* has knowledge of the transaction, and is under no disability, and his right to demand and have the funds has accrued, the statute of limitations will run against his claim.[99] The statute does not begin to run against a trust till it has been openly disavowed by the trustee, insisting on an adverse right and interest, clearly and unequivocally made known to the *cestui que trust.*[1] Limitations run against a suit to establish a trust in lands, in which the trustee has a life estate, only from the time the *cestui que trust* ascertains that he claims a greater estate than one for life.[2] Limitations will not run in favor of a trustee against his beneficiary until there is some manifestation of a hostile purpose by the trustee, notice of which is brought home to the beneficiary.[3]

enforce the trust created by such conveyance on the date complainant acquired knowledge that L. repudiated the trust. Mantle v. Speculator Min. Co., 27 Mont. 473, 71 Pac. 665.

98. Crowley v. Crowley, 72 N. H. 241, 56 Atl. 190.

In an action by a widow against the heirs of her deceased husband to establish a resulting trust in her favor in lands purchased by the husband with her money, the title being taken in his name without her knowledge, the constructive notice imparted by the recording of the deed by the husband will not start limitations running against the wife, where during the transaction the husband acted as the agent of the wife and concealed from her the fact that the title was not taken in her name. Hinze v. Hinze, 76 Kan. 169, 90 Pac. 762.

99. Ward v. Ward, 12 O. C. D. 59.

In 1846 legal limitations were not applied as between trustee and *cestui que trust* until after there had been an open repudiation of the trust brought home to the *cestui que trust.* Moton v. Dewell, 32 Ohio Cir. Ct. R. 35.

1. Levy v. Ryland, 32 Nev. 460, 109 Pac. 905. A suit to impress money as a trust, filed as an amended petition in 1911 to an action begun in 1907 for money paid by mistake, is barred by limitations, where the trust had been disavowed in 1903 with notice to all interested. Nicholson v. Nicholson, 94 Kan. 153, 146 Pac. 340.

2. Preston v. Preston, 202 Pa. 515, 52 Atl. 192.

3. Home Inv. Co. v. Strange (Tex. Civ. App.), 152 S. W. 510.

In case of a resulting trust, the statute does not begin to run against an action by the *cestui que trust* till repudiation of the trust by the trustee, and notice to the *cestui que trust* thereof. Tennison v. Palmer (Tex. Civ. App.), 142 S. W. 948.

Where defendant received money in trust, to be loaned pursuant to a continuing trust, limitations would not run against his liability to account and pay over the balance until he had repudiated the trust, and such repudiation had been brought home to the *cestui que trust*. Watson v. Dodson (Tex. Civ. App.), 143 S. W. 329.

See also, as to notice of repudiation of trust:

N. Y.—*In re* Smith's Estate, 66 App. Div. 340, 72 N. Y. Supp. 1062, order aff'd 179 N. Y. 563, 71 N. E. 1140.

S. C.—Montague v. Priester, 82 S. C. 492, 64 S. E. 393.

Tenn.—Fennell v. Loague, 107 Tenn. 239, 63 S. W. 1121.

Tex.—Campbell v. Shifflett (Tex. Civ. App.), 154 S. W. 664; Wood v. Dean (Tex. Civ. App.), 155 S. W. 363; Japhet v. Pullen (Tex. Civ. App.), 133 S. W. 441; Bond v. Poindexter (Tex. Civ. App.), 116 S. W. 395; Woodward v. San Antonio Traction Co. (Tex. Civ. App.), 95 S. W. 76; Davis v. Harwick, 43 Tex. Civ. App. 71, 94 S. W. 359; Hall v. Semple (Tex. Civ. App.), 91 S. W. 248; McCarthy v. Woods (Tex. Civ. App.), 87 S. W. 405; Laguerenne v. Farrar, 25 Tex. Civ. App. 404, 61 S. W. 953; Gregory v. Montgomery, 23 Tex. Civ. App. 68, 56 S. W. 231; Davis v. Davis, 20 Tex. Civ. App. 310, 49 S. W. 726; Scott v. Farmers' & Merchants' Nat. Bank (Tex. Civ. App.), 66 S. W. 485, 67 S. W. 343, rev'd 97 Tex. 31, 75 S. W. 7, 104 Am. St. Rep. 835; Rice v. Ward (Tex. Civ. App.), 54 S. W. 318, judg. rev'd 93 Tex. 532, 56 S. W. 747.

Wash.—New York Security & Trust Co. v. City of Tacoma, 30 Wash. 661, 71 Pac. 194.

Wis.—Hill v. True, 104 Wis. 294, 80 N. W. 462.

CHAPTER XXI.

MORTGAGOR AND MORTGAGEE.

§ 221. Relation of, to the property.

Strictly speaking, by a mortgage conveyance the mortgagee is invested with the legal title to the estate, while the mortgagor retains only the equitable title, which gives to him the right to reinvest himself with the legal title upon performance of the conditions imposed by the conveyance. In other words, the mortgagee takes the legal title subject to a condition, unless, as is the case in some of the States, the statute regulates the character of the relative estates.[1]

1. In some of the Western States, when the statute bars the debt, it discharges the mortgage. See *e. g.* Leeds Lumber Co. v. Haworth, 98 Iowa 463, 67 N. W. 383, 60 Am. St. Rep. 199; Cook v. Prindle, 97 Iowa 464, 66 N. W. 781, 59 Am. St. Rep. 424. But this is not the view taken in most of the Eastern States, or probably in a majority of the States.

There is much confusion in the cases as to the precise relation of a mortgagor and mortgagee to the estate;[2] but this results mainly from a difference in the form of the mortgages under which the decisions have arisen, and in some instances from the peculiar provisions of statutes relating to the matter.[3] The mortgagor has sometimes been treated as a tenant at will to the mortgagee, or as a mere tenant at sufferance; but at the present day, until condition broken and foreclosure, a mortgagor is treated both at law and in equity, as the legal owner of the estate, the mortgage being only a security, and the mortgagee having only a lien upon the land, as a security for his debt.[4]

But in some of the States it is held that a mortgage in fee

See 2 Jones on Mortgages (5th Ed.), § 1203 *et seq.;* McKisson v. Davenport, 83 Mich. 211, 47 N. W. 100, 10 L. R. A. 507, and note; Kulp v. Kulp, 51 Kan. 341, 32 Pac. 1118, 21 L. R. A. 550 and note. Where, as in Kentucky, there is no statute of limitations as to liens, then if the instrument shows no different intent, they are only valid and enforceable so long as the debt they secure is a valid and enforceable obligation. Craddock v. Lee, 22 Ky. Law Rep. 1651, 61 S. W. 22, 24. As to deeds of trust, see Fuller v. Oneal, 82 Texas, 417, 18 S. W. 479, 481; McGovney v. Gwillim, 16 Col. App. 284, 65 Pac. 346; Angell on Limitations (6th Ed.), § 468.

2. A mortgagor, says Parke, B., "can be described only by saying he is a mortgagor." Litchfield v. Ready, 20 L. J. Exch. 51.

3. "A mortgagor is not properly tenant at will to the mortgagee, for he is not to pay him rent. He is only *quodam modo*. Nothing is more apt to confound than a simile. When the court or counsel call a mortgagor a tenant at will, it is barely a comparison. He is like a tenant at will." Moss v. Gallimore, Doug. 279.

4. Elfe v. Cole, 26 Ga. 197; Casborne v. Scarfe, 1 Atk. 603; Jackson v. Lodge, 36 Cal. 28; Thayer v. Cramer, 1 McCord (S. C.) Ch. 395; McMillan v. Richards, 9 Cal. 365; United States v. Athens Armory, 35 Ga. 344; Fay v. Cheney, 31 Mass. (14 Pick.) 399; Caruthers v. Humphrey, 12 Mich. 270; Bryan v. Butts, 27 Barb. (N. Y.) 503; Hall v. Savill, 3 Iowa 37. But in some of the States the legal title is held to pass for some purposes. Thus, in Glass v. Ellison, 9 N. H. 69, it was held that, for the protection of the interests of the mortgagee, and in order to give him the full benefits of his security, the legal estate passes, but that for other purposes the mortgage is in general held to operate only as a mere security for the debt. See also, to same effect, Clark v. Reyburn, 1 Kan. 281. In many of the States, as between the mortgagor and mortgagee, it is held that the title passes, but not as to third persons. Terry v. Rosell, 32 Ark. 478.

passes both the legal and equitable estate, defeasible by the performance of the condition according to its legal effect.[5] The preponderance of authority, however, relative to ordinary mortgages, is in favor of the doctrine that the title remains in the mortgagor, at least until after condition broken (and in many of the States until after foreclosure);[6] and in England, while the

5. Blaney v. Bearce, 2 Me. 132; Briggs v. Fish, 2 D. Chip. (Vt.) 100; Carter v. Taylor, 40 Tenn. (3 Head) 30; Erskine v. Townsend, 2 Mass. 495; Wood's Landlord & Tenant, 183 *et seq.*

6. Whitemore v. Shiverick, 3 Nev. 288; Jackson v. Lodge, 36 Cal. 28; McMillan v. Richards, 9 Cal. 365; Goodenow v. Ewer, 16 Cal. 461; Boggs v. Hargrave, Cal. 559; Fogarty v. Sawyer, 17 Cal. 589; Dutton v. Warschauer, 21 Cal. 609; Bludworth v. Lake, 33 Cal. 265; Davis v. Anderson, 1 Ga. 176; Ragland v. Justices, etc., 10 Ga. 65; Elfe Ass'n v. Cole, 26 Ga. 197; United States v. Athens Armory, 35 Ga. 344; Seals v. Cashin, 2 Ga. Dec. 76; Hall v. Savill, 3 G. Greene (Iowa) 37; Chick v. Willetts, 2 Kan. 384; Caruthers v. Humphrey, 12 Mich. 270; Bryan v. Butts, 27 Barb. (N. Y.) 503; Thayer v. Cramer, 1 McCord (S. C.) Ch. 395.

In Alabama, a mortgage is regarded as possessing a dual nature, bearing one character in a court of law and another in a court of equity, but the legal estate is treated as remaining in the mortgagor until condition broken, when it at once vests in the mortgagee, leaving only an equity of redemption in the mortgagor. Welsh v. Phillips, 54 Ala. 309.

In Arkansas, the legal estate, as between the mortgagor and mortgagee, is treated as being in the latter, but as to third persons it is in the mortgagor. Terry v. Rosell, 32 Ark. 478; Collins v. Torry, 7 Johns. (N. Y.) 278, 5 Am. Dec. 273; Blanchard v. Brooks, 29 Mass. (12 Pick.) 47. In Kansas, Life Association v. Cook, 20 Kan. 19; Michigan, Wagar v. Stone, 36 Mich. 364; Nebraska, Harley v. Estes, 6 Neb. 386; California, Jackson v. Lodge, *supra*; Georgia, Rayland v. Justices, 10 Ga. 65; Nevada, Whitmore v. Shiverick, 3 Nev. 288; and, indeed, in most of the States, a mortgage is held to be a mere security, vesting no estate in the mortgagee until after foreclosure, Myers v. White, 1 Rawle (Pa.) 353; State v. Laval, 4 McCord (S. C.) 336; Cheever v. Railroad Co., 39 Vt. 363; while in Rhode Island, Connecticut, New Hampshire, Minnesota, Indiana, North Carolina, Mississippi, Missouri, and Massachusetts, the common law rule, with some limitations, prevails. It is a mere incident of the debt, and falls with it. Morris v. Bacon, 123 Mass. 58; Benton v. Bailey, 50 Vt. 137.

In New York, by statute, an action of ejectment by a mortgagee is abolished, and, in the absence of any contract for possession, the mortgagor is entitled thereto, and to the rents and profits of the estate, unless, upon a proper showing as to the in-

mortgagor is in possession, or in receipt of the rents and profits, he is treated as a freeholder, and as such is entitled to vote in the election of members of Parliament,[7] and is entitled to retain possession until the mortgagee enters or brings ejectment,[8] and is not liable to the mortgagee for the rents or profits of the premises.[9] The right of the mortgagor to retain possession of the premises, and consequently his right to lease the same after mortgage, is generally upheld, but must depend largely upon the language of the mortgage, and upon the statutes relating thereto in the several States, although the instances are very rare where a mortgagee takes possession before condition broken, or even before foreclosure and final decree. But, without stopping to discuss the relation of the parties to the estate further, it may be said that the tenant can acquire no greater rights than the mortgagor himself had, but may defend his title under the lease to the same extent that the mortgagor could, and may even redeem the estate to protect his term.[10]

adequacy of the security, and the irresponsibility of the mortgagor, the courts will appoint a receiver of the rents. Astor v. Turner, 11 Paige (N. Y.) Ch. 436; Sea Ins. Co. v. Stebbins, 8 id. 565. But after sale, a tenant who went in under the mortgagor, and was made a party to the proceedings, is bound to attorn to the purchaser. Lovett v. Church, 9 How. Pr. (N. Y.) 226.

7. 3 & 4 Will. IV., c. 45, § 23.

8. Rex v. Edington, 1 East 293; Keech v. Hall, 1 Doug. 21; Bree v. Holbech, 2 id. 655; Reading of Judge Trowbridge, 8 Mass. 551; Clark v. Reyburn, 1 Kan. 281.

9. Renard v. Brown, 7 Neb. 449. The mortgagor's right to lease and take the rents continues until it is divested by some positive interference of the mortgagee. Dunn v. Tillery, 79 N. C. 497; Chadbourn v. Henderson, 61 Tenn. (2 Baxter) 460; Gibson v. Farley, 16 Mass. 280.

10. Rogers v. Moore, 11 Conn. 553. As to tenant's right to redeem, see Averill v. Taylor, 8 N. Y. 44. In Walker v. King, 44 Vt. 601, it was held that a mortgagee who has never taken possession under his mortgage, but has permitted the assignee of the mortgagor to remain in possession, has no greater claim against him for rents and profits than he would have against the mortgagor; and it is well settled that he has no claim upon the mortgagor therefor, either at law or in equity. *Ex parte* Wilson, 2 V. & B. 252; Hele v. Bexley, 20 Beav. 127; Walmsley v. Milne, 7 C. B. N. S. 115; Moss v. Gallimore, 1 Doug. 279; Trent v. Hunt, 9 Exch. 14; Jolly v. Arbuthnot, 28 L. J. Ch. 547; Cole

The mortgagor is now generally treated, at least in equity, as retaining both the legal and the equitable title, and the mortgagee as only holding under his mortgage a conditional title or lien upon the land for the payment of the debt it is given to secure.[11] But whatever may be the true relation of the parties

on Ejectment, 38, 473. In Georgia, the mortgagor is entitled to all the rents and profits of the land, until he is sold out and dispossessed by foreclosure proceedings Vason v. Ball, 56 Ga. 268. In Kentucky, unless the rents and profits are specially pledged, the same rule prevails, and the mortgagee cannot claim them as a legal incident of the estate. A court of equity may, after the debt becomes due, if the property is inadequate to secure the debt, in an action to foreclose the mortgage, appoint a receiver of the rents. But if there is no deficiency, they go to the mortgagor. Douglass v. Cline, 75 Ky. (12 Bush) 608. In Mississippi, the mortgagor retains the legal title and right of possession until condition broken, and the mortgagee cannot interfere therewith, nor can the mortgagee take the rents and profits unless so agreed. Myers v. Estell, 48 Miss. 373; Black v. Payne, 52 Miss. 271. In North Carolina, the mortgagor is treated as having an equitable freehold. State v. Ragaland, 75 N. C. 12. In Tennessee, the mortgage to the extent of the mortgage debt is *pro tanto* a sale, giving the mortgagee all the rights of a *bona fide* purchaser. 2 Tenn. Ch. 531. So in Iowa. Hewitt v. Rankin, 41 Iowa 35. In Vermont, after condition broken, he may enter and take possession without previous notice, if he can do so peacefully. Fuller v. Eddy, 49 Vt. 11. So in Maine, he may enter and harvest the crops, unless the mortgagor is occupying by agreement, as tenant. Gilman v. Wills, 66 Me. 273. In Pennsylvania, the mortgagee is treated as having the title and right of possession to hold until payment, and may enter and hold the lands and receive the rents and profits until the mortgage debt is paid. Tryon v. Munson, 77 Pa. 250. These conflicting doctrines are, however, only applicable to ordinary mortgages, and the parties may, by special provision, entirely change the respective rights of the parties under the mortgage.

11. Carpenter v. Bowen, 42 Miss. 28; Trimm v. Marsh, 54 N. Y. 599; Fletcher v. Holmes, 32 Ind. 497; Buchanan v. Munroe, 22 Tex. 537; Williams v. Beard, 1 S. C. 309; Johnston v. Houston, 47 Mo. 227; Fletcher v. Holmes, 32 Ind. 497; Elfe Ass'n v. Cole, 26 Ga. 197; Mack v. Wetzlar, 39 Cal. 247; Priest v. Wheelock, 58 Ill. 114. Although in form a conveyance in fee upon condition, yet, in effect, even after condition broken, it is a mere security for a debt, and the title reverts without a reconveyance, whenever the debt is paid. Pease v. Pilot Knob Iron Co., 49 Mo. 124; and, before foreclosure, is not subject to levy and sale, Buckley v. Daley, 45 Miss. 338. And until condition broken he is entitled to possession, unless otherwise provided in

to the property, it is held that, whichever may be in possession he holds the possession for the other, until condition broken, and neither can set up an adverse claim against the other until that

the mortgage, and is in by right and by virtue of his title, and not as a tenant at sufferance. Hooper v. Wilson, 12 Vt. 695; Crippen v. Morrison, 13 Mich. 23; Kidd v. Temple, 22 Cal. 255. And if a mortgagee takes a lease of the mortgagor of the same lands, he will be treated as holding under the lease until he has made his election to hold under the mortgage. Wood v. Felton, 26 Mass. (9 Pick.) 171. And after condition broken he may hold under his mortgage without first surrendering possession under the lease. Shields v. Lozear, 34 N. J. L. 496. The mortgagor's interest is an estate of inheritance in no wise affected by the mortgage before entry and foreclosure. White v. Rittenmeyer, 30 Iowa 268. See Miner v. Beekman, 11 Abb. Pr. N. S. (N. Y.) 147; Norcross v. Norcross, 105 Mass. 265; O'Dougherty v. Felt, 65 Barb. (N. Y.) 220. And even after the debt is due he is not entitled to the rents and profits unless the security is insufficient. Myers v. Estell, 48 Miss. 373. As to the nature of mortgagor's estate, see Kline v. McGuckin, 24 N. J. Eq. 411; Hill v. Hewitt, 35 Iowa 563; Trimm v. Marsh, 54 N. Y. 599; Annapolis, etc., R. R. Co. v. Gantt, 39 Md. 115. The mortgage is but a security, and the freehold still remains in the mortgagor. Jackson v. Willard, 4 Johns. (N. Y.) 41. He is seised and is the legal owner. Orr v. Hadley, 36 N. H. 575; Hitchcock v. Harrington, 6 Johns. (N. Y.) 290; Runyan v. Mersereau, 11 id. 534. The mortgagee, before condition broken at least, has no estate in the land distinct from the debt. Aymar v. Bill, 5 Johns. Ch. 570. When out of possession he cannot be treated as the proprietor of the estate. Norwich v. Hubbard, 22 Conn. 587. It is only a security, and the mortgagor has the same rights to the estate that he ever had, except against the mortgagor. Wilkins v. French, 20 Me. 111; Orr v. Hadley, 36 N. H. 575. And as against him, until he has legally entered for condition broken, Kennett v. Plummer, 28 Mo. 142; under foreclosure proceedings, or as a judgment of a court of law, or by the consent of the mortgagor, Hooper v. Wilson, 12 Vt. 695; Crippen v. Morrison, 13 Mich. 23; Pierce v. Brown, 24 Vt. 195; Hill v. Robertson, 24 Miss. 368; Pratt v. Skolfield, 45 Me. 386. Lord Mansfield, in The King v. St. Michael's, 2 Doug. 631, very clearly defines the relations of the mortgagor and mortgagee to the lands. He says: "A mortgagor in possession gains a settlement because the mortgagee, notwithstanding the form, has but a chattel, and the mortgage is only security. It is an affront to common sense to say that the mortgagor is not the real owner." See Martin v. Weston, 2 Burr. 978. In Eaton v. Jaques, 2 Doug. 455, a term for years was assigned by way of mortgage with a clause of redemption, and it was held by the court that the lessor could not sue the mortgagee as assignee of all the estate, right, title, interest, etc., of the mortgagor even

event has transpired.[12] The rule is that the mortgagor and his vendee hold in subordination to the title of the mortgagee, not adversely to him; and the statute of limitations does not run, even after the law-day is past, as in favor of the mortgagor or his vendee, without some overt act throwing off allegiance; for it cannot be known otherwise that the mortgagor or his vendee is not quietly enjoying the possession of the equity of redemption, at all times acknowledging the rights of the mortgagee; and if, in an action by the second mortgagee against the mortgagor, he recover the property, and purchase subsequently at his own sale, the first mortgagee is not barred, by limitation, until six years from the sale, of his right of foreclosure.[13] "One is much at a

after the mortgage had been forfeited, unless the mortgagee had taken actual possession. See also, Walker v. Reeves, 2 Doug. 461, note 1. In The King v. Eddington, 1 East 288, it was held that the object of a mortgage is merely to secure a debt, and that the legal estate still remains in the mortgagor; and it was held also that the husband of a woman who had an estate in a term for ninety-nine years, but which had been by her and her first husband mortgaged to secure a loan, gained a settlement by a residence upon the estate for forty days, under a statute which enabled a person owning a freehold estate in a parish, who resided upon it for the period of forty days, to acquire a settlement therein; and the court adopted the rule as stated by Lord Mansfield in The King v. St. Michael's, *supra*. See opinion of Grose, J. The legal estate of the mortgagor is not divested by condition broken or entry therefor by the mortgagee, but he retains such an estate therein that it may be levied upon and sold under execution. Trimm v. Marsh, 54 N. Y. 599; Gorham v. Arnold, 22 Mich. 247. But *contra*, see Buckley v. Daly, 45 Miss. 338. In Kennett v. Plummer, 58 Mo. 142, it was held that, until after condition broken and entry by the mortgagee, the mortgagor continues owner, and may lease the estate, and in every respect deal with it as owner. M'Kircher v. Hawley, 16 Johns. (N. Y.) 289; Partington v. Woodcock, 5 N. & M. 672; Watts v. Coffin, 11 Johns. (N. Y.) 495; Rogers v. Humphreys, 4 Ad. & El. 299; Partington v. Woodcock, 5 N. & M. 672; Peters v. Elkins, 14 Ohio 344; Rogers v. Moore, 11 Conn. 553.

12. Gould v. Newman, 6 Mass. 239; Sweetser v. Lowell, 33 Me. 446; Colton v. Smith, 11 Pick. 28 Mass. 311; McGuire v. Shelby, 20 Ala. 456.

13. Boyd v. Beck, 29 Ark. 703; Jamison v. Perry, 38 Iowa 14; Rockwell v. Servant, 63 Ill. 424; Parker v. Banks, 79 N. C. 480; Medley v. Elliott, 62 Ill. 532; Martin v. Jackson, 27 Pa. 504.

loss," says Patterson, J.,[14] "as to the proper terms in which to describe the relation of mortgagor in possession to the mortgagee. In one case[15] such mortgagor is held to be tenant to the mortgagee; sometimes he is said to be the bailiff of the mortgagee; and in a late case Lord Tenterden said that his situation was of a peculiar character. But it is clear that his possession is, at all events, not adverse to the title of the mortgagee."[16] It has sometimes been thought that the mortgagee occupies the position of a trustee to the mortgagor; but as there is no trust expressed in the mortgage, if he can be said to be a trustee at all, it is only by implication, and in subordination to the main purposes of the contract. His right is qualified and limited, yet he has a distinct and beneficial interest in the estate which may in a certain contingency become absolute and perpetual, and may be enforced against the mortgagor. It is a general rule that a trustee is not allowed to deprive his *cestui que trust* of the possession; but a court of equity never interferes to prevent the mortgagee from assuming the possession. In this respect, it will be perceived that there is a marked difference in the contract between mortgagor and mortgagee, and trustee and *cestui que trust*. A trustee is estopped in equity from dispossessing his *cestui que trust,* because such dispossession would be a breach of trust. A mortgagee cannot be estopped, because in him it is no breach of trust, but in conformity to his contract. On the same principle a mortgagee is not prevented, but assisted in equity, when he has recourse to a proceeding which is not only to obtain the possession, but the absolute title to the estate, by forclosure. There is no resemblance, in this respect, to the character of a trustee, but to a character directly opposite; and it is in this opposite character that the mortgagee accounts for the rents and profits when in possession, and when he is not, receives the interest of his mort-

14. Jones v. Williams, 5 Ad. & El. 291.

15. Partridge v. Bere, 5 B. & Ald. 604.

16. Wilkinson v. Flowers, 37 Miss. 579, 75 Am. Dec. 78.

gage debt. The ground, therefore, on which a mortgagee is in any case and for any purpose considered to have a character resembling that of a trustee is the partial and limited right, which, in equity, he is allowed to have in the whole estate, legal and equitable. And hence, although as a general rule the statute will not apply to a direct trust, yet a mortgagee is allowed to set up lapse of time as a bar to the equity of redemption.[17] After the mortgage debt has been paid, if the mortgagee is in possession from that time, he holds the premises as trustee for the mortgagor, and he cannot set up his possession as adverse until he has done some act which shows that his possession and claim is adverse.[18]

§ 222. Distinction between note or bond, and the mortgage given to secure its payment—Periods of limitation as to, in the several states.

The fact that a note or other security is recited in the mortgage which is given to secure its payment does not raise the note or other debt from the character of a simple contract to a specialty, or in anywise affect or change the operation of the statute of limitations thereon; nor, on the other hand, generally, does the circumstance that the statute has run upon the note or debt affect the mortgage given to secure it, or destroy the lien which it imposes upon the land for the payment of such debt.[19] In some of the States, as California,[20] Nevada,[21]

17. Cholmondeley v. Clinton, 2 J. & W. 1.

18. Green v. Turner, 38 Iowa 112; Hammond v. Hopkins, 11 Tenn. (3 Yerg.) 525; Yarbrough v. Newell, 18 Tenn. (10 Yerg.) 376.

19. As against the foreclosure of a mortgage, the statute runs only from the maturity of the note which it secures, although the mortgage contains a stipulation that the whole principal and interest shall become immediately due upon a default in paying the interest, or any part thereof, according to the tenor of the note, such stipulation being regarded as a penalty for the creditor's benefit, and he waives all advantage he might gain from the default if he thereafter accepts interest. Mason v. Luce, 116 Cal. 232, 48 Pac. 72; Moline Plow Co. v. Webb, 141 U. S. 616, 12 Sup. Ct. 100, 35 L. Ed. 879;

Nebraska,[22] Illinois,[23] Iowa,[24] Texas,[25] and Kansas,[26] the debt is regarded as the principal, and the mortgage as a mere incident, and, consequently, when the debt is barred, the remedy upon the mortgage is also barred. This peculiar doctrine, however, is due to the statutes in those States, rather than to the introduction of a new principle by the courts. In most of the States the statute runs upon the note or debt, which is merely a simple contract, within a shorter period than it does upon the mortgage, which is a specialty; but while the debt itself, because of the statute bar, ceases to be enforceable as a personal claim, yet the lien created by the mortgage, as well as the right to enforce it, still remains, and, if enforced before it is also barred, continues as a valid security for the debt and for the interest accruing thereon even after the debt itself is barred by the statute,—the rule being, that, where the security for a debt is a lien on property, real or personal, the lien is not impaired in consequence of the running of the statute of limitations upon the debt.[27] The debt is not

Watts v. Creighton, 85 Iowa 154, 52 N. W. 32.

An unexplained delay of sixteen or seventeen years in seeking to avoid a foreclosure sale is such laches as will bar a suit in equity brought for that purpose. Fennyery v. Ransom, 170 Mass. 303, 49 N. E. 620. And, as all suits must be prosecuted with reasonable diligence in order to have the doctrine of *lis pendens* apply, an unexplained delay for over twenty years to proceed with a foreclosure suit is such laches as disables the mortgagee from enforcing the mortgage. Taylor v. Carroll, 89 Md. 32, 42 Atl. 920, 44 L. R. A. 379.

20. Lord v. Morris, 18 Cal. 482.

21. Henry v. Confidence Gold M. Co. 1 Nev. 619.

22. Hurley v. Estes, 6 Neb. 386.

23. Harris v. Mills, 28 Ill. 44; Hagan v. Parsons, 67 Ill. 170.

24. Gower v. Winchester, 33 Iowa 303; Clinton Co. v. Cox, 37 Iowa 570.

25. Ross v. Mitchell, 28 Tex. 150; Duty v. Graham, 12 Tex. 427.

26. Schmucker v. Sibert, 18 Kan. 104, 26 Am. Rep. 765.

27. Chamberlain v. Meeder, 16 N. H. 381. The general rule that a discharge of the debt discharges the mortgage lien given to secure it does not apply where the debt is merely barred by the statute of limitations or by a certificate in bankruptcy. Buck v. Cooper, 26 Miss. 599. The rule relative to the extinguishment of the mortgage under such circumstances is, that the mortgage is not extinguished by an extinguishment of the mere personal liability of the

extinguished, but the remedy is taken away by the statute.[28] A mortgage, being a specialty, is barred by the lapse of the period, after it becomes due, fixed upon by statute for that class of obligations; and where specialties are not specially provided for, they are left subject to the operation of the common-law

mortgagor by operation of law or by agreement of the parties, even if there is no intention to extinguish the debt itself. Donnelly v. Simonton, 13 Minn. 301; holding that the mortgage is not extinguished by the running of the statute upon the note or obligation which it is given to secure. In Higgins v. Scott, 2 B. & Ald. 413, this principle is illustrated in the case of an attorney's lien upon a judgment, which it was held might be enforced, although his remedy for the debt itself was barred. Potter v. Stransky, 48 Wis. 235; Thayer v. Mann, 36 Mass. (19 Pick.) 535; Townsend v. Jennison, 50 U. S. (9 How.) 413, 13 L. Ed. 194; Belknap v. Gleason, 11 Conn. 160; M'Elmoyle v. Cohen, 38 U. S. (13 Pick.) 312, 10 L. Ed. 177; Spears v. Hartley, 3 Esp. 81; Pratt v. Huggins, 29 Barb. (N. Y.) 277; Crane v. Page, 58 Mass. (4 Cush.) 483; Smith v. Washington City, etc., R. R. Co., 33 Gratt. (Va.) 617; Browne v. Browne, 17 Fla. 607, 35 Am. Rep. 96; Union Bank v. Stafford, 53 U. S. (12 How.) 340, 13 L. Ed. 1008; Eastman v. Forster, 49 Mass. (8 Met.) 19; Sturgess v. Crowninshield, 17 U. S. (4 Wheat.) 122, 4 L. Ed. 529; Hughes v. Edwards, 22 U. S. (9 Wheat.) 489, 6 L. Ed. 142; Harris v. Vaughn, 2 Tenn. Ch. 483; Elkins v. Edwards, 8 Ga. 325; Waltermire v. Westover, 14 N. Y. 16; Myer v. Beal, 5 Oreg. 130; Trotter v. Erwin, 27 Miss. 772; Cookes v. Culbertson, 9 Nev. 199; Henry v. Confidence Gold M. Co., 1 Nev. 619; Nevit v. Bacon, 32 Miss. 212; Wilkinson v. Flower, 37 id. 579, 75 Am. Dev. 78; Read v. Edwards, 2 Nev. 262; Gary v. May, 16 Ohio 66; Fisher v. Mossman, 11 Ohio St. 42; Wood v. Augustine, 61 Mo. 46; Longworth v. Taylor, 2 Cin. (Superior Ct. Ohio) 39; Kennedy v. Knight, 21 Wis. 340; Kellar v. Sinton, 53 Ky. (14 B. Mon.) 307; Richmond v. Aiken, 25 Vt. 324; Ohio L. & T. Ins. Co. v. Winn, 4 Md. Ch. 253; Cleveland v. Harrison, 15 Wis. 670. "It is well settled," says Hinman, C. J., in Hough v. Bailey, 32 Conn. 288, "that the mere fact that a debt is barred at law by the statute of limitations does not constitute a defense to a bill for the foreclosure of a mortgage given to secure it, or to an action of ejectment to recover possession of the mortgaged estate. In order to bar the mortgagee's right of foreclosure, or a suit at law to recover possession, the mortgagor must have been permitted to remain in possession of the premises for fifteen years at least, without payment of any portion of the debt or the performance of any act recognizing the continued existence of the mortgage." Jarvis v. Woodruff, 22 Conn. 548; Haskell v. Bailey, 22 Conn. 569.

28. Low v. Allen, 26 Cal. 141; Sichel v. Carrillo, 42 Cal. 493; Beckford v. Wade, 17 Ves. 87.

presumption of payment arising from the lapse of twenty years, without the payment of any part of the principal or interest, after it becomes due.[29] In some of the States the statute provides that unless a specialty is paid, either wholly or in part, within the period of twenty years, it shall be presumed to be paid; and these statutory presumptions, although only a re-enactment of the common-law rule by the legislature, are nevertheless treated as deriving increased vigor by such enactment, and operate as an absolute bar to a recovery thereon, after the lapse of the period

29. The presumption that a mortgage is paid only arises at the expiration of twenty years from the last payment of principal or interest. Peck v. Mallams, 10 N. Y. 509; People v. Wood, 12 Johns. (N. Y.) 242. Consequently, if within that time payments have been made by the mortgagor on account of the mortgage, the presumption cannot arise, New York Life Ins. & Trust Co. v. Covert, 3 Abb. Dec. (N. Y.) 350, 6 Abb. Prac. (N. S.) 154; or even if he has admitted the legal existence of the mortgage, Heyer v. Pruyn, 7 Paige (N. Y.) Ch. 465, 34 Am. Dec. 355. And an admission by a purchaser from the mortgagor and a promise to pay it within twenty years will rebut the presumption of payment both as against the purchaser and his judgment creditors. Park v. Peck, 1 Paige (N. Y.) Ch. 477; Belmont v. O'Brien, 12 N. Y. 394; Jackson v. Pierce, 10 Johns. (N. Y.) 414; Newcomb v. St. Peter's Church, 2 Sandf. (N. Y.) Ch. 636; Marvin v. Hotchkiss, 6 Cow. (N. Y.) 401. But this presumption cannot be rebutted by mere proof of non-payment in fact. Fisher v. New York, 67 N. Y. 73. "It is perfectly settled," says Sir William Grant, in Barron v. Martin, 19 Ves. 327, "that twenty years' possession by the mortgagee is *prima facie* a bar to the right of redemption." Crawford v. Taylor, 42 Iowa 260; Moore v. Cable, 1 Johns. (N. Y.) Ch. 385; Blake v. Foster, 2 B. & B. 402; Demarest v. Wynkoop, 3 Johns. (N. Y.) Ch. 129; Hall v. Denckla, 28 Ark. 506; Johnson v. Mounsey, 40 L. T. N. S. 234; Hoffman v. Harrington, 33 Mich. 392; Amory v. Lawrence, 3 Cliff. 523; Bates v. Conrow, 11 N. J. Eq. 137; Ayres v. Waite, 64 Mass. (10 Cush.) 72; Roberts v. Littlefield, 48 Me. 61; Howland v. Shurtleff 43 Mass. (2 Metc.) 26, 35 Am. Dec. 384; Randall v. Bradley, 65 Me. 43; Slicer v. Bank of Pittsburgh, 57 U. S. (16 How.) 571; 14 L. Ed. 1063; Bailey v. Carter, 42 N. C. (7 Ired. Eq.) 282; Slee v. Manhattan Co., 1 Paige (N. Y.) Ch. 48; Hughes v. Edwards, 22 U. S. (9 Wheat.) 489, 6 L. Ed. 142; Dexter v. Arnold, 1 Sumn. (U. S.) 109; Knowlton v. Walker, 13 Wis. 264; Cook v. Finkler, 9 Mich. 131; Ross v. Norvell, 1 Wash. (Va.) 17; Gunn v. Brantley, 21 Ala. 633; Montgomery v. Chadwick, 7 Iowa 114; Hallesy v. Jackson, 66 Ill. 139; McNair v. Lot, 34 Mo. 285.

fixed by statute, unless the operation of the statute has been saved by some one of the modes provided in the statute; and a court of equity will decree the satisfaction of a mortgage which has been permitted to lie dormant during the entire period fixed by statute for the maturing of this presumption;[30] whereas, under the common-law presumption, while a court of equity in analogy to the statute will not enforce a mortgage, which has been permitted to lie dormant for the period requisite under the statute to acquire the title to land by adverse possession, neither, on the other hand, will it ordinarily decree its satisfaction unless payment in fact is proved,—the mere lapse of time, of itself, not being regarded as a sufficient ground for its interference,[31] and the presumption raised by the lapse of such period is liable to rebuttal by evidence which fairly raises a contrary presumption.[32] It may be said that the special reasons which will let a mortgagor in to redeem after the lapse of such period must come within some one of the exceptions named in the statute;[33] and if the mortgagor or those claiming under him is under any disability at the time when the mortgage debt matures, or the condition thereof is broken, neither the statute nor the presumption applies until such disability is removed.[34] There is another circumstance to be con-

30. Kellogg v. Woods, 7 Paige (N. Y.) Ch. 578.

31. Coates v. Roberts, 2 Phila. (Pa.) 244.

32. Ayres v. Waite, 64 Mass. (10 Cush.) 72, where it was held that, where no entry to foreclose a mortgage has been made in compliance with the statute, a bill to redeem may be brought by a mortgagor at any time within twenty years, and that if the mortgagee has been in peaceable possession after condition broken for that period, no interest having been paid, the right to redeem is not favored in equity, and in analogy to the statute the mortgagor will not, except for special reasons, be admitted to redeem. See Robinson v. Fife, 3 Ohio St. 551.

33. Limerick v. Voorhis, 9 Johns. (N. Y.) 129; Demarest v. Wynkoop, 3 Johns. Ch. (N. Y.) 129.

34. Beckford v. Wade, 17 Ves. 87; Price v. Copner, 1 S. & S. 347; Jenner v. Tracey, 3 P. Wms. 287, note; White v. Ewer, 2 Vent. 340; Belch v. Harvey, 3 P. Wms. 287, note; Lamar v. James, 3 H. & M. (Md.) 328; Demarest v. Wynkoop, *supra*. The instances where a mortgagee or mortgagor are under disabilities must be extremely rare, as usually neither will be under a disability at

sidered in determining the right of the mortgagor to redeem after the mortgagee has been in possession for the requisite statutory period, and that is, whether during the entire period his possession has been adverse to the mortgagor, because, if he has misled the mortgagor by assuming any obligation to him as a return for his being let into possession or otherwise, whereby the mortgagor has been induced to lie by without redeeming the land, a court of equity will not treat the possession as adverse.[35] In those States where special statutory provisions are made [36] that a failure to bring proceedings to redeem mortgaged premises within a certain number of years after entry by the mortgagee shall forever bar the mortgagor, of course a court of equity has no power to override the statute and let the mortgagor in to redeem, where the time has run and the statute fairly applies; but where no statutory provision is made, courts of equity adopt the period prescribed by the statute for the acquisition of a title by possession as the period requisite to bar a right of entry by a mortgagor or mortgagee.[37]

the date of the mortgage. But instances may arise where a disability intervenes between the date of the mortgage and the accruing of a right of action under it, as where either party becomes insane.

35. Demarest v. Wynkoop, *supra;* Rafferty v. King, 1 Keen 601; Hyde v. Dillaway, 2 Hare 528.

36. As in California, New Jersey, Kentucky, Mississippi, and North Carolina.

37. Jarvis v. Woodruff, 22 Conn. 548; Crittendon v. Brainard, 2 Root (Conn.) 485; Skinner v. Smith, 1 Day (Conn.) 124. In Haskell v. Bailey, 22 Conn. 569, Waite, J., says: "Where the right of entry upon lands is, by statute, limited to a period of twenty years, a mortgagor who has suffered the mortgagee to remain in possession of the mortgaged premises during that period cannot afterwards sustain a bill to redeem without showing such circumstances as will relieve his case from the operation of the general rule. As in this State the right of entry upon lands is limited to a period of fifteen years, our courts, proceeding upon the same principle, have repeatedly held that the mortgagor under such circumstances must bring his bill within fifteen years, and is not allowed twenty years for that purpose. And they have said that it may be adopted as a rule that the mortgagee being in possession, a mortgagor shall not have more than fifteen years to redeem after his equitable right has accrued, unless the delay shall be accounted for by statute disabilities, or

§ 223. Statutory provisions relative to mortgages.

The same rule prevails as to mortgage debts as prevails in reference to other debts—that the statute simply defeats the remedy, but does not extinguish the debt; but as there are distinct remedies upon the debt, and the mortgage given to secure it,[38] and the nature of the remedies depends upon the character of the respective instruments, it would seem to follow that, in the absence of an express statute to the contrary in those States where a distinction is made between simple contracts and instruments under seal, the circumstance that the statute has run upon the one would not prevent or bar the remedy upon the other, upon which the statute has not run;[39] and, as we have before seen, except

other special circumstances that may be considered equivalent." Skinner v. Smith, 1 Day (Conn.) 127; Lockwood v. Lockwood, id. 295; Jarvis v. Woodward, *supra.*

In Maine, it is held that the right of redemption is not lost by lapse of time when the mortgagor retains possession for himself alone and not for the mortgagee; that while lapse of time may either bar the mortgagee's right to redeem or give rise to a presumption of payment in his favor, yet, as both these facts cannot exist as to the same mortgage at the same time, the question which of them will prevail depends upon the possession for the requisite lapse of time. Bird v. Keller, 77 Maine, 270, 273; Hemmenway v. Lynde, 79 id. 299, 9 Atl. 620. In New York, where a mortgage is merely a personal security, and does not pass the fee, a tender need not be made in order to extinguish the lien of a mortgage; the tender must be kept good, although it need not be kept good as between debtor and creditor when, upon payment, the debtor is entitled to the possession of his property. See Watkins v. Vrooman, 51 Hun (N. Y.) 175, 5 N. Y. Supp. 172; Nelson v. Loder, 55 Hun 173, 7 N. Y. Supp. 849; Exchange F. Ins. Co. v. Norris, 74 Hun 527, 26 N. Y. Supp. 823; Foster v. Mayer, 70 Hun 265, 24 N. Y. Supp. 46; 4 Kent Com. (14th Ed.) 188, and n. 1; McManaman v. Hichley, 82 Minn. 296, 84 N. W. 1018.

38. Lent v. Shear, 26 Cal. 361; Law v. Allen, 26 Cal. 141.

39. Hough v. Bailey, 32 Conn. 288; Heyer v. Pruyn, 7 Paige (N. Y.) Ch. 465, 34 Am. Dec. 355; Myer v. Beal, 5 Oreg. 130; Crain v. Paine, 58 Mass. (4 Cush.) 483. Sustaining this doctrine, see Hayes v. Frey, 54 Wis. 503; Whittington v. Flint, 51 Ark. 504, 51 Am. Rep. 572; Buckner v. Street, 15 Fed. 365; Nichols v. Briggs, 18 S. C. 473. In Hardin v. Boyd, 113 U. S. 765, 5 Sup. Ct. 771, 28 L. Ed. 1141, Harlan, J., says: "An action to recover the debt may be barred by limitation, yet the right to enforce the lien for purchase money may still exist." Coldcleugh v. Johnson, 34 Ark. 312; Lewis v.

where the statute expressly or by fair inference destroys the remedy upon the mortgage, at the same time that the remedy is destroyed as to the debt, it may be enforced after the statute has run upon the debt, unless the same statutory period is applicable to both. Thus, in California, no distinction exists between simple contracts and those under seal, but the statute runs upon all contracts, obligations, etc., founded upon an instrument of writing, except a judgment or decree, etc., in four years; and, as the courts do not regard a mortgage as a conveyance of real estate, they hold that when the debt is barred, the mortgage is also extinguished, because, being a mere incident of the debt, it cannot exist independently of its principal, which is the debt. The same rule prevails in several of the new States, where the old theories relative to real estate and the effect of sealed instruments are not adopted to their full extent, as in Iowa,[40] Nevada,[41] Nebraska,[42] Texas,[43] Illinois,[44] and Kansas;[45] and such, indeed,

Hawkins, 90 U. S. (23 Wall.) 119, 23 L. Ed. 113; Birnie v. Main, 29 Ark. 591; Cheney v. Cooper, 14 Neb. 415; Crook v. Glenn, 30 Md. 55; Bird v. Keller, 77 Me. 270; Locke v. Caldwell, 91 Ill. 417; Chouteau v. Burlando, 20 Mo. 482; Elsberry v. Boykin, 65 Ala. 336; Mich. Ins. Co. v. Brown, 11 Mich. 265; Browne v. Browne, 17 Fla. 607, 35 Am. Rep. 97; McNair v. Lot, 34 Mo. 285; Arrington v. Liscom, 34 Cal. 365; Bizzell v. Nix, 60 Ala. 281; Waldo v. Rice, 14 Wis. 286; Lingan v. Henderson, 1 Bland (Md.) 236; Cheney v. Janssen, 20 Neb. 128; Edmands v. Tipton, 85 N. C. 459; Earnshaw v. Stewart, 64 Md. 513; Christy v. Dana, 42 Cal. 174; Clough v. Rowe, 63 N. H. 562; Smith v. Woolfolk, 115 U. S. 143, 5 Sup. Ct. 1177, 29 L. Ed. 357; Allen v. Early, 24 Ohio St. 97; Tryon v. Munson, 77 Pa. 250; Potter v. Stransky, 48 Wis. 235; Fuller v. Eddy, 49 Vt. 11; Fisk v. Stewart, 26 Minn. 365; Green v. Mizelle, 54 Miss. 220; Baltimore & Ohio R. R. Co. v. Trimble, 51 Md. 99; Cape Girardeau County v. Harbison, 58 Mo. 90; Wood v. Augustine, 61 Mo. 46.

40. Clinton County v. Cox, 37 Iowa 570; Green v. Turner, 38 id. 112; Gower v. Winchester, 33 id. 303.

41. Henry v. Confidence Gold M. Co., 1 Nev. 619.

42. Hurley v. Estes, 6 Neb. 386; Kyger v. Ryley, 2 Neb. 20.

43. Ross v. Mitchell, 28 Tex. 150; Duty v. Graham, 12 Tex. 427.

44. Hagan v. Parsons, 67 Ill. 170. But in this State a distinction exists between a sealed instrument and one not under seal; but as the debt is treated as the principal, and the mortgage as an incident, they both fall together, unless the mortgage contains a covenant for the payment of the debt, in which case the mort-

would seem to be the necessary rule where this theory relative to the nature and effect of mortgages prevails. In some of the States, express limitations are provided as to the period within which an action for the enforcement or redemption of a mortgage must be brought. Thus, in New York,[46] it is provided that an action for the redemption of a mortgage, either with or without an account for rents and profits may be maintained, unless the mortgagee or those claiming under him have continuously maintained an adverse possession of the premises for twenty years;[47] and such a provision, in effect, exists in the New Jersey statute.[48] In Illinois,[49] it is provided that a mortgage shall be barred in ten years after a right of action accrued thereon. In Kentucky,[50] the remedy of a mortgagor for the redemption of a mortgage is barred when the mortgagee, or any person claiming under him, has been in the continuous adverse possession of the premises for fifteen years. In Mississippi,[51] the right of redemption is barred in ten years, and the remedy upon the mortgage is barred when the debt is.[52] In Minnesota,[53] a remedy upon a mortgage is

gage is not barred until the period for the limitation of sealed instruments has expired. Harris v. Mills, 28 Ill. 44.

45. Chick v. Willetts, 2 Kan. 384; Schmucker v Sibert, 18 Kan. 104, 26 Am. Rep. 765.

46. Appendix, New York.

47. The New York Code of Civil Procedure, §§ 380, 381, limiting actions upon sealed instruments to twenty years, applies to an action to foreclose a mortgage; and if a mortgagor has paid nothing for twenty years on the mortgage debt, but certain grantees of a part of the premises, have assumed the debt, and made payments thereon, this does not stop the running of limitations in favor of the grantee of another parcel, who has paid nothing, and who has not assumed the mortgage. Mack v. Anderson, 165 N. Y. 529, 59 N. E. 289. See also, Murdock v. Waterman, 145 N. Y. 55, 39 N. E. 829, 27 L. R. A. 418; Boughton v. Van Valkenburgh, 61 N. Y. S. 574, 46 App. Div. 352. In general, the agreement of a mortgagor's vendee to assume the mortgage, when made before the note is barred by limitation, is a new promise continuing the note. Daniels v. Johnson, 129 Cal. 415, 61 Pac. 1107, 79 Am. St. Rep. 123. See Robertson v. Stuhlmiller, 93 Iowa 326, 61 N. W. 986.

48. Appendix, New Jersey.

49. Appendix, Illinois.

50. Appendix, Kentucky.

51. Appendix, Mississippi.

52. Appendix, Mississippi.

53. Appendix, Minnesota.

barred in ten years after the cause of action accrued; and such, also, is the provision in North Carolina,[54] both as to the foreclosure and redemption of a mortgage.[55] In California,[56] an action to redeem a mortgage is barred in five years. In the other States, the period of limitations is made to depend upon the period requisite to bar an entry upon lands, or, in most of the new States and some of the old ones,[57] upon the period provided for the limitation of actions upon contracts in writing, or of instruments under seal. In New Hampshire, by statute,[58] the note is kept on foot as long as an action may be maintained upon the mortgage, which is twenty years from the time when the debt becomes due.[59] In Pennsylvania and Wyoming, the period of limitation is twenty-one years, adopting, as is generally the case, the period requisite to bar a right of entry upon lands, and treating the mortgage as a conveyance of land. In Maine, Rhode Island, Massachusetts, New Jersey, New York, Georgia, Indiana, Delaware, South Carolina, Wisconsin, and Dakota, the mortgage is barred in twenty years from the time when the obligation it is given to secure matures. In Vermont, Connecticut, Kentucky, Virginia, and Kansas, the limitation is fifteen years. In Alabama, Iowa, Oregon, North Carolina, West Virginia, Texas, Nebraska, Missouri, Minnesota, and New Mexico, ten years; in Tennessee, Florida, and Utah, seven years; in Colorado, six years; in Arkansas, California, and Idaho, five years; in Nevada, four years; in Montana, three years. Where a creditor has an election of remedies for the same debt, one of which is barred and the other not, he may maintain an action on the one not barred. Thus, where a note is given as collateral security for an account, an action may be maintained upon the note, although the statute has run aainst the account[60] and the same rule prevails where there is a note and mortgage. The note may be barred, but an action to recover the

54. Appendix, North Carolina.
55. Id.
56. Appendix, California.
57. Rhode Island, Oregon.
58. Appendix, New Hampshire.
59. Id.
60. Shipp v. Davis, 78 Ga. 201.

amount secured by the mortgage may be maintained until the statute has run against that.

§ 224. When statute begins to run in favor of or against the mortgagor.

The statute begins to run in favor of the mortgagor from the time when the mortgagee's right of action accrues against him, under the mortgage,[61] or, in other words, from the time of condition broken, so that the mortgagee may foreclose fully;[62] and, as the proceedings are *in rem*, the fact that the defendant is out of the State during the whole period does not save the mortgage from the operation of the statute.[63] When the mortgagee enters into the possession of the mortgaged premises for condition broken, the statute begins to run against the mortgagor from the time of such entry.[64] But if the mortgagee enters under an

61. Nevitt v. Bacon, 32 Miss. 212.

62. Wilkinson v. Flowers, 37 Miss. 579, 75 Am. Dec. 78; Trayser v. Trustees, 39 Ind. 556; Hale v. Pack, 10 W. Va. 145; Gladwyn v. Hitchman, 2 Vern. 134; Gillett v. Balcom, 6 Barb. (N. Y.) 370.

63. Anderson v. Baxter, 4 Oreg. 105.

64. Bailey v. Carter, 42 N. C. (7 Ired. Eq.) 282; Montgomery v. Chadwick, 7 Iowa 114; Waldo v. Rice, 14 Wis. 286; Hubbell v. Sibley, 50 N. Y. 468; Miner v. Beckman, 50 N. Y. 337; Peabody v. Roberts, 47 Barb. (N. Y.) 41; Knowlton v. Walker, 13 Wis. 264.

In Massachusetts the possession of the mortgaged premises by the mortgagor, and those claiming under him, for more than twenty years after the debt has matured, and without any recognition thereof, affords presumptive proof of payment. Kellogg v. Dickinson, 147 Mass. 432, 18 N. E. 223, 437, 1 L. R. A. 346, and note. And after an entry of foreclosure, the mortgagor and those claiming under him become tenants at sufferance of the mortgagee, and during the next three years they are assumed to hold under him, in the absence of any evidence of an adverse holding. Cunningham v. Davis, 175 Mass. 213, 222, 56 N. E. 2. In Massachusetts it is settled in favor of the mortgagor that the day of the entry to foreclose is to be excluded from the statutory three years, while the mortgagee is not allowed the corresponding benefit with regard to the last day. Jager v. Vollinger, 174 Mass. 521, 523, 55 N. E. 458.

In Missouri, it is held that, in order to bar a foreclosure, there must have been, for the required period, an adverse possession of the property; that the relation of the mortgagor and mortgagee, being in its inception friendly, as created by their volun-

agreement expressed in the mortgage, or entered into subsequently, that he shall take possession and reimburse himself the mortgage debt from the rents and profits, the statute does not begin to run against the mortgagor until the debt is fully satisfied from such rents and profits, or he asserts title in himself, and gives the mortgagor distinct notice thereof.[65] But if the agreement is that the mortgagee shall enter and have the rents and profits for a distinct or definite period, the statute will not begin to run against the mortgagor until such period has elapsed;[66] as in such case a court of equity would restrain the mortgagor from setting up a legal title to the land in himself, or from disturbing the mortgagee in his possession until the debt is satisfied.[67] When a mortgage is payable by installments, the statute attaches to each installment as it becomes due, but the mortgagor's possession does not become adverse until the last installment has matured.[68] Nothing short of actual possession by the mortgagee, continued for the entire statutory period, without recognition of the right of the mortgagor to redeem, will operate to convert his estate into an absolute title in equity,[69] and mere constructive possession is not sufficient;[70] nor is payment of taxes

tary contract, is presumed so to continue until the mortgagor by his acts or declarations repudiates the mortgage, of which the mortgagee must have notice enough, at least, to put him upon inquiry. Eyermann v. Piron, 151 Mo. 107, 117, 52 S. W. 229. Also, that a grantee of a mortgagor with constructive notice of the mortgage is in no better situation than his grantor, and can only avail of the presumption of payment from lapse of time when the mortgagor could do so, under the same circumstances. Ibid; Lewis v. Schwenn, 93 Mo. 26, 2 S. W. 391, 3 Am. St. Rep. 511.

In England, as to the effect of the statute 1 Vict., c. 28, by which a payment of interest upon a mortgage gives a new starting point for the running of limitation against a mortgagee out of possession, see 7 Law Quarterly Rev. 43.

65. Frink v. Le Roy, 49 Cal. 315; Anding v. Davis, 38 Miss. 574.

66. Frink v. Le Roy, *supra.*

67. *Id.*

68. Parker v. Banks, 79 N. C. 480.

69. Miner v. Beekman, 50 N. Y. 337; Demarest v. Wynkoop, 3 Johns. (N. Y.) Ch. 129.

70. Slee v. Manhattan, 1 Paige (N. Y.) Ch. 48; Moore v. Cable, 1 Johns. (N. Y.) Ch. 385.

for the statutory period, without actual possession, enough to cut off the mortgagor's right to redeem;[71] and the rule is not varied by the circumstance that the lands are wild and uncleared.[72] Where a right to redeem is not cut off by foreclosure proceedings, it seems that the statute does not begin to run in favor of the purchaser until the expiration of the period fixed in the decree for redemption.[73]

§ 225. Right of redemption barred, when.

When a mortgagee has been in possession of mortgaged premises after condition broken, for the period requisite to acquire a title to lands by adverse possession, without the payment to him of any part of the principal or interest due upon the mortgage, in the absence of any statute fixing the period within which the mortgagor may redeem, courts of equity, acting in analogy to the statute, treat the lapse of such period as *prima facie* a bar to his right to redeem,[74] unless the mortgagor or those claiming under him, during that period, were under some of the disabilities specified in the statute as suspending the statute, in which case proper allowance is made therefor,[75] which, in the absence of any provision in the statute itself, is usually ten years after the removing of such disabilities in analogy to the Stat. 21 James I.;[76] but if the statute makes specific provision as to the period within which

71. Bollinger v. Chouteau, 20 Mo. 89.

72. Moore v. Cable, *supra.*

73. Rockwell v. Servant, 63 Ill. 424.

74. Barron v. Martin, 19 Ves. 397; Crawford v. Taylor, 42 Iowa 260; Robinson v. Fife, 3 Ohio St. 551; Demarest v. Wynkoop, 3 Johns. (N. Y.) Ch. 129; Blake v. Foster, 2 B. & B. 402; Montgomery v. Chadwick, 7 Iowa 114; Howland v. Shultleff, 42 Mass. (2 Metc.) 26, 35 Am. Dec. 384; Dexter v. Arnold, 1 Sumner (U. S.) 109; Hoffman v. Harrington, 33 Mich. 392; Slee v. Manhattan Co., 1 Paige (N. Y.) Ch. 48; Hall v. Denckla, 28 Ark. 506; Phillips v. Sinclair, 20 Me. 269; Slicer v. Bank of Pittsburg, 57 U. S. (16 How.) 571, 14 L. Ed. 1063; Knowlton v. Walker, 13 Wis. 264; Gunn v. Brantley, 21 Ala. 633.

75. Price v. Copner, 1 S. & S. 347; Beckford v. Wade, 17 Ves. 87; White v. Ewer, 2 Vent. 340; Demarest v. Wynkoop, *supra.*

76. Lamar v. Jones, 3 H. & McH. (Md.) 328.

action may be brought after the removal of such disabilities, such statutory period would be adopted. As we have already seen in New York, New Jersey, Mississippi, Minnesota, and North Carolina, by statute, the right of redemption is barred in ten years, in Kentucky in fifteen, and in California, in five years. In all the other States the right is left subject to the common-law rules which have grown up under the statutes. But, as has been stated, this bar is only *prima facie,* and in order to be operative the mortgagee's possession must have been adverse during the respective periods;[77] and if his possession is consistent with the rights of the mortgagor, this *prima facie* bar does not attach,[78] as, if he recognizes the mortgagor's right to redeem by accepting a part payment of the principal or interest upon the mortgage,[79] or recognizing such right, by acknowledging the mortgagee as such, and the commencement of foreclosure proceedings, either under a statute or in equity, is sufficient to let the mortgagor in to redeem;[80] or, indeed, any acknowledgment in writing sufficient to take an ordinary debt out of the operation of the statute would be sufficient;[81] but a mere parol acknowledgment would not be sufficient, as now in nearly all the States and territories of this country except those previously named, as in England, an acknowledgment of a debt to be sufficient must be in writing, signed by the person to be charged. Where there are two or more mortgagees, all must sign the acknowledgment, as only those who do sign will be bound thereby[82] in those States where pro-

77. Hyde v. Dallaway, 2 Hare, 528.

78. Wallen v. Huff, 24 Tenn. (5 Humph.) 91; Rockwell v. Servant, 64 Ill. 424; Waldo v. Rice, 14 Wis. 286; Humphrey v. Hurd, 26 Mich. 44; Crawford v. Taylor, 42 Iowa 260; Yarbrough v. Newell, 18 Tenn. (10 Yerg.) 376; Quint v. Little, 4 Me. 495; Kohlheim v. Harrison, 34 Miss. 457; Frink v. Le Roy, 49 Cal. 315; Teulon v. Curtis, 1 Younge, 610; Morgan v. Morgan, 10 Ga. 297; Knowlton v. Walker, 13 Wis. 264.

79. Knowlton v. Walker, *supra.*

80. Calkins v. Isbell, 20 N. Y. 147; Jackson v. Slater, 5 Wend. (N. Y.) 295; Robinson v. Fife, *supra;* Cutts v. York Mfg. Co., 18 Me. 140; Jackson v. De Lancey, 11 Johns. (N. Y.) 365.

81. Stansfield v. Hobson, 3 De G. M. & G. 620; Price v. Cover, 1 S. & S. 347; Lake v. Thomas, 3 Ves. 17.

82. Richardson v. Young, L. R. 10 Eq. Cas. 275.

vision is made that the acknowledgment of one joint contractor, etc., shall not be binding upon the others. The acknowledgment, to be operative, must be made by and to the proper party. It is not the naked possession, but the nature of it, which determines his right.[83] The possession must not only be adverse, but it must also be actual; and mere constructive possession will not avail,[84] nor will an occasional occupation be sufficient. It must be continuous and without interruption, and adverse to the mortgagor's right to redeem. Payment of taxes on wild land of itself does not amount to a possessory act,[85] but accompanied with actual possessory acts, such as the premises are susceptible of, and which constitute a badge of ownership, it would doubtless be held sufficient.

§ 226. When mortgagor is in possession of a part of the premises.

When the mortgagor is in possession of a part of the premises, and the mortgagee is in possession of the other part, it seems that no length of time will bar the mortgagor's right to redeem, because, so long as the right to redeem any part of the estate remains, it exists as to the whole under the rule that, except in special instances, there can be no redemption of separate parts of the mortgaged estate,[86] and the same rule prevails when the mortgagor is constructively in possession.[87]

§ 227. Liability of mortgagee in possession.

If a bill to redeem is brought by a mortgagor before the mortgagee has been in possession for the period requisite to bar the mortgagor's right, he will be compelled to account for the rents

83. Reynolds v. Green, 10 Mich. 355; Robinson v. Fife, 3 Ohio St. 551; Blethen v. Dwinal, 35 Me. 556; Hurd v. Coleman, 42 Me. 182.

84. Milner v. Beekman, 50 N. Y. 337.

85. Bollinger v. Chouteau, 20 Mo. 89.

86. Rakestraw v. Brewer, Sel. Cas. temp. King, 55; Burke v. Lynch, 2 B. & B. 426. But see Lake v. Thomas, 3 Ves. 17.

87. Archbold v. Scully, 9 H. L. 360; Drummond v. Sant, L. R. 6 Q. B. 763.

and profits of the estate during his occupancy. He is not obliged to lay out money any further than to keep the estate in necessary repair; but on a bill to redeem he will be made to account for all loss and damage occasioned by his gross negligence in respect of bad cultivation and non-repair.[88] He will also be charged, not only for all rents received, but also for all rents which but for his willful neglect or default he might have received.[89] A mortgagee in possession has been held not chargeable as for willful default in declining to defend an action of replevin brought by the owner of goods distrained on the premises by such mortgagee.[90] If he has expended any sum in supporting the right of the mortgagor to the estate, where his title has been impeached, the mortgagee may certainly add that to the principal of his debt; and it shall carry interest. Where a mortgagee has been put to expense in defending the title to the estate, the defense being for the benefit of all parties interested, he is entitled to charge such expenses against the estate; but if his title to the mortgage only is disputed, the costs of his defense should not be borne by the estate as against parties interested in the equity of redemption, unless they can be shown to have concurred or assisted in the litigation.[91] If the estate lies at such a distance that the mortgagee must employ an agent to collect the rents, what he pays to the agent shall be allowed; but not where he does or may receive the rents himself. It is the settled practice in the Court of Chancery not to take an account against a mortgagee in possession with annual rests, where, at the time of his entering into possession, there is an arrear of interest.[92] A mortgagee of leaseholds may take possession, even where there is no arrear of interest due, under circumstances which may not render him liable to account with annual rests; as where he enters in order to prevent a forfeiture

88. Wragg v. Denham, 2 Y. & C. 117; Fisher, §§ 901-909; Wood's Landlord & Tenant, 198-199.

89. Fisher, §§ 873, 894, 895; Brandon v. Brandon, 10 W. R. 287.

90. Cocks v. Gray, 1 Giff. 77.

91. Parker v. Watkins, 1 Johns. 133.

92. Nelson v. Booth, 3 De G. & J. 119.

for non-payment of ground-rent or for non-insurance.[93] The Court of Chancery will not suffer, in a deed of mortgage, any stipulation to prevail, that the estate should become an absolute purchase in the mortgagee upon any event whatsoever.[94] A court of common law has no power to compel a reconveyance of a mortgaged estate after payment of the mortgage debt, interest, and costs.[95] The statute does not run against the mortgagor's right to have an account, until his right to redeem is lost.

§ 228. Welsh mortgages.

Welsh mortgages are effected by a conveyance of property to a mortgagee, coupled with occupation by him on the understanding that he is to pay himself the interest of the money lent by receiving the profits of the land. The land may be redeemed at any time on repayment by the mortgagor of the money lent; and the mortgagee cannot foreclose,[96] though now equity would probably compel an account against the mortgagee.[97] The reason for this is, that the receipt of the rents and profits in reduction of the debt operates as a constant renewal of the mortgage.[98] If a mortgagee after repayment of the mortgage debt continues to hold the property twenty years, the mortgagor will, it appears, be barred his right to recover it.[99] Any arrangement for securing repayment of a loan by demise, or granting annuities possessing characteristics similar to those above mentioned, is considered in the nature of a Welsh mortgage.[1] When no time of payment is fixed, as is the case in this class of mortgages, it is perhaps true that a redemption will

93. Patch v. Wild, 30 Beav. 99.

94. Bonham v. Newcomb, 1 Vern. 8, 232; Toomes v. Conset, 3 Ark. 261; Vernon v. Bethell, 2 Eden 110; Fisher, § 126; Powell on Mortgages, 116 *a*, note (H).

95. Gorely v. Gorely, 1 H. & N. 144.

96. Talbot v. Braddil, 1 Vern. 395; Lawley v. Hooper, 3 Atk. 280; Yates v. Hambly, 2 id. 237.

97. Fulthrope v. Foster, 1 Vern. 477.

98. Orde v. Heming, 1 Vern. 418; Marks v. Pell, *supra;* Fenwick v. Reed, 1 Mer. 114.

99. Fenwick v. Reed, 1 Mer. 119.

1. Teulon v. Curtis, 1 Younge, 610.

be decreed at any time;[2] but this right may be lost by a subsequent agreement of the parties;[3] so, too, by an express notice given by the mortgagee to the mortgagor that he claims adversely.[4]

§ 229. Presumption of payment—Effect of part payment.

Courts of equity, although not strictly bound by the statute of limitations, except in those States where express provision to that effect is made, nevertheless, as we have seen,[5] usually adopt a period in analogy to the statute as sufficient to raise a presumption against the right sought to be enforced; and where it is sought to enforce a mortgage after the lapse of the statutory period, when the mortgagor has been in possession and there has been no payment thereon within that period, or express recognition of the rights of the mortgagee, the courts will presume that the debt has been paid and the mortgage lien satisfied;[6] and this

2. Orde v. Heming, 1 Vern. 418; Fenwick v. Reed, 1 Mer. 114.

3. Hartpole v. Walsh, 5 Bro. P. C. 267.

4. Talbot v. Braddil, 1 Vern. 395; Yates v. Hambly, 2 Atk. 360; Alderson v. White, 2 De G. & J. 97; Longuet v. Scawen, 1 Ves. 403.

5. See Chap. VI., Equitable Actions.

6. Reynolds v. Green, 10 Mich. 355; Bacon v. McIntire, 49 Mass. (8 Metc.) 87; Martin v. Bowker, 19 Vt. 526; Hoffman v. Harrington, 33 Mich. 392; Newcomb v. St. Peter's Church, 2 Sandf. (N. Y.) Ch. 636; Donald v. Sims, 3 Ga. 383; McNair v. Lot, 34 Mo. 285. The possession of the mortgagor before condition broken is not hostile to that of the mortgagee, but after that event, if no payments are made upon the mortgage for the entire statutory period, the presumption that the mortgage has been satisfied is well sustained, although until the entire statutory period has elapsed the mortgagee is treated as constructively in possession. Atkinson v. Patterson, 46 Vt. 750; Doe v. Williams, 5 Ad. & El. 291; Hall v. Doe, 5 B. & Ald. 687; Pitzer v. Burns, 7 W. Va. 63; Howland v. Shurtleff, 42 Mass. (2 Metc.) 26, 35 Am. Dec. 384; Martin v. Jackson, 27 Pa. 504; Bates v. Conrow, 11 N. J. Eq. 137; Boyd v. Beck, 29 Ala. 703; Sheafe v. Gerry, 18 N. H. 245; Higginson v. Mein, 4 Cranch (U. S.) 415; Benson v. Stewart, 30 Miss. 49; Roberts v. Littlefield, 48 Me. 61; Chick v. Rollins, 44 Me. 104; Inches v. Leonard, 12 Mass. 379; Drayton v. Marshall, Rice (S. C.) Eq. 373; Downs v. Sooy, 28 N. J. Eq. 55. And a less period than that fixed by the statute for barring similar rights at law will not be sufficient to raise a presumption of payment. Boon v. Pierpont, 28 N. J. Eq. 7.

furnishes a good defense to an action of ejectment or a bill to foreclose brought by the mortgagee.[7] This presumption is not irrebuttable, but may be overcome by proof of a part payment of principal or interest, or a direct recognition of the mortgagee's rights, sufficient under the statute to amount to an acknowledgment,[8] which acknowledgment or recognition, in those States

7. Jackson v. Pratt, 10 Johns. (N. Y.) 381; Jackson *ex dem.* People v. Wood, 12 Johns. (N. Y.) 242, 7 Am. Dec. 315; Howland v. Shurtleff, *supra;* Martin v. Bowker, 19 Vt. 526; Hughes v. Edwards, 22 U. S. (9 Wheat.) 498, 6 L. Ed. 142; Reynolds v. Green, 10 Mich. 355; Field v. Wilson, 45 Ky. (6 B. Mon.) 479; Hoffman v. Harrington, 33 Mich. 892; Wilkinson v. Flowers, 37 Miss. 579, 75 Am. Dec. 78; McNair v. Lot, 34 Mo. 285.

8. Jarvis v. Albro. 67 Me. 310. And where the mortgagee is in possession, the mortgagor may avail himself of a part payment to save the statute as against him. Ford v. Ager, 2 H. & C. 279; Palmer v. Eyre, 17 Q. B. 366. This presumption may be overcome by circumstances which fairly overthrow it. Snavely v. Pickle, 29 Gratt. (Va.) 27; Brobst v. Brock, 77 U. S. (10 Wall.) 519, 19 L. Ed. 1002; Leman v. Newham, 1 Ves. 51; Hale v. Pack, 10 W. Va. 145. Where a mortgage was executed, in 1706, to a resident of Great Britain, who remained there, and never was in possession of the land mortgaged, and the mortgagor had, in 1741, devised the lands to his sons—*held,* that no presumption could arise that the mortgage had been satisfied, before the year 1780, in favor of a person with fifty years' exclusive possession, who did not derive his title under the mortgage. Owing v. Norwood, 2 Har. & J. (Md.) 96. When a mortgagor has retained possession of the mortgaged premises for more than twenty years after the execution of the mortgage, but has acknowledged the debt and paid interest upon it within twenty years there is no presumption that the debt is discharged. Howard v. Hildreth, 18 N. H. 105; Wright v. Eaves, 10 Rich. (S. C.) Eq. 582. But unexplained possession of mortgaged premises for less than twenty years by the mortgagor may be left to the jury in connection with the partial payments and other evidence, as tending to show that the debt was fully paid. Gould v. White, 26 N. H. 178. The retention of mortgaged property after the law-day has passed is not *prima facie* evidence of fraud, nor does it authorize a legal presumption of payment. Steele v. Adams, 21 Ala. 534; Clark v. Johnson, 5 Day (Conn.) 373. But a mortgage given to secure the title to land sold and conveyed will be presumed extinguished after a lapse of from thirty to fifty-six years, and the enjoyment of the land under the title conveyed. Murray v. Fishback, 44 Ky. (5 B. Mon.) 403; Inches v. Leonard, 12 Mass. 379. Mere lapse of time raises no presumption in favor of a stranger against the title of a mortgagee; and in this case the stranger was in adverse pos-

where parol acknowledgments are ineffectual, must be in writing and signed by the mortgagor; and if there are two of them both must sign it, or it will be ineffectual to bind the entire estate.[9] Mere silence on the part of the mortgagor, where demands for payment are made upon him by the mortgagee, does not of itself amount to such a recognition of the mortgagee's rights as will save the statute.[10] Any act of the mortgagor which operates to keep the mortgage debt on foot, also operates to keep up the mortgage lien, as an acknowledgment of the debt by the mortgagor[11] in the mode and with the formalities required by law. A part payment of principal or interest made by the mortgagor or his agent revives the mortgage, and gives it a new lease of validity from the date of such payment; and a payment by one of two or more mortgagors, while the mortgage is still operative, it seems, will keep up the right of entry against all.[12] But, in

session at the commencement of the action. Appleton v. Edson, 8 Vt. 241. But as between the parties, the presumption of the payment of a mortgage becomes absolute after the lapse of fifteen years, if there is no entry, or payment of interest; and being a presumption of law, it is in itself conclusive, unless encountered by distinct proof. Whitney v. French, 25 Vt. 663.

9. Richardson v. Younge, L. R. 6 Ch. 478. In Cheever v. Perley, 93 Mass. (11 Allen) 584, it was held that this presumption is not conclusive, but that, where parol evidence is relied upon to control it, it should clearly show some positive act of unequivocal recognition of the debt within the statutory period.

10. Cheever v. Perley, 93 Mass. (11 Allen) 584.

11. See Hough v. Bailey, 32 Conn. 289; Hart v. Boyd, 54 Miss. 547.

12. Pears v. Laing, L. R. 12 Eq. Cas. 41; Roddam v. Morley, 1 De G. & J. 1. Payments of interest made by tenant for life have been held sufficient as against the remainderman. Toft v. Stephenson, 1 De G. M. & G. 28; Pears v. Laing, L. R. 12 Eq. 51; Roddam v. Morley, *supra*. So a payment by the mortgagor's solicitor. Ward v. Carter, L. R. 1 Eq. 29. But in order to make a payment by a person other than the mortgagor operative to keep the mortgage on foot, either express authority must be established, or the payment must be made by a person so situated in reference to the property and the mortgagor that the law will imply authority. Chinnery v. Evans, 11 H. L. Cas. 115.

On a testator's simple or mortgage contract debt carrying interest, payment of the interest by a devisee for life so acknowledges the debt as to keep alive the right of action against the remaindermen. *In re* Hollings-

order to have that effect, the payment must be made while the mortgagor owns the equity of redemption, and a payment made after he has parted with the same does not revive or keep on foot the mortgage security, as, from the time when he parts with his interest in the land, his power to bind it in any manner is gone, either as to past or future debts. The payment of interest on a mortgage debt by the mortgagor repels the presumption of payment arising from the lapse of time.[13]

§ 230. Effect of acknowledgment or new promise upon the mortgage.

So long as the debt which a mortgage is given to secure is kept on foot, the mortgage lien remains in full force. Therefore, any acknowledgment or promise of the debtor sufficient to prevent the statute from running against the debt, equally prevents the statute from running upon the mortgage;[14] and, as we have seen, such also is the effect of a part payment, either of principal or interest made upon the mortgage.[15] But where the rights of subsequent mortgagees intervene, or where the mortgagor has sold the premises, an acknowledgment or payment afterwards made by the mortgagor after the statute bar has become

head, 37 Ch. D. 651; Barclay v. Owen, 60 L. T. 220, 222.

13. Hughes v. Blackwell, 69 N. C. (6 Jones Eq.) 73; Howard v. Hildreth, 18 N. H. 105; Wright v. Eaves, 10 Rich. (S. C.) Eq. 582.

14. Hart v. Boyd, 54 Miss. 547. See Cheever v. Perley, 93 Mass. (11 Allen) 584; Jarvis v. Albro, 67 Me. 310, as to the effect of acknowledgment in repelling presumption of payment. In California, it is held that after the rights of third parties have intervened, the mortgagor cannot, by any act of his, either suspend the running of the statute, or revive the debt after the statute has run upon it. Wood v. Goodfellow, 43 Cal. 185; Sichele v. Carrillo, 42 Cal. 493; Lent v. Shear, 26 Cal. 361; Barber v. Babel, 36 Cal. 11. But this doctrine, so far as the mortgagor's power to suspend the running of the statute is concerned, does not find any support in the courts of other States. Waterson v. Kirkwood, 17 Kan. 9; Clinton Co. v. Cox, 37 Iowa 570.

15. Roddam v. Morley, 1 De G. & J. 1; Pears v. Laing, L. R. 12 Eq. 51; Hough v. Bailey, 32 Conn. 288; Ayres v. Waite, 64 Mass. (10 Cush.) 72; Baton v. McIntire, 49 Mass. (8 Met.) 87; Clinton Co. v. Cox, 37 Iowa 570.

complete, does not revive the mortgage so as to defeat any of the rights of such subsequent mortgagee or grantee.[16] But so far as his own interests are concerned he may revive the mortgage by such acts, but not so as to impair or defeat the rights of other parties who, previous to such acts, acquired an interest in the premises.[17] Where a subsequent grantee or mortgagee agrees to pay the mortgage, and the mortgagor, either by suit or otherwise, insists upon his performance of this contract, a payment of either principal or interest made by such grantee or mortgagee upon the mortgage, will keep it on foot not only as against him, but also as against his grantor or mortgagor.[18] It seems that, when the statute has run upon a prior mortgage, the holder of a subsequent mortgage is entitled to have the prior mortgage cancelled as against a mortgagee out of possession, and a court of equity, upon proper proceedings to that end, will direct its cancellation on the ground of such bar.[19]

§ 231. Effect of fraud on part of mortgagee.

When the mortgagee has been guilty of fraud, either at the time the mortgage was made or subsequently, which has prevented the mortgagor from redeeming, a court of equity will let the mortgagor in to redeem, although more than the statutory period has elapsed since the mortgagee went into possession.[20] In an English case [21] the mortgage contained a provision that it should be redeemed with the mortgagor's own money. The court held that the words signified nothing where the money was to be repaid, "for the

16. New York Life Ins. & Trust Co. v. Covert, 29 Barb. (N. Y.) 435, reversed 3 Abb. Dec. (N. Y.) 350, 6 Abb. Prac. (U. S.) 154.

17. Schmucker v. Sibert, 18 Kan. 104, 26 Am. Rep. 765.

18. Cucullu v. Hernandez, 103 U. S. 105, 26 L. Ed. 322.

19. Fox v. Blossom, 17 Blatchf. (U. S. C. C.) 352.

20. In Reigal v. Wood, 1 Johns. (N. Y.) Ch. 402, this rule was applied in a case where a judgment was revived by fraud and imposition. Rakestraw v. Brewer, Sel. Cas. temp. King, 55; Marks v. Pell, 1 Johns. (N. Y.) Ch. 594.

21. Ord v. Smith, Sel. Ch. temp. King, 9.

borrower being necessitated, and so under the lender's power, the law makes a benign construction in his favor," and the imposition of such terms was held to amount to a fraud in its creation, and therefore that the mortgage was redeemable at any time.

§ 232. Distinction between equitable lien for purchase-money and mortgage.

While the statute does not run upon a mortgage until the lapse of the period requisite to bar an entry upon lands, yet it is held in New York and Mississippi that an equitable lien in favor of the vendor of land for the purchase money is barred when the debt itself is barred.[22] "There is," says Bowen, J.,[23] "a material distinction between a mortgage and an equitable lien for the purchase price of land given by law, and also between an action to foreclose a mortgage and one to enforce a lien." A lien created by law must coexist with the debt, and cannot survive it.[24] In the case last cited it was held that, while a vendor's lien has the incidents of, it is not a mortgage, but consists solely in debt, and must be subject to all the incidents of the debt, and cannot be enforced when the debt cannot be, and therefore that, when a purchase-money note is barred by the statute, the remedy to enforce the equitable lien is also barred. "It is," say the court, "a secret equity, and is not recognized as against the rights of a purchaser from the vendee without notice."[25] Upon principle and the weight of authority, the fact that the debt is barred appears not to destroy

22. Trotter v. Erwin, 27 Miss. 772; Littlejohn v. Gordon, 32 Miss. 235.

23. Borst v. Corey, 15 N. Y. 505.

24. Borst v. Corey, *supra;* Trotter v. Erwin, *supra.*

25. In Borst v. Corey, *supra,* the court say: "The action to foreclose a mortgage is brought upon an instrument under seal which acknowledges the existence of the debt to secure which the mortgage is given; and by reason of the seal the debt is presumed not to have been paid until the expiration of twenty years after it becomes due and payable. The six years' limitation has no application to a mortgage. * * * The equitable lien is neither created nor evidenced by deed, but arises by operation of law, and is of no higher nature than the debt which it secures. It must coexist with the debt, and cannot survive it."

the lien which the law gives to the vendor of lands for the purchase money, but it remains liable to be enforced in equity, until the lapse of such a period as, by the statutes of the State, is requisite to give a title by possession. This doctrine is sustained by the courts of Maryland,[26] Virginia,[27] Connecticut,[28] and Alabama.[29]

26. Magruder v. Peter, 11 G. & J. (Md.) 217.

27. Lingan v. Henderson, 1 Bland (Md.) 236, 282; Hopkins v. Cockerell, 2 Gratt. (Va.) 88.

28. In this State the question was not directly passed upon, but the rule stated in the case sustains the general doctrine announced in the text. Belknap v. Gleason, 11 Conn. 160.

29. Driver v. Hudspeth, 16 Ala. 348; Relfe v. Relfe, 34 Ala. 500. In Bizzell v. Nix, 60 id. 281, 31 Am. Rep. 38, a bill was brought to enforce a vendor's lien for the unpaid purchase money of land. The statute had run against the notes given therefor, and as a consequence it was insisted that the lien was destroyed. But the court held otherwise, Brickell, C. J., saying: "The authorities, which doubtless induced the decree of the Chancellor, and which are now relied on to support it, are Driver v. Hudspeth, 16 Ala. 348, and Relfe v. Relfe, 34 Ala. 500. The first was a proceeding under the statute then in force in the Orphans' Court, at the instance of a vendee holding a bond for title, to compel the personal representatives of the vendor, who had died, to make him title. The purchase money had not been paid, but an action at law on the notes given for it was barred by the statute of limitations. It was held that a vendor retaining the legal titles, and entering into bond for its conveyance only on payment of the purchase money, had a lien in the nature of a mortgage; that this lien the court would not divest until the purchase money was paid, and that it was not impaired, because an action at law for the recovery of the purchase money was barred by the statute of limitations. The court say: 'The fact that the notes were barred by the statute of limitations does not destroy the lien, which is regarded in the nature of a mortgage. If the vendor whose notes are barred, or his heirs after his death, should bring ejectment to recover the land, and thus drive the purchaser into a court of equity to enjoin the action, it is clear to my mind that the Court of Chancery would not interfere until he had paid up the purchase money, the remedy to recover which, at law, had been barred by the statute of limitations. The court of equity would not decree a specific performance in favor of one who withholds the compensation he stipulated to pay, upon the ground that the legal remedy to recover it is barred. The vendor is not bound to sue upon his note, but may rest upon the security furnished by his lien.' The contract of sale, in Relfe v. Relfe, was by parol, and, so far as is shown by the report of the case, the vendor had not conveyed. It was held that

§ 233. Distinction between a pledge and a mortgage—Difference in application of statute to the one and the other.

A wide distinction exists between a pledge of personal property and a transaction that amounts to a mortgage thereof. Thus, where property is deposited as collateral security with a creditor, with no understanding or agreement that he may sell the same and apply the proceeds in liquidation of the debt, it is a pledge merely, and the title to the property remains in the pledgor until he is divested thereof by due process of law; but where property is

the lien for the payment of the purchase money was not lost or destroyed, because the statute of limitations had operated a bar for its recovery in an action at law. It was further held that the lien could not be regarded as a stale demand within less than twenty years after the sale. It is said by the court: 'The principle which preserves liens, notwithstanding the bar of the debt, is neither confined to those secured by a conveyance, as for example a mortgage, nor to those secured by a sealed instrument, nor even to those provided by an express contract.' Again: 'The principle is, the statute of limitations does not extinguish the debt, but merely bars the remedy by action at law, and there is no inconsistency in the prosecution of another remedy after the action at law is barred.' The court was referred to the New York and Mississippi decisions, to which the appellant now refers, and declined to follow them, 'These decisions are not correct expositions of the law.' We are not inclined to depart from these decisions. The general principle, that when the security for a debt is a lien on property, personal or real, the lien is not impaired, because the remedy at law for the recovery of the debt is barred, is not, as is very emphatically and clearly stated in Relfe v. Relfe, confined to liens created by contract, or by instruments under seal, or by mortgages which convey a legal estate and confer a right of entry. The debt is not extinguished, though the statute of limitations may have barred legal remedies for its recovery. The bar of the statute may be removed by a subsequent promise or acknowledgment which is supported by the debt as a consideration, and the consideration rests on the moral obligation to pay, which statutes cannot obscure or impair. Cook v. Bramel (Ky.), 45 L. R. A. 212. The debt not being extinguished, the lien for its security remains, and though legal remedies are barred, the equitable remedy to enforce the security is unaffected. 'It is not necessary further to pursue a discussion of the question. We cannot regard it as *res integra.* The discussion was exhausted, and is foreclosed by the decisions to which we have referred, and on their authority we are content to rest." See Higgins v. Scott, 2 B. & Ad. 413; Spears v. Hartley, 3 Esp. 81; Hopkins v. Cockerell, 2 Gratt. (Va.) 68.

deposited with a creditor to be sold, and the proceeds applied in discharge of the debt, the transaction amounts to a mortgage, and the title to the property vests in the creditor. The distinction, as far as the operation of the statute is concerned, is, that in the former case the statute does not begin to run against the pledgor until he has paid or offered to pay the debt, while in the latter case the statute begins to run against the debtor's right to redeem at once upon the maturity of the debt, and is fully barred by the lapse of the statutory period requisite to bar the debt it was given to secure.[30]

30. Huntington v. Mather, 2 Barb. (N. Y.) 538. Edmonds, J., who delivered the opinion of the court, said: "It seemed to be conceded on the argument that unless the original transaction between these parties was a pledge of the stock in question, the plaintiff's bill could not be sustained; and therefore it was that so much of the argument was directed to that point. One consideration very strenuously urged was the expression used in the note that the stock had been 'deposited as collateral security,' which it was insisted conveyed the idea of a pledge, and that alone. But such an expression is not of itself sufficient to determine the character of the transaction; for it has been held that even the use of the word 'pledge' has not that effect, *ex vi termini;* and where it is the clear intent of the parties that the possession of the goods, etc., shall remain in the debtor until default in payment, it will be regarded as a mortgage, even if the word 'pledge' is used. Langdon v. Buel, 9 Wend. (N. Y.) 80; Reeves v. Capper, 5 Bing. N. C. 136; Ferguson v. Union Furnace Co., 9 Wend. (N. Y.) 345.

"There are two leading considerations to be regarded in determining whether the transaction is a pledge or a mortgage; namely, the title and the possession. If it is a mortgage, the legal title passes to and is vested in the creditor. Story on Bailm., § 287; Langdon v. Buel, *supra;* Patchen v. Pierce, 12 Wend. (N. Y.) 61. With a pledge it is different; the legal title, until a sale on default of payment or redemption, continuing in the pledgor. Story on Bailm., *supra;* Cortolyou v. Lansing, 2 Caines Cas. (N. Y.) 200. The pawnee has indeed a qualified property in the article pledged, but upon a tender to him of the debt he becomes divested even of that qualified property, and becomes a wrong-doer if after that he persists in retaining the article pledged, from the pawnor. Story on Bailm., §§ 339, 341; Coggs v. Bernard, 2 Ld. Raym. 916. The essential difference as to matter of right is, that the title passes, and in the other it does not. But the difference in substance and fact is, that in the case of a pawn or pledge the possession must pass out of the pawnor, but in the case of a mortgage it need not. In this case the possession and title both passed out of the debtor."

§ 234. Discharge of mortgage debt, effect of.

As a general rule, the discharge of the debt which a mortgage is given to secure operates as a discharge of the mortgage; but this rule does not apply where the personal liability of the mortgagor merely is discharged, without intending to extinguish the debt,[31] nor does it apply where the debt is merely barred by the statute of limitations.[32]

§ 235. Mortgagee in possession.

Where a mortgagee is in possession of the premises for the full statutory period after condition broken, the mortgagor's right of redemption is forever barred, unless within that period the mortgagee has accepted from him some portion of the principal or interest of the mortgage debt, or in some other legally effectual way acknowledged the right of the mortgagor to redeem. This may be done by settling the account of the rents and profits of the premises within that period, as the principal objection urged by courts of equity against letting the mortgagor in to redeem after that period is the difficulty of settling the accounts between the parties for so long a period; and where this objection is obviated by a settlement made by the parties themselves, the mortgagor will be admitted to redeem partly upon that ground, and partly upon the ground that such settlement operates as an admission of the mortgagor's right. Thus, in an English case,[33] a mortgage was held to

31. Donnelly v. Simonton, 13 Minn. 301. See Hayden v. Smith, 53 Mass. (12 Met.) 511.

32. Chamberlain v. Meeder, 16 N. H. 381; Bush v. Cooper, 26 Miss. 599.

33. Conway v. Shrimpton, 5 Bro. P. C. 187; Blake v. Foster, 2 B. & B. 387; Chapman v. Corpe, 41 L. T. N. S. 22; Guthrie v. Field, 21 Ark. 379; Gunn v. Brantley, 21 Ala. 633; Arrington v. Liscom, 34 Cal. 366; Taylor v. McClain, 60 Cal. 651, 64 id. 513; Bunce v. Wolcott, 2 Conn. 27; Morgan v. Morgan, 10 Ga. 297; Hallesy v. Jackson, 66 Ill. 139; Montgomery v. Chadwick, 7 Iowa 114; Crawford v. Taylor, 42 id. 260; Roberts v. Littlefield, 48 Me. 61; Hertle v. McDonald, 2 Md. Ch. 128; Crook v. Glenn, 30 Md. 55; Stevens v. Dedham Inst., 129 Mass. 547; Reynolds v. Green, 10 Mich. 355; Hoffman v. Harrington, 38 id. 392; McNair v. Lot, 34 Mo. 285; Tripe v. Marcy, 39 N. H. 439; Miner v. Beekman, 50 N. Y. 337; Bailey v. Carter, 42 N. C. (7 Ired. Eq.) 282; Yarbrough v. Newell, 18 Tenn. (10 Yerg.) 376;

be redeemable where the mortgagee had been in possession for forty years, upon the foot of a stated account and an agreement for turning interest into principal.[34]

Any act of the mortgagee by which he acknowledges the transaction to be still a mortgage, any time within twenty years before a bill to redeem is brought, is held sufficient to keep the mortgagor's right to redeem on foot. Thus, if the mortgagee, in his will, disposes of the money "in case the mortgage is redeemed," [35] or by any other deliberate acts admits that he is mortgagee as to the estate, a bill to redeem will lie;[36] or where the mortgagee enters under an agreement to reimburse himself out of the profits.[37] Before the statutes required acknowledgments to be in writ-

Knowlton v. Walker, 13 Wis. 264; Ross v. Norvell, 1 Wash. (Va.) 14; Hughes v. Edwards, 22 U. S. (9 Wheat.) 489, 6 L. Ed. 142; Fox v. Blossom, 17 Blachf. (U. S. C. C.) 352; Amory v. Lawrence, 3 Cliff (U. S. C. C.) 523; see Doe v. De Veber, 3 Allen (N. B.) 23; Miner v. Beekman, 14 Abb. Pr. N. S. (N. Y.) 1; Hammonds v. Hopkins, 11 Tenn. (3 Yerg.) 525; Wood v. Jones, 19 Tenn. (Meigs) 513; Anding v. Davis, 38 Miss. 574.

34. Cholmondeley v. Clinton, 2 J. & W. 188; Giles v. Baremore, 5 Johns. (N. Y.) Ch. 545. In Proctor v. Cowper, 2 Vern. 377, a bill was brought to redeem a mortgage made in 1642. The mortgagee entered into possession in 1650, and there were three descents on the defendant's part and four on the part of the plaintiff; but the length of time being unsevered for the greatest portion of the time by infancy or coverture, and because the mortgagee, in 1686, brought a bill to foreclose, and an account was then made up by the mortgagee, the court decreed a redemption and an account from the foot of the account in 1686.

35. Cruise's Digest, 156. See Hauselt v. Patterson, 124 N. Y. 349.

36. Perry v. Marston, 2 Bro. Ch. 397; Ross v. Norvell, 1 Wash. (U. S. C. C.) 18; Marks v. Pell, 1 Johns. (N. Y.) Ch. 594; Whiting v. White, 2 Cox 290. A recognition of the mortgage incidently in any conveyance or other instrument is sufficient. Pender v. Jones, 2 N. C. (2 Hayw.) 294; Price v. Copner, 1 S. & S. 347; Hansard v. Harvey, 18 Ves. 455; Conway v. Shrimpton, *supra;* Ord v. Smith Sel. Cas. temp. King, 9; Hodle v. Healey, 1 V. & B. 536; Vernon v. Bethell, 2 Eden 110; Elmendorf v. Taylor, 23 U. S. (10 Wheat.) 152, 6 L. Ed. 289. See Turlock v. Roby, 12 Scott, 87; Lucas v. Dennison, 7 Jur. 1122.

37. Marks v. Pell, *supra.* Acknowledgments by a mortgagee in possession have been held sufficient to remove the statute bar in numerous cases, as stating an account of the rents and profits of the land. Barron v. Martin, Cooper's Ch. 189; Palmer

ıg, it was seriously questioned whether any form of parol acknowlǀgment would be sufficient, and in an early case in this country,[38] tory, J., in a very able opinion in which he carefully reviewed ıe cases, held that such an acknowledgment or admission would ot be sufficient.[39]

. Jackson, 3 Bro. P. C. 194; Ley v. 'eter, 3 H. & N. 101; Kalheim v. [arrison, 34 Miss. 457, or the execuıon of a written promise; Snavely . Pickle, 29 Gratt. (Va.) 27; Hall . Felton, 105 Mass. 516; Lyon v. IcDonald, 51 Mich. 435; Haywood . Ensley, 27 Tenn. (8 Humph.) 60; Murphy v. Coates, 6 Stew. Eq. N. J.) 424; Kerndt v. Porterfield, 6 Iowa 412; Wells v. Harter, 56 Cal. 42; Schmucker v. Sibert, 18 Kan. 04; 26 Am. Rep. 765, or a eed to third persons; Cape Girrdeau County v. Harrison, 58 Io. 90; Randall v. Bradley, 65 Ie. 43; Biddel v. Brizzolara, 56 Cal. 74; or by an acceptance of interest r a part of the principal debt; Winhester v. Ball, 54 Me. 558; Stump . Henry, 6 Md. 201; Fisk v. Stewrt, 24 Minn. 97; Pears v. Laing, L. L. 12 Eq. 41; or by bringing a bill o foreclose, or any proceeding to enorce payment of the mortgage debt; lobinson v. Fife, 3 Ohio St. 551; Dexter v. Arnold, 1 Sumner (U. S.) 09; Erskine v. North, 14 Gratt. Va.) 60; Giles v. Baremore, 5 Johns. Ch. (N. Y.) 545; Johnson v. Johnon, 81 Mo. 331; Cleveland v. Harrion, 15 Wis. 870; Martin v. Bowker, 9 Vt. 526; Ricker v. Blanchard, 45 I. H. 39; and purposely absenting r concealing himself so as to preent a tender of the amount due on he mortgage has been held sufficient. Valdo v. Rice, 14 Wis. 286. See Wallace v. Stevens, 66 Me. 190; Cunningham v. Hawkins, 24 Cal. 403.

As to the effect of mere parol admissions, see Green v. Cross, 45 N. H. 574; Cheever v. Perley, 93 Mass. (11 Allen) 584; Hough v. Bailey, 32 Conn. 288; Morgan v. Morgan, 10 Ga. 297; Wimmer v. Ficklin, 77 Ky. (14 Bush) 193; Shepperd v. Murdock, 7 N. C. (3 Murph.) 218.

38. Dexter v. Arnold, 3 Sumn. (U. S. C. C.) 160, where Story, J., comments on the case of Perry v. Marston, 2 Bro. Ch. 357, where it has been supposed (though it is not, perhaps, certain) that Lord Thurlow thought parol evidence admissible, and sufficient to give the plaintiff a decree for redemption, but he, in fact, decided against it on another ground. See Reeks v. Postlethwaite, Cooper's Eq. 160; Barron v. Martin, 19 Ves. 326; Marks v. Pell, 1 Johns. (N. Y.) Ch. 594.

39. See also, Whiting v. White, 2 Cox 290.

A mortgagee of land, while disseised by a stranger, cannot make a valid assignment of his mortgage; but exclusive possession by a mortgagor and those claiming under him, with a claim of exclusive ownership, does not so disseise the mortgagee as to invalidate a transfer of the mortgage title, or the execution of a power of sale contained in the mortgage. Dadmun v. Lamson, 91 Mass. (9 Allen) 85; Murphy v. Welch, 128

§ 236. Absolute conveyances, but in fact mortgages.

If the parties to an instrument, at the time of its execution, intend it as a security, whatever may be its form, equity will consider it as a mortgage, and no terms or words used in it will be allowed to change its character, and cut off the right of redemption;[40] and this is the case even though the conveyance on its face is absolute, and there is nothing to indicate that it was intended as a security for a loan or a pre-existing debt;[41] and parol evidence

Mass. 489; Holmes v. Turner's Falls Co., 150 Mass. 535, 547, 23 N. E. 305, 6 L. R. A. 283. See 1 Encyc. of Law and Proc., p. 1069; 3 Kerr on Real Property, § 2104; Longstreet v. Brown (N. J. Eq.), 37 Atl. 56.

As to who is a "person claiming under a mortgage" under the English Real Property Limitation Act, 1874, § 9, see Thornton v. France (1897), 2 Q. B. 143.

As stated *supra*, § 219, possession subject to a vendor's lien is like possession subject to a mortgage, and is not adverse. Lewis v. Harkins, 90 U. S. (23 Wall.) 119, 127, 23 L. Ed. 113; Wheeling Bridge & T. Ry. Co. v. Reymann Brewing Co., 90 Fed. 189, 195. See Morgan v. Mueller, 107 Wis. 241, 83 N. W. 313; Milnes v. Van Gilder, 197 Pa. 347, 47 Atl. 197, 80 Am. St. Rep. 828; Cochran v. Linville Impr. Co., 127 N. C. 386, 37 S. E. 496; Watson v. Heyn, 62 Neb. 191, 86 N. W. 1064; Chase v. Cathright, 53 Ark. 358, 14 S. W. 90, 22 Am. St. Rep. 207, and note; 32 Am. L. Reg. (N. S.) 859.

40. Robinson v. Farrelly, 16 Ala. 472; Richardson v. Barrick, 16 Iowa 407; Howe v. Russell, 36 Me. 115; Artz v. Grove, 21 Md. 456; Bank of Westminster v. Whyte, 1 Md. Ch. 536; Parks v. Hall, 19 Mass. (2 Pick.) 211; Steel v. Steel, 86 Mass. (4 Allen) 417; Vasser v. Vasser, 1 Cush. (Miss.) 378; Davis v. Clay, 2 Mo. 161; Wilson v. Drumrite, 21 Mo. 325; Somersworth v. Roberts, 38 N. H. 22; De Camp v. Crane, 19 N. J. Eq. 166; Holliday v. Arthur, 25 Iowa 19; Phoenix v. Gardner, 13 Minn. 430; Bingham v. Thompson, 4 Nev. 224; Cotterell v. Long, 20 Ohio 464; Miami, etc., Co. v. United States Bank, Wright (Ohio) 249; Pattison v. Horn, 1 Grant (Pa.) Cas. 301, 304; Halo v. Schick, 57 Pa. 319; Nichols v. Reynolds, 1 R. I. 30; Bennett v. Union Bank, 24 Tenn. (5 Humph.) 612; McCan v. Marshall, 26 Tenn. (7 Humph.) 121; Webb v. Patterson, id. 431; Hinson v. Partee, 30 Tenn. (11 Humph.) 587; Yarbrough v. Newell, 18 Tenn. (10 Yerg.) 376; Delahay v. McConnel, 5 Ill. 156; Nichols v. Cabe, 40 Tenn. (3 Head) 92; Nickerson v. Toney, id. 655; Yates v. Yates, 21 Wis. 473; Catlin v. Chittenden, Brayt. (Vt.) 163; Campbell v. Worthington, 6 Vt. 448; Mott v. Harrington, 12 Vt. 119; Wright v. Bates, 13 Vt. 341; Rogan v. Walker, 1 Wis. 527.

41. Kellum v. Smith, 33 Pa. 158; Holmes v. Grant, 8 Paige (N. Y.) Ch. 243; Parmalee v. Lawrence, 44 Ill. 405; Baxter v. Deas, 24 Tex. 17;

is admissible to show that it was intended as a mortgage,[42] or that the defeasance was omitted by fraud or mistake.[43] Upon this

Mills v. Darling, 43 Me. 565; Crassen v. Swoveland, 22 Ind. 427; Barkelew v. Taylor, 8 N. J. Eq. 206; Chaires v. Brady, 10 Fla. 133.

42. Babcock v. Wyman, 60 U. S. (19 How.) 289, 15 L. Ed. 644; Rogan v. Walker, 1 Wis. 527; Bishop v. Bishop, 13 Ala. 475; Bryan v. Cowart, 21 Ala. 92; Blakemore v. Byrnside, 7 Ark. 505; Jordon v. Fenno, 13 Ark. 593; Pierce v. Robinson, 13 Cal. 116; Jones v. Jones, 38 Tenn. (1 Head) 105; Guinn v. Locke, id. 110; People v. Irwin, 14 Cal. 428; Johnson v. Sherman, 15 Cal. 287; Cunningham v. Hawkins, 27 Cal. 603; Hopper v. Jones, 29 Cal. 18; Trucks v. Lindsey, 18 Iowa 504; Jackson v. Lodge, 36 Cal. 28; Washburn v. Merrill, 1 Day (Conn.) 139; Marks v. Pell, 1 Johns. (N. Y.) Ch. 594; Collins v. Tillou, 26 Conn. 368; Hovey v. Holcomb, 11 Ill. 660; Shaver v. Woodward, 28 Ill. 277; Roberts v. McMahan, 4 Greene (Iowa) 34; Green v. Ball, 67 Ky. (4 Bush) 586; Whitney v. Batchelder, 32 Me. 313; Emerson v. Atwater, 7 Mich. 12; Johnson v. Huston, 17 Mo. 58; Carlyon v. Lannan, 4 Nev. 156; Condit v. Tichenor, 19 N. J. Eq. 43; Crane v. Buchanan, 29 Ind. 570; Key v. McCleary, 25 Iowa 191; Phoenix v. Gardner, 13 Minn. 430; Bingham v. Thompson, 4 Nev. 224; Walton v. Cronly, 14 Wend. (N. Y.) 63; Swart v. Service, 21 id. 36; Webb v. Rice, 1 Hill (N. Y.) 606; Hodges v. Tennessee, etc., Ins. Co., 8 N. Y. (4 Seld.) 416; Kimborough v. Smith, 2 Dev. (N. C.) Eq. 558; Couch v. Sutton, 1 Grant (Pa.) Cas. 114; Pattison v. Horn, id. 301, 304; Stamper v. Johnson, 3 Tex. 1; Mead v. Randolph, 8 Tex. 191; Hannay v. Thompson, 14 Tex. 142; Mann v. Falcon, 25 Tex. 271; Plato v. Roe, 14 Wis. 453. See Fitzpatrick v. Smith, 1 Desaus (S. C.) 340. To the contrary, Hale v. Jewell, 7 Me. 435; Bryant v. Crosby, 36 Me. 562; Watson v. Dickens, 20 Miss. 608.

43. Taylor v. Luther, 2 Sumn. (U. S. C. C.) 228; Morris v. Nixon, 42 U. S. (1 How.) 118, 11 L. Ed. 69; Slee v. Manhattan Co., 1 Paige (N. Y.) Ch. 48; Whittrick v. Kane, 1 id. 202; Van Buren v. Olmstead, 5 id. 1; Strong v. Stewart, 4 Johns. (N. Y.) Ch. 167; Ross v. Norvell, 1 Wash. (Va.) 14; Anon. 2 N. C. (2 Hayw.) 26; M'Laurin v. Wright, 37 N. C. (2 Ired. Eq.) 94; Hudson v. Isbell, 5 Stew. & P. (Ala.) 67; English v. Lane, 1 Port. (Ala.) 328; Craft v. Bullard, S. & M. (Miss.) Ch. 366; Murphy v. Trigg, 17 Ky. (1 T. B. Mon.) 72; Lewis v. Robards, 19 Ky. (3 T. B. Mon.) 406; Lindley v. Sharp, 23 Ky. (7 T. B. Mon.) 248; Overton v. Bigelow, 11 Tenn. (3 Yerg.) 513; Miami Exporting Co. v. United States Bank, Wright (Ohio) 249; Blair v. Bass, 4 Blackf. (Ind.) 539; Delahay v. McConnel, 5 Ill. 156; Wadsworth v. Loranger, Harr. (Mich.) 113; Lane v. Dickerson, 18 Tenn. (10 Yerg.) 373; Conwell v. Evill, 4 Blackf. (Ind.) 67; Scott v. Britton, 10 Tenn. (2 Yerg.) 215; May v. Eastin, 2 Port. (Ala.) 414; Aborn v. Burnett, 2 Blackf. (Ind.) 101; Bank of Westminster v. Whyte, 1 Md. Ch. 536;

class of mortgages it has been held that the statute does not begin to run until a tender of the money which it was given to secure, and a refusal to reconvey.[44] But there is no question but that a court of equity would refuse to enforce a right to redeem, where the grantee had slept upon his rights until his claim had become stale.[45]

Lokerson v. Stillwell, 13 N. J. Eq. 357. To the contrary, Streator v. Jones, 5 N. C. (1 Murph.) 449; Thompson v. Patton, 15 Ky. (5 Litt.) 74.

44. Wilson v. Richards, 1 Neb. 342.

45. Neglect by a grantee for thirty years to enforce any right under a deed absolute on its face does not preclude the claim that such deed was in fact a mortgage only. Mott v. Fiske, 155 Ind. 597, 58 N. E. 1053; Porter v. White, 128 N. C. 42, 38 S. E. 24. See Johnson v. Prosperity L. & B. Assoc., 94 Ill. App. 260.

CHAPTER XXII.

DISABILITIES IN PERSONAL ACTIONS.

§ 237. Saving clauses in statutes in favor of plaintiff.

In the seventh section of the statute of James it is provided that, if at the time when a cause of action accrued any person entitled to bring the same shall be within the age of twenty-one years, *feme covert, non compos mentis,* imprisoned, or beyond the seas,[1] such person shall be at liberty to bring the same action within the time limited by the statute after his disability has terminated; and substantially the same provision is incorporated into the statutes of most of the States. In Maine,[2] these and other exceptions are made, the words "married woman" and "insane" being substituted for "*feme covert*" and *non compos mentis;* so, also, in Vermont, but the statute of which State also contains the additional exceptions existing in the Maine statute, except that in cases where a debtor is out of the State at the time when an ac-

1. See Appendix, Maine Rev. Stats. (1903), ch. 83, 95, 96, 106, § 91.

2. In America the phrase "beyond the seas" means out of the State, or out of the jurisdiction. Maurice v. Worden, 52 Md. 283, 291; Mason v. Union Mills Co., 81 Md. 446.

tion accrues, or after it accrues, the exception does not apply if the debtor has within the State known property which, by the common and ordinary processes of law, could be attached; so, also, by section 1564 (1212), of the statute of Vermont, whenever the commencement of an action is stayed by an injunction of any court of equity, the time during which such injunction is in force is not to be taken as any part of the time limited for the commencement of the suit enjoined.[3] In New Hampshire, substantially the same exceptions exist as in the statute of James, except that the words "insane person" are substituted for *non compos mentis;* no exception is made in favor of persons imprisoned or out of the United States;[4] and substantially the same exception is made as in Maine in the case of the absence of the debtor, the exception being that, if the defendant at the time the cause of action accrued, or afterward, "was absent from and residing out of the State," the time of such absence shall be excluded. In Massachusetts,[5] an exception is made in favor of infants, insane persons or persons imprisoned, alien citizens of a country at war with the United States, and also where the defendant at the time when the cause of action accrued or after it had accrued, resided out of the State. In Connecticut,[6] as to actions of account, debt due by book or on simple or implied contract, or upon any contract in writing, not under seal, except promissory notes not negotiable, persons legally incapable to bring any such action at the accruing thereof may bring the same at any time within three years after becoming legally capable to do so; and the same exception exists as to specialties, except that four years are given after the party becomes capable of suing; where a person dies before the statute bar has become complete, his executor or administrator shall have one year from the time of such decease in which to bring an action thereon. In Rhode Island,

3. Vermont Stats. (1906), § 1560 (1208) *et seq.*

4. New Hampshire Public Stats. (1901), ch. 217, §§ 2, 7, 8.

5. Massachusetts Public Stats. (1902), ch. 202, §§ 7-9 (P. S. 197, §§ 9-11).

6. Connecticut Gen. Stats. 1902, ch. 79, § 1108 *et seq.;* (1888), ch. 98, § 1370 *et seq.*

substantially the same provision exists as in Maine, except as to absence from the State, and in that respect the provision is substantially the same as in Vermont;[7] and in all cases of adverse possession no exception is made in favor of a married woman because of her coverture.[8] In New York,[9] infancy or insanity creates a disability, and so does imprisonment on a criminal charge or in execution upon conviction of a criminal offense for a term less than for life; but the time for bringing an action cannot be extended more than five years by any such disability except infancy, nor in any case more than one year after the disability ceases. As to absence from the State when the right of action accrues, substantially the same provision exists as in the New England States. In New Jersey,[10] an exception is made in cases of infancy and insanity, but not in the case of coverture. In Pennsylvania, the same provisions exist as in the statute of James, and the provision as to persons "beyond sea" is construed as meaning persons "without the United States."[11] In Delaware,[12] exception is made in favor of persons "under disability of infancy, coverture, or incompetency of mind." In Maryland, exceptions exist in cases of infancy and insanity, but not in the case of imprisonment or coverture, and "absence from the State" is substituted for "beyond the seas."[13] In Virginia,[14] exception is made in favor of infants, married women, and insane persons; but the section "does not apply to a married woman having the right to make an entry on or bring an action to recover land which is her separate estate." In South Carolina,[15] substantially the same exceptions exist as in New York; so, in North

7. Rhode Island Gen Laws 1909, ch. 284, § 5; (1896), ch. 234, § 5.

8. Ibid. ch. 256, § 3 (1896), ch. 194, § 17.

9. Bliss's N. Y. Ann. Code (4th Ed.), § 396.

10. New Jersey Comp. Stats. 1911, § 4.

11. 2 Stewart's Purdon's Digest, 1910, p. 2266; Gonder v. Estabrook, 33 Pa. 374.

12. Delaware Laws (1893), ch. 122, §§ 13, 14.

13. Maryland Am. Civ. Code, 1911, art. 57, §§ 4, 5.

14. Pollard's Am. Virginia Code, 1904, § 2931.

15. South Carolina Cowe, 1912, §§ 133 (111), 108, 148 (124), 122.

Carolina,[16] except that married women are also included in the exception, as also are those "imprisoned on a criminal charge, or in execution upon conviction of a criminal offense." In Alabama, persons under the disability of infancy, insanity, or imprisonment on a criminal charge for less than for life, are given three years, or the period allowed by law for the bringing of such action if it be less than three years, after such disability is removed to bring an action, provided that no disability shall extend the period of limitation beyond twenty years from the time when the cause of action accrued.[17] In Georgia, infants, idiots or insane persons, or persons imprisoned, who are such when the cause of action accrues, are given the full statutory period after such disability is removed, to bring an action;[18] and substantially the same provision exists in Arkansas, except that "idiots" are not expressly included, and imprisonment does not constitute a disability, unless it occurs "beyond the limits of the State."[19] So in Colorado, the disabilities are substantially the same as in Georgia, except as to "idiots," and the statute also includes married women and persons who at the time when the action accrued were absent from the United States.[20] In Florida, a saving exists in favor of infants, insane persons, persons imprisoned, and seven years is given after the removal of such disability, or after the death of such person, in which to bring an action or to make an entry or defense.[21] In Indiana,[22] the disabilities are not specifically stated, but two years are given to any person "under legal disabilities[23] when the cause of action accrues" in which

16. Pell's Revisal N. C. Code, 1908, §§ 362, 363 (148).

17. Alabama Civil Code, 1907, §§ 4846 (2807).

In actions to recover land, here limited to seven years, persons under disability have, after it is removed, and after the seven years have elapsed, three years in which to sue. Kirby's Digest of Arkansas Statutes (1904), §§ 5056 (4815).

18. Georgia Code (1911), §§ 4374 (3779).

19. Appendix, Arkansas, Kirby's Digest (1904), §§ 5075 (4833).

20. Colorado, 2 Mills' Ann. Stats. 1912, §§ 4641 (2914).

21. Florida Rev. Stats. 1914, §§ 1723 (1292).

22. Indiana Stats. (1914, by Burns), §§ 298 (297).

23. This clause, "under legal dis-

to bring an action "after such disability is removed." In Iowa, non-residence is excepted, and one year after the removal of the disability is given to minors and insane persons.[24] In Illinois, an exception is made in favor of minors, or if a female, within the age of eighteen years, insane persons or persons imprisoned on a criminal charge, and two years after such disability is removed is given.[25] In Kentucky,[26] infancy, coverture, or unsoundness of mind constitute a disability, and the period of three years after its removal is given; by section 2534 an exception exists in favor of an alien and a citizen of a country at war with the United States, by section 2535 the time during which an action is enjoined is not to be computed; and by section 2536 the time during which the plaintiff is confined in the penitentiary is not to be computed.[27] In Mississippi, infancy and unsoundness of mind constitute the only disabilities.[28] In Missouri, the provision as to disabilities applies to infants, insane persons, married women, and persons imprisoned on a criminal charge, or in execution under sentence of a criminal court for a period less than his natural life;[29] so, also, in Minnesota, except that in the latter State the period of limitation cannot be extended more than five years, except in the case of infancy, nor in any case longer than one year after the disability ceases.[30] In Ohio, the exceptions are substantially the same as in

abilities," does not embrace non-residence, but does include absence from the United States, and also coverture. Bauman v. Grubbs, 26 Ind. 419; Smith v. Bryan, 74 Ind. 515; Royse v. Turnbaugh, 117 Ind. 539, 20 N. E. 485. Since 1881 married women are not under disability in Indiana. Indianapolis v. Patterson, 112 Ind. 344, 14 N. E. 551. As to cumulative disabilities, see *supra*, § 6 and note 69; *infra*, § 251; Miller v. Texas & Pac. Ry. Co., 132 U. S. 662, 10 Sup. Ct. 206, 33 L. Ed. 487; Davis v. Coblens, 174 U. S. 719, 19 Sup. Ct. 832, 43 L. Ed. 1147; Gaines v. Hammond, 6 Fed. 449, aff'd 111 U. S. 395, 4 Sup. Ct. 426, 28 L. Ed. 466; Oliver v. Pullam, 24 Fed. 127; East Tenn. & Coal Co. v. Wiggin, 68 Fed. 446, 15 C. C. A. 510.

24. Iowa Ann. Code (1897), §§ 3451, 3453.

25. Illinois Rev. Stats. (1912, by Hurd), ch. 83, Par. 7216 (§ 21).

26. Kentucky Stats. (1909, by Carroll), § 2506.

27. Ibid.

28. Mississippi Rev. Code, 1906, §§ 3106 (2746).

29. Missouri Rev. Stats. 1909, §§ 1894 (4279).

30. Minnesota Stats. 1913, §§ 7710 (5147).

Massachusetts, except as to aliens and the defendant's absence from the State.[31] In California, infants, insane persons, persons imprisoned on a criminal charge, or in execution under sentence of a criminal court for a period less than for life, and a married woman when her husband is a necessary party with her in commencing an action, are within the saving of the statute.[32] In Oregon, the provisions are the same as in California, except that the qualification as to married women is general, and except that the period within which action shall be brought shall not be extended more than five years, nor more than one year after the disability ceases.[33] In Michigan, infants, insane persons, persons imprisoned, married women, and persons absent from the United States (unless within the British Provinces of North America), are within the saving of the real property statute.[34] In Wisconsin, the same disabilities exist as in New York; but action must, except in the case of infancy, be brought within five years, and within one year after the disability ceases.[35] In Nevada, the same disabilities exist as in Wisconsin, but the period of five years, or after the death of a person while under such disability, after their removal is given, and married women are included.[36] In Nebraska, the exceptions apply to infants, insane persons and persons imprisoned.[37] In Tennessee, the saving is in favor of infants, persons of unsound mind, married women, and persons beyond the limits of the United States or the territories thereof;[38] and action may be brought within the statutory period after such disability is removed, unless it exceeds three years, and in that event within three years. In Texas, infants, married women, until they reach

31. Page & Adams' Ann. Ohio Gen. Code, 1910, §§ 11229, 11232 (4986, 4989).

32. California Code of Civil Procedure, 1908, §§ 328, 352.

33. 1 Oregon Laws (1910, by Lord), ch. 2, § 17.

34. 5 Michigan Am. St. (Howell), 1913, §§ 14123 (9718); as to personal actions, see §§ 14140 (9733).

35. 2 Wisconsin Statutes (1913, Sanborn & Berryman), § 4233.

36. Nevada Revised Laws, 1912, §§ 4966, 4976 (3716, 3717).

37. Nebraska Civil Code, 1913, Par. 7576, § 17.

38. Tennessee Code (1896, by Shannon), § 4448.

the age of twenty-one, persons of unsound mind, and persons imprisoned, are saved from the operation of the real property statute.[39] In Kansas, persons "under any legal disability" may bring an action within two years after the disability is removed,[40] in the case of real property, and within one year in other cases except penalties and forfeitures. In West Virginia, a saving exists in favor of infants, married women, and insane persons, except in cases where married women hold real estate in their sole right.[41] In Arizona, the exceptions are in favor of infants, persons of unsound mind, and persons imprisoned.[42] In North and South Dakota,[43] the exceptions are the same as in Oregon; but the period cannot be extended more than five years, except in case of infancy, nor in any case more than one year after the disability ceases. In Idaho, the same disabilities exist as in California.[44] In Montana, the same disabilities exist, but ten years are allowed in real actions after the disability ceases, or the death of the party disabled, and in personal actions five years' disability only is allowed, except in the case of infancy, or one year after the disability ceases.[45] In New Mexico, minors, insane persons, or persons "under any legal disability," are given one year after its removal in which to bring an action.[46] In Utah, the disabilities are the same as in California, but married women are not included, and actions lie for one year after disability ceases.[47] In Wyoming, a saving exists in favor of infants, insane persons, and persons imprisoned, and in personal actions the full statutory period after such disability is removed is given in which to bring an action, while in real actions ten years are allowed after "any legal disability" is removed.[48]

39. Texas Civ. Stats. 1913, §§ 5684 (3352); see §§ 5708 (3373).

40. Kansas Gen. Stats. (1909, by Dasslee), §§ 5609, 5611 (4261, 4263).

41. 2 Hogg's West Virginia Code, 1913, ch. 104, §§ 4416, 4429 (3, 16).

42. Arizona Rev. Stats. §§ 707, 729 (2307, 2330).

43. No. Dak. Code of Civil Procedure, 1913, §§ 7372, 7385; So. Dak. Comp Laws, 1910, § 70.

44. 2 Idaho Rev. Codes 1908, §§ 4046, 4070.

45. 2 Montana Code of Civ. Procedure, 1907, §§ 6442, 6459 (493, 542).

46. New Mexico Compiled Laws, 1897, § 2922.

47. Utah Comp. Laws, 1907, §§ 2872, 2889.

48. Wyoming Comp. Stats. 1910, §§ 4296, 4304 (2375, 2377).

It will be observed that these saving clauses, given here for convenience of comparison and reference, are substantially the same as those contained in the statute of James, except that in most of them,[49] instead of an exception in favor of persons *non compos mentis,* it only exists in favor of "insane persons;" a distinction which is of great importance, and excludes from its saving operation idiots, imbeciles, etc., who are properly embraced under the head of *non compotes.* In Connecticut, the saving exists in favor of persons "legally incapable" to sue, and this applies, therefore, only in favor of infants and *femes covert,* and such persons as by the common or statute law are incapable of bringing an action at law, and does not embrace persons imprisoned or beyond seas. In Delaware, instead of an exception in favor of persons *non compos mentis,* it exists in favor of persons under the disability of "incompetency of mind," which is substantially the same thing, and in Kentucky "unsoundness of mind;" so, also, in Tennessee, Mississippi, and Texas. In Iowa, there are no exceptions in favor of any disabilities, and no saving except as to minors and insane persons; while in Georgia, in addition to minors, insane persons, and married women, idiots are expressly included. In Pennsylvania and Maryland, the statute excepts persons *non compos mentis.* In Indiana, none but "legal" disabilities are excepted.[50]

49. Vermont, New Jersey, New Hampshire, Colorado, Rhode Island, Virginia, New York, Alabama, Illinois, Michigan, Wisconsin, Missouri, Arkansas, California, Massachusetts, Oregon, North Carolina, South Carolina, Minnesota, Kansas, Georgia, Nevada, Nebraska, Florida, Ohio, West Virginia, Arizona, Montana, Idaho, New Mexico, Utah, and Wyoming.

50. See Young v. Harris, 65 L. T. 45; Bent v. Thompson, 138 U. S. 114, 11 Sup. Ct. 238, 34 L. Ed. 902; Westmeyer v. Gallenkamp, 154 Mo. 28, 55 S. W. 231, 77 Am. St. Rep. 747; Carney v. Hennessey, 74 Conn. 107, 53 L. R. A. 699, 92 Am. St. Rep. 199, 49 Atl. 910; King v. Carmichael, 136 Ind. 20, 35 N. E. 509, 43 Am. St. Rep. 303; Landry v. Landry, 105 La. 362, 29 S. E. 900. In Moore v. Calvert, 69 Ky. (6 Bush) 356, it was held that when a right of action accrues to parceners or joint tenants, if some of them are under disability, the statute runs as to all, notwithstanding the coverture or infancy of the others. In Pope v. Brassfield, 110

§ 237a(1). Disabilities in general.

It is the general rule that, when the statute of limitations once begins to run, it is not suspended by intervening disabilities of the plaintiff or his privies in interest.[51] Limitations run against persons under disability, unless there is an express saving in the statute in their favor.[52] Arizona Laws 1913, No. 16, providing that certain actions shall be barred in one year, do not repeal Civ. Code Ariz. 1901, par. 2970, declaring that in cases of infancy, unsoundness of mind, or imprisonment the time of disability shall not be counted as a part of the time limited.[53] An adjudication in bankruptcy under the Bankruptcy Act of 1898, as amended, does not put the creditor under a "legal disability," within the meaning of Okl. Rev. Laws 1910, § 4658, as to an action in a state court on a provable claim.[54] The confirmation of a guardianship settlement being a special proceeding, Kirby's Dig. Ark., § 5075, extending the time within which persons under disability of minority or insanity may bring any action, does not refer thereto.[55] The Kentucky thirty-year statute of limitations bars all claims, without regard to disability, where there was a right of action in the claimants.[56] There being no saving clause in Missouri Rev. St. 1899, §

Ky. 128, 61 S. W. 5, 7, it was queried whether this case would be followed under the present statutes.

51. Larue v. C. G. Kershaw Contracting Co., 177 Ala. 441, 59 So. 155.

52. McGraw v. Rohrbough (W. Va.), 82 S. E. 217.

53. Silvas v. Arizona Copper Co., 213 Fed. 504 (U. S. D. C.).

54. Simpson v. Tootle, Wheeler & Motter Mercantile Co., 42 Okl. 275, 141 Pac. 448.

55. Nelson v. Cowling, 89 Ark. 334, 116 S. W. 890.

56. Dixon v. Harris, 32 Ky. Law Rep. 275, 105 S. W. 451; Rose v. Ware, 115 Ky. 420, 24 Ky. Law Rep. 2321, 74 S. W. 188; 25 Ky. Law Rep. 947, 76 S. W. 505.

Under Ky. St. 1903, § 2505, an action for the recovery of land can only be brought within 15 years after the accrual of the cause of action, and under section 2506, if, when the action first accrues, the person entitled to bring it is under disability, he may, though 15 years has expired, bring it within three years after the disability is removed; the purpose of section 2506 is not to extend the limitation three years, except where the disability is not removed more than three years before the expiration of 15 years. Dukes v. Davis, 30 Ky. Law Rep. 1348, 101 S. W. 390. See also, Young v. Ashland Coal & Iron Ry. Co., 19 Ky. Law Rep. 491, 41 S. W. 313.

4267, the right to sue is barred in ten years, except as to persons suffering from disabilities specifically mentioned in section 4265, and they are barred in twenty-four years, whether the disabilities have been removed or not.[57] The rule that, where the trustee is bound by the statute of limitations, the *cestui que trust* is also bound, is not applicable where, if there were no trustee intervening, the statute would not operate against the *cestui que trust,* as where the *cestui que trust* is a minor or otherwise disabled from suing on his own account.[58]

§ 237a(2). Disability of part of several jointly interested.

If an action not severable is not barred as to one of the parties on account of his infancy at the time the cause of action arose, it is not barred as to either of the other parties.[59] In joint actions to recover land, it is error to charge that, if the action was commenced by the plaintiffs at any time within the statute after the youngest became of age, they would not be barred; the true rule being that the action is barred as to each of the plaintiffs within the

57. De Hatre v. Edmunds, 200 Mo. 246, 98 S. W. 744.

See also, Tapley v. McPike, 50 Mo. 589; Gray v. Yates, 67 Mo. 601; Robinson v. Allison, 192 Mo. 366, 91 S. W. 115, as to the effect of disabilities.

58. Ward v. Ward, 12 O. C. D. 59.

See, as to effect of disabilities under other statutes:

La.—Sallier v. St. Louis, W. & G. Ry. Co., 114 La. 1090, 38 So. 868; Meyer v. Moss, 110 La. 132, 34 So. 332; Succession of Oormier, 52 La. Ann. 876, 27 So. 293.

Wis.—Brown v. City of Baraboo, 98 Wis. 273, 74 N. W. 223.

59. Beresh v. Supreme Lodge Knights of Honor, 166 Ill. App. 511, judg. aff'd 255 Ill. 122, 99 N. E. 349. See also, Williams v. Merritt, 109 Ga. 213, 34 S. E. 312.

Where heirs to whom a right of entry has descended were all under disability at the death of their ancestor, they have the time allowed by statute after the removal of such disabilities from all to make their entry or bring their action; but, if one or more of the heirs were free from disability at the death of the ancestor, the disabilities of the other heirs do not prevent the statute from running, nor bring any of them within its saving. Collier v. Davis, 4 Ky. Law Rep. (abstract) 981. The fact that one of the beneficiaries of a fund lent under order of court is an infant does not extend the time of limitation as to the surety in the bond executed therefor. Bowen v. Helm, 19 Ky. Law Rep. 486, 41 S. W. 289.

statutory period after coming of age.[60] Since adult heirs have no right to the possession of the homestead of the decedent until the termination of the homestead interest of a minor heir, which occurs on his reaching majority, limitations of two years within which to sue to set aside a void tax deed of the homestead do not begin to run against the adult heirs until the infant heir reaches his majority.[61]

§ 238. Infancy.

An infant, in law, is a person who by reason of his tender years is regarded as incapable of contracting, and who can neither sue or be sued thereon. In most of the States all male persons under the age of twenty-one years, and all females under the age of eighteen years, are infants, within the meaning of the term as used under this head.

Persons who have not attained the age of majority are infants, and in those States where infancy is within the saving clause of the statute, the statute does not begin to run against him or her, even though he or she has a guardian who might sue the claim in question;[62] nor even though other persons are jointly interested

60. Napier v. Little, 137 Ga. 242, 73 S. E. 3.

See also, Pickens v. Stout, 67 W. Va. 422, 68 S. E. 354; Allen v. Leflore County, 80 Miss. 298, 31 So. 815; Learned v. Ogden, 80 Miss. 769, 32 So. 278, 92 Am. St. Rep. 621.

Owing to the statutory modification of the common law rule, which no longer requires that all joint tenants shall unite in suits affecting the joint property, the infancy of some of several joint tenants does not prevent the running against the others of Code, § 2915, barring an action for the recovery of land in 15 years after the right of entry accrues. Redford v. Clark, 100 Va. 115, 4 Va. Sup. Ct. Rep. 36, 40 S. E. 630.

Where limitations barred a male heir from recovering his half interest in land, but not his sister—she being a married woman—a conveyance by the brother to his sister of his interest did not stop the statute, and an action by her to recover such interest more than seven years after the statute began to run was barred. McFarlane v. Grober, 70 Ark. 371, 69 S. W. 56, 91 Am. St. Rep. 84. And see Wolf v. Hess, 107 Fed. 194 (U. S. C. C. Ark.).

61. Harris v. Brady, 87 Ark. 428, 112 S. W. 974.

62. Moore v. Wallis, 18 Ala. 458; Grimsby v. Hudwell, 76 Ga. 378, 2 Am. St. Rep. 46. Infancy is within

in the claim, who are of full age,[63] until he or she attains the age of majority.[64] The fact that a guardian or the infant himself brings a suit before the disability is removed does not operate as a waiver of the saving clause in favor of the disability.[65] But while, as previously stated, the fact that an infant has a guardian who might maintain an action for a claim does not change the rule,[66] yet the minority of a claimant at the time when the claim

the saving clause of all the statutes except in Iowa, where there is no exception in favor of any disability except in the case of real actions, in reference to which an exception is made in favor of minors, and they are given one year after becoming of full age in which to bring an action.

63. Pendergrast v. Gullatt, 10 Ga. 218. In Milner v. Davis, 16 Ky. (Litt. Sel. Cas.) 436, it was held that the infancy of one plaintiff in an action of trover would not prevent the statute from running against all. But in Kentucky it is held that the infancy of one tenant in common will not prevent the running of the statute against a co-tenant. Thomas v. Machir, 7 Ky. (4 Bibb) 412; Moore v. Capps, 9 Ill. 315.

64. Merrill v. Tevis, 32 Ky. (2 Dana) 162; Shannon v. Dunn, 8 Blackf. (Ind.) 182; Hawkins v. Hawkins, 28 Ind. 66. And the common law presumption of payment does not run against an infant. Wilkinson v. Dunn, 52 N. C. (7 Jones) 125.

65. Jackson *ex dem.* Bunt v. Ransom, 10 Johns. (N. Y.) 407. In Chandler v. Vilett, 1 Saund. 120, it was held that the privileges by reason of infancy and other impediments are saved in an action on the case in assumpsit by the statute 21 James I. c. 16, and, although in that case it was claimed that the infant should have waited until he became of full age before suit was brought, yet the court held that he might pursue his action at any time within age, although the six years are elapsed. Cotton's Case, 2 Inst. 519; Stowel v. Zouch, Plowd. 366a. The meaning of the saving clause is, that the right of persons laboring under disabilities shall not suffer in consequence of such disabilities; and, therefore, where personal property of an infant is illegally disposed of, or permitted to pass into the hands of persons who are not entitled to it, by a guardian or other trustee, the statute does not begin to run against the infant until he is twenty-one years of age, and he may recover in a case where an action by the guardian or other trustee would be barred. Bacon v. Gray, 23 Miss. 140. See Layton v. The State, 4 Harr. (Del.) 8. No disability, arising after the disability of infancy has expired, can be added to it, to defeat the operation of the statute of limitations. Stevens v. Bomar, 28 Tenn. (9 Humph.) 546. It is no answer to a plea of the statute of limitations to a writ of error, that within five years next after one of the plaintiffs had arrived at full age the writ was prosecuted. Shannon v. Dunn, 8 Blackf. (Ind.) 182.

66. Bacon v. Gray, 23 Miss. 140.

accrued will not bring him within the exception of the statute, if at that time the legal right of action upon it was vested in a trustee who was under no disability, for his benefit.[67] In Kentucky, it has been held that where the executor has a right of action the statute will not be prevented from running by reason of the disability of the heir.[68]

§ 238a(1). Infancy—In general.

The cases holding that a State statute of limitations may be deemed suspended by causes preventing a suit not enumerated in the statute,[69] rest on the grounds that the creditor has been disabled to sue by a superior power and without any default of his own, and therefore none of the reasons which induced the enactment of the statute apply to his case; and unless the statute ceases to run during the continuance of the disability, he is deprived of a portion of the time during which the law contemplated he might sue. Hence the implied suspension should continue no longer than the

67. In Wilmerding v. Russ, 33 Conn. 67, Hinman, J., said: "The petitioners say that the fact that they were minors brings them within the exception of the statute. But the residuary estate is, by the will, vested in the trustees, who were under no legal disabilities, and this is a sufficient answer to the claim." Wych v. East India Co., 3 P. Wms. 309. The same rule prevails where the legal title to land is vested in a trustee. Brady v. Walters, 55 Ga. 25. In Hall v. Bumstead, 37 Mass. (20 Pick.) 2, it was held that the statute limiting suits against executors and administrators is an absolute bar, and that the fact that the plaintiff was under the disability of infancy during the time that the estate of the deceased was under administration will not prevent his claim from being barred by the lapse of the period fixed for limiting such actions. In this case, it is proper to state that actual fraud on the part of the executor was not shown, and, amounting only to constructive fraud, it was held that the statute applied. See Robinson v. Hook, 4 Mas. (U. S.) 151; Bickford v. Wade, 19 Ves. 88; Murray v. Coster, 20 Johns. (N. Y.) 576. In Howell v. Leavitt, 95 N. Y. 617, it was held that possession of real estate by a mortgagee, acquired by force or fraud, against the will and consent of the owner, and without color of legal authority, is not a defense to an action or ejectment brought by such owner.

68. Darnall v. Adams, 52 Ky. (13 B. Mon.) 273.

69. Hopkirk v. Bell, 7 U. S. (3 Cranch) 454, 2 L. Ed. 497, 73 U. S. (6 Wall.) 532, 18 L. Ed. 497.

actual disability prevented a suit. Only that period of time during which the party was actually prevented from bringing suit by the cause which he claims to have suspended the statutes should be allowed to be deducted from the term limited by the statute for suing.[70] The exemptions from the operation of statutes of limitation usually accorded to infants do not rest upon any fundamental doctrine of the law, but only upon express provision therefor in such statutes. It is competent for the Legislature to put infants and adults upon the same footing in this respect, and this is the effect of a statute containing no saving clause exempting infants.[71] For the construction of provisions in the statutes of limitations of the several States exempting minors from the operation of the statute, see the cases cited in the note below.[72] The doctrine that a person has a reasonable time after reaching majority in which to disaf-

70. Braun v. Sauerwein, 77 U. S. (10 Wall.) 218, 19 L. Ed. 895.

71. Schauble v. Schulz, 137 Fed. 389, 69 C. C. A. 581.

Alabama Code 1907, §§ 4846, 4860, operate to extend limitations in favor of minors only when the limitations had never commenced to run against their predecessor. Richardson v. Mertins, 175 Ala. 15, 57 So. 720.

No exceptions can be claimed in favor of minors in a statutory provision limiting the time of commencing actions given by such statute, unless they are expressly mentioned in the statute as excepted. Indiana Cent. Ry. Co. v. Oakes, 20 Ind. 9; De Moss v. Newton, 31 Ind. 219.

All persons are barred by statutes of limitations, unless excepted by a saving clause, even those under the disability of infancy. Favorite v. Booher's Adm'r, 17 Ohio St. 548.

72. *Ala.*—Richardson v. Mertins, 175 Ala. 309, 57 So. 720.

Ark.—Harris v. Brady, 87 Ark. 428, 112 S. W. 974; Rowe v. Allison, 87 Ark. 206, 112 S. W. 395.

Del.—Traverse's Adm'r v. Cain, 2 Har. 97.

Ga.—Edenfield v. Milner, 138 Ga. 402, 75 S. E. 319; Grimsby v. Hudnell, 76 Ga. 378, 2 Am. St. Rep. 46; Jordan v. Ticknor, 62 Ga. 123; Atlanta & West Point R. Co. v. Coleman, 142 Ga. 94, 82 S. E. 499.

Ill.—A female must bring a cause of action within three years after she arrives at the age of 18 years in order to avoid the effect of the statute of limitations. Davis v. Hall, 92 Ill. 85; Kilgour v. Cockley, 83 Ill. 109.

Ind.—Davidson v. Bates, 111 Ind. 391, 12 N. E. 687; Bryson v. Collmer, 33 Ind. App. 494, 71 N. E. 229; Breeding v. Shinn, 8 Ind. 125.

Iowa.—Tucker v. Stewart, 147 Iowa 294, 126 N. W. 183; Rice v. Bolton, 126 Iowa 654, 100 N. W. 634, modified on rehearing 102 N. W. 509, under the express provisions of Code, § 3453, limitations do not run

firm or ratify acts performed during infancy does not give an infant a time other than that specified by limitations to attack a constructive fraud of his guardian in purchasing the trust prop-

against an infant, save for penalties and forfeitures, until one year after majority.

Ky.—Willson v. Hodges' Guardian, 6 Ky. Law Rep. 295, 7 Ky. Law Rep. 525; Pool v. Allinsworth, 6 Ky. Law Rep. 594; Gibson v. Gibson, 25 Ky. Law Rep. 1332, 77 S. W. 928, the statute of limitations does not run against an infant.

La.—Prescription of 10 years does not run against a minor. Scovell v. St. Louis S. W. Ry. Co., 117 La. 459, 41 So. 723; George v. Delaney, 111 La. 760, 35 So. 894; Rocques' Heirs v. Levecque's Heirs, 110 La. 306, 34 So. 454; Cox v. Von Ahlefeldt, 105 La. 543, 30 So. 175; Messick v. Mayer, 52 La. Ann. 1161, 27 So. 815.

Minn.—Martz v. McMahon, 114 Minn. 34, 129 N. W. 1049.

Mich.—Keating v. Michigan Cent. R. Co., 94 Mich. 219, 53 N. W. 1053.

Miss.—Learned v. Ogden, 80 Miss. 769, 32 So. 278, 92 Am. St. Rep. 621; Adams v. Torrey's Ex'rs, 26 Miss. 499.

Mo.—Elliott v. Landis Mach. Co., 236 Mo. 546, 139 S. W. 356.

N. H.—Forest v. Jackson, 56 N. H. 357.

N. Y.—Decisions under Code Civ. Proc., § 396: *In re* Pond's Estate, 40 Misc. Rep. 66, 81 N. Y. Supp. 249; *In re* Irvin's Estate, 68 App. Div. 158, 74 N. Y. Supp. 443; Hyland v. New York Cent., etc., R. Co., 24 App. Div. 417, 48 N. Y. Supp. 416, 5 N. Y. Ann. Cas. 159; Norton v. City of New York, 16 Misc. Rep. 303, 38 N. Y. Supp. 90; Jagau v. Goetz, 11 Misc. Rep. 380, 32 N. Y. Supp. 144. Under Code Civ. Proc., § 1822: *In re* Brooks, 65 Misc. Rep. 439, 121 N. Y. Supp. 1092; *In re* Cashman, 62 Misc. Rep. 598, 116 N. Y. Supp. 1128, Niagara City Charter; Winter v. City of Niagara Falls, 119 App. Div. 586, 104 N. Y. Supp. 39, 82 N. E. 1101. See also, *In re* Becker, 28 Hun 207; Miller v. Parkhurst, 9 N. Y. St. Rep. 759; Danziger v. Iron Clad Realty & Trading Co., 80 Misc. Rep. 510, 141 N. Y. Supp. 593.

N. C.—Cameron v. Hicks, 141 N. C. 21, 53 S. E. 728, 7 L. R. A. (N. S.) 407.

Ohio.—Jaeger v. Herancourt, 1 Wkly. Law Bul. 10; Slater v. Cave, 3 Ohio St. 80.

R. I.—Bliven v. Wheeler, 23 R. I. 379, 50 Atl. 644.

S. C.—Fricks v. Lewis, 26 S. C. 237, 1 S. E. 884; Clark v. Smith, 13 S. C. 585; Thomson v. Gaillard, 3 Rich. Law 418, 45 Am. Dec. 778.

Tenn.—Gaugh v. Henderson, 39 Tenn. (2 Head) 628; Aiken v. Smith, 33 Tenn. (1 Sneed) 304; Nelson v. Allen, 9 Tenn. (1 Yerg.) 360.

Tex.—Japhet v. Pullen (Tex. Civ. App.), 133 S. W. 441; Schneider v. Sellers, 98 Tex. 380, 84 S. W. 417, modifying (Civ. App.) 81 S. W. 126; Ferguson v. Morrison (Tex. Civ. App.), 81 S. W. 1240; Behan v. Long (Tex. Civ. App.), 30 S. W. 380; Hampton v. Hampton, 9 Tex. Civ. App. 497, 29 S. W. 423.

Va.—Brown v. Lambert's Adm's 33 Grat. 256.

erty at foreclosure sale.[73] As to the application of the statutes of limitations of different States to actions against former guardians and trustees, see authorities cited in note below.[74]

§ 238a(2). Personal actions.

Under the Arkansas statute, giving an action for wrongful death, and providing that action therefor shall be begun within two years after the death of such person, in the absence of any saving clause, the infancy of plaintiff at the time the cause of action accrued does not postpone the running of the statute.[75] In California, the time within which an action may be brought by a female for her own seduction does not commence to run until she has arrived at the age of majority.[76] In Georgia, where plaintiff was a minor at the time a trespass was committed on her land, her right of action was suspended until her arrival at the age of twenty-one years.[77] In Illinois, in an action by minors to recover money due, defendant cannot invoke the statute of limitations, since under the statute of limitations such plea is not good.[78] In Indiana,

73. Cahill v. Seitz, 93 App. Div. (N. Y.) 105, 86 N. Y. Supp. 1009.

74. *Ark.*—Wallace v. Swepston, 74 Ark. 520, 86 S. W. 398, 109 Am. St. Rep. 94.

Ind.—Wilkinson v. Wilkinson, 33 Ind. App. 540, 71 N. E. 169; Lambert v. Billheimer, 125 Ind. 519, 25 N. E. 451; Peelle v. State, 118 Ind. 512, 21 N. E. 288.

Ga.—Lane v. Lane, 87 Ga. 268, 13 S. E. 335; Byne v. Anderson, 67 Ga. 466; Hobbes v. Cody, 45 Ga. 478.

La.—Succession of Richmond, 35 La. Ann. 858; Sewell v. McVay, 30 La. Ann. 673.

Md.—State v. Reilly, 88 Md. 63, 41 Atl. 121; State v. Henderson, 54 Md. 332.

Miss.—Fearn v. Shirley, 31 Miss. 301, 64 Am. Dec. 575.

Mo.—State, to the use of Coleman v. Willi, 46 Mo. 236.

Pa.—Wyant v. Dieffendaffer, 2 Grant Cas. 334; Appeal of Bones, 27 Pa. (3 Casey) 492.

S. C.—Long v. Cason, 4 Rich. Eq. 60.

Tenn.—Jackson v. Crutchfield, 111 Tenn. 394, 77 S. W. 776.

Va.—Magruder v. Goodwyn's Adm'r, 2 Pat. & H. 561.

75. Anthony v. St. Louis, etc., Ry. Co., 108 Ark. 219, 157 S. W. 394; Kirby's Dig. Ark. § 6290.

76. Morrell v. Morgan, 65 Cal. 575, 4 Pac. 580.

77. Cobb v. Wrightsville & T. R. Co., 129 Ga. 377, 58 S. E. 862.

78. Matt v. Matt, 182 Ill. App. 312; Hurd's Rev. Ill. St. 1913, c. 83, §

a prosecution for bastardy must be begun within two years from the time of the birth of the child.[79] To a complaint for slander, alleging the infancy of the plaintiff, it is not a good answer that the defendant has not been guilty within two years next before the commencement of the action.[80] In Iowa, an infant injured on a defective sidewalk must sue within three months, the same as other persons, where no notice has been served on the municipality, since the section of the general statute of limitations, providing that the times limited for actions shall be extended in favor of infants, etc., does not apply.[81] In Kansas, a cause of action in favor of an infant, for personal injuries sustained, may be brought at any time during infancy, and will in no event be barred by the two-year limitation until one year after the disability of infancy has been removed.[82] An infant who becomes possessed of a note before maturity may prosecute an action for the recovery of the amount due thereon at any time prior to the expiration of one year from the date of the removal of the disability of infancy.[83] In Kentucky, one who is an infant when a right of action accrues has the same length of time to sue after becoming of age that he would have had had he been of age when the cause of action accrued; the statute expressly providing as to infants entitled to sue that action may be brought within a like number of years after removal of their disability that is allowed to a person having no such impediment.[84] In Louisiana, the prescription of one year,

21 (Jones & A. Ann. St. 1913, par. 7216).

79. State v. Pavey, 82 Ind. 543.

80. Sunman v. Brewin, 52 Ind. 140.

81. Cushing v. City of Winterset, 144 Iowa 260, 122 N. W. 915.

82. Missouri Pac. Ry. Co. v. Cooper, 57 Kan. 185, 45 Pac. 587.

83. Tinsley v. Pitts, 10 Kan. App. 321, 62 Pac. 536.

84. Low v. Ramsey, 135 Ky. 333, 122 S. W. 167, Ky. St. § 2525 (Russell's St. § 191); Jones v. Comer, 25 Ky. Law Rep. 773, 76 S. W. 392, rehearing denied 25 Ky. Law Rep. 1104, 77 S. W. 184; Webb v. Webb, 25 Ky. Law Rep. 1476, 78 S. W. 166, rehearing 23 Ky. Law Rep. 1057, 64 S. W. 839, denied; Louisville & N. R. Co. v. Sanders, 86 Ky. 259, 5 S. W. 563.

Rents accruing during the minority of the landlord are not barred by lapse of time. Pugh's Heirs v. Bell's Heir's, 24 Ky. (1 J. J. Mar.) 398.

Plaintiff's action having been brought soon after he became of age, he is not limited to a recovery for

in an action for damages under Civ. Code, art. 3541,[85] and the prescription of three years, on a claim for services,[86] runs against minors, reserving, however, to them, their recourse against their tutors or curators. Notes payable to the order of minors, not being transferable by indorsement or delivery so long as the minority lasts, are not subject to the prescription of five years.[87] In Massachusetts, the statute authorizing the taking of land for the abatement of a nuisance and providing for the recovery of damages makes no exceptions in favor of minors.[88] In Michigan, where a person, soon after coming of age, sues for an assault during infancy, he is not at fault for not suing while under disability.[89]

In New York, under Code Civ. Proc., § 383, subd. 5, providing that an action for negligent personal injury must be brought within three years after the accrual of the cause of action, and section 396, providing that the time of the disability of infancy is not a part of the time limited for commencing the action, except that the time so limited cannot be extended more than one year after the

services rendered within five years before the action was brought, as limitation did not run against him during his minority. Myers v. Korb, 21 Ky. Law Rep. 163, 50 S. W. 1108.

85. Goodwin v. Bodcaw Lumber Co., 109 La. 1050, 34 So. 74.

86. Copse v. Eddins, 15 La. Ann. 528.

87. Bird v. Pate, 4 La. Ann. 225.

88. Sweet v. City of Boston, 186 Mass. 79, 71 N. E. 113.

A note given by an infant, and signed in the presence of an attesting witness, is barred by the statute of limitations (Rev. St. c. 120, § 4), if the action is brought thereon by the original payee. The fact of the maker being an infant does not take the case out of the statute. Earle v. Reed, 51 Mass. (10 Metc.) 387.

89. Thurstin v. Luce, 61 Mich. 292, 28 N. W. 103.

Where a father, who is the proper person to sue for the seduction of his adopted daughter, himself seduces her, her right of action extends for six years after she reaches her majority. Watson v. Watson, 53 Mich. 168, 18 N. W. 605, 51 Am. Rep. 111.

How. St. § 6332, limiting the liability of sureties on guardian's bonds to actions commenced within four years from the discharge of the guardian, has no application to conditional orders for such discharge; and, if at the time of such discharge the ward is an infant, he may bring such suit at any time within four years after attaining his majority. Landon v. Cornet, 62 Mich. 80, 28 N. W. 788.

disability ceases, an infant, reaching full age before the three-year limitation has expired, must commence his action for a personal injury either before the expiration of that period, or within one year after reaching full age, and the statutes do not add a year to the regular period of limitation.[90] The common-law presumption of payment does not begin to run against one until he becomes of age, in North Carolina.[91] In Mississippi, the rule that the statute of limitations does not run against actions on official bonds of trustees during the infancy of the beneficiaries applies equally to actions at law and in equity.[92] The Pennsylvania statute, providing that every action for personal injuries not resulting in death must be brought within two years from the injury, and making no exceptions in favor of persons under disability, applies to infants.[93] In Texas, an infant has a right to bring an action for personal injury within two years after attain-

90. Preusse v. Childwold Park Hotel Co., 134 App. Div. 383, 119 N. Y. Supp. 98.

In case of infancy the running of the limitation of one year provided by laws 1886, c. 572, § 1, as to an action against a city for negligent personal injuries, is suspended by reason of the exception contained in Code Civ. Proc., § 396. Conway v. City of New York, 139 App. Div. 446, 124 N. Y. Supp. 660.

The 10-year statute of limitation against an action to set aside a judgment begins to run from the time of the sale of the property, and not from the date of the majority of infant defendants, whose right of action would be extended only one year after their majority by Code Civ. Proc., § 396. Ford v. Clendenin, 137 N. Y. Supp. 54, judg. aff'd 140 N. Y. Supp. 1119.

A cause of action accrues on a voidable obligation of an infant for a debt contracted during minority when he elects to ratify it after he becomes of age, and not until then will the statute begin to run against the claim. Halsey v. Reid, 4 Hun 777.

91. Wilkerson v. Dunn, 52 N. C. 125.

92. Pearson v. McMillan, 37 Miss. 588.

As to rule in different States as to actions on the official bonds of administrators, executors, and trustees, see:

Md.—Welch v. State, 5 Har. & J. 369.

Mo.—State *ex rel.* Farley v. Welsh, 175 Mo. App. 303, 162 S. W. 637.

N. C.—Threadgill v. West, 35 N. C. 310; Lafferty v. Young, 125 N. C. 296, 34 S. E. 444.

S. C.—Lanier v. Griffin, 11 S. C. 565.

93. Peterson v. Delaware River Ferry Co., 190 Pa. 364, 42 Atl. 955.

ing his majority.[94] And in New Hampshire, a right of personal action accruing to an infant is not barred by the statute of limitations until two years after the disability ceases.[95] In Missouri, suit may be begun by a child after attaining his majority, if within one year.[96] In Washington, under a statute providing that the three-year limitation for an action for seduction shall not commence to run while the person entitled to bring the action is under the "age of twenty-one years," a female may bring such an action at any time within three years after she becomes twenty-one years of age, though by another statute a female reaches her majority at eighteen years.[97]

§ 238a(3). Actions for recovery of real property.

In Alabama, where a claim of ownership of land by defendants was not set up until after the death of plaintiffs' ancestor, through whom they claimed title, and at that time plaintiffs were minors, the bar of the statute of limitations would not become effective until three years after the removal of the minors' disability.[98] In Arkansas, the statutes of limitation, in actions for the recovery of lands, do not begin to run against minors until they become of age, and they may bring their action within three years after full age.[99] In California, where a right of action to recover land accrues during the minority of the owner, the statute of limitations does

94. Missouri, etc., Ry. Co. v. Scarborough, 29 Tex. Civ. App. 194, 68 S. W. 196.

95. Frost v. Eastern R. Co., 64 N. H. 220, 9 Atl. 790, 10 Am. St. Rep. 396; N. H. Gen. Laws, c. 221, § 7.

96. Rutter v. Missouri Pac. Ry. Co., 81 Mo. 169; Mo. Rev. St. 1879, §§ 2121, 2125.

97. Gates v. Shaffer, 72 Wash. 451, 130 Pac. 896; Wash. Rem. & Bal. Code, §§ 159, 8743.

98. Bradford v. Wilson, 140 Ala. 633, 37 So. 295; Code 1896, § 2807. See Riggs v. Fuller, 54 Ala. 141.

99. Kessinger v. Wilson, 53 Ark. 400, 14 S. W. 96; Simms v. Cumby, 53 Ark. 418, 14 S. W. 623; Falls v. Wright, 55 Ark. 562, 18 S. W. 1044, 29 Am. St. Rep. 74; Thomas v. Sypert, 61 Ark. 575, 33 S. W. 1059; Harris v. Brady, 87 Ark. 428, 112 S. W. 974; Carroll v. Carroll, 92 Ark. 625, 121 S. W. 947. Females of the age of 18 years are considered as of full age for all purposes. Brake v. Sides, 95 Ark. 74, 128 S. W. 572. See also, Martin v. Conner (Ark.), 171 S. W. 125.

not begin to run against the action until the owner attains majority, when he may convey the land, and the grantee may maintain an action against the disseisor, entering during the minority of the owner, at any time within five years after the disability terminates.[1] Under Georgia Code, § 2686, an infant cannot disaffirm his deed when more than seven years have passed since he attained majority.[2] The limitation act of Illinois runs against minors, unless within three years after becoming of age or attaining majority (eighteen years of age in the case of females) they bring suit to recover the land and refund the taxes paid thereon.[3] The Indiana statute, which relieves a party from a judgment taken against him through excusable neglect, must be considered with the statute, which provides that any person under legal disability may bring his action within two years after the disability is removed, and an infant defendant in a proceeding to foreclose a tax

1. Le Roy v. Reeves, 5 Sawy. (U. S.) 102.

2. Nathans v. Arkwright, 66 Ga. 179.

3. Safford v. Stubbs, 117 Ill. 389, 7 N. E. 653; Hodgen v. Henrichsen, 85 Ill. 259.

After the death of a married woman owning land, her children had no right of entry or of action for the land until the death of the husband, and the termination of his estate by the curtesy, and before that time the statute of limitations did not run against them, and laches was not imputable to them; and, by platting a town on the land, the husband and his grantees could convey no greater interest than he possessed, and the possession of the streets by the corporation during his life was not adverse to the right of the heirs. Orthwein v. Thomas, 127 Ill. 554, 21 N. E. 430, 4 L. R. A. 434, 11 Am. St. Rep. 159.

Infant remainder-men who are grantees of the life tenant may recover the land, against persons in adverse possession, within two years after becoming of age, under Hurd's Rev. St. 1897, p. 1048, though, before conveyance to them, the statute of limitations would have barred the life tenant's right of recovery, as the statute does not transfer the title, but merely bars a right to recover the land. Field v. Peeples, 180 Ill. 376, 54 N. E. 304.

Where an administratrix purchases land at her own sale, and remains in open, exclusive, and adverse possession for 24 years, a bill for relief brought by an heir six years after he attained his majority was barred by 2 Starr & C. Ann. St. 1896, p. 2620, par. 8, requiring such actions to be brought within three years after attainment of majority. Mason v. Odum, 210 Ill. 471, 71 N. E. 386, 102 Am. St. Rep. 180.

lien may within two years after majority proceed by motion under the former statute to set aside a default judgment and sales resulting therefrom and redeem the property.[4] The provision of the Iowa statute, providing that the "limitation of actions for the recovery of real property shall not apply to minors, so far as to prevent them from having at least one year after their majority within which to commence such actions," does not operate to suspend the statute of limitations as to such actions during infancy, but merely gives one year after majority to bring suit if the period has expired;[5] and they have more time if the law would give it to an adult.[6] In Kansas, an action to recover real property of a minor must be brought within two years after the disability of infancy is removed.[7] Under the Kentucky statute, one who is an infant when his right of action to recover real property accrues, may bring his action within three years after his disability is removed.[8] In Louisiana, the statute, prescribing in five years, as

4. Macy v. Lindley, 49 Ind. App. 469, 99 N. E. 790.

Where the grantee in a deed absolute on its face, but intended as a mortgage, fraudulently conveys the lands to another having knowledge of the facts, the 15-year statute of limitation applies to an action for partition brought by the widow and heirs of the deceased grantor in such deed, in which she joined, but cannot be pleaded against the minor heirs of such grantor. Caress v. Foster, 62 Ind. 145.

5. Mathews v. Stephens, 39 Iowa 279; Hubbird v. Goin, 137 Fed. 822, 70 C. C. A. 320. See also, Lloyd v. Bunce, 41 Iowa 660.

6. Campbell v. Long, 20 Iowa 382.

7. Howbert v. Heyle, 47 Kan. 58, 27 Pac. 116; Delashmutt v. Parrant, 39 Kan. 548, 18 Pac. 712; Scantlin v. Allison, 32 Kan. 376, 4 Pac. 618.

A right of action in ejectment for the recovery of land sold by an administrator, brought by an heir of a deceased person, is saved, under Gen. St. 1897, c. 95, § 11, to a minor who may sue within two years after the disability of infancy has been removed. Thompson v. Burge, 60 Kan. 549, 57 Pac. 110, 72 Am. St. Rep. 369.

8. Salyer v. Johnson, 32 Ky. Law Rep. 709, 107 S. W. 210; Ky. St. 1903, § 2506; Vincent v. Blanton, 27 Ky. Law Rep. 489, 85 S. W. 703; Sharp v. Stephens' Committee, 21 Ky. Law Rep. 687, 52 S. W. 977; Call v. Phelps' Adm'r, 20 Ky. Law Rep. 507, 45 S. W. 1051; Willson v. Louisville Trust Co., 102 Ky. 522, 19 Ky. Law Rep. 1590, 44 S. W. 121; Hoffert v. Miller, 86 Ky. 572, 6 S. W. 447; Gates v. Jacob, 40 Ky. (1 B. Mon.) 306; Pugh v. Bell, 18 Ky. (2 B. Mon.) 125, 15 Am. Dec. 142.

An infant's cause of action to set

to all persons, actions to set aside public sales on account of any informalities connected with them, and barring an action to rescind a partition, runs against minors from the time of their majority.[9] Under the express provisions of the Missouri statute, persons who were minors when the statute of limitations began to run had three years after they reached the age of twenty-one in which to sue for the recovery of lands.[10] Occupation of land for three years by a purchaser at tax sale is no bar to an action of ejectment by a minor to recover his interest in the land, in Mississippi.[11] In Nebraska, the statute of limitations as to adverse possession does not run against persons while under disability, such as minors; and an action to recover real estate, brought within ten years after such minors arrive at age, is commenced in time.[12] In New York, an action to recover an interest in real estate, which

aside a deed on the ground of infancy accrued when she attained her majority, though she was only a remainderman. Henson v. Culp, 157 Ky. 442, 163 S. W. 455.

Under Ky. St. § 2525, children of a devisee taking a remainder are entitled to 10 years from the time they arrived at age to have the will probated in that State. Thompson v. Penn, 149 Ky. 158, 148 S. W. 33.

9. Doucet v. Fenelon, 120 La. 18, 44 So. 908; Sewall v. Hebert, 37 La. Ann. 155; Fraser v. Zylicz, 29 La. Ann. 534; Gayoso de Lemos v. Garcia, 1 Mart. N. S. (La.) 324. But the prescription against attacks on partition sales has no application to the sale of the interests of a minor alone, in property held in common with others; such sale being invalid. Fahey v. Fahey, 128 La. 503, 54 So. 973. Act No. 53 of 1912, relating to actions to annul a private sale of realty, applies to minors. McNamara v. Marx, 136 La. 159, 66 So. 764.

10. Hinters v. Hinters, 114 Mo. 26, 21 S. W. 456; Ogle v. Hignet, 161 Mo. 47, 61 S. W. 596, Rev. St. 1889, § 6767.

Possession of land taken during disability of infants is insufficient to support a plea of the statute of limitations. Slicer v. Owens, 241 Mo. 319, 145 S. W. 428.

Under Rev. St. 1909, § 11, 506a, minors have the right to sue within two years after the removal of their disability to recover lands sold at a tax sale. Gulley v. Waggoner, 255 Mo. 613, 164 S. W. 557.

11. Wolfe v. Brown (Miss.), 11 So. 879.

As to application of the statute to a bill to enforce a trust in land, see Tippin v. Coleman, 59 Miss. 641. As to application of the 10-year statute bar from suing for partition, see Anglin v. Broadnax (Miss.), 52 So. 865.

12. Albers v. Kozeluh, 68 Neb. 522, 97 N. W. 646, aff'g 68 Neb. 522, 94 N. W. 521; Howe v. Blomenkamp, 88 Neb. 389, 129 N. W. 539.

accrued to the plaintiff during infancy, is not barred by the statute of limitations, if commenced within twenty years after the plaintiff became of age, though more than ten years thereafter and more than twenty years after the cause of action accrued.[13] Thus, where a right of action against an elevated railway for injuries to property abutting on a street resulting from the construction and operation of the railway in the street accrued on December 30, 1878, to infant owners of the property, the oldest of whom became of age August, 20, 1881, the right to bring the action was not on February 21, 1899, barred by the twenty-year statute of limitations, Code Civ. Proc., § 375, providing that if a person who might maintain an action to recover real property, etc., is, when his cause of action first accrues, within the age of twenty-one years, the time of such a disability is not a part of the time limited in this title for commencing the action, except that the time so limited cannot be extended more than ten years after the disability ceases.[14] In North Carolina, though an infant, after accrual of her cause of

13. Darrow v. Calkins, 154 N. Y. 503, 49 N. E. 61, 48 L. R. A. 299, 61 Am. St. Rep. 637, aff'g order 6 App. Div. 28, 39 N. Y. Supp. 527; Howell v. Leavitt, 95 N. Y. 617; Hoepfner v. Sevestre, 56 Hun 640, 10 N. Y. Supp. 51.

14. Muller v. Manhattan Ry. Co., 195 N. Y. 539, 88 N. E. 1126, aff'g judgs. 124 App. Div. 295, 108 N. Y. Supp. 852, and 53 Misc. Rep. 133, 102 N. Y. Supp. 454. See also, Goggin v. Manhattan Ry. Co., 124 App. Div. 644, 109 N. Y. Supp. 83, modifying judg. 54 Misc. Rep. 472, 104 N. Y. Supp. 548; Taggart v. Manhattan Ry. Co., 57 Misc. Rep. 184, 109 N. Y. Supp. 38.

Code Civ. Proc., §§ 375, 396, do not apply to an action to set aside a deed executed during infancy, since the cause of action therefor accrued only after the infant attained his majority. O'Donohue v. Smith, 130 App. Div. 214, 114 N. Y. Supp. 536, aff'g judg. 57 Misc. Rep. 448, 109 N. Y. Supp. 929.

Where executors holding land in trust for infants make a void deed thereof, and the grantee takes possession, if the executors do not continue to hold the legal title the infants may at once maintain an action for the land; and, under limitations provided by Code Civ. Proc., §§ 365, 375, the action cannot be maintained when the grantee has been in possession more than 20 years in all, and more than 10 years after the infants reached majority. Brown v. Doherty, 93 App. Div. 190, 87 N. Y. Supp. 563, aff'd 185 N. Y. 383, 78 N. E. 147, 113 Am. St. Rep. 915.

action for real estate, had a guardian for seven years before her marriage, which was before her majority, she is not barred by failure to sue for the land while under guardianship; it being provided by Code, § 148, that if one entitled to sue for real estate is under twenty-one years of age, or is a married woman, such person may, notwithstanding the statute of limitations, commence action within three years after full age or discoverture.[15] In Ohio, a person entitled to bring an action for the recovery of real estate, who is, at the time the cause of action accrues, within the age of minority, etc., may after the expiration of twenty-one years, bring such action within ten years after such disability is removed.[16] In Oklahoma, where the purchaser of land at a void guardian's sale went into possession and he and those claiming under him remained continuously in possession thereafter, an action by the minor to recover such land is barred, if not brought within five years after the recording of the guardian's deed, or within two years after the removal of plaintiff's disability.[17]

In Pennsylvania it is held that the uniform doctrine of the cases on the statutes of limitation which follow Act 21 James I., c. 16, § 2, in allowing a person under disability when a right of action for real property accrues, or his heirs, to sue within ten years after expiration of the twenty-one years prescribed for ordinary plaintiffs, is that, if twenty years have elapsed since the right of action accrued, and ten of those years have been free from disability, the right of entry is barred. In other words, the owner is not entitled to twenty years after the disability ceases within which to bring his action, but to ten years only if, at the expiration of the latter period, twenty years have elapsed since the right of entry or action first accrued; and if the owner dies, the heirs, if under disability, have no longer time for bringing the action or making

15. Cross v. Craven, 120 N. C. 331, 26 S. E. 940; Clayton v. Rose, 87 N. C. 106.

16. Lanning v. Brown, 84 Ohio St. 385, 95 N. E. 921; Walker v. Knight, 12 Ohio St. 209. See also, Paschall v. Hinderer, 28 Ohio St. 568.

17. Dodson v. Middleton, 38 Okl. 763, 135 Pac. 368; Comp. Laws 1909, §§ 5547-5549.

the entry than he would have had if he had lived.[18] The South Carolina statute provides that, if a person who is entitled to commence an action for the recovery of real property was laboring under the disability of infancy at the time the action accrued, the time during which such disability shall continue shall not be deemed any portion of the ten years limited for the commencement of the action.[19] It is held under the Tennessee statute that, where the owner of land in possession of another was a minor, such disability did not prevent the initiation of adverse possession during minority, but only authorized suit within three years after he became of age, so that where the full seven years possession had terminated before the removal of the disability, the owner's right would be barred, unless suit was brought within three years after the termination of the disability, regardless of whether the adverse possession was continued of not.[20] In Texas, a minor who delays suit more than ten years after attaining majority is bar-

18. Henry v. Carson, 59 Pa. (9 P. F. Smith) 297.

The infancy of the beneficiaries does not prolong the time within which an action to enforce a resulting trust in land may be brought under Act 1856, § 6. Way v. Hooton, 156 Pa. 8, 26 Atl. 784.

19. Maccaw v. Crawley, 59 S. C. 342, 37 S. E. 934; Rice v. Bamberg, 59 S. C. 498, 38 S. E. 209; Code Civ. Proc., § 108. See Goforth v. Goforth, 47 S. C. 126, 25 S. E. 40; Johnson v. Cobb, 29 S. C. 372, 7 S. E. 601.

Under Code 1873, § 111, as amended (15 St. at Large, p. 497), an action for possession of land vested in a minor must have been brought within five years after his disability was removed. Glover v. Floyd, 76 S. C. 292, 57 S. E. 25.

Code 1902, § 426, providing that no action to recover land sold by a sheriff shall be brought after two years is affected by the disability of infancy of plaintiffs. Jones v. Boykin, 70 S. C. 309, 49 S. E. 877.

20. Dewey v. Sewanee Fuel & Iron Co., 191 Fed. 450; Code Tenn. 1858, §§ 2763, 2764, as amended by Acts Tenn. 1895, c. 38, §§ 1, 2 (Shannon's Code, §§ 4456, 4457) and § 2757 (4448).

The legal title to the lands of a minor is in the minor, and not in the guardian, and the minor's right of action to recover the land from one who had illegally purchased it from the guardian accrues the moment the wrongful act is committed, and continues during minority, and the statutory period thereafter, and its accrual is not postponed until the termination of the guardianship. Hale v. Ellison (Tenn. Ch. App.), 59 S. W. 673.

red of the right to recover land.[21] In Vermont, the statute of limitations runs against an infant having only color of title to land.[22] In Washington, the ten-year statute of limitations, governing actions for the recovery of real property, is unavailable to defeat the claim of one who is a minor at the time his right of action accrued, and who asserts such claim within the prescribed period after attaining his majority.[23] Under the Wisconsin statute providing that any person under disability may commence an action for the recovery of realty within five years after the disability ceased, an infant is not entitled to such period after attaining his majority, within which to commence an action to cancel an administrator's deed, as such an action is not one for the recovery of realty.[24] The three-year limitation prescribed by the Utah statute, within which an action may be brought by a person claiming under a decedent to set aside an executor's conveyance

21. Wiess v. Goodhue, 98 Tex. 274, 83 S. W. 178; McMasters v. Mills, 30 Tex. 591.

Where an appeal in an action of trespass to try title is dismissed by a judgment rendered during the minority of the plaintiffs, limitation begins to run against them from the date of the removal of their disability. Martin v. Wayman, 38 Tex. 649.

22. Soule v. Barlow, 49 Vt. 329.

23. May v. Sutherlin, 41 Wash. 609, 84 Pac. 585; Ballinger's Ann. Codes & St., §§ 4796, 4797, 4809.

Plaintiff in ejectment is not limited in recovery of damages to the six years next before the commencement of the action, where, at the time defendant wrongfully took possession of the land in suit, plaintiff was a minor. Mabie v. Whittaker, 10 Wash. 656, 39 Pac. 172.

Exemptions of infants from the operation of statutes of limitations depends upon express statutory provisions, and not upon any constitutional provisions requiring such exemptions, and hence the Legislature could enact laws requiring actions for land possessed adversely by another under a title from one authorized to sell under an order or decree of court to be brought within seven years, without excepting infants from its operation. Schlarb v. Castaing, 50 Wash. 331, 97 Pac. 289.

24. Gibson v. Gibson, 108 Wis. 102, 84 N. W. 22.

An action to recover real estate in the adverse possession for 10 years of one claiming under color of title is barred, though brought by minors, or those under guardianship, or because of fraud. Steinberg v. Salzman, 139 Wis. 118, 120 N. W. 1005, under Wis. St. 1898, §§ 4211, 3212. 4215.

in probate proceedings, runs during the minority of the complainant.[25]

§ 238a(4). Effect of marriage.

In Kentucky, a cause of action by a minor female ward against her guardian for a settlement of his accounts accrues on her marriage with an adult husband capable of suing to enforce her rights;[26] and the wife's coverture is no bar to limitations against the right of both to an accounting and settlement.[27] In Louisiana, emancipation by marriage does not terminate the suspension of prescription as to minors, which continues until the actual majority of such minor;[28] but, where a minor has been emancipated by judgment of court, under Code, art. 385, prescription against his right of action against his tutor for a settlement begins from the date of his emancipation, and not from his majority.[29] In South Carolina, persons under the age of twenty-one are allowed by the statute to bring personal actions within four years after coming of age, and the marriage of the *feme* infant will not merge the disability of infancy in that of coverture, so as to require her and her husband to bring their action within five years after marriage.[30] In Texas, on the marriage of a female under twenty-one years of age, she becomes of full age, and the statute then begins to run against her;[31] and begins to run in her guardian's favor.[32]

§ 238a(5). Effect of absence or nonresidence.

Lapse of time does not operate against minors, and the statute

25. Williamson v. Beardsley, 137 Fed. 467, 69 C. C. A. 615.

26. Finnell v. O'Neal, 76 Ky. (13 Bush) 176.

27. Mouser v. Nunn, 142 Ky. 656, 134 S. W. 1148.

28. Barrow v. Wilson, 39 La. Ann. 403, 2 So. 809.

29. Proctor v. Hebert, 36 La. Ann. 250.

30. Robertson v. Wurdeman, 2 Hill (S. C.) 324.

31. White v. Latimer, 12 Tex. 61; Thompson v. Cragg, 24 Tex. 582; Smith v. Powell, 5 Tex. Civ. App. 373, 23 S. W. 1109; Taylor v. Brymer, 17 Tex. Civ. App. 517, 42 S. W. 999, the statute of limitations as to land cannot run against a woman until she becomes of age, or until she marries. D. Sullivan & Co. v. Ramsey (Tex. Civ. App.), 155 S. W. 580.

32. Parish v. Alston, 65 Tex. 194.

of limitations does not run against them, during the time they reside in a different state, and having no knowledge of their rights.[33] In Ohio, where, at the time a will is admitted to probate, a person entitled to contest its validity is under the disabilities of infancy and absence from the State, his action is not barred until the expiration of the statutory period after the longer continuing disability is removed.[34] In Louisiana, the Code suspends prescription during minority and it does not except from suspension the prescription of fifteen years. This suspension extends to nonresidents, as well as to resident, minors.[35] In South Carolina, minors have five years after their coming of age to prosecute their claims to land and four years to prosecute personal actions, whether within or out of the State when coming of age.[36] Under the Kentucky statute, where a distributee was a nonresident infant at the time of distribution, he may enforce his rights to distribution by action on the executor's official bond within five years after arriving at the age of twenty-one.[37]

§ 238a(6). Effect of action during disability.

Under New York Code Civ. Proc., § 396, declaring that if the person entitled to maintain an action is, when the cause of action accrues, a minor, insane, or imprisoned, the time of such disability is not a part of the time limited for commencing an action, except that the time limited cannot be extended more than five years by any such disability, except infancy, or in any case more than a year after the disability ceases, commencement of an action by an infant's guardian does not set the statute running.[38] Under the

33. Ware v. Brush, 1 McLean (U. S.) 533, affirmed Brush v. Ware, 40 U. S. (15 Pet.) 93, 10 L. Ed. 672; Killmer v. Wuchmer, 74 Iowa 359, 37 N. W. 778.

34. Powell v. Koehler, 52 Ohio St. 103, 39 N. E. 195, 49 Am. St. Rep. 705, 26 L. R. A. 480.

35. Smith v. McWaters, 7 La. Ann. 145; Leonard v. Fluker, 4 Rob. (La.) 148.

36. Edson v. Davis, 1 (McCord) S. C. 555; Papot v. Trowell, 8 Rich. Law (S. C.) 234.

37. Smith v. Hardesty, 26 Ky. Law Rep. 1266, 83 S. W. 646; Ky. St. 1903, §§ 2521, 2550.

38. Geibel v. Elwell, 91 Hun (N. Y.) 550, 36 N. Y. Supp. 238.

New Jersey statute, authorizing suing for an injury to a minor child at any time between the accrual of the cause of action and the expiration of two years after its majority, the bringing of an action during minority, which was dismissed, did not start the statute to running, so as to bar another action in two years thereafter.[39] Under the Kentucky statute, an infant may sue at any time after slanderous words are uttered until the expiration of one year after arriving at the age of twenty-one years; and because the infant fails to sue within one year after the slanderous words are uttered, she is not obliged to wait and sue as an adult.[40] In Mississippi, where minors who have sued by their next friend attain their majority after the next friend's death, complainants may appear as adults and prosecute the suit, and, the suit having been pending all the time, proceedings therein by complainants are not affected by any statute of limitations, though nothing was done for many years after the death of the next friend.[41] In Tennessee, a person injured when an infant may elect to sue by *prochein ami* at any time during minority, or alone within a year after majority.[42] In Texas, the bringing of an action by the next friend of a minor, and the dismissal thereof, does not cause limitations against a subsequent action to commence to run, since it does not remove the disability of the minor, as he has no control over the suit.[43]

39. Snare & Triest Co. v. Friedman, 169 Fed. 1, 94 C. C. A. 369. See 2 Gen. St. N. J. 1895, p. 1975, § 4.

In Alabama, where an infant brings an action by next friend which is dismissed for failure to answer interrogatories, such infant was held not barred by the one-year statute of limitations by such dereliction on the part of the next friend, being protected by Code 1907, § 4846. McLaughlin v. Beyer, 181 Ala. 427, 61 So. 62.

Under the Michigan statute (How. Ann. St., § 8718), saving the running of the statute of limitations as against infants, neither the appointment of a next friend, nor the actual commencement of an action which is afterwards discontinued, will operate to set the statute running. Keating v. Michigan Cent. R. Co., 94 Mich. 219, 53 N. W. 1053.

40. Hopkins v. Virgin, 74 Ky. (11 Bush) 677; Kentucky Gen. St. art. 4, c. 71, § 2.

41. Tucker v. Wilson, 68 Miss. 693, 9 So. 898.

42. Whirley v. Whiteman, 38 Tenn. (1 Head) 610.

43. Galveston, etc., Ry. Co. v. Washington, 25 Tex. Civ. App. 600,

§ 239. Insane persons, Non Compotes, etc.

Where the statute excepts from its operation claims in favor of a person who is insane, it does not begin to run until he or she is restored to sanity and knowledge of the existence of the claim.[44] Persons who are deaf and dumb, and have been so from birth, are *prima facie non compos,* and the statute of limitations, where that class are excepted, does not run against them, unless they are shown to have sufficient intelligence to know and comprehend their legal rights and liabilities.[45] In order to be effectual to suspend the operation of the statute, the insanity must have existed at the time when the right of action first accrued;[46] and if the statute began to run upon the claim before the plaintiff became *non compos,* its operation is not checked because he subsequently became insane.[47] Thus, in a case where, at the time a cause of action

63 S. W. 538, judg. aff'd 94 Tex. 510, 63 S. W. 534, the bringing of such an action does not create the relation of guardian and ward, so as to start the running of limitations against the minor. See Tex. Rev. St. art. 3498u.

44. Dicken v. Johnson, 7 Ga. 484; Clark's Ex'r v. Trail's Adm'rs, 58 Ky. (1 Met.) 35; Little v. Downing, 37 N. H. 355. In Sasser v. Davis, 27 Tex. 656, it was held that the statute requiring all actions for personal injury to be brought within one year, did not apply to a case where by the injury the person injured was rendered insane, and his insanity prevented him from originating a suit within the period named. See De Arnaud v. United States, 151 U. S. 483, 14 Sup. Ct. 374, 38 L. Ed. 244, 29 Ct. Cl. 555; Rugan v. Sabin, 53 Fed. 415, 3 C. C. A. 578, 10 U. S. App. 519; Grady v. Wilson, 115 N. C. 344, 20 S. E. 518, 44 Am. St. Rep. 461; Moore's Lessee v. Armstrong, 10 Ohio 11, 36 Am. Dec. 63, 71, n. Those who fraudulently deal with the estate of a lunatic or idiot can derive no advantage from the mere lapse of time while they continue the fraud, if the disability continues, and the laches of an imbecile's next friend in failing to bring suit promptly is not imputable to him. Kidder v. Houston (59 N. J. Eq.), 47 Atl. 336.

45. Oliver v. Berry, 53 Me. 206, 87 Am. Dec. 547.

46. In Allis v. Moore, 84 Mass. (2 Allen) 306, it was held that, if the owner of land has been disseised, his subsequent insanity does not prevent the disseisor's title from maturing by an adverse occupancy for the statutory period. See also, Adamson v. Smith, 2 Mill (S. C.) Const. 269, 12 Am. Dec. 665, where it was held that the statute was not checked in its operation on a note because, after it became due, the payee became *non compos.*

47. Clark's Ex'r v. Trail's Adm'rs,

accrued, the person in whose favor it existed was insane, it was held that the statute did not begin to run during the existence of such insanity, but that immediately upon his restoration to sanity the statute attached to the claim, and having once begun to run thereon, it was not checked by the circumstance that before the bar became complete his lunacy returned.[48]

§ 239a(1). Insanity and other incompetency.

Where a vendor has been induced to sell by fraud, and has failed to rescind the sale after discovery, the facts that he was at the time credulous, and so feeble in mind and body that he was unfit to transact business, are not sufficient to prevent the running of the statute, since such disability is not included among those to which the statute expressly gives this effect.[49] In Alabama, under the direct provisions of the statute fixing a three-year limitation for entries on land and for action similar thereto, the period of disability of one *non compos mentis* is exempted.[50] In Arizona, an action by an executor to set aside the fraudulent transfer of property of a corporation, in which testator was stockholder, was not barred, where testator was of unsound mind when the fraudulent transaction took place, and continued so until his death.[51] In Colorado, where a grantor was insane at the time of the execution of the deed and continuously thereafter until his death, limitations against an action to recover the land would not run as

supra; Allis v. Moore, *supra;* Adamson v. Smith, *supra.*

48. Clark's Ex'r v. Trail's Adm'rs, *supra.*

49. Rugan v. Sabin, 53 Fed. 415, 3 C. C. A. 578, 10 U. S. App. 519.

50. Bradley v. Singletary, 178 Ala. 106, 59 So. 58, under Code 1907, § 4846; Fowler v. Prichard, 148 Ala. 261, 41 So. 667.

Where both the trustee and beneficiary have been out of possession of lands held adversely to them for the length of time necessary to perfect the bar of the statute of limitations, the beneficiary will be barred, even though he was all the time under the disability of insanity; and this applies as well to his equitable as to his legal interests. Molton v. Henderson, 62 Ala. 426.

51. Fleming v. Black Warrior Copper Co. Amalgamated, 15 Ariz. 1, 136 Pac. 273, under Rev. St. 1901, par. 2949, as amended by Laws 1903, No. 16, and par. 2970.

against him during his lifetime.[52] In Georgia, a widow, insane at the date of her husband's death, is not barred of her right to apply for dower until seven years after the removal of her disability.[53] In Illinois, it is held that the fact that a person was peevish and peculiar on occasions either in private or public does not constitute insanity, within the meaning of the statute.[54] In Indiana, an habitual drunkard for whom a guardian has been appointed is not under legal disabilities as a person of "unsound mind" so as to be within the statute of limitations, authorizing persons under legal disabilities when their action accrued to sue within two years after the disability is removed.[55] In Iowa it is held that the statute of limitations begins to run when the cause of action accrues, notwithstanding the insanity of the party, and, in case he dies insane within one year before the statutory period expires, such period is merely extended until one year after his death;[56] and if a special statute of limitations contains no exemption of insane persons, no exemption exists.[57] In Kansas, limitations will not run in favor of a person claiming under a deed made by one mentally unsound and under the undue influence of the grantee;[58] and an insane person is under disability, within the meaning of the stat-

52. Parker v. Betts, 47 Colo. 428, 107 Pac. 816.

53. La Grange Mills v. Kener, 121 Ga. 429, 49 S. E. 300, under Acts 1855-56, p. 234, § 13.

54. Calumet Electric St. Ry. Co. v. Mabie, 66 Ill. App. 235.

Where the saving clause of a statute authorizes persons under a disability of insanity to avoid the bar of a statute of limitations within three years after the disability ceases, no reason is perceived why they may not do the same thing during the continuance of such disability through those who can legally act for them. Milliken v. Marlin, 66 Ill. 13.

55. Makepeace v. Bronnenberg, 146 Ind. 243, 45 N. E. 336.

Where a person, who was and remained of unsound mind and not under guardianship, executed a deed to land in 1876, and the grantee held adversely thereunder until the death of the grantor in 1898, the right of the heirs of the insane person to recover was not barred by the statute of limitations, as the deed was voidable only, and the right of action did not accrue until after disaffirmance. Downham v. Holloway, 158 Ind. 626, 64 N. E. 82, 92 Am. St. Rep. 330.

56. McNeil v. Sigler, 95 Iowa 587, 64 N. W. 604.

57. Collier v. Smaltz, 149 Iowa 230, 128 N. W. 396.

58. Howard v. Carter, 71 Kan. 85, 80 Pac. 61. And see Jenkins v. Jen-

ute of limitations, though the question of his sanity has never been adjudicated by the probate court.[59] In Kentucky, under the statute providing that limitations do not bar the rights of one of unsound mind while the disability continues, limitations do not bar an action by a committee of an incompetent to set aside his deed on the ground of incompetency, where the mental condition of the incompetent was congenital and there had been no change in his mental condition since the conveyance was made.[60] An action by an insane ward by his guardian, brought more than six years after the date when the transaction in question occurred, is not barred by the statute of limitations, in Massachusetts, if it comes within the provisions of Pub. St. c. 197, § 9.[61] In Mississipppi, a person shown to have been a lunatic for many years is presumed to continue such until his death, and the statute begins to run against his heirs at his death only.[62] Under the substantially direct provisions of Missouri Rev. St. 1909, § 1881, one who was insane

kins, 94 Kan. 263, 146 Pac. 414, under Gen. Laws 1909, §§ 5609, 5611 (Code Civ. Proc., §§ 16, 18).

59. Lantis v. Davidson, 60 Kan. 389, 56 Pac. 745.

The running of limitations in an action for damages from inducing plaintiff to become a user of morphine is not wholly suspended by the fact that the morphine so affects plaintiff mentally as to render her incapable of protecting her own interest; and such action is barred under Code Civ. Proc., § 18 (Gen. St. 1909, § 5611), when not brought within one year after the disability is removed. Gillmore v. Gillmore, 91 Kan. 293, 137 Pac. 958, judg. modified on rehearing 91 Kan. 707, 139 Pac. 386.

60. Collins v. Lawson's Committee, 140 Ky. 510, 131 S. W. 262, under Ky. St., §§ 2506, 2525 (Russell's St., §§ 213, 191).

The deed of a person of unsound mind being void, the 10-year statute of limitations applicable to actions for relief from fraud does not apply to set aside such a deed; and it seems that nothing short of adverse possession sufficient to give the grantee title to the land, if that could ever be, can bar such an action. Spicer v. Holbrook, 23 Ky. Law Rep. 1812.

Persons *non compos mentis* are not affected by the statutes of limitation until two years after the disability is removed. Lackey v. Lackey, 47 Ky. (8 B. Mon.) 107.

The statute of limitations runs against a devisee in favor of the sureties in the executor's bond, although the devisee be of unsound mind. Willson v. Hodge's Guardian, 7 Ky. Law Rep. 525 (abstract).

61. Hervey v. Rawson, 164 Mass. 501, 41 N. E. 682.

62. Jeffries v. Dowdle, 61 Miss. 505.

when he executed a trust deed and at all times thereafter, had twenty-four years from the time when defendants entered upon the land claiming ownership under their alleged purchase upon foreclosure of the trust deed, within which to commence an action to set aside the trust deed and the deed made at the sale and recover the land.[63] Limitations do not begin to run, in New Jersey, against an infant or a lunatic until after the infant reaches twenty-one years or the lunatic is restored to sound mind; and a person suffering under either of these disabilities may commence his action during the continuance thereof, or within six years after it ceases.[64]

Legal liabilities may be enforced against idiots and lunatics, in New York, whether the mental incompetency has been judicially determined or not. The idiocy, therefore, of the debtor does not take a claim out of the operation of the statute of limitations during his lifetime, but the statute begins to run against the claim the same as if he were of sound mind.[65] In North Carolina, the insanity of a debtor does not suspend the statute of limitations;[66] limitations do not run against an idiot, by reason of the saving clause in Code, § 163, excepting them from their operation;[67] but a deaf mute is not necessarily an idiot, or *non compos mentis*, within the intent of the statute.[68] In Pennsylvania, when a deed is voidable for insanity of the grantor, a right of action to avoid it accrues to such grantor immediately, which right, and that of the persons claiming under him, are barred, after thirty years from such date, under the statute.[69] In Rhode Island, a person of un-

63. Faris v. Moore, 256 Mo. 123, 165 S. W. 311.

64. Smith v. Felter, 61 N. J. Law 102, 38 Atl. 746.

65. Sanford v. Sanford, 62 N. Y. 553, 2 Hun 94.

Under Code Civ. Proc., § 388, an action to cancel a deed must be begun within ten years, though, if the grantor be insane, the time is extended five years by section 396, subd. 3. German Savings Bank v. Wagner, 149 N. Y. Supp. 654.

66. Grady v. Wilson, 115 N. C. 344, 20 S. E. 518, 44 Am. St. Rep. 461.

67. Outland v. Outland, 118 N. C. 138, 23 S. E. 972.

68. Christmas v. Mitchell, 38 N. C. 535.

69. Boyd v. Weber, 193 Pa. 651, 44 Atl. 1078, under Act April 22,

sound mind is not within the operation of either the statute of possession or of that of limitations, although he may have a guardian who might have brought suit for him.[70] In Tennessee, where an insane person has conveyed his property, negligence of his friends for a long period of time to have a guardian appointed, and take steps to avoid the conveyance, will not prejudice his rights.[71] In Texas, the statute of limitations does not run against a person of unsound mind so long as he remains insane.[72] The same rule obtains in Vermont.[73] In Virginia, where after one was adjudged a lunatic his land was sold in an action by a creditor against his committee, limitations on an action by the lunatic to recover the land commenced to run when he was discharged as restored to sanity, and continued to run notwithstanding a recurrence of insanity nine years later.[74] In Washington, proceedings to set aside a judgment rendered against a person of unsound mind are not barred until the expiration of one year from the removal of the disability.[75] In Wisconsin, it is held that the word

1856 (P. L. p. 532, § 1), declaring that no exception in any act of assembly respecting the limitation of actions in favor of persons *non compos mentis* shall stand, so as to permit any person to maintain any action for the recovery of land after 30 years shall have elapsed since the right of entry thereto accrued to any person within the exception aforesaid.

70. Bourne v. Hall, 10 R. I. 139.

71. Alston v. Boyd, 25 Tenn. (6 Humph.) 504.

72. Moore v. City of Waco, 85 Tex. 206, 20 S. W. 61.

Limitations could not run against plaintiff's action to set aside a judgment for fraud together with certain sales of land thereunder, during the time plaintiff was insane, nor until his sanity was restored. McLean v. Stith (Tex. Civ. App.), 112 S. W. 355.

Limitation does not begin to run against one's right to recover land when actual possession is taken by others, if he is in fact insane, the suspension of the statute not depending upon an adjudication of insanity. Kaack v. Stanton (Tex. Civ. App.), 112 S. W. 702.

Possession under a claim of title which begins after the owner has been adjudged a lunatic cannot ripen into title by limitations; the statute not running against a lunatic. Mitchell v. Stanton (Tex. Civ. App.), 139 S. W. 1033.

73. Chamberlain v. Estey, 55 Vt. 378.

74. Howard v. Landsberg's Committee, 108 Va. 161, 60 S. E. 769.

75. Curry v. Wilson, 45 Wash. 19, 87 Pac. 1065, under the express provisions of Ballinger's Ann. Codes & St., § 5156.

"insane," as used in the statute of limitations, is not restricted to persons wholly without understanding, but applies to every person who is *non compos*, or in the words of the statute of wills, "of unsound or deranged mind."[76] In Minnesota, where a personal injury caused by the negligence of defendant and resulting insanity occur on the same day, the two events are legally simultaneous, as the law will not take notice of fractions of a day, and the disability of insanity existed at the time the cause of action accrued within the meaning of the statute of limitations.[77]

§ 239a(2). Removal of disability.

Where a person of unsound mind to whom a cause of action has accrued has a lucid interval, it is held, in Kentucky, that limitation does not begin to run against him until the interval lasts sufficiently long for him to look into his rights in the matter and take steps toward their assertion.[78] In Georgia, it has been held that title by prescription might be asserted against one setting up the disability of insanity where such person was not continuously insane, and different lucid intervals amounted to the period of prescription.[79] In North Carolina, when a party claims a title in himself, under a conveyance from one *non compos mentis*, and has possession under such alleged title, he does not hold as bailee; but, although the original owner is not barred by such adverse possession on account of his incapacity, when his incapacity is removed, or he dies leaving an executor, the statute will begin to run.[80] In South Carolina, where, in an action of trespass to try title, it appeared that plaintiff was insane at the time he was dis-

76. Burnham v. Mitchell, 34 Wis. 117.

77. Nebola v. Minnesota Iron Co., 102 Minn. 89, 112 N. W. 880.

See Langer v. Newmann, 100 Minn. 27, 110 N. W. 68, holding an action to recover consequential damages for tort resulting in personal injury was not saved by the disability of the plaintiff.

78. Duncan v. Vick, 7 Ky. Law Rep. (abstract) 756, wherein the action was held barred.

79. Verdery v. Savannah, etc., Ry. Co., 82 Ga. 675, 9 S. E. 1133.

80. Arnold v. Arnold, 35 N. C. 174, 55 Am. Dec. 434.

seised of his land, his right of action was saved by the statute of limitations during his insanity, and for one year thereafter.[81]

§ 240. Coverture.

At the common law a woman's identity, both legal and otherwise, was merged in the husband immediately upon her marriage. She could neither sue or be sued, nor exercise any of the legal rights which she possessed while a *feme sole,* consequently so long as coverture existed she was under even greater legal disabilities than an infant; and this anomalous and unwarranted legal position led to the creation of an exception in her favor in the statute of limitations to save legal rights that existed in her behalf at the time of coverture, or which accrued to her subsequently; and this exception still exists in most of our statutes, although in very many of them the rights of married women have been greatly extended by statute, and she is clothed with the power to sue and be sued the same as a *feme sole.*[82] In most of the statutes the exception of married women is made in terms, and even where the exception is simply of "person under legal disabilities," it is held to include married women.[83] In those States in which married women are excepted from the operation of the statute, the circumstance that they are by statute clothed with the power of suing and being sued, or even endowed with all the privileges, rights, and liabilities of a *feme sole,* would hardly seem to be sufficient to change the rule, or deprive them of the benefits of the disability if they choose to avail themselves of it; and the circumstance that the legislature has clothed them with these rights, without making any change in

81. Cleveland v. Jones, 3 Strob. (S. C.) 479, note.

82. Morrison v. Norman, 44 Ill. 477.

83. Bauman v. Grubbs, 26 Ind. 419; Hawkins v. Hawkins, 28 Ind. 66. But *quaere,* If a married woman is given the right to sue and be sued, does not this take her out of the exception of such a clause?

As to coverture, see also Stubblefield v. Menzies, 11 Fed. 268; Partee v. Thomas, 11 Fed. 769; Elder v. McClaskey, 70 Fed. 529, 17 C. C. A. 251, 37 U. S. App. 1, 199, 163 U. S. 685, 16 Sup. Ct. 1201, 41 L. Ed. 315; Fink v. Campbell, 70 Fed. 664; Moore's Lessee v. Armstrong, 10 Ohio 11, 36 Am. Dec. 63, 69, n.

the statute of limitations with respect to them, indicates an intention on the part of the legislature that they shall still remain within the exception contained therein. This is still unquestionably the rule in reference to all matters where the wife is not capacitated to sue or be sued; but it is held in California [84] and in Maine [85] that in cases where a married woman is authorized by statute to sue alone, the saving in the statute of limitations is abrogated as to her. But in New York [86] it is held that the removal of a married woman's disability to sue does not deprive her of the benefit of the saving clause in the statute, unless, as is now the case in that State, the statute omits her from the saving clause; and in Massachusetts the saving clause is extended to infants, insane persons, and persons "disabled by marriage," [87] which would seem to apply only to cases where, by coverture, a woman cannot sue. It may be stated as a general proposition that where coverture is made a disability, the statute of limitations never begins to run against a married woman while she is covert.[88] But if the statute had begun to run upon her claim

84. Cameron v. Smith, 50 Cal. 303. In Massachusetts, Gen. Stat. 1882, the saving is restricted to those "disabled by marriage." See chap. 202, § 7, Rev. Laws 1902, where this clause is now omitted.

85. Brown v. Cousens, 51 Me. 301.

86. Clark v. McCann, 18 Hun (N. Y.) 13.

87. 2 Rev. Stat. p. 1115, § 9. See 2 Rev. L. 1910, p. 1718, § 7.

88. Jones v. Reeves, 6 Rich. (S. C.) 132; Sledge's Adm'rs v. Clopton, 6 Ala. 589; Wilson v. Wilson, 36 Cal. 447, 95 Am. Dec. 194; McLane v. Moore, 51 N. C. (6 Jones L.) 520; Michan v. Wyatt, 21 Ala. 813; McLean v. Jackson, 34 N. C. (12 Ired.) 149; Fatheree v. Fletcher, 31 Miss. 265; Fearn v. Shirley, 3 Miss. 301; Meegan v. Boyle, 60 U. S. (19 How.) 130, 15 L. Ed. 577; Gage v. Smith, 27 Conn. 70; Watson v. Watson, 10 Conn. 77; Drennen v. Walker, 21 Ark. 539; Caldwell v. Black, 27 N. C. (5 Ired. L.) 463; Randall v. Raab, 2 Abb. Pr. (N. Y.) 307; Willson v. Betts, 4 Den. (N. Y.) 201; Dunham v. Sage, 52 N. Y. 229. The statute of limitations does not run against a married woman, to whom property had been left in trust, after her coverture, she being within the exception in the statute in favor of *femes covert*, in a case where she and her husband are suing in equity for the recovery of the property. Flynt v. Hatchett, 9 Ga. 328. In Manchester v. Tibbetts, 121 N. Y. 219, it was held that when a wife establishes an indebtedness of her husband to her, she can enforce a security given for

before her marriage, her subsequent coverture does not suspend its operation.[89] But while as to the wife the operation of the statute is suspended, yet it is not, on that account, saved to the husband, or the grantee of the husband and wife, as to rights which he acquires in the wife's property.[90] The rule is, that

payment of the debt, like any other creditor. As against such an indebtedness, the husband is not obliged, by any duty he owes his other creditors, to interpose the statute of limitations as a defense.

89. Wellborn v. Weaver, 17 Ga. 267; Mitchell v. Berry, 58 Ky. (1 Met.) 602; Killian v. Watt, 7 N. C. (3 Murph.) 167. In Becton v. Alexander, 27 Tex. 659, it was held that the fact that some of the plaintiffs are *femes covert* and infants, at the commencement of the suit, does not deprive the defendants of the benefits of their limitation as to the others, and that to prevent it from being operative against the *femes covert*, etc., it must be shown that the disability preceded the commencement of the action. See also, Pendergrast v. Gullatt, 10 Ga. 218. In Killian v. Watt, *supra*, the court held that where a cause of action accrues to the wife before marriage, her subsequent coverture does not bar the statute of limitations. This ruling follows the settled rule that where the statute has once begun to run, no subsequent disability can suspend its operation. Cole v. Runnells, 6 Tex. 272; Chevallier v. Durst, 6 Tex. 239; Den v. Richards, 15 N. J. L. 347; Peck v. Randall, 1 Johns. (N. Y.) 165; Lynch v. Cox, 23 Pa. 265; Pearce v. House, 4 N. C. (Term Rep.) 305; McCoy v. Nichols, 5 Miss. 31; Fewell v. Collins, 3 Brev. (S. C.) 286; Fitzhugh v. Anderson, 2 H. & M. (Va.) 289; Faysoux v. Prather, 1 N. & McC. (S. C.) 296; Parsons v. M'Cracken, 9 Leigh (Va.) 495; Stowel v. Zouch, 1 Plowd. 353a; Duroure v. Jones, 4 T. R. 300; Cotterell v. Dutton, 4 Taunt. 826; Bunce v. Walcott, 2 Conn. 27. When the statute has once commenced to run, it runs over all subsequent disabilities and intermediate acts and events, and there is no distinction between a disability or impediment on the part of the plaintiff, and where it arises from some change or event that has happened to the debtor; or, in this respect, between a voluntary and an involuntary disability. Dekay v. Darrah, 14 N. J. L. 288. Where an adverse possession commenced during the life of the ancestor, it is not suspended by the title descending to a *feme covert*. Jackson v. Robins, 15 Johns. (N. Y.) 169; Fleming v. Griswold, 3 Hill (N. Y.) 85. This question was considered in Griswold v. Butler, 3 Conn. 227, and the rule established, that there is no saving in the statute of limitations for any disability in the heir supervenient to the disability of the person to whom the right of entry first accrued.

90. Carter v. Cantrell, 16 Ark. 154. In Gregg v. Tesson, 1 Black. (U. S.) 510, where a married woman was the owner of land in which, by force of the law of the State, her husband had a life interest, the grantee of the

where the husband sues in right of his wife, he cannot avail himself of her disability.[91] The disability that saves a claim from the operation of the statute is of a personal character, and can only be set up by the party in whose favor it exists, and those claiming under him;[92] nor is it available to a person claiming under such disabled person, if he has, at all times since the disability accrued, been in a position to assert and enforce the right; and for this reason the husband cannot avail himself of the wife's disability as to rights which he acquired by coverture over, to, or in her estate.[93] But this must be understood as applying only to that class of claims which the husband could have enforced during coverture.[94] If the wife's property is taken upon execution upon her husband's debts, or illegally sold, the statute does not begin to run against her until her husband's death;[95] but it begins to run against her heirs immediately upon her death, except as to such property as by law the husband is entitled to a life estate in.[96] In Pennsylvania [97] it was held that where a sale of land on execution against a deceased debtor has been acqui-

husband and wife was not saved from the operation of the statute by the wife's disability, because he might have brought ejectment counting on his interest immediately upon acquiring the right. McDowell v. Potter, 8 Pa. 189.

91. McDowell v. Potter, 8 Pa. 189.

92. Watson v. Kelly, 16 N. J. L. 517; Thorpe v. Corwin, 20 N. J. L. 311.

93. Gregg v. Tesson, *supra*. In Carter v. Cantrell, 16 Ark. 154, it was held that a right of action for the recovery of slaves belonging to the wife is not, on account of the wife's disability to sue for the same in her own name, saved to the husband in an action by husband and wife, after the statute would have otherwise attached.

94. State v. Layton, 4 Harr. (Del.) 8.

95. McDonald v. McGuire, 8 Tex. 361; Meanor v. Hamilton, 27 Pa. 137; Culler v. Motzer, 13 S. & R. (Pa.) 356. If a married woman loans money to her husband during coverture, the statute does not run upon her claim until his death. Towers v. Hayner, 3 Whart. (Pa.) 18. And the same rule prevails where she loans money to a firm of which the husband is a member. Kutz's Appeal, 40 Pa. 90.

96. Carpenter v. Schermerhorn, 2 Barb. Ch. (N. Y.) 314; Marple v. Myers, 12 Pa. 122; Lenhart v. Ream, 74 Pa. 59; Henry v. Carson, 59 Pa. 297.

97. Meanor v. Hamilton, *supra*.

esced in for thirty or forty years by the family of the decedent, a jury should not disturb the purchaser's title, except upon the most overwhelming proof of fraud, and that, although the disabilities of coverture or infancy have not been removed long enough to make the statute bar complete, yet that the long silence of husbands and guardians is entitled to weight as evidence of such an acquiescence as to protect the purchaser's title. But it is hardly believed that this doctrine can stand. To permit the circumstance that a husband or guardian has acquiesced in an improper interference with the property of the ward, to overcome the protection which the statute is intended to afford to persons under such disabilities, is an assumption by the court of authority to abrogate the clear and unequivocal provisions of a statute, and that, too, for the very reasons that led to the adoption of the statute itself.[98] In Ohio, it has been held that equity will refuse relief in a case where some of the applicants for relief are under no disability, even though some of them are under the disability of coverture, where they are all adults, and have slept upon their rights for so many years that the granting of the relief prayed for would operate as a fraud upon the defendants. But in such a case the parties under disability, upon the removal thereof, can stand upon their legal rights.[99] In New York, married women being given control over their own property, and the right to sue in their own name, no provision is made saving their rights from the operation of the statute; and the repeal of the saving clause in their favor is held to apply to claims existing before the repeal. Thus, where a woman, married in November, 1857, when a bond and mortgage became due to her, neglected to bring an action thereon until December, 1877, the saving clause as to married women having been omitted from the statute in 1870, it was held that her remedy was barred by the lapse of twenty years.[1] In

98. Piatt v. Smith, 12 Ohio St. 561.

99. Hansford v. Elliott, 9 Leigh (Va.) 79.

1. Acker v. Acker, 81 N. Y. 143, reversing the same case in 16 Hun (N. Y.) 173.

/isconsin, no exception is made in favor of married women, the :atute of that State in this respect being the same as in New 'ork. In Iowa, coverture is not within the saving clause. In [assachusetts, the statute only saves the rights of married women 'here they are disabled by coverture; that is, where they are not .othed with authority to prosecute their rights by suits in their wn name. In California and Indiana, married women are not ithin the saving clause of the statute, except as to those rights ır the enforcement of which the husband is a necessary party. ı West Virginia, coverture is within the exception of the statute, xcept in those cases where a married woman holds lands as her ıle and separate property. In all the other States, coverture is ithin the saving clause of the statute; and the circumstance that married woman is clothed with the power to sue in her own ame does not defeat the exception, because, although she may ɔt be within the reason of the statute, she is nevertheless within s letter, and the legislature not having seen fit to repeal the savıg clause as to her, the courts have no power to do so.

240a(1). Coverture—In general.

As stated in the last preceding section, where coverture is made disability, statutes of limitation do not run against a married oman so long as coverture continues.[2] Where a special statute of

2. *Ark.*—Vaughan v. Parr, 20 Ark. ю.

Ga.—Scott v. Haddock, 11 Ga. 258.

Ind.—Caress v. Foster, 62 Ind. 145; ennick v. Chandler, 59 Ind. 354; ırnett v. Harshbarger, 105 Ind. .0, 5 N. E. 718; Sims v. Smith, 86 ıd. 577; Sims v. Bardoner, 86 Ind. ', 44 Am. Rep. 263; De Armond v. lasscock, 40 Ind. 418.

Ky.—Smith v. Cox's Committee, :6 Ky. 118, 160 S. W. 786; Deıurcy's Adm'r v. Dicken, 1 Ky. Law ɛp. (abstract) 260; Priest v. Warn, 70 Ky. (7 Bush) 633; Grundy's Heirs v. Grundy, 51 Ky. (12 B. Mon.) 269.

Mo.—Graham v. Wilson, 168 Mo. App. 185, 153 S. W. 83; Witte v. Storm, 236 Mo. 470, 139 S. W. 384; Elliott v. Landis Mach. Co., 236 Mo. 546, 139 S. W. 356; Roberts v. St. Louis Merchants' Land Imp. Co., 126 Mo. 460, 29 S. W. 584; Franklin v. Cunningham, 187 Mo. 184, 86 S. W. 79; Reaume v. Chambers, 22 Mo. 36; Hinkle v. Lovlace, 204 Mo. 208, 102 S. W. 1015; Dubowsky v. Binggeli, 184 Mo. App. 361, 171 S. W. 12.

limitations contains no saving clause in favor of persons under disability of marriage, it runs as well against married women as other persons, and the courts cannot write into the statute a disability which the law has not provided for.[3] In Illinois, limitations do not run against the liability of the husband to support his wife, and do not operate to bar the right to relief by separate maintenance.[4] Coverture does not bring the wife within the exception in favor of persons under legal disabilities contained in the present statute.[5] The repeal of the disability of coverture by the North Carolina Act of 1899 was not retroactive, but, by its terms, no adverse possession prior to February 13, 1899, could be counted against a married woman.[6] In Arkansas, married women are not

N. H.—Little v. Downing, 37 N. H. 355; Pierce v. Dustin, 24 N. H. (4 Fost.) 417.

N. J.—Carey v. City of Paterson, 47 N. J. Law 365, 1 Atl. 473; Collins v. Babbitt, 67 N. J. Eq. 165, 58 Atl. 481, the statute of limitations does not apply as between husband and wife.

N. C.—Briggs v. Smith, 83 N. C. 306; Uzzle v. Wood, 54 N. C. 226.

Ohio.—Mathers v. Hewitt (Super. Ct. Cin.), 9 Wkly. Law Bul. 63.

Pa.—Etter v. Greenawalt, 98 Pa. 422; Offerman v. Packer, 26 Leg. Int. 205; Hill v. Goodman, 1 Woodw. Dec. 207; Beal v. Stahley, 21 Pa. (9 Harris) 376; Matlock v. Mutual Life Ins. Co., 5 Pa. Dist. R. 113, 37 Wkly. Notes Cas. 526.

S. C.—Payne v. Harris, 3 Strob. Eq. 39.

Tenn.—Brown v. Crawford, 28 Tenn. (9 Humph.) 164; Weisinger v. Murphy, 39 Tenn. (2 Head) 674; Fitzsimmons v. Johnson, 90 Tenn. (6 Pickle) 416, 17 S. W. 100.

Tex.—Estes v. Turner, 30 Tex. Civ. App. 365, 70 S. W. 1007; Crouch v. Crouch, 30 Tex. Civ. App. 288, 70 S. W. 595; Harrison v. City of Sulphur Springs (Tex. Civ. App.), 50 S. W. 1064; Smith v. McElyea, 68 Tex. 70, 3 S. W. 258; Roemilie v. Leeper, 2 Posey Unrep. Cas. 535. See Taylor v. Bland, 60 Tex. 29.

3. State *ex rel.* O'Malley v. Musick, 165 Mo. App. 214, 145 S. W. 1184, adopting opinion 145 Mo. App. 33, 130 S. W. 398.

4. Glynn v. Glynn, 139 Ill. App. 185.

5. Sedwick v. Ritter, 128 Ind. 209, 27 N. E. 610 (1891).

6. Norcum v. Savage, 140 N. C. 472, 53 S. E. 289.

As a guardian's possession of the ward's choses in action on her marriage in 1865 was transferred to the husband, so that he alone could maintain an action to recover them, or their value if converted, limitations began to run against him from the date of the marriage as to any action on the guardian's bond. Fowler v. McLaughlin, 131 N. C. 209, 42 S. E. 589.

excepted from the operation of the statute of limitation as to judicial sales.[7]

§ 240a(2). Effect of separate acts.

In Arkansas, it is held that the act giving married women exclusive control of their separate property, removing the disability of coverture, and authorizing them to sue in their own names, does not repeal by implication the saving clause, in their favor in the statute of limitations, exempting married women from the operation of limitations, and giving them three years after discoverture in which to bring a suit for lands.[8] In Georgia, as the act in regard to married women authorizes them to bring suit in respect to their separate estates, the statute of limitation runs against such suits, the same as against other causes of action.[9] In Illinois, since the passage of the married woman's Act of 1861, the saving clause in favor of married women in the statute of limitations has no force, and since that time the statute of limitations applies against a married woman equally as against an unmarried woman.[10] The Indiana statute of 1881 removed the "disabilities of married women," in the sense in which that phrase is used in the statute, giving a person "under legal disabilities" two years in which to bring an action after the disability is removed.[11] Un-

7. McGaughey v. Brown, 46 Ark. 25.

8. Memphis & L. R. R. Co. v. Organ, 67 Ark. 84, 55 S. W. 952; Rowland v. McGuire, 64 Ark. 412, 42 S. W. 1068. *Contra*: Garland County v. Gaines, 47 Ark. 558, 2 S. W. 460.

9. Perkins v. Compton, 69 Ga. 736. See also, Sparks v. Roberts, 65 Ga. 571.

10. Safford v. Stubbs, 117 Ill. 389, 7 N. E. 653; Geisen v. Heiderich, 104 Ill. 537; Enos v. Buckley, 94 Ill. 458; Castner v. Walrod, 83 Ill. 171, 25 Am. Rep. 369; Hayward v. Gunn, 82 Ill. 385. *Contra*: Harrer v. Wallner, 80 Ill. 197; Noble v. McFarland, 51 Ill. 226; Morrison v. Norman, 47 Ill. 477.

11. City of Indianapolis v. Patterson, 112 Ind. 344, 14 N. E. 551. See also, Rosa v. Prather, 103 Ind. 191, 2 N. E. 575; Royse v. Turnbaugh, 117 Ind. 539, 20 N. E. 485.

As, under Rev. St. 1881, § 254, a married woman can sue alone in her own name in regard to her separate property, her claim to such property may be barred by limitation. Irey v. Markey, 132 Ind. 546, 32 N. E. 309.

der the Kentucky Statute, 1903, § 2525, providing that if a person entitled to sue was, at the time the cause of action accrued, a married woman, the action may be brought within the number of years after the removal of such disability that is allowed to a person having no impediment to bring the same, limitations do not run against a married woman during her coverture, regardless of her ability to maintain suit during that time.[12] Since the enactment of the Michigan married women's property act of 1855, enabling such women to sue and be sued, the statute of limitations may run against a woman during her marriage.[13] It is held in Mississippi that mere ability to sue imposes no obligation to do so, and a married woman is not barred by limitation by the fact that she might have sued, either with or without her husband, after her marriage.[14] Likewise in Missouri it is held that the statute permitting a married woman to sue and be sued in her own name, the same as a *feme sole,* does not by implication repeal the statute that exempts a married woman from the running of the statute of limitations, since mere ability to sue does not impose an obligation to

12. Henson v. Culp, 157 Ky. 442, 163 S. W. 455; Dukes v. Davis, 30 Ky. Law Rep. 1348, 101 S. W. 390; Terrell v. Maupin, 26 Ky. Law Rep. 1203, 83 S. W. 591. The statute applies, though the plaintiff might, under Civ. Code Prac., § 34, have sued alone during coverture, if her husband refused to unite in the action. Onions v. Covington, etc., Bridge Co., 107 Ky. 154, 53 S. W. 8, 21 Ky. Law Rep. 820.

Limitations did not run during the life of the husband against her action to recover rents and profits collected by the husband from the wife's separate estate. Smith's Ex'r v. Johns, 154 Ky. 274, 157 S. W. 21.

Ky. St. 1899, § 2506, providing that if, at the time the right of any person to bring an action for the recovery of real property accrued, such person was a married woman, she may, though the period of 15 years has expired, bring an action within three years after such disability is removed, is not repealed by section 2128, providing that a married woman may take, acquire, and hold property, make contracts, and sue and be sued, as a single woman, etc. Sturgill v. Chesapeake & O. Ry. Co., 116 Ky. 659, 25 Ky. Law Rep. 912, 76 S. W. 826; Higgins v. Stokes, 116 Ky. 664, 25 Ky. Law Rep. 919, 76 S. W. 834.

13. King v. Merritt, 67 Mich. 194, 34 N. W. 689; Dougless v. Dougless, 72 Mich. 86, 40 N. W. 177; Curbay v. Bellemer, 70 Mich. 106, 37 N. W. 911.

14. North v. James, 61 Miss. 761.

do so.[15] Since the enactment in 1871 of the Nebraska married woman's act, permitting married women to sue in the same manner as if they were unmarried, the statute of limitations runs against women during coverture.[16]

By Laws 1870, c. 741, § 5, amending the New York Code Civ. Proc., § 88, striking married women from the list of persons against whom the statute of limitations does not run, a married woman, as to the commencement of actions, was placed on the same footing as other persons, and thereafter she was bound to commence her action within the time specified after the cause of action accrued, although it had accrued prior to the amendment.[17] The provisions of the North Carolina Code allowing a *feme covert* to sue or be sued alone, regarding her separate property, does not remove the disability of coverture, so as to allow the statute of limitations to bar her right of action.[18] The Ohio Act of 1861, constituting the real and personal property of a married woman her separate estate, and the provisions of the Civil Code, authorizing her to sue and be sued alone, do not repeal by implication the saving clause in the statute of limitations in favor of married women;[19] and the Act of 1883, removing the disabilities of coverture as to rights of action concerning a married woman's separate estate, did not affect the statute of limitations then in effect as to causes of action that

15. Lindell Real Estate Co. v. Linde, 142 Mo. 61, 43 S. W. 368.

16. Murphy v. J. H. Evans City Steam Laundry Co., 52 Neb. 593, 72 N. W. 960. The act applies to married women, both residents and nonresidents. Linton v. Heye, 69 Neb. 450, 95 N. W. 1040, 111 Am. St. Rep. 556.

17. Clarke v. Gibbons, 83 N. Y. 107; Acker v. Acker, 81 N. Y. 143, rev'g 16 Hun 173.

18. Campbell v. Crater, 95 N. C. 156; Lippard v. Troutman, 72 N. C. 551.

A married woman is not excluded from the benefit of the exception in the statute of limitations, providing that the statute shall not run against a married woman during coverture, by reason of the fact that she registered herself as a free trader during coverture, as authorized by Code, § 1827. Wilkes v. Allen, 131 N. C. 279, 42 S. E. 616. See Cherry v. Cape Fear Power Co., 142 N. C. 404, 55 S. E. 287.

19. Ashley v Rockwell, 43 Ohio St. 386, 2 N. E. 437; Hurlbut v. Wade, 40 Ohio St. 603.

had then accrued.[20] The Pennsylvania Act of June 3, 1887, conferring on a married woman the same rights concerning her own property as possessed by a *feme sole* repealed Act March 27, 1713, excepting from the running of the statute women under the disability of coverture.[21] Under the West Virginia statute, excepting a married woman from disabilities as to her sole and separate property, adverse possession will run against a married woman as to land owned by her in her sole right.[22] The Wyoming statute permitting a married woman to sue and be sued does not, by implication, repeal the statute providing that a cause of action accruing to her shall not be barred by the statute of limitations so long as the disability of coverture exists.[23]

§ 240a(3). Nature of property or cause of action involved.

Limitations do not run against a note to a married woman while coverture disables her from suing thereon.[24] The fact that the holder of a note is under the disability of coverture does not prolong the time within which suit must be brought in order to hold the surety liable.[25] Under the Missouri statute, exempting married women from the operation of the statute of limitations during coverture, the statute does not run against a wife's right of action for alienation of her husband's affections until termination of the coverture.[26] Under the North Carolina Code, providing that limitations shall not begin to run against a right of action accruing in favor of a married woman until the termination of her coverture, a wife's right of action for a trespass on land held by herself and her husband in entirety is not barred until the statu-

20. Yocum v. Allen, 58 Ohio St. 280, 50 N. E. 909.

21. *In re* Hick's Estate, 7 Pa. Super. Ct. 274, 42 W. N. C. 117; Nissley v. Brubaker, 192 Pa. 388, 43 Atl. 967, 44 W. N. C. 425. See as to effect of married woman's act of 1848, Dexter v. Billings, 110 Pa. 135, 1 Atl. 180.

22. Randolph v. Casey, 43 W. Va. 289, 27 S. E. 231.

23. Bliler v. Boswell, 9 Wyo. 57, 59 Pac. 798, 61 Pac. 867.

24. Taylor v. Slater, 21 R. I. 104, 41 Atl. 1001.

25. Reid v. Hamilton, 11 Ky. Law Rep. (abstract) 524.

26. Linck v. Linck, 104 Mo. App. 368, 79 S. W. 478.

tory period after her husband's death.[27] Where a husband and wife reside on land after the execution of a void deed thereof by the wife to the husband, and their marital relations are uninterrupted, the husband's possession is not adverse, and the statute of limitations does not run in his favor prior to her death.[28] Where a debt is due a married woman, and, she being incapable of holding the same, the debtor is allowed by agreement by her husband to hold the amount of the debt in trust for her, the statute of limitations begins to run against her on the death of her husband.[29]

§ 240a(4). Claim by wife against husband.

The statute of limitations does not run against claims existing between husband and wife during the continuance of the marital relation.[30] Where a wife loaned her husband money from her sole and separate estate, limitations ran against the loan as in the case of a transaction between strangers.[31] Where the only evidence in support of a wife's claim against her husband's estate is that she handed him a sum of money more than five years before her claim was filed in the probate court, the claim is barred by the Illinois statute of limitations.[32] Transactions between husband and wife are not regarded as contracts in a strict legal sense, and their contracts are not within the general statute of limitations, in Indiana.[33] In Iowa, limitations run against a claim in favor of a wife against her husband as in other cases; Code, § 3447, providing that actions may be brought within the times specified after their

27. Spruill v. Branning Mfg. Co., 130 N. C. 42, 40 S. E. 824.

28. Berkowitz v. Brown, 3 Misc. Rep. (N. Y.) 1, 23 N. Y. Supp. 792.

29. *In re* Neilley, 95 N. Y. 382.

30. Hamby v. Brooks, 86 Ark. 448, 111 S. W. 277.

31. Wagner v. Mutual Life Ins. Co. of New York, 88 Conn. 536, 91 Atl. 1012.

32. Bromwell v. Bromwell's Estate, 139 Ill. 424, 28 N. E. 1057.

33. Barnett v. Harshbarger, 105 Ind. 410, 5 N. W. 718.

Limitations do not run, during the continuance of the marital relations, against notes made by a husband to his wife before their marriage, and which were due, but not barred, at the date of the marriage. Fourthman v. Fourthman, 15 Ind. App. 199, 43 N. E. 965.

causes accrue, and not afterwards, except when otherwise specially declared, and the statute containing no exception in behalf of married women.[34] The Kentucky statute does not begin to run against a note executed by the husband to the wife until the husband's death, though the money for which the note was given was by virtue of an ante-nuptial agreement, the wife's separate estate.[35] Under the Mississippi Code of 1880, the constitution of 1890, and the Code of 1892, the statute of limitations will bar a debt owed by a husband to a wife.[36] In Missouri, limitations run against a cause of action in favor of a married woman against her husband only when she becomes discovert, subject, however, to the proviso of Rev. St. 1909, § 1881, that it may not be commenced more than twenty-four years after accrual.[37] In Louisana prescription does not run against a debt due by the husband to the wife during the marriage.[38] In Maine, an action on a note given by a husband to

34. *In re* Deaner's Estate, 126 Iowa 701, 102 N. W. 825, 106 Am. St. Rep. 374.

Under the Code of 1851, which provides that, in case the wife does not recover during the life of her husband property left under his control, she shall then have a remedy against his estate, her right of action therefor does not accrue until the husband's death. Lower v. Lower, 46 Iowa 525.

See Wallace v. Wallace, 137 Iowa 37, 114 N. W. 913, as to action by the wife to set aside a conveyance made by the husband previous to marriage in fraud of her rights.

35. Biggerstaff's Adm'r v. Biggerstaff's Adm'r, 19 Ky. Law Rep. 371, 40 S. W. 671.

36. Wyatt v. Wyatt, 81 Miss. 219, 32 So. 317.

37. Graham v. Wilson, 168 Mo. App. 185, 153 S. W. 83.

An action by a wife against her husband to recover realty may accrue during coverture, but if she dies under coverture, whether limitations have run or not, an action is saved to her heirs or those claiming by or under her, which may be brought within three years after her death, as expressly provided by Rev. St. 1899, § 4267. Smith v. Settle, 128 Mo. App. 379, 107 S. W. 430; Reed v. Painter, 145 Mo. 341, 46 S. W. 1089.

Where a husband received money belonging to his wife without her consent in writing, the period of limitations against her action to recover it began to run from the day the husband received the money, but, the wife having died under coverture, her personal representative was entitled to sue within one year from her death, as provided by Rev. St. 1899, §§ 4279, 4281. Smith v. Settle, *supra;* Rosenberger v. Mallerson, 92 Mo. App. 27.

38. Sewell v. McVay, 30 La. Ann. 673.

his wife is not barred, if begun within six years after her decease, and within two years and six months after notice of the appointment of his executor; the statute authorizing married women to sue not applying to actions against her husband.[39] In Maryland, the receipt of money under such circumstances as would make the husband liable therefor merely creates a debt due by him to his wife, and against such a debt the statute of limitations runs, and it will be barred, unless sued for or claimed in due time after disability of coverture removed.[40] In New Jersey limitation does not run during the coverture on the note of a husband to his wife.[41]

In Pennsylvania, since the married woman's act does not authorize a suit by a married woman against her husband, limitations do not run against a note given to a wife by her husband.[42] In Tennessee, where the right of a wife to sue, by her next friend, her husband and the holder of her inheritance in realty to recover the same, is barred by limitations, the running of limitations against the curtesy interest of the husband does not operate as a bar to her right to the fee on the death of her husband, if she sues within the time fixed by the statute.[43] In West Virginia, a claim of a wife against her husband is not barred during coverture, if at all, until twenty years from its inception or written renewal.[44] In Wisconsin, limitations do not run against a wife, as between herself and husband, so as to bar her claim against his estate for money loaned to him.[45] In North Carolina, in the absence of any ex-

39. Morrison v. Brown, 84 Me. 82, 24 Atl. 672.

40. Sabel v. Slingluff, 52 Md. 132.

41. Alpaugh v. Wilson, 52 N. J. Eq. (7 Dick.) 424, 28 Atl. 722.

42. *In re* Wilkinson's Estate, 192 Pa. 117, 43 Atl. 466.

In an action by an administrator of a married woman against her husband on a note, the period of the wife's coverture is properly excluded in ascertaining the time at which the presumption of payment on the note arose. Gillan v. West, 232, Pa. 74, 81 Atl. 128.

See also, Kennedy v. Knight, 174 Pa. 408, 34 Atl. 585.

43. Murdock v. Johnson, 47 Tenn. (7 Cold.) 605.

44. Righter v. Riley, 42 W. Va. 633, 26 S. E. 357.

45. Gudden v. Gudden's Estate, 113 Wis. 297, 89 N. W. 111; Brader v. Brader, 110 Wis. 423, 85 N. W. 681.

ception in favor of the wife holding a claim against her husband, the statute of limitations runs against the wife during coverture.[46]

§ 240a(5). Claim to real property in general.

In Arkansas, the statute of limitations against an action for the recovery of land, the separate property of a *feme covert,* does not run during coverture;[47] and title to land by adverse possession for seven years cannot be built up against a married woman, such person being exempted from the operation of the statute.[48] In Connecticut, a married woman, who executes a mortgage of her land with her husband, is not saved by her coverture from the running of the statute of limitations against her title in favor of the mortgagee.[49] In the District of Columbia, an action of ejectment to recover from an adverse holder the land of a married woman whose title vested prior to the passage of the statute defining the separate property rights of married women, is barred ten years after the removal of the disability of coverture, where the adverse possession has continued for ten years prior to the removal of such disability.[50] In Indiana, a person under the disability of coverture has two years after the disability is removed in which to bring an action to recover land, although the full period prescribed by the statute has expired; but such a person is not entitled to have the time the statute begins to run fixed at the date of the removal of the disability.[51] Under the Kentucky statute, providing that if, when the right to bring an action for realty first accrued, the person entitled was a married woman, she or one claiming through her

46. Graves v. Howard, 159 N. C. 594, 75 S. E. 998, under the Constitution, Revisal 1905, § 2093, and Laws of 1899, c. 78.

47. McKneely v. Terry, 61 Ark. 527, 33 S. W. 953. See also, Anders v. Roark, 108 Ark. 248, 156 S. W. 1018; Brasher v. Taylor, 109 Ark. 281, 159 S. W. 1120.

48. Harvey v. Dougless, 73 Ark. 221, 83 S. W. 946; Rowland v. McGuire, 67 Ark. 320, 55 S. W. 16; McFarlane v. Grober, 70 Ark. 371, 69 S. W. 56, 91 Am. St. Rep. 84; Cooper v. Newton, 68 Ark. 150, 56 S. W. 867. And see Martin v. Conner (Ark.), 171 S. W. 125.

49. Hanford v. Fitch, 41 Conn. 486.

50. Davis v. Coblens, 12 App. D. C. 51.

51. Wright v. Kleyla, 104 Ind. 223, 4 N. E. 16.

may bring the action within three years after such disability is removed, though the period of fifteen years has expired, limitations would not run against a married woman's right of action to recover realty; but thirty years' adverse possession of land owned by a married woman bars an action for its recovery by her heirs, notwithstanding her coverture, when the adverse possession began and continued until her death.[52] In Missouri, an action to recover land is governed by the statute providing that, if a person entitled to bring an action specified in the article (Limitation of Real Actions), be at the time of the accrual of the right of action a married woman, the time of such disability shall not be any portion of the time limited for beginning the action, but her action will not be barred for twenty-four years from the time it accrues; and if such married woman die intestate, while under the same coverture and within twenty-four years after the cause of action accrued, her heirs may commence such action within three years after her death.[53] In Maine, where the wife became entitled to the premises as heir at law during her coverture, and her husband conveyed his life estate therein, and his grantee continued in possession for more than thirty years, the husband still living, she may, after the decease of her husband, make an entry and recover the land.[54] Under the Massachusetts statute, a married woman was barred of her right of entry unless she made entry within thirty years next after the right accrued.[55] In New York, where

52. Kentucky Stave Co. v. Page (Ky.), 125 S. W. 170; Trail v. Turner, 22 Ky. Law Rep. 100, 56 S. W. 645. See also, Bankston v. Crabtree Coal Min. Co., 95 Ky. 455, 25 S. W. 1105; Conner v. Downer, 67 Ky. (4 Bush) 631; Sharp v. Head, 50 Ky. (11 B. Mon.) 277; Riggs v. Dooley, 46 Ky. (7 B. Mon.) 236; Marshall v. McQueen, 13 Ky. (3 Litt.) 468; Big Sandy Co. v. Ramey, 162 Ky. 236, 172 S. W. 508, a married woman, executing a deed alone, cannot recover the land after three years after the death of her husband.

53. McKee v. Downing, 224 Mo. 115, 124 S. W. 7; Rutter v. Carothers, 223 Mo. 631, 122 S. W. 1056; Graham v. Ketchum, 192 Mo. 15, 90 S. W. 350; Shumate v. Snyder, 140 Mo. 77, 41 S. W. 781; Snyder v. Elliott, 171 Mo. 362, 71 S. W. 826. See also, Bucher v. Hohl, 199 Mo. 320, 97 S. W. 922; Hatre v. Edmunds, 200 Mo. 246, 98 S. W. 744.

54. Mellus v. Showman, 21 Me. (8 Shep.) 201.

55. Atherton v. Hitchings, 78 Mass.

a wife joins in a purchase money mortgage on land purchased in her husband's name, her right to redeem is not suspended until the death of her husband, but accrues immediately on the sale, and is barred in twenty years thereafter.[56] In North Carolina, where one was in actual adverse possession, under color of title, of land of a married woman, for seven years before the death of her husband, and she failed to bring her action therefor within the three years after his death allowed by the statute, her heirs are barred by adverse possession and limitations from recovering it.[57] In Pennsylvania, a person under coverture must make entry or bring suit to recover lands within thirty years after her right of entry accrues, notwithstanding her coverture.[58] In Tennessee, a wife who, during coverture, has with her husband been disseised of her land, is limited to three years after his death within which to bring her action for its recovery.[59] In South Carolina, an action to recover real property, where the ancestor under whom plaintiff claimed and who owned the land in fee by marriage before the adoption of the constitution of 1868 vested in her husband an interest in her real estate, predeceased him, begun within ten years after the removal of disability of coverture, was not barred.[60] In Texas, where Act April 1, 1895, provides that limitations shall not begin to run against married women until they arrive at twenty-one years of age, and that their disability shall continue one year after the passage of the act, and that they shall have thereafter the same time to sue as is allowed others by the pro-

(12 Gray) 117; Melvin v. Proprietors of Locks and Canals, 46 Mass. (5 Metc.) 15, 38 Am. Dec. 384.

56. McMichael v. Russell, 74 N. Y. Supp. 212, 68 App. Div. 104, under Code Civ. Proc., § 379, limiting actions to redeem from mortgagees in possession, or those claiming under them, to 20 years.

57. Swift v. Dixon, 131 N. C. 42, 42 S. E. 458. See also, Gaskins v. Allen, 137 N. C. 426, 49 S. E. 919; Berry v. W. M. Ritter Lumber Co., 141 N. C. 386, 54 S. E. 278, as to actions for the recovery of land; Crump v. Thompson, 31 N. C. 491.

58. Hogg v. Ashman, 83 Pa. 80, under Act April 22, 1856.

59. King v. Nutall, 66 Tenn. (7 Baxt.) 321; Murdock v. Johnson, 47 Tenn. (7 Cold.) 605.

60. Stokes v. Murray, 99 S. C. 221, 83 S. E. 33.

visions thereof, where a woman was under coverture at the time the act took effect, the five-year statute of limitations against an action to recover land did not begin to run until one year after the act of 1895 took effect.[61] In Virginia, where the person is under disability when the cause of action arises, no action can be brought to recover land but within twenty years next after the time at which such right of action accrued.[62] In West Virginia, where adverse possession of a married woman's land, not her separate estate, beginning during coverture and continuing for the term of the statute of limitations, has barred her rights and those of her husband during coverture, the wife, or those claiming under her, has five years after the coverture ends to sue for the land.[63]

§ 240a(6). Recovery of property disposed of by husband.

In Alabama, the statute of limitations does not bar a married woman from recovering her separate property, sold under execu-

61. Beale's Heirs v. Johnson (Tex. Civ. App.), 99 S. W. 1045.

See also, as to the effect of coverture under this act: Hymer v. Holyfield (Tex. Civ. App.), 87 S. W. 722; Wren v. Howland, 33 Tex. Civ. App. 87, 75 S. W. 894; Broom v. Pearson (Tex. Civ. App.), 81 S. W. 753, modified 98 Tex. 469, 85 S. W. 790, and rehearing denied 98 Tex. 469, 86 S. W. 733; Surghenor v. Taliaferro (Tex. Civ. App.), 98 S. W. 648; Harry v. Hamilton (Tex. Civ. App.), 154 S. W. 638; Gibson v. Oppenheimer (Tex. Civ. App.), 154 S. W. 694.

Prior to 1895, the statute of limitations for the recovery of land did not run against a married woman during coverture. Byne v. Wise (Tex. Civ. App.), 31 S. W. 1069; Halbert v. Brown, 9 Tex. Civ. App. 335, 31 S. W. 535; Hardy v. Dunlap, 7 Tex. Civ. App. 339, 26 S. W. 852; Eddie v. Tinnin, 7 Tex. Civ. App. 371, 26 S. W. 732; Corley v. Renz (Tex. Civ. App.), 24 S. W. 935; Storer v. Lane, 1 Tex. Civ. App. 250, 20 S. W. 852; Tevis v. Collier, 84 Tex. 638, 19 S. W. 801; Norwood v. Gonzales County, 79 Tex. 218, 14 S. W. 1057; Hunton v. Nichols, 55 Tex. 217.

When female children were married and of legal age when their brother obtained a deed from the parents and took possession and set up an adverse claim to common family property, limitations ran against the female children by the removal of disability of coverture. Ryman v. Petruka (Tex. Civ. App.), 166 S. W. 711.

62. McMurray v. Dixon, 105 Va. 605, 54 S. E. 481, under Va. Code 1904, § 2918.

63. Waldron v. Harvey, 54 W. Va. 608, 46 S. E. 603, 102 Am. St. Rep. 959.

tion against her husband, when her title accrued during coverture;[64] if the husband sell or dispose of his wife's separate personal property without her consent, express or implied, her right of action is suspended during coverture only;[65] and where a husband and wife enter on land in her right, and by their joint occupation acquire title by adverse possession, limitations will not begin to run against heirs of the wife in favor of vendees of the husband until after the husband's death.[66] In Arkansas, where a husband conveys in fee land of the wife in which he has curtesy, limitations will not run against the vendee of the wife until the husband's death.[67] In Kentucky, the right of a married woman to bring suit for the recovery of land which was her separate estate and was sold by the husband, is not barred until the expiration of fifteen years after the death of her husband.[68] Under the Tennessee Code, providing that a husband and wife shall not be dispossessed of the real estate of the wife by any judgment against the husband, where a stranger has taken possession of the land of the wife, and a joint action by the husband and wife is barred by limitation, the wife can sue in her own name, and need not wait until the death of her husband to enforce her right.[69] In Louisiana, prescription does not run against the wife for purchasers of her property from her husband, though she be separated in property.[70] In Texas, limitations run against a married woman's right to recover a community homestead conveyed by her husband in direct hostility to her home-

64. Michan v. Wyatt, 21 Ala. 813.

65. Jenkins v. McConico, 26 Ala. 213.

66. McLeod v. Bishop, 110 Ala. 640, 20 So. 130.

67. Jones v. Freed, 42 Ark. 357.

Where the husband wrongfully sells the separate property of the wife, a cause of action accrues to her at the time of the sale and delivery of the property; and in a suit by her for the property, after the death of the husband, the statute of limitations will commence to run against her from the same time, unless she sets up the disability in reply. Gray v. Adams, 19 Ark. 289.

68. Stephens v. McCormick, 68 Ky. (5 Bush) 181. See also, Louisville & N. R. Co. v. Thompson, 105 Ky. 190, 20 Ky. Law Rep. 1110, 48 S. W. 990.

69. Key v. Snow, 90 Tenn. (6 Pickle) 663, 18 S. W. 251.

70. Prudhomme v. Dawson, 3 Mart. N. S. (La.) 161.

stead rights.[71] In Pennsylvania, where a husband conveyed without his wife joining in the conveyance, limitation will not run against her right until the death of her husband.[72] In South Carolina, a purchaser from the husband alone of the wife's inheritance will not be protected by the statute of limitations, as against the wife, until the statutory period has run out after the husband's death.[73]

§ 240a(7). Recovery of property purporting to have been conveyed by wife.

In Illinois, where a husband and wife executed a deed of land belonging to the wife under such circumstances that the title of the wife did not pass, but merely the husband's estate by curtesy, the statute of limitations did not run against the estate in fee remaining in the wife during the existence of the husband's life estate.[74] In Kentucky, where two of the grantors in a deed were married women, and the deed was void as to them for failure of their husbands to join therein, limitations did not run in favor of the grantee in possession of the land as against them during coverture.[75] Plaintiff's right of action for the recovery of her interest in land, which she claims by inheritance, accrues when a vendee

71. Sanders v. Word (Tex. Civ. App.), 110 S. W. 205; Hussey v. Moser, 70 Tex. 42, 7 S. W. 606. As to the disposition of exempt property of the wife, see Alsup v. Jordan, 69 Tex. 300, 6 S. W. 831, 5 Am. St. Rep. 53.

72. Culler v. Motzer, 13 Serg. & R. (Pa.) 356, 15 Am. Dec. 604.

73. Jones v. Reeves, 6 Rich. Law (S. C.) 132.

See as to the rule in other States:

Mo.—Bradley v. Missouri Pac. Ry. Co., 91 Mo. 493, 4 S. W. 427.

N. C.—Summerlin v. Cowles, 101 N. C. 473, 7 S. E. 881; Leggett v. Coffield, 58 N. C. 382.

W. Va.—Merritt v. Hughes, 36 W. Va. 356, 15 S. E. 56.

74. Higgins v. Crosby, 40 Ill. 260.

75. Furnish's Adm'r v. Lilly, 27 Ky. Law Rep. 226, 84 S. W. 734.

Where a wife, in attempting to convey her land, fails to convey title, owing to the recital in the certificate of acknowledgment that she merely releases her dower, her coverture does not prevent the running of limitations against her from the time the grantee takes possession of the land, claiming the absolute title. Brown v. Swango (Ky.), 28 S. W. 156.

to whom she has joined with her husband in conveying the title in fee simple enters into possession, claiming title, and her recovery is barred by the Kentucky statute, limiting, even to persons laboring under disability, the right to sue for recovery of real property to thirty years.[76] The Louisiana statute of limitation begins to run against an action by a widow to set aside a sale under a mortgage given by her to secure her husband's debts at the date of the dissolution of the marriage.[77] In North Carolina, where a married woman joined in a deed with her husband, but there was no privy examination of her, there was no adverse possession, as against her heir, until after the death of her husband.[78] In Pennsylvania, a married woman who with her husband is a beneficiary in a conveyance of land, and who reconveys it to the grantor, may enforce her title herself or through the trustee, the reconveyance being adjudged invalid; and she is not within the exception of the statute, extending the period of limitation in favor of persons under disability.[79] In South Carolina, where the inheritance of a married woman has been conveyed, but not in accordance with law, a suit by her to recover the land after the death of her husband will not be barred by the statute until five years after his death.[80] In Tennessee, where the husband and wife join in a conveyance of the wife's land, which is void as to the wife, she has seven years after she becomes discovert within which to bring her action;[81] and adverse possession under a registered deed of a married woman is, with or without privy examination, and disregarding infancy or coverture, a bar to any suit by the wife or those claiming through her.[82] In Texas, it has been held that where a married woman ex-

76. Bradley v. Burgess, 87 Ky. 648, 10 S. W. 5. See also, Mantle v. Beal, 82 Ky. 122; Stephens v. McCormick, 68 Ky. (5 Bush) 181; Gill v. Fauntleroy's Heirs, 47 Ky. (8 B. Mon.) 177.

77. Brownson v. Weeks, 47 La. Ann. 1042, 17 So. 489.

78. Kincaid v. Perkins, 63 N. C. 282.

79. Thompson v. Carmichael, 122 Pa. 478, 15 Atl. 867.

80. Brown v. Spand, 2 Mill, Const. (S. C.) 12.

81. King v. Nutall, 66 Tenn. (7 Baxt.) 221.

82. Shields v. Riverside Imp. Co., 90 Tenn. (6 Pickle) 633, 18 S. W. 258.

ecutes a power of attorney to her husband to convey her land, and he sells and executes a deed of such land under such power in 1872, and dies in 1889, and she does not commence an action to recover the land until more than four years after the act of 1895, which removed the exception which prevented limitations from running against married women, her action is barred by the ten-year statute of limitations, as against such purchaser and his grantees, who have had continued possession since 1872.[83] In West Virginia, where a wife owning land in fee, not her separate estate, makes a deed purporting to convey the land in fee, which deed is void because of the nonjoinder of her husband, the grantee's possession is adverse to her and her husband, and twenty years of such possession will bar her right, though she may have remained married during the whole twenty years; but she may maintain a suit during coverture to recover the land, though ten years of such possession may have elapsed.[84]

§ 240a(8). Effect of separation from husband.

In Missouri, the fact that a husband and wife are living apart under such circumstances as to constitute an abandonment of the wife by the husband, which would authorize her to sue for the possession of her real estate, does not impose an obligation on her to sue therefor, and the statute of limitations does not begin to

83. Williams v. Bradley (Tex. Civ. App.), 67 S. W. 170.

The provision deferring the running of the statute of limitations "if during coverture a sale of the lands of the wife be illegally effected," does not apply to a case where a deed is void as not having been properly acknowledged by the wife. Harris v. Wells, 85 Tex. 312, 20 S. W. 68.

84. Merritt v. Hughes, 36 W. Va. 356, 15 S. E. 56.

Where husband and wife, by a deed void as to the wife, for want of a proper certificate of her examination and acknowledgment, convey land to a purchaser, and put him in possession, such purchaser is entitled to hold that possession until the death of the husband, and the wife and her heirs, or any one claiming under them, have no right of entry until the husband's death, and right of action does not accrue to them, nor does the statute of limitations run against them, until his death. Central Land Co. v. Laidley, 32 W. Va. 134, 9 S. E. 61, 25 Am. St. Rep. 797, 3 L. R. A. 826.

run against her on that account.[85] The Kentucky statute authorizes a wife abandoned by her husband to sue and be sued only after being empowered by equity, and the three-year limitation of a married woman's right to sue to recover real property, after the disability is removed, commences to run from the date of the judgment, and not from the date of the abandonment.[86] In Louisiana, a wife's paraphernal funds having first gone into the partnership of which her husband was a member, and afterwards into the corporation of which he was and is a stockholder, and been used in its business, the indebtedness to the wife remains absolutely imprescriptable in so far as the husband is concerned, so long as the marriage exists, though she be judicially separate from him.[87] In Washington it has been held that, after the lapse of three years, a married woman, who had remained in Dakota after her husband had left to take up his residence in Washington, cannot maintain an action in Washington for the wrongful taking of her personal property in Dakota after the departure of her husband, as her residence in Dakota at the time of the taking, in matters relative to her separate property rights, was not affected by the change in the husband's residence, and as the Dakota statute limits the time of bringing such actions to three years.[88]

§ 240a(9). Effect of disability on joint action of husband and wife.

In California, where a married woman may sue without joining her husband, limitations run against her; but, where the husband is a necessary party, she is, under the Code, deemed under disability, and limitations cannot be urged.[89] In Georgia, where the husband is the only person who can legally bring suit for land, the

85. Graham v. Ketchum, 192 Mo. 15, 90 S. W. 350; Throckmorton v. Pence, 121 Mo. 50, 25 S. W. 843.

86. McDanell v. Landrum, 87 Ky. 404, 9 S. W. 223, 12 Am. St. Rep. 500.

87. *In re* Leeds & Co., 49 La. Ann. 501, 21 So. 617.

88. McCain v. Gibbons, 7 Wash. 314, 35 Pac. 64.

89. Moody v. Southern Pac. Co., 167 Cal. 786, 141 Pac. 388; Code Civ. Proc., § 352.

title to which was derived through the wife, the statute of limitations runs during the coverture.[90] In Kentucky, actions by husband and wife, as to lands granted to her during coverture, are barred by the seven-year law, though not actions by the wife after his decease.[91] In Maine, where a wife, acquiring land by inheritance, was disseised, with her husband, during coverture, they could enter at once, and hence limitation ran against them both from that time.[92] In Maryland, a *feme covert* is within the saving clause of the statute, and the plea of limitations is no bar to an action by husband and wife on an executor's bond, to recover a legacy given the wife, who was covert at the time of the probate of the will, though brought more than twelve years after the passing of the bond.[93] In North Carolina, the statute of limitations is no defense to an action by a husband and wife to recover land under a lost deed which is alleged to have conveyed to them the fee simple in the land in question, since the husband has no interest or estate separable from the wife's, and since her right cannot be barred because she is under the disability of coverture.[94] In an action in which husband and wife are plaintiffs, in Pennsylvania, for a libel on the wife, the statute of limitations cannot be pleaded during her coverture.[95] In Tennessee, if there be a disseisin during coverture, it is of the entire joint estate, and the husband and wife must jointly bring suit to recover the possession. If they neglect to sue for seven years, during which period there is an adverse possession of the land, their joint right of action will be barred.[96] In Texas, in an action against a railroad company for

90. Shipp v. Wingfield, 46 Ga. 593.

91. Neal v. Robertson, 32 Ky. (2 Dana) 86.

Where a woman was a *feme covert* before possession of her lands was taken by defendant, and has been ever since, the statute of limitations is no bar to a suit by the husband and wife. Marshall v. McQueen, 13 Ky. (3 Litt.) 468.

92. Mellus v. Snowman, 21 Me. (8 Shep.) 201.

93. Knight v. Brawner, 14 Md. 1.

94. Johnson v. Edwards, 109 N. C. 466, 14 S. E. 91, 26 Am. St. Rep. 580. See also, as to the effect of coverture: Wheeler v. Piper, 56 N. C. 249; Williams v. Lanier, 44 N. C. 30; Caldwell v. Black, 27 N. C. 463; Allen v. Gentry, 4 N. C. 411.

95. Bailey v. Reed, 14 Phila. (Pa.) 167.

96. Weisinger v. Murphy, 39 Tenn. (2 Head) 674.

personal injuries inflicted on plaintiff and his wife while travelling as passengers on defendant's road, a plea of limitations to an amended petition making the wife a party to the suit is not available, conceding that it set up a new cause of action, because pleaded against a married woman; the exception of such a woman from the operation of the statute applying in this case, as in others arising thereunder.[97]

§ 240a(10). Effect on husband of wife's disability.

The Connecticut statute of limitations does not run in favor of the husband against the claim of his wife for her separate property, placed by her in his hands to manage, invest, and account for.[98] In Missouri, where the right to the possession of the separate estate of the wife is vested in the husband, limitations will begin to run against him from the accrual of the right, in spite of the disability of the wife to sue, and though his interest is not liable for his sole debts, and his wife's joinder in a conveyance of the land is necessary.[99] In New York, where defendant and wife, at the time residing in France, agreed in a marriage contract to mortgage a certain estate, situated in New York, as security for their daughter's dowry, the statute of limitations did not run against an action on the agreement during the coverture of the daughter.[1] In Pennsylvania, since a husband cannot maintain an action against

Where a husband and wife joined in an action for personal injuries to the wife, the cause of action being barred unless the wife's coverture saved her right to sue, the action being essentially that of the wife, as recognized by the statute, and the husband being a mere formal party, her coverture suspended the bar of the statute, though on the recovery of judgment the husband might reduce it to possession subject to the wife's equity. Thompson v. Cincinnati, etc., Ry. Co., 109 Tenn. 268, 70 S. W. 612.

97. Texas & P. Ry. Co. v. Gwaltney, 2 Willson Civ. Cas. Ct. App. (Tex.) 684.

A suit by a husband and wife on a note was held barred by the statute of limitations, as the wife's disability did not prevent the joint action. Wells v. Cockrum, 13 Tex. 127.

98. Appeal of Comstock, 55 Conn. 214, 10 Atl. 559.

99. Arnold v. Willis, 128 Mo. 145, 30 S. W. 517.

1. De Pierres v. Thorn, 17 N. Y. Super. Ct. (4 Bosw.) 266.

his wife, limitations do not begin to run against a claim by him against her until after her death.[2]

§ 240a(11). Effect on husband's right to wife's property.

In Georgia, the husband may sue for his minor wife's land at any time within three years after her becoming of age.[3] In Kentucky, a husband in right of his wife, or in his own right, may collect money due his wife on final settlement by an administrator of her former husband, and the coverture does not prevent the running of the statute.[4] In Mississippi, choses in action of the wife, accruing during coverture, vest immediately in the husband the right to sue for them, and therefore the statute then begins to run, notwithstanding the coverture.[5] In Missouri, the right of a husband to the possession of his wife's real estate, prior to the Act of 1889, giving her a right to sue for the possession of her realty, was a right against which limitations ran.[6] In Ohio, a husband and wife, barred by the statute of limitations from recovering the wife's land in an action for ejectment after twenty-one years' adverse enjoyment, are not helped by the statute relating to the interest of husbands in the estates of their wives.[7]

§ 240a(12). Effect on wife's heirs of surviving husband's interest.

Where a husband made partition of his wife's land, the running of the statute of limitations against her heirs, as to the lands not partitioned to her, did not begin at the date of her death, but was suspended during the continuance of the husband's estate by the curtesy.[8] In Arkansas, the statute of limitations does not com-

2. *In re* Gracie's Estate (Orph. Ct.), 24 Pittsb. Leg. J. (N. S.) 9; Appeal of Union Trust Co., Id., affirmed 158 Pa. 521, 27 Atl. 1083.

3. Bush v. Lindsey, 14 Ga. 687.

4. Hargis v. Sewell's Adm'r, 87 Ky. 63, 7 S. W. 557.

5. Cook v. Lindsey, 34 Miss. 451.

6. Vanata v. Johnson, 170 Mo. 269, 70 S. W. 687. See also, Glasgow v. Missouri Car & Foundry Co., 229 Mo. 585, 129 S. W. 900.

7. Thompson's Heirs' Lessee v. Green, 4 Ohio St. 216.

8. Seawell v. Berry, 55 Fed. 731. See also, Beattie v. Wilkinson, 36 Fed. 646.

mence to run against the heirs of a deceased wife, as against a husband, having an estate by curtesy, who sells the entire estate, until the termination of the curtesy.[9] In Connecticut, the statute of limitations regarding lands does not commence running until after the right of entry accrues. Hence, where a married woman dies seized of land, the statute of limitations does not begin to run against her heirs till the death of her husband, who was tenant by curtesy.[10] In Kentucky, limitation does not commence to run against the heirs of the wife, as to her realty, until the death of the husband, who is tenant by curtesy.[11] In Missouri, as against the heir of a married woman, whose husband survives her and is entitled to an estate in her lands as tenant by the curtesy, the statute of limitations runs from the expiration of his estate, and not from her death.[12] In New York, the statute of limitations cannot be set up in bar to a recovery against the grandchildren of a person dying seised, against whom there was no adverse possession, where, at his death, the mother of the lessors, through whom the estate descended to them, was under coverture, against whom the statute had not begun to run, and the action is brought within ten years after the decease of their father, the tenant by the custesy.[13] In North Carolina, where a married woman joined in a deed with her husband, but there was no privy examination of her, there was no adverse possession as against her heir, until after the death of her husband.[14] In Ohio, heirs of a wife are not entitled to bring an action to recover her land, which her husband

9. Banks v. Green, 35 Ark. 84.

10. Clark v. Vaughan, 3 Conn. 191.

11. Meraman's Heirs v. Caldwell's Heirs, 47 Ky. (8 B. Mon.) 32, 46 Am. Dec. 537; Butler v. McMillan, 88 Ky. 414, 11 S. W. 362. See also, Gudgell Tydings (Ky.), 10 S. W. 466; Baseman's Heirs v. Batterton, 31 Ky. (1 Dana) 432.

12. Dyer v. Brannock, 66 Mo. 391, 27 Am. Rep. 359; Dyer v. Wittler, 89 Mo. 81, 14 S. W. 518, 58 Am. Rep. 85, overruling Valle v. Obenhause, 62 Mo. 81; Smith v. Patterson, 95 Mo. 525, 8 S. W. 567.

13. Moore v. Jackson, 4 Wend. (N. Y.) 58.

14. Kincaid v. Perkins, 63 N. C. 282. Decedent having been seised of land during coverture, her husband's estate by the curtesy for his life suspended limitations as a bar to her heirs during its continuance. Hill v. Lane, 149 N. C. 267, 62 S. E. 1074.

had conveyed without her joining, until after the death of the husband, surviving his wife.[15] In Pennsylvania, where the husband dies in possession of land in right of his wife, an action then accrues to her heirs, and the statute of limitations does not begin to run until then.[16] In Tennessee, where the husband acquired land in the right of his wife, and conveyed the same by deed, and delivered the possession thereof, the wife not uniting in the conveyance, the statute of limitations did not commence to run against the heirs of the wife until the death of the husband.[17]

§ 241. Imprisonment.

Under the statute of James, the disability arising from imprisonment relates to a restraint of one's liberty under process or color of law, or an involuntary restraint that prevents the person from fully availing himself of the remedies provided for the enforcement of his legal rights. Thus, in this country it has been held that a person held in slavery is imprisoned, within the meaning of the term as used in these statutes,[18] and that the disability does not cease until he is emancipated.[19] In New York, the saving is restricted to persons imprisoned on a criminal charge, or in execution under the sentence of a criminal court for a term less than life; and the provision is the same in Wisconsin, Missouri, California, Oregon, Minnesota, Nevada, North Carolina, South Carolina, Arizona, Dakota, Idaho, Montana and Utah; while in Maine, Vermont, Massachusetts, Rhode Island, Alabama, Colorado, Florida, Georgia, Ohio, Pennsylvania, Maryland, Nebraska, Texas, and Wyoming this disability applies to any person

15. Cracraft v. Roach, 5 Ohio Dec. 467. See also, Koltenbrock v. Cracraft, 36 Ohio St. 584.

16. Ege v. Medlar, 82 Pa. 86; Shallenberger v. Ashworth, 25 Pa. (1 Casey) 152; Marple v. Myers, 12 Pa. (2 Jones) 122.

17. Royston v. Wear, 40 Tenn. (3 Head) 8.

18. Matilda v. Crenshaw, 12 Tenn. (4 Yerg.) 299; Berry v. Berry's Adm'r, 22 S. W. 654, 15 Ky. Law Rep. 865. See also, Downs v. Allen, 78 Tenn. (10 Lea) 652; Ponder v. Cox, 26 Ga. 485.

19. Price v. Slaughter, 1 Cin. R. (Ohio) 429. See also, Moore's Lessee v. Armstrong, 10 Ohio 11, 36 Am. Dec. 63; 72, n., as to the general rule stated in the text.

"imprisoned," and therefore applies in all those instances to which the statute of James applied, and embraces persons imprisoned upon civil as well as criminal processes, or deprived of their liberty by any process of law or statute. In Illinois, in order to be within the saving of the statute, the person must be imprisoned upon a criminal charge; in Michigan, in the State prison; and in Arkansas, imprisoned "beyond the limits of the State." In Connecticut, New Hampshire, Iowa, Kansas, New Jersey, Kentucky, Mississippi, Tennessee, Delaware, Virginia, West Virginia, and New Mexico, imprisonment is not recognized as constituting a disability, and no saving exists in favor of persons restrained of their liberty.[20]

In those States in which imprisonment constitutes a disability, the circumstance that the plaintiff might have commenced an action upon a claim existing at that time, but did not, does not deprive him of the saving of the statute,[21] as it is well settled that the statute does not prevent a person under a disability from suing if he elects to do so;[22] nor is he obliged to sue simply because he can; nor even if he should bring an action while the disability existed, and failed in it upon technical grounds, would he be deprived of the saving of the statute when the disability is removed.

In Texas it has been held that one is "a person in prison," within the statute, stopping the running of the statute as to such

20. As to what constitutes imprisonment, see State v. Calhoun, 50 Kan. 523, 32 Pac. 38, 34 Am. St. Rep. 141, 18 L. R. A. 838, holding that the phrase "under legal disability" includes a person imprisoned; Wood v. Ward, Fed. Cas. No. 17,965.

It has been held in Massachusetts that the statute of limitations begins and continues to run while the debtor is within the commonwealth, although brought here under a warrant for crime, and then imprisoned here. Turner v. Shearer, 72 Mass. (6 Gray) 427.

Under the Michigan statute of 1897, § 9733, postponing limitations while plaintiff is in the State prison, it has been held that the London, Ontario Insane Asylum is not the State prison contemplated by the statute. Alexander v. Thompson, 195 Fed. 31.

21. Piggott v. Rush, 4 Ad. & El. 912.

22. Chandler v. Villett, 2 Saund. 117k, 120.

person, when the sheriff after arresting him wrongfully moves him before his broken leg is in proper condition, and while he is confined in jail awaiting trial, and while he is absent from the jail as an attached witness, in the custody of the sheriff.[23]

§ 242. Alien enemy.

In Maine, Vermont, Massachusetts, New York, North Carolina, Kentucky, Missouri, South Carolina, Michigan, Wisconsin, California, Oregon, Minnesota, Alabama, Nevada, Arizona, Dakota, Idaho, and Utah, the statutes contain an exception in favor of a person who is a citizen of a country at war with the United States, providing that during the continuance of such hostilities the statute shall be suspended and not considered as a part of the period limited for the commencement of an action. In Nevada, it is provided, however, that a citizen of a State in rebellion against the United States government shall not be treated as an alien. None of the statutes of the other States contain this exception, and consequently in none of the other States is there any saving in favor of an alien enemy.[24]

§ 242a(1). Disability intervening after accrual of cause of action. In general.

After the statute of limitations has commenced to run, no subsequent disability will interrupt it.[25] The rule is universal, with

23. Lasater v. Waites (Tex. Civ. App.), 67 S. W. 518, judgment rev'd Lasater v. Waits, 95 Tex. 553, 68 S. W. 500.

24. By the strict rule of the common law, where the statute makes no exception, the courts can make none. Amy v. Watertown, 130 U. S. 320, 9 Sup. Ct. 537, 32 L. Ed. 953. But a disability "happening by an inevitable necessity" is now recognized as constituting an exception to the statute of limitations, though not specified therein, though this is not allowed to extend beyond necessity arising from war or death. 130 U. S. 326; Murray v. Chicago & N. W. Ry. Co., 92 Fed. Rep. 868, 871, 35 C. C. A. 62; Hill v. Phillips, 14 R. I. 93. See *supra*, § 6, n. 4.

25. *D. C.*—Gibson v. Ruff, 8 App. D. C. 262.

Ky.—Loyd v. Loyd's Adm'r, 20 Ky. Law Rep. 347, 46 S. W. 485.

W. Va.—Mynes v. Mynes, 47 W. Va. 681, 35 S. E. 935.

the exceptions provided in the statute itself, and certain cases where the statute is suspended when it becomes impossible under the law for plaintiff to begin his action, that, when the period of limitation has once begun to run, it cannot be postponed, suspended, or interrupted by any subsequent condition.[26] Limitation, having begun to run against the ancestor, continues to run against the heir under disability.[27] Any disability of heirs to whom title to land descends after commencement of adverse possession against the ancestor does not extend their time for bringing ejectment therefor beyond the twenty years limited to the ancestor.[28] Where a right of action for the possession of land held adversely accrues while the holder of the legal title is a resident of the county, in the absence of a statutory provision therefor, the running of limitations is not arrested by any intervening disabilities of the parties.[29] Where adverse possession starts before plaintiff's predecessor secures title that such predecessor wills the property as a life estate to claimant's mother, with the remainder in fee to claimant, does not postpone the running of the statute in favor of the one holding by adverse possession during the existence of the life estate.[30] After limitation has begun to run against a note, it continues to run, though the note is transferred to one under disability.[31] The loss of the ability of the creditor to sue a municipal corporation by reason of the repeal of its charter suspends the operation of the statute of limitations until its successor, organized under a new charter, takes benefits from the property of the old corporation.[32]

26. Congregational Church Bldg. Soc. v. Osborn, 153 Cal. 197, 94 Pac. 881.

27. Loyd v. Loyd's Adm'r, *supra;* Doty v. Jameson, 29 Ky. Law Rep. 507, 93 S. W. 638; Shaffer v. Detie, 191 Mo. 377, 90 S. W. 131.

28. Messinger v. Foster, 115 App. Div. 689, 101 N. Y. Supp. 387.

29. Milton v. Pace, 85 S. C. 373, 67 S. E. 458.

30. Roe v. Doe *ex dem.* Rowe, 159 Ala. 614, 48 So. 1033.

31. Meyer v. Christopher, 176 Mo. 580, 75 S. W. 750.

32. Broadfoot v. City of Fayetteville, 124 N. C. 478, 32 S. E. 804, 70 Am. St. Rep. 610.

§ 242a(2). Infancy.

A statute of limitations having begun to run against one is not interrupted by the succession of a minor to his right.[33] The fact that certain plaintiffs, in an action to quiet title, or in an action to redeem from a mortgage foreclosure sale, are minors, who claim title through descent, does not toll the statute of limitations, where it had commenced to run during the lifetime of their ancestor.[34] Where limitations against the recovery of real property commenced running in a person's lifetime, the running of the statute was not suspended after his death during the infancy of such person's heir.[35] Where the mother of infant complainants, under whom they claimed as heirs in an action to recover land held adversely, did not die until after the statute of limitations had commenced to run, the statute was not arrested by the provision excepting infants from the operation of the statute; and hence, where no action was brought to recover the property until after the bar of the statute had become complete, the infant's right was barred.[36] Where infancy exists when a cause of action accrues, the time for commencing the action is extended for a certain period after the infant becomes of age; but, if the statute has already begun to run against the ancestor, it is not interrupted by his death and the supervening disability of his infant heirs, in the absence of provisions to the contrary.[37] Where limitations began to run against an administrator by reason of adverse possession of land, a pos-

33. Munroe v. Wilson, 68 N. H. 580, 41 Atl. 240; Wilson v. Harper, 25 W. Va. 179.

34. McNeill v. Schumaker, 94 Neb. 544, 143 N. W. 845; Lyons v. Carr, 77 Neb. 883, 110 N. W. 705.

35. Fore v. Berry, 94 S. C. 71, 78 S. E. 706; Satcher v. Grice, 53 S. C. 126, 31 S. E. 3.

36. Dawson v. Edwards, 189 Ill. 60, 59 N. E. 590.

37. Scallon v. Manhattan Ry. Co., 185 N. Y. 359, 78 N. E. 284, rev'g judg. 112 App. Div. 262, 98 N. Y. Supp. 272, under Code Civ. Proc., §§ 375 and 408.

Under Code Civ. Proc., § 375, providing that, if a person who might sue to recover real property or defend an action brought against him for that purpose is, when his title descends, within the age of 21 years, the time of such disability is not a part of the time limited for commencing the action, the fact that the statute has commenced to run against the mother at the time of her death, and devolution of her title on her

thumous heir of the intestate, born after the administrator's appointment, could not avail himself of the disability of infancy to stop the running of the statute.[38] The running of the statute against the right of action of a married woman is not interrupted by her death, where her infant child takes only such right of action as she had.[39] The running of limitations against a person is not interrupted by his death, but continues to run against his heirs, though they be infants, the heirs in such instance not being within the saving clause of West Virginia Code 1906, c. 104, § 3.[40]

§ 242a(3). Coverture.

As stated in a previous section, when the statute of limitations has once begun to run, it is not interrupted by the subsequent disability of coverture.[41] Coverture does not stop the running of limitations against a married woman taking a note after maturity.[42] Limitations having begun to run against a trustee or an undisclosed agent acting as a principal, are not suspended by the subsequent coming forward of a married woman as *cestui que trust* or as the undisclosed principal.[43] Under Kentucky Statutes, § 2525, the running of limitations on a cause of action for fraud is not interrupted by plaintiff's marriage after the accrual of the right of action.[44] Where a wife paid

then infant child, does not affect the right of the child to assert her disability of infancy as a ground for the suspension of the statute. Mills v. Thompkins, 95 N. Y. Supp. 962, 47 Misc. Rep. 455, judgment rev'd Mills v. Tompkins, 97 N. Y. Supp. 9, 110 App. Div. 212. See also, Meiggs v. Hoagland, 74 N. Y. Supp. 234, 68 App. Div. 182.

38. Jenkins v. Jensen, 24 Utah 108, 66 Pac. 773, 91 Am. St. Rep. 783.

39. Patton v. Dixon, 105 Tenn. 97, 58 S. W. 299.

40. Pickens v. Stout, 67 W. Va. 422, 68 S. E. 354. See also, Talbott v. Woodford, 48 W. Va. 449, 37 S. E. 580.

41. See § 240, *supra*. State v. Macy, 72 Mo. App. 427. Where the act of limitations begins to run against a *feme sole*, her marrying will not suspend its operation. Anonymous, 2 N. C. 416.

42. Causey v. Snow, 122 N. C. 326, 29 S. E. 359; Graves v. Howard, 159 N. C. 594, 75 S. C. 998.

43. Barden v. Stickney, 132 N. C. 416, 43 S. E. 912, rehearing, 130 N. C. 62, 40 S. E. 842, denied.

44. Fox v. Hudson's Ex'x, 150 Ky. 115, 150 S. W. 49.

a mortgage on the homestead, which her husband had assumed, in order to prevent foreclosure, without intending to relinquish her right to repayment, the statute of limitations having already begun to run against the mortgagee's right to foreclose, it was not suspended as to her right of subrogation because of her coverture, but was barred in twenty years after the mortgagee's right to foreclose accrued, as provided by statute.[45] Though Mills' Ann. St. Colo., § 2941, provides that, where the person to whom a cause of action on notes accrues is a married woman, the statute of limitations does not run until the disability of coverture is removed, the subsequent marriage of a woman who was single when her right to sue on notes accrued does not prevent the running of the statute; and hence, under Wyo. Rev. St., § 3464, providing that a cause of action is barred in this state if barred in the state where it arose, plaintiff, after the time limited by the Colorado statute, cannot maintain an action on a note executed to decedent, when the cause arose in Colorado while decedent was single, though she married before the action was barred.[46]

§ 242a(4). Insanity.

The provision suspending, in favor of idiots, lunatics, insane persons, and persons beyond seas, the operation of the six-year statute of limitations in respect to claims cognizable in the court of claims, is restricted to persons laboring under such disabilities at the time their claims accrued, and cannot be invoked by one whose disabilities subsequently arose.[47] Where the statute of limitations

The object of the statute of limitations of 1814, containing distinct provisions in favor of infants and *femes covert*, was to give increased efficacy to an adverse possession, and diminish the savings in the Act of 1796; but it gives no protection to the *feme covert* unless she derived her title by descent or devise during coverture. Boyce's Heirs v. Dudley, 47 Ky. (8 B. Mon.) 511.

45. Charmley v. Charmley, 125 Wis. 297, 103 N. W. 1106, 110 Am. St. Rep. 827.

46. Bliler v. Boswell, 9 Wyo. 57, 61 Pac. 867, 59 Pac. 798.

47. De Arnaud v. United States, 151 U. S. 483, 14 Sup. Ct. 374, 38 L. Ed. 244; Oliver v. Pullam, 24 Fed. 127.

has begun to run, subsequent insanity will not interrupt it.[48] Iowa Code, § 3453, providing that the times limited for actions shall be extended in favor of insane persons, so that they shall have a year after termination of disability, applies only where plaintiff is insane when the cause of action accrues, and not where he becomes insane a few hours after the injury for which he sues, though on the same day, and as a result of the injury.[49] A statute providing that, if a person entitled to bring a certain suit "is, at the time the cause of action accrued" under certain disabilities, as insanity, "the time of such disability is not a part of the time limited for the commencement of the action," refers only to disability existing at the time the cause of action accrued.[50]

§ 243. Injunction.

Except in those States where a saving is expressly made in favor of parties, where the commencement of an action is enjoined, the fact that an injunction has been procured preventing the bringing of an action upon a certain claim does not save it from the operation of the statute; nor can a court of equity make any order which will prevent the running of the statute during such period, but the remedy of the party is through an application to the court for an injunction to restrain the party from pleading the statute.[51] But in Vermont, New York, Arkansas, Iowa, Illinois, Kentucky, Missouri, Minnesota, North Caro-

48. Calumet Electric St. Ry. Co. v. Mabie, 66 Ill. App. 235. See also, Hale's Heirs v. Ritchie, 142 Ky. 424, 134 S. W. 474; McCutchen v. Currier, 94 Me. 362, 47 Atl. 923.

49. Roelefsen v. City of Pella, 121 Iowa 153, 96 N. W. 738.

Where the holder of a matured note became insane within the statutory period, his guardian was not entitled to maintain suit thereon more than 10 years after the note matured, since section 3453 applies only to actions accruing during disability. Black v. Ross, 110 Iowa 112, 81 N. W. 229.

50. Kelly v. Gallup, 67 Minn. 169, 69 N. W. 812.

51. Barker v. Millard, 16 Wend. (N. Y.) 572; Robertson v. Alford, 21 Miss. (13 Smedes & M.) 509; Ingraham v. Regan, 23 Miss. 213; Rice's Heirs v. Lowan, 5 Ky. (2 Bibb) 149; Doughty v. Doughty, 10 N. J. Eq. 347. In Dekay v. Darrah, 14 N. J. L. 288, it was held that, while the

lina, and South Carolina, it is provided that, when the commencement of an action is enjoined, the time during which the injunction "is in force" shall not be deemed a part of the time limited for the commencement of the action. In Alabama, California, Oregon, Wisconsin, Nevada, Arizona, North Dakota, South Dakota, Idaho, Montana, and Utah, the same exception is made not only where the commencement of an action is prevented by injunction, but also where it is prevented by any statutory prohibition. In Mississippi, the same provision is made where the commencement of an action is prohibited by law, or restrained or enjoined by the order, decree, or process of any court of the State. In Michigan, no exception is made where an action is enjoined, but it is provided that the time during which any case in chancery, commenced by any debtor, has or may be pending and undetermined, shall not be computed as constituting any part of the time limited, as to the particular debt or subject-matter of such proceeding in chancery.

It will be noticed by the language of these statutes that the suspension only exists while the injunction is in force, therefore the circumstance that an application has been made for an injunction, and is pending, will not save the statute, whether the in-

circumstances that the bringing of an action has been enjoined will not save the statute as to the claim involved, yet that a court of equity under such circumstances may enjoin a party from setting up the statute in bar of the action. In Van Wagonen v. Terpenning, 122 N. Y. 222, 25 N. E. 254, 46 Hun 423, it was held that an injunction order will not be construed to restrain acts beneficial or not injurious to the rights of the party in whose behalf it was obtained, unless its words clearly have that important effect; and that the injunction does not stay the commencement of the action, as it did not deny to plaintiff the right to protect his possession of the property against the acts of others, and so it did not, under the Code, suspend the operation of the statute. Fincke v. Funke, 25 Hun 616; Stubbs v. Ripley, 39 Hun 626; McQueen v. Babcock, 41 Barb. 337; 3 Keys 428; 3 Abb. App. Dec. 129, distinguished. In Brehm v. City of New York, 104 N. Y. 186, 10 N. E. 158, where the plaintiff was prohibited from bringing suit until after the lapse of thirty days from the presentation of the claim, the running of the statute was held suspended during the thirty days. See Dickinson v. Mayor, etc., 92 N. Y. 584.

junction is or is not subsequently granted; and if the statute runs upon a claim while a petition for an injunction is pending, but before it is granted or denied, the claim is barred, as the suspension exists only while an injunction is actually in force.[52]

§ 244. Absence of defendant from state, statutory provisions as to.

In several of the States the statute contains a provision that if at the time a cause of action accrues against a person he shall be out of the State, the action may be commenced within the time limited after he comes into the State, and that if after a right of action has accrued against a person he shall be absent from and reside out of the State, the time of his absence shall not be taken as any part of the time limited for the commencement of the action. This is substantially the provision existing in the statutes of Maine, Vermont, New Hampshire,[53] Massachusetts,[54] Rhode

52. That a resident in one State may there be enjoined from inequitably relying in another State upon a foreign statute of limitations, see Eingartner v. Illinois Steel Co., 94 Wis. 70, 68 N. W. 664, 34 L. R. A. 503, 59 Am. St. Rep. 859, 879, 885, n. And generally, as to enjoining a party from setting up the statute in defense in cases of fraud and concealment, see Holloway v. Appleget, 55 N. J. Eq. 583, 40 Atl. 27, 62 Am. St. Rep. 827; 12 Harvard L. Rev. 220. As to enjoining reliance upon a confession of judgment when the original debt is barred by limitation, see Cheek v. Taylor, 22 Ga. 127; Brown v. Parker, 28 Wis. 21; Lockhart v. Fessenich, 58 Wis. 588, 17 N. W. 302; Harner v. Price, 17 W. Va. 523; Shriver v. Garrison, 30 W. Va. 456, 4 S. E. 660.

53. In New Hampshire, the statutory provision is: "If the defendant in a personal action was absent from and residing out of the State at the time the cause of action accrued, or afterward, the time of such absence shall be excluded in computing the time," etc. Public Stats. (1900), ch. 217, § 8. In Vermont, Vt. Stats. 1906, §§ 1563 (1211), in addition to the provisions stated in the text, after the words "is absent from and resides out of the state," the provision, "and has no known property within the State which can by the common process of law be attached, the time of his absence shall not be taken as part of the time limited for the commencement of the action;" and substantially the same provision exists in Rhode Island. General Laws (1909), ch. 234, § 5.

54. Under Mass. Pub. Stats. c. 197, § 11, in computing the period of limitation, the time of the debtor's absence from the State is not excluded

Island, Florida, Missouri, Minnesota, South Carolina,[55] California, Michigan,[56] Nevada, Tennessee, Arizona, Dakota, Idaho, Montana, Utah, New York, [57] and Mississippi as to the second clause only,[58] and Texas as to the first clause only. In New Jersey, the provision is substantially the same, but does not apply in all actions.[59] In Alabama, the exception is, "when any person is absent from the State during the period within which a suit might have been brought," such period is not to be computed;[60] and substantially the same provision exists in Connecticut.[61] In Delaware, the provision is the same as in Vermont, except that if at the time when the cause of action accrues the defendant is out of the State, action

unless it is of such a character as to work a change of his domicil. Slocum v. Riley, 145 Mass. 370, 14 N. E. 174, Whitton v. Wass, 109 Mass. 40.

55. See Maccaw v. Crawley (S. C.), 37 S. E. 934.

56. In Michigan, the exception in 3 Comp. Laws, 1897, § 9736, as to commencing personal actions, when the defendant is absent from the State, applies by analogy to the limitation of ten years prescribed by section 9751 on a judgment creditor as to enforcing the judgment. Newlove v. Pennock, 123 Mich. 260, 82 N. W. 54.

57. In New York, section 401 of the Code was amended in 1888 by providing that if, after a cause of action has accrued against a person, he departs from and resides without the State, and remains continuously absent therefrom for the space of one year or more, the time of his absence is not to be counted as part of the time limited for the commencement of the action. Under this provision it is held that both non-residence and continuous absence for a year must concur in order to stop the running of the statute. Hart v. Kip, 148 N. Y. 306, 42 N. E. 712; Costello v. Downer, 19 App. Div. 434, 46 N. Y. Supp. 713; Connecticut Trust, etc., Co. v. Wead, 69 N. Y. Supp. 518, 58 App. Div. 493. See Palmer v. Bennett, 83 Hun 220, 31 N. Y. Supp. 567, 1 N. Y. Ann. Cases, 208, and n., aff'd 152 N. Y. 621, 46 N. E. 1150.

In this State, however, the second clause of the statute, section 401, is extended to cases where, after the cause of action has accrued, the defendant "remains continuously therefrom (the State) for the space of one year or more." Bliss's Ann. Code (4th Ed.), § 401. In Arizona, see Rev. Stats. (1887) § 2324.

58. In this State the language of the statute is, "If, after any cause of action has accrued in this State," the defendant "be absent from and reside out of the State." Code (1892), § 2748.

59. 3 New Jersey Comp. Stats. 1911, p. 3166, § 8.

60. Alabama Civil Code, 1907, § 4844.

61. Connecticut Gen. Stats. 1902, § 1125.

may be commenced within the time limited therefor "after such person shall come into the State in such manner that, by reasonable diligence, he may be served with process.[62] In Georgia, if the defendant removes from the State before the statute has run, "the time of his absence from the State, and until he returns to reside," is not counted.[63] In Indiana, the time during which the defendant is "a nonresident of the State or absent on public business" is not counted; but if he resides in another State until by the laws thereof the statute has run, he may set up the bar to any cause of action which did not arise in Indiana.[64] In Iowa, the time during which a person is a nonresident is not computed.[65] In Illinois, if the defendant is absent from the State when the cause of action accrues, the action may be brought within the time limited "after his coming into or return to the State;" and if after the cause of action accrues, he departs from and resides out of the State, the time of his absence is not to be counted;[66] but this section does not apply when, at the time the cause of action accrued or shall accrue, neither the party against nor in favor of whom the same accrued or shall accrue were or are residents of the State.[67] In Kentucky,[68] if, when a cause of action accrues against a resident of the State, he is absent therefrom, the period of limitation is computed from his return to the State, and when a resident of the State at the time when a cause of action accrues against him, "by departing therefrom, or by absconding or concealing himself, or by any other indirect means obstructs the prosecution of the action," the time of such absence or obstruction is not computed as any part of the period within which the

62. Delaware Amended Code (1893), p. 889, § 14.

63. 1 Georgia Code, 1911, §§ 4378 (2783).

64. 1 Indiana Stats. 1914, §§ 299 (298).

65. Iowa Ann. Code (1897), § 3451.

66. Illinois Rev. Stats. 1912, Vol. 4, Par. 7213, ch. 83, § 18.

67. Living in another State for a sufficient time to there bar the action is not a defense when sued on returning home. Wooley v. Yarnell, 142 Ill. 442, 32 N. E. 891.

68. Kentucky Stats. (1909, by Carroll), §§ 2531, 2532.

action may be commenced. In Kansas, if when a cause of action accrues against a person he is out of the State, or has absconded or concealed himself, the statute does not begin to run "until he comes into the State, or while he is so absconded or concealed;" and if he leaves the State, or absconds or conceals himself, after the cause of action accrues, the time of his absence or concealment is not computed;[69] and this is substantially the provision in Ohio.[70] In Oregon, the provision is virtually the same, except that it does not expressly apply to absconding debtors.[71] In Nebraska, the provision is the same as in Kansas;[72] so, also, substantially in Wyoming.[73] In North Carolina, the provision is substantially the same as in New York, except that it expressly applies to "judgments rendered or docketed," and provides for their enforcement after the debtor's return to the State.[74] In Maryland,[75] by section 4 of the statute, "no person absenting himself from this State, or that shall remove from county to county after any debt contracted, whereby the creditor may be at an uncertainty of finding out such person or his effects, shall have any benefit of any limitation herein contained; but nothing contained in this section shall debar any person from removing himself or family from one county to another for his convenience, or shall deprive any person leaving this State, for the time herein limited, of the benefit thereof, he leaving effects sufficient and known for the payment of his just debts in the hands of some person who will assume the payment thereof to his creditors." And by section 5 "if any person liable to any action shall be absent out of the State at the time when the cause of action may arise or accrue against him, he shall have no benefit of the limitation herein contained, if the person who has the cause of action

69. Kansas Gen. Stats. (1909, § 5613 (4265).

70. 2 Ohio Stats. (1910, by Page & Adams), 1123.

71. 1 Oregon Laws (1910, by Lord), § 16.

72. Nebraska Rev. Stats. § 7577.

73. Wyoming Comp. Stats. 1910, §§ 4307 (3463).

74. North Carolina Code, 1908, § 366 (162).

75. 2 Md. Ann. Civ. Code, 1911, art. 57.

shall commence the same after the presence in this State of the person liable thereto within the terms herein limited." In Wisconsin, the provision is the same as in Michigan, except that when the defendant is out of the State when the cause of action accrues the statute does not begin to run until he returns or removes to the State.[76] In Virginia, "where any right shall accrue against a person who by departing without this State, or by absconding or concealing himself, or by continuing to reside without this State, or by any other indirect ways or means shall obstruct the prosecution of such right, the time that such obstruction may have continued shall not be computed as any part of the time within which the said right might or ought to have been prosecuted. But this section shall not avail against any other person than him so obstructed, notwithstanding another might have been jointly sued with him, if there had been no such obstruction. And upon a contract which was made and was to be performed in another State or country, by a person who then resided therein no action shall be maintained after the right of action thereon is barred by the laws of such State or country;"[77] and a similar provision exists in West Virginia.[78] In New Mexico, if a defendant removes from the Territory after a cause of action accrues, the time he is so a nonresident is not computed.[79] In Louisiana, Pennsylvania, and Colorado, no saving exists because of the defendant's absence from the State.

76. 2 Wisconsin Stats. (1913, by Nash & Belitz), ch. 177, § 4231.

See Amy v. Watertown, 130 U. S. 320, 326, 9 Sup. Ct. 537, 32 L. Ed. 953.

77. Virginia Code (1904, Pollard), § 2933.

78. West Virginia Ann. Code (1913, by Hogg), § 4431, ch. 104, § 18.

See Fisher's Ex'rs v. Hartley, 48 W. Va. 339, 37 S. E. 578, 86 Am. St. Rep. 39, 54 L. R. A. 215.

79. New Mexico Comp. Laws (1897), § 2921.

As to what constitutes an absence from this state, see the following cases:

Iowa.—Jenks v. Shaw, 99 Iowa 604, 68 N. W. 900, 61 Am. St. Rep. 256.

Md.—Mason, Chapin & Co. v. Union Mills Co., 81 Md. 446, 32 Atl. 311, 29 L. R. A. 273.

Mass.—Converse v. Johnson, 146 Mass. 20, 14 N. E. 925.

Minn.—Kerwin v. Sabin, 50 Minn.

§ 245. What constitutes an absence from the state.

Under the statute of Maine, and the other States whose statutes accord therewith, it is an important question whether a mere temporary absence of the defendant when the right of action accrued, as, for a day or week, constitutes such an absence as prevents the statute from attaching in his favor; and it may be said that even in such a case the statute does not begin to run until his return to the State, unless the circumstances existing during the period of such temporary absence were such that the service of legal process against him could have been made so that the plaintiff could obtain a judgment against him personally.[80] The evident purpose of this clause of the statute is to insure to a plaintiff the full statutory period within which to commence his action against a defendant; and if he is temporarily absent from the State when the right of action accrues, so that process cannot at that time be served upon him, so that the plaintiff cannot obtain a personal judgment against him, the saving clearly applies in favor of the plaintiff; and this construction is strengthened by the language of the succeeding clause in the same section, which provides that if, after a right of action has accrued against a person, "he shall be absent from and reside out of the State," the time of such absence shall not be taken as any part of the time limited for the commencement of an action; thus

320, 52 N. W. 642, 36 Am. St. Rep. 645, 17 L. R. A. 225 and n.

Neb.—Omaha & F. Land & Trust Co. v. Parker, 33 Neb. 775, 51 N. W. 139, 29 Am. St. Rep. 506.

Ohio.—Powell v. Koehler, 52 Ohio St. 103, 39 N. E. 195, 49 Am. St. Rep. 705, 26 L. R. A. 480, 40 Cent. L. J. 187 and n.; Stanley v. Stanley, 47 Ohio St. 225, 24 N. E. 493, 21 Am. St. Rep. 806, 8 L. R. A. 333 and n.

Pa.—Bates v. Cullum, 177 Pa. 633, 35 Atl. 861, 55 Am. St. Rep. 753, 34 L. R. A. 440.

S. C.—Latimer v. Trowbridge, 52 S. C. 193, 29 S. E. 634, 68 Am. St. Rep. 893.

Tenn.—Turcott v. Yazoo & M. V. R. Co., 101 Tenn. 102, 45 S. W. 1067, 40 L. R. A. 768, 70 Am. St. Rep. 661.

Tex.—Wilson v. Daggett, 88 Tex. 375, 31 S. W. 618, 53 Am. St. Rep. 766.

80. Palmer v. Shaw, 16 Cal. 93; Vanlandingham v. Huston, 9 Ill. 125; Chenot v. Lefevre, 8 Ill. 637; Penley v. Waterhouse, 1 Iowa 498; Ward v. Cole, 32 N. H. 452, 64 Am. Dec. 378; Hill v. Bellows, 15 Vt. 727.

clearly showing that in the one case the legislature intended that the words "if he shall be out of the State" were to be construed literally, and apply to a temporary absence, while in the other not merely absence from, but residence out of, the State by the defendant is essential to save the plaintiff's cause of action from the operation of the statute. In some States this language is qualified by a provision which deprives the plaintiff of the saving, if the defendant left known property in the State which, by the common and ordinary processes of law, could be attached; and in the States where this provision exists, where the defendant sets up the statute in bar of an action, and the plaintiff replies, the defendant's absence when the cause of action accrued, or his subsequent absence from and residence out of the State, he must also negative the fact that the defendant had any known property within the State which, by the common and ordinary processes of law, could be attached, or his replication will be bad.[81] In order to bar a claim, the defendant must show that he has resided in the State for the full statutory period.[82]

It is held in Virginia, and it would seem that this is the general rule, that where the removal from the State antedates the contract sued upon, and before the cause of action accrued, the provision as to absent debtors has no application.[83]

It is not the domicile but the residence out of the State which suspends the statute. Thus in a New York case,[84] where the defendant retained his domicile in New York, but actually resided

81. In Stevens v. Fisher, 30 Vt. 200, a replication to a plea of the statute stated that before and after the cause of action accrued the defendant was out of the State, and that the action was brought when he for the first time returned into it, which was within eight years before the commencement of the action. It being found that the defendant had been, since and before the action was commenced, a resident of New York, it was held that the replication and proof were both defective, because not bringing the defendant within all the exceptions of the statute.

82. Bohannan v. Chapman, 13 Ala. 641.

83. Ficklin's Ex'r v. Carrington, 31 Gratt. (Va.) 219; Embrey v. Jemison, 131 U. S. 336, 9 Sup. Ct. 776, 33 L. Ed. 172; Dorr's Adm'r v. Rohr, 82 Va. 359, 3 Am. St. Rep. 106.

84. Haggart v. Morgan, 5 N. Y.

for three years in New Orleans, it was held, that he was to be deemed a nonresident within the meaning of the statute.

A mere temporary absence from the State upon business or other purposes, without any intention of remaining permanently, at least for a time, is not regarded as an absence within the meaning of the term as implied in these statutes.[85]

The law gives a creditor six years continued presence of his debtor within the State after his cause of action has accrued; and if he is continuously a resident of the State for the statutory period of six years after the debt is created and becomes due, the statute runs in his favor, although he is living under an assumed name and purposely conceals himself.[86]

422, 55 Am. Dec. 350. See also, Weitkamp v. Loehr, 53 N. Y. Super. Ct. (21 Jones & S.) 79, 11 Civ. Proc. R. 36; Burroughs v. Bloomer, 5 Denio (N. Y.) 532; Cole v. Jessup, 10 N. Y. 96, 10 How. Prac. (N. Y.) 515, Seld. Notes, 220; Satterthwaite v. Abercrombie, 23 Blatch. (U. S.) 308, 24 Fed. 543.

85. *In re* Wrigley, 8 Wend. (N. Y.) 134; Frost & Dickinson v. Brisbin, 19 Wend. (N. Y.) 11, 32 Am. Dec. 423; Armfield v. Moore, 97 N. C. 34, 2 S. E. 347; Boardman v. House, 18 Wend. (N. Y.) 512; Tomes v. Barney, 35 Fed. 112. But in Tennessee under the Code the rule is otherwise. Kempe v. Bader, 86 Tenn. 189, 6 S. W. 126. In Barney v. Oelrichs, 138 U. S. 529, 11 Sup. Ct. 414, 34 L. Ed. 1037, it was held that the words "reside out of the State" in section 100 of the New York statute of limitations, must be taken to mean the taking up of an actual abode or dwelling-place elsewhere, and not a mere temporary sojourn for transient purposes; and that mere temporary absences from the State, without any intention to remain permanently, upon business or for other purposes, could not be deducted from the statutory period to extend it beyond the six years.

A foreign ambassador at London or Washington is so far "absent" and a non-resident, that, as he cannot be sued while holding such office, the statute of limitations does not run in his favor against his creditors. Magdalena Steam Nav. Co. v. Martin, 2 E. & E. 94; Musurus Bey v. Gadban (1894), 2 Q. B. 352, 356.

86. Engel v. Fischer, 102 N. Y. 400, 7 N. E. 300, 55 Am. Rep. 818; Rhoton v. Mendenhall, 17 Or. 199, 20 Pac. 49. In some cases it is held that the return must be open and notorious, and under such circumstances that the creditor could with reasonable diligence find his debtor and serve him with process. Little v. Blunt, 33 Mass. (16 Pick.) 359; Hill v. Bellows, 15 Vt. 727; Hysinger v. Baltzell, 3 Gill & J. (Md.) 158; Didier v. Davison, 2 Barb. Ch. 477; Ford v. Babcock, 4 N. Y. Super. Ct. (2 Sandf.) 518; Cole v. Jessup, 10 N.

The question what constitutes a resident is one which has been often considered by the courts, and upon which no definite rule can be said to exist. It is mainly a question of fact to be determined by the jury.[87] In the United States Supreme Court,[88] where a traveling saleman residing in St. Louis (Mo.), who sent his wife and children to Brooklyn (N. Y.), where they took up their residence and commenced to keep house and have since resided, was held not to become a resident of New York when he sent his family into that State, nor until he joined them there, it was held, that by retaining his residence for purposes of business in St. Louis, he did not become a resident of New York, within the meaning of its statutes of limitation, until he changed his actual residence to that State, although his domicile might be there. In these statutes the word "residence" is not synonymous with "domicile."[89]

§ 245a. Absence at time of accrual of cause of action.

The absence or removal of defendant from the State is a statu-

Y. 96, 10 How. Prac. 515, Seld. Notes 220; Dorr v. Swartwout, 1 Blatchf. (U. S.) 179; 3 Pars. Cont. (6th ed.) 96; Ang. Lim. (2d ed.) 216. See Sleght v. Kane, 1 Johns. Cas. (N. Y.) 76; Poillon v. Lawrence, 77 N. Y. 207. In Rhoton v. Mendenhall, 17 Or. 199, 20 Pac. 49, it was held that under the statute, the word "conceal," as used therein, means some affirmative act done in the State, such as passing under an assumed name, change of occupation, or some other act which will prevent the community in which he lives from knowing who he is or where he came from. In several of the States, as Virginia, West Virginia, and Nebraska, the statute provides, as it does in Oregon, that if a person shall be absent from the State, or conceal himself, etc., the statute shall not run. Indeed, in most of the States, the statutes differ in their provisions under this head, and should be examined to ascertain the application of a decision thereunder.

87. See Frost & Dickinson v. Brisbin, 19 Wend. (N. Y.) 11, 32 Am. Dec. 423.

88. Penfield v. Chesapeake, etc., R. Co., 134 U. S. 351, 10 Sup. Ct. 566, 33 L. Ed. 940.

89. *In re* Thompson, 1 Wend. (N. Y.) 45; Bell v. Pierce, 51 N. Y. 12; Union Hotel Co. v. Hersee, 79 N. Y. 454, 35 Am. Rep. 536; Tazewell Co. v. Davenport, 40 Ill. 197; Strang v. Smith, 43 Miss. 499; Reg. v. University of Oxford, L. R. 7 Q. B. 471; Blackwell v. England, 8 El. & El. 549; Hewer v. Cox, 3 El. & El. 428; Atty.-Gen. v. McLean, 1 H. & C. 750.

tory and not a judicial exception to the running of limitations.[90] Unless there is an exception in the statute, limitations will begin to run at the time of the accrual of the action, regardless of the presence or absence of the debtor or creditor.[91] When a cause of action arises, limitations in the country where the obligor resides immediately begin to run, and, if in another country than the State of Kansas, it is held in that State that an action on a contract is not barred by limitations under the statute of that State, unless the bar of limitations has fallen in such other country.[92] It is also held in Kansas that where defendant, against whom a cause of action for fraud accrued, was at that time absent in another State, limitations did not begin to run as to him until his return to that State;[93] and that the running of limitations, as against a grantee assuming a mortgage debt, may be suspended by the absence of the grantee from the State.[94] In Ohio the plea of the statute is not good as against a nonresident defendant absent when the right of action accrued. The statute does not begin to run until he comes into the State or enters his appear-

90. Weaver v. Davis, 2 Ga. App. 455, 58 S. E. 786.

Where a limitation statute contained no exception saving from its operation suits against defendants who had removed from the State, no such exception can be implied as to actions falling within its terms. Id.

91. Rock Island Plow Co. v. Masterson, 96 Ark. 446, 132 S. W. 213.

92. Hays Land & Investment Co. v Bassett, 85 Kan. 48, 116 Pac. 475.

Where a resident of Oklahoma bought goods in Kansas in January, 1907, and resided in Oklahoma until the action was barred there, and the account was assigned to a Kansas bank, which sued in Kansas in 1911, as defendant was at no time a resident of Kansas, the action was not barred by Code Civ. Proc., §§ 20, 21 (Gen. St. 1909, §§ 5613, 5614), relating to limitation of actions between nonresidents. Stock Exchange Bank v. Wykes, 88 Kan. 750, 129 Pac. 1131.

A cause of action on a note cannot be maintained in Kansas under Code Civ. Proc., § 22 (Gen. St. 1901, § 4450), where both plaintiff and defendant were nonresidents of Kansas when the cause of action accrued, and defendant resided in a foreign State until the cause of action was barred by the laws of that State. Brunner v. Martin, 76 Kan. 862, 93 Pac. 165. See Nickel v. Vogel, 76 Kan. 625, 92 Pac. 1105.

93. Sherman v. Havens, 86 Kan. 99, 19 Pac. 370.

94. Hendricks v. Brooks, 80 Kan. 1, 101 Pac. 622.

ance by pleading.[95] Under the Texas statute it is held that when a defendant resides out of the State at the time a cause of action arises, such absence will not interrupt the running of limitations;[96] and that a judgment on which execution has been issued is not a cause of action within the purview of the statute, stopping the running of limitations during the absence from the State of one against whom plaintiff has a cause of action.[97] Under the Idaho

Though one who assigns a mortgage note and guaranties payment within two years of maturity can stand in place of the maker, and, like him, invoke the statute of limitations, it is unavailing where the running of the statute has been suspended by the continuous absence of the maker from the State from the time of giving the note. Spink v. Newby, 64 Kan. 883, 67 Pac. 437.

Under section 15, c. 95, Gen. St. 1897, providing that if, when a cause of action accrues against a person he be out of the State, the statute shall not begin to run until he comes into the State, the fact of personal presence in the State, and not of domicile, controls the question of limitation. Investment Securities Co. v. Bergthold, 60 Kan. 813, 58 Pac. 469; Hoggett v. Emerson, 8 Kan. 262. The last mentioned section of the Code applies to a defendant in ejectment claiming title by adverse possession, though he had possession through a tenant during such absence. Ard v. Wilson, 60 Kan. 857, 56 Pac. 80, aff'g 8 Kan. App. 471, 54 Pac. 511.

The statute of limitations does not run on a cause of action for the recovery of real property, while the person who claims title thereto is absent from the State. Ard v. Wilson, *supra;* Corby v. Moran, 58 Kan. 278, 49 Pac. 82. The absence from the State of the owner of real estate upon which there is a mortgage, but for which he is not personally liable, will not prevent the statute of limitations from running against the mortgage lien. Hogaboom v. Flower, 67 Kan. 41, 72 Pac. 547.

95. Marriott v. Columbus S. & H. Ry. Co., 30 Ohio Cir. Ct. R. 419.

96. Jaffray Realty Co. v. Solomon's Estate (Tex. Civ. App.), 157 S. W. 170, since an action to revive a judgment did not accrue until the judgment had become dormant, where at the time the debtor had left the State, his nonresidence did not suspend limitations against a proceeding to administer his estate in Texas after an action to revive was barred. See also Habermann v. Heidrich (Tex. Civ. App.), 66 S. W. 106, 795. The fact that the judgment defendant had not resided in Texas for 10 years next before the bringing of an action upon the judgment of a foreign State does not prevent the operation of the statute of limitations. Tourtelot v. Booker (Tex. Civ. App.), 160 S. W. 293.

97. Spiller v. Hollinger (Tex. Civ. App.), 148 S. W. 338; Tex. Rev. St. 1895, art. 3367.

In view of Rev. St. 1895, arts.

statute, providing that, if a person be absent from the State when a cause of action accrues against him, the action may be commenced within the time limited after his return, the cause or nature of the absence from the State is held to be immaterial as affecting limitations.[98] Under the express provisions of the Illinois limitation act, the bar of the statute of limitations is not available to defendants out of the State when the action accrued, who have not since come into the State;[99] and the Florida statute has no reference to defendants who reside out of the State when the cause of action accrued.[1]

In California a mortgagor's absence from the State, while suspending the running of the statute of limitations as against the mortgagee's right to foreclose the mortgage, will not prevent the attachment of other liens after the time limited has elapsed, so as to give the liens priority over the mortgage;[2] and on the recording of a deed of the property prior to the maturity of the note, limitations begin to run immediately on the maturity of the note, not-

2326a, 3361, a judgment on which no execution has been issued within 12 months after rendition is a cause of action under article 3367, stopping the running of limitation on any cause of action when defendant is without the jurisdiction. Id. Under Rev. St. 1895, arts. 1664, 2326a, 3358, a judgment on which execution was first issued within 12 months after its rendition becomes a dormant judgment after the lapse of 10 years, and so is a cause of action within the purview of article 3367.

Where the first of a number of notes of which the defendant had assumed the payment fell due February 1, 1891, at which time the maker, who was also a defendant, was absent from the State, continuing absent until the fall of 1893, suit brought January 27, 1896, was not barred by the four years' limitations. Liner v. J. B. Watkins Land and Mort. Co., 29 Tex. Civ. App. 187, 68 S. W. 311.

98. Anthes v. Anthes, 21 Idaho 305, 121 Pac. 553.

99. Janeway v. Burton, 201 Ill. 78, 66 N. E. 337, aff'g 102 Ill. App. 403.

1. Haviland, Clark & Co. v. Hargis, 9 Fla. 15.

2. Brandenstein v. Johnson, 140 Cal. 29, 73 Pac. 744.

Although under Cal. Code Civ. Proc., § 351, a nonresident mortgagor cannot plead the two-year limitations of section 339, subd. 1, if he has not been in the State, such is not true as to one who has acquired the interest of the mortgagor through an execution sale. Foster v. Butler, 164 Cal. 623, 130 Pac. 6.

withstanding the mortgagor continued absent from the State after the note's maturity.[3] In North Dakota an action to foreclose a mortgage on realty is held to be an action *in personam,* within the statute, excepting from period of limitations the time during which defendant was absent from the State;[4] while in Utah such an action is held under the statute to be essentially one *in rem,* in which personal service is not necessary except to support judgment for a deficiency after sale, and since such deficiency may be sued for as a personal debt of the mortgagor, the mortgagor's absence from the State would not extend the period of limitations in favor of a first mortgagee, so as to prevent a junior mortgagee from interposing the statute of limitations against the senior mortgage.[5] In North Carolina the time when defendant was absent from the State it is held should not be reckoned against heirs of a mortgagor suing in equity to redeem land sold under the mortgage.[6] Where a widow begins an action for dower more than twenty years after her husband's death, the cause of action is not exempted from the limitations of the New York Code Civ. Proc., § 1596, by section 401, providing that if, when a cause of action accrues, a person is without the State, the action may be commenced within the time limited

3. Filippini v. Trobock, 134 Cal. 441, 66 Pac. 587, rev'g 62 Pac. 1066, so held since, under Code Civ. Proc., § 726, the grantee of mortgaged property, whose deed is recorded, is a necessary party to the foreclosure proceedings.

4. Colonial & United States Mortg. Co. v. Northwestern Thresher Co., 14 N. D. 147, 103 N. W. 915, 116 Am. St. Rep. 642; Colonial & United States Mortg. Co. v. Flemington, 14 N. D. 181, 103 N. W. 929, 116 Am. St. Rep. 670; Paine v. Dodds, 14 N. D. 189, 103 N. W. 931, 116 Am. St. Rep. 674.

5. Boucofski v. Jacobsen, 36 Utah 165, 104 Pac. 117, while the running of limitations as against a subsequent claimant was not suspended by the mortgagor's absence from the State, it was suspended as between the prior mortgagee and the mortgagor.

6. McFarland v. Cornwell, 151 N. C. 428, 66 S. E. 454, where the personal presence of a defendant is essential to the granting of relief, Revisal 1905, § 366, providing that the time of a person's absence from the State for one year or more after a cause of action accrues against him shall not be deemed or taken as any part of the time limited for commencing action, applies, and the time of his absence is not to be counted.

after his return, by the fact that the defendants have not been in the State since the husband's death, as by section 441, subd. 1, the general provisions of the Code as to limitations do not apply to a case where a different limitation is specially prescribed by law.[7]

The Michigan statute providing for a deduction from the period of limitation of the time the debtor is absent from and resides out of the State, applies to every cause of action mentioned in the chapter, which includes debtors by judgment recovered in courts of record, as well as those recovered in courts not of record.[8] The Minnesota statute providing that, if when a cause of action accrues the defendant is out of the State, the action may be brought within the time limited after his return, and that the time of his absence is not part of the time limited for the commencement of the action, applies to actions the subject-matter of which arises or originates in the State, and where the debtor is out of the State when the cause of action accrues or departs therefrom.[9] That section of the Code of Alaska, which provides that the statutory term of limitation may be extended when the cause of action lies against a person "out of the district therein at the time when it accrues," applies only to a state of facts or a condition wherein the cause of action matures against a person or persons whose status is that of a resident or residents of Alaska.[10] If when a cause of action

7. Wetyen v. Fick, 178 N. Y. 223, 70 N. E. 497, aff'g 90 App. Div. 43, 85 N. Y. Supp. 592.

8. Conrad v. Nall, 24 Mich. 275; Mich. Comp. Laws, § 5369.

Where, in an action on a note executed in another State brought against the maker nearly 20 years after its maturity, during which time he had resided in Michigan, it was admitted that no payment had been made on the note, and no proof was offered to show that the action was not barred by the statute of limitations, it was held that plaintiff could not recover. Howard v. Coon, 93 Mich. 442, 5 N. W. 513.

9. Powers Mercantile Co. v. Blethen, 91 Minn. 339, 97 N. W. 1056; Mich. Gen. St. 1894, § 5145.

10. Murray v. Farrell, 2 Alaska 360.

For the application of various statutes, see Willis v. Rice, 157 Ala. 252, 48 So. 397, holding that Ala. Code 1896, c. 72, § 2805, is confined to limitations provided for in that chapter; Beatty v. Lewis (N. J. Ch.), 68 Atl.

accrues in favor of a resident of Wisconsin against a nonresident thereof, the latter be out of the State, the statute of limitations of that State upon the enforcement of such cause of action there will not run against the former while the latter remains so absent.[11] Under the Montana statute, absence from the State of the debtor's personal representative after his death does not suspend the running of limitations.[12]

§ 245b. Departure after accrual of cause of action.

Under the express provision of the New York Code of Civil Procedure, § 401, the running of limitations is suspended during the time of continuous absence of over a year's duration from the State.[13] The amendment of 1888, changing this section so that it reads, " departs from *and* resides without the State and remains continuously absent therefrom " instead of "*or* remains continuously absent therefrom," does not alter the rule that nonresidence is absence, and that casual visits to the State do not destroy the continuity of such absence.[14] So in West Virginia where a judg-

95, holding that N. J. Gen. St., p. 1975, § 15, applies only to the cases designated in the seven preceding sections of the statute; Casey v. American Bridge Co., 116 Minn. 461, 134 N. W. 111, holding that the limitation in Okla. St. 1893, § 435, is qualified by the tolling provision of section 21 of the same act; Jamieson v. Potts, 55 Or. 292, 105 Pac. 93, showing the application of Or. B. & C. Comp., § 16; Williams v. Iron Belt Building & Loan Ass'n, 131 N. C. 267, 42 S. E. 607, showing the application of N. C. Code, § 162.

11. Adkins v. Loucks, 107 Wis. 587, 83 N. W. 934.

12. Smith v. Smith, 210 Fed. 947; Rev. Codes Mont., § 6458. This is held to be so especially in view of section 6214, abolishing the rule that statutes in derogation of the common law are to be strictly construed.

13. Miller v. Warren, 87 N. Y. Supp. 1011, 94 App. Div. 192, judg. aff'd in 182 N. Y. 539, 75 N. E. 1131.

14. Connecticut Trust & Safe Deposit Co. v. Wead, 172 N. Y. 497, 65 N. E. 261, 92 Am. St. Rep. 756, modifying order, 69 N. Y. Supp. 518, 58 App. Div. 493, modifying judgment, 67 N. Y. Supp. 466, 33 Misc. Rep. 374; Lawrence v. Hogue, 93 N. Y. Supp. 998, 105 App. Div. 247, 16 N. Y. Ann. Cas. 298.

Where in December, 1889, a New York debtor gave up his house, stored his furniture, and went to Florida for the recovery of his son's health; he returned in April, 1890, remained a little over a month at an hotel, and then went to Europe for the

ment debtor departs from the State to reside, the time of his absence may be deducted from the limitation period within which the judgment lien may be enforced, though he occasionally visits or attends to business within the State.[15]

Under Idaho Rev. Codes, § 4069, providing that, if a person departs from the State after a cause of action accrues and the statute begins to run, the time of his absence is not a part of the time limited, the cause or nature of the absence from the State has been held immaterial as affecting limitations.[16] The rule in Texas is that where a person resides in the State at the time of the accrual of an action against him, and then permanently removes from the State, the running of limitations is suspended and remains suspended until he returns to the State, though he remains away more than the full period of limitation.[17] The

same purpose, finally returning to New York in June, 1893, it was held that, although he may have been continuously "domiciled" in New York, he "resided" without the State during such absences, within Code Civ. Proc., § 401, and hence they were not a part of the time limited for suing on the debt. Bennett v. Watson, 47 N. Y. Supp. 569, 21 App. Div. 409; 44 N. Y. Supp. 247, 26 Civ. Proc. R. 128, 19 Misc. Rep. 260.

Neither the period of five years after discovery of ground for action of absolute divorce, limited by Code Civ. Proc., § 1758, for the bringing of such an action, nor the general statute of limitations, runs while the defendant is without the jurisdiction of the court, so that process cannot be served upon him. Gouch v. Gouch, 69 Misc. Rep. (N. Y.) 436, 127 N. Y. Supp. 476.

15. Batten v. Lowther (W. Va.), 81 S. E. 821; W. Va. Code 1913, c. 104, § 18 (section 443).

16. Anthes v. Anthes, 21 Idaho 305, 121 Pac. 553.

17. Bemis v. Ward, 37 Tex. Civ. App. 481, 84 S. W. 291.

Under Rev. St. 1895, art. 3367, providing that, if a person is absent from the State during any of the time that an action might be brought against him, the period of such absence shall not be counted as part of the time limited for bringing the action, the running of the statute is interrupted whenever the defendant leaves the State either on business or pleasure, though he does not change his residence. Id. It is immaterial whether or not the debtor is within the State at the time of the accruing of the action where he leaves before it is barred. Dignowity v. Sullivan (Tex. Civ. App.) 109, S. W. 428.

In Texas, under Sayles' Ann. Civ. St. 1897, art. 3367, the statute of limitations, with reference to actions for land, is suspended during the absence of the defendant from

absence from the State contemplated by the Missouri statute has been held to be such an absence as would for a considerable period render it impossible to obtain such service of process as would support a general judgment.[18] And where a person, after the accrual of a cause of action against him, left the State and went to another State, returning to the State left by him occasionally until his death, but retained his ownership of his homestead in the State left by him, it has been held that there was not a departure from and residence out of the State by him within the meaning of the Wisconsin statute.[19]

The absence from the State referred to in the North Dakota statute is held to be absence by one who has not established a residence out of the State.[20] Under the statute of Washington, providing that the time that a person shall reside out of the State shall not be a part of the time limited for the commencement of an action, a temporary return to the State does not deprive one who has removed therefrom of his status as a nonresident.[21] And under a similar statute in New Mexico it has been held that the defendant must be a resident of the State when the cause of action accrues, and depart therefrom.[22] While a mere temporary

the State. Tate v. Waggoner (Tex. Civ. App.) 149, S. W. 737.

18. State *ex rel* Shipman v. Allen, 124 Mo. App. 465, 103 S. W. 1090; Mo. Rev. St. 1899, § 4282 (Am. St. 1906, p. 2356). See also same case, 132 Mo. App. 98, 111 S. W. 622.

19. *In re* Taylor's Estate, 132 Wis. 38, 111 N. W. 229; Taylor v. Thieman, Id.; Wis. Stat. 1898, § 4231.

20. Paine v. Dodds, 14 N. D. 189, 103 N. W. 931, 116 Am. St. Rep. 674; N. D. Rev. Codes 1899, § 5210.

Under North Dakota Rev. Codes 1905, § 6796, the absence of the judgment debtor from the State tolls the limitations prescribed by section 6786; and the judgment will support an action against the judgment debtor after 10 years have elapsed. Union Nat. Bank of Grand Forks v. Ryan, 23 N. D. 482, 137 N. W. 449.

21. Dignam v. Shaff, 51 Wash. 412, 98 Pac. 1113; Ballinger's Ann. Codes & St., § 4808 (Pierce's Code, § 292).

Under Rem. & Bal. Code, § 226, providing that service of summons may be made upon the defendant personally or by leaving it at the house of his usual abode, with some person of suitable age, etc., the actual whereabouts of a husband is immaterial, so long as he maintains a home at which service may be made, when it appears that his absence was of a temporary or casual nature. Crowder v. Morphy, 61 Wash. 626, 112 Pac. 742.

22. Lindauer Mercantile Co. v.

absence of a debtor from the State on a visit, or even on business, should not have the effect of suspending the statute of limitations, yet where a debtor departs from the State for the purpose of engaging, and does engage, in business in another State, the time he is thus absent should not be computed in estimating the time in which, under the statute, the action may be brought; and this though he may never have intended to forfeit his citizenship in the State he thus leaves.[23]

Where a resident, against whom a cause of action has accrued, removes his residence to another State, but continues his business in the former State and comes to the State openly and regularly

Boyd, 11 N. M. 464, 70 Pac. 568; N. M. Comp. Laws 1897, § 2921.

Where plaintiff, an employe residing in California, was injured in New Mexico, where the laws require action for such injuries to be brought within one year, it was held that, even if they annulled plaintiff's common law right to sue, the provisions would not affect his rights unless he and defendant continued to reside in New Mexico during the full period of limitation, so that it could act both on the parties and the cause of action. Atchison, etc., Ry. Co. v. Mills (Tex. Civ. App.), 116 S. W. 852.

In a Delaware case a cause of acion for personal injuries was held barred where the action was not brought until after one year from the date on which the injuries were sustained, though defendant, immediately upon the accrual of the cause of action, removed from the State and until the commencement of the action was absent therefrom, and that the act of 1897 (Del. Laws, p. 712, c. 594), requiring such action to be brought within one year, was not subject to the exception contained in Rev. Code 1852, amended in 1893, c. 123, § 14, providing for the suspension of the running of limitations where the party had departed from and resided out of the State. Lewis v. Pawnee Bill's Wild West Co., 6 Penneville (Del.) 316, 66 Atl. 471, aff'g 61 Atl. 868.

23. Nunez v. Taylor, 11 Ky. Law Rep. (abstract) 677, as the defendant in this case was temporarily in the State on numerous occasions after his departure from the State, it was held to be a question of fact for the jury whether his presence was of such duration or the circumstances such as to have afforded the plaintiff an opportunity to sue, and thus to have removed the obstruction occasioned by the departure, so as to take the case out of the proviso or exception to the statute.

The absence from the State of devisees stops the running of limitations during the period of absence as to claims against the estate for which the land devised is liable. Withers' Adm'r v. Withers' Heirs, 30 Ky. Law Rep. 1099, 100 S. W. 253.

each business day during working hours, he is not absent from the State, within the Nebraska statute, providing that the time of absence from the State shall not be computed as any part of the period within which the action must be brought.[24] A plaintiff suing for injuries to his land caused by the operation by defendant of a quarry on adjacent land is entitled, under the North Carolina Revisal 1905, § 366, to recover damages for acts done within three years before the commencement of the action, excluding from the computation the time defendant was absent from the State.[25] In South Carolina, where the right of action for the possession of land held adversely accrued while the holder of the legal title resided in the county, his subsequent absence from the State is not a disability suspending the running of limitations.[26]

§ 246. Joint debors, absence of one, effect of.

Where there are two or more joint debtors, one of whom is absent, the statute does not run in favor of the absent debtor, although it has run in favor of the other;[27] nor, upon the other hand, does the circumstance that one of the joint debtors is absent from the

24. Webster v. Citizens' Bank, 2 Neb. (Unof.) 353, 96 N. W. 118; Neb. Code Civ. Proc. § 20.

25 Arthur v. Henry, 157 N. C. 438, 73 S. E. 206.

While in ejectment the absence of the owner from the State does not suspend limitations where there is a tenant in possession, against whom the action may be brought, ejectment being a possessory action, a suit to vacate a mortgage foreclosure sale for fraud is equitable, and the mortgagees making the sale, of whom an accounting for rents and profits is sought, are necessary parties, so that the absence of one of them from the State would stay limitations; Revisal 1905, § 391, subsec. 4, requiring an action for the redemption of a mortgage where the mortgagee has been in possession to be brought within 10 years, applying. Owens v. Hornthal, 156 N. C. 19, 72 S. E. 5.

26. Milton v. Pace, 85 S. C. 373, 67 S. E. 458.

27. Bogert v. Vermilya, 10 N. Y. 447; Cutler v. Wright, 22 N. Y. 472; Denny v. Smith, 18 N. Y. 567; Brown v. Delafield, 1 Denis (N. Y.) 445. Thus in Bell v. Lamprey, 57 N. H. 168, it was held as to a claim upon which the statute ran in six years, that the defendant, in order to avail himself of the statute, must show that he has resided in the State six full years, of three hundred and sixty-five days in common years, and three hundred and sixty-six days in leap years.

State prevent the statute from running in favor of the others. Under the Virginia statute, providing that where a right has accrued against a person who had before resided in that State, if such person shall, by departing without the same, obstruct the prosecution of such right, the time that such obstruction may have continued shall not be computed as any part of the time within which the said right ought to have been prosecuted, where a claim for money furnished by decedent in a partnership business had been incurred a sufficient length of time to be barred by limitations, the fact that decedent's copartner was not a resident of the State, and traveled most of the time in Europe, but had frequently been within the State, did not prevent the running of the statute.[28]

§ 247. Residence need not be continuous.

In order to avail himself of the benefit of the statute of limitations, the party must have resided in the State, either actually or constructively, for the full statutory period. But the residence need not be continuous. If it is actual, different periods may be tacked together to make out the full period;[29] and if he actually dwells in the State for the requisite period, the circumstance that his wife and family have resided in another State will not deprive him of the benefit of the statute.[30] But the fact that a person does business in one State, but resides with his family in another, although he spends most of his time in the State where he does business, will not entitle him to the benefit of the statute of such State.[31]

28. Lovett's Adm'r v. Perry, 98 Va. 604, 37 S. E. 33, 2 Va. Sup. Ct. Rep. 507.

29. Crocker v. Clements's Adm'r, 23 Ala. 296.

30. Seymour v. Street, 5 Neb. 85.

31. Bennett v. Cook, 43 N. Y. 537, 3 Am. Rep. 727. This rule was also held in Bassett v. Bassett, 55 Barb. (N. Y.) 505, where the defendant, after the note was given, removed to another State, but continued to do business in New York, and came daily to his office there. Occasionally coming into the State is held not to put the statute in motion where a person, after the cause of action accrues, is absent from and resides out of the State. Hacker v. Everett, 57 Me. 548. In Lane v. National Bank of the Metropolis, 6 Kan. 74, where a citizen of Kansas was personally

Under the second clause of those statutes, which provide that where a debtor after a cause of action accrues against him, "shall be absent from and reside out of the State," the time of such absence shall not be taken as a part of the time limited, neither absence from the State, nor residence out of it, alone, will suspend the statute. Both must concur.[32] And it has been held that, under this clause, where the absence from the State has not been continuous the different occasions when the debtor has been within the State may be taken together, and during the periods so computed the statute will run, provided the plaintiff by due diligence might have obtained service of process upon the defendant.[33] Except where the statute expressly so provides, the fact that the defendant had property subject to attachment in the State will not prevent the suspension of the statute during the period he is actually absent therefrom, as the statute follows the person and not the property.[34] Under those statutes in which provision is made that if a person obstructs the service of process upon him, or the prosecution of an action pending, the "time during which he so obstructs such service or the prosecution of such action shall not be computed," it is held that absence from the State amounts to such obstruction.[35]

absent from the State in which his residence was, it was held that the statute did not run in his favor, although he kept a furnished house in his usual place of residence, which was occupied by his family. See also, Conrad v. Nall, 24 Mich. 275, where it was held erroneous to charge that the defendant's stay in another State, while his family resided in the State of the forum, was not a residence in such other State, as the residence of the defendant's family does not of itself, as a matter of law, determine the place of the husband's residence.

32. In Campbell v. White, 22 Mich 178, it was held that the residence out of the State contemplated by the legislature must be something more than having a mere place of abode out of the State.

33. Campbell v. White, *supra.*

34. Fisher v. Fisher, 43 Miss. 212.

35. Poston v. Smith, 8 Bush (Ky.) 589. See Barney v. Oelrichs, 138 U. S. 529, 11 Sup. Ct. 414, 34 L. Ed. 1037, stated *supra,* § 245, where the court said: "In Penfield v. Chesapeake, O. & S. W. R. Co., 134 U. S. 351, 10 Sup. Ct. 566, 33 L. Ed. 940, we had occasion to consider when a person might be properly held to be a resident of the State of New York and entitled to bring an action which

§ 247a(1). Nonresidence—In general.

The words, "when a cause of action has arisen," in a foreign State, as used in the Kansas statute of limitations, mean when the plaintiff has a right to sue the defendant in the courts of such foreign State, and have no reference to the origin of the transaction

would have otherwise been barred by the laws of the defendant's residence, and this involved an examination of the decisions in that State in the construction of the words 'resident' and 'residence,' as contained in its statutes." Citing *Re* Thompson, 1 Wend. (N. Y.) 43; Frost v. Brisben, 19 Wend. (N. Y.) 11; Haggart v. Morgan, 5 N. Y. 422, and Meitkamp v. Loehr, 21 Jones & S. (N. Y.) 79; Burroughs v. Bloomer, 5 Denio (N. Y.) 532; Ford v. Babcock, 2 Sandf. (N. Y.) 518; Cole v. Jessup, 10 N. Y. 96; Satterthwaite v. Abercrombie, 23 Blatchf. 308, and Engel v. Fischer, 102 N. Y. 400. See *In re* Wrigley, 4 Wend. (N. Y.) 602, 8 Wend. 134. In Frost v. Brisbin, 19 Wend. (N. Y.) 11, it is said that the word "inhabitant" implied a more permanent and fixed abode than the word "resident" and "frequently imports many privileges and duties which a mere resident cannot claim or be subject to" and that "the transient visit of a person for a time at a place does not make him a resident while there—that something more is necessary to entitle him to that character." See Bartlett v. New York, 5 Sandf. (N. Y.) 44; Douglas v. New York, 2 Duer (N. Y.) 110; Bell v. Pierce, 51 N. Y. 12. As to the statute of limitations there were two exceptions to its operation: (1) Where the debtor was absent from the State when the cause of action accrued; (2) where the debtor, after the cause of action had accrued, departed from and resided out of the State. Under the first exception absence was sufficient to avert the bar, because the statute did not commence to run until the return of the debtor into the State, and such return, it was decided, must be open and notorious, so that a creditor might with reasonable diligence find his debtor and serve him with process. Engel v. Fischer, 102 N. Y. 400, 7 N. E. 300, 55 Am. Rep. 818. But to bring a case within the second exception something more than absence was essential to be shown. In Wheeler v. Webster, 1 E. D. Smith, 1, Judge Ingraham said that "it was necessary to prove that the debtor departed from the State, and also that he resided out of the State. The evidence did not tend to show this. For aught that is in proof before us, the absence may have been merely temporary; excursions for pleasure or business, with a return to this State as the residence of the debtor. Mere presence was not tantamount to residence under the statute, nor mere absence equivalent to residence elsewhere. And the occasional absences of a resident of the State continuing to reside therein were not to be deducted in computing the statutory term. Ford v. Babcock, 4 N. Y. Super. Ct. (2 Sandf.) 518, 529. Apparently, because this was obviously so, the legislature of New York, by

out of which the cause of action arose.[36] Limitations in Michigan apply to a right of action which accrued without the State between parties who were at the time nonresidents.[37] The statute of limitations as contained in Mansfield's Digest of the Laws of Arkansas, put in force in Indian Territory by Act of Cong. May 2, 1890, applies to and runs in favor of nonresidents as well as residents.[38] A nonresident cannot invoke the Texas statutes of limitation, relating to actions for the recovery of real estate, notwithstanding he had tenants in possession of the land, and had paid all taxes thereon.[39] The words, "return to the State," in Idaho Rev. St. 1887, § 4069, apply to a nonresident debtor who enters into a

an act passed April 25, 1867 (Laws N. Y. 1867, p. 1921), amended section 100 by adding after the words "and reside out of this State," the following, "or remain continuously absence therefrom for the space of one year or more." Absence for the time specified was thus provided to be deducted from the time limited for the commencement of actions, so that, whether the defendant resided out of the State or not, such absence would suspend the running of the statute. We hold that the residence out of the State which operated to suspend the running of the statute under section 100 as originally framed was a fixed abode entered upon with the intention to remain permanently, at least for a time, for business or other purposes, and as there was no evidence tending to establish such a state of fact here, the judgment must be reversed. The same conclusion has been reached in effect by many of the State courts, and reference to decisions in Massachusetts, Maine, Vermont, and New Hampshire, will be found in the well-considered opinion of the Supreme Court of Illinois in Pells v. Snell, 130 Ill. 379, where the terms of the statute were nearly identical with those of that of New York, and the court approved the definition of "residence" as given in *Re* Wrigley, 8 Wend. (N. Y.) 134; Frost v. Brisbin, 19 Wend. (N. Y.) 11; and Boardman v. House, 18 Wend. (N. Y.) 512.

36. Bruner v. Martin, 76 Kan. 862, 93 Pac. 165; Kan. Code Civ. Proc. § 22; Gen. St. 1901, § 4450.

37. Belden v. Blackman, 118 Mich. 448, 5 Detroit Leg. N. 567, 76 N. W. 979.

38. Schwab Clothing Co. v. Cromer, 1 Ind. Tex. 661, 43 S. W. 951, under Mansf. Dig. § 4490

39. Beale's Heirs v. Johnson (Tex. Civ. App.), 99 S. W. 1045, under Sayles' Rev. Civ. St. art. 3367.

In an action to correct a certificate of acknowledgment to a deed, the nonresidence of the parties did not prevent the running of limitations, whether such action could have been brought and jurisdiction over defendants therein obtained in the State or not. Veeder v. Gilmer, 103 Tex. 458, 129 S. W. 595, rev'g judg. (Civ. App.) 120 S. W. 584.

contract in a foreign State, and thereafter comes into the State, as well as to a citizen who enters into a contract within the State, and subsequently departs therefrom.[40] Arizona Civ. Code 1901, par. 2964, does not operate to prevent limitations from running against a nonresident's cause of action.[41] Where the plaintiff's right to proceed by attachment depended upon the nonresidence of the defendant, and the allegation that the defendant was a nonresident was not stricken out by amendment, and could not have been stricken out without resulting in dismissal of the case, the absence or nonresidence of the debtor who had never resided within the State, is no reply to the defense of limitations.[42]

§ 247a(2). Persons entitled to sue.

Under Iowa Code, § 3451, excluding from computation of limitations the time while defendant is a nonresident, plaintiff's residence is immaterial.[43] Under New York Code Civ. Pro., § 1502, plaintiff's right to sue defendant for real property occupied by the latter is not suspended by nonresidence of the defendant, so as to prevent her acquisition of title by adverse possession.[44] The Rhode Island statute of limitations is not suspended during plaintiff's nonresidence.[45] The "absence" spoken of in Louisiana Civ. Code 1838, art. 3508, relating to prescription, is the absence of the creditor from the domicile of his debtor; and, where the debtor and creditor have always lived in the same place, although that place be out of the limits of the State, the creditor cannot be viewed in regard to the debtor as an absentee.[46] Where a deed to a city for a money consideration recited that the grantee should hold the land for burial purposes and no other, and after an aband-

40. West v. Theis, 15 Idaho, 167, 96 Pac. 932.

41. Work v. United Globe Mines, 12 Ariz. 339, 100 Pac. 813.

42. Cooper v. P. P. Most Nursery Co., 10 Ga. App. 351, 73 S. E. 414.

43. McNamara v. McAllister, 150 Iowa, 243, 130 N. W. 26.

44. French v. Wray, 151 N. Y. Supp. 1015.

45. Griffin v. Woodhead, 30 R. I. 204, 74 Atl. 417.

46. Surget v. Stanton, 10 La. Ann. 319.

onment of such purpose the grantors sued in equity for a reconveyance and accounting or an injunction, the fact that complainants were nonresidents was of no avail to them as against the ten-year statute of limitations.[47] Under the Washington statute, plaintiff's right of action on notes made to him by defendant in another State, of which both were residents, was not barred by the limitations of the State where the notes were made, since the cause of action did not arise until the maturity of the notes, at which time plaintiff was a resident of Washington.[48] The purpose of South Dakota Code Civ. Proc., § 69, is to protect from loss through lapse of time rights for the enforcement of which a party has a right of action in the State courts.[49]

§ 247a(3). Persons liable.

Under the statute of Iowa, as construed by its supreme court, limitation does not run in favor of a defendant during the time he is a nonresident of the State.[50] Alabama Code, § 2805, applies to a contract made in a foreign State, though the defendant was

47. Thornton v. City of Natchez, 88 Miss. 1, 41 So. 498.

48. Freundt v. Hahn, 24 Wash. 8, 63 Pac. 1107, 85 Am. St. Rep. 939, modified 28 Wash. 117, 68 Pac. 184, under Ballinger's Ann. Codes & St. § 4818.

Where defendant, while a resident of Missouri, executed four notes, and after maturity of the first note and before maturity of the other three he left the State and never returned thereto, and had not acquired a fixed abode elsewhere, he was not a non-resident of Missouri when the causes of action on the last three notes accrued, and hence limitations did not run against them under the first clause of section 6781, Rev. St. Mo., so that both parties being non-residents, an action thereon was not barred in Washington, under Rem. & Bal. Code Wash., § 178. McElroy v. Gates, 64 Wash. 249, 116 Pac. 845.

49. Froelich v. Swafford (S. D.), 150 N. W. 476, and where the remedy for the enforcement of a right is unaffected by the absence of defendant, his absence does not, under Code Civ. Proc. § 69, extend the time within which the action must be brought.

The general provisions of the Indiana statutes of limitations do not govern suits under Burns' Ann. St. Ind. 1901, § 609, and hence sections 297 and 298 have no application therein. Hollenback v. Posten, 34 Ind. App. 481, 73 N. E. 162.

50. City of Davenport v. Allen, 120 Fed. 172 (C. C., Iowa).

a nonresident, and absent from the State until shortly before the institution of the suit.[51] The statute of limitations of Alaska cannot begin to run until there is found some one within the jurisdiction of the forum capable of being sued.[52] An action on a special bail bond executed in an action in Connecticut is not barred in one year after judgment in the action, where the sureties have not resided in Connecticut after accrual of the cause of action, and have not been in Connecticut, except for occasional trips therein by automobile.[53] Kentucky statute 1899, § 2531, providing for the suspension of the statute of limitations during the debtor's absence from the State, does not apply to nonresident debtors.[54] By the common law a statute of limitations is suspended during the defendant's nonresidence.[55] In New York, the plea of limitations is ineffectual to a defendant who has continually resided without the State.[56] In Oklahoma, where a cause of action arose in another State, limitations do not begin to run against it until the debtor becomes a resident of the territory.[57] Under the Indiana statute, where it appears that all of the defendants, from the time that the cause of action accrued to the beginning of the suit, were nonresidents, they therefore were not in a position to invoke as a defense the statute of limitations.[58] Under the Texas statute, the

51. Steen v. Swadley, 126 Ala. 616, 28 So. 620.

52. Van Schuyver v. Hartman, 1 Alaska, 431.

53. Isenberg v. Rainier, 70 Misc. Rep. 498, 127 N. Y. Supp. 411, under Conn. Gen. St. 1902, § 1122.

54. Clarke v. Seay, 21 Ky. Law Rep. 394, 51 S. W. 589. See also Bybee's Ex'r v. Poynter, 117 Ky. 109, 25 Ky. Law Rep. 1251, 77 S. W. 698; Tabor v. Hardin, 9 Ky. Law Rep. 491.

55. Cobb v. Houston, 117 Mo. App. 645, 94 S. W. 299.

56. Moloney v. Tilton, 22 Misc. Rep. 682, 51 N. Y. Supp. 19.

57. Keagy v. Wellington Nat. Bank, 12 Okl. 33, 69 Pac. 811.

58. Watson v. Lecklinder, 147 Ind. 395, 45 N. E. 72, under Burns' Rev. St. 1894, § 298 (Rev. St. 1881, § 297).

As to persons liable, in other jurisdictions, see:

U. S.—Horner v. Perry, 112 Fed. 906 (C. C., Mo.), applying Kansas and Missouri statutes; Stern v. Compagnie Generale Transatlantique, 110 Fed. 996 (D. C., N. Y.); St. N. J. 1848 (1 Gen. St. p. 1188).

S. D.—McConnell v. Spicker, 15 S. D. 98, 87 N. W. 574.

Wash.—Omaha Nat. Bank v. Lindsay, 41 Wash. 531, 84 Pac. 11.

departure from the State of a nonresident who had been temporarily present in the State does not suspend the running of limitations against a cause of action against him.[59]

§ 247a(4). Nature of residence.

Under Mass. Rev. Laws, c. 202, § 9, excluding from the time of limitation the time during which the debtor resides out of the State, which is substantially the same as Pub. St. 1882, c. 197, § 11, the time of the debtor's absence is to be excluded only if it is such as to work a change of domicile.[60] The residence out of the State which suspends the running of the Illinois statute of limitations is the fixed abode entered into with the intention to remain permanently at least for a time for business or other purposes.[61] The terms "residence" and "domicile" are not identical for all purposes, and their meaning is different under the rule suspending limitations by absence from the State.[62]

Wis.—National Bank of Oshkosh v. Davis, 100 Wis. 240, 75 N. W. 1005; Weyburn & Briggs v. Bemis, 122 Wis. 321, 99 N. W. 1050.

59. Pollard v. Allen (Tex. Civ. App.), 171 S. W. 530.

60. Nichols v. Vaughan, 217 Mass. 548, 105 N. E. 376.

A decision by the United States Supreme Court that due process of law, under Const. U. S. Amend. 14, prevents a personal judgment against one not personally served within the State, even though a resident thereof, does not change this construction of Rev. Laws, c. 202, § 9. Id.

And see Converse v. Johnson, 146 Mass. 20, 14 N. E. 925.

61. Fidelity & Deposit Co. v. Sheahan, 37 Okl. 702, 133 Pac. 228.

To constitute a "residence out of the State" sufficient to suspend the running of the Illinois statute of limitations, it was not necessary that there should be an actual change of domicile in the strict legal sense, but it was necessary that a fixed and permanent abode or dwelling place out of that State should have been acquired at least for the time being. Id.

The 10-year statute of Illinois bars an action on a promissory note where more than 10 years have elapsed between its maturity and the institution of suit thereon, notwithstanding the defendant lived from time to time in different jurisdictions and had not remained in any one jurisdiction a sufficient length of time to bar such note. Warren v. Clemenger, 120 Ill. App. 435.

62. McDowell v. Friedman Bros. Shoe Co., 135 Mo. App. 276, 115 S. W. 1028.

§ 247a(5). Actions relating to specific property or interest therein.

Despite the two-year limitation prescribed by California Code Civ. Proc., § 339, limitations in foreclosure of a mortgage of a nonresident do not begin to run under section 351 until he comes within the State.[63] Under Burns' Rev. St. Indiana 1909, § 298, providing that limitations do not run while the defendant is a nonresident, where a personal judgment has been procured, the statute does not bar a subsequent action to subject to the payment of the judgment property which has been fraudulently conveyed by the judgment debtor to nonresidents, though more than six years have passed.[64] Under Iowa Code 1873, § 2533, providing that the time during which defendant is a nonresident of the State shall be excluded, in computing periods of limitation, the right to bring an action to set aside a fraudulent conveyance to a nonresident grantee was not barred by the statute, where it was brought within five years after the grantee's conveyance of the property in controversy to a resident of the State.[65] An action of ejectment by a

63. San Diego Realty Co. v. Hill, 168 Cal. 637, 143 Pac. 1021.

Where a debt secured by deed executed out of the State was due when the deed was executed, December 11, 1875, and the debtor came into the State early in 1876, and remained there until his death, any action on the debt or mortgage deed was barred December 11, 1877, under Code Civ. Proc. §§ 312, 339, barring an action on a contract or liability, not founded on a writing, or founded on a writing executed out of the State, two years after the cause of action shall have accrued. Sanford v. Bergin, 156 Cal. 43, 103 Pac. 333.

Under Code Civ. Proc. § 336, subd. 1, prescribing a five-year limitation for actions on foreign judgments, and section 351, providing that absence from the State is no part of such period, action on a foreign judgment against defendant who had resided in the State no more than two and one-half years was not barred. Chappell v. Thompson, 21 Cal. App. 136, 131 Pac. 82.

64. Balph v. Magaw, 33 Ind. App. 399, 70 N. E. 188.

Burns' Ann. St. 1908, § 299, providing that the time of non-residence of defendant shall not be computed in the period of limitation, does not apply to persons who at all times have been non-residents. Sinclair v. Gunzenhauser, 179 Ind. 78, 98 N. E. 37.

65. Applegate v. Applegate, 107 Iowa, 312, 78 N. W. 34.

tax deed holder out of possession does not become barred by the Kansas two-year statute of limitations, while occupied by tenants, agents, or employes of a nonresident owner.[66] The nonresidence of parties to a mortgage does not prevent the running of the Tennessee statute of limitations (Acts 1885, p. 49, c. 9), since the only exception therein contained relates to those under disability.[67] Under Mississippi Code, § 2748, where a note was given in the State, secured by a mortgage on land therein, the period of the debtor's subsequent absence from the State should not be computed as part of the time limited for the enforcement of the security against the land.[68] Under South Dakota Code Civ. Proc., § 69, nonresidence of the purchaser at foreclosure sale and her successive grantees owning the land until within ten years toll the statute, so that a junior mortgagee's action to redeem was not barred.[69]

Suit to enforce the personal liability of mortgagors after their conveyance to a third party was not barred by limitations where the note matured July, 1910, and suit was brought December, 1902, though service was not had on the mortgagors until July, 1910, where in the meantime they had been non-residents of the State for four years and ten months. Schafer v. Jackson, 155 Iowa, 108, 135 N. W. 622.

66. Gibson v. Hinchman, 72 Kan. 382, 83 Pac. 981.

The statute excluding the time when defendant is absent from the State applies to an action of ejectment by a judgment debtor against a purchaser at a sheriff's sale. Morrell v. Ingle, 23 Kan. 32. Limitation does not run against a mortgage foreclosure suit against a non-resident, though the plaintiff is in possession of the mortgaged premises as grantee of the mortgagor. Smith v. Perkins, 10 Kan. App. 577, 63 Pac. 297.

67. Christian v. John, 111 Tenn. 92, 76 S. W. 906.

Shannon's Code, § 4455, suspending limitations while defendant is without the State, does not apply to a suit to set aside a deed for fraud and to recover certain land, in which plaintiff may obtain complete relief by service of publication. Boro v. Hidell, 122 Tenn. 80, 120 S. W. 961.

68. Hunt v. Belknap, 78 Miss. 76, 28 So. 751.

69. Froelich v. Swofford, 33 S. D. 142, 144 N. W. 925.

Where a grantee in a tax deed was at the time a non-resident, and remained so until he conveyed the property, the period of his absence was not to be considered in determining whether the statute of limitations had run in a suit by the original owner to determine adverse claims. Burleigh v. Hecht, 22 S. D. 301, 117 N. W. 367.

§ 247a(6). Effect of agency within jurisdiction.

Ownership of property in the State does not make a nonresident corporation or individual a "resident" so as to put in force the statute of limitations which is suspended by North Carolina Revisal 1905, § 366, as to nonresident defendants; neither does the appointment of a local agent on whom process can be served have that effect.[70] Limitations on a cause of action against a nonresident who has an office or agency in the county, out of the business carried on in which the cause of action accrued, where process may be served under Shannon's Code, Tenn., §§ 4516, 4542, 4546, are not tolled by defendant's nonresidence.[71] The statute of limitations is not suspended, as against a nonresident defendant who has an office in the State at which he does business practically every day of the year, with the exception of Sundays and holidays, and who lives in the State half the time during each year.[72]

§ 247a(7). Corporations.

Foreign corporations come within the California statutes which prevent the running of limitations in favor of absent debtors while they are out of the State.[73] A foreign corporation is a person "out of the State," within Kansas Gen. St. 1901, § 4449,[74] and within Wisconsin Rev. St., § 4231, providing for the running of limitations after his return.[75] Limitations do not run in favor

70. Volivar v. Richmond Cedar Works, 152 N. C. 34, 67 S. E. 42, judg. rev'd 68 S. E. 200. Revisal 1905, § 366, suspending limitations against non-residents, by its terms does not apply to a cause of action which accrued prior to August 24, 1868. Johnson v. Eversole Lumber Co., 144 N. C. 717, 57 S. E. 518.

71. Green v. Snyder, 114 Tenn. 100, 84 S. W. 808.

72. Holt v. Hopkins, 63 Misc. Rep. 537, 117 N. Y. Supp. 177, judg. aff'd 136 App. Div. 940, 121 Supp. 1136.

73. O'Brien v. Big Casino Gold Min. Co., 9 Cal. App. 283, 99 Pac. 209.

74. Williams v. Metropolitan St. Ry. Co., 68 Kan. 17, 74 Pac. 600, 64 L. R. A. 794, 104 Am. St. Rep. 377.

75. Travelers' Ins. Co. v. Fricke, 99 Wis. 367, 74 N. W. 372, 41 L. R. A. 557.

A foreign corporation which has acquired a domicile in the State for the purposes of litigation is not a non-resident, so as to suspend the operation of limitations. Travelers' Ins.

of a foreign corporation which has failed to comply with Oklahoma Const., art. 9, § 43, and become a resident.[76] The appointment of a local agent on whom process can be served by a foreign corporation put in force the statute of limitations, which is suspended by North Carolina Revisal 1905, § 366, as to nonresident defendants.[77] Mississippi Code 1906, § 3108, applies only where a cause of action accrues in the State and the person against whom it has accrued goes from and resides out of the State, and does not apply where a nonresident alien corporation claimed adverse possession of land when such possession was by tenants against whom ejectment might at any time have been instituted.[78] South Dakota Code Civ. Proc., § 69, prevents limitations running against a nonresident corporation until it is brought within the reach of the process of the state courts.[79] The rule that a foreign corporation cannot avail itself of the statute of limitations under Rem. & Bal. Washington Code, § 168, does not apply to a contract limitation contained in a foreign indemnity company's bond.[80] Under the statute of limitations of Nevada (Gen. St. Nev., § 3651), a foreign corporation cannot plead limitation as a bar to a suit to foreclose a

Co. of Hartford v. Fricke, 99 Wis. 367, 78 N. W. 407, 41 L. R. A. 557, denying rehearing 74 N. W. 372. An insurance corporation not organized under the laws of the State, which, in compliance with the statute, maintains an attorney within the State upon whom process can be served in actions commenced in its courts, is nevertheless a non-resident, within the meaning of section 4231, Rev. St., and not entitled to the benefit of the statutes of limitations. State v. National Acc. Soc. of New York, 103 Wis. 208, 79 N. W. 220.

76. Oklahoma Nat. Bank v. Chicago, R. I. & P. Ry. Co. (Okl.), 146 Pac. 716; Hale v. St. Louis & S. F. R. Co., 39 Okl. 192, 134 Pac. 949. See also Johnson & Larimer Dry Goods Co. v. Cornell, 4 Okl. 412, 46 Pac. 860; Tiller v. St. Louis & S. F. R. Co., 189 Fed. 994 (C. C., Okl.).

77. Voliva v. Richmond Cedar Works, 152 N. C. 656, 68 S. E. 200, rev'g judg. Volivar v. Same, 67 S. E. 42; Bennett v. Western Union Telegraph Co., 68 S. E. 202. See Green v. Hartford Life Ins. Co., 139 N. C. 309, 51 S. E. 887, 1 L. R. A. (N. S.) 623; Southern Ry. Co. v. Mayes, 113 Fed. 84, 51 C. C. A. 70 (C. C. A., N. C.).

78. Scottish American Mortgage Co. v. Butler, 99 Miss. 56, 54 So. 666.

79. Reeves & Co. v. Block, 31 S. D. 60, 139 N. W. 780.

80. Ilse v. Aetna Indemnity Co., 69 Wash. 484, 125 Pac. 780.

mortgage on property situated in the State, executed to secure an indebtedness of the corporation, since, having been out of the State, the debt is not barred.[81] Where defendant, a foreign corporation, was licensed to do business in Missouri, and there maintained an office and agent on whom service of process might be obtained at any time, under Mo. Rev. St. 1889, §§ 570, 1007, it was not a nonresident within section 4282, providing for the suspension of limitations as against a debtor who was a resident at the time the action accrued and thereafter departed from the State.[82]

§ 247b. Return and residence after absence.

When the person against whom a cause of action exists is a nonresident of the State of New York when it accrues, but at that time, and for more than six years thereafter, comes into the State on every business day, and remains during business hours, attending at his office within the State, where, by the use of reasonable diligence, he could be found, the statute of limitations begins to run in his favor, upon the first day of his coming into the State, after the cause of action accrues, and its running is not thereafter suspended, since he is not continuously absent from the State for a year.[83] Under Delaware Rev. Code, p. 889, c. 128, § 14, limitations are not set running on a cause of action against a nonresident by his coming into the State, unless such coming was open and notorious, without attempt to prevent the creditor from ascertaining his presence, and for such length of time as to enable process to be served on him by the exercise of reasonable diligence.[84] Under California Code Civ. Proc., § 351, a person leaving the State after a cause of action accrues against him cannot have reckoned in

81. Hanchett v. Blair, 100 Fed. 817, 41 C. C. A. 76 (C. C. A., Nev.).

82. Sidway v. Missouri Land & Live Stock Co., 187 Mo. 649, 86 S. W. 150.

83. Costello v. Downer, 19 App. Div. 434, 46 N. Y. Supp. 713.

A debtor who returns to New York after absence from the State is not shown to have concealed his return by the fact that he did not put his name in the city directory. Campbell v. Post, 20 Misc. Rep. 339, 45 N. Y. Supp. 919.

84. Morrow v. Turner, 2 Marv. (Del.) 332, 43 Atl. 166.

his favor the time of any secret or fraudulently contrived visit to his former residence; but, where he returns openly, the statute runs against the claim during his stay, although the creditor does not know of his presence before his departure.[85] Under Kansas Code Civ. Proc., § 21 (Gen. St. 1901, § 4449), before a debtor who is absent from the State when a cause of action accrues, and who makes occasional visits to the State during the period of limitation, can set up a bar of the statute, the time of his temporary presence in the State must aggregate the statutory period.[86] Where a debtor had departed from the State, and resided elsewhere and had no place of abode in the State, his temporary return and presence at court did not continue the operation of the Missouri statute of limitations.[87] The word "return," in Utah Rev. St. 1898, § 2888, as applied to absent debtors, includes nonresidents as well as citizens of the State who have gone abroad and returned to the State, the words "return to the State" being equivalent to "come into the State."[88] The removal of a debtor from the State suspends the running of the Kentucky statute of limitations in his favor, and his subsequently coming temporarily into the State does not cause the statute to begin to run again in his favor.[89]

§ 248. Absconding debtors.

In those States where the statute is only saved when the debtor absconds from the State, in order to avail himself of the saving of the statute, it is incumbent upon the plaintiff to show that the defendant actually absconded from the State, that is, left is secretly;

85. Stewart v. Stewart, 152 Cal. 162, 92 Pac. 87.

And see McKee v. Dodd, 152 Cal. 637, 93 Pac. 854. The rule is the same under the Texas statute. See Gleen v. McFaddin (Tex. Civ. App.), 143 S. W. 234.

86. Gibson v. Simmons, 77 Kan. 461, 94 Pac. 1013. It is not necessary that such visits shall be made so as to give the creditor an opportunity to serve summons on him, but he is entitled to credit for all the time spent in the State unless he conceals himself. Baxter v. Krause, 79 Kan. 851, 101 Pac. 467.

87. State *ex rel.* Shipman v. Allen, 132 Mo. App. 98, 111 S. W. 622.

88. Lawson v. Tripp, 34 Utah 28, 95 Pac. 520.

89. Chiles, Bean & Co. v. McClure, 11 Ky. Law Rep. (abstract) 676.

and if he left openly the statute is not saved, although the debtor does not return to the State again.

§ 249. Concealment.

The concealment of a debtor, which saves the statute in those States where a provision of that kind exists, need not be fraudulent, but a change of residence several times by the debtor, without informing his creditor, has been held sufficient.[90]

§ 249a(1). Concealment of person or residence—In general.

Conspiracy on the part of city officials to prevent the service of process in an action against the city furnishes no excuse for not commencing the action within the time limited by statute, in the absence of a statute creating it an exception.[91] The Arkansas statute refers to absconding debtors and persons who fraudulently conceal themselves to prevent the commencement of an action against them, and in such case limitations do not begin until the residence of the absconder has been discovered, and the commencement of the action for that reason no longer prevented, and they do not apply to a foreign corporation doing business in the State without designating an agent, where the corporation claims the benefit of section 5057 by paying taxes on lands to which it has color of title.[92] The Alaska statute applies only to a state of facts or a condition wherein the cause of action matures against a person

90. Harper v. Pope, 9 Mo. 402.

91. Amy v. City of Watertown, 130 U. S. 320, 9 Sup. Ct. 537, 32 L. Ed. 953; Spaulding v. City of Watertown, 130 U. S. 327, 9 Sup. Ct. 539, 32 L. Ed. 946.

92. Rachels v. Stecher Cooperage Works, 95 Ark. 6, 128 S. W. 348, under Kirby's Dig. §§ 5077, 5088, providing that limitations do not apply to absconding debtors until the creditor becomes apprised of the residence of the absconding debtor, etc.

Under section 5088, limitations are suspended from the time defendant escaped from the penitentiary until he was pardoned; he, as an escaped convict, before pardon, having no usual place of abode at which service on him could be made under the statute. Reeder v. Cargill, 102 Ark. 518, 145 S. W. 223.

Under Sand. & H. Dig. §§ 4835, 4846, one who has a right of action for damages, and the person against whom such right exists, are debtor and creditor, and a concealment before the cause of action accrues does

whose status is that of a resident of Alaska.[93] In California, living in the State under an assumed name will not prevent one, when sued on a foreign judgment from pleading limitations.[94] In Illinois, concealment of identity of a party liable is not a ground recognized by the statute of limitations for the postponement of its running.[95] In Iowa, it has been held that the facts that the debtor had changed his residence from Ohio, where the contract relied on was executed, to Iowa, where the action was brought, and lived there under an assumed name, and that the creditor did not know his residence, although he had made diligent inquiry to ascertain it, did not prevent the statute from running.[96] The Kansas statute does not apply to a cause of action arising in another State from which defendant absconded to Kansas, where he made no effort to conceal his whereabouts while within the State.[97] In Louisiana, if a debtor abandon his residence to avoid his creditors, prescription does not run in his favor.[98] In Missouri, the ab-

not extend the time for suit. Keith v. Hiner, 63 Ark. 244, 38 S. W. 13.

93. Murray v. Farrell, 2 Alaska, 360, under Code Alaska, c. 2, § 15, providing that the statutory term of limitation may be extended when the cause of action lies against a person concealed in the district at the time when it accrues.

94. St. Paul Title & Trust Co. v. Stensgaard, 162 Cal. 178, 121 Pac. 731.

95. Proctor v. Wells Bros. Co. of New York, 181 Ill. App. 468, judg. aff'd 262 Ill. 77, 104 N. E. 186. Mere silence or concealment by defendant without affirmative misrepresentation does not toll the statute of limitations. Id.

96. Miller v. Lesser, 71 Iowa, 147, 32 N. W. 250, the only exceptions in the Iowa statute being in § 2530, which provides that, in the case of fraud, mistake, or trespass, the statute shall not run until the discovery of the same.

97. Myers v. Center, 47 Kan. 324, 27 Pac. 978, under Kan. Civ. Code, § 21, which provides that, when a cause of action accrues against a person who has "absconded or concealed" himself, the period limited for the commencement of the action shall not begin to run while he is so absconded or concealed. See also Swickard v. Bailey, 3 Kan. 507.

The word "conceal," as used in the statute, applies to acts of a party in Kansas. Frey v. Aultman, Miller & Co., 30 Kan. 181, 2 Pac. 168.

A mere nonuser of all corporate powers is not a concealment of the corporation, such as to suspend the running of the statute. City of Ft. Scott v. Schulenberg, 22 Kan. 648.

98. Martin v. Jennings, 10 La. Ann. 553; Blossman v. Mather, 5 La. Ann. 335.

sconding or concealing must be of such a character as to prevent the commencement of an action, and a judgment debtor who merely concealed his name from an assignee of the judgment, and stated that he did not know where the debtor resided, and offered a nominal sum for the judgment, did not prevent an action on the judgment and was not guilty of absconding or concealing himself, or other improper act, so as to toll the statute.[99] The concealment or absconding which, under the Nebraska statute, suspends the operation of the statute, must be such as affects the commencement of judicial proceedings in that State.[1] In New York, where the debtor is continually in the State for more than six years after the cause of action accrues, the statute relating to absence from the State has no application, and the statute of limitations will operate, even though he conceals his abode from his creditor, who is thus unable to discover and serve him with process, and even if he changes his name for the purpose of eluding his creditor.[2] One who clandestinely leaves a distant State and settles in Oregon, but makes no effort there to conceal his identity or place of residence, is not "concealed" in the State, within the exception of the Oregon statute.[3] "Departing without the State" within the meaning of the Virginia statute, relating to limitation of actions, is a removal from the State with the intention of changing one's residence, and the burden of proving such removal is on the plaintiff.[4]

99. Davis v. Carp, 258 Mo. 686, 167 S. W. 1042, under Mo. Rev. St. 1909, § 1905. See also Harman v. Looker, 73 Mo. 622; Nelson v. Beveridge, 21 Mo. 22; Bobb v. Shipley, 1 Mo. 229.

The statute does not apply to concealments or improper acts by other persons than the debtor. Wells v. Halpin, 59 Mo. 92.

1. Talcott v. Bennett, 49 Neb. 569, 68 N. W. 931, under Code Civ. Proc. § 20. See also Thomas v. Brewer, 55 Iowa, 227, 7 N. W. 571.

2. Engel v. Fischer, 102 N. Y. 400, 7 N. E. 300, 55 Am. Rep. 818, rev'g 51 N. Y. Super. Ct. (19 Jones & S.) 71, 15 Abb. N. C. 72, under Code Civ. Proc. § 401.

3. Rhoton v. Mendenhall, 17 Or. 199, 20 Pac. 49, under Hill's Ann. Code, § 16.

4. Brown v. Butler, 87 Va. 621, 13 S. E. 71, under Va. Code, § 2933.

§ 249a(2). Ignorance of person entitled to sue.

Where suit was brought in Michigan on a bond made in New Jersey, plaintiff's ignorance of the fact that the maker of the bond had removed to Michigan will not arrest the running of limitations.[5] In New York, the statute of limitations does not run in favor of a nonresident debtor who comes into the State clandestinely, and with intent to defraud his creditor, by setting the statute to running, and then departing.[6] In Maryland, the presence of the debtor within the State must be such as to enable the creditor to avail himself of it. A secret presence, of which the creditor could not take advantage, is not sufficient.[7] Proof that plaintiff inquired for defendant, and could not find where he was, so as to sue, prevents the statute of limitations from running, in Missouri.[8] In Vermont, where a debtor, nonresident when the cause of action accrued, comes to reside in the State, it is not necessary for the creditor to know of his arrival in order for the statute of limitations to begin to run.[9] In Iowa, the running of the statute of limitations on a claim against a foreign corporation is not dependent on plaintiff's knowledge or lack of knowledge of the presence of the general agent in the State.[10] As to the effect of ignorance of the person entitled to sue upon the running of the statute of limitations in other jurisdictions, see authorities cited in note below.[11]

5. Home Life Ins. Co. v. Elwell, 111 Mich. 689, 70 N. W. 334, 3 Detroit Leg. N. 853.

A foreign plaintiff is not relieved from the force of the statute of limitations because he is ignorant that defendant has removed to this State. Dowse v. Gaynor, 155 Mich. 38, 118 N. W. 615, 15 Detroit Leg. N. 897.

6. Fowler v. Hunt, 10 Johns. (N. Y.) 464.

7. Hysinger v. Baltzell, 3 Gill & J. (Md.) 158.

8. Bobb v. Shipley, 1 Mo. 229.

9. Davis v. Field, 56 Vt. 426. See also Mazozon v. Foot, 1 Aikens (Vt.) 282, 15 Am. Dec. 679.

10. Winney v. Sandwich Mfg. Co., 86 Iowa 608, 53 N. W. 421, 18 L. R. A. 524.

11. *U. S.*—Patterson v. Safe Deposit & Trust Co. of Baltimore, 148 Fed. 787, 78 C. C. A. 453; Cadmus v. Polhamus, Fed. Cas. No. 2,282a.

Ala.—State Bank v. Seawell, 18 Ala. 616.

Me.—Crosby v. Wyatt, 23 Me. (10 Shep.) 156.

Tex.—Montgomery v. Brown, 9 Tex. Civ. App. 127, 28 S. W. 834.

§ 249b. Concealment of property involved or liable.

Removal or concealment of property, to avoid its recovery by an action of replevin, will not postpone the running of the statute of limitations against an action of trover for its conversion.[12] When there is no fraudulent concealment of the fact that a right of action exists, but a concealment merely of the existence of property from which a judgment might be satisfied, the operation of the statute of limitations is not suspended.[13] Where property has been within the State during the period of limitation, in order to take the case out of the statute there must have been such notoriety to this ownership that the creditor might, with common and ordinary diligence, have secured his debt, or by attachment have given jurisdiction to the court, so that judgment could have been had, and his claim preserved in force.[14] Where a husband, having funds of his wife in his hands, loaned them with other money of his own, taking a mortgage as security, in the absence of evidence to the contrary, it would be presumed that the security was taken by the husband with the consent of the wife; and hence the husband was not guilty of conversion of her money, so as to set the statute of limitations running as against her claim for reimbursement.[15] The Oklahoma statute of limitations, as to personalty stolen and removed from the jurisdiction, is suspended by § 4502, and begins to run in favor of an innocent purchaser so as bar replevin by the true owner from the time the property is returned to the jurisdiction in Oklahoma and held openly for three years.[16]

12. Chapman v. Hudson, 46 Ark. 489.

One taking up an estray without advertising it as required by Kirby's Dig. c. 149, subd. 2, §§ 7833-7868, but converting the animal to his own use, and claiming in bad faith to own it, is guilty of fraudulently concealing it from the owner, within section 5088, and limitation did not begin to run against the owner until discovery of the fraud. Conditt v. Holden, 92 Ark. 618, 123 S. W. 765.

13. Humphreys v. Mattoon, 43 Iowa, 556.

14. Dow v. Sayward, 12 N. H. 271.

15. *In re* Fraser, 92 N. Y. 239.

16. Vaught v. Gatlin, 31 Okl. 394, 120 Pac. 273. See Mansf. Dig. §§ 4478, 4502 (Ind. T. Ann. St. 1899, §§ 2945, 2969).

§ 249c. Effect as to parties jointly or severally liable, guarantors, and sureties.

The absence of a principal debtor from the State will not suspend the statute of limitations in favor of his surety,[17] nor will the absence from the State of the principal suspend the statute in favor of the sureties on an administrator's bond; they are severally liable, and are severally entitled to the protection of the statute.[18] Absence of a mortgagor from the state will not prevent limitations running in favor of his grantee, who is not obligated to pay the debt;[19] and the absence of the mortgagee from the State, after he has parted with the title, does not prevent the running of limitations in favor of his grantee.[20] The right to subject land to the payment of the purchase money depending upon the enforcement of a judgment against the purchaser, the absence of a grantee of such purchaser from the State does not operate to suspend the statute of limitations, and this though the grantee assumed payment, such assumption not having been accepted.[21] The absence of a mortgagor from the State does not suspend the statute of limitations against a resident who assumed payment of the mortgage.[22]

17. Mozingo v. Ross, 150 Ind. 688, 50 N. E. 867, 41 L. R. A. 612, 65 Am. St. Rep. 387. The statute of limitations does not run against a surety on a sealed note, who pays it, during the absence of the principal from the State. Smith v. Swain, 7 Rich. Eq. (S. C.) 112.

18. Davis v. Clark, 58 Kan. 454, 49 Pac. 665.

19. George v. Butler, 26 Wash. 456, 67 Pac. 263, 57 L. R. A. 396, 90 Am. St. Rep. 756.

Where a mortgagor died intestate before the mortgage debt was due, and left four heirs, only one of whom was resident, no administrator was ever appointed, and nearly fourteen years after the debt was due, the heirs conveyed the land to defendant, an action to foreclose was barred as to one-fourth of the land, but was not barred as to the remaining three-fourths. Colonial & United States Mortg. Co. v. Flemington, 14 N. D. 181, 103 N. W. 929, 116 Am. St. Rep. 670.

20 Colonial & United States Mortgage Co. v. Northwest Thresher Co., 14 N. D. 147, 103 N. W. 915, 116 Am. St. Rep. 642.

21. Miller v. Anders, 21 Tex. Civ. App. 72, 51 S. W. 897.

22. Robertson v. Stuhlmiller, 93 Iowa, 326, 61 N. W. 986.

Where a mortgage is given as collateral security for the bond of a third person, and obligor in the bond joins in the mortgage, though he has no interest in the mortgaged land,

The absence from the State of one of several joint debtors suspends the statute of limitations as to all.[23] Where one of two joint debtors absents himself from the State, the statute is suspended as to him, but runs as to the other.[24] A debt may be barred by the statute of limitations as to a partner residing in the State, notwithstanding it continues in force against his absent copartners.[25] When a cause of action against the agent of an undisclosed principal is barred by the statute of limitations, no action can be brought against the principal when discovered.[26]

§ 250. Foreign corporations.

Foreign corporations, although having general agents and transacting business in a State, come within the provisions of those statutes which make a saving as to absent debtors;[27] for although by comity, they may transact business in another State, yet they are "citizens," so to speak, of the State under the laws of which they are created, and, except by comity, have no legal existence elsewhere, and consequently are "absent," within the meaning of the term as used in these statutes, from every State except the one in

the absence of the mortgagor from the State does not stop the running of the statute of limitations against the mortgage. Fowler v. Wood, 78 Hun 304, 28 N. Y. Supp. 976.

23. Reybold v. Parker, 7 Houst. (Del.) 526, 32 Atl. 981; Casey v. Kimball, 7 Ohio Dec. 584, 4 Wkly. Law Bul. 78.

24. Brewster v. Bates, 81 Hun, 294, 30 N. Y. Supp. 780; Caswell v. Engelmann, 31 Wis. 93. And see § 246, *supra.*

25. Spaulding v. Ludlow Woolen Mill, 36 Vt. 150; Town v. Washburn, 14 Minn. 268, 100 Am. Dec. 219.

The return of one of several partners, who, while out of the State, contracted a debt to creditors within the State, did not set the statute running as to the others. Davis v. Kinney, 1 Abb. Prac. (N. Y.) 440.

26. Ware v. Galveston City Co., 111 U. S. 170, 4 Sup. Ct. 337, 28 L. Ed. 393.

27. Robinson v. Imperial, etc., Mining Co., 5 Nev. 44; Rathbun v. Northern Central R. Co., 50 N. Y. 656; Olcott v. Tioga R. Co., 20 N. Y. 210; Thompson v. Tioga R. Co., 36 Barb. (N. Y.) 79; Mallory v. Tioga R. R. Co., 3 Keyes (N. Y.) 354. In New York, in Faulkner v. Delaware, etc., Canal Co., 1 Den. (N. Y.) 441, a contrary doctrine was held, but was overruled. Olcott v. Tioga R. Co., *supra.* And the doctrine of the latter case now prevails in that State.

which they have their situs.[28] The rule above stated, however, would have no application in Vermont, when the corporation had attachable property in the State; because the statute of that State does not save a debt from the operation of the statute where the debtor has known property in the State, which, by the ordinary process of law, might be attached.[29]

Defendant foreign corporation, having no other representatives in Maryland, than mere selling agents, was not subject to service of process as affecting limitations under a Maryland statute, which provides that, if any person liable to suit shall be absent from the State when the cause of action accrues against him, he shall have no benefit of the statute of limitations.[30] A foreign corporation suing a Kansas shipper to recover for an alleged balance due according to the legal rates, cannot, to a counterclaim for damages to the property transported, plead the statute of limitations.[31]

§ 251. Cumulative disabilities.

Except where the statute otherwise so provides, one disability cannot be tacked to another, nor the disabilities of an ancestor to those of the heir, to protect a party from the operation of the statute;[32] nor can a party avail himself of several disabilities, un-

28. See Turcott v. Railroad, 101 Tenn. 102, 45 S. W. 1067, 40 L. R. A. 768, 70 Am. St. Rep. 661, and n. As to the right of a foreign corporation to plead the statute of limitations, see Winney v. Sandwich Mfg. Co., 86 Iowa 608, 53 N. W. 421, 18 L. R. A. 524, and n., 38 Cent. L. J. 275. See also as to foreign corporations, Larson v. Aultman & Taylor Co., 86 Wis. 281, 56 N. W. 915, 39 Am. St. Rep. 893; Clarke v. Bank of Mississippi, 10 Ark. 516, 52 Am. Dec. 248, and n.

29. Hull v. Vermont, etc., R. R. Co., 28 Vt. 401.

30. Duryee v. Sunlight Gas Mach. Co., 132 N. Y. Supp. 407, 74 Misc. Rep. 440.

31. Oregon R. & Nav. Co. v. Thisler, 90 Kan. 5, 133 Pac. 539.

32. Clark v. Jones, 55 Ky. (16 B. Mon.) 121; Parsons v. McCracken, 9 Leigh (Va.) 495; Martin v. Letty, 57 Ky. (18 B. Mon.) 573; Boyce v. Dudley, 47 Ky. (8 B. Mon.) 511; Jackson v. Wheat, 18 Johns. (N. Y.) 40; McDonald v. Johns, 12 Tenn. (4 Yerg.) 258. Cumulative disabilities are of no avail against the statute of limitations. Fritz v. Joiner, 54 Ill. 101; Mercer v. Selden, 42 U. S. (1 How.) 37; 11 L. Ed. 38; Thorp v. Raymond, 57 U. S. (16 How.) 247, 14 L. Ed. 923; Ashbrook v. Quarles, 54 Ky. (15 B. Mon.) 20; White v. Latimer, 12 Tex. 61; Currier v.

less they all existed at the time when the right of action accrued.[33] Thus, if a right of action accrues to a female infant, and she afterwards marries, the coverture does not create an additional disability; but, notwithstanding the coverture, an action must be brought within the specified period after she becomes of age, or the claim will be barred,[34] as no supervenient disability can have the

Gale, 85 Mass. (3 Allen) 328; Dessaunier v. Murphy, 33 Mo. 184, where, at the time the right of action accrued, the plaintiff was insane, but subsequently recovered; and before the statute had run upon the claim he again became insane, it was sought to avoid the effect of the statute under this second disability; but the court held that, as the statute began to run from he time of his recovery from his lunacy, it was not arrested by a return of the disability. Clark v. Trail, 58 Ky. (1 Metc.) 35. The disability of minor children cannot be added to the disability of the mother, under whom they claim. Mitchell v. Berry, 58 Ky. (1 Metc.) 602; Mercer v. Selden, 42 U. S. (1 How.) 37; Starke v. Starke, 3 Rich. (S. C.) 438; Thorp v. Raymond, 57 U. S. (16 How.) 247; Dease v. Jones, 23 Miss. 133; Caldwell v. Thorp, 8 Ala. 25; Tyson v. Britton, 6 Tex. 222; Stevens v. Bomar, 28 Tenn. (9 Humph.) 546.

33. Bunce v. Wolcott, 2 Conn. 27. In Bradstreet v. Clarke, 12 Wend. (N. Y.) 602, it is held that cumulative disabilities cannot be allowed either in real or personal actions. Rankin v. Tenbrook, 6 Watts (Pa.) 388; Kendal v. Slaughter, 1 A. K. Mar. (Ky.) 375. A few cases have here applied this rule in personal actions, Butler v. Howe, 13 Me. 397; and there can be no question but that in this country this rule is applicable in either real or personal actions. In England there is no actual decision upon this question; but in Borrows v. Ellison, L. R. 6 Exch. 128, there are *dicta* which intimate a contrary rule from that held in this country; but such a doctrine hardly seems warranted by a fair construction of the English statutes, and it is extremely doubtful whether, if a case involving the question should arise, it would be applied. In Bunce v. Wolcott, 2 Conn. 32, where an application was made to redeem a mortgage by the heirs of a mortgagor, more than fifty years after his death, because of certain irregularities, and it was sought to avoid the effect of the statute of limitations as to the heirs by tacking the disability of infancy and coverture together. But the court held that this could not be done, although it was permitted in an early case in that State. Eaton v. Sanford, 2 Day (Conn.) 523.

34. Clark v. Jones, *supra;* Fewell v. Collins, Const. Rep. (S. C.) 202; Wellborn v. Weaver, 17 Ga. 267; Mitchell v. Berry, 58 Ky. (1 Metc.) 602. The disability of coverture cannot be united with that of infancy to avoid the effect of the statute. Parsons v. McCracken, 9 Leigh (Va.) 495; Martin v. Letty, 57 Ky. (18 B. Mon.) 573; Manion v. Titsworth, id. 582; Billon v. Larimore, 37 Mo. 375;

effect to suspend the operation of the statute.[35] It will be observed

Carlisle v. Stitler, 1 Pa. 6; Dugan v. Gittings, 3 Gill (Md.) 138, 43 Am. Dec. 306. In Findley v. Patterson, 41 Ky. (2 B. Mon.) 76, it was held that an action for slaves held adversely to the wife on her marriage in infancy, must be brought within the statutory period after she became of age, and that the fact that the wife died before that time did not change the rule, and that the disability of infancy could not be lapped on to that of coverture so as to prolong the statutory saving against the legal effect of the lapse of time. Riggs v. Dooley, 46 Ky. (7 B. Mon.) 236. In Texas, a female infant upon her marriage immediately becomes of age, and the statute then begins to run against a previously existing claim. Thompson v. Cragg, 24 Tex. 582; White v. Latimer, 12 Tex. 61. But the rule is generally otherwise, and the statute does not begin to run until she becomes of age. Wilson v. Kilcannon, 7 Tenn. (4 Hayw.) 182. But in North Carolina it is held otherwise. Davis v. Cooke, 10 N. C. (3 Hawks) 608. But see Duckett v. Crider, 50 Ky. (11 B. Mon.) 188, where it was held that a woman under age was entitled to her action to recover possession of a slave. She married before she came of age, and it was held that the two disabilities of nonage and coverture could be joined for the purposes of deferring the bar of the statute of limitations. See Boyce v. Dudley, 47 Ky (8 B. Mon.) 511, where a contrary rule was adopted; and Martin v. Letty, 57 Ky. (18 B. Mon.) 573; Clark v. Jones, 55 Ky. (16 B. Mon.) 121; and see Wellborn v. Finley, 52 N. C. (7 Jones L.) 228, where it was held that the disability of nonage and coverture could not be joined to prevent the operation of the statute. In Keil v. Healey, 84 Ill. 104, it was held that the statute is not arrested by cumulative disabilities, as where a female is not married until five months after age, her coverture does not create a disability as to matters accruing before coverture; and the same doctrine was adopted in Cozzens v. Farnan, 30 Ohio St. 491, adopting the invariable rule that the disability which arrests the running of the statute must exist at the time when the right of action accrued. Hinde v. Whitney, 31 Ohio St. 53; Hogan v. Kurtz, 94 U. S. 773, 24 L. Ed. 317; Bozeman v. Browning, 31 Ark. 364; Roberts v. Moore, 3 Wall. Jr. (U. S. C. C.) 292; Hull v. Deatly, 70 Ky. (7 Bush) 687; Fritz v. Joiner, 54 Ill. 101; Harris v. McGovern, 2 Sawyer (U. S.) 515; Rogers v. Brown, 61 Mo. 187; Swearingen v. Robertson, 39 Wis. 462.

35. Bunce v. Wolcott, 2 Conn. 32. A party cannot avail himself of any disability to bring himself within the saving of the statute, except such as existed at the time when the cause of action accrued. McCoy v. Nichols, 5 Miss. 31. And no after accruing disability can stop the statute after it has once commenced to run. Parsons v. McCracken, 9 Leigh (Va.) 495; Fitzhugh v. Anderson, 2 H. & M. (Va.) 289; Hudson v. Hudson, 6 Munf. (Va.) 352; McDonald v. Johns., 12 Tenn. (4 Yerg.) 358. In Demarest v. Wynkoop, 3 Johns. (N. Y.) Ch. 129, the court held that a disability to relieve a party from the operation of the statute limiting real

that the saving clause in the statute of James, as well in all our statutes, is limited expressly to such disabilities as existed at the time the right of action accrued; consequently, if, at the time when a right of action accrues, a man is of full age, the fact that he shortly afterwards became insane will not save his claim from the operation of the statute.[36] Nor if a right of action accrues in

actions must exist when the right first accrues, and that although before the termination of the first disability another commences, the statute begins to run from the termination of the first. In Lewis v. Marshall, 30 U. S. (5 Pet.) 469, 8 L. Ed. 195, it was held, under a former statute of limitations of Kentucky limiting the right of action against one in the adverse possession of land to twenty years, provided that persons under disability may, although said twenty years are expired, maintain his action, or make his entry, within ten years next after such disabilities removed, or the death of the person so disabled, that if an adverse possession of land commenced during the disability of a claimant, who died during such disability, the ten years began to run against his heirs from the time of his death; but if the right of such claimant descended to his heirs before the commencement of the adverse possession, the statute did not operate against them until their disability was removed. In Texas, by statute, a female infant, upon her marriage, becomes of full age although in fact a minor; and this is held to deprive her of both the disabilities of infancy and coverture as to all rights of action which accrued before her marriage. Thompson v. Cragg, 24 Tex. 582. The provisions in the statute exempting certain persons subject to specified disabilities until ten years after their removal, only applies where some one of such disabilities exists in the person entitled to the estate at the commencement of the adverse possession; and if there be a succession of such disabilities, whether in the person then entitled, or in him or those who succeed to his title, such person or persons are protected by the proviso only for ten years after the removal of the first disability. Clarke v. Cross, 2 R. I. 440. Disabilities which may bring a person within the exceptions cannot be piled one upon another, but only the disability in existence at the time the cause of action accrued applies. When there are two or more coexisting disabilities in the same person at the time the cause of action accrues, as, for instance, infancy and coverture, the statute does not run till both or all are removed. But if at the time the cause of action accrues only one disability exists, others which arise afterwards cannot be tacked to the first disability so as to prevent the operation of the statute. Scott v. Haddock, 11 Ga. 258; Young v. Mackall, 4 Md. 362.

36. In Adamson v. Smith, 2 Mill. Const. (S. C.) 269, 12 Am. Dec. 665, where a person who was under no disability at the time when a note given to him became due shortly

favor of a female of full age, and she soon afterwards marries, will the disability of coverture save her rights from being barred by the lapse of the statutory period.[37] This is in obedience to the universal rule, before stated, that when the statute once begins to run no subsequent disability can stop its operation,[38] unless specially so provided in the statute. It may be stated as a general rule, to which there are no exceptions, that, except when the statute otherwise provides, disabilities which bring a person within the exceptions of the statute cannot be tacked one upon another, and that a party can only avail himself of such disability or disabilities as existed when the right of action accrued.[39] If a right of action accrues to a married woman during

afterwards became *non compos mentis*, the court held that this supervenient disability did not check the operation of the statute.

37. Carlisle v. Stitler, 1 Penn. 6.

38. Crozier v. Gano, 1 Bibb (Ky.) 257; Faysoux v. Prather, 1 Nott & Mc (S. C.) 296; Rogers v. Hillhouse, 3 Conn. 398; Peck v. Randall, 1 Johns. (N. Y.) 165; Ruff v. Bull, 7 Har. & J. (Md.) 14, 16 Am. Dec. 290. Dillard v. Philson, 5 Strobh. (S. C.) 213; Sevenson v. McReary, 20 Miss. 9 Byrd v. Byrd, 28 id. 144; Pendergrast v. Foley, 8 Ga. 1; Smith v. Newby, 13 Mo. 159; Parsons v. M'Cracken, 9 Leigh (Va.) 495; Hudson v. Hudson, 6 Munf. (Va.) 352.

39. McFarland v. Stone, 17 Vt. 165; Mercer v. Selden, 42 U. S. (1 How.) 37; White v. Latimer, 12 Tex. 61; South v. Thomas, 23 Ky. (7 T. B. Mon.) 59; M'Donald v. Johns. 12 Tenn. (4 Yerg.) 258; Thorp v. Raymond, 16 How. (U. S.) 247; Starke v. Starke, 3 Rich. (S. C.) 438; Rankin v. Tenbrook, 6 Watts (Pa.) 388; Doe v. Barksdale, 2 Brock. (U. S. C. C.) 436; Scott v. Haddock, 11 Ga. 258; Demarest v. Wynkoop, 3 Johns. (N. Y.) 129; Dease v. Jones, 23 Miss. 133; Den v. Richards, 15 N. J. L. 347; Bradstreet v. Clarke, 12 Wend. (N. Y.) 602; Jackson v. Wheat, 18 Johns. (N. Y.) 40. This rule, says Hosmer, J., in Bunce v. Wolcott, 2 Conn. 34, "avoids the inconvenience of accumulated successive disabilities, which, for an interminable period, might subvert titles apparently well established, and produce the most ruinous instability." 3 Bac. Abr. 206; Stowel v. Zouch, Plowd. 356; Duroure v. Jones, 4 T. R. 300; George v. Jesson, 6 East 80; Eager v. Commonwealth, 4 Mass. 182. In Minnesota, Oregon, New York, and California, it is specially provided that no person shall avail himself of a disability unless it existed when the action accrued, and that if two or more disabilities existed when the cause of action arose, the statute shall not begin to run until all are removed. In all the States except Texas, Mississippi, and Indiana, the disability is expressly restricted to the time when the cause

coverture, and she becomes discovert, and before the statute has run upon her claim marries again, her second marriage does not prevent the statute from running upon the claim, because the statute, having once attached to the claim, overrides all after-accruing disabilities.[40] When several disabilities exist at the time when a right of action accrues, as, if a woman should be both an infant and a *feme covert,* or a *feme covert* and insane, she may elect to avail herself of either of the disabilities, and, if no election is made, the court would give her the advantage of the one most available to defeat the statute; and in the language of Edmund, J.,[41] "It will always be a sufficient answer to an objector to such an election to say, 'the disability on which I rely is pointed out by the proviso. It existed at the time my right or title accrued. I have prosecuted my claim within the time allowed after its discontinuance, and come within both the letter and spirit of the law.'"[42] The disabilities are not merged, but each remains distinctly until it is extinguished by lapse of time;[43] and, as we have already stated, either may be set up to defeat the statute as the party may elect.

§ 251a. Coexisting disabilities.

When there are two or more coexisting disabilities in the same

of action accrues; but in those States the words "when the right of action accrues," or "when the cause of action arises," are not used in the statute, and in those States cumulative disabilities may doubtless be tacked. In Texas it is held that the statute relates to such disabilities only as existed when the right of action arose. White v. Latimer, 12 Tex. 61.

40. Downing v. Ford, 39 Ky. (9 Dana) 391; McDonald v. McGuire, 8 Tex. 361; Den v. Moore, 3 Wall. Jr. (U. S.) 292; Mitchell v. Berry, 58 Ky. (1 Met.) 602.

41. Bunce v. Wolcott, 2 Conn. 34. In Dugan v. Gittings, 3 Gill (Md.) 138, 43 Am. Dec. 306, the same doctrine was held. In Allis v. Moore, 84 Mass. (2 Allen) 306, it was held that, where an owner of land has been disseised, his subsequent insanity will not prevent the disseisor's title from maturing by twenty years' adverse possession.

42. Butler v. Howe, 13 Me. 397; Keeton's Heirs v. Keeton's Adm'r, 20 Mo. 530; Sturt v. Mellish, 2 Atk. 616; Jordan v. Thornton, 7 Ga. 517.

43. Martin v. Letty, *supra;* Robertson v. Wurdeman, 2 Hill (S. C.) 324; Layton v. State, 4 Harr. (Del.) 8; Carter v. Cantrell, 16 Ark. 154.

person, when his right of action accrues, he is not obliged to act until the last is removed.[44] When the disabilities of infancy and coverture exist at the execution of a deed, the right to disaffirm continues until both disabilities are removed, and through the ordinary limitations thereafter, whatever time elapses between the date of the deed and its disaffirmance.[45] When there are two or more coexisting disabilities in the same person, at the time the cause of action accrues,—as, for instance, infancy and coverture,—the statute of limitations does not run until both or all are removed.[46]

§ 251b. Tacking successive disabilities.

As has been stated in a preceding section,[47] tacking or cumulating disabilities under the statutes of limitations, as a general rule, is not allowable.[48] One disability cannot be tacked onto another to

44. Wilson v. Branch, 77 Va. 65, 7 Va. Law J. 161, 46 Am. Rep. 709.

The omission of a married woman to exercise her right to sue alone cannot operate to her prejudice, so as to allow the statute of limitations to bar her action. Under Battle's Revisal, c. 17, § 28, the statute "shall not begin to run until the termination of the latest disability," in case minority and coverture coexist. Lippard v. Troutman, 72 N. C. 551.

Under the Michigan Married Women's Act of 1855, a married woman is relieved from all disability to sue, and the statute of limitations will run against her, though she was married while an infant, and had remained married up to the time of the action. Douglass v. Douglass, 72 Mich. 86, 40 N. W. 177.

45. Blake v. Hollandsworth, 71 W. Va. 387, 76 S. E. 814.

Limitations do not run against the right of an infant *feme covert* to disaffirm a conveyance during marriage. Fox v. Drewry, 62 Ark. 316, 35 S. W. 533.

46. *Ga.*—Scott v. Haddock, 11 Ga. 258.

Me.—Butler v. Howe, 13 Me. (1 Shep.) 397.

Md.—Dugan v. Gittings, 3 Gill 138, 43 Am. Dec. 306.

Miss.—North v. James, 61 Miss. 761. See Watts v. Gunn, 53 Miss. 502.

Mo.—Keeton's Heirs v. Keeton's Adm'r, 20 Mo. 530.

N. Y.—Jackson v. Jackson, 5 Cow. 74, 15 Am. Dec. 433.

47. See § 251, *supra*.

48. Rutter v. Carothers, 223 Mo. 631, 122 S. W. 1056.

Mo. Rev. St. 1899, § 4265, provides that, if any person entitled to commence an action for the recovery of real estate be under disability when the cause of action accrues, the time during which such disability shall continue shall not be deemed a portion of the time limited for the com-

avoid the operation of the statute.[49] The disability of coverture cannot be added to that of infancy to prevent the running of the statute.[50] The disability of minority cannot be tacked onto the disability of coverture of the ancestor of the minors.[51] Where one who was an infant when his cause of action accrued afterwards

mencement of the action, but that such person may bring the action after the time so limited and within three years after removal of disability, provided that no such action shall be commenced by any person under disability after 24 years after the accrual of the cause of action. Section 4267 provides that, if any person entitled to commence any action die during the continuance of any disability specified in section 4265, and no determination or judgment be had of the title or right of action to him accrued, his heirs may commence such action after the time limited and within three years after his death, but not after that period. It was held that disabilities cannot be cumulated, and where an infant, having a cause of action, died before his majority, his heir could not commence an action after three years from the death, though the heir was under disability at the time of the death; the heir not being entitled to the provisions of section 4265. Robinson v. Allison, 192 Mo. 366, 91 S. W. 115. So, where a person entitled to commence an action was insane at the time of her death, the disability of a devisee who was under coverture at the time the descent was cast on her could not be tacked to that of the ancestor, in order to avoid limitations. De Hatre v. Edmunds, 200 Mo. 246, 98 S. W. 744.

The marriage of a woman after reaching her majority does not interrupt the running of the statute of limitations against her right to disaffirm a deed made during her minority. Priddy v. Boice, 201 Mo. 309, 99 S. W. 1055.

49. Knippenberg v. Morris, 80 Ind. 540; Williams v. Dongan, 20 Mo. 186; Hancock v. Hutcherson, 76 Va. 609.

50. Knippenberg v. Morris, *supra;* Eager v. Commonwealth, 4 Mass. 182; Quick v. Rufe, 164 Mo. 408, 64 S. W. 102; Franklin v. Cunningham, 187 Mo. 184, 86 S. W. 79; Buttery v. Brown (Tenn. Ch. App.), 52 S. W. 713; Hale v. Ellison (Tenn.), 59 S. 673; Louisiania & T. Lumber Co. v. Lovell (Tex. Civ. App.), 147 S. W. 366; York v. Hutcheson, 37 Tex. Civ. App. 367, 83 S. W. 895; Reed v. Money (Ark.), 170 S. W. 478.

51. Elcan v. Childress, 40 Tex. Civ. App. 193, 89 S. W. 84; Laird v. Murray (Tex. Civ. App.), 111 S. W. 780, under the express provisions of Rev. St. 1895, art. 3376.

Where a right of action to recover certain real estate accrued to a married woman during coverture, and she died while the right of action existed, leaving minor heirs, such heirs could not set up their disability of infancy as an excuse for not having brought their action within the time limited by the statute. Lamberida v. Barnum (Tex. Civ. App.), 90 S. W. 698.

became of unsound mind, this disability cannot be added to that of infancy, to extend the time for bringing suit.[52] Under St. 21 James I, c. 16, in force in Maryland, providing that no person shall make entry into lands but within twenty years next after his right or title shall accrue, and in default thereof such persons not entering and their heirs shall be utterly excluded and disabled from any entry thereafter, provided that if, at the time the right or title first descended, the person having the same shall be within the age of twenty-one years, such person may make entry within ten years after his full age, the persons protected in the proviso cannot avail themselves of successive or cumulative disabilities, so that, where a disability ceases while the period of twenty-year limitations in running, the ten years given to the person subject to the disability will run concurrently with the twenty years, and not successively to it.[53] Though the owner of land was an infant just born when adverse possession of it began, and died before his right of action to recover was barred, leaving infant heirs, their right of action, as his would have been, is barred, if there was no other disability than infancy, when the possession has continued thirty-one years; N. Y. Code Civ. Proc., § 375, providing that if a person, who might maintain an action to recover real estate, is, when his

52. Sharp v. Stephens' Committee, 21 Ky. Law Rep. 687, 52 S. W. 977.

Ky. St. 1903, § 2506, provides that if, at the time the right of any person to bring an action to recover real property first accrued, such person was an infant or married woman, such person may, though 15 years have expired, bring the action within three years after removal of disability. Section 2508 provides that the period within which an action for the recovery of real estate may be brought shall not in any case be extended beyond 30 years by the existence or continuance of any disability. It was held that an action to recover land was not barred, where it appeared that plaintiff's father sold it when she was an infant, and that, though the purchaser went into possession, plaintiff was a married woman when she reached her majority, and was still under the disability of coverture, and that 30 years had not elapsed. Smith v. Cornett, 30 Ky. Law Rep. 302, 98 S. W. 297.

53. Wickes v. Wickes, 98 Md. 307, 56 Atl. 1017; Stevens v. Wickes, Id.

Limitations give the heir of a person under disability only 10 years from the death of the ancestor to sue for land of which the ancestor was out of possession. Baumeister v. Silver, 98 Md. 418, 56 Atl. 825.

cause of action first accrues, either under the age of twenty-one years, or insane, or imprisoned, the time of such disability is not a part of the time limited for commencing the action, except that the time so limited cannot be extended more than ten years after the disability ceases, or after the death of the person so disabled.[54]

§ 252. Disability must be one provided for by statute.

The statute of limitations begins to run against a party immediately upon the accrual of a right of action, unless at that time he was under some of the disabilities named in the statute; and a saving or exception not found in the statute will not be implied, however much it may be within the reason of other exceptions.[55]

54. Messinger v. Foster, 101 N. Y. Supp. 387, 115 App. Div. 689.

55. Warfield v. Fox, 53 Pa. 382; Howell v. Hair, 15 Ala. 194; Favorite v. Booher, 17 Ohio St. 548; Pryor v. Ryburn, 16 Ark. 671; Bucklin v. Ford, 5 Barb. (N. Y.) 393; Wells v. Child, 94 Mass. (12 Allen) 333; The Sam Slick, 2 Curt. (U. S.) 480; Gaines v. Williams, 25 N. C. (3 Ired. L.) 481; Dozier v. Ellis, 28 Miss. 730; Sacia v. De Graaf, 1 Cow. (N. Y.) 356; Harrison v. Harrison, 39 Ala. 489. In Carrier v. Chicago, etc., R. Co., 79 Iowa 80, there is a *dictum* to the effect that the specification by the legislature of exceptions to the statute of limitations will not preclude the court from applying exceptions to such statute which are recognized by the common law, other than those prescribed by the legislature. While this *dictum* and this doctrine were wholly unnecessary to the decision, there was a class of cases in which it was held, although the statute made no exception upon that ground, that where a cause of action had been fraudulently concealed from the person in whose favor the right of action existed, the statute did not begin to run until the fraud was discovered, although this doctrine never found much support in the courts of this country or of England. Indeed, independent of the statute making them, no exceptions to the operation of the statute existed, except in equity, nor even in that court where the statute was in express terms made applicable to courts of equity, as well as to courts of law. The court, upholding Boomer Dist. Twp. v. French, 40 Iowa 601, and later cases, said: "These cases measured by the statute alone, are clearly barred; but in that case this court held the rule to be that 'where the party against whom a cause of action existed in favor of another, by fraud or actual fraudulent concealment prevented such other from obtaining knowledge thereof, the statute would only commence to run from the time the right of action was discovered, or might, by the means of diligence, have been discovered.'" It was said in Heiserman v. Burlington, C. R. &

Thus, the circumstance that the debtor is insolvent, and that a suit against him would be fruitless, or that the plaintiff had not the means to bring an action, does not create a bar to the legal remedy of the creditor.[56] Nor will the bankruptcy of a creditor excuse delay in bringing an action beyond the statutory period.[57] In Louisiana, however, when an insolvent has surrendered his

N. R. Co., 63 Iowa 736, that 'railroad companies are public carriers, and those who employ them are in their power, and must bow to the rod of authority which they hold over consignors and consignees of property transported by them. The reason for the rule requiring disclosures and fair dealing applies to this defendant with the same force that it did to French. The appellant contends that when exceptions are provided to a general statute it excludes all others than those expressed, and that courts are not at liberty to ingraft other exceptions than those expressed upon such a statute. This claim finds strong support in the following cases cited by counsel: Chemical Nat. Bank v. Kissanne, 32 Fed. 429; Engel v. Fischer, 102 N. Y. 400, 3 Cent. Rep. 303; Fee v. Fee, 10 Ohio 470; Amy v. Watertown, 130 U. S. 320, 9 Sup. Ct. 537, 32 L. Ed. 953, 22 Fed. 418; Bank of Alabama v. Dalton, 50 U. S. (9 How.) 526, 13 L. Ed. 242; Kendall v. United States, 107 U. S. 123, 2 Sup. Ct. 277, 27 L. Ed. 437, 19 Ct. Cl. 758; Favorite v. Booher, 17 Ohio St. 548; Woodbury v. Shackleford, 19 Wis. 55; Somerset Co. v. Veghte, 44 N. J. L. 509; Demarest v. Wynkoop, 3 Johns. Ch. 129; Miles v. Berry, 1 Hill L. 296; Troup v. Smith, 20 Johns. 33. These questions were presented and passed upon in a number of those cases, holding that the general statute excludes all others, and that when the legislature has made exceptions the courts can make none, Campbell v. Long, 20 Iowa 382; Shorick v. Bruce, 21 Iowa 307; Relf v. Eberly, 23 Iowa 469; Gebhard v. Sattler, 40 Iowa 152; Miller v. Lesser, 71 Iowa 147. Boomer Dist. Twp. v. French finds strong support in the authorities cited in the opinion. Sherwood v. Sutton, 5 Mason 143, wherein Judge Story reviews many cases, shows a diversity of rulings on this question by the courts of different States. Boomer Dist. Twp. v. French was approved. Humphreys v. Mattoon, 43 Iowa 556; Findley v. Stewart, 46 Iowa 655; Brunson v. Ballou, 70 Iowa 34; Bradford v. McCormick, 71 Iowa 129; Wilder v. Secor, 72 Iowa 161; Shreves v. Leonard, 56 Iowa 74. We think there is no sufficient reason for now reversing the conclusion there announced.

56. Mason v. Crosby, Davies (U. S.) 303. But in this case the pecuniary embarrassments of the plaintiff were held sufficient in equity to excuse delay not beyond the period of legal limitation in bringing his bill, to relieve his claim from the imputation of staleness, and especially where his embarrassments were occasioned by the defendant.

57. Harwell v. Steel, 17 Ala. 372.

property, prescription is suspended as to his creditors; but this is held not to apply to successions, whether solvent or insolvent.[58] So, too, in that State it is held that the prescription of a judgment interrupts prescription against the hypothecary action on the judgment.[59] In North Carolina, it has been held that, where a note is deposited in the hands of a master by order of a court of equity, the acts of limitation are thereby suspended.[60] It may be safely said that the courts have no authority to make any exceptions in favor of the party, to protect him from the consequences of the statute, unless they come clearly within the letter of the saving clauses therein contained, and that the exercise of any such authority by the courts is a usurpation of legislative powers by it which is wholly unwarranted, and which courts should never resort to. By making the exceptions which exist in the statute the legislature has exercised its prerogative power, and the fact that no others were made clearly indicates that it intended that no others should exist, and the courts have no power to add any, however much the ends of justice in a particular case may demand it.[61]

58. Succession of Flower, 12 La. Ann. 216; West v. Creditors, 1 id. 365.

59. Van Wickle v. Garrett, 14 La. Ann. 106.

60. Kendal v. United States, 107 U. S. 123, *supra;* The Sam Slick, 2 Curt. (U. S.) 480; Leffingwell v. Warren, 2 Black (U. S.) 599; United States v. Muhlenbrink, 1 Woods (U. S.) 569; Fisher v. Harnden, 1 Paine (U. S.) 55; Amy v. Watertown, 130 U. S. 320, *supra.* There can be no exception unless expressly named in the statute, Bank of Alabama v. Dalton, 50 U. S. (9 How.) 522; Dupleix v. De Roven, 2 Vern. 540; McIver v. Ragan, 2 Wheat. (U. S.) 25; Hall v. Weyborn, 8 Salk. 420; Beckford v. Wade, 17 Ves. 87, and the rule is the same although it is claimed that the party setting up the statute has been guilty of fraud. Bucklin v. Ford, 5 Barb. (N. Y.) 393; Humbert v. Trinity Church, 24 Wend. (N. Y.) 587; Leonard v. Pitney, 5 Wend. (N. Y.) 30; Conner v. Goodman, 104 Ill. 365; United States v. Maillard, 4 Ben. (U. S.) 459; Gaines v. Miller, 111 U. S. 395, 4 Sup. Ct. 426, 28 L. Ed. 466; Wood v. Carpenter, 101 U. S. 135, 25 L. Ed. 807.

61. Vance v. Grainger, Cam. & N. (N. C.) 71.

§ 253. Disability of defendants.

It will be perceived that there is not in any of the statutes any saving in favor of the plaintiff on account of any disability of the defendant, and, consequently, that the mere circumstance that the person against whom a right of action accrues to a plaintiff, himself under no legal disability, is under a legal disability, does not save his claim from the operation of the statute because the defendant is an infant, *non compos mentis*, a *feme covert*, or alien enemy; and this was also the case under the statute of James.[62] The reason for this is hardly apparent, in view of the fact that the plaintiff, in the case of his own disability, is so carefully considered, especially in cases where the defendant, by reason of disability on his part, cannot be made a proper party to an action.[63] But while in the statute of James, as is also the case in the statute of several of the States of this country, if the plaintiff "is beyond seas," when his right of action accrued to him, his remedy is saved to him until his return into the country, yet his right of action is not saved by reason of the defendant's absence "beyond seas;" and unless provision is made by statute for the service of process upon an absent defendant, who has no known residence, place of business, or property in the State, a plaintiff's claim would be lost because of the impossibility of making service upon him.

62. Jones v. Turberville, 2 Ves. Jr. 11; Fladong v. Winter, 19 Ves. 196; Fannin v. Anderson, 7 Q. B. 811; Story v. Fry, 1 Y. & C. Ch. 603; Williams v. Jones, 13 East 439.

63. Banning on Limitations, 85.

CHAPTER XXIII.

PENDENCY OF LEGAL PROCEEDINGS, INJUNCTION, OR STAY.

§ 253a(1). Pendency of action or other proceeding—In general.

Statutes of limitation are statutes of repose, based on the likelihood that inaction for a protracted period would not occur unless a settlement had been made; and while litigation is going on, and the parties are using legal proceedings to effect a settlement, it would be at variance with the principles underlying limitations to hold that such statutes were then running.[1] Limitations do not run against an action by a receiver to enforce the liability of a shareholder of a national bank while proper liquidation proceedings are pending in a court of equity.[2] When a person is prevented from exercising his legal remedy by some paramount authority, the time during which he is thus prevented should not be counted against him in determining whether limitations have barred his

1. Klumpp v. Thomas, 162 Fed. 853, 89 C. C. A. 543 (C. C. A., Pa.).

2. King v. Pomeroy, 121 Fed. 287, 58 C. C. A. 209 (C. C. A., Kan.).

In order that the pendency of other proceedings may toll the statute of limitations, the proceedings must be such as to prevent the enforcement of the remedy by action. Harrison v. Scott, 77 Kan. 637, 95 Pac. 1045. See also, Walterscheid v. Bowdish, 77 Kan. 665, 96 Pac. 56; Steffins v. Gurney, 61 Kan. 292, 59 Pac. 725; City of Hutchinson v. Hutchinson, 92 Kan. 518, 141 Pac. 589.

right.[3] While an action against one claiming by adverse possession would stop the running of limitations pending the action, the rule will not apply to stop the running of limitations against a subsequent action, where the suit resulted in no change of possession.[4] Where contractors who laid a pavement were refused payment on the ground that it was not in compliance with the contract and were defeated in actions for the contract price and on the *quantum meruit,* the pendency of those actions tolled the statute of limitations as to their right to remove the pavement.[5] In view of Missouri Rev. St. 1909, § 2391, referring to actions in ejectment against several defendants, a previous suit against defendant who occupied land adversely, though praying cancellation of the deed to him, was held identical with a subsequent action of ejectment, and to toll the statute of limitations.[6] Where, in a proceeding before the New York State board of claims for allowance of a claim for work and materials furnished for the construction of a State asylum, under a contract with the managers, plaintiff sought to avoid the bar of the statute of limitations of six years by showing various efforts to collect the claim before it was barred, it was held that a mandamus proceeding against the managers to compel

3. St. Paul, etc., Ry. Co. v. Olson, 87 Minn. 117, 91 N. W. 294, 94 Am. St. Rep. 693. And see Downer v. Union Land Co., 103 Minn. 392, 115 N. W. 207.

4. Martin v. Hall, 152 Ky. 677, 153 S. W. 997. See also, as to pendency of action or other proceeding: City of Louisville v. Meglemery, 107 Ky. 122, 21 Ky. Law Rep. 751, 52 S. W. 1052; City of Louisville v. Hornsby's Ex'r, 23 Ky. Law Rep. 1238, 64 S. W. 996; Hyatt v. Anderson's Trustee, 25 Ky. Law Rep. 132, 74 S. W. 1094; 25 Ky. Law Rep. 711, 76 S. W. 337.

Under Ky. St., §§ 2519, 2544, efforts of a debtor to defeat liability, delaying judgment, do not extend the time for bringing suit to subject property voluntarily transferred without consideration, to the payment of the judgment. Graham's Adm'r v. English, 160 Ky. 375, 169 S. W. 836. A void judgment against the assignor on a note will not suspend the running of limitations in his favor against an action against him on the note. Arnett v. Howard, 156 Ky. 458, 161 S. W. 531.

5. Snouffer & Ford v. City of Tipton, 161 Iowa 223, 142 N. W. 97.

6. Norton v. Reed, 253 Mo. 236, 161 S. W. 842. See also, Estes v. Nell, 140 Mo. 639, 41 S. W. 940; De Both v. Rich Hill Coal-Min. Co., 141 Mo. 497, 42 S. W. 1081; Sanford v. Herron, 161 Mo. 176, 61 S. W. 839, 84 Am. St. Rep. 703.

them to measure stone furnished as provided in the contract did not stop the running of the statute, since the State was not a party, and the managers were not authorized to represent the State in any litigation, and such proceeding was not a necessary preliminary to the presentation of the claim to the State board of audit.[7]

7. Bissell v. State, 70 App. Div. 238, 73 N. Y. Supp. 1105, judg. aff'd, 177 N. Y. 540, 69 N. E. 1120.

See, generally, as to the effect of the pendency of an action or other proceeding on the operation of statutes of limitation:

Ala.—Taber v. Royal Ins. Co., 124 Ala. 68, 26 So. 252.

Ark.—Cole v. Hall, 85 Ark. 144, 107 S. W. 175.

Cal.—Clyne v. Easton, Eldredge & Co., 148 Cal. 287, 83 Pac. 36, 113 Am. St. Rep. 253; Earle v. Bryant, 12 Cal. App. 553, 107 Pac. 1018.

Colo.—Patterson v. Fort Lyon Canal Co., 36 Colo. 175, 84 Pac. 807; Altvater v. First Nat. Bank, 45 Colo. 528, 103 Pac. 378, the mere filing of a claim against the estate of a decedent in the county court did not arrest the running of the statute of limitations.

Conn.—The law calls for no one to perform a nugatory act, and a suit which could not be maintained would be useless to prevent running of limitations as to a cause of action. Appeal of Beardsley, 83 Conn. 34, 75 Atl. 141.

Ind.—Fast v. Swisher, 182 Ind. 501, 107 N. E. 6.

La.—Succession of Williams, 132 La. 865, 61 So. 852; Rees v. Sheridan, 135 La. 7, 64 So. 923, a reconventional demand interrupts prescription during pendency of the action; *In re* Southern Wood Mfg. Co., 49 La. Ann. 926, 22 So. 39; Woodcock v. Baldwin, 110 La. 270, 34 So. 440.

Md.—Williams v. Watters, 97 Md. 113, 54 Atl. 767; Williams v. Taylor, 99 Md. 306, 57 Atl. 641, applying Act Va. Dec. 22, 1897 (Acts 1897-98, p. 6, c. 20).

Neb.—Patrick v. National Bank of Commerce, 63 Neb. 200, 88 N. W. 183.

N. C.—Governor v. Franklin, 7 N. C. 213; Davis v. Pierce, 167 N. C. 135, 83 S. E. 182.

Ohio.—Mills, Spellmire & Co. v. Whitmore, 12 O. C. D. 338, 22 Ohio Cir. Ct. R. 467; Bray v. Darby, 82 Ohio 47, 91 N. E. 861, the allowance of a claim by an administrator suspends the right of the creditor to sue thereon, and thus arrests the running of limitations.

Tenn.—Weaver v. Ruhm (Ch. App.), 47 S. W. 171.

Tex.—Cates v. Field (Tex. Civ. App.), 85 S. W. 52; Holland v. Shannon (Civ. App.), 84 S. W. 854; Robinson v. Thompson (Civ. App.), 52 S. W. 117, rev'd Thompson v. Robinson, 93 Tex. 165, 54 S. W. 243, 77 Am. St. Rep. 843; Hanrick v. Gurley (Civ. App.), 48 S. W. 994, modified 93 Tex. 458, 54 S. W. 347, and 93 Tex. 458, 55 S. W. 119, 56 S. W. 330; Maes v. Thomas (Civ. App.), 140 S. W. 846.

Va.—Sipe v. Taylor, 106 Va. 231, 55 S. E. 542; Robinett's Adm'r v. Mitchell, 101 Va. 762, 45 S. E. 287,

§ 253a(2). Pendency of action on different cause or in different forum.

In an action under Illinois Rev. St. c. 68, § 15, providing that the expenses of the family are chargeable upon the property of both husband and wife or either of them, and in relation thereto they may be sued jointly or severally, the running of the statute of limitations is not tolled as against the wife by the fact that a judgment had been obtained against her husband.[8] Prescription on the notes of a corporation is not interrupted by a suit brought against certain of the stockholders upon the theory of their being bound as commercial partners, in consequence of failure to effect legal incorporation, though the receiver of the corporation may have attempted to consolidate such suits with the receivership.[9] The pendency of an action against a deputy sheriff for seizure of plaintiff's property under a writ against another does not suspend the running of limitations in favor of the sheriff.[10] That defendants were sued by other parties for the land in controversy during the time necessary to complete the period of limitations in favor of defendant as against plaintiff did not interrupt the statute as between them.[11] Where residuary devisees execute a power of at-

99 Am. St. Rep. 928; Gunnell's Adm'rs v. Dixon's Adm'r, 101 Va. 174, 43 S. E. 340; Callaway's Adm'r v. Saunders, 99 Va. 350, 38 S. E. 182; Covington v. Griffin's Adm'r, 98 Va. 124, 34 S. E. 974; Repass v. Moore, 96 Va. 147, 30 S. E. 458; Harvey's Adm'r v. Steptoe's Adm'r, 17 Grat. 289.

W. Va.—Woods v. Douglass, 52 W. Va. 517, 44 S. E. 234; Rowan v. Chenoweth, 49 W. Va. 287, 38 S. E. 544, 87 Am. St. Rep. 796; Keck v. Allender, 42 W. Va. 420, 26 S. E. 437.

Wis.—Maldaner v. Beurhaus, 108 Wis. 25, 84 N. W. 25.

8. Staver Carriage Co. v. Beaudry, 138 Ill. App. 147. As to partition suit, see Spencer v. Wiley, 46 Ill. App. 585.

9. Taylor v. Vossburg Mineral Springs Co., 128 La. 364, 54 So. 907.

10. Lyman v. Holmes (Vt.), 92 Atl. 829.

11. Paterson v. Rector (Tex. Civ. App.), 91 N. E. 861. And see, as to the effect of the pendency of action on different causes on limitations, under Texas statutes: Noel v. Clark, 25 Tex. Civ. App. 136, 60 S. W. 356; Herr v. Rodriguez (Civ. App.), 50 S. W. 487; Hays v. Tilson, 18 Tex. Civ. App. 610, 45 S. W. 479; Bowen v. Kirkland, 17 Tex. Civ. App. 346; Robb v. Henry (Civ. App.), 40 S.

torney, authorizing the attorney to sell and convey all their interest in the real estate of the decedent, and the land is thereafter sold under such power, proceedings in the Surrogate's Court for the settlement of the personal estate of the testator, in which the devisees were defendants, did not prevent them from asserting any remedies they might have for the moneys collected under the power of attorney, so as to prevent the running of the statute.[12] Where the court has refused to entertain jurisdiction of a suit to recover lands because a controversy concerning them was then pending between the parties in the land department of the United States, limitations do not begin to run against the right to recover the lands until after the termination of such controversy.[13] An action to foreclose a mortgage does not suspend the running of limitations as to an action on the notes secured by the mortgage.[14]

W. 1047; City of Dallas v. Kruegel, 95 Tex. 43, 64 S. W. 922.

12. Yates v. Wing, 42 App. Div. 356, 59 N. Y. Supp. 78. Code Civ. Proc., § 405, authorizing actions to be brought after the period limited, where a prior action has been brought within such period, applies to an action for wrongful death required by section 1902 to be commenced within two years after the death. Hoffman v. Delaware & H. Co., 148 N. Y. Supp. 509.

13. Frink v. Hoke, 35 Or. 17, 56 Pac. 1093.

14. Hinchman v. Anderson, 32 Wash. 198, 72 Pac. 1018, under 2 Ballinger's Ann. Codes & St. Wash., § 5893.

Prior to Nebraska Act of 1897 (Laws of 1897, p. 378, c. 95) the institution of a suit to foreclose a mortgage and for personal judgment against the makers of notes tolls the statute of limitations on the liability of the makers on the notes. Carstens v. Eller, 5 Neb. (Unoff.) 149, 97 N. W. 631; Harris v. Nye & Schneider Co., 3 Neb. (Unoff.) 169, 91 N. W. 250.

As to the effect on limitations of the pendency of an action or other proceeding on a different cause or in a different forum, in other jurisdictions, see the following cases:

Ark.—Jacoway v. Hall, 67 Ark. 340, 55 S. W. 12.

D. C.—Gibson v. Ruff, 8 App. D. C. 262.

Ga.—Schofield v. Woolley, 98 Ga. 548, 25 S. E. 769, 58 Am. St. Rep. 315.

Iowa.—Freeburg v. Eksell, 123 Iowa 464, 99 N. W. 118.

Kan.—McDonald v. Symns Grocer Co., 64 Kan. 529, 67 Pac. 1111.

Ky.—Masonic Temple Co. v. Pflanz, 21 Ky. Law Rep. 583, 52 S. W. 821; Turner v. Everett, 5 Ky. Law Rep. (abstract) 325; Dugan's Adm'r v. Mitchell, 5 Ky. Law Rep (abstract) 181.

§ 253b. Pendency of appeal.

The running of the statute against an action on an appeal undertaking given on appeal to the general term of the superior court of the city of New York is not affected by the taking of a further appeal from the judgment of the general term to the court of appeals.[15] An action for specific performance of an agreement to transfer property to an attorney in consideration of his services is properly brought within four years from the judgment on appeal in the action in which the services were rendered.[16] The

Mich.—O'Toole v. Hurley, 115 Mich. 517, 4 Detroit Leg. N. 965, 73 N. W. 805.

Minn.—St. Paul, M. & M. Ry. Co. v. Olson, 87 Minn. 117, 91 N. W. 294, 94 Am. St. Rep. 693.

Mo.—Tower v. Compton Hill Imp. Co., 192 Mo. 379, 91 S. W. 104.

Mont.—Mantle v. Speculator Min. Co., 27 Mont. 473, 71 Pac. 665.

N. J.—Ware v. Weatherby's Ex'rs (N. J. Sup.), 45 Atl. 914.

N. Y.—Bissell v. State, 70 App. Div. 238, 73 N. Y. Supp. 1105, judg. aff'd, 177 N. Y. 540, 69 N. E. 1120.

Tenn.—Grayson v. Harrison (Tenn. Ch. App.), 59 S. W. 438.

Va.—Caperton v. Gregory, 11 Grat. 505.

15. Howard Ins. Co. of New York v. Silverberg, 94 Fed. 921, 36 C. C. A. 549, aff'd judg., 89 Fed. 168 (C. C. A., Cal.).

An appeal from a decree confirming a foreclosure sale suspends the running of limitations against an application for a deficiency judgment. Brand v. Garneau, 3 Neb. (Unoff.) 879, 93 N. W. 219.

The filing and approval of a supersedeas bond in an error proceeding from a judgment of the district court suspends the lien of the judgment and limitations against the lien. Ebel v. Stringer, 4 Neb. (Unoff.) 43.

An appeal from the final order and judgment of the district court to the supreme court, in the absence of a supersedeas, does not suspend limitations. Bank of Stockton v. Weins, 12 Okl. 502, 71 Pac. 1073.

Petitioning for a writ of error is but a continuation of the original suit, and not the commencement of a new one, so far as limitations are concerned. Duke v. Helms, 100 Tenn. 249, 46 S. W. 761.

Though a judgment is suspended pending appeal, it is not thereby so vacated as to allow limitations to continue to run after its rendition, in a suit to recover lands held adversely. Miller v. Gist, 91 Tex. 335, 43 S. W. 263, modifying judg., Gist v. East, 16 Tex. Civ. App. 274, 41 S. W. 396.

If an appeal bond has been duly filed with the justice rendering the judgment, the running of the statute is tolled until the final disposition of such appeal. Rosenberg v. Pritzker, 156 Ill. App. 463.

16. Archer v. Harvey, 164 Cal. 274, 128 Pac. 410.

Limitation against a receiver's right to recover his compensation and

right to sue for malicious prosecution of a civil action accrues from the rendition of a judgment for defendant and is barred if not brought within one year after such judgment, though a proceeding in error may have intervened.[17] A right of action accrues on plaintiff's undertaking in replevin when he fails to comply with the judgment rendered against him, and the statute begins to run from the rendition of the judgment even though plaintiff prosecutes a proceeding in error, without giving a supersedeas bond, to reverse the judgment.[18] Where an insurer, which has procured reinsurance, contests payment on the original policy in good faith, limitations do not run against its right of action against the reinsurer until final judgment against it in the appellate court.[19] Since a suit to set aside an alleged fraudulent conveyance can be prosecuted notwithstanding an appeal from the judgment in the original suit against the debtor, the pendency of such appeal did not suspend the statute of limitations against the suit to set aside such conveyance.[20]

expenses from the plaintiff in the action in which he was appointed is suspended pending an appeal from the settlement of his final account. Ephraim v. Pacific Bank, 129 Cal. 589, 62 Pac. 177.

17. Levering v. National Bank of Morrow County, 87 Ohio 117, 100 N. E. 322. As to an appeal from an action to recover from a stockholder in another State of an insolvent corporation, under Rev. St. Ohio, 1908, § 3260d, see Irvine v. Bankard, 181 Fed. 206 (C. C., Md.).

18. Delay v. Yost, 59 Kan. 496, 53 Pac. 482. As to an appeal from a judgment of conviction for unlawful sale of intoxicants, see State v. Alexander, 84 Kan. 393, 114 Pac. 241.

19. Insurance Co. of State of Pennsylvania v. Telfair, 27 Misc. Rep. 247, 57 N. Y. Supp. 780, rev'd 45 App. Div. 564, 61 N. Y. Supp. 322.

20. State v. Osborn, 143 Ind. 671, 42 N. E. 921. But where plaintiff could not maintain an independent action for the recovery of damages for the taking of his property by a city by condemnation while an appeal was pending from the condemnation proceedings, the statute of limitations did not run against him during that time. City of Ft. Wayne v. Hamilton, 132 Ind. 487, 32 N. E. 324, 32 Am. St. Rep. 263.

As to the effect on limitations of the pendency of an appeal, in other jurisdictions, see the cases below:

La.—Slawson v. McCaffery, Man. Unrep. Cas. 313.

Mo.—Moore v. Gibson, 130 Mo. App. 590, 109 S. W. 1056.

Tex.—Britton v. Matlock, 40 Tex. Civ. App. 275, 89 S. W. 1092; Bostick v. Heard (Civ. App.), 164 S. W. 34.

§ 253c. Suspension or stay in general.

Whenever the law requires a delay in legal proceedings, it also suspends the running of limitations.[21] The rule that, when a person is prevented from exercising his legal remedy by some paramount authority, the time for which he is thus prevented must not be counted in determining the running of limitations, applies only where such authority is invoked by the debtor.[22] Where defendant, who agreed to diligently prosecute plaintiff's application to patent, did not use diligence in accordance with the agreement, and the same was rejected prior to the date fixed for the payment of money by defendant, the statute of limitations was not tolled by an agreement extending the time for deposit of the money.[23]

§ 253d. Supersedeas or stay of proceedings.

The statutory provision allowing judges to enlarge the time within which a proceeding in an action after its commencement must be done does not authorize an order allowing a plaintiff, who has at the time no cause of action against defendant, to postpone indefinitely the service of complaint in the action for the purpose of preventing the statute of limitations from running against some cause of action which might thereafter be determined to exist.[24] If, as required by statute, a claim against a city is

Wash.—Green v. Spokane County, 55 Wash. 308, 104 Pac. 510.

21. Hume v. Perry (Tex. Civ. App.), 130 S. W. 594.

Under Kentucky statute, § 2544 (Russell's St., § 210), providing that, where the doing of an act necessary to save any right is lawfully restrained, the time of such restraint shall not be estimated in the application of any statute of limitation, the time between the overruling of plaintiff's motion in the United States Circuit Court to dismiss the action without prejudice, and such dismissal by that court pursuant to the mandate of the United States Circuit Court of Appeals, should not be counted in determining whether limitations had run against plaintiff's right to thereafter bring the action in the State court. Knight's Adm'r v. Illinois Cent. R. Co., 143 Ky. 418, 136 S. W. 874.

22. Lagerman v. Casserly, 107 Minn. 491, 120 N. W. 1086.

23. Dilg v. Strauss, 158 App. Div. 718, 143 N. Y. Supp. 948.

24. Mercantile Nat. Bank v. Corn Exchange Bank, 68 Hun (N. Y.) 95, 22 N. Y. Supp. 643.

presented to the city comptroller before the bar of the statute of limitations has attached, but, under the statute thirty days must elapse before action can be commenced, this is a stay by "statutory prohibition," within the meaning of that term as used in section 406, New York Code of Civil Procedure, excepting such period from the computation of time, and the running of the statute is suspended during the thirty days.[25] A stipulation to stay proceedings on a claim against an estate, given in pursuance of an order requiring it, is, in effect an order for a stay, under Code Civ. Proc., § 406, providing that, where the commencement of an action has been stayed by an order, the time of the stay is not a part of the time limited for the commencement of an action, and the time of such stay should be excluded in computing the time within which an action must be commenced under section 1822, which bars a claim presented against an estate and rejected, unless action is brought thereon six months after rejection.[26] The running

25. Brehm v. City of New York, 104 N. Y. 186, 10 N. E. 158.

Where, on appeal to this court judgment was reversed, and plaintiff, under Code, § 104, had a year after the reversal to commence a new action, and defendant took an appeal to the Court of Appeals, and gave an undertaking to stay proceedings on the judgment of this court, the commencement of a new action was stayed by statute prohibition, within section 105 of the Code, providing that the time of the continuance of the prohibition shall not be part of the time limited for the commencement of the action. Worster v. Forty-Second St., etc., R. Co., 6 Daly (N. Y.) 528.

26. Wilder v. Ballou, 63 Hun (N. Y.) 118, 17 N. Y. Supp. 625.

Where, in an action on certain obligations it appeared that, some years before, defendant corporation obtained a judgment in replevin against plaintiff for these obligations, which judgment was afterwards reversed, the statute of limitations did not cease to run in favor of defendant while the possessory judgment in its favor was in force; such a judgment not being an order staying the commencement of an action, which, under Code Civ. Proc., § 406, prevents the running of the statute. Best v. Davis Sewing Mach. Co., 65 Hun (N. Y.) 72, 19 N. Y. Supp. 731, 22 Civ. Proc. R. 362.

Where a creditor of an incompetent properly brought suit against him prior to the appointment of a committee, and the committee applied for a stay of the prosecution of the action a few days within the expiration of the statute of limitations, an order granting a stay did not affect limitations; the creditor, on his claim not being paid in full, being at

of the statute of limitations against a judgment against a township will be suspended during the operation of a supersedeas bond in favor of the township staying the issuance of execution thereon.[27] The statute of limitations does not run against the issuance of an execution on a sale bond during the period for which defendants have obtained a stay.[28] While a creditors' bill has the effect to stay during its pendency the running of the statute of limitations, it has that effect only as to such debts as are brought into the suit and kept alive while it is pending, and, after the conclusion of the suit, the statute continues to run.[29]

Where, in an action by a builder for the contract price, defendant, after answer, applied for a stay of proceedings pending the determination of a suit in another court by a subcontractor to establish a lien on the building, and an order was entered reciting the subcontractor's suit, and ordering that the further progress of the builder's suit be stayed until the further order of the court, it was held that the stay was merely to prevent the case from coming to trial until the question of the subcontractor's lien was determined, and did not preclude the filing of an amended petition, and hence did not prevent the running of the statute of limitations as to claims for extras not mentioned in the original petition.[30]

liberty, after the discharge of the committee, to continue the action for any unpaid balance. Grant v. Humbert, 100 N. Y. Supp. 44, 114 App. Div. 462.

27. Ware v. Pleasant Grove Tp., 9 Kan. App. 700.

Where execution was issued on a valid judgment, levy made on the debtor's real estate, and the execution returned as satisfied, and afterwards, for irregularities, the execution and levy were vacated on *audita querela*, the statute of limitations did not begin to run on the judgment until the time such execution and levy were vacated. Fairbanks v. Devereaux, 58 Vt. 359, 3 Atl. 500.

28. Preston v. Breckinridge, 86 Ky. 619, 6 S. W. 641.

29. Prince's Adm'r v. McLemore, 108 Va. 269, 61 S. E. 802.

The entry, in an action for the settlement of a trust estate, of a decree requiring all creditors thereof to present their claims therein, and restraining the prosecution by claimants of separate actions, stops the running of the statute of limitations against judgments previously obtained against such estate. Houck's Adm'r v. Dunham, 92 Va. 211, 23 S. E. 238.

30. Taub v. Woodruff (Tex. Civ. App.), 134 S. W. 750.

§ 253e. Pendency of arbitration or reference.

Where a statute (Joint Resolution No. 34) recites the matters in controvesy between the State and the general government, and authorizes certain officers on behalf of both parties "to compromise, adjust, and settle all such claims, and to report any balance arising therefrom to the governor of the State and to Congress," it is sufficient to prevent the running of the statute of limitations.[31] The reference by the senate to the court of claims of a bill for the relief of a claimant does not invest that court with jurisdiction, relieved from the limitations prescribed by Rev. St., § 1069, or that of two years established by the captured and abandoned property act of March 12, 1863.[32] A statute limiting the time for bringing an action is not defeated or its operation retarded by negotiations for a settlement, or for a reference, pending between the parties, provided there be no agreement for delay, and defendant has done nothing to mislead plaintiff.[33] But reference of a suit to arbitrators takes the subject-matter referred out of the statute of limitations.[34] Where a suit was begun before the right to sue was barred, and was adjourned to a day after the six years had expired, and on that day the parties agreed in writing to an arbitration, whereupon the suit was discontinued, and defendant afterwards revoked the submission, he could not interpose the plea of the statute to another suit begun for the same cause of action.[35] While a defendant cannot avail himself of the bar of the statute of limitations if he did anything to induce the plaintiff to delay bringing suit, a mere agreement to arbitrate and the selection of an arbitrator, not followed up by any steps by the plaintiff to have the matter submitted, or any act of the defendant to prevent submission, will not estop the defendant from relying on the statute.[36] The rule that the mere submission to arbitration of matters on

31. Louisville & N. R. Co. v. United States, 47 Ct. Cl. (U. S.) 129.

32. Ford v. United States, 116 U. S. 213, 6 Sup. Ct. 360, 29 L. El. 608.

33. Gooden v. Amoskeag Fire Ins. Co., 20 N. H. 73.

34. Colkings v. Thackston, 1 N. C. 312.

35. Anderson v. Sibley, 28 Hun (N. Y.) 16.

36. Hornblower v. George Washington University, 31 App. D. C. 64.

which the arbitrators never acted would not prevent the running of the statute of limitations during the continuance of the submission is not affected by the fact that, pending the submission, the right of action was suspended.[37] When, in a creditors' suit in equity against an administrator and the heirs, the court takes into its own hands the administration of the assets, by referring the cause to a commissioner to take an account of the debts of the intestate, the statute of limitations ceases to run against the creditors, not formal parties to the bill, the bill not being in form a creditors' bill, from the date of such decree.[38]

§ 253f. Property in custody of the law.

That the subject of an action is held *in custodia legis* in another action, to which defendant is neither a party nor in privity with a party, and over which he has no control, will not suspend the running of the statute of limitations in his favor.[39] Whether a debt sought to be proved against an insolvent beneficiary corporation is barred by time depends upon its status when decree was made sequestrating the corporation's assets.[40] The mere appointment of a receiver does not affect the running of limitations.[41] In

37. Cowart v. Perrine, 21 N. J. Eq. (6 C. E. Green) 101.

38. Woodyard v. Polsley, 14 W. Va. 211. See also, where the reference to a commissioner was by consent of parties. Fowler v. Lewis' Adm'r, 36 W. Va. 112, 14 S. E. 447.

39. Hawkins v. Brown, 78 Kan. 284, 97 Pac. 479.

40. Attorney General v. Supreme Council A. L. H., 196 Mass. 151, 81 N. E. 966.

41. Cain v. Seaboard Air Line Ry., 138 Ga. 96, 74 S. E. 764.

Under Ga. Civ. Code 1910, § 4497, an action for personal injuries, brought more than two years from the injury, is barred, though during a portion of that time the assets and business of the defendant were in the hands of a receiver. Id.

Where an action at law was begun against a railroad corporation while it was in the hands of a receiver, and afterwards the receiver was substituted as defendant in place of the corporation, it was held that the chancery court appointing the receiver would grant plaintiff permission to proceed against the receiver, and would restrain the receiver from setting up the statute of limitations, it appearing that the claim was not outlawed when the original suit was begun. Lehigh Coal & Nav. Co. v. Central R. Co., 42 N. J. Eq. (15 Stew.) 591, 8 Atl. 648.

In Arkansas, a tenant who has pur-

North Carolina, where a note is deposited in the hands of a master, by order of a court of equity, the acts of limitation are thereby suspended;[42] but where commissioners in insolvency, under order of the court, loan money of the estate, a note taken as security therefor is not a fund in the hands of the court, and hence is subject to limitations.[43] In Missouri, it is held that, if an individual partner's interest in real estate standing in his name but bought with the firm's money was as personal property in the probate court's custody, on insolvency of defendant, yet it was real estate in fact, so that such custody would not defeat the operation of the statute of limitations and the doctrine of laches.[44] In Louisiana, an executor is a judicial depositary of property of the estate he represents, and his possession is that of the creditors, for whom he is *quasi* mandatory. Hence his custody of succession effects, continued by the assent and acquiescence of the heirs, suspends the running of the statute of limitations in favor of the creditors whose claims have been acknowledged.[45] By the Virginia attachment law, the fund is in custody of the law, and the statute

chased the property occupied by him at a sale for taxes holds it subject to the control of the court, and may be compelled by rule to surrender possession thereof to the receiver; and, as to such proceeding, the statute of limitations as to actions does not apply. Waggener v. McLaughlin, 33 Ark. 195.

42. Vance v. Grainger's Ex'rs, 1 N. C 291.

43. Causey v. Snow, 122 N. C. 326, 29 S. E. 359.

Pending administration the statute of limitations will not run, as to funds in the hands of an administrator, in favor of the decedent's heir at law, and against creditors who have reduced their claims to judgment against the personal representatives; such funds being held in trust for the creditors until the estate is settled. Phifer v. Berry, 110 N. C. 463, 15 S. E. 1.

The statute of limitations does not run against a debt during the life of the debtor's estate of homestead, if the homestead has been laid off, and if the debt is one affected by the allotment. Morton v. Barber, 90 N. C. 399.

44. Troll v. City of St. Louis, 257 Mo. 626, 168 S. W. 167, holding also that the equitable right of a partnership in land purchased with its funds for partnership use by one of the partners and standing in his name is not within the custody of the probate court in its administration of partnership assets for the benefit of creditors.

45. Morris v. Cain's Ex'rs, 39 La. Ann. 712, 1 So. 797, 2 So. 418. See also, Norres v. Hays, 44 La. Ann

of limitations does not run while the suit is pending, and a suit brought against the executor of the garnishee after the termination of the principal suit in sufficient time is not barred by the general statute of limitations.[46] The Maryland tax law does not apply where a court of equity has taken jurisdiction of the property liable for taxes.[47] In Tennessee, the statute of limitations has no application to a note executed to a clerk of a court, for property sold in the progress of a cause, while the note is in the custody of the law.[48]

§ 253g. Pendency of proceedings under assignment for creditors or in insolvency or bankruptcy.

Proceedings in bankruptcy under the Federal laws suspend the operation of the statute of limitations, as to all parties properly in the bankrupt proceedings, but the pendency of bankrupt proceedings against certain defendants does not have the effect of interrupting prescription as to one who was not a party to the bankruptcy proceedings.[49] The running of the statute of limitations against an open account is not tolled by the mere filing of a petition in bank-

907, 11 So. 462; McKnight v. Calhoun, 36 La. Ann. 408.

Where an insolvent corporation is in process of liquidation in the hands of a liquidator appointed under the law, prescription does not run in favor of the corporation during the term of the liquidation. Gaslight & Banking Co. v. Haynes, 7 La. Ann. 114.

See Succession of Marchand, 116 La. 207, 40 So. 637, as to effect of a sheriff's sale under a writ of *fi. fa.* on the running of prescription as to other seizing creditors.

46. Mattingly v. Boyd, 61 U. S. (20 How.) 128, 15 L. Ed. 845.

47. Hebb v. Moore, 66 Md. 167, 7 Atl. 255.

48. Tyner v. Fenner, 72 Tenn. (4 Lea) 469.

Where a person has been compelled by a decree in chancery to give security for the forthcoming of a slave, during the pendency and operative force of such proceeding, the slave is in the custody of the law; and the operation of the statute of limitations is arrested as between the parties thereto. Moore v. Crockett, 29 Tenn. (10 Humph.) 365.

49. Horton v. Haralson, 130 La. 1003, 58 So. 858 (1912). Where the plaintiff sold defendant a bill of goods in 1904, and a month later defendant was adjudged a bankrupt, and plaintiff procured an allowance of its claim and participated in the dividends of the bankrupt estate, an action in the State court for the price in 1909 was barred by the three-year statute of limitations. Simpson v. Tootle, Wheeler & Motter Mercantile Co., 42 Okl. 275, 141 Pac. 448.

ruptcy.[50] The statute of limitations does not operate between the time of proving a debt against a bankrupt and the termination of the proceedings in his failure to get a discharge.[51] The period of suspension of a right of action, through pendency of proceedings, is not to be counted as part of the time prescribed by the statute of limitations to bar the action.[52] Under New York Code Proc., § 105, and under the provisions of the Federal Bankrupt Act, the running of the statute of limitations is suspended during the pendency of the bankruptcy proceedings; and whether the bankruptcy court had jurisdiction is immaterial, if it in fact entertained the proceedings, and the bankrupt applied for a discharge.[53] In Massachusetts, the pendency of proceedings under the insolvent laws does not suspend the statute of limitations upon debts provable in insolvency, since such proceedings do not prevent

50. Nonotuck Silk Co. v. Pritzker, 143 Ill. App. 644 (1908).

51. Hawes v. Fette, 42 Ark. 370 (1883).

52. Hoff v. Funkenstein, 54 Cal. 233 (1880).

53. Rosenthal v. Plumb, 25 Hun (N. Y.) 336 (1881).

After an adjudication in bankruptcy, the statute of limitations does not run against a creditor's claim that was not then barred thereby. The assignee stands as trustee for the creditors. Von Sachs v. Kretz, 72 N. Y. 548, aff'g 10 Hun 95 (1878).

The bankruptcy of the maker of a note does not suspend the operation of the statute of limitations. Harwell v. Steele, 17 Ala. 372 (1850).

The pendency of proceedings in bankruptcy, under Act Cong. March 2, 1867, against a debtor, does not suspend the operation of the statute of limitations in his favor. Doe v. Erwin, 134 Mass. 90 (1883).

Where a debt is proved in bankruptcy, the running of the limitations is not suspended by the pendency of the proceedings in bankruptcy. Appeal of Milne, 99 Pa. 483 (1882).

Formal, but defective, proof of a mortgage debt was offered in bankruptcy before the statute of limitations had run against it. The sufficiency of the proof was not objected to. By leave of the court, and by agreement with the debtor, the claim was withdrawn, to be enforced in a State court. At the time of the beginning of suit there, the statute of limitations had run. It was held that it could not be pleaded. Wofford v. Unger, 53 Tex. 634 (1880).

Bankruptcy statutes do not generally suspend the right of a creditor to commence an action, but only prevent him from prosecuting it to final judgment until the bankrupt has the opportunity to obtain his discharge. Porter v. Cummings, 108 Ga. 797, 33 S. E. 986 (1899).

the creditor from bringing an action upon his debt.[54] In Maryland, a claim against an insolvent's estate not barred by the statute at the time of filing with the auditor cannot become so afterwards.[55] In Michigan, an assignment for the benefit of creditors made by a debtor does not prevent the running of the statute of limitations against his creditor.[56] In New York, the statute of limitations ceases to run against claims against an insolvent estate on the appointment of a receiver.[57] In Pennsylvania, the discharge of an insolvent's person, under the law, does not prevent the statute of limitations from running against the claim of a creditor.[58] In South Carolina, a debtor who has taken the benefit of the insolvent debtor's act cannot afterwards plead the statute of limitations to a debt which existed, unbarred, at the time of his discharge, although contracted after the filing of the petition for the benefit of the act.[59] In Tennessee, the statute of limitations is not restrained by the insolvency of the estate, nor by the pendency

54. Richardson v. Thomas, 79 Mass. (13 Gray) 381, 74 Am. Dec. 636; Stoddard v. Doane, 73 Mass. (7 Gray) 387; Collester v. Hailey, 72 Mass. (6 Gray) 517. So it has been held that the representation of the estate of a deceased person as insolvent and the appointment of commissioners do not suspend the operation of the statute limiting actions against administrators to two years from the time of their giving bonds. Tarbell v. Parker, 106 Mass. 347; Richardson v. Allen, 116 Mass. 447.

55. Hignutt v. Garey, 62 Md. 190. Under the insolvent laws, the property of the insolvent is vested in the trustee appointed by the court. The trust thus created is an express trust for the benefit of the creditors of the insolvent, who are such at the date of his application, and their claims, unless then barred by the statute of limitations, are not afterwards, during the execution of the trust, affected by the lapse of time. *In re* Leiman's Estate, 32 Md. 225, 3 Am. Rep. 132.

56. Parsons v. Clark, 59 Mich. 414, 26 N. W. 656.

57. Ludington v. Thompson, 38 N. Y. Supp. 768, 4 App. Div. 117, aff'd 153 N. Y. 499, 47 N. E. 903.

58. Shoenberger v. Adams, 4 Watts (Pa.) 430; Gest v. Heiskill, 5 Rawle (Pa.) 134; Sletor v. Oram, 1 Whart. (Pa.) 106; Appeal of Feather, 1 Pen. & W. (Pa.) 322, overruled.

The statute of limitations as to a corporation stops running from the time of the sheriff's sale of all the property and franchises thereof. Shamokin Valley & P. R. Co. v. Malone, 85 Pa. 25.

59. Hagood v. Robinson, 7 Rich. Law (S. C.) 43; Sinclair's Ex'rs v. Lynah, 1 Speers (S. C.) 244.

of an insolvent bill, nor by the orders or notices for the filing of claims.[60] In Texas, an assignment for the benefit of creditors does not suspend the running of the statute of limitations against a matured debt mentioned in the assignment during the time the estate remains in the hands of the assignee, since the assignment does not interrupt the creditor's right of action; but the statute will run against such debt from the date of the assignment.[61] In Virginia, in a creditor's suit for the administration of assets, where a decree for an accounting was made, it was held that the statute of limitations ceased to run against all debts of the debtor from the date of the decree.[62]

In Illinois, a voluntary assignment for the benefit of creditors and the appointment of an assignee does not toll the running of the statute of limitations against an open account.[63] In Maine, before the statute of 1887, the subsequent insolvency of defendant did not interrupt the running of limitation, and action on a claim provable in insolvency was barred by the general limitation of six years.[64] In California, the time during which insolvency proceedings are pending is excluded from the period of limitations, although the insolvency act authorizes the maintenance of suits for certain purposes by leave of court.[65] The appointment of a receiver does not in any way effect the running of the statute of limitations.[66] The appointment of a receiver or the existence of a receivership does not interrupt prescription of claims against the corporation to which the receiver was appointed.[67] Upon the appointment of a receiver in a proceeding for the voluntary dissolution of a corporation, he becomes a trustee for the creditors of

60. Todd v. Wright, 59 Tenn. (12 Heisk.) 442.

61. Meusebach v. Half, 77 Tex. 185, 13 S. W. 979.

62. Ewing's Adm'r v. Ferguson's Adm'r, 33 Grat. (Va.) 548.

63. Geddes-Brown Shoe Co. v. Suttle, 145 Ill. App. 407.

64. Trafton v. Hill, 80 Me. 503, 15 Atl. 64.

65. Union Collection Co. v. Soule, 141 Cal. 99, 74 Pac. 549, under the Insolvency Act of 1895 (St. 1895, p. 152, c. 143) and Code Civ. Proc., § 356.

66. White v. Meadowcraft, 91 Ill. App. 293; Ellicott v. United States Ins. Co., 7 Gill (Md.) 307.

67. Taylor v. Vossburg Mineral Springs Co., 128 La. 364, 54 So. 907.

such corporation, whether or not their status as such creditors is then ascertained; and the statute of limitations does not thereafter run against the claims of such creditors, so long as the trust is open and continuing.[68] The appointment of a receiver for the settlement of partnership affairs at the suit of the personal representative of a deceased partner, with power to collect and receive all moneys and property of the firm, and out of the proceeds to pay the debts of the firm, is for the benefit of all firm creditors, and, in analogy with a creditors' bill, suspends the running of the statute of limitations in equity against claims by firm creditors for the payment of partnership debts out of the firm assets in the receiver's hands.[69]

§ 253h. Injunction.

A debtor who procures and keeps in force an injunction against the collection of a debt which he ought to pay, until it is barred at law by the statute of limitations, will not be allowed to avail himself of the bar in a court of equity.[70] In California, the running of the statute of limitations against an action for the wrongful issuing of an execution on a satisfied judgment is not suspended by injunction proceedings restraining the enforcement of the execution.[71] An injunction on a *fieri facias* suspends the running of the statute of limitations, in Georgia.[72] In Illinois, when the commencement of an action is stayed by injunction, order of a judge or court, or statutory prohibition, the time of the continu-

68. Ludington v. Thompson, 153 N. Y. 499, 47 N. E. 903, aff'g 4 App. Div. 117, 38 N. Y. Supp. 768.

69. Kirkpatrick v. McElroy, 41 N. J. Eq. (14 Stew.) 539, 7 Atl. 647.

70. Union Mut. Life Ins. Co. v. Dice, 14 Fed. 523, 11 Biss. 373.

71. Wood v. Currey, 57 Cal. 208.

Where a seller of shares of stock to be issued by a corporation was unable to perform his contract because the issuance of the stock was enjoined, an action to recover the purchase money, brought within the statutory period after demand, was not barred. Rose v. Foord, 96 Cal. 152, 30 Pac. 1114.

72. Cox v. Montford, 66 Ga. 62.

The statute of limitations does not run against the State during the time the Comptroller-General is enjoined by a Federal court from issuing any executions for taxes on certain property. Georgia R. & Banking Co. v. Wright, 124 Ga. 596, 53 S. E. 251.

ance of the injunction or prohibition is no part of the time limited for the commencement of the action.[73] In Kentucky, when an injunction does not stay an action, but only prescribes where and how it shall be instituted, the time of the continuance of the injunction is not to be excluded in determining whether the right to sue is barred by the statute of limitations.[74] In Louisiana, the restraining of the execution of a judgment by a writ of injunction sued out by the judgment debtor does not interrupt the current of prescription.[75] In Maryland, the running of the act of limitations is suspended by an injunction.[76] In Michigan, the running of limitations is interrupted by an injunction preventing an action within the statutory period, the statute indicating the legislative policy to preserve rights which individuals may be prevented from exercising by a paramount power without their own fault.[77] The Minnesota statutory provision suspending the running of limitations while the beginning of an action is stayed by injunction applies only between parties to the suit.[78] In Mississippi, during the time of an injunction, by the debtor preventing execution for the

73. Tanton v. Boomgaarden, 89 Ill. App. 500; Wild v. People, 92 Ill. App. 66.

An injunction in a suit by one in possession, restraining the owner of the paramount title to land from setting up or insisting on any title or interest therein, affords a sufficient ground in equity for not allowing the statute of limitations to become a bar of such owner's right during the time such injunction was in force. Kelly v. Donlin, 70 Ill. 378.

74. Biggs v. Lexington & B. S. R. Co., 79 Ky. 470.

A decision of the Court of Appeals held not a "lawful restraint," within Ky. St., § 2544. Bank of Commerce v. Stone, 108 Ky. 427, 22 Ky. Law Rep. 70, 56 S. W. 683.

75. Yale v. Randle, 23 La. Ann. 579.

76. Little v. Price, 1 Md. Ch. 182.

77. Steele v. Bliss, 166 Mich. 593, 132 N. W. 345, so that, under Comp. Laws, § 9754, an injunction which prevented the sale of realty under an execution levy would stay the running of Comp. Laws, § 9233, providing that all execution liens shall be void after five years from the levy, unless the realty be sooner sold.

An injunction issued with reference to certain real property in a suit to which plaintiff was not a party *held* not to suspend the statute of limitations against plaintiff's right to recover the land in ejectment. West Michigan Park Ass'n v. Pere Marquette R. Co., 172 Mich. 179, 137 N. W. 799.

78. Lagerman v. Casserly, 107 Minn. 491, 120 N. W. 1086.

debt, the statute does not run against the debt.[79] In New York, the operation of the statute of limitations is suspended during the time within which the bringing of suits is enjoined.[80] The same rule prevails in Nevada,[81] in North Carolina,[82] and in North Dakota.[83]

An injunction against the commencement of an action does not save the running of the statute of limitations unless the statute so provides, and no such provision is found in the statutes of Ohio or Florida.[84] In South Carolina,[85] and Tennessee,[86] by

79. Wilkinson v. Flowers, 37 Miss. 579, 75 Am. Dec. 78.

Where a debt is secured by a trust deed which the creditor is enjoined from foreclosing, the statute of limitations is suspended during the operation of the injunction. Tishimingo Sav. Inst. v. Buchanan, 60 Miss. 496.

80. Fincke v. Funke, 25 Hun (N. Y.) 616.

But an injunction obtained by a wife, restraining her husband from disposing of, or interfering with, her property, does not interrupt the running of the statute of limitations against his right of bringing an action to recover it, or its full value, when wrongfully taken from his possession by a third person. Van Waggonen v. Terpenning, 122 N. Y. 222, 25 N. E. 254.

To a limitation of the time within which an action may be brought, prescribed by contract, Code, § 406, saving the rights of parties under the statute of limitations when they are stayed by injunction, does not apply. Wilkinson v. First Nat. Ins. Co., 72 N. Y. 499, 28 Am. Rep. 166, aff'g 9 Hun 522.

81. Wells, Fargo & Co. v. Vansickle, 112 Fed. 398.

82. Walton v. Pearson, 85 N. C. 34, mere irregularity in the granting of an injunction will not render it a nullity so as to prevent the suspension of the statute of limitations, under Code, § 46, during the pendency of the injunction.

83. The commencement of an action on a judgment is not stayed within the meaning of Rev. Codes, § 5215, during the time the judgment creditor is required to obtain leave of court in order to bring suit thereon. Osborne v. Lindstrom, 9 N. D. 1, 81 N. W. 72, 46 L. R. A. 715.

84. Hunter v. Niagara Fire Ins. Co., 73 Ohio St. 110, 76 N. E. 563, 3 L. R. A. (N. S.) 1187, 112 Am. St. Rep. 669. See Treasurer of Brown County v. Martin, 50 Ohio St. 197, 33 N. E. 1112.

85. McLure v. Melton, 34 S. C. 377, 13 S. E. 615, 27 Am. St. Rep. 820, 13 L. R. A. 723, an order enjoining creditors from prosecuting actions at law against an estate, and fixing a time for proving their claims in the action in which the injunction was granted, will not suspend the running of the statute of limitations against a creditor who brings suit on a simple contract claim more than six years after the time so fixed.

86. Terrell v. Ingersoll, 78 Tenn.

statute, when the commencement of an action is stayed by injunction, the time of the continuance of the injunction is not to be counted, in computing the running of the statute of limitations. In Texas, where plaintiff obtained an injunction restraining sale under a trust deed, equity will not suspend the running of the statute for the time the injunction was in force, in favor of the executors of the beneficiary in the deed who were not parties when the injunction was granted, and were in no wise prevented from bringing suit on the notes within the statutory period.[87] In Virginia, the statute of limitations to judgments does not run while an injunction to the judgment is pending.[88]

§ 253i. Stay laws.

The stay laws passed during the Rebellion interposed no obstacle to the institution of a suit to fix the liability of indorsers.[89] The stay law of 1861, forbidding the service of any process for the collection of money until after the expiration of the first session of the next general assembly, and providing that the operation of the statute of limitations shall be suspended while the act was in force, applied to actions on contracts then existing, and suspended the statute of limitations in such actions, during its continuance and successive renewals.[90] The running of the statute of limitations in favor of an adverse occupant against the owner

(10 Lea) 77, the statute does not apply to an injunction in a suit to which the debtor is not a party. See also, Latta v. Sumerow, 72 Tenn. (4 Lea) 486; Bibb v. Tarkington, 70 Tenn. (2 Lea) 21.

87. Davis v. Andrews, 88 Tex. 524, 30 S. W. 432, 2 Am. & Eng. Dec. in Eq. 587, 596, note. And see Converse v. Davis, 90 Tex. 462, 39 S. W. 277, rev'g (Tex. Civ. App.) 37 S. W. 247; Yzaguirre v. Garcia (Tex. Civ. App.), 172 S. W. 139.

88. Hutsonpiller's Adm'r v. Stover's Adm'r, 12 Grat. (Va.) 579. See Braxton v. Harrison's Ex'r, 11 Grat. (Va.) 30.

In Kansas, where legal proceedings restrain one party from exercising a legal remedy against another, the running of limitations is postponed or suspended during such restraint. City of Hutchinson v. Hutchinson, 92 Kan. 518, 141 Pac. 589.

89. Jopling v. Turner, 32 Tex. 281.

90. Wradlaw v. Buzzard, 15 Rich. L. (S. C.) 158, 94 Am. Dec. 148.

of land was suspended by the stay law of 1865 during the continuance of that act.[91] A stay law which merely suspends the creditor's right to issue execution without interfering with his right of action, does not suspend the running of the statute of limitations.[92]

§ 253j. Suspension of statute of limitations.

The Act of Congress of June 11, 1864 (13 Stat. 123), suspending the statute of limitations during the Rebellion as to any action accruing against a person who, because of the conflict, was beyond the reach of process, was not unconstitutional as applied to actions in the State courts as well as in the Federal courts.[93] Where a statute imposing a liability for wrongful death provides for suit to enforce the same within a specified time, such limitation operates on the liability, and not on the remedy alone; and hence suit must be brought within that time, regardless of other statutes suspending the operation of the statutes of limitation.[94] Where a right had accrued before the passage of the Tennessee Code, § 4464, suspending limitations from May 6, 1861, to January 1, 1867, the right was not affected or impaired thereby, or by the constitutional provision on the same subject.[95] Where the statute of limitations was suspended by law as to taxes due a State or county, mere lapse of time could not be set up to defeat their recovery.[96]

91. Pegues v. Warley, 14 S. C. 180.

92. Kirkland v. Krebs, 34 Md. 93.

As to the effect on limitations of other State laws, see Bates v. Gregory, 89 Cal. 387, 26 Pac. 891; Mahone v. Central Bank, 17 Ga. 111; Hudson v. Carey, 11 Serg. & R. (Pa.) 10.

93. Mayfield v. Richards, 115 U. S. 137, 5 Sup. Ct. 1187, 29 L. Ed. 334.

94. Kavanagh v. Folsom, 181 Fed. 401.

95. Breckenridge Cannel Coal Co. v. Scott, 121 Tenn. 88, 114 S. W. 930.

See § 6, *supra*, and cases cited there as to the effect of statutes of the different States suspending statutes of limitation during the Civil War.

96. State v. Gibson, 21 Tex. Civ. App. 355, 65 S. W. 690.

CHAPTER XXIV.

ADVERSE POSSESSION AND REAL ACTIONS.

§ 254. Title by, under statutes.

The acquisition of the title to land by adverse user [1] is referable to and predicated upon the statutes of limitations in force in the several States, which, in effect, provide that an uninterrupted occupancy of lands by a person who has in fact no title thereto, for a certain number of years, shall operate to extinguish the title of the true owner thereto, and vest a right to the premises absolutely in the occupier.[2] The object of these statutes is to quiet the titles

1. This important and extensive topic will be found fully discussed in the following recent authorities: 1 Cyclopedia of Law and Proc., p. 908; Atkyns v. Horde, 3 Smith's Lead. Cas. (9th Am. ed.), pp. 1869, 1983, n.; Gray v. Bond, 25 Ruling Cases, 339, 344, n.; Preble v. Maine Cent. R. Co., 85 Me. 260, 27 Atl. 149, 21 L. R. A. 829, and n.; Baker v. Oakwood, 123 N. Y. 16, 25 N. E. 312, 10 L. R. A. 387, and n.; 1 Am. and Eng. Encyc. of Law (2d ed.), p. 787; 1 Jones on Real Property, ch. 7; 1 Abbott's N. Y. Cyclopedic Digest, p. 216; Riggs v. Riley, 113 Ind. 208, 15 N. E. 253, 27 Cent. L. J. 87, and n.

The claimant by adverse possession does not abandon or impair his own title by purchasing an outstanding claim of title from a third person. Warren v. Bowdran, 156 Mass. 280, 31 N. E. 300. The characteristic of such title is always that it is acquired without the consent and against the will of the former owner. Marshall v. Taylor (1895), 1 Ch. 641, 650; Middlesex Co. v. Lane, 149 Mass. 101, 21 N. E. 228, 14 Harvard L. Rev. 149. The elder of different possessions prevails when neither party has the legal title. Reddick v. Long, 24 Ala. 260, 27 So. 402. The statute, when a bar to a direct proceeding by the original owner, cannot be defeated by indirection within the jurisdiction where it is the law. Chapin v. Freeland, 142 Mass. 382, 386, 8 N. E. 128, 56 Am. Rep. 701.

2. Trim v. McPherson, 47 Tenn. (7 Coldw.) 15. In Hopkins v. Calloway, id. 37, it was held that an adverse possession under a conveyance from the State of North Carolina, for the statutory period, not only bars the remedy of the party out of possession, but vests an absolute estate in fee-simple in the party in possession; but that where a person without color of title occupies land for the statutory period, so that the claimant's right is barred, such possession does not take away the claimant's right, but simply bars his remedy; and no subsequent action can be brought by the claimant, either at law or in equity, to question the title of the occupier. When the bar of the statute is complete, the right of the person entitled to its benefits is as perfect as though he was actually invested with the title by deed; and as against him the holder of the paramount title cannot use it for either recovery or defense until he has destroyed the bar, either by purchase or limitation. Hale v. Gladfelder, 52 Ill. 91. In New Jersey, by statute,

to land, and prevent that confusion relative thereto which would necessarily exist if no period was limited within which an entry upon lands could be made; and they are believed to be of even more importance to the interests of society than those relating to personal actions. The effect of these statutes generally is, not to transfer the fee to lands from the true owner to the occupier, but to destroy the remedy of the true owner for their recovery by action, and to vest an absolute right of exclusive possession in the occupier as against the true owner and all the world, and a right which is transferable and vests in his grantees a right to the lands as full and complete as could be conferred by the owner of the fee. In a word, it vests in the occupier a title to the premises by possession, which is in every respect equal to a conveyance of the fee.[3] But while the fee does not pass under a naked adverse possession for the requisite period yet, when a person enters into possession under color of title, and occupies adversely for the requisite period, he is treated as being clothed with the title to the premises, in fee-simple.[4] The title acquired in such cases is predicated upon the presumption that the party in possession is the real owner, or that the real owner has surrendered or abandoned his claim to the premises, or he would have asserted his claim thereto within the requisite period, to save his right.[5] The first statute enacted to settle the title to lands which were in the adverse occupancy of a person other than the real owner, for a long period of time, was enacted during the reign of Henry VIII., (Stat. 32 Henry VIII., c. 2). This statute fixed the period of occupancy requisite to quiet titles at sixty years, and was

sixty years' continuous possession vests a full and complete title in the occupier. See Appendix, New Jersey, sec. 23. In Missouri, it is held that there is no need of presuming a deed from possession for the statutory period, as such possession by itself alone is evidence of an estate in fee, and equivalent to an absolute title. Warfield v. Lindell, 38 Mo. 561.

3. Trim v. McPherson, 47 Tenn. (7 Coldw.) 15.

4. Hopkins v. Calloway 47 Tenn. (7 Coldw.) 37; Hale v. Gladfelder, 52 Ill. 91.

5. Abell v. Harris, 11 G. & J. (Md.) 367; Cooper v. Smith, 9 S. & R. (Pa.) 26.

regarded with great favor. The period was materially lessened by Stat. 21 James I., c. 27, and twenty years' adverse occupancy was fixed upon as sufficient to defeat the true owner's right of entry, except when he was as the time under some one of the disabilities named in the statute. In this country, the period within which a right of entry is barred is fixed by the statute of each State. In Maine, Massachusetts, New Hampshire, New York, Alabama, Delaware, Indiana, Illinois, Minnesota, North Carolina, South Carolina, Oregon, Maryland,[6] Wisconsin and Dakota, the period is twenty years; in Ohio, Pennsylvania and Wyoming, twenty-one years; in Vermont, Connecticut, Michigan, Kentucky, Kansas and Virginia, fifteen years; in Missouri, Mississippi, Nebraska, Texas, West Virginia and New Mexico, ten years; in Florida, Tennessee, Arkansas and Utah, seven years; and in California, Colorado, Nevada, Arizona, Idaho and Montana, five years. It will be observed that the shortest periods are adopted in the new States and the Territories, and the wisdom of this course is not doubtful. In some of the States different periods are adopted according to the character of the estate occupied, or the nature of the occupancy. Thus, in New Jersey, sixty years' possession is ordinarily necessary; but thirty years' occupancy is sufficient when the possession commences or is founded on a proprietary right duly laid thereon, and recorded in the surveyor-general's office.[7] In Indiana, a purchaser of lands

6. In Maryland, the statute does not extend to any possession except where "land shall be taken up under a common or special warrant, or warrant of resurvey, escheat, or proclamation warrant."

7. In Arkansas, when the plaintiff does not claim title to the land, and neither he nor his intestate has been in possession for five years, his right of entry is barred. Where a person claims as, or under, a purchaser of lands at a judicial sale, his title cannot be impeached after five years, unless the person claiming the right of entry was a minor or of unsound mind when the sale was made, and in that case three years after the removal of the disability is given; and persons holding under a sheriff's or auditor's sale for the non-payment of taxes, or who have redeemed the same from the State auditor under the statute, or who hold the same under the auditor's deed, are protected, unless the plaintiff, his ancestor, predecessor, or grantor, was seized or possessed of the lands in question

under an execution, as well as all persons claiming under him, are protected after ten years from the sale; and purchasers, etc., from executors, administrators, guardians, or commissioners, who have sold under a judgment of a competent court directing the sale, are protected, unless action is brought within five years.[8]

These provisions, however, do not apply to lands owned by the State or the United States, nor where the person having an adverse title to the lands is under any of the disabilities specified in the statute, and commences an action for the recovery of the lands within three years after such disabilities are removed.[9]

within two years next before the action was commenced.

8. In Illinois, a person actually residing on lands for seven consecutive years, having a connected title in law or equity, deducible of record from the State or the United States, or from any public officer or person authorized to sell the same, is protected against all claims of title upon which action is not brought within that period; and where a person is in the actual possession of lands under color of title, made in good faith for seven consecutive years, and during such period pays all taxes assessed thereon, he is adjudged the legal owner of such lands to the extent and according to the purport of his paper title; and the same provision exists in favor of a person having color of title made in good faith to vacant and unoccupied lands, who during the period of seven years pays the taxes thereon, unless some person having a better title within that time pays the taxes thereon assessed for one or more years during such period.

9. So long as the title to public land is in the United States, no adverse possession of it can, under a State statute of limitations, confer a title which will prevail in a Federal court against the legal title under a patent from the United States. Redfield v. Parks, 132 U. S. 239, 10 Sup. Ct. 83, 33 L. Ed. 327. Hence, between rival individual claimants of land acquired from the general government, the statute of limitations does not begin to run in favor of an adverse claimant in possession, until the entryman becomes entitled to a patent, by a full compliance with the law. Ibid.; Stephens v. Moore, 116 Ala. 397, 22 So. 542; Denver & R. G. R. Co. v. Wilson, 28 Colo. 6, 62 Pac. 843. As to acquiring minerals and mining lands by adverse occupancy, see Risch v. Wiseman, 36 Oregon, 484, 59 Pac. 1111, 78 Am. St. Rep. 783; Wood v. Etiwanda Water Co., 122 Colo. 52, 54 Pac. 726; 1 Am. and Eng. Encyc. of Law (2d ed.), p. 874; Houser v. Christian, 108 Ga. 469, 34 S. E. 126, 75 Am. St. Rep. 72.

"Prescription or a statute of limitations may give a good title against the world and destroy all manner of outstanding claims without any notice or judicial proceeding at all. Time and the chance which it gives the owner to find out that he is in danger of losing rights are due pro-

In Kentucky, possession for seven years under a title of record from the Commonwealth vests the title in the occupier against all adverse claimants under or by virtue of interfering surveys or patents, except where the claimant at the time a cause of action accrued was under some one of the disabilities named in the statute. In Kansas, an action for the recovery of land sold for taxes is barred in two years from the time when the deed is

cess of law." Holmes, Ch. J., in Tyler v. Court of Registration, 175 Mass. 71, 73, citing Wheeler v. Jackson, 137 U. S. 245, 258, 11 Sup. Ct. 76, 34 L. Ed. 659. "Speaking for myself, I see no reason why what we have said as to proceedings *in rem* in general should not apply to such proceedings concerning land. In Arndt v. Griggs, 134 U. S. 316, 327, 10 Sup. Ct. 557, 33 L. Ed. 918, it is said to be established that 'a State has power by statute to provide for the adjudication of titles to real estate within its limits as against nonresidents who are brought into court only by publication.' In Hamilton v. Brown, 161 U. S. 256, 274, 16 Sup. Ct. 585, 40 L. Ed. 691, it was declared to be within the power of a State 'to provide for determining and quieting the title to real estate within the limits of the State and within the jurisdiction of the court, after actual notice to all known claimants, and notice by publication to all other persons.' I doubt whether the court will not take the further step when necessary, and declare the power of the States to do the same thing after notice by publication alone." Holmes, C. J., in Tyler v. Court of Registration, *supra*, p. 75, citing Huling v. Kaw Valley R. & Impr. Co., 130 U. S. 559, 564, 9 Sup. Ct. 603, 32 L. Ed., 1045; Parker v. Overman, 59 U. S. (18 How.) 137, 140, 15 L. Ed. 318. In Tyler v. Court of Registration, *supra*, Lathrop, J., says (p. 92), in his dissenting opinion: "The reference made in the opinion of the majority of the court to the statute of limitations makes it necessary to state in passing that the registration act cannot be supported on the grounds on which the statute of limitations quiets titles against all the world, or on any grounds deducible therefrom. It is unquestionably within the constitutional power of the legislature to quiet the title to property by a statute of limitations. The principle of such a statute is that one, who is dispossessed of his property, must assert his ownership thereto by action within a specified time or be barred thereof; that is to say, cease to be such owner. But no statute was ever passed providing that an owner in possession of his property could be dispossessed thereof by any lapse of time, and no principle is deducible from the statute of limitations, which can justify such a statute, or a statute providing that, without naming him as a defendant, or without giving him notice, a court can by decree alone, unaided by the subsequent lapse of time, transfer his property to another."

recorded, for lands sold on execution within five years from the recording of the deed, and for lands sold by executors, administrators, or guardians, within three years from the time when the deed is recorded; in all other cases within fifteen years from the time when the right of action or entry accrued. In North Carolina, the State is barred when a person has been in the adverse occupancy of lands belonging to it under visible lines or boundaries, for thirty years. Where a person has been in the possession of lands with visible lines and boundaries under colorable title for seven years, such possession is a perpetual bar against all persons except such as are under some one of the statutory disabilities, and railroad, turnpike, or canal companies. In all other cases twenty years' occupancy under known or visible boundaries is a bar. In South Carolina, the State is barred in forty years, where, during that period, it has not received any rent for, or profits from, the land. In Michigan, where the title to land is claimed by or through some deed made by an executor, administrator, guardian, sheriff, or other proper ministerial officer under the order, decree, or process of a competent court, five years' occupancy under such deed constitutes a bar against all persons claiming title thereto; and an occupancy of ten years under a deed made by some officer of the State or of the United States authorized to make deeds upon the sale of land for taxes assessed thereon and levied within the State, makes a complete bar; but in all other cases fifteen years' occupancy is necessary. In Nevada, a person in possession of mining claims, and working the same in the usual and customary manner is protected by two years' possession. In Tennessee, a continuous adverse possession for twenty years of lands, held under a conveyance from husband and wife executed upon valuable consideration without fraud upon the wife, and registered more than twenty years before any suit commenced, is an absolute bar to the husband and wife and all persons claiming title by or through them.[10] In

10. Tennessee Code (1896, by Shannon), § 4460.

Texas, a person holding peaceable and adverse possession of land, cultivating, using or enjoying the same for five years, paying the taxes, and claiming under a deed duly registered, is protected, unless the deed was forged or executed under a forged power of attorney;[11] in other cases ten years' possession is necessary; but where a person has had peaceable and uninterrupted possession of lands for three years under title or color of title, as defined by section 3341, such possession constitutes a complete bar. In Virginia, a distinction is made between lands lying on the east side of the Allegheny mountains and those upon the west side. As to the former, fifteen years' possession is required; as to the latter, only ten years' possession is necessary. In some of the States, a distinction is made as to the quality of the estate acquired, where the occupant enters and holds under a color of title, and where he merely holds by naked possession. So, too, in several States a distinction is made between the character of occupancy required in the two cases; but it will be unnecessary to refer to that matter at length in this place, as this distinction will be developed in another part of this chapter.

§ 255. Statutory provisions as to adverse possession.

In New York, for the purpose of constituting adverse possession under a claim of title founded upon a written instrument, the premises are deemed to have been possessed and occupied in either of the following cases: First, where it has been usually cultivated and improved; second, where it has been protected by a substantial enclosure; and third, where, although not enclosed, it has been used for supply of fuel, or of fencing timber for the purposes of husbandry, or for the ordinary use of the occupant. And where a known farm or a single lot has been partly improved, the other portion, if used according to the usual course and custom of the adjoining country, is treated as within the possession of such occupant. Under this statute it is held that the

11. Texas Civ. Stats. (1913), §§ 5672-5675 (3340-3343).

occupancy need not be under a valid deed, but that if the deed covers the land, and there has been an occupancy under it for the requisite period, although the person executing the deed has no authority to do so, it is sufficient.[12] Substantially the same provision exists in the statutes of Florida, South Carolina, California, Wisconsin, Nevada, Arizona, Dakota, Idaho, Montana, and Utah. In New York and in all these States,[13] it is also provided that where a person claims title not founded on a written instrument, judgment, or decree, such land shall be deemed to have been occupied and possessed, first, where it has been protected by a substantial fence; and, second, where it has been usually cultivated and improved.

Under these statutes, specifically defining what possession shall be regarded as adverse, the possession, in order to be operative, must be shown to be by some one of the modes stated in the statute, or it will be no protection, however long such possession may have been continued.[14] Under these statutes, in order to acquire a title by possession on account of an enclosure, the

12. Bishop's Ann. Code (4th ed. 1895), §§ 369-372; Hilton v. Bender, 2 Hun (N. Y.) 1.

It is not enough in New York to claim title, but the defendant must claim under some specific title, and this must be disclosed so that the court may see that it is adverse to that of the grantor in the deed assailed. Dawley v. Brown, 79 N. Y. 390, 396; Heller v. Cohen, 154 N. Y. 299, 48 N. E. 527. See Knellar v. Lang, 137 N. Y. 589, 33 N. E. 555; Sanders v. Reidinger, 43 N. Y. Supp. 127; De St. Laurent v. Gescheidt, 45 N. Y. Supp. 730. In the case of co-tenants, if no explicit notice is given of the denial of the right of one, the occupant must make his possession so visibly hostile and notorious, and so apparently exclusive and adverse, as to justify an inference of knowledge on the part of the tenant sought to be ousted, and of laches if he fails to discover and assert his rights. Culver v. Rhodes, 87 N. Y. 348. Equity will prevent a threatened cloud on title when there is a determination to create such cloud, and a real danger. King v. Townshend, 141 N. Y. 358, 36 N. E. 513.

13. Wisconsin Stats., § 4212. But in this State, where the possession is under a written title, or upon a judgment, ten years' occupancy in this manner constitutes a bar; but in all other cases twenty years' occupancy is required.

14. East Hampton v. Kirk, 68 N. Y. 459; Cleveland v. Crawford, 7 Hun (N. Y.) 616.

party claiming must show that he has maintained during the requisite period a substantial enclosure and an actual occupancy, definite, positive, and notorious;[15] and merely keeping up a fence already built by a neighbor does not constitute a sufficient enclosure, within the statute.[16] If cultivation and improvement are relied upon to give title, both must be shown; and merely reaping, of itself, is not cultivation; nor does the mowing of grass or the cutting of brush alone amount to an improvement, within the meaning of the statute.[17] Where land is entered upon under a claim of, but without written title, there must be a *pedis possessio,* or an enclosure. But this does not necessarily contemplate an artificial fence. If the possession is actual, visible, exclusive, and notorious, so far as the actual occupancy extends by actual cultivation and improvement for the ordinary purposes of agriculture for the requisite period, a title may be acquired, but cannot, as in the case of an actual fence or color of title, be extended by construction to embrace lands not so actually cultivated and improved.[18] Occasionally taking wood and timber from a wood-lot, or using it for a pasture, does not amount to cultivation and improvement, within the meaning of the statute, so as to give title by possession, in the absence of an enclosure.

§ 256. What constitutes a disseisin under these statutes.

Except where the statute defines the species of possession which

15. Jackson v. Schoonmaker, 2 Johns. (N. Y.) 230; McFarlane v. Kerr, 10 Bosw. (N. Y.) 249.

16. Doolittle v. Tice, 41 Barb. (N. Y.) 181. Where a lot was inclosed on one side by a highway, on two sides by a fence, and on the other side by a distinct line of marked trees extending from corner stake to corner stake, it was held that the lot was not protected by a substantial inclosure, within the meaning of the Code. Pope v. Hanmer, 8 Hun (N. Y.) 265.

17. Doolittle v. Tice, *supra.*

18. Becker v. Van Valkenburgh, 29 Barb. (N. Y.) 319; Jackson v. Halstead, 5 Cow. (N. Y.) 216; Jackson v. Camp, 1 id. 605; Sharp v. Brandow, 15 Wend. (N. Y.) 597; Jackson v. Woodruff, 1 Cow. (N. Y.) 276. In Pope v. Hanmer, 8 Hun (N. Y.) 265, these questions were fully considered, reference being specially made to the Code, §§ 369, 372; Doolittle v. Tice, 41 Barb. (N. Y.) 181; Hallas v. Bell, 53 id. 247; Lane v. Gould, 10 id. 254; Jackson v. Woodruff, 1 Cow. (N. Y.) 276; Crary v. Goodman, 22 N. Y. 170.

shall be regarded as adverse, so as to bar a right of entry, the question is left for settlement by the courts, in view of the language of the statute under which the question arises. In Maine,[19] the language of the statute is, "No person shall commence any real or mixed action for the recovery of lands, or make an entry thereon, unless within twenty years after the right to do so first accrued; or within twenty years after he, or those under whom he claims, were seised or possessed of the premises;"[20] and this is practically the provision in Vermont, New Hampshire, Connecticut, Massachusetts, Arkansas, Delaware,[21] Illinois, Mississippi,[22] Minnesota, North Carolina, Ohio,[23] Oregon, Michigan,[24] Nebraska, Tennessee, Virginia, West Virginia, New Mexico,

19. Rev. Stats. (1883), ch. 105, § 1.

20. This provision does not apply to an action of dower which is not barred until twenty years and one month after demand. Chase v. Alley, 82 Me. 234, 19 Atl. 397; Hastings v. Mace, 157 Mass. 499, 32 N. E. 668; Robie v. Flanders, 33 N. H. 524; Munroe v. Wilson, 68 id. 580; Long v. Kansas City Stock Yards Co., 107 Mo. 298, 17 S. W. 656.

21. In Indiana, the statute provides "for the recovery of the possession of real estate twenty years," which is practically the same, as under this statute the right of action does not accrue until there has been a disseisin. 1 Ind. Stats. (1894, by Burns), § 294, Ch. 6. This limitation applies to an action for breach of the covenant of warranty in a deed. Hyatt v. Mattingly, 68 Ind. 271. Color of title not being necessary to an adverse possession, it is sufficient if there is, for the prescribed period, assertion of ownership and unbroken possession. Collett v. Commissioners, 119 Ind. 27; 21 N. E. 329, 4 L. R. A. 321; Herff v. Griggs, 121 Ind. 471, 23 N. E. 279. In Kentucky, the provision is, "An action for the recovery of real property can only be brought within fifteen years after the right to institute it first accrued." Ky. Stats. (1899, by Carroll), § 2805.

22. In this State the language is not the same, but its effect is identical, and the statute in this respect is expressly applied to courts of equity as well as courts of law. Code (1892), §§ 2730, 2731.

In this State, as elsewhere, a claim of title under a parol gift or purchase, accompanied by entry and adverse holding, may ripen into an indefeasible title by the lapse of the statutory period of limitations. Davis v. Davis. 68 Miss. 478, 10 So. 70.

23. In this State the language is, "An action for the recovery of the title or possession of real property can only be brought within twenty-one years after the cause of such action accrues." Sec. 4977.

24. In this State the statute specifies when the right of action shall be treated as having accrued; but the provisions in this respect do not vary

and Wyoming. The language of the statute in all of these States is not identical with that of the Maine statute, nor is the period of limitation; but the practical effect is the same, and in none of them is there any provision as to what shall be deemed an adverse possession sufficient to bar a suit or entry. From this summary of the statutes it will be observed that the statute will not commence to run until a cause of action has arisen in favor of the person having the rightful title; in other words, until he has been disseised by the person in possession or those in privity with him in the possession. And a person who enters upon the land of another, with the intention of usurping the possession, and carries that intention into effect by retaining the exclusive possession of the premises, actually disseises the owner;[25] and this is so whether the entry and possession are contrary to the will of the owner or not, because, as we shall see hereafter, it is immaterial whether the owner knows of the disseisin or not;[26] nor is it necessary that the entry should be wrongful, because, although a person enters lawfully, yet if, after entry, he calls the owner's title in question, and claims the land as his own, or usurps dominion over it, either by words or acts, he is a disseisor;[27] and if suffered to remain in possession under such circumstances, without entry or action by the owner, for the requisite statutory period, he acquires a title thereto by possession. But where the possession commences by the permission of the owner, there can be no disseisin or adverse possession until there has been a disclaimer by the assertion of an adverse title, and notice thereof, either actual or constructive.[28] There are two kinds

essentially from those which exist where no such provisions are made. Compiled Laws (1897), § 9714 *et seq.*

25. Towle v. Ayer, 8 N. H. 57; Melvin v. Proprietors, 46 Mass. (5 Met.) 15; Co. Litt. 279.

26. Brown v. King, 46 Mass. (5 Met.) 173; Poignard v. Smith, 23 Mass. (6 Pick.) 172.

27. Walker v. Wilson, 4 N. H. 217.

28. Hudson v. Putney, 14 W. Va. 461; Foulke v. Bond, 41 N. J. L. 527. See Legg v. Horn, 45 Conn. 415; Wiseman v. Lucksinger, 84 N. Y. 31; Coleman v. Pickett, 31 N. Y. S. 480; Morse v. Sherman, 155 Mass. 222, 29 N. E. 523; Prescott v. Prescott, 175 Mass. 64, 66, 55 N. E. 805; Bond v. O'Gara, 177 Mass. 139, 58 N. E. 275,

of disseisin: one a disseisin in fact, and the other a disseisin by election.[29] A disseisin in fact is one whereby the original owner is divested of his seisin, and of all right in relation thereto, except his right of entry and of property, or of action for its recovery. A disseisin by election is when an act is done upon or in relation to lands, which is equivocal, and may be treated either as a trespass or a disseisin according to the intention with which it was done, in which case the law will not permit the wrong-doer to qualify his own wrong, and claim it to be a mere trespass, unless the owner elects to so regard it.[30] It frequently occurs that the courts fail to observe the proper distinction between these two classes of disseisins; but for the purposes of the application of the statute, and ascertaining the period from which it begins to run, this distinction is important, and quite apparent, because there can be no disseisin in fact, except by the wrongful entry of a person claiming the freehold, and an actual ouster or expulsion of the true owner, or by some other act which

83 Am. St. Rep. 265; Coffrin v. Cole, 67 Vt. 226; Great Falls W. W. Co. v. Gt. Northern Ry. Co., 21 Mont. 487; Thoemke v. Fiedler, 91 Wis. 386; Yeager v. Woodruff, 17 Utah 361, 53 Pac. 1045. In the absence of evidence of what claim the original entry was made under, it is always presumed to have been made in subordination to the legal title. Sanders v. Riedinger, 51 N. Y. S. 937, 940 aff'd 164 N. Y. 564, 58 N. E. 1092; Lucy v. Tenn. & Coosa R. Co., 92 Ala. 246, 250. An entry so made is presumed to continue subordinate to the legal title until notice is by some means brought home to the original owner. Ross v. Veech, 22 Ky. Lew Rep. 578, 58 S. W. 475; Whieney v. Wheeler Cotton Mills, 151 Mass. 396, 407, 24 N. E. 774, 7 L. R. A. 613. And all presumptions are *prima facie* in favor of the true owner. Illinois Steel Co. v. Bilot, 109 Wis. 418, 85 N. W. 402, 406, 83 Am. St. Rep. 905; Heermans v. Schmaltz, 10 Biss (U. S.) 323, 7 Fed. 566. The fact that such owner is absent from home, and does not see or know of the claimant's hostile acts, is immaterial. Talbott v. Woodford, 48 W. Va. 499, 37 S. E. 580. As to the notoriety required to support a claim by adverse user, see Gould on Waters, § 337; De Frieze v. Quint, 94 Cal. 653, 28 Am. St. Rep. 151, and n.

29. This species of disseisin is recognized in Atkyns v. Horde, 2 Cowp. 689, also in 2 Inst. 412. But it seems that, in order to enable the owner to elect to treat an act as a disseisn, the entry must be *injuste et sine judicio.*

30. Prescott v. Nevers, 4 Mas. (U. S.) 326; Blunden v. Baugh, Cro. Car. 302.

is tantamount thereto;[31] and the claim or color of title must exist at the commencement, and any other entry is a mere trespass;[32] and the person who is put out of possession may maintain ejectment or trespass against the wrong-doer, at his election.[33] Of course, where the statute defines the species of possession requisite to bar the claim of the true owner, for the purposes of this statute, such a possession only will amount to a disseisin. There are loose *dicta* in the cases upon this question where the statute does not define the species of possession required, and many misstatements of the true doctrine or rules that control in determining whether there has been a disseisin and a sufficient adverse possession to divest the true owner of his title to lands, and as to the character of the possession requisite to work this result. But the whole matter hinges upon the circumstance whether there has been a disseisin in fact, and an actual expulsion of the true owner for the full statutory period; and in all cases where there has been, the possession is adverse, and the true owner is barred, both as to his right of entry upon, and his remedy for the recovery of, the land; and this has been held to be the case under these statutes in Connecticut and Michigan, where the original entry is wrongful, although the person entering does not claim title in himself, or deny the title of the legal owner if he usurps dominion over the land at the time of entry, and uses and occupies it excusively and continuously as his own for the requisite statutory period, as in such a case, as in instances where there is entry under a conveyance, the law presumes that the holding was adverse, where the possession is accompanied with acts which are the usual insignia of ownership.[34] In other words, any entry

31. Varick v. Jackson, 2 Wend. (N. Y.) 166.

32. Co. Litt. 153 *b;* 4 Bouvier's Law Dic. 558.

33. Wheeler v. Bates, 21 N. H. 640; Bateman v. Allen, Cro. Eliz. 437; Allen v. Rivington, 2 Saund. 111; Clute v. Voris, 31 Barb. (N. Y.) 511; Jackson v. Harder, 4 Johns. (N. Y.) 202.

34. Ingersoll, J., in Bryan v. Atwater, 5 Day (Conn.) 181; French v. Pearce, 8 Conn. 442. In Bryan v. Atwater, *supra*, an adverse possession is defined by Ingersoll, J., to be "a possession not under the legal

upon lands without the consent of the true owner, and continuous occupancy thereof by the person entering, as his own, which excludes the possession, actual or constructive, of such owner, for the full statutory period, is held by the courts of the States named to be adverse, within the meaning of the statute, and divests the legal owner of all right to such lands, whether such entry was made under a claim of title or not.[35] This doctrine is in strict accordance with the definition of a disseisin given by Littleton.[36] "A disseisin," saye he, "is where a man entereth into any lands or tenements where his entrance is not congeable, and ousteth him who has the freehold;" and of Coke, who says:[37] "A disseisin is the putting a man out of possession, and ever implieth a wrong. But dispossession or ejectment is a putting out of possession, and may be by right or by wrong." [38] Under this definition it would seem to follow that, if the entry was made by the permission of the owner, possession, however long con-

proprietor, but entered into without his consent, either directly or indirectly given. It is a possession by which he is disseised and ousted of the lands so possessed."

35. See Kennebeck Purchase v. Laboree, 2 Me. 275. In Kennebeck Purchase v. Springer, 4 Mass. 416, Parsons, C. J., said: "To constitute an actual ouster of him who was seised, the disseisor must have the actual exclusive occupation of the land claiming to hold it against him who was seised, or he must actually turn him out of possession." In Patterson v. Reigle, 4 Pa. 201, it was held that one who enters upon the land of an unknown owner, with intent to hold until the real owner appears, has an adverse possession which will ripen into a title by the lapse of the statutory period. See Stokes v. Berry, 2 Salk. 421; Hellings v. Bird, 11 East, 49; Walton v. Ogden, 1 Johns. (N. Y.) 156; Griswold v. Bond, 5 id. 230; Bound v. Sharp, 9 id. 162; Hinkley v. Crouse, 125 N. Y. 730. In Michigan, in Campau v. Dubois, 39 Mich. 274, it was held that no claim of title is necessary to perfect an adverse holding.

36. Co. Litt. 279.

37. Co. Litt. 153.

38. "Disseisin," he continues, "is a personal trespass, or tortious ouster of the seisin," and Aston, J., gives full countenance to the definition of a disseisin by Littleton, and agrees with him and Coke that to operate a disseisin two elements must concur, to wit, an entry which is not made under the title of the true owner, and an actual ouster of the owner under such entry; and he says, "Every entry is not a disseisin, unless there be likewise an ouster of the freehold." Atkyn v. Horde, 2 Cowp. 689.

tinued, will be treated as the possession of such owner, and in subservience to his title, until the person in possession has disclaimed, and set up an adverse title thereto in himself or some third person, and given the owner notice thereof, actual or constructive;[39] but that an adverse user may be presumed from a long possession without the payment of rent or other recognition of the owner's title, or an account for the rents or profits of the land.[40] But while, as already stated, it is held in those States that the entry need not necessarily be made under a claim of title, yet whether it is so made or not is treated as an important element in the determination of the question whether there has in fact been an adverse user, and an actual ouster of the true owner; but the real question as to whether there has been an actual ouster of the true owner and a consequent disseisin is one which depends upon all the circumstances, and may be solved in favor of the occupant, although no claim of title in himself is shown to have existed.[41] It is the fact of exclusive occupancy, using and enjoying the land as his own, in hostility to the true owner, for the full statutory period, which enables the occupant to acquire an absolute right to the land under these statutes.[42] The motive of the occupant is not material, provided his occupancy is actual and exclusive, and after the manner of the owner of the fee.[43]

While, strictly speaking, as held in Connecticut and some other States, it may not be necessary that the entry or possession should, in all cases, be under a pretense or claim of title by the occupant in himself, yet it is an indispensable requisite that the entry and possession, or the possession where the entry is not wrongful, should be hostile to the true owner;[44] and a person who

39. See sec. 265, Landlord and Tenant; sec. 266, Co-tenants; Atkyns v. Horde, 2 Cowp. 689.

40. Fishar v. Prosser, 1 Cowp. 217.

41. Johnson v. Gorham, 38 Conn. 521; Patterson v. Reigle, 4 Pa. 201.

42. French v. Pearce, 8 Conn. 439. See Johnson v. Gorham, 38 id. 513.

43. French v. Pearce, *supra*.

44. Griswold v. Bard, 4 Johns. (N. Y.) 320. A naked possession without any claim of title is not sufficient, Brandt v. Ogden, 1 Johns. (N. Y.) 156; Humbert v. Trinity Church, *supra;* nor is an entry by the permission of the owner, with the expec-

merely claims the improvements upon land cannot acquire a title

tation that the land will be conveyed to him as a gift, Howard v. Howard, 17 Barb. (N. Y.) 663; Pease v. Lawson, 33 Mo. 35. It is not indispensable that the entry should be adverse in its inception. Jackson v. Brink, 5 Cow. (N. Y.) 483. If an adverse claim is subsequently set up, either by taking a deed of the land or otherwise by unequivocal acts of ownership, it is enough. Jackson v. Smith, 13 Johns. (N. Y.) 406; Jackson v. Frost, 5 Cow. 346. There must be an assertion of a right to the exclusion of every other person. Sherry v. Frecking, 4 Duer (N. Y.) 452. And it must be under a claim of the entire title, and which excludes every presumption of title in another. Hoyt v. Dillon, 19 Barb. (N. Y.) 644. See Jackson v. Sharp, 9 Johns. (N. Y.) 163. In Pepper v. O'Dowd, 39 Wis. 538, it was held that to make the actual adverse possession of a part of a tract of farming land, which was once possessed and used as several farms by several owners, constructive adverse possession of the whole tract, it must be shown that the whole tract is included in some of the claimant's title papers, and that the several farms have been joined together in one known farm before the entry under which the claim exists was made. An adverse possession must not be a mere trespass. It must be visible and notorious, and exclude the exercise of ownership by the other party, and must be hostile in such sense as to indicate intent to occupy exclusively. Miller v. Platt, 5 Duer (N. Y.) 272. The person having the legal title to land has the constructive possession of it. To overcome that possession, and perfect title by limitation, or create the presumption of a grant to such land, there must be an actual possession of some part of the land in dispute. Snoddy v. Kreutch, 40 Tenn. (3 Head) 301; Foster v. Grizzle, 41 Tenn. (1 Coldw.) 530. A mere adverse claim to the land for the period required to form the bar is not sufficient. Smith v. Lee, 41 Tenn. (1 Coldw.) 549. To make a possession adverse, there must be an entry under a color of right claiming title hostile to the true owner and the world, and the entry must be followed by the possession and appropriation of the premises to the occupant's use, done publicly and notoriously. Dixon v. Clark, 47 Miss. 220. The adverse character of the possession must be proved as a fact; it cannot be assumed as a matter of law from mere exclusive possession, however long continued. Russell v. Davis, 38 Conn. 562. And the proof must be clear that the party held under a claim of right, and with intent to hold adversely. Grube v. Wells, 34 Iowa, 148; Washburn v. Cutter, 17 Minn. 361; Baker v. Swan, 32 Md. 355. A mere possession without claim of title can afford no presumption of right from lapse of time. Taggart v. Stanbery, 2 McLean (U. S.) 543; Stillman v. White Rock Mfg. Co., 3 W. & M. (U. S.) 539; Peyton v. Stith, 30 U. S. (5 Pet.) 485, 8 L. Ed. 200. In Wilkes v. Elliot, 5 Cranch, C. C. 611, it was held that there must be an entry under claim of title, or a subsequent claim of hos-

by any length of possession.[45] In some of the States it is expressly provided that where the possession is not held under any writing,[46] it must be under a claim of title, that is, that the person must occupy and claim the premises as his own; and practically in all the States there must be an entry or possession under a claim of title, or such a user of the premises as raises a presumption of such a claim, and in many of the States a claim of title, as well as exclusive and continuous occupancy, is held to be indispensable;[47] and generally it may be said that the intention of the occupant is a material element in determining whether or not the possession is adverse in such a sense as to operate as an actual ouster of the true owner and defeat his right of entry.[48] It is well settled that, where there is no claim of title in the occupant, his possession cannot be adverse to the true title, upon the principle that, where a person is in possession, making no claim whatever to the premises, his title, in presumption of law, is in amity with and subservience to the true title.[49] Indeed, the courts in Georgia

tile title and possession under it. In Ewing v. Burnett, 36 U. S. (11 Pet.) 41, 9 L. Ed. 624, it was held that an entry operates as an ouster, or not, according to the intent with which the act was done.

45. Davenport v. Sebring, 52 Iowa 364. Where one of several heirs took exclusive possession of land belonging to a number of heirs, and improved it, without interference from them, although they lived in the immediate neighborhood, and no action was brought by them for more than twenty-five years, it was held that ejectment would not lie; also that the heir in possession had acquired a title to the land by adverse possession for the requisite period, and that no claim of title was necessary to perfect an adverse holding. Campau v. Dubois, 39 Mich. 274.

46. Mississippi, New York, Florida, Louisiana, Colorado, South Carolina, California, Wisconsin, Nevada, Texas, Arizona, Utah, Dakota, Idaho, and Montana.

47. Hale v. Glidden, 10 N. H. 397; Hunter v. Chrisman, 45 Ky. (6 B. Mon.) 463; Kincheloe v. Tracewells, 11 Gratt. (Va.) 587, 605; Ewing v. Burnett, 36 U. S. (11 Pet.) 41, 9 L. Ed. 624; Harvey v. Tyler, 2 Wall. (U. S.) 328.

48. Brown v. Gay, 3 Me. 126; Howard v. Rudy, 29 Ga. 154; Brown v. Cockerell, 33 Ala. 45. In Simmons v. Nahant, 85 Mass. (3 Allen) 316, the court held that, in order to gain a possessory title to land lying in common and undivided, there must be proof of acts of ownership done with the intention of asserting a title thereto.

49. Harvey v. Tyler, *supra;* Kincheloe v. Tracewells, *supra;* Jackson

have extended this rule so far as to hold that, where a person goes into possession under such circumstances, he holds as tenant at will to the true owner, and cannot, by secretly attorning to another, change the character of his possession so as to make it adverse.[50] Although such naked possession is treated as held in subservience to the legal title, yet it implies no privity of contract with the legal owner, or duty towards him or the estate; and while his possession, unless its character is changed, may not ripen into an adverse title, upon the principle that, unless adverse in its inception, it will be presumed to continue as it began, yet this does not preclude the occupant from setting up an adverse claim at any time he chooses, either by taking a conveyance under a tax title or any conveyance, or by any act which changes the character of his occupancy from amicable to adverse.[51]

It is the intention to claim title which makes the possession adverse; but this intention must be evinced and effectuated by the manner of occupancy;[52] and neither a mere claim of title with-

v. Waters, 12 Johns. (N. Y.) 365; Jackson v. Howe, 14 id. 405; Johnston v. Irwin, 3 S. & R. (Pa.) 291; Markley v. Amos, 2 Bailey (S. C.) 603; Jackson v. Thomas, 16 Johns. (N. Y.) 293. A person under such circumstances is a mere intruder. "*Intrusio est ubi quis, cui nullum jus competit in re nec scintilla juris, possessionem vacuam ingreditur, quae nec corpore nec animo possidetur, sicut hereditatum jacentum.*" Bracton, Book IV., ch. 2, fol. 160. In Book II., ch. 17, fol. 39, possession is called "*nuda, ubi quis nil juris habet in re, nec aliquam juris scintillam, sed tantum nudum pedum possessionem.*" As previously stated, such possession has always been treated as in subservience to the true title. Jackson v. Porter, 1 Paine (U. S. C. C.) 457; Jackson v. Camp, 1 Cow. (N. Y.) 605. See Story, J.: "No ouster can be presumed in favor of such a possession." Society v. Pawlet, 29 U. S. (4 Pet.) 480.

50. Gay v. Mitchell, 35 Ga. 139. See Link v. Doerfer, 42 Wis. 391, where it is intimated that a person so possessing land may subject the tenant to some form of action for the profits. But this is mere *obiter*.

51. Blackwood v. Van Vleit, 30 Mich. 118; Bowman v. Cockrill, 6 Kan. 311; Blakeley v. Bestor, 13 Ill. 708; Moss v. Shear, 25 Cal. 38; Link v. Doerfer, 42 Wis. 407; Hamilton v. Wright, 30 Iowa 480; Stubblefield v. Borders, 92 Ill. 279.

52. Jackson v. Porter, 1 Paine (U. S.) 457; Bartholomew v. Edwards, 1 Houst. (Del.) 17. In Campau v. Dubois, 39 Mich. 274, it was held that no claim of title is necessary to perfect a title by adverse holding.

out occupancy,[53] nor a mere occupancy without an intent to claim title, are sufficient.[54] " It is not the possession alone," says Thompson, J.,[55] " but that it is accompanied with the claim of the fee, which, by construction of law, is deemed *prima facie* evidence of such an estate." The intention need not be expressed, but may be inferred from the manner of occupancy;[56] and in one case, where the possession was shown to have been in fact adverse, it was held that the statute barred an entry after the lapse of the requisite period, although the occupant practiced deceit, and lulled the owner into the belief that he did not intend to claim adversely.[57]

§ 257. Entry or possession without color of title.

It is well settled that, when a person relies upon naked possession as the foundation for an adverse claim, there must be a *pedis possessio*, or an actual occupancy, and the possession cannot be extended by construction beyond the limits of his actual occupation;[58] and it must not only be actual, but also visible, continu-

53. Abell v. Harris, 11 G. & J. (Md.) 637; Cooper v. Smith, 9 S. & R. (Pa.) 26.

54. Brown v. Gay, 3 Me. 126; Allen v. Holton, 37 Mass. (20 Pick.) 458; Betts v. Brown, 3 Mo. App. 20; McNamara v. Seaton, 82 Ill. 498; Skinner v. Crawford, 54 Iowa 119.

55. Jackson v. Porter, 1 Paine (U. S.) 457.

56. Conyers v. Kenan, 4 Ga. 308.

57. Strange v. Durham, 1 Brev. (S. C.) 83; and see Patterson v. Reigle, 4 Pa. 201. In Pennsylvania, it is held that, where an entry is made without the permission of the owner, the possession is presumed to be adverse, until the contrary is shown. Neel v. McElhenny, 69 Pa. 300.

As to mistake in boundary lines, see 6 Harvard L. Rev. 385. When possession is to be inferred from equivocal acts, the intention with which they are done is all important. See Leigh v. Jack, 5 Ex. D. 264; Littledale v. Liverpool College [1900], 1 ch. 19. The mere user of land, without claiming it, and under the belief that the real owner does own it, is not adverse. Pearson v. Adams, 129 (Ala.) 157, 29 So. 977.

58. Coburn v. Hollis, 44 Mass. (3 Met.) 125; Jackson v. Hardenburgh, 2 Johns. (N. Y.) 234; Hale v. Glidden, 10 N. H. 397; Ferguson v. Peden, 33 Ark. 150; Wilson v. McEwan, 7 Oreg. 87; Schneider v. Botsch, 90 Ill. 577; Peterson v. McCullough, 50 Ind. 35; Wells v. Jackson Manuf. Co., 48 N. H. 491. In Alabama, the title in such cases is restricted to lands inclosed and under cultivation. Hawkins v. Hawkins, 45 Ala. 482; Ege v. Medlar, 82 Pa. 86; Clarke v. Wagner, 74 N. C. 791; Bristol v. Carroll County, 95 Ill. 84; Humphries v.

ous, notorious, distinct, and hostile,[59] and of such a character as to indicate exclusive ownership in the occupant.[60] No definite rule as to what constitutes sufficient possessory acts can be given, as the matter must necessarily depend largely upon the nature and character of the property, and must be determined from the circumstances of each case, and is for the jury. A substantial fence erected around land is a sufficient evidence of disseisin,[61] and the limit and extent of the occupant's claims; but the fence must be substantial, and a brush fence,[62] or a fence made merely by lapping trees one upon another,[63]—although the person claim-

Huffman, 33 Ohio St. 333; Foster v. Letz, 86 Ill. 412. Where a person acquires a title by naked occupancy upon a river, his title cannot be extended by construction to the centre of the river. Riley v. Jameson, 3 N. H. 23; Coming v. Troy Iron Co., 34 Barb. (N. Y.) 529. But a person may so use the river as to acquire title to the land lying under it. Wickes v. Lake, 25 Wis. 71. But in Hawkins v. Hudson, 45 Ala. 482, where a person went into possession of land under a parol gift, and actually occupied only a part of the lot, it was held that his title could not be extended beyond his actual occupancy, as against a *bona fide* purchaser from the owner of the legal estate. A person going into possession without color of title, but as a mere intruder, acquires possession "inch by inch" of the part which he occupies, and he cannot extend his title beyond his actual occupation for any distance. Prescptt v. Johnson, 9 Martin (La.) 123; Brooks v. Clay, 10 Ky. (3 A. K. Mar.) 545. See Miller v. Shaw, 7 S. & R. (Pa.) 143; Royer v. Benlow, 10 S. & R. (Pa.) 303.

59. In Sparrow v. Hovey, 44 Mich. 63, a refusal of the court to charge that when title is claimed by an adverse possession it should appear that the possession had been "actual, continued, visible, notorious, distinct, and hostile," but merely charging the jury that the possession "must be actual, continued, and visible," was held erroneous, although in fact the possession was held under a tax title which rendered it necessarily hostile to the owner of the original title.

60. Soule v. Barlow, 49 Vt. 329.

61. Ringold v. Cheney, 4 Hall's L. J. (Md.) 128; Miller v. Shaw, 7 S. & R. (Pa.) 129; Munshower v. Pattan, 10 id. 334; Hawk v. Senseman, 6 id. 21; Burns v. Swift, 2 id. 436; Mercer v. Watson, 1 Watts (Pa.) 330; Smith v. Hosmer, 7 N. H. 436. If a person enters under a deed, and fences in more land than his deed covers, he will hold the whole if he keeps up the fence for the full statutory period. Levettenham v. Leary, 18 Hun (N. Y.) 284.

62. Hale v. Glidden, 10 N. H. 397.

63. Coburn v. Hollis, 44 Mass. (3 Met.) 125; Parker v. Parker, 83 Mass (1 Allen 245; Slater v. Jepherson, 60 Mass. (6 Cush.) 129; Jackson v. Schoonmaker, 2 Johns. (N. Y.) 230.

ing the land occasionally entered upon it and cut wood and timber,[64] and sold a part of the land,—have been held not sufficient to continue a disseisin, although done with the knowledge of the owner.[65] A fence erected merely for convenience in working a farm, and not for the purpose of making the boundaries according to the title, is of no weight in determining acts of possession.[66] A fence must not only be substantial, but it must also extend around the whole lot, and one built only on three sides of it has been held insufficient;[67] but the rule would be otherwise where upon one side there is a natural substitute for a fence, as a ledge of rocks,[68] or other natural obstruction that renders a fence unnecessary, and in connection with the fence actually constructed forms a sufficient boundary and *indicia* or badge of ownership of the lot claimed. The rule is that where an enclosure consisting partly of natural and partly of artificial obstructions is relied upon as in itself establishing a *possessio pedis,* it is for the jury, upon all the proofs, and considering the quantity, locality, and character of the land, to decide whether the artificial barriers were sufficient to notify the public that the land was appropriated, and to impart to the appropriation the notoriety and *indicia* of ownership.[69]

Where land was enclosed by a river and a fence and road, and a disseisor occupied as near it as was convenient, it was held that this might be, if so intended by the occupant, a possession of the whole lot, although there was a narrow strip uncultivated.[70]

64. Hale v. Glidden, *supra;* Slater v. Jepherson, *supra.*

65. Slater v. Jepherson, *supra;* Parker v. Parker, *supra.*

66. Soule v. Barlow, 49 Vt. 329. In Allen v. Holton, 43 Mass. (26 Pick.) 458, it was held that the building of a fence upon a part of another's land, for the purpose of protecting his crops, and with no intention to exclude the owner from the lot, although the person building it occasionally cut wood and brush from the lot inclosed, did not constitute a disseisin.

67. Armstrong v. Risteau, 5 Md. 256. But see Dennett v. Crocker, 8 Me. 239; Pope v. Hanmer, 74 N. Y. 240.

68. St. Louis v. Gorman, 29 Mo. 593.

69. Brumagim v. Bradshaw, 39 Cal. 24.

70. Allen v. Holton, 37 Mass. (20 Pick.) 458. And where land was claimed by actual possession and in-

Where the party relies upon a fence to establish his title to land, he cannot extend his possession beyond its limits,[71] except by an actual occupancy of the land outside of the limits of the fence for the full statutory period.[72] Unless expressly made so by

closure by a fence, and was bounded on one side by a pond and on the other by lands owned by the claimant, it was held that although his fences did not surround the land in question on all sides except that next to the pond, yet it was proper to submit the facts to the jury to determine whether they were erected for the purpose of inclosing the land in controversy, or merely for the protection of his own land. Dennett v. Crocker, 8 Me. 239. See also Soule v. Barlow, *supra*.

71. Ringold v. Cheney, *supra;* Hall v. Gittings, 2 H. & J. (Md.) 380; Goewey v. Urig, 8 Ill. 238.

72. In Hull v. Gittings, *supra*, where a claimant to land, who had inclosed a hundred acres of land and cultivated it for fifteen years, subsequently inclosed fifty acres additional, and occupied it in connection with the other for six years, it was held that he only had title to the hundred acres. Adverse possession is made out by the coexistence of two distinct ingredients: the first, such a title as will afford color; and, second, such possession under it as will be adverse to the right of the true owner; and whether these two essentials exist is in all cases, a question of law, to be determined by the court, though the facts upon which they are founded are for the finding of the jury. Baker v. Swan, 32 Md. 355. Wickes v. Lake, 25 Wis. 71. To defeat an action of ejectment, the possession must have been an open, notorious, and continuous occupancy of the land, or some part thereof, under color of title to the whole, and must be taken in good faith under a claim adverse to plaintiff and those from whom he derives title, Turner v. Hall, 60 Mo. 271; and must be such as operates as a notice of the claim of title to all parties. Wilder v. Clough, 55 N. H. 359. Under this rule, to prevent the establishment of a right to maintain across one lot of land a drain leading from another lot, by adverse use continued for twenty years, the testimony of a person who within that time owned the first lot is admissible; and that during the time he owned it, and with ample opportunities, if visible, he never knew of the existence of the drain. Hannefin v. Blake, 102 Mass. 297. A claim of title based on continuous possession is not impaired by occasional occupancy by persons not distinctly shown to be in under the claimant if the same is not positively proved to have been adverse, nor the claim at any time to have been abandoned. Rayner v. Lee, 20 Mich. 384. Compare Whalley v. Small, 29 Iowa 288. The building of a shed, quarrying rock, erecting a limekiln, and cutting wood, to burn it for the purpose of making lime on the land in dispute, continued uninterruptedly for more than seven years, constitute such a possession as will give a good title to the person claiming adversely under it. Moore

statute, the mere circumstance that a person erected a fence around a lot, however substantial, is not of itself sufficient evidence of exclusive occupation; it must also be shown that the person claiming not only held the land adversely, but also that he had the exclusive occupation of the land surrounded by the fence for the entire statutory period.[73]

v. Thompson, 69 N. C. 120. It is for the jury to say whether one who does acts of ownership upon wild land, and afterwards buys it, was in possession before his conveyance, and under the grantor or adverse to him, possession at that time under color of the grantor's title being necessary to support a plea of the statute, and the grantor never having been personally in possession, the land being wild, and his claim a tax title. Wiggins v. Holley, 11 Ind. 2. An exclusive possession and occupancy for ten years, under a claim of absolute title, and where there is no adverse showing, is sufficient evidence for a jury to infer a title in fee simple in the occupant, on an appeal from the appraisement and assessment of county commissioners, of land taken for a railroad. Gulf R. R. Co. v. Owen, 8 Kan. 409. The acceptance of a lease from the owner of the title interrupts the running of limitation. Under a lease, during the term there can be no adverse possession by the tenant, unless by some act creating an adverse possession if done by a tenant who entered under a lease. Abbey Homestead Assoc. v. Willard, 48 Cal. 614.

73. See Russell v. Davis, 38 Conn. 562; Walsh v. Hill, 41 Cal. 571.

The evidence necessary to prove adverse possession varies with the character of the land. Bowen v. Guild, 130 Mass. 121, *infra*, § 267. A title to land by disseisin and adverse possession up to the line of an ancient fence is evidence of title to that line. Holloran v. Holloran, 149 Mass. 298, 21 N. E. 374; Houghton v. Wilhelmy, 157 Mass. 521, 32 N. E. 861; Beckman v. Davidson, 162 Mass. 347, 39 N. E. 38; Northern Counties Inv. Trust v. Enyard, 24 (Wash.) 366, 64 Pac. 516; Pittsburg, etc., R. Co. v. Stickley (2d), 58 N. J. 192; Bell v. Whitehead (Tenn. Ch. App.) 62 S. W. 213; Daughtrey v. New York & T. Land Co. (Tex. Civ. App.) 61 S. W. 947. See McAvoy v. Cassidy, 8 Misc. Rep. 595, 29 N. Y. S. 321. No particular kind of inclosure is requisite; the boundaries may be artificial in part and natural in part, if the circumstances clearly indicate that it marks the bounds of the adverse occupancy. Trustees v. Kirk, 84 N. Y. 215; Illinois Steel Co. v. Bilot, 109 (Wis.) 418, 85 N. W. 402, 406, 83 Am. St. Rep. 905; Polk v. Beaumont Pasture Co. (Tex. Civ. App.) 64 S. W. 58. Thus, the claim need not be evidenced by fencing on every side; a natural boundary, like a stream, will suffice on one side, if the other sides are inclosed. Sanders v. Riedinger, 30 App. Div. 277, 51 N. Y. S. 937, aff'd 164 N. Y. 564, 58 N. E. 1092. But the building of a temporary or inadequate fence, not fitted or intended to inclose the land in dispute, so as to exclude its free,

§ 258. Occupancy where premises are not enclosed.

As previously stated, the question whether an alleged possession is marked by the characteristics requisite to make it adverse, and the foundation for a title by occupancy, is not wholly a question of law, and is a question for the jury, under proper instructions from the court.[74] The question as to what constitutes adverse

unlimited use by the owner or others, nor to utilize the land within it for any practical purpose, is not such an "inclosure" as the law contemplates. Helton v. Strubbe, 22 Ky. Law Rep. 1919, 62 S. W. 12.

74. Webb v. Richardson, 42 Vt. 465. Lord Mansfield, in Taylor v. Horde, 1 Burr. 60, said that "disseisin is a fact to be found by the jury." This rule has been adopted in our courts; and it is invariably held that the question as to whether an occupancy was with an adverse intent must be found by the jury. Poignard v. Smith, 23 Mass. (6 Pick.) 172; Hale v. Dewey, 10 Vt. 593; Jackson v. Joy, 9 Johns. (N. Y.) 102; Bradstreet v. Huntington, 30 U. S. (5 Pet.) 402; Kinsell v. Daggett, 11 Me. 309; Jackson v. Stephens, 13 Johns. (N. Y.) 496; Coburn v. Hollis, 44 Mass. (3 Met.) 125; Gayetty v. Bethune, 14 Mass. 49; Hopkins v. Robinson, 3 Watts (Pa.) 205; Brandt v. Ogden, 1 Johns. (N. Y.) 156; Jackson v. Sharp, 9 id. 163; Jackson v. Wheat, 18 id. 40; Jackson v. Waters, 12 id. 365; Jackson v. Ellis, 13 id. 118; Smith v. Burtis, 9 id. 174; Jackson v. Newton, 18 id. 355; Jackson v. Thomas, 16 id. 293; Jones v. Porter, 3 P. & W. (Pa.) 132; McClung v. Ross, 14 U. S. (5 Wheat.) 124, 5 L. Ed. 46; Iler v. Routh, 3 How. (Miss.) 276; Cummings v. Wyman, 10 Mass. 464; Wallace v. Duffield, 2 S. & R. (Pa.) 527; Schwartz v. Kuhn, 10 Me. 274; Atherton v. Johnson, 1 N. H. 34; Munshower v. Patton, 10 S. & R. (Pa.) 334; Overfield v. Christie, 7 id. 172; Bolling v. Petersburg, 3 Rand. (Va.) 563; Malson v. Frye, 1 Watts (Pa.) 433; Bell v. Hartley, 4 W. & S. (Pa.) 32; McNair v. Hunt, 5 Mo. 300; Rogers v. Madden, 2 Bailey (S. C.) 321; Mill Dam Corp. v. Bullfinch, 6 Mass. 229; Bracken v. Martin, 11 Tenn. (3 Yerg.) 55; Warren v. Childs, 11 Mass. 222; Read v. Goodyear, 17 S. & R. (Pa.) 350; Pray v. Pierce, 7 Mass. 383; Stevens v. Dewing, 2 Aik. (Vt.) 112. The proof to establish adverse possession must be clear and positive, and not left to inference. Weaver v. Wilson, 48 Ill. 125; Jackson v. Berner, id. 203. But when once established, it is presumed to continue, in the absence of proof of abandonment, or of possession by another under claim of title. Marston v. Rowe, 43 Ala. 271. Upon a trial involving such a title, the claimant may introduce the record of proceedings and judgment in an action of trespass previously brought by him against a third person in respect of the same premises. Such record is not evidence of his title, but is evidence that his possession was under claim of title, which is material. Hollister v. Young, 42 Vt. 403. Where a claimant relies upon his possession to defeat the lien of a judgment,

possession, as well as what evidence is necessary to establish it, is for the court; but the question as to whether the possession in a given case is adverse, or under the owner's title, is for the jury, and the person setting up the claim takes the burden of establishing all the requisites to make his title by occupancy complete.[75]

he must prove actual possession, and it is not sufficient to prove that he had such possession as a deed gave, without proving by the deed itself or otherwise, the character and extent of the possession which the deed gave, or what occupation was had under the deed. Eagle &. M. Co. v. Bank of Brunswick, 55 Ga. 44. An actual possession of some part of the premises must be shown; and if an easement is claimed by prescription, the use of the right is the only evidence of the extent to which it was acquired. Peterson v. McCullough, 50 Ind. 35. And where, while the right was being exercised, and before the statutory period had elapsed, the owner asserts his rights by an action for the injury resulting from such use, it cannot ripen into a right. Cobb v. Smith, 38 Wis. 21. But mere verbal objections to, or denial of, the right of user is not such an interruption as will prevent an acquisition of the right by prescription. Kimball v. Ladd, 42 Vt. 747. The occasional cutting of timber and boiling of sugar on the land of another, by the occupier of an adjoining tract, and the extension of his lines so as to include a small portion of the meadowland, is not such a possession as will give title under the statute of limitations. In such cases the statute only extends to the ground actually included in the interference. Washabaugh v. Entriken, 36 Pa. St. 513; Hole v. Rittenhouse, 23 Pa. St. 490. Evidence of occupation of wild, uninclosed land, by cutting firewood and bushes, and trimming the trees thereon, and, in one instance, within twenty years, by cutting off the entire growth of wood upon the land, and leaving it to grow over again, is held insufficient in Massachusetts to establish a title by possession, although such acts are within the knowledge of the owner. Parker v. Parker, 83 Mass. (1 Allen) 245. Occupancy through a tenant is sufficient. Smith v. Jackson, 76 Ill. 254. Fencing in a small portion of the highway, not sufficient to seriously obstruct public travel, although done by an adjoining land-owner under claim of title, does not constitute an adverse possession which can ripen into title. Brooks v. Riding, 46 Ind. 15. Evidence that a house and granary were built upon the forty acres in controversy, and that one-half of the tract was cultivated and inclosed—held, to warrant a finding that the occupant was in possession of the whole forty. Teabout v. Daniels, 38 Iowa, 158. It is not necessary that the adverse character of the possession should be actually brought home to the knowledge of the plaintiff by affirmative proof, if it was adverse to all others, open, notorious, and held under claim of title. Scruggs v. Scruggs, 43 Mo. 142.

75. Herbert v. Hanrick, 16 Ala. 581; Rung v. Schoneberger, 2 Watts

But the court may decline to submit the question of adverse possession to the jury, where, from the undisputed facts, as a matter of law, no such possession exists.[76] The character of the possession requisite to establish a title by adverse possession has already been adverted to, and from what has been said it will be readily understood that the possession must be of a different character from that which marks the conduct of a mere trespass,—it must be so open, notorious, and important as to operate as a notice to all parties that it is under a claim of right; that the right of the true owner is invaded and denied with an intention on the part of the occupant to assert a claim of title adverse to him;[77] that is, a person must possess, use, and occupy the land as owner, and as an owner would do; and an occasional exercise of dominion by broken and unconnected acts of ownership over lands which may be made productive is in no respect calculated to assert to the world a claim of right, but, says Taylor, C. J.,[78] "such conduct bespeaks the fitful invasions of a conscious trespasser rather than the confident claims of a rightful owner." There can be no hardship in limiting the claims of a wrong-doer to his actual occupancy, or in requiring him to occupy in such a decisive manner as to indicate his claim of ownership; and the distinction between the claim of a person under naked possession and one who claims under color of title, both as to the extent of his claim and the kind or quality of possession requisite to establish it, must not be lost sight of.[79]

(Pa.) 23; Jones v. Porter, 2 P. & W. (Pa.) 132; Gill v. Fauntleroy, 47 Ky. (8 B. Mon.) 177; Baker v. Swan, 32 Md. 355; Washburn v. Cutter, 17 Minn. 361.

76. Argotsinger v. Vines, 82 N. Y. 308; Bowie v. Brahe, 3 Duer (N. Y.) 35; Nearhoff v. Addleman, 31 Pa. 279.

77. Beatty v. Mason, 30 Md. 409; Carroll v. Gillion, 33 Ga. 539; Thomas v. Babb, 45 Mo. 384; Soule v. Barlow, 49 Vt. 329; Paine v. Hutchins, 49 Vt. 314.

78. Jones v. Ridley, 2 N. C. 400.

79. In North Carolina an actual, open adverse possession, even of a small part of a large tract of land, will mature title to all the tract embraced within the boundaries of the adverse holder's claim, but possession of one tract cannot give constructive possession of an adjoining tract with the distinct boundaries. Scaife v.

Under the rule as above stated, an adverse entry upon land, and digging a canal and felling trees,[80] or turning cattle upon unenclosed land to pasture,[81] paying taxes upon it [82] and survey-

Western North Carolina Land Co., 90 Fed. 238, 33 C. C. A. 47; Basnight v. Meekins, 121 N. C. 23, 37 S. E. 992; Allen v. Boggess, 94 Tex. 83, 58 S. W. 833. In Missouri and most of the States, actual possession, in the absence of color of title, only extends to the part which has been inclosed. Carter v. Hornback, 139 Mo. 238, 245, 40 S. W. 893; Boynton v. Hodgdon, 59 N. H. 247; Penn. R. Co. v. Breckenridge, 60 N. J. L. 583, 38 Atl. 740; Fullman v. Foster, 68 Vt. 590, 35 Atl. 484; Norris v. Ile, 152 Ill. 190, 38 N. E. 762, 43 Am. St. Rep. 233; Ely v. Brown, 183 Ill. 575, 596, 56 N. E. 181; Wilson v. Johnson, 145 Ind. 40, 38 N. E. 38, 43 N. E. 930; Barber v. Robinson, 78 Minn. 193; Nicklase v. Dickerson, 65 Ark. 422, 46 S. W. 945; Brown v. Watkins, 98 Tenn. 454, 40 S. W. 480; Parkersburg Ind. Co. v. Schultz, 43 W. Va. 470, 27 S. E. 255; Sulphur Mines Co. v. Thompson, 93 Va. 293, 25 S. E. 232. As used in this connection, "actual" possession depends upon the nature and location of the property and all the circumstances of the particular case. Ozark Plateau Land Co. v. Hays, 105 Mo. 143, 152, 16 S. W. 957; Illinois Steel Co. v. Bilot, 109 Wis. 418, 84 N. W. 855, 83 Am. St. Rep. 905, 85 N. W. 402. The rule appears to be now settled that, after an entry on land under color of title by deed, the possession is deemed to extend to the bounds of the deed, although the actual settlement and improvements are on a small parcel only of the land; and, as to the owner of the better legal title who occupies only in part, another claimant's junior paper title has no effect to extend the latter's right beyond the bounds of his actual possession under that junior title. Hunnicutt v. Peyton, 102 U. S. 333, 26 L. Ed. 113; Smith v. Gale, 144 U. S. 509, 526, 12 Sup. Ct. 674, 36 L. Ed. 521; Ozark Plateau Land Co. v. Hays, *supra;* Sholl v. German Coal Co., 139 Ill. 21, 33, 28 N. E. 748; Johns v. McKibben, 156 Ill. 71, 40 N. E. 449. And clearly there can be no constructive possession of land which is in the actual and hostile possession of another. New York Cent. & H. R. R. Co. v. Brennan, 24 App. Div. 343, 48 N. Y. S. 675, 678, aff'd 163 N. Y. 584, 57 N. E. 1119.

80. McCarty v. Foucher, 12 Martin (La.) 4, 114; Prevost v. Johnson, 9 id. 123.

81. Andrews v. Mulford, 1 Hawy. (N. C.) 311. In Sepulveda v. Sepulveda, 39 Cal. 13, such a use of land was held not such as would enable the owner to maintain an action, consequently could not be construed into a disseisin.

82. The fact that taxes on the land have been uninterruptedly paid by the occupant or his ancestors for more than twenty years has been considered strong evidence of a claim of right to all the property taxed. Fletcher v. Fuller, 120 U. S. 534, 552, 7 Sup. Ct. 667, 30 L. Ed. 759; Holtzman v. Douglas, 168 U. S. 278, 284, 18 Sup. Ct. 65, 42 L. Ed. 466; St. Louis Public Schools v. Risley, 40

ing it,[83] or surveying and marking the lines around it, and the occasional cutting of grass [84] or wood and timber for use and sale,[85] a survey which is not accompained by any other act of user or occupation,— is not sufficient to establish an ouster, or prove that the party went upon the land to claim title;[86] nor does an entry upon lands, cutting wood and splitting rails,[87] or occasional entries at long intervals, at one time to cut timber and at another to make bricks,[88] tend to establish a title to land by adverse occupancy. Indeed, in Massachusetts [89] it is held that there can be

Mo. 356. On the other hand, if the adverse holder has not paid the taxes, this is evidence that his possession is not under a claim of title. Todd v. Weed, 84 Minn. 4, 86 N. W. 756. Such payment of taxes does not, apart from statute, constitute possession though accompanied by pasturing the land; it is merely evidence of a claim of ownership. Carter v. Hornback, 139 Mo. 238, 40 S. W. 893; McVey v. Carr, 159 Mo. 648, 653, 60 S. W. 1034; Nye v. Alfter, 127 Mo. 529, 30 S. W. 186; Millett v. Mullen, 95 Me. 400, 49 Atl. 871; Whitman v. Shaw, 166 Mass. 451, 44 N. E. 333; Harrison v. Dolan, 172 Mass. 395, 52 N. E. 513; Lewis v. Pleasants, 143 Ill. 271, 30 N. E. 323, 32 N. E. 384; Johns v. McKibben, 156 Ill. 71; Osburn v. Searles, 156 Ill. 88, 40 N. E. 452; Anderson v. Canter, 10 Kan. App. 167, 63 Pac. 285; Fuller v. Jackson (Tenn.), 62 S. W. 274; Wood v. Chapman, 24 Col. 134, 49 Pac. 136. In California and Texas the payment of taxes is made an element of adverse possession by statute. See Lucas v. Provines, 130 Cal. 270, 62 Pac. 509; Standard Quicksilver Co. v. Habishaw, 132 Cal. 115, 64 Pac. 113; Gillum v. Fuqua (Tex. Civ. App.), 61 S. W. 938. In New York the payment of taxes is not evidence of possession, actual or constructive; and in a suit against a city to determine title, its assessment and levy of taxes on the land are not admissible on the issue of adverse user. Archibald v. New York Cent. & H. R. R. Co., 157 N. Y. 574, 583, 52 N. E. 567; Consolidated Ice Co. v. New York, 166 N. Y. 92, 59 N. E. 713.

83. Paine v. Hutchins, 49 Vt. 314; Miller v. Long Island R. R. Co., 71 N. Y. 380.

84. Kennebeck Purchase v. Springer, 4 Mass. 416. See Miller v. Long Island R. Co., 71 N. Y. 380, where it was held that an occasional entry upon woodland was not sufficient to maintain an action for an injury to the freehold.

85. Slater v. Jepherson, 60 Mass. (6 Cush.) 129; Parker v. Parker, 83 Mass. (1 Allen) 245; Hale v. Glidden, 10 N. H. 397; Washburn v. Cutter, 17 Minn. 361.

86. Beatty v. Mason, 30 Md. 409.

87. Carroll v. Gillion, 33 Ga. 539.

88. Williams v. Wallace, 78 N. C. 354.

89. Morrison v. Chapin, 97 Mass. 72; Morris v. Callanan, 105 Mass. 129.

no adverse claim to wild or wood land by a naked entry, without an actual enclosure built by the person claiming title or those under whom he claims; and if the entry is under color of title, the claimant must either enclose the land, or in some way manifest his exclusive occupation, which must be of such a character as to disseise the owner,[90] and whether or not he has so occupied is a question of fact for the jury.[91] But in that State it has been held that a title to flats may be made by an appropriate occupation, by entering upon and filling them up, or by building a wharf and using the flats adjoining for laying vessels, and that is such case the occupant will acquire an adverse title not only to the land covered by the wharf, but also as to so much of the land under the water (as in this case eighty feet) as was used for the purpose of laying vessels.[92] But as the use of navigable waters for the passage of vessels to and from a wharf is a usage of common right, the title was restricted to the portion of the flats used for laying the vessels, and did not embrace that portion of them lying beyond and between the outer limits of the eighty-feet strip and that portion of the shore where the title of the State terminated.[93] The exercise of a common right, however long

90. Bates v. Norcross, 31 Mass. (14 Pick.) 224; Coburn v. Hollis, 44 Mass. (3 Met.) 125.

91. Cummings v. Wyman, 10 Mass. 464; Parker v. Locks and Canals, 44 Mass. (3 Met.) 91. The exercise of a right, for however long a time, under circumstances which are not inconsistent with the exercise of the same right by others, will not establish a prescriptive right to an exclusive use thereof, although no other person did in fact exercise the privilege. State v. Cincinnati Gas Light Co., 18 Ohio St. 262. See Indianapolis, etc., R. Co. v. Ross, 47 Ind. 25.

92. Wheeler v. Stone, 55 Mass. (1 Cush.) 313. See also, Nichols v. Boston, 98 Mass. 39.

93. Wheeler v. Stone, *supra*. In Wilson v. McEwan, 7 Oreg. 87, it was held that a person who claimed several blocks of land, and occupied one adversely, could not claim title to the others simply because he had paid the taxes and warned off trespassers.

As to adverse possession of land under water, see Atty.-Gen. v. Portsmouth, 25 W. R. 559; Jones v. Williams, 2 M. & W. 326; Illinois Steel Co. v. Bilot, 109 Wis. 418, 84 N. W. 855, 83 Am. St. Rep. 905, 85 N. W. 402; De Lancey v. Hawkins, 23 App. Div. 8, 49 N. Y. S. 469, aff'd 163 N. Y. 587, 57 N. E. 1108; Merrill v. Tobin, 30 Fed. 738; Ludlow Manuf. Co. v. Indian Orchard Co., 177 Mass.

continued, cannot operate a disseisin.[94] The fact that a person passes over flats with vessels and anchors them there, or uses the flats for the purposes of access and egress from a wharf,[95] or sails over them with boats or vessels for a long period, for the purposes of navigation,[96] does not amount to possessory acts sufficient to give title under the statute; nor does the cutting of grass every

61, 58 N. E. 181. A riparian proprietor, being entitled to accretions made by the water, if barred, or partially barred, by the statute of limitations as to the river bank, is barred also as to the accretions, whether they be new or old. Campbell v. Laclede Gas Co., 84 Mo. 352, 372, aff'd 119 U. S. 445, 7 Sup. Ct. 278, 30 L. Ed. 459. As to prescriptive rights in artificial water courses, see Gould on Waters (3d ed.), §§ 225, 340, 352, 13 Harv. Rev. 608.

94. Green v. Chelsea, 41 Mass. (24 Pick.) 71; Drake v. Curtis, 55 Mass. (1 Cush.) 395. See Tracy v. Norwich, etc., R. Co., 39 Conn. 382; and East Hampton v. Kirk, 68 N. Y. 459, where the same rule was adopted where the only possessory acts were such as existed as a common right. Tappan v. Burnham, 90 Mass. (8 Allen) 65, also Drake v. Curtis, 55 Mass. (1 Cush.) 395.

As to adverse possession against the government or the public, see Gould on Waters (3d ed.), §§ 22, 37, 121; Schneider v. Hutchinson, 35 Or. 253, 57 Pac. 324, 76 Am. St. Rep. 474, and n.; Meyer v. Graham, 33 Neb. 566, 50 N. W. 763, 29 Am. St. Rep. 500, 18 L. R. A. 146, and n. "It has sometimes been suggested that the comparative amount of rightful private use (of a way) and of the public use which is without absolute right is an important element in determining whether such public use is under a claim of right. No doubt the amount of such unauthorized use may be considered as tending to show a use under the belief that the way is a public one; but the final test is, not whether it is greater or less in amount than the rightful private use, but whether it is of such a character as to show the assertion or assumption of a right so to use the way, or a use under the belief that such use is a matter of public right. See Weld v. Brooks, 152 Mass. 297, 25 N. E. 719; Taft v. Commonwealth, 158 id. 526, 552, 33 N. E. 1046." And while it is not necessary for each traveller to claim a right of way as one of the public, yet "the fact must exist that the way is used as a public right, and it must be proved by some evidence which distinguishes the use relied on from a rightful use by those who have a right to travel over the private way, and also from a use which is merely casual, or incidental, or permissible." Sprow v. Boston & Albany R. Co., 163 Mass. 330, 340, 39 N. E. 1024. See Franz v. Mendonca, 131 Cal. 205, 63 Pac. 361.

As to limitation in matters of eminent domain, see 2 Lewis on Eminent Domain (2d ed.), ch. 30, 38 Am. L. Reg. (N. S.) 184, 410.

95. Wheeler v. Stone, *supra*.

96. Drake v. Curtis, *supra*.

year upon flats partly covered with water,[97] or the entry upon an open beach for a long period of time and gathering and removing the seaweed, because these acts are consistent with the rights of the rest of the public, and afford no evidence of an adverse claim.[98] An entry upon land and erecting a building or buildings thereon operates as a disseisin to the extent of the actual occupancy, but title to adjacent lands occasionally used in connection with the buildings cannot be acquired by such use;[99] but if the use of adjoining land is of such a character that it can be said to be continuous, as where a house was extended over a part of the land, and the rest was cultivated as a garden under a claim of title the use operates as a disseisin of the whole.[1] Of course, an entry upon land, and improving or cultivating it, continued for the requisite statutory period, even though the person entering has no color of title, will give title to all the land actually cultivated or improved, but no more.[2] So, using land for mining purposes or quarrying stone,[3] and cutting wood for a lime-kiln,[4] clearing and cultivating new fields, turning out old ones and cutting wood promiscuously, has been held sufficient.[5]

§ 259. Entry and possession with color of title.

But while a person entering upon lands adversely, without any deed or color of title, is thus restricted to the land actually occupied by him, and takes nothing beyond the limits of his actual occupancy, and is required to occupy the land for the purposes of improvement or cultivation, yet where a person goes into possession under color of title, duly recorded, in which the boundaries of the lot are defined, this operates as constructive notice to all

97. Commonwealth v. Roxbury, 75 Mass. (9 Gray) 451.

98. Tappan v. Burnham, *supra;* East Hampton v. Kirk, *supra.*

99. Poignard v. Smith, 25 Mass. (8 Pick.) 272.

1. Hastings v. Merriam, 117 Mass. 245.

2. Miller v. Shaw, 7 S. & R. (Pa.) 129; M'Caffrey v. Fisher, 4 W. & S. (Pa.) 181; Hall v. Powel, 4 S. & R. (Pa.) 456.

3. Bell v. Denson, 56 Ala. 444.

4. Moore v. Thompson, 69 N. C. 120.

5. Wallace v. Maxwell, 32 N. C. (10 Ired.) 110.

the world, of his claim, and also of its extent, so that not only does a sufficient occupancy of a part of the lot carry with it, by construction, the possession of the entire premises described by his conveyance, where the boundaries are well defined,[6] but also dispenses with the rule as to *pedis possessio,* and only requires from him such an occupancy as the nature and character of the premises admit of.[7] The rule is well stated in an Illinois case,[8]

6. Stevens v. Hollister, 18 Vt. 294; Bank v. Smyers, 2 Strobh. (S. C.) 24; Lenoir v. South, 32 N. C. (10 Ired.) 237; Johnson v. McMillan, 1 Strobh. (S. C.) 143; Jackson v. Oltz, 8 Wend. (N. Y.) 440; Simpson v. Downing, 23 id. 316; Golson v. Hook, 4 Strobh. (S. C.) 23; Janes v. Patterson, 62 Ga. 527; Coleman v. Billings, 89 Ill. 183; Waggoner v. Hastings, 8 Pa. 300; Ament v. Wolf, 1 Grant's Cas. (Pa.) 518; Jackson v. Porter, 1 Paine (U. S. C. C.) 457; Ware v. Johnson, 55 Mo. 300; Chapman v Templeton, 53 Mo. 463; Wellborn v. Anderson, 37 Miss. 155; Bynum v. Thompson, 25 N. C. (3 Ired.) 578; Kile v. Tubbs, 23 Cal. 431; Webb v. Sturtevant, 2 Ill. 181; Shackleford v. Smith, 35 Ky. (5 Dana) 232; Jackson v. Vermilyea, 6 Cow. (N. Y.) 677; Prevost v. Johnson, 9 Mart. (La.) 123; Jackson v. Smith, 13 Johns. (N. Y.) 406; Poignard v. Smith, 25 Mass. (8 Pick.) 272; Waldron v. Tuttle, 4 N. H. 371; Sparhawk v. Bullard, 42 Mass. (1 Met.) 95; Higbee v. Rice, 5 Mass. 344; Pearsal v. Thorp, 1 D. Chip. (Vt.) 92; Read v. Eifert, 1 N. & McCord (S. C.) 374, n.; King v. Smith, 1 Rice (S. C.) 14; McEvoy v. Lloyd, 31 Wis. 143; Ralph v. Bayley, 11 Vt. 521; Thompson v. Cragg, 24 Tex. 582; McRae v. Williams, 52 N. C. (7 Jones L.) 430; Crary v. Goodman, 22 N. Y. 170; Cline v. Catron, 22 Gratt. (Va.) 378; Hawkins v. Robinson, 3 Watts (Pa.) 205; Bowie v. Brahe, 3 Duer (N. Y.) 35; Finnlay v. Cook, 54 Barb. (N. Y.) 9; Downing v. Miller, 33 id. 383; Munro v. Merchant, 28 N. Y. 9; Hubbard v. Austin, 11 Vt. 129; M'Call v. Neely, 3 Watts (Pa.) 70; Hollinshead v. Nauman, 45 Pa. 140; Alden v. Grove, 18 Pa. 377; Fitch v. Mann, 8 Pa. 503; Ege v. Medlar, 82 Pa. 86; Sholly v. Stahl, 2 W. N. C. (Pa.) 418; Nearhoff v. Addleman, 31 Pa. 279; McCall v. Coover, 4 W. & S. (Pa.) 151; Heiser v. Riehle, 7 Watts (Pa.) 35; Saxton v. Hunt, 20 N. J. L. 487; Bowman v. Bartlett, 10 Ky. (3 A. K. Mar.) 99; Cheney v. Ringgold, 2 H. & J. (Md.) 87; Stanley v. Turner, 5 N. C. (1 Murph.) 14; Crowell v. Bebee, 10 Vt. 33; Chiles v. Conley, 39 Ky. (9 Dana) 385; Alston v. Collins, 2 Speers (S. C.) 450.

7. Royer v. Benlow, 10 S. & R. (Pa.) 303. See Robinson v. Swett, 3 Me. 316. Whenever an instrument by apt words of transfer from grantor to grantee, whether the grantor acts under the authority of judicial proceedings or otherwise, in form passes what purports to be the title, it gives to the grantee color of title, even should the instrument be considered as invalid. Hall v. Law, 102 U. S. 461, 26 L. Ed. 217.

8. Coleman v. Billings, 89 Ill. 183; Fisher v. Bennehoff, 121 Ill. 426.

that a person who enters into possession of land under a conveyance, although from a person having no title, is presumed to enter according to the description in the deed; and his occupancy of a part, claiming the whole, is construed as a possession of the entire tract.[9] But in order to entitle a party to the benefits of

See Austin v. Rust, 73 Ill. 491; Scott v. Delany, 87 Ill. 146; Hubbard v. Kiddo, 87 Ill. 578; Cairo, etc., R. R. Co. v. Woolsey, 85 Ill. 370. In the main case (Fisher v. Bennehoff) it was held that testimony is admissible to show *who* was in possession during the period, or any portion thereof, when title by possession was being acquired.

9. A deed without a seal which purports to convey a title is sufficient as color of title. Kruse v. Wilson, 79 Ill. 233; Hamilton v. Boggess, 63 Mo. 233. So is a void deed. Mason v. Ayers, 73 Ill. 121. Executor's deeds, valid or not, are sufficient as color of title. King v. Merritt, 67 Mich. 194. A deed by the husband of a life tenant, after her decease, may, under some circumstances, be good as a color of title. Forest v. Jackson, 56 N. H. 357. So a bond for a deed. Spitter v. Scofield, 43 Iowa 571. So a deed obtained from a person who has no title may be good as color of title. Russell v. Mandell, 73 Ill. 136; McCamy v. Higdon, 50 Ga. 629; Nowlin v. Reynolds, 25 Gratt. (Va.) 137; Payne v. Blackshear, 52 Ga. 637; Fagan v. Rosier, 68 Ill. 84. It was held in some early cases in New York, that possession taken under a grant from a foreign government does not constitute a sufficient color of title. Jackson v. Ingraham, 4 Johns. (N. Y.) 163. See also, Jackson v. Waters, 12 id. 365. But in view of the general doctrine that every possession under pretense or claim of right is protected, without regard to whether the title was from a valid source, the distinction made in these early cases seems not to be recognized. Barney v. Sutton, 2 Watts (Pa.) 37; La Frombois v. Jackson, *supra*. See, as to the effect of what may be termed Indian deeds, that is deeds from the aborigines, Jackson v. Porter, 1 Paine (U. S. C. C.) 457; Johnson v. McIntosh, 17 U. S. (8 Wheat.) 543, 571, 5 L. Ed. 681; Thompson v. Gotham, 9 Ohio 170; Jackson v. Hudson, 3 Johns. (N. Y.) 384. Continued, open, and exclusive possession for the statutory period, under claim and color of title, is sufficient to give a good title thereto, without regard to the regularity and validity of the colorable title, or to the defects or insufficiency of the instruments confirming it. Grant v. Fowler, 39 N. H. 101; Farrar v. Fessenden, 39 N. H. 268; Elliott v. Pearce, 20 Ark. 508; Cofer v. Brooks, 20 Ark. 542; St. Louis v. Gorman, 29 Mo. 593. And an entry upon and continued occupation of a portion of a lot, under a deed describing the whole by metes and bounds, gives possession of all the lands embraced in the title under which the entry is made and the occupation continued. It need not commence or be continued under valid and effectual deeds. See Farrar v. Fessenden, *supra*. Imperfections and irregularities in any part of the claim

an extension of his possession by construction, it is essential that the deed or writing should describe and include the land not actually occupied;[10] and if the land is not described in the writing in such a manner that it can be readily identified, the doctrine relative to constructive possession cannot apply, and the party must stand or fall by his actual occupancy.[11] Indeed, color of title has been aptly described as any writing which purports to convey the title to land by apt words of transfer, and clearly defines the extent of the claim;[12] and a party cannot claim lands by constructive possession which are not embraced within the description of the deed under which he claims;[13] but as to lands outside his boundaries, but contiguous thereto, he is put to his claim of actual occupancy.[14] It is not essential in all cases that the land should be described by metes and bounds; but it must be described in such a manner that the limits and extent of the claim can be readily ascertained.[15] It is sufficient if the instru-

of title from which color is derived do not of themselves afford evidence of bad faith. Dawley v. Van Court, 21 Ill. 460; Edgerton v. Bird, 6 Wis. 527. An administrator's deed void as against heirs for want of notice, they being minors, will give color of title, under which, if the premises be held adversely during the statute period after the heirs attain their majority, their right of action will be barred. Vancleave v. Milliken, 13 Ind. 105. But a deed which does not describe the land is not color. Kilpatrick v. Sneros, 23 Tex. 113. If a deed is intended to convey all the land which the grantor owned in a certain tract, and the grantor had marked a line beyond the one conveyed to as the line of the lot conveyed, it has been held that the grantee might hold to the line so marked. Mayse v. Lafferty, 38 Tenn. (1 Head) 60.

10. Woods v. Banks, 14 N. H. 111; Thompson v. Cragg, 24 Tex. 583; Jackson v. Camp, 1 Cow. (N. Y.) 605.

11. Jackson v. Woodruff, 1 Cow. (N. Y.) 276.

12. Hall v. Law, 102 U. S. 461, 26 L. Ed. 217; Bank v. Smyers, 2 Strobh. (S. C.) 24; Johnson v. McMillan, 1 id. 143; Lynde v. Williams, 68 Mo. 360. In the first of these cases cited in this note, the court also held that it was immaterial whether the grantor acts under judicial proceedings or otherwise, or whether the title was actually conveyed or not, provided the grantee went into possession under the deed and occupied for the requisite statutory period.

13. Pope v. Hanmer, 74 N. Y. 240.

14. Slaughter v. Fowler, 44 Cal. 195.

15. In Henley v. Wilson, 81 N. C.

ment relied on purports upon its face to convey the lands in question, and describes them with such definiteness that they can be easily identified,[16] although in fact it is invalid and insufficient to pass the title,[17] or actually void,[18] or one that is voidable, as a deed from an infant,[19] or from an officer who had no authority in fact to convey the land,[20] or although such authority, if he had any, is not shown,[21] or although made under a sale which was subsequently invalidated by individual or judicial action.[22] A tax-

405, where, in an action of trespass to land, the judge instructed the jury that a will, devising "all my lands on both sides of Haw River, in Chatham County, and all the mills and appurtenances and improvements thereto, said property being known as the McClenahan Mills," gave color of title, provided the jury found that the tract was well known throughout the country by that name, and that the boundaries were all ascertainable and visible, and the plaintiff was in actual adverse possession, was sufficient to enable him, by an occupancy of part of the land, to claim the whole, was held correct. In Congdon v. Morgan, 14 S. C. 587, an entry under a deed, and marking out the claim by survey and stakes, and building a wharf and boat-sheds, were held to be possessory acts under color of title.

16. Jackson v. Frost, 5 Cow. (N. Y.) 346; Hall v. Law, 102 U. S. 461, 26 L. Ed. 217; Lynde v. Williams, 68 Mo. 360; Wales v. Smith, 19 Ga. 8; Dobson v. Murphy, 18 N. C. (1 D. & B.) 586; Coleman v. Billings, *supra*.

17. La Frombois v. Jackson, 8 Cow. (N. Y.) 589; Mason v. Ayers, 73 Ill. 121; Forest v. Jackson. 56 N. H. 357; Fagan v. Rosier, 68 Ill. 84; McCamy v. Higdon, 50 Ga. 629; Russell v. Mandell, 73 Ill. 136; Nowlin v. Reynolds, 25 Gratt. (Va.) 137; Payne v. Blackshear, 52 Ga. 637.

18. Ewing v. Burner, 36 U. S. (11 Pet.) 41, 9 L. Ed. 624; Moody v. Fleming, 4 Ga. 115.

19. Murray v. Shanklin, 20 N. C. (4 D. & B.) 288.

20. Hester v. Coats, 22 Ga. 56.

21. Ibid.; Riggs v. Dooly, 46 Ky. (7 B. Mon.) 236; North v. Hammer, 34 Wis. 425; Northrop v. Wright, 7 Hill (N. Y.) 476; Brien v. Sargent, 13 La. Ann. 198; Bailey v. Doolittle, 24 Ill. 577.

22. Hamilton v. Wright, 30 Iowa 480. But see Presley v. Holmes, 33 Tex. 476, where it was held that where a title under which an occupant holds is subsequently invalidated by judicial action, his possession from that time becomes tortious. To constitute color of title, some act must have been done conferring some title, good or bad, to a parcel of land of definite extent; a mere disseisor cannot resort to the metes and bounds of the tract upon which he wrongfully enters. St. Louis v. Gorman, 29 Mo. 593. An unrecorded deed is good color of title. Hardin v. Barrett, 51 N. C. (6 Jones L.) 159. An administrator's deed is void on account of

collector's deed,[23] a paper purporting to be a will,[24] a deed from a

defects in the order of sale. Root v. McFerrin, 37 Miss. 17. So a deed void as to the grantor's creditors. Harper v. Tapley, 35 Miss. 506. But it is held that a deed which disclaims any title in the grantor on its face is not good color, as the execution of a bond for a deed signed "A. B., Agent." Simmons v. Lane, 25 Ga. 178. If real estate is held in common, and one tenant assumes to convey the entire land, or any specific part of it, by metes and bounds, his deed will be a color of title, and possession under it for the statutory period will be adverse to the title of the cotenants, and bar their right to recover the land conveyed. Weisinger v. Murphy, 39 Tenn. (2 Head) 674. Though a tax sale of land be irregular and invalid, the collector's deed in connection with proof of the actual possession of the land by the purchaser, and those claiming under him, during the whole period of limitation, is sufficient to entitle him to have his possession protected and his title quieted. Elliott v. Pearce, 20 Ark. 508; Cofer v. Brooks, 20 Ark. 542. A judgment of the county court in proceedings to settle the estate of a person who, though represented to be dead, proves to be living, cannot support a claim by adverse occupation, under the statute authorizing such claim when founded on "the judgment of some competent court;" such proceedings in administering are absolutely void for all purposes. Melia v. Simmons, 45 Wis. 334. A deed made by a clerk or master in equity, after he goes out of office, on a sale made by him while in office, is color of title, though not otherwise operative. Williams v. Council, 49 N. C. (4 Jones L.) 206. A sheriff's deed, accompanied with possession under it, gives a color of title without proof of the judgment and execution, and affords a starting-point for the statute of limitations to run. Hester v. Coats, 22 Ga. 56. The universal legatee cannot set up the will of the testator as a just title, and make it the basis of the prescription of ten years. Griffon v. Blanc, 12 La. An. 5. A title by descent is an assurance of title. Hubbard v. Wood, 33 Tenn. (1 Sneed) 279. An administrator is within the description of "other person authorized to sell land," so as to give title by seven years' actual residence. If the foundation or source of the title by which a party claims under the limitation act is of record, the title is "deducible of record," within the meaning of that statute. Collins v. Smith, 18 Ill. 160. A void and worthless deed is sufficient as foundation of an adverse possession. Roberts v. Pillow, Hemp. (U. S.) 624.

When one claims under color of title, the nature and extent of his claim, as well as his possession, must be made known, but color of title need not necessarily consist of recorded instruments. Ozark v. Plateau Land Co. v. Hays, 105 Mo. 143, 150, 16 S. W. 957; Bellefontaine Imp. Co. v. Niedringhaus, 181 Ill. 426, 55 N. E. 184, 72 Am. St. Rep. 269; Donohue v. Whitney, 133 N. Y. 178, 30 N. E. 848; Fullam v. Foster, 68 Vt. 590, 35 Atl. 484; Moore v. Hinkle, 151 Ind. 343, 50 N. E. 822; Davis v.

mortgagee,[25] or an unrecorded deed, is good color of title.[26] It has been intimated that there may be color of title without any conveyance in writing, and that it may be created by an act *in pais*, as by a verbal gift of land, with a survey and surrender of

Davis, 68 Miss. 478, 10 So. 70; Zundel v. Baldwin, 114 Ala. 328, 21 So. 420; Furgerson v. Bagley, 95 Ga. 516, 20 S. E. 241; Libbey v. Young, 103 Iowa 258, 72 N. W. 520; Hebard v. Scott, 95 Tenn. 467, 32 S. W. 390. Circumstances which show sufficient notoriety of claim, and of its extent and nature, may sometimes impart to an unrecorded or even void document the effect of color. Ibid.; Nelson v. Cooper, 108 Fed. 919, 48 C. C. A. 140; Northern Pac. Ry. Co. v. Ely, 25 Wash. 384, 65 Pac. 555, 54 L. R. A. 526, 87; Power v. Kitching, 10 N. D. 254, 86 N. W. 737, 88 Am. St. Rep. 691; Nye v. Alfter, 127 Mo. 529, 30 S. W. 186. See Jones on Real Property, § 122 *et seq.;* 1 Am. & Eng. Encyc. of Law (2d ed.), p. 846; 1 Encyc. of Law & Proc., p. 1082. Thus, one whose house is on adjoining land, who, cultivating the land in dispute, is known to claim under an unrecorded and unauthorized guardian's deed thereof to him, has color of title thereto, especially when the real owner lives near by and knows the circumstances. Plaster v. Grabeel, 160 Mo. 669, 61 S. W. 589. So, in Washington, it is held that a void deed, accompanied by actual occupation, is sufficient to set the statute in motion, though as to short statutes in relation to sales of realty for taxes a different view has been expressed. Hurd v. Brisner, 3 Wash. 1, 28 Pac. 371, 28 Am. St. Rep. 17; Ward v. Huggins, 7 Wash. 617, 624. 32 Pac. 740, 1015, 36 Pac. 285; Redfield v. Parks, 132 U. S. 239, 10 Sup. Ct. 83, 33 L. Ed. 327; Dibble v. Bellingham Bay Land Co., 163 U. S. 63, 72, 16 Sup. Ct. 939, 41 L. Ed. 72.

It is essential to color of title that the premises be described with the same degree of certainty as is required in deeds relied upon as absolute conveyances. Allmendinger v. McHie, 189 Ill. 308, 316, 59 N. E. 517; see O'Brien v. Goodrich, 177 Mass. 32, 58 N. E. 151. The fact that the use of the granted premises is limited, by the deed thereof, to a particular purpose, does not interfere with its constituting color of title. Petit v. Flint & Pere Marquette R. Co., 119 Mich. 492, 78 N. W. 554, 75 Am. St. Rep. 417.

One taking possession under color of title may set up in defense a supposed outstanding title in a third person, without connecting himself therewith, because his possession is good against all but the true owner; but a mere trespasser cannot show a continuity of the adverse holding by setting up such a title. Lucy v. Tennessee & C. R. Co., 92 Ala. 246, 249, 8 So. 806.

23. Rivers v. Thompson, 43 Ala. 633.

24. McConnell v. McConnell, 64 N. C. 342.

25. Stevens v. Brooks, 24 Wis. 326.

26. See Nowlin v. Reynolds, 25 Gratt. (Va.) 137.

possession by the donor to the donee.[27] In one case,[28] it was said that an entry under a *bona fide* claim originating under a parol contract for the purchase of land and payment of the purchase-money, where the boundaries of the land are well defined, invests the purchaser with all the benefits of constructive possession, the same as though there had been a contract in writing describing the lands.[29] A deed made under a sale of a life estate only, does not constitute sufficient color of title to become the basis of an adverse possession, because it does not purport to convey the fee.[30] But a deed executed after her decease, by a husband, of lands in which his wife had only a life estate, if it purports to convey the fee, will be a sufficient color to build an adverse possession upon;[31] because, as a rule, although the statute will not run against a remainderman,[32] yet it may run against him

27. Rannels v. Rannels, 52 Mo. 108.

28. M'Call v. Neely, 3 Watts (Pa.) 69. A defendant in ejectment, desiring to rely on a deed as color of title for the purpose of establishing title by prescription, need not show affirmatively that the person who made the deed had either title or possession, apart from fraud. A written agreement to divide lands owned or claimed in common, though made by the administrator of one of the tenants in common without an order from court for the partition thereof, is admissible in evidence as color of title, and though such an agreement does not prescribe the line with great certainty. McMullin v. Erwin, 58 Ga. 427; McNamara v. Seaton, 82 Ill. 498. A title bond, whether the purchase-money be paid or not, save as against the vendor, is, if connected with the sovereignty of the soil, title, or color of title, under which a defendant may maintain his defense under the statute of limitations of three years. Elliott v. Mitchell, 47 Tex. 445. But in Georgia, to make an execution showing levy upon, and sale of, certain land, admissible as color of title, there must be proof that a deed was executed in accordance with such sale. Baird v. Evans, 58 Ga. 350. In all cases, in order to a disseisin of the true owner by adverse possession under a defective deed, such possession must be exclusive. Bellis v. Bellis, 122 Mass. 414.

29. Brown v. King, 46 Mass. (5 Met.) 173; Magee v. Magee, 37 Miss. 138; Robertson v. Wood, 15 Ark. 1.

30. Dewey v. McLain, 7 Kan. 126.

31. Forest v. Jackson, 56 N. H. 357.

32. Jackson v. Schoonmaker, 4 Johns. (N. Y.) 390; 3 Cruise's Dig. 403; Cheseldine v. Brewer, 4 H. & McH. (Md.) 487; Hall v. Vandegift, 3 Binn. (Pa.) 374; Henderson v. Griffin, 30 U. S. (5 Pet.) 150, 8 L. Ed. 79; Litchfield v. Ready, 1 Eng. L. & Eq. 460; Bradstreet v. Huntington, 30 U. S. (5 Pet.) 40.

after the estate falls in;[33] and where a husband sells the fee of an estate of which he is only seised as tenant by curtesy, while the statute will not be put in motion as to the wife or the heirs of the wife until after her death, yet from that period the statute begins to run.[34] As previously stated, any writing which on

33. See Arnold v. Garth, 106 Fed. 13; Matson v. Abbey, 141 N. Y. 179, 36 N. E. 11; Meacham v. Bunting, 156 Ill. 586, 41 N. E. 175, 28 L. R. A. 618, 47 Am. St. Rep. 239; Clark v. Parsons, 69 N. H. 147, 39 Atl. 898, 76 Am. St. Rep. 157; Lumley v. Haggerty, 110 Mich. 552, 68 N. W. 243, 64 Am. St. Rep. 364; Bowen v. Brogan, 119 Mich. 218; Whitaker v. Whitaker, 157 Mo. 342, 58 S. W. 5; Chambers v. Chambers, 139 Ind. 111, 38 N. E. 334 Hanson v. Ingwaldson, 77 Minn. 533, 80 N. W. 702, 77 Am. St. Rep. 692; Lamar v. Pearre, 82 Ga. 354, 9 S. E. 1043, 19 Am. St. Rep. 168; Hoskins v. Ames, 78 Miss. 986, 29 So. 828; Robinson v. Pierce, 118 Ala. 273, 24 So. 984, 45 L. R. A. 66, 72 Am. St. Rep. 160; Anderson v. Northrop, 30 Fla. 612, 12 So. 318; *In re* Owen (1894), 3 Ch. 220; Tichborne v. Weir, 67 L. T. 735; Morrow v. James, 69 Ark. 539, 64 S. W. 269; Jeffries v. Butler, 108 Ky. 531, 56 S. W. 979, 22 Ky. Law Rep. 226; Allen v. De Groodt, 98 Mo. 159, 11 S. W. 240, 14 Am. St. Rep. 626, and note; Gindrat v. Western Ry. of Alabama, 96 Ala. 162, 11 So. 372, 19 L. R. A. 839, and note. When, however, equitable as well as legal remedies are barred by the statute, if a trustee or administrator is barred of his remedy; his *cestui que trust* are also barred, even though they include remaindermen. Partee v. Thomas, 11 Fed. 769, 778; Lloyd v. Ball, 77 Fed. 365; East Rome Town Co. v. Cothran, 81 Ga. 359, 8 S. E. 737; Weems v. Simpson, 93 Ga. 364, 20 S. E. 548; Barclay v. Goodloe, 83 Ky. 493, 5 Ky. Law Rep. (abstract) 936.

As a rule, a payment by a tenant for life binds the remainderman. Leahy v. De Moleyns (1896), 1 I. R. 206; see Barcroft v. Murphy, id. 590.

34. Miller v. Schackleford, 33 Ky. (3 Dana) 289; Constantine v. Van Winkle, 6 Hill (N. Y.) 177; Meraman v. Caldwell, 47 Ky. (8 B. Mon.) 32; Mellus v. Snowman, 21 Me. 201; Bruce v. Wood, 42 Mass. (1 Met.) 542. Where the wife joins with the husband in the deed in the conveyance of an estate in the wife in tail, the statute runs from the date of the deed and possession under it, against the children. Giddings v. Smith, 15 Vt. 344. But if the conveyance is in the name of the husband, and the wife signs the deed, "in token of the relinquishment of all her right in the bargained premises," it has been held that the wife is not barred of her entry after the husband's decease, Bruce v. Wood, *supra;* upon the general doctrine that the remainderman cannot be barred until the estate falls in. See Gill v. Fauntleroy, 47 Ky. (8 B. Mon.) 177; May v. Hill, 15 Ky. (5 Litt.) 313; Patrick v. Chenault, 45 Ky. (6 B. Mon.) 315; Cook v. Danvers, 7 East 299; Wallingford v. Hearl, 15 Mass. 471; Jackson v. Johnson, 5 Cow. (N. Y.) 74; Wells

its face purports to convey certain lands affords sufficient color of title for the purposes of the statute, although fraudulent on the

v. Prince, 9 Mass. 508; Jackson v. Sellick, 8 Johns. (N. Y.) 262; Heath v. White, 5 Conn. 228. Where there are two separate rights of entry, the loss of one by lapse of time does not impair the other; and if a person acquires a second right, he is allowed a new period in which to pursue his remedy, although he has neglected his first. 2 Cruise's Dig. 498; Goodright v. Forrester, 8 East 551; Hunt v. Bourne, 1 Salk 339. A remainder-man expectant on an estate for life or years, who has a right to enter because of the forfeiture of the tenant, is not bound to avail himself of the forfeiture, and his neglect to enter at that time does not bar him of his entry on the limitation of the estate by efflux of time or the death of the tenant. Stowel v. Zouch, 1 Plowd. 374; Salmons v. Davis, 29 Mo. 176; Woodson v. Smith, 38 Tenn. (1 Head.) 276; Stevens v. Winship, 18 Mass.) (1 Pick.) 318; Bell v. McCawley, 29 Ga. 355; Miller v. Ewing, 60 Mass. (6 Cush.) 34; Gibson v. Jayne, 37 Miss. 164; Gwynn v. Jones, 2 G. & J. (Md.) 173; Wells v. Prince, 9 Mass. 508; Allen v. Blakeway, 5 C. & P. 563. This rule accorded with the maxim of the old civil law, *quando duo jura concurrunt in una persona aequum est ac si essent in diversis.* According to Plowden, in Stowel v. Zouch, Plowd. 374, when there were three separate rights in the same person, he was entitled to the benefits of all of them the same as though they existed in three different persons. But in England, by statute, this old principle is abolished, except in cases where the same person who has the reversion has also the particular estate. Johnson v. Liversedge, 11 M. & W. 517; Hall v. Moulsdale, 16 M. & W. 689. But after the estate has fallen in, the reversioner must enter upon the land within the statutory period. Altemas v. Campbell, 9 Watts (Pa.) 28; Berrington v. Parkhurst, 13 East 489; Ridgely v. Ogle, 4 H. & McH. (Md.) 123; Goodright v. Cator, 1 Doug. 477; Doe v. Danvers, 7 East 299; Harbaugh v. Moore, 11 G. & J. (Md.) 283; Jackson v. Haviland, 13 Johns. (N. Y.) 229; Brown v. Porter, 10 Mass. 93; or bring an action for the recovery of the possession, in which case the confession of lease, entry, and ouster dispense with an entry, 3 Cruise's Dig. 383; Den v. Moore, 8 N. J. L. 6; Bond v. Hopkins, 1 Sch. & Lef. 413; Jackson v. Cairns, 20 Johns. (N. Y.) 301. In order to make an entry effectual, it must be made upon the land. Anonymous, Skinn. 412; Kennebec Purchase v. Laboree, 3 Me. 275; Robinson v. Sweet, 3 Me. 316; and if it lies in two or more counties, entry must be made in each county. Jackson v. Lunn, 3 Johns. (N. Y.) Cas. 109. But if an actual entry is prescribed by force or fraud, then his intention to enter, made as near the land as possible, has been held sufficient as an equivalent for an entry. Jackson v. Haviland, 13 Johns. (N. Y.) 229; Jackson v. Schoonmaker, 4 id. 389; 2 Cruise's Dig. 289. The entry must be made *animo clamandi* and must be indicated either by acts or words

part of the grantor,[35] or defective,[36] or invalid,[37] or void,[38] or a deed from one having no title or authority to convey,[39] or a quitclaim deed which conveys no interest.[40] Thus, a deed executed by an attorney without authority,[41] or by an officer upon a tax sale which was invalid,[42] or by an administrator which was void for want of notice to the heirs,[43] or a quitclaim deed from a person who had no interest,[44] and, in a word, however groundless the supposed title may be, if the writing purports to convey it, it affords color of title, and a proper basis for an adverse possession under it.[45] Indeed, it has been held that any instrument having a grantor and grantee, and containing a description of the lands intended

accompanying the act, Robinson v. Swett, 3 Me. 316; and must bear on its face an unequivocal challenge of the occupant's right, Altemas v. Campbell, *supra;* and whether so made or not is a question for the jury, Miller v. Shaw, *supra;* Dillon v. Mattox, 21 Ga. 113; Holtzapple v. Phillibaum, 4 Wash. (U. S.) 356; Brown v. M'Kinney, 9 Watts (Pa.) 565; Hooper v. Garner, 15 Pa. 517. The entry may be made by the reversioner in person or by his agent, Hinman v. Cranmer, 9 Pa. 40; Ingersoll v. Lewis, 11 Pa. 212; or even an entry made by a person not authorized may be ratified so as to make it operative, Hinman v. Cranmer, *supra.*

As to the estate by the curtesy, as the husband is the one entitled to sue for the possession, the statute runs against the wife or her descendants only when such estate terminates. Dawson v. Edwards, 189 Ill. 60, 59 N. E. 590.

35. Griffin v. Stamper, 17 Ga. 108; Gregg v. Sayre's Lessee, 33 U. S. (8 Pet.) 244, 8 L. Ed. 932. A deed, although not recorded, which purports to convey title, no matter on what founded, is held to amount to color of title. Lea v. Polk County Copper Co., 62 U. S. (21 How.) 493, 16 L. Ed. 203; Hanna v. Renfro, 32 Miss. 125; Dickenson v. Breeden, 30 Ill. 279. It has been held that color of title may be given without any writing. McClellan v. Kellogg, 17 Ill. 498.

36. McClellan v. Kellogg, 17 Ill. 498.

37. Cofer v. Brooks, 20 Ark. 542; Elliott v. Pearce, 20 Ark. 508.

38. Whitesides v. Singleton, 19 Tenn. (1 Meigs) 207; Cornelius v. Giberson, 25 N. J. L. 1; Vancleve v. Wilkinson, 13 Ind. 105; Ewing v. Burnett, 36 U. S. (11 Pet.) 41, 9 L. Ed. 624; Livingston v. Pendergast, 34 N. H. 544.

39. Hill v. Wilson, 6 N. C. (2 Murph.) 14; Munro v. Merchant, 28 N. Y. 9; Farrow v. Edmundson, 43 Ky. (4 B. Mon.) 605.

40. Minot v. Brooks, 16 N. H. 374; McCamy v. Higdon, 50 Ga. 629.

41. Hill v. Wilson, *supra.*

42. Elliott v. Pearce, *supra.*

43. Vancleve v. Wilkinson, *supra.*

44. Minot v. Brooks, 16 N. H. 374.

45. La Frombois v. Jackson, 5 Cow. (N. Y.) 589.

to be conveyed, and apt words for their conveyance, gives color of title.[46] The rule which is generally adopted, and which seems to be the only one resting upon any accurate basis, is, that color of title is that which in appearance is title, but which in reality is no title; and the question as to what is color of title is merely a question of law for the court, leaving the question of occupancy under it, and of *bona fides* in those States where by statute it is required to be established, for the jury.[47] A valid and perfect title is not required;[48] and a deed without a seal,[49] or one that is not recorded,[50] is sufficient.[51]

46. Brooks v. Bruyn, 35 Ill. 392; Childs v. Showers, 18 Iowa 261. A *bona fide* claim by color of title is not disparaged by the claimant's knowledge that the boundary lines are uncertain, and the title disputed. Cornelius v. Giberson, 25 N. J. L. 1. Color of title is anything in writing, connected with the title, which serves to define the extent of the claim. Walls v. Smith, 19 Ga. 8. Where one is in possession, claiming title under and pursuant to a state of facts, which of themselves show the character and extent of his claim, such facts perform sufficiently the office of color of title. Bell v. Longworth, 6 Ind. 273. That color may be given for title without any writing, and commence in trespass, and when founded on writing it is not essential that it should show on its face a *prima facie* title, but it may be good as a foundation for color, however defective, see McClellan v. Kellogg, 17 Ill. 498. A written instrument is not always necessary to constitute color of title, but there must in all cases be some *indicia* or visible acts of ownership, which are apparent to all, showing the extent of the boundaries of the land claimed. Cooper v. Ord, 60 Mo. 420. Color of title is that which is a title in appearasce, but not in reality; and possession under an invalid deed draws to it the protection of the statute. Wright v. Mattison, 59 U. S. (18 How.) 50, 15 L. Ed. 280; Arrowsmith v. Burlingame, 4 McLean (U. S.) 490; Holden v. Collins, 5 id. 189; Barger v. Miller, 4 Wash. (U. S.) 280. In California, "radeo" boundaries are equivalent to notorious evidence of possession. Boyreau v. Campbell, 1 McAll. (U. S.) 119. The sale by an administrator of a solvent estate of his intestate's land under license does not give color of title, unless a deed is executed. Livingston v. Pender gast, 34 N. H. 544. See also Hester v. Coats, 22 Ga. 56.

47. Hanna v. Renfro, 32 Miss. 125; Dickinson v. Brown, 30 Ill. 299; Wright v. Mattison, *supra;* Wales v. Smith, 19 Ga. 8; Lea v. Polk County Copper Co., 62 U. S. (21 How.) 493, 16 L. Ed. 203.

48. Close v. Samm, 27 Iowa 503; Hines v. Robinson, 57 Me. 324; Field v. Boynton, 33 Ga. 239.

49. Barger v. Hobbs, 67 Ill. 592.

50. Rawson v. Fox, 65 Ill. 200.

51. The belief of the occupant that

In Louisiana, by statute, good faith on the part of the occupant is made an essential element; but while in some of the early cases in some of the States the courts seem to hold that good faith on the part of the grantee is a material element in determining whether a conveyance operates as color of title or not, yet it is not easy to understand how that question can be of any sort of importance, except where it is made a necessary element by statute. One of the very essentials of color of title is that it shall be raised by an instrument which appears to convey a title, but in reality conveys none; and it would seem almost ridiculous that it could be of any sort of importance for the purpose of acquiring title under such a conveyance, whether the grantee acted in good faith in obtaining it or not. His act in entering into possession is a wrong, and his possession continues wrongful until it ripens into a right by virtue of a continuance of the wrong for the requisite statutory period. Without any title whatever, except a naked claim resting in parol, and which the person making knows to be groundless, it is universally held that a title may be acquired to the extent of the actual occupancy. Now, by what process of reasoning is any *bona fides* dispensed with in the former case, and insisted upon when a person enters under a color of title? True, in the latter case, the occupant is not restricted to his actual occupancy, but is treated, under proper limitations, as constructively in possession of all the land that is described in and *prima facie* conveyed by the conveyance to him. It has never been intimated that the doctrine of constructive possession was extended to such cases because of the good faith of the occupant in taking his conveyance, but it is predicated entirely upon the ground that the conveyance marks the limit of his claim, and operates as notice to everybody of its limit and extent, and it is upon this ground alone that the doctrine rests, subject to the condition that there is an actual, open, visible,

his title is absolute, when in fact it is only a life estate, does not make his occupation adverse. Mixter v. Woodcock, 154 Mass. 535, 28 N. E. 907.

uninterrupted, and hostile occupancy of a part of the premises conveyed for the full statutory period.[52]

52. The strictest proof of the hostile inception of the possession is required. As to the supervening change of possession, that must be proved by an accession of another title, and other circumstances furnishing a motive for exclusive claim. See United States v. Arredondo, 31 U. S. (6 Pet.) 743, 691, 8 L. Ed. 547; Clarke's Lessee v. Courtney, 30 U. S. 354, 8 L. Ed. 140; Jackson *ex dem.* Bradstreet v. Huntington, 30 U. S. (5 Pet.) 402, 8 L. Ed. 170; M'Iver v. Ragan, 15 U. S. (2 Wheat.) 29, 4 L. Ed. 175; Kirk v. Smith, 22 U. S. (9 Wheat.) 241, 288, 6 L. Ed. 81; La Frombois v. Jackson, 8 Cow. (N. Y.) 589; Gittens v. Lowry, 15 Ga. 336; Jackson v. Potter, 1 Paine (U. S.) 457; Markley v. Amos, 2 Bailey, 603; Ray v. Barker, 40 Ky. (1 B. Mon.) 364; Moore v. Moore, 21 Me. 350; Lamb v. Foss, id. 240; Millay v. Millay, 18 id. 387; Hamilton v. Paine, 17 id. 219; Read v. Thompson, 5 Pa. 327; Dikeman v. Parrish, 6 id. 210; Hall v. Stephens, 50 Mass. (9 Met. 418; Moore v. Johnston, 2 Speers (S. C.) 288; Rogers v. Hillhouse, 3 Conn. 398; Borrets v. Turner, 2 N. C. (2 Hayw.) 114; Armour v. White, id. 69; Grant v. Winborne, id. 56; Anonymous, id. 134; Hatch v. Hatch, id. 34; Tasker v. Whittington, 1 H. & McH. (Md.) 151. The statute ripens no possession into title which is unaccompanied with a color of title, but there need not be a rightful title. Jackson v. Wheat, 18 Johns. (N. Y.) 44; Jackson v. Newton, id. 355; Smith v. Lorillard, 10 id. 356; Smith v. Burtis, 9 id. 180; Jackson v. Woodruff, 1 Cow. (N. Y.) 276; Jackson v. Camp, id. 605. An entry under color or claim of title is sufficient and it is immaterial whether the title afterwards turns out to be valid or invalid. Nor is it material, when the entry is made under a conveyance, whether such conveyance does or does not contain covenants of warranty. Jackson v. Newton, 18 Johns. (N. Y.) 355. The fact that the purchaser from the sheriff is afterwards induced to doubt the validity of his title under the sheriff's sale, where he continues in possession under the same, it seems, will not destroy the adverse character of that possession. Northrop v. Wright, 7 Hill (N. Y.) 476. A sheriff's deed is held admissible in evidence as color of title, although unaccompanied by the execution under which the property was sold, and the sheriff sold without authority. Burkhalter v. Edwards, 16 Ga. 593. A sheriff's deed which recited the execution under which the sheriff sold the land, tested and signed by the deputy clerk instead of the clerk himself, inures as color of title, although the State constitution requires all writs to bear *teste* and be signed by the clerks of the respective courts. Den v. Putney, 7 N. C. (3 Murph.) 562. One who enters into possession of land under a deed purporting to convey to him an estate in fee, claiming to be sole and exclusive and absolute owner in fee thereof, may be regarded as holding adverse to all the world. Bradstreet v. Huntington, 30 U. S. (5 Pet.) 401.

We think that the weight of authority sustains the rule that any instrument which purports to convey lands, and describes

A deed purporting to be executed by virtue of a power of attorney from the owner of the land, which power is not proved, affords sufficient color of title on which to found an adverse possession, if there has been a good constructive possession under it. Monro v. Merchant, 28 N. Y. 9. To give color of title does not require the aid of a written conveyance or other evidence in writing; but it is only necessary that the entry be made under a *bona fide* and not a pretended claim of title existing in another. La Frombois v. Jackson, 8 Cow. (N. Y.) 589; M'Call v. Neely, 3 Watts (Pa.) 70. Even if the grantor in deeds be justly chargeable with fraud, but the grantees did not participate in it, and when they received their deeds had no knowledge of it, but accepted the same in good faith, the deeds upon their face purporting to convey a title in fee, and showing the nature and extent of the premises, there can be no doubt the deeds give color of title under the statute of limitations. Gregg v. Sayre's Lessee, 33 U. S. (8 Pet.) 244, 8 L. Ed. 932. It is settled that, however wrongful or fraudulent the possession, or defective the title, an entry under claim of exclusive title, founding such claim upon a written conveyance, accompanied by a continued possession for the requisite period, constitutes an effective adverse possession. The muniment is but one circumstance by which to make out an adverse possession. An oral claim of exclusive title or any other circumstances by which the absolute owner of land is distinguished from the naked possessor, are equally admissible, and may be equally satisfactory. Humbert v. Trinity Church, 24 Wend. (N. Y.) 587. *Bona fides* is not requisite to adverse possession, although there are some cases in which the idea is intimated that fraud may be received as an answer to the statute, when it is interposed against a legal claim. But those cases generally arose under the statutes concerning champetry and maintenance. Jackson v. Andrews, 7 Wend. (N. Y.) 152; Livingston v. Peru Iron Co., 9 id. 511. After the statutory limit, it is always dangerous to open an inquiry upon the *bona fides* of the defendant's claim. See Den v. Leggat, 7 N. C. (3 Murph.) 539. This accords with the general tenor of all the cases, and as early as the reign of Queen Elizabeth the English courts recognized the doctrine. See Stowell v. Lord Zouch, Plowden 358, 371; Maddock v. Bond, 1 Irish T. R. 332, 340. Some of these cases arose under statutes of short limitation, and the strict doctrine laid down is more appropriate in cases of long than those of short limitation. See Cholmondeley v. Clinton, 2 J. & W. 1, 139, 155. In all cases, unless a statute intervenes and establishes a different doctrine a possession to be adverse need only to be under color or claim of title, that is, inconsistent with the title of the claimant who is out of possession. Northrup v. Wright, 7 Hill (N. Y.) 476; Bogardus v. Trinity Church, 4 Sandf. (N. Y.) Ch. 633, 712, 738. It is the office of the statute to mature a possession, in itself wrongful, if accompanied by even a

them definitely, and upon its face appears to be a valid deed or conveyance of the premises, is a sufficient color of title, regardless of the question of *bona fides* or *mala fides* on the part of the grantee under it. The office of such conveyances is to mark the limits of the occupant's claim, and they are admitted in evidence, not necessarily to prove title, but merely to indicate the extent of an occupant's claim, and as a defense under the statute of limitations in connection with proof of the requisite period of occupancy.[53] In Louisiana, the statute makes a distinction between a person who enters in good faith and a just title and one who does not. In the former case possession is acquired in ten years, but lands are prescribed for in thirty years without any need of good faith or title. In most of the other States the statute is silent upon this point, and indeed in most of them the entire doctrine relative to constructive possession is the outgrowth of judicial decisions.

§ 260. Executory contracts, etc.—Possession under.

When an instrument is executed to a person which on its face shows that the entry is not under a claim of title in himself, but that it is in another, it follows as a necessary consequence that it does not afford color of title, and that no length of possession under it can ripen into an adverse title; and under this rule it follows that a possession and claim of land under an executory contract of purchase is not such an adverse possession as will render a deed from the true owner void for champerty or maintenance; nor is it such an adverse possession as, if continued for the requisite period, will bar an entry within the statute of limitations; and especially it is in no sense adverse as to the one with whom the contract is made.[54]

pretense of title, into a legal right. In some of the States, as in Georgia, it was provided by statute that no possession is adverse unless evidenced by written evidence of title, and any forged or fraudulent title will not be evidence of adverse possession. But this is contrary to the general rule. Tyler on Ejectment, 861.

53. Finlay v. Cook, 54 Barb. (N. Y.) 9.

54. Jackson v. Johnson, 5 Cow. (N.

To constitute an adverse possession, it must not only be hostile in its inception, but the possessor must claim the entire title; for if it be subservient to, and admits the existence of, a higher title, it is not adverse to that title.[55] But where a contract is made for the sale of land upon the performance of certain conditions, and the purchaser enters into possession under the contract, his possession from the time of entry is adverse to all except his vendor,[56] and it seems now to be well settled that, after the performance by him of all the conditions of the contract, he from that time holds adversely to the vendor, and full performance is treated as a sale, and the party in possession may acquire a good title as against the vendor by the requisite period of occupancy.[57]

Y.) 74; Higginbotham v. Fishback, 8 Ky. (1 A. K. Mar.) 506; Wilkinson v. Nichols, 40 Ky. (1 B. Mon.) 36; Richardson v. Broughton, 2 N. & McC. (S. C.) 417; Fowke v. Darnall, 15 Ky. (5 Litt.) 316; Chiles v. Bridges, 16 Ky. (Litt. Sel. Cas.) 420; Kirk v. Smith, 22 U. S. (9 Wheat.) 241, 6 L. Ed. 81; Jackson v. Hotchkiss, 6 Cow. (N. Y.) 401.

55. Botts v. Shield, 13 Ky. (3 Litt.) 34; Proprietors v. M'Farland, 12 Mass. 324; Knox v. Hook, id. 329.

56. Whitney v. Wright, 15 Wend. (N. Y.) 171; Woods v. Dille, 11 Ohio 455. See sec. 219.

57. Ridgeway v. Holliday, 59 Mo. 444; Clapp v. Bromagham, 9 Cow. (N. Y.) 530; Briggs v. Prosser, 14 Wend. (N. Y.) 228; *Ex parte* Department of Public Parks, 73 N. Y. 560; La Frombois v. Jackson, *supra;* Vrooman v. Shepherd, 14 Barb. (N. Y.) 441; Fain v. Garthright, 5 Ga. 6; Brown v. King, 46 Mass. (5 Met.) 173; Catlin v. Delano, 38 Conn. 262; Stark v. Starr, 1 Sawyer (U. S. C. C.) 15; M'Call v. Neely, 3 Watts (Pa.) 69; Hunter v. Parsons, 2 Bailey (S. C.) 59; Bank v. Smyers, 2 Strobh. (S. C.) 24; Fowke v. Beek, 1 Speers (S. C.) 291. Any possession which is accompanied by the recognition of a superior title still existing cannot be adverse. Griswold v. Butler, 3 Conn. 246. But where a person enters under an agreement to purchase, whether by parol or otherwise, and pays for the land, or takes a deed which is defective, the possession from that time, *prima facie* becomes adverse. So, School Dist. v. Blakeslee, 13 Conn. 235; French v. Pearce, 8 id. 439; Bryan v. Atwater, 5 Dey (Conn.) 181. In such a case, after the requisite statutory period, the jury may presume a conveyance. Maltonner v. Dimmick, 4 Barb. (N. Y.) 566. Specific performance of such a contract will not be denied, even though thirty years have elapsed since the right to have it matured. Somerville v. Trueman, 4 H. & McH. (Md.) 43; Ripley v. Yale, 18 Vt. 220; Appleby v. Obert, 16 N. J. L. 336; Ellison v. Cathcart, 1 McMull. (S. C.) 5; Pendergrast v. Gullatt, 10 Ga. 218; Magee v. Magee,

But an entry cannot become adverse where it is made upon a condition to be performed by the person entering until it is performed. Thus, where a person goes into possession of land under an agreement to exchange, and to pay a balance thereon, a conveyance to be made when such balance is paid, the possession cannot become adverse until such balance is paid.[58] The fact that a vendee under a contract to purchase, who went into possession under it, abandons the possession of the land, and subsequently goes into possession under a lease from another, will not make his possession adverse to his vendor. His second entry and possession relates back to, and continues the possession under, the original possession, and will not create a new and adverse possession.[59] This is also the rule as to all permissive entries upon land, as under a license, etc., so long as the license remains unrevoked, there can be no adverse occupancy, but possession continued after the license has expired may become adverse.[60] And the same rule holds as to any permissive entry. So long as the occupation is under such permission, the possession cannot be adverse; but when the permission is withdrawn, or terminates by efflux of time, or the occupant disclaims, and gives notice of such disclaimer to the person under whom he entered, he may hold adversely.[61] The rule that to make an entry adverse it must be

37 Miss. 138; Drew v. Towle, 31 N. H. 531; McQueen v. Ivey, 36 Ala. 308; Lander v. Rounsaville, 12 Tex. 195; Paxson v. Bailey, 17 Ga. 600. But while the contract is unperformed on the part of the vendee, and he is in possession, he is treated as a tenant at will to the vendor, and not as a disseisor. Brown v. King, *supra;* Stamper v. Griffin, 20 Ga. 312; Van Blarcom v. Kip, 26 N. J. L. 351; Judger v. Barnes, 48 Tenn. (1 Heisk.). 570; Ormond v. Martin, 1 Ala. Sel. Cas. 526.

58. See Adams v. Fullam, 47 Vt. 558.

59. Pratt v. Canfield, 67 Mo. 50.

60. Babcock v. Utter, 32 How. Pr. (N. Y.) 439; Luce v. Carley, 24 Wend. (N. Y.) 451; Farsh v. Coon, 40 Cal. 33.

61. See *post,* sec. 235, Landlord and Tenant; White v. Hapeman, 43 Mich. 267; Thompson v. Felton, 54 Cal. 547. A claim of title by adverse possession must have been under a claim of title; but a possession originally permissive will never become adverse. Adams v. Guice, 30 Mass. 397. And the possession must be held by the claimant, or some one in privity with him; if it is held by a person with

hostile in its inception,[62] is subject to the exception that a party so entering may disclaim, and from the time when notice of such disclaimer is brought home to the person under whom he entered his possession becomes adverse, but that he takes nothing by his previous occupancy.[63] An entry under a parol gift of

whom the claimant resides, the possession is not adverse. See Snodgrass v. Andrews, 30 Miss. 472. Evidence that an administrator entered into the possession of land of his intestate, upon a sale under a license, at which the land was struck off to himself, that he considered himself the owner, had the land surveyed and the lines around it marked, let a neighbor mow over a part of it, and cut three or four pine timber trees upon it, during an occupation of about three years, is not evidence of such possession, marked by definite boundaries, as is necessary to render it adverse to the title of the legal owner. Livingston v. Pendergast, 34 N. H. 544. An administrator's possession of the estate of the intestate, continued for a long time after the period limited by law for closing the administration and distributing the property, does not, by the mere lapse of time, change the original character of the possession, and make it adverse against those entitled to distribution, or create any right or title in the administrator under the statute. Harriet v. Swan, 18 Ark. 495. An administrator's deed may confirm the title of the heirs, and not be adverse to it. See Livingston v. Pendergast, 34 N. H. 544.

62. McGee v. Morgan, 8 Ky. (1 A. K. Mar.) 62; Brandt v. Ogden, 1 Johns. (N. Y.) 156; Jackson v. Parker, 3 Johns. Cas. (N. Y.) 124; Kirk v. Smith, 22 U. S. (9 Wheat.) (U. S.) 241, 6 L. Ed. 81; Jackson v. Berner, 48 Ill. 203.

63. Hamilton v. Wright, 30 Iowa 486; Huls v. Buntin, 47 Ill. 397. An entry by one man on the land of another is an ouster of the legal possession arising from the title, or not, according to the intention with which it is done; if made under claim or color of right adverse to the legal title, it is an ouster; otherwise it is a mere trespass, as the intention guides the entry and fixes its character. The doctrine of adverse possession is taken strictly, and is not made out by inference. Brandt v. Ogden, 1 Johns. (N. Y.) 156; Jackson v. Sharp, 9 id. 163; Jackson v. Parker, 3 Johns. Cas. (N. Y.) 124; Gay v. Moffit, 5 Ky. (2 Bibb.) 507; McGee v. Morgan, 8 Ky. (1 A. K. Mar.) 62. Where a party occupied land as the tenant of the owner until the death of the latter, and after that held possession in right of his wife, who was an heir of the deceased owner, during which he acquired the interest of several of the other heirs, he always recognizing their claims, his possession after the death of the owner was held not adverse to the remaining heirs. Busch v. Huston, 75 Ill. 343. See Kille v. Ege, 79 Pa. 15. The quality and extent of the right acquired by possession of lands depends upon the claim accompanying it; and to be adverse there must be

certain lands, the extent of which is definitely fixed, is adverse to the donor, and ripens into a title after the lapse of the requisite

a claim of title in fee. Bedell v. Shaw, 59 N. Y. 46. The adverse possession of a tenant is notice to all the world that he can maintain whatsoever title he has against all the world. Jeffersonville, etc., R. Co. v. Oyler, 60 Ind. 383. Where lands of a married woman are sold by her husband, the possession of the grantee does not become adverse to the wife until the marriage is terminated. Stephens v. McCormick, 68 Ky. (5 Bush.) 181. The possession, to give title, must be adversary; and it cannot be adversary unless it is hostile to the true title. Kirk v. Smith, 22 U. S. (9 Wheat.) (U. S.) 241, 288, 6 L. Ed. 81. Adverse possession sufficient to defeat the legal title where there is no paper title must be hostile in its inception and is not to be made out by inference, but by clear and positive proof; and the possession must be such as to show clearly that the party claims the land as his own, openly and exclusively. Jackson v. Birner, 48 Ill. 128. A possession taken under a grant from the French Canadian government, before the conquest of Canada by the British, of land in the State of New York, is not hostile to any private or individual right, but is and must be considered as held in subordination to title conveyed by a patent of the State. Jackson v. Waters, 12 Johns. (N. Y.) 365; Jackson v. Ingraham, 4 id. 163. Where a party did not originally enter into the possession of the land under a title hostile to the title of the owner, it will be intended that he entered under his title. Jackson v. Thomas, 16 Johns. (N. Y.) 293. If a man enters on land, without claim or color of title, and no privity exists between him and the real owner, he may afterward acquire such a title to the land as the law will, *prima facie*, consider a good title, and from that moment his possession becomes adverse. Jackson v. Thomas, *supra;* Jackson v. Frost, 5 Cow. (N. Y.) 346. Where a party is in possession of lands in privity with the rightful owner, nothing short of an open and explicit disavowal and disclaimer of a holding under that title, and assertion of title in himself, brought home to the owner, will satisfy the law. Floyd v. Mintsey, 7 Rich. (S. C.) 181. The doctrine has been maintained that a party in possession of lands confessedly in subordination to the title of the owner is incapable in law of imparting, by any act of his own, an adverse character to his possession; also that, in order to deny or dispute the title, he must first surrender the possession, and place the owner in the condition in which he stood before the possession was taken under him. This doctrine was supposed to govern the rights of trustee and *cestui que trust*, landlord and tenant, vendor and vendee, tenants in common, and the like, and by it no lapse of time would support a statute bar to the right of entry by reason of an adverse possession between parties standing in this relation, or others of like privity. The law, however, has been settled otherwise. The statute does not operate until the

statutory period.[64] There are cases in which a contrary doctrine is held;[65] but the weight of authority, as well as common sense and the principles applicable to adverse possession, seem to support the rule as stated, because a person entering under such circumstances enters as owner, and occupies under a claim of ownership, and every attribute requisite to acquire a title by adverse possession exists.[66]

possession, before consistent with the title of the real owner, becomes tortious and wrongful by the disloyal and notorious acts of the tenant.

In an action of ejectment the court charged the jury that: "Notice of the disclaimer puts the true owner under the same obligation to reclaim the possession within the fixed period, as if no trust had ever existed; and it matters not whether the trust began by the voluntary act of the trustee, or the law made him a trustee against his will, as the result of his situation or conduct;" and the Supreme Court of the United States, on writ of error, sustained the charge of the judge. Zeller's Lessee v. Eckert, 45 U. S. (4 How.) 289, 11 L. Ed. 979. This doctrine, however, does not impair the rule that a possession to be adverse must be hostile in its inception. In the cases last referred to the party may be said to have held possession under different claims, at different dates, the last of which was hostile, and hence adverse, and the first was in subservience to the true title, and not adverse. The possession must be hostile in its inception. Jackson v. Camp, 1 Cow. (N. Y.) 605. A possession and claim of land, under an executory contract of purchase is not adverse, as to the one with whom the contract is made. But when one enters under a contract for a deed with one party, and afterward takes a deed from another party, his possession from this time is adverse to the first vendee, and, if continued the statutory period, will bar his entry. Jackson v. Johnson, 5 Cow. (N. Y.) 74; Jackson v. Bard, 4 Johns. (N. Y.) 231. After performance of a contract of purchase, and an equitable title to a deed of the premises acquired, there is no good reason why the vendee's possession may not become adverse. Briggs v. Prosser, 14 Wend. (N. Y.) 228.

64. Clark v. Gilbert, 39 Conn. 94; Graham v. Craig, 81 Pa. 465; School District v. Blakeslee, *supra;* Sumner v. Stephens, 47 Mass. (6 Met.) 337; Moore v. Webb, 41 Ky. (2 B. Mon.) 282; Outcalt v. Ludlow, 32 N. J. L. 239; Steel v. Johnson, 86 Mass. (4 Allen) 425.

65. Watson v. Tindal, 24 Ga. 494; Jackson v. Rogers, 1 Johns. (N. Y.) Cas. 36.

66. As to specific performance special provisions of a contract of sale may require or imply that the purchaser is to have a good title by the record, but it is not yet settled in Massachusetts that in no case will a purchaser be compelled in equity to take a title which rests on adverse possession. See Noyes v. Johnson, 139 Mass. 436, 31 N. E. 767; Conley v. Finn, 171 Mass. 70, 73, 50 N. E.

§ 261. Mixed possession.

The rule is, that where there is a mixed possession,—that is, where there are two or more persons in possession, each under a separate conveyance or color of title,—the possession will be treated as being in him who has the better title, upon the ground that the seisin is in him who has the best title, and, as all cannot be seised, the possession follows the title.[67] The rule is well settled that title

460, 68 Am. St. Rep. 399; 33 Am. L. Rev. 357. Such a title is sufficient to support a petition for damages to land caused by the discontinuance of a highway, or by the taking of the land by a railroad corporation. Andrew v. Nantasket Beach R. Co., 152 Mass. 506, 25 N. E. 966.

67. Langdon v. Potter, 3 Mass. 219; Gilman v. Wilson, 10 id. 151; Cushman v. Blanchard, 3 Me. 266; Bellis v. Bellis, 122 Mass. 414; Crispen v. Hannavan, 50 Mo. 536. When two persons are in possession of land at the same time, under different claims of right, he has the seisin in whom the legal title is vested. Winter v. Stevens, 91 Mass. (9 Allen) 526. If the holders of two hostile titles to the same land each occupy a small portion within the exterior boundaries of the tract, the constructive possession follows the true title, and limitation does not run in favor of the holder of the invalid title, except as to his actual possession. Semple v. Cook, 50 Cal. 26. One who has the title to land, but fails to take actual possession of it for twenty years, is not barred by the statute, because the title carries with it the seisin. Mylar v. Hughes, 60 Mo. 105. Ordinarily, the possession of one who does not hold the true title can extend only to the land in actual occupancy. If a written instrument is relied upon as giving color of title the entry and occupation must be open and notorious, and the true owner must have actual or constructive notice of the instrument under which claimant enters of the actual possession, and of extent and boundary of the claim, which can only be known by the paper. In cases of mixed possession, where both claimants actually occupy parts, under adverse claims to the whole, the true title will prevail against the one merely colorable, and the adverse claimant will be confined to the portion actually occupied. Crispen v. Hannavan, 50 Mo. 536. A possessory title to land, though for less than twenty years, is good against one who subsequently enters, claiming by no higher title. Thoreau v. Pallies, 83 Mass. (1 Allen) 425; Wolcott v. Ely, 84 Mass. (2 Allen) 338; Currier v. Gale, 91 Mass. (9 Allen) 522. If the inhabitants of a town, through their committee, survey a portion of land lying in common and undivided, put up stakes as monuments, marked with the name of the town, and afterwards, through one of their selectmen, proceed to erect a fence about the same, which is removed by others before its completion, this is enough to give them a possessory title to the same as against strangers. Simmons v. Nahant, 85 Mass. (3 Allen), 316.

draws to it the possession, and it remains with the owner of the legal title until he is divested of it by an actual, adverse possession;[68] and, while he is in possession of a part of the premises, his possession is entitled to the benefit of the constructive possession, and can only be ousted by, and to the extent of, the actual occupation of a mere intruder.[69] "Although," says Parsons, C. J.,[70] "there may be concurrent possession, there cannot be a concurrent seisin of land; and one only being seised, the possession must be adjudged to be in him, because he has the best right."[71]

68. Davidson v. Beatty, 3 H. & McH. (Md.) 621; Hammond v. Ridgely, 5 H. & J. (Md.) 245; Dow v. Stephens, 18 N. C. (1 D. & B.) 5; Hall v. Powel, 4 S. & R. (Pa.) 465; Orbison v. Morrison, 8 N. C. (1 Hawks) 468; Burns v. Swift, 2 S. & R. (Pa.) 433.

69. Id.; Barr v. Gratz's Heirs, 17 U. S. (4 Wheat.) 213, 4 L. Ed. 553; Cushman v. Blanchard, 3 Me. 266.

70. Langdon v. Potter, *supra*. "There would appear to be no clearer principle of reason and justice," said Duncan, J., in Hall v. Powell, 4 S. & R. (Pa.) 465, "than that if the rightful owner is in possession of a part of his tract, by himself or his tenant, he is in the constructive and legal possession and seisin of the whole, unless he is disseised by actual occupation and dispossession. If this were not so, the possession by wrong would be more favored than the rightful possession. * * * In this kind of mixed constructive possession the legal seisin is according to the title. Title draws possession to the owner. It remains until he is dispossessed, and then no further than actual dispossession by a trespasser, who cannot acquire a constructive possession, which always remains with the owner." See Calk v. Lynn, 8 Ky. (1 A. K. Mar.) 346; Jackson v. Vermilyea, 6 Cow. (N. Y.) 677; Miller v. Shaw, 7 S. & R. (Pa.) 143; Royer v. Benlow, 10 id. 303.

71. Livingston v. Peru Iron Co., 9 Wend. (N. Y.) 511; Brimmer v. Proprietors of Long Wharf, 22 Mass. (5 Pick.) 131; Hunnicutt v. Peyton, 102 U. S. 333, 26 L. Ed. 113, it was held that the possession of a person who under color of title enters upon vacant lands and holds adversely, is construed to hold so much as is within the boundaries of his title, and to that extent the legal owner is disseised. But, if the legal owner is in actual possession of any part of the land whereon the entry is made, his constructive seisin extends to all not in fact occupied by the intruders. See also, Scott v. Elkins, 83 N. C. 424. The rule seems settled that two persons representing separate interests cannot have constructive possession of the same land at the same time, consequently the benefit of constructive possession necessarily and rightfully belongs to the legal owner, and all others are confined to their actual occupancy. Hodges v. Eddy, 38 Vt. 344; Stevens v. Hollister, 18

Where the rightful owner is in the actual occupancy of a part of his land he is treated as being in the constructive and legal possession and seisin of the whole, unless he is disseised by actual occupation and dispossession, and where the possession is mixed it is invariably the rule that the legal seisin is in accordance with the legal title. In order to dispossess a person whose title covers an entire tract of land, there must be an actual disseisin by actual possession and occupancy during the entire statutory period.[72]

The rule may be said to be that when a person enters upon unoccupied land under a deed or title, and holds adversely, his possession is construed to be coextensive with his deed or title, and the true owner will be deemed to be disseised to the extent of the boundaries described in that title, although his possession beyond the limits of his actual occupancy is only constructive. But if the true owner is at the same time in actual possession of a part of the land, claiming title to the whole, he has the constructive possession of all the land not in the actual possession of the intruder, and this, although the owner's actual possession is not within the limits of the defective title. The reason for this rule is that both parties cannot be seised at the same time of the same land under different titles. The law therefore holds the seisin of all that is not in the actual occupancy of the adverse party to be in him who has the better title.[73]

Vt. 294; Whittington v. Wright, 9 Ga. 23; Codman v. Winslow, 10 Mass. 146. And the occupation necessary to disseise him as to any part of the land must be actual, visible, notorious, distinct, and hostile. Robinson v. Lake, 14 Iowa 424.

72. Deputron v. Young, 134 U. S. 241, 10 Sup. Ct. 539, 33 L. Ed. 923; Hunnicutt v. Peyton, 102 U. S. 333, 26 L. Ed. 113; Barr v. Gratz's Heirs, 17 U. S. (4 Wheat.) 313, 4 L. Ed. 553.

73. Clarke's Lessee v. Courtney, 30 U. S. (5 Pet.) 319, 8 L. Ed. 140. In Altemus v. Long, 4 Pa. 254, it was held that, although actual possession under a junior title of part of a tract of land which interfered with an older grant gave possession of the whole to the holder of the junior title, yet that a subsequent entry of the true owner upon any part of the land was an ouster of the intruder from what he had in constructive possession merely; and this may be said to be the rule generally adopted.

In Pennsylvania, where, by statute as well as by the courts, much force is given to surveys by a person going into the adverse possession of lands, it is held that in the case of interfering surveys the possession will be adjudged to be in him who has the elder title, and the possession of a person holding a junior survey, unaccompanied by an actual entry upon the interference, takes nothing by construction, and acquires no title in the lands within the interference,[74] following in this respect the rule existing in all cases of mixed possession. But where a person lays a new survey on parts of older surveys, the interior lines of which are not marked, and takes actual possession of a part of the land, and exercises dominion over all, and establishes his lines and pays taxes on the whole, he acquires title thereto.[75] But he will not acquire possession beyond his marked lines, even though embraced within his survey;[76] and if his survey interferes with others, his constructive possession will be broken by the entry of the owner of the warrant upon any part of the land within the bounds of his survey;[77] and if the evidence in the case of interfering surveys is equally balanced, the preference is given to the oldest survey.[78]

§. 262. Limits upon the operation of possession by construction. The doctrine of constructive possession under color of title is subject to certain limitations and, cannot be extended to whole townships of land,[79] nor to large tracts of land not taken for the ordinary purposes of cultivation and occupation;[80] nor does it

74. Cluggage v. Duncan, 1 S. & R. (Pa.) 111; McArthur v. Veitchen, 77 Pa. 62; Washabaugh v. Entriken, 36 Pa. 513; Altemus v. Trimble, 9 Pa. 232; O'Hara v. Richardson, 46 Pa. 385; Beaupland v. McKeen, 28 Pa. 124; Hole v. Rittenhouse, 25 Pa. 491.

75. Nearhoff v. Addleman, 31 Pa. 279; Heiser v. Riehle, 7 Watts (Pa.) 35; Kite v. Brown, 5 Pa. 291; Hatch v. Smith, 4 Pa. 109.

76. Reland v. Eckert, 23 Pa. 215.

77. Altemus v. Long, 4 Pa. 254.

78. Hull v. Wilson, 11 Pa. 515.

79. Chandler v. Spear, 22 Vt. 388; Hunter v. Chrisman, 45 Ky. (6 B. Mon.) 463.

80. Sharp v. Brandow, 15 Wend. (N. Y.) 397; Chandler v. Spear, *supra;* Hunter v. Chrisman, *supra;* People v. Livingston, 8 Barb. (N. Y.) 253. In ejectment the defense of twenty years' adverse possession, in order to countervail a legal title,

apply unless the lands actually possessed have some necessary connection with the other portion, as by use with it or subservience to it.[81] The doctrine of the case last cited arises under the peculiar statute of New York, and for that reason does not

must be supported by twenty years' actual occupancy, or a substantial inclosure of the premises by the defendant, or by him and those through whom he derives title. A cultivation of part of the premises for that time, with a claim of title to the whole, will not constitute a defense beyond the portion actually improved. And even where such possession is under a deed or paper title, for a large tract of land, and only a small part is improved, with a claim of title to the whole, this is not an adverse possession beyond the actual improvement. In Dervient v. Lloyd, decided October term, 1820, but not reported, where the defendant had a deed for Lot 4, but took possession of Lot 5, adjoining, believing it to be Lot 4, and claiming it as such, and improving a part, it was held that his adverse possession did not extend beyond his actual improvements. The doctrine of the constructive adverse possession of land by the cultivation of part accompanied by a claim of the whole under a deed, does not apply to large tracts of land not purchased for the purpose of actual cultivation. The doctrine is in general applicable to a single farm or lot of land only, purchased for the purpose of actual cultivation. A constructive adverse possession must be founded on a deed or paper title, though such title need not be a rightful one. Gilliland v. Woodruff, 1 Cow. (N. Y.) 276; Miller v. Dow, 1 Root (Conn.) 412. See Ten Eyck v. Richards, 6 Cow. (N. Y.) 623; Jackson v. Woodruff, 1 Cow. (N. Y.) 276.

81. In Thompson v. Burhaus, 79 N. Y. 93, which was an action of ejectment to recover five-sixteenth of four thousand acres of land, divided into quarter-sections, the plaintiff, hearing that the defendants intended to enter upon certain lands, caused a shanty without a roof to be erected thereon, also a barn, and cut logs from about a quarter of an acre of the land, the court held that the recovery must be limited to the land actually occupied, to wit, one-quarter of an acre, and that the circumstance that the plaintiff, after the action was commenced, built roads and cut a large quantity of logs upon the lot in dispute, was immaterial upon the question of constructive possession. The court disapproved Wood v. Banks, 14 N. H. 101, holding that an entry upon a lot with a view of taking possession of it by spotting the trees around it, is a sufficient possession of land as against one not having a better right to enter upon the land, and held that such acts, of themselves, or taken in connection with the acts detailed, could not extend the plaintiff's possession by construction to such spotted lines. Reversing Thompson v. Burhaus, 15 Hun (N. Y.) 580. Bare possession of land, and exercising acts of ownership over it, is sufficient to put all persons on inquiry as to the occupant's claim. Franklin v. Newsom, 53 Ga. 580; Morgan v. Taylor, 55 Ga.

seem to accord with the rule that a possession of a part of premises under a deed purporting to pass the title of land, with definite boundaries, is extended by construction to the whole tract conveyed, except as against the owner of the legal title, who is also in possession,[82] unless it is put upon the ground, as it really was, that the land claimed by construction had no necessary connection with the part actually possessed, by use or as being subservient to it.[83]

A distinction is also made by many of the courts between lands laid out into distinct lots and those which are not, and in the former case it is held that an entry upon and possession of one lot, under a conveyance which embraces several, cannot be extended by construction to other lots not actually occupied. There must necessarily be limitations imposed upon the application of the doctrine of constructive possession, or the consequences might be disastrous; and the tendency of the courts is to hold, as previously stated, that it can only be held to extend to lands taken for the ordinary purposes of cultivation and occupation.[84] And some of the cases hold that where a person claims the benefit of this doctrine under color of title and by adverse possession of a part of the land, it must be restricted to a single farm or lot for the purposes of ordinary cultivation or improvement.[85] Of course, in those States where the statute provides what shall be the effect of color of title and occupancy of a part, the statute will control; but in New York and the other States before referred to, as fixing the effect of such colorable title, and what shall constitute possession, title by construction, where land is divided into dis-

224; Havens v. Bliss, 26 N. J. Eq. 363. And this applies to levies upon execution, judgment liens, etc. Morgan v. Taylor, *supra*. A prior possession, although short of the statutory period, is sufficient against a subsequent adverse possession, and enables the occupant to maintain his claim against everybody except the owner, or those claiming under him. Martin v. Bousack, 61 Mo. 556. Adams v. Guerard, 29 Ga. 651.

82. Scott v. Elkins, 83 N. C. 424.

83. People v. Livingston, *supra*; Wilson v. McEwen, 7 Oreg. 87.

84. Chandler v. Spear, *supra*.

85. Jackson v. Woodruff, 1 Cow. (N. Y.) 277; Jackson v. Richards, 6 id. 617; Sharp v. Brandow, 15 Wend. (N. Y.) 597.

tinct lots, is expressly confined to one lot;[86] but where no such division is made, and the land is not in the actual adverse possession of a person who entered before he did, the title would, by force of the statute, embrace all that was described in the conveyance.[87]

§ 263. Possession by mistake.

The question whether a party can set up an adverse possession where lands have been occupied by him by mistake, has been often before the courts; and the rule has been adopted in some of the States, that where a person takes possession of land, and through inadvertence or ignorance as to the true line, takes and holds possession of land not covered by his deed, with no intention of claiming or occupying beyond his actual boundaries, such possession will not support a plea of the statute against the real owner,[88] because in such a case the possession lacks an essential requisite, viz., an intention to claim adversely, which is an indispensable ingredient to constitute a disseisin.[89] This doctrine, however, has been denied in Connecticut;[90] and in all cases if a person under a mistake as to the boundaries enters and occupies land not embraced in his title, claiming it as his own for the requisite statutory period, he thereby becomes invested with the title thereto by possession,[91]

86. Appendix, New York, § 369.

87. Munro v. Merchant, 28 N. Y. 9.

88. Skinner v. Crawford, 54 Iowa, 119; Smith v. Morrow, 15 Ky. (5 Litt.) 210; McKinney v. Kenney, 8 Ky. (1 A. K. Mar.) 460; Thompson v. Babb, 45 Mo. 384; Brown v. Cockerell, 33 Ala. 38; Howard v. Reedy, 29 Ga. 154; Dow v. McKenney, 64 Me. 138; Robinson v. Kline, 70 N. Y. 147; Haux v. Battin, 68 Mo. 84; Grube v. Wells, 34 Iowa, 148.

89. Ross v. Gould, 5 Me. 204; Brown v. Gay, 3 Me. 126.

90. Pearce v. French, 8 Conn. 439, reviewing Brown v. Gay, 3 Me. 126; Ross v. Gould, 5 Me. 204. See also Swettenham v. Leary, 18 Hun (N. Y.) 284; Cole v. Parker, 70 Me. 372; Crary v. Goodman, 22 N. Y. 170; Melvin v. Proprietor's, etc., 46 Mass. (5 Met.) 33; Seymour v. Carli, Minn. (S. C.) July, 1883; Enfield v. Day, 7 N. H. 457.

91. Ricker v. Hibbard, 73 Me. 300; Abbott v. Abbott, 51 Me. 584; Hitchings v. Morrison, 72 Me. 331; Wallbrun v. Batten, 68 Mo. 164. See Bunce v. Bidwell, 43 Mich. 542. See White v. Hapeman, 43 Mich. 267, as to occupancy under an agreement relative to lines. As to whether a party can set up an adverse possession to lands occupied by him under a mistake sup-

although his entry and possession may have been founded upon a mistake. But where a person enters upon a lot not covered by his title, through mistake, he takes nothing by construction, and is limited to his actual occupancy.[92] To the extent of his actual occupancy, which, in case a substantial fence is erected around it, includes the whole lot, he will hold, unless there is evidence that he did not intend to do so.[93]

The rule may be said to be, according to the decided cases, that if a person enters upon land under color of title, and takes possession of lands not embraced therein, with the intention of possessing the whole, he is treated as being in possession of the whole; but if he enters upon a certain part, with the intention of possessing such part only, his possession is confined to that part.[94] But a very important question arises as to whether the intention of the occupant is to be determined from his acts, or from his secret determination in that respect. If the former, then from the fact of exclusive use for the requisite period the adverse character of the occupancy is to be presumed, and the burden is

posing the same to belong to him, when in point of fact they are outside of his real claim, the doctrine evidently is that, where a grantee, in taking possession under his deed, goes unintentionally and by mistake beyond his proper boundaries, and enters upon and actually occupies and improves lands not included in the deed, claiming and supposing it to be his, this occupation is to be deemed adverse within the meaning of the statute of limitations, and, if continued the requisite length of time, will bar the right of the true owner. See Enfield v. Day, 7 N. H. 457; Hale v Glidden, 10 N. H. 397; Crary v. Goodman, 22 N. Y. 170; McKinney v. Kenny, 8 Ky. (1 A. K. Mar.) 460. And see Smith v. Morrow, 15 Ky. (5 Litt.) 210; Hunter v. Chrisman, 45 Ky. (6. B. Mon.) 463. The general doctrine of the courts upon this subject is, undoubtedly, in accordance with the rule before stated.

92. Napier v. Simpson, 1 Tenn. 453.

93. Holton v. Whitney, 30 Vt. 410; St. Louis University v. McConn, 28 Mo. 481; Miner v. Mayor, etc., of New York, 37 N. Y. Superior Ct. 171; Robinson v. Phillips, 1 T. & C. (N. Y.) 151.

94. Bodley v. Cogshill, 10 Ky. (3 A. K. Mar.) 615; Mode v. Loud, 64 N. C. 433; Bowman v. Bartlett, 3 N. C. 99; Schneider v. Botsch, 90 Ill. 577. A person who takes possession under a claim without intending to intrude on another, but accidentally does so, acquires no interferring possession. Smith v. Morrow, *supra;* McKinney v. Kenny, *supra.*

upon the legal owner to show that it was not adverse in fact. If the latter, then the whole matter rests upon the integrity of the occupant. Where adjoining owners enter into possession and actually occupy to erroneous lines, under an agreement that the true lines may be afterwards ascertained, no length of occupancy to wrong lines under such agreement will be adverse, as the occupancy is in recognition of the owner's title.[95] But where two conterminous owners agree upon what shall constitute the true line, and occupy up to it for the requisite statutory period, although it is not the true line, such line becomes established as the true line, and cannot afterwards be disturbed.[96]

§ 264. Grantor in possession.

Where a grantor remains in possession after a conveyance by him, his possession is presumed to be adverse to that of the grantee, where it has continued for a long time after the grant is made, and is inconsistent with its terms, and knowledge of possession by a subsequent purchaser affords some notice of the grantor's rights;[97] and by remaining in possession for the full statutory period adversely to the grantee he becomes reinvested with the title.[98]

95. White v. Hapeman, 43 Mich. 267; Irvine v. Adler, 44 Cal. 559; Devyr v. Schaefer, 55 N. Y. 446. So where, for convenience of cultivation or the protection of his crops or fields, lands of adjoining owners are divided by fences not placed upon the true lines, inasmuch as the occupancy was not adverse in its inception, it cannot become so by any length of possession, unless the other owner is notified of an intention to claim adversely. Betts v. Brown, 3 Mo. App. 20; McNamara v. Seaton, 82 Ill. 498; Soule v. Barlow, 49 Vt. 329.

96. Tanner v. Kellogg, 49 Mo. 118.

97. Brinkman v. Jones, 44 Wis. 498.

98. Furlong v. Garrett, 44 Wis. 111.

Mass. Stat., 1891, c. 354, providing that "notwithstanding disseisin or adverse possession, any conveyance of real estate otherwise valid shall be as effective to transfer title as if the owner of the title were actually seized and possessed of such real estate, and shall vest in the grantee the rights of entry and of action for recovery of the estate incident to such title," is not unconstitutional. McLoud v. Mackie, 175 Mass. 355, 56 N. E. 714.

§ 265. Landlord and tenant.

It is a well-settled general rule that a lessee cannot deny the title of his landlord,[99] and this rule applies whether the tenant was

99. Miller v. McBrian, 14 S. & R. (Pa.) 382; Shepard v. Martin, 31 Mo. 492; Cranz v. Kroger, 22 Ill. 74; Plumer v. Plumer, 30 N. H. 558; Walden v. Bodley, 39 U. S. (14 Pet.) 156, 10 L. Ed. 398; Tewksbury v. Magraff, 33 Cal. 237; Cody v. Quarterman, 12 Ga. 386; Atwood v. Mansfield, 33 Ill. 452. And especially is this so in an action for rent. Codman v. Jackson, 14 Mass. 93; Allen v. Chatfield, 8 Minn. 435; Watson v. Alexander, 1 Wash. (Va.) 340; Perkins v. Governor, Minor (Ala.) 352. And if there are two or more lessors, he cannot deny the title of either of them. Wood v. Day, 7 Taunt. 646; Delaney v. Fox, 1 C. B. N. S. 166; Friend v. Eastabrook, 2 W. Bl. 1152; Langford v. Selmes, 3 Kay & J. 220; Beckett v. Bradley, 7 M. & G. 994. The rule not only extends to the lessee, but to his assignee or undertenant. Kluge v. Lachenour, 34 N. C. (12 Ired. L.) 180; Blackeney v. Ferguson, 20 Ark. 547; McCrancy v. Ransom, 19 Ala. 430; Lunsford v. Alexander, 20 N. C. (4 Dev. & B. L.) 40; Millhouse v. Patrick, 6 Rich. (S. C.) 350; Rose v. Davis, 11 Cal. 133. A stranger even, who comes into possession through the tenant, though by a purchase of the land, is subject to the rule. Newman v. Mackin, 21 Miss. 383; Lockwood v. Walker, 3 McLean (U. S.) 431; Farley v. Rogers, 8 Ky. (1 A. K. Mar.) 245; Phillips v. Rothwell, 7 Ky. (4 Bibb) 33. The rule applies to a mortgagor and mortgagee, trustee and *cestui que trust*, and generally in all cases where one obtains possession by a recognition of the landlord's title. Willison v. Watkins, 28 U. S. (3 Pet.) 43, 7 L. Ed. 596. And whether the lease is by deed, in writing or oral, or even though he is in under an agreement for a lease merely, or under a contract of purchase. Love v. Edmonston, 23 N. C. (1 Ired, L.) 152; Dubois v. Mitchell, 33 Ky. (3 Dana) 336; Williams v. Cush, 27 Ga. 507. In an action on a bond for rent of certain premises recited in the condition, to be demised by indenture at a certain rent, the defendant is estopped from saying that by the indenture a less rent than that mentioned in the condition was reserved. Lainson v. Tremere, 1 Ad. & El. 792. In an ejectment for mines against a member of a mining company, it was held that the defendant was estopped from disputing the title of the lessor of the plaintiff who had leased the mines to the company, of which the lessor was a partner at the time of the action, but not at the time he granted the lease. Francis v. Harvey, 4 M. & W. 331. The lessee may, however, show that his landlord's title has expired. Neave v. Moss, 1 Bing. 363; England v. Slade, 4 T. R. 682; Jackson v. Ramsbotham, 3 M. & S. 516; Strode v. Seaton, 2 C. M. & R. 728; Downes v. Cooper, 2 Q. B. 256; Agar v. Young, 1 Car. & M. 78; Claridge v. Mackenzie, 4 M. & G. 143; Leeming v. Skirrow, 7 Ad. & El. 157. But where a defendant, in an action for use and occupation, had occupied apartments in a house belonging to

in possession before the lease was made or not.[1] So long as he re-

a wife, and had paid rent to the husband, who subsequently, with the knowledge of the defendant, granted a lease of the whole house to the plaintiff, it was held that, having occupied with notice of the lease, he could not impeach its validity, nor controvert the plaintiff's title. Rennie v. Robinson, 1 Bing. 147. Upon an information to set aside a lease of charity lands, it was held in chancery that the lessees could not dispute the title by setting up an adverse title whilst they retained possession. Atty.-Gen. v. Hotham, 3 Russ. 415. The interest of a tenant for life and a reversioner are the same and therefore a lessee who has paid rent to the first cannot set up title in another person as an answer to an action by the latter after the death of the former. Doe v. Whitroe, 1 Dow & Ry. (N. P.) 1. A lessee, by executing an indenture of lease, admits a will under which it is recited that the lease was granted. Bringloe v. Goodson, 5 Bing. N. C. 738. A lessee of tolls, under an instrument signed by two persons as trustees, admits they are trustees. Willington v. Brown, 8 Q. B. 169. An assignee is estopped by the deed which estops his assignor. Taylor v. Needham, 2 Taunt. 278; Barwick v. Thompson, 7 T. R. 488; Bryan v. Winwood, 1 Taunt. 208. And an assignor, by executing the assignment in which the original lease is recited, is precluded in an action by the assignee from calling upon him to prove the lease. Nash v. Turner, 1 Esp. 217. So an assignee of a void lease by a tenant for life is estopped from disputing the title of the remainderman, though his assignment was after the death of the tenant for life, and payment to and acceptance of rent by the remainderman, and with notice of that fact. Johnson v. Mason, 1 Esp. 89. So where a lease was granted by A. and B. as granting parties, and reserved the rent and right of re-entry to a close, it was held that the assignee of the lessor was estopped from showing that A. had no interest in the premises. Parker v. McLaughlin, 1 Ir. L. R. N. S. 186. In defense of an action of ejectment it may be shown that the parties under whom the plaintiff claims had no title when they conveyed to him, although the defendant himself claims by a conveyance from the same parties, if the latter conveyance was subsequent to that which the defendant seeks to impeach. Oliver v. Powell, 1 Ad. & El. 531. Where a lease granted under a power contained in a settlement recited the title of the lessor, and showed that he had only an equitable interest, the lessee was held not to be estopped from disputing the title of the lessor so disclosed in the lease. Greenway v. Hart, 14 C. B. 348. Estoppel in such cases rests on the ground of the advantage derived by the tenant from being let into possession by the landlord, which would make it unjust and inequitable for him to use his portion thus acquired to undermine or defeat the landlord's rights, Fuller v. Sweet, 30 Mich. 237; and hence the rule that a tenant cannot set up a superior title acquired by him until he has first surrendered possession, Freeman v. Heath, 35 N. C. (13 Ired. L.) 498.

1. Richardson v. Harvey, 37 Ga.

mains in undisturbed possession he is estopped from attacking the

224; Patterson v. Hansel, 67 Ky. (4 Bush) 654; Thayer v. Society, 20 Pa. St. 60; McConnell v. Bowdry, 20 Ky. (4 T. B. Mon.) 392; Hockenbury v. Snyder, 2 W. & S. (Pa.) 240. But in California the rule is otherwise, Franklin v. Merida, 35 Cal. 558; Peralta v. Ginochio, 47 Cal. 459; and in New York, Jackson v. Leek, 12 Wend. (N. Y.) 105; Virginia, Alderson v. Merrill, 15 Gratt. (Va.) 279; Tennessee, Washington v. Conrad, 21 Tenn. (2 Humph.) 562; and in South Carolina, Givens v. Mollyneaux, 4 Rich. (S. C.) 590, it was held that a person in possession is not estopped from subsequently disclaiming holding under such title, if the original entry is not under the person whose title is acknowledged. And this is so in all the States, if such acknowledgment was induced by fraud, Gleim v. Rise, 6 Watts (Pa.) 44; Jackson v. Harper, 5 Wend. (N. Y.) 246; Byrne v. Beeson, *supra;* or was the result of mistake or misapprehension, Miller v. Williams, 15 Gratt. (Va.) 213; Swift v. Dean, 11 Vt. 323; Cramer v. Carlisle Bank, 2 Grant's Cas. (Pa.) 267; Smith v. McCurdy, 3 Phila. (Pa.) 488. The rule adopted in California is certainly just, and does not seem to trench upon the general rule.

When the possession is clearly subservient to a lease, the presumption is that the occupation was under the lease. Bradt v. Church, 110 N. Y. 537, 18 N. E. 357; Church v. Wright, 4 App. Div. 312, 38 N. Y. S. 701, 39 id. 989; Peakin v. Peakin [1895], 2 I. R. 359; Stark v. Mansfield, 178 Mass. 76, 59 N. E. 643. In New York, under section 373 of the Code of Civil Procedure, the tenant's possession in subordination to the landlord's title continues not only during the term, but is presumed to be such, and to continue unchanged, until twenty years after the end of the term, even though the tenant or his successors may claim a hostile title. Whiting v. Edmunds, 94 N. Y. 309; Church v. Schoonmaker, 115 N. Y. 570, 22 N. E. 575.

The rule as to landlord and tenant is but one phase of the general rule that, to set the statute in motion, the relation of the parties must be hostile; so long as their interests are common, or their relations fiduciary, the statute does not begin to run, and this is equally true in the case of landlord and tenant, guardian and ward, vendor and vendee, tenants in common, or trustee and *cestui que trust.* New Orleans v. Warner, 175 U. S. 120, 130, 20 Sup. Ct. 44, 44 L. Ed. 96; Frishmuth v. Farmers' Loan & Trust Co., 95 Fed. 5, 10; Bissing v. Smith, 85 Hun 564, 33 N. Y. S. 123. As to adverse possession between husband and wife, see Gafford v. Strauss (89 Ala. 283), 7 So. 248, 7 L. R. A. 568, 18 Am. St. Rep. 111, and n.; 1 Am. and Eng. Encyc. of Law (2d ed.), p. 820. As to tenants from year to year, see Molony v. Molony, [1894] 2 I. R. 1; Jackson v. McMaster, 28 L. R. Ir. 176. As to tenants at will and at sufferance, see Peakin v. Peakin, [1895] 2 I. R. 359; Lyebrook v. Hall, 73 Miss. 509, 19 So. 348.

When a lessor, claiming land under a deed, leases it the lessee's posses-

title under which he entered,[2] unless his entry was induced by the

sion is his possession to the farthest boundaries contained in the deed. Worth v. Simmons, 121 N. C. 357, 361, 28 S. E. 528; Cochran v. Linville Imp. Co., 127 N. C. 386, 37 S. E. 496.

If intending lessors are unable legally to get possession of their land, the statute of limitations will not apply. Warren v. Murphy, [1894] 2 Q. B. 648; Eccl. Com'rs v. Treemer, [1893] 1 Ch. 166.

2. Paquetel v. Gauche, 17 La. Ann. 89. He cannot controvert the title of him under whom he holds, and whose title he has recognized, Bremer v. Bigelow, 8 Kan. 497; Burnett v. Rich, 45 Ga. 211; Jackson v. Wheldon, 1 E. D. Sm. (N. Y. C. P.) 141; Ingraham v. Baldwin, 9 N. Y. 45, Seld. Notes, 167; Stout v. Merrill, 35 Iowa, 47; even by taking a lease from another after his term is ended, Jackson v. Stiles, 1 Cow. (N. Y.) 575; Jackson v. Hinman, to 10 Johns. (N. Y.) 292; Phelps v. Taylor, 23 La. An. 585; Simmons v. Robertson, 27 Ark. 527. If he denies the title, the landlord may, at his election, treat it as a disseisin. It is in law a termination of the tenancy, and equivalent to notice to quit. Hall v. Davey, 10 Vt. 593; Currier v. Earl, 13 Me. 216; Tillotson v. Doe, 5 Ala. 407; Stearns v. Godfrey, 16 Me. 158; Fusselman v. Worthington, 14 Ill. 135. In an action of ejectment or for rent, the defendant, by admitting that he is the plaintiff's tenant, admits the plaintiff's title. Millhaller v. Jones, 7 Ind. 715; Russell v. Erwin, 38 Ala. 40; Ingraham v. Baldwin, 9 N. Y. 45, Seld. Notes, 167. The fact that the lease is void does not change the rule, or enable the tenant to dispute the title; but, after the relation has ceased, his right to do so is not impaired because he neglected to do so before. Bryne v. Beeson, 1 Dougl. (Mich.) 179; Heath v. Williams, 25 Me. 209; King v. Murray, 28 N. C. (6 Ired. L.) 62; Ankeny v. Pierce, 1 Ill. 202. He cannot set up a title acquired by adverse use while he was occupying either as tenant or licensee. Corning v. Troy Nail Factory, 34 Barb. (N. Y.) 485; Brown v. Keller, 32 Ill. 151; Bryne v. Beeson, 1 Dougl. (Mich.) 179; Hatch v. Pendergast, 15 Md. 251. In order to gain such a title he must first disclaim. Walden v. Bodley, 39 U. S. (14 Pet.) 156, 10 L. Ed. 398; Duke v. Harper, 14 Tenn. (6 Yerg.) 280; and surrender the property before he will be permitted to assert it, Reed v. Shepley, 6 Vt. 602; Tompkins v. Snow, 63 Barb. (N. Y.) 525; Hershey v. Clark, 27 Ark. 525; Brown v. Keller, *supra;* Ryerson v. Eldred, 18 Mich. 12; Greeno v. Munson, 9 Vt. 37; Moshier v. Redding, 12 Me. 478. Statements of his own title will not be evidence unless brought home to the landlord. Ingram v. Little, 14 Ga. 173. And a tenant at will will not be permitted to set up an inconsistent title without surrender or eviction by the owner of a paramount title or its equivalent. Town v. Butterfield, 97 Mass. 105. He cannot avail himself of the purchase of an outstanding title to defeat the title of his landlord. Clemm v. Wilcox, 15 Ark. 102; Russell v. Titus, 3 Grant's Cas. (Pa.) 295; Elliott v. Smith, 23 Pa. 131. See Gallagher v. Bennett, 38 Tex. 291. In order to create this estoppel, the re-

fraud of the landlord or by a mistake in the execution of the

lation of landlord and tenant must exist. It does not apply to a tortfeasor or one who has not recognized the landlord's title. But if he has distinctly recognized the landlord's title, so that he can be said to hold under him, or in subserviency to his title, the rule applies. The best evidence of such recognition is the payment of rent or the taking of a lease; but these are not indispensable. Hood v. Mathias, 21 Mo. 308; Plumer v. Plumer, 30 N. H. 558; Morse v. Roberts, 2 Cal. 515. In Maine, it is held that there must be an actual surrender of the premises, and that notice to the landlord is not sufficient. Longfellow v. Longfellow, 61 Me. 590. If a tenant holds over after the termination of his lease, he cannot, by surrendering part of the premises, acquire a right to dispute the title of the landlord to the remainder. Longfellow v. Longfellow, 54. Me. 240; stoops v. Delvin, 16 Mo. 162. A subtenant cannot dispute the title of his lessor or of his assignee. Stagg v. Eureka Tanning Co. 56 Me. 317; Dunshee v. Grundy, 81 Mass. (15 Gray) 314; Earle v. Hale, 31 Ark. 470; Prevat v. Lawrence, 51 N. Y. 219. A tenant at sufferance is bound by this estoppel. Griffin v. Sheffield, 38 Miss. 359. Nor can a lessee of a tenant at will dispute the title of his lessor or of the landlord. Hilbourn v. Fogg, 99 Mass. 11. Nor can the lessee for life at law set up a conveyance by the intestate to a third person, of which he was ignorant when they leased to him. Hawes v. Shaw, 100 Mass. 187. A tenant contracting to pay the taxes upon the premises cannot, by permitting the lands to be sold for taxes, and purchasing them at such sale, acquire any title thereto as against his landlord. Carithers v. Weaver, 7 Kan. 110. But a tenant at will may at any time abandon his tenancy, and then take the same property by purchase from another, so as to avail himself of the statute of limitations; but the abandonment must be brought home to the knowledge of his landlord. Hudson v. Wheeler, 34 Tex. 356. A person who was in possession of land when the lease was made is estopped from setting up that the lessor holds the title merely as his trustee, Lucas v. Brooks, 85 U. S. (18 Wall.) 436, 21 L. Ed. 779. For instances where, according to the rule in California, a tenant may set up a paramount title when he was in possession when the lease was made, see Peralta v. Ginochio, 47 Cal. 459; Holloway v. Galliac, id. 474; Franklin v. Mereda, 35 Cal. 558; Tewksbury v. Magroff, 33 Cal. 237. The rule only extends to the lessor and his privies in blood or estate; as against a stranger, the tenant may set up title in himself or a third person. Cole v. Maxfield, 13 Minn. 235. A person in possession of premises which are sold or set off upon an execution against him, becomes so far a *quasi* tenant as to be precluded from disputing the title of the purchaser upon execution while he is in possession, but not if he is not in possession. Wood v. Turner, 26 Tenn. (7 Humph.) 517. A person who enters as sub-tenant, although he subsequently acquires a perfect title to the lands, cannot set up such title against his lessor without first surrendering possession to him. He

lease,[3] or unless the lease was made for purposes in violation of law, or of improvements upon public lands specially reserved from sale so that the lessor's possession was unlawful.[4] The fact that the lease is void,[5] or that the lessor had no title whatever,[6] or that the title was really in the lessee, and he was ignorant of the fact when

must give up the advantage which he derived under the tenancy by being let into possession, before the estoppel is removed. Callender v. Sherman, 27 N. C. (5 Ired. L.) 711; Freeman v. Heath, 35 N. C. (13 Ired. L.) 498; Millhouse v. Patrick, 6 Rich. (S. C.) 350. The rule applies where a party takes an undivided half of premises as purchaser, and the other half as tenant. In such a case he is estopped from denying the title of his lessor to the half leased to him. Clark v. Crego, 47 Barb. (N. Y.) 599.

3. Lively v. Ball, 41 Ky. (2 Mon.) 53. See Mays v. Dwight, 84 Pa. 462; Hamilton v. Marsden, 6 Binn. (Pa.) 45; Brown v. Dysenger, 1 Rawle (Pa.) 408; Baskin v. Seechrist, 6 Pa. St. 154. If a person falsely represents himself to be the owner of premises, and thus induces a person to take a lease from him, the tenant is not estopped from denying such person's title. Gleim v. Rise, 6 Watts (Pa.) 44. See Jenckes v. Cook, 9 R. I. 520. See Gallagher v. Bennett, 38 Tex. 291; Alderson v. Miller, 15 Gratt. (Va.) 279; Pearce v. Nix, 34 Ala. 183; Alderson v. Miller, 15 Gratt. (Va.) 279. If it is shown that the tenant was induced to attorn to the plaintiff as landlord, in consequence of the plaintiff's fraud or misrepresentation, he is not estopped. Schnetz v. Arratt, 32 Mo. 172; Tison v. Yawn, 15 Ga. 491. Indeed, the rule may be said to be that the tenant is never estopped from showing that the tenancy was induced by fraud, misrepresentation, or misapprehension, Swift v. Dean, 11 Vt. 233, Cramer v. Carlisle Bank, 2 Grant's Cas. (Pa.) 267; Smith v. McCurdy, 3 Phila. (Pa.) 488; or otherwise unfairly obtained. Brown v. Dyserger, *supra;* Isaac v. Clarke, 2 Gill (Md.) 1; Miller v. Bonsadon, 9 Ala. 317. See Satterlee v. Matthewson, 13 S. & R. (Pa.) 133.

4. Dupas v. Wassell, 1 Dill. (U. S.) 213.

5. Bryne v. Beeson, 1 Dougl. (Mich.) 179; Heath v. Williams, 25 Me. 209; King v. Murray, 28 N. C. (6 Ired. L.) 62. See Shriver v. Shriver, 86 N. Y. 575; Miner v. Beekman, 50 N. Y. 337.

6. Bowdish v. Dubuque, 38 Iowa, 341. A tenant under a lease from one having possession and control of the premises but no title to them (which lease contains a clause that, in case lessors should cease to control or own the property, no rent should be paid unless their successors should in writing confirm the lease), by holding under and paying rent to the successive assignees of the owner, is estopped from denying that they are assignees of his original lessor, and continues bound to pay rent to them in that character, or as having, by the instruments of confirmation, become new lessors. Whalin v. White, 25 N. Y. 462; Flanders v. Train, 13 Wis. 596; Jackson v. Wheedon, 1 E. D. Sm. (N. Y. C. P.) 141.

the lease was made, will not change the rule.[7] Nor is the rule changed although the lease was made to defraud the landlord's creditors.[8] But, in order to subject a party to this rule, the relation of landlord and tenant must exist. By this it is not meant that the party must be in under a lease, or that he must pay rent; but if he is in possession by the permission of the owner, and has recognized his title in any way, it is enough.[9] A tenant in law, as a tenant by dower, elegit, or curtesy, is estopped whenever the person from whom his title is derived would have been;[10] and the rule also applies to a person who goes in under an agreement for a lease, or under a contract for the purchase of the premises, or under any arrangement which operates as a recognition of the landlord's title, and as holding under, or in subserviency to it.[11] When the estate which the landlord held vests in the lessee, whether by purchase from the lessor or by purchase under valid leal proceedings, the tenant may set up this title in defense to any action brought against him by the lessor, either to recover possession of the premises, or to recover after-accruing rent;[12] and indeed in all cases it is competent for the

7. In Baker v. Noll, 59 Mo. 265, the tenant took a lease of the plaintiff who held the lands as trustee of the tenant's wife, but of which fact the tenant was ignorant when the lease was made. The court held that he was estopped. In Abbott v. Cromartie, 72 N. C. 292, the tenant was, in fact, entitled to the lands as a homestead, but he was ignorant of the fact when the lease was made. The court held that he was estopped. But *contra*, see Cain v. Gimon, 36 Ala. 168; Shultz v. Elliott, 30 Tenn. (11 Humph.) 183.

8. Steen v. Wadsworth, 17 Vt. 297.

9. See Downer v. Ford, 16 Cal. 345; Ward v. McIntosh, 12 Ohio St. 231; Flanders v. Train, 13 Wis. 596; Wyoming, etc., Co. v. Price, 81 Pa. 156.

10. Love v. Dennis, Harp. (S. C.) 70; Bufferlow v. Newsom, 12 N. C. (1 Dev. L.) 208; Gorham v. Brenon, 13 N. C. (2 Dev. L.) 174. The tenant of a tenant by dower is estopped from disputing the title of the intestate. Clarke v. Clarke, 51 Ala. 498. A tenant in possession under a lessor whose lands are sold on execution may, however, set up the title of the purchaser, in defense to an action for the rent accruing after the sale. Lancashire v. Mason, 75 N. C. 455.

11. Dubois v. Mitchell, 33 Ky. (3 Dana) 336; Love v. Edmston, 23 N. C. (1 Ired. L.) 152.

12. Ryder v. Manzell, 66 Me. 197; Shields v. Lozear, 34 N. J. L. 496, 3 Am. Rep. 256.

tenant to show that the landlord's title has terminated, as, that the premises have been sold under forclosure proceedings,[13] under execution,[14] or for taxes,[15] or indeed that the title of the

13. It is competent for him to show that they were sold upon a mortgage given to himself, and that he became the purchaser at such sale, or that the condition upon which the mortgage to him was given is broken, Shields v. Lozear, *supra;* Pope v. Biggs, 9 B. & C. 245; Watson v. Lane, 11 Exch. 769; or where his title has been extinguished in any manner subsequent to the making of the lease, Camp v. Camp, 5 Conn. 291; Jackson v. Rowland, 6 Wend. (N. Y.) 666; Wheelock v. Warschauer, 21 Cal. 309; Randolph v. Carlton, 8 Ala. 606; McDevitt v. Sullivan, 8 Cal. 592; Devacht v. Newsom, 3 Ohio 57; Walls v. Mason, 5 Ill. 84; Lawrence v. Miller, 1 Sandf. (N. Y.) 516; Tilghman v. Little, 13 Ill. 239; Ryers v. Farwell, 9 Barb. (N. Y.) 615; Kinney v. Doe, 8 Blackf. (Ind.) 350; Hoag v. Hoag, 35 N. Y. 469; Casey v. Gregory, 52 Ky. (13 B. Mon.) 346; Gregory v. Crab, 41 Ky. (2 B. Mon.) 234; Homer v. Leeds, 25 N. J. L. 106; Hintz v. Thomas, 7 Md. 346; Giles v. Ebsworth, 10 Md. 333; Howell v. Ashmore, 22 N. J. L. 261; Wolf v. Johnson, 30 Miss. 513; England v. Slade, 4 Johns. (N. Y.) 682; Russell v. Allard, 18 N. H. 222; Purtz v. Cuester, 41 Mo. 447. After a judgment of eviction against the tenant, he may, without the landlord's consent, attorn to the successful party, although he has not actually been evicted, Moffat v. Strong, 9 Bos. (N. Y. Sup. Ct.) 57; Lunsford v. Turner, 28 Ky. (5 J. J. Mar.) 104; Foster v. Morris, 10 Ky. (3 A. K. Mar.) 609; or he may show that the premises have been sold under a mortgage, execution, or for taxes, Shields v. Lozear, 34 N. J. L. 496; Doe v. Ashmore, 261. And if the sale is subsequently set aside, he may dispute the title of the purchasers and attorn to his original landlord. Miller v. Williams, 15 Gratt. (Va.) 213. This is upon the principle that if one in possession, under claim of title, is, by fraud or mistake, induced to believe that another has a better title, and thereupon to take a lease from him, the tenant will not be estopped. Alderson v. Miller 16 Gratt. (Va.) 279.

14. Doe v. Ashmore, 22 N. J. L. 162. And he may set up the title of the purchaser under execution against the landlord in any action brought by the landlord, for matters accruing or occurring after such sale. Lancashire v. Mason, 75 N. C. 455.

15. If the lessee buys in the whole or a part of the lessor's title at a tax or execution sale, or by private purchase, it is a proportionate defense to a suit for rent or ejectment. Nellis v. Lathrop, 22 Wend. (N. Y.) 121; Elliott v. Smith, 23 Pa. 131; George v. Putney, 58 Mass. (4 Cush.) 358; Bettison v. Budd, 17 Ark. 546; Carnley v. Stanfield, 10 Tex. 546. But if the tenant contracted to pay the taxes, he cannot set up a tax title against the landlord. Carithers v. Weaver, 7 Kan. 110.

landlord has, from any cause, expired.[16] So a tenant is not estopped when he has been induced to take a lease from the landlord by his fraud or misrepresentation,[17] or under a misapprehension or mistake.[18] Neither is he estopped from setting up a paramount title in another, where he has been evicted, or a judgment of eviction has been obtained against him,[19] nor when the payment of rent by him was merely grauitous.[20] The estoppel only exists during his tenancy, express or implied. After that is ended, whether by surrender or otherwise, he may set up title in himself or in a third person,[21] and, as a tenant for years holding over after his term is treated as holding upon the terms of the former lease, he remains subject to the estoppel.[22]

§ 266. Co-tenants.

Prima facie, the possession of one tenant in common is the possession of all,[23] consequently acts done upon the common prop-

16. Doe v. Seaton, 2 Cr. M. & R. 728.

17. Gleim v. Rise, 6 Watts (Pa.) 44; Swift v. Dean, 11 Vt. 323; Baskin v. Seechrist, 6 Pa. 154.

18. Schultz v. Elliott, 30 Tenn. (11 Humph.) 183.

19. Moffatt v. Strong, 9 Bos. (N. Y. Sup. Ct.) 57; Foster v. Morris, 10 Ky. (3 A. K. Mar.) 609; Fletcher v. McFarlane, 12 Mass. 43; Allen v. Thayer, 17 Mass. 299.

20. Shelton v. Carrol, 16 Ala. 148.

21. Page v. Kinsman, 43 N. H. 328; Carpenter v. Thompson, 3 N. H. 204. If there is no tenancy, there is no estoppel. Hughes v. Clarksville, 31 U. S. (6 Pet.) 369, 8 L. Ed. 430; Foust v. Trice, 53 N. C. (8 Jones L.) 290; Head v. Head, 52 N. C. (7 Jones L.) 620.

22. Stoops v. Delain, 16 Mo. 162; Longfellow v. Longfellow, 54 Me. 240; Wilson v. James, 79 N. C. 349; Wood's Landlord and Tenant, 368 *et seq.*

23. Peaceable v. Reed, 1 East, 568; Doe v. Hellings, 11 id. 49; Atkyns v. Horde, 1 Burr, 111; Ewer v. Lowell, 75 Mass. (9 Gray) 76; Higbee v. Rice, 5 Mass. 351; Whiting v. Dewey, 32 Mass. (15 Pick.) 428; Jackson v. Brink, 5 Cow. (N. Y.) 484; Strong v. Cotter, 13 Minn. 82; Story v. Saunders, 27 Tenn. (8 Humph.) 663. The possession of one tenant in common is never presumed to be adverse, but the contrary. Berthold v. Fox, 13 Minn. 501; Owen v. Morton, 24 Cal. 373; Small v. Clifford, 28 Me. 213; White v. Wilkinson, 2 Grant (Pa.) 249; Buckmaster v. Needham, 22 Vt. 617; Challefoux v. Ducharme, 4 Wis. 554; Cunningham v. Robertson, 31 Tenn. (1 Swan) 138; Van Bibber, v. Frazer, 17 Md. 136. But from a long period of exclusive occupation disseisin may be presumed. Purcell v. Wilson, 4 Gratt. (Va.) 16.

erty by one co-tenant, which if done by a stranger to the title would amount to a disseisin, are susceptible of explanation consistently with the true title; and mere acts of ownership exercised by one co-tenant are not, of themselves, necessarily acts of disseisin, nor do they warrant a presumption of ouster.[24] But if one tenant in common enters upon the whole land, and takes the entire profits, claiming and holding exclusively for the full statutory period, an actual ouster of his co-tenants may be presumed.[25] But the mere pernancy of the profits for that period, of itself, does not amount to conclusive evidence of an ouster,[26] because that is susceptible of explanation consistently with his rights as co-tenant. In order to set the statute in motion in his favor, he must absolutely deny the title of his co-tenants,[27] or by other notorious acts indicate his intention to claim and hold the estate exclusively. There must not only be an exclusive possession, but the possession must be under a claim of title to the whole estate, either brought home to the knowledge of the other tenant, or so notorious that his knowledge of such adverse claim can be presumed.[28] And the evidence must be much stronger than would be required to establish a title

24. Parker v. Locks & Canals, 44 Mass. (3 Met.) 9; Bolton v. Hamilton, 2 W. & S. (Pa.) 294; Calhoun v. Cook, 9 Pa. 226; Brown v. McCoy, 2 W. & S. (Pa.) 307, n.; Phillips v. Gregg, 10 Watts (Pa.) 158; Hart v. Gregg, 10 Pa. 185; Keyser v. Evans, 30 Pa. 507; Forward v. Deetz, 32 Pa. 69.

25. Frederick v. Gray, 10 S. & R. (Pa.) 182; Susquehanna, etc., R. R. Co. v. Quick, 61 Pa. 328; Rider v. Maul, 46 Pa. 376; Mehaffy v. Dobbs, 9 Watts (Pa.) 363; Workman v. Guthrie, 29 Pa. 495; Law v. Patterson, 1 W. & S. (Pa.) 184; Cummings v. Wyman, 10 Mass. 464.

26. Higbee v. Rice, 5 Mass. 351; Bolton v. Hamilton, 2 W. & S. (Pa.) 294; Calhoun v. Cook, *supra*. But pernancy of the profits for a long period, as forty years, is evidence from which an adverse claim may be inferred. Chambers v. Pleak, 36 Ky. (6 Dana) 426.

27. Kathau v. Rockwell, 16 Hun (N. Y.) 96.

28. Van Bibber v. Frazer, 17 Md. 136; Andres v. Andres 31 N. C. (9 Ired.) 214; Forward c. Deetz, 32 Pa. 69; Crane v. Robinson, 21 Conn. 379; Larman v. Hoey, 52 Ky. (13 B. Mon.) 436; Colburn v. Mason, 25 Me. 434; Gill v. Fauntleroy, 47 Ky. (8 B. Mon.) 177; Abercrombie v. Baldwin, 15 Ala. 363; Peck v. Ward, 18 Pa. 506; Meredith v. Andres, 29 N. C. (7 Ired.) 5; Johnson v. Tuolumne, 18 Ala. 50; Newall v. Woodruff, 30 Conn. 492.

by possession by a stranger.[29] What constitutes an actual ouster is a mixed question of law and fact. If one co-tenant goes into possession of the entire estate under a notorious claim of title to the whole, and resists or denies the right of his co-tenant to enter and persistently and notoriously excludes him from the enjoyment of the premises, this is an ouster.[30] So, too, if one co-tenant erects a building upon the estate without the knowledge or consent of the other, and occupies it exclusively, and does, upon the estate, acts such as clearly and unequivocally indicate a claim of exclusive ownership, this is an ouster of his co-tenant.[31] So it has been held that the erection of a dam upon the sole estate of one tenant, which floods the lands of the joint estate, is an ouster.[32] But a mere cutting of trees and converting them to his own use,[33] or cutting the grass and removing fences,[34] the plowing up of crops,[35] the removal of fixtures,[36] or, indeed, the doing of any acts which may be referred to his right, are not regarded as amounting to an actual expulsion, or as an ouster.[37] So, if one defendant executes a mortgage of the entire estate,[38] or a deed of his interest, it is not an ouster,[39] But a conveyance by one of the

29. Barrett v. Coburn, 60 Ky. (3 Met.) 510; Newell v. Woodruff, 30 Conn. 492.

30. Thomas v. Pickering, 13 Me. 337; Forward v. Dietz, 32 Pa. 69.

31. Bennett v. Clemence, 88 Mass. (6 Allen) 10.

32. Jones v. Wetherbee, 4 Strob. (S. C.) 50.

33. Wait v. Richardson, 33 Vt. 190.

34. Booth v. Adams, 11 Vt. 156.

35. Harman v. Gardiner, Hemp. (S. C.) 430.

36. Gibson v. Vaughn, 2 Bailey (S. C.) 389; McPherson v. Seguine, 14 N. C. (3 Dev.) 153.

37. Booth v. Adams, *supra*.

38. Wilson v. Callinshaw, 13 Pa. 276; Harman v. Hannah, 9 Gratt. (Va.) 146.

39. Porter v. Hill, 9 Mass. 34; Roberts v. Morgan, 30 Vt. 319. Where one tenant does an act amounting to a destruction of a portion of the estate, or a serious injury thereto, his co-tenant may have an action on the case against him therefor, but cannot maintain trespass, Anders v. Meredith, 20 N. C. (4 D. & B.) 199; Odiorne v. Lyford, 9 N. H. 502; Gt. Falls Co. v. Worcester, 15 id. 412; Cowles v. Garrett, 30 Ala. 341; Gynther v Pettijohn, 28 N. C. (6 Ired.) 388; as for the erection of a dam on his own estate which floods the joint estate, Jones v. Wetherbee, 4 Strob. (S. C.) 50; Odiorne v. Lyford, *supra;* Gt. Falls Co. v. Worcester, *supra;* Hutchinson v. Chase, 39 Me. 508; or for diverting water from a mill owned

entire estate,[40] or devising it by will,[41] or, indeed, any act which clearly indicates an intention on his part to usurp the entire estate to himself, is an ouster;[42] and the question as to whether his acts accrue to the benefit of the joint estate, or as an ouster and disseisin of the others, is a question for the jury.[43]

§ 267. What possession will sustain constructive possession.

In all cases, in order to entitle a person to the benefit of the doctrine of constructive possession who claims under a color of title, there must be an entry upon, and an actual possession of, some part of the land covered by his title, with the palpable intention to claim and hold the land as his own;[44] and an actual possession of adjoining land will have no effect to entitle a person to the benefits of a constructive possession.[45] There must in all

by two in common, Pillsbury v. Moore, 44 Me. 144.

40. Marcy v. Marcy, 47 Mass. (6 Met.) 360; Kittredge v. Locks & Canals, 34 Mass. (17 Pick.) 246; Bigelow v. Jones, 27 Mass. (10 Pick.) 161.

41. Miller v. Miller, 60 Pa. 16.

42. Cummings v. Wyman, 10 Mass. 464.

43. Lefavour v. Homan, 85 Mass. (3 Allen) 354; Parker v. Locks & Canals, *supra;* Cummings v. Wyman, *supra.*

As a deed from one tenant in common of a part of the common estate by metes and bounds is not absolutely void, but may be good by way of estoppel against the grantor and his heirs, and is valid against all persons unless avoided by the co-tenants, a deed taking effect only as the deed of a disseisor is good, although the title, but for the disseisin, is in him and another as tenants in common. Frost v. Courtis, 172 Mass. 401, 404, 52 N. E. 515. See Old South Society v. Wainwright, 156 Mass. 115, 120, 30 N. E. 476; Kimball v. Com'th Ave. St. Ry. Co., 173 Mass. 152, 53 N. E. 274; Robinson v. Robinson, 173 Mass. 233, 53 N. E. 854.

44. Altemus v. Campbell, 9 Watts (Pa.) 28. An adverse possession of land cannot be extended by construction beyond the limits of the land actually covered by the conveyance. Pope v. Hanmer, 74 N. Y. 240; Enfield v. Day, 7 N. H. 457; Hale v. Glidden, 10 id. 397. As to any lands outside the limits of the conveyance, an actual possession must be shown, Pope v. Hanmer, *supra;* even though the occupant went into the possession of a wrong lot and improved it under a mistake, Hale v. Glidden, *supra;* Johnson v. Lloyd (N. Y.), MSS. case cited in Pope v. Hanmer, *supra.*

45. Hale v. Glidden, *supra;* Pope v. Hanmer, *supra;* Johnson v. Lloyd, *supra;* Tritt v. Roberts, 64 Ga. 156; Peyton v. Barton, 53 Tex. 298; David-

cases be an actual entry upon the land *animo clamandi possessionem,* and a visible, notorious, distinct, and hostile possession of a part of it, continued for the entire statutory period.[46] The kind of possession which will be sufficient must depend largely upon the character of the land, the locality, and the purposes to which it can be put. Thus, an entry upon woodland by a person holding a deed, and clearing off a part of it, with an intention of soon making other improvements, has been held sufficient.[47] In Maine,[48] the doctrine was asserted at an early day, that, in the case of "wild and uncultivated land, the jury were not to expect the same evidence of occupancy which a cultivated farm would present to them." And where the land is so situated as not to admit of any permanent useful improvement, neither residence,

son v. Beatty, 3 H. & McH. (Md.) 621. A., the owner of a tract of land, sold the western half to B., by metes and bounds. The whole tract was subsequently sold under a void judgment for taxes, and C. became the purchaser. He placed a tenant on the eastern half, who remained in possession seven years, claiming the whole tract by virtue of the tax sale. There was no visible open possession of the western half by C. It was held that the statute did not bar the right of B., and that the constructive possession of B. was not disturbed by C.'s occupation of the eastern half. Stewart v. Harris, 28 Tenn. (9 Humph.) 714. The occupation of pine land by annually making turpentine on it is such an actual possession as will oust a constructive possession by one claiming merely under a superior paper title. Bynum v. Carter, 27 N. C. (4 Ired. L.) 310. Where a party is in actual possession, and has a right to possession under a legal title which is not adverse, but claims the possession under another title which is adverse, the possession will not in law be deemed adverse. Nichols v. Reynolds, 1 R. I. 30. In Tritt v. Roberts, 64 Ga. 156, it was held that possession of a part of one lot, embraced in the same deed with other distinct lots, could not be extended by construction to the other lots, unless the deed was on record, and that prescription as to those lots would only begin to run from the date of the record.

46. Stanley v. White, 14 East 332; Doe v. Campbell, 10 Johns. (N. Y.) 477; Ewing v. Burnet, 36 U. S. (11 Pet.) 41, 9 L. Ed. 624; De Lany v. Mulcher, 47 Iowa 445; Scott v. Delany, 87 Ill. 146.

47. Scott v. Delany, 87 Ill. 146. See Thompson v. Burhaus, 79 N. Y. 97.

48. Robinson v. Swett, 3 Me. 316. See Miller v. L. I. R. R. Co., 71 N. Y. 380; Wheeler v. Spinola, 54 id. 377; Miller v Downing, id. 631; Argotsinger v. Vines, 82 N. Y. 308.

cultivation, nor actual occupation are necessary where the continued claim to the premises is evidenced by notorious acts of ownership, such as a person would not exercise over lands which he did not own.[49]

It is not necessary that the occupation should be such that a mere stranger, passing by the land, would know that some one was asserting title to a dominion over it. It is not necessary that the land be cleared or fenced, or that any building be put upon it.[50]

The possession of land cannot be more than the exercise of exclusive dominion over it. This possession or dominion cannot be the same or uniform in every case, and there may be degrees even in the exclusiveness of the exercise of ownership. The owner cannot literally occupy a whole tract; he cannot stand upon all of it or hold it in his hands. His possession must be indicated by other acts, and these acts must vary according to the circumstances of each case. When one enters upon land under color of title and with claim of ownership, any acts of user which are continuous and which indicate unequivocally to the neighborhood in which the land is situated that it is appropriated exclusively to his individual use and ownership, such entry is sufficient to render the possession adverse.[51]

An indispensable requisite to the acquisition of title under statutes of limitation is that the possession must be both adverse and continuous.[52]

49. Baldwin, J., in Ewing v. Burnet, *supra*; Ellicott v. Pearl, 10 id. 412; Moss v. Scott, 2 Dana (Ky.) 275. In Ewing v. Burnett, *supra*, the exclusive and notorious use of a valuable sand-bank was held sufficient to give title by adverse possession, and that the erection of a fence or the making of improvements was not necessary, but that any acts under a claim of right, visible and notorious, are sufficient, and the nature of the acts required must depend upon the uses to which the land is adapted.

50. Ellicott v. Pearl, 10 Pet. (U. S.) 412; Davis v. Easley, 13 Ill. 192; Brooks v. Bruyn, 24 id. 372; Booth v. Small, 25 Iowa 177; Langworthy v. Myers, 4 id. 18; Ewing v. Burnett, 11 Pet. 41.

51. Morse, J., in Murray v. Hudson, 9 Western Rep. (Mich.) 347.

52. Albut v. Nilson, 89 Mo. 536.

The ground upon which the statute proceeds is, that the owner of the legal title has been ousted of his possession, and has acquiesced therein; and the acts necessary to sustain this presumption must be of such a visible, notorious, and hostile character as to operate as a notice to all parties that the person is in possession as owner.[53] And it would seem, under the theory relative to the acquisition of such title by constructive possession, that the extent of his claim must be clearly indicated by some of the insignia of boundaries, as marked trees upon the lines, the erection of a fence, the establishment of corners by stakes and stones, or some other equally decisive evidence of the limits of his claim, or that his deed must accurately describe the premises and be recorded; as in no other way could publicity be given to the limits of the possession, or the extent of the claim be ascertained.[54] Actual residence by the claimant or his tenant upon the land is not necessary to continue possession or occupancy. It is only necessary that the claimant should maintain continuous dominion over the land, manifested by continuous acts of ownership according to the purposes for which the land is adapted, and according to the custom of the country.[55] Thus, the open, notorious, and

53. Blood v. Wood, 42 Mass. (1 Met.) 528. Thompson v. Burhaus, 79 N. Y. 101, questions the doctrine of Wood v. Banks, 14 N. H. 101, that an entry upon a lot, with a view of taking possession of it under a claim of title, and marking the lines of it by spotting the trees around it, is a sufficient possession against one who has no better right. Passing around land or over it, asserting title ever so loud, does not give possession; and in Lynde v. Williams, 68 Mo. 360, it was held that posting a notice upon land, that a certain person claimed it, did not amount to a possessory act. Although in one case it was said that the claimant "must keep his flag flying." Stephens v. Leach, 19 Pa. St. 265, yet it is hardly believed that that would be sufficient, if it was simply nailed to a tree on the land. Either the claimant or his agent would be required to stay on the land, and wave it continuously, until the statutory period has elapsed.

54. In Tritt v. Roberts, *supra*, it was held that the record of the conveyance is necessary in some cases to support constructive possession. Doe v. Campbell, 10 Johns. (N. Y.) 477. See Riley v. Jameson, 3 N. H. 23. See Corning v. Troy Iron Co., 34 Barb. (N. Y.) 529.

55. Coleman v. Billings, 89 Ill. 183; Thompson v. Burhaus, *supra;* Ford v. Wilson, 35 Miss. 490; Miller v.

exclusive use of a valuable sand bank for the purpose of getting sand is held sufficient.[56] So, surveying the land and setting up stakes to indicate the lines and corners, and the erection of a wharf and boat sheds.[57] The mere payment of taxes upon land, while it indicates a claim of ownership, and the extent of the claim, does not of itself amount to possession, nor operate as a substitute therefor.[58] In Illinois, however, by statute, an entry under color of title and payment of taxes for seven years is

Platt, 5 Duer (N. Y.) 272. Where the entry on land was originally in a fiduciary character as agent, it requires some decisive act or declaration to render the possession adverse. Giving receipts for rent in one's own name is not such an act. Martin v. Jackson, 27 Pa. St. 504. Whether possession is adversary or not depends on the circumstances under which it was taken and held, especially the *animus* of the party holding; and whether with a claim of title, or without any such claim, is a question of fact for the jury. Early v. Garland, 13 Gratt. (Va.) 1. If acts of ownership and possession relied upon as proof of a title by disseisin and not of a nature to work a disseisin, they cannot be made more effectual for that purpose, by proof that they were known and not objectd to by the legal owner. Cook v. Babcock, 65 Mass. (11 Cush.) 206. An obstruction of part of a space, over all which A. claims a right of way by adverse user, does not defeat A.'s right to pass over the way as reduced in width. Putnam v. Bowker, 65 Mass. (11 Cush.) 542. Occupation by the grantee in a deed, with the consent of the grantor, of premises more extensive than those conveyed to him by the deed, for a less period than that required by the statute to bar all claims, does not give the grantee any title as to the land not included in the deed. Clark v. Baird, 9 N. Y. 183. The burden of proving an adverse possession is on the party claiming the easement. Hammond v. Zehner, 23 Barb. (N. Y.) 473. Possession taken under color of title is in law possession of all the land described in the deed conferring such color of title, lying in the same tract; but, in order to make such possession effectual to the party claiming title under it, it must be open, visible, exclusive, and notorious, calculated to give notice to the owner of an adverse claim thereby to the land. Little v. Downing, 37 N. H. 355.

56. Ewing v. Burnet, 36 U. S. (11 Pet.) 41, 9 L. Ed. 624.

57. Congdon v. Morgan, 14 S. C. 587.

58. Cornelius v. Giberson, 25 N. J. L. 1; Sorber v. Willing, 10 Watts (Pa.) 141; Reed v. Field, 15 Vt. 672; Naglee v. Albright, 4 Whart. (Pa.) 291; Chapman v. Templeton, 53 Mo. 463; Hockenbury v. Snyder, 2 W. & S. (Pa.) 240; Paine v. Hutchins, 49 Vt. 314. Taken in connection with other acts, the payment of taxes is a fact proper to go to the jury, as tending to establish adverse possession. Draper v. Shoot, 25 Mo. 197.

sufficient to perfect a title under the statute; and, indeed, it would doubtless be held in all the States that if the owner has abandoned his land, and permits another, under color of title for the requisite statutory period, without objection, and without entry upon the land, to pay the taxes thereon, that circumstance, accompanied by proof of an actual entry made by the claimant, and possession of some part of the premises, and the establishment of well-defined boundaries, would be treated as such actual possession as would overcome the constructive possession of the owner of the legal title.[59] Thus, where a person entered upon lands under color of title, made a survey, marked his lines, paid taxes, and used a part of the woodland for erecting a saw-mill, it was held that he, by such acts, acquired a title by adverse possession co-extensive with his boundaries.[60] But such constructive possession may be restricted and reduced by acts and declarations of the occupant, that he does not claim title extensive with his survey. The record of a survey affords no evidence of title or possession, nor does the marking of trees around the land as surveyed;[61] but it is evidence of the claim of the person for whom it was made;[62] and the same is true as to the payment of taxes upon land. That circumstance of itself, however, has no tendency to prove an adverse possession of the land, but it is evidence of an adverse claim thereto;[63] and even in Illinois, although the payment of taxes for seven years under color of title gives title under certain circumstances, yet it is held that unless it is shown that the lands were vacant and unoccupied during that period the claimant must prove actual occupancy by himself or others in his behalf.[64]

59. Farrar v. Fessenden, 39 N. H. 268; Royer v. Benlow, 10 S. & R. (Pa.) 303.

60. Heiser v. Riehle, 7 Watts (Pa.) 35. See also Shally v. Stahl, 2 W. N. C. (Pa.) 418; Thompson v. Milford, 7 Watts (Pa.) 442; McCall v. Coover, 4 W. & S. (Pa). 151; Paine v. Hutchins, 49 Vt. 314.

61. Oatman v. Fowler, 43 Vt. 462.

62. Oatman v. Fowler, *supra*.

63. Thompson v. Burhaus, 79 N. Y. 101. But the uninterrupted payment of taxes for a long period, as in this case twenty-four years, was held to afford strong evidence of a claim of right. Ewing v. Burnet, *supra*.

64. Whitney v. Stevens, 89 Ill. 53.

Actual residence, the erection of fences around the lot, the making of improvements upon the land, and the use of it for any purpose to which such land is usually devoted in the section of country in which the land is situated, continuously for the full statutory period, will be sufficient; but no definite rule can be given which will be applicable in all cases, as the question must necessarily depend upon such a variety of circumstances that the same state of facts which would be held sufficient in one case would be held insufficient in another. In the case of entry and possession under a conveyance, whether recorded or not,[65] the

65. When a man enters on, improves, fences, and occupies part of another man's tract of land, and has the boundaries of his claim surveyed and marked, including woodland not inclosed, and for twenty-one years openly and exclusively uses the woodland as his own, in connection with his improvements, as farmers ordinarily do, this is not a constructive, but an actual, possession of the woodland, and excludes the constructive possession usually attributed to the title, and to the owner's actual possession of the rest of his tract. Ament v. Wolf, 33 Pa. 331; Wolf v. Ament, 1 Grant's Cases (Pa.) 150. Actual possession or cultivation of part of a tract of land, use of the uninclosed portions as woodland, and payment of taxes on the whole for the statutory period, may constitute title to the whole. Murphy v. Springer, 1 Grant's Cases (Pa.) 73. So in cases of interference of lines, "inclosing and cultivating part of the interference, and using the residue as adjacent woodland is customarily enjoyed, is actual possession of the whole." In such cases the possession of the real owner, be it actual or constructive, is ousted by inclosing and cultivating part of the interference, and using the residue as adjacent woodland is customarily enjoyed; and after the statutory period the title is changed. Ament v. Wolf, 1 Grant's Cases (Pa.) 518; Beedy v. Dine, 31 Pa. 13; Nearhoff v. Addleman, id. 279. If the possession of a trespasser is interrupted, the possession of the real owner is renewed, and that without actual entry. Cornelius v. Giberson, 25 N. J. L. 1. See Byrne v. Lowry, 19 Ga. 27. Entering upon land at intervals, cutting down trees, deadening timber, and fencing in a cow-pen, nor even the renting of a small part of the lot, does not necessarily draw after it the possession of the whole lot, even if it can be said to be sufficient as to any part of it. Denham v. Holeman, 26 Ga. 182. That merely cutting wood is not enough, see Keller v. Dillon, 26 Ga. 701; Long v. Young, 28 id. 130. The occasional cutting of wood and boiling sugar on the land has been held not sufficient. Washabaugh v. Entriken, 34 Pa. 74. But see Green v. Kellum, 23 id. 254, where such acts under color of title were held sufficient. To support a title by adverse possession, it suffices that

conveyance itself, and entry under it, is sufficient evidence of the adverse character of the entry and possession; and if the deed is recorded, it is also evidence of the extent of the claim and of its notoriety; but, except in the case of gores and other vacant lands, it affords no evidence of possession, actual or constructive, upon which a title can be predicated by the lapse of the statutory period.[66] The constructive possession which is extended over

visible and notorious acts of ownership are exercised over the premises for the time limited by the statute, and the kind of acts required depends upon the nature and situation of the premises; less evidence will be required when the entry was under a claim of right than when it is a mere intrusion. Draper v. Shoot, 25 Mo. 197. The possession of a vendee after the purchase-money is due is adverse, and if he holds possession for the requisite period, claiming under the purchase, as evidenced by the bond, it is adverse. Ray v. Goodman, 33 Tenn. (1 Sneed) 586. (Totten, J., dissented.)

66. In Taylor v. Public Hall Co., 35 Conn. 430, the court held that a deed, although it conveyed no title, characterized the possession, and rendered it adverse against all the world from its date. An entry upon land under a deed, and possession by leasing parts of it, and occasionally cutting wood upon it during the period required by the statute, although for a few years no acts of ownership were exercised, is a sufficient possession to constitute title. Menkens v. Ovenhouse, 22 Mo. 70. See Beaupland v. McKean, 28 Pa. 124; Watts v. Griswold, 20 Ga. 732. Where two parties are in joint possession of land, mutually conceding each other's title to respective moieties, limitation cannot run in favor of the one having legal title to the whole. McCammon v. Petit, 35 Tenn. (3 Sneed) 242. One who enters as tenant for life does not hold adversely to the remainderman. Turman v. White, 53 Ky. (14 B. Mon.) 560. Where one is in possession, claiming an adverse title, with only the naked possession to evidence his claim, his title is limited to that portion over which he exercises palpable and continuous ownership. Bell v. Longworth, 6 Ind. 273. It is against the policy of the statutes of fraud and limitations to allow a mere intruder, without color or claim of title, to acquire rights on easier terms than those who hold under adverse possession. Ball v. Cox, 7 Ind. 453. Possession, to be adverse, must be clearly proved, and must be with such circumstances as are capable in their nature of notifying mankind that the party is on the land, claiming it as his own, openly and exclusively. McClellan v. Kellogg, 17 Ill. 498. And a possession is not subordinate, but adverse, to the title of the true owner, wherever it is inconsistent with the idea of paramount title in another. Morrison v. Hays, 19 Ga. 294. Where a tenant in possession dies, adverse possession cannot commence to run against his title

lands covered by his deed, as an incident to actual possession of a part of the land, cannot be extended to lands adjoining which are not embraced within the conveyance;[67] but if adjoining owners recognize a particular line as the true line between their lands, when in fact it is not, such acquiescence for the requisite period is binding upon them, if either had a continued, although only a constructive possession of his lot, as such mutual recognition of the line operates as a sufficient color of title.[68] In order to defeat the right of the public in the use of lands which have been dedicated for public use as a common or highway, the lands must not only be enclosed, but also must be used adversely to the public for the full statutory period.[69]

until the appointment of his administrator. Miller v. Surls, 19 Ga. 331. The acts of going yearly, for a few weeks at a time, to get rails and other timber from land, though only valuable for timber, do not amount to such an exercise of ownership as will ripen a defective title, or give an action of *quare clausum fregit*. Bartlett v. Simmons, 49 N. C. (4 Jones L.) 295. Nor is an entry for survey. Dillon v. Mattox, 21 Ga. 113. To constitute an adverse possession, there need not be an exclusive claim to the entire title, nor one necessarily excluding the idea of title in another person. Wicklow v. Lane, 37 Barb. (N. Y.) 244. In Maryland, before the present statute was adopted, actual inclosure for twenty years was essential to the possession of a *tortfeasor* to divest the title of the true owner. The act of 1852 provided that "actual inclosure shall not be necessary to prove possession, but acts of user and ownership other than inclosure may be given in evidence to prove possession." It was held that this last, without having a retroactive operation, could have a constitutional effect as a change of remedy. Thistle v. Frostburg Coal Co., 10 Md. 129. The entry of a person not having a perfected title, and collecting rent, will not operate as an interruption of the occupant's possession. Donahue v. O'Connor, 45 N. Y. Superior Ct. 278.

67. Shedd v. Powers, 28 Vt. 652; Grimes v. Ragland, 28 Ga. 123.

68. Clark v. Tabor, 28 Vt. 222; Brown v. Cockerell, 33 Ala. 38.

69. Covington v. McNickle, 57 Ky. (18 B. Mon.) 262. The character of the user must be such as does not comport with the public easement. Hatch v. Vt. Central R. R. Co., 28 Vt. 142. In such a case there must be proof of acts of ownership done with an intent to assert title thereto. Simmons v. Nahant, 85 Mass. (3 Allen) 316. See Lane v. Kennedy, 13 Ohio St. 42. The use, by the owner of the adjoining estate, of the land between his own and the traveled part of the way, by removing a wall and bank and building another, planting trees, cutting brushwood, digging

§ 268. How adverse possession may be proved.

In determining the question of adverse possession, the jury may take into consideration the nature and situation of the land. And the placing of deeds on record, passing over the tract, employment of agents living in the neighborhood to look after it and prevent trespassers upon it, payment of taxes continuously under claim of title, and the like, may be considered by them; and it is not always necessary to prove actual occupation by the claimant; but the acts referred to would not be sufficient of themselves to establish title by reason of adverse possession, unless the land was unsusceptible of more definite and actual possession, or such acts were known to the party holding the legal title, and known to have been done under claim of adverse title.[70] Where the defendants held under a deed executed less than twenty years before the commencement of an action to recover possession of the land, it was held that evidence to show that more than twenty years before the action was commenced they entered into possession under an executory contract for the purchase of the premises, which sale was afterwards consummated by deed, was admissible for the purpose of establishing an adverse possession.[71] A person may acquire title by adverse user, by the occupancy of a tenant, or any person who occupies for him and in recognition of his title.[72]

the soil, and placing wood and wagons upon it, is not an adverse possession, such as to found an action of trespass *quare clausum* against an intruder. Smith v. Slocumb, 77 Mass. (11 Gray) 280.

70. Turner v. Hall, 60 Mo. 271; Clement v. Perry, 34 Iowa 564; Washburn v. Cutter, 17 Minn. 361. Proof of a general inclosure of a large tract of land is not sufficient to constitute an actual, exclusive possession of a specific parcel within it, when it appears that much of the land within the inclosure is not claimed, and much of it is in the actual occupancy of parties claiming and holding adversely. Walsh v. Hill, 41 Cal. 571. Nor is the mere fact that a person built a fence around lands evidence of any possession or occupation, but the motive and claim under which he acted should be shown. Russell v. Davis, 38 Conn. 562.

71. Howland v. Newark Cemetery Ass'n, 66 Barb. (N. Y.) 366. See Soule v. Barlow, 48 Vt. 132.

72. Price v. Jackson, 91 N. C. 11. In North Carolina possession of part

§ 269. Continuity of possession.

The possession must be continuous during the entire statutory period, and uninterrupted, and the question as to whether or not it has been kept up will depend largely upon the situation and character of the land, and is a mixed question of law and fact. "If there be one element more distinctly material than another in conferring title, where all are so, it is the existence of a continuous adverse possession for the statutory period;" and if this continuity is broken, no title can be gained under the statute.[73] So absolute is this rule,

of the land described in a deed is superior to that of any person who has not superior title. Staton v. Mullis, 92 N. C. 623. In Garrett v. Ramsey, 26 W. Va. 345, where an elder grantee is in the actual possession of part of his land outside of an interlock and the junior grantee is in the actual possession of a part of the interlock claiming the whole to the extent of his boundaries, the latter will not be limited in his possession by the possession of the former, but will not be regarded as in possession of all the land in the interlock; but where the deed does not contain definite boundaries, no title of adverse user can be acquired, where the statute makes the occupancy requisite to obtain title dependent upon an occupancy under "known and visible boundaries." Elliott v. Dycke, 78 Ala. 150; Groft v. Weakland, 34 Pa. 304.

73. Unbroken continuity of possession is an essential element of an adverse holding, such as will ripen into a title under the statute, except when it is interrupted by mere intruders, who are ejected by a prompt resort to legal remedies. Beard v. Ryan, 78 Ala. 37. If the property is of a character to admit of permanent useful improvement, the possession should be kept up during the statutory period by actual residence, or by continued cultivation or inclosure, Johnston v. Irwin, 3 S. & R. (Pa.) 291; Royer v. Benlow, 10 id. 303; Jackson v. Schoonmaker, 2 Johns. (N. Y.) 230; either of which will do. Hoey v. Furman 1 Pa. 295. Occasional occupancy with payment of taxes will not answer. Sorber v. Willing, 10 Watts (Pa.) 141; Ridd v. City of Philadelphia, 11 Phila. Leg. Int. 84. But if the land is not such as to admit of residence or improvement, such use and occupation of it as from its nature it is susceptible of, with claim of ownership, is an actual possession. West v. Lanier, 28 Tenn. (9 Humph.) 762. But intention will not be. "He must keep his flag flying." Stephens v. Leach, 19 Pa. 265. The effect given to claim under color of title is, perhaps, not the same in all the States. See Hill v. Saunders, 6 Rich. (S. C.) 62; 2 Smith's Lead. Cas. H. & W.'s notes, 563. Possession must be continuous and adverse, to give title under the statute. Holcombe v. Austell, 19 Ga. 604; Harrison v. Cachelin, 23 Mo. 117; Sharp v. Johnson, 22 Ark. 79; Trapnall v. Burton, 24 Ark. 371;

that even a military order which directs all persons of a certain nationality to leave the State within a certain time will not save the benefits of a previous possession to one who falls within the terms of the order, during the period of such enforced absence, although the *animus revertendi* remains, as the courts can make no saving which the statute has omitted.[74] The mere erection of a fence around a lot, which it not kept up, is not sufficient to preserve the continuity of possession required. So where one entered on land, and cut logs, split boards, and otherwise prepared for building a house on the land, but returned to his home, which was in another county, and at the end of the succeeding year came back and finished the house, and put his family in it, no other person having had possession during said interval, it was held that the statute of limitations did not run in his favor during such absence.[75] So where a person enters upon land, splits a few hundred rails, encloses and ploughs an acre and a half, then abandons the premises for three years, but at the end of that time returns and occupies the same continuously for four years, he cannot be considered as having maintained such a continuous adverse possession for seven years as is necessary to perfect a title under the statute of limitations.[76] Where a person goes into adverse possession, but subsequently, before the statute has run

Smith v. Chapin, 31 Conn. 530; Denham v. Holeman, 26 Ga. 182; Stump v. Henry, 6 Md. 201; Wheeler v. Moody, 9 Tex. 372; Story v. Saunders, 27 Tenn. (8 Humph.) 663; Miller v. Platt, 5 Duer (N. Y.) 272.

74. Halliday v. Cromwell, 37 Tex. 437. Where evidence was offered that a fence consisting of small posts with two rails fastened on them was placed round a lot of land by the plaintiff, but there was no evidence of his actual occupation or use of the land, and it appeared that the fence was suffered to go to decay in a year or two, and to become insufficient to keep out cattle, it was held that that was not sufficient to constitute *prima facie* evidence of title to land by adverse possession at common law, or under the provisions of the California statute of limitations, or under the Van Ness ordinance, as against a party who entered into possession and occupation of a part of the land after the fence had been suffered to become broken down and decayed. Borel v. Rollins, 30 Cal. 408.

75. Bryne v. Lowry, 19 Ga. 27.

76. Joiner v. Borders, 32 Ga. 239. See Virgin v. Land, 32 Ga. 572.

in his favor, under threats from the owner that he would commence legal proceedings against him, he is induced to surrender possession, such surrender breaks the continuity of his possession, and should he go into possession again, the owner having entered in the meantime, the time of his previous possession would go for nothing.[77] A mere removal from the land, without any intention of abandonding the possession, or the claim to the land, is not necessarily a waiver of a previous adverse possession.[78] The question whether there has been such an abandonment of possession as to break the continuity thereof depends upon the question whether the premises were vacant for such a length of time and under such circumstances that the constructive possession of the owner can be said to have reasserted itself; and where the defendant's grantor vacated the premises a short time before the latter took possession, and it did not appear that during such time he exercised any control or ownership over the land, it was held that

77. Shaffer v. Lowry, 25 Pa. 252; Pederick v. Searle, 5 S. & R. (Pa.) 236. Every element of a title by adverse possession must exist; otherwise the possession will not confer title, under the statute of limitations. If there be one element more distinctly material than another in conferring title, where all are so, it is the existence of a continuous adverse possession for the requisite statutory period. Groft v. Weakland, 34 Pa. 304. Where the owner of a house put lumber and other materials on an adjoining lot while building his house; erected steps on the lot for access to his house; used it in going in and out of his house, and for drying clothes; held, not a sufficient possession to give title under the statute of limitations. Brolaskey v. McClain, 61 Pa. 146.

78. Harper v. Tapley, 35 Miss. 506; see Ford v. Wilson, id. 490. A short and reasonable time between the outgoing and incoming of persons whose continuous possession in succession is necessary does not break the adverse possession, De la Vega v. Butler, 47 Tex. 529; nor does a temporary absence from the premises for a special purpose. Cunningham v. Patton, 6 Pa. 355; Sailor v. Hertzogg, 10 id. 296. But an abandonment of the premises, for however short a period, although with the *animus revertendi*, will destroy the continuity. Susquehanna, etc., R. Co. v. Quick, 68 Pa. 189. Where in an action to recover land, it appeared that the plaintiff, under color of title, had made occasional entries upon the land, at long intervals, for the purpose, at one time, of cutting timber, at another, of making bricks, etc., the plaintiff was held not entitled to recover. Williams v. Wallace, 78 N. C. 354.

the possession was not continuous, and that the defendant could not avail himself of the possession of his grantor.[79] It is settled that a possession which can ripen into a title must not only be notorious, but continued without entry or action by the legal owner for the full statutory period;[80] and, as indicated by the cases already cited, a person who enters upon premises and commits trespasses and then leaves, without keeping up the *indicia* of claim and ownership, does not destroy the effect of the constructive possession of the legal owner, but stands rather in the light of a trespasser than of an occupier under a claim of

79. Tegarden v. Carpenter, 36 Miss. 404.

The landowner is not required to battle continuously and successfully for his rights; in the case of an easement it is sufficient to interrupt its acquisition by adverse user that he assert his claim by an overt act affording a cause of action. Brayden v. New York, etc., R. Co., 172 Mass. 225. But previous possession cannot avail after it has been interrupted. Chicago & Alton R. Co. v. Keegan, 185 Ill. 70. In general, a slight variation in the user, or a brief interruption in the enjoyment of the easement to its full extent, as when the right to flow another's land is claimed, and the dam is heightened or strengthened from time to time, or the water is occasionally let off through the dam, does not break the continuity of use. Alcorn v. Sadler, 71 Miss. 634. See Chicago & Alton R. Co. v. Keegan, 185 Ill. 70; Dean v. Goddard, 55 Minn. 290; Elyton Land Co. v. Denny, 108 Ala. 553. But the occupation must be always substantially continuous, and such acts as the carrying on of lumbering operations, necessarily casual and intermittent, are insufficient to establish a disseisin, though supported by defective tax deeds of the land. Fleming v. Katahdin Pulp & Paper Co., 93 Me. 110; Barr v. Potter (Ky.), 57 S. W. 478. And a purchase of the property by the demandant at a tax sale is immaterial if the possession is not changed. Harrison v. Dolan, 172 Mass. 395. See 12 Harv. L. Rev. 569.

The period of time required to acquire an easement by adverse use is usually the same as that provided for gaining a title to the land itself by adverse possession. Alcorn v. Sadler, 71 Miss. 634; Hodgkins v. Farrington, 150 Mass. 535, 547; Cole v. Bradbury, 86 Me. 380; Jones on Easements, ch. 7.

80. Hood v. Hood, 2 Grant's Cas. (Pa.) 229; Andrews v. Mulford, 1 Hawy. (N. C.) 320; Park v. Cochran, 1 id. 180; Wickliffe v. Ensor, 48 Ky. (9 B. Mon.) 253; Taylor v. Burnside, 1 Gratt. (Va.) 165; Merriam v. Hays, 19 Ga. 294; Melvin v. Proprietors, etc., 46 Mass. (5 Met.) 15; Christy v. Alford, 58 U. S. (17 How.) 601, 15 L. Ed. 256; Moore v. Collinshaw, 10 Pa. 224.

title.[81] The possession must also continue as to the same premises;[82] in other words, the locality of the possession must remain the same throughout the entire period.[83] But when the statute has once run in favor of the occupant, the title acquired is indefeasible, and is not affected by a subsequent neglect to keep up possession, and neither the legal owner nor a purchaser from him without notice of such adverse title acquire any rights, legal or equitable, from such neglect.[84] The benefits of a constructive possession may be lost, where a person, before the statute has run in his favor, sells the part of the land which he actually occupied, and retains the balance. In that case, his possession of the part sold goes for nothing, as to the part occupied, and the grantee does not succeed to it.[85]

§ 270. How the continuity of the possession may be broken.

The continuity of possession may be broken by an entry of the legal owner, by an abandonment of the possession by the occupant, by a subsequent recognition of the owner's title, or an acknowledgment made before the statute has run in his favor that he has and claims no title to the lands occupied.

First, an entry by the legal owner upon the land breaks the continuity of an adverse possession, when it is made openly with the intention of asserting his claim thereto, and is accompanied with acts upon the land which characterize the assertion of title

81. Bryne v. Lowry, *supra;* Borel v. Rollins, *supra.*

82. Potts v. Gilbert, 3 Wash. (U. S.) 475.

83. Griffith v. Schwenderman, 27 Mo. 412.

84. Schall v. Williams Valley R. Co., 35 Pa. 191. In Georgia it has been held that if, after having held possession for the statutory period, the occupant voluntarily abandons the possession of the premises, the presumption arises that his holding was not adverse. Vickery v. Benson, 26 Ga. 582; Russell v. Slaton, 26 id. 193.

85. Chandler v. Rushing, 38 Tex. 591. If a person has written evidence of title and the premises are occupied by a tenant, and he subsequently sells an undivided half of the land to the tenant, who remains in possession of his half as owner, and of the other half as tenant, the tenant's possession is the possession of the landlord, and preserves his possession. Hanks v. Phillips, 39 Ga. 550.

or ownership;[86] and a mere naked entry, which is made for the purpose of ascertaining whether or not there is any adverse occupancy, is not sufficient to break or interrupt the possession.[87] The entry must be made openly, with the purpose of asserting his claim thereto, and must be accompanied by acts of ownership which characterize and effectuate the claim; and an entry upon land and cutting wood or timber therefrom, or to plough, to sow, or to reap or to gather the crops thereon, would be such acts.[88] Of

86. Henderson v. Griffin, 30 U. S. (5 Pet.) 151, 8 L. Ed. 79. But the entry must be made by the owner. The interruption of mere trespassers, if unknown, will not affect the possession; but if known, and repeated, without legal proceedings being instituted, it is said they become *legitimae interruptiones*, and are converted into adverse assertions of right, which, if not promptly and effectually litigated, defeat the claim of rightful prescription. Doe v. Eslava, 11 Ala. 1028; Henderson v. Griffin, *supra*. The mere intrusion of trespassers, not continuing long enough to raise a presumption that it was known to the one in possession, does not break the continuity of his possession. Bell v. Dinson, 56 Ala. 444. Nor is it broken by negotiating with other claimants, if there is no waiver or nonclaim on the occupant's part. 40 Mich. 595. Nor by a forcible entry of the legal owner when the restitution is made by law, and the period during which the owner held possession will not be deducted from the occupant's possession. Ferguson v. Bartholomew, 67 Mo. 212. But where the legal owner interrupts possession, and the occupant does not regain possession by legal proceedings, his possession must begin *de novo*. Steeple v. Downing, 60 Md. 478. Where a person purchases land, and the grantor's title failing, he sues for and recovers back the money paid therefor, he cannot set up the possession held by him under such conveyance to defeat the title of the true owner. Davenport v. Sebring, 52 Iowa 364; Piper v. Sloneker, 2 Grant's Cas. (Pa.) 113.

87. Bowen v. Guild, 130 Mass. 121.

88. Thus, where an owner of land which was in the adverse occupancy of another went thereon with a purchaser to show him the land and to ascertain the quantity, quality, and value of the wood thereon, accompanied by the subsequent execution of deed to the person so entering with him, was held a sufficient entry to break the continuity of the adverse occupant's possession, Brickett v. Spofford, 80 Mass. (14 Gray) 514; and where an entry was made upon land by the owner, and a deed of the premises was there by him delivered to a purchaser, it was held that the disseisin was so far purged by the entry as to give operation to the deed, although the grantee knew that the land was claimed adversely. Oakes v. Marcy, 27 Mass. (10 Pick.) 195; Knox v. Jenks, 7 Mass. 488; Warner v. Bull, 54 Mass. (13 Met.) 1. The rule relative to entries under these stat-

course, the bringing of an action of ejectment and a recovery therein, accompanied by an entry, breaks the continuity of possession.[89] An entry made by the legal owner, with "high hand" and forcibly, does not defeat the continuity of the possession of an adverse occupant, if he subsequently regains possession by an action for forcible entry and detainer.[90] In some of the States, by statute, no entry is sufficient to toll the statute, unless it is followed by an action within one year from the time it was made;[91] and in Texas "peaceable possession" is defined to be that which is continuous, and not interrupted by action.[92] In Massachusetts and Michigan,[93] an entry must be followed by possession for one year, or by an action brought within one year from the time entry was made. In Kentucky,[94] Virginia,[95] and West

utes is thus stated: "When a party is once dispossessed, it is not every entry upon the premises without permission that would disturb the adverse possession. He may tread upon his own soil, and still be as much out of the possession of it there as elsewhere. He must assert his claim to the land, perform some act which would reinstate him in possession, before he can regain what he has lost. It is evident, therefore, that an entry by stealth, under circumstances that go to show that the party claimed no right to enter, or any entry for other purposes than those connected with a right to enter, would not be sufficient to break the continuity of exclusive possession in another." Burrows v. Gallup, 32 Conn. 493. An entry upon land in the possession of another, in order to work a legal interruption of such possession, must be so made as to enable the party in possession, by the use of reasonable diligence, to ascertain the right and claim of the party making the entry. Wing v. Hall, 47 Vt. 182. A claim based on adverse constructive possession under a tax-deed for the three years limited by the statute, may be avoided by the owner by proof of actual use and occupation for any portion of the statutory period. Such occupation may be established by proof of his rental of the land to neighboring farmers. Wilson v. Henry, 35 Wis. 241.

89. Groft v. Weakland, 34 Pa. 304. The statute is not suspended by an unsuccessful action of ejectment not leading to a change of possession. Workman v. Guthrie, 29 Pa. 495; Kennedy v. Reynolds, 27 Ala. 364.

90. Cary v. Edmunds, 71 Mo. 523.

91. Appendix, New York, § 367; North Carolina, § 144; South Carolina, § 103; Pennsylvania, § 16; Wisconsin, § 4209; Missouri, § 6765; California, § 320; Nevada, § 6; Idaho, § 4038; Montana, § 31; Arizona, § 5; Dakota, § 43.

92. Appendix, Texas.

93. Appendix, Massachusetts, § 8; Michigan, § 8.

94. Appendix, Kentucky.

95. Appendix, Virginia.

Virginia,[96] no continual claim upon or near real property preserves the right to bring an action therefor. After a party has been evicted under a recovery in ejectment, the continuity of his possession is destroyed, and he cannot keep it up by the payment of taxes on the land, or the assertion of any other claim thereto.[97] Instances may arise where the facts are not controverted, where the question as to whether the possession has been interrupted by entry is properly a question of law for the court, but generally it is a question for the jury in view of all the circumstances.[98]

Second, the continuity of possession may also be broken by an acknowledgment by the occupant of the owner's title, before the statute has run in his favor, but not after it has run.[99] In Georgia it has been held that such an acknowledgment made by a tenant in possession, either before or after the statutory period has elapsed, prevents the running of the statute against the owner of the fee.[1] The ground upon which these cases proceed is, that such an admission rebuts the allegation of adverse possession; but where the possession is shown to have been adverse in fact, and the bar to have become complete before an acknowledgment of title in the legal owner is made, it can have no such effect, especially if it is by parol. A parol acknowledgment of title made while the statute is running must be such as to show that the occupant no longer intends to hold adversely,[2] and must refer to the title set up by the occupant.[3] Thus, where the statutory

96. Appendix, West Virginia.

97. Groft v. Weakland, 34 Pa. 304.

98. Stevens v. Taft, 77 Mass. (11 Gray) 33; O'Hara v. Richardson, 46 Pa. 385; Groft v. Weakland, 34 id. 304; Jackson v. Joy, 9 Johns. (N. Y.) 102; Beverly v. Burke, 9 Ga. 440; Van Gorden v. Jackson, 5 Johns. (N. Y.) 440; Jackson *ex dem.* People v. Wood, 12 Johns. (N. Y.) 242, 7 Am. Dec. 315; Fisher v. Prosser, Cowp. 217; Mayor of Hull v. Horner, id. 102; Peaceable v. Reed, 1 East 568.

99. Bradford v. Guthrie, 4 Brewst. (Pa.) 351; London v. Lyman, 1 Phila. (Pa.) 465. In Bell v. Hartley, 4 W. & S. (Pa.) 32, an acknowledgment made twenty-one years before ejectment was brought was held not admissible.

1. Long v. Young, 28 Ga. 130; Cook v. Long, 27 id. 280.

2. Sailor v. Hertzog, 4 Whart. (Pa.) 259; Ingersoll v. Lewis, 11 Pa. 212; Moore v. Collinshaw, 10 id. 224. See Ley v. Peter, 3 H. & N. 101.

3. Farmers' & Mechanics' Bank v. Wilson, 10 Watts (Pa.) 261.

bar was sought to be rebutted by proof of a lease executed by the occupier and the claimant, it was held that it might be shown that the latter held the legal title as trustee for the former, in order to explain the apparent admission of title.[4] An admission or declaration of a person that he went into possession by permission of the owner, or in the exercise of a legal right, and that the owner leased or devised it to him during life, negatives any adverse possession.[5] So where a person admits that he holds for the true owner,[6] or agrees even by parol to surrender the possession to the legal owner,[7] or to hold possession for or under him,[8] the continuity of possession is broken. So if the tenant of a mere intruder, without color of title, takes a conveyance from the legal owner, and gives a mortgage for the purchase-money, it has been held that this breaks the continuity of the possession, at least as against the holder of the mortgage.[9] So if a person in possession of lands adversely under a warrant procures it to be assessed to him in less quantity than is called for in the survey, it is held that the continuity of his possession is thereby broken by detaching from it the landmarks which had sustained it.[10] So the occupier must continue his possession for the whole period on the same claim; and if before the statute has run he sets up another and different claim, the continuity of his possession is broken, and must begin *de novo*. And where a party is in the adverse occupancy of land under a statute which gave possession in seven years, where the taxes, etc., are paid by him, he must fully comply with the statutory requirement; and if he permits the land to be sold for taxes during the running of the statute, and afterwards redeems the land under such sale, his possession can only date from the time of redemption.[11] The continuity of possession is broken by a decree directing the occupant to convey

4. Neele v. McElhenny, 69 Pa. 300.

5. Breidegam v. Hoffmaster, 61 Pa. 223.

6. Criswell v. Altemus, 7 Watts Pa. 565.

7. Moore v. Small, 9 Pa. 194.

8. Read v. Thompson, 5 Pa. 327.

9. Koons v. Steele, 19 Pa. 203.

10. Clarke v. Dougan, 12 Pa. 87.

11. Wettig v. Bowman, 47 Ill. 17; Austin v. Bailey, 37 Vt. 219.

the land, although the possession is not disturbed, as the decree has the effect of a voluntary conveyance.[12]

Third, the continuity of possession may be broken by a recognition of the owner's title during the period that the statute was running.[13] And this may arise in a variety of ways, as by taking a lease from him of the land, or offering to hold the land under him;[14] offering to purchase or surrender it;[15] or asserting that he gave him the use of the land for a term or for life; or in any way which admits the superiority of the owner's title, and that the occupant holds under, for, or in subservience to him; [16] or when he, in fact, holds under a title which does not give him the fee, although he supposes that it does, and disposes of the estate under that misapprehension.[17] Thus, where a widow remains in possession of her husband's lands after his decease, her possession is not adverse to the heirs,[18] even though she buys in an outstanding title; [19] nor is the possession of the husband adverse to the wife during her lifetime;[20] nor of an agent to his principal,[21]— because in all these cases the occupant holds in recognition of a superior title, and in subservience to it. When a person enters by the permission of the owner, or is let in by operation of law in subservience to the title of another, his occupation cannot become adverse without the clearest evidence of a repudiation by him of the owner's title, and of a claim to hold in hostility to it.[22] When a person has entered by the permission of another, and thus be-

12. Gower v. Quinlan, 40 Mich. 572.

13. Koons v. Steele, 19 Pa. 203.

14. Read v. Thompson, 5 Pa. 327. And in this case it was held that this may be shown by admission to strangers.

15. Moore v. Small, 9 Pa. 194.

16. Criswell v. Altemus, 7 Watts (Pa.) 565; Dikeman v. Parrish, 6 id. 210.

17. Tullock v. Worrall, 49 Pa. 133.

18. Cook v. Nicholas, 2 W. & S. (Pa.) 27; Hall v. Mathias, 4 id. 331.

19. Idding v. Cairns, 2 Grant's Cas. (Pa.) 88.

20. Kille v. Ege, 79 Pa. 15.

21. Comegys v. Carley, 3 Watts (Pa.) 280.

22. Cadwallader v. App, 81 Pa. 194; McGinnis v. Porter, 20 id. 86. And a tenant who holds over does not hold adversely until he in some manner gives the landlord notice of such an intention. Schuylkill, etc., R. Co. v. McCreary, 58 Pa. 304.

comes a tenant of such person, either by sufferance or at will, even though without rent, every presumption is in favor of a continued holding in that capacity, and he cannot set up an adverse claim until he has in some manner brought the knowledge of his intention home to the person under whom he entered;[23] and a relaxation of this rule cannot consistently be made.[24]

§ 271. Tacking possession.

The successive possession of several distinct occupants of land, between whom no privity exists, cannot be united to make up the period required to perfect title by possession.[25] But if a successive

23. McGinnis v. Porter, *supra;* McMasters v. Bell, 2 P. & W. (Pa.) 181; Hood v. Hood, 2 Grant's Cas. (Pa.) 229; Martin v. Jackson, 27 Pa. 504. And even if rent was agreed to be paid, but is not for many years, that circumstance does not defeat the owner's right of entry. Buller's N. P. 104; Saunders v. Annesly, 2 Sch. & Lef. 106; Orrel v. Maddox, Runnington on Eject., Appendix, 1; Doe v. Danvers, 7 East 299. See Jackson v. Davis, 5 Cow. (N. Y.) 123. The right of a tenant to set up the statute to defeat the title of his landlord does not depend upon the landlord's right to receive rent, but upon his right to enter. Failing v. Schenck, 3 Hill (N. Y.) 344. See Williams v. Annapolis, 6 H. & J. (Md.) 529. In Moore v. Turpin, 1 Speers (S. C.) 32, it was held that, after a great lapse of time, and an omission to pay rent, it might be presumed that the relation of landlord and tenant existed.

24. Collins v. Johnson, 57 Ala. 304.

25. Pegues v. Warley, 14 S. C. 180; Rutherford v. Hobbs, 63 Ga. 243; Schrack v. Zubler, 34 Pa. 38. But in South Carolina the right to tack successive possessions is confined to cases between landlord and tenant, and disseisors and their heirs. King v. Smith, Rice (S. C.) 11. In Potts v. Gilbert, 3 Wash. (U. S.) 475, it was held that there could be no tacking of possession to make out title by adverse use, because, as he insisted, such a possessor has nothing to convey. But this case has never been recognized as embodying the true doctrine. Moore v. Small, 9 Pa. 194. See Overfield v. Christie, 7 S. & R. (Pa.) 177; Durel v. Tennison, 31 La. Ann. 538. If the continuity be broken, either by fraud or a wrongful entry, the protection given by the statute is lost; and a party cannot add to his own possession that of the one who preceded him, when he did not enter into possession under or through such predecessor. San Francisco v. Fulde, 37 Cal. 349. There must be privity of grant or descent, or some judicial or other proceedings which shall connect the possessions so that the latter shall apparently hold by right of the former; but not even a writing is necessary if it appears that the holding is continuous and under the

privity exists between them, the last occupant may avail himself of the occupancy of his predecessors.[26] Thus, where one of two joint tenants, after the death of the other, purchased the land at partition sale under an order of court, and paid the amount of his bid, but took no deed, it was held [27] that his possession thereafter might be added to the time of the joint possession of him and his co-tenant to make up an adverse possession of the necessary length to bar an entry.[28] But even an innocent purchaser cannot tack to his own

first entry; and this doctrine applies not only to actual but constructive possession under color of title. Crispen v. Hannavan, 50 Mo. 536.

26. In such case the occupant has merely to prove that the possession has been legally continued from one holder to another, as the term of enjoyment is deemed uninterrupted from ancestor to heirs, and from vendor to vendee. Cole v. Bradbury, 86 Me. 380, 383; Leonard v. Leonard, 89 Mass. (7 Allen) 280; Kepley v. Scully, 185 Ill. 52; Smith v. Reich, 30 N. Y. S. 167; Sutton v. Clark (S. C.), 38 S. E. 150; Davock v. Nealon, 58 N. J. L. 21; Reid v. Anderson, 13 App. D. C. 30; Costello v. Harris, 162 Pa. 397; Hickman v. Link, 97 Mo. 482; Adair v. Mette, 156 Mo. 496; Robinson v. Allison (Ala.), 27 So. 461; Collier v. Couts, 92 Tex. 234, 14 Harv. L. Rev. 72. So when a disseisor leases the land to a tenant who continues to occupy it under his lease, the tenant's adverse possession may be tacked to the landlord's, his possession being that of the landlord. Holmes v. Turner's Falls Co., 150 Mass. 535, 547.

27. Congdon v. Morgan, 14 S. C. 587. A party cannot connect his possession of the land previous to obtaining a deed with his subsequent possession under a deed, to make out the seven years. Barnes v. Vickers, 59 Tenn. 370. A son's possession of land after the death of his father may be presumed to be for the benefit of the father's estate. Alexander v. Stewart, 50 Vt. 87. From an adverse possession of land for thirty years, the law presumes a grant from the State, without a privity or connection among the successive tenants. Davis v. McArthur, 78 N. C. 357. Actual possession by prior occupants claiming title, although having no color of title, will avail a subsequent occupant under color of title, claiming under such prior occupants, in making out a possessory title in himself. Day v. Wilder, 47 Vt. 584. See Shuffleton v. Nelson, 2 Sawyer (U. S.) 540.

28. In Durel v. Tennison, 31 La. An. 538, it was held that a claimant might tack to his own possession that of his grantor to make out prescription. In Texas, if the possession of two or more parties in succession, holding in privity with each other, under title or color of title, make out the prescribed term, the bar is complete. Christy v. Alford, 58 U. S. (17 How.) 601, 15 L. Ed. 256. So, also, in Tennessee. Lea v. Polk County Copper Co., 62 U. S. (21 How.) 494, 16 L. Ed. 203; Doswell v. De la Lanza, 61 U. S. (20 How.) 29, 15 L.

possession that of his grantor, which originated in fraud of the true owner,[29] nor the possession of a person which was not adverse. In order to create the privity requisite to enable a subsequent occupant to tack to his possession that of a prior occupant, it is not necessary that there should be a conveyance in writing. It is sufficient if it is shown that the prior occupant transferred his possession to him, even though by parol.[30] So, too, the posses-

Ed. 824; Benson v. Stewart, 30 Miss. 49; Morrison v. Hays, 19 Ga. 294; Chouquette v. Barada, 23 Mo. 331; Shaw v. Nicholay, 30 Mo. 99; Chadbourne v. Swan, 40 Me. 260. A wife has no such privity of estate with her husband, in land of which he died in an adverse possession to the real owner, that her continued adverse possession after his decease can be tacked to his, to give her a complete title by disseisin. Sawyer v. Kendall, 64 Mass. (10 Cush.) 241. See Holton v. Whitney, 30 Vt. 405. One who purchases at an administrator's sale land which the decedent occupied, used, and cultivated claiming it as his own, but without color of title, or deed on record, may, in pleading the ten years' limitation, tack said decedent's possession to his own. Cochrane v. Faris, 18 Tex. 850. So a purchaser even by parol contract may tack his possession to that of his vendor. Cunningham v. Potter, 6 Pa. 355; Caston v. Caston, 2 Rich. (S. C.) Eq. 1; Doe v. Eslava, 11 Ala. 1028. See Dikeman v. Parrish, 6 Pa. 210; Adams v. Tiernan, 5 Dana (Ky.) 394; Chilton v. Wilson, 28 Tenn (9 Humph.) 399; Overfield v. Christie, 7 S. & R. (Pa.) 173; Valentine v. Cooley, 19 Tenn. (Meigs) 613. A purchaser under an execution sale may tack the possession of the judgment debtor to his own. Schutz v. Fitzwalter, 5 Pa. 126. But see Bullen v. Arnold, 31 Me. 583, where it was held that the title must pass by contract in order that the possession may be tacked. But in Moffitt v. McDonald, 30 Tenn. (11 Humph.) 457, it was held that the possession of an administrator might be tacked to that of his intestate. And in Cleveland Ins. Co. v. Reed, 65 U. S. (24 How.) 284, 16 L. Ed. 686, it was held that the title of the assignee in bankruptcy may be tacked to that of his grantee. See also, Fanning v. Willcox, 3 Day (Conn.) 258, and Smith v. Chapin, 31 Conn. 530, holding that no privity of estate between successive occupants need be shown, but that a continuous and uninterrupted possession for the requisite period, whether by one or more persons, is sufficient where such was the understanding of the parties.

29. Farrow v. Bullock, 63 Ga. 360.

30. Weber v. Anderson, 73 Ill. 439. In Smith v. Chapin, 31 Conn. 530, evidence that certain land which the plaintiff's grantor held adversely was omitted by mistake from the conveyance, was held admissible to show the relation of the possession taken to that relinquished, and to enable the defendant to tack his possession to that of his predecessor. It is sufficient if there is an adverse possession continued uninterruptedly for

sion of a prior occupant may be passed by operation of law, as of an execution debtor to a purchaser of the land on execution sale,[31] and of an intestate to that of an administrator,[32] and of an assignee in bankruptcy to that of a purchaser from him,[33] and of a tenant under the ancestor to that of the heirs,[34] and in all cases where the interest of the occupant passes by contract or by operation of law.[35] But such possession of a previous occupant cannot be tacked to that of a subsequent one, where there is no privity. Thus, it is held that the possession of the husband cannot be tacked to that of the widow,[36] unless the husband claimed the land

fifteen years, whether by one or more persons. Ibid.; Fanning v. Willcox, 3 Day (Conn.) 258. See Jackson v. Moore, 13 Johns. (N. Y.) 513; Cunningham v. Patton, 6 Pa. 355; Valentine v. Cooley, *supra.* The privity requisite to be established may be by will, Haynes v. Boardman, 119 Mass. 414; or by descent, Currier v. Gale, 91 Mass. (9 Allen) 522; or it may be continued by an administrator. Peele v. Cheever, 90 Mass. (8 Allen) 89. Where the holder of color of title held possession and paid taxes on the land for four years, and then gave a contract to sell the land to another, who went into possession and paid taxes for five years more, the payment of the last five years' taxes was held a payment under the title of the holder of the color of title, inuring to establish the bar. Kruse v. Wilson, 79 Ill. 233.

31. Schutz v. Fitzwalter, *supra.* In order that the possession of successive occupants may be so continuously adverse as to inure to the benefit of the last occupant, there must be a privity between them, either by contract or by operation of law. Shaw v. Nicholay, 30 Mo. 99.

32. Moffitt v. McDonald, *supra.*

33. Cleveland Ins. Co. v. Reed, *supra.*

34. Williams v. McAliley, Cheves (S. C.) 200. If a parent places a son in possession of land under a verbal gift, and the possession is held by the son adversely to the father and all other persons, the death of the father will not arrest the running of the statute. By the descent cast the heirs are placed exactly in the shoes of their ancestor; and the statute having commenced running against him in his lifetime, it continues to run without intermission against his heirs. Haynes v. Jones, 39 Tenn. (2 Head) 372.

35. Pederick v. Searle, *supra,* 2 S. & R. (Penn.) 240.

36. Sawyer v. Kendall, 64 Mass. (10 Cush.) 241.

In the recent case of Wishart v. McKnight, 178 Mass. 356, 59 N. E. 1028, the cited case of Sawyer v. Kendall is thus explained, and the rule made clear as to tacking: "Sawyer v. Kendall was a case where no continuity of possession had been made out by the tenant, and the decision was finally put upon that ground. * * * We are of opinion that that case is to be confined to the

to belong to his wife.[37] But in those States where the wife, by statute, is made an heir of her husband, the rule would be different, as in those cases she would hold in the double capacity of heir and widow. The possession of a son may be tacked to that of his father.[38] But in all cases the several occupancies must be so connected that they can be referred to the original entry, and the continuity of the possession must be unbroken; as, if there has been such a lapse in possession as to raise a presumption of abandonment, the constructive seisin of the owner of the legal title will apply and the possession must begin *de novo;* and whether there has been such a lapse or not is a question for the jury, in view of all the circumstances.[39] So, too, the successive occupants must claim through their predecessors;[40] and if they claim independently the continuity is broken, and each must stand upon his own possession.[41]

point actually decided, and cannot be held to be an authority for all the statements in the opinions in that case and in the cases cited. * * * Where possession has been actually and in each instance transferred by the one in possession to his successor, the owner of the record title is barred from maintaining an action to recover the land. In some cases this conclusion has been reached on the ground that in such a case there is the necessary privity, or, more properly, continuity of possession, between the successive trespassers, within the doctrine on which Sawyer v. Kendall was decided." See also Faloon v. Simshauser, 130 Ill. 649; Vandall v. St. Martin, 42 Minn. 163; Adkins v. Tomlinson, 121 Mo. 487; Coogler v. Rogers, 25 Fla. 853, 882; Rowland v. Williams, 23 Oregon, 515; Shuffleton v. Nelson, 2 Sawyer, 540. Other cases go further still. See Willis v. Howe, [1893] 2 Ch. 545, 553; Chapin v. Freeland, 142 Mass. 383, 387; Harrison v. Dolan, 172 Mass. 395, 397; McNeely v. Langan, 22 Ohio St. 32; Frost v. Courtis, 172 Mass. 401; 13 Harv. L. Rev. 52.

37. Holton v. Whitney, 30 Vt. 405. But the husband may tack the possession of his wife to his own. Steel v. Johnson, 86 Mass. (4 Allen) 425; Smith v. Garza, 15 Tex. 150. And the possession of a son-in-law may be tacked to that of his father-in-law, where he occupied for him. St. Louis v. Gorman, 29 Mo. 193.

38. King v. Smith, 1 Rice (S. C.) 10.

39. Hood v. Hood, 2 Grant's Cas. (Pa.) 229; Andrews v. Mulford, 1 Hayw. (N. C.) 320.

40. Johnston v. Nash, 15 Tex. 419.

41. Menkens v. Blumenthal, 27 Mo. 198; Taylor v. Burnside, 1 Gratt. (Va.) 165; Wickliffe v. Ensor, 48 Ky. (9 B. Mon.) 253; Doe v. Eslava, 11 Ala. 1028.

§ 272. Effect of bringing ejectment.

Although the adverse possession of a defendant in ejectment cannot, during the pendency of the suit, ripen into an absolute title under the operation of the statute of limitations, yet the effect of the statute is neutralized only in respect to the particular suit, and the plaintiff therein. And after the termination of that suit, the statutory limitation having meanwhile expired, no subsequent action can be brought, either at law or in equity, to question that title or possession;[42] and if the plaintiff fails therein, the period during which the action was pending is not deducted from the period requisite to gain a title by possession.

§ 272a(1). Recovery of real property in general—Lmitations applicable.

An action to establish a resulting trust in land, and compel the legal title to be transferred to the equitable owner, in which the petition does not allege that defendants are in possession of the property, or that plaintiff is entitled to possession thereof, is not an action for the recovery of real property within the meaning of the Kansas statute.[43] The Colorado statute providing seven years' limitation for actions to recover real property in possession by actual residence, is a defense only where defendant has been an actual resident for seven years and having a connected title.[44] Iowa Code, § 4198, limiting the right to recover for the use and occupation of premises to five years prior to the commencement of an action to recover real property, has no application to a suit to quiet title.[45] Where defendant, on taking possession of the bed

42. Hopkins v. Calloway, 47 Tenn. (7 Coldw.) 37.

43. Main v. Payne, 17 Kan. 608, under Civ. Code Kan. § 16 (Gen. St. 1868, p. 632), allowing 15 years in which to bring such actions.

44. Poage v. E. H. Rollins & Sons, 24 Colo. App. 537; 135 Pac. 990, under Mills' Ann. St. Rev. Supp. § 2923c.

Colo. Rev. St. 1908, § 4073, limiting the time within which to sue for fraud or in cases of trust, has no application to actions affecting realty only. Wells v. Brown, 23 Colo. App. 190, 128 Pac. 869.

45. German v. Heath, 139 Iowa, 52, 116 N. W. 1051. See also Empire Real Estate & Mortgage Co. v. Beechley, 137 Iowa 7, 114 N. W. 556.

of a non-navigable lake, had not held it adversely for seven years, riparian owners were not barred from suing for its recovery.[46] In Kentucky, under the direct provisions of the Constitution, § 251, claimants under a prior patent who have failed for fifteen years to bring their action against those in possession of lands claiming under a patent are barred.[47] In Missouri, where, in an action to quiet title to certain land, plaintiff had held the legal title for more than thirty years, but no one had ever been in possession of the land and had never paid any taxes thereon for more than thirty years, plaintiff's action was not barred by the thirty years' statute of limitations.[48] Trusts arising from an implication of law are within the operation of the Idaho statute of limitations, providing that actions for the recovery of real estate cannot be maintained unless plaintiff or his ancestors were seized or possessed of the land within five years before action brought.[49] In South Carolina, where property is conveyed to satisfy a mortgage by husband

The statute of limitations contained in Oklahoma St. 1893, § 5668, relating to actions to recover possession of realty, does not apply to an action to quiet title. Lowenstein v. Sexton, 18 Okl. 322, 90 Pac. 410.

46. Rhodes v. Cissell, 82 Ark. 367, 101 S. W. 758.

47. Steele v. Jackson, 140 Ky. 821, 131 S. W. 1032.

Where a banking corporation held for more than five years while it continued in business real estate not necessary for its business and its charter then expired, so that it existed only to wind up its business under Ky. St. § 561 (Russell's St. § 2147), an action to escheat property being an action only for recovery of real estate was barred in 15 years under Ky. St. § 2505 (Russell's St. § 212), after the expiration of the charter. Louisville Banking Co. v. Commonwealth, 142 Ky. 690, 134 S. W. 1142.

The 10-year limitation applies to an action to set aside a deed on the ground of infancy. Henson v. Culp, 157 Ky. 442, 163 S. W. 455.

48. Haarstick v. Gabriel, 200 Mo. 237, 98 S. W. 760. Mo. Rev. St. 1899, § 4268. Rev. St. 1899, § 4262, providing a 10-year limitation for actions for the recovery of lands, applies to land claimed as a homestead. Joplin Brewing Co. v. Payne, 197 Mo. 422, 94 S. W. 896, 114 Am. St. Rep. 770.

49. Ames v. Howe, 13 Idaho, 756, 93 Pac. 35, under Rev. St. 1887, § 4036.

Under the statute of limitations (Rev. Codes, § 4054, subd. 1 and §§ 4037, 4038, 4060), an action to have ordinances vacating streets and alleys of a city declared null and void, and to compel the removal of obstructions from the streets, should have been commenced within at least

and wife, but without a release by the wife after the lapse of more than twenty years from the date of the mortgage, it is presumed paid, and is barred by the twenty-year statute of limitations.[50] Interest which the State took by escheat from alien heirs of a decedent is an interest in real estate within the forty-year limitation prescribed by New York Code Civ. Proc., § 362, par. 1.[51] An action by the grantee in an executed contract transferring title to land, or by his heirs against the grantor to determine adverse claims and compel a conveyance is not barred by the Minnesota six-year statute of limitation.[52] Under the Massachusetts statute, a purchaser's uninterrupted possession for twenty years or more, after performance by the vendor was due, and the vendor had refused a deed, bars a writ of entry.[53] Limitations prescribed in Oregon B. & C. Comp., §§ 3128, 3146, do not apply to suits to remove a cloud, for

five years from the time the cause of action arose. Canady v. Coeur d'Alene Lumber Co., 21 Idaho, 77, 120 Pac. 830.

50. Gainey v. Anderson, 87 S. C. 47, 68 S. E. 888, under Civ. Code 1902, § 2449.

As to the application of the statutes to an action brought by a minor in a federal court after his disability ceased to recover real property, see Cheatham v. Evans, 160 Fed. 802, 87 C. C. A. 576 (U. S. C. C. A., S. C.).

51. Stappenbeck v. Mather, 73 Misc. Rep. 434, 133 N. Y. Supp. 482.

The right given by Buffalo City Charter, Laws 1891, c. 105, § 406, reenacting Laws 1870, c. 519, tit. 9, § 17, giving compensation to owners of property abutting on a street for damages caused by alterations in its grade, is in the nature of a grant or an easement in the street that the grade will remain unchanged, and where the grade crossing commissioners, created by Laws 1888, c. 345, as amended by Laws 1890, c. 255, lowered the grade of a street without compensation to the abutting owners, it invaded their property rights and violated the grant existing between the city and the owners, and the only way the city could destroy the easement was by adverse holding for 20 years, and the right to claim compensation was not barred by the six-year statute of limitations. *In re* Grade Crossing Com'rs of City of Buffalo, 138 App. Div. 349, 122 N. Y. Supp. 922.

See Bergman v. Klein, 89 N. Y. Supp. 624, 97 App. Div. 15, as to the limitation of actions to recover possession of land upon which the walls of abutting buildings stand, under Code Civ. Proc., § 1499.

52. Coates v. Cooper, 121 Minn. 11, 140 N. W. 120, nor by the 15-year limitation; it not appearing that defendants have for that period asserted any adverse, hostile claim.

53. Endicott v. Haviland, 220 Mass. 48, 107 N. E. 394, under Mass Rev. Laws, c. 179, § 2, and chapter 202, §§ 20, 22.

by their terms they only apply to suits to recover property.[54] An action to remove a cloud created by a devise of land which the testator had previously conveyed is not an action to set aside or construe the will, within Illinois Wills Act., § 7, limiting the time for bringing such action.[55] In Washington, one having the record or paper title to land is not barred by the seven-year statute of limitations; the ten-year statute applying in his case.[56] A suit to reform a deed and to quiet title is one "for lands," governed as to limitations by Shannon's Code Tenn., § 4458, and not barred thereunder where defendants had never been in possession of the land.[57] In Texas, an action for the "recovery of real estate," within Rev. St. 1879, art. 3207, excepting such actions from the four-years statute of limitations, includes only actions on a title which would sustain an action of trespass to try title, not actions to enforce a mere equity, though judgment for the land might be rendered on the establishment of such equity.[58] But when the allegations of a petition are to the effect that a sale by a trustee is null and void, and that it conveyed no title to the land, and the primary purpose of the suit is to recover the land, and not to cancel the deed by the trustee, and the deed, as alleged, bears on its face the evidence of its invalidity, the four-years statute of limitations cannot be pleaded in bar to the action.[59]

54. Martin v. White, 53 Or. 319, 100 Pac. 290.

55. Thurston v. Tubbs, 257 Ill. 465, 100 N. E. 947.

56. Johnson v. Ingram, 63 Wash. 554, 115 Pac. 1073.

An action against the widow of plaintiff's deceased partner to recover an undivided interest in certain tide lands to which plaintiff claimed an equitable title, is not a suit to establish a trust, but an action to recover real estate, and not barred by limitations. Lehman v. Heuston, 73 Wash. 154, 131 Pac. 825.

An action brought in the State of Washington to recover land which had been occupied and used by a railroad company for 18 years as a right-of-way, held barred by limitations. Nielsen v. Northern Pac. R. Co., 184 Fed. 601, 106 C. C. A. 581 (U. S. C. C. A., Wash.).

57. Williams v. American Ass'n, 197 Fed. 500, 118 C. C. A. 1 (Tenn.).

58. Campbell v. Durst, 15 Tex. Civ. App. 522, 40 S. W. 315, and hence an action by devisees to set aside an administrator's sale of land which is voidable only, and to establish their title in the land, is not for the recovery of real estate, and is barred by the four-year statute.

59. Chandler v. Peters (Tex. Civ. App.), 44 S. W. 867.

§ 272a(2). Actions at law in general.

An action at law, under South Dakota Rev. Code Civ. Proc., § 675, providing that an action may be brought by any person against another who claims an interest in real property adverse to him for the purpose of determining such adverse claim, is governed by the statutory sections providing for a limitation of actions.[60] In Texas, in trespass to try title to recover land in possession of another, no limitation is available except that which affects the right to recover real estate.[61] In a suit to recover land pursuant to

Where the owner of land conveyed the same under circumstances whereby the equitable title remained in him and thereafter he conveyed the land to plaintiff, who sued in trespass to try title to recover from those claiming under the deed which created the trust, the only limitation applicable was that applying to actions for land and not the four years' limitation as against the cancellation of a deed, the ten years against specific performance, or the limitation of stale demand. Craig v. Harless, 33 Tex. Civ. App. 257, 76 S. W. 594.

60. Burleigh v. Hecht, 22 S. D. 301, 117 N. W. 367.

61. Hoffman v. Buchanan (Tex. Civ. App.), 123 S. W. 168.

Trespass to try title, in which plaintiff claims on the theory that the debt secured by an ancient deed, accompanied by written defeasance, is to be presumed satisfied, is not in the nature of a suit for specific performance of the defeasance, so as to be subject to the bar of limitations. Turner v. Cochrane, 30 Tex. Civ. App. 549, 70 S. W. 1024. The four years' statute of limitations does not apply to trespass to try title. Watson v. Harris (Tex. Civ. App.), 130 S. W. 237.

Where a deed of land was a mortgage, and the equitable title remained in the grantor, so that he could sue for a recovery of the land, a suit by him for a cancellation of the deed and for an accounting was in effect an action to recover the land, so that limitations as to actions for real estate applied, and not the four-year statute (Rev. St. 1895, art. 3358), which applies to other actions than for the recovery of land, for which no limitation is provided. Smith v. Olivarri (Tex. Civ. App.), 127 S. W. 235. The three-year statute of limitations held without application in an action of trespass to try title. Fidelity Cotton Oil & Fertilizer Co. v. Martin (Tex. Civ. App.), 136 S. W. 533.

An answer seeking affirmative relief and indorsed as required for a suit in trespass to try title, but which relied upon mistake in the deed to plaintiff's grantor of which plaintiff had knowledge, alleged a suit for the reformation of the deed, which was barred in four years by Rev. St. 1911, art. 5690, and not a suit to recover the land. Hamilton v. Green (Tex. Civ. App.) 166 S. W. 97.

See also Bell County v. Felts (Tex. Civ. App.), 120 S. W. 1065, rehearing denied, 122 S. W. 269; Sherman v. Pickering (Tex. Civ. App.), 121 S. W. 536.

an alleged constructive trust, only those statutes of limitation which affect actions to recover realty are applicable.[62] In Georgia, an action by a widow and minor child to recover possession of a homestead, being an action at law, is not barred by intervention of sixteen years between the eviction and institution of the suit.[63] In Ohio, an action under the statute to recover possession of realty, plaintiff relying on a mortgage to prove title, is not an action on the mortgage itself, and is not barred in less than twenty-one years.[64] To an action in effect to determine title to one-half cubic foot per second of water, claimed by plaintiff under a deed, but possession of which defendant has at all times had, defendant's defense of mistake is not barred by California Code Civ. Proc., § 338, subd. 4, prescribing a three-years limitation for an action for relief on the ground of mistake, but only by section 318, prescribing a five-years limitation for recovery of real property or the possession thereof.[65] The three-years possession which may be pleaded in bar to an action for forcible entry and detainer, under the Oregon statute, does not bar an action for ejectment.[66]

§ 272a(3). Equitable actions.

A suit by a creditor to have set aside a fraudulent conveyance by the debtor is a suit in equity for the recovery of land, and is

62. Nuckols v. Stanger (Tex. Civ. App.), 153 S. W. 931.

By its express terms the four-year statute of limitations (Rev. St. 1895, art. 3358) does not apply to actions to recover real estate. Broussard v. Cruse (Tex. Civ. App.), 154 S. W. 347.

The three-year statute of limitations is not applicable in an action to quiet title by an heir who had not joined in conveying the land. Woodburn v. Texas Town Lot & Improvement Co. (Tex. Civ. App.), 153 S. W. 365.

63. Hughes v. Purcell, 135 Ga. 174, 68 S. E. 1111, the statute of limitations does not apply to suits to recover land; lapse of time being only available in aid of any prescriptive title which defendant may set up.

64. Hall v. Bradfield, 21 Ohio Cir. Ct. R. 184, 12 O. C. D. 339.

65. South Tule Independent Ditch Co. v. King, 144 Cal. 450, 77 Pac. 1032.

66. Malony v. Adsit, 20 Sup. Ct. 115, 175 U. S. 281, 44 L. Ed. 163, under Hill's Code Or. § 3524.

See Myers v. Mathis, 2 Ind. T. 3, 46 S. W. 178; Sittel v. Wright, 3 Ind. T. 684, 64 S. W. 576, as to when an action for the recovery of realty is barred under Mansf. Dig. § 4476

governed by the statute of limitations of ten years.[67] A suit to reform a deed is one for the recovery of real property, the correction of the deed being merely incidental, and is therefore within the five years' limitation prescribed by Code Civ. Proc. Cal., § 318, for actions for the recovery of real property, and not within section 338, subd. 4, limiting actions for relief from fraud or mistake to three years.[68] Where a city in 1888 established a building line on property in a proceeding of which the owner had no notice, and of which she apparently had no knowledge until 1907, but the city had never entered on her land, her suit to enjoin its enforcement is not within the equity of Conn. Gen. St. 1902, § 1109, providing that no person shall make entry on land except within fifteen years next after his title shall first accrue, and no entry shall be sufficient unless action be commenced thereupon and prosecuted to effect within one year.[69] Actions by grantors of real property, about five years after the youngest of them came of age, to have the deed set aside, are not "proceedings to recover real property or the possession thereof," within New York Code

(Ind. T. Ann. St. 1899, § 2943), providing a limitation of five years for such actions.

67. Washington v. Norwood, 128 Ala. 383, 30 So. 405; Van Ingen v. Duffin, 158 Ala. 318, 48 So. 507.

68. Union Ice Co. v. Doyle, 6 Cal. App. 284, 92 Pac. 112.

Code Civ. Proc., § 318, providing that no action for the recovery of real property can be maintained unless it appear that the plaintiff, his ancestor, predecessor, or grantor, was seized or possessed of the property in question within five years before the commencement of the action, is applicable to a suit by the widow of an intestate to recover property conveyed during the lifetime of the intestate through the fraudulent representations and undue influence of the grantee. Page v. Garver, 146 Cal. 577, 80 Pac. 860. See also Murphy v. Crowley, 140 Cal. 141, 73 Pac. 820, rev'g judg. 70 Pac. 1024.

Action to establish a trust, in land, and for an award of possession is an action to recover real property and its possession, within Code Civ. Proc., § 318. Bradley Bros. v. Bradley, 20 Cal. App. 1, 127 Pac. 1044.

But an "action" to reform a deed as to the description for mutual mistake is not within Code Civ. Proc., § 318, but is within Civ. Code, § 3399, authorizing an action to reform a contract, which because of mistake does not express the intent of the parties. Hart v. Walton, 9 Cal. App. 502, 99 Pac. 719.

69. Northrop v. City of Waterbury, 81 Conn. 305, 70 Atl. 1024.

Civ. Proc., § 365, and fall within the ten-year limitation of section 338.[70] Whether a deed is fraudulent and void as to creditors may be examined and decided in an action to recover real estate, and, in such cases, the Indiana statute of limitations is twenty years.[71] The twenty-year limitation fixed by the North Dakota statute, relating to the recovery of real property and the causes of action founded on the title to real property, does not apply to equitable causes of action in favor of a mortgagor against the mortgagee in possession.[72] The Virginia statute, limiting the time within which suit may be brought to recover land, has no application to the suit of a judgment creditor to enforce his lien against the land.[73] Where plaintiff, knowing of a mistake in the description of a deed sought to be reformed, remained silent for nearly sixteen years before suit was brought, he was barred from obtaining relief under the Iowa statute, limiting actions founded on written contracts and those brought for the recovery of real property to ten years.[74] The interest acquired by a locator in possession of a mining claim prior to his compliance with provisions of United States statutes entitling him to a patent is mere personalty, and not an interest in real property, within the Oregon statute, providing that a suit for the determination of an interest in real property shall be deemed within the limitations of actions for the recovery of real

70. O'Donohue v. Smith, 109 N. Y. Supp. 929, 57 Misc. Rep. 448.

71. Vanduyn v. Hepner, 45 Ind. 589, the limitation of six years for relief against frauds has no application.

A suit by an administrator to reform a deed to certain land sold by him under order of court, on the ground that by mutual mistake the description included more land than was intended to be sold or purchased, and that the additional land was needed to pay debts of the deceased, was not a suit to recover real property sold by him as administrator, and was therefore not within the five years' statute of limitations. Pierce v. Vansell, 35 Ind. App. 525, 74 N. E. 554.

72. Nash v. Northwest Land Co., 15 N. D. 566, 108 N. W. 792, under Rev. Codes N. D. 1899, §§ 5188, 5189 (Rev. Codes 1905, §§ 6774, 6775).

73. Flanary v. Kane, 102 Va. 547, 46 S. E. 312, rehearing denied, 102 Va. 547, 46 S. E. 681, under Va. Code 1887, § 2915.

74. Garst v. Brutsche, 129 Iowa, 501, 105 N. W. 452, under Iowa Code, §§ 3747, 3748.

property, and hence such statute has no application to an action for specific performance of a contract to convey such mining claims.[75] In Texas, an action to recover land held by defendants under a deed void for want of delivery is not one to cancel a deed so as to be barred in four years.[76]

§ 272a(4). Partition.

The bar of the statute of limitations relating to real actions is not confined to the action of ejectment, but applies also to a bill for partition, in equity as well as at law.[77] In an action for partition, where an interest in land was sold under the power contained in a mortgage, and conveyed to plaintiff one year after the right to sell under the power accrued, but the mortgagor was in possession ever since that time, the fact that over ten years have elapsed since the mortgage matured is not a bar to the prosecution of the action.[78] Where, in an action for a division of land, plaintiff claimed a half interest, but his share had been sold by his agent thirty-five years before to the owner of the remaining interest, who with his grantees have been in actual, continuous possession ever since, and within four years after the sale, plaintiff, when asked to clear the title, said he had received his pay and had no interest in the land, plaintiff's claim was barred by the statute of limitations.[79] The New York statute of limitations does not apply either to partition actions or accounting therein.[80] Under the Washington statute, declaring that actions for the recovery of real property must be begun within ten years after the accrual of the cause of action, an action for partition against one who, together with his predecessors in interest, has exercised dominion over and claimed the property adversely against the world for over ten years, is barred.[81]

75. Herron v. Eagle Min. Co., 37 Or. 155, 61 Pac. 417, under Hill's Ann. Laws, Or. § 382.

76. McCelvey v. McCelvey, 15 Tex. Civ. App. 105, 38 S. W. 473.

77. Smith v. Clark, 248 Ill. 255, 93 N. E. 727; Kotz v. Belz, 178 Ill. 434, 53 N. E. 367.

78. Call v. Dancy, 144 N. C. 494, 57 S. E. 220.

79. Godsey v. Standifer, 31 Ky. Law Rep. 44, 101 S. W. 921.

80. *In re* Wood's Estate, 123 N. Y. Supp. 574, 68 Misc. Rep. 267.

81. Hyde v. Britton, 41 Wash. 277,

Where property in which plaintiff was interested was sold under mortgage foreclosure September 15, 1886, and she was then of age, but asserted no rights until July, 1907, her right to partition, on the ground that the judgment was void as against her, was barred by the twenty-year statute of limitations prescribed for actions to recover real property or the possession thereof by New York Code Civ. Proc., § 365.[82] The thirty-year prescription provided for by Louisiana Civ. Code, art. 1305, applies to partition suits and not to petitory actions.[83]

§ 272a(5). Foreclosure of mortgage or deed for security.

Limitations will not run against the foreclosure of a mortgage on lands until there is a presumption that the debt is satisfied, in the absence of adverse possession.[84] Under the Arkansas statute, which provides that in suits to foreclose mortgages it shall be a sufficient defense that they have not been brought within the period of limitation prescribed by law for a suit on the debt for the security of which they were given, where the five-years limitation had not run against the note at the mortgagor's death, the general statute then ceased to run against the debt, and was succeeded by the two-year statute of nonclaims, which, as it does not begin to run before administration of an estate, never commenced running, so that foreclosure of the mortgage was not barred.[85] In New Jersey,

83 Pac. 307, under 2 Ballinger's Ann. Codes & St. Wash. § 4797.

Under La. Civ. Code, arts. 1791, 3542, an action by an heir of an interdict to recover property partitioned held barred by prescription. Hamilton v. Hamilton, 130 La. 302, 57 So. 935.

82. Hope v. Seaman, 119 N. Y. Supp. 713, judg. modified Hope v. Shevill, 122 N. Y. Supp. 127, 137 App. Div. 86.

83. Vestal v. Producers' Oil Co., 135 La. 984, 66 So. 334.

In a petitory action by parties claiming to own undivided interests in an immovable against parties possessing and claiming to hold in indivision the whole immovable, defendants can plead the prescription of 10 years, the prescription relating to an action for partition not applying. Ogden v. Leland University, 49 La. Ann. 190, 21 So. 685.

84. Shockley v. Christopher, 180 Ala. 140, 60 So. 317.

85. A. R. Bowdre & Co. v. Pitts, 94 Ark. 613, 128 S. W. 57, under Kirby's Dig. Ark., § 5399.

Prior to Kirby's Dig., § 5399, seven

the statute of limitations applies to a suit in equity to foreclose a mortgage, under the rule that the right to foreclose ceases when the legal right of entry is barred.[86] In Indiana, where a mortgage was executed in June, 1895, and in March, 1901, a purchaser of the mortgaged premises agreed for a valuable consideration to assume an undivided part of the mortgage debt, a suit to foreclose the mortgage instituted in April, 1904, was not barred by limitations.[87] In Illinois, in a suit to foreclose as a mortgage a deed absolute on its face, where the defendants pleaded limitations of sixteen years, it was held that, the defendants being in possession of the premises, they were tenants at will, and the only limitation law that could be invoked was that of twenty years' adverse possession.[88] Where defendants acquired title to real property of a corporation under mortgage foreclosure, and by sale in satisfaction of a deficiency judgment, the corporation after a change of control, fifteen years thereafter, could not recover the land in ejectment for alleged invalidity of the mortgage, under the Michigan statute, limiting the time in which to sue to recover real property or the possession thereof to five years.[89] In Wisconsin, the

years' continuous adverse possession was necessary to bar an action to foreclose a mortgage on real property and to make limitations available either by the mortgagor or a subsequent grantee or mortgagee. Wadley v. Ward, 99 Ark. 212, 137 S. W. 808.

86. Wallace v. Coward, 79 N. J. Eq. 243, 81 Atl. 739.

87. Union Trust Co. v. Scott, 170 Ind. App. 666, 83 N. E. 1031, transferred to Supreme Court, 85 N. E. 481.

Under Prac. Act, § 211, cl. 5, it was formerly held that the statute of limitations of 15 years did not apply to the foreclosure of a mortgage, but the time of limitation in such a case was 20 years. Catterlin v. Armstrong, 79 Ind. 514.

88. Reed v. Kidder, 70 Ill. App. 498.

Mortgage notes which had been due for upward of 18 years, where nothing had been paid on them, and there had been no promise to pay, are barred by the statute of limitations. Watts v. Rice, 192 Ill. 123, 61 N. E. 337.

89. West Michigan Park Ass'n v. Pere Marquette R. Co., 172 Mich. 179, 137 N. W. 799.

In a suit by the purchaser of lands from the mother and guardian of minor children by regular probate proceedings, the guardian's right to insist that as to one of the descriptions sold she did not sell her dower interest therein was barred by the five-year statute of limitation of actions to recover land (Comp. Laws 1897, §

rights of plaintiff, who was beneficiary under a mortgage, were held barred by the twenty-year statute of limitations.[90] The enforcement in equity of mortgages and deeds of trust of real estate is governed by the statute of limitations applicable to possessory actions at common law for the recovery of real estate, which statute in the District of Columbia is that of 21 James I., c. 16, prescribing twenty years within which such actions must be instituted.[91] In an action in ejectment by a mortgagee, after condition broken, the statutory bar of fifteen years, as provided by Ohio Rev. St., § 4980, in an action on a specialty, does not apply, but the bar is twenty-one years, as provided by section 4977.[92] In South Dakota, the six-year limitation does not apply to an action to foreclose a mortgage, and such action can only be barred by the ten-year statute.[93] In Texas, the three, five, and ten years' statutes of limitations are not available to bar foreclosure of a trust deed, as they apply only to suits for land.[94] In West Virginia, the right to enforce the lien of a trust deed being an equitable remedy the statute of limitations has no direct operation on the right, but the general rule in equity as to the limit of time for the enforcement of such lien is by analogy to the right of entry at law, namely, that twenty years' possession by the grantor after default, without any acknowledgment or recognition of the lien, will be a bar.[95] The Wyoming statute, limiting the time within which suit may be brought for the recovery of the possession of lands, cannot be applied to an action to foreclose a mortgage, since the object of such action is not to recover the land, but to realize the amount of the debt by selling the security.[96]

9714. Hunt v. Stevens, 174 Mich. 501, 140 N. W. 992.

90. Wetutzke v. Wetutzke, 158 Wis. 305, 148 N. W. 1088.

91. Sis v. Boarman, 11 App. D. C. 116. And see Cropley v. Eyster, 9 App. D. C. 373.

92. Bradfield v. Hale, 67 Ohio St. 316, 65 N. E. 1008.

93. Bruce v. Wanzer, 20 S. D. 277, 105 N. W. 282.

94. Williams v. Armistead, 41 Tex. Civ. App. 35, 90 S. W. 925.

95. Camden v. Alkire, 24 W. Va. 674.

96. Balch v. Arnold, 9 Wyo. 17, 59 Pac. 434, under Wyo. Rev. St. 1887, § 2366.

§ 272a(6). Redemption from mortgage or deed for security.

A mortgagor's right to redeem from a void foreclosure sale is barred after ten years, in Alabama;[97] and, a bill in equity to establish as a mortgage an absolute deed intended only as a mortgage is barred by the statute of limitations of ten years.[98] In South Dakota, the ten-year limitation applies to an action to redeem from a mortgage.[99] The right to foreclose and the right to redeem are reciprocal, and an action to redeem may be brought at any time before the statutory bar of ten years is complete, under the Nebraska statute.[1] The Missouri statute, which limits the time within which an action may be brought for the recovery of lands or tenements to ten years, and which, under the decisions of the State courts, applies to all suits, whether legal or equitable, in their nature, may be invoked by a purchaser in possession under a deed executed upon a foreclosure sale against a suit by the mortgagee to redeem, where the possession of the defendant was adverse to the complainant.[2] An action seeking to have the value of mortgaged lands sold to a *bona fide* purchaser treated as the land itself, and redemption had accordingly, is not on a money demand, and hence limitations, applicable thereto, are no bar to such an action.[3] An action to have a deed declared a mortgage and to redeem is barred in five years under the Idaho statute.[4]

97. Summerford v. Hammond, 187 Ala. 244, 65 So. 831.

98. Richter v. Noll, 128 Ala. 198, 30 So. 740.

A cross-bill by an administrator, asking that the amount of a lien chargeable, by agreement, upon the interests of the heirs in the land be considered in determining the amount each should contribute for redemption of the land from a mortgage, seeks to enforce a lien on the land, and not a right to recover the indebtedness, and is not barred until the lapse of 20 years. Caldwell v. Caldwell, 183 Ala. 590, 62 So. 951.

99. West v. Middlesex Banking Co., 33 S. D. 465, 146 N. W. 598.

1. Dickson v. Stewart, 71 Neb. 424, 98 N. W. 1085, 115 Am. St. Rep. 596; Dorsey v. Conrad, 49 Neb. 443, 68 N. W. 645, under Neb. Code Civ. Proc., § 6.

2. Stout v. Rigney, 107 Fed. 545, 46 C. C. A. 459 (Mo.), under Rev. St. Mo. 1899, § 4262.

3. Mooney v. Byrne, 163 N. Y. 86, 57 N. E. 163, rev'g judg. 44 N. Y. Supp. 1124, 15 App. Div. 624.

4. Fountain v. Lewiston Nat. Bank, 11 Idaho, 451, 83 Pac. 505, under Rev. St. Idaho, 1887, §§ 4036, 4037.

§ 272a(7). Title under forced sale.

The right of a mortgagor to have a sale under a power set aside in equity, because the debt had been theretofore paid, is barred in ten years, and not in two, as is a bill to redeem.[5] An action to remove a cloud from the title to land sold for taxes is not to recover land, within the statute requiring actions to recover land sold at judicial sale to be brought within five years.[6] The Kansas five-year statute of limitations, against actions for the recovery of real property sold on execution brought by the execution debtor or any person claiming under him by title acquired after the judgment, applies to all sales, void and voidable.[7] Where the real

5. Liddell v. Carson, 122 Ala. 518, 26 So. 133.

6. Streett v. Reynolds, 63 Ark. 1, 38 S. W. 150, under Sand. & H. Dig. § 4818.

The plea of the five-year statute of limitations against recovery of land sold at a judicial sale by a purchaser at a probate sale to pay debts is unavailing, where the sale was wholly void for the insufficiency of the description of the land sold in the petition; such insufficiency depriving the court of jurisdiction, and rendering the sale and confirmation wholly void. Jennings v. Bouldin, 98 Ark. 105, 134 S. W. 948. See also Indiana & Arkansas Lumber & Mfg. Co. v. Brinkley, 164 Fed. 963 (U. S. C. C. A. Ark.), holding Kirby's Dig. Ark., § 5060, inapplicable where the court which ordered the sales never acquired any jurisdiction to make them.

7. James v. Logan, 82 Kan. 285, 108 Pac. 81, under Code Civ. Proc. Kan. (Gen. St. 1909, § 5608). It does not apply to an action to recover land sold by one as guardian, who was not so appointed. Harrison v. Miller, 87 Kan. 48, 123 Pac. 854.

Where the holder of a valid tax deed, before the two-year limitation has barred his right to rocover possession under it, obtains the actual and peaceable possession of the land, the statute is satisfied, and, if he thereafter loses possession, his right to recover it continues until barred by the general statute of limitations. Buckner v. Wingard, 84 Kan. 682, 115 Pac. 636. See Martin v. Cochran, 81 Kan. 602, 106 Pac. 45, as to when the two-year statute of limitations is a bar.

The five-year statute of limitations does not apply to a sheriff's deed executed prior to its passage. Ogden v. Walters, 12 Kan. 282. It applies to actions brought to recover lands sold under execution issued by the probate court against an administratrix to enforce an order requiring her to pay an allowed claim; Cheesebrough v. Parker, 25 Kan. 566; and to an action by an heir to set aside a sale of land made by the administrator, though the irregularity complained of is that proper notice of the sale was not given. Young v. Walker, 26 Kan. 242.

owner of property procured the holder of the nominal title to convey to a trustee, without consideration, and subsequently a prior mortgage was foreclosed, the real owner of the land was an "execution debtor" within the Indiana statute, providing that actions to recover real property, sold on execution, brought by the execution debtor, are barred in ten years.[8] Under Ky. St., § 458, defining "real estate," "personal estate," and "land," the right of action to enforce the lien acquired by an execution creditor purchasing at a sale of incumbered real property passes to his personal representative, and hence is not an action affected by the limitation of section 2505 as to actions to recover land.[9] The Missouri statute, which limits the time within which an action may be brought for the recovery of lands to ten years, and which under the decisions of the State Supreme Court applies to all suits, whether legal or equitable, may be invoked in a Federal court by a purchaser in possession under a deed executed on a foreclosure sale in a suit by the mortgagor to redeem, where the possession of the defendant was not adverse.[10] In Nebraska, where the lands of

8. Sinclair v. Gunzenhauser, 179 Ind. 78, 98 N. E. 37, an action to quiet title is barred by the 15-year limitation (Burns' Ann. St. 1908, § 295, subd. 3). See as to 10-year statute of limitations: Hutchens v. Lasley, 11 Ind. 456; Wood v. Sanford, 23 Ind. 96; Wright v. Wright, 97 Ind. 444.

The statute of limitations relative to the recovery of land applies to defective titles and imperfect sales. Hawley v. Zigerly, 135 Ind. 248, 34 N. E. 219. The statute of limitations providing that an action to recover real estate sold on execution must be brought within 10 years applies to a sheriff's sale of land in pursuance of a mortgage foreclosure decree. Moore v. Ross, 139 Ind. 200, 38 N. E. 817.

9. Due v. Bankhardt, 151 Ky. 624, 152 S. W. 786.

10. Clapp v. Leavens, 164 Fed. 318 (U. S. C. C. A., Mo.), under Rev. St. Mo. 1899, § 4262 (Ann. St. 1906, p. 2335).

Mo. Rev. St. 1909, § 1879, requiring all suits to recover lands or their possession to be brought within 10 years, would include an action to set aside a trustee's deed made at a sale under a deed of trust and to recover possession of the land, and to redeem from the trust lien and for an accounting for rents. Faris v. Moore, 256 Mo. 123, 165 S. W. 311.

Where a trustee, in 1898, took title to land by sheriff's deed and conveyed the land in 1899, a suit by the beneficiaries, commenced in 1907, to set aside the deed from the trustee for fraud was not barred by limitations; the ten-year's statute (Rev. St. 1909, § 1879) being applicable to the case.

a resident of the State are sold under a decree entered on service by publication, no appearance being made by or on behalf of such party, an action to quiet his title may be brought at any time within ten years from the recording of the deed, made on a sale under the decree, or taking possession thereunder.[11] In New Jersey, the right of a purchaser of land for a term for unpaid water rents to take possession at the expiration of the period of redemption is a right of entry authorizing ejectment against the person in possession under the legal title, and is therefore barred after twenty years, under the statute.[12] An action of trespass for injuries to land is not an action for the recovery of the land within the meaning of the Pennsylvania statute, which provides that "no action for recovery of said land shall lie, unless the same be brought within five years after the sale thereof for taxes as aforesaid."[13] In North Carolina, the right of a devisee, not made a party to a proceeding resulting in a judgment directing a sale of the testator's realty to pay debts, to maintain ejectment against the purchaser, is not barred by any time other than that prescribed by the statute of limitations.[14] A suit by the holder of a Buffalo tax sale certificate to obtain actual possession of the premises by an action at law, authorized by Buffalo City Charter (Laws 1891, c. 105), § 112, may be brought within twenty years from accrual of the cause of action.[15] In Louisiana, an action to annul a sheriff's sale is barred, when not brought within five years after the sale.[16]

Summers v. Abernathy, 234 Mo. 156, 136 S. W. 289.

11. Hill v. Chamberlain, 91 Neb. 610, 136 N. W. 999; Payne v. Anderson, 80 Neb. 216, 114 N. W. 148.

12. Beatty v. Lewis (N. J. Ch.), 68 Atl. 95, under Gen. St., p. 1977, § 23, providing that no person having right of entry on any lands shall make entry therein, but within 20 years next after such right shall have accrued and such person shall be barred from any entry thereafter.

13. Trexler v. Africa, 33 Pa. Super. Ct. 395, under Act April 3, 1804, § 3 (4 Smith's Laws, p. 201). The act of 1804 has no application where the title based upon a tax sale is void.

14. Card v. Finch, 142 N. C. 140, 54 S. E. 1009.

15. Cary v. Koener, 200 N. Y. 253, 93 N. E. 979, aff'g order and answering certified question Cary v. Koener, 124 N. Y. Supp. 501, 139 App. Div. 811.

16. Vinton Oil & Sulphur Co. v. Gray, 135 La. 1049, 66 So. 357. See

§ 272a(8). Establishment of lost deed.

The Kentucky statute prescribing the limitation of actions for the recovery of real estate applies by analogy to actions to supply lost deeds to real estate.[17] While a suit to supply evidence of a lost deed and to perpetuate testimony will be barred by laches, if not brought within a reasonable time after the loss of the deed, an action for the land, and to establish title through the lost deed, will only be barred by a limitation barring recovery of land.[18] An action to establish a lost or concealed deed of trust to secure payment of a note given for the purchase price of land is not an action for the recovery of land, but is within the statute, declaring that every action for which no limitation is prescribed shall be brought within four years next after the right to bring the same has accrued.[19]

§ 272a(9). Enforcement of vendor's lien.

Where for seventy years a purchaser and his grantees continued in the actual adverse possession of the land purchased, without any effort on the part of the vendor or his only heir at law to make

Foreman v. Francis, Man. Unrep. Cas. (La.) 357.

The prescription of five years against informalities connected with, or arising out of, public sales, is inapplicable to sales affected with jurisdictional defects. Brewer v. Yazoo & M. V. R. Co., 128 La. 544, 54 So. 987. The prescriptive term of three years contained in Const. 1898, art. 233, has no application to attempted sale of public property by tax collectors for alleged delinquent taxes. Cordill v. Quaker Realty Co., 130 La. 933, 58 So. 819. An action which is not brought by a creditor, but by one claiming title, whether it is to set aside a tax sale or is petitory, is not a revocatory action, and the prescription of one year does not apply. Howcott v. Petit, 130 La. 791, 58 So. 574.

See as to title under forced sale:

Mich.—Potter v. Martin, 122 Mich. 542, 81 N. W. 424, 6 Detroit Leg. N. 865.

Miss.—Moores v. Flurry, 87 Miss. 707, 40 So. 226.

Tex.—Green v. Robertson, 30 Tex. Civ. App. 236, 70 S. W. 345.

Wash.—Krutz v. Isaacs, 25 Wash. 566, 66 Pac. 141.

17. Brandenburg v. McGuire, 105 Ky. 10, 19 Ky. Law Rep. 1598, 44 S. W. 96; Ky. Gen. St. c. 71, art. 1, §§ 1, 2, 4.

18. Shepard v. Cummings' Heirs, 44 Tex. 502.

19. Farmers' Loan & Trust Co. v. Beckley, 93 Tex. 267, 54 S. W. 1027.

a deed to the purchaser, as stipulated in the title bond on payment of the balance of the purchase price due, and more than fifty years elapsed since the purchaser promised to pay the balance of the purchase price, without any attempt on the part of the sole heir to recover the same or to recover the land, the statutes of limitation of both fifteen and thirty years barred an action by the sole heir to recover the land.[20]

§ 272b(1). Title to or possession of real property in general—Accrual of right of action.

A State statute of limitations for the recovery of real property does not begin to run in favor of a railway company as against a settler, under the homestead laws of the United States, until patent has issued.[21] Land dedicated to the public for use as a cemetery is dedicated for a public or charitable use and is within the Missouri statute, providing that nothing contained in any statute of limitations shall extend to lands given to any public, pious, or charitable use.[22] The statute of limitations of Texas may not be invoked against title to land emanating from Texas, while the boundary between the United States and Mexico, as observed by the political authorities of the United States and Texas, left the land in Mexico, though the boundary line *de jure* placed the land within Texas.[23] A creditor's cause of action to avoid a fraudulent conveyance made after his debt matured accrued when the conveyance was made.[24] The twenty-year provision of the Illinois statuate commences to run in favor of a tenant when he refuses to

20. Doty v. Jameson, 29 Ky. Law. Rep. 507, 93 S. W. 638.

21. Northern Pac. Ry. Co. v. Slaght, 205 U. S. 122, 27 Sup. Ct. 442, 51 L. Ed. 738; 205 U. S. 134, 27 Sup. Ct. 446, 51 L. Ed. 742, aff'g judg. Slaght v. Northern Pac. Ry. Co., 39 Wash. 576, 81 Pac. 1062.

22. Tracy v. Bittle, 213 Mo. 302, 112 S. W. 45, under Mo. Rev. St. 1899, § 4270 (Ann. St. 1906, p. 2344).

23. Reese v. Cobb (Tex. Civ. App.), 135 S. W. 220.

24. Van Ingen v. Duffin, 158 Ala. 318, 48 So. 507, under Ala. Code 1907, §§ 4832, 4834, par 2, requiring suit for land to be brought within 10 years after accrual of the cause of action.

The action is one for the recovery of real estate, which under Burns' Ann. St. Ind. 1908, § 295, subd. 6, may be brought within 20 years, and

attorn or to pay for the premises in question.[25] Where defendant, in peaceable possession of land under a deed, knew that plaintiffs had by fraud obtained a second deed from her grantor to the same land, defendant's failure to have the second deed declared invalid will not start the running of limitations so long as no rights are asserted thereunder.[26] Prescription does not run against an action or exception attacking the validity of a sale of land, where the vendor was at all times in possession of the land.[27] Where a landowner granted a parol license to maintain a flume across his land, his right of action to recover possession did not accrue until the revocation of the license.[28]

§ 272b(2). Nature of entry or possession.

The statute of limitations does not begin to run until the right of action accrues, and, in the case of a claim to the possession of real estate, the right of action does not accrue until there is a right of entry.[29] The statute of limitations with respect to the recovery

not one for relief from fraud, subject to a shorter limitation, though the complaint, praying for possession and damages for detention, and complying with section 1100, prescribing the contents of a complaint to recover possession, in addition, sets out the history of plaintiff's title, and charges that defendant is unlawfully in possession claiming title under a forged deed. Stevens v. Neiman, 43 Ind. App. 317, 87 N. E. 153.

25. Plock v. Plock, 139 Ill. App. 416.

26. Turner v. Pool, 97 S. C. 446, 81 S. E. 156.

27. Hamilton v. Moore, 136 La. 631, 67 So. 523.

The want of power to appoint an agent to convey real estate is a defect *de hors* the title of a bona fide purchaser, and is curable by the prescription of 10 years *acquirendi causa.* Westerfield v. Cohen, 130 La. 533, 58 So. 175.

28. Gustin v. Harting, 20 Wyo. 1, 121 Pac. 522.

As to the application of statutes of limitation to actions for the recovery of real property in general, see:

U. S.—Maytin v. Vela, 216 U. S. 598, 30 Sup. Ct. 439, 54 L. Ed. (U. S., Porto Rico).

Iowa—Mead v. Illinois Cent. R. Co., 112 Iowa 291, 83 N. W. 979.

Mo.—Hudson v. Cahoon, 193 Mo. 547, 91 S. W. 72.

Neb.—City of Omaha v. Redick, 61 Neb. 163, 85 N. W. 46.

Tex.—Pope v. Riggs (Tex. Civ. App.), 43 S. W. 306.

29. Wright v. Tichenor, 104 Ind. 185, 3 N. E. 853.

of real estate begins to run at the commencement of adverse possession.[30] According to the modern rule, the commencement of a suit in ejectment by a grantor after condition broken takes the place of a formal entry and demand of possession; and where a grantee, on condition subsequent, has clearly manifested his intention not to perform the condition, so that his holding thereafter may be deemed to be adverse, the statute of limitations will run from that time against a suit by his grantor.[31] The statute of limitations runs against the title of a pre-emptor of public land from the date of his compliance with all the requisites to entitle him to a patent in favor of one who holds adverse possession.[32] Where a husband and wife conveyed premises in which they had a life interest to a third person by deed, professing to convey the fee on the death of the wife, the life tenant's right of entry accrued, and limitations began to run from that date, and their rights were

There can be no ouster or running of limitations against a person's rights in land until he has a right of entry. Lynch v. Brookover, 72 W. Va. 211, 77 S. E. 983. A cause of action against one who entered upon land under an adverse claim accrued when the entry was made. Hickman v. Ferguson (Tex. Civ. App.), 164 S. W. 1085.

30. Vail v. Jacobs, 7 Mo. App. 571, memorandum.

What is not such hostile or exclusive possession against other joint owners as will invoke the operation of the statute of limitations. See Nickels v. Hand in Hand Cornet Band in Manayunk, 52 Pa. Super. Ct. 145, 151.

31. Union Pac. Ry. Co. v. Cook, 98 Fed. 281, 39 C. C. A. 86 (Neb.).

In ejectment, where no possession in defendant is shown, the cause of action did not accrue until defendant obtained a deed to the property. Smith v. Algona Lumber Co., 73 Or. 1, 143 Pac. 921.

Where complainants alleged that their mother, in 1878, while of unsound mind, conveyed to nonresident purchasers the land in dispute, and that in 1900 the land was conveyed to defendant, and that their mother died in an insane hospital in 1891, as ejectment might have been brought by complainants when the lands were held by nonresident owners, the statute of limitations began to run in favor of the persons in possession in 1891, and it was not postponed until the year 1900. Beresford v. Marble, 95 Miss. 461, 50 So. 68.

32. Eastern Banking Co. v. Lovejoy, 81 Neb. 169, 115 N. W. 857.

Statutes of limitations do not begin to run against the patentee of public land until the patent has been issued to him. Haggerty v. Annison, 133 La. 338, 62 So. 946.

barred at the end of seven years.[33] Defendant having joined with his mother, a widow, in a deed of certain community property, in exchange for certain lots, after which the mother and her grantees for more than five years repudiated any claim on the part of defendant to the lots received in exchange, and held the title and paid taxes, was not excused, because his mother was occupying the property as a homestead, for his failure to sue to establish his interest within the period of limitations.[34] One having equitable title to land was not bound to assert it till repudiation of his right, and limitations did not begin to run against him till then.[35]

§ 272b(3). Title to support action in general.

Where at the time of the accrual of an interest in realty by inheritance, the heir is a married woman, having living issue by her husband, so that curtesy initiate in him attaches, he alone can sue to recover the property, and hence the statute of limitations does not commence to run against the wife's interest until the husband's death, and the consequent termination of his intervening estate.[36] Where executors sold land of their testator, but only one of them executed the deed, and the grantee went into possession, a right of action in ejectment accrued at once in their favor, and limitations began to run against them, under New York Code Civ.

33. Cherry v. Cape Fear Power Co., 142 N. C. 404, 55 S. E. 287.

Where land was conveyed in trust to collect the rents and profits and pay the same to W. and permit him to occupy the premises as a home for life, the ouster of W. was the ouster of his trustees, and started limitations against both which barred their right to recover after seven years. Webb v. Borden, 145 N. C. 188, 58 S. E. 1083. See also as to title under trust deed, Bernhardt v. Hagamon, 144 N. C. 526, 57 S. E. 222.

34. Williamson v. Williamson (Tex. Civ. App.), 116 S. W. 370.

35. Stonehouse v. Stonehouse, 156 Mich. 43, 16 Detroit Leg. N. 21, 120 N. W. 23. And see Bower v. Earl, 18 Mich. 367.

See, as to nature of entry or possession:

Mo.—Tower v. Compton Hill Imp. Co., 192 Mo. 379, 91 S. W. 104; Hoke v. Central Tp. Farmers' Club, 194 Mo. 576, 91 S. W. 394.

Tex.—Dyer v. Pierce (Tex. Civ. App.), 60 S. W. 441.

36. Dawson v. Edwards, 189 Ill. 60, 59 N. E. 590.

Proc., § 415, from that time.[37] Limitations begin to run against a cause of action to establish an involuntary trust in land, and to secure possession, only from the time plaintiff lost possession.[38] Where a grantor of land imposed restrictions against alienation by his grantee and the grantee conveyed the coal under the land, limitations do not begin to run against the right of the grantor to set aside the conveyance so long as his grantee remains in undisturbed possession.[39] Where plaintiff, to whom deceased had agreed to leave specified realty on her remaining with and caring for him during

37. Brown v. Doherty, 93 App. Div. 190, 87 N. Y. Supp. 563, aff'd 185 N. Y. 383, 78 N. E. 147, 113 Am. St. Rep. 915.

A tenant in common, who conveyed his interest to his co-tenant in consideration of the latter's agreement to furnish him with a home for the rest of his life, has a continuing right of action to set aside the deed or enforce the lien which was reserved to protect the grantor. Curran v. Hosey, 153 App. Div. 557, 138 N. Y. Supp. 910.

Where one who executed a deed during infancy disaffirmed the conveyance within the statutory period of 10 years after arriving at age, no limitation applies to an action by him to set aside the deed until claimants under the grantee take possession. O'Donohue v. Smith, 130 App. Div. 214, 114 N. Y. Supp. 536, aff'g. judg. 57 Misc. Rep. 448, 109 N. Y. Supp. 929.

Under Code Civ. Proc. § 362, providing that the State could not bring an action with respect to title to lands unless the cause of action accrued within 40 years, limitations do not start to run at the death of a citizen owner intestate and without heirs, but only upon the transition of the title to the State, which would not be until after proceedings instituted for inquest of office. Hamlin v. People, 155 App. Div. 680, 140 N. Y. Supp. 643.

38. Bradley Bros. v. Bradley, 20 Cal. App. 1, 127 Pac. 1044, under Code Civ. Proc. § 318. As to action to foreclose a lien on real estate, see Congregational Church Bldg. Soc. v. Osborn, 153 Cal. 197, 94 Pac. 881. The "right or title," under Code Civ. Proc. § 315, refers to the "right or title" of the State to sue and not to the "right or title" on which a right to sue is based. People v. Banning Co., 167 Cal. 643, 140 Pac. 587.

39. Pond Creek Coal Co. v. Runyon, 161 Ky. 64, 170 S. W. 501.

The statute of limitations is not a bar to the correction of a deed, where the vendee has been in possession of the land, under Ky. St. 1903, § 2543, providing that limitation shall not apply to an action by a vendee in possession for a conveyance. Hill v. Clark, 32 Ky. Law Rep. 595, 106 S. W. 805. See also Vanover v. Maggard, 157 Ky. 743, 164 S. W. 94. As to action to have a conveyance by mistake corrected, see Jenkins v. Taylor, 22 Ky. Law Rep. 1137, 59 S. W. 853.

his declining years, was in possession claiming to own the property, limitations did not run against her right of action against the administrator of the deceased to compel specific performance of the contract.[40] Limitations do not begin to run in favor of one claiming an interest in real estate until he has taken possession thereof, or has exercised such dominion as amounts to notice to the real owner of his adverse possession.[41] The cause of action in a formal action of trespass to try title to recover possession arose when defendant wrongfully took possession of the premises, and that having been done at least eight years before suit was filed, and the deed under which defendant claimed being duly recorded and all taxes paid, plaintiff's right to recover is barred by the five-year statute.[42]

40. Clow v. West (Nev.), 142 Pac. 226.

41. Stephenson v. Murdock, 88 Neb. 796, 130 N. W. 578.

The cloud upon a title to land created by a recorded deed obtained by duress is a continuing one, while the title owner retains possession, and the right of action for its removal is also continuous during such time, and may be brought at any time within four years after the claimant under such deed has taken possession of the land claiming title under his deed. Dringman v. Keith, 86 Neb. 476, 125 N. W. 1080.

42. Hoffman v. Buchanan (Tex. Civ. App.), 123 S. W. 168.

Where, in trespass to try title, wherein plaintiff asked that the deed, under which defendants claimed, be canceled as a cloud on her title, it appeared that defendants had never had possession or claimed title under the deed prior to the commencement of the action, the statute of limitations was not available as a defense, since the right to have a cloud on the title removed is a continuing right. Pannell v. Askew (Tex. Civ. App.), 143 S. W. 364.

The running of limitations against a grantee's right of action to correct a mistake in a deed was not interrupted by his sale of the land. Durham v. Luce (Tex. Civ. App.), 140 S. W. 850.

Where a purchaser of the timber on school lands filed prior to the removal of the timber an application to purchase the land, and paid the price at the same time, he became entitled under the statute to the land, and his cause of action against an adverse claimant accrued at that time, and not at the time of a subsequent award of the land to him; that being mere evidence of his existing right to the land. Houston Oil Co. of Texas v. McGrew (Tex. Civ. App.), 143 S. W. 191.

An absolute grantor is not entitled to a suit to try title more than 10 years after notice of a conveyance by her grantee. Kennon v. Miller (Tex. Civ. App.), 143 S. W. 986.

§ 272b(4). Title under forced or judicial sale.

Limitations do not begin to run against a purchaser at a foreclosure sale until the delivery of the deed.[43] Limitations do not begin to run against a mortgagor's right to redeem, until possession is taken under the mortgage or the foreclosure.[44] Where land is levied on under an execution, but it is sold and possession given by the judgment debtor before sheriff's sale, the statute of limitations runs against the purchaser at sheriff's sale from the time the deed of the execution debtor is delivered, and not merely from the time the sheriff's deed is delivered.[45] An action to cancel a commissioner's deed and recover the land, brought within five

See also, as to title to support action:

Ky.—Watkins v. Pfeiffer, 29 Ky. Law Rep. 97, 92 S. W. 562.

Tenn.—Anthony v. Wilson (Tenn. Ch. App.), 62 S. W. 340.

Tex.—Gillean v. City of Frost, 25 Tex. Civ. App. 371, 61 S. W. 345.

Wash.—Gasaway v. Ballin, 57 Wash. 355, 106 Pac. 905.

43. McDonald v. McCoy, 121 Cal. 55, 53 Pac. 421. See also Group v. Jones (Okl.), 144 Pac. 377.

Where one purchased from the State swamp lands after a void tax sale, the land not being subject to taxation, the seven years' statute of limitations was set in motion by the conveyance to the purchaser as against the holder under the tax sale. Brinneman v. Scholem, 95 Ark. 65, 128 S. W. 584. When land is sold under tax foreclosure, the statute of limitations does not begin to run against the prior owner until the expiration of two years within which he could redeem. Young v. Jackson (Tex. Civ. App.), 110 S. W. 74.

44. Essex v. Smith, 97 Neb. 649, 150 N. W. 1022.

45. Watt v. Killibrew, 156 Ala. 454, 47 So. 83.

Where plaintiff received a sheriff's deed for vacant and unimproved property within seven years before commencement of an action, his right is not barred under a statute providing that no action for real property can be maintained unless the plaintiff was in possession within seven years before the commencement thereof, because defendants held possession a few years before the commencement of the action; the deed carrying constructive possession with it. Ives v. Grange, 42 Utah, 608, 134 Pac. 619.

A creditor of a debtor executing fraudulent conveyances may wait until the last day for suing on the debt, and on procuring judgment may wait until about the expiration of the period within which execution must issue before procuring execution, and on purchasing at execution sale, he may wait almost five years before suing to set aside the conveyance, though the debtor died before judgment. Scholle v. Finnell, 166 Cal. 546, 137 Pac. 241.

years after the final determination of the attachment suit, is not barred by limitations.[46] An action of ejectment by one claiming title to real estate by purchase at a sale under a deed of trust is not barred under the statute of limitations, when it is brought within ten years after the last payment was made on a note secured by the deed of trust, and within ten years after the premises were sold to plaintiff under it.[47] The right of parties interested in the assigned estate to impeach a sale of part of the property on mortgage foreclosure to the assignee is available from the day of the sale, and the statute of limitations commences to run from that date.[48]

§ 272b(5). Title or right of parties to mortgage or deed as security.

One who enters upon land under a trustee's deed which purports to convey an absolute title, and which was executed upon a sale by the trustee in a mortgage, the purpose of which was to bar the mortgagor's equity of redemption, must be regarded as holding adversely to the mortgagor from the time his deed is recorded, and possession is taken thereunder, although the sale made by the trustee was irregular or premature; and no actual notice to the mortgagor of the adverse nature of his claim is necessary to invoke the running of the statute of limitations for its protection.[49] Limitations run

46. Spicer v. Seale, 106 Ky. 246, 20 Ky. Law Rep. 1869, 50 S. W. 47.

The statute of limitations runs against the right of action of an execution creditor, who purchases at a sale of incumbered real property, to forceclose his lien, thereby acquired, from the time of his purchase. Due v. Bankhardt, 151 Ky. 624, 152 S. W. 786.

47. Rines v. Mansfield, 96 Mo. 394, 9 S. W. 798.

48. Smith v. Hamilton, 43 App. Div. 17, 59 N. Y. Supp. 521.

See also, as to title under forced or judicial sale: Cheesebrough v. Parker, 25 Kan. 566; White v. Pingenot (Tex. Civ. App.), 90 S. W. 672.

49. Stout v. Rigney, 107 Fed. 545, 46 C. C. A. 459 (Mo.).

Where a mortgagee enters into possession of the mortgaged premises under a void foreclosure he is presumed to hold as mortgagee in possession, and limitation does not run in his favor, or in favor of his grantees, against a suit by the mortgagor to enforce the right of redemption, and to an accounting, which is a continuing right, unless there is an actual notice

against a bill to declare a deed absolute in form a mortgage, in favor of a grantee in possession, from the time such possession became adverse to the grantor's title.[50] A mortgagor's right to redeem will not be barred by any claim of possession by a mortgagee, etc., unless the possession is adverse.[51] A mortgagor's right of action to quiet

to the mortgagor that they claim to hold in some other right, adverse to the mortgage. Rigney v. De Graw, 100 Fed. 213 (C. C., Mo.).

50. Minick v. Reichenbach, 97 Neb. 629, 150 N. W. 1001.

A grantor who claims that a deed, absolute in form, is a mortgage, must proceed to enforce his claim within five years from the time the grantee asserts his adverse holding, whether the debt secured by the deed be paid or not. Cal. Code Civ. Proc. § 346. Peshine v. Ord, 119 Cal. 311, 51 Pac. 536, 63 Am. St. Rep. 131.

While plaintiff was in actual possession of land conveyed by absolute deed which was intended as a mortgage, he had the right to regard the deed simply as security until such time as the grantee or successors in interest deprived him, or attempted to deprive him, of possession on the ground that the deed was absolute, and until that time the statute of limitations would not begin to run against an action to have the deed declared a mortgage. Brown v. Spradlin, 136 Ky. 703, 125 S. W. 150.

The statute of limitations did not run against an action to have a deed declared a mortgage while the grantor was making repeated demands for a reconveyance, and the grantee was promising to comply therewith. Clark v. Shoesmith, 91 Kan. 797, 139 Pac. 426

Where a party suing in 1894 to have a deed made in 1878 declared a mortgage was in continuous possession from 1870, the statute of limitations had no application. Porter v. White, 128 N. C. 42, 38 S. E. 24.

51. West v. Middlesex Banking Co., 33 S. D. 465, 146 N. W. 598.

Where a mortgagee takes possession of real estate under an agreement with the mortgagor to collect the rents and apply them on the debt, limitations will not begin to run against the mortgagor's right to redeem until the mortgagee, with notice to the mortgagor asserts title in himself. Hunter v. Coffman, 74 Kan. 308, 86 Pac. 451.

A cause of action of an owner of a fee to redeem from a mortgage which has been foreclosed, in a proceeding in which he was not served with process, accrued when the mortgage matured. Dorsey v. Conrad, 49 Neb. 443, 68 N. W. 645.

Where one in good faith claims title under a void foreclosure sale, and takes possession, such adverse possession puts the statute of limitations in motion against the remedies of the mortgagor. Nash v. Northwest Land Co., 15 N. D. 566, 108 N. W. 792.

Where a grantee of lands conveyed by deeds operating as mortgages entered into possession of the lands at the time of the conveyance under an agreement with the grantor that he should hold them as security for a debt not then due, such possession does not constitute a continuing fore-

title, recover possession, and redeem from the lien of the mortgage accrues when the mortgagee takes possession with color of title to the fee and claim of ownership, and the ten year limitation will then begin to run.[52] Where the interest of a junior mortgagee is acquired before the debt secured by a first mortgage has matured, the statute of limitations begins to run in favor of the junior mortgagee from the time the right of action of the senior claimant against the mortgagor accrues.[53]

§ 272b(6). Rights of heirs and devisees.

The Arkansas five-year statute of limitations from a judical sale in which to sue the purchasers does not apply to an action by heirs for land sold at administrator's sale, the land having been allotted to his widow as dower, the sale being inoperative as to her dower, and the heirs not being entitled to assert their right to the land till after death of the doweress, which was after the five years.[54] Where testator devised his real estate to his wife for life,

closure, so as enable the grantor to maintain an action to redeem at any time during its continuance, free from limitations, since the right to foreclose did not accrue until the debt was due, and the right to redeem was contemporaneous therewith. Adams v. Holden, 111 Iowa, 54, 82 N. W. 468.

52. Jackson v. Rohrberg, 94 Neb. 85, 142 N. W. 290.

A suit to redeem from foreclosure is barred in 15 years from its accrual at the expiration of the year for statutory redemption. Sinclair v. Gunzenhauser, 179 Ind. 78, 98 N. E. 37. A mortgagor held not precluded by the statute of limitations from enforcing her rights under the mortgage. McKenney v. Page, 146 Ky. 682, 143 S. W. 382. Where the mortgage sued on contained no independent agreement to pay the money secured, it was barred after five years. Allen v. Shepherd, 162 Ky. 756, 173 S. W. 135.

53. Boucofski v. Jacobsen, 36 Utah 165, 104 Pac. 117.

See, as to limitations in action to foreclose a mortgage, Wallace v. Coward, 79 N. J. Eq. 243, 81 Atl. 739.

54. Martin v. Conner (Ark.), 171 S. W. 125.

As adult heirs have no right to the possession of the homestead of the decedent until the termination of the homestead of a minor heir, which occurs on his reaching full age, limitations within which to sue for the possession of the homestead do not begin to run until the homestead right of the minor heir ceases. Smith v. Scott, 92 Ark. 143, 122 S. W. 501.

Limitations begin to run against an action by the heirs to recover possession from an adverse holder of a homestead abandoned by the widow,

limitations did not run against his heirs for the recovery of the property during her lifetime as against her grantee under a deed purporting to convey the fee.[55] In Illinois, limitations run against the right of the children of a deceased person to recover his homestead, to which they were entitled as remaindermen, the widow being the life tenant, from the time that the widow released her dower and homestead rights in the premises to a purchaser thereof at an administrator's sale to pay decedent's debts.[56] Limitations do not commence to run, in Indiana, against heirs of a widow entitled to an interest in her husband's realty until her death, as they can maintain no action for its recovery until such event.[57] In Maryland, where a will, which appointed no executor, directed the sale of all of testator's property, and after certain deductions that the proceeds be placed at interest for the support of testator's wife during her life, the legal title at once vested in the heirs at law, against whom limitations was not tolled by reason of the life estate of the widow.[58] In Mississippi, under a devise of an undivided interest in lands in trust for the distributee until he has become a temperate and prudent man, and remained such for five years, whereupon the lands shall vest in him in fee, limitations do not run against his right to have the lands partitioned, and to re-

and of which they had notice, not from the widow's death, but from the time it was abandoned by her. Killeam v. Carter, 65 Ark. 68, 44 S. W. 1032; Griffin v. Dunn, 79 Ark. 408, 96 S. W. 190, the statute does not run in favor of the heirs during occupancy by the widow.

55. Winters v. Powell, 180 Ala. 425, 61 So. 96.

56. Robb v. Howell, 180 Ill. 177, 54 N. E. 324.

Where a wife, having an interest by inheritance in certain realty, dies after having living issue by her husband, so that his life estate by courtesy becomes consummate, the statute of limitations does not begin to run against her heirs entitled to the remainder until her husband's death, notwithstanding his life estate becomes barred during his life by the statute of limitations, since such bar does not terminate the life estate so as to merge it in the remainder, or vest the remainder in possession before the life tenant's death. Dawson v. Edwards, 189 Ill. 60, 59 N. E. 590.

57. Bell v. Shaffer, 154 Ind. 413, 56 N. E. 217; Haskett v. Maxey, 134 Ind. 182, 33 N. E. 358, 19 L. R. A. 379.

58. Baumeister v. Silver, 98 Md. 418, 56 Atl. 825.

cover his share, until he has for five consecutive years remained temperate, since his interest does not vest until then.[59] In Missouri, where a widow conveyed her right to quarantine in the house and plantation of her deceased husband, and dower was not assigned to the widow, limitations did not begin to run against an action by a remainderman to recover the property from the grantee until the widow's death.[60] In Oregon, where testator left all his property by an invalid will to his wife, and she transferred the land in question to defendant under a deed in fee simple, and he took possession of it, the right of action by the heirs to recover the property is not postponed until the death of the widow, although the deed might have transferred the widow's unassigned right of dower, as, before assignment, the right of dower does not give any right to possession.[61] In South Carolina, the title of a devisee vests immediately on testator's death, and hence it is from that time that the statute of limitations commences to run against his right to recover the land.[62] In Tennessee, the existence of a widow's unallotted right to dower in land will not prevent the running of the statute of limitations against the heirs, who have conveyed in fee their undivided shares of the land subject to the dower, especially where the dower right has been conveyed to the same purchaser.[63] In Texas, where testator devised to his wife an estate in

59. Millsaps v. Shotwell, 76 Miss. 923, 25 So. 359.

60. Graham v. Stafford, 171 Mo. 692, 72 S. W. 507; Holmes v. Kring, 93 Mo. 452, 6 S. W. 347, where dower is not assigned, a right of action on the part of the heirs does not accrue until the widow's death; unless she abandoned her right of dower. Quick v. Rufe, 164 Mo. 408, 64 S. W. 102.

Limitations do not begin to run against a devisee of leased land, until the expiration of the lease. Sutton v. Dameron, 100 Mo. 141, 13 S. W. 497.

61. Neal v. Davis, 53 Or. 423, 101 Pac. 212, rehearing, 99 Pac. 69, denied.

See Clarke v. Bundy, 29 Or. 190, 44 Pac. 282, holding that the running of the statute of limitations for recovery of land of decedent by an heir, pending administration, is not suspended, as against the heir, unless the administrator took actual possession thereof.

62. Satcher v. Grice, 53 S. C. 126, 31 S. E. 3.

63. Jackson v. Hodges, 2 Tenn. Ch. 276.

land which was to terminate on her remarriage, and the widow, for herself and as independent executrix of the estate of testator, executed a deed to the land, the statute of limitations did not begin to run against an action by the heirs to recover the land from the purchaser until the remarriage of the widow.[64] In Colorado, limitations commence to run against the heirs of a decedent to set aside a conveyance on the ground of mental incompetency from the time of the ancestor's death.[65] In California, where a father, on receiving the custody of a minor child, orally agreed that such child should share equally with his only other child, a daughter, the right to set aside a conveyance to the daughter, made before his death, did not accrue until the death of the father without complying with the agreement.[66] In Iowa, limitations begin to run against a suit by heirs of a decedent to set aside probate of his will and quiet title in plaintiffs from the accruing of the cause of action upon the ancestor's death.[67] In Kentucky, limitations do not run against children with a right in property until the death of a grantee, who took for life under a parol agreement to convey to them at her death.[68]

§ 272b(7). Tacking successive possession or right.

A grantee of mortgaged premises may add to the time limitations have run in his favor since he acquired the land the time it had run in favor of his grantors, in order to make up the aggregate period

64. Haring v. Shelton (Tex. Civ. App.), 114 S. W. 389.

Where the land set apart to an heir in the partition proceedings was afterwards sold as being a part of the estate, to satisfy claims of creditors, and such sale was invalid, the statute commenced to run in her favor from the date of the judgment in partition, and not from the date of the invalid sale. Hardin v. Clark, 1 Tex. Civ. App. 565, 21 S. W. 977.

Where heirs, prior to intestate's death, could not have maintained an action for his lands, limitations do not run against them until after his death. Wilson v. Fields (Tex. Civ. App.), 50 S. W. 1024.

65. Parker v. Betts, 47 Colo. 428, 107 Pac. 816.

66. Rogers v. Schlotterback, 167 Cal. 35, 138 Pac. 728.

67. Cooley v. Maine, 163 Iowa 117, 143 N. W. 431.

68. Becker v. Neurath, 149 Ky. 421, 149 S. W. 857.

required to bar the action to foreclose.[69] A naked trespasser without color of title cannot transmit his right to a successor, so as to enable the latter to couple the two possessions to make out the bar of the statute. But those having color of title may transfer their possession and convey their right, by conveyance, so as to enable the holder to connect the successive conveyances and possessions with his own right and possession.[70]

§ 272b(8). Forcible entry and detainer.

Where one wrongfully or unlawfully enters on the possession of another, the wrongful entry is consummated the moment the entry is made, and the right to maintain the action of forcible entry and detainer vests at once in him whose possession is thus invaded.[71] Limitations against an action of forcible entry and detainer against a tenant holding at sufferance begins to run against the landlord on the termination of the tenancy.[72] The right of action in a forcible entry and detainer case between adverse claimants of a homestead accrues when the contest is finally adjudicated in the land office.[73] If defendants in unlawful detainer attorned to the plaintiff within three years before the bringing of the suit, the statute of limitations was not available to them.[74]

§ 272c. Recent English decisions.

In the notes to this section a summary of late English case law, showing the application made by the courts of England of the statutes of limitations to actions relating to land and actions on specialties and for legacies, will be found. It covers the construc-

69. Paine v. Dodds, 14 N. D. 189, 103 N. W. 931, 116 Am. St. Rep. 674.

70. Nelson v. Trigg, 72 Tenn. (4 Lea) 701.

See Shortall v. Hinckley, 31 Ill. 219; Bentley v. Newlon, 9 Ohio St. 489, as to tacking successive possessions.

71. Nauman v. Burch, 91 Ill. App. 48.

72. Clark v. Tukey Land Co., 75 Neb. 326, 106 N. W. 328.

73. Cope v. Braden, 11 Okl. 291, 67 Pac. 475.

74. Barnewell v. Stephens, 142 Ala. 609, 38 So. 662.

tion of the statutes and subject matters to which they relate;[75] the application of the statutes to particular persons, such as landlord and tenant,[76] joint tenants and tenants in common,[77] trustee

75. Land Tax—Redemption by lessee—Money paid as consideration—Annual sum payable by way of interest—Sum of money "charged upon" land—"Rent." Skene v. Cook, 71 L. J., K. B. 446; (1902) 1 K. B. 682; 86 L. T. 319; 50 W. R. 506; 18 T. L. R. 431—C. A.

Unclaimed dividends—Reduction of capital—Return of moneys to shareholders—Sanction of court—Moneys not claimed—Statutory period of limitation. Artizans' Land & Mortgage Corporation, *In re,* 73 L. J., Ch. 581; (1904) 1 Ch. 796; 52 W. R. 330; 12 Manson 98.

Smith v. Cork & Bandon Railway, Ir. R. 5 Eq. 65, and Drogheda Steam Packet Co., *In re,* (1903) 1 Ir. R. 512, followed. Ib.

Vesting of real estate—Title—Legal estate—Private partnership—"Company duly constituted by law"—Registration — Trustee — Possession. Cussons, Ltd., *In re,* 73 L. J., Ch. 296; 11 Manson 192.

Kibble v. Fairthorne, 64 L. J., Ch. 184; (1895) 1 Ch. 219, applied.

Restrictive covenant—Possessory title—Constructive notice—Purchaser. Nisbet and Potts' Contract, *In re,* 75 L. J., Ch. 238; (1906) 1 Ch. 386; 94 L. T. 297; 54 W. R. 286; 22 T. L. R. 233—C. A.

London & Southwestern Railway v. Gomm, 51 L. J., Ch. 530, 532; 20 Ch. D. 562, 582 and Cox and Neve's Contract, *In re,* (1891) 2 Ch. D. 109, 117, applied. Ib.

Dower—Action for assignment of dower—Time for ascertaining value. Williams v. Thomas, 78 L. J., Ch. 473; (1909) 1 Ch. 713; 100 L. T. 630—C. A. Marshall v. Smith, 34 L. J., Ch. 189; 5 Giff. 37, considered and overruled in part.

Lease of minerals—Severance of reversion—No apportionment of rent—Payment to one reversioner. Mitchell v. Mosley, 108 L. T. 326; 57 S. J. 340; 29 T. L. R. 273. Affirmed, 58 S. J. 218; 30 T. L. R. 29—C. A.

Mines and minerals—Land subject to mining lease—Conveyance of part of land—Conveyance of reversion—Severance of reversion—Apportionable rent. Mitchell v. Mosley, 83 L. J., Ch. 135; (1914) 1 Ch. 438; 109 L. T. 648; 58 S. J. 218; 30 T. L. R. 29—C. A.

76. Invalid lease by municipal corporation—Agreement to surrender existing lease in exchange for continuance of existing lease—Estoppel. Canterbury Corporation v. Cooper, 100 L. T. 597; 73 J. P. 225; 7 L. G. R. 908; 53 S. J. 301—C. A.

Tenant of land—Adverse possession—Arrears of rent. Jolly, *In re;* Gathercole v. Norfolk, 69 L. J., Ch. 661; (1900) 2 Ch. 616; 83 L. T. 118; 48 W. R. 657; 16 T. L. R. 521—C. A.

Tenancy at will—Determination—Creation of fresh tenancy. Jarman v. Hale, 68 L. J., Q. B. 681; (1899) 1 Q. B. 994—D.

Determination of tenancy at will—Entry by landlord to repair. Lynes v. Snaith, 68 L. J., Q. B. 275; (1899) 1 Q. B. 486; 80 L. T. 122; 47 W. R. 411; 15 T. L. R. 184—D.

77. A tenant in common who has been in actual possession of part of

and *cestui que trust*,[78] mortgagor and mortgagee,[79] executors, administrators, devisees, legatees and heirs,[80] persons claiming under

a coal mine must be treated, as against his co-tenants, as a stranger in possession of a separate tenement so far as regards the undivided shares of his co-tenants. The Real Property Limitation Act, 1833, therefore applies, and after twelve years gives him a statutory title to so much of the coal as he has actually gotten, but to no more, unless the court finds that there is just reason for inferring constructive possession of a wider area. Glyn v. Howell, 78 L. J., Ch. 391; (1909) 1 Ch. 666; 100 L. T. 324; 53 S. J. 269. Job v. Potton, 44 L. J., Ch. 262; L. R. 20 Eq. 84, considered.

Next of kin remaining in possession. Smith v. Savage, (1906) 1 Ir. R. 469; Coyle v. McFadden, (1901) 1 Ir. R. 298.

78. Trustee ceasing to be executor—Breach of trust—Account—Real Property Limitation Act. Timmis, *In re;* Nixon v. Smith, 71 L. J., Ch. 118; (1902) 1 Ch. 176; 85 L. T. 672; 50 W. R. 164.

79. Mortgage of reversionary estate in realty—Action on covenant. Kirkland v. Peatfield, 72 L. J. K. B. 355; (1903) 1 K. B. 756; 88 L. T. 472; 51 W. R. 544; 19 T. L. R. 362. Sutton v. Sutton, 52 L. J., Ch. 333; 22 Ch. D. 511, followed.

Mortgage—Real estate—Trust for sale—Proceeds of sale. Fox, *In re;* Brooks v. Marston, 82 L. J., Ch. 393; (1913) 2 Ch. 75; 108 L. T. 948. Hazeldine's Trusts, *In re,* 77 L. J., Ch. 97; (1908) 1 Ch. 34, and Kirkland v. Peatfield, *supra,* followed.

Mortgagor and mortgagee—Claim for account and recovery of rents by second mortgagee against first mortgagee. Ocean Accident & Guarantee Corporation v. Collum, (1913) 1 Ir. R. 328.

Foreclosure—Recovery of land—Payment of interest by mortgagor or his agent—Person bound as between himself and mortgagor to pay. Bradshaw v. Widdrington, 71 L. J., Ch. 627; (1902) 2 Ch. 430; 86 L. T. 726; 50 W. R. 561—C. A.

Action for recovery of land—Mortgage—Payment of interest by mortgagor—Mortgagee and trespasser. Ludbrook v. Ludbrook, 70 L. J., K. B. 552; (1901) 2 K. B. 96; 84 L. T. 485; 49 W. R. 465; 17 T. L. R. 397.

Equity of redemption—Freeholds, Copyholds and Policy of Insurance. Charter v. Watson, 68 L. J., Ch. 1; (1899) 1 Ch. 175; 47 W. R. 250; 79 L. T. 440.

Foreclosure action by *puisne* mortgagee—Entry of prior mortgagee during running of statutory period—Future estate or interest—Suspension of period. Johnson v. Brock, 76 L. J., Ch. 602; (1907) 2 Ch. 533; 97 L. T. 294. *Dictum* in Kibble v. Fairthorne, 64 L. J., Ch. 184; (1895) 1 Ch. 219, not followed.

Mortgage—Inclusion in deed of power of sale. Cronin, *In re,* (1914) 1 Ir. R. 23.

Presumption of payment of interest—Owner of portion of lands being also owner or tenant for life of mortgage. Finnegan's Estate, *In re,* (1906) 1 Ir. R. 370.

Acknowledgment in writing after bar of statute. Beamish v. Whitney, (1909) 1 Ir. R. 360.

80. Express trustees — Executors.

land clauses acts,[81] and persons under disabilities;[82] possession

In the absence of special circumstances, executors are not, prior to the Executors' Act, 1830, regarded by courts of equity as express trustees, and the trusteeship created by that Act was not intended to be different in its nature from that which previously existed. Lacy, *In re;* Royal General Theatrical Fund Association v. Kydd, 68 L. J., Ch. 488; (1899) 2 Ch. 149; 80 L. T. 706; 47 W. R. 664. Salter v. Cavanagh, 1 Dr. & Wal. 668, and Patrick v. Simpson, 59 L. J., Q. B. 7; 24 Q. B. D. 128, distinguished.

Administration — Executors — Right of one only of several executors to receive and give discharge—Recovery of fund. Pardoe, *In re;* McLaughlin v. Penny, 75 L. J., Ch. 161; (1906) 1 Ch. 265; 94 L. T. 88; 54 W. R. 210. Reversed on facts, 75 L. J., Ch. 748; (1906) 2 Ch. 340; 95 L. T. 512.

Will—Action to recover legacy—Express trust. Mackay, *In re;* Mackay v. Gould, 75 L. J., Ch. 47; (1906) 1 Ch. 25; 93 L. T. 694; 54 W. R. 88.

Action to recover legacy. The period of limitation is 12 years from the death of the testator, not from the expiration of one year after his death. Waddell v. Harshaw, (1905) 1 Ir. R. 416—C. A.

Real Estate—Mortgage containing covenants for the payment of principal and interest—Specific devise subject to mortgage—Payment of interest by devisee—Effect of payment—Other specifically devised real estate—Right to administration. Lacey, *In re;* Howard v. Lightfoot, 76 L. J., Ch. 316; (1907) 1 Ch. 330; 96 L. T. 306; 51 S. J. 67—C. A.

Roddam v. Morley, 26 L. J., Ch. 438; 1 DeG. & J. 1, and Leahy v. De Moleyns, (1896) 1 Ir. R. 206, applied. Dickinson v. Teasdale, 32 L. J., Ch. 37; 1 DeG. J. & S. 52, and Coope v. Cresswell, 36 L. J., Ch. 114; L. R. 2 Ch. 112, discussed and not followed. Bradshaw v. Widdrington, 71 L. J., Ch. 627; (1902) 2 Ch. 430, considered. Ib.

Executor *de son tort*—Chattels real—Next of kin—Administrator. Doyle v. Foley, (1903) 2 Ir. R. 95—K. B. D.

Will—Money charge on land—Contribution between specific and residuary devisees—Unity of possession—Presumption of payment of interest on charge by tenant for life. Allen, *In re;* Bassett v. Allen, 67 L. J., Ch. 614; Bassett v. Allen, 67 L. J., Ch. 614; (1898) 2 Ch. 499; 79 L. T. 107; 47 W. R. 55.

England, *In re;* Steward v. England, 65 L. J., Ch. 21; (1895) 2 Ch. 820.

81. Land purchased for undertaking—Tunnel—Superfluous land—Discontinuance of possession—Possession of surface by stranger—Telegraph wires over tunnel—Title to surface and space above. Midland Railway v. Wright, 70 L. J., Ch. 411; (1901) 1 Ch. 738; 84 L. T. 225; 49 W. R. 474.

82. Bailiff for infants—Change of possession. Maguire & McClelland's Contract, *In re,* (1907) 1 Ir. R. 393—C. A.

Infancy—Adverse possession—Subsequent accruer of infant's title. Garner v. Wingrove, 74 L. J., Ch. 545; (1905) 2 Ch. 233; 93 L. T. 131; 53 W. R. 588. Murray v. Watkins, 62 L. T. 796, followed.

Copyholds—Custom of manor--Title

generally,[83] consecutive,[84] and adverse;[85] right of entry;[86] charges

—Possession—Married woman—Disability—Husband suing in right of wife — Will — Construction — "Estate." Hounsell v. Dunning, 71 L. J., Ch. 259; (1902) 1 Ch. 512; 86 L. T. 382.

83. Purchase by railway—Expiration of powers.

A railway company can purchase minerals after the expiration of its statutory powers to purchase if such purchase is reasonably incident to its business. Thompson v. Hickman, 76 L. J., Ch. 254; (1907) 1 Ch. 550; 96 L. T. 454; 23 T. L. R. 311.

Wrongful working—No title by statute of limitations.

Where a mine owner wrongfully works an adjoining seam of coal for more than 12 years before action brought, he acquires no title to such seam under the statute of limitations. Ashton v. Stock, 6 Ch. D. 719, followed. Ib.

Wrongful working of coal—Tenants in common—Actual possession—Constructive possession—Adverse possession. Glyn v. Howell, 78 L. J., Ch. 391; (1909) 1 Ch. 666; 100 L. T. 324; 53 S. J. 269.

84. Title by possession—Devisable interest—Ejectment.

A person in possession of land without any title thereto has a devisable interest, and a statutory title may be acquired by the possession of the testator and his devisees. Calder v. Alexander, 16 T. L. R. 294.

85. Accrual of right of action. Connolly v. Leahy, (1899) 2 Ir. R. 344—Q. B. D.

Land—Acts of possession—Dispossession of true owner—Right of way—Equivocal acts. Littledale v. Liverpool College, 69 L. J., Ch. 87; (1900) 1 Ch. 19; 81 L. T. 564; 48 W. R. 177; 16 T. L. R. 44—C. A.

Will—Purported disposition of realty—Incapacity to dispose. Anderson, *In re;* Pegler v. Gillatt, 74 L. J., Ch. 433; (1905) 2 Ch. 70; 92 L. T. 725; 53 W. R. 510.

The principle of Board v. Board, 43 L. J., Q. B. 4; L. R. 9, Q. B. 48, does not apply to the case of a person who has a good title to property, but is not competent to dispose of it. Paine v. Jones, 43 L. J., Ch. 787; L. R. 18 Eq. 320, applied. Ib.

Trespass to Land—Adjoining Owners—Wall within Boundary Line—Strip Outside Wall—Abandonment—Adverse possession—Acts of Ownership.—When a person claims to have acquired a possessory title in law under the Real Property Limitation Act, 1833, upon the abandonment of possession by the original owner, he must prove not only a discontinuance of possession by the original owner for the statutory period, but also acts of possession by himself. Norton v. London & Northwestern Ry., 13 Ch. Div. 268, and Marshall v. Taylor, 64 L. J. Ch. 416; (1895) 1 Ch. 641, followed. Kynoch, Lim. v. Rowlands, 81 L. J., Ch. 340; (1912) 1 Ch. 527; 106 L. T. 316—C. A. The mere straying of cattle over a known boundary by reason of there being no fence is not an act of such exclusive possession as will enable the trespasser whose cattle has so strayed on to land of an adjoining owner to acquire a statutory title as against the true owner. Ib.

Discontinuance of.—Acts of ownership—Intention to exclude owner—

on land;[87] ecclesiastical and charitable property;[88] concealed fraud;[89] and arrears of rent and interest.[90] The manner and extent to which the rules and principles of the older authorities, elsewhere cited herein, have been approved and followed, or modified, distinguished, or reversed, is also shown.

Foreshore. Philpot v. Bath, 21 T. L. R. 634—C. A.

User of land.—Vernon's Estate, *In re*, (1901) 1 Ir. R. 1.

86. "Particular estate"—"Future estate or interest"—Reversion expectant on a term of years—Surrender of term—Accrual of right of entry. Walter v. Yalden, 71 L. J., K B. 693; (1902) 2 K. B. 304; 87 L. T. 97; 51 W. R. 46; 18 T. L. R. 668—D.

Real Property—Accrual of right of action—Trustee—*Cestui que trust* of lessee—Accretion to demised property. East Stonehouse Urban Council v. Willoughby, 71 L. J., K. B. 873; (1902) 2 K. B. 318; 87 L. T. 366; 50 W. R. 698.

87. Equitable charge on lands appointed in certain shares—Interest. Young v. Lord Waterpark, 8 L. J., Ch. 214, distinguished. Power's Estates, *In re*, (1913) 1 Ir. R. 530.

Rentcharge—Covenant to pay—Remedy on covenant barred—Remedy against land. Shaw v. Crompton, 80 L. J., K. B. 52; (1910) 2 K. B. 370; 103 L. T. 501—D.

Settlement—Term of years—Money charged upon land—Express trust. Williams v. Williams, 69 L. J., Ch. 77; (1900) 1 Ch. 152; 81 L. T. 804; 48 W. R. 245.

Charity. Drake's Estate, *In re*, (1909) 1 Ir. R. 136—C. A.

Commissioners of Charitable Donations and Bequests v. Wybrants, 2 Jo. & Lat. 182, not followed. Hughes v. Coles, 53 L. J., Ch. 1047; 27 Ch. D. 231, disapproved. Ib.

88. Rent—Charity—Express trust. Montalt's Estate, *In re*, (1909) 1 Ir. R. 390. Drake's Estate, *In re*, (1909) 1 Ir. R. 136, distinguished. Hughes v. Coles, 53 L. J., Ch. 1047; 27 Ch. D. 231, followed. Ib.

Title rent charge—Discontinuance of receipt—Subsequent receipt from person not liable. Winter's Estate, *In re*, (1908) 1 Ir. R. 529—C. A.

89. Real property—Possession. McCallum, *In re;* McCallum v. McCallum, 70 L. J., Ch. 206; (1901) 1 Ch. 143; 83 L. T. 717; 49 W. R. 129; 17 T. L. R. 112—C. A.

90. Administration of real and personal estate—Claim upon covenant in mortgage deed—Amount of interest recoverable. Thompson v. Hurly, (1905) 1 Ir. R. 588—M. R.

CHAPTER XXV.

DOWER.

§ 273. Not within the statute, unless made so expressly.

Except where specially so provided, a widow's right to dower is not barred by the statutes of limitations in the several States.[1] The writ of dower *unde nihil habet* is a real action, which lies for the recovery of dower where none has been assigned.[2] So, too, courts of equity have concurrent jurisdiction with courts of law, and can both assign dower to the widow and assess and award damages;[3] and in some of the States courts of probate are by statute invested with this power, and this statutory remedy has taken the place of the common-law remedy. The writ of dower was not within either the statute of Henry VIII. or James I., and the only method of avoiding it was by a fine levied by the husband, or his alienee or heir, which, under the statute of non-claims, barred the wife unless she brought her action within five years after her title accrued, and the removal of her disabilities, if any.[4] It will not be profitable to review the office, purposes, and nature of writs of dower, as that is not germane to our subject, and also

1. Barnard v. Edward, 4 N. H. 107, 17 Am. Dec. 403; Bordly v. Clayton, 5 Harr. (Del.) 154; May v. Rumney, 1 Mich. 1; Mitchell v. Payas, 1 N. & McCord (S. C.) 85; Wakeman v. Roache, Dudley (Ga.) 123; Parker v. O'Bear, 48 Mass. (7 Metc.) 24; Owen v. Campbell, 32 Ala. 521; Tooke v. Hardeman, 7 Ga. 20.

2. Booth on Real Actions, 166; and according to this author there is still another writ, called the writ of right of dower, which, however, is obsolete, or at least seldom employed in practice, although it was formerly used in cases where a part of the dower had been received.

3. 4 Kent's Com. 71, 72.

4. Park on Dower, 311.

because they have been so generally superseded by statutory and equibtale remedies, that they are not generally resorted to in practice. In many of the States, a widow's claim to dower is expressly brought within either the general statute of limitations, or a special limitation is imposed by the statute providing for dower. This is the case in Georgia, where the widow's application is limited to seven years after the husband's death;[5] but prior to the act of 1839 her right was not within the statute, and was not barred by the mere lapse of time.[6] In Iowa, by statute, the right of dower is not destroyed, but the remedy for its admeasurement in the County Court is barred in ten years; but it is held that courts of equity may assign it after that time.[7] In Indiana, the widow's right of dower is barred in twenty years after her disabilities, if any, are removed.[8] Such, also, is the provision in Ohio, except that the limitation is twenty-one years.[9] In New Hampshire, the period of limitation is twenty years, and the statute attaches from the time when the widow's right to a writ of dower accrues after demand, and not from the time of her husband's death.[10] In North Carolina, it is held that the statute does not apply until dower is assigned,[11] and the same rule also prevails in Missouri.[12] In Pennsylvania, the statute runs against a claim for dower, by action of dower, *unde nihil habet.*[13] In New York, a claim for dower is barred absolutely in twenty years.[14] In New Jersey, actions for dower are held to be within the statute.[15] So in South Carolina.[16] In Michigan, it is held

5. Tooke v. Hardeman, 7 Ga. 20.

6. Chapman v. Schroeder, 10 Ga. 321.

7. Starry v. Starry, 21 Iowa 254.

8. Harding v. Third Presbyterian Church, 20 Ind. 71.

9. In Tuttle v. Willson, 10 Ohio 24, it was held that by the lapse of twenty-one years the right of dower was not only barred at law, but also in equity.

10. Robie v. Flanders, 33 N. H. 524.

11. Spencer v. Weston, 18 N. C. (1 Dev. & B.) 213.

12. Johns v. Fenton, 88 Mo. 64; Littleton v. Paterson, 32 Mo. 337.

13. Care v. Keller, 77 Pa. 487.

14. Westfall v. Westfall, 16 Hun (N. Y.) 541.

15. Berrian v. Conover, 16 N. J. Law 107; Conover v. Wright, 6 N. J.

that as dower, like other landed interests, can be reached only by the statutory action of ejectment, it is barred by the statutory limitation upon that action.[17] In Arkansas, it is held that the statute does not run against a widow's claim for dower while the heirs of her husband are in possession of his land, but that the rule is otherwise where a purchaser is in possession.[18] In Alabama, the statute applies to a suit or proceedings for dower, whether the application is made by the widow or by an heir.[19] In Massachusetts, dower is now within the statute.[20] In Maryland, where until quite recently the statute was almost identical with the statute of James, dower was held not to be within the statute;[21] but it is within the present statute. In England, un-

Eq. 613, 47 Am. Dec. 213, reversing the same case, id. 482, in which it was held that the statute did not apply to dower.

16. Wilson v. McLenagan, 1 McMul. Eq. (S. C.) 35; Ramsay v. Dozier, 3 Brev. (S. C.) 246. But see Mitchell v. Poyas, 1 N. & McCord (S. C.) 85, *contra.*

17. Proctor v. Bigelow, 38 Mich. 282; Beebe v. Lyle, 73 Mich. 114, 40 N. W. 944.

18. Livingston v. Cochran, 33 Arkansas, 294.

19. Farmer v. Ray, 42 Ala. 125, 94 Am. Dec. 633.

20. Pub. Stats., c 124, § 14. The case of Parker v. Obear, 48 Mass. (7 Metc.) 24, was decided in 1848, before this statute was adopted.

Mass. Pub. Stats., c. 124, § 13, enabling a widow to claim her interest after occupying in common with the heirs, was held, in Hastings v. Mace, 157 Mass. 499, 32 N. E. 668, not to bar a widow who had for more than twenty years occupied with his heirs land of which her husband died seised, and she was held entitled to petition for the assignment of her dower when, after the expiration of twenty years, the heirs sought to hold the land in severalty. But where the widow had not continued to occupy the lands with the heirs or devisees of her deceased husband, or to receive her share of the rents, issues, and profits, and where the land has passed into the hands of a *bona fide* purchaser for value without notice of her claim or right, or of the fact that she occupied or received the rents with her husband's heirs or devisees, her action cannot be maintained unless commenced within twenty years after her husband's death. O'Gara v. Neylon, 161 Mass. 140, 36 N. E. 743. See Smith v. Shaw, 150 Mass. 297; Osborn v. Weldon, 146 Mo. 185; Winters v. De Turck, 133 Pa. 359, 19 Atl. 354, 7 L. R. A. 658; Lyebrook v. Hall, 73 Miss. 509; Thompson v. McCorkle, 136 Ind. 484, 34 N. E. 813, 36 N. E. 211, 43 Am. St. Rep. 334.

21. Watts v. Beall, 2 G. & J. (Md.) 468; Kiddall v. Trimble, 1 Md. Ch.

der the statute 3 and 4 Wm. IV., c. 27, no suit for dower can be maintained unless brought within twenty years after the death of the husband, and no action for an account of the rents and profits of the dowable land after six years.

§ 273a(1). Proceedings for assignment or recovery of dower—Limitations applicable.

An action by a mortgagor's widow to recover dower in the land against one holding under a foreclosure sale is subject to the Arkansas seven-year statute of limitations.[22] In Missouri, an action for enforcement of dower is barred by the thirty-one-year statute of limitations, where no person under whom plaintiff claimed had been in possession for thirty years, and no such person had paid any taxes on the premises for thirty-one years.[23] Under the Iowa statute, providing that actions for the recovery of real property must be brought within ten years after the accrual of the cause of action, an action for partition by a widow against a stranger claiming the entire title under a deed from the husband, under which he has been in actual possession not only as against him for the statutory period, but also as against the widow for more than ten years after the death of the husband, is barred by limitations.[24] The right to dower is unlike any other right to land known to the law, and its peculiar nature is such as to exempt it from the operation of all general statutes of limitations, however broad and comprehensive, in which it is not named, or by unavoidable implication included.[25] Under the Nebraska statute, limiting the time within which actions for the recovery of realty may be brought to ten years, an action for dower must be brought within ten years from

143; Sellman v. Bowen, 8 G. & J. (Md.) 50, 29 Am. Dec. 524.

22. Fourche River Lumber Co. v. Walker, 96 Ark. 540, 132 S. W. 451, and is not subject to Kirby's Dig., § 5060, declaring that all actions against a purchaser, his heirs or assigns, to recover land sold at judicial sale shall be brought within five years from the date of the sale.

23. Jodd v. Mehrtens, 262 Mo. 391, 171 S. W. 322.

24. Britt v. Gordon, 132 Iowa 431, 108 N. W. 319, under Iowa Code, § 3447, subd. 7.

25. May v. Rumney, 1 Mich. (Man.) 1.

the time it accrued.[26] Under the Indiana statute, which provides that a widow shall not have dower as against a purchase money mortgage, though she did not join in it, the right of foreclosure is not barred against her by lapse of time until the expiration of the twenty-year statute of limitation, which applies to a party to the mortgage.[27] In Kentucky, an action to recover dower is barred within fifteen years after the cause of action accrues.[28] The lapse of seven years after the death of the widow of a vendor of land is a bar to an action by the heirs of the grantee and their privies, to recover that part of the land assigned to her as dower.[29] A suit brought by a widow to set aside an instrument by which she elected to accept certain provisions of the will in lieu of dower is not a proceeding for the recovery of dower, within the provision of the New York Revised Statutes requiring her to take such a proceeding within a year.[30] A suit brought by a widow to set aside a surrender of her homestead and certain subsequent deeds to the property, and to have her homestead rights therein declared, is an action to recover real property, and is barred by California Code Civ. Proc., § 318, providing a limitation of five years for such an action.[31]

§ 273a(2). Actions for dower—Limitations and laches.

In New York, it is now held that section 1596 of the Code of Civil Procedure, which provides that an action for dower must be

26. Beall v. McMenemy, 63 Neb. 70, 88 N. W. 134, 93 Am. St. Rep. 427, under Neb. Code Civ. Proc., § 6.

Under West Virginia Code 1899, c. 104, § 1, limiting the time within which actions to recover land shall be brought, the statutory bar to an action by a widow to recover dower is 10 years from the death of her husband, unless she is in possession and taking the rents and profits in common with the heirs. Sperry v. Swiger, 54 W. Va. 283, 46 S. E. 125.

27. Leonard v. Binford, 122 Ind. 200, 23 N. E. 704, under Rev. St. Ind. 1881, § 2495.

28. Anderson's Trustee v. Sterritt, 79 Ky. 499, 3 Ky. Law Rep. 277, under Ky. Gen. St. c. 21, § 3, and Gen. St. c. 71, § 9, art. 3.

29. Burns v. Headerick, 85 Tenn. (1 Pickle) 102, 2 S. W. 259.

30. Chamberlain v. Chamberlain, 43 N. Y. 424.

31. Daniels v. Dean, 2 Cal. App. 421, 84 Pac. 332.

A charge on land for the benefit of a widow is barred by limitation in 21 years in Pennsylvania, under Act April 27, 1855 (P. L. 368). *In re* DeHaven's Estate, 25 Pa. Super. Ct. 507.

brought within twenty years of the husband's death, is an exclusive statute of limitations in actions for dower, and section 401 of the Code, providing limitations generally, does not apply.[32] In Iowa,[33] Missouri,[34] Kentucky,[35] a wife's right of action for assignment of her dower accrues immediately upon the death of her husband and the statute of limitations does not begin to run against the dower interest of the wife until the husband's death. In Alabama, it has been held that a widow's right of dower was not barred by statutory limitations, though her action was not brought within twenty years after her husband's death, the ten-year limitation provision of the Code 1907, § 3837, not going into effect until 1907.[36] In Arkansas, it is held that the duty of the heirs of a husband to assign dower is a continuing one, and the fact that they remain in possession after his death does not set the statute of limi-

32. Wetyen v. Fick, 178 N. Y. 223, 70 N. E. 497, aff'g judg. 90 App. Div. 43, 85 N. Y. Supp. 592, and the statute is not prevented from running because the life tenant and owners in fee were nonresidents.

33. Lucas v. White, 120 Iowa 735, 95 N. W. 209, 98 Am. St. Rep. 380; Lucas v. Whitacre, 121 Iowa 251, 96 N. W. 776.

A widow occupying a homestead for more than 10 years after her husband's death is not precluded from asserting her right to dower, which she has elected to take in lieu of homestead, by Iowa Code, § 3369, which limits the time within which application for dower may be made to 10 years, since the remedy therein provided is not exclusive. Wold v. Berkholtz, 105 Iowa 370, 75 N. W. 329. Section 3369 does not apply to an action in equity or for the partition of a distributive share, and the general statute of limitations applies to such an action. Britt v. Gordon, 132 Iowa 431, 108 N. W. 319.

Where a wife is induced by fraud to execute an antenuptial agreement waiving her dower rights, limitations do not begin to run in favor of her husband's estate and against her action to set aside the agreement until her right of dower has ripened; but the rule is otherwise as to third persons. Rankin v. Schiereck, 166 Iowa 10, 147 N. W. 180.

34. McCrillis v. Thomas, 110 Mo. App. 699, 85 S. W. 673; Joplin Brewing Co. v. Payne, 197 Mo. 422, 94 S. W. 896, 114 Am. St. Rep. 770.

A dower right not asserted for 10 years after the death of the husband is barred by limitations. Id.; Jodd v. St. Louis, etc. Ry. Co., 168 S. W. 611; Harrison v. McReynolds, 183 Mo. 533, 82 S. W. 120.

Limitations do not run against the heirs' action to have dower assigned, in favor of one claiming under the widow, until her death. Carey v. West, 139 Mo. 146, 40 S. W. 661.

35. Winchester v. Keith, 24 Ky. Law Rep. 1033, 70 S. W. 664.

36. Vaughn v. Vaughn, 180 Ala. 212, 60 So. 872.

tations in motion against the widow.[37] It is held in West Virginia that the right of a widow to sue for dower accrues on her husband's death, so that her right of action under the statute is barred in ten years after his death.[38]

Until dower has been allotted to a widow, limitations do not run against her cause of action to recover the possession of the same.[39] Limitations begin to run against a widow claiming under dower under the Kansas statute, when the husband makes a conveyance of such property without the wife joining therein and the grantee takes adverse possession thereof.[40]

37. Brinkley v. Taylor, 111 Ark. 305, 163 S. W. 521. See also, Grober v. Clements, 71 Ark. 565, 100 Am. St. Rep. 91.

An action by a widow to recover dower in the mortgaged lands of her husband after foreclosure, being an action to enforce a legal right, laches is not available as a defense thereto. Fourche River Lumber Co. v. Walker, 96 Ark. 540, 132 S. W. 451. See as to the rules as to laches in New Jersey, Turner v. Kuehnlye, 71 N. J. Eq. 466, 64 Atl. 478. Inaction for 18 months does not constitute laches in Illinois which will bar the right to a widow's award. Fick v. Armstrong, 136 Ill. App. 26. See also, Brumback v. Brumback, 198 Ill. 66, 64 N. E. 741, holding that a widow in joint possession with others cannot be precluded by laches from maintaining an action for dower.

For the rule as to laches in Rhode Island, see Hunt v. Reilly, 23 R. L. 471, 50 Atl. 833.

38. Morris v. Roseberry, 46 W. Va. 24, 32 S. E. 1019.

Limitations do not run against the dower right of a testator's widow while in possession under a will devising land to her, to hold until his youngest child attains majority. Sperry v. Swiger, 54 W. Va. 283, 46 S. E. 125.

39. Bartee v. Edmunds, 29 Ky. Law Rep. 872, 96 S. W. 535.

Where judgment creditors, to whom a deed had been made in an equitable action, had an action to recover possession of a lot when the deed was made in 1881, but the wife of the judgment debtor had a dower interest in the lot until her death in 1905, an action to recover the lot, not brought until 1911, was barred as to two-thirds thereof, but not as against the one-third dower interest. Garrison v. Clark, 151 Ky. 565, 152 S. W. 581. And see Dixon v. Harris, 32 Ky. Law Rep. 275, 105 S. W. 451.

40. French v. Poole, 83 Kan. 281, 111 Pac. 488, under Kan. Gen. St. 1901, § 2510, providing that one-half in value of all the realty in which a husband at any time during marriage had a legal or equitable interest which has not been sold on judicial sale, and is not necessary for payment of debts, and of which the wife has made no conveyance, shall, under the direction of the probate court, be set apart by the executor as her property, upon the death of her husband, if she survives him.

CHAPTER XXVI.

FRAUD, IGNORANCE, MISTAKE, AND CONCEALMENT OF CAUSE OF ACTION.

§ 274. Statutory provisions as to fraud.

In many of the States it is now expressly provided that, where the cause of action is fraudulently concealed, or where it arises from fraud, the statute shall not begin to run except from the time of its discovery, as in Maine, Massachusetts, Connecticut, Alabama, Georgia, Indiana, Illinois, Mississippi, Maryland, Michigan, and New Mexico. In New Mexico, however, the saving is restricted to cases where the cause of action originated in or arises out of a trust. In Iowa, Colorado, Florida, Kentucky, North Carolina, South Carolina, Wisconsin, Kansas, Missouri, Minnesota, New York, Ohio, Nebraska, Nevada, California, Arizona, Dakota, Utah, Idaho, Montana, New Mexico, and Wyoming provision is made that in bills or actions for relief on the ground of fraud the cause of action shall not be deemed to have accrued until the discovery of the fraud. In the first eleven States named, the questions growing out of the fraudulent concealment of the cause of action are set at rest by the statute. But in the last-named States and Territories, inasmuch as the statute makes express provision for a saving only in cases where a court of equity, or courts of law clothed with equitable powers, can give relief, and only in favor of bills and actions for such relief, it would seem to follow, under the well-settled rules for the construction of statutes, that the fraudulent concealment of the cause of action, or the non-discovery of the fraud for which an action would lie, affords no excuse for the delay of the plaintiff in an action at law in bringing his action, and that he can only obtain relief through the interposition of a court of equity, or the equitable powers of courts of law, in such cases as come within the scope of equitable relief. In Vermont, Rhode Island, New Hampshire, Louisiana, New Jersey, Arkansas, Delaware, Pennsylvania, Texas, and Tennessee, no statutory provision upon this subject exists. In Virginia and West Virginia the statute provides that if a person shall, etc., "or by any other indirect means obstruct the prosecution of such right," etc. And it is held that, when the facts upon which the action is founded are exclusively within the knowledge of the defendant, and he fraudulently concealed them, he thereby obstructs the prosecution of the right within the meaning of the statute.[1] But in Missouri, under a somewhat similar statute, it was held that the statute did not apply to concealment or improper acts by other persons than the debtor.[2]

1. Vanbibber v. Bierne, 6 W. Va. 168.

2. Wells v. Halpin, 59 Mo. 92.

In some of the other States in which no statutory provision exists upon this subject, it has been held that in the case of fraud, and the willful suppression of the truth, the statute does not begin to run at law until its discovery.[3] But the statute is put in motion as soon as the fraud is discovered, although its full extent or all the facts are not known.[4] In Massachusetts, before the present statutory exception existed, the fraudulent concealment of a cause of action was held to be a good replication to a plea of the statute.[5] In Maine, also, this rule was adopted.[6] The doctrine of these cases was predicated upon a *dictum* of Lord Mansfield, in an English case;[7] but this *dictum* seems never to have been followed in the English cases in actions at law,[8] nor

3. Pennock v. Freeman, 1 Watts (Pa.) 401; Jones v. Conaway, 4 Yeates (Pa.) 109; Rush v. Barr, 1 Watts (Pa.) 110; Morgan v. Tener, 83 Pa. 305; Wickersham v. Lee, 83 Pa. 416; Peck v. Bank of America, 16 R. I. 710; Thompkins v. Hollister, 60 Mich. 470; Moyle v. Landers, 83 Cal. 579; Norris v. Haggin, 136 U. S. 386, 10 Sup. Ct. 942, 34 L. Ed. 424; Purdon v. Seligman, 78 Mich. 132, 43 N. W. 1045; Lawrence v. Norreys, L. R. 15 App. Cas. 210; Teall v. Slaven, 40 Fed. 774; Fisher v. Tuller, 122 Ind. 31, 23 N. E. 523; Fitts v. Beardsley, 8 N. Y. Sup. 567; Carrier v. Chicago, etc., R. R. Co., 79 Iowa 80, 44 N. W. 203, 6 L. R. A. 799.

4. Ferris v. Henderson, 12 Pa. 49; Bricker v. Lightner, 40 Pa. 199. In Miller v. Wood, 41 Hun 600, 5 N. Y. St. Rep. 214, aff'd 116 N. Y. 351, 22 N. E. 553, an action, brought to recover money as damages on the ground of fraud, was held barred by limitation if not brought within six years after the perpetration of the fraud. It is within the exception in the provision declaring that "in an action to procure a judgment, other than for a sum of money, on the ground of fraud," the cause of action "is not deemed to have accrued until the discovery by the plaintiff, or the person under whom he claims, of the facts constituting the fraud."

5. Massachusetts Turnpike Co. v. Field, 3 Mass. 201; Farnam v. Brooks, 26 Mass. (9 Pick.) 212; Wells v. Fish, 20 Mass. (3 Pick.) 74; Homer v. Fish, 18 Mass. (1 Pick.) 435. See also, Douglas v. Elkins, 28 N. H. 26; Way v. Cutting, 20 N. H. 187; Campbell v. Vining, 23 Ill. 525; Hugh v. Jones, 35 Ga. 40.

6. Cole v. McGlathry, 9 Me. 131; McKown v. Whittemore, 31 Me. 448.

7. Bree v. Holbech, Doug. 654. See also, Brown v. Howard, 3 B. & B. 73.

8. Brooksbank v. Smith, 2 Y. & C. 58; Imperial Gas Light Co. v. London Gas Co., 10 Exch. 39. See, in this country, Pyle v. Beckwith, 24 Ky. (1 J. J. Mar.) 445; Wilson v. Ivey, 32 Miss. 233; Callis v. Waddy, 2 Munf. (Va.) 511; Rice v. White, 4 Leigh (Va.) 474; Cox v. Cox. 6 Rich. (S. C.) Eq. 275; York v. Bright, 23 Tenn. (4 Humph.) 312; Hamilton v. Smith, 7 N. C. (3 Murph.) 115.

do the American cases before cited seem to have been generally followed in this country. The courts of New York repudiated this doctrine at an early day, so far as it made fraud a replication to the statute in courts of law;[9] and such also was the case in Kentucky,[10] Mississippi,[11] Virginia,[12] Tennessee,[13] North Carolina,[14] and South Carolina.[15] In England, this question is decisively put at rest by a provision of the statute,[16] to the effect that the right of a party to bring a suit in equity for the recovery of

9. Troupe v. Smith, 20 Johns. (N. Y.) 33; Leonard v. Pitney, 5 Wend. (N. Y.) 30; Humbert v. Trinity Church, 24 id. 587; Allen v. Mille, 17 id. 202. In Bosley v. Nat. Machine Co., 123 N. Y. 550, 25 N. E. 990, it was held that the provision of the statute of limitation, declaring that "an action to procure a judgment, other than for a sum of money, on the ground of fraud, in a case which was cognizable by the Court of Chancery, is not deemed to have accrued until the discovery by the plaintiff, or the person under whom he claims, of the facts constituting the fraud," applies to all cases formerly cognizable by the Court of Chancery, whether the jurisdiction therein was exclusive or concurrent with that of courts of law; that it applies when any remedy or relief is sought for, aside from a mere money judgment, and which a court of law could not give, although as a mere part of the relief sought a money judgment is demanded; and that the fact that in such an action the plaintiff asks for a money judgment for the amount paid him on subscribing, does not take it out of said provision, and the statute does not commence to run until after the discovery of the fraud.

10. Pyle v. Beckwith, 24 Ky. (1 J. J. Mar.) 445; Salve v. Twing, 62 Ky. (1 Duv.) 271. In Ellis v. Kelso, 57 Ky. (18 B. Mon.) 296, where a clerk made a fraudulent entry upon his employer's books, it was held that the statute ran from the date of entry.

11. In Wilson v. Ivey, 32 Miss. 233, the court held that, in case of fraud, the statute begins to run from the time of its commission, and not from the time the injury arising from it is established.

12. In Rice v. White, 4 Leigh (Va.) 474, an action for deceit was held to arise from the time of its commission. Callis v. Waddy, 2 Munf. (Va.) 511.

13. York v. Bright, 23 Tenn. (4 Humph.) 312. See also, to same effect, Smith v. Bishop, 9 Vt. 110; Fee v. Fee, 10 Ohio 469.

14. Hamilton v. Smith, 7 N. C. (3 Murph.) 115.

15. In Miles v. Berry, 1 Hill (S. C.) 296, where the maker of a note secretly and fraudulently obtained possession of it, and kept it until the statute had run upon it, it was held that the fraud of the maker did not save the statute.

16. See Appendix, 3 & 4 Wm. IV., § 26.

any land or rent of which he or any person through whom he claims may have been deprived by such fraud, shall be deemed to have accrued at, and not before, the time when such fraud by reasonable diligence might have been discovered. It is unfortunate that in this country the legislature of all the States have not put this question at rest by some decisive provision instead of leaving it to judicial legislation, because, when the courts engraft upon these statutes exceptions which the statute does not make or warrant, its action is nothing more nor less than an assumption of legislative functions. The cause of action, except where the statute otherwise provides, in cases of fraud, arises from the time of its commission; and when courts of law hold to the contrary, it is by force of a judicial exception engrafted upon the statute, by the assumption of legislative and equitable powers, and is not warranted by any principle or rule of law, nor can it be supported by any known rule for the construction of statutes.[17]

§ 275. Equitable rule in cases of concealed fraud.

Courts of equity, independently of any statute, will relieve against fraud, if proceedings are seasonably brought after its discovery.[18] Indeed, to use the language of Lord Cottenham, a court of equity will wrest property fraudulently acquired, not only from the perpetrator of the fraud, but "from his children and his children's children," or, as was said in another English case,[19] "from any persons to whom he may have parcelled out the fruits of his fraud." But the party seeking relief must state in his bill or complaint the non-discovery of the fraud until within the proper period.[20]

17. See opinion of Spencer, J., in Troupe v. Smith, *supra.*

18. Hovenden v. Lord Annesley, 2 Sch. & Lef. 629; South Sea Co. v. Wymondsell, 3 P. Wms. 143; Shields v. Anderson, 3 Leigh (Va.) 729; Longworth v. Hunt, 11 Ohio St. 194; Prescott v. Hubbell, 1 Hill (S. C.) 210; Donnelly v. Donnelly, 47 Ky. (8 B. Mon.) 113; Heywood v. Marsh, 14 Tenn. (6 Yerg.) 69; Currey v. Allen, 34 Cal. 234; Croft v. Arthur, 3 Desaus. (S. C.) 223; Mattock v. Todd, 25 Ind. 128; Stocks v. Van Leonard, 8 Ga. 511; Sears v. Shafer, 6 N. Y. 268.

19. Hueguenin v. Beasley, 14 Ves. 273. See also, Bridgman v. Green, Wilmot's notes, 58.

20. South Sea Co. v. Wymondsell,

The equity jurisdiction of the courts of the United States is the same as that of the High Court of Chancery in England, is not subject to limitation or restraint by State legislation, and is uniform throughout the different States of the Union.[21] And in those courts it is an established rule of equity that where relief is asked on the ground of actual fraud, especially if the fraud has been concealed, that time will not run in favor of the defendant until the discovery of the fraud, or until, with reasonable diligence, it might have been discovered.[22] The equitable jurisdiction of these courts over controversies between citizens of different States cannot be impaired by the laws of the State which prescribe the modes of redress in their courts, or which regulate the distribution of their judicial power.[23] And while legal remedies are sometimes modified to suit the changes in the laws of the States and the practice of their courts, it is not so with equitable remedies.[24] The equity practice of the Federal courts is the same

supra; Sublette v. Tinney, 9 Cal. 423. Thus, in Lott v. De Graffenreid, 10 Rich. (S. C.) Eq. 346, it was held that a creditor's bill to set aside fraudulent conveyances of the debtor is barred by the lapse of four years from the execution of the deeds, unless it be averred in the bill that the fraud was not discovered till within four years before the bill was filed. The statute runs against a suit in equity by creditors, to set aside a voluntary conveyance, by their debtor, from the time of notice to them of the conveyance, and the want of consideration. Eigleberger v. Kibler, 1 Hill (S. C.) Ch. 113; White v. Poussin, 1 Bailey (S. C.) Ch. 458. Where a broker falsely represented to a party for whom he undertook to invest money upon a good bond, well secured by mortgage, that the security was ample, it was held that the right of action arose when it was discovered and the insecurity of the bond and mortgage ascertained, and that no suit in law or equity could be maintained after the time limited for such suits by the statute of limitations. Turnbull v. Gadsden, 2 Strobh. (S. C.) Eq. 14. Upon a bill brought to set aside a sheriff's deed on the ground that the purchase was fraudulent, the statute was held to run from the date of the purchase. Cox v. Cox, 6 Rich. (S. C.) Eq. 275.

21. Robinson v. Campbell, 16 U. S. (3 Wheat.) 212, 4 L. Ed. 372; Kirby v. Lake Shore, etc., R. Co., 120 U. S. 130, 7 Sup. Ct. 430, 30 L. Ed. 569.

22. Meader v. Norton, 78 U. S. (11 Wall.) 442, 20 L. Ed. 184; Kirby v. Lake Shore, etc., R. Co., *supra.*

23. Payne v. Hook, 74 U. S. (7 Wall.) 425, 430, 19 L. Ed. 260.

24. Harlan, J., in Kirby v. Lake Shore, etc., R. Co., *supra.*

in every State, and they demonstrate the same system of equity rules and equity jurisdiction throughout the whole of the United States, without regard to State laws.[25] In California, it is held that the statute operates a saving in favor of actions for relief on the ground of constructive fraud.[26] The species of fraud against which a court of equity will give relief, although an action therefor is barred at law, must be distinct in its characteristics.[27] In England, under the statute of 3 and 4 Wm. IV., it has been held that a possession through a conveyance from a lunatic is not necessarily fraudulent,[28] but that the rule is otherwise where *mala fides* on the part of the purchaser is shown;[29] but the mere fact that the grantee is aware of a flaw in his title is not such a case of fraud as takes the case out of the statute.[30] In equity, where there is a fraudulent concealment of a cause of action, the statute commences running from the time it is discovered; but where the right depends on recorded instruments, there must be such misrepresentations as to prevent an examination of the records.[31] Nor, generally, will equity interfere in a case where the party seeking relief might, by the exercise of proper diligence, have discovered the fraud.[32] Where an estate was intentionally omitted

25. Payne v. Hook, *supra;* Green's Adm'x v. Creighton, 64 U. S. (23 How.) 90, 16 L. Ed. 419; Rosenthal v. Walker, 111 U. S. 185, 4 Sup. Ct. 382, 28 L. Ed. 395; United States v. Howland, 17 U. S. (4 Wheat.) 108, 4 L. Ed. 526.

26. Boyd v. Blankman, 29 Cal. 19.

27. Dean v. Thwaite, 21 Beav. 621; Petre v. Petre, 1 Drew. 397.

28. Price v. Berrington, 3 Mac. & G. 486; Manby v. Bewickle, 3 K. & J. 342.

29. Lewes v. Thomas, 3 Hare 26. See also, Crowther v. Rowlandson, 27 Cal. 376, where it was held that the statute does not commence to run against the right to have a deed set aside on the ground of the grantor's insanity, and fraud on the part of the grantee, until the grantor recovers his reason. Arrington v. McLemon, 33 Ark. 759.

30. Langley v. Fisher, 9 Beav. 90; Bellamy v. Sabine, 2 Phil. 425.

31. Haynie v. Hall, 24 Tenn. (5 Humph.) 220.

32. Thus, where a register-book containing a certificate of marriage, which formed a principal link in the title of the plaintiff, had been fraudulently mutilated, it was held upon demurrer that as the fraud could have been discovered earlier with proper diligence, the bill was too late. In this case, the claim had, in fact, lain dormant for nearly one hundred and fifty years. Chetham v. Hoare, L. R. 9 Eq. 571.

from an insolvent's schedule, it was considered an instance of concealed fraud.[33] The court will not enter into the question how far a fraud has been in effect concealed, owing to the exceptional dullness of the lawful claimant's intellect;[34] and where the question of fraud is raised, but there is a doubt of its existence, the court will not be inclined to presume it at a great distance of time, but will require strong *prima facie* evidence.[35] The reason why, if fraud has been concealed by one party, and until it has been discovered by the other, the statute should not operate as a bar, is, that it ought not in conscience to run; the conscience of the party being so affected that he ought not to be allowed to avail himself of the length of time.[36] In many of the States, a certain period

33. Sturgis v. Morse, 24 Beav. 541.

34. Manby v. Bewicke, 3 K. & J. 342; Bridgman v. Gill, 24 Beav. 302.

35. Charter v. Trevelyan, 4 L. J. N. S. Ch. 239, 11 Cl. & Fin. 714; Bonney v. Ridgard, cited in 17 Ves. 97. "Length of time," said Story, J., "necessarily obscures all human evidence; and as it thus removes from the parties all the immediate means to verify the nature of the original transaction, it operates by way of presumption in favor of innocence and against the imputation of fraud." Prevost v. Gratz, 19 U. S. (6 Wheat.) 481, 5 L. Ed. 311. In Marquis of Clanricarde v. Henning, 30 Beav. 175, a bill to impeach a purchase by a solicitor from his client was deemed too late after forty years.

36. Hovenden v. Annesley, *supra*.

Under section 26 of this statute, it is not enough in England to prove concealed fraud, but the plaintiff must also show that it was intentionally concealed, resulting in depriving him of the land sought to be recovered, and that the fraud could not have been known or discovered by reasonable diligence during the statutory period before suit is brought. Lawrence v. Norreys, 15 A. C. 210; Moore v. Knight (1891), 1 Ch. 547; Willis v. Howe (1893), 2 Ch. 545; Betjemann v. Betjemann (1895), 2 Ch. 474; *Re* Arbitration Between the Ashley and Tildesley Coal Cos., 80 L. T. 116. See Amy v. Watertown, 130 U. S. 320, 324, 9 Sup. Ct. 537, 32 L. Ed. 953. "Concealed fraud" under the above section 26, must be the fraud of the person who set up the statute, or of some one through whom he claims. *In re* McCallum (1901), 1 Ch. 143.

The statute of limitations has no application even at law to a secret stealing of coal by a wilful, underground trespass, prior to its discovery. Bulli Coal Mining Co. v. Osborne (1899), A. C. 351; Lewey v. H. C. Fricke Coke Co., 166 Pa. 536, 31 Atl. 261, 28 L. R. A. 283, 45 Am. St. Rep. 684, and n. See *supra*, § 178, n. (a). In some of the States, as, e. g., in Ohio, such underground trespasses are specially provided for in the limitation acts; the Ohio provision (§ 4982) is that "in an action for trespass underground or in-

after the discovery of the fraud is fixed within which an action for relief must be brought; but where no period is fixed a delay beyond the statutory period will be fatal.[37]

jury to mines, the action shall not be deemed to have accrued until the wrong-doer is discovered."

In the recent case of Dean v. Ross, 178 Mass. 397, 60 N. E. 119, where the plaintiff had a verdict for $10,-493, for the conversion of fifteen bonds of the par value of $500 each by the defendant, a spiritualist medium, the court said: "We do not agree with the defendant's contention that if a defendant, who falsely represents that the spirit of a dead husband speaks through the defendant's lips, and thereby obtains the plaintiff's property, is successful in continuing the deception for six years next after the last cent of the plaintiff's property was obtained by the defendant, the plaintiff is without remedy when her eyes are opened; on the contrary, we are of opinion that, in such a case, there is concealment of the fraud, and the plaintiff can sue within six years after she discovers that she has been duped. Manufacturers' Nat. Bank v. Perry, 144 Mass. 313, 11 N. E. 81. It does not lie in the mouth of a defendant who has fraudulently succeeded in bringing a plaintiff under such a delusion to set up that the plaintiff had means of ascertaining the truth."

Although the equity rule that, in cases of fraud, limitation begins to run not at the time of its perpetration, but at the time of its discovery, cannot be maintained to the same extent in actions at law, yet there appears to be no good reason why equity and law should be so far apart as to forbid a court of law taking the same starting point, when active additional fraud has prevented such discovery. See Reynolds v. Hennessy, 17 R. I. 169, 178, 20 Atl. 307, 23 Atl. 639.

In the case of official bonds, defalcation and concealed fraud on the principal's part will deprive his surety as well as himself of the benefit of the statute of limitations, which, as to both, begins to run only when the fraud is discovered. Lieberman v. First Nat. Bank, 8 Del. Ch. 519, 2 Pennewill, 416, 48 L. R. A. 514, 82 Am. St. Rep. 414, 45 Atl. 901, 904. As to fraudulent concealment of the cause of action, see also, Shellenberger v. Ransom, 41 Neb. 631, 59 N. W. 935, 25 L. R. Ann. 564, and n.; Peck v. Bank of America, 16 R. I. 710, 7 L. R. A. 826, and n., 19 Atl. 369; Manufacturers' Nat. Bank v. Perry, 144 Mass. 313, 11 N. E. 81; Abbott v. North Andover, 145 Mass. 484, 14 N. E. 754; Sanborn v. Gale, 162 Mass. 412, 38 N. E. 710, 26 L. R. A. 864; Graham v. Stanton, 177 Mass. 321, 58 N. E. 1023; Lewey v. Fricke Coke Co., *supra;* Dorsey Machine Co. v. McCaffrey, 139 Ind. 545, 38 N. E. 208, 47 Am. St. Rep. 290; Toole v. Johnson, 61 S. C. 34, 39 S. E. 254; Cox v. Von Ahlefeldt, 105 La. 542, 30 So. 175; 34 Am. L. Reg. (N. S.) 462; *infra,* § 276, n. (a).

37. In Bailey v. Glover, 88 U. S. (21 Wall.) 342, 347, 22 L. Ed. 636, the court said: "To hold that by concealing fraud or by committing a fraud in a manner that concealed it

In the United States courts the equity jurisdiction of those courts is not subject either to limitation or restraint by State legislation, and is uniform throughout the different States of the Union.[38]

The statute of New York upon limitations does not, in view of these authorities, says Harlan, J., in a case previously cited, affect the power and duty of the court below—following the settled rules of equity—to adjudge that time did not run in favor of defendants, charged with actual concealed fraud, until after such fraud was or should with due diligence have been discovered. Upon any other theory the equity jurisdiction of the courts of the United States could not be exercised according to

self until such time as the party committing the fraud could plead the statute of limitations to protect it, is to make the law which was designed to prevent fraud the means by which it is made successful and secure." See Traer v. Clews, 115 U. S. 528, 1 Sup. Ct. 155, 29 L. Ed. 467. In Kirby v. Lake Shore, etc., R. Co., 120 U. S. 130, 7 Sup. Ct. 430, 30 L. Ed. 569, Harlan, J., says: "It is an established rule of equity, as administered in the courts of the United States, that where relief is asked on the ground of actual fraud, especially if such fraud has been concealed, time will not run in favor of the defendant until the discovery of the fraud, or until with reasonable diligence it might have been discovered." See Meader v. Norton, 78 U. S. (11 Wall.) 442, 20 L. Ed. 184; Prevost v. Gratz, 19 U. S. (6 Wheat.) 481, 5 L. Ed. 311; Michoud v. Girod, 45 U. S. (4 How.) 503, 11 L. Ed. 1076; Veazie v. Williams, 49 U. S. (8 How.) 149, 12 L. Ed. 1018; Brown v. Buena Vista, 95 U. S. 157, 24 L. Ed. 422; Rosenthal v. Walker, 111 U. S. 185, 190, 4 Sup. Ct. 382, 28 L. Ed. 395.

38. Robinson v. Campbell, 16 U. S. (3 Wheat.) 212, 4 L. Ed. 372; Boyle v. Zacharie, 31 U. S. (6 Pet.) 648, 8 L. Ed. 532; Livingston v. Story, 34 U. S. (9 Pet.) 632, 656, 9 L. Ed. 255; Stearns v. Page, 48 U. S. (7 How.) 819, 12 L. Ed. 928; Russell v. Southard, 53 U. S. (12 How.) 139, 147, 13 L. Ed. 927, 147; Neves v. Scott, 54 U. S. (13 How.) 268, 272, 14 L. Ed. 140; Barber v. Barber, 21 id. 572; Green's Adm'r v. Creighton, 64 U. S. (23 How.) 90, 105, 16 L. Ed. 419; Kirby v. Lake Shore, etc., R. Co., 120 U. S. 130, 7 Sup. Ct. 430, 30 L. Ed. 569. In Burke v. Smith, 83 U. S. (16 Wall.) 390, 401, 21 L. Ed. 361, where the local statute prescribed six years for the commencement of actions for fraud, the court said: "We think a court of equity will not be moved to set aside a fraudulent transaction at the suit of one who has been quiescent during a period longer than that fixed by the statute of limitations, after he had knowledge of the fraud, or after he was put upon inquiry with the means of knowledge accessible to him."

rules and principles applicable alike in every State. It is undoubtedly true, as announced in adjudged cases, that courts of equity feel themselves bound, in cases of concurrent jurisdiction, by the statutes of limitation that govern courts of law in similar circumstances, and that sometimes they act upon the analogy of the like limitation at law. But these general rules must be taken subject to the qualification that the equity jurisdiction of the courts of the United States cannot be impaired by the laws of the respective States in which they sit. It is an inflexible rule in those courts, when applying the general limitation prescribed in cases like this, to regard the cause of action as having accrued at the time the fraud was or should have been discovered, and thus withhold from the defendant the benefit, in the computation of time, of the period during which he concealed the fraud. It results that even if this be not an action "to procure a judgment, other than for a sum of money, on the ground of fraud," within the meaning of the New York Code of Procedure, the limitation of six years, being applied here, does not, as adjudged below, commence from the commission of the alleged frauds.

Without inquiring whether the plaintiff was not guilty of such gross laches, in applying for relief, as deprived him of all right to the aid of equity, and giving him the benefit of the limitation of six years, to be computed from the discovery of the fraud, there seems to be even then no escape from the conclusion that the suit was not brought in time. Seven years, lacking only seven days, elapsed after the discovery of the frauds by the plaintiff's testator before suit was brought.

§ 276. Instances in which the statute will not run until fraud is discovered.

In order to avail himself of the rule as to concealed fraud, to excuse delay in bringing an action, the bill or complaint should set forth the nature of the transaction fully, and also the acts of concealment, and the time of its discovery.[39]

39. State v. Giles, 52 Ind. 356. If at the time of the discovery of a

The provision that if a person liable to an action shall conceal the fact from the knowledge of the person entitled thereto, the action may be commenced at any time within the period of limitation after the discovery of the cause of action, applies to causes of action for fraud, as well as to other causes of action; but the concealment contemplated by the statute is something more than mere silence; it must be of an affirmative character, and must be alleged and proved so as to bring the case clearly within the meaning of the statute.[40] Something more than mere silence is necessary, unless the relationship of the parties is such that the

fraud, the party injured has a legal capacity to act and to contract, his right of action accrues and the statute of limitations begins to run against it, irrespective of his intelligence, or of his freedom from undue influence, or his ability to resist it. Piper v. Hoard, 107 N. Y. 67, 13 N. E. 632, 1 Am. St. Rep. 785.

40. Wynne v. Cornelison, 52 Ind. 312; Township of Boomer v. French; 40 Iowa, 601; Stanley v. Stanton, 36 Ind. 445. A request by one of two indorsers of a note that suit be delayed against him, or that the other indorser be sued first, is no case for the interference of a court of equity. Bank of Tenn. v. Hill, 29 Tenn. (10 Humph.) 176. So where, in an account settled between the parties, the plaintiff has erroneously credited the defendants with an amount which, for that reason, he would be entitled to recover. Brown v. Edes, 37 Me. 492. Nor is a denial on the part of the defendant that he was part owner in a vessel, made when a portion of an account for repairs was presented to him, such a fraudulent concealment as to prevent him from availing himself of the plea of the statute. Rense v. Southard, 39 Me. 404. But where the delay of the plaintiff to seek relief was occasioned, in part at least, by the promise of the defendant to rectify certain errors, the existence of such errors came to the knowledge of the plaintiff gradually, and the circumstances were such that the defendant could suffer nothing by the delay, it was held that the plaintiff was not precluded from relief on the ground that he had not sought it within reasonable time. Callender v. Colegrove, 17 Conn. 1. And where it is agreed between the assignor and assignee of a promissory note, at the time of the assignment, that the assignee need not demand payment of the maker before a certain time, it is not laches in the assignee not to commence suit on the note before that time. Nance v. Dunlavy, 7 Blackf. (Ind.) 172. When the limitation is by agreement, as in an insurance policy, it is generally held that conduct on the part of the insurers which leads the insured to delay, is a waiver of the limitation. Black v. Winnishiek Ins. Co., 31 Wis. 74; Fullam v. N. Y. Union Ins. Co., 73 Mass. (7 Gray) 61; McKown v. Whitman, 31 Me. 448; Buckner v. Calcote, 28 Miss. 432.

party is bound to speak;[41] it is necessary that some effort to conceal the fraud should have been made, either by preventing an investigation, or by misleading the party making inquiry, or that misrepresentations were made by the party which were calculated to mislead him. In other words, some affirmative acts to conceal the fraud must be shown,[42] and, according to the case last cited, the party seeking to avoid the statute must have exercised proper diligence.[43] Mere silence or passiveness, there being no fidu-

41. Miller v. Powers, 119 Ind. 79, 21 N. E. 455, 4 L. R. A. 483; Jackson v. Buchanan, 59 Ind. 390; Wynne v. Cornelison, 52 Ind. 312.

42. Stone v. Brown, 116 Ind. 78, 18 N. E. 392.

43. See Rhoton v. Mendenhall, 17 Or. 199, 20 Pac. 49.

See St. Paul, etc., Ry. Co. v. Sage, 49 Fed. 315; Clark v. Van Loon, 108 Iowa, 250, 79 N. W. 88, 75 Am. St. Rep. 219; Lady Washington Consol. Co. v. Wood, 113 Cal. 482, 45 Pac. 809; Hart v. Church, 126 Cal. 471, 59 Pac. 296, 77 Am. St. Rep. 195; Thomas v. Rauer, 62 Kan. 568, 64 Pac. 80; Stearns v. Hochbrunn, 24 Wash. 206, 64 Pac. 165. When fraud is not proved, the statute runs from the time when the wrongful act was committed. Trotter v. Maclean, 13 Ch. D. 574; *In re* Crosley, 35 Ch. D. 266; Moore v. Knight, [1891] 1 Ch. 547; Wilkinson v. Verity, L. R. 6 C. P. 206; Miller v. Dell, [1891] 1 Q. B. 468; Carter v. Eighth Ward Bank, 33 Misc. Rep. 128, 67 N. Y. Supp. 300. It is often material to distinguish between actual and constructive fraud, especially in relation to trusts, since, for instance, the statute of limitations applies to constructive trusts, but not to express trusts while continuing. See Patrick v. Sampson, 24 Q. B. D. 128; Speidel v. Henrici, 120 U. S. 377, 7 Sup. Ct. 610, 30 L. Ed. 718; Alsop v. Riker, 155 U. S. 448, 460, 15 Sup. Ct. 162, 39 L. Ed. 218; Whitney v. Fox, 166 U. S. 637, 17 Sup. Ct. 713, 41 L. Ed. 1145; McMonagle v. McGlinn, 85 Fed. 88; Cooper v. Hill, 94 id. 582; Mount v. Mount, 35 Misc. Rep. 62, 71 N. Y. S. 199, rev'd 68 App. Div. 144, 74 N. Y. Supp. 148; Seitz v. Seitz, 59 App. Div. 150, 69 N. Y. S. 170; Currier v. Studley, 159 Mass. 17, 33 N. E. 709; Fuller v. Cushman, 170 Mass. 286, 49 N. E. 63; St. Paul's Church v. Atty.-Gen., 164 Mass. 188, 199, 41 N. E. 231, *supra*, § 58, and n. Within this rule a solicitor whom trustees, employing him for the trust, allow to collect and retain the trust funds, is an express trustee, though he is guilty of concurring in the trustee's breach of trust in so receiving the money. Soar v. Ashwell, [1893] 2 Q. B. 390. See *In re* Lands Allotment Co., [1894] 1 Ch. 616; Heynes v. Dixon, [1900] 2 Ch. 561; Municipal Freehold Land Co. v. Pollington, 63 L. T. 238; *In re* Bowden, 45 Ch. D. 444. But a mortgagee, on receiving the cash proceeds of the sale of the mortgaged property is not the trustee of an express trust so as to suspend the statute. Mills v. Mills, 115 N. Y. 80, 21 N. E. 714. While equity will regard with suspicion an attempt to establish a constructive re-

ciary relation or act of the party calculated to deceive or lull inquiry, is not a fraudulent concealment within the meaning of the statute.[44] The rule that the "concealment" which prevents

sulting trust after such lapse of time as thirty years, yet when the evidence, though oral, is clear, it may establish such a trust, though denied by the defendant's answer. McIntire v. Pryor, 173 U. S. 38, 19 Sup. Ct. 352, 43 L. Ed. 606; Condit v. Maxwell, 142 Mo. 266, 44 S. W. 467; Cooksey v. Bryan, 2 App. D. C. 557; Robb v. Day, 90 Fed. 337, 33 C. C. A. 84; Lemoine v. Dunklin County, 51 Fed. 487, 2 C. C. A. 343.

44. Tillison v. Ewing, 91 Ala. 467, 8 So. 404, holding that if due inquiry for a certificate of entry filed in the proper governmental department to obtain a patent would have led to information of its issuance, which is the only fact claimed to have been discovered, the concealment or destruction of the patent will not constitute such fraud which, under the statute, prevents the accrual of a cause of action, until its discovery. In Wisconsin actual notice of the facts is held necessary, and constructive notice will not put the statute in motion, under a statute providing that a cause of action for relief on the ground of fraud does not accrue until the discovery of the facts constituting the fraud. Fox v. Zimmerman, 77 Wis. 414, 46 N. W. 533. In New York an action to rescind a purchase of stock in a corporation, induced by fraud, does not accrue until the discovery of the fraud by the plaintiff or the person under whom he claims. Bosley v. National Mach. Co., 123 N. Y. 550, 25 N. E. 990. The statute does not run as to a claim against a firm of solicitors for money sent them to invest, but which is embezzled by their clerk, until discovery of that fact, where they represent that it has been invested and continue to pay interest on it. This rule is unaffected by the English Trustee Act, 1888. Moore v. Knight, [1891] 1 Ch. 547. In Louisiana it is held that prescription against an action to annul a judgment for fraud only runs from the date of discovery of the fraud. Lazarus v. McGuirk, 42 La. Ann. 194. The statute does not begin to run against the claim of a shipper to recover back excessive payments of freight charges so long as he has no knowledge of his rights, owing to the fraudulent concealment of the cause of action by the carrier. Cook v. Chicago, R. I. & P. R. Co., 81 Iowa 551, 46 N. W. 1080, 9 L. R. A. 164, 25 Am. St. Rep. 512. The statute does not apply to an action to cancel a sheriff's deed of land sold under a judgment which had been purchased and held by one who, acting under a trust, had collected funds for its satisfaction to such purchaser, and to remove the incumbrance of the judgment from the property. Wilson v. Brookshire, 126 Ind. 497, 25 N. E. 131, 9 L. R. A. 792. In Kentucky it is held that the statute runs against an action by a creditor to subject his debtor's lands to the payment of his debt, although the creditor lived in a distant county and did not know of a conveyance by his debtor and a record of the deed in the county where the debtor lived. Cock-

the running of the statute must be of a positive and affirmative character was applied in Indiana, where one sued for criminal conversation had persuaded the plaintiff's wife to deny the same for two years; and the court held that such denial or procurement thereof was no "concealment."[45] Living with a woman without marriage to her, and publicly acknowledging her as the wife of defendant, does not constitute a case of concealment of the crime of fornication, such as will take the offense out of the statute of limitations.[46] In Iowa, the provision of the code as to fraud is held to apply only in cases of equitable cognization; and is a case where B. conveyed to his son, who died shortly afterwards, leaving an illegitimate son whom he had recognized, and after the death of his son, B. again conveyed the property to another, in fraud of the rights of the grandson, who had no knowledge of the existence of the estate of his father until twenty years afterwards, whereupon he immediately commenced his action, it was held that it was barred by the statute.[47] In Maryland, it is held that where one practices fraud, to the injury of

rill's Ex'r v. Cockrill, 13 Ky. L. Rep. 10, 15 S. W. 1119. The statute only begins to run against an action to charge a trustee for the trust property which has been fraudulently purchased at a judicial sale for his benefit, from the discovery, by the *cestui que trust*, of the facts constituting fraud. Lewis v. Welch, 47 Minn. 193, 48 N. W. 608, 49 N. W. 665. A creditor, by admitting that he was informed by his debtor that he conducted his business in his wife's name to prevent his creditors from hampering him, acknowledges that he then had notice of the fraud, so as to set the statute running from that date against an action by him against the wife. Osborne v. Wilkes, 108 N. C. 651, 13 S. E. 285. In Ohio the statute begins to run against an action to reform a written instrument on the ground of mistake, upon the execution of the instrument, and not upon the discovery of the mistake. Bryant v. Swetland, 48 Ohio St. 194, 27 N. E. 100. But in Nebraska it is held that the statute begins to run against a suit to correct a mistake in the drafting or recording of a deed, where the correction involves no change of actual possession or disturbance of investments, upon the discovery of the mistake, or of facts placing one on inquiry. Ainsfield v. More, 30 Neb. 385, 46 N. W. 828, 1 Neb. L. J. 202.

45. Jackson v. Buchanan, 59 Ind. 390.

46. Robinson v. State, 57 Ind. 113.

47. Brown v. Brown, 44 Iowa 349.

another, the subsequent concealment of it from the injured party is in itself a fraud; and if he is thereby kept in ignorance of his cause of action, he is kept in ignorance by "the fraud of the adverse party," within the meaning of the statute regarding the right of action "to have first accrued at the time at which such fraud shall, or with usual and ordinary diligence might, have been known or discovered."[48] In Illinois, it is held that there is no rule which requires a trustee or *cestui* to execute and record any instrument to counteract the record of a forged release of the trust deed. Nor is the owner of land limited to any particular period for commencing proceedings, at law or in equity, against a forger of title to his land, to vindicate his good title against the fraudulent claim of the forger, or one claiming under him. He may bide his time, and trust to the strength of his title.[49] In Minnesota, it is held that, under the statute, time commenced to run for a fraudulent conversion from the time of its discovery.[50] In Louisiana, an action by a judgment creditor, to annul a mortgage on the ground that it was fraudulent, was held to be barred by the statute in one year.[51] In West Virginia, the statute is held to run against a suit to set aside a conveyance as fraudulent against creditors, founded on the charge that its provisions are such as to render it voidable, as matter of law, from the time when the deed was made; but that it does not run against a suit founded on the charge of a fraudulent intent, in fact, except from the time of discovering the fraud.[52] In Iowa, an action by a ten-

48. Wear v. Skinner, 46 Md. 347. See also Findley v. Stewart, 46 Iowa 655.

49. Chandler v. White, 84 Ill. 435. Where parties secured the legal title of a Mexican grant, by presenting to the land commissioners a worthless document, as a transfer of the grantee's interest, whereby a fraud was committed upon the heirs of the grantee, it was held that the patentees would, in equity, be converted into trustees, and that limitation did not run, in such case, against the right of the heirs, until their discovery of the fraud. Hardy v. Harbin, 4 Sawyer (U. S.) 536. See Bescher v. Paulus, 58 Ind. 271.

50. Commissioners v. Smith, 22 Minn. 97.

51. Brewer v. Kelly, 24 La. Ann. 246; Powell v. O'Neill, id. 522.

52. Hunter v. Hunter, 10 W. Va. 123.

ant in common to recover possession of the common property which is fraudulently held by his co-tenant, and to which the latter has acquired a tax deed, is held not to be barred at the expiration of five years from the recording of the deed.[53] In Arkansas, under the code of practice, when courts can exercise equitable and legal jurisdiction, if the administrator pleads the statute of limitations in a suit founded on a cause of action accruing in the lifetime of his intestate, fraudulent conversion and concealment by the intestate may be given in evidence in answer to such plea.[54]

It is an invariable rule, says Miller, J., that the fraud must have been one which was concealed from the plaintiff by the defendant, or which was of such a character as necessarily implied concealment. And the acts which are claimed to constitute the fraud are evidenced by public record or by judicial proceedings, and it cannot be claimed that there was such a concealment as would prevent the operation of the statute.[55]

The omission to disclose to the owner a trespass upon land, if there is no fiduciary relation between the parties, and the owner has the means of discovering the facts, and nothing has been done to prevent him from discovering them, is not a fraudulent concealment, within the statute.[56] But where an agent or officer of a corporation falsely represents that he has paid a debt of his principal or of the corporation, and thereby induces the payment of the amount to him, the cause of action does not arise until the fraud is discovered.[57] The fraudulent concealment must have

53. Austin v. Barrett, 44 Iowa, 488; Muir v. Bozarth, id. 499.

54. Meyer v. Quarteman, 28 Ark. 45.

55. Norris v. Haggen, 136 U. S. 386, 10 Sup. Ct. 942, 34 L. Ed. 424. See Way v. Cutting, 20 N. H. 187; Bricker v. Lightner, 40 Pa. 199; Livermore v. Johnson, 27 Miss. 284; Vigus v. O'Bannon, 118 Ill. 334, 346, 8 N. E. 778; Atlantic National Bank v. Harris, 118 Mass. 147; Wear v. Skinner, 46 Md. 257; Wilson v. Ivy, 32 Miss. 233.

56. Nudd v. Hamblin, 90 Mass. (8 Allen) 130.

57. Atlantic Bank v. Harris, 118 Mass. 147. But the procuring of the settlement and discharge of an existing cause of action by fraudulent means is not such fraudulent concealment within the statute. Penobscot R. R. Co. v. Mayo, 65 Me. 566.

been that of the party sought to be charged, and a mere allegation or proof that it was the act of his agent will not be sufficient, unless he is in some way shown to have been instrumental in, or cognizant of, the fraud;[58] and in all cases the plaintiff takes the burden of establishing the fraud, so as to bring his case within the statute.[59] So, too, it must relate to the cause of action, and does not apply to the concealment of property, so that it cannot be reached upon execution.[60] Except where made so by statute, mere ignorance of one's rights does not prevent the operation of the statute.[61]

58. Stevenson v. Robinson, 39 Mich. 160.

59. Evans v. Montgomery, 50 Iowa 325. Proof of a mere non-user of corporate powers is not a concealment of the corporation such as to suspend the running of the statute. Fort Scott v. Schulenberg, 22 Kan. 648. So where a guardian refused to settle with his ward, and put him off for several years, saying that he had the matter fixed, it was held not such fraud as would take the case out of the statute. Jones v. Strickland, 61 Ga. 356. In an action by a judgment plaintiff induced by one in collusion with the debtor to sell the judgment for half its amount, it was held that the six years' limitation of the Indiana statute to "an action for relief against frauds" commenced to run when the fraud was perpetrated. Wood v. Carpenter, 101 U. S. 135, 25 L. Ed. 807. See also Mercantile Nat. Bank v. Carpenter, 101 U. S. 567, 25 L. Ed. 815; Sweet v. Hentig, 24 Kan. 497.

From fraudulent concealment of a cause of action a new promise will not be inferred, nor does such concealment estop the defendant from setting up at law the bar of the statute; and even when such concealment is not an answer to the statute in an action at law, relief therefrom may still be gained in equity. Freeholders of Somerset v. Veghte, 44 N. J. Law 509; Sanborn v. Gale, 162 Mass. 412, 38 N. E. 710, 26 L. R. A. 864; Coffing v. Dodge, 169 Mass. 459, 48 N. E. 840. And there is no reason why a court of equity may not, by injunction, disarm a defendant from using the statute fraudulently in an action at law. Holloway v. Appelget, 55 N. J. Eq. 583, 40 Atl. 27, 62 Am. St. Rep. 827. See Parsons v. Hartman, 25 Oregon 547, 42 Am. St. Rep. 803, 37 Pac. 61, 30 L. R. A. 98, 142, n.

60. Humphreys v. Mattoon, 43 Iowa 556. In Rice v. Burt, 58 Mass. (4 Cush.) 208, the concealment of property by an insolvent from his assignee, and his concealment from a creditor of fraudulent acts, which if known would have enabled the creditor to avoid the debtor's discharge, were held not a fraudulent concealment of the plaintiff's cause of action. In Fleming v. Culbert, 46 Pa. 498, the investment of money in bonds, etc., by an attorney in fact, instead of remitting it to his client, was held not a fraudulent concealment suspending the statute. See also Munson v. Hallowell, 26 Tex. 475.

61. Foster v. Rison, 17 Gratt. (Va.)

§ 276a(1). Fraud as ground of relief—In general.

The statute does not begin to run in favor of one who falsely certifies to a purchaser of corporate bonds that they were secured by a mortgage, and who afterwards executed another mortgage on behalf of the company, and received part of the proceeds, until the bonds become due.[62] That a freight agent has told a shipper that he will be charged the same rates as others, and will be notified of any additional concession made to others, is not fraudulent conduct such as will prevent the running of limitations against the shipper's action for subsequent unlawful discrimination in allowing rebates to other shippers.[63] Limitations run against a cause of action arising out of fraud, unless the cause of action has been fraudulently concealed.[64] An action to recover money paid on

321; Campbell v. Long, 20 Iowa 382; Bassand v. White, 9 Rich. (S. C.) Eq. 483; Bank v. Waterman, 26 Conn. 324; Abell v. Harris, 11 G. & J. (Md.) 367; Martin v. Bank, 31 Ala. 115; Davis v. Cotten, 55 N. C. (2 Jones Eq.) 430.

62. Miles v. Roberts, 76 Fed. 919 (C. C., N. Y.).

Repetition of the fraudulent representations by which a contract to marry was procured does not give a new cause of action, so as to interrupt the running of limitations against an action for the fraud. Reilly v. Sabater, 43 N. Y. Supp. 383, 26 Civ. Proc. R. 34.

63. Mitchell Coal & Coke Co. v. Pennsylvania R. Co., 241 Pa. 536, 88 Atl. 743. That the coal freight agent of a railroad company promised a coal company that in the future it would be given as favorable rates as were given to any other shipper, which promise was not kept, but lower rates were afterward given to other competing companies, did not constitute fraud which would prevent the running of limitations against an action to recover damages for the unlawful discrimination. Mitchell Coal & Coke Co. v. Pennsylvania R. Co., 181 Fed. 403, dismissed for want of jurisdiction, 183 Fed. 908 (C. C., Pa.). See Franklin v. Franklin, 22 Pa. Super. Ct. 463, wherein an alleged fraud was held insufficient to overcome the plea of the statute of limitations.

64. Plant v. Humphries, 66 W. Va. 88, 66 S. E. 94.

Acts between the purchaser and strangers to the contract of sale will not constitute such fraud as will prevent limitations from running against the vendor's cause of action arising out of a mutual mistake as to the amount of purchase money, in a settlement between vendor and purchaser, even though they may have tended to conceal the cause of action. Craig v. Gauley Coal Land Co., 73 W. Va. 624, 80 S. E. 945. The fact that money is obtained by fraud will not prevent the running of the statute of limitations, under Code 1906,

insurance policies within the statutory period, on the ground that the beneficiaries in the policies made false representations when the policies were issued, more than ten years prior to the commencement of the action, is not barred by the ten-year statute of limitations, since the statute runs from the date the payment was made, which marked the consummation of the fraud.[65] The claim of a vendee against the vendor of real estate for damages for fraudulent representations as to title accrues immediately on the perpetration of the fraud, and is not postponed to such time as he sustains actual loss.[66] The statute of limitations begins to run in favor of the third person to whom it is claimed partnership funds have been fraudulently diverted immediately upon such fraudulent diversion, if the injured partners have knowledge of it.[67] Right of action by a vendor against a purchaser for falsely stating to vendor that no broker employed by vendor was concerned in the transaction is founded on the fact that because of the false representations vendor was persuaded to sell for less than he would have otherwise received, and right of action became complete as soon as the vendor conveyed to the purchaser for such price.[68] The Missouri statute, providing that, if a party by improper conduct prevents the commencement of an action, it may be begun within the period of limitation after the obstacle is removed, is not applicable

§ 3511, against an action to recover the same from the consummation of the transaction, unless investigation is prevented by affirmative acts of the wrongdoer, and mere silence is not sufficient. Boyd v. Beebe, 64 W. Va. 216, 61 S. E. 304. Where a cause of action arises out of a fraud, the statute runs from its perpetration. This does not apply to fraudulent transfers. Thompson v. Whataker Iron Co., 41 W. Va. 574, 23 S. E. 796.

65. Johnson v. Equitable Life Assur. Society of United States, 137 Ky. 437, 125 S. W. 1074. In no case does an action for fraud lie after 10 years from the making of the contract or perpetration of the fraud. Lyms v. Henderson, 6 Ky. Law Rep. (abstract) 219.

66. Burling v. Allvord's Estate, 77 Neb. 861, 110 N. W. 683. See, as to action against a county clerk for excess fees collected: State v. Boyd, 49 Neb. 303, 68 N. H. 510.

67. Stone v. Baldwin, 127 Ill. App. 563, judg. aff'd 226 Ill. 338, 80 N. E. 890.

68. Brackett v. Perry, 201 Mass. 502, 87 N. E. 903.

where a surety on a note prior to judgment against the maker and sureties made himself insolvent by a fraudulent transfer of his land; such conduct not preventing suit against him for contribution by a co-surety, but only going to defeat an execution on a judgment against him.[69] A claim of fraud in a conveyance is barred both as stale and by limitations where over forty years has elapsed since the facts claimed to constitute the fraud arose.[70] Constructive fraud will not prevent the running of limitations to a claim growing out of a payment by mistake in excess of that to which the creditor was entitled, where the debtor was guilty of laches in not sooner discovering the mistake under which the parties acted.[71] Fraud sufficient to suspend limitations, under the Maryland statute, may be either an actual concealment of facts, or of such a nature as to conceal itself, whereby plaintiff remains in ignorance without any lack of diligence on his part.[72] Under the Wisconsin statute, ignorance of the existence of a cause of action, though produced by fraud, does not delay limitations, unless, prior to the code of limitations, the cause of action would be for relief on the ground of fraud.[73]

69. Certified from the Court of Appeals. See 117 Mo. App. 385, 93 S. W. 888. Burrus v. Cook, 215 Mo. 496, 114 S. W. 1065, under Rev. St 1899, § 4290 (Ann. St. 1906, p. 2359). The "improper act" in Rev. St. 1909, § 1905, must be one in the nature of a fraud that will prevent the commencement of an action, and a judgment debtor, who merely concealed his name from the assignee of the judgment, did not commit an improper act which prevented suit. Davis v. Carp, 258 Mo. 686, 167 S. W. 1042.

70. Adams v. Hopkins, 144 Cal. 19, 77 Pac. 712.

71. Maxwell v. Walsh, 117 Ga. 467, 43 S. E. 704.

72. Schuck v. Bramble, 122 Md. 411, 89 Atl. 719, under Code Pub. Civ. Laws, art. 57, § 14.

73. Ott v. Hood, 152 Wis. 97, 139 N. W. 762, under St. 1911, § 4222, subd. 7.

See, as to the application of statutes of limitation in other jurisdictions, where fraud is the ground for relief:

La.—Olivier, Voorhies & Lowrey v. Majors, 133 La. 764, 63 So. 323, under Civ. Code, art. 1994.

Tex.—Vernor v. D. Sullivan & Co. (Civ. App.), 126 S. W. 641; Jackson v. Martin, 37 Tex. Civ. App. 593, 84 S. W. 603; O'Neal v. Clymer (Civ. App.), 61 S. W. 545.

Va.—Liskey v. Paul, 100 Va. 764, 42 S. E. 875; Stokes v. Oliver, 76 Va 72.

§ 276a(2). Fraud in obtaining possession of or title to property.

Where land is held in fee, the statute of limitations begins to run against an action for relief from fraud practiced in procuring a conveyance thereof from the delivery of the deed.[74] Limitations, as to an action to subject to a judgment against an insolvent property accumulated by him in conducting a business under his wife's apparent proprietorship, began to run from the time when the business was first established, when its alleged fraudulent character could have been tested by a judicial inquiry.[75] The Kentucky ten-year statute of limitations applicable to actions for relief from fraud or mistake does not operate to perfect the title of the grantee in a voluntary conveyance who has never been in possession, so as to enable him to recover the land conveyed from a subsequent purchaser for value without actual notice of his claim, as the statute, as affects property, does not apply in favor of one not in possession.[76] Where the vendor of goods accepts security under false representations as to its value, such fraud will not prevent the operation of the statute of limitations against the debt.[77] The statute commences to run against an action for money obtained by fraud from the time the transaction is completed by the receipt

74 Chambers v. Chambers, 139 Ind. 111, 38 N. E. 334.

75. Shircliffe v. Casebeer, 122 Iowa 618, 98 N. W. 486. As to an action to recover from a guardian the proceeds of a sale of the ward's property, see Blakeney v. Wyland, 115 Iowa 607, 89 N. W. 16.

76. Sewell v. Nelson, 113 Ky. 171, 23 Ky. Law Rep. 2438, 67 S. W. 985; Potter v. Benge, 24 Ky. Law Rep. 24, 67 S. W. 1005. See also, as to actions for fraud in obtaining possession of or title to property. Row v. Johnston, 25 Ky. Law Rep. 1799, 78 S. W. 906; Lyms v. Henderson, 6 Ky. Law Rep. (abstract) 219.

Under Ky. St. § 2519, where a debtor made a voluntary transfer in trust, and subsequently purchased land with the trust funds in the name of the beneficiary, suit to subject the land to the payment of a judgment on the debt, more than 10 years after the transfer in trust, could not be maintained. Graham's Adm'r v. English, 160 Ky. 375, 169 S. W. 836.

77. Rouss v. Ditmore, 122 N. C. 775, 30 S. E. 335.

As to an action by the sureties on a bond to set aside a deed as a fraud on their rights of indemnity, see: Graeber v. Sides, 151 N. C. 596, 66 S. E. 600.

of the money, where nothing is thereafter done by the person receiving it to prevent inquiry and discovery of the fraud.[78]

§ 276a(3). Cancellation of instrument.

The recording of a deed starts limitations running, as to the grantors, as to any fraud in procuring the deed.[79] In Kentucky, an action to set aside a deed for fraud or mistake cannot be maintained after the expiration of ten years from the time of its execution.[80] Under New York Code, § 91, a suit to set aside a deed obtained by fraud was required to be brought within six years from the time of the discovery of the fraud. Where an action was brought accordingly, and defendant, by the exercise of undue influence, induced plaintiff to discontinue, and sixteen years afterwards, when the undue influence came to an end, another suit was brought, it was held barred by the statute, and that equity could not afford a remedy.[81] Where a grantee went into possession and dealt with the property as his own, the right of the grantors to sue to set aside the deed for fraud was barred by limitations, where the grantors took no action during their lifetime, though they lived more than five years, in the absence of anything to show that they did not know of the fraud at the execution of the deed.[82]

78. Smith v. Blachley, 198 Pa. 173, 47 Atl. 985, 53 L. R. A. 849.

As to the application of limitation laws in other jurisdictions to actions wherein relief is sought from fraud in obtaining possession of or title to property, see:

U. S.—Thayer v. Kansas Loan & Trust Co., 100 Fed. 901, 41 C. C. A. 106 (C. C. A., Kan.).

Ark.—Salinger v. Black, 68 Ark. 449, 60 S. W. 229.

Cal.—Matteson v. Wagoner, 147 Cal. 739, 82 Pac. 436.

Colo.—Arnett v. Berg, 18 Colo. App. 341, 71 Pac. 636.

Miss.—Thornton v. City of Natchz, 88 Miss. 1, 41 So. 498.

Neb.—Aldrich v. Steen, 71 Neb. 33, 98 N. W. 445, 100 N. W. 311.

N. J.—Markley v. Camden Safe Deposit & Trust Co. (N. J. Ch.), 69 Atl. 1100.

Va.—Williams v. Blakey, 76 Va. 254.

79. McDonald v. Bayard Sav. Bank, 123 Iowa 413, 98 N. W. 1025.

80. Combs v. Noble, 22 Ky. Law Rep. 736, 58 S. W. 707; Buckler's Adm'x v. Rogers, 22 Ky. Law Rep. 1, 53 S. W. 529; 21 Ky. Law Rep. 1265, 54 S. W. 848.

81. Piper v. Hoard, 65 How. Prac. (N. Y.) 228, 107 N. Y. 67, 13 N. E. 632, 1 Am. St. Rep. 785.

82. Ryman v. Petruka (Tex. Civ. App.), 166 S. W. 711.

§ 276b(1). Discovery of fraud — In general.

Limitations do not commence to run against an action for fraud till the discovery of the fraud, or of facts sufficient to put an ordinarily intelligent person on inquiry.[83] Where plaintiff sued defendants for a conspiracy to injure it in its business, in violation of the Sherman Anti-Trust Act, limitations did not begin to run until plaintiff discovered the existence of the conspiracy and its right to sue.[84] Under the express provisions of the California statute, the period of limitations in actions for relief on the ground of fraud does not begin to run until the fraud is discovered.[85] Under the Kansas statute, where the evidence, in an action by trustees for relief on account of fraud, fails to show that such fraud was known to one of the plaintiffs, or their predecessors, more than two years prior to the commencement of the action, plaintiffs cannot recover.[86] The Maryland statute does not refer to a fraud inde-

83. *Ind.*—Dorsey Machine Co. v. McCaffrey, 139 Ind. 645, 38 N. E. 208, 47 Am. St. Rep. 290. And see Day v. Dages, 17 Ind. App. 228, 46 N. E. 589.

Mo.—Thomas v. Mathews, 51 Mo. 107.

Neb.—Raymond v. Schriever, 63 Neb. 719, 89 N. W. 308; Cole v. Boyd, 68 Neb. 146, 93 N. W. 1003; Forsyth v. Easterday, 63 Neb. 887, 89 N. W. 407; Weckerly v. Taylor, 74 Neb. 84, 103 N. W. 1065, or of such facts as are indicative of fraud, and which, if followed up, would lead to the discovery.

Pa.—Smith v. Blachley, 188 Pa. 550, 41 Atl. 619, 43 Wkly. Notes Cas. 201, 68 Am. St. Rep. 887; Kalin v. Wehrle, 36 Pa. Super. Ct. 305, where money was fraudulently taken from the possession of its owner; Semple v. Callery, 184 Pa. 95, 41 W. N. C. 356, 39 Atl. 6, where the seller, by agreement, kept bonds in his possession, and improperly converted them to his use.

Utah.—Larsen v. Utah Loan & Trust Co., 23 Utah, 449, 65 Pac. 208.

84. American Tobacco Co. v. People's Tobacco Co., 204 Fed. 58.

85. People v. Perris Irr. Dist., 142 Cal. 601, 76 Pac. 381; Fogg v. Perris Irr. Dist., 142 Cal. xviii.

Where plaintiff knew that a corporation's directors had fraudulently assessed his stock, and sold the same under the assessment, his failure to discover other frauds perpetrated by them, without seeking to inspect the corporation's books, did not delay the running of limitations, since he would be presumed to know all that reasonable diligence would have disclosed to him. Marks v. Evans, 129 Cal. xviii, 62 Pac. 76.

86. Manley v. Robertson, 6 Kan. App. 921, 51 Pac. 795.

A defense in which it is sought to avoid a written agreement and re-

pendent of the original fraud, for the purpose of keeping the injured party in ignorance, but where one practices fraud the subsequent concealment of it from the injured party is a keeping in ignorance by fraud.[87] In New York, where a contract is induced by fraud, action for damages accrues immediately, and limitations begin to run against recovery immediately on its execution or discovery of the fraud.[88] In Texas, a cause of action for fraud accrues at the time of the discovery of the fraud, or when it should have been discovered by the use of ordinary diligence, and limitations begin to run at that time.[89] In Missouri, limitations are no defense to a suit against defendant member of a real estate loan firm for his absconded associate's fraud in a partnership transaction, brought within the period of limitations after actual discovery of the fraud, where plaintiff was not negligent in failing earlier to discover the fraud.[90] In Virginia, in an action

form the same, on the ground of fraud, is barred after two years from the discovery of the fraud. McCormick Harvesting Mach. Co. v. Hayes, (Kan. App.), 49 Pac. 632.

87. New England Mut. Life Ins. Co. v. Swain, 100 Md. 558, 60 Atl. 469.

88. Isman v. Loring, 130 App. Div. 845, 115 N. Y. Supp. 933.

A cause of action for fraud in procuring a contract to marry accrues when the contract is made, not when the fraud is discovered. Reilly v. Sabater, 43 N. Y. Supp. 383, 26 Civ. Proc. R. 34.

89. Howell v. Bank of Snyder (Tex. Civ. App.), 158 S. W. 574.

In cases of fraud when the means of discovery are at hand, diligence must be exercised to discover the fraud, but the statute does not run until there is some circumstance or fact to arouse suspicion. Smalley v. Vogt (Tex. Civ. App.), 166 S. W. 1. See also Coleman v. Ebeling (Civ. App.), 138 S. W. 199; Clement v. Clement (Civ. App.), 99 S. W. 138; Stanford v. Finks (Civ. App.), 99 S. W. 449; Martinez v. Gutierrez's Heirs (Civ. App.), 172 S. W. 766; Boren v. Boren, 38 Tex. Civ. App. 139, 85 S. W. 48; Pitman v. Holmes, 34 Tex. Civ. App. 485, 78 S. W. 961; West v. Clark, 28 Tex. Civ. App. 1, 66 S. W. 215; Cetti v. Dunman, 26 Tex. Civ. App. 433, 64 S. W. 787; American Freehold Land Mortg. Co. of London v. Pace, 23 Tex. Civ. App. 222, 56 S. W. 377.

90. Monmouth College v. Dockery, 241 Mo. 522, 145 S. W. 785.

Failure to discover fraud will not toll the statute, unless defendant did some act which prevented the discovery. State *ex rel.* O'Malley v. Musick, 165 Mo. App. 214, 145 S. W. 1184, adopting opinion 145 Mo. App. 33, 130 S. W. 398.

Rev. St. 1909, § 1889, subd. 5, governs a suit by a stockholder for the benefit of the corporation for an accounting and for profits growing out

at law to recover an overpayment by reason of fraud, limitations run from the date of the settlement and payment; but in equity only from the discovery of the fraud.[91] In Wisconsin, where a stockholder at the time stock was wrongfully transferred by the corporation, had a legal remedy and an equitable remedy for the same wrong, the statute of limitations ran upon the equitable remedy and barred it when it had run upon the legal remedy; the Wisconsin statute as to accrual of cause of action not applying.[92] Under the Kentucky statute, ignorance of, or failure to discover, the existence of a transfer in fraud of creditors, does not prevent the running of the ten-year limitation against actions for relief for fraud.[93]

§ 276b(2). What constitutes cause for relief on ground of fraud.

The fact that a deed is withheld from record or is otherwise concealed is a badge of fraud, and when accompanied by other evidence of fraudulent intent will prevent the statute of limitations from running in favor of a grantee against a suit affecting the property during its concealment.[94] Where defendant's title to certain land in controversy was of record, and the validity thereof could have been ascertained by an examination, his mere statement that he owned a particular title to the land prior to his conveyance thereof to the plaintiff, was not such fraud as would suspend the statute of limitations, reasonable effort not having been made by plaintiff to ascertain the source of such title.[95] The Cali-

of an alleged fraud perpetrated on the corporation, and limitations begin to run from the date of transaction alleged by the stockholder to constitute a fraud on the corporation. Johnson v. United Rys. Co. of St. Louis, 243 Mo. 278, 147 S. W. 1077.

91. Grove v. Lemley, 114 Va. 202, 76 S. E. 305; Senseny's Adm'r v. Boyd's Adm'r, 114 Va. 308, 76 S. E. 280.

92. Casper v. Kalt-Zimmers Mfg. Co., 159 Wis. 517, 149 N. W. 754, under St. 1913, § 4222, subd. 5.

93. Graham's Adm'r v. English, 160 Ky. 375, 169 S. W. 836, under Ky. St. § 2519.

94. Linn & Lane Timber Co. v. United States, 196 Fed. 593, 116 C. C. A. 267, aff'g United States v. Smith, 181 Fed. 545. And see United States v. So. Pac. Co., 225 Fed. 197.

95. Wilson v. Le Moyne, 204 Fed. 726, 123 C. C. A. 30, under Code Pub. Gen. Laws Md. 1904, art. 57, § 14.

In suits in equity, where relief is sought on the ground of fraud, and the party injured remained in ignor-

fornia statute applies to all actions for relief against fraud, whether legal or equitable, and the cause of action does not accrue until the actual discovery of the fraud, from which time limitations begin to run.[96] Under the Alabama statute, in the absence of a fiduciary relation, imposing a duty to disclose, there must be some act calculated to mislead or to lull inquiry before the exception to the statute can be invoked.[97] In Georgia, where the basis of an action is actual fraud, limitations do not run against the right of action until the fraud is discovered, or could have been discovered by ordinary diligence.[98] In Kentucky, it has been held that where the insured could have discovered by inspection whether life policies delivered to him conformed to the preliminary contract, his right of action to have the policies corrected accrued at the time of their delivery to him, from which date the statute began to run.[99] The Iowa statute is applicable only to suits solely cognizable in equity.[1] The Idaho statute applies only to actions for fraud within the common acceptance of those terms and the cause of action does not accrue until the discovery of the facts constituting the fraud.[2] In Kansas, a cause of action, founded on fraud, for damages is deemed to have accrued when the fraud was discovered, and the

ance of the fraud, without fault or want of diligence on his part, limitation does not begin to run until the fraud is discovered, although there are no special circumstances, and no effort on the part of the party committing the fraud to conceal it. Board of Levee Com'rs of Tensas Basin Levee Dist. v. Tensas Delta Land Co., 204 Fed. 736, 123 C. C. A. 40.

96. Lightner Mining Co. v. Lane, 161 Cal. 689, 120 Pac. 771. See also, Osmont v. All Persons, 165 Cal. 587, 133 Pac. 480; McMurray v. Bodwell, 16 Cal. App. 574, 117 Pac. 627; Vance v. Supreme Lodge of Fraternal Brotherhood, 15 Cal. App. 178, 114 Pac. 83.

97. Van Ingen v. Duffin, 158 Ala. 318, 48 So. 507.

98. American National Bank of Macon v. Fidelity & Deposit Co. of Maryland, 131 Ga. 854, 63 S. E. 622; Garbutt Lumber Co. v. Walker, 6 Ga. App. 189, 64 S. E. 698.

99. Provident Saving Life Assur. Society of New York v. Withers, 132 Ky. 541, 116 S. W. 350. The statute does not apply to actions for malicious prosecution. Hutchings v. Fraser, 4 Ky. Law Rep. (abstract) 448.

1. Daugherty v. Daugherty, 116 Iowa, 245, 90 N. W. 65.

2. Burch v. Nicholson, 157 Iowa 502, 137 N. W. 1066; Havirdo v. Lung, 19 Idaho 790, 115 Pac. 930.

statute does not apply to an action founded on contract.[3] In Massachusetts, the time limited by statute within which a corporation must sue a promoter for secret profits made in selling property to the corporation does not begin to run until the facts have or ought to have been discovered; for the liability of the promoter is based on his breach of trust, and his duty required him to disclose the facts on which the cause of action rests.[4] The Nebraska statute applies to actions for fraud affecting the title to real estate as well as to actions affecting the title to personalty.[5] In New Jersey a claim in equity against a legatee to charge him as trustee *ex malificio,* of which claim complainant had knowledge before she became of age, which was not prosecuted within twenty years after becoming of age, is barred by limitations.[6] New York Code Civ. Proc., 382, subd. 5, providing that a cause of action for fraud does not accrue until discovery of the facts, governs actions in which the fraud complained of is the essential fact, and does not apply to an action against a corporation wrongfully transferring stock on a forged power of attorney.[7] The North Carolina stat-

3. Sherman v. Havens, 86 Kan. 99, 119 Pac. 370; Mateer v. Great Western Land Co., 91 Kan. 349, 137 Pac. 786; Gillmore v. Gillmore, 91 Kan. 293, 137 Pac. 958; 91 Kan. 707, 139 Pac. 386, an action for damages from inducing plaintiff to become a user of morphine in ignorance of its nature is not within the statute; Atchison, etc., Ry Co. v. Atchison Grain Co., 68 Kan. 585, 75 Pac. 1051, 70 Pac. 933; Nelson v. Stull, 65 Kan. 585, 70 Pac. 590, 68 Pac. 617; Rizer v. Board of Com'rs of Geary County, 58 Kan. 114, 48 Pac. 586.

4. Old Dominion Copper Mining & Smelting Co. v. Bigelow, 203 Mass. 159, 89 N. E. 193. See, as to circumstances under which fraud cannot be presumed, Colby v. Shute, 219 Mass. 211, 106 N. E. 1006.

5. Kohout v. Thomas, 4 Neb. (Unof.) 80, 93 N. W. 421.

6. Heinisch v. Pennington (N. J. Ch.), 73 Atl. 1118, aff'g 68 Atl. 233.

7. Glover v. National Bank of Commerce of New York, 156 App. Div. 247, 141 N. Y. Supp. 409. For other instances where Code Civ. Proc. N. Y., subd. 5 has been applied see the following cases:

Gabriel v. Gabriel, 79 Misc. Rep. 346, 139 N. Y. Supp. 778; Finnegan v. McGuffog, 203 N. Y. 342, 96 N. E. 1015, aff'g judg. 139 App. Div. 899, 123 N. Y. Supp. 539, action to enforce a constructive trust; Slayback v. Raymond, 93 App. Div. 326, 87 N. Y. Supp. 931, aff'g judg. 40 Misc. Rep. 601, 83 N. Y. Supp. 15; Kelley v. Pratt, 41 Misc. Rep. 31, 83 N. Y. Supp. 636; Talmadge v. Russell, 74

ute applies only in actions for fraud or mistake, and the statute runs from the discovery of the facts and not from the discovery by a party of rights theretofore unknown to him.[8] The Ohio statute includes actions to set aside deeds fraudulent as to creditors.[9] The Utah statute applies to the fraud of a bank in loaning the money of a depositor in a different manner than he directs, for the benefit of the bank, though the fraud is not intentional.[10] The Washington statute applies to causes of action for embezzlement of funds and issuance of illegal warrants by a county auditor.[11] Under the express provisions of the Wisconsin statute, an equitable action for relief on the ground of fraud does not accrue until discovery by the aggrieved party of the facts constituting the fraud.[12]

§ 276b(3). Fraud in obtaining possession of or title to property.

Where petitioners were led by the grantee to believe that a deed was to him as guardian for them, and were content that the land should be so held that their mother might have a home on the

App. Div. 7, 76 N. Y. Supp. 854; Libby v. Vanderzee, 176 N. Y. 591, 68 N. E. 1119, aff'g judg. 80 App. Div. 494, 81 N. Y. Supp. 139, an action by a ward against the executors of his deceased guardian to compel an accounting; Mason v. Henry, 152 N. Y. 529, 46 N. E. 837; Seitz v. Seitz, 59 App. Div. 150, 69 N. Y. Supp. 170.

8. Bonner v. Stotesbury, 139 N. C. 3, 51 S. E. 781.

9. Stivens v. Summers, 68 Ohio St. 4,21, 67 N. E. 884.

10. Larsen v. Utah Loan & Trust Co., 23 Utah, 449, 65 Pac. 208.

11. Skagit County v. American Bonding Co. of Baltimore, 59 Wash. 1, 109 Pac. 197. See, as to other actions: Johnstone v. Peyton, 59 Wash. 436, 110 Pac. 7; Conaway v. Co-operative Home Builders, 65 Wash. 39, 117 Pac. 716.

12. Boon v. Root, 137 Wis. 451, 119 N. W. 121. For cases in which the statute has been applied, see: Foote v. Harrison, 137 Wis. 588, 119 N. W. 291; Steinberg v. Salzman, 139 Wis. 118, 120 N. W. 1005; State v. Chicago & N. W. Ry. Co., 132 Wis. 345, 112 N. W. 515; State v. Chicago, etc., Ry. Co., 132 Wis. 364, 112 N. W. 522; Pietsch v. Milbrath, 123 Wis. 647, 68 L. R. A. 945, 107 Am. St. Rep. 1017, 101 N. W. 388, 102 N. W. 842.

As to what constitutes cause for relief on the ground of fraud under the statutes of other states, see:

Miss.—Jones v. Rogers, 85 Miss. 802, 38 So. 742.

Mo.—Ruff v. Milner, 92 Mo. App. 620.

Mont.—Chowen v. Phelps, 26 Mont. 524, 69 Pac. 54.

S. C.—Lenhardt v. French, 57 S. C. 493, 35 S. E. 761.

Tex.—Dean v. A. G. McAdam Lumber Co. (Tex. Civ. App.), 172 S. W. 762.

same, a suit to cancel the deed, soon after they discovered that it vested an absolute title in the grantee, was not barred by limitations, though the deed had been executed for twenty-nine years.[13] In an action to set aside a deed on the ground of fraud, the cause of action will not be deemed to have accrued at the time of the delivery of the deed, but at the time of the discovery of the fraud by means of which the grantor was induced to execute and deliver the same.[14] An action to set aside a deed on the ground that it was procured by fraud was not barred by limitations, though brought more than five years after the deed was made, where it was brought within five years from the time the grantor discovered the fraud, and the evidence authorized the conclusion that the grantor could not by the exercise of ordinary care, have discovered the fraud sooner.[15] Fraud of the vendee of goods sold and delivered, first discovered after action for the price is barred by limitations, will not revive it.[16] Where a man, by fraudulently representing himself as single, married defendant, and obtained from her a conveyance of her land without consideration other than the relationship existing between them, limitations do not begin to run as to her right to cancel such conveyance until she discovers the fraud.[17] Limitations will not begin to run against an action by a county to recover a road tax, refunded to a taxpayer in reliance on a fraudulent

13. Albritton v. Giddings, 140 Ga. 169, 78 S. E. 723.

14. Brown v. Brown, 62 Kan. 666, 64 Pac. 599. Where defendant induced plaintiff to sign a deed of land to him, she supposing it to be a power of attorney, an action for relief is not barred until two years after the discovery of the deception. Kahm v. Klaus, 64 Kan. 24, 67 Pac. 542.

15. Potter v. Benge, 24 Ky. Law Rep. 24, 67 S. W. 1005. See also Graves v. Trimble's Assignee, 1 Ky. Law Rep. (abstract) 416; Morgan v. Combs, 32 Ky. Law Rep. 1205, 108 S. W. 272; 33 Ky. Law Rep. 817, 111 S. W. 294, an action for the reformation of a deed for fraud.

16. Rouss v. Ditmore, 122 N. C. 775, 30 S. E. 335.

17. Hodges v. Hodges, 27 Tex. Civ. App. 537, 66 S. W. 239.

A vendee, who purchases land, knowing at the time that children of the vendor have an equity therein, participates with the vendor in a fraud on them, so that the statute does not run in his favor against them until they discover, or should discover, the same. Worst v. Sgitcovich (Tex. Civ. App.), 46 S. W. 72.

certificate that the tax had been worked out, until the refunding of the money and the detection of the fraud by the county.[18] An action for fraud, in that defendant made misrepresentations as to the title to land, the growing timber on which was sold to plaintiff, is barred, under the Alabama statute, where it is shown that the fraud was discovered by plaintiff more than a year before commencement of the action.[19] An action by an administrator to recover the value of land conveyed by deceased on the ground that the deed was procured by fraud or undue influence, where the facts constituting the same are discovered by the heirs, and the administrator appointed and a suit commenced more than seven years after such discovery, is barred by limitations, under the Minnesota statute.[20] A suit to enforce a constructive trust in a mining claim arising out of the fraudulent acts of plaintiff's co-owner was subject to the limitations prescribed by the Montana statute.[21] Where complainant employed her brother to obtain restitution of certain land which she had been induced to convey by fraudulent representations, complainant's right of action was barred at the expiration of seven years after the brother acquired knowledge of the fraud, under the Tennessee statute.[22] In Texas, a cause of action by a chattel mortgagee for conversion accrues on the discovery of the fraud participated in by the person converting the mortgaged chattels.[23] Under the Utah statute, a city is not entitled more than three years after judgment quieting title to land as against it to bring suit to set aside the judgment for fraud, consisting of the plaintiff's knowledge of the city's title and its own lack of title.[24]

18. Walla Walla County v. Oregon R. & Nav. Co., 40 Wash. 398, 82 Pac. 716.

19. Christian v. Denmark, 156 Ala. 390, 47 So. 82.

20. Howard v. Farr, 115 Minn. 86, 131 N. W. 1071.

21. Delmoe v. Long, 35 Mont. 38, 88 Pac. 778.

22. Boro v. Hidell, 122 Tenn. 80, 120 S. W. 961.

23. Port Arthur Rice Milling Co. v. Beaumont Rice Mills, 105 Tex. 514, 143 S. W. 926, rev'g judg. 141 S. W. 349, 148 S. W. 283. See, as to action for conversion of a special deposit by a bank, Prosser v. First Nat. Bank of Del Rio (Tex Civ. App.), 134 S. W. 781.

24. Salt Lake City v. Salt Lake Inv. Co., 43 Utah 181, 134 Pac. 603.

§ 276b(4). Fraud in obtaining judgment.

Under California Code Civ. Proc., §§ 1327, 1333, providing that any person interested may contest a will within a year after its probate, an heir who was absent from the State when a fraudulent will was probated, and for more than a year thereafter, and who did not discover the fraud until after the expiration of such year, was nevertheless barred from contesting the will after the expiration of the statutory limitation.[25] In Louisiana, an action to annul a judgment for fraud is prescribed in one year from the discovery of the fraud, and the burden is on plaintiff in nullity to show when such discovery was made.[26] In Texas, limitations commence to run against an action to set aside a judgment, on account of the fraud of plaintiff's attorneys representing him at the time it was rendered, from the time when the fraud is discovered or should have been;[27] and to suspend the running of limitations so as to permit an attack on a judgment for taxes after the expiration of four years there must not only have been fraud in obtaining the judgment, but it must have been coupled with such concealment of the fraud as to prevent the attacking party from ascertaining the fraud by the use of reasonable diligence.[28]

25. *In re* Davis' Estate, 136 Cal. 590, 69 Pac. 412.

A complaint to modify a decree on the ground that, as made, it was procured by fraud, is bad, where it shows that plaintiffs knew of the decree within the six months allowed by Code Civ. Proc., § 473, for moving to modify or vacate judgments. Heller v. Dyerville Mfg. Co., 116 Cal. 127, 47 Pac. 1016.

26. Succession of Dauphin, 112 La. 103, 36 So. 287.

27. Watson v. Texas & P. Ry. Co. (Tex. Civ. App.), 73 S. W. 830.

28. Dunn v. Taylor, 42 Tex. Civ. App. 241, 94 S. W. 347.

A suit to open and alter a partition decree for fraud is barred in four years after rendition of the decree, though the fraud was not discovered until a short time before the suit, where no reason is shown why it was not discovered sooner. Woodhouse v. Cocke (Tex. Civ. App.), 39 S. W. 948. See also East Texas Land & Improvement Co. v. Graham, 24 Tex. Civ. App. 521, 60 S. W. 472, holding that there was a failure to show such diligence in discovering fraud in the judgment sought to be set aside as would relieve plaintiff from the charge of laches, or prevent the running of the statute.

§ 276b(5). Action for deceit.

Where fraud relied on as the basis of an action for deceit is concealed by the defendant, the statute of limitations does not begin to run until it is discovered, or might have been discovered by plaintiff in the exercise of reasonable diligence.[29] In New York, limitations run against a cause of action for damages for deceit by which plaintiff was induced to purchase corporate stock from the consummation of the fraud, and not from the discovery thereof.[30] In Minnesota, where a complaint shows that plaintiff began suit for deceit within a reasonable time after discovering the fraud, and it does not appear that he was guilty of laches, the action is not barred by limitations.[31] The Florida statute, prescribing limitations in actions for relief on the ground of fraud, applies to an action for deceit, wherein defendant " ought to have known " the falsity of his representations, as well as in a case where he actually knew their falsity.[32] In Texas, limitations do not commence to run against a cause of action for deceit until the discovery

29. Gamet v. Haas, 165 Iowa 565, 146 N. W. 465.

In view of Code, § 3447, par. 6, requiring actions for relief on the ground of fraud in cases theretofore solely cognizable in a chancery court, to be commenced within five years, section 3448 providing that, in actions for relief on the ground of fraud, etc., the cause of action shall not be deemed to have accrued until the fraud is discovered, applies only to cases of fraud for which relief may be obtained in equity, so that an action for damages for false representations inducing a sale, being merely a common-law action for deceit, accrued when the transaction was consummated so as to set limitations running, and not when the fraud was discovered by the party aggrieved. McKay v. McCarthy, 146 Iowa 546, 123 N. W. 755, rehearing denied and opinion modified (Iowa), 125 N. W. 207.

30. Ball v. Gerard, 160 App. Div. 619, 146 N. Y. Supp. 81. See Coffin v. Barber, 115 App. Div. 713, 101 N. Y. Supp. 147, wherein plaintiff was held charged with knowledge of the falsity of defendant's representations at a date which barred the action by limitations.

31. Newstrom v. Turnblad, 108 Minn. 58, 121 N. W. 236; Norrbom v Turnblad, 108 Minn 521, 121 N. W. 236.

32. Watson v. Jones, 41 Fla. 241, 25 So. 678, under Rev. St. 1894, § 1294, prescribing a limitation of three years in action for relief on the ground of fraud, the cause of action not to be deemed to have accrued until the discovery by the aggrieved party of the facts constituting the fraud.

of the fraud, where the failure to discover the fraud sooner was not due to any negligence.[33]

§ 276b(6). Fraud in sale of property.

Defendant in an action for balance of purchase price of a fruit farm is not barred by limitations from defending, and recovering by cross complaint money paid, on the ground of fraudulent representations; not having till then discovered the misrepresentation as to amount of land, and become convinced of the falsity of plaintiff's representation as to the amount of profits he had realized from the land, and his representation, repeated year after year, that the reason defendant did not obtain such profits was due to his want of experience.[34] Where a vendor makes fraudulent misrepresentations as to the condition of the title of the land sold, the cause of action for such fraud accrues on the discovery of the fraud, though the falsity of the representations could have been discovered by an examination of the record.[35] An action *quanti minoris,* which by reason of the fact that the seller knew the vice of the thing he sold and omitted to declare it falls under the provisions of Louisiana Civ. Code, art. 2545, is governed by the prescription of one year after discovery of the vice.[36] An action for damages for misrepresentations in the sale of a bond is not affected by limitations, where the falsity of the representations was only discovered by plaintiff about a year previous to the trial of the case.[37] In a suit

33. Western Cottage Piano & Organ Co. v. Griffin, 41 Tex. Civ. App. 76, 90 S. W. 884. Limitations will not begin to run against an action for false representations until the falsity of the representations is discovered, or should have been discovered by the use of ordinary diligence. Harris v. Cain, 41 Tex. Civ. App. 139, 91 S. W. 866.

34. Evans v. Duke (Cal. App.), 69 Pac. 688, rev'd 140 Cal. 22, 73 Pac. 732.

35. Claggett v. Crall, 12 Kan. 393. The rule that, if an examination of the public records would reveal a fraud, the records are constructive notice sufficient to set limitations in motion, does not obtain in favor of a vendee who procured his conveyance by fraudulent representations as to the state of the record on which the vendor relied. Hutto v. Knowlton, 82 Kan. 445, 108 Pac. 825.

36. George v. Shreveport Cotton Oil Co., 114 La. 498, 38 So. 432.

37. Edwards v. Noel, 88 Mo. App. 434.

for fraud because of the shortage in acreage in land transferred to plaintiff, an action not brought for thirteen years, during ten of which plaintiff lived on the land, was barred by Missouri Rev. St. 1909, § 1889, barring such an action in five years from the discovery of facts constituting the fraud.[38] Where a grantor fraudulently misrepresented the number of acres conveyed, neither the Texas two-years nor the four-years statute of limitations will begin to run against an action for damages for shortage, until the fraud is discovered or could have been discovered.[39] Under the South Carolina statute, limitations begin to run against a person seeking to set aside a sale under execution because of chilling the bidding, from the time of the discovery of the fraud.[40] Where a seller by mistake drew on the purchasers for less than the price, the failure of the purchasers to notify him of the mistake was not legal fraud, within the Washington statute, providing that, in an action for relief on the ground of fraud, the cause of action shall not be deemed to have accrued until the discovery of the facts constituting the fraud.[41]

§ 276b(7). Fraud of person acting in official or fiduciary capacity.

Under Georgia Civ. Code 1910, § 3084, fixing the limitation of proceedings for an accounting by guardian after settlement, and section 4380, before plaintiff can fix a new point for the running of limitations for concealed fraud, he must exercise reasonable diligence to detect the fraud.[42] The bar of the statute of limita-

38. Powell v. White, 170 Mo. App. 598, 157 S. W. 111.

In an action for the value of stock and for an accounting, for fraud in representing that stock transferred to plaintiff was his pro rata share of that held by defendant as trustee for plaintiff and others, the facts were held insufficient to bring the case within Rev. St. 909, § 1889, subd. 5, providing that causes of action for fraud are not deemed to have accrued until the discovery of the fraud. Heisler v. Clymer, 179 Mo. App. 110, 161 S. W. 337.

39. Powell v. March (Tex. Civ. App.), 169 S. W. 936.

40. Toole v. Johnson, 61 S. C. 34, 39 S. E. 254, under Code, § 112, subd. 6.

41. Evert v. Tower, 51 Wash. 514, 99 Pac. 580.

42. Bennett v. Bird, 139 Ga. 25, 76 S. E. 568. An action by a vendee

tions is removed where it appears that defendant practiced a fraud on the plaintiff while standing in a fiduciary relation to the plaintiff, and concealed the real facts.[43] When property is fraudulently sold, by the administrator of a partnership, to pay debts of the partnership, for which purpose he has in his hands other partnership assets, which he conceals and applies to his own use, such administrator is chargeable with the rents and profits of such property from the date of the sale; such recovery not being barred by the three-year statute of limitations, concerning implied contracts, since the cause of action dates from the discovery of the fraud.[44] Knowledge of trustees, appointed to hold property upon the termination of a prior trust, of the fraudulent concealment by the former trustee of trust property, or want of ordinary diligence to discover such fraud, is imputed to the beneficiaries or those claiming under them, so as to bar an action to compel a reaccounting on the ground of fraud, within the statutory time, under the Maryland statute of limitations.[45] Under the Kentucky statute,

against a vendor to recover damages for a deficiency in quantity of the land sold, based on fraud of the vendor, of which plaintiff was kept in ignorance because of the fiduciary relation existing between defendant and her, was within Code, § 2931, providing that, if defendant is guilty of fraud by which plaintiff was deterred from his action, the limitation shall run only from the discovery of the fraud. Kirkley v. Sharp, 98 Ga. 484, 25 S. E. 562.

43. Barnes v. Huffman, 113 Ill. App. 226. But the bar of the statute will not be removed where title to the land in dispute was a matter of record and had passed to innocent third parties, holding the land in good faith upon the validity of the title they had received. Smith v. Clark, 248 Ill. 255, 93 N. E. 727.

44. Branner v. Nichols, 61 Kan. 356, 59 Pac. 633. But see Walline v. Olson, 84 Kan. 37, 113 Pac. 426, where, in an action against defendants on the ground of fraud of the administrator of an estate on whose bond they were sureties, the records of the probate court involving the transactions complained of were held constructive notice of the alleged fraud sufficient to set in motion the two-year statute of limitation.

Where a county clerk fraudulently draws county warrants for a sum in excess of the amount allowed by the board of county commissioners, the cause of action against him and his bondsmen does not accrue until discovery of the fraud. Allen v. State, 6, Kan. App. 915, 51 Pac. 572.

45. Reeder v. Lanahan, 111 Md. 372, 74 Atl. 575; under Acts 1868, p. 646, c. 357 (Code Pub. Gen. Laws 1904, art. 57, § 14), requiring such

an action to surcharge a false settlement between a sheriff and his deputy made in 1899 was barred February 9, 1911, though the fraud was discovered within the statutory period prior to the latter date.[46] An action in equity being maintainable against a thief's administrator for an accounting because of the thief's fraud in concealing the property, its sale, and the receipt of its proceeds, the action under New York Code Civ. Proc., § 382, subd. 5, is not barred till six years after discovery of the fraud, though the ultimate relief sought is a money judgment.[47] The statute does not begin to run against an action by a *cestui que trust* till the time of the discovery by the latter of fraud or mistake on which it is based.[48] Under the general rule that, where one person represents both sides of conflicting claims, limitations do not run, a suit by one trust estate to recover from another for funds stolen by a common trustee, and applied to the benefit of defendant estate, is properly brought within six years after discovery of the embezzle-

suits to be brought within three years from the time the action accrues, provided that, where one having a cause of action has been kept in ignorance by the adverse party, the right of action shall be deemed to have accrued when the fraud is, or, with ordinary diligence could have been, discovered.

46. Alexander v. Alexander, 154 Ky. 773, 159 S. W. 583, denying rehearing 154 Ky. 324, 157 S. W. 377, under Ky. St. § 2519, providing that an action for relief on the ground of fraud or mistake may be brought within five years after discovery, but no action shall be brought more than ten years after the perpetration of the fraud.

47. Lightfoot v. Davis, 132 App. Div. 452, 116 N. Y. Supp. 904, order rev'd 198 N. Y. 261, 91 N. E. 582.

48. Levy v. Ryland, 32 Nev. 460, 109 Pac. 905.

Where a widow sought to rescind a contract of settlement with the trustees of her deceased husband because of fraud in procuring it, the statute of limitations (Rev. St. 1898, § 4222) commenced to run from the time that she knew of the fraud constituting the ground of her cause of action, or might have known thereof by the exercise of ordinary care. Ludington v. Patton, 111 Wis. 208, 86 N. W. 571.

Ballinger's Ann. Codes & St. § 4800, subd. 4, relieves a *cestui que trust*, whose trustee converts the trust property, and conceals the fact from the former, from the duty of using diligence to discover such fraud, and limitations do not commence to run until he has received actual knowledge thereof. Irwin v Holbrook, 26 Wash. 89, 66 Pac. 116.

ment.[49] Where an administrator of his wife's estate falsely and fraudulently informs the widow of his son that she has no interest in the decedent's estate, although as a matter of fact she is entitled to a share therein as the heir of her own deceased child, and distribution is made without her sharing in it, the statute of limitations begins to run in favor of the administrator or his estate only from the date when the fraud was discovered.[50] Where intestate was trustee of a secret trust, so far as complainant was concerned, limitations did not begin to run against his administratrix to recover for alleged breaches of trust until the right of action accrued on discovery of the fraud.[51]

§ 276b(8). Fraud of agent or attorney.

The statute of limitations does not begin to run against an agent, for misappropriation, until discovery by the principal of the defalcation.[52] Limitations do not run against a principal and in

49. Bremer v. Williams, 210 Mass. 256, 96 N. E. 687.

Suit by wards to avoid the sale of their lands by their guardian indirectly to herself is not barred as a stale claim, though not brought within the 10 years of their attaining full age, the limitation fixed by Rev. Laws, c. 202, § 24, for recovery of land; they having brought it soon after learning of the fraud, and having exercised reasonable diligence. Sunter v. Sunter, 190 Mass. 449, 77 N. E. 497.

50. *In re* Roseburg's Estate, 47 Pa. Super. Ct. 255.

Where money was deposited with testator for investment, and the securities purchased therewith were misappropriated by him, and he rendered detailed statements to the depositor of investments alleged to have been made, and paid her from time to time money stated to have been derived therefrom, and after his death, the executors, who had full knowledge of the facts, continued such statements and payments, limitations did not begin to run against the depositor's claim until discovery by her of the facts. *In re* Claghorn's Estate, 181 Pa. 609, 37 Atl. 921.

51. Russel v. Huntington Nat. Bank, 162 Fed. 868, 89 C. C. A. 558 (W. Va.).

52. San Pedro Lumber Co. v. Reynolds, 121 Cal. 74, 53 Pac. 410; Guernsey v. Davis, 67 Kan. 378, 73 Pac. 101.

Where an officer misappropriates money intrusted to him and fraudulently conceals his default, limitations will not begin to run until the discovery of the fraud and of the breach of the conditions of his bond. McMullen v. Winfield Building & Loan Ass'n, 64 Kan. 298, 67 Pac. 892, 56 L. R. A. 924, 91 Am. St. Rep. 236.

favor of an agent, who has misappropriated the funds of the principal, until the misappropriation has been discovered, if reasonable diligence has been used.[53] Where a married woman intrusted her property to the management of agents, and such agents, by fraud, acquired the title to the property, the statute of limitations has no application to an action brought by her after the fraud was discovered, for Rev. St. Mo., 1909, § 1889, provides that an action for relief on the ground of fraud shall not be deemed to have accrued until the discovery of the fact constituting the fraud.[54] Where an attorney wrongfully dismissed an action he was engaged to prosecute, representing to his client that the case had been decided adversely, limitations begin from the time of the dismissal, notwithstanding Rem. & Bal. Code, Wash., § 159, subd. 4, declaring that, in actions based on fraud, the cause shall not be deemed to have accrued until the discovery of the fraud.[55] Where plaintiff sued defendant for fraud in investing her money as her agent, in accepting a second mortgage security, which he fraudulently represented to her was the first mortgage on the property, limitations did not begin to run against plaintiff's right of action until she actually discovered the fraud, or until such time as she might have discovered it by the exercise of ordinary care.[56] Where a principal

The statute does not begin to run against an action for false representations of authority to contract until discovery of the fraud. Pierson v. Holdridge, 92 Kan. 365, 140 Pac. 1032.

53. Ash v. A. B. Frank Co. (Tex. Civ. App.), 142 S. W. 42. See also, Arkins v. Arkins, 20 Colo. App. 123, 77 Pac. 256.

54. Witte v. Storm, 236 Mo. 470, 139 S. W. 384.

55. Cornell v. Edsen, 78 Wash. 662, 139 Pac. 602.

An action against a broker for fraudulently converting to his own use moneys of plaintiff is one for relief on the ground of fraud, within the statute of limitations (2 Ballinger's Ann. Codes & St. § 4800, subd. 4). Stearns v. Hochbrunn, 24 Wash. 206, 64 Pac. 165.

56. Faust v. Hosford, 119 Iowa 97, 93 N. W. 58, and the agent's subsequent silence as to the fact that the mortgage was a second mortgage amounted to a continuance of the original fraud, sufficient to suspend the statute of limitations, as against an action against the agent for the fraud, until plaintiff became aware thereof, or by the exercise of ordinary care could have discovered it.

sends a horse to an agent to sell, and the latter sells the horse, but not only conceals the fact of the sale from the principal, but also attempts to make the principal believe that the horse had been killed, and the principal does not learn these facts until he is barred by the statute from bringing suit against the purchaser, the statute of limitations does not run in favor of the agent against his principal from the date of the sale of the horse, but only from the discovery of the fraud.[57] Limitations do not run against the right of action by a purchaser of a note, falsely purporting to be secured by a vendor's lien, against the agent through whom he purchased the note, until his discovery of the agent's interest in the proceeds of the sale thereof.[58]

§ 276b(9). Actions to open account or settlement.

Limitations do not run against an action to set aside a partnership accounting until the discovery of the fraud.[59] A suit to set aside a settlement and release, and an order approving a guardian's final report on the ground that the release was obtained by fraud, was not barred, though it was not brought within five years after plaintiff's majority, where she did not learn of the fraud

57. Cloyd v. Reynolds, 52 Pa. Super. Ct. 365. Evidence that the agent had not in fact been paid for the horse is immaterial, as is also that a new agreement was substituted for the original agreement, after the sale of the horse, if it appears that the principal entered into the new agreement without knowledge of the fraud and concealment which had been practiced upon him; and it is also immaterial in such a case whether the purchaser of the horse was solvent or insolvent. Id.

58. Young v. Barcroft (Tex. Civ. App.), 168 S. W. 392.

An action for fraud committed by defendant employed to sell plaintiff's land for a part of the proceeds, based on defendant making sales and appropriating the proceeds, was not barred by limitations, where it was brought within two years after plaintiff learned the facts by an independent investigation. Thomason v. Rogers (Tex. Civ. App.), 155 S. W. 1040.

Where a purchaser sued the broker of the vendor for fraud inducing the purchase, the action was barred by the four-years limitations; the failure to discover the fraud not being excused. Gordon v. Rhodes & Daniel (Tex. Civ. App.), 117 S. W. 1023, certified questions answered 116 S. W. 40.

59. Johnston v. Johnston, 107 Minn. 109, 119 N. W. 652.

alleged until shortly before bringing the suit.[60] Under Code Civ. Proc. New York, § 382, limiting actions for relief on the ground of fraud to six years from the discovery of the fraud, as construed by the highest court of the State, the limitation begins to run against an action to open and resettle an account from the time the account was settled, and not from the time of the discovery of facts showing that such settlement was fraudulently made.[61] A cause of action to impeach a settlement on the ground of fraud is barred by the Ohio statute of limitations, unless an action is commenced thereon within four years after the discovery of the fraud.[62] In New Jersey, against a suit in equity to open accounts after a settlement, and for an accounting, on the ground of fraud on the part of defendant in procuring the settlement, limitations do not begin to run until the fraud is discovered, or until complainant is in a situation where by the exercise of reasonable diligence he can discover it.[63] In South Carolina where a ward, after attaining his majority, settles with the guardian, the statute then begins to run against his suit to set aside the settlement; he then having notice

60. Witt v. Day, 112 Iowa 110, 83 N. W. 797.

Where a ward sued the guardian, within a year after the discovery of the fraud, for the value of land fraudulently concealed from her by her guardian on a settlement had with him after she arrived of age, and for the rents and profits therefrom, the action was held not barred by limitations. Short v. Mathis, 107 Ga. 807.

Under Ky. St. § 2519, an action to surcharge a guardian's settlement for fraud or mistake must be brought, in any event, within 10 years after the ward arrived at age. Blake v. Wolfe, 105 Ky. 380, 49 S. W. 19, 20 Ky. Law Rep. 1212.

Circumstances of fraud and concealment held not sufficient to remove from the operation of limitations an action for relief brought by a ward against a guardian. Black v. Black, 64 Kan. 689, 68 Pac. 662; Stewart v. Robbins, 27 Tex. Civ. App. 188, 65 S. W. 899. And see Scoville v. Brock, 79 Vt. 449, 65 Atl. 577, wherein it was held that the statute did not begin to run until something occurred to raise a doubt in the mind of the ward as to the guardian's conduct.

61. Kirby v. Lake Shore & M. S. R. Co., 14 Fed. 261 (C. C., N. Y.).

62. Railroad Co. v. Smith, 48 Ohio St. 219, 31 N. E. 743, and the statute applies as well where the cause of action is set up by answer in an action brought for the balance found due on the settlement.

63. Lincoln v. Judd, 49 N. J. Eq. (4 Dick.) 387, 24 Atl. 318.

sufficient to put him on inquiry concerning the fraud on which he relies.[64]

§ 276b(10). Cancellation of instruments.

The limitation of six years prescribed by Act March 3, 1891, § 8, for suits by the United States to annul patents to lands, is subject to the equitable rule that, where the basis of the suit is fraud which has been concealed, the statute does not begin to run until the discovery of the fraud by the Interior Department,[65] and knowledge acquired incidentally by a special agent of the Land Office cannot be attributed to the Department.[66] The statute of limitations does not run in favor of one who receives a mere voluntary conveyance for the purpose of enabling the grantor to defraud his creditor, unless it be shown that the creditor had knowledge of the fraud.[67] An action to set aside, as fraudulent, conveyances of realty, where more than three years had elapsed after all the transactions had taken place and were known to plaintiffs, is barred by limitations, in California.[68] The Colorado statute, providing that bills for relief on the ground of fraud shall be filed within three years after the discovery thereof, does not apply to an action to have the foreclosure of a trust deed set aside for fraud.[69] An action to confirm plaintiff's title under a conveyance to

64. Owens v. Watts, 24 S. C. 76.

65. United States v. Exploration Co., 203 Fed. 387, 121 C. C. A. 491, rev'g decree (C. C.) 190 Fed. 405; United States v. American Smelting & Refining Co., 203 Fed. 393, 121 C. C. A. 497; Linn & Lane Timber Co. v. United States, 203 Fed. 394, 121 C. C. A. 498, amending decree on rehearing, 196 Fed. 593, 116 C. C. A. 267. See also United States v. Southern Pac. Co., 225 Fed. 197.

66. United States v. Lee, Wilson & Co., 214 Fed. 630 (D. C.); Act March 3, 1891, c. 561, § 8, 26 Stat. 1099 (U. S. Comp. St. 1901, p. 1521).

67. Farrar v. Bernheim, 75 Fed. 136, 21 C. C. A. 264.

68. Tully v. Tully, 137 Cal. 60, 69 Pac. 700.

By the express provisions of Code Civ. Proc., § 338, an action to rescind certain instruments on the ground of fraud is not barred, though the instruments were executed more than three years before its commencement, where it is shown that the fraud relied on was discovered within a year of the filing of the complaint. Richards v. Farmers' & Mechanics' Bank, 7 Cal. App. 387, 94 Pac. 393.

69. Barlow v. Hitzler, 40 Colo. 109, 90 Pac. 90, under Mills' Ann. St. § 2911.

her and to set aside subsequent fraudulent conveyances is solely cognizable in equity, and the statute of limitations does not begin to run, under Iowa Code, §§ 3447, 3448, until the fraud is actually discovered.[70] In an action by a creditor for relief on the ground of fraud of his debtor, it is necessary to establish the ignorance of the fraud until the time within the period limited for the commencement of an action to remove the bar of limitations.[71] Where a father conveyed land to his son without any change of possession, and the son did not render the land for taxation, and there was nothing in the way in which the property was held to put a creditor of the father, who lived in an adjoining county, on notice, limitations did not bar her rights; she having no actual notice of the conveyance until just prior to suit brought.[72] Under the six-year limitation prescribed by New York Code Civ. Proc., § 382, an action brought May 1, 1909, by a trustee in bankruptcy to avoid an assignment made September 29, 1900, as being fraudulent as to creditors, was barred where plaintiff was chargeable with knowledge of the assignment, and the consideration for it as early as December 17, 1900, and where the assignor was adjudged a bankrupt October 15, 1900.[73]

70. Mullen v. Callanan (Iowa), 149 N. W. 516.

71. Fuller v. Horner, 69 Kan. 467, 77 Pac. 88.

72. Chinn v. Curtis, 24 Ky. Law Rep. 1563, 71 S. W. 923.

The payment of annual premiums would not suspend the running of the statute of limitations against an action against an insurance company for rescission of a contract of insurance on the ground of misrepresentations as to what insured would be entitled to receive under the policy, the misrepresentations, and not the payment or receipt of premiums, being the fraud complained of. Schoolfield v. Provident Savings Life Assur. Society, 158 Ky. 687, 166 S. W. 207.

73. Beattys v. Straiton, 142 App. Div. 369, 126 N. Y. Supp. 848.

Under Code Civ. Proc., § 382, subd. 5, providing that an action to procure a judgment on the ground of fraud must be brought within six years after the discovery of the fraud, an action to set aside an assignment of a trust fund to the trustee for fraud is not barred until six years after discovery of the fraud. Anderson v. Fry, 116 App. Div. 740, 102 N. Y. Supp. 112. An action by a trustee in bankruptcy to set aside a fraudulent transfer of property made by the bankrupt before the institution of proceedings in bankruptcy may be brought at any time within

§ 276b(11). Diligence in discovering fraud.

The rule that the statute of limitations does not begin to run, or that a party cannot be charged with laches, until the discovery of the fraud, does not mean that one can shut his eyes to obvious facts.[74] A mere allegation that plaintiff "had no knowledge or notice" of an alleged fraudulent conversion of property, on which the action is based, until a later date, is insufficient to avoid the bar of limitations; no facts showing either concealment by defendant or diligence on the part of plaintiff being alleged.[75] While a cause of action to cancel a trust deed for fraud is deemed not to have accrued until the discovery of the facts constituting the fraud,

four years from the discovery of the fraud. Nye v. Hart, 22 Ohio Civ. Ct. Rep. 427, 12 O. C. D. 419.

For the rule maintained in other jurisdictions as to application of statutes of limitations to action for the cancellation of instruments on the ground of fraud, see:

U. S.—Eddy v. Eddy, 168 Fed. 590, 93 C. C. A. 586 (C. C. A., Mich.).

La.—Kinder v. Scharff, 129 La. 218, 55 So. 769, action by bankrupt's trustee to set aside a fraudulent conveyance of the bankrupt.

Minn.—Brasie v. Minneapolis Brewing Co., 87 Minn. 456, 92 N. W. 340, 67 L. R. A. 865, 94 Am. St. Rep. 709.

Neb.—Westervelt v. Filter, 2 Neb. (Unoff.) 731, 89 N. W. 994.

Ohio.—Boies v. Johnson, 25 Ohio Cir. Ct. Rep. 331.

S. C.—Tucker v. Weathersbee, 98 S. C. 402, 82 S. E. 638.

Tenn.—Green v. Huggins (Ch. App.), 52 S. W. 675.

Tex.—Stern v. Marx, 23 Tex. Civ. App. 439, 56 S. W. 93.

Wash.—Fidelity Nat. Bank v. Adams, 38 Wash. 75, 80 Pac. 284.

74. Shelby County v. Bragg, 135 Mo. 291, 36 S. W. 600; Goggins v. Risley, 13 Pa. Super. Ct. 316.

75. School Dist. of City of Sedalia, Mo., v. Deweese, 93 Fed. 602 (C. C., Mo.). One must exercise due diligence to discover a fraud complained of, and where he does not do so limitations run against his cause of action therefor; one who wrongs another by fraud, and who then further wrongs him by a later fraud calculated to disarm the former of suspicion and prevent an investigation, may not charge the former with negligence or laches in not making an investigation and discovering the fraud. McLain v. Parker, 229 Mo. 68, 129 S. W. 500. There must have been some act done by defendant to lull plaintiff into nonaction or prevent him from discovering the fraud, and concealment of the facts by mere silence is not enough. State *ex rel.* O'Malley v. Musick, 145 Mo. App. 33, 130 S. W. 398, where plaintiff could have discovered the fraud at any time by examining the public record of an option of purchase. Scott v. Boswell, 136 Mo. App. 601, 118 S. W. 521.

it must also appear that the discovery could not sooner have been made by the exercise of reasonable diligence; plaintiff being presumed to have known all that reasonable diligence would have disclosed.[76] Fraud is deemed to be discovered, within the statute of limitations, when, in the exercise of reasonable diligence, it could have been discovered; and where a creditor knew of the execution of a deed, which he supposed named his debtor as grantee, reasonable diligence would have required an examination of the record, which would have disclosed the fact that it was executed to the debtor's wife.[77] Under Kentucky St., § 2515, in an action for relief on the ground of fraud, plaintiff must establish a state of facts showing that he could not, with ordinary or reasonable diligence, have discovered the fraud within the statutory period of limitation before the action was instituted.[78] In Minnesota, it is incumbent on the plaintiff to allege and prove not merely that he did not discover the facts constituting the fraud within the statutory period of limitation, but also that his failure to discover them sooner was consistent with reasonable diligence on his part, and not the result of his own negligence.[79] In Georgia, ignorance of fraud, which by use of due diligence might have been discovered, will not bar the running of the statute of limitations.[80] In New York, knowledge of the facts constituting a fraud, within the meaning of Code Civ. Proc., § 382, subd. 5, will be imputed to the plaintiff, where the circumstances are such as to suggest to a person of ordi-

76. Shiels v. Nathan, 12 Cal. App. 604, 108 Pac. 34, under Cal. Code Civ. Proc., § 338, subd. 4; Loeffler v. Wright, 13 Cal. App. 224, 109 Pac. 269.

77. Donaldson v. Jacobitz, 67 Kan. 244, 72 Pac. 846; Duphorne v. Moore, 82 Kan. 159, 107 Pac. 791.

78. Exchange Bank v. Trimble, 108 Ky. 230, 21 Ky. Law Rep. 1681, 56 S. W. 156; Nave v. Price, 108 Ky. 105, 21 Ky. Law Rep. 1538, 55 S. W. 882; Wilhoit v. Musselman, 24 Ky. Law Rep. 2011, 72 S. W. 1112; Clarke v. Seay, 21 Ky. Law Rep. 394, 51 S. W. 589; Zackay's Adm'r v. Hicks, 7 Ky. Law Rep. (abstract) 755.

79. Duxbury v. Boice, 70 Minn. 113, 72 N. W. 838; First Nat. Bank v. Strait, 71 Minn. 69, 73 N. W. 645.

80. Freeman v. Craver, 56 Ga. 161; Sutton v. Dye, 60 Ga. 449; Edmond's Ex'rs v. Goodwyn, 28 Ga. 38; Little v. Reynolds, 101 Ga. 594, 28 S. E. 919.

nary intelligence the probability that he has been defrauded, and he omits to make inquiry which would have developed the truth.[81] In Texas, the plaintiff is not entitled to the benefit of the exception in the statute suspending the running of limitations till discovery of the fraud, where he could have discovered it by reasonable diligence.[82] In Alabama, in the absence of a fiduciary relation, imposing a duty to disclose, there must be some act calculated to mislead or to lull inquiry before the exception to the statute of limitations can be invoked; and one suing to set aside a fraudulent conveyance to avoid the statute could not rely upon the fact that he did not discover the fraud until just before suit.[83] A client employing an attorney to sue upon a promissory note was held not guilty of laches, in Texas, in not discovering the attorney's fraud in not bringing such action until after such attorney's death, nearly four years after the action had become barred by limitations, where the attorney had represented to him that suit had been brought and judgment obtained, and that he was taking steps to collect the judgment.[84]

§ 276b(12). What constitutes discovery of fraud.

The word "discovery" as used in California Code Civ. Proc., § 338, subd. 4, providing that a cause of action for relief on the

81. Higgins v. Crouse, 147 N. Y. 411, 42 N. E. 6, rev'g judg. 71 Hun 615, 24 N. Y. Supp. 1080; 63 Hun 134, 17 N. Y. Supp. 696.

82. Boren v. Boren, 38 Tex. Civ. App. 139, 85 S. W. 48; Missouri, K. & T. Ry. Co. v. Smith, 28 Tex. Civ. App. 565, 68 S. W. 543; Moore v. Brown, 27 Tex. Civ. App. 208, 64 S. W. 946; Vodrie v. Tynan (Tex. Civ. App.), 57 S. W. 680; Cleveland v. Carr (Tex. Civ. App.), 40 S. W. 406.

83. Van Ingen v. Duffin, 158 Ala. 318, 48 So. 507.

84. Shuttleworth v. McGee (Tex. Civ. App.), 105 S. W. 823.

As to facts sufficient to show reasonable diligence in discovering fraud or the reverse, see the following cases:

U. S.—Martin v. Smith, 1 Dill, 85

Cal.—Bills v Silver King Min. Co., 106 Cal. 9, 39 Pac. 43; Burling v. Newlands (Cal.), 39 Pac. 49; Simpson v. Dalziel, 135 Cal. 599, 67 Pac. 1080.

Miss.—Murphy v. Reedy (Miss.), 2 So. 167; Matthews v. Southeimer, 39 Miss. 174.

Ohio.—Bohm v. Cunningham, 7 Ohio Dec. 382, 2 Wkly. Law Bul. 274.

Tex.—Alston v. Richardson, 51 Tex.

ground of fraud, is not deemed to have accrued until discovery of the facts constituting such fraud, is not equivalent to "knowledge" and plaintiff must show that the acts of fraud were committed under such circumstances that he would not be presumed to have knowledge of them.[85] Mills' Ann. St. Colorado, § 2911, requiring bills for relief on the ground of fraud to be filed within three years after discovery of the fraud, bars such suits three years after the discovery of facts which would awaken a person of ordinary prudence to an inquiry, which, if pursued with reasonable diligence, would lead to a discovery of the fraud.[86] In Nebraska, an action for fraud must be commenced within four years after discovery of the facts constituting fraud, or facts sufficient to put an ordinary person on inquiry.[87] Under the New York statute of limitations (Code Civ. Proc., § 382, subd. 5), providing that actions for judgments other than for money, on the ground of fraud, must be commenced in six years from the discovery of the "facts" constituting the fraud, the limitations against a right of action to vacate a release of a general guardian procured by fraudulent representations begin to run from the moment they are made, where the party executing the release does not believe them, and is not deceived thereby, and not from the time of the discovery of evidence to establish the fraud.[88] Silence by the promoters of a corporation, acting as its agents, as to the price paid by them for land afterwards sold to the corporation at an advanced price is fraudulent concealment, and will be deemed to avoid the statute

1; Kuhlman v. Baker, 50 Tex. 630; Stanford v. Finks (Tex. Civ. App.), 99 S. W. 449; Clement v. Clement (Tex. Civ. App.), 99 S. W. 138.

85. Davis v. Hibernia Savings & Loan Society, 21 Cal. App. 444, 132 Pac. 462. And see Smith v. Martin, 135 Cal. 247, 67 Pac. 779; Archer v. Freeman, 124 Cal. 528, 57 Pac. 474; Nicholson v. Tarpey, 124 Cal. 442, 57 Pac. 457.

86. Redd v. Brun, 157 Fed. 190, 84 C. C. A. 638 (C. C. A., Colo.); Swift v. Smith, 79 Fed. 709, 25 C. C. A. 154 (C. C. A., Colo.). See also, Rose v. Dunklee, 12 Colo. App. 403, 56 Pac. 342.

87. Coad v. Dorsey, 96 Neb. 612, 148 N. W. 155; Raymond v. Schriever, 63 Neb. 719, 89 N. W. 308. See also, State Bank of Pender v. Frey, 3 Neb. (Unof.) 83, 91 N. W. 239.

88. Stevens v. Reed, 60 N. Y. Supp. 726.

An action to recover money only is not within said section, which ap-

of limitations, within Iowa Code, § 3448.[89] Where a party defrauded had the means at hand to readily discover the fraud, and such means of information would have been used by a person of ordinary care in the transaction of his own business, he will be held, as a matter of law, to have had due notice of everything which a proper use of such means would have disclosed.[90]

plies only to equitable causes for other than the recovery of money only. East River Sav. Inst. v. Barrett, 23 Misc. Rep. 423, 52 N. Y. Supp. 81.

Where a grandson of the grantor learned in 1893 of defendant's fraud in procuring the deed, under Code Civ. Proc., § 382, subd. 5, his time to sue for cancellation was, despite section 396, limited to six years from that date, although he was then only 20 years old. Gabriel v. Gabriel, 160 App. Div. 901, 144 N. Y. Supp. 1117, aff'g judg. 79 Misc. Rep. 346, 139 N. Y. Supp. 778.

Under Code Civ. Proc., § 1743, subds. 4 and 5, and section 1752, an action to annul a marriage for physical incapacity cannot be brought within section 382, subd. 5, relative to actions on the ground of fraud, within six years after the discovery of the fraud, by alleging fraudulent representations. Deitch v. Deitch, 162 App. Div. 25, 146 N. Y. Supp. 1019, leave to appeal granted 147 N. Y. Supp. 1106.

The ten years' limitations will not commence to run against an equitable action against the pledgees for an accounting as to a sale of the pledged property, without foreclosure of the lien or notice, until the pledgor learns of such sale. Beugger v. Ashley, 161 App. Div. 576, 146 N. Y. Supp. 910.

89. Chaffee v. Berkley, 141 Iowa 344, 118 N. W. 267. See also, E. B. Piekenbrock & Sons v. Knoer, 136 Iowa 534, 114 N. W. 200, as to what facts constitute discovery of fraud.

90. Boren v. Boren, 38 Tex. Civ. App. 139, 85 S. W. 48.

See also, as to what constitutes discovery of fraud, within the statutes of the several States:

Kan.—Eaton v. Elliott, 9 Kan. App. 882, 57 Pac. 243; Donaldson v. Jacobitz, 67 Kan. 244, 72 Pac. 846.

Ky.—Johnson v. Equitable Life Assur. Society of United States, 137 Ky. 437, 125 S. W. 1074; Brown v. Spradlin, 136 Ky. 703, 125 S. W. 150; Meehan v. Peck, 28 Ky. Law Rep. 446, 89 S. W. 491.

Md.—Shuck v. Bramble, 122 Md. 411, 89 Atl. 719.

Mich.—Comfort v. Robinson, 155 Mich. 143, 15 Detroit Leg. N. 951, 118 N. W. 943.

Mo.—Callan v. Callan, 175 Mo. 346, 74 S. W. 965; Loomis v. Missouri Pac. Ry. Co., 165 Mo. 469, 65 S. W. 962.

Pa.—Braddock Trust Co. v. Guarantee Trust & Safe-Deposit Co., 180 Pa. 529, 37 Atl. 101.

Wash.—Griffith v. Seattle Consol. St. Ry. Co., 36 Wash. 627, 79 Pac. 314; Wickham v. Sprague, 18 Wash. 466, 51 Pac. 1055; Uhlbright v. Mulcahy, 78 Wash. 9, 138 Pac. 314.

§ 276b(13). Constructive notice of fraud.

The phrase "until discovery of the fraud," as used in the Kansas and Oklahoma statutes of limitations, does not mean actual notice, as constructive notice is sufficient; and, where the means of discovery lie in public records required by law to be kept, they are sufficient to set the statute in motion.[91] The existence of public records of deeds, access to which is easy, and which would disclose that a trustee's representation that he had sold trust property worth $2,200 so as to net less than $600 was fraudulent, is such notice to the *cestui que trust* as to start limitations.[92] The recording of a fraudulent deed is not of itself sufficient to charge all parties with knowledge of the fraud; but, when accompanied with circumstances sufficient to put a person on inquiry, which if pursued would lead to the discovery of the fraud, limitations begin to run from the recording of the deed, but not otherwise.[93] In Iowa, the recording of a deed alleged to be fraudulent gives such notice of its character as will bar an action to set it aside unless the action is commenced within five years.[94] But, in Kentucky, the con-

91. Black v. Black, 64 Kan. 689, 68 Pac. 662; Board of Com'rs of Garfield County v. Renshaw, 23 Okl. 56, 99 Pac. 638. Plaintiff residing in New York was not charged with notice of fraud practiced on her by her attorney in Nebraska, so as to start the statute of limitations because the records of the Nebraska courts would show fraud, where the attorney was acting for her in the matter concerning which the record was made, and she had no means of ascertaining what the records would show, except from her attorney. Mohr v. Sands (Okl.), 133 Pac. 238.

92. Irwin v. Holbrook, 32 Wash. 349, 73 Pac. 360. See also, Deering v. Holcomb, 26 Wash. 588, 67 Pac. 240, applying the rule to an action to set aside a transfer made in fraud of creditors, where the attorney of the creditor had knowledge of the transfer, although the creditor did not have such knowledge till within the statutory period of limitation; *In re* Dunavant, 96 Fed. 542 (D. C., N. C.), wherein the knowledge of the attorney was held imputable to his client, and the debtor could plead the statute.

93. Jones v. Danforth, 71 Neb. 722, 99 N. W. 495; Forsyth v. Easterday, 63 Neb. 887, 89 N. W. 407. See also, State Bank of Pender v. Frey, 3 Neb. (Unof.) 83, 91 N. W. 239; Coulson v. Galtsman, 1 Neb. (Unof.) 502, 96 N. W. 349.

94. Fuller & Johnson v. McMahon (Iowa), 94 N. W. 205; Clark v. Van Loon, 108 Iowa 250, 79 N. W. 88, 75 Am. St. Rep. 219; Brooks v. Jones, 114 Iowa 385, 82 N. W. 434, modified on rehearing 86 N. W. 300.

structive notice from the mere recording of a fraudulent deed is insufficient to set the statute of limitations, as affecting an action to set it aside, in motion;[95] and in Ohio, a cause of action to set aside a fraudulent deed does not accrue when it is filed for record, unless plaintiff then received actual notice of its execution and of the circumstances which render it fraudulent.[96] In Pennsylvania, the record of a deed is not notice to the grantor of the fraudulent inclusion therein of land which he continues to occupy, so as to set the statute of limitations running against him.[97] In Michigan, the fact that conveyances of land were matters of public record did not put a creditor of the grantor on notice that there was no real consideration.[98]

Under the New York recording act, a recorded deed is not constructive notice to an owner in possession, who does not claim title through any party to the deed.[99] Under the Colorado statute, a creditor is not chargeable with constructive notice of his debtor's fraud in making a conveyance by the recording of the conveyance

95. Chinn v. Curtis, 24 Ky. Law Rep. 1563, 71 S. W. 923.

But an action brought by creditors to set aside a deed as fraudulent, more than five years after it was recorded, is barred by limitation, it appearing that plaintiffs, who resided in the town where the deed was recorded, and who were from time to time becoming the sureties of the grantor, might, by reasonable diligence, have discovered the deed at any time after it was recorded. Poynter v. Mallory, 20 Ky. Law Rep. 284, 45 S. W. 1042. And see McGehee v. Cox, 22 Ky. Law Rep. 619, 58 S. W. 532; Cotton v. Brown, 3 Ky. Law Rep. 679. An action to set aside a deed as fraudulent cannot be brought after the lapse of 10 years from the time the deed was made and recorded. Blake v. Wolfe, 105 Ky. 380, 20 Ky. Law Rep. 1212, 49 S. W. 19.

96. Stivens v. Summers, 68 Ohio St. 421, 67 N. E. 884.

97. Davis v. Monroe, 187 Pa. 212, 41 Atl. 44, 67 Am. St. Rep. 581.

98. Lant v. Manley, 75 Fed. 627, 21 C. C. A. 457 (C. C. A., Mich.).

99. Seely v. Seely, 150 N. Y. Supp. 66.

An equitable action seeking a money judgment, not as damages, but as a substitute for land upon which plaintiff might have impressed a trust, had not defendant sold it to a *bona fide* purchaser, is within Code Civ. Proc., § 382, subd. 5, as an action to procure a judgment for money on the ground of fraud, so that the statute did not begin to run until plaintiff's discovery of the fraud. Id.

showing that it was voluntary.[1] In Texas, where an insolvent debtor conveys lands to a relative for an insufficient consideration, and the deed is recorded, and the grantee takes possession thereunder, such facts constitute sufficient information to the grantor's creditors to put them on inquiry as to his intent to defraud them; and hence the statute of limitations begins to run against the creditors' action to set aside the conveyance from the date of the record of the deed.[2] In Virginia, where plaintiff seeks to avoid a conveyance made by his creditor on the ground that it was voluntary, the statute of limitations runs as to such action from the date of recording the deed, and not from plaintiff's knowledge that it was without consideration, unless his ignorance of such fact proceeded from the fraud of the grantee.[3]

§ 276c(1). Ignorance of cause of action—In general.

Code Civ. Proc. N. Y., § 410, as construed by the courts of the State, operates to shield clients from the effect of the six-years statute of limitations in actions growing out of the receipt and detention of money by attorneys, when the client does not have knowledge of the facts which entitle him to dispense with a demand, and to set the statute in operation only from the time he acquires such knowledge.[4] Mere ignorance of the existence of a cause of action does not prevent the running of the statute of limi-

1. Rose v. Dunklee, 12 Colo. App. 403, 56 Pac. 342.

2. Vodrie v. Tynan (Tex. Civ. App.), 57 S. W. 680.

Where defendant sold land to plaintiff, and afterwards conveyed the same land to another, who recorded his deed before plaintiff, the statute of limitation runs against plaintiff's right to recovery, from the time he has actual notice of such second conveyance, and not from the date it was recorded. Mitchell v. Simons (Tex. Civ. App.), 53 S. W. 76.

See, as to rule in other jurisdictions:

Miss.—North American Trust Co. v. Lanier, 78 Miss. 418, 28 So. 804, 84 Am. St. Rep. 635.

Mo.—Hudson v. Cahoon, 193 Mo. 547, 91 S. W. 72.

3. Vashon v. Barrett, 99 Va. 344, 3 Va. Sup. Ct. Rep. 227, 38 S. E. 200. And see McCue's Trustees v. Harris, 86 Va. 687, 10 S. E. 981.

4. Birckhead v. De Forest, 120 Fed. 645, 57 C. C. A. 107 (N. Y.).

Where an undivided interest in land is conveyed under an agreement

tations unless there has been fraudulent concealment on the part

that the purchaser will recover the vendor's interest from persons claiming adversely, and the purchaser wholly fails to perform the agreement, and allows the vendor's interest to be sacrificed, an action by the vendor against the purchaser for an accounting is within Code Civ. Proc., § 410, subd. 1. Cornwell v. Clement, 10 App. Div. 446, 42 N. Y. Supp. 295.

Where a grantee is in possession claiming to own the land by virtue of his deed, limitations will not run against his right to seek a reformation of the deed to make his title effective, until he knows of the flaw in his title deed, or of an adverse claim to the land. Perrior v. Peck, 39 App. Div. 390, 57 N. Y. Supp. 377, judg. aff'd 167 N. Y. 582, 60 N. E. 1118.

A declaration of an express trust made by a lessee in favor of the children of a former lessee who had been evicted for nonpayment of rent, and recorded in the office of the register of the county, is, as affecting the running of the statute of limitations against enforcement of the trust, constructive notice of its own existence to the *cestuis que trust*, and to the widow of the declarant who continued to occupy the premises after her husband's death, under the term granted to her husband and renewal terms, secured by her in her own name in accordance with the provision of the lease to her husband. Finnegan v. McGoffog, 203 N. Y. 342, 96 N. E. 1015, aff'g judg. 139 App. Div. 899, 123 N. Y. Supp. 539.

The statute does not run against the right of remaindermen in trust property to sue for the recovery of part of the property converted by the life beneficiary until they have actual knowledge of the facts upon which their right depends. Putnam v. Lincoln Safe Deposit Co., 191 N. Y. 166, 83 N. E. 789, rev'g judg. 118 App. Div. 463, 104 N. Y. Supp. 4, which modifies 49 Misc. Rep. 578, 100 N. Y. Supp. 101.

Where the title to stock pledged to secure a disputed debt was not divested, and the owner's right to possession depended on his satisfaction of the debt, his right to sue to redeem the stock in the hands of a transferee of the pledgee accrued on his obtaining knowledge of the transfer. Treadwell v. Clark, 190 N. Y. 51, 82 N. E. 505, aff'g judg. 114 App. Div. 493, 100 N. Y. Supp. 1.

Where imported merchandise is sold by the importer "in bond, actual duty" and all refunds of duties belonging to the purchaser, the importer becomes his agent for their collection; and, since the purchaser cannot recover them from his agent without demand, limitation does not begin to run till he has knowledge that they have been collected by the importer. Schmid v. Dohan, 167 Fed. 804 (C. C. A., N. Y.).

Limitations (Code Civ. Proc., § 382) commence to run against an action for the conversion of corporate bonds from the time the bonds were converted, and not from the discovery of the person who converted them. Lightfoot v. Davis, 132 App. Div. 452, 116 N. Y. Supp. 904.

of those invoking the benefit of the statute.[5] Under Ky. St., § 2519 (Russel's St., § 229), it was no answer to a plea of limitations, in a suit by a ward for an accounting against the heirs of her deceased guardian more than ten years after the right to such accounting accrued, that she did not know, and could not by reasonable diligence have discovered, sooner than she did, that her guardian was indebted to her.[6] The mere ignorance of a plaintiff of his cause of action will not prevent the running of the statute, but there must have been some concealment of the facts which ordinary diligence could not discover.[7] Ignorance of right does not prevent the running of limitations.[8] The rule that courts of equity ordinarily apply rules of limitation which will bar remedies at law is not applicable where the person seeking relief

5. Hibben v. Malone, 85 Ark. 584, 109 S. W. 1008; Bridge v. Connecticut Mut. Life Ins. Co., 167 Cal. 774, 141 Pac. 375; Davis v. Boyett, 120 Ga. 649, 48 S. E. 185, 66 L. R. A. 258, 102 Am. St. Rep. 118. See also, Lester & Haltom v. Bemis Lumber Co., 71 Ark. 379, 74 S. W. 518; Hibernia Savings & Loan Society v. Farnham, 153 Cal. 578, 96 Pac. 9.

Mere want of knowledge of executors' sale did not excuse plaintiff's delay of 20 years after reaching her majority to bring an action to set aside the sale, nor prevent action being barred by Code Civ. Proc., §§ 1573, 1574. Bagley v. City & County of San Francisco, 19 Cal. App. 255, 125 Pac. 931; Ruland v. All Persons, 10 Cal. App. 275, 125 Pac. 939.

A father's cause of action for the seduction of his daughter arises when the act of seduction is complete, and not when he discovers that his daughter has been seduced. Davis v. Boyett, *supra*.

6. Mouser v. Nunn, 142 Ky. 656, 134 S. W. 1148. And see Metropolitan Life Ins. Co. v. Trende, 21 Ky. Law Rep. 909, 53 S. W. 412; Covington v. Morton, 6 Ky. Law Rep. (abstract) 219, 352; Willis v. Brassfield, 8 Ky. Law Rep. (abstract) 353.

7. Clapp v. Leavens, 164 Fed. 318 (C. C. A., Mo.).

See McMurray v. McMurray, 180 Mo. 526, 79 S. W. 701; Dye v. Bowling, 82 Mo. App. 587; Arnold v. Scott, 2 Mo. 13, 22 Am. Dec. 433.

Limitations begin to run against an action on a trust arising, by operation of law, from the discovery by the *cestui que trust* of the facts from which it arises. Graham v. Wilson, 168 Mo. App. 185, 153 S. W. 83.

8. Garrett v. Olford, 152 Iowa 265, 132 N. W. 379.

And see Mather v. Rogers, 99 Iowa 292, 68 N. W. 700, wherein it was held that the complaint did not show such diligence in discovering fraud as would relieve plaintiff from the bar of the statute; The Telegraph v. Loetscher, 127 Iowa 383, 101 N. W. 773, wherein the evidence was held sufficient to excuse plaintiff's failure to discover the cause of action.

has no knowledge of the necessity of taking action to protect his interest, and is not chargeable with negligence, and the rights of third parties have not been prejudiced.[9] In the absence of fraud, neither ignorance of the right to sue nor mere silence of a person liable prevents the running of limitations.[10] Where ignorance of facts was relied on to arrest the running of limitations, a party is chargeable with knowledge of the facts, where the circumstances were such as should have induced inquiry, and the means of ascertaining the truth were readily available on such inquiry, but he neglects to make it.[11] That a person entitled to an action has no knowledge of his right to sue, or of the facts out of which his right arises, does not postpone the period of limitation.[12] Limitations begin to run on a cause of action against an abstractor from the time the abstract is furnished rather than from discovery of the errors or omissions.[13] Where the owner of land has no knowledge that coal is being taken from under his land by a trespasser, the statute of limitations does not begin to run against him until the time of actual discovery of the trespass, or the time when discovery was reasonably possible.[14] In a suit by an heir to set aside a deed of his ancestor, the averments as to discovery of the cause of action, in order to avail the heir as against limitations, must state a case for relief on the ground of fraud.[15]

9. Nichols v. Nichols, 79 Conn. 644, 66 Atl. 161.

10. Coe v. Sloan, 16 Idaho 49, 100 Pac. 354. See Stoltz v. Scott, 23 Idaho 104, 129 Pac. 340.

11. Ater v. Smith, 245 Ill. 57, 91 N. E. 776. See also, Cunningham v. Cunningham's Estate, 220 Ill. 45, 77 N. E. 95.

12. Craven v. Craven, 181 Ind. 553, 103 N. E. 333.

Whether a board of commissioners of a county had knowledge of a cause of action so that limitations would run was not affected by charge in the personnel of the members of the board. State v. Jackson, 52 Ind. App. 254, 100 N. E. 479.

13. E. T. Arnold & Co. v. Barner, 91 Kan. 768, 139 Pac. 404.

14. Gotshall v. J. Langdon & Co., 16 Pa. Super. Ct. 158; Trustees of Proprietors of Kingston v. Lehigh Valley Coal Co., 241 Pa. 469, 88 Atl. 763. See, as to other actions: Guarantee Trust & Safe Deposit Co. v. Farmers' & Mechanics' Nat. Bank, 202 Pa. 94, 51 Atl. 765; Mifflin County Nat. Bank v. Fourth St. Nat. Bank, 199 Pa. 459, 49 Atl. 213.

15. Thomas v. McKay, 143 Wis. 524, 128 N. W. 59.

§ 276c(2). Want of diligence by person entitled to sue.

The running of limitations against a suit involving title to land held adversely to complainants was not prevented by complainants' ignorance of their title to the land until after the expiration of the

In construing St. 1898, § 984, requiring actions on official bonds to be brought within three years after a municipality acquires knowledge of default, mere definitions of particular words used in different connections are of little value, but the intent of the particular legislation must be gathered; knowledge of a sentient person being quite different from that of a corporation; a county is not charged with knowledge of a treasurer's defalcation where it could not be discovered by the county board in their audit of his account. Oconto County v. McAllister, 155 Wis. 286, 143 N. W. 702; Oconto County v. Lindgren, 155 Wis. 303, 143 N. W. 707.

As to effect of ignorance of cause of action on limitations in other jurisdictions, see:

Ala.—Bromberg v. Sands, 127 Ala. 411, 30 So. 510, action against an attorney for money collected.

Del.—Lieberman v. First Nat. Bank, 8 Del. Ch. 229, 40 Atl. 382, action upon a bond given by an officer to a corporation.

La.—Hamilton v. Moore, 136 La. 631, 67 So. 523; Breaux v. Albert Hanson Lumber Co., 125 La. 421, 51 So. 444, action for unlawful cutting of timber; Woodward-Wight & Co. v. Engel Land & Lumber Co., 123 La. 1093, 49 So. 719, action to avoid contract and recover price paid; Christie & Lowe v. Pennsylvania Iron Works, 128 La. 208, 54 So. 742; Cox v. Von Ahlefeldt, 105 La. 543, 30 So. 175; Boagni v. Wartelle, 50 La. Ann. 128, 23 So. 206.

Mich.—Bates v. Boyce's Estate, 135 Mich. 540, 98 N. W. 259, 10 Detroit Leg. N. 868, 106 Am. St. Rep. 402, action by stockholder for conversion of his interest in the corporation.

Minn.—Everett v. O'Leary, 90 Minn. 154, 95 N. W. 901, in an action for breach of contract to insure, ignorance of violation of the contract will not prevent the running of the statute.

Neb.—Webster v. Bates Mach. Co., 64 Neb. 306, 89 N. W. 789.

N. J.—James v. Aller, 66 N. J. Eq. 52, 57 Atl. 476, rev'd 68 N. J. Eq. 666, 62 Atl. 427, 111 Am. St. Rep. 654, action by a father to set aside an unreasonable settlement of his property on his children.

N. H.—Rowell v. Sanborn, 76 N. H. 520, 85 Atl. 665.

Tenn.—Daniels v. Pickett (Ch. App.), 59 S. W. 148; Harris v. Thomas (Ch. App.), 52 S. W. 706.

Tex.—Yeaman v. Galveston City Co. (Tex.), 167 S. W. 710; First State Bank of Seminole v. Shannon (Civ. App.), 159 S. W. 398, action for the proceeds of a draft sent for collection; Dashner v. Wallace, 29 Tex. Civ. App. 151, 68 S. W. 307, suit to enjoin a judgment; Gerfers v. Mecke, 28 Tex. Civ. App. 269, 67 S. W. 144; Meyer Bros. Drug Co. v. Fry (Civ. App.), 48 S. W. 752; Moore v. Waco Bldg. Ass'n, 19 Tex. Civ. App. 68, 45 S. W. 974; Rice v. Ward, 92 Tex. 704, 51 S. W. 844.

limitation period, where complainants were, during that period, adults, and there was no concealment, deceit, or misrepresentation as to their rights by any party in possession, and none of the parties in possession occupied any fiduciary relation toward complainants.[16] A party cannot defer the running of limitations by his own negligence.[17] But, ordinarily, neglect or laches of public officials is not chargeable to the public, as barring a suit by lapse of time, where no intervening right of a third person is to be affected.[18] Under the Texas statute, an action to enjoin the execution of a judgment is barred at the expiration of four years after the existence of the judgment is discovered, or by reasonable diligence might have been discovered.[19]

Utah.—Snow v. Rich, 22 Utah 123, 61 Pac. 336.

Va.—Bickle v. Chrisman's Adm'x, 76 Va. 678; Virginia Hot Springs Co. v. McCray, 106 Va. 461, 56 S. E. 216, action for the pollution of a stream by sewage.

Wash.—Northwestern Lumber Co. v. City of Aberdeen, 44 Wash. 261, 87 Pac. 260, 35 Wash. 636, 77 Pac. 1063; Christianson v. King County, 203 Fed. 894, aff'g judg. 196 Fed. 791 (C. C. A., Wash.), an action of ejectment; Chilberg v. Siebenbaum, 41 Wash. 663, 84 Pac. 598, suit to enforce unpaid stock subscriptions; Gove v. City of Tacoma, 34 Wash. 434, 76 Pac. 73.

16. Steele v. Steele, 220 Ill. 318, 77 N. E. 232; Waterman Hall v. Waterman, 220 Ill. 569, 77 N. E. 142, 4 L. R. A. (N. S.) 776.

17. Ryan v. Woodin, 9 Idaho 525, 75 Pac. 261.

Where a city ordinance, imposing a license tax only on milk venders by means of wagons and vehicles, was unconstitutional on its face, plaintiff was not excused from refusing to comply therewith, and from testing its validity, by the fact that he was ignorant of the law, and his legal rights, but was bound to exercise ordinary diligence to discover the same, and hence he was barred by the five-year statute of limitations from recovering license fees paid for a longer period, on the ordinance being subsequently declared unconstitutional. City of Louisville v. Weikel, 137 Ky. 784, 127 S. W. 147; 128 S. W. 587.

18. Alexander v. Owen County, 136 Ky. 420, 124 S. W. 386. See Schroer v. Central Kentucky Asylum for Insane, 113 Ky. 288, 24 Ky. Law Rep. 150, 68 S. W. 150. Ignorance of one's rights will not prevent the statute of limitations from running, even though such ignorant person be guilty of neither fraud nor deceit. Berryman's Adm'r v. Garnett's Ex'r, 4 Ky. Law Rep. (abstract) 358.

19. Foust v. Warren (Tex. Civ. App.), 72 S. W. 404. See also, Warren v. Foust, 36 Tex. Civ. App. 59, 81 S. W. 323; Tex. Rev. St. art. 3358.

The fact that a grantor in a deed

§ 276d(1). Mistake as ground for relief—In general.

Where defendants, to secure the payment of notes, gave plaintiff a lien on land, which, by inadvertence, was incorrectly described, plaintiff's right to have the contract reformed accrued as soon as the mistake occurred, and he was not compelled to wait until default in the payment of the notes.[20] The recording of a deed is not required to charge the parties thereto with notice of its contents; the recording of certain deeds containing a mutual mistake is not of itself constructive notice to the grantors of the mistake, but is only to be considered with other facts and circumstances in determining whether the grantors had notice thereof, either actual or constructive.[21] In the absence of fraud, limitations run from the date of settlement against a vendor's cause of action arising out of a mutual mistake as to the amount of purchase money, in a settlement between vendor and purchaser.[22] Where a warranty in a deed did not cover the quantity of land, plaintiff's right to recover a portion of the consideration for a deficiency in quantity was in assumpsit for money paid under mistake and was barred in five years after the discovery of the mistake.[23] Where a vendor sold land under a *bona fide* belief that he had a legal right to do so,

containing a misdescription had an opportunity to investigate and discover the mistake was not sufficient to charge him with notice or knowledge thereof, in the absence of facts exceeding a mere suspicion that would cause an ordinarily prudent person to make an investigation which, if pursued, would have disclosed the mistake. Isaacks v. Wright (Tex. Civ. App.), 110 S. W. 970.

Limitations began to run against the assignee of a note when he knew that the money had been collected, or should, by reasonable diligence, have known it. Vernor v. D. Sullivan & Co. (Tex. Civ. App.), 126 S. W. 641. See Camp Mfg. Co. v. Durham Fertilizer Co., 150 N. C. 417, 64 S. E. 188, as to bar of limitations on an assigned judgment.

20. Stark v. Zehnder, 204 Mo. 442, 102 S. W. 992.

21. American Mining Co. v. Basin & Bay State Mining Co., 39 Mont. 476, 104 Pac. 525.

22. Craig v. Gauley Coal Land Co., 73 W. Va. 624, 80 S. E. 945.

23. Burton v. Cowles' Adm'x, 156 Ky. 100, 160 S. W. 782.

Under Ky. St. § 2519, providing that no action for relief on the ground of mistake shall be brought ten years after the time of making the contract, a mistake in a policy of life insurance, in naming as the beneficiary a person other than the beneficiary named in the application, can-

the fact that his title was not good did not constitute a mistake, within North Carolina Code Civ. Proc., § 155 (9), providing that a cause of action for fraud or mistake shall not be deemed to have accrued until the discovery of the fraud or mistake.[24] Where a wife demanded a deed to land she had purchased and which had by mistake been deeded to her husband from him as soon as she knew the property stood in his name, and he promised to give it, a delay for over two years was not enough to bring the statute of limitations into operation.[25] The right of the original purchaser to recover in equity the value of a deficiency in the land conveyed is not affected by the lapse of five years, where the mistake was not discovered until after the land was sold by him, and the suit was brought in about one year after an award of arbitrators establishing his liability to his grantee because of the same deficiency.[26] An action by an independent school district against another independent school district to recover money erroneously paid by the county treasurer to defendant as taxes on property situate within the limits of plaintiff district is an action for money had and received, and not for relief on the ground of mistake, and limitations commenced to run as to each payment made by the treasurer at the time of the payment, and not at the time of the discovery of the mistake.[27] The statute of limitations begins to run against the cause of action to reform a deed on the ground of mistake at the time of the delivery of the deed, and not at the time of the discovery of the mistake.[28]

not be corrected after the lapse of 10 years from the date of the policy. Webb v. Webb, 23 Ky. Law Rep. 1057, 64 S. W. 839. And see Elam v. Hadden (Ky.), 51 S. W. 455.

24. Barden v. Stickney, 130 N. C. 62, 40 S. E. 842, rehearing denied 132 N. C. 416, 43 S. E. 912. This provision of the Code has no application to a case of adverse possession of land for 20 years; defendant having pointed out the boundary line claimed by him and which plaintiff believed to be correct, no fraud being charged. Pittman v. Weeks, 132 N. C. 81, 43 S. E. 582.

25. Olinger v. Shultz, 183 Pa. St. 469, 38 Atl. 1024.

26. Hull v. Watts, 95 Va. 10, 27 S. E. 829.

27. Independent School Dist. of Union in Indiana Tp. v. Independent School Dist. of Union in Washington Tp., 123 Iowa 455, 99 N. W. 106.

28. Exkorn v. Exkorn, 1 App. Div. 124, 37 N. Y. Supp. 68. See also,

§ 276d(2). Discovery of mistake.

That the holder of a mortgage, which, by mistake, set out an incorrect copy of the note it was given to secure, had possession of the mortgage, and therefore had opportunity to discover the mistake, does not import such lack of diligence as would bar an action for reformation in three years from its date, instead of within three years from the discovery of the mistake.[29] Under Iowa Code, § 3448, providing that in actions for relief on the ground of fraud or mistake the cause of action shall not be deemed to have accrued till the fraud or mistake shall have been discovered by the party aggrieved, the statute commences to run against a cause of action arising from a pure mistake from the time when the mistake might, in the exercise of ordinary diligence, have been discovered.[30]

Mastin v. Mastin, 49 Hun 609, 1 N. Y. Supp. 746; Bryant v. Swetland, 48 Ohio St. 194, 27 N. E. 100; Norton v. Davis, 83 Tex. 32, 18 S. W. 430.

The statute of limitations will not run against an action to reform a deed for mistake until discovery thereof, or until the time when it might reasonably have been discovered. Duvall v. Simpson, 53 Kan. 291, 36 Pac. 330.

29. Tarke v. Bingham, 123 Cal. 163, 55 Pac. 759, under Code Civ. Proc., § 338, subd. 4. See Banks v. Stockton, 149 Cal. 599, 87 Pac. 83, holding an action not within section 338, subd. 4. Limitations did not begin to run against a suit to set aside a distribution decree for mistake until the mistake was discovered. Bacon v. Bacon, 150 Cal. 477, 89 Pac. 317.

Record of conveyance of water rights is not constructive notice to a subsequent grantee of a mistake in the amount of water conveyed within Civ. Code, § 19, so as to bar an action to reform the conveyance within three years thereafter under Code Civ. Proc., § 338, subd. 4. Lillis v. Silver Creek & Panoche Land & Water Co., 21 Cal. App. 234, 131 Pac. 344.

Where no duty is imposed by law on one to make inquiry, the mere fact that means of knowledge are open to him, and he did not avail himself of them, does not bar him of relief, on making actual discovery; where there was nothing to excite any suspicion of a mistake in a deed, and there was nothing to show that the grantee and his purchaser acted without ordinary prudence, that the mistake was not discovered sooner by the grantee and his purchaser did not defeat an action to reform the deed, on discovery of the mistake, though the grantee owed a duty to his purchaser to ascertain whether the deed was correct. Hart v. Walton, 9 Cal. App. 502, 99 Pac. 719.

30. West v. Fry, 134 Iowa 675, 112 N. W. 184; Bottorff v. Lewis, 121 Iowa 27, 95 N. W. 262. See also, Sioux City & St. P. Ry. Co. v. O'Brien County, 118 Iowa 582, 92 N. W. 857;

Under Ky. St. 1903, § 2515, requiring actions for relief on the ground of fraud or mistake to be commenced within five years after the accrual thereof, and section 2519, providing that the cause of action shall not be deemed to have accrued until the discovery of the fraud or mistake, but further providing that no action shall be brought after ten years from the making of the contract or the perpetration of the fraud, limitations on actions for mistake begin to run from the time the mistake should, by ordinary diligence, have been discovered.[31] In Nebraska, limitations do not begin to run against an action to reform a conveyance by correcting an alleged mistake in the drafting of a deed until the mistake is discovered.[32] In New York, the statute of limitations does not begin to run against a cause of action by the grantor in a deed, to reform the description, until he has knowledge that some one, claiming under it, is asserting some right not intended to be embraced in the instrument, and not apparent from its terms.[33]

Baird v. Omaha & Council Bluffs Ry., etc., Co. of Nebraska, 111 Iowa 627, 82 N. W. 1020; Lonsdale v. Carroll County, 105 Iowa 452, 75 N. W. 332; Clapp v. Greenlee, 100 Iowa 586, 69 N. W. 1049. Code, § 3448, does not apply to a case where the clerk of a court omits to enter and index a judgment transcript; and the action is governed by Code, § 3447, providing that actions against officers for neglect must be brought within three years. Lougee v. Reed, 133 Iowa 48, 110 N. W. 165.

31. German Security Bank v. Columbia Finance & Trust Co., 27 Ky. Law Rep. 581, 85 S. W. 761.

A cause of action on the ground of mistake is barred, under §§ 2515, 2519, after a lapse of 10 years, irrespective of the time of its discovery. Blakley v. Hanberry, 137 Ky. 283, 125 S. W. 703.

The statute of limitations began to run against the right of a county to surcharge a sheriff's tax collection settlement when a mistake therein was discoverable by the exercise of reasonable diligence. Alexander v. Owen County, 136 Ky. 420, 124 S. W. 386. See also, City of Louisville v. Anderson, 79 Ky. 334, 2 Ky. Law Rep. 344, 42 Am. Rep. 220, an action to recover illegal taxes paid on mistake; Mayes v. Payne, 22 Ky. Law Rep. 1465, 60 S. W. 710, action to correct mistake in a title; Swinebroad v. Wood, 29 Ky. Law Rep. 1202, 97 S. W. 25, an action to have a deed reformed; Burton v. Cowles' Adm'x, 156 Ky. 100, 160 S. W. 782, to recover money paid under mistake; Eversole & Co. v. Burt & Brabb Lumber Co., 160 Ky. 477, 169 S. W. 846.

32. Carter v. Leonard, 65 Neb. 670, 91 N. W. 574; Pinkham v. Pinkham, 60 Neb. 600, 83 N. W. 837, aff'd 61 Neb. 336, 85 N. W. 285.

33. De Forest v. Walters, 153 N.

Under the direct provisions of North Carolina Revisal 1905, sub-sec. 9, the three-year period in which a suit may be brought for the reformation of a deed on the ground of a mistake does not begin to run until the discovery of the mistake, or when the mistake should have been discovered by the exercise of ordinary diligence.[34] Idaho Rev. Codes, § 4054, subdiv. 4, applies only to actions for mistake within the common acceptance of those terms, and has no application to the action for taking, detaining, or injuring goods or chattels, the period for commencing which is prescribed by the third subdivision of the section.[35] Where, by mutual mistake, land was purchased and sold as containing a greater number of acres than it did, limitations do not begin to run upon the purchaser's right to recover on the deficiency until his discovery of the shortage.[36] While the lapse of time will bar equitable relief against a mistake in describing land conveyed, limitations will not run till the discovery of the mistake, or the time at which, by reasonable diligence, it might have been discovered.[37] Under the Texas statute, a suit to correct a mistake in a deed must be brought

Y. 229, 47 N. E. 294, aff'g judg. 78 Hun 611, 28 N. Y. Supp. 831.

Where a wife took out a 20-year endowment policy on the life of her husband, and the insurer by mistake made it payable to the husband in case he survived until its maturity, limitations did not begin to run against the wife, who did not discover the error for more than 10 years, where the policy had not matured and the husband had asserted no rights thereunder. Ulman v. Newman, 161 App. Div. 708, 146 N. Y. Supp. 696. An action to cancel the discharge of a mortgage covering two tracts, and to reform it so that only one should be released, on the ground that plaintiff supposed she was releasing only the one tract, was not barred until 10 years from the time plaintiff acquired knowledge of the mistake. Perry v. Williams, 40 Misc. Rep. 57, 81 N. Y. Supp. 204.

34. Pelletier v. Interstate Cooperage Co., 158 N. C. 403, 74 S. E. 112; Peacock v. Barnes, 142 N. C. 215, 55 S. E. 99; Jefferson v. Roanoke R. & Lumber Co., 165 N. C. 46, 80 S. E. 882.

35. Havirdo v. Lung, 19 Idaho 790, 115 Pac. 930.

36. Hall v. Graham, 112 Va. 560, 72 S. E. 105.

Limitations do not run until discovery of mistake. Senseny's Adm'r v. Boyd's Adm'r, 114 Va. 308, 76 S. E. 305. In an action at law to recover overpayment by mistake, limitation runs from the payment; but in equity it runs only from discovery of the mistake. Grove v. Lemley, 114 Va. 202, 76 S. E. 305.

37. Jackson-Walker Coal & Ma-

within four years after the mistake was discovered, or should have been discovered by the exercise of reasonable care.[38]

§ 276e. Duress as ground for relief.

Limitations do not commence to run against an action for relief on the ground of duress by threats while the mind of the aggrieved party continues to be dominated by the threats.[39] Limitations against an action by a wife or her heirs to avoid a deed which she was induced to execute under duress, to prevent a threatened prosecution of her husband for embezzlement, did not begin to run until his death, since while he was alive the duress was still in force.[40]

§ 276f(1). Concealment of cause of action—In general.

Where fraud, forming the basis of a suit in equity, has been concealed and kept from the knowledge of complainant until limitations have run, the court will disregard the statute.[41] Conceal-

terial Co. v. Miller, 88 Kan. 763, 129 Pac. 1170. See also, Nicholson v. Nicholson, 94 Kan. 153, 146 Pac. 340.

38. Durham v. Luce (Tex. Civ. App.), 140 S. W. 850; Wright v. Isaacks, 43 Tex. Civ. App. 223, 95 S. W. 55. And see: Harris v. Flowers, 21 Tex. Civ. App. 669, 52 S. W. 1046; Oldham v. Medearis, 90 Tex. 506, 39 S. W. 919.

The recording of a mortgage does not put the mortgagor on inquiry to discover the mistake in the description. American Freehold Land Mortg. Co. of London v. Pace, 23 Tex. Civ. App. 222, 56 S. W. 377.

In case of mistake, when the means of discovery are at hand, diligence must be exercised to discover the mistake, but the statute does not run until there is some circumstance or fact to arouse suspicion. Smalley v. Vogt (Tex. Civ. App.), 166 S. W. 1.

But see Patterson v. Rector (Tex. Civ. App.), 127 S. W. 561, as to deed of school lands.

39. Eureka Bank v. Bay, 90 Kan. 506, 135 Pac. 584.

40. Allen v. Leflore County, 78 Miss. 671, 29 So. 161.

41. Newberry v. Wilkinson, 199 Fed. 673, 118 C. C. A. 111, aff'g decree Newberry v. Wilkinson, 190 Fed. 62.

Acts of defendants in managing a corporation, so as to prevent it from doing business and using its patents in competition with another corporation, held incapable of concealment, so as to sustain a reply to a defense of limitations that the acts had been fraudulently concealed from the corporation's trustee until within the statutory period. Strout v. United Shoe Machinery Co., 208 Fed. 646.

The statute of limitations does not

ment and fraud constitute an implied exception to the statute of limitations, and a party who wrongfully conceals material facts, and thereby prevents a discovery of his wrong, or the fact that a cause of action has accrued against him, is not allowed to take advantage of his own wrong by setting up the statute.[42] An action cognizable either at law or in equity, or at law alone, is not barred by the statute, where the defendant deliberately concealed from the plaintiff her right of action, and she had no knowledge of facts putting her upon inquiry.[43] The fraudulent concealment by a

begin to run until the person entitled to sue has discovered facts, entitling him to sue, which were concealed from him by defendant's fraud. Boyer v. Barrows, 166 Cal. 757, 138 Pac. 354; Vance v. Supreme Lodge of Fraternal Brotherhood, 15 Cal. App. 178, 114 Pac. 83.

If the cause of action be fraudulently concealed from the plaintiff, the statute does not begin to run until the existence of the cause of action is discovered by the plaintiff. Pratt v. Worthington, 169 Ill. App. 533.

42. Earnhart v. Robertson, 10 Ind. 8; Atchison, etc., Ry. Co. v. Atchison Grain Co. (Kan.), 70 Pac. 933, modified 68 Kan. 585, 75 Pac. 1051.

Under Burns' Ann. St. Ind. 1908, §§ 302, 2924, 2925, where a guardian was discharged on final report in 1869 and failed to charge himself with money received, of which the ward had no knowledge until 1903, an action therefor begun in 1904 was not barred. Campbell v. First's Estate, 49 Ind. App. 639, 97 N. E. 954. See also, Roberts v. Smith, 165 Ind. 414, 74 N. E. 894, where a female ward married a man of full age.

Where limitations do not begin to run against an officer of a corporation because of the concealment of his fraud, the surety on his bond cannot invoke the aid of the statute on the ground that he was innocent of fraud. McMullen v. Winfield Building & Loan Ass'n, 64 Kan. 298, 67 Pac. 892, 56 L. R. A. 924, 91 Am. St. Rep. 236.

One seeking to toll the statute of limitations by reason of the fraudulent concealment of the facts out of which his action arises must exercise reasonable diligence, and a delay of 20 years without explanation is unreasonable. Lewis v. Duncan, 66 Kan. 306, 71 Pac. 577.

See also, Zinkeisen v. Lews, 63 Kan. 590, 66 Pac. 644; Gano v. Martin, 10 Kan. App. 384, 61 Pac. 460, as to other instances of concealment.

43. Mullen v. Callanan (Iowa), 149 N. W. 516.

Where there is a fraudulent concealment of the facts giving a cause of action the statute does not begin to run till discovery thereof. Cress v. Ivens, 155 Iowa 17, 134 N. W. 869.

An action by a shipper against a carrier for unjust discrimination in the imposition of freight charges paid by plaintiff lies at common law, regardless of fraud, and the carrier's fraudulent concealment of the cause of action does not bring it within Code Iowa, § 2530, providing that, in

notary of false acknowledgment certified by him postponed the running of limitations, not only as against him, but as against the sureties on his bond as well.[44] The defendant cannot defeat a suit to compel him to account for the proceeds of corporate stock intrusted to him for sale on the theory that a suit in equity did not lie and action at law was barred by limitations, where he fraudulently concealed the fact of sale.[45] Where there has been a fraudulent concealment of a cause of action, limitations do not, as a general rule, even in the absence of statute, begin to run until the discovery of the fraud.[46] The statute of limitations does not run against a claim for unpaid alimony, where there has been merely a fraudulent concealment of property.[47] An appeal in a previous action against a policeman which protracted the litigation past the seven-year period of limitation will not stop the running of limitations in favor of the sureties.[48] Where a bank, believing a forged indorsement to be genuine, paid a check to a person other than the drawee, and delivered the canceled check to the drawer as a voucher, the statute of limitations did not operate until the drawer's discovery of the wrongful payment.[49] Where defendant's

actions for relief on the ground of fraud, the cause of action does not accrue until the fraud is discovered. Murray v. Chicago & N. W. Ry. Co., 92 Fed. 868, 35 C. C. A. 62.

See Cole v. Charles City Nat. Bank, 114 Iowa 632, 87 N. W. 671, where plaintiff sued to recover money deposited in a bank without his knowledge to his credit.

44. State *ex rel.* Barringer v. Hawkins, 103 Mo. App. 251, 77 S. W. 98.

Limitation does not begin to run against an action to recover from an agent for converting to his own use money and property of his principals, who resided in a distant State, where he fraudulently represented to them in his letters that he had not received such money or property until they discovered the fraud. Bracken v. Milner, 104 Fed. 522 (C. C., Mo.).

45. Clarke v. Gilmore, 149 App. Div. 445, 133 N. Y. Supp. 1047.

46. Conditt v. Holden, 92 Ark. 618, 123 S. W. 765.

One obtaining from a carrier goods held not guilty of fraudulent concealment so as to prevent the running of limitations against the carrier's right to recover for a wrongful delivery. Tedford Auto Co. v. Chicago, R. I. & P. Ry. Co. (Ark.), 172 S. W. 1006.

47. Gilbert v. Hayward (R. I.), 92 Atl. 625, under Gen. Laws R. I. 1909, c. 284, § 7.

48. McGovern v. Rectanus, 32 Ky. Law Rep. 364, 105 S. W. 965.

49. Masonic Benefit Ass'n of Stringer Grand Lodge v. First State

grantee who purchased the land in suit under a contract to discharge a vendor's lien thereon concealed his assumption of the debt so that the plaintiff could not have discovered it by any diligence, the grantee's active fraud will prevent the running of the statute of limitations.[50] Where a cause of action is fraudulently concealed from complainant, the statute of limitations is suspended until complainant discovers the fraud.[51]

§ 276f(2). What constitutes concealment.

Mere silence by the person liable is not concealment, but there must be some affirmative act or representation designed to prevent, and which does prevent, the discovery of the cause of action.[52] Concealment of a cause of action preventing the running of limitations must consist of some trick or artifice preventing inquiry, or calculated to hinder a discovery of the cause of action by the use of ordinary diligence, and mere silence is insufficient.[53] There

Bank of Columbus, 99 Miss. 610, 55 So. 408, under Miss. Code 1906, § 3109.

50. Raley v. D. Sullivan & Co. (Tex. Civ. App.), 159 S. W. 99.

Where defendant received money belonging to plaintiff, and concealed the fact from him, limitations would not run against plaintiff's right to recover the same except from such time as plaintiff discovered the fact, or by the exercise of reasonable diligence would have discovered it. Holland v. Shannon (Tex. Civ. App.), 84 S. W. 854.

51. Boro v. Hidell, 122 Tenn. 80, 120 S. W. 961.

In the absence of fraud, neither ignorance of his right to sue nor mere silence of a person liable prevents running of limitations. Coe v. Sloan, 16 Idaho 49, 100 Pac. 354.

See State v. Chicago & N. W. Ry. Co., 132 Wis. 345, 112 N. W. 515, and action by the State against a railroad for license fees imposed by Wis. St. 1898, § 1213; Wolkins v. Knight, 134 Mich. 347, 10 Detroit Leg. N. 453, 96 N. W. 445, an action to recover for a payment upon an account fraudulently alleged to have been made, but which in fact was not made.

52. Lancaster v. Springer, 239 Ill. 472, 88 N. E. 272; Fortune v. English, 226 Ill. 262, 80 N. E. 781, aff'g 128 Ill. App. 537; Cunningham v. Dougherty, 121 Ill. App. 395.

A party is chargeable with knowledge of the facts, where the circumstances are such as would have induced inquiry, and the means of ascertaining the truth were readily available on such inquiry, but he neglects to make it. Ater v. Smith, 245 Ill. 57, 91 N. E. 776.

53. State v. Jackson, 52 Ind. App. 254, 100 N. E. 479; Board of Com'rs

must be something actually said or done which is directly intended to prevent discovery.[54] Mere silence or concealment by a debtor may not, without affirmative misrepresentation, toll the running of the statute. Where, however, a debtor by actual fraud keeps his creditor in ignorance of the cause of action, the statute does not begin to run until the creditor had knowledge, or was put upon inquiry with means of knowledge that such cause of action had accrued.[55] Fraudulent concealment must consist of affirmative acts of misrepresentation, mere silence being insufficient.[56] The fraud which will relieve the bar of the statute must be of that character which involves moral turpitude, and must have the effect of debarring or deterring the plaintiff from his action.[57] A cause of action cannot be said to be concealed from one who has a personal knowledge of the facts which create it, although he may have no other means of establishing his case than his own testimony.[58] For facts which have been held by the courts to be sufficient or insufficient to show a fraudulent concealment of a cause of action, reference may be had to the cases cited in the note below.[59]

of Monroe County v. Hall, 51 Ind. App. 475, 99 N. E. 1009.

The acts constituting a fraudulent concealment must ordinarily be subsequent to the accruing of the cause of action, but may be concurrent or coincident with it, or even precede it, if they are of such a nature as to operate after the cause of action arose, and thereby prevent its discovery, and were intended by the concealor to so operate. Caldwell v. Ulsh (Ind. App.), 103 N. E. 879.

54. State *ex rel.* Bell v. Yates, 231 Mo. 276, 132 S. W. 672; Same v. Bell, 132 S. W. 676; Smith v. Settle, 128 Mo. App. 379, 107 S. W. 430.

55. Cloyd v. Reynolds, 44 Pa. Super. Ct. 81.

56. Glover v. National Bank of Commerce of New York, 156 App. Div. 247, 141 N. Y. Supp. 409.

57. Anderson v. Foster, 112 Ga. 270, 37 S. E. 426.

58. Sanborn v. Gale, 162 Mass. 412, 38 N. E. 710, 26 L. R. A. 864.

59. *U. S.*—Darnold v. Simpson, 114 Fed. 368; Despeaux v. Pennsylvania R. Co., 87 Fed. 794.

Ill.—Gunton v. Hughes, 79 Ill. App. 661, aff'd 181 Ill. 132, 54 N. E. 895; Parmelee v. Price, 105 Ill. App. 271, aff'd 208 Ill. 544, 70 N. E. 725; Athey v. Hunter, 65 Ill. App. 453.

Ind.—Jackson v. Jackson, 149 Ind. 238, 47 N. E. 963; Bower v. Thomas, 22 Ind. App. 505, 54 N. E. 142; State v. Walters, 31 Ind. App. 77, 66 N. E. 182, 99 Am. St. Rep. 244; Lemster v. Warner, 137 Ind. 79, 36 N. E. 900.

Iowa.—Mereness v. First Nat. Bank, 112 Iowa 11, 83 N. W. 711, 51 L. R. A. 410, 84 Am. St. Rep. 318.

Kan.—Stewart v. Bank of Indian

§ 276f(3). Concealment by agent or third person.

The rule that the time limited for beginning an action for fraud shall not commence to run while defendant conceals it does not apply when the concealment is by a third person.[60] A person against whom a cause of action has arisen on account of the fraudulent conduct of his agent is not guilty of fraudulent concealment of the cause of action, so as to prevent the statute of limitations from running, by the fact that his said agent conceals the fraud.[61] Where a company assigned accounts and sold goods to a bank to apply the proceeds on the company's notes to the bank, and the bank's president concealed such facts from it, and took possession of the property and applied the proceeds to other debts of the company, of which he was a stockholder, the statute did not, during such concealment, run against the bank's right of action for an ac-

Territory, 68 Kan. 755, 75 Pac. 1055.

Ky.—Isaacs v. Murphy, 1 Ky. Law Rep. (abstract) 409.

Mass.—Graham v. Stanton, 177 Mass. 321, 58 N. E. 1023.

Mich.—Allen v. Conklin, 112 Mich. 74, 3 Detroit Leg. N. 813, 70 N. W. 339; First Nat. Bank v. Steel, 146 Mich. 308, 13 Detroit Leg. N. 762, 109 N. W. 423.

Miss.—Hudson v. Kimbrough, 74 Miss 341, 20 So. 885; McCarlie v. Atkinson, 77 Miss. 594, 27 So. 641, 78 Am. St. Rep. 540.

Mo.—Central Bank of Kansas v. Thayer, 184 Mo. 61, 82 S. W. 142; Spuryer v. Hardy, 4 Mo. App. 573; Aultman, Miller & Co. v. Loring, 76 Mo. App. 66.

N. C.—Dunn v. Beaman, 126 N. C. 766, 36 S. E. 172.

Okl.—Waugh v. Guthrie Gas, Light, etc., Co., 37 Okl. 239, 131 Pac. 174.

Pa.—Taylor v. Hammel, 201 Pa. 546, 51 Atl. 316.

Tenn.—Woodfolk v. Marley, 39 S. W. 747, aff'd 98 Tenn. 467, 40 S. W. 479.

Tex.—Vernor v. D. Sullivan & Co. (Civ. App.), 126 S. W. 641; Presnall v. McLeary (Civ. App.), 50 S. W. 1066; Ward v. Marion County, 26 Tex. Civ. App. 361, 62 S. W. 557, 63 S. W. 155.

60. Hayden v. Thompson, 71 Fed. 60, 17 C. C. A. 592, 36 U. S. App. 361.

The "fraudulent concealment" which will take a claim out of the statute must be that of the person sought to be charged, and not of his clerk, without his fault. Stevenson v. Robinson, 39 Mich. 160.

The concealment of a right by one whose duty it is to disclose it prevents the running of limitations in favor of the party succeeding to his rights, in default. Hoyle v. Jones, 35 Ga. 40, 89 Am. Dec. 273.

61. Wood v. Williams, 142 Ill. 269, 31 N. E. 681, 34 Am. St. Rep. 79, aff'g 40 Ill. App. 115; Wilson v. Williams (Ill.), 33 N. E. 884, aff'g 42 Ill. App. 612.

counting.[62] Where an attorney advised his client that the land was unincumbered, and the client bought it, and suit was brought under a mortgage existing at the time of the purchase, the attorney's representation to the client that the land was not subject to the mortgage, and that he could successfully defend the foreclosure proceeding, was not such a fraudulent concealment of the client's cause of action for his negligence in approving the title at the time the purchase was made as would stay the running of limitations, in the absence of a showing that the attorney knew his misrepresentations to be untrue.[63] Where an officer of a bank, by agreement, conceals the defalcation of another officer, his knowledge of the transaction is not chargeable to the bank, so as to set running the statute of limitations, as against a claim against the defaulting officer for the amount of the loss.[64] Where a person through whose negligence another has suffered an injury places the injured party in the care of a doctor who has previously been the physician of both, and the physician misleads his patient as to the extent of his injuries by false and fraudulent misrepresentations, such misrepresentations will not prevent the statute of limitations from running.[65] The fact that a plaintiff is ignorant of facts necessary to enable him to bring a suit, through the fraud or concealment of one for whose acts the defendant is not responsible, will not avail to defeat a plea of limitation.[66]

62. Huntington Nat. Bank v. Huntington Distilling Co., 152 Fed. 240 (C. C., W. Va.), under Code W. Va. 1906, § 3511.

63. Fortune v. English, 226 Ill. 262, 80 N. E. 781, aff'g judg. 128 Ill. App. 537, under Rev. St. Ill. 1874, c. 83, § 22.

64. Vance v. Mottley, 92 Tenn. 310, 21 S. W. 593.

The statute does not begin to run in favor of an agent, and against his principal, until the principal has knowledge of some wrong committed by the agent inconsistent with his rights as principal. Perry v. Smith, 31 Kan. 423, 2 Pac. 784; Perry v. Wade, 31 Kan. 428, 2 Pac. 787.

65. Chamberlain v. Chicago, B. & Q. R. Co., 27 Fed. 181.

66. School Dist. of City of Sedalia, Mo. v. De Weese, 100 Fed. 705 (C. C., Mo.).

CHAPTER XXVII.

MUTUAL ACCOUNTS, ACCOUNTS IN GENERAL, ETC.

§ 277. Statutory provisions as to mutual accounts.

Formerly the doctrine relative to mutual accounts was predicated upon the rule advanced in Catling *v.* Skoulding,[1] that the statute only attached from the date of the last item on either side of the account. This rule was generally adopted in this country.[2] In most

1. Catling v. Skoulding, 6 T. R. 189. See also Cranch v. Kirkman, Peake's Cas. 164.

2. Hutchinson v. Pratt, 2 Vt. 149; Wood v. Barney, 2 id. 369; Davis v. Smith, 4 Me. 337; Penn's Adm'r v. Watson, 20 Mo. 13; Cogswell v. Dolliver, 2 Mass. 217, 3 Am. Dec. 45; Belles v. Belles, 12 N. J. Law 339; Pridgen v. Hill, 12 Tex. 374; Van Swearingen v. Harris, 1 W. & S. (Pa.) 356; Thomson v. Hopper, id. 467; Chambers v. Marks, 25 Pa. 296; Sickles v. Mather, 20 Wend. (N. Y.) 72, 32 Am. Dec. 521; Coster v. Murray, 5 Johns. (N. Y.) Ch. 522; Ramchander v. Hammond, 2 id. 200; Union Bank v. Knapp (3 Pick.), 20 Mass. 96, 15 Am. Dec. 181; Tucker v. Ives, 6 Cow. (N. Y.) 193; Chamberlin v. Cuyler, 9 Wend. (N. Y.) 126; Edmonstone v. Thompson, 15 id. 559; Bass v. Bass, 23 Mass. (6 Pick.), 364; Ashley v. Hill, 6 Conn. 246; McClellan v. Croften, 6 Me. 308; App. v. Dreisbach, 2 Rawle (Penn.) 287; Brady v. Calhoun, 1 Pa. 140; Moore v. Munro, 4 Rand. (Va.) 488; New-

of the States this rule has now been adopted by positive enactment. Thus, in Maine the statute [3] provides that "in all actions of debt or assumpsit to recover the balance due, in cases where there have been mutual dealings between the parties, the items of which are inserted, whether kept or proved by one party or both, the cause of action shall be deemed to accrue at the time of the last item proved in such account;" and a similar provision exists in the

some v. Persons, 3 N. C. (2 Hayw.) 242; Davis v. Tiernan, 2 How. (Miss.) 786; Fitch v. Hilleary, 1 Hill (S. C.) 292; Taylor v. McDonald, 2 Mill's Const. (S. C.) 178; Kimball v. Brown, 7 Wend. (N. Y.) 322; Hay v. Kramer, 2 S. & W. (Pa.) 137; Ingram v. Sherard, 17 S. & R. (Pa.) 347; Beltzhoover v. Yewell, 11 G. & J. (Md.) 212; Turnbull v. Strohecker, 4 McCord (S. C.) 210; Buntin v. Lagow, 1 Blackf. (Ind.) 573; Hibler v. Johnston, 18 N. J. Law 266; Knipe v. Knipe, 3 Blackf. (Ind.) 300; McNaughton v. Norris, 1 Hayw. (N. C.) 216; Sumter v. Morse, 2 Hill (S. C.) 92; Mandeville v. Wilson, 5 Cranch (U. S.) 15; Toland v. Spring, 12 Peters (U. S.) 300; Smith v. Ruecastle, 7 N. J. Law 357. But in New Hampshire this doctrine is denied. Blair v. Drew, 6 N. H. 235; Hannan v. Englemann, 49 Wis. 278; Turnbull v. Storhecker, 4 McCord (S. C.) 210; Mauney v. Coit, 86 N. C. 463; Waffle v. Short, 25 Kan. 503; Keller v. Jackson, 58 Iowa, 629; Chambers v. Chambers, 78 Ind. 400; Gunn v. Gunn, 74 Ga. 555, 58 Am. Rep. 447; Flournoy v. Wooten, 71 id. 168; Ford v. Clark, 72 id. 760; Kutz v. Fleisher, 67 Cal. 93, 7 Pac. 195; Ware v. Manning, 86 Ala. 238. See Gage v. Dudley, 64 N. H. 271, 9 Atl. 786 (where the accounts were hardly mutual), and Livermore v. Rand, 26 N. H. 85, where this doctrine is denied, following the rule adopted in Blair v. Drew, 6 N. H. 235. See also Perry v. Chesley, 77 Me. 393, and Lancey v. R. R. Co., 72 id. 34, where it is held that the last item of an account does not save the statute unless there are other items within six years. The theory upon which the doctrine as to mutual accounts rests, is, that there is a mutual understanding between the parties, either express or implied, that they will continue to credit each other until one signifies a contrary intention, when the balance, being ascertained, becomes due and payable. Gunn v. Gunn, 74 Ga. 555; Dunn v. Fleming, 73 Wis. 545; Kutz v. Fleisher, 67 Cal. 93; Roots v. Mason, etc., Co., 27 W. Va. 483; Webster v. Byrnes, 32 Md. 86; Chapman v. Goodrich, 55 Vt. 354; Hodge v. Manly, 25 id. 210, 60 Am. Dec. 253; Dyer v. Walker, 51 Me. 104; Mattern v. McDivett, 113 Pa. 402, 6 Atl. 83; Parker v. Schwartz, 136 Mass. 30; Adam v. Carroll, 85 Pa. 209; Abbay v. Hill, 64 Miss. 340; Appeal of Stewart, 105 Pa. 307; Hollywood v. Reed, 55 Mich. 308; Adams v. Patterson, 35 Cal. 122; Lark v. Cheatha, 80 Ga. 1; Ford v. Clark, 72 id. 760; Dickinson v. Williams, 11 Cush. (Mass.) 258; Wooley v. Osborne, 39 N. J. Eq. 54.

3. Appendix, Maine.

statute of Massachusetts, New York, Alabama, Arkansas, Colorado, Delaware, Florida, Indiana, Iowa, Mississippi, Missouri, Minnesota, North Carolina, South Carolina, Oregon, California, Michigan, Wisconsin, Nevada, Tennessee, Arizona, Dakota, Idaho, Montana, New Mexico, and Utah. In Rhode Island, New Jersey, Kentucky, Maryland, Virginia, West Virginia, and Pennsylvania, the provision is substantially the same as in the statute of James. In Virginia and West Virginia an action must be brought upon any store account for goods charged therein within two years. In Texas, in all accounts except between merchant and merchant, their factors and agents, the respective time or date of the delivery of each article charged must be specifically stated, and the statute runs against each item from the date of delivery, unless otherwise agreed. In Louisiana, the accounts of retailers of provisions and liquors, and the accounts of all merchants, whether selling by retail or wholesale, are barred within three years from the time when the articles charged shall have been furnished, but upon open accounts the statute does not run until five years.

§ 278. What are mutual accounts.

Mutual accounts are made up of matters of set-off, or, in other words, are accounts between parties who have a mutual and alternate course of dealings,[4] under an implied agreement that one account may and shall be offset against the other, *pro tanto*. In the language of Earl, J.,[5] in an able opiinion, " The very theory upon which this statute is based is that the credits are mutual, and that the account is permitted to run with the view of ultimate adjustment by a settlement and payment of the balance; and this theory is recognized in the statute, as it mentions an action brought to recover a balance due upon an account." The action, however, need not be for the balance due upon the account. It is suffi-

4. Robarts v. Robarts, 1 M. & P. 487; Ingram v. Sherard, 17 S. & R. (Penn.) 347.

5. Green v. Disbrow, 79 N. Y. 1, 35 Am. Rep. 496.

cient if such is its purpose and legal effect.[6] If the account is all upon one side, and the statute has run upon some of the items, the account is not mutual, and only those upon which the statute has not run can be recovered;[7] and this is so, although entries of payments are made upon the account, the rule being that mere technical payments of money on account, made by one to another, for which credit is given, do not make the accounts mutual so as to prevent the statutory bar from attaching.[8] In such a case, the accounts are said to lack the essential attributes to the creation of mutual accounts, the express or implied agreement to set off the one against the other, and, instead, that the payment instantly goes in reduction of the debt, *pro tanto.*[9] Such accounts,

6. Penniman v. Rotch, 44 Mass. (3 Met.) 216. "In ordinary cases," said Redfield, J., "of mutual dealings no obligation is created in regard to each particular item, but only for the balance; and it is the constantly varying balance which is the debt." Abbott v. Keith, 11 Vt. 525. See also Hodge v. Manley, 25 Vt. 210, 60 Am. Dec. 253.

7. Robarts v. Robarts, *supra;* Ashby v. James, 11 M. & W. 542; Smith v. Forty, 4 C. & P. 126.

8. Webster v. Byrnes, 32 Md. 86; Adams v. Carroll, 85 Pa. 209; Prenatt v. Runyan, 12 Ind. 174; Dyer v. Walker, 51 Me. 104; Weatherwax v. Cosumnes Valley Mill Co., 17 Cal. 344; Adams v. Paterson, 35 Cal. 122; Peck v. N. Y., etc., Mail S. S. Co., 5 Bosw. (N. Y.) 226; Fraylor v. Sonora, Min. Co., 17 Cal. 594; Lark v. Cheatham, 80 Ga. 1.

9. In Gold v. Whitcomb (14 Pick.), 31 Mass. 188, where it appeared that the defendant kept no account with the plaintiff. In this case a shopkeeper's account containing charges and credits more than six years before action brought, and only two small charges within six years, was held not an account current or mutual account, so that the last two items should draw the others out of the statute.

In order to prove a mutual and open account current, it is sufficient to prove mutual dealings between the parties, consisting of sales made, or services performed, by each party, to or for the other, creating mutual debts, and which by mutual agreement or understanding are to be set off against each other. Corinne Mill Co. v. Toponce, 152 U. S. 405; *In re* Huger, 100 Fed. Rep. 805; Safford v. Barney, 121 Mass. 300; Eldridge v. Smith, 144 Mass. 35; Kingsley v. Delano, 169 Mass. 285; *In re* Hovey's Estate (Penn.), 48 Atl. 311; Dunavant v. Fields (Ark.) 60 S. W. 420; McFarland v. O'Neil, 155 Penn. St. 260; Haffner v. Schmuck, 63 N. Y. S. 55. Mere credits, not proved to have been actually made, have no effect on the running of the statute. *In re* Gladke, 60 N. Y. Supp. 869, 45 App. Div. 625. An item which

instead of being mutual, are one-sided,[10] and lack the essential attribute of mutuality.[11] In Pennsylvania,[12] it is held that an account is not rendered mutual by a payment, either of goods or money, and the reason is stated to be that a mutual account is when each has a demand or right of action against the other; and that this is not so when the sale is by one to the other, whether it is to be paid for in cash or in kind, and that the manner of payment can make no difference. But the doctrine of these cases is questioned in New York, and it is held that where there are charges upon both sides of the account for property other than money, although the account is kept by one of the parties only, and consists of debits on one side, and credits for merchandise upon the other, the account is a mutual account, within the mean-

is merely a payment made by the defendant on account of items charged against him by the plaintiff does not make the account a mutual and open one within the meaning of the statute, as it is not a matter of separate and individual charge, but is merely a partial extinguishment of an existing indebtedness. Day v. Mayo, 154 Mass. 472. There must be evidence of an intention on the debtor's part to apply such payments, if not more than sufficient to cover recent items, to the older items already barred by limitation. Miller v. Cinnamon, 168 Ill. 447, 456. In Minnesota the question simply is whether the part payment was voluntary and unconditional; if it was, it operates, if the defendant has admitted the correctness of the account against him, to renew from its date, for the statutory period, the right of action upon the balance remaining. Clarkin v. Brown, 80 Minn. 361. When an account is closed by settlement or otherwise, it becomes an account stated; this gives a new and original cause of action, and the statute of limitations begins to run only from its date. King v. Davis, 168 Mass. 133, 46 N. E. 418; Porter v. Chicago, etc., Ry. Co., 99 Iowa 351; Morse v. Minton, 101 Iowa 603, 70 N. W. 691; and cases cited *infra*, § 280, n. 41.

10. Ingram v. Sherard, 17 S. & R. (Pa.) 347; Lowber v. Smith, 7 Pa. 381.

11. Hay v. Kramer, 2 W. & S. (Pa.) 137; Coster v. Murray, 5 Johns. (N. Y.) Ch. 522; Edmonstone v. Thomson, 15 Wend. (N. Y.) 554; Belles v. Belles, 12 N. J. Law 339; Gulick v. Turnpike Co., 14 id. 545.

12. "As, for example," says Rogers, J., "where A. and B. dealing together, A. sells B. an article of furniture or any other commodity, and afterwards B. sells A. property of the same or a different description, this constitutes a reciprocal demand, because A. and B. have a demand or right of action against each other." Lowber v. Smith, 7 Pa. 381; Adams v. Carroll, 85 id. 209.

ing of the statute.[13] And this view is adopted in California;[14] and in Georgia [15] and Michigan [16] it has been carried still further, and credits for labor upon one side, and payments of money upon the other, have been held sufficient to render the accounts mutual. In England, it is also held that the balance of an account may be carried forward and become an item in a new account.[17] But in Massachusetts [18] a contrary doctrine was held.

The advantage of bringing an account under the head of mutual accounts is, that an item upon either side within the statutory period draws after it all other items beyond that period;[19] whereas,

13. Green v. Disbrow, 79 N. Y. 1. Cash payments made and received to be applied on general account, and on account of actual or supposed indebtedness, extinguish *pro tanto* the indebtedness, and, if made in advance, will apply to extinguish the next indebtedness, and the statute of limitations has no application. Raux v. Brand, 90 N. Y. 309.

14. Norton v. Larco, 30 Cal. 126, where the delivery of articles to be applied on account was held to be a sale, and not a payment *pro tanto*.

15. Where a running account for a series of years is kept between an employer and his employee, for work on the one hand and payments upon the other, the statute does not run thereon so long as the last item of such account is within the statute; but if there has at any time been an accounting and settlement between the parties, monthly or otherwise, whereby the account is sifted and stated, or liquidated either by cash or note for the balance due, or the carrying forward of such balance to the next month's account, such settlement will become a new departure, and the items within the statute will draw without its operation only that part of the account made since such settlement, with such balance, if any, brought forward. Schall v. Eisner, 58 Ga. 190.

16. Payne v. Walker, 26 Mich. 60.

17. Farrington v. Lee, 1 Mod. 270.

18. Where the defendant was a depositor in the plaintiff bank, and his deposits were erroneously footed at $1,000 too much, and the balance so erroneously ascertained was struck and carried to his credit on the bank books, the checks being annulled, and the same error was repeated monthly for more than six years, during which the dealings of the parties continued, when to an action by the bank to recover back the amount the defendant pleaded the statute, it was held that as to the $1,000, the account was not an open, mutual, and running account, but had become a settled and stated account each month, although the balance due the defendant was not then paid in cash, but was carried forward as the first item in the subsequent month's account. Union Bank v. Knapp, 20 Mass. (3 Pick.) 96, 15 Am. Dec. 181. See also Belchertown v. Bridgman, 118 Mass. 486.

19. Hallock v. Losee, 3 N. Y. Super. Ct. (1 Sandf.) 220; Judd v.

if the account is not mutual, and the items upon one side are mere cash payments upon the items on the other, the payments so made will only keep that portion of the account on foot which accrued within six years from the time such payment was made.[20]

§ 278a. What are mutual accounts—Recent decisions.

The New York rule, as set forth in the last preceding section, that there must be items on both sides, other than cash payments, to make applicable Code of Civil Procedure, § 386, providing that the cause of action for a balance due on a mutual, open, and current account, where there have been reciprocal demands between the parties, accrues from the time of the last item, has been applied in a number of recent cases.[21] In California, where prac-

Sampson, 13 Tex. 19; Guichard v. Superveile, 11 Tex. 522; Turnbull v. Strohecker, 4 McCord (S. C.) 214; Cotes v. Harris, Buller's N. P. 149; Mt. Nebo Anthracite Coal Co. v. Martin, 86 Ark. 608, 112 S. W. 882; *In re* Holloway's Estate, 89 Neb. 403, 131 N. W. 606.

20. Tucker v. Ives, 6 Cow. (N. Y.) 193; Bennett v. Davis, 1 N. H. 19; Buntin v. Lagow, 1 Blackf. (Ind.) 373; Miller v. Colwell, 5 N. J. Law 577; Kimball v. Brown, 7 Wend. (N. Y.) 322; McCullough v. Judd, 20 Ala. 703; Prewett v. Runyan, 12 Ind. 174; Adams v. Patterson, 35 Cal. 122. If personal property is delivered to a creditor, to be applied towards payment of the debt, the transaction is not a mutual account, consisting of "reciprocal demands" between the parties, within the meaning of section 17 of the Nevada statute. Warren v. Sweeney, 4 Nev. 101. Items in an account, charged within six years, do not take items charged more than six years before suit out of the statute of limitations, unless there are mutual accounts between the parties. Bennett v. Davis, 1 N. H. 19; Kimball v. Brown, 7 Wend. (N. Y.) 322; Miller v. Colwell, 5 N. J. Law 577; Buntin v. Lagow, 1 Blackf. (Ind.) 373; Tucker v. Ives, 6 Cow. (N. Y.) 193. Items, in mutual accounts, within six years next before action brought, do not admit an unsettled account extending beyond six years, nor show a promise to pay the balance, so as to take the case out of the statute of limitations. Blair v. Drew, 6 N. H. 235.

21. John Klein Wagon Works v. Hencken-Willenbrock Co., 123 N. Y. Supp. 119, 67 Misc. Rep. 425, where plaintiff having merely a demand for various items of work and materials, a subsequent item of payment by defendant was held not to affect the bar as to any of plaintiff's items; Miller v. Longshore, 131 N. Y. Supp. 1041, 147 App. Div. 214, where an account of a miller for supplies furnished on the credit of a physician, pursuant to his orders, and an account of the physician for professional services ren-

tically the same rule prevails, it has recently been held that a mutual account, within Code Civ. Proc., § 344, providing that an action thereon is deemed to have accrued from the time of the last item proved in the account on either side, implies an account in which there is a reciprocity of dealing between the parties made up of matters of set-off, whereon each party has a right of action against the other.[22] In Georgia, it is now held that, in order for such mutuality of account to exist as will arrest the bar of limita-

dered the miller and his family during the period of the furnishing of the supplies, were held to consist of reciprocal demands constituting a mutual current account; Lowenthal v. Resnick, 110 N. Y. Supp. 1045, where an account between a liquor seller and a customer, consisting merely of debits on one side and payments made solely in cash and credits for the return of the demijohns in which he purchased his liquors on the other, was held not to be a mutual current account, where there have been reciprocal demands by the parties; Pulver v. Esselstyn, 50 N. Y. Supp. 756, 22 Misc. Rep. 429, where it was a tenant's duty, under his lease, to market the hay raised on the farm, half the proceeds of which belonged to the landlord, applying the landlord's portion of the proceeds on a debt due by the landlord to the tenant, without the landlord's authority, was held not to make the debt a mutual open account, so as to keep it from being barred by the statute of limitations. See also Fennell v. Black, 53 N. Y. Supp. 797, 24 Misc. Rep. 728; McDonald v. Jaffa, 65 N. Y. Supp. 1059, 53 App. Div. 484; Leahy v. Campbell, 75 N. Y. Supp. 72, 70 App. Div. 127; Meehan v. Figliuolo, 88 N. Y. Supp. 920.

22. Flynn v. Seale, 2 Cal. App. 665, 84 Pac. 263; Santa Rosa Nat. Bank v. Barnett, 125 Cal. 407, 58 Pac. 85, where a depositor borrows money from a bank by means of overdrafts, and occasionally deposits money, which is applied to the overdrafts, the transaction is not a mutual account, and the statute of limitations runs from the date of each loan, notwithstanding the transaction opens with a credit to the depositor; Copriviza v. Rilovich, 4 Cal. App. 26, 87 Pac. 398, moneys which are advanced by a debtor to third parties at the request of a creditor, upon which demands arise by the debtor against the creditor, and which are charged on an account between them, render the account an open, mutual, and current account, an action on which is not barred until the expiration of the period of limitation from the time of the last item thereof proved. See also Dillon v. Cross, 5 Cal. App. 766, 91 Pac. 439, where it was held that an action for an accounting could not be defeated by limitations, where Code Civ. Proc., § 440, providing that, where cross-demands have existed between persons under such circumstances that, if one had sued the other, a counterclaim could have been set up, the two demands shall be deemed compensated so far as they equal each other, applies.

tions, each party to the account must extend credit to the other on the faith of an admitted indebtedness, and to bring an account, otherwise barred, within such exception, it is not enough to show that there are two accounts, but it is necessary to show the indebtedness of each party was the result of a course of dealing in which credit was extended on the faith of the indebtedness to him.[23] In Michigan, it is now held that a "mutual and open account current" means a course of dealing where each party furnishes credit to the other on the reliance that on settlement the accounts will be allowed, so that one will reduce the balance due on the other.[24] The latest cases in Pennsylvania hold to the rule stated in the last preceding section that where there are mutual accounts, if any of the items of the account be within six years before the commencement of the suit, such item is equivalent to a subsequent promise reviving the debt; but the mutual accounts must on both sides relate to trade in merchandise, labor, or something that is

23. Mobley, Ward & Davis v. Pendegrast, 8 Ga. App. 565, 70 S. E. 18; Smith v. Hembree, 3 Ga. App. 510, 60 S. E. 126; Bank of Blakely v. Buchannon, 13 Ga. App. 793, 80 S. E. 42; Reid v. Wilson, 109 Ga. 424, 34 S. E. 608, the existence of an indebtedness by A to B and an extension of credit by B to A, by reason thereof, constitute a mutual account against which the statute of limitations runs only from the date of the last item on either side thereof. This rule applies where there has been no liquidation or accounting by which a new point was established. Youmans v. Moore, 11 Ga. App. 66, 74 S. E. 710.

In Iowa, the claim of one county against another for the amount of charges paid an insane hospital to which a patient was committed has been held to be one on an open, continuous, current account within the general statute of limitation of that State. Buena Vista County v. Woodbury County, 163 Iowa, 626, 145 N. W. 282.

24. *In re* Hiscock's Estate, 79 Mich. 537, 44 N. W. 947; Stoner v. Riggs, 128 Mich. 129, 8 Detroit Leg. N. 557, 87 N. W. 109, where plaintiff had charge of the loaning and collecting of defendant's money for a series of years, and, on submitting an account of the business, defendant promised to pay him for his services, the claim therefor became a part of the mutual account, unaffected by the general statute of limitations, though it was not entered on the books, and the value of the services was not agreed upon. But see the earlier cases of Hollywood v. Reed, 55 Mich. 308, 21 N. W. 313; White v. Campbell, 25 Mich. 463; Campbell v. White, 22 Mich. 178, holding payments of money on account to be sufficient to render the accounts mutual, as stated in the last preceding section.

provable by books of original entries.[25] In South Dakota, where the Code provision is practically the same as in New York, the rule is maintained the same as in New York that an account consisting entirely of charges on one side and a payment on account on the other is not such a mutual account as the statute contemplates.[26] In Massachusetts it has been held that where one cotenant receives rents and pays for repairs, insurance, and taxes, the account is a "mutual and open account current," within the provisions of the statute of that State.[27]

In mutual accounts and dealings, the obligations arise, not out of the various items, but out of the balance, which is the debt, and so the statute of limitations begins to run only from the date of the last item.[28] A mutual, open account is not terminated, until a final balance is arrived at, which balance constitutes an independent debt, and from the date thereof the statute of limitations begins to run.[29] Where parties by their mutual dealings by some item of debit or credit have extended the time of operation of the statute of limitations on the balance of the account, the debtor cannot shorten the time by making specific payment of debit items.[30]

25. *In re* Radenbach's Estate, 52 Pa. Super. Ct. 461; Hudson v. Hudson, 21 Pa. Super. Ct. 92.

Money being not a proper subject of book account, to take a running account out of the statute of limitations there must be mutual accounts for other items. Kline v. Mohry, 4 Walk. (Pa.) 279.

An action for an accounting is not barred by limitations, where there exists an open account between the parties and a duty to account at the commencement of the action. Hurst v. Brennen, 239 Pa. 216, 86 Atl. 778.

26. McArthur v. McCoy, 21 S. D. 314, 112 N. W. 155.

27. Robinson v. Robinson, 173 Mass. 233, 53 N. E. 854. The mere lapse of the period of limitations after the division of property between devisees does not bar an action for the stating of an account between them, where there was an open running account between the parties, and the divisions made were only *pro tanto*, and the final distribution was to be made in the future. Moseley v. Perry, 201 Mass. 135, 87 N. E. 606.

28. Messier v. Messier, 34 R. I. 233, 82 Atl. 996.

29. Louisville & N. R. Co. v. United States, 47 Ct. Cl. (U. S.) 129.

30. Rogers v. Davis, 103 Me. 405, 69 Atl. 618. See Hagar v. Springer, 63 Me. 506, as to what constitutes a mutual account.

In Missouri, it has been held that where plaintiff performed services and paid money for defendant at its request at divers times during a period of three years, and during the same time defendant paid to plaintiff generally divers sums, which were credited generally on the account, and paid a claim against him at his request, there was an open, mutual account, and limitations did not commence to run until the date of the last item.[31] Where a partnership transaction as to land had extended over a long term of years, and was not terminated when suit was brought, it has been held in Nebraska that neither party could complain by pleading limitations, that the other had not sooner called for an accounting and settlement.[32]

§ 279. Merchants' accounts.

There is an exception in favor of merchants' accounts, or accounts between merchants, etc., in some of the statutes, as in Texas, Kentucky, New Jersey, Rhode Island, Virginia, and West Virginia; and while an account to come within the saving under this head, must be for merchandise or money growing out of the trade of merchandise between merchants,[33] yet in other respects they resemble mutual accounts, and must be reciprocal demands;[34] and in some English cases it was intimated[35] that in such accounts mere time would

31. Lancieri v. Kansas City Improved Street Sprinkling Co., 95 Mo. App. 319, 69 S. W. 29. See also Mabary v. Mabary, 173 Mo. App. 437, 158 S. W. 690, holding that an account of an adult son against the estate of his deceased father and an account of the executrix against the son are not mutual, and do not save items from the statute of limitations; Vogel v. Kennedy, 127 Mo. App. 228, 104 S. W. 1151.

32. Hanson v. Hanson, 78 Neb. 584, 111 N. W. 368.

An account between a corporation and an officer rendering services as general manager held a mutual, open account, within Washington Code, § 166. Blom v. Blom Codfish Co., 71 Wash. 41, 127 Pac. 596.

33. Bass v. Bass, 25 Mass. (8 Pick.) 187; Mandeville v. Wilson, 9 U. S. (5 Cranch) 15, 3 L. Ed. 23; Wilson v. Mandeville, 1 Cranch (U. S. C. C.) 433; Bond v. Jay, 11 U. S. (7 Cranch) 350.

34. Atwater v. Fowler, 1 Edw. (N Y.) Ch. 417; Hussy v. Burgwyn, 6 Jones (N. C.) L. 385; Chew v. Baker, 4 Cranch (U. S. C. C.) 696.

35. Catling v. Skoulding, 6 T. R. 189.

never be a bar, while in others [36] the difference between merchants' accounts and others was said to be that a continuation afterwards will prevent the statute from running against the former, but will be a bar to all articles before six years in other accounts. In Pennsylvania,[37] a single transaction is held not to be within the exception of the statute, although it happens to be between merchants; and accounts when stated cease to be merchants' accounts;[38] and accounts, the items of which are all on one side, are not merchants' accounts, because not mutual.[39] The question whether accounts do concern the trade of merchandise between merchant and merchant is for the jury.[40]

§ 280. Stated accounts.

As soon as an account ceases to be open, and the balance is ascertained and assented to, it becomes a stated account, and the balance is at once subject to the operation of the statute;[41] and an account becomes a stated account when it is furnished to another, and he retains it for a long time without objection,

36. Martin v. Heathcote, 2 Eden, 169. See also Dyott v. Letcher, 29 Ky. (6 J. J. Marsh.) 541.

37. Marseilles v. Kenton, 17 Pa. 238.

38. Thompson v. Fisher, 13 Pa. 310; Bevan v. Cullen, 7 id. 281.

39. Fox v. Fisk, 7 Miss. (6 How.) 328; Coster v. Murray, 5 Johns. (N. Y.) Ch. 322.

40. Bass v. Bass, *supra*.

41. Waller v. Lacey, 1 M. & G. 54; Williams v. Griffith, 2 Cr. M. & R. 45; Mills v. Fowkes, 7 Scott, 444; Clark v. Alexander, 8 id. 147; Cottam v. Partridge, 4 M. & G. 271.

"An account stated is merely an agreement between persons who have had previous transactions fixing the amount due as the result of an accounting." Jorgensen v. Kingsley, 60 Neb. 44, 82 N W. 104; Spellman v. Muehlfeld, 166 N. Y. 245, 59 N. E. 817; Harrison v. Henderson, 67 Kan. 202, 72 Pac. 878; Porter v. Chicago, etc., Ry. Co., 99 Iowa, 351, 69 N. W. 724; Peirce v. Peirce, 199 Pa. 4, 48 Atl. 689. It "cannot be made the instrument *per se* to create a liability where none before existed," and there must be an agreement by the parties. Davies v. Seattle Nat. Bank, 19 Wash. 65, 72, 52 Pac. 526; Hughes v. Smithers, 49 N. Y. S. 115, 23 App. Div. 590, aff'd 57 N. E. 1112; Bradley Fertilizer Co. v. South Pub. Co., 17 N. Y. Supp. 587; Howell v. Johnson, 38 Or. 571, 64 Pac. 659. It need not be in writing. Watkins v. Ford, 69 Mich. 357, 37 N. W. 300; Lallande v. Brown, 121 Ala. 513, 25 So. 997.

as well as where the parties mutually agree upon a balance. Except in those States where the statute requires that a new promise or acknowledgment shall be in writting, the statute begins to run from the date of the account stated,[42] as the stating of an account, accompained by an express promise to pay it, or an acquiescence in the account as stated sufficiently long to rebut any presumption that there are objections thereto, raises an implied promise to pay the balance found, and changes the character of the account from a mutual to a stated account, so that assumpsit will lie for its recovery, even though the remedy originally might have been by debt or covenant.[43] But in those States where the statute re-

42. Little v. Blunt, 26 Mass. (9 Pick.) 488. When parties make out an itemized account of their mutual dealings, and the balance is then ascertained and paid, the items are no longer unsettled, although one item was omitted by mistake. And if in such case, six years thereafter, on discovering the omission, an action on the entire account is brought to recover the real balance, the statute will bar the recovery. Lancey v. Maine Central R. Co., 72 Me. 34. The leading English case upon mutual accounts between parties other than merchants is Catling v. Skoulding, 6 T. R. 189, in which it was held that if there be any mutual account between the parties for any item of which credit has been given within six years, that is evidence of acknowledgment of there being such an open account current between them and of a promise to pay the balance, so as to take the case out of the statute. That decision was cited and followed in Cogswell v. Dolliver, 2 Mass. 217. And the court in this State adopted the same doctrine, citing the above cases, and calling it a reasonable judicial construction of the statute. Davis v. Smith, 4 Me. 337. See also *Mc-Lellan* v. Crofton, 6 Me. 307; Therbold v. Stinson, 38 Me. 149; Dyer v. Walker, 51 Me. 104. The settlement changes the character of the account; the items become discharged by the payment of the agreed balance which resulted from setting off against each other the counter items. The discharge of the items is a consideration to sustain a promise to pay the balance. May v. King, 12 Mod. 538; s. c., 1 Ld. Raym. 680; Callander v. Howard, 10 C. B. 290. If one of the items of the account was overlooked, the settled account, after six years, can afford no aid in taking it out of the statute of limitations. Union Bank v. Knapp, 20 Mass. (3 Pick.) 96, 15 Am. Dec. 181.

43. Moravia v. Levy, 2 T. R. 483, n.; Foster v. Alanson, 2 id. 479. An account stated may be recovered although the original contract out of which the account grew was void by the statute of frauds, Cocking v. Ward, 1 C. B. 858; Seago v. Dean, 3 C. & P. 170; as the action is upon the account stated, and not for the original indebtedness. Milward v. Ingram, 2 Mod. 43.

quires that an acknowledgment or new promise shall be in writing, the stating of an account does not, either with an express parol promise or an implied promise to pay it, fix a new period from which the statute starts to run; and if the statute had begun to run upon the original account, or any of the items thereof, before the account was stated, it continues to do so, notwithstanding the stating of the account, unless there is a promise in writing to pay the account as stated.[44] It is true the rule is generally that, when a party indebted upon an account receives and retains it beyond such time as is reasonable under the circumstances, and according to the usage of the business, for examining and returning it, without communicating any objections, he is considered to acquiesce in its correctness, and he becomes bound by it as an account stated;[45] and a court of equity will not open it, except in cases where there have been mutual mistakes, omissions, fraud, or undue advantage, so that the balance stated is in truth vitiated, and in equity ought not to stand.[46] But these rules relative to stated accounts are held not sufficient to enable a party to start the statute afresh, by stating his account, where the statute expressly ignores the force of a

See Ibid.; King v. Davis, 168 Mass. 133, 46 N. E. 418; Fair v. Mevey, 56 N. Y. S. 414, 28 Civ. Proc. R. 245; Gordon v. Frazer, 13 App. D. C. 382; American Brewing Co. v. Berner-Mayer Co., 83 Ill. App. 446. The limitation prescribed by a statute as to open accounts cannot be applied to stated accounts. Carter v. Fischer, 127 Ala. 52, 28 So. 376. And so of agreements classified as specialities. Searles v. Lum, 81 Mo. App. 607.

44. Chace v. Trafford, 116 Mass. 529, 17 Am. Rep. 171; Sperry v. Moore's Estate, 42 Mich. 353, 4 N. W. 13.

45. Freeland v. Heron, 7 Cranch (U. S.) 147; Langdon v. Roane, 6 Ala. 518, 41 Am. Dec. 60; Terry v. Sickles, 13 Cal. 427; White v. Hampton, 10 Iowa 238; Mansell v. Payne, 18 La. Ann. 124; Wood v. Gault, 2 Md. Ch. 433; Brown v. Vandyke, 8 N. J. Eq. 795; Coopwood v. Bolton, 26 Miss. 212; Murray v. Toland, 3 Johns. (N. Y.) Ch. 569; Consequa v. Fanning, id. 587; Atwater v. Fowler, 1 Edw. (N. Y.) Ch. 417; Phillips v. Belden, 2 id. 1; Lockwood v. Thorne, 11 N. Y. 170; Bruen v. Hone, 2 Barb. (N. Y.) 586; Dows v. Durfee, 10 id. 213; Beers v. Reynolds, 12 id. 288; Towsley v. Denison, 45 id. 490; Pratt v. Weyman, 1 McCord (S. C.) Ch. 156; Tharp v. Tharp, 15 Vt. 105.

46. Farnam v. Brooks, 26 Mass. (9 Pick.) 212; Roberts v. Totten, 13 Ark. 609; Goodwin v. United States Ins. Co., 24 Conn. 591.

new promise to pay such balance implied from such statement, without objection, to raise a new promise to overcome the force of the statute of limitations, as such action by a party, if permitted, would place it within the power of parties to abrogate the provisions of the statute in reference to the effect of parol acknowledgments.[47]

§ 280a(1). Accounts in general—Limitations applicable.

Where plaintiff in an action on account alleged that defendants were a mercantile firm, and plaintiff a merchant, and that the dealings were a sale between merchant and merchant, the limitation of the action was five years, under the express terms of Ky. St. 1899, § 2515.[48] Where neither the buyer nor seller of logs to be paid for on receipt of scale bills kept an account, an action by the seller on the common counts in assumpsit and a special count for the price of logs delivered under the contract more than six years before was barred by the Michigan six-year statute of limitation.[49] In Louisiana, a right of action for goods sold and delivered on open account is barred by the prescription of three years.[50] In Nebraska, an action on an account is barred in four years;[51] and,

47. Reed v. Smith, 1 Idaho 533; Weatherwax v. Consumnes Valley Mill Co., 17 Col. 344.

48. Fennell v. Myers, 25 Ky. Law Rep. 589, and a plea of the two-year statute relating to merchants' accounts was not good.

Where a third person paying a mortgage did not take an assignment either of the mortgage or the note so as to acquire a lien on the land, any claim that he may have had was barred by the five-year statute of limitations. Letton's Adm'r v. Rafferty, 154 Ky. 278, 157 S. W. 35.

49. Hebinger v. Ross, 175 Mich. 241, 141 N. W. 629.

50. Interstate Trust & Banking Co. v. United States Fidelity & Guaranty Co., 133 La. 781, 63 So. 354.

Where payments of interest have been made and imputed with plaintiff's sanction, and over 12 months have elapsed since they were made, they fall within the prescription of 12 months directed against actions for the recovery of interest paid on settlement of an account. Glennon v. Vatter, 109 La. 942, 33 So. 930. The prescription of 12 months bars recovery of amounts on defendant's indebtedness. Dannenmann & Charlton v. Charlton, 113 La. 276, 36 So. 965.

51. Mizer v. Emigh, 63 Neb. 245, 88 N. W. 479. An action for an accounting for rents and profits against a tenant in common is not barred until four years from the accrual thereof. Schuster v. Schuster, 84 Neb. 98, 120 N. W. 948.

in Texas, a petition on an account made in mutual current trade between merchant and merchant is governed by the four-years statute.[51a] In Illinois, where no suit was brought to compel an agent to account for claims accruing out of his agency within five years after the principal's death, the claim, in the absence of fraudulent concealment, was barred by limitations.[52] In South Carolina, an action to recover money paid to another to be used in paying margins on contracts for future delivery of grain is barred in six years.[53] In Mississippi, the three-year limitations do not apply to an action based upon a written contract.[54]

§ 280a(2). What constitutes accounts.

A contract, in writing or not, which is definite in all its terms, and which leaves nothing for future adjustment, is not a mere open account within the Alabama three-years' statute of limitations (Code 1907, § 4338).[55] An account of loans between the lender and the borrowing firm, kept on the firm's books or on slips of paper, does not constitute a "mutual, open, and current account," within Code Civ. Proc. N. Y., § 386, providing that in an action to recover a balance due on a mutual, open, and current account, where there have been reciprocal demands between the parties, the cause of action is deemed to have accrued from the time of the last item proved in the account on either side.[56] A claim of an

51a. Willard v. Guttman (Tex. Civ. App.), 43 S. W. 901.

52. Lancaster v. Springer, 239 Ill. 472, 88 N. E. 272.

53. V. P. Randolph & Co. v. Walker, 78 S. C. 157, 59 S. E. 856, under Civ. Code S. C. 1902, § 2312.

54. Vicksburg Water Works Co. v. Yazoo & M. V. R. Co., 102 Miss. 504, 59 So. 825.

55. Union Naval Stores Co. v. Patterson, 179 Ala. 525, 60 So. 807, a contract of sale of rosin and turpentine, based on the Savannah market, fixes the price, and is not an open account.

The three-year statute of limitations is not a good defense to an action for the price of a horse sold. Moore v. Crosthwait, 135 Ala. 272, 33 So. 28. An action for contribution by a maker of a note, who has paid it, against a co-maker, is not an action on an open account, within the meaning of the statute of limitations, though partial payments may have been made by the defendant. Truss v. Miller, 116 Ala. 494, 22 So. 863.

56. *In re* Girvin, 160 Fed. 197 (U. S. D. C., N. Y.).

A current account kept by a husband of his transactions with his

interstate carrier for under freight charges on interstate shipment is not an " account " within Civil Code La., art. 3538, prescribing a prescription of three years for all accounts.[57] A claim for money paid a physician for services to a decedent, and for money paid for an invalid chair for his use, is an " account " within the Indiana six-year statute as to accounts.[58] Where a materialman delivered materials to a government contractor for use in the performance of the contract in California, the materialman's right to recover on the contractor's bond to the government was barred by the California statute, limiting actions on accounts to two years, and was not within the four-year statute relating to actions on written contracts.[59] A tax is not a debt in the sense that it will be barred by a statute of limitations against actions upon open account.[60] Where a contractor's bond is conditioned to pay for the labor and material used in digging a well for a city, the promise to pay for the labor and material does not rest on the account between

wife's money does not constitute a "mutual account," nor is an account mutual where it simply contains items of money received and paid, nor one in which there were but three items of credit during a period of five years; cash items being also held to form no part of a mutual, open, and running account. Id.

57. Illinois Cent. R. Co. v. Segari & Co., 205 Fed. 998 (U. S. D. C.).

The accounting due by the agent to his principal does not fall within the prescription of three years. Means v. Ross, 106 La. 175, 30 So. 300.

58. Hildebrand v. Kinney, 172 Ind. 447, 87 N. E. 832, rev'g judg. 83 N. E. 379, funeral and burial expenses not arising under contract, but by statute, are not debts of decedent, and hence accounts against him and his estate barred by six-year limitation.

That funeral expenses are incurred before administration does not distinguish them from costs thereof, which cannot be regarded as accounts within the statute; for, when the administrator's appointment is made, it relates back to the death to preserve rights in favor of the estate, one of which is that of Christian burial. Id.

59. United States v. Axman, 152 Fed. 816 (U. S. C. C., Cal.).

60. Georgia R. & Banking Co. v. Wright, 124 Ga. 596, 53 S. E. 251.

The term "running account," when used in a statute of limitations, means an open, mutual account. Brock v. Wildey, 125 Ga. 82, 54 S. E. 195.

Notwithstanding Conn. Gen. St. 1902, § 2407, providing that taxes shall become a debt against the person assessed, a tax is not within section 1110, limiting actions on account or for debt. Town of Cromwell v. Savage, 85 Conn. 376' 82 Atl. 972.

the contractor and the laborers and materialmen, but the bond creates a promise to pay for the labor and material, and hence an action thereon is not barred by the Missouri statute, limiting actions on accounts to five years.[61] Where a firm of merchants acts as a factor for a similar firm, and numerous items of debit and credit resulting from such transactions have never been agreed on as an account stated, such account is a mutual account current between merchants, within the Texas statute, providing that causes of action arising on such accounts shall be brought in four years.[62] A petition by a surveyor to have proceedings for the establishment of a drainage district which have been dismissed redocketed, so that the surveyor's fees may be taxed therein as costs, is an action on account, within the Indiana statute.[63] The Georgia statute, providing a limitation of four years for actions on open accounts, does not apply to an action by a trustee in bankruptcy, under Bankruptcy Act, § 60b, against a transferee for value of goods received from the bankrupt in payment of a preexisting debt less than four months prior to the filing of the petition.[64]

§ 280a(3). Account stated.

Where a statement of account was rendered and its correctness verbally admitted, it constituted a stated account and created a new cause of action not founded upon an instrument in writing, and was barred by limitation under California Code Civ. Proc., § 339, after two years; the term "open account," as used in Code Civ. Proc., § 337, being in opposition to a stated account the correctness of which is admitted.[65] In Texas, an amount due on an

61. Miner v. Howard, 93 Mo. App. 569, 67 S. W. 692, under Rev. St. Mo. 1899, § 4273.

62. Dwight v. Matthews, 94 Tex. 533, 62 S. W. 1052, rev'g judg. (Tex. Civ. App.) 60 S. W. 805, under Rev. St. Tex. art. 3356, subd. 3.

63. Fast v. Swisher (Ind.), 107 N. E. 6, under Burns' Ann. St. Ind. 1914, § 294.

64. Arnold Grocery Co. v. Schackelford, 140 Ga. 585, 79 S. E. 470, under Civ. Code Ga. 1910, §§ 4362, 4368. See Collier on Bankruptcy, 10th Ed., pp. 280-282, and cases there cited.

65. National Lumber Co. v. Tejunga Valley Rock Co., 22 Cal. App. 726, 136 Pac. 508.

account stated is barred by limitations after two years.[66] In Pennsylvania, accounts stated are governed by the statute of limitations from the date when rendered, and are not affected by the statute relating to accounts concerning the trade of merchandise between merchants, their factors or servants.[67] In Alabama, the three-year statute of limitations applicable to actions on open accounts is not a good defense to an action on an account stated.[68] Under the Louisiana statute, the prescription of three years is extended to accounts stated and verbally or tacitly acknowledged as well as to the open accounts, to which it had previously applied.[69] Where the balance in a mutual account current between parties is stated, the Wisconsin six-year statute of limitations commences to run as to the transactions included in the account up to that time.[70]

§ 280a(4). Partnership accounts.

In Michigan, an action between partners for an accounting is barred in ten years where the partnership agreement is under seal; and where there is no partnership agreement under seal, in six years.[71] In North Carolina, where a partnership was dissolved in 1899, and no debts remained to be collected or paid, the claim of one partner against his copartner for advancements to the firm will be barred in 1911 by the statute of limitations.[72] In Virginia, persons engaged as partners in the business of farming,

66. Stacy v. Parker (Tex. Civ. App.), 132 S. W. 532.

67. Morgan v. Lehigh Valley Coal Co., 215 Pa. 443, 64 Atl. 633.

68. Moore v. Crosthwait, 135 Ala. 272, 33 So. 28.

Where the statute (Ala. Civ. Code, § 2796) provided that actions on an account stated could be brought at any time within six years, a plea of the statute of limitations in an action on an account stated, setting up the period of three years applicable to actions on open accounts, is bad on demurrer. Carter v. Fischer, 127 Ala. 521, 28 So. 376.

69. Sleet v Sleet, 109 La. 302, 33 So. 322, under Acts 1888, No. 78, amending and re-enacting La. Rev. Civ. Code, art. 3538.

70. Figge v. Bergenthal, 130 Wis. 594, 110 N. W. 798, rehearing 130 Wis. 594, 109 N. W. 581, denied.

71. Dowse v. Gaynor, 155 Mich. 38, 15 Detroit Leg. N. 897, 118 N. W. 615.

72. Moore v. Westbrook, 156 N. C. 482, 72 S. E. 842.

distilling, and purchasing and selling cattle, cannot properly be considered merchants within the meaning of the exception in the statute of limitations excepting such accounts as concerns the trade of merchandise between merchants.[73]

§ 280b(1). Accounts in general — Accrual of right of action.

Action for the whole amount due on a book account is not barred until the statutory period after the latest item.[74] Where some items of an account are within the statute of limitations, and others are not, the latter are not barred.[75] If the last item of an account is not barred, the whole account is saved, though all the items are against one party.[76] On a continuous dealing the statute runs from the last item.[77] One item of an account proven to exist within six years of the bringing of suit will not draw after it other items of more than six years' standing, so as to prevent a bar by limitations, unless there were mutual accounts and reciprocal demands between the parties.[78] Where a contract is a continuing one to furnish building material for twenty houses, and materials are furnished from time to time thereunder and prices thereof entered into a running account, upon which payments are made from time to time, the account will be considered as one account, with the element of mutuality running throughout the whole transaction; and the statute of limitations will not begin to run until the date of the last item appearing in the account.[79] In the

73. Coalter v. Coalter, 1 Rob. (Va.) 79, the exception made by the statute prevents the statute from barring an action on such accounts when there has been a cessation of dealings between the parties for five years.

74. Carpenter v. Plagge, 192 Ill. 82, 61 N. E. 530, modifying decree 93 Ill. App. 445.

75. Grand Rapids & I. R. Co. v. McAnnally, 98 Ind. 412.

76. Roberts v. Neal, 134 Mo. App. 612, 114 S. W. 1120, where it is fairly inferable from the conduct of the parties, while an account is accruing, that it is to be taken as such, it will be so regarded by the courts in computing the period of limitation. See also, Hammer v. Crawford (Mo. App.), 93 S. W. 348; Morrison v. The Burns, 41 Mo. 491. See Roeder v. Studt, 12 Mo. App. 566, memorandum.

77. McNaughton & Co. v. Norris, 2 N. C. 216.

78. Elwood v. Hughes, 109 N. Y. Supp. 25.

79. Smith v. Ross, 31 App. D. C. 348.

case of an entire account, limitations begin to run from the date of the last item in the account.[80] When an account ceases to be open, and the balance is ascertained and assented to, it becomes a stated account, and the balance is at once subject to the operation of the statute of limitations.[81] Where goods were sold under an agreement by which they were to go as payment on account, limitation did not begin to run as against the bill of goods as long as anything remained due on the account to which they were to be applied as payments. The statute does not apply to payments made.[82] Where, in an action for royalties, there was evidence that certain charges were items of an open running account on which payments had been made within six years prior to the commencement of the suit, the court did not err in refusing to charge that the items arising more than six years prior to the suit were barred.[83]

80. Wimbush v. Curry, 8 Ga. App. 223, 68 S. E. 951. See Godley v. Hopkins, 126 Ga. 178, 54 S. E. 974.

Limitations begin to run against an account from the date of the last item. Walsh v. Welsh, 46 Colo. 344, 104 Pac. 399. A counterclaim for rent is barred after 8 years where the transactions were not an open running account. MacFaddin v. Bice, 58 Colo. 173, 146 Pac. 244.

81. Visher v. Wilbur, 5 Cal. App. 562, 90 Pac. 1065, rehearing denied 91 Pac. 412.

Where the balances of accounts stated were each year carried forward into the next year's current account as a part thereof, with the consent of the debtor, who assented to the balances each year, none of the balances ever became more than one year old before they were supported by a new promise, when the account was stated at the end of the next year, and the balances did not stand as a distinct cause of action within the statute of limitations. Brown & Manzanares Co. v. Guise, 14 N. M. 282, 91 Pac. 716.

A statement by plaintiff, at the time an account was stated, that he was to "carry the debt" without any proof as to the length of time credit was to be extended, would not take the case out of the general rule with reference to limitations concerning debts payable on demand. Stacy v. Parker (Tex. Civ. App.), 132 S. W. 532.

82. Butcher v. Daniel, 10 Ky. Law Rep. (abstract) 406.

83. Brazel v. Thompson Smith's Sons, 141 Mich. 628, 12 Detroit Leg. N. 599, 104 N. W. 1097. And see Hillebrands v. Nibbelink, 40 Mich. 646.

Tacking transactions or accounts after cessation.— Where services are rendered from 1870 to 1884 and from 1890 to 1893, those rendered during

§ 280b(2). Nature of account in general.

A statutory provision that limitation shall begin to run against an indebtedness on account, where there is a mutual running account between the parties, only from the date of the last item in such account, does not apply to an indebtedness which was not entered in such account until after the death of the party charged, and after the statutory period of limitation from the date of the transaction had expired.[84] A claim for sums of money lent to a bankrupt at different times, for which no notes were taken, does not constitute a running account; but each item is a separate and distinct transaction, unaffected by any other, so far as relates to the running of limitations against it.[85] Where an open account is kept by one person against another, each particular item charged is a distinct and substantive cause of action, barred when limitations have run against it.[86] Where, in an action for money loaned, defendant set up a counterclaim for board furnished plaintiff, which demand plaintiff claimed was barred by limitations, and it appeared that the board was furnished at different widely disconnected periods covering a number of years, the court properly regarded each time plaintiff was entertained by defendants as an independent transaction, and refused to charge the law of limitations as applied to a continuous account.[87] The statute of limita-

the first period are not items of a mutual account current which will prevent the running of limitations. Graham v. Stanton, 177 Mass. 321, 58 N. E. 1023.

Where defendant ran an open store account with plaintiff from 1885 to 1888, but from that date until 1894 there were neither credit nor debit entries made therein, and plaintiff sold out his mercantile business and commenced a different business, and in 1894 sold clover and timothy seed to defendant's husband, and the price thereof was entered on the account as cash, the latter transaction was not a continuation of the old account, so as to prevent the running of limitations. Moore v. Blackman, 109 Wis. 528, 85 N. W. 429.

84. *In re* Huger, 100 Fed. 805 (U. S. C. C., S. C.).

85. *In re* Wooten, 118 Fed. 670 (U. S. D. C., N. C.).

86. Moore v. Morris, 1 Pennewill (Del.) 412.

A claim for legal services became barred by limitations three years after the date of each item. Parker v. Carter, 91 Ark. 162, 120 S. W. 836.

87. Hendelman v. Kahan, 50 Wash. 247, 97 Pac. 109.

tions does not apply to a running account with a payment within the period of limitation; and an account for board at so much per week is a continuous account, and does not accrue at the end of each month, so as to bar all months prior to the five-year period of limitation.[88] Items in a claim case on a decedent's estate, which were separate and distinct transactions, occurring more than five years before beginning of action, and formed no part of a continuous, open, current account, are barred by limitations, in the absence of an agreement to defer payment.[89] An open account

A claim for labor and materials advanced to a railroad from time to time on claimant's credit between January, 1892, and August, 1893, under an agreement to thereby furnish such labor and materials for its operating expenses, constituted a single legal demand, and the bar of a three-year statute of limitations is not complete in June, 1895. Bellingham Bay Imp. Co. v. Fairhaven & N. W. Ry. Co., 17 Wash. 371, 49 Pac. 514.

In an action on a written guaranty of any and all indebtedness of a third party to a bank, whether then existing or thereafter contracted, where such indebtedness was in part for money borrowed and in part on open accounts containing items of debit and credit, the entire account therefor is to be treated as a single current and mutual account for the purpose of the statute of limitations, and under Pierce's Code Wash., § 290 (Ballinger's Ann. Codes & St. § 4806), limitations commenced to run in favor of the original debtor at the time of the last item, and also, unless a demand was necessary under his contract, in favor of the guarantor. Gill v. Waterhouse, 175 Fed. 805 (U. S. C. C., Wash.).

88. Beeler v. Finnel, 85 Mo. App. 438.

In an action on account where it appears that all the items in the account previous to a certain period were contracted with plaintiff's predecessors in business, and it is not shown that there was any agreement by which the account with plaintiff's predecessors was to be treated as an open account between plaintiff and defendant, the continuity is broken, and limitations will run against the earlier account. Bust v. Long, 75 Mo. App. 103.

Where merchants, who sold lumber and did weighing, six months after they ceased to sell a customer lumber did weighing for him, charging the same on open account, and there had been other mutual accounts between such dealings, a finding that the weighing was not a part of the lumber account, so as to avoid the bar of limitations as to the lumber, was erroneous. Gibson v. Jenkins, 97 Mo. App. 27, 70 S. W. 1076.

89. Hickey v. Hickey (Iowa), 81 N. W. 152.

Where lumber is ordered at different times during a period of several years, and is used for distinct and separate improvements on land, and

within the statute of limitations is one in which some term of the contract is not settled, whether the account consists of one or many items, and it is immaterial whether it is stated or reduced to writing, but a demand which is certain in all its terms never constitutes an open account. Freight charges do not constitute an open account between the railroad company and a consignee, within the statute of limitations applicable to open accounts, since the law fixes freight rates, and also the duty of the company to deliver the freight and of the consignee to pay the charges, and a contract of shipment is thus certain in all its terms.[90]

§ 280b(3). Services rendered.

In Arkansas, accounts for work are divisible, and rights of action accrue thereon, in the absence of evidence to the contrary, as the work is performed.[91] Where, in an action for services, plaintiff's claim was not the subject of a book account, but he testified that within three months prior to the trial he had gone through over 3,000 letters between defendant and himself, from which

the amount due is computed and settled from time to time, and at each of the settlements a note is given by the purchaser for the balance then due, the continuity of the account is broken; and, as to lumber furnished under the earlier contracts, the statute of limitations as to the enforcement of mechanics' liens begins to run from the date of the last item furnished under the last contract. Hoag v. Hay, 103 Iowa 291, 72 N. W. 525.

90. Northern Alabama Ry. Co. v. Wilson Mercantile Co., 9 Ala. App. 269, 63 So. 34, holding also that an action to recover freight charges was not barred by the statute of limitations against an action on an open account (Ala. Code 1907, § 4838), where it was not shown that it had been more than three years since the last charge for freight between the parties, under a custom of presenting such bills for settlement every two weeks.

Where plaintiff had made shipment over defendant's railroad during several years, and settled the freight bills presented by defendant, and in each of the bills the company had charged plaintiff over weight, the several items of money paid defendant as freight on the excessive weight constituted an open account within the statute of limitations. Higley v. Burlington, etc., Ry. Co., 99 Iowa 503, 68 N. W. 829, 61 Am. St. Rep. 250.

91. St. Louis, etc., Ry. Co. v. Love, 74 Ark. 528, 86 S. W. 395.

he had made up a statement of the charges sued on, running over a period of twenty years, plaintiff's claim was not a current account within Missouri Rev. St. 1899, § 4278, providing that a cause of action on a current account shall be deemed to have accrued from the date of the last item on the adverse side.[92] Where deceased employed plaintiff to render services for him in his business in 1884, and she continued to render such services until his death in March, 1902, and from September, 1887, to 1900, deceased kept a book in which entries of payments to plaintiff were made, plaintiff's claim for the balance due her was not barred by limitations.[93]

92. Sidway v. Missouri Land & Live Stock Co., 187 Mo. 649, 86 S. W. 150. What constitutes a running account. See Murphy v. People's Ry. Co., 15 Mo. App. 595, memorandum. In a suit to recover for services rendered decedent in his lifetime, a charge that all the items which had accrued five years before the commencement of the suit were barred by limitations was properly refused; the account being a running and continuous one, and it being fairly inferable from the conduct of the parties that the whole was regarded as one account. Moore v. Renick, 95 Mo. App. 202, 68 S. W. 936. Where there is a running account, though all the items are on one side, none of the items are barred by the statute, unless all are. Bowman v. Shelton, 175 Mo. App. 696, 158 S. W. 404.

That the first items of an account against an estate for services in caring for decedent were charged for at a different rate than the later services did not change the claim from one for a continuous running account to a claim for two accounts so as to bar the first items by limitations. Hyde v. Honiter (Mo. App.), 158 S. W. 83.

Where plaintiff, who had previously contributed her wages to the support of her mother, ceased to do so in 1899, and after her marriage in 1900 made her mother only one or two presents of small amounts, all right of action to recover her wages was barred by a lapse of more than five years; the small gratuities to her mother not tolling the statute of limitations. McGrath v. Talty's Estate (Mo. App.), 156 S. W. 826.

93. Greenwood v. Judson, 109 App. Div. 398, 96 N. Y. Supp. 147.

The payment by an employer of six dollars per month in the years 1886 to 1888 on account of services rendered continuously from 1878 to 1893, when the employer died, makes the account a continuing one, and prevents eight years' limitations being a bar to any part of a claim duly presented to the executor for such services for the entire period. Hay v. Peterson, 6 Wyo. 419, 45 Pac. 1073, 34 L. R. A. 581.

Where items of services rendered, as disclosed in a cross-petition, antedated April 28, 1895, and of the 10 items 7 were for services rendered prior to 1895, and the dates of two were not given, and the other was

§ 280b(4). Partnership.

Closed transactions and similar matters between partners are in the nature of accounts stated, and therefore subject to the bar of the statute of limitations.[94] Limitations do not begin to run against a claim by one partner against another, arising out of the partnership business, until after the dissolution of the partnership, though for a considerable period before dissolution the firm had not been actively engaged in the prosecution of its business, but had placed its assets in the hands of an agent for the purpose of collecting the same and paying the partnership debts.[95] Where a

for services in an action rendered between December 21, 1892, and February 28, 1896, and cross-petitioner alleged his inability to more specifically state the exact date at which the service was rendered, his claims could not be regarded as a continuous account as a matter of law, so as to suspend limitations until the date of the last item. Novak v. Novak, 137 Iowa 519, 115 N. W. 1.

Monthly payments for services are not an open account, under Mass. Rev. Laws, c. 202, § 6, tolling the six-year limitations prescribed by section 2, upon an action to recover an overpayment. Harding v. Covell, 217 Mass. 120, 104 N. E. 452.

94. Garretson v. Brown, 185 Pa. 447, 40 Atl. 293.

Limitations run against a claim against a firm, acquired by one of the members to be used by him as a set-off against his partner, where, if he had paid the claim as a partner, it would not have run against his claim on account thereof. Ahl v. Ahl, 186 Pa. 99, 40 Atl. 405.

95. Harris v. Matthews, 107 Ga. 46, 32 S. E. 903.

A partner cannot sue on a particular item of the partnership business, but must provoke a settlement of the entire partnership and sue for the balance on account, and hence prescription does not commence to run until dissolution of the firm. Burbank v. Oglesby, 35 La. Ann. 1201.

The statute of limitations, if applicable to a partner's right to an accounting on dissolution of the firm, is suspended by dealings in the shape of a showing of balances within six years. Near v. Lowe, 49 Mich. 482, 13 N. W. 825.

Where plaintiff and defendant orally entered into a partnership to buy and sell cattle, and after being in business for about a year defendant executed to plaintiff a bill of sale of his interest, and four months after the execution of the bill of sale plaintiff sent defendant a letter, stating the amount defendant owed plaintiff in regard to their transactions, and setting out the partnership indebtedness and credits thereon specifically, to which letter defendant never replied, in an action for the balance due on such partnership account, the letter was an account stated, the partnership having been dissolved, and hence the statute of limitations began to run against such action from

partnership was dissolved and no debts remained to be collected or paid, the statute of limitations will begin to run immediately upon dissolution against the claim of one partner against his copartner for advancements to the firm.[96] Where a partner in a general firm, without any fixed limit as to its duration, terminates it by notice to his copartner, limitations begin thereupon to run against the right of the copartner to an accounting; but where the firm is to run for a specific time, and it is dissolved prior to that time by the wrongful act of one partner, there may be equities between the partners that will require adjustment before limitations begin to run.[97] The charging of overdrafts by a partner to profit and loss, and the striking of the balance due from him, which was carried forward to the following year, was not an account stated, and the statute of limitations does not begin to run against an action for such overdrafts until the dissolution of the firm.[98]

the date of the letter. Lendholm v. Bailey, 16 Colo. App. 190, 64 Pac. 586.

96. Moore v. Westbrook, 156 N. C. 482, 72 S. E. 842.

97. Beller v. Murphy, 139 Mo. App. 663, 123 S. W. 1029, holding also that an action by a partner wrongfully excluded from the firm for an accounting, brought within three years from the expiration of the period for which the partnership should continue, is not barred by limitations.

Where the retiring partner from a firm owned a patent on a lamp, and it was agreed that the remaining partner would sell the lamp indefinitely and account for the proceeds, limitations did not start to run on the patent owner's right of action, until the partner selling the lamp had made a statement of the business and delivered it to the other; nor did limitations run against the retiring partner's right to recover for electric toy wheels, and the like, which were left with the remaining partner to be sold in the course of business, until the rendering of the account; and the fact that the remaining partner furnished the retiring partner with different items, the claim for the last of which on its face was barred by limitations, would not defeat the remaining partner's right to counterclaim for the articles furnished, since there was a running account between them, and, the last item of the retiring partner's claim not being barred until the account was rendered, the items of the counterclaim were thereby saved. Somerville v. Missouri Glass Co., 144 Mo. App. 463, 129 S. W. 474.

98. McMahon v. Brown, 219 Mass. 23, 106 N. E. 576, under Mass. Rev. Laws, c. 202, § 2.

§ 280b(5). Principal and agent.

In the case of a running account between principal and agent, covering continuous dealings, no action can be brought against the agent until the termination of the relation of principal and agent, and the statute of limitations runs only from the time of such termination.[99] Generally limitations, in cases where the agency is a general and continuing one, begin to run on the principal's right of action against his agent from the time of the termination of the agency, or from the time the agent has rendered an accounting to his principal and offered to settle, or from the time the principal has made a demand on the agent for an accounting and the latter has refused or neglected to render it.[1] Limitations do not begin to run in favor of an agent for collection and care of the funds of another, whose duties are those of a steward or factor, running from year to year, till he has rendered an account, accompanied by an offer to settle, or the principal has demanded settlement, and he refused, or there has been an expressed repudiation of the agency or such a change in their relation as would warrant the inference that the confidential agency has in fact ceased.[2]

99. Appeal of Ritchey, 8 Pa. Super. Ct. 527, 43 W. N. C. 194.

1. Somerville v. Missouri Glass Co., 144 Mo. App. 463, 129 S. W. 474; Knowles v. Rome Tribune Co., 127 Ga. 90, 56 S. E. 109.

2. Greer v. Andrews, 133 Ga. 192, 65 S. E. 416; Andrew v. Greer, Id.

Under Ky. St., § 2520, providing for the recovery of a balance upon a mutual account between merchant and merchant, the five-year statute runs as to a commission merchant's account for advances made on shipments of tobacco, not from the date of the last credit of proceeds of sales, but from the date when the last of the tobacco should with reasonable diligence have been sold, or, at most, after allowing a reasonable period after such time in which to have made up and rendered a statement of the balance due. Seibert's Assignee v. Albritton, 101 Ky. 241, 19 Ky. Law Rep. 402, 40 S. W. 698.

As to action by the administratrix of the deceased owner of a judgment against the executrix of the administrator of one who, as attorney for such owner, had it in his hands to collect, to recover the amount collected by such executrix. See McClaren v. Williams, 132 Ga. 352, 64 S. E. 65.

§ 280c(1). Mutual accounts—Necessity for mutuality of accounts.

In an action on a note, where defendant counterclaimed for a board bill, there was no mutuality of account or reciprocity of dealing, causing items within the period of limitations to withdraw items beyond the period from the operation of the statute.[3] Where the statute of limitations had commenced to run against a certain item in an account, which the plaintiff sought to save by showing credits in favor of the deceased, to prevent the statute from running against said item, there must have existed some credit given by deceased within the six years prior to his death.[4]

§ 280c(2). Effect of mutuality of accounts.

The statute of limitations runs against an open mutual account from the date of the last entry.[5] Limitations do not run against any item of mutual and running accounts while they continue open and current.[6] An action brought on an account within six years from the date of the last payment thereon is not barred by the statute of limitations.[7] Where transactions between the presi-

3. Beach v. Bennett, 16 Colo. App. 459, 66 Pac. 567.

4. Kimball v. Kimball, 16 Mich. 211. And see Rickard v. Geach, 26 Nev. 444, 69 Pac. 861.

5. *Del.*—Moore v. Morris, 1 Pennewill 412, 41 Atl. 889.

Ga.—Brock v. Wildey, 125 Ga. 82, 54 S. E. 195, under Civ. Code 1895, § 3769; Adams v. Holland, 101 Ga. 43, 28 S. E. 434.

Utah.—E. & H. T. Anthony & Co. v. Savage, 2 Utah 466.

6. Moore v. Morris, *supra;* Myers v. Patterson, 14 Ky. Law Rep. (abstract) 143.

7. Ernest Ochs v. Frey, 47 App. Div. 390, 62 N. Y. Supp. 67.

Plaintiff having alleged the rendition of services for a period of nine years at a certain agreed amount per month, that a certain balance is due thereon, on which defendant is entitled to a credit of a certain amount loaned, the statute of limitations applicable to a loan pleaded by defendant as made by her to plaintiff during that period is Code Civ. Proc., § 386, providing that in an action for balance on a mutual, open and current account, where there have been reciprocal demands between the parties, the cause of action is deemed to have accrued from the time of the last item proved in the account on either side. Haffner v. Schmuck, 49 App. Div. 193, 63 N. Y. Supp. 55, judg. aff'd 168 N. Y. 649, 61 N. E. 1130.

Under Me. Rev. St. 1857, c. 81, §

dent and a corporation arose out of mutual charges and credits, and did not cease until his official connection with the company ended, limitations will not begin to run until such time.[8] Where, in partition, transactions between parties with respect to the land in question have extended over a long term of years, and have not yet terminated, limitations are not pleadable.[9]

§ 280c(3). Closing accounts.

In an action on an account stated, consisting of a series of monthly statements, showing items and balance due, rendered to and accepted by defendant, the defense of the statute of limitations is not available as to separate items entering into such statements of account.[10] Where a debt is not barred at the time an account is orally stated, the statute begins to run as to the cause of action on the account stated from the date thereof.[11] Where there has been a running account between two parties, it is not divided, and a new account started, by the mere fact that the creditor renders the debtor a statement up to a certain date, but afterwards lets the debtor have other items, which are charged on the account.[12] When a running account is balanced and adjusted by one of the parties thereto, with the knowledge of the other, it becomes an account stated, and its items become subject to the statute of limitations,

99, as amended by Pub. Laws 1867, c. 117, it is sufficient for plaintiff in assumpsit on an account annexed, in order to remove the statutory bar, to show mutual dealings between the parties, and that the last item on either side of the account was within six years of the commencement of the action. Hagar v. Springer, 63 Me. 506.

8. Danville, H. & W. R. Co. v. Kase, 41 W. N. C. (Pa.) 411, 39 Atl. 301.

9. Hanson v. Hanson, 4 Neb. (Unof.) 880, 97 N. W. 23.

10. Sayward v. Dexter, Horton & Co., 72 Fed. 758, 19 C. C. A. 176, 44 U. S. App. 176.

11. Baird v. Crank, 98 Cal. 293, 33 Pac. 63.

Where a stated account, apparently barred by limitation, is not intended as a separate cause of action, but as a part of a subsequent stated account, not barred, which is made the basis of the action, the first account is not affected by limitation, where it was not barred when included in the subsequent account. Ready v. McDonald, 128 Cal. 663, 61 Pac. 272, 79 Am. St. Rep. 76.

12. Boyd v. Ernest, 36 Ill. App. 583.

though the balance is not paid, but is transferred to a succeeding account, the balance in such case being treated as an item of a new running account.[13] A settlement of mutual demands, whereby a balance is found to be due to one of the parties from the other, is the foundation of a new cause of action, and the statute of limitations begin to run from that time.[14] Where an account has been of long standing and the last item in it entered more than six years, still, if there has not been an actual settlement, it is a running account, and not barred by the statute of limitations.[15] No statement of account can have the effect of stopping the running of limitations on the separate items of the account stated, and which would otherwise be barred, unless there be a writing, signed by the party to be charged or his agent, expressly promising to pay the balance thus ascertained.[16]

13. Estes v. Hamilton-Brown Shoe Co., 54 Mo. App. 543.

14. Agan v. File, 84 Hun 607, 32 N. Y. Supp. 1066.

15. Franklin v. Camp's Ex'rs, 1 N. J. Law (Coxe) 196.

A bill to account under defendant's agreement to pay complainant one-eighth of the profits realized by defendant in his contract with H to build a railroad, is not barred by the statute of limitations; it not beginning to run until date of final settlement between defendant and H. Colver v. Culver, 31 N. J. Eq. (14 Stew.) 448.

16. Magarity v. Shipman, 93 Va. 64, 24 S. E. 446.

CHAPTER XXVIII.

SET-OFF, RECOUPMENT AND DEFENSES IN GENERAL.

§ 281. Set-off, when statute begins to run against.

The statute of limitations is not only applicable to a claim that is the subject-matter of the action against which it is pleaded, but it is also applicable to a set-off that is pleaded by a defendant; and where a demand upon which the statute has run is set up in bar of an action, or in diminution of the principal debt, the plaintiff may plead the statute thereto; or, if the set-off is given in evidence under a notice, the statute may be set up against it on the trial.[1] If a defendant pleads a set-off, the plaintiff may reply the statute; but a set-off is available as a simultaneous cross-action

1. Hicks v. Hicks, 5 East 16; Harwell v. Steel, 17 Ala. 372; Ruggles v. Keeler, 3 Johns. (N. Y.) 263; Caldwell v. Powell, 65 Tenn. (6 Baxter) 82; Gorham v. Buckley, 49 Conn. 91; Nolin v. Blackwell, 31 N. J. Law 170, 86 Am. Dec. 206; Chapman v. Hogg, 135 Mo. App. 654, 116 S. W. 492. In Trimyer v. Pollard, 5 Gratt. (Va.) 460, it was held that where the defendant does not plead a set-off, but files his account and gives notice of a set-off, as the plaintiff cannot reply the statute, he is at liberty to rely upon it at the trial. Hinkley v. Walters, 8 Watts (Pa.) 260. A debt which upon its face appears to be barred cannot be used as a set-off without evidence to take it out of the statute. Taylor v. Gould, 57 Pa. 152; Watkins v. Harwood, 2 G. & J. (Md.) 307; Shoenberger v. Adams, 4 Watts (Pa.) 430; Levering v. Rittenhouse, 4 Whart. (Pa.) 130.

would be, and, if it is to be barred at all, must be barred at the time of the commencement of the action. In other words, the bringing of an action by one party saves from the operation of the statute all such claims of the defendant against the plaintiff as are properly the subject of set-off, and which are in fact pleaded as a set-off in that action.[2] Where there are cross-demands between the parties, which accrued at nearly the same time, both of which would be barred by the statute, and the plaintiff has saved the statute by suing out process, but the defendant has not, it has been held that, nevertheless, the defendant may set off such demands.[3]

§ 281a. Set-offs, counterclaims, and cross-actions—Limitations applicable.

The statute of limitations may be pleaded to a set-off.[4] In

2. In Walker v. Clements, 15 Q. B. 1046, the plaintiff, to a plea of set-off, replied that the cause of set-off "did not accrue within six years" of the plea; this was held bad, because not alleging that the cause of the set-off did not accrue within six years before the commencement of the action. In an action to foreclose a mortgage, the defendant may plead in set-off an account against a firm of which the plaintiff is a member, and that the statute of limitations is not a bar to the set-off. Allen v. Maddox, 40 Iowa, 124.

See McDougald v. Hulet, 132 Cal. 154, 64 Pac. 278; Beecher v. Baldwin, 55 Conn. 419, 3 Am. St. Rep. 57, 12 Atl. 401 and n.. Under the Alabama and California statutes the defendant's answer may set up a counterclaim which was not barred at the commencement of the action. Perkins v. West Coast Lumber Co., 120 Cal. 27, 52 Pac. 118; Dunham Lumber Co. v. Holt, 124 Ala. 181. In West Virginia limitation runs against a set-off from the time when it is filed. Rowan v. Chenoweth, 49 W. Va. 287, 38 S. E. 544, 87 Am. St. Rep. 796; Boyd v. Beebe 64 W. Va. 216, 61 S. E. 304.

3. The demands were similar, and relate to the principal claim. Ord v. Ruspini, 2 Esp. 569; Mann v. Palmer, 41 N. Y. (2 Keyes) 177, 3 Abb. App. Dec. (N. Y.) 162.

4. *Ala.*—Conner v. Smith, 88 Ala. 300, 7 So. 150; Harwell v. Steel, 17 Ala. 372.

Conn.—Gorham v. Bulkley, 49 Conn. 91.

N. J.—Nolin v. Blackwell, 31 N. J. Law (2 Vroom) 170, 86 Am. Dec. 206.

Ohio.—Irwin v. Garretson, 1 Cin. R. 533; Cole v. Kerr, Wright, 675.

Pa.—Keim v. Kaufman, 15 Pa. Co. Ct. R. 539, 4 Pa. Dist. R. 234; Hutchinson v. Hutchinson, 4 Lanc. Law Rev. 3.

Massachusetts, in an action by the assignee of an insolvent debtor on a debt due to the insolvent, debts due and payable from the insolvent more than six years before the commencement of the action, but less than six years before the commencement of the proceedings in insolvency, may be set off.[5] In New York, in an action by a partner against his copartner for an accounting, a counterclaim for damages arising from a breach by plaintiff of the partnership agreement is not an independent cause of action, and cannot be defeated by a plea of the statute of limitations.[6]

A claim, an action on which would be barred by the statute of limitations, cannot be set off.[7] A demand barred by the statute of limitations, but afterwards revived by a new promise, is no set-off to an action commenced during the time that the demand was barred.[8] In Texas, it is held that the rule that limitations do not affect defenses which are properly applicable to the plaintiff's cause of action does not apply to cross-actions which are not pleaded as a defense.[9] And in an action upon a contract, where defendant's claims against plaintiff are unliquidated, they

5. Parker v. Sanborn, 73 Mass. (7 Gray). 191.

6. Campbell v. Hughes, 73 Hun (N. Y.) 14, 25 N. Y. Supp. 1021.

7. *Ala.*—Washington v. Timberlake, 74 Ala. 259.

Ky.—Williams v. Gilchrist, 6 Ky. (3 Bibb) 49; Gilchrist v. Williams, 10 Ky. (3 A. K. Marsh.) 235.

Mass.—Tyler v. Boyce, 135 Mass. 558.

Okla.—Theis v. Board of County Com'rs of Beaver County, 22 Okla. 333, 97 Pac. 973; Richardson v. Penny, 10 Okl. 32, 61 Pac. 584; McClure v. Johnson, 10 Okl. 663, 65 Pac. 103.

Pa.—Reed v. Marshall, 90 Pa. 345; Appeal of Milne, 99 Pa. 483.

S. C.—Madden v. Madden, 2 Mill, Const. 350; Turnbull v. Strohecker, 4 McCord, 210.

Tex.—Campbell v. Park, 11 Tex. Civ. App. 455, 33 S. W. 754.

8. Lee v. Lee, 31 Ga. 26, 76 Am. Dec. 681.

Where, in an action on a note, defendant sets up by way of set-off open accounts which are barred on their face by limitations, it is error to overrule a demurrer to such defense. Brewer v. Grogan, 116 Ga. 60, 42 S. E. 525. A defendant cannot set off usurious payments barred by the statute. Finney v. Brumby, 64 Ga. 510.

9. Smith v. Fairbanks, Morse & Co. (Tex.), 102 S. W. 908, aff'g Fairbanks, Morse & Co. v. Smith (Tex. Civ. App.), 90 S. W. 705.

Where plaintiff's claim is based on a note, and defendant's cross-claim on a balance of account, the civil-law principle of compensation cannot be invoked to extinguish the claims, and

do not extinguish *pro tanto* the claim sued on, for a set-off is not effected, as a matter of law, where it is for unliquidated damages; and hence limitations continue to run against such claims, despite the action, until pleaded.[10] In Colorado, where a note is interposed as a set-off in justice's court before it is barred by limitations, on appeal to the county court it is error to exclude the note as evidence on the ground that it has become barred in the meantime.[11] Where plaintiff seeks to have a judgment obtained by him set off against a judgment in favor of a defendant, he is seeking to recover on his judgment, within the meaning of the New York statute of limitations.[12] In Iowa, under Code, § 3457, providing that a counterclaim may be pleaded as a defense, though barred by limitations, if it was the property of the party pleading it at the time it became barred, and was not barred at the time the claim sued on originated, where defendant owned the claims set out in the counterclaim, before they were barred by limitations, and they did not become barred until after the claim sued on by plaintiff had originated, the counterclaim was not barred.[13] In

limitations will run against the set-off. Walker v. Fearhake, 22 Tex. Civ. App. 61, 52 S. W. 629.

10. Nelson v. San Antonio Traction Co. (Tex. Civ. App.), 142 S. W. 146.

11. Engel v. Samuels, 9 Colo. App. 338, 339, 48 Pac. 276.

12. Dieffenbach v. Roch, 112 N. Y. 621, 20 N. E. 560, 2 L. R. A. 829, holding that an action to compel a set-off of a justice's judgment, docketed in the county clerk's office, against a judgment of a court of record, was not maintainable after the lapse of six years from the time of its rendition.

13. Richardson v. Richardson, 134 Iowa 242, 111 N. W. 934. See Mann v. Gordon, 15 N. M. 652, 110 Pac. 1043, under N. M. Comp. Laws, § 2927, a similar provision to that contained in the Iowa statute.

In an action against a grantee on a verbal promise to pay a mortgage on land conveyed by plaintiff to defendant, defendant's counterclaim for false representations respecting the land while barred as an original cause of action was available as a defense under Code, § 3457. Bradley v. Hufferd, 138 Iowa 611, 116 N. W. 814.

In an action upon a foreign judgment based upon a note for the price of land, defendant could interpose a counterclaim for fraud in the sale, though it was barred by limitations, or could not be the basis of an independent suit. Secor v. Siver, 165 Iowa 673, 146 N. W. 845. The party pleading the counterclaim cannot recover judgment, except for costs. Folsom v. Winch, 63 Iowa 477, 19 N. W. 305.

Arkansas, in an action on a note for the final payment of a building, defendant's counterclaim, either as a recoupment of unliquidated damages for breach of contract, or for failure of consideration, is not barred by limitations, though barred as a ground of affirmative action.[14] In Louisiana, a claim on which suit cannot be brought, because prescribed, may still be pleaded in compensation.[15] In Kentucky, the statute of limitations does not apply to, or run against, debts which, by operation of law, are set off one against the other.[16] In Nebraska, the defense of recoupment arising out of the same transaction as a note survives as long as the cause of action on the note exists, though an affirmative action on the defense may be barred by limitations.[17] In Oklahoma, a counterclaim pleaded as a defense, or a set-off pleaded for the purpose of liquidating the whole or a part of plaintiff's claim, is not barred by the statute of limitations until the claim or demand of the plaintiff is barred.[18] In Pennsylvania, limitations may be set up against a set-off where it could be set up against the claim if sought to be enforced in assumpsit.[19] In New Jersey, a cross

14. Stewart v. Simon, 111 Ark. 358, 163 S. W. 1135.

15. Nichols v. Hance, 2 La. 382.

An indorser, when sued on the note, may plead in compensation notes acquired before the maturity of the note sued on, provided the notes were not prescribed when acquired, though prescribed at the time they were pleaded in compensation, for compensation took place by mere operation of law the moment the notes were held by the two parties, as provided by Civ. Code, art. 2208. Lewy v. Wilkinson (La.), 64 So. 1003. See also, Riddell v. Gormley, 4 La. Ann. 140; Boeto v. Laine, 3 La. Ann. 140.

16. Cooper's Adm'r v. Cooper, 8 Ky. Law Rep. (abstract) 528.

17. Williams v. Neely, 134 Fed. 1, 67 C. C. A. 171 (U. S. C. C. A. Neb.).

Though limitations may bar the right of purchasers of land to cancel their overdue purchase money notes and a mortgage executed as a part consideration for the alleged fraud of the vendors, the purchasers may set up by way of recoupment their damages in any action prosecuted by the payees of the notes or any person claiming title to those instruments to recover thereon or to foreclose the mortgage. Kaup v. Schinstock, 88 Neb. 95, 129 N. W. 184.

18. Stauffer v. Campbell, 30 Okl. 76, 118 Pac. 391.

19. Woodland Oil Co. v. A. M. Byers & Co., 223 Pa. 241 72 Atl. 518; Enterline v. Miller, 27 Pa. Super. Ct. 463; Trustees of State Hospital for Insane v. Philadelphia County, 205 Pa. 336, 54 Atl. 1032.

bill by a township to recover of a street railway company compensation required of it for a location for its tracks by the ordinance granting such location has been held barred as to compensation accruing more than six years before the date of the filing of the bill.[20] In Maine, in an action on a note given by defendant to plaintiff, an account in favor of defendant and against plaintiff, growing out of an entirely separate transaction, action for the recovery of which is barred by limitation, though arising after the giving of the note, cannot be proved as a set-off.[21] In Illinois, the statute of limitations is no defense by a distributee to the setting off against his share of an advance received by him from the testator whose estate is in process of administration.[22] In Indiana, a set-off is barred by the statute of limitations only when the original claim is barred.[23] In Missouri, where a decedent's alleged indebtedness to a surviving partner for payments by him is barred, such surviving partner, in settlement of the partnership estate, cannot retain a fund as against the decedent's heirs as in partial settlement of such indebtedness.[24] In Oregon, the statute of limitations is not a bar to a suit in the nature of a cross-

20. Asbury Park & S. G. Ry. Co. v. Township Committee of Neptune Tp., 73 N. J. Eq. 323, 67 Atl. 790.

In a suit on a bond against the widow and heirs of the deceased obligor, where the defense was payment of the bond by an account of the obligor against the obligee for board furnished him, under an agreement that it should be applied to reduce the bond, the statute of limitations was no bar to such a defense, although more than six years had elapsed after most of the account had accrued. King v. King, 9 N. J. Eq. 91 Stoct. 44.

21. Nason v. McCulloch, 31 Me. 158.

22. *In re* Esmond's Estate, 154 Ill. App. 357.

But a defendant may plead a set-off or counterclaim barred by the statute of limitations, while held and owned by him, to any action the cause of which was owned by the plaintiff, or person under whom he claims, before such set-off or counterclaim was so barred. Neville v. Brock, 91 Ill. App. 140.

23. Peden v. Cavins, 134 Ind. 494, 34 N. E. 7, 39 Am. St. Rep. 276; Warring v. Hill, 89 Ind. 497; Armstrong v. Ceasar, 72 Ind. 280; Fankboner v. Fankboner, 20 Ind. 62; Fox v. Barker, 14 Ind. 309. See also, Zink v. Zink (Ind. App.), 106 N. E. 381.

24. Cogswell's Heirs v. Freudenau, 93 Mo. App. 482, 67 S. W. 744.

action to correct public records and to enjoin the prosecution of an action at law theretofore commenced to recover the possession of real property, since such suit is invoked as a shield.[25] In South Dakota, in an action by a national bank upon a usurious contract the statute of limitations applies to a counterclaim for the usurious interest.[26] In Utah, where money paid in excess of what should have been paid on a debt could not be recovered because of the bar of limitations, a counterclaim for the overpayment did not sustain a judgment therefor.[27]

§ 281b. Set-offs and counterclaims—Accrual of right of action or defense.

In Michigan, a debt alleged by way of set-off is not barred by the statute of limitations unless the statutory period had run against it before the accruing of the claim on which suit is brought.[28] The statute does not run against a defense by way of recoupment for breach of warranty, in Minnesota, so long as the right of action for the price continues.[29] In Oklahoma, a proper defense, set-off, or counterclaim is not barred by limitations until the claim of plaintiff is also barred.[30] In New York, where in an action on an account which had accrued in 1868 and 1869, defendant claimed to offset an account against plaintiff running from 1855, but of which the last item accrued in 1863, it was held that there was a mutual running account between the parties and the offset was not barred by the statute of limitations.[31] In Maryland, where in

25. Hall v. O'Connell, 51 Or. 225, 94 Pac. 564.

26. First Nat. Bank v. McCarthy, 18 S. D. 218, 100 N. W. 14.

27. Utah Commercial & Savings Bank v. Fox, 40 Utah 205, 120 Pac. 840; 44 Utah 323, 140 Pac. 660, under Comp. Laws 1907, § 2971, providing that when cross-demands exist, the two demands shall be compensated so far as they equal each other.

28. Busch v. Wilcox, 106 Mich. 514, 64 N. W. 485, under 2 How. St., § 8731.

29. C. Aultman & Co. v. Torrey, 55 Minn. 492, 57 N. W. 211.

30. Advance Thresher Co. v. Doak, 36 Okl. 532, 129 Pac. 736, under Comp. Laws 1909, § 5635.

31. Helms v. Otis, 5 Lans. (N. Y.) 137.

an action on an open account there was a replication of the statute of limitations to a plea of set-off, it was held that the fact that one item in the account current, pleaded as set-off, was within the statutory limit, did not withdraw the whole account from the operation of the statute.[32] Where a stockholder of a bank indorsed a note for the bank's accommodation he did not become a creditor of the bank until he was reqnired to perform his obligation as indorser, and limitations did not begin to run against his right to set off the amount so paid against his statutory liability as a stockholder until such payment was made.[33] Where it was agreed in a foreclosure proceeding that the mortgaged property should be taken at the sale in full satisfaction of the judgment, and the debtor accordingly failed to claim for certain payments he had made, it was held that the statute of limitations would not run against the counterclaim until after the repudiation of the agreement.[34] If it appears that the possession of a vendor was under an understanding that he should be considered the tenant of the purchaser, the latter's claim for an injury to the property during such occupancy, or for rent for such period, is a matter of set-off to an action on the bond for the purchase money, which will be barred by the lapse of time fixed by the statute.[35] It is held in Texas, that if, when plaintiff filed his suit, defendant owed a subsisting counterclaim, which was not barred by the two-year limitation of the statute, that the bar was completed before the counterclaim was pleaded will not prevent defendant from setting off the counterclaim at any time pending suit, though, if he did not assert it until after two years from its accrual, he could not recover any excess over plaintiff's demand.[36]

32. Sprogle v. Allen, 38 Md. 331.

33. Strauss v. Denny, 95 Md. 690, 53 Atl. 571.

34. Savery v. Sypher, 39 Iowa, 675.

35. Patterson v. Hulings, 10 Pa. (10 Barr) 506.

36. Shaw v Faires (Tex. Civ. App.), 165 S. W. 501, under Texas Rev. Civ. St. 1911, art. 5687, subd 2.

For other instances of the application of statutes of limitation to set-offs, see Collins v. Loyd, 31 Ga. 128; Upham v. Wyman, 89 Mass. (7 Allen) 499; Verrier v. Gullion, 97 Pa. 63.

§ 282. Bringing of action suspends statute as to defendant's claims which go to reduce plaintiff's claim.

The bringing of an action by the plaintiff stops the running of the statute upon all demands due from him to the defendant, which, in that action, are the proper subject of a set-off,[37] and which are in fact pleaded as required by statute.[38] Also, it seems that is revives a claim which is actually barred, but which is the proper subject of recoupment in the action, as damages growing out of the same transaction. Thus, in an action to recover the price of goods sold, unsoundness may be set up by way of defense, although an action to recover damages therefor is barred.[39] So in

37. Walker v. Clements, 15 Q. B. 1046; Moore v. Lobbin, 26 Miss. 304; McElwig v. James, 36 Ohio St. 384. But see Gilmore v. Reed, 76 Pa. 462; King v. Coulter, 2 Grant's Cas. (Pa.) 77. In Pennsylvania the statute runs against the plaintiff until the issuing of his writ, and against the defendant until the filing of his plea. McClure v. McClure, 1 Grant's Cas. (Penn.) 222.

38. Trimyer v. Pollard, 5 Gratt. (Va.) 460. Under the West Virginia Code the statute of limitations runs against a set-off until it is filed. Rowan v. Chenoweth, 49 W. Va. 287, 38 S. E. 544, 87 Am. St. Rep. 796; Boyd v. Beebe, 64 W. Va. 216, 61 S. E. 304; Hurst v. Hite, 20 W. Va. 183.

39. Riddle v. Kreinbiehl, 12 La. Ann. 297. This follows from the rule that a person seeking to enforce a claim must take his rights subject to all counter rights of the defendant incident to the same claim. The same rule is also applied to a defendant, who, when he insists upon the allowance to him of claims upon which the statute has run, is held to be precluded from setting up the statute against similar demands put in by the plaintiff, especially when there is an implied agreement that one shall go in discharge of the other *pro tanto*, as in matters of book accounts. Gulick v. Turnpike Co., 14 N. J. Law 545. In Massachusetts, the filing of a claim in set-off commences an action thereon, so far as regards limitation, and, if the plaintiff discontinues his action, the defendant may sue thereon within three months thereafter, although the time of limitation has expired, the same as a plaintiff may do when his action has failed because of some defect in process, etc. Hunt v. Spaulding, 35 Mass. (18 Pick.) 521.

In general, so long as a party in the peaceable possession of land is not attacked, the statute of limitations does not run to prevent him, when sued, from setting up any equity he has in defense of his possession; and likewise, in an action of ejectment, such person may prove any equitable defenses in favor of his right of possession. Staley v. Housel, 35 Neb. 160, 52 N. W. 888; Pinkham v. Pinkham, 60 Neb. 600, 83 N. W. 837; De Guire v. St. Joseph Lead Co., 38 Fed. 65.

Georgia, it has been held that in an action on a note the defendant is not precluded from setting up a failure of consideration, or a parol warranty of the property for which the note was given, and a breach thereof, although an action upon such warranty is barred.[40] So, too, the statute does not defeat a defense of partial payment, although the statute might be a bar to an action to recover therefor if it stood alone.[41] So it has been held in Englan that a debt otherwise barred may be a good set-off, where there has been an express agreement that the debt should be applied upon the demand in suit.[42]

§ 283. Executor may deduct debt due estate, when.

It has also been held that an executor may retain a debt due by a legatee, which is barred by the statute as a set-off against the legacy to him;[43] and the same rule has been applied as to administrators, and it has been held that they may set off a similar debt against the debtor's share under an intestacy, on the ground that one of the next of kin of an intestate can take no share of the estate until he has discharged his obligation to it, and paid the debt in full.[44]

40. Munroe v. Hanson, 9 Ga. 398. Thus, where an action was brought upon a bond, it was held that a defense of payment by board furnished to the obligee, under an agreement that it should go in reduction of the bond, was admissible, although the statute had run upon most of the account. See also Evans v. Yongue, 8 Rich. (S. C.) 113, where, in an action upon a bond given for the price of land, a defense that there was a deficiency in the quantity of land, and a consequent partial failure of the consideration, was held admissible, although an action to recover therefor would have been barred. See also Richardson v. Bleight, 48 Ky. (8 B. Mon.) 580.

41. King v. King, 9 N. J. Eq. 41.

42. Smith v. Winter, 12 C. B. 487; Rowley v. Rowley, 1 Q. B. D. 463.

When, by a pledgee's negligence, the collection of collateral securities has been lost under the statute of limitations, and such statutory defense has become perfect, the pledgor may by counterclaim recover the value of his collateral, though it is not known that the debtor will, when sued on such collateral, plead the statute in defense. Hawley Bros. Hardware Co. v. Brownstone, 123 Cal. 643, 649; First Nat. Bank v. O'Connell, 84 Iowa 377, 35 Am. St. Rep. 313, and n. See *supra*, § 183 (*ad finem*).

43. Courteney v. Williams, 3 Hare, 539.

44. *In re* Cordwell's Estate, L. R. 20 Eq. 644. That an heir who is

§ 284. Statutory provisions as to set-offs.

In Wisconsin, by statute, the commencement of an action by the plaintiff is treated as the commencement of an action by the defendant upon any debt or contract which can properly be alleged by way of set-off, and the time of the limitation of such debt is to be computed in the same manner as though an action had been commenced thereon at the time when the plaintiff's action was commenced; and if the statute had run upon the set-off at that time, it is barred the same as the principal debt would be, and if the plaintiff's action is discontinued or dismissed, the time between the commencement of the action and its termination is not computed as any part of the time for the running of the statute upon the matter alleged by way of set-off.[45] So, also, in Arkansas, the statute is expressly applied to any debt or simple contract set up as a set-off, whether by plea, motion or otherwise.[46] In Michigan, a similar provision to that contained in the statute of Wisconsin exists;[47] likewise in Massachusetts [48] and Vermont,[49] and also in Maine, where the statute further provides that if the plaintiff's action fails by the nonsuit or other acts of the plaintiff, the defendant alleging the set-off, he may commence a new action thereon within six months from the termination of the suit.[50] But these statutory provisions are only confirmatory of the doctrine previously stated, as held under statutes which contained no such exceptions. The wisdom of inserting them in the statute is manifest, in that the rule is thus made permanent, and not subject to question or exception.

§ 284a(1). Defenses in general—Limitations applicable.

The Arkansas statute to quiet land titles, declaring that no ac-

claiming a share of an intestate's estate may set up the statute in bar of a claim due from him to the estate, was held in Drysdale's Appeal, 14 Pa. 531. See Rose v. Gould, 21 L. J. Ch. (N. S.) 360, *contra*, which case seems supported by those above cited.

45. See Appendix, Wisconsin.

46. Appendix, Arkansas.

47. Appendix, Michigan.

48. Appendix, Massachusetts.

49. Appendix, Vermont; see Sargeant v. Sargeant's Ex'rs, 18 Vt. 330.

50. Appendix, Maine.

tion for the recovery of any land against any person, his heirs or assigns, holding under a donation deed from the State, shall be maintained, unless plaintiff, his ancestor, or grantor, was seized or possessed within two years next before the commencement of the action, is available as a defense to one who holds under a donation deed good on its face, though perhaps invalid for reasons not there appearing.[51] In California, the plea of limitations may be interposed, in an action at law on a contract, to a defense based on an equitable cause of action for the reformation of the contract.[52] In Georgia, where in a suit on a note long past due defendant pleaded payment alleging that plaintiff had accepted lumber in satisfaction of the note, such defense is not barred by limitations, though such time may have elapsed that it would be too late to sue for the value of the lumber or to set up its delivery as a counterclaim.[53] In Colorado, where the answer in an action to quiet title against the holder of a trust deed alleges that the debt is valid and indisputable, that the trust deed constitutes a lien superior to that of plaintiff, and that defendant had a right to sell the property thereunder and apply the proceeds to the debt, the bar of the statute of limitations may be pleaded against such affirmative allegations.[54] In Kentucky, the statute of limitations applies alone to plaintiff's cause of action, and, so long as the courts will hear plaintiff's case, time cannot bar the defense.[55] In

51. Sims v. Cumby, 53 Ark. 418, 14 S. W. 623.

52. Bradbury v. Higginson, 167 Cal. 553, 140 Pac. 254.

53. Blackshear v. Dekle, 120 Ga. 766, 48 S. E. 311.

Where a debt was created in 1866, and in 1884 it was sought by cross-bill to subject a trust estate on the ground that the debt was created for the benefit thereof, the demand was stale, and became barred by the statute of limitations. Saulsbury v. Iverson, 73 Ga. 733.

54. Foot v. Burr, 41 Colo. 192, 92 Pac. 236, 13 L. R. A. (N. S.) 1210.

55. Aultman & Taylor Co. v. Meade, 121 Ky. 241, 28 Ky. Law Rep. 208, 89 S. W. 137, 123 Am. St. Rep. 193. See also Grover's Ex'rs v. Tingle, 21 Ky. Law Rep. 885, 53 S. W. 281; Fuller v. Wallace Ex'r, 6 Ky. Law. Rep. (abstract) 742; Edwards v. McKinsey's Adm'r, 14 Ky. Law Rep. (abstract 925; Weakley v. Meriwether, 156 Ky. 304, 160 S. W. 1053, the statute of limitations is not applicable to a mere defense.

The statute of limitations has no application to an action seeking the

Louisiana, an opposition filed to a syndic's tableau of distribution is a suit to establish a money demand, and any defense, such as usury, or want of consideration, etc., cannot be barred by prescription.[56] In Missouri, the purpose of the statute of limitations is held to be to quiet the assertion of old, stale and antiquated demands, but a ground of defense never becomes stale or barred by the statute.[57] In Nebraska, where the title of a person in the undisputed possession of land is challenged, he may set forth any equitable defense in favor of his right to the property, and the statute of limitations will not run so as to prevent him from setting forth such defense.[58] In South Carolina, to an action of debt on bond given for the price of a tract of land, a defense of partial failure of consideration because of a deficiency in quantity is not subject to the plea of the statute of limitations.[59] In Texas, limitations do not bar a defense against a legal action brought by another, nor preclude the introduction of competent evidence to establish the defense pleaded.[60] In Washington, it is held that the fact that a city's right to affirmatively attack judgments obtained against it by collusion was barred by the statute of limitations did not prevent it from impeaching the judgments, in defense of an action founded upon them, since equitable defenses are barred

surrender of a note executed by plaintiff to defendant in renewal of certain other notes, which, without plaintiff's knowledge, had been paid by the collection by defendant of an attorney's fee, to one-half of which plaintiff was entitled. Avritt v. Russell, 22 Ky. Law Rep. 752, 58 S. W. 811.

56. Walling v. His Creditors, 14 La. Ann. 670.

57. Butler v. Carpenter, 163 Mo. 597, 63 S. W. 823; Sebree v. Patterson, 92 Mo. 451, 5 S. W. 31; Williamson v. Brown, 195 Mo. 313, 93 S. W. 791; Redman v. Hampton, 26 Mo. App. 504.

58. Pinkham v. Pinkham, 60 Neb. 600, 83 N. W. 837, aff'd 61 Neb. 336, 85 N. W. 285. In trespass to try title, proof of an equitable claim by defendant in possession is not subject to limitation. Gilmore v. O'Neil (Tex.), 173 S. W. 203.

59. Evans' Ex'rs v. Yongue, 8 Rich. Law (S. C.) 113.

60. Snow v. Gallup (Tex. Civ. App.), 123 S. W. 222.

The plea of usury in an action on a note is not a suit to recover money paid on a usurious contract, to which the statute of limitations applies. Smith v. Mason (Tex. Civ. App.), 39 S. W. 188.

by neither the statute of limitations nor laches.[61] In Vermont, the statute of limitations does not apply to pleas in bar alleging payment.[62]

§ 284a(2). Fraud as a defense.

The California statute, requiring one to bring an action for the rescission of a contract for fraud within three years after discovery of the fraud does not preclude him from interposing fraud as a defense in an action on such contract, brought by the person guilty of the fraud more than three years after the former had discovered the fraud.[63] The South Carolina statute, limiting the time in which an action may be brought for fraud, does not limit the time in which one may defend against a deed procured by fraud.[64] In Kentucky, where, to an action on a note, defendant pleaded a discharge in bankruptcy, which plaintiff sought to avoid on the ground that the note was procured by fraud; and, under section 17 of the Bankruptcy Act of 1898, was therefore unaffected by the discharge, defendant could not set up Kentucky statute 1903, §§ 2515, 2519, limiting the time of commencement of actions for relief on the ground of fraud, as the statute applies to actions and not defenses, and defendant's plea went not to the cause of action, but to the defense, *i. e.*, to the effect of the discharge in bankruptcy.[65] The Indiana statute, providing that actions for relief against frauds shall be commenced within six years after the cause of action has accrued, does not apply to matters set up as a defense.[66] In Louisiana, a vendee, sued for the price, may except

61. State v. Tanner, 45 Wash. 348, 88 Pac. 321.

62. Tinkham v. Smith, 56 Vt. 187.

63. Hart v. Church, 126 Cal. 471, 58 Pac. 910, 77 Am. St. Rep. 195.

Code Civ. Proc., § 338, subd. 4, providing that an action for relief on the ground of fraud is barred within three years, does not apply to fraud pleaded as an equitable defense against a judgment which was without consideration, though the court rendering the same had jurisdiction. McColgan v. Muirhead, 2 Cal. App. 6, 82 Pac. 1113.

64. Cannon v. Baker, 97 S. C. 116, 81 S. E. 478.

65. Louisville Banking Co. v. Buchanan, 117 Ky. 975, 25 Ky. Law Rep. 2167, 80 S. W. 193.

66. Wilhite v. Hamrick, 92 Ind. 594; Robinson v. Glass, 94 Ind. 211; Ind. Rev. St. 1881, § 292.

that the consideration has failed through the redhibitory defects of the thing, though the redhibitory action be prescribed.[67]

§ 284b. Defenses in general—Accrual of right of action or defense.

A defense to an action by a son against his father's estate for rents and profits received by the father from the son's land, that such rents and profits were used in improving the land, is not barred by limitations, since it might be properly made whenever suit was brought on the claim for the income of the property.[68] One who is invested with the equitable title by the face of an instrument entitled to record need not sue for specific performance of the agreement for a deed, and is not therefore barred by limitations from setting up such instrument against plaintiff in trespass to try title.[69] The ten years after the cause of action has accrued, within which, under the New York statute, bills for relief must be brought, does not apply to an equitable defense set up under the New York practice.[70] Matters of defense, though pleaded in the form of a set-off or counterclaim, may be set up at any time before trial, without being subject to the running of the statute of limitations during the pendency of the action.[71]

§ 284c. Effect of subsequent accrual of new cause of action.

On the entry of judgment on a bond, before action was barred on the bond, the statute of limitations thereafter runs from the date of the judgment, and not of the bond.[72] Where, shortly after plaintiff's animal was struck by a train, plaintiff filed a claim for

67. Thompson v. Milburn, 1 Mart. N. S. (La.) 468.

68. Rhea v. Bagley, 66 Ark. 93, 49 S. W. 492.

69. Tompkins v. Broocks (Tex. Civ. App.), 43 S. W. 70.

70. Bartlett v. Judd, 21 N. Y. 200, 78 Am. Dec. 131, aff'g 23 Barb. 262.

71. Nelson v. San Antonio Traction Co. (Tex. Civ. App.), 142 S. W. 146.

72. Stockley v. Bewley, 5 Houst. (Del.), 587.

Where personalty is conveyed in fraud of sureties on the grantor's bond, a new right does not accrue against the grantee on rendition of judgment against the sureties, or payment of money by them. Howell v. Thompson, 95 Tenn. (11 Pickle) 396, 32 S. W. 309.

damages for injuring the animal, the fact that suit was not brought within a year after the presentation of such claim was no bar to plaintiff's right to recover the value of the animal, which died from the injuries sustained within a year prior to suit brought.[73]

Where it was declared by Pennsylvania Const. 1874, art. 16, § 8, that municipal corporations shall make just compensation for property injured by the enlargement of their works, "which compensation shall be paid or secured before such taking, injury," etc.; and Act 1878 (P. L. 129), provided a proceeding for the recovery for such injury, but contained no clause limiting the time in which to bring such proceeding, it was held that the Act 1878 did not create a new cause of action for an injury which occurred before its enactment or the adoption of the constitution of 1874, but only a remedy, so that the general statute of limitations commenced to run from the passage of the act.[74] An heir may maintain a writ of right on the seisin of his ancestor at any time within thirty years from the commencement of the disseisin, although the ancestor had been disseised more than twenty years at the time of his decease.[75]

73. Jones v. Texas & P. Ry. Co., 125 La. 542, 51 So. 582.

74. Croft v. Borough of South Chester, 3 Del. Co. R. 8, 2 Pa. Co. Ct. R. 508; Beck v. Borough of Bethlehem, 3 Lanc. Law Rev. 386, 2 Pa. Co. Ct. R. 511.

75. Moason v. Walker, 14 Me. (2 Shep.) 163.

CHAPTER XXIX.

CO-CONTRACTORS, ETC.

§ 285. Statutory provisions as to.

The doctrine of Whitcomb v. Whiting,[1] that an acknowledgment, new promise, or payment, made by one of two or more joint contractors, will remove the statute bar as to all, has practically but little force at the present day, as in many of the States [2] the legislature has expressly overridden it by providing that no acknowledgment, promise, or part payment made by one joint debtor shall deprive the others of the benefit of the statute; while in others [3] the same result is practically reached by a provision that no acknowledgment or promise shall be sufficient to revive a debt, unless it is made in writing, under the hand of the party to be charged thereby; and in others, the courts, without any express legislation, have repudiated the doctrine as unsound, predicated upon erroneous reasoning, and opposed to the spirit of these statutes.[4] Especially

1. Whitcomb v. Whiting, Doug. 652.

2. Maine, Vermont, Massachusetts, Arkansas, Colorado, Georgia, Indiana, Mississippi, Missouri, North Carolina, Michigan, Wisconsin, Virginia, and West Virginia.

3. New York, Alabama, Iowa, Minnesota, Kansas, South Carolina, Ohio, California, Oregon, Nevada, Nebraska, Texas, Arizona, Dakota, Idaho, Montana, Utah, and Wyoming.

4. As to the provision of the Mercantile Law Amendment Act, 1856, § 14, that no contractor or co-debtor shall lose the benefit of that enactment by reason of the payment of any principal or interest by a co-contractor or co-debtor, see *In re* Frisby, 43 Ch. D. 106.

Under the Michigan statutes a joint maker of a note does not lose the benefit of the statute by payments made by another joint maker. Rog-

is this the case in New Hampshire,[5] Pennsylvania,[6] Tennessee,[7]

ers v. Anderson, 40 Mich. 290. And so as a payment made by a husband without his wife's authority. Curtiss v. Perry, 126 Mich. 600, 85 N. W. 1131, 8 Detroit Leg. N. 123.

5. Exeter Bank v. Sullivan, 6 N. H. 124; Kelly v. Sanborn, 9 N. H. 46; Whipple v. Stevens, 22 N. H. 219. In Massachusetts, Cady v. Shepherd, 28 Mass. (11 Pick.) 400, 22 Am. Dec. 379; Sigourney v. Drury, 31 Mass. (14 Pick.) 387; Connecticut, Clark v. Sigourney, 17 Conn. 511; Maine, Parker v. Merrill, 6 Me. 41; Shepley v. Waterhouse, 22 Me. 497; Vermont, Wheelock v. Doolittle, 18 Vt. 440, 46 Am. Dec. 163; North Carolina, Mc-Intire v. Oliver, 9 N. E. (2 Hawks) 209, 11 Am. Dec. 760; Virginia, Rhode Island, New Jersey, and Delaware,—the doctrine of Whitcomb v. Whiting, has been approved and followed; but in all those States except Connecticut, New Jersey, Rhode Island, and Delaware, the legislature has repudiated the doctrine and forced the courts to recede from it. But in Pennsylvania, Kentucky, New York, New Hampshire, Tennessee, Indiana, Alabama, Kansas, Nebraska, Illinois, Florida, Ohio, Maryland, Georgia, South Carolina, and North Carolina, the doctrine was repudiated by the courts, either wholly, or except as to partners, before the legislature in any of them had placed any restraint upon the courts in that respect.

6. Levy v. Cadet, 17 Serg. & R. (Pa) 126, 17 Am. Dec. 650; Searight v. Craighead, 1 Pen. & W. (Pa.) 135; Reppert v. Colvin, 48 Pa. 248; Bush v. Stowell, 71 Pa. 208, 10 Am. Rep. 694. Van Keuren v. Parmalee, 2 N. Y. 523, 51 Am. Dec. 322, is a leading case in opposition to Whitcomb v. Whiting, *supra*, where Bronson, J., said in part: "If the promise is not express, the case must be such that it can be fairly implied. There must, at the least, be a plain admission that the debt is due, and that the party is willing to pay it. Allen v. Webster, 15 Wend. (N. Y.) 284; Stafford v. Richardson, id. 302; Bell v. Morrison, 26 U. S. (1 Pet.) 351, 7 L. Ed. 174. It is the new promise and not the mere acknowledgment that revives the debt and takes it out of the statute. Rosevelt v. Mark, 6 Johns. (N. Y.) Ch. 290. This doctrine is sustained by many decisions in other States. The case of Whitcomb v. Whiting has, to a limited extent, been followed in Massachusetts, Cady v. Shepherd, 28 Mass. (11 Pick.) 400; Bridge v. Gray, 31 Mass. (14 Pick.) 55; Sigourney v. Drury, 31 Mass. (14 Pick.) 387, 391, 392; Vinal v. Burrill, 33 Mass. (16 Pick.) 401; in Connecticut, Bound v. Lathrop, 4 Conn. 336, 10 Am. Dec. 147; Coit v. Tracy, 8 Conn. 268, 20 Am. Dec. 110; Austin v. Bostwick, 9 Conn. 496, 25 Am. Dec. 42; Clark v. Sigourney, 17 Conn. 511; in Maine, Parker v. Merrill, 6 Me. 41; Pike v. Warren, 15 Me. 390; Dinsmore v. Dinsmore, 21 Me. 433; Shepley v. Waterhouse, 22 Me. 497; and in Vermont, Joslyn v. Smith, 13 Vt. 353; Wheelock v. Doolittle, 18 Vt. 440. But I think the judgment under review would not be upheld in either of those States. In North Carolina it has been held that the acknowledgment of the debt by one partner, though after the dissolution, will prevent the operation of the statute. McIntire v. Oliver, 9 N. C. (2

Kansas,[8] Florida,[9] Maryland,[10] Illinois,[11] and by the United States Supreme Court;[12] while in Connecticut, New Jersey, Rhode Island, and Delaware the doctrine of Whitcomb v. Whiting is still adhered to. It is not necessary to discuss the accuracy of this doctrine, as it has been attacked and also sustained by some of the ablest judges in this country; and the judgment of the profession, as well as of the people generally, as to the wisdom of the doctrine is best evidence by the circumstance that it has been nearly obliterated by legislative and judicial action.

Hawks) 209, 11 Am. Dec. 760. And the same has been decided in Georgia, provided the new promise is made before the action is barred; but not when the new promise is made afterwards, as it was in the case before us. Brewster v. Hardeman, Dudley (Ga.) 138. It has been decided by the Court of Appeals, in South Carolina, that a promise by one partner made after the dissolution, and after the statute had run, will not charge the other partner. Steele v. Jennings, 1 McMull. (S. C.) 297. In the Exeter Bank v. Sullivan, 6 N. H. 124, the authority of Whitcomb v. Whiting was wholly denied; and the court held that a payment by one of the joint makers of a promissory note did not take the case out of the statute as to the other. In Alabama, a promise by the principal debtor will not revive the demand against a codebtor, who is a surety. Lowther v. Chappel, 8 Ala. 353, 42 Am. Dec. 364. In Tennessee, a promise by one partner, after the dissolution of the partnership, to pay a note made by the firm, does not take the case out of the statute of limitations as to the other partner. Belote v. Wynne, 15 Tenn. (7 Yerg.) 534; Muse v. Donelson, 21 Tenn. (2 Humph.) 166, 36 Am. Dec. 309. This is also the rule in Pennsylvania. Levy v. Cadet, 17 Serg. & R. (Pa.) 126; Searight v. Craighead, 1 Pen. & W. (Pa.) 135. It is also held in Indiana that the power of one partner to bind the other by the admission of a debt ceases with the partnership. Yandes v. Lefavour, 2 Blackf. (Ind.) 371. And in Bell v. Morrison, 26 U. S. (1 Pet.) 351, 7 L. Ed. 174, the United States Supreme Court followed the decisions in Kentucky, and held that this dissolution of the partnership put an end to the authority of the partners to bind each other by any new engagement; and consequently that the acknowledgment of a debt by one partner, after the dissolution, would not take the case out of the statute of limitations."

7. Belote v. Wynne, 15 Tenn. (7 Yerg.) 534; Muse v. Donelson, 21 Tenn. (2 Humph.) 166.

8. Steele v. Souder, 20 Kan. 39.

9. Tate v. Clements, 16 Fla. 339, 26 Am. Rep. 709.

10. Schindel v. Gates, 46 Md. 604, 24 Am. Rep. 526.

11. Kallenbach v. Dickinson, 100 Ill. 427, 39 Am. Rep. 47.

12. Bell v. Morrison, 26 U. S. (1 Pet.) 351, 7 L. Ed. 174.

§ 286. Grounds upon which doctrine of Whitcomb v. Whiting is predicated.

The ground upon which the doctrine of Whitcomb v. Whiting was predicated is, that in the case of co-contractors each is, with reference to the joint debt, the agent of the others. "Payment by one," said Lord Mansfield, "is payment for all, the one acting virtually as the agent of the rest; and in the same manner an admission by one is an admission by all; and the law raises the promise to pay when the debt is admitted to be due." However this might be in the case of partners, it is difficult to understand upon what ground, in the case of co-sureties and other joint indebtedness, one can be said to be an agent for the others, as to that transaction, or upon what ground an implied agency can be raised.[13] "There is nothing in the relation of joint debtors," said Bronson, J., in the case last cited, "from which such an agency can be inferred. A joint obligation is the only tie which links them together; and from the nature of the case, payment of the debt is the only thing which one has authority to do for all." It is held in New York that one joint debtor cannot by a payment made by him upon the joint debt, before the statute has run upon the debt, as to them, suspend the operation of the statute,[14] and much less after the statute has run,[15] unless such payment was made by one of the joint debtors, by the direction of the other, so that a direct agency is established as to such payment.[16]

§ 287. Present doctrine in this country.

Except in the four States already referred to, the doctrine in reference to joint debtors—except partners—may be said to be, that one co-debtor can neither suspend nor remove the statute bar by

13. See Van Keuren v. Parmalee, 2 N. Y. 523, 51 Am. Dec. 322; Smith v. Caldwell, 15 Rich. (S. C.) 365; Vent v. Hart, 8 Pa. 337; Sigourney v. Drury, 31 Mass. (14 Pick.) 387; Rucker v. Frazier, 4 Strobh. (S. C.) 93; Cleveland v. Harrison, 15 Wis. 670.

14. Shoemaker v. Benedict, 11 N. Y. 176, 62 Am. Dec. 95; Dunham v. Dodge, 10 Barb. (N. Y.) 566.

15. Payne v. Slate, 39 Barb. (N. Y.) 634.

16. Haight v. Avery, 16 Hun (N. Y.) 252.

an admission of, or promise to pay, the joint debt, nor by a partial payment thereof, out of his own funds, without the direction, assent, or subsequent ratification of his co-debtors.[17] In reference to partners more conflict exists, and inasmuch as, without question, while the partnership exists each partner is agent for the

17. Exeter Bank v. Sullivan, 6 N. H. 124; Bell v. Morrison, 26 U. S. (1 Pet.) 351, 7 L. Ed. 174; Whipple v. Stevens, 22 N. H. 219; Levy v. Cadet, 17 Serg. & R. (Pa.) 126, 17 Am. Dec. 650; Van Keuren v. Parmalee, 2 N. Y. 523, 51 Am. Dec. 322. In United States v. Wilder, 80 U. S. (13 Wall.) 254, 20 L. Ed. 681, it was held that when a debtor admits a certain sum to be due by him, and denies that a larger sum claimed is due, a payment of the exact amount admitted cannot be converted by the creditor into a payment on account of the larger sum denied, so as to take the claim for such larger sum out of the statute. See also, Exeter Bank v. Sullivan, 6 N. H. 124; Kelly v. Sanborn, 9 N. H. 46; Whipple v. Stevens, 22 N. H. 219; Levy v. Cadet, 17 Serg. & R. (Pa.) 126, 17 Am. Dec. 650, holds that payment on account, or an acknowledgment, by one of two or more joint debtors, will not take the case out of the statute as to the others. See also Coleman v. Forbes, 22 Pa. 156; Searight v. Craighead, 1 Pen. & W. (Pa.) 135; Houser v. Irvine, 3 W. & S. (Pa.) 345; Schoneman v. Fegley, 7 Pa. 208. In Yandes v. Lefavour, 2 Blackf. (Ind.) 371, it was held that an acknowledgment of a debt made by one partner, after the dissolution of the partnership, is not sufficient to take a case out of the statute as to the others. See Shoemaker v. Benedict, 11 N. Y. 176, 62 Am. Dec. 95; Winchell v. Hicks, 18 N. Y. 558; Kallenbach v. Dickinson, 100 Ill. 427, 39 Am. Rep. 47. In Lowther v. Chappell, 8 Ala. 353, 42 Am. Dec. 364, it was held that "a payment by one of several joint debtors, before the statute has completed a bar, will not prevent the completion of the bar as to the others, at the expiration of the time within which the statute required suit to be brought on the original evidence of debt, relied on to sustain the action." Myatts v. Bell, 41 Ala. 222; Knight v. Clements, 45 Ala. 89; Belote v. Wynne, 15 Tenn. (7 Yerg.) 534; follows Bell v. Morrison, as does Muse v. Donelson. 21 Tenn. (2 Humph.) 166. See also Palmer v. Dodge, 4 Ohio St. 21. More recently, in Kansas, Nebraska, and Florida, the doctrine of Whitcomb v. Whiting is repudiated, and that of Bell v. Morrison followed. Steele v. Souder, 20 Kan. 39; Mayberry v. Willoughby, 5 Neb. 368, 25 Am. Rep. 491; Tate v. Clements, 16 Fla. 339, 26 Am. Rep. 709. Like reasoning will also be found in Steele v. Jennings, 1 McMull. (S. C.) 297; Foute v. Bacon, 24 Miss. 156; Briscoe v. Anketell, 28 Miss. 361. The earlier decisions in New York following Whitcomb v. Whiting (see Johnson v. Beardslee, 15 Johns. (N. Y.) 3; Patterson v. Choate, 7 Wend. (N. Y.) 441), were overruled in 1849, in Van Keuren v. Parmalee, 2 N. Y. 523, 51 Am. Dec. 322.

others, it is held in all the States that, while the partnership exists, one partner can bind the others by an admission or part payment where it is made according to the requirements of the statute, and in the name and on behalf of the firm; and where the admission or payment is made in reference to a partnership transaction, it is treated as having been made on behalf of the firm. But as, when the partnership is dissolved, the agency of each partner to act for the firm is generally treated as having been revoked, it is held in most of the States that an admission or payment made after such dissolution does not have the effect to revive the debt against the firm;[18] while in others it is held that such admissions

18. Van Keuren v. Parmalee, *supra;* Tate v. Clements, 16 Fla. 339, 26 Am. Rep. 709; Yandes v. Lefavour, 2 Blackf. (Ind.) 371; Palmer v. Dodge, 4 Ohio St. 21; Foute v. Bacon, 24 Miss. 156; Briscoe v. Anketell, 28 Miss. 361; Whipple v. Stevens, 22 N. H. 219; Bush v. Stowell, 71 Pa. 208, 10 Am. Rep. 694; Schoneman v. Fegley, 7 Pa. 433; Knight v. Clements, 45 Ala. 89; Kallenbach v. Dickinson, 100 Ill. 427, 39 Am. Rep. 47. In Bell v. Morrison, 26 U. S. (1 Pet.) 351, 7 L. Ed. 174, the statute of limitations had run before the promise or admission by one of the partners was made. See 3 Kent's Com., Lect. 48; Hackley v. Patrick, 3 Johns. (N. Y.) 536; Walden v. Sherburne, 15 Johns. (N. Y.) 424; Baker v. Stackpoole, 9 Cow. (N. Y.) 420, 18 Am. Dec. 508. The decision in Whitcomb v. Whiting, *supra*, is said to have been in direct conflict with Bland v. Haselrig, 2 Vent, 151. In Shoemaker v. Benedict, 11 N. Y. 176, 62 Am. Dec. 95, where payments were made by one of several joint makers of a note before the statute of limitations had run upon it, it was held that such payments did not affect the defense of the statute as to the other debtors. In Tennessee, Pennsylvania, Indiana, Illinois, Florida, Kentucky, New Hampshire, Alabama, Kansas, and Nebraska this doctrine would seem to be held, carrying out the principle of decided cases. After a joint debt has been barred by the statute, part payment by one joint debtor does not revive the debt as to the others. Biscoe v. Jenkins, 10 Ark. 108; Mason v. Howell, 14 Ark. 199. And this rule holds as to a payment made by one partner after the partnership is dissolved. Myatts v. Bell, 41 Ala. 222. In Emmons v. Overton, 54 Ky. (18 B. Mon.) 643, it was held that a part payment made by a surety *after* all right of action upon the note is barred does not renew the note as to the balance. Where the maker and indorser of a note are sued jointly, proof that the indorser made payments at different times within six years will not vary or affect the liability of the maker, or deprive him of the advantages of the bar of the statute. Bibb v. Peyton, 19 Miss. 275. Nor will a payment made by one of two sureties remove the statute bar as to the other. Exeter Bank v. Sul-

or part payments made after the dissolution, but before the statute has run, will be operative as against the others.[19] In others it has been held that a part payment made by one partner after the dissolution, and after the statute has run, will bind all.[20] From this conflict it will be seen that it is impossible to formulate any general rule relative to the power of one copartner to

livan, 6 N. H. 124. In New York an acknowledgment or promise to pay a debt, or a part payment made by one of several partners after dissolution of a firm, or by one of two joint and several debtors, will not renew the debt against the others, under the statute of limitations. New York Life Ins. Co. v. Covert, 29 Barb. (N. Y.) 435. Payment of interest on a note by one of two joint makers, at the request of the other, is sufficient to take the debt out of the statute of limitations, as against both the makers. Munro v. Potter, 34 Barb. (N. Y.) 58. See also Searight v. Craighead, 1 Pa. 135; Brewster v. Handman, Dudley (Ga.) 138; Levy v. Cadet, 17 Serg. & R. (Pa.) 126; Yandes v. Lefavour, 2 Blackf. (Ind.) 371; Belote v. Wynne, 15 Tenn. (7 Yerg.) 534.

19. Mayberry v. Willoughby, 5 Neb. 368, 25 Am. Rep. 491; Schindel v. Gates, 46 Md. 604, 24 Am. Rep. 526; Beardsley v. Hall, 36 Conn. 270; Green v. Greensboro Female College, 83 N. C. 449; Merritt v. Day, 38 N. J. Law 32. But in North Carolina, though the power of one partner to bind the others by an admission or part payment is expressly taken away by statute, the power of one joint maker of a note to bind the others by an admission or payment before the statute has run is retained. The court, in Schindel v. Gates, *supra*, seems to assent to the doctrine of Whitcomb v. Whiting; referring to Ellicott v. Nichols, 7 Gill (Md.) 85, 48 Am. Dec. 546, it said: "The court, in Ellicott v. Nichols, fully recognized the decision of Whitcomb v. Whiting, and said that the part payment of principal and the payment of interest relied on to take the case out of the bar was made within the legal time and before the statute had attached. The rule thus laid down has been the accepted law of this State for nearly thirty years, and, in the absence of legislation to the contrary, it is not to be questioned. The same rule has received the sanction of the highest courts in other States. Selltey v. Selltey, 2 Hill (S. C.) 496; Steele v. Jennings, 1 McMull. (S. C.) 297; Goudy v. Gillam, 6 Rich. (S. C.) 28; McIntire v. Oliver, 9 N. C. (2 Hawks) 209, 11 Am. Dec. 760; Walton v. Robinson, 5 Ired. (N. C.) 341; Emmons v. Overton, 54 Ky. (18 B. Mon.) 643. In regard to the supposed hardship of the rule as against sureties to a note, the answer is, that it is always in their power to inquire whether it has been paid, and, if it remains unpaid, to compel the holder to proceed against the principal, or to pay the note and proceed in their own name."

20. Mix v. Shattuck, 50 Vt. 421. And this seems also to be the rule in England. See Goodwin v. Parton, 42 L. T. N. S. 568.

revive a debt as to the others, but that the doctrine held in a given State must be consulted.[21]

§ 287a. Present doctrine in this country—Recent decisions.

The New York doctrine as to joint contractors, as expressed in the latest decisions of its highest court, is thus stated: "It is the settled law of this State that payments made by one joint contractor cannot save from the statute of limitations a claim against another joint contractor, and that payments made by the principal debtor cannot save from the statute a claim against the surety; and it makes no difference that the payments were made with the knowledge of the other party liable for the same debt. To make payments effective against a party to save a claim from the statute, they must have been made by him, or for him by his authorized agent. One joint contractor may make payments as agent for all the contractors, or the pricipal debtor may make payments for and in the name of his surety as his agent, or payments may thus be made in the name of all the joint contractors, or of the surety without previous authority, but be subsequently ratified, and in all such cases the running of the statute may be prevented. But in all cases to make the payments effective they must by previous authorization or subsequent ratification be the payments of the party sought to be affected by them." [22] An acknowledgment

21. See Smith v. Ludlow, 6 Johns. (N. Y.) 267; Burnett v. Snyder, 45 N. Y. Super. Ct. 577.

22. Hoover v. Hubbard, 202 N. Y. 289, 95 N. E. 702 rev'g 118 N. Y. Supp. 1114, 134 App. Div. 909; McMullen v. Rafferty, 89 N. Y. 456; First Nat. Bank of Utica v. Ballou, 49 N. Y. 155. In Hoover v. Hubbard, *supra,* the court said: "There has been a controversy in some jurisdictions as to the legal consequences of a payment made upon an indebtedness by one of two or more joint debtors, so far as it affects the running of the statute of limitations against the debtors other than the person making the payment. In Shoemaker v. Benedict, 11 N. Y. 176, 62 Am. Dec. 95, referring to payments made by one of several makers of a promissory note before the statute of limitations had barred an action thereon, it was said that 'Before the decision of Van Keuren v. Parmalee, 2 N. Y. 523, 51 Am. Dec. 322, it would have been considered very well settled upon authority that such payments did operate to prevent the statute of limitations from attaching to the demand.' It was, however, by Shoemaker v. Benedict, *supra,* clearly settled in this

by a joint debtor does not remove the bar of the statute as to his co-debtor.[23] Substantially the same rule as is maintained in New

State that a payment made by one of the joint and several makers of a promissory note, either before or after an action upon it is barred by the statute of limitations and within six years before suit brought does not affect the defense of the statute as to the others. There have been many cases in this court approving and confirming the authority of that case. Among the most recent of the reported decisions is Brooklyn Bank v. Barnaby, 197 N. Y. 210, 90 N. E. 834, rev'g 126 App. Div. 936, 110 N. Y. Supp. 1123, in the opinion in which case the authority of Shoemaker v. Benedict, *supra*, is again referred to, approved and reasserted." See also, Cohen v. Diamond, 132 N. Y. Supp. 355, 74 Misc. Rep. 444; Security Bank of New York v. Finkelstein, 135 N. Y. Supp. 640, 76 Misc. Rep. 461; Union Nat. Bank of Franklinville v. Dean, 139 N. Y. Supp. 835, 154 App. Div. 869; Clute v. Clute, 197 N. Y. 439, 90 N. E. 988; aff'g 116 N. Y. Supp. 1133, 132 App. Div. 938; Mott v. Ingalsbe, 120 N. Y. Supp. 151, 136 App. Div. 140; Akin v. Van Wirt, 108 N. Y. Supp. 327, 124 App. Div. 83; Ulster County Sav. Institution v. Deyo, 191 N. Y. 505, 84 N. E. 1122, aff'g 101 N. Y. Supp. 263, 116 App. Div. 1. *In re* Neher's Estate, 109 N. Y. Supp. 1090, 57 Misc. Rep. 527, where a payment was made on a firm note by an assignee for the benefit of creditors of a surviving partner after the death of one partner; Security Bank of New York v. Finkelstein, 145 N. Y. Supp. 5, 160 App. Div. 315, part payment, to prevent running of limitations, if not made by the debtor, must be made by his agent authorized to disclaim for him any intention to have the payment given the effect which by legal inference or presumption would otherwise attach thereto, or must be ratified by the debtor.

23. Connecticut Trust & Safe Deposit Co. v. Wead, 67 N. Y. Supp. 466, 33 Misc. Rep. 374, judg. modified 69 N Y. Supp. 518, 58 App. Div. 493, modified 172 N. Y. 497, 65 N. E. 261, 92 Am. St. Rep. 756; Matteson v. Palsner, 67 N. Y. Supp. 612, 56 App. Div. 91, 31 Civ. Proc. Rep. 198, modified 173 N. Y. 404, 66 N. E. 110.

Where defendants were obligors on a bond given as collateral to a bond and mortgage, payments by the trustees who gave the mortgage did not constitute an acknowledgment by the defendants stopping the running of limitations, even though they were beneficially interested in the property; nor did defendants' endorsement of notes, the proceeds of which were used by the mortgagor to pay the interest on the mortgage on which they were sureties, stop the running of limitations as against them. Mutual Life Ins. Co. of New York v. United States Hotel Co., 144 N. Y. Supp. 476, 82 Misc. Rep. 632. An attorney cannot be presumed to have authority to acknowledge a debt already barred by the statute of limitations. Id.

Where a life tenant of mortgaged property, in order to protect her life estate, from time to time made payments of principal and interest on the mortgage, which was past due, each payment of interest operated as a new admission of indebtedness, sufficient to postpone the running of the stat-

York obtains in Minnesota,[24] Kansas,[25] Ohio,[26] Illinois,[27] Montana,[28]

ute of limitations against the life tenant's right, on paying the debt in full and being subrogated to the mortgagee's rights, to foreclose the mortgage as against the remaindermen; since in making such payments the tenant represented the whole estate and all interested therein. Bonhoff v. Wiehorst, 108 N. Y. Supp. 437, 57 Misc. Rep. 56.

24. Woodcock v. Putnam, 101 Minn. 1, 111 N. W. 639, holding that to prevent the running of limitations, a payment on a debt must be voluntarily made by the debtor in person or by one having authority, or for him and in his name by one without authority with subsequent ratification by the debtor; Atwood v. Lammers, 97 Minn. 214, 106 N. W. 310, holding that partial payment on a note by one of two joint makers will not prevent the running of limitations as to the other maker; Northwest Thresher Co. v. Dahltorp, 104 Minn. 130, 116 N. W. 106, partial payments by the principal debtor will not prevent the running of limitations as to the guarantor of a note, unless the contract of guaranty expressly so provides; Pfenninger v. Kokesch, 68 Minn. 81, 70 N. W. 867, where one of two joint and several debtors makes a payment in his own behalf, the mere fact that the other debtor, after knowledge of such payments, verbally promises to pay the balance, will not constitute a ratification of the payments as having been made for him or in his behalf.

25. Elmore v. Fanning, 85 Kan. 601, 117 Pac. 1019, where one of two joint makers of a note makes a payment thereon after it is due as the agent of the other and with his money, and states that the money belongs to his co-obligor for whom he is paying it, it does not affect the operation of limitations as to himself.

26. Keel v. Rudisell, 13 Ohio Cir. Ct. Rep. 199, 7 O. C. D. 464, a partial payment on a note by one of two joint makers will not prevent the running of limitations as to the other maker.

27. Payments made by one joint debtor with the knowledge, consent, or subsequent ratification of the other, arrest the running of the statute as to both joint debtors. Adams v. Douglass, 128 Ill. App. 319; McDonald v. Weidmer, 103 Ill. App. 390; Granville v. Young, 85 Ill. App. 167; Howe v. Stratton, 107 Ill. App. 281. But one joint debtor cannot, by a partial payment made without knowledge, assent, or subsequent ratification of the other, bind him, so as to authorize the inference of a new promise on the part of the latter and avoid the effect of the statute of limitations. Id.

Notwithstanding a joint note is, as to one of the joint debtors, barred by the statute of limitations, a mortgage given to secure the same may be foreclosed as against both of the joint debtors. Payments made by one joint debtor upon a note so secured, while not binding the joint debtor so that he may be proceeded against personally, have the effect of keeping alive the security with respect to such note. Ritzmuller v. Neuer, 130 Ill. App. 380.

28. Monidah Trust v. Kemper, 44 Mont. 1, 118 Pac. 811; First Nat.

Maine,[29], Michigan,[30] North Dakota,[31] Washington,[32] and Wisconsin.[33] The rule is different in Colorado,[34] Missouri,[35] Oregon,[36] and the District of Columbia.[37]

§ 288. Assent of a co-contractor to a part payment by another—Effect of.

While in most of the States a part payment made by one joint debtor will not suspend or remove the statute bar as to the others, yet, even where the statute provides that an acknowledgment or part payment made by one joint debtor shall not remove the statute bar as to the others, it is held that where such part payment is made by the direction or at the request of the others, they are all equally bound thereby, as in such case the one making the payment acts as the agent of the others.[38] The

Bank v. Bullard, 20 Mont. 118, 49 Pac. 658; Oleson v. Wilson, 20 Mont. 544, 52 Pac. 372, 63 Am. St. Rep. 639.

29. Medomak Nat. Bank v. Wyman, 100 Me. 556, 62 Atl. 658, 4 L. R. A. (N. S.) 562; McKenney v. Bowie, 94 Me. 397, 47 Atl. 918.

30. Godde v. Marvin, 142 Mich. 518, 12 Detroit Leg. N. 786, 105 N. W. 1112; Borden v. Fletcher's Estate, 131 Mich. 220, 9 Detroit Leg. N. 285, 91 N. W. 145.

31. Grovenor v. Signor, 10 N. D. 503, 88 N. W. 278.

32. Old Dominion Mining & Concentrating Co. v. P. A. Daggett & Co., 38 Wash. 675, 80 Pac. 839; Hanna v. Kasson, 26 Wash. 568, 67 Pac. 271.

33. State Bank of West Pullman v. Pease, 153 Wis. 9, 139 N. W. 767.

34. Torbit v. Heath, 11 Colo. App. 492, 53 Pac. 615.

35. Kemble *ex rel.* Rosenberg v. Logan, 79 Mo. App. 253.

36. *In re* Smith's Will, 43 Or. 595, 75 Pac. 133.

37. White v. Connecticut Life Ins. Co., 34 App. D. C. 460.

See § 116b (2), *supra.*

38. See Haight v. Avery, 16 Hun (N. Y.) 252; Pitts v. Hunt, 6 Lans. (N. Y.) 146; National Bank of Delavan v. Cotton, 53 Wis. 31, 9 N. W. 926. In Winchell v. Hicks, 18 N. Y. 558, where sureties on a joint and several note were called upon for payment, and they directed the holder to call for payment upon the principal, who made a payment on the note, it was held such an acknowledgment as to arrest the running of the statute against him. In Huntington v. Ballou, 2 Lans. (N. Y.) 120, where the maker paid interest on the note, reciting in the receipt that it was made by an accommodation indorser, by the hand of the maker, and the indorser, when afterwards shown the receipt by the holder, examined it and expressed his approval of it, it was held that the payment took the case out of the statute, as to such indorser. See First Nat. Bank of

assent of a surety to a part payment by the principal may be inferred.[39] And it seems that where money is paid by a surety in the presence of the principal, and the latter does not dissent thereto, or say anything, his silence may be treated as an acquiescence in such payment, so as to remove the statute bar as to both.[40] If one co-contractor procures a payment to be made by his co-debtor, it is sufficient to bind him.[41] But even though the money is paid by one co-contractor *for another, with funds of the other, and as his agent, and he so informs the creditor, at the time,* he is not bound thereby; and such payment does not remove the statute bar as to him.[42] But the question as to whether there has been an assent by one co-debtor to a payment made upon the joint debt by another is a mixed question of law and fact, to be determined in view of all the circumstances attending the transaction.

Utica v. Ballou, 49 N. Y. 155, approving this case, and holding that the requirement of the statute, that an acknowledgment or promise to take a case out of the operation of the statute must be in writing, does not alter the effect of a payment of principal or interest. The case of Harper v. Fairley, 53 N. Y. 442, depended simply on the question whether the maker of the note had knowledge of and assented to the payment made upon it by another.

39. If a debtor and his surety go to the creditor together, for the express purpose of making a payment, and for that alone, and both apparently co-operate in the transaction, though the debtor alone handles the money, the creditor may consider it a joint payment binding the surety under the statute of limitations, unless the surety notifies him that it is not so. Mainzinger v. Mohr, 41 Mich. 685. The admissions of one joint debtor are not evidence against the others. Rogers v. Anderson, 40 Mich. 290.

40. Whipple v. Stevens, 22 N. H. 219. But see Quimby v. Putnam, 28 Me. 419, where it was held that a payment by one of two joint debtors, in the presence of the other, is not evidence of a new promise made by both. See also Patch v. King, 29 Mo. 448. Payments authoritatively made by the treasurer of a partnership or joint-stock company, from the partnership funds, and by him indorsed on a note executed by the partnership, take the note out of the statute. Walker v. Wait, 50 Vt. 668.

41. McConnell v. Merrill, 53 Vt. 149, 38 Am. Rep. 663.

42. Bailey v. Corliss, 51 Vt. 366.

CHAPTER XXX.

JUDICIAL PROCESS.

§ 289. When action is treated as commenced.

The question as to when an action is commenced, within the meaning of the statute, is one which has been variously decided. In some of the States, the statute itself settles this question, but where the statute is silent upon this point, it may be said that an action is commenced when the writ is issued. That is, when it is filled out and completed with an intention of having it served.[1] In any event, the issue of a process and giving it to an officer for service, or depositing it in a place designated or provided by an officer for that purpose, clearly amounts to a commencement of an action.[2]

1. Jackson v. Brooks, 14 Wend. (N. Y.) 649; Lowry v. Lawrence, 1 Caines (N. Y.) 69, Colem. & C. Cas. 170; Ross v. Luther, 4 Cow. (N. Y.) 158, 15 Am. Dec. 341; Burdick v. Green, 18 Johns. (N. Y.) 14; Cheetham v. Lewis, 3 id. 43; Fowler v. Sharp, 15 id. 323; Cox v. Cooper, 3 Ala. 256; Schroeder v. Merchants' Ins. Co., 104 Ill. 71; Feazle v. Simpson, 2 Ill. 30; Ford v. Phillips, 18 Mass. (1 Pick.) 202; Seaver v. Lincoln, 38 Mass. (21 Pick.) 267; Mason v. Cheney, 47 N. H. 24; Parker v. Colcord, 2 N. H. 36; Society for Propogating the Gospel v. Whitcomb, 2 id. 227; Hardy v. Corliss, 21 N. H. 356; Day v. Lamb, 7 Vt. 426; Hail v. Spencer, 1 R. I. 17; Johnson v. Farwell, 7 Me. 372, 22 Am. Dec. 203; Updike v. Ten Broock, 32 N. J. Law 105.

2. Michigan Ins. Bank v. Eldred, 130 U. S. 693, 9 Sup. Ct. 690, 32 L. Ed. 1080.

See Gough v. McFall, 52 N. Y. Supp. 221, 31 App. Div. 578; McKee v. Allen, 94 Ill. App. 147. The running of the statute of limitations is stopped by the filing of a creditor's

Formerly the question as to when an action could be said to have been commenced, so as to save a debt from the operation of the statutes, was one of great importance, and over which there was some confusion and conflict of doctrine. But the general rule adopted was, and is, except where otherwise provided by statute, that the statute is suspended from the time of the suing out of the writ, and its *bona fide* delivery to a proper officer for service.[3] The writ may be sent to the sheriff for service by mail, and if it fails to reach him without any fault on the part of the plaintiff, that is, if it was seasonably deposited by him or some person for him in the post-office, and except for unusual delay or accident in the transmission of the mail it should have seasonably reached the sheriff, the plaintiff will not be prejudiced.[4]

bill and a decree thereon, or by a valid assignment for creditors, as to creditors who come in under its terms. Richmond v. Irons, 121 U. S. 27, 7 Sup. St. 788, 30 L. Ed. 864; Thompson v. German Ins. Co., 76 Fed. 892; Fidelity Ins. Co. v. Roanoke Iron Co., 81 id. 439, 452. See McDonald v. Nebraska, 101 id. 171, 41 C. C. A. 278; Peabody v. Tenney, 18 R. I. 498, 30 Atl. 456; Taber v. Royal Ins. Co., 124 Ala. 681, 26 So. 252, 689; Richardson v. Whitaker, 103 Ky. 425, 45 S. W. 774, 20 Ky. Law Rep. 121.

3. Beckman v. Satterlee, 5 Cow. (N. Y.) 519; Evans v. Gallaway, 20 Ind. 479; Lowry v. Lawrence, 1 Caines (N. Y.) 69; Kinney v. Lee, 10 Tex. 155; Hail v. Spencer, 1 R. I. 17; Cheetham v. Lewis, 3 Johns. (N. Y.) 42; Burdick v. Green, 18 id. 14; Jackson v. Brooks, 14 Wend. (N. Y.) 649; Sharp v. Maguire, 19 Cal. 577; Pimental v. City of San Francisco, 21 id. 351; State v. Groome, 10 Iowa 308. See Clare v. Lockard, 122 N. Y. 263, 25 N. E. 391, 9 L. R. A. 547, under the New York Code. See also, McGhee v. City of Gainesville, 78 Ga. 790, 3 S. E. 670; Hampe v. Schaffer, 76 Iowa 563, 41 N. W. 315; Knowlton v. City of Watertown, 130 U. S. 327, 9 Sup. Ct. 539, 32 L. Ed. 956, 130 U. S. 334, 9 Sup. Ct. 542.

4. Jewett v. Greene, 8 Me. 447. In some of the States express provision is made for saving the rights of parties where the writ fails of proper service by accident. See next note.

From the time when a claim is submitted to the jurisdiction of a court, the common statute of limitations and the analogous bars and presumptions in equity and at law cease to operate for all the purposes of the pending litigation. Smith v. Crater, 43 N. J. Eq. 636, 12 Atl. 530; Forman v. Brewer, 62 N. J. Eq. 748, 48 Atl. 1012, 90 Am. St. Rep. 475.

As to sureties on a bond for costs, the statute runs only from the time when the decree is actually entered; and a *nunc pro tunc* entry, as of an earlier date, has no effect on the operation of the statute of limita-

§ 290. Statutory provisions relating to.

In many of the States provision is now made in the statute as to what shall be deemed the commencement of an action. Thus, in Maine, "the time when a writ is actually made with an intention of service" is the commencement of the suit;[5] and this is practically the provision in Alabama, whether the writ is executed or not, if it is continued by an *alias,* or recommenced at the next term of the court.[5a] In Kentucky, the action is deemed to be commenced at the date of the first summons or process issued in good faith from the court or tribunal having jurisdiction in the action. In North Carolina, the action is deemed to be commenced as to each defendant when the summons is issued against him. In Ohio, at the date of the summons which is actually served on the defendant, and when service by publication is proper, from the date of

tions. Borer v. Chapman, 119 U. S. 587, 602, 7 Sup. Ct. 342, 30 L. Ed. 532; Fewlass v. Keeshan, 88 Fed. 573, 576.

A cause of action against an abstracter of titles for giving a wrong certificate of title, though amounting to an implied contract for skill and care, does not rest on the contract itself, but on tort for negligence; it accrues at the date of the delivery, and not when the negligence is discovered or consequential damages arise. See Lattin v. Gillette, 95 Cal. 317, 30 Pac. 545, 29 Am. St. Rep. 115; Yore v. Murphy, 18 Mont. 342, 45 Pac. 217; Russell & Co. v. Polk County Abstract Co., 87 Iowa 233, 54 N. W. 212, 43 Am. St. Rep. 381; Provident Loan Trust Co. v. Walcott, 5 Kan. App. 473, 47 Pac. 8. See Shackelford v. Staton, 117 N. C. 73, 23 S. E. 101; Daniel v. Grizzard (State v. Grizzard), id. 105, 23 S. E. 93; *supra,* § 179, n. In general, as to contracts, the statute begins to run when there is a breach of contract, express or implied, though the damages resulting from the original wrong mainly develop later. Campbell v. Culver, 67 N. Y. S. 469, 56 App. Div. 591. As to the time for bringing suit under the conditions of insurance policies, see Rogers v. Home Ins. Co., 95 Fed. 109, 35 C. C. A. 402, 404, n.; *supra,* § 100 and notes. That a motion in bankruptcy may be equivalent to an action in this respect, see *Re* Mansell, 66 L. T. 245.

5. In Maine, it is also provided that "when a writ fails of a sufficient service or return, by unavoidable accident, or default or negligence of the officer to whom it was delivered or directed," etc., a new action may be commenced within six months thereafter. In Vermont, a similar provision exists, except that one year is given. In Connecticut a provision similar to that in Vermont exists. so also in Massachusetts, Colorado, Iowa, and some other States.

5a. Southern Ry. Co. v. Dickens, 163 Ala. 114, 50 So. 109.

the first publication; so also in Wyoming. In California, when the complaint is filed. So in Arizona, Utah, Idaho, and practically in New Mexico. In Oregon, when the complaint is filed and served on one or more of the defendants. In Wisconsin, when the summons is served on one of the defendants. In Nevada, when the complaint is filed in the proper court, and a summons issued and placed in the hands of the sheriff of the county or other person authorized to serve the same. In Tennessee, the suing out of a summons, whether it is executed or not, if it is continued by the issuance of an *alias* process from term to term, or recommenced within one year after the failure to execute. In Florida, when the summons is issued to the proper officer or filed in the proper office. In New York, South Carolina, and Dakota, when the summons is served on one or more of the defendants.[6] In Connecticut, the action is deemed to be commenced from the date of the service of the writ.[7] In Vermont, the making of a writ,[8] or the issue of a summons and order of notice, is the commencement of an action;[9] and such, also, is the rule in Massachusetts;[10] and the filling up and dating of a writ before the statute has run has been held sufficient to save the statute.[11] In Pennsylvania, the issue of a summons suspends the statute if an *alias* summons is issued within six years;[12] and it is not necessary to enter continuances to save the bar;[13] and if the proper persons are sued, the statute is suspended, notwithstanding the firm name is erroneously given, and the process is subsequently amended.[14] But the issue of a summons which is not served will not save the statute, unless an *alias* is taken out and

6. In New York, provision is made for saving the plaintiff's rights when he attempts to commence an action. And a provision similar to that in section 399 exists in South Carolina and Dakota.

7. Sandford v. Dick, 17 Conn. 213.

8. Allen v. Mann, 1 D. Chip. (Vt.) 94.

9. Blain v. Blain, 45 Vt. 538.

10. Woods v. Houghton, 67 Mass. (1 Gray) 580.

11. Gardner v. Webber, 34 Mass. (17 Pick.) 407.

12. McClurg v. Fryer, 15 Pa. 293.

13. Schlosser v. Lesher, 1 Dall. (Pa.) 411, 1 L. Ed. 200.

14. Nichols v. Fox, 2 W. N. C. 196.

served within six years.[15] In Pennsylvania, the practice is to issue the original writ before the statute has run, and to continue it by an *alias, plus,* and *pluries,* even after the intervention of more than one term;[16] and as the writ which commences the action states the ground thereof, it is sufficient to set it forth without the continuances.[17] In South Carolina, however, an *alias* must be issued within one year from the time the original issued, and must also be regularly delivered to the sheriff, or it does not operate as a continuance of the original writ.[18] In New York, under the old practice, the issuing of a *capias* to any county would save the statute,[19] even though the plaintiff directed the sheriff to return it *non est;*[20] but it was required to be kept on foot by continuances, which could be entered at any time.[21] The fact that the *ad damnum* is laid at a different sum from that in the original process, or that the venue was laid in a different county, will not defeat its effect in suspending the statute, if the action is transitory, and it is averred that both actions were predicated on the same claim, nor even that the actions are different in form, if both are for the same cause.[22] If the action is commenced in season, the statute is saved without any reference to the question whether the plaintiff used any diligence in its prosecution.[23]

§ 291. Date of writ not conclusive.

The date of the writ is not conclusive, but is a fact which may be contested, and the rule may be said to be that it is not enough that the writ bears date before the expiration of the statutory period, but both the *bona fides* of the plaintiff in taking it out and

15. Curcier's Estate, 28 Pa. 261.

16. Pennock v. Hart, 8 Serg. & R. (Pa.) 369.

17. Schlosser v. Lesher, 1 Dall. (Pa.) 411, 1 L. Ed. 200.

18. State Bank v. Baker, 3 McCord (S. C.) 281.

19. Jackson v. Brooks, 14 Wend. (N. Y.) 649.

20. Beckman v. Satterlee, 5 Cow. (N. Y.) 519.

21. Baskins v. Wilson, 6 Cow. (N. Y.) 471.

22. Young v. Davis, 30 Ala. 213.

23. King & Houston v. State Bank, 13 Ark. 269. But see Clark v. Kellar, 66 Ky. (3 Bush) 223; where a different doctrine was held.

the exact time may be averred and shown, notwithstanding the *teste*.[24] The date of the writ is only *prima facie* evidence of the time of its issue;[25] and whenever the exact time of its issue, even to the hour, becomes necessary, the defendant may, if he can, show it, even though it contradicts the *teste* of the writ. "It would be most extraordinary and inequitable," said Lord Mansfield,[26] "not to allow the presumption, that the plaintiff commenced his process seasonably, to be rebutted by the defendant, by showing that in real truth the time was run before he took any step."

§ 292. Filing claim before commissioners—Pleading, set-off, etc.

Filing a claim with the commissioners of a deceased insolvent estate has been held equivalent to commencing an action.[27] And in New York the entry of an order to refer a claim against the estate of a decedent is held to be the commencement of an action, within the meaning of the statute.[28] The filing of a claim in set-off operates as a suspension of the statute as to it, so that, even though the plaintiff's action fails, and the set-off cannot be enforced therein, the defendant may, by a suit brought within a reasonable time thereafter, preserve his rights.[29]

§ 293. Mistaken remedy, etc.

If the plaintiff mistakes his remedy, in the absence of any statutory provision, saving his rights, and during the pendency of the action the statute runs upon his claim, his remedy is barred;[30] and the same rule prevails where, from any cause, the plaintiff becomes nonsuit,[31] or the action abates or is dismissed, or judgment therein

24. Comyn's Digest, 539; Lester v. Jenkins, 8 B. & C. 339; Allen v. Portland Stage Co., 8 Me. 207; Chauncey v. Rutter, 3 Neb. 313; Henderson v. Baker, 2 Burr, 950; Hanway v. Merrey, 1 Vent. 28; Morris v. Pugh, 3 Burr. 1241.

25. Gardner v. Webber, 34 Mass. (17 Pick.) 407; Society for Propogating the Gospel v. Whitcomb, 2 N. H. 227; Johnson v. Farwell, 7 Me. 372, 22 Am. Dec. 203.

26. Henderson v. Baker, *supra*.

27. Guild v. Hale, 15 Mass. 455.

28. Hultslander v. Thompson, 5 Hun (N. Y.) 348.

29. Hunt v. Spaulding, 35 Mass. (18 Pick.) 521. See chapter on Set-off.

30. Appeal of Todd, 24 Pa. 429.

is reversed or set aside, the statute bars another action brought for the same claim, unless as is the case in several of the States, provision is made to save the remedy.[32]

§ 294. Amendment of process.

An amendment of the process which does not change the remedy does not affect the statutory suspension; but where a party obtains leave to amend his summons and complaint after the statute has fully run, and does so by bringing in new parties defendant, the parties so brought in may set up the statute in bar of the action as to them;[33] and it would seem that the bringing in of such new parties would be so far equivalent to bringing a new action,[34] that such new defendants may rely upon the statute as a defense,[35] especially where the new complaint does not advert to the former proceedings so as to connect the former with the latter.[36] Of course,

31. Harris v. Dennis, 1 Serg. & R. (Pa.) 236.

32. Williamson v. Wardlaw, 46 Ga. 126; Memphis & C. R. Co. v. Orr, 52 Miss. 541.

33. Newman v. Marvin, 12 Hun (N. Y.) 236.

34. McMahon v. Allen, 3 Abb. (N. Y.) 89, 1 Hilt. 103. See also, Magaw v. Clark, 6 Watts (Pa.) 528; Brown v. Goolsby, 34 Miss. 437. In Bradford v. Andrews, 20 Ohio St. 208, 5 Am. Rep. 645, it was held that a new defendant brought in was in as of the date of the original process, although the statute had run in his favor before he was brought in.

35. See Shaw v. Cock, 12 Hun (N. Y.) 173, aff'd 78 N. Y. 194.

36. Sands v. Burt, 1 Abb. L. J. 124. Where new plaintiffs were substituted who claimed to be entitled to be subrogated to the rights of the original plaintiff, the court held that by such substitution a new action was virtually commenced, and that the statute was a bar thereto, although the original action was seasonably commenced. Sweet v. Jeffries, 67 Mo. 420. See Bennington v. Dinsmore, 2 Gill (Md.) 348; Gray v. Trapnall, 23 Ark 510.

As to amendments of the declaration or complaint, the general rule is that, if such amendments do not present a new or different cause of action, and the original pleading alleged a good cause of action, the statute of limitations does not bar the amendment. See *supra*, § 7, n.; Chicago City Ry. Co. v. Hackendahl, 188 Ill. 300, 58 N. E. 930; Chicago Gen. Ry. Co. v. Carroll, 189 Ill. 273, 59 N. E. 551; Belden v. Barker, 124 Mich. 667, 83 N. W. 616; City of Detroit v. Hosmer, 125 Mich. 634, 7 Detroit Leg. N. 655, 85 N. W. 1; Bank of Stockham v. Alter, 61 Neb. 359, 85 N. W. 300; Cincinnati, etc., Ry. Co. v. Gray, 101 Fed. 623, 41 C. C. A. 535, 50 L. R. A. 47; Frishmuth v. Farmers' Loan & T. Co., 107 id. 169,

an amendment of a complaint or declaration so as to present a new cause of action which was barred at the time of the amendment, but which was not barred when the action was brought, will not defeat the operation of the statute as to such new matter,

46 C. C. A. 222; Moles v. Crozier, 31 Pitts. L. J. (N. S.) 316; *In re* Ibert, 62 N. Y. S. 1051, 48 App. Div. 510; Woodcock v. Bostic, 128 N. C. 243, 38 S. E. 881; Cicero & P. St. Ry. Co. v. Brown, 89 Ill. App. 318, aff'd 193 Ill. 274, 61 N. E. 1093; Chicago North Shore St. Ry. Co. v. Payne, 94 id. 466, aff'd 192 Ill. 239, 61 N. E. 467; City of Elgin v. Anderson, Ill. App. 527; Kent v. San Francisco Savings Union, 130 Cal. 401, 62 Pac. 620; Alabama Gt. Southern R. Co. v. Thomas, 89 Ala. 294, 7 So. 762, 18 Am. St. Rep. 119; Chambers v. Talladega Real-Estate, etc., Assoc., 126 Ala. 296, 28 So. 636; Galveston, etc., Ry. Co. v. English (Tex. Civ. App.), 59 S. W. 626; Beaty v. Atlantic & W. P. R. Co., 100 Ga. 123, 28 S. E. 32; Service v. Farmington Sav. Bank, v. Cobb, 88 Maine 488, 34 Atl. 277, 62 Kan. 857, 62 Pac. 670; Flanders v. Cobb, 88 Maine 488, 34 Atl. 277, 51 Am. St. Rep. 410, 431, n.; 57 Albany L. J. App., p. 16. As to the effect of amendments in actions for conversion, see *supra*, § 183, n. 49.

In some States, as, e. g., in Ohio and West Virginia, it is provided by statute that an attempt to commence an action shall be deemed equivalent to the commencement thereof, enabling a plaintiff who becomes nonsuit to bring a new action within a specified time, as one year, without becoming amenable to the statute of limitations. See Pittsburg C. C. & St. L. Ry. Co. v. Bemis, 64 Ohio St. 26, 59 N. E. 745; Wiggins Ferry Co. v. Gardner, 91 Ill. App. 20; Hamilton v. Royal Ins. Co., 156 N. Y. 327, 50 N. E. 863, 42 L. R. A. 485; Gough v. McFall, 31 App. Div. 578, 52 N. Y. Supp. 221; Hooper v. Atlanta, K. & N. Ry. Co., 106 Tenn. 28, 60 S. W. 607, 53 L. R. A. 931; Manuel v. Norfolk & W. Ry. Co., 99 Va. 188, 3 Va. Sup. Ct. Rep. 110, 37 S. E. 957; Ketterman v. Dry Fork R. Co., 48 W. Va. 606, 37 S. E. 683; Smith v. Herd, 110 Ky. 56, 22 Ky. Law Rep. 1596, 60 S. W. 841, 1121; Irwin v. Lloyd, 20 Ohio Cir. Ct. R. 339, 11 O. C. D. 212. The Iowa statute (§ 2537), allows this when, after commencing an action, "the plaintiff for any cause, except negligence in its prosecution, fails therein." This exception of negligence has been held to apply where a plaintiff, having ground for a continuance, did not apply therefor, but voluntarily dismissed the action. Pardey v. Town of Mechanicsville, 112 Iowa 68, 83 N. W. 828. And see Boyce v. Snow, 187 Ill. 181.

If when actions at law were originally brought the cause of action sued on was not barred by limitation, but was barred when a motion to consolidate the actions and to convert them into a bill in equity was made, the plaintiff's claim against the defendants in the original actions at law is not barred, but as against those defendants, who were first made parties by the filing of the bill in equity, it is barred. Smith v. Butler, 176 Mass. 38, 57 N. E. 322.

because as to it the statute was not suspended until the amendment was made.[37] But as to all amendments of the complaint which do not change the remedy or the original ground of action as stated therein, they are treated as relating back to the time of the commencement of the action.[38]

§ 295. Must be action at law.

The commencement of a bill in chancery does not suspend the statute, and if pending such bill the statute runs upon the claim, it is barred so that an action at law cannot be maintained thereon, although the bill is dismissed, even where the statute makes provision for the bringing of a fresh action, when the original action was brought in season, and was abated or dismissed, etc.[39] An action in the nature of a creditor's bill to recover property of a judgment debtor, and to have the same applied in payment of the judgment, does not operate to extend the lien beyond the statutory period. Such an action is not, in any proper sense, an action brought upon the judgment as a cause of action, in order to obtain a new judgment, but simply an action ancillary to and for the purpose of obtaining satisfaction of an existing judgment. It has been repeatedly held that a pending levy of an execution made during the life of a judgment will not operate to continue the life or lien of a judgment beyond the statutory period; that a judgment creditor must sell the property levied on within the statutory period of the life of the lien of the judgment; that a levy during that period neither creates a new lien nor extends the judgment lien; that nothing but a renewal within the life of the judgment will continue the lien of the judgment; that if an execution is issued at so late a day that a sale cannot be made within the life of the judgment, it should be accompanied by a *scire facias* or renewal.[40]

37. Lagow v. Neilson, 10 Ind. 183.

38. Agee v. Williams, 30 Ala. 636. See Wing v. De la Rionda, 125 N. Y. 678, 25 N. E. 1064.

39. Roland v. Logan, 18 Ala. 307; Gray v. Berryman, 4 Munf. (Va.) 181.

40. Tenney v. Hemenway, 53 Ill. 97; Gridley v. Watson, id. 186; Isaac v. Swift, 10 Cal. 71, 70 Am. Dec. 698;

§ 296. Abatement of writ, dismissal of action, reversal of judgment, etc.

Except where the statute expressly makes a saving of the rights of a plaintiff, on the failure of the original suit, for any cause, whether by reason of the plaintiff becoming nonsuit, the abatement or dismissal of the action, or the reversal of the judgment, a new action cannot be brought for the same cause against which the statute will not be a bar.[41] In many of the States, the statute provides that when a writ fails of a sufficient service or return by unavoidable accident, or default, or negligence of the officer to whom it was delivered or directed, or is abated, or the action otherwise defeated for any matter of form, or by the death of either party, or if a judgment for the plaintiff is reversed on a writ of error, the plaintiff may commence a new action on the same demand within six months after the abatement or determination of the original suit, or reversal of the judgment; and if he dies, and the cause of action survives, his executor or administrator may

Bagley v. Ward, 37 Cal. 121, 99 Am. Dec. 256; Rogers v. Druffel, 46 Cal. 654; Dickinson v. Collins, 1 Swan 516; Davis v. Ehrman, 20 Pa. 256; Rupert v. Dantzler, 20 Miss. (12 S. & M.) 697; Bierne v. Mower, 21 Miss. (13 S. & M.) 427; Graff v. Kip, 1 Ed. Ch. (N. Y.) 619; Tufts' Adm'r v. Tufts, 18 Wend. (N. Y.) 621; Little v. Harvey, 9 id. 157; Roe v. Swart, 5 Cow. 294; Newall v. Dart, 28 Minn. 248, 9 N. W. 732.

As to the effect of renewing writs under the present English practice, see Hewett v. Barr (1891), 1 Q. B. 98; Magee v. Hastings, 28 L. R. Ir. 288.

41. Dennistoun v. Rist, 9 La. Ann. 464; Walker v. Peay, 22 Ark. 103; Mahon v. The Justices, Ga. Dec. 201; Gray v. Trapnall, 23 Ark. 510; Robinson v. Robinson, 5 Harr. (Del.) 8. An action voluntarily abandoned cannot be made available to save a subsequent suit for the same cause, from the operation of the statute. *Ex parte* Hanks, 1 Cheves (S. C.) Eq. 209; Null v. White Water Valley Canal Co., 4 Ind. 431. It is no bar to the statute that the plaintiff commenced an action seasonably, which failed for informality. Callis v. Waddy, 2 Munf. (Va.) 511. In Vermont, where the statute saves the rights of a plaintiff when his action fails for any matter of form, for one year thereafter, it was held that this did not extend to a case where the first suit was terminated by a nonsuit occasioned by the inability of the plaintiff, through poverty, to comply seasonably with an order, made by the court, that he furnish additional security by way of recognizance for the defendant's costs. Hayes v. Stewart, 23 Vt. 622.

commence such new action within said six months. Under such statutes, the rights of a party are saved where his original action is defeated for any of the reasons stated, or within the spirit of the saving clause, as a nonsuit,[42] or a failure of the action by reason of the absence of the justice before whom it was brought.[43] So, where the summons is set aside for defective service,[44] or is dismissed by reason of an accidental omission of the clerk to enter it seasonably on the docket.[45] But a voluntary dismissal of the action does not save the remedy,[46] nor indeed, in any case where there was a voluntary abandonment of the action, can it be relied upon to check the operation of the statute.[47]

42. Freshwater v. Baker, 52 N. C. (7 Jones L.) 225; Spear v. Newell, 13 Vt. 288; Skillington v. Allison, 9 N. C. (2 Hawks) 347.

43. Where a plaintiff brought a suit before a justice of the peace who once continued the cause, but at the second time appointed he was absent, whereby the plaintiff was necessarily driven to a nonsuit, it was held that, under a similar statute, he might bring a new action within the time named therein, and the statute would not be a bar thereto unless it had run before the commencement of the first suit. Phelps v. Wood, 9 Vt. 399; Spear v. Curtis, 40 Vt. 59.

44. Meisse v. McCoy, 17 Ohio St. 225. See Bullock v. Dean, 53 Mass. (12 Metc.) 15.

45. Allen v. Sawtelle, 73 Mass. (7 Gray) 165.

46. Walker v. Peay, 22 Ark. 103.

47. Null v. White Water Valley Canal Co., 4 Ind. 431.

CHAPTER XXXI.

COMMENCEMENT OF ACTION OR OTHER PROCEEDING.

§ 297. Mode of computation of time limited.

The time of the statute is computed from the accruing of the action to the commencement of the suit.[1] Where, in trespass to try title, limitations are relied on as a defense, the running of the statute should be reckoned from the date of the deeds under which the parties in possession claim title until the beginning of the suit against them to recover possession.[2] In Arkansas, in computing the time of the running of the statute, the day on which the right of action accrues should be included, and the day when the summons was issued excluded.[3] In California, a note drawn payable "one day after" the happening of a particular event is not due until the day after the event happens. The maker has all of that day in which to pay the money, and an action commenced during that day would be premature; hence an action on it is not barred until the lapse of the term allowed by the statute, after such day, and not including it.[4] In the District of Columbia, under a statute providing that suits shall be brought "within three years ensuing the cause of such action, and not after," the day on which the cause of action accrues is to be excluded.[5] In Illinois, the statute of five years begins to run as to trespass from the time it was committed.[6] In Kansas, in an action on an account, the period of limitation should be computed by excluding the day on which the last item was furnished and including the last day of the period

1. Withers v. Richardson, 21 Ky. (5 T. B. Mon.) 94, 17 Am. Dec. 44; Stewart v. Durrett, 19 Ky. (3 T. B. Mon.) 113. See also Computation of Time, Ch. V, *supra*.

2. Wade v. Goza, 78 Ark. 7, 96 S. W. 388.

3. Shinn v. Tucker, 33 Ark. 421.

4. Hathaway v. Patterson, 45 Cal. 294.

The time of one's minority is calculated from the first minute of the day on which he was born to the first minute of the day corresponding which completes the period of minority; and, in calculating the time within which he may thereafter sue for an interest in land, the latter day is to be considered the first day of the five years allowed. Ganahl v. Soher (Cal.), 5 Pac. 80.

5. Baker v. Ramsburg, 4 Mackey (D. C.) 1.

6. Krug v. Outhouse, 8 Ill. App. 304, and hence, where a trespass was committed on June 21, 1873, and suit begun therefor on June 21, 1878, the cause of action was barred, the five years having elapsed before the action was brought.

of limitation.[7] Under the Kentucky statute providing for setting aside certain mortgages and transfers of property made in fraud of creditors where the action therefor is brought "within six months after" the instrument is placed on record, in computing the time for bringing the action, the day on which the instrument is placed on record should be included.[8] In Louisiana, under the Code provision requiring that prescription shall only be acquired after the last day allowed by law has elapsed, the one-year prescription for an action for tort is computed from and after the day of the commission of the tortious act.[9] In New Jersey, when, on the issue of limitation, the time is to be computed from a date, the day is excluded; and, when it is to be computed from an event or an act, the day is included; and the day on which the cause of action accrued is not to be counted.[10] In Minnesota, in determining whether a cause of action is barred by limitations, the day on which it occurred is excluded.[11] Under North Carolina Code, § 152, declaring that actions on judgments shall be commenced "within ten years after the date of the rendition of said judgment," action begun October 20, 1883, on a judgment rendered October 20, 1873, was begun too late.[12] Under Tennessee Code, § 2281, providing that a married woman may bring suit within one year after her discoverture, where plaintiff's husband died November 9, 1869, and her bill was filed Novmeber 9, 1870, the suit was brought in time, as the law does not take account of fractions of a day.[13] In Texas, in computing the time by which an action is barred by Rev.

7. Hook v. Bixby, 13 Kan. 164, under Code provision that an action on contract must be brought "within three years after the cause of action shall have accrued" and statutory provision that "the time within which an act is to be done shall be computed by excluding the first day and including the last."

8. Lebus v. Wayne Ratterman Co. (Ky.), 21 S. W. 652.

9. Wartelle v. King, 10 La. Ann. 655. The 10 years prescription against an action to set aside a deed elapses at the last hour of the last day of the tenth year. Breaux v. Broussard, 116 La. 215, 40 So. 639.

10. McCulloch v. Hopper, 47 N. J. Law (18 Vroom) 189, 54 Am. Rep. 146, 7 N. J. Law J. 336.

11. Nebola v. Minnesota Iron Co., 102 Minn. 89, 112 N. W. 880.

12. Cook v. Moore, 95 N. C. 1.

13. Rogers v. Etter, 67 Tenn. (8 Baxt.) 13. See Elder v. Bradley, 34 Tenn. (2 Sneed) 247.

St., art. 3203, which provides that certain actions shall be brought "within two years after the cause of action shall have accrued," the day on which a cause of action accrues is not counted.[14] Under the Vermont statute, providing that, when time is to be reckoned from a day or date, such day or date shall not be included in the computation, the day on which payment was made on a promissory note is excluded in determining whether the statute of limitations is a bar.[15]

§ 298(1). Proceedings constituting commencement of action in general.

A suit to establish a personal judgment as an equitable lien, being on a separate and distinct cause of action, does not relate back to the commencement of the original action, and is subject to the defense of limitation.[16] Where certain defendants seek to enforce demands against a codefendant, the action will be deemed commenced as to such demands at the time the answers setting them up are filed.[17] An action prematurely brought prevents the running of limitations.[18]

§ 298(2). Filing pleadings.

In the District of Columbia, when a declaration is filed with directions, either express or implied, by the plaintiff or his attorney to the clerk to issue process thereon, and nothing remains to be done but that the clerk should proceed, and plaintiff has otherwise complied with all the requirements of the law, such as the

14. Smith v. Dickey, 74 Tex. 61, 11 S. W. 1049. See also, Texas & P. Ry. Co. v. Goodson, 2 Willson, Civ. Cas. Ct. App. § 27.

In estimating a period of limitation running against a person from the date of his majority, the day on which he attained it must be computed, and, in ascertaining the date of his majority, his age is computed by including the date of his birth. Ross v. Morrow, 85 Tex. 172, 19 S. W. 1090, 16 L. R. A. 542.

15. Hicks' Estate v. Blanchard, 60 Vt. 673, 15 Atl. 401.

16. Lang v. Choctaw, O. & G. R. Co., 198 Fed. 38, 117 C. C. A. 146.

17. German Fire Ins. Co. v. Bullene, 51 Kan. 764, 33 Pac. 467.

18. St. Louis & S. F. Ry. Co. v. Kinman, 9 Kan. App. 633, 58 Pac. 1037.

payment of necessary fees and the like, the suit must be deemed to be then commenced so far as to arrest the running of the statute of limitations.[19] In California, an answer in partition setting up a mortgage, and asking that it be declared a lien on the land, and its payment provided for, is equivalent to an action to foreclose, and the question of the bar of limitations or of laches decided as if the action was begun when the answer was filed.[20] In Colorado, the filing of a complaint within two years after the accrual of the cause of action, and the issuance of a summons against defendant, is the commencement of an action tolling limitations.[21] In Georgia, the filing of the petition is treated as the commencement of the suit only when followed by due and legal service. If there is no process and no service, and the plaintiff is guilty of laches, the writ becomes abortive, and the court loses jurisdiction to issue process or to have service perfected.[22] In Delaware, the commencement of an action in a justice's court, that will arrest the running of limitations, is not the order for summons or attachment, the two kinds of process provided for in such court, but the issuance thereof, so that filing a praecipe before the justice, commanding the issuance of summons or attachment, is not a "commencement of action" with such effect.[23] In Illinois, the mere appearance of a subcontractor to a bill to enforce a mechanic's

19. Huysman v. Evening Star Newspaper Co., 12 App. D. C. 586.

20. Sanford v. Bergin, 156 Cal. 43, 103 Pac. 333.

21. Kingsley v. Clark, 57 Colo. 352, 141 Pac. 464, under Mills' Ann. Code, § 32, even though defendant was not served within the six-year period prescribed by Rev. St. 1908, § 4061, as the time within which such actions should be begun.

An attempted suit by a foreign corporation doing business within the State without having paid the fee required by law would not suspend the running of limitations, since a corporation not complying with the statutes cannot institute suit in this State. Western Electrical Co. v. Pickett, 51 Colo. 415, 118 Pac. 988.

22. Cox v. Strickland, 120 Ga. 104, 47 S. E. 912. See also, Jordan v. Bosworth, 123 Ga. 879, 51 S. E. 755; Nicholas v. British American Assur. Co., 109 Ga. 621, 34 S. E. 1004; Bentley v. Reid, 133 Fed. 698, 66 C. C. A. 528 (Ga.).

23. McMullin v. Beck, 3 Boyce's (26 Del.) Rep. 116, 80 Atl. 524. But see Gatta v. Philadelphia, B. & W. R. Co., 1 Boyce's (24 Del.) Rep. 293, 76 Atl. 56.

lien, pursuant to an allegation made by complaint that he had been informed that the subcontractor appearing claimed some interest, is not the equivalent of "filing a petition" or "commencing a suit" or filing an answer, intervening petition, or cross-bill, arresting the running of the statute limiting the time within which a subcontractor can enforce a lien.[24] In Indiana, the filing of a declaration is not the commencement of a suit.[25] In Iowa, the record alone must be looked to, to determine when notice of the beginning of an action was delivered to the sheriff, or when the action was instituted, as affecting limitations.[26] In Michigan, the statute includes in the things constituting commencement of suit by declaration the service of a copy personally on defendant.[27] In Minnesota, the filing of complaints in an action by creditors against an insolvent corporation, exhibiting their claims against it, tolls the statute of limitations both as to it and its stockholders.[28] In Missouri, the filing of the petition with the clerk of the court before limitations have run is the bringing of a suit within the Code, though summons be not issued until after that time.[29] Un-

24. Galloy v. Sparrow, 166 Ill. App. 197. And see Miller v. Rich, 204 Ill. 444, 68 N. E. 488.

25. State v. Clark, 7 Ind. 468.

26. Cooley v. Maine, 163 Iowa, 117, 143 N. W. 431. And see Klingman v. Madison County, 161 Iowa 422, 143 N. W. 426.

In Louisiana, a plea of prescription filed in the Supreme Court will be overruled where it appears from the record that plaintiff's suit was instituted and defendant excepted to the demand and answered within the prescription period. Sharp v. McBride, 134 La. 249, 63 So. 892.

27. Wilton v. City of Detroit, 138 Mich. 67, 11 Detroit Leg. N. 467, 100 N. W. 1020.

28. London & N. W. American Mortg. Co. v. St. Paul Park Imp. Co., 84 Minn. 144, 86 N. W. 872. See also, Downer v. Union Land Co., 103 Minn. 392, 115 N. W. 207. The filing of an answer in proceedings under the Torrens Act by defendant, setting up a mechanic's lien, is not equivalent to an action to foreclose, and does not continue the lien in force beyond the period fixed by the statute of limitations. Reed v. Siddall, 94 Minn. 216, 102 N. W. 453.

29. State *ex rel.* Brown v. Wilson, 216 Mo. 215, 115 S. W. 549; McCormick v. Clopton, 150 Mo. App. 129, 130 S. W. 122, unless plaintiff directed the clerk not to issue until further orders; in which latter case the suit is to be treated as not commenced till a purpose to proceed with it is manifested by causing the summons to actually issue.

A suit in equity is commenced by the filing of the bill with intent to

der the Montana Code Civ. Proc., § 66, providing that civil actions are commenced by filing a complaint, a complaint to revive a judgment filed within six years confers jurisdiction, though the summons is not served within that time.[30] In Oregon, by statute, an action is commenced when the complaint is filed and summons served, and suit is commenced so as to stop limitations when defendant voluntarily appears in the action by demurring to the complaint.[31] Under the Texas statute the filing of the petition is the commencement of the suit if there is a *bona fide* intention of the plaintiff to prosecute the suit, and he uses reasonable diligence to have process issued and served.[32] In Washington, the date of the filing of a complaint marks the commencement of the action in so far as the limitations are concerned.[33] To constitute the

prosecute the same, if there is no unreasonable delay in the issue or service of the subpoena. Armstrong Cork Co. v. Merchants' Refrigerating Co., 184 Fed. 199, 107 C. C. A. 93, modifying judg. 171 Fed. 778 (C. C. A., Mo.).

Whether an action has been commenced within the statute is determined by whether plaintiff complied with Rev. St. 1909, § 1756, providing that the filing of a petition and suing out process shall be deemed the commencement of the action. Hinshaw v. Warren's Estate, 167 Mo. App. 365, 151 S. W. 497.

30. Haupt v. Burton, 21 Mont. 572, 55 Pac. 110, 69 Am. St. Rep. 698.

Pleading a lien on land by a judgment creditor, in an action by the executor to sell the land for the payment of debts, is not the commencement of an action, within Ohio Rev. St., § 6113. Ambrose v. Byrne, 61 Ohio St. 146, 55 N. E. 408.

In South Dakota, a reply, when filed, relates back to the commencement of the action, and may be filed after the expiration of the limitation period, where the action is commenced within that period. State v. Coughran, 19 S. D. 271, 103 N. W. 31.

31. Hawkins v. Donnerberg, 40 Or. 97, 66 Pac. 908. See also, Smith v. Day, 39 Or. 531, 64 Pac. 812, judg. aff'd 39 Or. 531, 65 Pac. 1055.

32. Wigg v. Dooley, 28 Tex. Civ. App. 61, 66 S. W. 306; City of Belton v. Sterling (Tex. Civ. App.), 50 S. W. 1027; Wood v. Mistretta, 20 Tex. Civ. App. 236, 49 S. W. 236; Wood v. Gulf, etc., Ry. Co., 15 Tex. Civ. App. 322, 40 S. W. 24; Gulf, etc., Ry. Co. v. Flatt (Tex. Civ. App.), 36 S. W. 1029; Hutcheson v. Chandler (Tex. Civ. App.), 104 S. W. 434.

The statute of limitations is suspended by the institution of a suit, service on defendant, and its appearance and answer. Forbes Bros. Teas & Spice Co. v. McDougle, Cameron & Webster (Tex. Civ. App.), 150 S. W. 745.

33. Lara v. Sandell, 52 Wash. 53, 100 Pac. 166; Blalock v. Condon, 51

"commencement of a suit" in equity in a federal court, which will stop the running of the statute of limitations, there must be the filing of a bill and the due issuance of a writ of subpoena, which must come to the hands of the serving officer with intent that it be served, and there must be a *bona fide* attempt to serve it, followed, if unsuccessful, by reasonable diligence to procure service through further or additional process.[34]

§ 299(1). Issuance and service of process—Issuance of process.

A suit in equity in a Federal court is commenced, so as to stop the running of limitations, by the suing out of the appropriate process and a *bona fide* attempt to serve it. *Bona fides* requires an effort to proceed according to law, and to employ the means which the law prescribes.[35] In Arkansas, where, in a suit to foreclose a mortgage, plaintiff suffered a nonsuit, but thereafter he caused a summons to be issued and served on the defendants, such issuance and service was equivalent to the commencement of a new

Wash. 604, 99 Pac. 733; Petree v. Washington Water Power Co., 64 Wash. 636, 117 Pac. 475; Service v. McMahon, 42 Wash. 452, 85 Pac. 33; Hayton v. Beason, 31 Wash. 317, 71 Pac. 1018; Cresswell v. Spokane County, 30 Wash. 620, 71 Pac. 195.

In Utah, an action is commenced by the filing of the complaint. Keyser v. Pollock, 20 Utah 371, 59 Pac. 87.

In West Virginia, where a judgment claim against a fraudulent grantor is impleaded in a suit attacking the fraudulent conveyance, limitations ceased to run against the judgment, though no answer has been filed asserting it. Davis v. Halstead, 70 W. Va. 572, 74 S. E. 725.

34. United States v. Miller, 164 Fed. 444 (C. C., Or.).

35. United States v. American Lumber Co., 85 Fed. 827, 29 C. C. A. 431, aff'g decree 80 Fed. 309 (C. C. A., Cal.). The issuance of a subpoena to be served outside the territorial jurisdiction of a federal court, and the service thereof, is a mere nullity, and not a commencement of the suit, which will stop the running of limitations. Id.

The issuance of a writ of *scire facias* to revive a judgment suspends the running of limitations against it for the purposes of the proceeding, and the fact that the judgment would have become ineffective for any purpose, by limitation, before the hearing, had the proceeding not been commenced, is no defense to a revival. Lafayette County v. Wonderly, 92 Fed. 313, 34 C. C. A. 360, aff'g judg. Wonderly v. Lafayette County, 77 Fed. 665 (C. C. A., Mo.).

suit within the statute.[36] Under the Kentucky statute, providing that an action shall be deemed to have been commenced at the date of the first summons issued in good faith, the filing of petition and issuing of summons against defendant stopped the running of the statute, though defendant was a nonresident, plaintiff city and its attorney being ignorant of that fact.[37] In Louisiana, prescription against an action to annul a judgment for fraud begins to run from the date of the service of the citation, and not from that of the filing of the suit.[38] Under the express provision of the Nebraska statute, an action was deemed commenced at the date of the summons which was served; under the Oklahoma statute, adopted from Indiana, a civil action was deemed commenced from the time of issuing summons.[39] In Texas, the issuance of a citation is the commencement of a suit in justices' courts.[40] In West Virginia, a suit begins with the issuance of the summons to answer the bill or declaration, and therefore the statute of limitations ceases to run at the date of the issue of the summons.[41] In North Carolina, under a rule that, when a summons issues, limitations are suspended, though the service is not made till later, a direction by the court that the owner of a judg-

36. Livingston v. New England Mortgage Security Co., 77 Ark. 379, 91 S. W. 752, under Kirby's Dig., § 5083.

37. Walston v. City of Louisville, 23 Ky. Law Rep. 1852, 66 S. W. 385, under Ky. St., § 2524. See also, as to the effect of the issuance of process: Lucas v. Commonwealth, 121 Ky. 423, 28 Ky. Law Rep. 372, 89 S. W. 292; Louisville & N. R. Co. v. Bowen, 18 Ky. Law Rep. 1099, 39 S. W. 31; Schwab v. Gutman, 9 Ky. Law Rep. (abstract) 765; Louisville & N. R. Co. v. Smith, 9 Ky. Law Rep. (abstract) 404; Ballou v. Wilmot, 9 Ky. Law Rep. (abstract) 774; Savings Bank of Louisville v. McAllister's Adm'r, 83 Ky. 149, 7 Ky. Law Rep. 81.

38. Duplessis v. Siewerd, 36 La. Ann. 779.

39. Schnell v. Jay, 4 Okl. 157, 46 Pac. 598. And see Greenamayer v. Coate, 12 Okl. 452, 72 Pac. 377.

40. Brown v. Been (Tex. Civ. App.), 54 S. W. 779; Moore v. Gulf, etc., Ry. Co. (Tex. Civ. App.), 46 S. W. 388. And see August Kern Barber Supply Co. v. Freeze, 96 Tex. 513, 74 S. W. 303.

41. Lawrence v. Winifrede Coal Co., 48 W. Va. 139, 35 S. E. 925; United States Blowpipe Co. v. Spencer, 46 W. Va. 590, 33 S. E. 342; Lambert v. Ensign Mfg. Co., 42 W. Va. 813, 26 S. E. 431.

ment against decedent be made a party to a suit to compel a sale of the judgment debtor's homestead to pay liens and that notice be issued to such judgment creditor effectually suspended limitations as against his judgment to the same extent as if a summons had been issued.[42]

§ 299(2). Delivery of process to officer.

The statute of limitations does not cease to run in favor of the holder of the legal title to land as against a suit by the United States to set aside the patent until he is made a party to the suit and process issued and placed in the hands of the marshal with a *bona fide* intent that it be served.[43] In Illinois, the issuance of a summons, at law, is deemed the commencement of the action, and is sufficient to prevent the running of the statute of limitations, notwithstanding it was never delivered to the sheriff for service.[44] An action is not commenced, within the meaning of the Iowa statute, by delivering the original notice for service to one who was not a sheriff or officer, and who did not serve it on any person on whom service was authorized, or by the delivery of it to the sheriff for service where, after it had been placed in the sheriff's

42. Town of Tarboro v. Pender, 153 N. C. 427, 69 S. E. 425.

Where summons is issued, but not given to an officer for service, and the suit is dismissed by plaintiff for want of service, with judgment against plaintiff for costs, no suit is commenced, within Shannon's Code Tenn., §§ 4445, 4446. East Tennessee Coal Co. v. Daniel, 100 Tenn. 65, 42 S. W. 1062.

Where an attorney received from a justice signed summons blanks, and filled one in with the proper entries for an action on a certain note, and delivered it to an officer on the last day of the period of limitations, and the officer served the paper two days thereafter, such proceedings were not sufficient to avoid the bar of limitations under Rev. St. Wis. 1898, § 4240. Johnson v. Turnell, 113 Wis. 468, 89 N. W. 515.

Where plaintiff made three successive attempts to serve defendant with summons in an action on a note commenced within the four years prescribed by Civ. Code Ariz. 1901, par. 2954, that it was over two years before defendant was found and served did not affect the suspension of the statute, caused by bringing the action. Bennett v. Ellison, 16 Ariz. 196, 141 Pac. 738.

43. United States v. Smith, 181 Fed. 545 (C. C., Or.).

44. Rich v. Scalio, 115 Ill. App. 166.

hands for service, he is unable to make service.[45] In Kentucky, the filing of a petition in the clerk's office, and the issuing of summons thereon, suspends the running of the statute of limitations, though the clerk may fail in his duty to see to the delivery of the summons to the sheriff.[46] In Michigan, the commencement of a suit consists of suing out the summons, and delivering or transmitting it to an officer, with the *bona fide* intention of having it served.[47] In Missouri, in a suit before a justice, the delivery of the writ to the constable to be served is the commencement of the action.[48] In New Jersey, an action is commenced when process, duly tested and issued, is put in the hands of the sheriff to be served.[49] In New York, where, in an action to recover money paid in excess of the legal interest under General Business Law, § 372, the summons, though delivered to the sheriff within a year after the cause of action accrued, was not served until after the year, the action must fail for failure to bring the action within the time limited.[50] Delivery in good faith of a summons from a justice court for service to a person incapable of making a valid

45. Lesure Lumber Co. v. Mutual Fire Ins. Co., 101 Iowa 514, 70 N. W. 761; Richardson v. Turner, 110 Iowa 318, 81 N. W. 593. And see Hawley v. Griffin, 121 Iowa 667, 92 N. W. 113.

46. Blackburn v. City of Louisville, 21 Ky. Law Rep. 1716, 55 S. W. 1075. But see Mullins v. Fidelity & Deposit Co. of Baltimore, Md., 30 Ky. Law Rep. 1077, 100 S. W. 256. Where plaintiff has filed his petition, and caused summons to issue, he could not be prejudiced by a mistake of the clerk. Casey c. Newport Rolling Mill Co., 156 Ky. 623, 161 S. W. 528.

47. Dedenbach v. City of Detroit, 146 Mich. 710, 13 Detroit Leg. N. 922, 110 N. W. 60.

48. Heman v. Larkin (Mo. App.), 70 S. W. 907.

49. County v. Pacific Coast Borax Co., 67 N. J. Law, 48, 50 Atl. 906.

An action is "commenced and sued" within the statute of limitations (3 Comp. St. 1910, p. 3162), § 1, when the summons is signed and sealed in good faith for immediate service, where that purpose is not afterwards abandoned. Wilson v. Clear, 85 N. J. Law 474, 89 Atl. 1031.

50. Landeker v. Property Security Co., 79 Misc. Rep. 157, 140 N. Y. Supp. 745, judg. aff'd 156 App. Div. 938, 141 N. Y. Supp. 1128. See Littlejohn v. Leffingwell, 34 App. Div. 185, 54 N. Y. Supp. 536, holding that mailing a summons on December 30th to an outgoing sheriff, who received it on January 1st, after his successor was entitled to the office, but before he had taken possession or served the certificate of his qualifica-

service is not an attempt to commence an action, within the Wisconsin statute, suspending limitations where an unsuccessful attempt to commence an action is made.[51]

§ 299(3). Service of process.

In Iowa, an action to subject property of a nonresident to the payment of a foreign judgment is commenced, within the statute of limitations, when the property is levied on under a writ of attachment, if not before, and the statute then ceases to run.[52] In Missouri, service of process in a suit against an executor on a demand against testator, made within two years after letters testamentary, stops the running of limitations, provided the service of process was within the time prescribed by the general statute of limitations.[53] In Nebraska, an action is not commenced within the meaning of the statute of limitations at the date of the issuance of the summons, unless such summons is served on the defendant; where a summons is issued but not served, and the defendant enters a voluntary appearance, the commencement of the action dates from the entry of the appearance.[54] Under the express

tion, is an attempt to commence an action, within section 399 of the Code Civ. Proc.

The owner of the premises and a contractor for work thereon are not joint contractors as to a subcontractor, or "otherwise united in interest," within Code Civ. Proc., § 399, providing that an attempt to commence an action is the commencement thereof against each defendant, when the summons is delivered to be served to officers of the county in which one of two codefendants, who are joint contractors or otherwise united in interest, resides. Martens v. O'Neill, 131 App. Div. 123, 115 N. Y. Supp. 260.

51. Moulton v. Williams, 101 Wis. 236, 77 N. W. 918, under Rev. St. 1898, § 4240, since that section applies to cases in which service may be made by publication of the summons.

52. Slater v. Roche, 148 Iowa 413, 126 N. W. 925, an action against a nonresident is not commenced until the completion of the process of service by publication, and, where the publication was not completed until after the running of the statute, a personal judgment could not be rendered, though the nonresident personally appeared after the claim was barred.

53. Knisely v. Leathe, 256 Mo. 341, 166 S. W. 257, under Rev. St. 1909, §§ 190-195.

54. Reliance Trust Co. v. Atherton, 67 Neb. 305, 96 N. W. 218, 93 N. W. 150; Hotchkiss v. Aukermann, 65 Neb. 177, 90 N. W. 949.

provisions of New York Code Civ. Proc., § 398, an action is commenced, for the purposes of the statute of limitations, when the summons is served.[55] Under Ohio Gen. Code, §§ 11230, 11231, providing that the date of the summons shall be deemed the commencement of an action, and an attempt to commence shall be equivalent to a commencement, where plaintiff diligently endeavors to procure service, there must have been a summons issued prior to the expiration of the period fixed by statute.[56] In Oregon, where in an action on an account, the complaint was filed and the summons delivered to the sheriff for service two days before the expiration of the statutory period, but no service was had or publication begun until ten months thereafter, the action was barred.[57] The Wisconsin statute fixes the service of the summons as a commencement of an action.[58] In Texas, in order to stop the running of the statute by the institution of a suit, not only must the petition be filed, but there must be shown a *bona fide* intention that the process shall at once be served upon the defendant.[59]

§ 299(4). Service on part of defendants.

The New York Code Civ. Proc., 398, providing that an action is commenced, within the statute of limitations, when the summons is served on defendant, "or on a codefendant who is a joint contractor or otherwise united in interest with him," applies to an action to determine the validity of a will under section 2653a,

Where all the parties are nonresidents, the issuance of an attachment and levy on real estate within four years after a fraudulent transfer will prevent the running of limitations, if the attachment proceedings are followed up with a creditors' bill. Coulson v. Galtsman, 1 Neb. (Unof.) 502.

55. Metz v. Metz, 45 Misc. Rep. 338, 90 N. Y. Supp. 340.

56. McLarren v. Myers, 87 Ohio St. 88, 100 N. E. 121. And see Baltimore & O. R. Co. v. Collins, 11 O. C. D. 334.

57. Dutro v. Ladd, 50 Or. 120, 91 Pac. 469. See Smith v. Day, 39 Or. 531, 64 Pac. 812, 65 Pac. 1055.

58. Gager v. Paul, 111 Wis. 638, 87 N. W. 875, under Rev. St. 1898, § 4239.

59. Faires v. Loessin (Tex. Civ. App.), 102 S. W. 924. A suit is not commenced in justice's court, so as to toll limitations, until the citation is issued. Hooks v. Gulf, etc., Ry. Co. (Tex. Civ. App.), 97 S. W. 516.

requiring such action to be commenced within two years after probate.[60] The service of a summons on one spouse in an action to enforce a mechanic's lien against community property is not the commencement of the action as to the other spouse, unless personal service is had on the latter within two years.[61] Under the South Carolina statute, an action is commenced on the day of issuing the summons, where the same was issued in good faith, and afterwards regularly returned as served on all the defendants, though one of the defendants was not actually served.[62]

§ 299(5). Substituted service.

The New York Code Civ. Proc., § 399, provides that "an attempt to commence an action in a court of record is equivalent to the commencement thereof, * * * within the meaning of each provision of this act which limits the time for commencing an action when the summons is delivered with the intent that it shall be actually served to the sheriff * * * followed within sixty days after the expiration of the time limited for the actual commencement of the action by personal service," or by the first publication. Substituted service, under sections 435, 437, being of equal force with the other methods in the support given to pro-

60. Croker v. Williamson, 208 N. Y. 480, 102 N. E. 588, aff'g order Croker v. Taylor, 154 App. Div. 930, 139 N. Y. Supp. 842. Reargument denied Croker v. Williamson, 209 N. Y. 591, 103 N. E. 1123.

Code Civ. Proc., § 398, also applies to an action on a partnership demand against the individual members. Bennett v. Watson, 21 App. Div. 409, 47 N. Y. Supp. 569. Partners are, as to a firm note, "joint contractors," Howell v. Dimock, 15 App. Div. 102, 44 N. Y. Supp. 271.

Vendor and purchaser in an executory contract for the sale of a lot are not "united in interest," so that an action brought against both to foreclose a mechanic's lien on a building erected by the purchaser will be deemed to have been commenced against the purchaser by service of the summons on his codefendant. Moore v. McLaughlin, 11 App. Div. 477, 42 N. Y. Supp. 256.

61. Powell v. Nolan, 27 Wash. 318, 68 Pac. 389, or by notice by publication within nine months after the filing of the complaint within two years; the action in the latter case being deemed to have been commenced on the filing of the complaint.

62. Montague v. Stelts, 37 S. C. 200, 15 S. E. 968, 34 Am. St. Rep. 736.

ceedings based thereon, is equivalent thereto, and, if had within the sixty days specified, will take the case out of the statute of limitations.[63] Acceptance of citation by a *curator ad hoc* of an absent defendant will not interrupt prescription as to the latter. The waiver allowed by Louisiana Code Prac., art. 177, can only be made by defendant personally, or an attorney whom he has employed.[64]

§ 299(6). Subsequent, alias, or pluries process.

Under the Kansas statute, where a petition is filed and summons issued thereon, though service is not obtained, but an *alias* summons is issued and properly served within sixty days, the action will be deemed to have been commenced when the petition was filed.[65] In Pennsylvania, where in an action on a note, a summons was issued within six years from maturity of the note and returned "Not found," and within six years from such return an *alias* summons was issued, and also returned "Not found," and a *pluries* summons was also returned served after six years from the return day of the original process, but within six years from the return of the *alias* summons, the action was not barred by limitations.[66] In Illinois, where a suit was begun and summons taken out, within the period of limitations, but was not put into the hands of the sheriff, nor was the declaration filed, and an *alias* summons, which was the one served on defendant, was not issued, nor was the declaration filed, until after the bar of the statute of

63. Clare v. Lockard, 122 N. Y. 263, 25 N. E. 391, 9 L. R. A. 547, 2 N. Y. Supp. 646, 16 N. Y. St. Rep. 739; Clark v. Lockard, 13 Civ. Proc. R. 278, 21 Abb. N. C. 173.

64. Hill v. Barlow, 6 Rob. (La.) 142. Service by handing citation to a person in charge of defendant's plantation held sufficient to interrupt prescription. Sharp v. McBride, 134 La. 249, 63 So. 892.

65. German Ins. Co. v. Wright, 6 Kan. App. 611, 49 Pac. 704, under Gen. St. 1889, § 4097.

Under Code Civ. Proc., § 19 (Gen. St. 1909, § 5612), where an alias summons was issued and served more than 60 days after confession of a motion to set aside a summons, the action was not begun until the date of the alias summons. Brock v. Francis, 89 Kan. 463, 131 Pac. 1179.

66. Bovaird & Seyfang Mfg. Co. v. Ferguson, 215 Pa. 235, 64 Atl. 513. And see Rees v. Clark, 213 Pa. 617, 63 Atl. 364; *In re* O'Neill's Estate, 29 Pa. Super. Ct. 415; Magaw v. Clark, 6 Watts (Pa.) 528.

limitations had arisen, the suit was begun by the issuing of the first summons, and was not barred.[67] In Michigan, the failure to take out the second summons for more than two months after the return of the first summons was held to interrupt the continuity of the action.[68] Under the New York Code Civ. Proc., § 2883, providing that, where it appears by the return of the constable to whom a summons was issued for service that it was not served, a second summons may be issued, and, on a like return thereof, a third summons may be issued, and that the second or third summons, as the case may be, relates back to the time when the first summons was issued, a third summons does not relate back unless the first and second were not served on defendant.[69] In Virginia, the suing out of the writ being the commencement of the action, where a writ issued contrary to the statute is quashed, and a new writ ordered, and served, the commencement of the action, so far as relates to the statute of limitations, dates from the issuance of the new writ.[70] In the Federal courts it has been held that, where there was a *bona fide* attempt by the marshal to make the service of a subpoena, and reasonable diligence was used in that behalf and in the issuance and service of the *alias* subpoena, for the purpose of arresting the running of limitations, the suit was commenced on the date of the filing of the bill.[71]

67. McKee v. Allen, 94 Ill. App. 147. See also Schroeder v. Merchants' & Mechanics' Ins. Co., 104 Ill. 71.

68. Colling v. McGregor, 144 Mich. 651, 15 Detroit Leg. N. 310, 108 N. W. 87. And see Johnson v. Mead, 58 Mich. 67, 24 N. W. 665.

69. Finan v. O'Dowd, 6 App. Div. 268, 40 N. Y. Supp. 969, 75 St. Rep. 371.

And see Quick v. Leigh, 59 Hun 616, 12 N. Y. Supp. 616, 20 Civ. Proc. R. 147.

70. Noel v. Noel, 93 Va. 433, 25 S. E. 242.

In Louisiana, it has been held that, though the first citation was defective, the original service of papers upon the mayor of a town in an action against the town, interrupted prescription on the claim. Gueble v. Town of Lafayette, 118 La. 494, 43 So. 63.

71. United States v. Miller, 164 Fed. 444 (C. C., Or.). See Armstrong Cork Co. v. Merchants' Refrigerating Co., 171 Fed. 778 (C. C., Mo.), wherein proceedings were held insufficient to constitute commencement of suit to foreclose a mechanics' lien, within the required time.

§ 300. Want of jurisdiction.

The running of the limitation of actions against New York City by Greater New York Charter, § 261, is not suspended under Code of Civil Procedure, § 405, by the commencement of an action in the City Court, of which it had no jurisdiction.[72] In Georgia, a suit brought in a court having jurisdiction of the subject matter though not of the person is not void, and, when the petition therein is seasonably served, tolls the statute.[73] A receiver appointed and residing in another State cannot sue in Texas; and hence, where a suit was brought by such a receiver in Texas, solely by virtue of the foreign appointment, and the insolvent filed an amended complaint on the termination of the receivership, limitation ran against the cause of action until the amended complaint was filed.[74] In Louisiana, the fact that the court in which a suit was brought had not jurisdiction does not defeat the effect of bringing suit as an interruption of prescription;[75] but a citation judicially held to be absolutely null, because defendant, a married woman, was not previously authorized to stand in judgment in the absence of her husband, is not sufficient to interrupt prescription running in favor of defendant.[76] In Texas, where the trial court has absolutely no jurisdcition under the pleadings, the filing of the petition cannot interrupt the running of limitations on the cause of action.[77]

§ 301(1). Defects as to parties in general.

The commencement of an action against one person or corporation upon a cause of action against another person or corporation

72. Gaines v. City of New York, 215 N. Y. 533, 109 N. E. 594, aff'g judg. 142 N. Y. Supp. 401, 156 App. Div. 789, aff'g judg. 137 N. Y. Supp. 964, 78 Misc. Rep. 126.

73. Atlanta, K. & N. Ry. Co. v. Wilson, 119 Ga. 781, 47 S. E. 366.

74. Kellogg v. Lewis, 16 Tex. Civ. App. 668, 40 S. W. 323.

75. Sorrell v. Laurent, 27 La. Ann. 70; Levy v. Calhoun, 34 La. Ann. 413. See Ealer v. Lodge, 36 La. Ann. 115.

76. Bertrand v. Knox, 39 La. Ann. 431, 2 So. 63.

77. Pecos & N. T. Ry. Co. v. Rayzor (Tex.), 172 S. W. 1103.

Where a petition is susceptible of two constructions, it is to be construed so as to give the court jurisdiction of the suit, so that filing the petition would interrupt the running of limitations. Id.

does not arrest the running of the statute of limitations against the latter.[78] The institution of an action against a concern alleged to be a corporation, but which was in fact a partnership, was not the commencement of an action against the individual owners and operators of such concern, so as to suspend the running of limitations as to them.[79] Where a corporation, knowing itself to be the wrongdoer which plaintiff intended to sue, answers ostensibly for a corporation mistakenly sued, the statute of limitations will cease to run from the time the real defendant appears and answers in the name of the nominal defendant.[80] Under the Tennessee statute, permitting ejectment against one in actual possession or against one claiming or exercising acts of ownership, the action is maintainable against one in possession as servant by a claimant having no knowledge of the relationship, and stops the running of limitations, and complainant may make the owner a party.[81] Where an action was brought against a corporation, but individuals forming a partnership having the name of the corporation appeared, stating the partnership and its members and answered by demurrer and general denial within two years from the time of the accrual of the cause of action, the action was pending from the time of the answer, within the statute of limitations.[82]

78. Proctor v. Wells Bros. Co. of New York, 262 Ill. 77, 104 N. E. 186, aff'g judg. 181 Ill. App. 468.

A mere change in parties, plaintiff or defendant, does not of itself change the cause of action, so as to make the defense of the statute of limitations available. Chesapeake & O. Ry. Co. v. Fish, 170 Ill. App. 359; Houghland v. Avery Coal & Mining Co., 152 Ill. App. 573, 246 Ill. 609, 93 N. E. 40; Stephens v. Collison, 249 Ill. 225, 94 N. E. 664.

79. Geneva Cooperage Co. v. Brown, 30 Ky. Law Rep. 272, 98 S. W. 279.

The bringing of action on a cause of action belonging to none of the parties does not stop the running of the statute. Boughner v. Sharp, 144 Ky. 320, 138, S. W. 375. The running of the statute of a year for an action for death is not stopped by the commencement of an action by the public administrator, under a reference to him of the estate, premature under Ky. St., § 3905. Fentzka's Adm'r v. Warwick Const. Co., 162 Ky. 580, 172 S. W. 1060.

80. Boehmke v. Northern Ohio Traction Co., 88 Ohio St. 156, 102 N. E. 700.

81. De Garmo v. Prater, 125 Tenn. 497, 146 S. W. 144.

82. Law Reporting Co. v. Texas Grain & Elevator Co. (Tex. Civ. App.), 168 S. W. 1001.

§ 301(2). Amendment of defects.

Where a person was sued by the name of John Doe, and his real name was thereafter substituted in the complanit, but not before the statute of limitations had run against the claim, recovery could nevertheless be had, since the defendant was a party to the action from its commencement.[83] A mere change in a party to a suit does not of itself change the cause of action, or ground of recovery, and, unless the cause of action is a new one, an amended declaration is not subject to the statute of limitations.[84] An amendment of a petition in an action for damages, by adding the name of a party plaintiff, made more than two years after the cause of action accrued, relates back to the date of the commencement of the action, and the cause of action is not for that reason barred by

Where a suit was brought against a corporation, which filed an answer in the corporate name, and subsequently an individual appeared and answered, alleging that she did business in the name of the corporation, and that there was no corporation, the commencement of the action stopped the running of limitations. Pickering Mfg. Co. v. Gordon (Tex. Civ. App.), 168 S. W. 14.

See also, as to defects of parties: Southern Contract Co.'s Assignee v. Newhouse, 119 Ky. 704, 23 Ky. Law Rep. 2141, 66 S. W. 730; Prichard v. McCord-Collins Co., 30 Tex. Civ. App. 582, 71 S. W. 303; McCord-Collins Co. v. Pritchard, 37 Tex. Civ. App. 418, 84 S. W. 388.

83. Hoffman v. Keeton, 132 Cal. 195, 64 Pac. 264. See also Fox v. Hale & Norcross Silver Min. Co. (Cal.), 53 Pac. 32.

84. Wilcke v. Henrotin, 241 Ill. 169, 89 N. E. 329, the amendment to the declaration by inserting the word "as" after the name of the defendant and before the word "receiver" did not set up a new cause of action, and was not subject to the statute of limitations.

Where an action is brought against several defendants as joint *tort feasors*, and, after the running of limitations, plaintiff amends his declaration by eliminating the names of two of the defendants, the amended declaration does not present such a new cause of action as to be subject to the bar of the statute. Ross v. Shanley, 185 Ill. 390, 56 N. E. 1105, aff'g judg. 86 Ill. App. 144.

Service of summons upon the proper party defendant, though under the wrong name, is sufficient to toll the statute. The power of amendment, however, does not extend to the length of substituting another defendant in lieu of the defendant answering and before the court, since such other defendant can be brought in only by summons, and the suit is not begun as to him until summons for him is issued. Proctor v. Wells Bros. Co. of New York, 262 Ill. 77, 104 N. E. 186, aff'g judg. 181 Ill. App. 468.

limitations.[85] In an action against the American Fire Insurance Company, the omission of the word "fire" in the petition and summons does not render the action ineffectual to stop the running of limitations, though the omission is not cured by amendment until after the expiration of the statutory period.[86] Where limitations have run, amendments introducing a new cause of action, or bringing in a new party or changing the capacity in which he is sued, will not be allowed.[87] Where plaintiff, doing business under the name "Kansas City View Company," a nonexistent corporation, brought suit in that name, it was proper for the court, after the running of limitations, to permit an amendment of the title substituting plaintiff's individual name, followed by the words "doing business as Kansas City View Company."[88] A

85. Hucklebridge v. Atchison, etc., Ry. Co., 66 Kan. 443, 71 Pac. 814.

86. American Fire Ins. Co. v. Bland, 19 Ky. Law Rep. 287, 40 S. W. 670.

An amendment striking out a middle initial in the name of defendant sued on a guardian's bond does not change the character of the action so as to render limitations available that were not so at the commencement of the action. State v. Reilly, 89 Md. 162, 43 Atl. 58.

Where a corporation, sued by the wrong name, has answered to the merits, that an amendment inserting its correct name was granted after the cause of action sued on would be barred by limitations was immaterial. Sentell v. Southern Ry. Co., 67 S. C. 229, 45 S. E. 155.

87. Mumma v. Mumma, 246 Pa. 407, 92 Atl. 504; Girardi v. Laquin Lumber Co., 232 Pa. 1, 81 Atl. 63, and where suit was brought against the "Laquin Lumber Company, a corporation," the record cannot be amended, after limitations had run, to name as defendant a partnership composed of six persons trading as the Laquin Lumber Company.

Where a corporation known as the copper "works" was sued by the wrong name, copper "company," an amendment to the record by striking out the word "company" and inserting the word "works," should have been allowed. Wright v. Eureka Tempered Copper Co., 206 Pa. 274, 55 Atl. 978.

88. Bowen v. Buckner, 171 Mo. App. 384, 157 S. W. 829.

An amendment by which one of several codefendants sued as partners, was dropped from the case, but leaving the case to stand against the remaining defendants as partners, does not change the cause of action, so as to permit the intervention of the statute of limitations. St. Charles Savings Bank v. Edwards, 243 Mo. 553, 147 S. W. 978.

Where a complaint against the M. Mill Company, a corporation, was amended by substituting as defendant V. J. H., doing business under the

petition against one defendant alone, filed on appeal more than two years after the filing of the original suit, and stating that this defendant was an equal joint owner of the lot sold and liable for one-half of the commission sued for, did not set up a new cause of action, and hence was not defeated by a plea of limitations.[89]

§ 302. Defects or irregularities in process or service.

Where, on a *praecipe* in trespass, the prothonotary by mistake issued a summons in assumpsit, the court may allow the record to be amended to show an action in trespass after the statutory period within which to bring such action had expired.[90] Where the city clerk was the proper officer on whom to serve the declaration in

name of the M. Mill Company, the statute of limitations was no defense where V. J. H. and the mill company were the same person. Manistee Mill Company v. Hobdy, 165 Ala. 411, 51 So. 871.

89. Grayson v. Hollingsworth (Tex. Civ. App.), 148 S. W. 1135.

Where defendant corporation, sued in the wrong name, voluntarily answered to the merits, it could not plead limitations after plaintiff had corrected the misnomer. Forbes Bros. Teas & Spice Co. v. McDougle, Cameron & Webster (Tex. Civ. App.), 150 S. W. 745.

See also, as to amendments of defects as to parties:

Iowa.—Padden v. Clark, 124 Iowa, 94, 99 N. W. 152, wherein an amendment was held not so materially different from the original cause of action as to render limitations a defense.

Neb.—Haas v. Mutual Life Ins. Co. of New York, 90 Neb. 808, 134 N. W. 937, wherein the amendment of a petition, summons, and return after the expiration of the period of limitation, in an action commenced within the period, was held proper and to relate back to the service of the summons.

Tex.—Martinez v. Dragna (Tex. Civ. App.), 73 S. W. 425; Texas Midland R. R. v. Cardwell (Tex. Civ. App.), 67 S. W. 157; Grand Lodge A. O. U. W. of Texas v. Bollman, 22 Tex. Civ. App. 106, 53 S. W. 829; Bickford v. Refugio Land & Irrigation Co. (Tex. Civ. App.), 143 S. W. 1188.

90. Wilkinson v. Northeast Borough, 215 Pa. 486, 64 Atl. 734.

Where, in an action on a municipal lien, a *scire facias*, issued within the time prescribed by law, proved ineffective because not served according to law, and the statutory period closed with the return of the writ, the lien was wholly lost, and defendant's general appearance to an *alias scire facias*, issued after the expiration of the statutory period, could not supply the existence of a legal claim to support such a *scire facias*, without which any action of the court would be a mere nullity. City of Scranton v. Genet, 232 Pa. 272, 81 Atl. 335.

an action against the city for personal injuries, service on a clerk in the office of the corporation counsel was a nullity, and did not stay the running of the statute of limitations.[91] Where a judicial demand has been served on the right person and conveys full information, a slight error in the description of the person intended to be sued which could mislead no one will not prevent its interrupting the prescription of the claim demanded.[92] Where, in an action for money only, the *praecipe* omitted to direct the clerk of the court to indorse on the summons the amount for which judgment would be taken on default, and the summons served bore no such indorsement, an amendment, by leave of court, allowing such indorsement and the service of an *alias* summons, will not relate back to the time of the original summons so as to stop the running of limitations.[93] A rendition of a judgment in favor of the receiver of an insolvent national bank against a guardian for the amount of an assessment on shareholders to pay debts, on which execution was directed to issue against the estate of the ward, even if construed as a personal judgment, if obtained by fraud or rendered without service of process, was equivalent to no judgment, and the statute of limitations would apply.[94] A summons issued in the name of an agent not an attorney, and requiring service of an answer on him, was allowed to be amended, where the statute of limitations would defeat the claim if the amendment were denied.[95]

91. Boyle v. City of Detroit, 152 Mich. 248, 15 Detroit Leg. N. 136, 115 N. W. 1056.

92. Babin v. Lyons Lumber Co., 132 La. 873, 61 So. 855.

Prescription is not interrupted by the service of citation on Saturday afternoon, a day of public rest, under Acts 1904, No. 3. Rady v. Fire Ins. Patrol of New Orleans, 126 La. 273, 52 So. 491.

The service of citation with a copy of the petition interrupts prescription, though the citation does not bear the impress of the seal of the court. King v. Guynes, 118 La. 344, 42 So. 959; Adams v. Guynes, 118 La. 348, 42 So. 960.

Prescription is not interrupted where the citation is not signed by the clerk, as provided by Code Prac., art. 179. Schwartz v. Lake, 109 La. 1081, 34 So. 96.

93. Elmen v. Chicago, B. & Q. R. Co., 75 Neb. 37, 105 N. W. 987.

94. Clark v. Ogilvie, 111 Ky. 181, 23 Ky. Law. Rep. 552, 63 S. W. 429.

95. Weir v. Slocum, 3 How. Prac.

§ 303. Defects or irregularities in pleadings or other proceedings.

The filing of a complaint defective only in that it is neither signed by the plaintiff nor his attorney tolls the running of the statute.[96] A petition, in a widow's action for the negligent killing of her husband by a train, was sufficient to constitute a commencement of the action within the statute of limitations, though it failed to allege that deceased was a nonresident and that by the laws of the State of his residence the widow was the only person entitled to bring the action.[97] The fact that when plaintiff corporation sued on notes it was not legally entitled to sue under the statute, because it had not paid its franchise tax, would not cause the action to be barred by the four-year limitation, though before an amended petition was filed showing compliance with the statute more than four years had elapsed since maturity of the last note.[98] An action was commenced when the petition was filed and the summons issued, although the petition was not vertified until subsequently.[99] Where an original petition, while it would have been open to attack by a special demurrer, was good on general demurrer, it stopped the running of limitations.[1]

(N. Y.) 397. See also, as to defects or irregularities in process or service: Bruen v. Bokee, 4 Denio (N. Y.) 56, 47 Am. Dec. 239; Vandenburgh v. Biggs, 3 How. Prac. (N. Y.) 316.

96. Canadian Bank of Commerce v. Leale, 14 Cal. App. 307, 111 Pac. 759.

97. Robinson v. Chicago, R. I. & P. Ry. Co., 90 Kan. 426, 133 Pac. 537.

Where a passenger on a train was injured, the filing of a petition praying a recovery of damages for such injuries stopped the running of limitations, even though the petition was defective in failing to allege that the action was maintainable only under a foreign statute, and that fact was supplied by an answer filed long after the period of limitation would have expired had not the petition been filed. Houston & T. C. R. Co. v. Fife (Tex. Civ. App.), 147 S. W. 1181.

98. Clegg v. Roscoe Lumber Co. (Tex. Civ. App.), 161 S. W. 944, under Rev. St. 1911, art. 7399.

99. City of Dayton v. Hirth, 121 Ky. 42, 27 Ky. Law Rep. 1209, 87 S. W. 1136.

1. Schmidt v. Brittain (Tex. Civ. App.), 84 S. W. 677.

And see generally as to defects or irregularities in pleadings or other proceedings: Chambers v. Talladega Real Estate & Loan Ass'n, 126 Ala. 296, 28 So. 636; Missouri Pac. Ry. Co. v. McCarthy, 97 Mo. 214, 11 S. W. 52; Howard v. Windom, 86 Tex. 560, 26 S. W. 483; Smith v. Farmers' Loan & Trust Co., 21 Tex. Civ. App. 170, 51 S. W. 515.

§ 304. Intervention or bringing in new parties.

The addition of a coplaintiff does not change the cause of action.[2] As to persons becoming parties to a pending suit by intervention, the suit is to be regarded as having been commenced at the time of their intervention.[3] Where an action in tort for injury to personalty is barred, it is thereafter too late for one sued on a contract to vouch another into court liable to him in tort.[4] A proceeding to contest a will commenced within two years after probate inures to the benefit of a party who intervenes after the statutory period, and the statute of limitations is not available as a defense to the intervening petition.[5] Where a mortgagee was not made a party to a suit to foreclose a mechanic's lien until after the expriation of the year for filing the complaint, the statutory bar was complete, and it was not avoided by the filing of an amended complaint making the mortgagee a party.[6] Where a father sues to recover for the death of his son, and it appears that the son died within a few hours after the accident and was unmarried, the record may be amended, after one year from the death of the son, by adding the name of his mother as a party plaintiff.[7] Under the Civil Code of Lower Canada, giving in case of wrongful death a right to decedent's consort and his ascendant and descendant relations, but only for a year after his death, to recover therefor, but providing that no more than one action can be brought in behalf of those entitled to indemnity, and that the judgment shall determine the proportion of such indemnity which each is to receive, the right given such persons being individual and personal, and the action being several, and not joint, the action being brought

2. Price v. Goodrich, 141 Ill. App. 568; Cousar v. Heath, 80 S. C. 466, 61 S. E. 973. Nor the substitution of a third party for the original plaintiff. State Bank of Gothenburg v. Carroll, 81 Neb. 484, 116 N. W. 276.

3. Mason v. City of Chicago, 163 Ill. 351, 45 N. E. 567.

4. Raleigh & G. R. Co. v. Western & A. R. Co., 6 Ga. App. 616, 65 S. E. 586.

5. Maurer v. Miller, 77 Kan. 92, 93 Pac. 596; Lyons v. Berlau, 67 Kan. 426, 73 Pac. 52.

6. Ward v. Yarnelle, 173 Ind. 535, 91 N. E. 7.

7. Sontum v. Mahoning & S. Ry. & Light Co., 226 Pa. 230, 75 Atl. 189.

by the consort only, the others may not be made plaintiffs after the end of the year.[8] New parties cannot be brought in after the statute of limitations has become a bar.[9] Where parties are brought in by amendment, the suit as to them is begun when the amendment is filed.[10]

8. Johnson v. Phoenix Bridge Co., 197 N. Y. 316, 90 N. E. 953, modifying order 118 N. Y. Supp. 88.

9. Bender v. Penfield, 235 Pa. 58, 83 Atl. 585; Wright v. Eureka Tempered Copper Co., 206 Pa. 274, 55 Atl. 978.

10. Hiller v. Schulte, 184 Mo. App. 42, 167 S. W. 461, in a suit to enforce a mechanic's lien, new parties defendant cannot be brought in by amendment so as affect their rights after the expiration of 90 days from the filing of the lien.

See also, as to intervention or bringing in new parties:

Ark.—Less v. English, 75 Ark. 288, 87 S. W. 447.

Cal.—John Bollman Co. v. S. Bachman & Co., 16 Cal. App. 589, 117 Pac. 690; Harrison v. McCormick, 122 Cal. 651, 55 Pac. 592.

Ga.—Taylor v. James, 109 Ga. 327, 34 S. E. 674.

Ill.—Houghland v. Avery Coal & Mining Co., 246 Ill. 609, 93 N. E. 40, aff'g judg. Stevenson v. Same, 152 Ill. App. 565; Hougland v. Same, Id. 573; Knickerbocker v. Benes, 195 Ill. 434, 63 N. E. 174, aff'g judg. 93 Ill. App. 305; Mosier v. Flanner-Miller Lumber Co., 66 Ill. App. 630.

Kan.—Anderson v. Atchison, etc., R. Co., 71 Kan. 453, 80 Pac. 946; Western Sash & Door Co. v. Heiman, 65 Kan. 5, 68 Pac. 1080; Toby v. Allen, 3 Kan. 399.

Ky.—Nunn v. City of Louisville, 31 Ky. Law Rep. 1293, 105 S. W. 119; Walker's Ex'r v. Luxon's Adm'r, 138 Ky. 14, 127 S. W. 489; City of Louisville v. Jacob, 27 Ky. Law Rep. 175, 84 S. W. 722; City of Louisville v. Kohnhorst's Adm'x, 25 Ky. Law Rep. 532, 76 S. W. 43.

La.—Geisenberger v. Cotton, 116 La. 651, 40 So. 929.

Mich.—Casserly v. Waite, 124 Mich. 157, 7 Detroit Leg. N. 143, 82 N. W. 841, 83 Am. St. Rep. 320.

Miss.—State v. Woodruff, 81 Miss. 456, 33 So. 78.

Mo.—Rumsey & Sikimeier Co. v. Pieffer, 108 Mo. App. 486, 83 S. W. 1027; City of St. Joseph *ex rel.* Forsee v. Baker, 86 Mo. App. 310; Jaicks v. Sullivan, 128 Mo. 177, 30 S. W. 890.

N. Y.—Brinkerhoof v. Bostwick, 34 Hun 352.

R. I.—Taylor v. Superior Court, 30 R. I. 560, 76 Atl. 644.

Tex.—Trinity &. V. Ry. Co. v. Doke (Tex. Civ. App.), 152 S. W. 1174; El Paso & S. W. R. Co. v. Harris & Liebman (Tex. Civ. App.), 110 S. W. 145; Bean v. Dove, 33 Tex. Civ. App. 377, 77 S. W. 242; Cable v. Jackson, 16 Tex. Civ. App. 579, 42 S. W. 136.

Wash.—Northwest Bridge Co. v. Tacoma Shipbuilding Co., 36 Wash. 333, 78 Pac. 996.

W. Va.—Jackson's Adm'r v. Hull, 21 W. Va. 601.

Wis.—Webster v. Pierce, 108 Wis. 407, 83 N. W. 938; Levy v. Wilcox, 96 Wis. 127, 70 N. W. 1109.

§ 305. Substitution of parties.

The amendment of the petition in an action by the sole surviving parent in her individual capacity to recover for the death of her unmarried son, without stating new facts, setting up the Employer's Liability Act April 22, 1908, is not the commencement of a new action within the two-year limitation prescribed by that statute.[11] Where an action to enforce pledged securities was properly brought by the pledgor before limitations had run, and pending suit, the securities were absolutely assigned to the pledgee, who was thereupon substituted as plaintiff by an amendment of the complaint after the limitation period had expired, the amendment

11. Missouri, K. & T. Ry. Co. v. Wulf, 226 U. S. 570, 33 Sup. Ct. 135, 57 L. Ed. 355, aff'g judg. 192 Fed. 919, 113 C. C. A. 665.

A recovery under the Employer's Liability Act April 22, 1908, and supplements, for the death of an employee of a railroad company, is for the benefit of the surviving spouse and children, and, if none, for the parents, and the personal representative is only a nominal party; and where decedent left no widow or children, but parents, the parents, under the act and Purdon's Dig. Pa. (13th Ed.), p. 3238, were the sole beneficiaries, and where they brought in their individual names an action within the statutory time they could be substituted as plaintiffs in their representative capacity. Bixler v. Pennsylvania R. Co., 201 Fed. 553 (U. S. D. C.).

Change of the capacity in which plaintiff sued for the wrongful killing of his son from that of an individual to that of his son's administrator, as required by Civ. Code Cal., § 1970, is not the commencement of a new suit, and was properly allowed by amendment, under Rev. St., § 954 (U. S. Comp. St. 1901, p. 696), though the time within which a new action could have been brought had expired. Reardon v. Balaklala Consol. Copper Co., 193 Fed. 189 (U. S. C. C.).

Under the Tennessee statute relating to actions for wrongful death (Mill. & V. Code, §§ 3130-3134), a suit in behalf of one beneficiary is a different suit from one in behalf of another, and an amendment of a declaration changing the beneficiary is in effect the beginning of a new suit, and is subject to a plea of limitations as such. Atlanta, K. & N. Ry. Co. v. Hooper, 92 Fed. 820, 35 C. C. A. 24. But see, to the contrary, Hooper v. Atlanta, K. & N. Ry. Co., 107 Tenn. 712, 65 S. W. 405.

Where the court allowed the petition to be amended by substitution of the name of the State, such amendment made no change in the cause of action, or, in fact, in the real parties; it related back to the commencement of the action for the purposes of the statute of limitations. McDonald v. State of Nebraska, 101 Fed. 171, 41 C. C. A. 278.

did not constitute a new action, and the action was therefore not barred.[12] A mere change in a party to a suit does not of itself change the cause of action, unless the cause of action is a new one, and the amended declaration is not subject to the statute of limitations.[13] An amendment of a petition substituting one party for another as plaintiff relates to the institution of the action and suspends limitations as to the substituted plaintiff from the time the action was begun and not from the date of the amendment.[14] Where plaintiff sued for injuries, and pending the suit the defendant corporation leased its property to another corporation, which assumed all obligations and liabilities of defendant, and plaintiff was allowed to amend her writ by substituting the lessee corporation, the fact that at the time of the amendment the action would have been barred by limitations, if no suit had been brought, did not prevent the allowance of the amendment.[15] Under New York Code Civ. Proc., § 723, authorizing the court at any stage of the action, in furtherance of justice, to amend any process or pleading, by adding or striking out the name of a person as a party, or by correcting a mistake in any respect, or where the amendment does not change substantially the claim or defense, by conforming the pleading or other proceeding to the facts proven, the cause of action for wrongful death being given decedent's

12. Merced Bank v. Price, 9 Cal. App. 177, 98 Pac. 383.

13. Beresh v. Supreme Lodge Knights of Honor, 255 Ill. 122, 99 N. E. 349, aff'g judg. 166 Ill. App. 511; Haldeman v. Schuh, 109 Ill. App. 259.

14. Harlan v. Loomis, 92 Kan. 398, 140 Pac. 845; Service v. Farmington Sav. Bank, 62 Kan. 857, 62 Pac. 670. A mere order of revivor is sufficient to prevent the running of limitations. McLean v. Parker, 88 Kan. 717, 129 Pac. 1140; Kansas City, etc., R. Co. v. Menager, 59 Kan. 687, 54 Pac. 1043.

15. McLaughlin v. West End St. Ry. Co., 186 Mass. 150, 71 N. E. 317.

Under the Massachusetts statute, where, pending an action against partners on a contract, one of them dies, and the administrators of his estate appear to defend, the court may permit the plaintiff to amend by discontinuing as to the other defendant, and then allowing the action to proceed against the administrators, though at the time of such discontinuance the special statute of limitations would have run against such administrators, but for their appearance. Philadelphia & R. Coal & Iron Co. v. Butler, 181 Mass. 468, 63 N. E. 949.

spouse individually and personally, and she having sued as his administratrix, amendment may be allowed before trial, though after expiration of the year for bringing the action, by striking from the summons and complaint the words indicating the bringing of the action in a representative capacity.[16] An amendment will not be allowed after a cause of action against an executor for decedent's negligence has been barred, making the executor a defendant individually as the sole devisee under decedent's will.[17]

16. Johnson v. Phoenix Bridge Co., 197 N. Y. 316, 90 N. E. 953, modifying order 133 App. Div. 807, 118 N. Y. Supp. 88. See Bowen v. Phoenix Bridge Co., 134 App. Div. 22, 118 N. Y. Supp. 93; Smith v. Phoenix Bridge Co., 134 App. Div. 909, 118 N. Y. Supp. 95.

Under the rule that the court may permit an amendment changing the capacity in which defendants are sued even if an action is barred by limitations, plaintiff, in a suit against defendants as executors, may, after the running of limitations, convert the action into an action against defendants individually as to those defendants personally served with process, but not as to a defendant not served. Helling v. Boss, 121 N. Y. Supp. 1013.

Where one was sued as trustee of the estate of a decedent for injuries sustained by plaintiff while examining a building being erected by defendant as trustee of the estate, an amendment of the complaint, whereby the action proceeded as against the defendant individually, did not amount to the bringing in of a new party, and hence limitations ceased to run against the action when the suit was first commenced and not when the amendment was made. Boyd v. United States Mortgage & Trust Co., 187 N. Y. 262, 79 N. E. 999, aff'g judg. 95 N. Y. Supp. 1115, 88 N. Y. Supp. 289, 94 App. Div. 413. And see Kerrigan v. Peters, 108 App. Div. 292, 95 N. Y. Supp. 723.

17. Bender v. Penfield, 235 Pa. 58, 83 Atl. 585.

Where a widow sued a railroad company in her own right to recover for the death of her husband, killed in New Jersey while in the employ of defendant company, it was too late to amend by adding the name of the widow as executrix of the deceased, as required by the New Jersey statute, after limitations had become a bar. La Bar v. New York, S. & W. R. Co., 218 Pa. 261, 67 Atl. 413.

In an action to recover damages for personal injuries against an electric railway company, a motion to amend by striking out the name of defendant and substituting the name of another as its lessee will be denied, where limitations have become a bar. Coyne v. Lakeside Electric Ry. Co., 227 Pa. 496, 76 Atl. 224.

See also, as to substitution of parties.

Ariz.—Motes v. Gila Val., G. & N. Ry. Co., 8 Ariz. 50, 68 Pac. 532.

Ark.—Buck v. Davis, 64 Ark. 345, 42 S. W. 534.

Colo.—Cochrane v. Parker, 12 Colo. App. 169, 54 Pac. 1027.

Fla.—Todd v. Louisville & N. R.

§ 306. Effect as to persons not parties.

The bringing of a suit for the cancellation of a patent to land does not suspend the running of limitations in favor of a grantee, who purchased prior to the suit, until he is made a party.[18] An action by a tenant of an abutting owner against an elevated railroad for injuries to easements, brought within twenty years after the commencement of the operation of the railroad, does not interrupt the running of limitations against the owner, and he cannot after the expiration of more than twenty years from the commencement of the operation of the railroad maintain an action for injury to easements.[19] Where, in a suit to foreclose a mortgage, one who had purchased the property was not made a party, the suit having been commenced against the mortgagors within the period of limitations, the purchaser could not avail himself of limitations as against the foreclosure.[20] Where a second mortgagee was not made

Co. (Fla.), 67 So. 41, in an agent's action in tort for injury to his principal's shipment, a refusal to permit the principal to be substituted as plaintiff after limitations had run was not error.

Mo.—Gewe v. Hanszen, 85 Mo. App. 136; McFaul v. Haley, 166 Mo. 56, 65 S. W. 995.

Neb.—Tecumseh Nat. Bank v. McGee, 61 Neb. 709, 85 N. W. 949.

Pa.—Comrey v. East Union Tp., 202 Pa. 442, 51 Atl. 1025.

18. United States v. Cooper, 217 Fed. 846.

Where suit is brought by a mail contractor, who has sublet a portion of his contract, to recover extra pay for services "dispensed with" before termination of the contract, the statute of limitations ceases to run as to all the parties interested at the time of the bringing of the suit. Garman v. United States, 34 Ct. Cl. (U. S.) 237.

19. Goldstrom v. Interborough Rapid Transit Co., 115 App. Div. 323, 100 N. Y. Supp. 911.

Under Code Civ. Proc., § 1937, providing that, after judgment against joint debtors, an action may be maintained against one or more of the defendants, who were not summoned in the original action, to procure a judgment charging his property with the sum remaining unpaid on the original judgment, in an action under the statute, a defense that the action was not brought within six years after the original cause of action had accrued was not available, where it did not exist when the former action was brought. Hofferberth v. Nash, 50 Misc. Rep. 328, 98 N. Y. Supp. 684, rev'd 117 App. Div. 284, 102 N. Y. Supp. 317. And see Kramer v. Schatzkin, 27 Misc. Rep. 206, 57 N. Y. Supp. 803, 29 Civ. Proc. R. 86.

20. Livingston v. New England Mortgage Security Co., 77 Ark. 379, 91 S. W. 752.

a party to a suit to foreclose the first mortgage, and, at the time suit was brought to foreclose the second mortgage, the time limited by law for suing on the first mortgage had fully elapsed, the second mortgagee was entitled to plead the statute of limitations as a complete defense to any rights acquired under the first mortgage.[21] An action for personal injuries, brought within the period of limitations, does not save the right to sue another company for the same injury, by a new writ, after limitations have run, even though the liabilities of defendants in both suits are indentical.[22] An action by a landlord to foreclose a lien on his tenant's property does not interrupt the running of limitations in favor of a purchaser of the property who was not made a party.[23] The fact that a note has been reduced to judgment has no effect on the defense of limitations, as against one not a party to the action therein.[24]

§ 307(1). Amendment of pleadings in general.

The original declaration, by fiction of law, relates back to the beginning of the suit. The amended declaration, if it presents a restatement of the cause of action set out in the original declara-

An action by a ward against her former guardian and a surety on his bond to falsify and surcharge the guardian's account was insufficient to toll the statute of limitations as against the heirs and administrator of a deceased surety not a party to the suit. Wallace v. Swepston, 74 Ark. 520, 86 S. W. 398, 109 Am. St. Rep. 94.

21. Frates v. Sears, 144 Cal. 246, 77 Pac. 905.

Under the California statutes, the action of the original plaintiff in partition is for the benefit of all persons interested in the property included in the complaint, and all such parties are actors from the commencement of the suit, so that the running of limitations as to them is stopped by the filing of the complaint. Adams v. Hopkins, 144 Cal. 19, 77 Pac. 712.

22. Peterson v. Delaware River Ferry Co., 190 Pa. 364, 30 Pittsb. Leg. J. (N. S.) 26, 42 Atl. 955.

23. Meyer Bros. Drug Co. v. Fry (Tex. Civ. App.), 48 S. W. 752.

24. Damon v. Leque, 17 Wash. 573, 50 Pac. 485, 61 Am. St. Rep. 927.

See also, as to effect as to persons not parties:

Iowa.—Clark v. Staber (Iowa), 98 N. W. 560, following Polly v. Walker, 60 Iowa 86, 14 N. W. 137.

Kan.—Demple v. Hofman, 9 Kan. App. 881, 57 Pac. 234, rev'g judg. 55 Pac. 558.

La.—E. J. Gay & Co. v. Suthon, Man. Unrep. Cas. 442; Segura v. Labit, Man. Unrep. Cas. 296.

Tex.—Houston & T. C. Ry. Co. v. McFadden. 91 Tex. 194, 40 S. W. 216.

tion, also relates back to the beginning of the suit. If the cause of action set out in the amended declaration is a new cause of action and not a mere restatement of the cause of action set out in the original declaration, the amended declaration does not relate back to the beginning of the suit so as to stop the running of the statute, but is the equivalent of a new suit on such cause of action, and the statute continues to run until the amended declaration is filed.[25] The statute of amendments does not cause an amendment to a pleading to relate back to the commencement of a suit, so as to defeat the bar of the statute of limitations against the cause stated in the amendment, but whether such amendment relates back is to be determined by the common-law rule against departures in pleading.[26] Within the statute of limitations, an amended complaint sets up a new cause of action composed of the right of plaintiff and the obligation, duty, or wrong of defendant, where the new allegation deprives defendant of any defense he had to the original action, where the evidence that would have proved the original complaint will not prove the new, where the new allegations, if in reply, would have amounted to a departure, where the amended complaint sets up a title not before asserted, or where a judgment on the first complaint would be no bar to a judgment on the amended complaint.[27] Under the settled law of Pennsylvania, a new cause of action cannot be introduced into a pending suit by amendment after the statute of limitations has run against it.[28]

25. *Ill.*—Klugman v. Sanitary Laundry Co., 141 Ill. App. 422; Walters v. City of Ottawa, 240 Ill. 259, 88 N. E. 651, rev'g judg. 144 Ill. App. 379; Lee v. Republic Iron & Steel Co., 241 Ill. 372, 89 N. E. 655.

Tex.—Texas & N. O. R. Co. v. McDonald (Tex. Civ. App.), 120 S. W. 494; Newsom & Johnson v. Sharman (Tex. Civ. App.), 119 S. W. 912.

26. Nelson v. First Nat. Bank, 139 Ala. 578, 36 So. 707, 101 Am. St. Rep. 52.

27. Raley v. Evansville Gas & Electric Light Co., 45 Ind. App. 649, 90 N. E. 783, rehearing denied, 91 N. E. 571. In general, an amendment to a complaint will not be permitted when it will operate to defeat a plea of limitations. Indiana Union Traction Co. v. Pring, 50 Ind. App. 566, 96 N. E. 180.

28. Mitchell Coal & Coke Co. v. Pennsylvania R. Co., 181 Fed. 403, dismissed for want of jurisdiction, 183 Fed. 908 (U. S. C. C., Pa.).

Where, in an action for the death of plaintiff's husband, the negligence

Under a special statute limiting the filing of claims for damages from the discontinuance of streets to six years, claims filed in time cannot, after the period of limitations has expired be increased.[29]

§ 307(2). Amendment restating original cause of action.

As a general rule, where an amendment to a petition, declaration, or complaint sets up no new matter or claim, but merely amplifies and restates with more certainty or in a different form the cause of action set out in the original pleading, it relates back to the commencement of the suit, and the statute of limitations is arrested at that point.[30] One of the tests for determining whether

charged is shown to be unfounded, plaintiff cannot amend by setting up a different theory charging different negligence after limitations have become a bar. Martin v. Pittsburg Rys. Co., 227 Pa. 18, 75 Atl. 837, 26 L. R. A. (N. S.) 1221.

29. *In re* Spuyten Duyvil Road, 116 N. Y. Supp. 857.

See also, as to amendment of pleadings in general:

Ark.—St. Louis, etc., Ry. Co. v. Love, 74 Ark. 528, 86 S. W. 395.

Fla.—Todd v. Louisville & N. R. Co. (Fla.), 67 So. 84.

Ga.—Roberts v. Leak, 108 Ga. 806, 33 S. E. 995; Southern Ry Co. v. Horine, 121 Ga. 386, 49 S. E. 285.

Ill.—Heffron v. Rochester German Ins. Co., 220 Ill. 514, 77 N. E. 262, aff'g judg. 119 Ill. App. 566, aff'g judg. Rochester German Ins. Co. v. Heffron, 89 Ill. App. 659.

Iowa.—Jones v. Clark, 34 Iowa 590.

Kan.—Anthony Inv. Co. v. Arnett, 63 Kan. 879, 64 Pac. 1024.

Ky.—City of Louisville v. Robinson's Ex'r, 119 Ky. 908, 27 Ky. Law Rep. 375, 85 S. W. 172; Norman v. Central Kentucky Asylum, 26 Ky. Law Rep. 71, 80 S. W. 781, denying rehearing 25 Ky. Law Rep. 1846, 79 S. W. 189; Stengel v. Preston, 89 Ky. 616, 11 Ky. Law Rep. 976, 13 S. W. 839.

Mo.—Long v. Long, 141 Mo. 352, 44 S. W. 341.

Tenn.—Crofford v. Cothran, 34 Tenn. (2 Sneed) 492.

Tex.—Prichard v. Foster (Tex. Civ. App.), 170 S. W. 1077; Cotton v. Barnes (Tex. Civ. App.), 167 S. W. 756; Schmidt v. Brittain (Tex. Civ. App.), 84 S. W. 677; Southern Cold Storage & Produce Co. v. A. F. Dechman & Co. (Tex. Civ. App.), 73 S. W. 545; Stewart v. Robbins, 27 Tex. Civ. App. 188, 65 S. W. 899; Hanrick v. Gurley, 93 Tex. 458, 54 S. W. 347, judg. modified 93 Tex. 458, 56 S. W. 330, modifying judg. (Tex. Civ. App.) 48 S. W. 994.

Va.—Morrison's Ex'r v. Householder's Adm'r, 79 Va. 627.

W. Va.—Kuhn v. Brownfield, 34 W. Va. 252, 12 S. E. 519, 11 L. R. A. 700.

30. *U. S.*—Bankers' Surety Co. v. Town of Holly, 219 Fed. 96; Illinois Surety Co. v. United States, 215 Fed. 334; Patillo v. Allen-West Commission Co., 131 Fed. 680, 65 C. C. A.

an additional count states a different cause of action from the ori-

508; Whalen v. Gordon, 95 Fed. 305, 37 C. C. A. 70; Marshalltown Stone Co. v. Louis Drach Const. Co., 123 Fed. 746; Crotty v. Chicago Great Western Ry. Co., 169 Fed. 593, 95 C. C. A. 91 (C. C. A., Iowa).

Ala.—Alabama Consol. Coal & Iron Co. v. Heald, 168 Ala. 626, 53 So. 162; Byrd v. Hickman, 167 Ala. 351, 52 So. 426, where the amendment referred to the same transaction, property, title, and parties as the original; Gaines v. Birmingham Ry., etc., Co., 164 Ala. 6, 51 So. 238, where the amendment referred to the same injury; St. Louis & S. F. R. Co. v. Hooker, 161 Ala. 312, 50 So. 56; Dallas Mfg. Co. v. Townes, 162 Ala. 630, 50 So. 157; Central of Georgia Ry. Co. v. Williams, 163 Ala. 119, 50 So. 328; Central of Georgia Ry. Co. v. Styrgis, 159 Ala. 222, 48 So. 810; Illinois Car & Equipment Co. v. Walch, 132 Ala. 490, 31 So. 470.

Ark.—Western Coal & Mining Co. v. Corkille, 96 Ark. 387, 131 S. W. 963; Smith v. Scott, 92 Ark. 143, 122 S. W. 501; Price v. Greer, 89 Ark. 300, 116 S. W. 676, judg. modified on rehearing, 118 S. W. 1009.

Ariz.—Kain v. Arizona Copper Co., 14 Ariz. 566, 133 Pac. 412; Arizona Eastern R. Co. v. Old Dominion Copper Mining & Smelting Co., 14 Ariz. 209, 127 Pac. 713; Hagenauer v. Detroit Copper Mining Co., 14 Ariz. 74, 124 Pac. 803; Bourdreaux v. Tocson Gas, etc., Co., 13 Ariz. 361, 114 Pac. 547.

Cal.—Ruiz v. Santa Barbara Gas. & Electric Co., 164 Cal. 188, 128 Pac. 330, where the amended complaint merely added matters essential to make the original cause of action complete; Union Lumber Co. v. J. W. Schouten & Co., 25 Cal. App. 80, 142 Pac. 910, where the amended count was on a different theory from the original complaint.

Del.—Gatta v. Philadelphia, B. & W. R. Co., 1 Boyce (24 Del.) 293, 76 Atl. 56, limitations cannot be invoked in bar of an action as based on an amended declaration, if deemed reasonable and allowed by the court.

Ill.—Maier v. Chicago City Ry., 166 Ill. App. 500; Beresh v. Supreme Lodge Knights of Honor, 255 Ill. 122, 99 N. E. 349, aff'g judg. 166 Ill. App. 511; Johnson v. Perkins, 167 Ill. App. 611; Lyons v. Sampsell, 168 Ill. App. 542; Christensen v. Oscar Daniels Co., 170 Ill. App. 59; Gassman v. Hetzel, 175 Ill. App. 404; Neroni v. Inland Steel Co., 178 Ill. App. 246, where the gist of the action was the same in the original and the amended declaration; McInerney v. Western Packing & Provision Co., 154 Ill. App. 559, judg. aff'd 249 Ill. 240, 94 N. E. 519; Asplund v. Conklin Const. Co., 154 Ill. App. 164; Jacobson v. Duffy, 154 Ill. App. 505; Bober v. City of Chicago, 155 Ill. App. 561; Joerg v. Atchison, etc., Ry. Co., 152 Ill. App. 229, a change in the form of the action from tort to contract does not constitute the setting up of a new cause of action where the claim is the same, governed and controlled by the same facts; Wilcke v. Henrotin, 146 Ill. App. 481, judg. aff'd 241 Ill. 169, 89 N. E. 329; Lee v. Republic Iron & Steel Co., 148 Ill. App. 585, judg. aff'd 89 N. E. 655; Monahan v. Fidelity Mut. Life Ins. Co., 242 Ill. 488, 90 N. E. 213, a change from covenant to assumpsit does not

ginal count, and is therefore barred by the statute of limitations,

amount to the commencement of a new suit; Maegerlein v. City of Chicago, 141 Ill. App. 414, judg. aff'd 237 Ill. 159, 86 N. E. 670; Byrne v. Marshall Field & Co., 142 Ill. App. 72, judg. aff'd 237 Ill. 384, 86 N. E. 748.

Ind.—Chicago & E. R. Co. v. Dinius, 180 Ind. 596, 103 N. E. 652; United States Health & Accident Ins. Co. v. Emerick, 55 Ind. App. 591, 103 N. E. 435; Harrod v. Bisson, 48 Ind. App. 549, 93 N. E. 1093; Ft. Wayne Iron & Steel Co. v. Parsell, 49 Ind. App. 565, 94 N. E. 770; Terre Haute & I. R. Co. v. Zehner, 166 Ind. 149, 76 N. E. 169; Springfield Engine & Thresher Co. v. Michener, 23 Ind. App. 130, 55 N. E. 32; Shroyer v. Pittenger, 31 Ind. App. 158, 67 N. E. 475.

Iowa.—Blake v. City of Bradford (Iowa), 151 N. W. 74; Knight v. Moline, etc., Ry. Co., 160 Iowa 160, 140 N. W. 839; Gordon v. Chicago, etc., Ry. Co., 129 Iowa 747, 106 N. W. 177.

Ky.—Cincinnati, etc., Ry. Co. v. Goode, 163 Ky. 60, 173 S. W. 329; Jones v. Scott, 5 Ky. Law Rep. (abstract) 858.

Md.—State v. Chesapeake Beach Ry. Co., 98 Md. 35, 56 Atl. 385.

Mass.—Regan v. Keyes, 204 Mass. 294, 90 N. E. 847.

Mich.—Pratt v. Montcalm Circuit Judge, 105 Mich. 499, 63 N. W. 506.

Minn.—Gilbert v. Gilbert, 120 Minn. 45, 138 N. W. 943.

Mo.—Bowen v. Buckner, 171 Mo. App. 384, 157 S. W. 829, amendments are liberally allowed to save a cause from the statute when the cause of action is not totally changed; Cytron v. St. Louis Transit Co., 205 Mo. 692, 104 S. W. 109; Bricken v. Cross, 163 Mo. 449, 64 S. W. 99.

Mont.—McAuley v. Casualty Co. of America, 39 Mont. 185, 102 Pac. 586; Clark v. Oregon Short Line R. Co., 38 Mont. 177, 99 Pac. 298.

Neb.—Witt v. Old Line Bankers' Life Ins. Co., 92 Neb. 763, 139 N. W. 639; Duffy v. Scheerger, 91 Neb. 511, 136 N. W. 724; First Nat. Bank v. Cooper, 91 Neb. 624, 136 N. W. 1023; McCague Savings Bank v. Croft, 87 Neb. 770, 128 N. W. 504, where the original petition contained two causes of action, which were improperly joined, and one of them was eliminated by an amended petition; Bush v. Tecumseh Bank, 64 Neb. 451, 90 N. W. 236; Chicago, etc., R. Co. v. Young, 67 Neb. 568, 93 N. W. 922; Tomson v. Iowa State Traveling Men's Ass'n, 88 Neb. 399, 129 N. W. 529.

N. J.—Duffy v. McKenna, 82 N. J. Law 62, 81 Atl. 1101.

Okl.—Z. J. Fort Produce Co. v. Southwestern Grain & Produce Co., 26 Okl. 13, 108 Pac. 386.

Pa.—Puritan Coal Mining Co. v. Pennsylvania R. Co., 237 Pa. 420, 85 Atl. 426. And see Barnett v. Cain, 51 Pa. Super. Ct. 642; Collins v. Philadelphia & R. Ry. Co., 244 Pa. 210, 90 Atl. 575.

Tex.—Maple v. Smith (Tex. Civ. App.), 166 S. W. 1196; Collin County Nat. Bank v. Turner (Tex. Civ. App.), 167 S. W. 165; Texarkana, etc., Ry. Co. v. Casey (Tex. Civ. App.), 172 S. W. 729; Lilly v. Yeary (Tex. Civ. App.), 152 S. W. 823; Eastern Ry. Co. of New Mexico v. Ellis (Tex. Civ. App.), 153 S. W. 701; Ft. Worth & D. C. Ry. Co. v. Mata-

is whether the same evidence will support the different counts.[31] In determining whether an amendment states a different or a new cause of action from that set forth in the original pleading the nature of the action in general must be considered.[32] The general rule above set forth has been applied by the courts in actions on contract,[33] actions for injuries to the person,[34] actions for causing

dor Land & Cattle Co. (Tex. Civ. App.), 150 S. W. 461; Texas & P. Ry. Co. v. Myers (Tex. Civ. App.), 151 S. W. 337; Western Union Tel. Co. v. Smith (Tex. Civ. App.), 146 S. W. 332; Galveston, etc., Ry. Co. v. Affleck (Tex. Civ. App.), 147 S. W. 288.

W. Va.—Shires v. Boggess, 72 W. Va. 109, 77 S. E. 542.

Wis.—Dittgen v. Racine Paper Goods Co., 164 Fed. 85 (C. C., Wis.).

31. Lakin v. South Side Elevated R. Co., 178 Ill. App. 76; Wasson v. Boland, 136 Mo. App. 622, 118 S. W. 663.

32. *Ala.*—Townes v. Dallas Mfg. Co., 154 Ala. 612, 45 So. 696.

Ark.—Gannon v. Moore, 83 Ark. 196, 104 S. W. 139.

Cal.—Nellis v. Pacific Bank, 127 Cal. 166, 59 Pac. 830.

D. C.—Columbia Heights Realty Co. v. MacFarland, 31 App. D. C. 112, condemnation proceedings; Beasley v. Baltimore & P. R. Co., 27 App. D. C. 595.

Ill.—Connell v. Crosby, 210 Ill. 380, 71 N. E. 350; Liebold v. Green, 69 Ill. App. 527; Bennett v. Baird, 67 Ill. App. 422.

Me.—Doe v. Littlefield, 99 Me. 317, 59 Atl. 438.

Mass.—Cogswell v. Hall, 185 Mass. 455, 70 N. E. 461.

N. C.—Woodcock v. Bostic, 128 N. C. 243, 38 S. E. 881.

Tex.—Ferguson v. Morrison (Tex. Civ. App.), 81 S. W. 1240; Cox v. Patten (Tex. Civ. App.), 66 S. W. 64; St. Louis Type Foundry v. Taylor, 27 Tex. Civ. App. 349, 65 S. W. 677; Orange Mill Supply Co. v. Goodman (Tex. Civ. App.), 56 S. W. 700.

33. *U. S.*—Patillo v. Allen-West Commission Co., 131 Fed. 680, 65 C. C. A. 508 (C. C. A., Ark.).

Cal.—Calloway v. Oro Min. Co., 5 Cal. App. 191, 89 Pac. 1070; Ball v. Lowe, 1 Cal. App. 228, 81 Pac. 1113; Frost v. Witter, 132 Cal. 421, 64 Pac. 705, 84 Am. St. Rep. 53; Stockton Combined Harvester & Agricultural Works v. American Fire Ins. Co., 121 Cal. 182, 53 Pac. 573.

Ga.—Sanders v. Allen, 135 Ga. 173, 68 S. E. 1102.

Ind.—Mitchelltree School Tp. of Martin County v. Carnahan, 42 Ind. App. 473, 84 N. E. 520.

Iowa.—Taylor v. Taylor, 110 Iowa 207, 81 N. W. 472.

Kan.—Bradley v. Pinney, 77 Kan. 763, 93 Pac. 585.

N. H.—Seely v. Manhattan Life Ins. Co., 72 N. H. 49, 55 Atl. 425.

Tex.—Green v. Loftus (Tex. Civ. App.), 132 S. W. 502; Booth v. Houston Packing Co. (Tex. Civ. App.), 105 S. W. 46; Texas & N. O. R. Co. v. Clippenger (Tex. Civ. App.), 106 S. W. 155; Borden v. Le Tulle Mercantile Co. (Tex. Civ. App.), 99 S. W. 128; Taylor v. Silliman (Tex.

death,[35] actions for slander or libel,[36] actions for injuries to or

Civ. App.), 108 S. W. 1011; El Paso & S. W. R. Co. v. Harris & Liebman (Tex. Civ. App.), 110 S. W. 145; Burton-Lingo Co. v. Beyer, 34 Tex. Civ. App. 236, 78 S. W. 248; Goodwin v. Simpson (Tex. Civ. App.), 136 S. W. 1190; Gilliland v. Ellison (Tex. Civ. App.), 137 S. W. 168; Schauer v. Schauer (Tex. Civ. App.), 138 S. W. 145; Jones v. Thompson (Tex. Civ. App.), 138 S. W. 623.

Wis.—Meinshausen v. A. Gettelman Brewing Co., 133 Wis. 95, 113 N. W. 408, 13 L. R. A. (N. S.) 250.

U. S.—Smith v. Atlantic Coast Line R. Co., 210 Fed. 761.

34. *Ala.*—Freeman v. Central of Georgia Ry. Co., 154 Ala. 619, 45 So. 898; Atlanta & B. Air Line Ry. v. Wheeler, 154 Ala. 530, 46 So. 262; Mobile Light & R. Co. v. Bell, 153 Ala. 90, 45 So. 56; Southern Ry. Co. v. Cunningham, 152 Ala. 147, 44 So. 658.

D. C.—District of Columbia v. Frazer, 21 App. D. C. 154.

Ill.—Carlin v. City of Chicago, 262 Ill. 564, 104 N. E. 905, rev'g judg. 177 Ill. App. 89; Horstman v. Staver Carriage Co., 153 Ill. App. 130; Ratner v. Chicago City Ry. Co., 233 Ill. 169, 84 N. E. 201; Lake Shore & M. S. Ry. Co. v. Enright, 227 Ill. 403, 81 N. E. 374, aff'g judg. 129 Ill. App. 223; McAndrews v. Chicago, etc., Ry. Co., 222 Ill. 232, 78 N. E. 603, aff'g judg. Chicago, etc., Ry. Co. v. McAndrews, 124 Ill. App. 166; Gilmore v. City of Chicago, 224 Ill. 490, 79 N. E. 596, rev'g judg. City of Chicago v. Gilmore, 125 Ill. App. 13; North Chicago St. Ry. Co. v. Aufmann, 221 Ill. 614, 77 N. E. 1120, 112 Am. St. Rep. 207; Town of Cicero v. Bartelme, 114 Ill. App. 9, judg. aff'd 212 Ill. 256, 72 N. E. 437; Chicago City Ry. Co. v. McMeen, 206 Ill. 108, 68 N. E. 1093, aff'g Judg. 102 Ill. 318; Chicago City Ry. Co. v. Leach, 182 Ill. 359, 55 N. E. 334, rev'g judg. 80 Ill. App. 354; Illinois Cent. R. Co. v. Weiland, 179 Ill. 609, 54 N. E. 300, aff'g judg. 67 Ill. App. 332; Griffin Wheel Co. v. Markus, 180 Ill. 391, 54 N. E. 206, aff'g judg. 79 Ill. App. 82; Illinois Cent. R. Co. v. Souders, 178 Ill. 585, 53 N. E. 408, 79 Ill. App. 41; Swift & Co. v. Foster, 163 Ill. 50, 44 N. E. 837, aff'g judg. 55 Ill. App. 280; Waters v. City of Ottawa, 175 Ill. App. 130.

Ind.—Indianapolis St. Ry. Co. v. Fearnaught, 40 Ind. App. 333, 82 N. E. 102; Cleveland, etc., Ry. Co. v. Bergschicker, 162 Ind. 108, 69 N. E. 1000.

Iowa.—Benson v. City of Ottumwa, 143 Iowa 349, 121 N. W. 1065; Russell v. Chicago, R. I. & P. Ry. Co., 160 Iowa 503, 141 N. W. 1077; Bacon v. Iowa Cent. Ry. Co., 157 Iowa 493, 137 N. W. 1011.

Kan.—Taylor v. Atchison, etc., Ry. Co., 64 Kan. 888, 68 Pac. 691; Missouri Pac. Ry. Co. v. Moffatt, 60 Kan. 113, 55 Pac. 837, 72 Am. St. Rep. 343.

Ky.—Williamson's Adm'r v. Norfolk & W. R. Co., 160 Ky. 158, 169 S. W. 613; Louisville & N. R. Co. v. Pointer's Adm'r, 113 Ky. 952, 24 Ky. Law Rep. 772, 69 S. W. 1108.

Mich.—Brown v. Detroit United Ry., 179 Mich. 404, 146 N. W. 278.

Neb.—Johnson v. American Smelting & Refining Co., 80 Neb. 250, 114 N. W. 144, judg. vacated on rehearing 116 N. W. 517.

wrongful dealings with property,[37] actions to enforce liens,[38] actions

R. I.—Chobanian v. Washburn Wire Co., 33 R. I. 289, 80 Atl. 394.

Tex.—Houston Chronicle Pub. Co. v. McDavid (Tex. Civ. App.), 173 S. W. 467; Ft. Worth & R. G. Ry. Co. v. Robertson (Tex. Civ. App.), 121 S. W. 202; Texas & N. O. R. Co. v. Clippenger (Tex. Civ. App.), 106 S. W. 155; Johnson v. Texas Cent. R. Co., 42 Tex. Civ. App. 604, 93 S. W. 433; Gulf, etc., Ry. Co. v. O'Neill, 32 Tex. Civ. App. 411, 74 S. W. 960; Caswell v. Hopson (Tex. Civ. App.), 47 S. W. 54; The Oriental v. Barclay, 16 Tex. Civ. App. 193, 41 S. W. 117.

Va.—Wise Terminal Co. v. McCormick, 107 Va. 376, 58 S. E. 584.

35. *U. S.*—Cincinnati, etc., Ry. Co. v. Gray, 101 Fed. 623, 41 C. C. A. 535, 50 L. R. A. 47.

Ala.—Alabama Consol. Coal & Iron Co. v. Heald, 154 Ala. 580, 45 So. 686; Woodstock Iron Works v. Kline, 149 Ala. 391, 43 So. 362; Nashville, etc., Ry. v. Hill, 146 Ala. 240, 40 So. 612.

Cal.—Barr v. Southern California Edison Co., 24 Cal. App. 22, 140 Pac. 47.

Del.—Philadelphia, B. & W. R. Co. v. Gatta (Del.), 85 Atl. 721.

Ga.—Atlanta, K. & N. Ry. Co. v. Smith, 1 Ga. App. 162, 58 S. E. 106.

Ill.—Byrne v. Marshall Field & Co., 142 Ill. App. 72, judg. aff'd 237 Ill. 384, 86 N. E. 748; Devine v. Chicago City Ry. Co., 262 Ill. 484, 104 N. E. 826; aff'g judg. 171 Ill. App. 349; South Chicago City Ry. Co. v. Kinnare, 216 Ill. 451, 75 N. E. 179, aff'g judg. 117 Ill. App. 1; Wolf v. Collins, 196 Ill. 281, 63 N. E. 638, aff'g judg. 94 Ill. App. 518.

Kan.—Robinson v. Chicago, R. I. & P. Ry. Co., 90 Kan. 426, 133 Pac. 537; Mott v. Long, 90 Kan. 110, 132 Pac. 998; Cunningham v. Patterson, 89 Kan. 684, 132 Pac. 198.

Ky.—Louisville & N. R. Co. v. Greenwell's Adm'r, 155 Ky. 799, 160 S. W. 479.

Md.—State v. Chesapeake Beach Ry. Co., 98 Md. 35, 56 Atl. 385.

Mich.—City of Detroit v. Hosmer, 125 Mich. 634, 7 Detroit Leg. N. 655, 85 N. W. 1.

Mo.—Walker v. Wabash R. Co., 193 Mo. 453, 92 S. W. 83.

N. Y.—Miller v. Erie R. Co., 109 App. Div. 612, 96 N. Y. Supp. 244.

N. C.—Lassiter v. Norfolk & C. R. Co., 136 N. C. 89, 48 S. E. 642.

Pa.—McArdle v. Pittsburg Rys. Co., 41 Pa. Super. Ct. 162; Herbstritt v. Lackawanna Lumber Co., 212 Pa. 495, 61 Atl. 101.

Tenn.—Love v. Southern Ry. Co., 108 Tenn. 104, 65 S. W. 475, 55 L. R. A. 471.

Tex.—St. Louis, etc., Ry. Co. v. Smith (Tex. Civ. App.), 171 S. W. 512; Texas & P. Ry. Co. v. Eberhart (Tex. Civ. App.), 40 S. W. 1060.

36. *Ky.*—Vest v. Norman, 1 Ky. Law Rep. (abstract) 317, action for slander.

Miss.—Yazoo & M. V. R. Co. v. Rivers, 93 Miss. 557, 46 So. 705, slander.

Mo.—Courtney v. Blackwell, 150 Mo. 245, 51 S. W. 668, action for slander.

S. C.—Bell v. Floyd, 64 S. C. 246, 42 S. E. 104, action for slander.

Tex.—Dickson v. Lights (Tex. Civ. App.), 170 S. W. 834, action for libel.

37. *Ala.*—Nashville, etc., Ry. v.

to contest the probate of wills,[39] and to amendments affecting the form of action or relief.[40]

§ 307(3). Amendment introducing new cause of action.

Where an amendment sets forth a new cause of action, limitation may be pleaded to the new matter.[41] Where an amended de-

Garth, 155 Ala. 311, 46 So. 583; Floyd v. Wilson, 171 Ala. 139, 54 So. 528.

Ga.—McGregor v. Witham, 126 Ga. 702, 56 S. E. 55.

Ill.—Chicago North Shore St. Ry. Co. v. Payne, 192 Ill. 239, 61 N. E. 467.

Iowa.—Anderson v. Atcheson, 132 Iowa 744, 110 N. W. 335.

Kan.—Fox v. Turner, 85 Kan. 146, 116 Pac. 233; Green v. Turner, 85 Kan. 877, 116 Pac. 234; Higman v. Quindaro Tp., 91 Kan. 673, 139 Pac. 403; Emporia Nat. Bank v. Layfeth, 63 Kan. 17, 64 Pac. 973.

Neb.—Gourley v. Prokop, 71 Neb. 607, 100 N. W. 949; rehearing 99 N. W. 243, denied.

Tex.—Kingsbury v. Phillips (Tex. Civ. App.), 142 S. W. 73; Rotan Grocery Co. v. Missouri, K. & T. Ry. Co. of Texas (Tex. Civ. App.), 142 S. W. 623; Hitson v. Hurt (Tex. Civ. App.), 101 S. W. 292; Parlin & Orendorff Co. v. Glover (Tex. Civ. App.), 99 S. W. 592; Worsham v. Vignal, 14 Tex. Civ. App. 324, 37 S. W. 17.

38. *Cal.*—Lemon v. Hubbard, 10 Cal. App. 471, 102 Pac. 554.

Ill.—Joseph N. Eisendrath Co. v. Gebhardt, 222 Ill. 113, 78 N. E. 22, aff'g decree 124 Ill. App. 325.

Ky.—City of Louisville v. Selvage, 26 Ky. Law Rep. 479, 66 S. W. 376.

Mo.—Mann v. Schroer, 50 Mo. 306; Woodson v. Schroer, 50 Mo. 308.

Neb.—Merrill v. Wright, 54 Neb. 517, 74 N. W. 955.

Tex.—Sexton Rice & Irrigation Co. v. Sexton (Tex. Civ. App.), 106 S. W. 728.

39. Hoffman v. Steffey, 10 Kan. App. 574, 61 Pac. 822; *In re* Sullivan's Estate, 40 Wash. 202, 82 Pac. 297, 111 Am. St. Rep. 895.

40. If an amendment to a complaint is not a departure from the original complaint, the fact that the former was based on a statute and the latter framed under the common law would not prevent the amendment from relating back to the complaint. Alabama Consol. Coal & Iron Co. v. Heald, 154 Ala. 580, 45 So. 686.

Where a petition in a broker's action for commissions alleged express contract, exceptions are properly sustained to paragraphs in an amended petition filed after limitations had run alleging conduct inducing plaintiff to believe that defendant was employing him. Prichard v. Foster (Tex. Civ. App.), 170 S. W. 1077.

41. *U. S.*—Hills & Co. v. Hoover, 211 Fed. 241; Alessandrelli v. Arbogast, 209 Fed. 126; United States v. Dwight Mfg. Co., 210 Fed. 79, 85; Weighel v. United States, 47 Ct. Cl. (U. S.) 528; De Valle Da Costa v. Southern Pac. Co., 167 Fed. 654 (C. C., Mass.).

Ala.—Age-Herald Pub. Co. v. Waterman (Ala.), 66 So. 16; Hess v.

claration, alleging for the first time an essential element of plain-

Birmingham Ry., etc., Co., 149 Ala. 499, 42 So. 595; Freeman v. Central of Georgia Ry. Co., 154 Ala. 619, 45 So. 898.

Ark.—Cottonwood Lumber Co. v. Walker, 106 Ark. 102, 152 S. W. 1005; Warmack v. Askew, 97 Ark. 19, 132 S. W. 1013. And see Martin v. H. T. Simon, Gregory & Co., 86 Ark. 280, 110 S. W. 1046.

Cal.—Rauer Law & Collection Co. v. Leffingwell, 11 Cal. App. 494, 105 Pac. 427.

Fla.—La Floridienne, J. Buttgenbach & Co., Societe Anonyme v. Atlantic Coast Line R. Co., 63 Fla. 208, 58 So. 186.

Ill.—Vogrin v. American Steel & Wire Co., 179 Ill. App. 245; Carlin v. City of Chicago, 177 Ill. App. 89; Gassman v. Hetzel, 175 Ill. App. 404; Kolber v. Frankenthal, 159 Ill. App. 382; Henderson v. Moweaqua Coal Mining & Mfg. Co., 145 Ill. App. 637; Heffron v. Concordia Fire Ins. Co., 138 Ill. App. 483; Chicago-Virden Coal Co. v. Bradley, 134 Ill. App. 234, judg. aff'd Bradley v. Chicago-Virden Coal Co., 231 Ill. 622, 83 N. E. 424; Bahr v. National Safe Deposit Co., 234 Ill. 101, 84 N. E. 717, aff'g judg. 137 Ill. App. 397; Richter v. Michigan Mut. Life Ins. Co., 66 Ill. App. 606.

Ind.—Williams v. Lowe, 49 Ind. App. 606, 97 N. E. 809; Fleming v. City of Anderson, 39 Ind. App. 343, 76 N. E. 266; Shroyer v. Pittenger, 31 Ind. App. 158, 67 N. E. 475; Blake v. Minkner, 136 Ind. 418, 36 N. E. 246.

Kan.—Elrod v. St. Louis & S. F. R. Co., 84 Kan. 444, 113 Pac. 1046; Union Pac. R. Co. v. Sweet, 78 Kan. 243, 96 Pac. 657; Thompson v. Beeler, 69 Kan. 462, 77 Pac. 100; Powers v. Badger Lumber Co., 75 Kan. 687, 90 Pac. 254.

Md.—Catanzaro Di Giorgio Co. v. F. W. Stock & Sons, 116 Md. 201, 81 Atl. 385.

Mich.—Van Cleve v. Radford, 149 Mich. 106, 112 N. W. 754.

Miss.—Cox v. American Freehold & Land Mortgage Co., 88 Miss. 88, 40 So. 739.

Mo.—Wasson v. Boland, 136 Mo. App. 622, 118 S. W. 663; Bricken v. Cross, 163 Mo. 449, 64 S. W. 99. And see Linn County Bank v. Clifton, 263 Mo. 200, 172 S. W. 388.

Neb.—Davis v. Manning, 97 Neb. 658, 150 N. W. 1019; Melvin v. Hagadorn, 87 Neb. 398, 127 N. W. 139; Buerstetta v. Tecumseh Nat. Bank, 57 Neb. 504, 77 N. W. 1094.

N. Y.—Serrell v. Forbes, 106 App. Div. 482, 94 N. Y. Supp. 805, judg. aff'd 185 N. Y. 572, 78 N. E. 1112; Nathan v. Woolverton, 149 App. Div. 791, 134 N. Y. Supp. 469; Dobbs v. Pearl, 118 N. Y. Supp. 485.

Pa.—Mitchell Coal & Coke Co. v. Pennsylvania R. Co., 241 Pa. 536, 88 Atl. 743; Bender v. Penfield, 235 Pa. 58, 83 Atl. 585, a new cause of action cannot be introduced, or new subject-matter presented, or material defects in pleadings corrected, after the statute of limitations has become a bar; Lane v. Sayre Water Co., 220 Pa. 599, 69 Atl. 1126, or new parties brought in; Lane v. Cayuta Wheel & Foundry Co., 220 Pa. 603, 69 Atl. 1127; Mahoney v. Park Steel Co., 217 Pa. 20, 66 Atl. 90.

Okl.—Butt v. Carson, 5 Okl. 160, 48 Pac. 182.

tiff's cause of action, is not filed until limitations would have barred a new action, if then brought, a plea of limitations is available to the declaration as amended.[42] The general rule, that an amendment to the complaint relates to the time of the filing of the original complaint, does not apply where the amendment sets up a title not previously asserted, and where the amended complaint sets up a new cause of action and is not presented until after the running of limitations the action therein is barred.[43] Amendments introducing a new cause of action, bringing in a new party, or changing the capacity in which a party is sued, cannot be allowed after limitations have run.[44] In the application of the above stated general rule, the nature of the action in general is given consideration in the cases.[45] It has been applied in actions on contract,[46]

Tenn.—Macklin v. Dunn, 130 Tenn. 342, 170 S. W. 588.

Tex.—Texas Co. v. Alamo Cement Co. (Tex. Civ. App.), 168 S. W. 62; Eagle Pass Lumber Co. v. Galveston, etc., Ry. Co. (Tex. Civ. App.), 164 S. W. 402; Quanah, A. & P. Ry. Co. v. Galloway (Tex. Civ. App.), 165 S. W. 546; Paris & G. N. Ry. Co. v. Robinson (Tex. Civ. App.), 127 S. W. 294; Kirby v. Hayden (Tex. Civ. App.), 125 S. W. 993.

42. Prouty v. City of Chicago, 250 Ill. 222, 95 N. E. 147.

When a cause of action is stated for the first time in an amended or additional count, the suit, so far as limitations as to such cause of action are concerned, is regarded as having been commenced at the time the amendment was filed. Devaney v. Otis Elevator Co., 251 Ill. 28, 95 N. E. 990.

The plea of the statute of limitations is a good defense to a declaration in an action against a city for negligence, amended after the statutory period had run, by reciting that the statutory notice was duly given. Penkala v. City of Chicago, 153 Ill. App. 337.

43. Raley v. Evansville Gas & Electric Light Co., 45 Ind. App. 649, 90 N. E. 783, rehearing denied 91 N. E. 571.

In determining whether a new cause of action is presented so as to render it subject to the defense of limitations, the court must look to the substantial nature of the claim introduced by the amendment, and not to the formal manner in which it is declared upon. Oolitic Stone Co. of Indiana v. Ridge, 174 Ind. 558, 91 N. E. 944.

44. Tonge v. Item Pub. Co., 244 Pa. 417, 91 Atl. 229; Mumma v. Mumma, 246 Pa. 407, 92 Atl. 504.

45. *U. S.*—Despeaux v. Pennsylvania R. Co., 133 Fed. 1009 (C. C., Pa.), an action for unlawful discrimination in the transportation of freight.

Cal.—Campbell v. Campbell 133 Cal. 33, 65 Pac. 134; Lambert v. McKenzie, 135 Cal. 100, 67 Pac. 6.

actions for injuries to the person,[47] actions for causing death,[48]

Ga.—Bentley v. Crummey & Hamilton, 119 Ga. 911, 47 S. E. 309; Burbage v. Fitzgerald, 98 Ga. 582, 25 S. E. 554.

Iowa.—O'Banion v. De Garmo, 121 Iowa 139, 96 N. W. 739.

Kan.—Walker v. Hester, 9 Kan. App. 201, 59 Pac. 662.

Ky.—Roush v. Vanceburg, etc., Turnpike Co., 120 Ky. 165, 27 Ky. Law Rep. 542, 85 S. W. 735; Norman v. Central Kentucky Asylum, 25 Ky. Law Rep. 1846, 79 S. W. 189, rehearing denied 26 Ky. Law Rep. 71, 80, S. W. 781; Fisher v. Mucick's Ex'r, 24 Ky. Law Rep. 1913, 72 S. W. 787.

Miss.—Cox v. American Freehold & Land Mortgage Co., 88 Miss. 88, 40 So. 739.

Mo.—Bricken v. Cross, 163 Mo. 449, 64 S. W. 99.

Neb.—Wigton v. Smith, 57 Neb. 299, 77 N. W. 772.

Nev.—Schwartz v. Stock, 26 Nev. 128, 65 Pac. 351.

Or.—Montgomery v. Shaver, 40 Or. 244, 66 Pac. 923.

Pa.—City of Philadelphia v. Hestonville, etc., Ry. Co., 203 Pa. 38, 52 Atl. 184.

Tex.—Stewart v. Robbins, 27 Tex. Civ. App. 188, 65 S. W. 899; Missouri, K. & T. Ry. Co. of Texas v. Levy, 23 Tex. Civ. App. 686, 57 S. W. 866; Estey v. Fisher (Tex. Civ. App.), 44 S. W. 555.

46. *U. S.*—United States v. Norton, 107 Fed. 412, 46 C. C. A. 387 (C. C. A., Tex.); Whalen v. Gordon, 95 Fed. 305, 37 C. C. A. 70 (C. C. A., Iowa).

Ala.—Nelson v. First Nat. Bank, 139 Ala. 578, 36 So. 707, 101 Am. St. Rep. 52.

Cal.—Merchants' Collection Agency v. Gopcevic, 23 Cal. App. 216, 137 Pac. 609; Rogers v. Byers, 1 Cal. App. 284, 81 Pac. 1123; Merchants' Nat. Bank of Santa Monica v. Bentel, 166 Cal. 473, 137 Pac. 25.

Ga.—McIntosh v. Thomasville Real Estate & Improvement Co., 141 Ga. 105, 80 S. E. 629.

Ill.—Pullman v. Secord-Hopkins Co., 73 Ill. App. 30, aff'd Secord-Hopkins Co. v. Lincoln, 173 Ill. 357, 50 N. E. 1074.

Ky.—Montague v. Bell, 14 Ky. Law Rep. 890; Clark v. Logan County, 138 Ky. 676, 128 S. W. 1079.

Md.—Hamilton v. Thirston, 94 Md. 253, 51 Atl. 42.

Pa.—Mumma v. Mumma, 246 Pa. 407, 92 Atl. 504.

Tex.—Phoenix Lumber Co. v. Houston Water Co. (Tex. Civ. App.), 59 S. W. 552, judg. aff'd 94 Tex. 456, 61 S. W. 707; Cotton v. Rand, 93 Tex. 7, 51 S. W. 838, rev'g judg. (Tex. Civ. App.) 51 S. W. 55; Modified on rehearing 93 Tex. 7, 53 S. W. 343; Nelson v. Brenham Compress Oil Mfg. Co. (Tex. Civ. App.), 51 S. W. 514; Fidelity & Casualty Co. of New York v. Allibone, 15 Tex. Civ. App. 178, 39 S. W. 632; Cotulla v. Urhahn, 104 Tex. 208, 135 S. W. 1159, rev'g judg. (Tex. Civ. App.) 126 S. W. 13.

47. *U. S.*—Tiller v. St. Louis & S. F. R. Co., 189 Fed. 994 (C. C., Okl.).

Ga.—Gainesville Midland Ry. v. Vandiver, 141 Ga. 350, 80 S. E. 997.

Ill.—Carlin v. City of Chicago, 177 Ill. App. 89; Sturonois v. Morris, 177 Ill. App. 514; Long v. City of Chicago, 178 Ill. App. 577; Chicago City Ry. Co. v. Leach, 80 Ill. App. 354, judg. rev'd 182 Ill. 359, 55 N. E. 334; Chicago City Ry. Co. v. Cooney, 95

actions for malicious prosecution or slander,[49] actions for injuries to or wrongful dealings with property,[50] and to amendments affecting the form of action or relief.[51]

Ill. App. 471, judg. aff'd 196 Ill. 466, 63 N. E. 1029; Wabash R. Co. v. Bhymer, 112 Ill. App. 225, judg. rev'd 214 Ill. 579, 73 N. E. 879; Jones v. Klawiter, 110 Ill. App. 31, judg. aff'd Klawiter v. Jones, 219 Ill. 626, 76 N. E. 673; Harper v. Illinois Cent. R. Co., 74 Ill. App. 74; Chicago & A. R. Co. v. Reilly, 75 Ill. App. 125; Chicago & A. R. Co. v. Scanlan, 67 Ill. App. 621, judg. aff'd 170 Ill. 106, 48 N. E. 826.

Ind.—Fleming v. City of Anderson, 39 Ind. App. 343, 76 N. E. 266.

Iowa.—Sachra v. Town of Manilla, 120 Iowa 562, 95 N. W. 198.

Neb.—Westover v. Hoover, 94 Neb. 596, 143 N. W. 946.

N. Y.—Hughes v. New York, O. & W. Ry. Co., 158 App. Div. 443, 143 N. Y. Supp. 603.

Pa.—Allen v. Tuscarora Valley R. Co., 229 Pa. 97, 78 Atl. 34.

Where the original declaration failed to allege any cause of action whatever, a subsequent amended declaration, setting up negligence of defendant, states a new cause of action, for the purpose of the statute of limitations. Eylenfeldt v. Illinois Steel Co., 165 Ill. 185, 46 N. E. 266, aff'g 62 Ill. App. 552; Illinois Cent. R. Co. v. Campbell, 170 Ill. 163, 49 N. E. 314, rev'g judg. 58 Ill. App. 275; Strojyn v. Griffin Wheel Co., 116 Ill. App. 550.

When an additional count filed to a declaration in an action for personal injuries sets up a new or different cause of action and is not filed within the time limited by the statute for commencing the action, such amended count is amenable to a plea of the statute of limitations. Dalton v. Chicago City Ry. Co., 93 Ill. App. 7; South Chicago City Ry. Co. v. Kinnare, 117 Ill. App. 1, judg. aff'd 216 Ill. 451, 75 N. E. 179.

48. *U. S.*—Boston & M. R. R. v. Hurd, 108 Fed. 116, 313 (C. C. A., Mass.), 47 C. C. A. 615, 56 L. R. A. 193 (C. C. A., N. H.); Hall v. Louisville & N. R. Co., 157 Fed. 464 (C. C., Fla.); De Valle Da Costa v. Southern Pac. Co., 160 Fed. 216, judg. rev'd Viscount De Valle Da Costa v. Southern Pac. Co., 176 Fed. 843, 100 C. C. A.

Ill.—Bahr v. National Safe Deposit Co., 137 Ill. App. 397, judg. aff'd 234 Ill. 101, 84 N. E. 717; Byrne v. Marshall Field & Co, 237 Ill. 384, 86 N. E. 748; St. Luke's Hospital v. Foster, 86 Ill. App. 282, judg. aff'd 191 Ill. 94, 60 N. E. 803.

Kan.—City of Kansas City v. Hart, 60 Kan. 684, 57 Pac. 938.

Neb.—Zitnik v. Union Pac. R. Co., 95 Neb. 152, 145 N. W. 344.

49. Brooks v. Seevers, 112 Iowa 480, 84 N. W. 517.

50. *U. S.*—United States v. Martinez, 195 U. S. 469, 25 Sup. Ct. 80, 49 L. Ed. 282.

Ill.—Doyle v. City of Sycamore, 81 Ill. App. 589, judg. aff'd 193 Ill. 501, 61 N. E. 1117.

Ky.—Kentucky Cent. R. Co. v. Campbell, 7 Ky. Law Rep. (abstract) 525.

Md.—Schuck v. Bramble, 122 Md. 411, 89 Atl. 719.

§ 308(1). New action after dismissal or nonsuit or failure of former action in general.

Under a statute of limitations, which permits the beginning of a new suit within a certain time after the failure of a former suit brought in due time on the same cause of action otherwise than on the merits, a second suit by an employe against a railroad company for a personal injury is for the same cause of action as a prior suit, where the parties and injury are the same, the facts pleaded are the same, and the negligence charged against the company is the same in legal effect, although it may be attributed to a different agent.[52] The Georgia statute, relating to the renewal of actions within six months, is a remedial statute, and should be so construed as to preserve the right to renew, when the previous suit has been disposed of on any ground other than one affecting the merits.[53] The Missouri statute, allowing another action on the same grounds to be brought within a year after a nonsuit, does not curtail, but extends, the time allowed bv other sections of the limitation law.[54] Under the Vermont statute, providing

Nev.—Schwartz v. Stock, 26 Nev. 155, 65 Pac. 357.

Tex.—Worsham v. Vignal, 14 Tex. Civ. App. 324, 37 S. W. 17; Griffin v. Allison (Tex. Civ. App.), 138 S. W. 623.

51. *Cal.*—Kent v. San Francisco Sav. Union, 130 Cal. 401, 62 Pac. 620.

D. C.—Howard v. Chesapeake & O. Ry. Co., 11 App. D. C. 300.

Ill.—Walker v. Warner, 179 Ill. 16, 53 N. E. 594, 70 Am. St. Rep. 85.

Miss.—Easter v. Riley, 79 Miss. 625, 31 So. 210.

N. Y.—Truman v. Lester, 71 App. Div. 612, 75 N. Y. Supp. 548, 10 N. Y. Ann. Cas. 478.

Tenn.—Crofford v. Cothran, 34 Tenn. (2 Sneed) 492.

Tex.—McLaury v. Watelsky, 39 Tex. Civ. App. 394, 87 S. W. 1045; Scanlon v. Galveston, etc., Ry. Co. (Tex. Civ. App.) 86 S. W. 930; International & G. N. R. Co. v. Dalwigh (Tex. Civ. App.), 56 S. W. 136; Ball v. Hagy (Tex. Civ. App.), 54 S. W. 915; Santleben v. Froboese, 17 Tex. Civ. App. 626, 43 S. W. 571.

52. Brown v. Erie R. Co., 176 Fed. 544, 100 C. C. A. 132.

53. Atlanta, K. & N. Ry. Co. v. Wilson, 119 Ga. 781, 47 S. E. 366, under Civ. Code 1895, § 3786. The institution of an action against a different defendant on the same cause of action as that involved in a suit dismissed was not a "renewal" of the action within Civ. Code 1910, § 4381; Floyd & Lee v. Boyd (Ga. App.), 84 S. E. 494.

54. Karnes v. American Fire Ins. Co. of Philadelphia, 144 Mo. 413, 46 S. W. 166, under Rev. St. 1889, §

that if, after verdict for plaintiff, the judgment is arrested, plaintiff may commence a new action for the same cause within a year, an arrest of judgment in favor of plaintiff does not bar a subsequent action for the same cause.[55] An unsuccessful action of ejectment which led to no change in the possession of the land did not stop the running of the statute of limitations.[56]

§ 308(2). Nature or form or identity of actions or proceedings.

The California statute, which provides that, if a judgment for plaintiff be reversed on appeal, the plaintiff may commence a new action within one year after the reversal, permits a new action of any kind, having for result the same relief as was obtained in the original action, to be brought within the year.[57] Under the

6784. And see Billion v. Walsh, 46 Mo. 492.

55. Baker v. Sherman, 77 Vt. 167, 59 Atl. 167, under V. S. 1214.

56. Nelson v. Triplett, 99 Va. 421, 3 Va. Sup. Ct. Rep. 293, 39 S. E. 150.

Where verdict had been rendered for defendant, and a new trial denied, the case has, without entry of judgment, which is only a ministerial act, been "decided" against plaintiff, within Pa. Act April 13, 1859 (P. L. 603), providing that no entry or action, without a recovery therein, shall "arrest the running of said statute in respect to another ejectment, unless it be brought within a year after the first shall have been nonsuited, arrested, or decided against the plaintiff therein." Crumley v. Lutz, 196 Pa. 559, 46 Atl. 901.

Actions within exception of statute. See

Ill.—Wiggins Ferry Co. v. Gardner, 91 Ill. App. 20; Lake Shore & M. S. Ry. Co. v. Dylinski, 67 Ill. App. 114.

Ind. T.—Turner v. Gonzales, 3 Ind. T. 649, 64 S. W. 565.

Kan.—McGlinchy v. Bowles, 68 Kan. 190, 75 Pac. 123; Berkley v. Tootle, 62 Kan. 701, 64 Pac. 620; Knox v. Henry, 8 Kan. App. 313, 75 Pac. 123.

Mass.—Tyndale v. Stanwood, 190 Mass. 513, 77 N. E. 481.

N. Y.—*In re* May's Estate, 24 Misc. Rep. 456, 53 N. Y. Supp. 710, 2 Gibbons 547, rev'd *In re* Schlessinger's Estate, 36 App. Div. 77, 55 N. Y. Supp. 514, 2 Gibbons 547.

N. C.—Meekins v. Norfolk & S. R. Co., 131 N. C. 1, 42 S. E. 333.

Tenn.—Stuber v. Louisville & N. R. Co., 113 Tenn. 305, 87 S. W. 411.

Va.—Manuel v. Norfolk & W. Ry. Co., 99 Va. 188, 3 Va. Sup. Ct. Rep. 110, 37 S. E. 957; Dawes v. New York, P. & N. R. Co., 96 Va. 733, 32 S. E. 778.

W. Va.—Hevener v. Hannah, 59 W. Va. 476, 53 S. E. 635.

Severance of action.—See Garman v. United States, 34 Ct. Cl. (U. S.) 237.

57. Kenney v. Parks, 137 Cal. 527, 70 Pac. 556, under Code Civ. Proc., § 355.

Georgia statute, granting the right to bring a new action within six months after discontinuance, dismissal, or nonsuit, the second suit does not have to be a literal copy of that dismissed, although it must be for substantially the same cause of action, by the same plaintiff or his legal representatives, and against all the defendants who were necessary parties to the first suit, or their legal representatives.[58] The Iowa statute, which provides that, where a plaintiff fails in any action for any cause except negligence in its prosecution, a new action commenced within six months, shall be deemed a continuance of the first, for the purpose of the statute of limitations, does not apply where the cause of action stated in the second action is different from that alleged in the first, though based on the same transaction.[59] The word "action" in the Illinois statute is not limited to actions at law, but includes suits in equity, and hence, where plaintiff was nonsuited in a chancery suit, and limitations ran against his claim during the pendency of such suit, he was entitled to commence an action at law on the claim within a year after the entry of the nonsuit.[60]

§ 308(3). Abatement or abandonment of former action.

The death of the defendant in ejectment abates the suit, but the statute of limitations does not run during the pendency of the suit; and under the Michigan statute, plaintiff may bring an action

58. Cox v. Strickland, 120 Ga. 104, 47 S. E. 912, under Civ. Code 1895, § 3786. And see Atlanta, K. & N. Ry. Co. v. Wilson, 119 Ga. 781, 47 S. E. 366.

59. Whalen v. Gordon, 95 Fed. 305, 37 C. C. A. 70, under Code Iowa 1897, § 3455.

60. Lamson v. Hutchings, 118 Fed. 321, 55 C. C. A. 245, under 2 Starr & C. Ann. St. Ill., p. 2642, c. 83, par. 25. See also, Gibbs v. Crane Elevator Co., 180 Ill. 191, 54 N. E. 200, aff'g judg. Gibbs v. Chicago Title & Trust Co., 79 Ill. App. 22.

See also, as to the rule in other jurisdictions:

Ark.—Covington v. Berry, 76 Ark. 460, 88 S. W. 1005.

Ky.—Commonwealth v. Elkins, 116 Ky. 303, 25 Ky. Law Rep. 485, 76 S. W. 25; Smith v. Herd, 110 Ky. 56, 22 Ky. Law Rep. 1596, 60 S. W. 841, 1121.

Okl.—Hatchell v. Hebeisen, 16 Okl. 223, 82 Pac. 826; Myers v. First Presbyterian Church of Perry, 11 Okl. 544, 69 Pac. 874.

for the same cause at any time within one year after the suit is thus abated.[61] The Maine statute, relative to the commencement of action within six months after abatement of the writ in a former action on the same demand, has no application to a case where the writ, contrary to law, was not made returnable at the first term after its issuance.[62] Where a county board sued its auditor to recover for illegal allowances received by him, and afterwards the action was compromised, and an action was then commenced by interested citizens to invalidate the settlement, the statute of limitations stopped running in favor of the auditor at the commencement of the first suit and remained so throughout both actions, under the Indiana statute.[63] Under the Kentucky statute, the institution by appellant of another action, which was dismissed on his own motion, cannot be regarded as an abandonment of the original action, so as to make the plea of limitations available.[64]

§ 308(4). Dismissal or nonsuit in general.

A voluntary dismissal without prejudice to a future action is a failure other than upon the merits within the Kansas Civ. Code, § 23, providing that if an action fails otherwise than on the merits, plaintiff may commence a new action within one year.[65] Under

61. McKenzie v. A. P. Cook Co., 113 Mich. 452, 4 Detroit Leg. N. 396, 71 N. W. 868, under How. Ann. St., § 8707.

Where a resident of Iowa died pending suit against him in Illinois, action on a claim filed against the estate in Iowa was a new suit, within the statute of limitations. Malone v. Averill, 166 Iowa 78, 147 N. W. 135.

62. Densmore v. Hall, 109 Me. 438, 84 Atl. 983, under Rev. St. c. 83, § 94.

63. Zuelly v. Casper, 46 Ind. App. 430, 92 N. E. 785, under Burns' Ann. St. 1908, § 301, providing that if the plaintiff fail in the prosecution for any reason except negligence, or the action abate, a new action may be commenced within five years after such determination, and be deemed a "continuation of the first" in order to prevent the running of the statute of limitations.

64. Johnson v. Barnes, 8 Ky. Law Rep. (abstract) 956, 4 S. W. 176.

See also, as to abandonment of suit: Raymond v. Conery, 50 La. Ann. 155, 23 So. 208; Mechanics' & Traders' Bank v. Theall, 8 La. Ann. 469.

65. Harrison v. Remington Paper Co., 140 Fed. 385, 72 C. C. A. 405, 3 L. R. A. (N. S.) 954; Draper v. Miller, 92 Kan. 275, 140 Pac. 890; Denton v. City of Atchison, 76 Kan. 89,

Georgia Civ. Code 1895, § 3786, providing that, if a plaintiff shall be nonsuited or shall discontinue or dismiss his case and shall recommence within six months, the second case shall stand upon the same footing as to limitations with the original case, the mere dismissal in general terms of a suit will not after the expiration of six months from such dismissal operate as a bar to the bringing of the second suit by the same plaintiff against the same defendant on the same cause of action when the cause of action is not barred by the statute of limitations applicable thereto at the time the second suit is brought.[66] Where the plaintiff in an action suffers an involuntary nonsuit, he is given by the Illinois statute of limitations one year from the date of suffering such nonsuit to begin his action anew; the section does not apply where a voluntary nonsuit has been taken.[67] In Iowa, where the plaintiff

90 Pac. 764, but where the new action is dismissed more than one year after the first dismissal, there is no authority for the bringing of another new action; Parker v. Dobson, 78 Kan. 62, 96 Pac. 472; Swift & Co. v. Hoblawetz, 10 Kan. App. 48, 61 Pac. 969; Hiatt v. Auld, 11 Kan. 176; McWhirt v. McKee, 6 Kan. 412.

Where in an action it was determined that plaintiff could not maintain the same, because of an oral agreement not to sue until other litigation was terminated, in an action after the termination of such other litigation defendants could not plead that limitations had barred the action; the decision in the first case suspending limitations until the action was determined. Dendy v. Russell, 84 Kan. 377, 114 Pac. 239.

66. Hackney v. J. R. Asbury & Co., 124 Ga. 678, 52 S. E. 886.

Civ. Code, § 3786, does not authorize the renewal of a writ of certiorari dismissed for want of proper affidavit. Hill v. State, 115 Ga. 833, 42 S. E. 286.

Where a suit is dismissed and a writ of error is sued out, the statutory period of six months within which a suit which has been dismissed may be renewed so as to prevent the running of limitations does not run while such writ of error is pending. Seaboard Air-Line Ry. v. Randolph, 126 Ga. 238, 55 S. E. 47.

Where a railroad created a nuisance, and a suit therefor resulted in a nonsuit, and the company was merged with another, a renewal of the suit against the new company within six months after the nonsuit was a renewal against the original company, within Civ. Code 1910, § 4381. Atlantic Coast Line R. Co. v. Knapp, 139 Ga. 422, 77 S. E. 568. See also, as to dismissal or nonsuit under § 4386, Piedmont Hotel Co. v. Henderson, 9 Ga. App. 672, 72 S. E. 51, and under § 3786, Southern Express Co. v. Sinclair, 135 Ga. 155, 68 S. E. 1113.

67. Koch v. Sheppard, 223 Ill. 172, 79 N. E. 52, aff'g judg. 124 Ill. App. 266; Wiehe v. Atkins, 126 Ill. App.

relies on Code, § 3455, providing that, if the plaintiff fails in a suit for any cause except negligence in its prosecution, a new suit brought within six months shall be deemed a continuation of the first, before such a suit can be held a continuation, the burden is on the plaintiff to allege in his petition in the second action facts showing that the dismissal of the first was not caused by any negligence on his part.[68] In Missouri, where plaintiffs, the owners of land, instituted an action before the running of the period of limitations, they could thereafter suffer a voluntary nonsuit, and within a year institute a new action, which would not be barred by limitations even though the period had then run, provided it involved the same issues as the first.[69] The Michigan statute, providing that if an action commenced within the time allowed there-

1; Boyce v. Snow, 187 Ill. 181, 58 N. E. 403, aff'g judg. 88 Ill. App. 402.

If, when a case is regularly called upon the docket, and the plaintiff not appearing, the court dismisses his action, he suffers an involuntary nonsuit, within the meaning of section 25 of the statute of limitations. Sehnert v. Schipper & Block, 168 Ill. App. 245.

The distinction between voluntary and involuntary nonsuits, as affecting the period of limitations within which an action for death may be brought, is material only when the nonsuit occurs after the period allowed by the statute for bringing suit, as the law does not limit the number of successive suits that may be brought within the year allowed by the injuries act. Heimberger v. Elliot Frog & Switch Co., 245 Ill. 448, 92 N. E. 297. And see Adams v. Holden, 111 Iowa 54, 82 N. W. 468, as to the application of Rev. St. Ill. c. 83, § 25.

68. Ceprley v. Incorporated Town of Paton, Greene County, 120 Iowa 559, 95 N. W. 179; Pardee v. Incorporated Town of Mechanicsville, 101 Iowa 266, 70 N. W. 189.

69. Norton v. Reed, 253 Mo. 236, 161 S. W. 842.

The dismissal of an action on plaintiff's motion without a trial on the merits is not a common law judgment of retraxit, so that plaintiff could again institute suit within one year after suffering such a nonsuit pursuant to statute. Johnson v. Metropolitan St. Ry. Co., 177 Mo. App. 298, 164 S. W. 128.

Rev. St. 1909, § 1900, providing that plaintiff may have one year additional time to bring suit after nonsuit does not apply where there was a final judgment on a demurrer to the merits. Johnson v. United Rys. Co. of St. Louis, 243 Mo. 278, 147 S. W. 1077. It has no application to an action to set aside a tax sale barred by the limitation section of a municipal charter. Meriwether v. Overly, 228 Mo. 218, 129 S. W. 1.

Plaintiff having a right to sue at once for an accounting on notice of an attempted forfeiture of his rights in a partnership, or to wait till ter-

for be defeated for any matter of form, or if, after verdict for plaintiff, the judgment be reversed, plaintiff may commence a new action for the same cause within one year, authorizes plaintiff to institute a new action within a year after a former suit was dismissed because of a mistake in the form of the remedy.[70] An action by a mortgagee against an insurance company having been dismissed pursuant to stipulation that his claim might be asserted in an action by the insured, was not a "voluntary discontinuance," within New York Code Civ. Proc., § 405, so that the claim was not barred, though the answer was not filed until more than twelve months after the accrual of such claim.[71] The dismissal of plaintiff's suit on account of his failure to file a declaration does not conclude his right of action, and hence a second suit, brought

mination of the time for which the partnership was formed, his commencement of a suit at once, which was dismissed before final judgment, did not start the statute of limitations running, so as to affect the time for bringing action after termination of the partnership. Steinbach v. Murphy, 143 Mo. App. 537, 128 S. W. 207. See also, as to dismissal or nonsuit in general: Harris v. Quincy, etc., Ry. Co., 124 Mo. App. 45, 101 S. W. 601; Missouri & S. W. Land Co. v. Quinn, 172 Mo. 563, 73 S. W. 184; Wetmore v. Crouch, 188 Mo. 647, 87 S. W. 954; Estes v. Fry, 166 Mo. 70, 65 S. W. 741.

70. McMillan v. Reaume, 137 Mich. 1, 11 Detroit Leg. N. 168, 100 N. W. 166, 109 Am. St. Rep. 666, under Comp. Laws, § 9738.

Where a demurrer to a declaration is sustained because the remedy is in equity, the action is defeated by a defect of form, within Pub. St. Mass. c. 136, § 12, providing that, if an action commenced against an executor or administrator before the expiration of two years from the time of his giving bond be defeated by a defect in the form of the writ or a mistake in the form of the proceeding, plaintiff may commence a new action for the same cause within one year thereafter. Taft v. Stow, 174 Mass. 171, 54 N. E. 506.

71. O'Neil v. Franklin Fire Ins. Co. of Philadelphia, 159 App. Div. 313, 145 N. Y. Supp. 432.

The commencement of an action against defendant for an injunction and damages, by reason of a viaduct constructed in a street and the operation of trains over the same, which action was voluntarily discontinued, was insufficient to interrupt the statute of limitations, so as to prevent the railroad company from acquiring a prescriptive right to use the viaduct, on the lapse of the statutory period. Foster v. New York Cent. & H. R. R. Co., 118 App. Div. 143, 103 N. Y. Supp. 531. And see, as to application of section 405, Conolly v. Hyams, 176 N. Y. 403, 68 N. E. 662.

within twelve months after dismissal of the first, is not barred by the Tennessee statute limiting the time in which the action may be brought to one year.[72] The North Carolina Revisal 1905, § 370, permitting a new suit within twelve months after nonsuit, does not abridge the statutes of limitation, and hence a suit for trespass to land is properly brought within three years from the date thereof, though more than one year after nonsuit on the same cause of action.[73] Under the Rhode Island statute, a nonsuit is not an adjudication on the merits, and plaintiff may, within a year thereafter, institute a new action.[74] Under the express pro-

72. Minton v. La Follette Coal, Iron & R. Co., 117 Tenn. 415, 101 S. W. 178. The statute applies to a voluntary nonsuit by the plaintiff. Hooper v. Atlanta, K. & N. Ry. Co., 106 Tenn. 28, 60 S. W. 607, 53 L. R. A. 931.

The Ohio statute does not entitle a plaintiff to bring a new action where his former action was dismissed on his own motion without trial. Irwin v. Lloyd, 20 Ohio Cir. Ct. R. 339, 11 O. C. D. 212.

73. Caldwell Land & Lumber Co. v. Hayes, 157 N. C. 333, 72 S. E. 1078.

Plaintiff having been nonsuited upon the ground that under the form of the pleadings, taken in connection with the evidence, a direct action to charge the land with indebtedness should have been brought instead of ejectment, he may bring another action within a year. Henderson v. Eller, 147 N. C. 582, 61 S. E. 446.

Kirby's Dig. Ark., § 5083, providing that plaintiff, suffering a nonsuit, may commence a new action within one year, does not limit, but extends, the period provided by the general statute of limitations applicable. Williford v. Williford, 102 Ark. 65, 143 S. W. 132; Love v. Kahn, 93 Ark. 215, 124 S. W. 259; Dressler v. Carpenter, 107 Ark. 353, 155 S. W. 108.

A dismissal of an action in justice's court, on motion of plaintiff, without any ruling on motion for judgment on the pleadings argued and submitted, is not on the merits, within Utah Comp. Laws 1907, § 2893; and an action commenced within one year after dismissal is not barred by limitations. Quealy v. Sullivan, 42 Utah 565, 132 Pac. 4. An action, voluntarily dismissed by plaintiff, fails "otherwise than on the merits," within section 2893. Luke v. Bennion, 36 Utah 61, 106 Pac. 712. Where a nonsuit is granted for any reason, an action fails otherwise than on the merits, within section 2893. Williams v. Nelson (Utah), 145 Pac. 39.

74. Sullivan v. John R. White & Son, Inc., 36 R. I. 488, 90 Atl. 738, under Gen. Laws 1909, c. 284, § 9. And see Pesce v. Mondare, 30 R. I. 247, 74 Atl. 913.

Where plaintiff sued upon a cause of action not yet barred, and judgment of nonsuit was entered, plaintiff was entitled under Rev. Codes Mont., § 6464, to commence an ac-

visions of the Oregon statute, the time during which an appeal from a voluntary nonsuit was pending should be excluded in computing the time for the commencement of a second action.[75] In West Virginia, where an action is dismissed, the time of its pendency is to be excluded from computation of limitations on a new suit for the debt.[76]

§ 308(5). New action in different forum.

Under the Georgia statute, granting the right to commence a new action within six months after discontinuance, dismissal, or nonsuit, the new action may be brought in any court having jurisdiction thereof in the State.[77] Under the North Carolina statute,

tion for the same cause within a year of dismissal, though limitations had run against the original action. Wilson v. Norris, 43 Mont. 454, 117 Pac. 100.

Where a party sues for relief on the ground of fraud within Wilson's Rev. & Ann. St. Okl. 1903, § 4216, and on the trial, by leave, dismisses the action without prejudice, more than two years after his right of action accrued, and brings a second action within a year from the dismissal of the first, the bar of the statute is not let in because of section 4221. Wilson v. Wheeler, 28 Okl. 726, 115 Pac. 1117.

A properly instituted claim or action which is voluntarily dismissed or abandoned cannot be used to save a subsequent action from being barred by limitations, under Burns' St. Ind. 1908, § 301. Pennsylvania Co. v. Good (Ind. App.), 103 N. E. 672.

In Texas, a suit voluntarily dismissed without a trial on the merits does not interrupt limitations. Mitchell v. Thomas (Tex. Civ. App.), 172 S. W. 715.

75. Hutchings v. Royal Bakery & Confectionary Co., 66 Or. 301, 131 Pac. 514.

An appeal from an *ex parte* order of the clerk admitting a will and codicil to probate as authorized by Va. Code 1904, § 2639a, is not a new suit within section 2934, authorizing the commencement of a new suit where limitations have run pending an original proceeding, so that a will contest under section 2544 having failed, the contestants could not appeal from the order of probate, after the original time for such appeal had expired. Tyson v. Scott, 116 Va. 243, 81 S. E. 57.

76. Hevener v. Hannah, 59 W. Va. 476, 53 S. E. 635.

77. Cox v. Strickland, 120 Ga. 104, 47 S. E. 912, under Civ. Code 1895, § 3786. But the Code provision does not apply where a suit brought in a State court is removed by defendant to a federal court, and there dismissed on plaintiff's motion, and applies only to a case pending in a State court. Webb v. Southern Cotton Oil Co., 131 Ga. 682, 63 S. E. 135.

the plaintiff taking a nonsuit in a case before the federal court could bring another suit for the same cause of action at any time within a year.[78] But, under the New York statute, providing that if an action is commenced within the time limited therefor, and the action is terminated in any other manner than by a voluntary discontinuance, or a dismissal, or a final judgment on the merits, plaintiff may commence a new action, where an alleged libellous article was published in October, 1896, an action commenced therefor in April, 1899, was barred, notwithstanding that an action filed in June, 1898, within the statutory period of limitation, in the United States circuit court to recover damages for the same libel had been dismissed for want of jurisdiction, since under the constitution the legislature had power to prescribe rules only for the courts of the State, and hence the Code relates only to such courts.[79] Where the jurisdiction given a federal court to enforce a remedy on a contractor's bond given for government work is exclusive, the commencement of an action on such bond in a State court of Colorado, which was afterwards dismissed, did not extend the time for bringing a new action in the federal court by virtue of the State statute.[80]

§ 308(6). Failure of action for want of jurisdiction.

Where plaintiff sues in a court having jurisdiction of the subject-matter, and after the bar of the statute has attached the same is dismissed, because of a ruling indicating that the court has no jurisdiction of the person of the defendant, the action may be renewed, under the Georgia statute, within six months, in another court of the State having jurisdiction of the person and of the subject-matter.[81] Where a plaintiff recovered judgment before a justice, and again on appeal to the district court, but

78. Fleming v. Southern Ry. Co., 128 N. C. 80, 38 S. E. 253, under Clark's Code (3d ed.), §§ 142, 166.

79. Solomon v. Bennett, 62 App. Div. 56, 70 N. Y. Supp. 856, 32 Civ. Proc., R. 104, under Code Civ. Proc., §§ 384, 405 and Const. 1846, art. 6, § 24.

80. United States v. Boomer, 183 Fed. 726, 730, 106 C. C. A. 164, 168.

81. Atlanta, K. & N. Ry. Co. v. Wilson, 119 Ga. 781, 47 S. E. 366, under Civ. Code 1895, § 3786.

such judgment was reversed and the action dismissed by the supreme court, on the ground that the amount involved was beyond the jurisdiction of the justice, the action "failed otherwise than upon the merits," and, under the Kansas statute, a second action is not barred if commenced within one year after such dismissal.[82] Where a proceeding was the commencement of an action, within the meaning of the Ohio statute, and the plaintiff failed otherwise than upon the merits, the cause being dismissed on the ground that the federal court in which the action was brought had no jurisdiction over the parties or subject-matter, he is entitled to commence a new action within a year from such date, though, under the statute, his action would be barred.[83] In an action for the death of a horse caused by an accident, for which the limitation prescribed by Greater New York Charter is one year, evidence of a prior action by the same plaintiff against the same defendant, which was dismissed on the ground of want of jurisdiction, without any showing that the former action was for the same cause, or that it was commenced within a year, does not entitle plaintiff to the benefit of Code Civ. Proc., § 405, providing that, if an action is commenced within the time limited therefor, the plaintiff may commence a new action for the same cause.[84] The commencement of an action in a court not having jurisdiction to try it does not suspend the running of the statute of limitations, in Tennessee.[85] Where executors bring a suit in equity to settle their accounts, setting up in their bill that one H. claims a debt against their decedent, and denying it, and asking the court to adjudicate as to

82. Ball v. Biggam, 6 Kan. App. 42, 49 Pac. 678, under Civ. Code, § 23.

83. Pittsburg, etc., Ry. Co. v. Bemis, 64 Ohio St. 26, 59 N. E. 745, under Rev. St. §§ 4983, 4991.

84. Thomas v. City of New York, 123 N. Y. Supp. 113, under Greater New York Charter (Laws 1901, c. 466), § 261, as amended by Laws 1906, c. 550.

85. Sweet v. Chattanooga Electric Light Co., 97 Tenn. 252, 36 S. W. 1090, under Mill. & V. Code, § 3449, providing that if an action is commenced within the time limited, but judgment is rendered against the plaintiff on any grounds not concluding his right of action, he may bring a new action within a year thereafter.

its validity, and H. files an answer setting up the debt and asking a decree for it against the estate, and the bill is dismissed for want of jurisdiction in equity, H. has one year after such dismissal to save a suit by him from limitations by force of the West Virginia statute.[86]

§ 308(7). Failure for defects as to parties.

The Virginia statute, which provides that where an action is brought against the wrong defendant, and judgment is rendered against the plaintiff solely on such ground, he may bring an action within one year thereafter, notwithstanding the expiration of the time within which the action must otherwise have been brought applies to any case where, through a misapprehension of the facts or for any other reason, without fraud, the action is brought against the wrong party, and is for that reason dismissed by the court.[87] Though a suit by individual members of a commercial firm for a tort committed to the damage of the firm has been dismissed, on the ground that it should have been brought in the firm name, the suit none the less interrupts the running of prescription, in Louisiana, against the partnership during its pendency.[88] The quashing of the service of summons because made by the coroner, authorized to serve process only where the sheriff is a party, based on the fact that the sheriff was improperly joined as a party, results in failure by plaintiff otherwise than on the merits, within the Wyoming statute providing that, where plaintiff in an action commenced in time fails otherwise than on the merits, he may commence a new action within one year thereafter,

86. Hevener v. Hannah, 59 W. Va. 476, 53 S. E. 635, under Code 1899, c. 104, § 19.

A party who has applied to chancery for relief and obtained a decree, when his remedy was exclusively at law, may, under the proviso of Ind. Acts 1838, § 11, regulating the practice in suits at law, at any time within a year after the reversal of such decree for error prosecute his action for the same matter at law. McKinney v. Springer, 3 Ind. 59, 54 Am. Dec. 470.

87. Norfolk & A. Terminal Co. v. Rotolo, 179 Fed. 639, 103 C. C. A. 197, under Code Va. 1904, § 2934.

88. B. J. Wolf & Sons v. New Orleans Tailor-Made Pants Co., 110 La. 427, 34 So. 590.

in which case the bar of limitations is not applicable.[89] A dismissal from an action of an unnecesssary and improper party defendant does not result in creating a new cause of action.[90]

§ 308(8). Failure of action for want of, or defects in, process or service thereof.

Failure of an officer to make return of a summons on the return day is negligence, within the Michigan statute, authorizing a new action within one year where the writ fails of a sufficient service by neglect, etc., of the officer.[91] As an action, commenced in justice court by filing of complaint, does not, under the Utah statutes, terminate for mere delay in serving the summons, it does not, till actually dismissed, "fail" within the statute, providing that if an action be seasonably commenced, and plaintiff fail therein otherwise than on the merits, and the time limited for the action shall have expired, plaintiff may commence a new action within a year after the failure.[92] Under the Vermont statute, providing that if, in an action commenced within the time limited by statute, the writ fails of sufficient service or return by unavoidable accident, the plaintiff may have one year after the determination of the original suit to commence a new action, an action is commenced when the writ is issued with the purpose on the plaintiff's part of having it served and proceeded with, although the writ fails of sufficient service through unavoidable mistake; an utter failure of service is as much within the contemplation of the statute as a case in which something is done toward service, but not

89. Clause v. Columbia Savings & Loan Ass'n, 16 Wyo. 450, 95 Pac. 54, under Rev. Ct. 1899, § 3465.

90. Patten v. Iroquois Furnace Co., 124 Ill. App. 1.

91. Ricaby v. Gentle, 122 Mich. 336, 6 Detroit Leg. N. 765, 80 N. W. 1093, under 3 Comp. Laws 1897, § 9738.

Section 9738 has no application to an action barred because the original service was on the wrong person, under a statute providing that an action against a city for negligent injury shall be commenced within a year from the time the injury is received. Wilton v. City of Detroit, 138 Mich. 67, 11 Detroit Leg. N. 467, 100 N. W. 1020.

92. Luke v. Bennion, 36 Utah 61, 106 Pac. 712, under Comp. Laws 1888, § 3544 *et seq.*, and Rev. St. 1898, § 2893.

enough to amount to a legal service.[93] An order to set aside a judgment on the ground that the summons was void is a final order within the Kansas statute, and terminates the action unless set aside on proceedings in error, and tolls the statute of limitations for one year, requiring the issuance of *alias* summons within that time to save the right of action if it was barred at the date of the entry of the order.[94]

§ 308(9). Failure of action for defects in pleading.

To bring within the Georgia statute an action which has been dismissed so as to make a new action stand on the same footing as to limitation as the original action, the declaration filed in the first instance must have been served upon defendant, and mere filing without serving is insufficient.[95] In Illinois, where a demur-

93. Tracy v. Grand Trunk Ry. Co., 76 Vt. 313, 57 Atl. 104, under V. S. 1214.

Under North Carolina Code 1883, § 166, which provides that, if an action be commenced within the time limited, and plaintiff be nonsuited, he may commence an action within one year after such nonsuit, where proceedings by an administrator for the sale of land of his intestate were set aside because of insufficient service of summons, such dismissal amounted to a nonsuit within the statute. Harris v. Davenport, 132 N. C. 697, 44 S. E. 406.

94. Bank of Topeka v. Clark, 69 Kan. 864, 77 Pac. 92, under Code Civ. Proc., §§ 542, 543 (Gen. St. 1901, c. 80, §§ 5019, 5027).

Under West Virginia Code, c. 104, § 19, providing that, if an action commenced within the time allowed by limitations be dismissed for any cause which could not be pleaded in bar of the action, another action may be brought within one year after the dismissal thereof, an action commenced by a summons which is void because it has a wrong return day is nevertheless effective to give one year after its dismissal for a new suit. Ketterman v. Dry Fork R. Co., 48 W. Va. 606, 37 S. E. 683.

An action for wrongful death, where service of summons upon defendant railway company was defective, and a later service was not made within 60 days from the attempted service, and not until after the expiration of the two years in which such action must be brought, is not within or saved by section 4991, Ohio Rev. St. providing that if, in an action commenced in due time, the plaintiff fail otherwise than upon the merits, a new action may be commenced within one year. Baltimore & O. R. Co. v. Collins, 11 O. C. D. 334.

95. McClendon v. Hernando Phosphate Co., 100 Ga. 219, 28 S. E. 152, under Code 1882, § 2932.

Plaintiff's postponing the mailing

rer was sustained to plaintiff's original declaration, on the ground that it failed to state a cause of action with certainty only, and plaintiff suffered an involuntary nonsuit by reason thereof, he was entitled to file a new suit within a year after such nonsuit, though the time within which the action could have been brought originally had expired during the pendency of the original action.[96] North Carolina Code, § 166, allowing a new action to be instituted within one year after a reversal of a former judgment obtained on a suit on such cause of action, authorizes the commencement of a new suit within such time, though the complaint in the first action is insufficient to state a cause of action.[97] One whose action, commenced within the time allowed by law, has been erroneously dismissed on a plea in abatement for variance between the writ and the declaration, after refusal to permit an amendment of the writ, may bring a new action having the same purpose as the one dismissed, within a year after the dis-

of his petition so that a slight interruption in the mail service prevented its receipt in time for filing on the date specified therefor in the original notice, thereby entitling defendant to dismissal of the action (Code 1873, § 2600), is negligence, within section 2537, declaring that, if plaintiff fail in his action through any cause except negligence in its prosecution, a new suit, if brought within six months, shall be deemed a continuance of the first. Conly v. Dugan, 105 Iowa 205, 74 N. W. 774.

A suit begun by the issuance of a summons, and dismissed at rules for the mere failure of the plaintiff to file his declaration, will not save a second suit for the same cause of action, brought within one year after such dismissal, from the statute of limitations. Lawrence v. Winifrede Coal Co., 48 W. Va. 139, 35 S. E. 925.

96. Hinchliff v. Rudnik, 212 Ill. 569, 72 N. E. 691, under Limitation Act, § 25.

Where a demurrer to a petition was sustained on the ground of misjoinder of causes, and without other pleading a judgment was entered that defendant was the owner and entitled to possession of the property in question, the plaintiff, having commenced his action in due time, failed therein otherwise than on the merits within Kansas Code Civ. Proc., § 22 (Gen. St. 1909, § 5615), authorizing a new action within one year after such failure. New v. Smith, 86 Kan. 1, 119 Pac. 380. And see Becker v. Atchison, etc., Ry. Co., 70 Kan. 193, 78 Pac. 408.

97. Woodcock v. Bostic, 128 N. C. 243, 38 S. E. 881; Webb v. Hicks, 125 N. C. 201, 34 S. E. 395, denying rehearing 123 N. C. 244, 31 S. E. 479.

missal, though after his right of action would have been barred by limitation, had the dismissed action not be instituted.[98]

§ 308(10). Identity of, or change in parties.

A plaintiff in a suit to redeem from a mortgage is not aided, as against the bar of limitation, by the fact that a prior suit to redeem, which was dismissed, was brought within the time limited, by a different party as plaintiff, although based on the same grounds.[99] Under the Ohio statute, providing that where an action is commenced in due time, and the plaintiff fails otherwise than upon the merits, and the time limited for the commencement of such action has expired, the plaintiff may commence a new action within one year after the date of such failure, a new action commenced within one year, but in which the parties are different from the first action, cannot be maintained, since the new action must be the same as the first.[1]

§ 308(11). Decisions on review.

The Illinois Limitation Act, providing that in certain cases where suit is brought within the required time, and the time expires during the pendency thereof, the plaintiff on reversal, nonsuit, etc., may commence a new action within one year thereafter,

98. Ryan v. Piney Coal & Coke Co., 69 W. Va. 692, 73 S. E. 330. And see Duty v. Chesapeake & O. Ry. Co., 70 W. Va. 14, 73 S. E. 331, where the declaration erroneously alleged the wrong state under the laws of which defendant was incorporated.

99. H. B. Claflin Co. v. Middlesex Banking Co., 113 Fed. 958 (C. C., Ark.).

The record in an equity suit to recover possession of land, which was dismissed without prejudice, is admissible to avoid the bar of limitation in an action of ejectment for the same land commenced within a year thereafter by the same plaintiffs, claiming in the same right, and against the successors in interest of the former defendant. Alexander v. Gordon, 101 Fed. 91, 41 C. C. A. 228, under Sand. & H. Dig. Ark. 1894, § 4841.

1. Larwill v. Burke, 19 Ohio Cir. Ct. Rep. 449, 513, 10 O. C. D. 605, under Rev. St., § 4991. See also, as to identity of, or change in parties: Anthony Inv. Co. v. Law, 62 Kan. 193, 61 Pac. 745, rev'g judg. 9 Kan. App. 890, 58 Pac. 1116; Meddis v. Wilson, 175 Mo. 126, 74 S. W. 984.

does not mean that a new action may be commenced within one year of judgment, etc., if the original declaration did not state a cause of action, but it applies to defects by which a party is defeated as stated therein.[2] Under New York Code, Civ. Proc., § 405, providing that, where an action is terminated by a judgment entered on a decision of the Appellate Division which reversed a judgment of the lower court without awarding a new trial, if such action was commenced within the time limited therefor, the plaintiff may commence a new action for the same cause after the expiration of the time so limited and within a year after such reversal or termination, and also declaring that if the prior action is terminated in any other manner than by a voluntary discontinuance, a dismissal of the complaint for neglect to prosecute, or a final judgment on the merits, such new action may be commenced on the same conditions, where plaintiff in former actions against the same defendants for the same cause recovered a judgment which was reversed and new trials were ordered by the appellate court, the actions were not terminated in any of the modes referred to in such section, and hence plaintiff was entitled to maintain new

2. Walters v. City of Ottawa, 175 Ill. App. 130.

Where a suit is brought in apt time, and a declaration filed imperfectly stating the cause of action, subsequent amendments, though filed after limitations against a new action have run, will not be barred, if they amount to not more than a restatement in a different form of the cause of action originally declared on; but, if they set up an entirely new and distinct cause of action, limitation will be successfully pleaded. George B. Swift & Co. v. Gaylord, 229 Ill. 330, 82 N. E. 299; Bradley v. Chicago-Virden Coal Co., 231 Ill. 622, 83 N. E. 424. And see McAndrews v. Chicago, etc., Ry. Co., 162 Fed. 856, 89 C. C. A. 546.

Where a judgment for plaintiff was reversed by the appellate court on a finding of facts different from that found by the trial court, which precluded a recovery, such judgment not appealed from was *res judicata* under section 88, and plaintiff was not entitled to bring a new suit under section 25, which has no application to a judgment of reversal with a finding of facts entered by the appellate court pursuant to Prac. Act, § 87. Larkins v. Terminal R. Ass'n, 221 Ill. 428, 77 N. E. 678, aff'g judg. 112 Ill. App. 366, and 122 Ill. App. 246.

Section 25 applies only to involuntary, not to voluntary, nonsuits. Koch v. Sheppard, 223 Ill. 172, 79 N. E. 52, aff'g decree 124 Ill. App. 266.

actions thereunder.[3] Alabama Code 1896, § 2806, providing for additional time to bring a second action after arrest or reversal of judgment on appeal, applies only to actions at law, and not to suits in chancery.[4] Under California Code Civ. Proc., § 355, providing that, if an action is commenced within the time prescribed therefor and a judgment for plaintiff is reversed on "appeal," the plaintiff may commence a new action within a year after reversal, the commencement of a suit and the bringing of an action within a year from the annulling of a decree therein on a "writ of review" does not prevent the bar of limitations.[5] Under the Missouri statute, where the Supreme Court has rendered a judgment merely reversing the judgment for plaintiff on the law and the facts, plaintiff cannot within a year bring another action on the same cause of action; such judgment not being equivalent to a nonsuit, the "reversal" mentioned in the statute meaning a

3. Bellinger v. German Ins. Co. of Freeport, 189 N. Y. 533, 82 N. E. 1124, aff'g judg. 113 App. Div. 917, 100 N. Y. Supp. 424, 51 Misc. Rep. 463.

And see Wooster v. Forty-Second St. & Grand St. Ferry Co., 71 N. Y. 471. Code Civ. Proc., § 405, applies to an action for wrongful death by an administrator for the next of kin, though section 1902 limits the time to bring such action to two years, in spite of section 414. Hoffman v. Delaware & Hudson Co., 147 N. Y. Supp. 475.

4. Wood-Dickerson Supply Co. v. Cocciola, 153 Ala. 555, 45 So. 192.

Code Ala., § 2623, applies only where the judgment of reversal is fatal to plaintiff's right to maintain the action in the form in which it was first brought rather than where it is reversed on the merits. Carroll v. Alabama G. S. R. Co., 60 Fed. 549 (C. C., Ala.).

5. Fay v. Costa, 2 Cal. App. 241, 83 Pac. 275.

Under Florida Gen. St. 1906, §§ 1715, 1725, a suit to reform and enforce a fire insurance policy is barred by limitations when not commenced within five years after the accrual of the right of action or within one year after a judgment for plaintiff on the policy has been reversed. Erickson v. Insurance Co. of North America, 66 Fla. 154, 63 So. 716.

The Kansas Gen. St. 1901, § 4451, providing for the commencement of a new action within one year after the reversal or failure of a prior action, applies to an action on a bond given by a contractor for public work under sections 5130, 5131, to secure payment for labor or material, required by such statute to be commenced within six months after completion of the work. Kansas City Hydraulic Press Brick Co. v. National Surety Co., 167 Fed. 496, rev'g judg. 157 Fed. 620 (C. C. A., Mo.).

reversal in which the merits were not passed on.[6] Under South Dakota Code Civ. Proc., § 73, a proceeding before a referee for the assessment of the damages caused defendant by an improvidently issued injunction constitutes the commencement of an action, and, such assessment having been reversed on appeal, defendant has one year after reversal to commence a new action, regardless of the fact that the statute of limitations had run before such action was commenced.[7] Where a complaint was dismissed, and exceptions, heard by the Appellate Division, overruled, and an appeal taken to the Court of Appeals, which affirmed, the year in which plaintiff could sue anew, under New York Code Civ.

6. Strottman v. St. Louis, etc., Ry. Co., 228 Mo. 154, 128 S. W. 187.

And see A. M. Stevens Lumber Co. v. Kansas City Lumber Co., 72 Mo. App. 248; Hewitt v. Steele, 136 Mo. 327, 38 S. W. 82.

Under the provisions of Montana Code Civ. Proc., § 547, an action having been terminated by a judgment of affirmance of a judgment of dismissal on the pleadings, which was not on the merits, a second action on such cause of action may be commenced within a year after such termination. Glass v. Basin & Bay State Min. Co., 34 Mont. 88, 85 Pac. 746.

Oklahoma Comp. Laws 1909, § 5555, providing that a new action may be commenced within one year after reversal or failure, is inapplicable to actions under section 5945, authorizing recovery for wrongful death in an action commenced within two years. Partee v. St. Louis & S. F. R. Co., 204 Fed. 970, 123 C. C. A. 292.

Under Shannon's Code Tenn., § 4446, a defendant, who secured a reversal because the action was improperly brought in a court of chancery, will be enjoined by the decree of reversal from setting up the defense of limitations against a new action begun within a year. Swift & Co. v. Memphis Cold Storage Warehouse Co., 128 Tenn. 82, 158 S. W. 480.

7. Quarnberg v. City of Chamberlain, 29 S. D. 377, 137 N. W. 405.

See, as to the rule as to decisions on review under the statutes of other jurisdictions:

Mich.—Pattridge v. Lott, 15 Mich. 251.

N. C.—Webb v. Hicks, 125 N. C. 201, 34 S. E. 395, denying rehearing 123 N. C. 244, 31 S. E. 479.

Pa.—Spees v. Boggs, 204 Pa. 504, 54 Atl. 346.

S. C.—Richardson v. Riley, 67 S. C. 53, 45 S. E. 104.

Utah.—Gutheil v. Gilmer, 27 Utah 496, 76 Pac. 628.

Va.—Bradley Salt Co. v. Norfolk Importing & Exporting Co. of Virginia, 101 Fed. 681, 41 C. C. A. 600.

Wash.—Ryno v. Snider, 58 Wash. 457, 109 Pac. 55.

Proc., § 405, began to run from the affirmance by the Court of Appeals.[8]

§ 308(12). Action on set-off or counterclaim or cause of action alleged as defense.

Limitation does not run against an action on a claim during the pendency of an action against the claimant, in which such claim is pleaded as a set-off, which action is eventually discontinued by the plaintiff.[9] But a statute providing that, where the defendant has set up a counterclaim, and the action is discontinued, the time intervening between the commencement of the action and its termination is not a part of the time limited for the commencement of an action by defendant on the counterclaim, does not apply to a defendant who has not actually filed his claim as a counterclaim.[10] Under the Wisconsin statute declaring that when a defendant has interposed an answer as a defense, the remedy upon which at the commencement of such action was not barred, and such complaint is dismissed, the time which intervenes between the commencement and the termination of the action shall be excluded in determining limitations on the cause of action interposed by the defendant, it has been held that the time which elapsed between the filing and the dismissal of a suit to quiet title was not a part of the time limited for bringing an action for ejectment on the cause of action alleged as a defense in the former suit.[11] But a statute giving one who has "suffered" a nonsuit a year within which to sue again has no application to one who has pleaded set-off, and has been thrown out of court by the dismissal of the main action.[12]

8. People *ex rel.* Nolan v. Prendergast, 150 N. Y. Supp. 683.

9. United States v. Gillies, 144 Fed. 991.

10. *In re* Schlesinger's Estate, 55 N. Y. Supp. 514, 36 App. Div. 77, 2 Gibbons, 547; May v. Schlesinger, Id., rev'g *In re* May's Estate, 53 N. Y. Supp. 710, 24 Misc. Rep. 456, 2 Gibbons, 547, so held as to New York Code Civ. Proc., § 412, and hence did not relieve a contestant of an executor's account, who obtained leave to file objections, but did not file them until after his claim was barred.

11. Preston v. Thayer, 127 Wis. 123, 106 N. W. 672.

12. Liebke v. Thomas, 24 Mo. App. 24.

§ 309. Civil proceedings other than actions in general.

A right of action against the government under a contract for cartage of imported goods in its custody, accrues as soon as the money becomes due, without prior presentation of the claim to the executive department for allowance; and hence the six-years limitation in the Act of March 3, 1887, begins to run from that time, and is not interrupted by such presentation of the claim, or while it is under investigation, or in course of auditing by executive officers.[13] The citation of a surety on a guardian's bond to appear and state the condition of his principal's account, the guardian having died, is not an action at law or in equity, within the meaning of the Illinois statute of limitations; and his appearance does not revive a right already barred to recover from such surety any balance due on the account.[14] In Kentucky, where an assignor for the benefit of creditors has a demand against one of his creditors, the assignment is, in legal effect, an appropriation by the assignor of the debt due to him to the satisfaction, *pro tanto,* of the debt due by him to his debtor, and as to this sum the statute of limitations does not apply.[15] In Louisiana, the institution of executory proceedings on a mortgage note will interrupt prescription of the note, unless the proceedings are dismissed on motion of plaintiff.[16] In New York, the presentation of a claim against the State to a

13. United States v. Utz, 80 Fed. 848, 26 C. C. A. 184.

See also, Mississippi Cent. R. R. v. United States, 23 Ct. Cl. (U. S.) 27; Ihrie v. United States, 21 Ct. Cl. (U. S.) 216.

The presentation of a claim against the United States to the treasury department for examination and allowance, as required by law, bars the running of the statute of limitations during the time consumed in such investigation. United States v. Lippitt, 100 U. S. 663, 25 L. Ed. 747, 15 Ct. Cl. 622, followed. Utz v. United States, 75 Fed. 648, reversed United States v. Utz, *supra.*

14. People v. Stewart, 29 Ill. App. 441.

15. Cooper's Adm'r v. Cooper, 8 Ky. Law Rep. (abstract) 528.

16. Tertrou v. Durand, 30 La. Ann. 1108.

Waiver by defendant in executory process of demand of payment and notice of process is an interruption of prescription. Borland v. Lawrence, Man. Unrep. Cas. (La.) 331.

An order of seizure does not interrupt prescription on the note and debt on which it is founded. Harrod v. Voorhies, 16 La. 254.

board appointed by the Legislature to examine into its merits is equivalent to the commencement of an action between citizens, so as to stop the running of limitations against the claim.[17] In Nebraska, where an action against a county upon a claim for a tort, or for unliquidated damages is commenced by filing a claim with the county board, and the claim is rejected by the board, and the claimant appeals from the board's action to the district court, his action will be deemed to have been commenced upon the date of his filing his claim with the board.[18] In New Jersey, the running of the statute of limitations is arrested, upon the filing of a bill asking for the sale of land, as to taxes properly assessed upon the land and not barred at the time, whether accruing before or after the filing of the bill.[19]

In Texas, merely posting notices of sale under a trust deed will not suspend the running of the statute of limitations.[20] In Wisconsin, the presentation to the proper board of county supervisors of a claim for moneys paid on void tax certificates is the commencement of an action, and, if made within six years after the issue of the certificate or its assignment by the county, will prevent the bar of the statute from attaching.[21]

§ 310. Presentation of claim against estate of decedent.

In New York, presentation to an executor of a claim against the estate and its allowance by him is a liquidation of the claim, and fixes a new date for the running of limitations as of the date of

17. Coxe v. State, 144 N. Y. 396, 39 N. E. 400.

See Corkings v. State, 99 N. Y. 491, 2 N. E. 454, where a claim before the State Board of Audit was held to have been prosecuted with due diligence, and therefore was not barred.

18. Wherry v. Pawnee County, 88 Neb. 503, 129 N. W. 1013.

19. Barnes v. Brown, 1 Tenn. Ch. App. 726, Shannon's Code, § 969, providing for a reference, before confirmation of sale of land sold under decree, to ascertain if there are any taxes which are a lien upon the real estate on the day of sale, and providing for the collection thereof from the fund realized by the sale, being in effect a proceeding for the collection of taxes.

20. Blackwell v. Barnett, 52 Tex. 326.

21. Marsh v. St. Croix County Sup'rs, 42 Wis. 355.

presentation.[22] On presentation of a claim against a decedent's estate, the entry of an order of reference is the commencement of an action for the purpose of determining the period of limitation.[23] The presenting of the petition for the sale of realty of an estate for the payment of debts is the commencement of a legal proceeding for the payment of the claim and limitation will not run against it pending the proceeding, though the proceeding be not instituted by the claimant, but by the administrator for his benefit.[24] In Illinois, the effect of filing a claim in the court of probate is to arrest the running of the statute against such claim.[25] In Kansas, a proceeding to establish a claim against an estate is begun whenever a notice containing a copy of the instrument or account on which founded, and stating that it will be presented for allowance to the probate court at a time named, is served on the personal representative, so as to stop running of limitations.[26] In Mississippi, limitations do not bar the claim of an administrator against the estate for an individual debt duly probated and not barred at his appointment.[27] In Massachussetts, the leaving of a claim against an estate with the register, and his indorsement before the expiration of two years, is a beginning of suit sufficient to avoid

22. *In re* Nelson, 118 N. Y. Supp. 673, 63 Misc. Rep. 627.

23. Leahy v. Campbell, 75 N. Y. Supp. 72, 70 App. Div. 127.

24. *In re* Sargent, 59 N. Y. Supp. 105, 42 App. Div. 301, 2 Gibbons 597; *In re* Bradley's Estate, Id., aff'g 54 N. Y. Supp. 555, 25 Misc. Rep. 261, 2 Gibbons 597.

25. DeClerque v. Campbell, 125 Ill. App. 357. See Viskniskki v. Bleakley, 88 Ill. App. 613.

But the making out of an account, swearing to it and presenting it to an administrator out of court, does not arrest the running of the statute with respect to the rights of the heirs in the real estate. Mayberry v. Moore, 137 Ill. App. 40.

26. Clifton v. Meuser, 79 Kan. 655, 100 Pac. 645, and the controversy need not be decided, or submitted for decision, before expiration of the limitation period, or even the day first set for a hearing fall within that period.

27. Oliver v. Smith, 94 Miss. 879, 49 So. 1; Sims v. Sims, 30 Miss. 333.

Where a creditor procures his claim to be registered, the statute of limitations ceases to run, regardless of whether or not the proof of the claim is sufficient to make it a voucher to the personal representative. Allen v. Hillman, 69 Miss. 225, 13 So. 871.

the bar of the statute, providing that no administrator shall be held to answer the suit of a creditor of his decedent unless it is commenced within two years from his giving bond.[28] In Missouri, the presentment to the probate court for classification of a judgment against a testator on which neither execution nor *scire facias* can issue is, in effect, the institution of a suit on the judgment against the executor, and limitation ceases to run on such judgment from presentation.[29] In North Carolina, the commencement of proceedings by an executor for leave to sell testator's land for the payment of debts is, as regards the statute of limitations, the commencement of an action against the testator's estate by the creditors, especially as to a claim which the executor acknowledges, and asks leave to pay.[30] In Pennsylvania, the running of the statute of limitations is barred by the presentation of the claim to the auditor appointed to audit the accounts of the decedent's executor, as provided by statute.[31] In Tennessee, if a claim is filed, and reported by the clerk of the county court, and his report is confirmed, this is itself the commencement of an action, and an adjudication sufficient to prevent the bar of the statute.[32] And in Washington, the presentation of a claim for allowance, to the administrator of a deceased debtor, as required by statute, is the

28. Robinson v. Robinson, 173 Mass. 233, 53 N. E. 854.

29. McFaul v. Haley, 166 Mo. 56, 65 S. W. 995.

Exhibition of a demand against an estate properly made, and the docketing thereof in the probate court, arrest the running of the statute of limitations against the demand. Nicholls-Shepard Co. v. Donavon, 67 Mo. App. 286.

30. Harris v. Davenport, 132 N. C. 697, 44 S. E. 406; Wyrick v. Wyrick, 106 N. C. 84, 10 S. E. 916.

Under Code, § 164, when a claim is filed with the personal representative within a year after the grant of letters, and the same is admitted by him, it is not necessary to bring an action to prevent the bar of the statute, as to the heirs as well as to the personal representative. Woodlief v. Bragg, 108 N. C. 571, 13 S. E. 211.

31. *In re* Agnew's Estate, 17 Pa. Super. Ct. 201. See also, *In re* Heller's Estate, 17 Pa. Co. Ct. R. 603, 5 Pa. Dist. R. 205; Appeal of Keyser, 124 Pa. 80, 16 Atl. 577, 23 W. N. C. 201, 2 L. R. A. 159; *In re* Irvin's Estate, 6 Pa. Co. Ct. R. 582; *In re* Shand's Estate, 1 Pa. Co. Ct. R. 600.

32. Treece v. Carr (Tenn. Ch. App.), 58 S. W. 1078. See Woods v. Woods, 99 Tenn. 50, 41 S. W. 345; Wharton v. Marberry, 35 Tenn. 603.

commencement of an action within the statute.[33] As to the effect of the presentation of claims against estates of decedents in other States on the statute of limitations, see the authorities cited in the note below.[34]

§ 311. Presentation of claim against estate of insolvent or bankrupt.

An adjudication that a judgment debtor is a bankrupt does not operate as a stay of proceedings so as to stop the running of the statute of limitations against the judgment creditor's right to maintain supplementary proceedings.[35] The statute of limitations is a good defense to the suit of a creditor, who has proved his claim in bankruptcy, but has neglected to bring his suit until a discharge in bankruptcy has been refused.[36] The limitation declared by section 2 of the bankrupt act, that a suit by or against an assignee, touching the property and rights of the bankrupt, must be brought within two years, does not extend to or include an application by the assignee for moneys paid into court, belonging, in part at least, to the bankrupt's estate, and directed to remain in court to answer an alleged claim against it, when established.[37] The commencement of an action to sequestrate the prop-

33. Frew v. Clark, 34 Wash. 561, 76 Pac. 85.

34. *Cal.*—*In re* Schroeder's Estate, Myr. Prob. (Cal.) 7.

Colo.—Fox v. Lipe, 14 Colo. App. 258, 59 Pac. 850.

Fla.—Barnes v. Scott, 29 Fla. 285, 11 So. 48; Deans v. Wilcoxon, 25 Fla. 980, 7 So. 163.

Iowa.—Fritz v. Fritz, 93 Iowa 27, 61 N. W. 169; Johnston v. Johnston, 36 Iowa 608.

Ky.—Beddow v. Wilson, 28 Ky. Law Rep. 661, 90 S. W. 228.

La.—Elmore v. Ventress, 24 La. Ann. 382.

N. J.—Smith v. Crater, 43 N. J. Eq. (16 Stew.) 636, 12 Atl. 530.

N. M.—Browning v. Browning, 3 N. M. (Gild.) 659, 9 Pac. 677.

Ohio.—Taylor v. Thorn, 29 Ohio St. 569.

S. C.—McMillin v. Brown, 2 Hill Eq. 457.

Va.—Crauford's Adm'r v. Smith's Ex'r, 93 Va. 623, 23 S. E. 235, 25 S. E. 657.

Wis.—Jones v. Keep's Estate, 23 Wis. 45.

35. Cleveland v. Johnson, 26 N. Y. Supp. 734, 5 Misc. Rep. 484.

36. Hill v. Phillips, 14 R. I. 93.

37. Phillips v. Helmbold, 26 N. J. Eq. (11 C. E. Green) 202 (1875).

erty of a corporation by a creditor, and his exhibiting his claim against it, tolls the statute of limitations, both as to the corporation and its stockholders.[38] The allowance and approval of claims in receivership proceedings prevents the running of the statute of limitations, and a subsequent motion of creditors for payment of their claims does not constitute the commencement of the action.[39] In Alabama, one who contests a claim against an insolvent estate, in order to avail himself of the statute of limitations, must show that after the maturity of the debt the statutory bar was complete before the claim was filed.[40] In Iowa, the depositing of a claim with an assignee for creditors within the time fixed by law is a commencement of an action on the claim.[41] In Maryland, the statute may be relied on against the claims of creditors in a creditors' suit, after the auditor has reported in favor of the claims to which the statute is set up as a bar, unless the party setting it up has before waived it, expressly or impliedly.[42] In Massachusetts, the statute of limitations does not run against a claim on an insolvent debtor, after the publication of the messenger's notice of the issuing of a warrant against the debtor, under the statute. A claim not barred by the statute when such publication is made, may be proved at a meeting of the creditors held after it would otherwise have been barred.[43] In New York, the exhitition of the claim of a creditor against an absent or absconding debtor to his trustees is equivalent to the commencement of a suit against

38. Potts v. St. Paul Athletic Park Ass'n, 84 Minn. 217, 87 N. W. 604; Stevens v. Hause, Id.

39. St. Louis Union Trust Co. v. St. Louis & S. F. Ry. Co. (Tex. Civ. App.), 146 S. W. 348, a receiver of a railroad company held to have saved claims of creditors against a plea of limitations by allowing and auditing them.

40. Woodruff v. Winston, 68 Ala. 412.

41. Lacey v. Newcomb, 95 Iowa 287, 63 N. W. 704, within Miller's Code, §§ 2017, 2018, which provide that a landlord's lien shall exist for one year only after the rent falls due, and that the lien shall be effected by the commencement of an action for the rent within that time.

42. Post v. Mackall, 3 Bland (Md.) 486. See also, Welch v. Stewart, 2 Bland (Md.) 37.

43. Minot v. Thatcher, 48 Mass. (7 Metc.) 348, 41 Am. Dec. 444, under St. 1838, c. 163. And see Guild v. Hale, 15 Mass. 455, under St. 1793, c. 75, § 3.

the debtor, so as to prevent the statute from attaching.[44] In Ohio, mere presentation of a claim to an assignee for allowance under the statute, regulating the presentation of claims to an assignee, does not prevent a statute of limitations from running, but approval is required.[45] In Texas, where the claims of creditors of assigning debtors are filed with the assignees within the time prescribed by law, no limitation can accrue thereafter while the estate is in process of settlement.[46]

§ 312. Proceedings in other court or tribunal.

An injunction granted in proceedings for limitation of liability restraining the further prosecution of pending actions for damages is in effect a removal of such actions into the admiralty court, where they are to be considered as continued for all purposes of the statute of limitations.[47] The commencement of a contest in the United States land department will not stop the running of the statute of limitations of the State.[48] Under Louisiana Civil Code, § 3484, providing that a legal prescription takes place when the possessor has been cited to appear before a court of justice, in a suit for damages arising from an obstruction on a sidewalk, suit previously brought in the circuit court of the United States interrupts prescription, though that court had no jurisdiction *ratione personae;* the plaintiff being a citation of Louisiana.[49] The Oregon statute, making the presentation of a State claim to the Legislature prevent its being barred by the statute of limitations, gives the claimant the right to sue after the passage of the act, and his claim is not barred for the lapse of the statutory time after the taking effect of the act, whether presented to the Legislature or not.[50] Where A. and B. are codefendants, and in the course

44. Peck v. Trustees of Randall, 1 Johns. (N. Y.) 165.

45. Burrows v. Hussong, 31 Ohio Cir. Ct. R. 211, under Ohio Rev. St. § 6352.

46. McCord v. Sprinkel, 105 Tex. 150, 141 S. W. 945, aff'g Sprinkel v. McCord (Civ. App.), 129 S. W. 379.

47. Union Steamboat Co. v. Chaffin's Adm'rs, 204 Fed. 412.

48. Southern Pac. R. Co. v. Whitaker, 109 Cal. 268, 41 Pac. 1083.

49. Blume v. City of New Orleans, 104 La. 345, 29 So. 106.

50. Ketchum v. State, 2 Or. 103.

of judicial inquiry the indebtedness of A. to B. is found, B., or his creditor pursuing his rights in B's name, may avail himself of this to repel the effect of lapse of time, or to defeat the operation of the statute of limitations, in a subsequent suit against A.[51] To a plea of the statute of limitations, the plaintiffs replied, setting forth an action against the same defendants, brought within the period of limitation by one of the present plaintiffs upon the same cause of action and arrest of judgment, and that the present action was brought within a year, it was held that the replication was bad, as all the plaintiffs did not join in the first action.[52]

§ 313. Excuses for delay.

Where plaintiff, one of two joint makers of a note, paid it at maturity, and the defendant requested him to " hold up the note until he could pay his part," this request was not a promise not to plead limitations, and plaintiff could not excuse his delay to sue upon that ground.[53] The plea of the statute of limitations cannot be defeated, for no other reason than that the plaintiff supposed, if he sued, he could not recover.[54] An action will not lie by the purchaser of land at execution sale to set aside an alleged fraudulent certificate of redemption, more than three years after the discovery of the fraud, such limitation being prescribed by statute for actions for relief on the ground of fraud, though, after the discovery of the fraud, the commencement of suit was delayed by negotiations with reference to settlements and owing to the ill health of plaintiff.[55] The fact that by the clerk's fault citation was not issued before the running of limitations did not bar the action.[56] Poverty and inability to bear litigation are no excuse for failure to bring suit to recover land.[57]

51. Fahs v. Taylor, 10 Ohio 104.

52. Crow v. State, 23 Ark. 684.

53. Liverman v. Cahoon, 156 N. C. 187, 72 S. E. 327.

54. Commissioners of Sinking Fund v. McDowell, 6 Ky. Law Rep. (abstract) 520.

55. Carroll v. Hill Tract Imp. Co., 44 Wash. 569, 87 Pac. 835.

56. Western Union Telegraph Co. v. Hill (Tex. Civ. App.), 162 S. W. 382.

57. Voight v. Raby, 90 Va. 799, 20 S. E. 824.

APPENDIX.

THE AMERICAN AND ENGLISH

STATUTES OF LIMITATIONS.

Space permits only the most important of these statutes being here printed, but the provisions here given are in their exact language, and all amendments are included down to date. The following topics are covered in the text and notes of this book: Absence, §§ 237, 244, 245; Acknowledgments, § 83; Accounts, §§ 277-280; Adverse Use and Right of Entry, §§ 254-256; Assumpsit, §§ 19, 23, 24; Co-contractors, § 285; Commencement of Action, § 290; Defendants' Estates, § 196; Disabilities, § 237; Dower, § 273; Effect of Foreign Statutes, § 8; Fraudulent Concealment, §§ 274-276; Injunction, § 243; Mortgages, § 223; Set-off, § 284; Simple Contracts, §§ 21, 23; Specialties, §§ 21, 30-32, 37, 172.

UNITED STATES.

UNITED STATES REVISED STATUTES.

Crimes.—For treason or other capital offence, wilfull murder excepted, *three years* [§ 1043]. For offences not capital, except as provided in § 1043, *three years* [§ 1044, as amended by the Act of April 13, 1876, chap. 56, 19 Statutes at Large, p. 32]. For crimes under the revenue laws, *five years* [§ 1046]. Suits or prosecutions for penalties and forfeitures under the laws of the United States, *five years* [§ 1047].

In civil prosecutions the Federal Courts follow the local State statutes of limitations. See *supra*, § 40*a*, n, 2, note 3. As to limitation in suits for the the infringement of patents, see *supra*, § 40*a*, n, 2.

ALABAMA.

CIVIL CODE (1907) CHAP. 108, ART. 1.

Section 4830. **No limitation to certain specified actions by the State to recover land.**—There s no lmitation of the time within which the State may bring actions for the recovery of any of the land mentioned in Section 3859 of this Code (lands of State, and educational or charitable institutions).

Sec. 4831. **No limitation to action by Municipal Corporation to recover land.** There is no limitation of the time within which counties and other municipal corporations may bring actions for the recovery of lands belonging to them.

Sec. 4832. (2793.) **Limitation of action.**—All other civil actions must be commenced after the cause of action has accrued within the period prescribed in this chapter and not afterwards.

Sec. 4833. (2794.) **Actions within Twenty Years.**—Actions upon a judgment or decree of any court of the State, of the United States, or of any State or Territory of the United States.

Sec. 4834. (2795.) **Actions to be brought within Ten Years.**—1. Actions founded upon any contract or writing under seal.

2. Actions for the recovery of lands, tenements, or hereditaments, or the possession thereof, except as herein otherwise provided.

3. Motions and other actions against sheriffs, coroners, constables, and other public officers, for nonfeasance, misfeasance, or malfeasance in office.

Sec. 4835. (2796.) **Six Years.**—1. Actions for any trespass to person or liberty, such as false imprisonment or assault and battery.

2. Actions for any trespass to real or personal property.

3. Actions for the detention or conversion of personal property.

4. Actions founded on a promise in writing not under seal.

5. Actions for the recovery of money upon a loan, upon a stated or liquidated account, or for arrears of rent due upon a parol demise.

6. Actions for the use and occupation of land.

7. Motions, and other actions against the sureties of any sheriff, coroner, constable, or any public officer, or actions against the sureties of executors, administrators, or guardians, for any misfeasance or malfeasance whatever of their principal, the time to be computed from the act done or omitted by their principal, which fixes the liability of the surety.

8. Motions and other actions against attorneys at law, for failure to pay over money of their clients, or for neglect or omission of duty.

9. Actions founded upon judgments obtained before justices of the peace of this State.

10. Actions upon any simple contract or specialty, not herein specifically enumerated.

Sec. 4836. (2797.) **Five Years.**—1. All actions founded on equities of redemption, where lands have been sold under a decree of the court of chancery, existing in any person not a party to the proceedings, who claims under the mortgagor or grantor in the deed of trust.

2. (Sec. 5214, 3171). Bills in equity to annual probate partitions.

Sec. 4837. (2798.) **Four Years.**—1. All actions or motions against any surety to any writ of error, appeal, replevy, or forthcoming bond, executed in any cause in any of the courts of the United States, or of any other State or country except the State of Alabama.

Sec. 4838. (2799.) **Three Years.**—1. Actions to recover money due by open or unliquidated account, the time to be computed from the date of the last item of the account, or from the time when, by contract or usage, the account is due.

Sec. 4839. (2800.) **Two Years.**—Actions by representatives to recover damages for wrongful act, omission or negligence causing death of the decedent, under sections 2486 (27) and 2485 (26).

Sec. 4840. (2801.) **One Year.**—1. Actions for malicious prosecutions.

2. Actions for criminal conversation, for seduction, or breach of marriage promise.

3. Actions *qui tam*, or for a penalty given by statute to the party aggrieved, unless the statute imposing it prescribes a different limitation.

4. Actions of libel or slander.

5. Actions for any injury to the person or rights of another, not arising from contract, and not herein specifically enumerated.

6. Proceedings in court for disbarring an attorney.

By section 3091 (674), the above provisions apply to suits in chancery. As to disabilities, see *supra*, section 237.

Sec. 4841. (2802.) **Agreement or Stipulation to Shorten Statute of Limitations void.**—Any agreement or stipulation, verbal or written, whereby the time for the bringing of any action is limited to a time less than that prescribed by law for the bringing of such actions, is void.

ALASKA.

CODE OF CIVIL PROCEDURE, §§ 835-845; COMPILED LAWS OF THE TERRITORY OF ALASKA (1913), PP. 379-382.

Sec. 836. (4.) **Actions to be brought within Ten Years.**—Actions for the recovery of real property, or for the recovery of the possession thereof.

Sec. 837. (5.) 1. An action upon a judgment. 2. An action upon a sealed instrument.

Sec. 838. (6.) **Six Years.**—1. An action upon a contract or liability, express or implied, excepting those mentioned in section 837.

2. An action upon a liability created by statute, other than a penalty or forfeiture.

3. An action for waste or trespass upon real property.

4. An action for taking, detaining, or injuring personal property, including an action for the specific recovery thereof.

Sec. 839. (7.) **Three Years.**—1. An action against a marshal, coroner, or constable, upon a liability incurred by the doing of an act in his official capacity or in virtue of his office; or by the omission of an official duty, including the non-payment of money collected upon an execution, but not including an action for an escape.

2. An action upon a statute for penalty or forfeiture, where the action is given to the party aggrieved, or to such person and the United States, except where the statute imposing it prescribes a different limitation.

Sec. 840. (8.) **Two Years.**—1. An action for libel, slander, assault, battery, seduction, false imprisonment, or for any injury to the person or rights of another not arising on contract, and not herein especially enumerated.

2. An action upon a statute for a forfeiture or penalty to the United States.

Sec. 841. (9.) **One Year.**—An action against the marshal or other officer for the escape of a person arrested or imprisoned on civil process.

Sec. 842. (10.) **Actions for penalties.**—Actions for penalties given to private individuals for prosecuting an offense, *one year* after its commission; or *two years*, if not so prosecuted, but prosecuted by the district attorney in behalf of the United States.

Sec. 843. (11.) **Other actions.**—Actions for any cause not here provided for, must be commenced *within ten years.*

ARIZONA

REVISED STATUTES 1913, CIVIL CODE, TITLE 6, PART 3.

CHAP. I.—LIMITATION OF ACTIONS FOR LAND.

(2297.) Sec. 695. (1.) **Suit against Possessor under Color of Title, Three Years.**—To recover real property as against any person in peaceable and adverse possession thereof under title or color of title, *three years.*

(2298.) Sec. 696. (2.) **"Title" and "color of title" defined.**

(2299.) Sec. 697. (3.) **Suit against Possessor under Deed; Forged Deed, Five Years.**—To recover real property as against any person having peaceable and adverse possession thereof, cultivating, using, or enjoying the same, and paying taxes thereon, if any, and claiming under a deed or deeds duly recorded, shall be instituted within five years next after the cause of action shall have accrued, and not afterwards: *provided* that this section shall not apply to any one in possession of land, who in the absence of this section would deraign title through a forged deed; *provided, further*, that no one claiming under a forged deed, or a deed executed under a forged power of attorney, shall be allowed the benefits of this section.

Sec. 698.—Any person who has a right of action for recovery of any lands, tenements, or hereditaments against another having peaceable and adverse possession thereof, cultivating, using and enjoying the same, shall institute his suit therefor within ten years next after his cause of action shall have accrued, and not afterward.

(2300.) Sec. 699. (4.) **Restriction to 160 acres.**—The peaceable and adverse possession contemplated in the preceding section as against the person having right of action shall be construed to embrace not more than one hundred and sixty acres, including the improvements or the number of acres actually enclosed, should the same be less than one hundred and sixty acres, but when such possession is taken under some written memorandum of title, other than a deed, which fixes the boundaries of the possessor's claim and is duly recorded, such peaceable possession shall be construed to be co-extensive with the boundaries specified in such instrument.

Sec. 700.—Town or City Lots.—Every suit instituted to recover any lot or lots situate in a city or town against a person having a recorded deed therefor, who claims the ownership thereof and who has paid the taxes thereon, shall be instituted within five years next after the cause of action accrued, and not afterwards; *provided*, that the one against whom the suit is instituted, by himself or his grantors, shall have such recorded deed or deeds on record, shall have claimed the ownership thereof and shall have paid the taxes thereon for at least five consecutive years next preceding the institution of such suit.

(2301.) Sec. 701. (5.) **Against Claimant by Right of Possession, Two Years.**— In all cases where the party in possession claims real property by right of possession, only suits to recover the possession from him shall be brought in *two years* after the right of action accrues and not afterwards, and in such case the defendant is not required to show title or color of title from and under the sovereignty of the soil as provided in the preceding section as against the plaintiff who shows no better right.

CHAP. II.—LIMITATION OF PERSONAL ACTIONS.

(2309.) Sec. 709. (13.) **One Year.**— All actions or suits, in court, of the following description:—

1. Actions for malicious prosecution, or for false imprisonment, or for injuries done to the character or reputation of another by libel or slander.
2. Actions for damages for seduction or breach of promise of marriage.
3. An action upon a liability created by statute, other than a penalty or forfeiture.

(2310.) Sec. 710. (14.) **Two Years.**—All actions or suits, in court, of the following description:—

1. Actions for injuries done to the person of another.
2. Actions of trespass for injury done to the estate or the property of another.
3. Actions for detaining the personal property of another and for converting such personal property to one's own use.
4. Actions for taking or carrying away the goods and chattes of another.
5. Actions for injuries done to the person of another where death ensued from such injuries; and the cause of action shall be considered as having accrued at the death of the party injured.

(2311.) Sec. 711. (15.) **Three Years.**—All actions or suits, in court of the following description:—

1. Actions for debt where the indebtedness is not evidenced by contract in writing.
2. Actions upon stated or open accounts other than such mutual and current accounts as concern the trade of merchandise between merchant and merchant, their factors or agents.

3. Actions for relief on the ground of fraud or mistake. The cause of action in such case need not be deemed to have accrued until the discovery by the aggrieved party of the facts constituting the fraud or mistake.

(2312.) Sec. 712. (16.) **Accounts not of Merchants, &c., from Date of Delivery.**—In all accounts except those between merchant and merchant, as aforesaid, their factors and agents, the respective times or dates of the delivery of the several articles charged shall after demand made in writing be particularly specified, and limitation shall run against each item from the date of such delivery, unless otherwise specifically contracted.

(2313.) Sec. 713. (17.) **Four Years.**—All actions or suits in court, of the following description:—

1. Actions for the penalty or for damages on the penal clause of a bond to convey real estate.

2. Actions by one partner against his copartner for a settlement of the partnership accounts; or upon mutual and current accounts concerning the trade of merchandise between merchant and merchant, their factors or agents, and the cause of action shall be considered as having accrued on a cessation of the dealings in which they were interested together.

3. Actions upon a judgment or decree of any court rendered without this State or upon an instrument in writing executed without this State.

(2314.) Sec. 714. (18.) **Action on Written Contract, Four Years.**—Actions for debt where the indebtedness is evidenced by or founded upon any contract in writing, executed within this State, shall be commenced and prosecuted within four years after the cause of action shall have accrued and not afterward.

(315.) Sec. 715. (19.) **Suit on Bond of Executor, or Guardian, Four Years.**—All suits on the bond of any executor, administrator, or guardian, shall be commenced and prosecuted within four years next after the death, resignation, removal, or discharge of such executor, administrator, or guardian and not thereafter.

(2316.) Sec. 716. (20.) **Other Personal Actions, Four Years.**—Every action other than for the recovery of real estate, for which no limitation is otherwise prescribed, shall be brought within four years next after the right to bring the same shall have accrued, and not afterward.

(2317.) Sec. 717. (21.) **Actions on foreign Judgments.**—Every action upon a judgment or decree rendered in any other State or Territory of the United States, in the District of Columbia, or in any foreign country, shall be barred, if by the laws of such State or country such action would there be barred, and the judgment or decree be incapable of being otherwise enforced.

(2318.) Sec. 718. (22.) **Action for Specific Performance, Four Years.**—Any action for the specific performance of a contract for the oonveyance of real estate, four years.

(2319.) Sec. 719. (23.) **Revivor, Five Years.—Proceeding against Sheriff.**—Where execution has issued and no return is made thereon, the party in whose favor the same was issued may move against any sheriff or other officer and his deputies for not returning the same within five years from the day on which it was returnable and not after.

(2321.) Sec. 720. (25.) **Forcible Entry or Forcible Detainer, Two Years.**—No action of forcible entry or forcible detainer, as provided for by law, shall be prosecuted at any time after two years from the commencement of the forcible entry or detainer.

(2322.) Sec. 721. (26.) **Contest of Will, One Year.**—Any person interested in any will which shall have been probated under the laws of this State, institute suit in the proper court to contest the validity thereof, within one year after such will shall have been admitted to probate, and not afterward.

Sec. 722. **Cancellation of Will for forgery or other fraud, One Year.**—Any heir at law of the testator or any person interested in his estate, may institute a suit in the proper court to cancel a will for forgery or other fraud within one year after the discovery of the forgery or fraud, and not afterward.

ARKANSAS.

KIRBY'S DIGEST OF THE STATUTES, 1904, CHAP. 102; CASTLE'S SUPPLEMENT TO KIRBY'S DIGEST, 1911.

Sec. 5056. (4815.) For the recovery of lands, tenements or hereditaments, *seven years;* as to disabilities, see *supra,* § 237, and n. 17.

Sec. 5060. (4818.) For the recovery of lands sold at judicial sales, *five years.*

Sec. 5064. (4822.) **Actions to be commenced in Three Years.**—*First,* All actions founded upon any contract or liability, express or implied, not in writing. *Second,* All actions for trespass on lands, or for libels. *Third,* All actions for taking or injuring any goods or chattels.

Sec. 5065. (4823.) **Within One Year.**—*First,* All actions for criminal conversation, assault and battery, and false imprisonment. *Second,* All actions for words spoken, slandering the character of another. *Third,* All words spoken, whereby special damages are sustained.

Sec. 5066. (4824.) **For Escape.**—All actions against sheriffs or other officers, for the escape of any person imprisoned on civil process within *one year.*

Sec. 5067. (4825.) **Sheriffs and Coroners.**—All actions against sheriffs and coroners, for other official misconduct, *one year.*

Sec. 5068. (4826.) **Penal Statutes.**—All actions upon penal statutes where the penalty or any part thereof goes to the State or any county or person suing for the same *two years.*

Sec. 5069. (4827.) **Instruments in Writing.**—Actions on promissory notes, and other instruments in writing, *five years.—Act Dec.* 14, 1844.

Sec. 5070. (4828.) **Writings under Seal.**—Actions on writings under seal, *five years.*

Sec. 5071. (4829.) **Official Bonds.**—Actions on the official bonds of sheriffs, coroners, and constables, *four years.—Act Dec.* 14, 1844, *and Rev. St. c.* 26, § 14.

Sec. 5072. (4830.) **Executors' Bonds.**—Action on the bonds of executors and administrators, *eight years.*—*Act Dec.* 14, 1844.

Sec. 5073. (4831.) **Judgments.**—Actions on all judgments and decrees, *ten years.*

[By the Act of April 19, 1895, chap. 135, claims against counties, *three years.*]

Sec. 5074. (4832.) **General Provision.**—All other actions, *four years.*

CALIFORNIA.

CODE OF CIVIL PROCEDURE. 1908.

PART II., TITLE II., CHAP. I.

Sec. 312. **Commencement of Civil Actions.**—Civil actions, without exception, can only be commenced within the periods prescribed in this title, after the cause of action shall have accrued, unless where, in special cases, a different limitation is prescribed by statute.

Sec. 315. **When the People will not Sue.**—The people of this State will not sue any person for or in respect to any real property, or the issues or profits thereof, by reason of the right or title of the people to the same, unless:

1. Such right or title shall have accrued within ten years before any action or other proceeding for the same is commenced; or,

2. The people, or those from whom they claim, shall have received the rents and profits of such real property, or of some part thereof, within the space of ten years.

Sec. 316. **When Action cannot be brought by Grantee from the State.**—No action can be brought for or in respect to real property by any person claiming under letters patent or grants from this State, unless the same might have been commenced by the people as herein specified, in case such patent had not been issued or grant made.

Sec. 317. **When Actions by the People or their Grantees are to be brought within Five Years.**—When letters patent or grants of real property issued or made by the people of this State, are declared void by the determination of a competent court, an action for the recovery of the property so conveyed may be brought, either by the people of the State, or by any subsequent patentee or grantee of the property, his heirs or assigns, within four years after such determination, but not after that period.

CHAP. II.—AS TO REAL PROPERTY.

Sec. 318. **Seizin within Five Years, when necessary.**—No action for the recovery of real property, or for the recovery of the possession thereof, can be maintained, unless it appear that the plaintiff, his ancestor, predecessor, or grantor, was seized or possessed of the property in question within five years before the commencement of the action.

Sec. 319. **Such Seizin, when necessary in action or defense arising out of title to or rents of real property.**—No cause of action, or defense to an action, arising out of the title to real property, or to rents or profits out of the same, can be effectual, unless it appear that the person prosecuting the action, or making the defense, or under whose title the action is prosecuted, or the defense is made, or the ancestor, predecessor, or grantor of such person was seized or possessed of the premises in question within five years before the commencement of the act in respect to which such action is prosecuted or defense made.

Sec. 320. **Entry on Real Estate.**—No entry upon real estate is deemed sufficient or valid as a claim, unless an action be commenced thereupon within one year after making such entry, and within five years from the time when the right to make it descended or accrued.

Sec. 321. **Possession, when presumed. Occupation deemed under legal title, unless adverse.**—In every action for the recovery of real property, or the possession thereof, the person establishing a legal title to the property is presumed to have been possessed thereof within the time required by law. And the occupation of the property by any other person is deemed to have been under and in subordination to the legal title, unless it appear that the property has been held and possessed adversely to such legal title, for five years before the commencement of the action.

Sec. 322. **Occupation under Written Instrument or Judgment, when deemed adverse.**—Whenever it appears that the occupant, or those under whom he claims, entered into possession of the property under claim of title, exclusive of other right, founding such claim upon a written instrument, as being a conveyance of the property in question, or upon the decree or judgment of a competent court, and that there has been a continued occupation and possession of the property included in such instrument, decree, or judgment, or of some part of the property under such claim, for five years, the property so included is deemed to have been held adversely, except that, when it consists of a tract divided into lots, the possession of one lot is not deemed a possession of any other lot of the same tract.

Sec. 323. **What constitutes Adverse Possession under Written Instrument or Judgment.**—For the purpose of constituting an adverse possession by any person claiming a title founded upon a written instrument, or a judgment or decree, land is deemed to have been possessed and occupied in the following cases: 1. Where it has been usually cultivated and improved. 2. Where it has been protected by a substantial inclosure. 3. Where, although not inclosed, it has been used for the supply of fuel, or of fencing timber for the purposes of husbandry, or for pasturage, or for the ordinary use of the occupant. 4. Where a known farm or single lot has been partly improved, the portion of such farm or lot that may have been left not cleared, or not inclosed according to the usual course and custom of the adjoining country, shall be deemed to have been occupied for the same length of time as the part improved and cultivated.

CHAP. III.—THE TIME OF COMMENCING ACTIONS OTHER THAN FOR THE RECOVERY OF REAL PROPERTY.

Sec. 335. **Periods of Limitation prescribed.**—The periods prescribed for the commencement of actions other than for the recovery of real property are as follows:

Sec. 336. **Within Five Years.**

1. An action upon a judgment or decree of any court of the United States, or of any State within the United States.

2. An action for mesne profits of real property.

Sec. 337. **Within Four Years.**

An action upon any contract, obligation, or liability, founded upon an instrument in writing executed within this State.

Sec. 338. **Within Three Years.**

1. An action upon a liability created by statute, other than a penalty or forfeiture.

2. An action for trespass upon real property.

3. An action for taking, detaining, or injuring any goods or chattels, including actions for the specific recovery of personal property.

4. An action for relief on the ground of fraud or mistake. The cause of action in such case not to be deemed to have accrued until the discovery, by the aggrieved party, of the facts constituting the fraud or mistake.

Sec. 339. **Within Two Years.**

1. An action upon a contract, obligation, or liability, not founded upon an instrument in writing, or founded upon an instrument of writing executed out of the State.

2. An action against a sheriff, coroner, or constable, upon a liability incurred by the doing of an act in his official capacity, and in virtue of his office, or by the omission of an official duty, including the non-payment of money collected upon an execution. But this subdivision does not apply to an action for an escape.

Sec. 340. **Within One Year.**

1. An action upon a statute for a penalty or forfeiture, when the action is given to an individual, or to an individual and the State, except when the statute imposing it prescribes a different limitation.

2. An action upon a statute, or upon an undertaking in a criminal action, for a forfeiture or penalty to the people of this State.

3. An action for libel, slander, assault, battery, false imprisonment, seduction, or for injury to, or for the death of one caused by the wrongful act or neglect of another, or by a depositor against a bank for the payment of a forged or raised check.

4. An action against a sheriff or other officer for the escape of a prisoner arrested or imprisoned on civil process.

5. An action against a municipal corporation for damages or injuries to property caused by a mob or riot.

Sec. 341. **Within Six Months.**

An action against an officer, or officer *de facto:*

1. To recover any goods, wares, merchandise, or other property seized by any such officer in his official capacity as tax-collector, or to recover the price or value of any goods, wares, merchandise, or other personal property so seized, or for damages for the seizure, detention, sale of or injury to any goods, wares, merchandise, or other personal property seized, or for damages done to any person or property in making any such seizure.

2. To recover stock sold for a delinquent assessment, as provided in section 347 of the Civil Code.

Sec. 342. **Action on Claims against Counties.**—Actions on claims against a county, which have been rejected by the board of supervisors, must be commenced within six *months* after the first rejection thereof by such board.

Sec. 343. **Actions for Relief not hereinbefore provided for.**—An action for relief not hereinbefore provided for, must be commenced within *four years* after the cause of action shall have accrued.

Sec. 348. **No Limitation.**—To actions brought to recover money or other property deposited with any bank, banker, trust company, or savings and loan society, there is no limitation.

The Act of Feb. 28, 1893, chap. 45, limits suits against the State on contract or for negligence to *two years,* except as to minors and persons insane or imprisoned.

COLORADO.

MILL'S ANNOTATED STATUTES, 1912, VOL. 2, CHAP. 99.

DIVISION I., PERSONAL ACTIONS.

Sec. 4627. (2900.) **Actions barred in Six Years.**

First. All actions of debt founded upon any contract or liability in action.

Second. All actions upon judgments rendered in any court not being a court of record.

Third. All actions for arrears of rent.

Fourth. All actions of assumpsit or on the case, founded on any contract or liability, express or implied.

Fifth. All actions for waste and for trespass on land.

Sixth. All actions of replevin, and all other actions for taking, detaining, or injuring goods or chattels.

Seventh. All other actions on the case, except actions for slanderous words, and for libels.

Sec. 4628. (2901.) **In One Year.**—All actions for assault and battery, and for false imprisonment, and all actions for slanderous words and for libels.

Sec. 4629. (2902.) **For Escape.**—All actions against sheriffs, or other officers for the escape of persons imprisoned on civil process, *six months.*

Sec. 4630. (2903.) **Against Sheriffs and Coroners.**—All actions against sheriffs and coroners, upon any liability incurred by them, by the doing of any act in their official capacity, or by the omission of any official duty, except for escapes, *one year*.

Sec. 4631. (2904.) **Action on Account.**—In all actions of debt or assumpsit, brought to recover the balance due upon a mutual and open account-current, from the time of the last item proved in such account.

Sec. 4632. (2905.) **Actions Barred in Three Years.**—All personal actions, on any account not limited by the foregoing sections, or by any other law in this State.

Sec. 4633. (2906.) **Set-off, how Limitation Computed on.**—All the provisions of this chapter shall apply to the case of any debt or contract, alleged, by way of set-off, on the part of a defendant; and the time of limitation of such debt shall be computed in like manner as if an action had been commenced therefor at the time when the plaintiff's action accrued.

Sec. 4634. (2907.) **Actions for Penalties and Forfeitures.**—All actions and suits, for any penalty or forfeiture of any penal statute brought by this State, or any person to whom the penalty or forfeiture is given, in whole or in part, *one year*.

Sec. 4635. (2908.) **Suits Limited by Statute.**—The preceding section shall not apply to any suit which is or shall be limited by any statute to be brought within a shorter time than is prescribed therein, but such suit shall be brought within the time that may be limited by such statute.

Sec. 4636. (2909.) **Limitations to Apply to Court of Equity, when.**—Whenever there is a concurrent jurisdiction in the courts of common law and in courts of equity, of any cause of action, the provisions of this chapter limiting the time for the commencement of a suit for such cause of action in a court of common law shall apply to all suits hereafter to be brought for the same cause in the court of chancery.

Sec. 4637. (2910.) **Not to Apply to Courts of Equity, when.**—The last section shall not extend to suits over the subject-matter of which a court of equity has peculiar and exclusive jurisdiction, and which subject-matter is not cognizable in the courts of common law.

Sec. 4638. (2911.) **Actions for Relief on Ground of Fraud.**—Bills of relief on the ground of fraud, *three years* after its discovery.

Sec. 4639. (2912.) **Trusts and other Cases.**—Bills of relief, in case of the existence of a trust not cognizable by the courts of common law, and in all other cases not herein provided for, *five years*.

Sec. 4642. (2915.) **What Actions Barred in Six Years.**—It shall be lawful for any person, against whom any action shall be commenced in any court of this State, wherein the cause of action accrued without this State, upon a contract or agreement expressed or implied, or upon any sealed instrument in writing, or upon a judgment or decree rendered in any court without this State, more than six years before the commencement of the action in this State, to plead the same in bar of the action in this State, *provided*, etc., [*as amended by the Act of* 1899, *c.* 113, *which repealed the prior amendment made by the Act of April* 29, 1895].

DIVISION II., CONCERNING REAL ESTATE.

Sec. 4650. (2923.) **Limitation—Twenty Years.**—That no person shall commence an action for the recovery of lands, or make an entry thereon, unless within twenty years after the right to bring such action or make such entry first accrued, or within twenty years after he or those from, by or under whom he claims, have been seized or possessed of the premises, except as hereinafter provided.

Sec. 4653. **Within Seven Years.**—Actions brought for the recovery of any lands, tenements, or hereditaments of which any person may be possessed by actual residence thereon for seven successive years, having a connected title in law or equity, deducible of record, from this State or the United States, or from any public officer or other person authorized by the laws of this State to sell such land for the nonpayment of taxes, or from any sheriff, marshal, or other person authorized to sell such land on execution, or under any order, judgment or decree of any court of record, shall be brought within seven years next after possession being taken as aforesaid; but when the possessor shall acquire such title after taking such possession, the limitation shall begin to run from the time of acquiring title.

Sec. 4656. (2924.) **Persons not Entitled to Benefits of Act.**—Whenever a person having color of title, made in good faith, to vacant and unoccupied land, shall pay all taxes legally assessed thereon for seven successive years, he or she shall be deemed and adjudged to be the legal owner of such vacant and unoccupied land, to the extent and according to the purport of his or her paper title. All persons holding under such taxpayer, by purchase, devise, or descent, before said seven years shall have expired, and who shall continue to pay the taxes as aforesaid, so as to complete the payment of the taxes for the aforesaid, shall be entitled to the benefit of this section: *Provided, however,* that if any person having a better paper title to said vacant and unoccupied land, shall, during the said term of seven years pay the taxes assessed on said land, for any one or more years during the said term of seven years, then, and in that case, such person seeking title under claim of taxes paid, his heirs and assigns, shall not be entitled to the benefit of this section. [As amended by § 7 of the above Act of 1893.]

Sec. 4657. (2925.) **Property to which Provisions of Act shall not extend.**—The two preceding sections shall not extend to lands or tenements owned by the United States, or of this State, nor to school or seminary lands, nor to land held for the use of any religious societies, nor to lands held for any public purpose. Nor shall they extend to any lands or tenements, when there shall be adverse title to such lands or tenements, and the holder of such adverse title is under the age of twenty-one years, insane, imprisoned, *feme covert*, or out of the limits of the United States, and in the employment of the United States or of this State: *Provided*, such person shall commence an action to recover such lands or tenements so possessed as aforesaid, within three years after the disabilities herein enumerated shall cease to exist, and shall prosecute such action to judgment, or in case of vacant and unoccupied land, shall within the time last aforesaid, pay to the person or persons who have paid the same, all the taxes, with interest thereon, at the rate of twelve per cent. per annum, that have been paid on said vacant and unoccupied land.

Sec. 4658. **Action within Two Years.**—If at the time when such right of entry or of action upon or for lands first accrues the person entitled to such entry or action is within the age of twenty-one years, or if a female of the age of eighteen years, or insane, imprisoned or absent from the United States, in the service of the United States, or of this State, such person or any one claiming from, by or under him or her, may make the entry or bring the action at any time within two years after such disability is removed, notwithstanding the time before limited in that behalf has expired.

Sec. 6160. (3706.) An **Action against a Railroad Corporation** for damages from fires must be brought within *three years.*

CONNECTICUT.

GENERAL STATUTES, 1902, CHAP. 79.

LIMITATIONS OF CIVIL ACTIONS.

Sec. 1108. (1370.) **Suits on Specialties.**—No action shall be brought on any contract under seal or promissory note not negotiable, but within *seventeen years* next after an action on the same shall accrue; but persons, legally incapable to sue thereon at the accruing of the right of action, may sue at any time within four years after their becoming legally capable to bring such action.

Sec. 1109. (1368.) **Ejectment. Reversionary or Remainder Interests.**—No person shall make entry into any lands or tenements, but within *fifteen years* next after his right or title to the same shall first descend or accrue, etc.

Sec. 1110. (1371.) **On Simple Contracts.**—No action for an account, or for a debt due by book to balance book accounts, or on any simple or implied contract, or upon any contract in writing, not under seal, except promissory notes not negotiable, shall be brought but within *six years* next after the right of action shall accrue; but persons legally incapable to bring any such action at the accruing of the right of action, may sue at any time within three years next after becoming legally capable to bring action. The provisions of this section shall not apply to actions upon judgments of any court of the United States nor of any court of any State within the United States.

Sec. 1112. **Limitation of Suit on Probate Bond; Exception.**—No action shall be maintained against the surety on any probate bond unless brought within six years from the final settlement of account of the principal in such bond and the acceptance of said account by the court of probate; but this provision shall not apply to minors who are parties in interest. (1893, Chap. 75.)

Sec. 1114. (1372.) **Oral Contracts.**—Excepting actions for a debt due by book, or actions founded on proper subjects of book debt, no action founded upon any express contract or agreement, not reduced to writing, or of which some note or memorandum shall not be made in writing, and signed by the party to be charged therewith or his agent, shall be brought but within three years next after the right of action shall accrue.

Sec. 1123. (1373.) **Limitation of Action on Note alleged to have been fraudulently obtained.**—No action shall be brought on a negotiable note, if the holder thereof has been notified in writing by the maker thereof, or his attorney or agent, that said note was obtained of the maker in pursuance of a conspiracy, or of a general intent to defraud, unless the same shall be brought within one year after such notice was given, or six months after such note became due, nor shall any claim be maintained against the estate of any deceased person or insolvent debtor, unless such claim shall be presented within the time above specified after notice as aforesaid. If any such note be negotiated after it is due, the provisions of this section shall be held to apply to any action or proceeding founded upon such note in as full a manner as if the plaintiff had been the holder of such note at the time when such notice was given.

Sec. 1113. (1374.) **Settlement of Partnership or Joint Accounts.**—In all cases of partnership, and of joint occupancy of real or personal estate, the court, before which any action for the settlement or adjustment of the partnership or joint account may be pending, shall take into consideration, in making such settlement, all the partnership or joint transactions since the time of the last settlement, although more than six years may have elapsed since said settlement.

Sec. 1111. (1375.) **Torts without Force.**—No action founded upon a tort unaccompanied with force and where the injury is consequential shall be brought but within *six years* next after the right of action shall accrue.

Sec. 1115. (1376.) **Trespass and Slander.**—No action for trespass to person or property, or for slanderous words, shall be brought but within *three years* next after the right of action shall accrue.

Sec. 1117. **Proceeding in error or for new trial limited to three years.** No writ of error, or petition for a new trial, shall be brought but within *three years* next after the rendition of the judgment or decree complained of.

Sec. 1119. **Action for personal injury and for death limited to one year.**—No action against a municipal or other corporation, to recover damages for injury to the person, or for causing the death of any person, or for an injury to personal property caused by negligence, shall be brought but within *one year* from the date of such injury, or from the decease of such person, as the case may be.

Sec. 1121. (1377.) **Scire Facias against Garnishee.**—No writ of *scire facias* against any garnishee shall be brought but within *one year* next after the right of bringing it shall accrue.

Sec. 1124. (1378.) **Forcible Entry and Detainer.**—No complaint for a forcible entry and detainer shall be brought, but within six months after the entry complained of.

Sec. 1120. (1379.) **Penal Forfeitures.**—No suit for any forfeiture, upon any penal statute, shall be brought, but within one year next after the commission of the offense.

Sec. 1122. (1380.) **Action on Bond or Recognizance for Costs.**—No action shall be brought against the surety on any bond or recognizance for costs only, given in any civil action, or on the appeal of any civil cause, or on any bail-bond, except within one year after final judgment has been rendered in the suit in which such bond or recognizance was given.

Sec. 1118. (1381.) **Against Officers for Neglect of Duty.**—No civil action shall be brought against any sheriff, sheriff's deputy, or constable, for any neglect or default in his office or duty, but within two years next after the right of action shall accrue.

Sec. 1116. (1382.) **Bastardy Process.**—No complaint of bastardy shall be brought after three years from the birth of the bastard.

Sec. 1119. (1383.) **Action for Personal Injury and for Death.**

Sec. 1125. **Defendant's absence from State to be excluded, when.**

Sec. 1126. **New action may be brought after time limited, when.**

Sec. 1127. (1386.) **Accidental failure of suit, when new action is allowed.** (Chap. 206, St. 1913).

Sec. 1128. **Limit for executor to bring personal action that survives.**

Sec. 1129. (1389.) **Cause of Action fraudulently concealed.**—If any person, liable to an action by another, shall fraudulently conceal from him the existence of the cause of such action, said cause of action shall be deemed to accrue against said person so liable therefor, at the time when the person entitled to sue thereon shall first discover its existence.

CHAP. 75.—RIGHTS OF WAY AND OTHER EASEMENT.

Sec. 1130. **Four Months' notice required in actions against railways.**

Sec. 1073. (1390.) **Easements.**—No person shall acquire a right of way, nor any other easement, from, in, upon, or over the land of another by the adverse use or enjoyment thereof unless such use has been continued uninterrupted for fifteen years.

Secs. 1074-1077. (1391-1394.) **How to prevent the acquisition.**—The owner of land over which such way or easement is claimed or used may give notice in writing to the person claiming or using the privilege, of his intention to dispute such right of way or other easement, and to prevent the other party from acquiring such right, and such notice, being served and recorded as provided in the two succeeding sections, shall be deemed an interruption of such use, and shall prevent the acquiring of a right thereto by the continuance of the use for any length of time thereafter, &c.

DELAWARE.

REVISED STATUTES OF 1852, AS AMENDED IN 1893.

TITLE 18, CHAP. 122.—LIMITATION OF REAL ACTIONS.

Sec. 1. **Right of Entry barred in Twenty Years.**—No person shall make an entry into any lands, tenements, or hereditaments, but within twenty years next after his right, or title, to the same, first descended, or accrued.

Sec. 2. **Actual Seisin within Twenty Years necessary.**—No person shall have, or maintain any writ of right, or action, real, personal, or mixed, for, or make any prescription, or claim, to, or in, any lands, tenements or hereditaments, of the seizing, or possession of him, his ancestor, or predecessor, and declare, or allege, in any manner whatever, any further seizing of him, his ancestor, or predecessor, but only an actual seizing of him, his ancestor or predecessor, of the premises sued for, or claimed, within twenty years next before such writ, or action.

Sec. 3. **Infancy. Coverture. Insanity. Duress.**—If at any time when such right or entry upon, or action for any lands or tenements shall first accrue, the person entitled to such entry, or action, shall be an infant, or a married woman, insane, or imprisoned, such person, or any one claiming from, by, or under him, may make the entry, or bring the action, at any time within ten years after such disability shall be removed notwithstanding the twenty years before limited in that behalf shall have expired.

Sec. 4. **Saving survives in Case of Death under Disability.**—If the person entitled to an entry, or action, die under any of the disabilities aforesaid, any other person claiming from, by, or under him, shall have the same benefit which the person first entitled would have had, by living till the removal of the disability.

Chap. 123.—Limitation of Personal Actions.

Sec. 6. **Certain Personal Actions. Three Years.**—No action of trespass, no action of replevin, no action of detinue, no action of debt not founded upon a record or specialty, no action of account, no action of assumpsit, and no action upon the case shall be brought after the expiration of *three years* from the accruing of the cause of such action; subject, however, to the provisions of the three next following sections.

Sec. 7. **Mutual Accounts.**—In the case of a mutual and running account between parties, the limitation shall not begin to run while such account continues open and current.

Sec. 8. **Promissory Notes, &c.**—When the cause of action arises from a promissory note, bill of exchange, or an acknowledgment under the hand of the party of a subsisting demand, the action may be commenced at any time within *six years* from the accruing of such cause of action.

Sec. 9. **Action for Mesne Profits, after Ejectment.**—When, after a recovery in ejectment, an action is brought for mesne profits, if such action be commenced within six months after the judgment, or if there be a writ of error, within six months after the affirmance of said judgment, or other determination of the proceeding in error, the action shall, so far as to avoid the intermediate operation of the sixth section, be deemed a continuation of the proceeding in ejectment; and the plaintiff shall not be debarred from recovering mesne profits for three years next preceding the commencement of the ejectment.

Sec. 10. **Action of Waste. Three Years.**

Sec. 12. **Penal Actions.**—No civil action for a forfeiture upon a penal statute, whether at the suit of the party aggrieved or of a common informer, or of the State, or otherwise, shall be brought after the expiration of one year from the accruing of the cause of such action.

SUPPLEMENTAL ACTS.

The Act of 1893, chap. 778, limited judgment liens upon real estate to *ten years*, &c.

The Act of 1897, chap. 594, limited actions for damages for personal injuries to *one year*.

Sec. 16. (2754.) **Set-off.**—The provisions of this chapter shall apply to any debt alleged by way of set-off on the part of a defendant; and the time of limitation of such debt shall be computed in like manner as if an action therefor had been commenced at the time when the plaintiff's action commenced.

FLORIDA.

REVISED STATUTES, 1914, 2D DIVISION, TITLE 1, CHAP. 26.

LIMITATION OF ACTIONS.

ARTICLE 2.—*Provisions Applicable to Real Actions.*

Sec. 1718. (1287.) **Actions for the Recovery of Real Property.**—No action for the recovery of real property, or for the recovery of the possession thereof, shall be maintained unless it appear that the plaintiff, his ancestor, predecessor, or grantor, was seized or possessed of the premises in question within seven years before the commencement of such action.

Sec. 1719. (1288.) **Action Founded on Title to Real Property.**—No cause of action or defence to an action founded upon the title to real property, or to rents, or to service out of the same, shall be effectual unless it appear that the person prosecuting the action, or making the defence, or under whose title the action is prosecuted or the defence is made, or the ancestor, predecessor, or grantor of such person was seized or possessed of the premises in question within *seven years* before the accruing of the right of action or defence in respect to which such action is prosecuted or defence made, or unless it appear that the title to such premises was derived from the United States or the State of Florida within seven years before the commencement of such action; and the period of limitation shall not begin to run until the passage of the title from the State or the United States.

Sec. 1720. (1289.) **Possession by Legal Owner, Presumed.**—In every action for the recovery of real property, or the possession thereof, the person establishing a legal title to the premises shall be presumed to have been possessed thereof within the time prescribed by law, and the occupation of such premises by any other person shall be deemed to have been under and in subordination to the legal title, unless it appear that such premises have been held and possessed adversely to such legal title for seven years before the commencement of such action.

Secs. 1721-1722. (1290-1291.) **Adverse Possession Defined.**

ARTICLE 3.—*Provisions Applicable to Actions Other Than Real Actions.*

Sec. 1725. (1294.) **Personal Actions.**—Actions other than those for the recovery of real property can only be commenced as follows:

1. *Within twenty years.*—An action upon a judgment or decree of a court of record in the State of Florida, and an action upon any contract, obligation, or liability founded upon an instrument of writing under seal.

2. *Within seven years.*—An action upon a judgment or decree of any court of the United States, or of any State or Territory within the United States, or of any foreign country.

3. *Within five years.*—An action upon any contract, obligation, or liability founded upon an instrument of writing not uder seal.

4. *Within four years.*—An action for relief not specifically provided for in this chapter.

5. *Within three years.*—1. An action upon a liability created by statute, other than a penalty or forfeiture; 2. an action for trespass upon real property; 3. an action for taking, detaining, or injuring any goods or chattels, including actions for the specific recovery of personal property; 4. an action for relief on the ground of fraud, the cause of action in such case not to be deemed to have accrued until the discovery by the aggrieved party of the facts constituting the fraud; 5. and an action upon a contract, obligation, or liability not founded upon an instrument of writing, including an action for goods, wares and merchandise, sold and delivered, and on store accounts.

6. *Within two years.*—An action by another than the State upon a statute for a penalty or forfeiture; an action for libel, slander, assault, battery, or false imprisonment.

7. *Within one year.*—An action by the State for a penalty or forfeiture under a penal act of the legislature. An action arising upon account of an act causing the wrongful death, and on account of wrongful death, of child.

In Cases of Mutual Account.—In an action brought to recover a balance due upon a mutual, open and current account, where there have been reciprocal demands between the parties, the cause of action shall be deemed to have accrued from the time of the last item proved in the account on either side.

SUPPLEMENTAL ACTS.

The Act of 1895, chap. 4412, provided "that no action for the recovery of real property or of its possession against a person without color of title shall be barred within twenty years next after the accruing of the right of action nor shall any occupation of the premises by a person without color of title for less than twenty years be deemed an adverse possession."

GEORGIA.

CODE, 1911, TITLE 8, CHAP. 7.

ART. 8. OF LIMITATION OF ACTIONS ON CONTRACTS.

SEC. I. *Periods of Limitations.*

Sec. 4354. (3760.) **On Foreign Judgment.**—All suits upon judgments obtained out of this State shall be brought within *five years* after such judgment is obtained.

Sec. 4355. (3761.) **Dormancy of Judgments.**— No judgment shall be enforced after *seven years* from its rendition, when no execution has been issued upon it and the same placed upon the execution docket, or when execution has been issued and seven years have expired from the time of the record, upon the execution docket of the court from which the same issued, of the last entry upon the execution made by an officer authorized to execute and return the same. Such judgments may be revived by *scire facias*, or be sued on within three years from the time they became dormant.

Sec. 4359. (3765.) **On Specialties.**—Actions upon bonds or other instruments under seal shall be brought within *twenty years* after the right of action accrues, but no instrument shall be considered under seal unless so recited in the body of the instrument.

Sec. 4360. (3766.) **Statutory Rights.**—All suits for the enforcement of rights accruing to individuals under statutes, acts of incorporation, or by operation of law, shall be brought within *twenty years* after the right of action accrues.

Sec. 4361. (3767.) **Simple Contracts.**—All actions upon promissory notes bills of exchange, or other simple contract in writing, shall be brought within *six years* after the same become due and payable.

Sec. 4362. (3768.) **Open Accounts.**—All actions upon account, or for the breach of any contract not under the hand of the party sought to be charged, or upon any implied assumpsit or undertaking, shall be brought within *four years* after the right of action accrues.

Sec. 4366. (3772.) **Suits against Executors, Administrators, etc.**—All actions against executors, administrators, guardians, or trustees, except on their bonds, must be brought within *ten years* after the right of action accrues.

Sec. 4368. (3774.) **Other Actions ex Contractu.**—All other actions upon contracts, express or implied, not hereinbefore provided for, must be brought within *four years* from the accrual of the right of action.

Sec. 4369. (3775.) **Limitations in Equity.**—The limitations herein provided apply equally to all courts; and, in addition to the above, courts of equity may interpose an equitable bar, whenever, from the lapse of time and laches of the complainant, it would be inequitable to allow a party to enforce his legal rights.

Sec. 4370. (3776.) **Suits by Informers.**—All actions by informers to recover any fine, forfeiture or penalty, shall be commenced within one year from the time the defendant's liability thereto was discovered, or by reasonable diligence could have been discovered.

Sec. 4371. (3777.) **Limitations to Operate against the State.**—When, by the provisions of the foregoing sections, a private person would be barred of his rights, the State shall be barred of her rights under the same circumstances.

Sec. 4382. (3787.) **Claims pleaded as Set-off.**—Where any matter has been pleaded as a set-off in a suit, and the suit is dismissed, or the case is otherwise disposed of without a hearing upon the merits of the set-off, such set-off shall not be barred until the expiration of six months next after the time of such disposition of such suit.

TITLE 7, CHAP. 6.—OF TITLE BY PRESCRIPTION.

Sec. 4168. (3588.) **Prescription by Twenty Years' Possession.**—Actual adverse possession of lands by itself, for *twenty years*, shall give title by prescription against every one, except the State, or persons laboring under the disabilities hereinafter specified.

Sec. 4169. (3589.) **Seven Years' Possession under Written Evidence of Title.**—Adverse possession of lands, under written evidence of title for *seven years*, shall give a like title by prescription. But if such written title be forged or fraudulent, and notice thereof be brought home to the claimant before or at the time of the commencement of his possession, no prescription can be based thereon.

Sec. 4170. (3590.) **Prescriptive Right to Easement.**—An incorporeal right which may be lawfully granted, as a right of way or the right to throw water upon the land of another, may be acquired by prescription.

Sec. 4172. (3592.) **Personalty.**—Adverse possession of personal property within this State for *four years* shall give a like title by prescription. No prescription arises if the property be concealed or removed out of the State, or otherwise is not subject to reclamation.

HAWAIIAN ISLANDS.

REVISED LAWS (1905), CHAP. 127.

STATUTE OF LIMITATIONS, PART I.—PERSONAL ACTIONS.

Sec. 1971. (1287.) **Actions to be Commenced within Six Years.**—1. Actions for the recovery of any debt founded upon any contract, obligation or liability, excepting such as are brought upon the judgment or decree of some court of record.

2. Actions upon judgments rendered in any court not being a court of record.

3. Action of debt for arrearages of rent.

4. Actions for trespass upon lands.

5. Actions for taking, detaining or injuring any goods or chattels, including actions of replevin.

6. Special actions on the case for criminal conversation, for libels, or for any other injury to the persons or rights of any, except as otherwise provided.

Sec. 1976. (1288.) **Four Years.**—Actions for the recovery of any debt founded upon any contract, obligation or liability, where the cause of action has arisen in any foreign country, except such as are brought upon the judgment or decree of a court of record.

Sec. 1974. (1289.) **Two Years.**—1. Actions for assault and battery.

2. Actions for false imprisonment.

3. Actions for words spoken slandering the character or title of any person.

4. Actions for words spoken whereby special damages are sustained.

5. Actions against the high sheriff, sheriffs or other officers, for the escape of prisoners, or upon any liability incurred by them by the doing any act in their official capacity, or by the omission of any official duty.

PART II.—REAL ACTIONS.

Sec. 1988. (1305.) No person shall commence an action to recover possession of any lands, or make any entry thereon, unless within *ten years* after the right to bring such action first accrued.

IDAHO.

REVISED CODE OF CIVIL PROCEDURE 1908, PART II.

TITLE II.—OF THE TIME OF COMMENCING CIVIL ACTIONS.

CHAP. 2.—FOF THE RECOVERY OF REAL PROPERTY.

Sec. 4036. **Seisin within Five Years, when necessary.**—No action for the recovery of real property, or for the recovery of the possession thereof, can be maintained, unless it appear that the plaintiff, his ancestor, predecessor, or grantor, was seized or possessed of the property in question within *five years* before the commencement of the action; and this section includes possessory rights to lands and mining claims.

Sec. 4037. **Seisin, when necessary in Action or Defense.**

Sec. 4038. **Entry on Real Estate.**—No entry upon real estate is deemed sufficient or valid as a claim, unless an action be commenced thereupon within one year after making such entry, and within five years of the time when the right to make it descended or accrued.

Sec. 4039. **Possession, when Presumed.**

Secs. 4040-4043. **Occupation and Adverse Possession.**

CHAP. 3.—*Actions* OTHER THAN FOR THE RECOVERY OF REAL PROPERTY.

Sec. 4050. **Periods of Limitation Prescribed.**—The periods prescribed for the commencement of actions other than for the recovery of real property are as follows:

Sec. 4051. **Within Six Years.**—1. An action upon a judgment or decree of any court of the United States, or of any State or Territory within the United States.

2. An action for mesne profits of real property.

Sec. 4052. **Within Five Years.**—An action upon any contract, obligation, or liability, founded upon an instrument of writing.

Sec. 4053. **Within Four Years.**—An action upon a contract, obligation, or liability, not founded upon an instrument of writing.

Sec. 4054. **Within Three Years.**—1. An action upon a liability created by statute, other than a penalty or forfeiture.

2. An action for trespass upon real property.

3. An action for taking, detaining, or injuring any goods or chattels, including actions for the specific recovery of personal property.

4. An action for relief on the ground of fraud or mistake. The cause of action in such case not to be deemed to have accrued until the discovery by the aggrieved party of the facts constituting the fraud or mistake.

Sec. 4055. **Within Two Years.**—1. An action against a sheriff, coroner, or constable, upon the liability incurred by the doing of an act in his official capacity, and in virtue of his office, or by the omission of an official duty, including the non-payment of money collected upon an execution.

2. An action upon a statute for a penalty or forfeiture, when the action is given to an individual, or to an individual and the Territory, except when the statute imposing it prescribes a different limitation.

3. An action upon a statute, or upon an undertaking in a criminal action, for a forfeiture or penalty to a county or to the people of the Territory.

4. An action to recover damages for the death of one caused by the wrongful act of another.

5. An action for libel, slander, assault, battery, false imprisonment, or seduction.

6. An action against a sheriff, or other officer, for the escape of a prisoner, arrested or imprisoned on civil process.

Sec. 4056. **Within One Year.**—An action against an officer, or officer *de facto.*

1. To recovery any goods, wares, merchandise, or other property, seized by any such officer in his official capacity as tax-collector, or to recover the price or value of any goods, wares, merchandise, or other personal property so seized, or for damages for the seizure, detention, sale of or injury to any goods, wares, merchandise, or other personal property seized, or for damages done to any person or property in making any such seizure.

2. For money paid to any such officer under protest, or seized by such officer in his official capacity as a collector of taxes, and which, it is claimed, ought to be refunded.

Sec. 4057. **Within Six Months.**—Actions on claims against a county, which have been rejected by the board of commissioners, must be commenced within six months after the first rejection thereof by such board.

Sec. 4058. **Mutual Accounts.**—In an action brought to recover a balance due upon a mutual, open, and current account, where there have been reciprocal demands between the parties, the cause of action is deemed to have accrued from the time of the last item proved in the account on either side.

Sec. 4059. **Deposits with Banks or Bankers.**—To actions brought to recover money or other property deposited with any bank, banker, trust company, on savings and loan society, no limitation begins to run until after an authorized demand.

Sec. 4060. **Actions for Relief not hereinbefore provided for.**—An action for relief not hereinbefore provided for must be commenced within four days after the cause of action shall have accrued.

ILLINOIS.

HURD'S REVISED STATUTES 1912, CHAP. 83.

LIMITATIONS.

An Act in regard to Limitations. [Approved April 4, 1872. In force July 1, 1872. L. 1871-72, p. 556; R. S. 1874, p. 673.]

Par. 7196. **Twenty Years.**—Sec. 1. Be it enacted, etc., that no person shall commence an action for the recovery of lands, nor make an entry thereon, unless within twenty years after the right to bring such action or make such entry first accrued, or within twenty years after he or those from, by, or under whom he claims, have been seised or possessed of the premises, except as hereinafter provided.

Par. 7197. **Time, how computed.**—Sec. 2. If such right or title first accrued to an ancestor or predecessor of the person who brings the action or makes the entry, or to any person from, by, or under whom he claims, the twenty years shall be computed from the time when the right or title so first accrued.

Par. 7198. **When Right of Entry or to bring Action Accrues.**—Sec. 3. The right to make an entry or bring an action to recover land shall be deemed to have first accrued at the times respectively hereinafter mentioned, that is to say:—

First. When any person is disseised, his right of entry or of action shall be deemed to have accrued at the time of such disseisin.

Second. When he claims as heir or devisee of one who died seised, his right shall be deemed to have accrued at the time of such death, unless there is a tenancy by the curtesy or other estate intervening after the death of such ancestor or devisor; in which case his right shall be deemed to accrue when such intermediate estate expires, or when it would have expired by its own limitations.

Third. When there is such an intermediate estate, and in all other cases when the party claims by force of any remainder or reversion, his right, so far as it is affected by the limitation herein prescribed, shall be deemed to accrue when the intermediate or precedent estate would have expired by its own limitation, notwithstanding any forfeiture thereof by which he might have entered at an earlier time.

Fourth. The preceding clause shall not prevent a person from entering when entitled to do so by reason of any forfeiture or breach of condition; but if he claims under such a title, his right shall be deemed to have accrued when the forfeiture was incurred or the condition was broken.

Fifth. In all cases not otherwise specially provided for, the right shall be deemed to have accrued when the claimant, or the person under whom he claims, first became entitled to the possession of the premises under the title upon which the entry of the action is founded.

Pars. 7199-7203. **Seven Years, with Possession and Record Title, or Color of Title, etc.**—Sec. 4.

Par. 7206. **Mortgage.**—Sec. 11. No person shall commence an action or make a sale to foreclose any mortgage or deed of trust in the nature of a mortgage, unless within ten years after the right of action or right to make such sale accrues.

PERSONAL ACTIONS.

Par. 7207. Sec. 12. The following actions can only be commenced within the periods hereinafter prescribed, except when a different limitation is prescribed by statute.

Par. 7208. **Slander and Libel.**—Sec. 13. Actions for slander or libel shall be commenced within *one year* next after the cause of action accrued.

Par. 7209. **Personal Injuries, Penalties, etc.**—Sec. 14. Actions for damages for an injury to the person, or for false imprisonment, or malicious prosecution, or for a statutory penalty, or for abduction, or for seduction, or for criminal conversation, shall be commenced within *two years* next after the cause of action accrued.

Par. 7210. **On Oral Contracts, Damages, etc.**—Sec. 15. Actions on unwritten contracts, expressed or implied, or on awards of arbitration, or to recover damages for an injury done to property, real or personal, or to recover the possession of personal property or damages for the detention or conversion thereof, and all civil actions not otherwise provided for, shall be commenced within five years next after the cause of action accrued.

Par. 7211. **On Writings, New Contracts.**—Sec. 16. Actions on bonds, promissory notes, bills of exchange, written leases, written contracts, or other evidences of indebtedness in writing, shall be commenced within *ten years* next after the cause of action accrued; but if any payment or new promise to pay shall have been made, in writing, on any bond, note, bill, lease, contract, or other written evidence of indebtedness, within or after the said period of ten years, then an action may be commenced thereon at any time within ten years after the time of such payment or promise to pay.

Par. 7212. **Set-off or Counterclaim.**—Sec. 17. A defendant may plead a set-off or counterclaim barred by the statute of limitation, while held and owned by him, to any action, the cause of which was owned by the plaintiff or person under whom he claims, before such set-off or counterclaim was so barred, and not otherwise: *Provided,* this section shall not affect the right of a *bona fide* assignee of a negotiable instrument assigned before due.

Par. 7217. **Fraudulent Concealment.**—Sec. 22. If a person liable to an action fraudulently conceals the cause of such action from the knowledge of the person entitled thereto, the action may be commenced at any time within five years after the person entitled to bring the same discovers that he has such cause of action, and not afterwards.

Par. 7218. **When Action stayed, Time does not run.**—Sec. 23. When the commencement of an action is stayed by injunction, order of a judge of court, or statutory prohibition, the time of the continuance of the injunction or prohibition is not part of the time limited for the commencement of the actions.

SUPPLEMENTAL ACT.

Par. 6185. By Chap. 70, Sec. 2. An **Action by the Representative of a decedent** for causing the death must be brought within *one year* after the death.

INDIANA.

BURN'S ANNOTATED STATUTES, 1914, CHAP. 2.

ART. VI.—*Actions, When Commenced.*

Sec. 294. (293.) **Six Years.**—*First.* On accounts and contracts not in writing.

Second. For use, rents, and profits of real property.

Third. For injuries to property, damages for any detention thereof, and for recovering possession of personal property.

Fourth. For relief against frauds.

Sec. 295. (294.) **Injury to Persons, etc.**

First. **Two Years.**—For injuries to person or character, and for a forfeiture or penalty given by statute, within *two years.*

Second. **Five Years.**—All actions against a sheriff or other public officer, or against such officer and his sureties on a public bond, growing out of a liability incurred by doing an act in an official capacity, or by the omission of an official duty, within *five years;* but an action may be brought against the officer or his legal representatives, for money collected in an official capacity, and not paid over at any time within six years.

Third. **Ten Years.**—For the recovery of real property sold on execution, brought by the execution debtor, his heirs, or any person claiming under him, by title acquired after the date of the judgment, within *ten years* after the sale.

Fourth. **Executors' Sales, etc., Five Years.**—For the recovery of real property sold by executors, administrators, guardians, or commissioners of a court, upon a judgment specially directing the sale of property sought to be recovered, brought by a party to the judgment, his heirs, or any person claiming a title under a party, acquired after the date of the judgment, within *five years* after the sale is confirmed.

Fifth. **Notes, etc., Ten Years.**—Upon promissory notes, bills of exchange, and other written contracts for the payment of money, hereafter executed, within *ten years: provided,* that all such contracts as have been heretofore executed may be enforced, under this act, within such time only as they have to run before being barred under the existing law limiting the commencement of actions, and not afterward.

Sixth. **Twenty Years.**—Upon contracts in writing other than those for the payment of money on judgments of a court of record, and for the recovery of the possession of real estate, within *twenty years.*

Sec. 296. (295.) **Actions not otherwise limited, Fifteen Years.**—All actions not limited by any other statute shall be brought within *fifteen years.* In special cases, where a different limitation is prescribed by statute, the provisions of this act shall not apply.

Sec. 297. (296.) **Mutual accounts.**—In an action brought to recover a balance due upon a mutual, open, and current account between the parties, the cause of action shall be deemed to have accrued from the date of the last item proved in the account on either side.

Sec. 298. (297.) **Legal Disabilities.**—Any person being under legal disabilities when the cause of action accrues, may bring his action within *two years* after the disability is removed.

Sec 302. (301.) **Concealment of Cause of Action.**—If any person liable to an action shall conceal the fact from the knowledge of the person entitled thereto, the action may be commenced at any time within the period of limitation, after the discovery of the cause of action.

Sec. 305. (304.) **Payment Memorandum.**—Nothing contained in the preceding sections shall take away or lessen the effect of any payment made by any person; but no indorsement, or memorandum of any payment made upon any instrument of writing, by or on behalf of the party to whom the payment shall purport to be made, shall be deemed sufficient to exempt the case from the provisions of this act.

Sec. 306. (305.) **State not barred, Sureties excepted.**—Limitation of actions shall not bar the State of Indiana, except as to sureties.

Sec. 307. (306.) **Judgments and Decrees deemed satisfied after Twenty Years.**—Every judgment and decree of any court of record of the United States, or of this or any other State, shall be deemed satisfied after the expiration of twenty years.

Sec. 308. (307.) **Joint Debtor not liable on Payment.**—Neither a joint debtor or his representatives, in whose favor the statute of limitations has operated, shall be liable to a joint debtor or surety, or their representatives, upon payment, by such joint debtor or surety, or their representatives, of the debt or any part of it.

CHAP. 6, ART. 9.

Sec. 2850. (2487.) **Action to recover Lands fraudulently Conveyed by Decedent.**—* * * No proceeding by any executor or administrator, to sell any lands so fraudulently conveyed, shall be maintained, unless the same shall be instituted within five years after the death of the testator or intestate.

ART. 16.

Sec. 2965. (2597.) **Creditors' Action against Distributees.—Disability.**—The heirs, devisees, and distributees of a decedent shall be liable, to the extent of the property received by them from such decedent's estate, to any creditor whose claim remains unpaid, who, six months prior to such final settlement, was insane, an infant, or out of the State; but such suit must be brought within *one year* after the disability is removed: *provided*, that suit upon the claim of any creditor out of the State must be brought within *two years* after such final settlement.

SUPPLEMENTAL ACTS.

By Chap. 2, Art. 29, Sec. 925. (892.) **A Creditor's Action on a Recognizance** of special bail must be brought within *two years* after final judgment against the principal.

By Chap. 2, Art. 41, Sec. 1196. (1153.) A **Relator's Action for his Damages** must be brought within *one year* after the judgment.

By Chap. 9, Art. 3, Sec. 3154. (2766.) An **Action to Contest the Validity of a Will** must be brought within *three years* after the offer of probate.

By Chap. 100, Sec. 8394. (7312.) **An Action on an Indenture** of apprenticeship must be brought within *two years* after expiration of the term of service.

INDIAN TERRITORY.

CARTER'S STATUTES (1899), CHAP. 45.

Sec. 2938. No person or persons, or their heirs, shall have, sue, or maintain any action or suit, either in law or in equity, for any lands, tenements, or hereditaments, but within *seven years* next after his, her or their right to commence, have or maintain such suit shall have come, fallen, or accrued; and all suits either in law or equity, for the recovery of any lands, tenements or hereditaments, shall be had and sued within *seven years* next after title or cause of action accrued, and no time after said seven years shall have passed: Provided, etc.

Sec. 2939. No entry upon lands or tenements shall be deemed sufficient or valid as a claim unless an action be commenced thereon within one year after such entry, and within *seven years* from the time when the right to make such entry descended or accrued.

Sec. 2941. **Five Years.**—For the recovery of lands sold at judicial sales.

Sec. 2945. **Three Years.**—*First.* All actions founded upon any contract or liability, express or implied, not in writing.

Second. All actions for trespass on lands or for libels.

Third. All actions for taking or injuring any goods or chattels.

Sec. 2946. **One Year.**—*First.* All actions for criminal conversation, assault and battery, and false imprisonment.

Second. All actions for words spoken, slandering the character of another.

Third. All words spoken whereby special damages are sustained.

Sec. 2947. **One Year.**—Against sheriffs or other officers, for escape of persons imprisoned on civil process.

Sec. 2948. **Two Years.**—Against sheriffs or coroners, for misconduct, except for escapes.

Sec. 2949. **Two Years.**—Actions upon penal statutes.

Sec. 2950. **Five Years.**—Actions upon promissory notes, and other instrument in writing, not under seal.

Sec. 2951. **Ten Years.**—Actions on writings under seal.

Sec. 2954. **Ten Years.**—Actions on judgments and decrees.

Sec. 2955. **Other actions—five years.**

IOWA.

REVISED ANNOTATED CODE, 1897, TITLE 18, CHAP. 2.

OF LIMITATION OF ACTIONS.

Sec. 3447. (2529.) **Period of.**—Actions may be brought within the times herein limited respectively after their causes accrue and not afterwards, except when otherwise specially declared:

1. **Three Months.**—Actions founded on injury to the person on account of defective roads, bridges, streets or sidewalks, within *three months*, unless written notice specifying the time, place and circumstances, of the injury shall have been served upon the county or municipal corporation to be charged within *sixty days* from the happening of the injury.

2. **One Year.**—Actions to enforce the payment of a penalty or forfeiture under an ordinance, within *one year.*

3. **Two Years.**—Actions founded on injuries to the person or reputation, including injuries to relative rights, whether based on contract or tort, or for a statute penalty, within *two years;* and those brought to set aside a will, within *five years* from the time the same is filed in the clerk's office for probate and notice thereof is given.

4. Actions to enforce a mechanic's lien, within *two years* from the expiration of the 30 or 90 days, as the case may be, for filing the claim as provided in the law relative to mechanic's liens.

5. **Three Years.**—Those against a sheriff or other public officer, growing out of a liability incurred by the doing of an act in an official capacity or by

the omission of an official duty, including the non-payment of money collected on execution, within *three years.*

6. **Five Years.**—Those founded on unwritten contracts, those brought for injuries to property, or for relief on the ground of fraud in cases heretofore solely cognizable in a court of chancery, and all other actions not otherwise provided for in this respect, within *five years.*

7. **Ten Years.**—Those founded on written contracts, or on judgments of any courts, except those courts provided for in the next subdivision and those brought for the recovery of real property, within *ten years.*

8. **Twenty Years.**—Those founded on a judgment of a court of record, whether of this or of any other of the United States, or of the federal courts of the United States, within *twenty years.*

Sec. 3448. (2530.) **Fraud. Mistake. Trespass.**—In actions for relief on the ground of fraud or mistake, and in actions for trespass to property, the cause of action shall not be deemed to have accrued until the fraud, mistake, or trespass complained of shall have been discovered by the party aggrieved.

Sec. 3449. (2531.) **Open Account.**—Where there is a continuous open current account, the cause of action shall be deemed to have accrued on the date of the last item therein, as proved on the trial.

Sec. 3450. (2532.) **Commencement of Action.**—The delivery of the original notice to the sheriff of the proper county with intent that it be served immediately which intent shall be presumed unless the contrary appears, or the actual service of that notice by another person, is a commencement of the action.

Sec. 3455. (2537.) **Failure of Action.**—If, after the commencement of an action, the plaintiff, for any cause except negligence in its prosecution, fails therein, and a new one is brought within six months thereafter, the second suit shall, for the purposes herein contemplated, be held a continuation of the first.

Sec. 3456. (2539.) **Admission in Writing.**—Causes of action founded on contract are revived by an admission in writing, signed by the party to be charged, that the debt is unpaid, or by a like new promise to pay the same.

Sec. 3457. (2540.) **Counterclaim.**—A counterclaim may be pleaded as a defense to any cause of action, notwithstanding the same is barred by the provisions of this chapter, if it was the property of the party pleading it at the time it became barred, and was not barred at the time the claim sued on originated; but no judgment thereon, except for costs, can be rendered in favor of the party so pleading the same.

Sec. 3458. (2541.) **Injunction or Statutory Prohibition.**—When the commencement of an action shall be stayed by injunction or statutory prohibition, the time of the continuance of such injunction or prohibition shall not be part of the time limited for the commencement of the action, except as herein otherwise provided.

Sec. 2852. (2542.) **School Fund.**—The provisions of this chapter shall not be applicable to any action brought on any contract for any part of the school fund.

TITLE 7, CHAP. 2.

Sec. 1448. (902.) **Action to recover Land sold for Taxes.**—No action for the recovery of real estate sold for the non-payment of taxes shall be brought after *five years* from the execution and recording of the treasurer's deed, unless the owner is at the time of such sale, a minor, insane person, or convict in the penitentiary, in which case such action must be brought within *five years* after such disability is removed.

TITLE 16, CHAP. 5.

Sec. 3212. (2265.) **Action to contest Guardian's Sale of Lands.**—The rule prescribed in the sale of real property by executors shall be observed in relation to the evidence necessary to show the regularity and validity of the sales of guardians; and no person can question the validity of any such sale after the lapse of five years from the time it was made.

TITLE 17, CHAP. 3.

Sec. 3332. (2401.) No action for the recovery of any real estate sold or mortgaged by an executor or administrator can be maintained by any person claiming under the deceased, unless brought within *five years* after the sale by him or under the foreclosure of such mortgage.

KANSAS.

DASSLER'S GENERAL STATUTES 1919, CHAP. 95, ART. 3.

Sec. 5608. (4260.) **Limitation of Action for Recovery of Real Property.**—§§ 15 (16). Actions for the recovery of real property, or for the determination of any adverse claim or interest therein, can only be brought within the periods hereinafter prescribed, after the cause of action shall have accrued, and at no time thereafter:

First. An action for the recovery of real property sold on execution, brought by the execution debtor, his heirs, or any person claiming under him, by title acquired after the date of the judgment, within *five years* after the date of the recording of the deed made in pursuance of the sale.

Second. An action for the recovery of real property sold by executors, administrators, or guardians, upon an order or judgment of a court directing such sale, brought by the heirs or devisees of the deceased person, or the ward or his guardian, or any person claiming under any or either of them, by title acquired after the date of the judgment or order, within *five years* after the date of the recording of the deed made in pursuance of the sale.

Third. An action for the recovery of real property sold for taxes, within *two years* after the date of the recording of the tax deed.

Fourth. An action for the recovery of real property not hereinbefore provided for, within *fifteen years.*

Fifth. An action for the forcible entry and detention, or forcible detention only, of real property, within *two years.*

Sec. 5610. (4262.) **Other Actions.**—§§ 17(18). Civil actions other than for the recovery of real property can only be brought within the following periods after the cause of action shall have accrued, and not afterwards:

First. Within five years: An action upon any agreement, contract, or promise in writing.

Second. Within three years: An action upon a contract, not in writing, express or implied; an action upon a liability created by statute, other than a forfeiture or penalty.

Third. Within two years: An action for trespass upon real property; an action for taking, detaining or injuring personal property, including actions for the specific recovery of personal property; an action for injury to the rights of another, not arising on contract, and not hereinafter enumerated; an action for relief on the ground of fraud. The cause of action in such case shall not be deemed to have accrued until the discovery of the fraud.

Fourth. Within one year: An action for libel, slander, assault, battery, malicious prosecution, or false imprisonment; an action upon a statute for penalty or forfeiture, except where the statute imposing it prescribes a different limitation.

Fifth. An action upon the official bond or undertaking of an executor, administrator, guardian, sheriff, or any other officer, or upon the bond or undertaking given in attachment, injunction, arrest, or in any case whatever required by statute, can only be brought within *five years* after the cause of action shall have accrued.

Sixth. An action for relief, not hereinbefore provided for, can only be brought within *five years* after the cause of action shall have accrued.

Seventh. Any agreement for a different time for the commencement of actions from the times in this act provided shall be null and void as to such agreement.

Sec. 5612. (4264.) **Commencement of Action.**—§§ 19(20). An action shall be deemed commenced within the meaning of this article, as to each defendant, at the date of the summons which is served on him, or on a co-defendant who is a joint contractor, or otherwise united in interest with him. Where service by publication is proper, the action shall be deemed commenced at the date of the first publication. An attempt to commence an action shall be deemed equivalent to the commencement thereof within the meaning of this article when the party faithfully, properly and diligently endeavors to procure a service; but such attempt must be followed by the first publication or service of the summons within sixty days.

Sec. 5614. (4266.) **Barred in Other State, barred here.**—§§ 21(22). Where the cause of action has arisen in another State or country, between non-residents of this State, and by the laws of the State or country where the cause of action arose an action cannot be maintained thereon by reason of lapse of time, no action can be maintained thereon in this State.

Sec. 5615. (4267.) **New action may be commenced, when.**—§§ 22(23). If any action be commenced within due time, and a judgment thereon for the plaintiff be reversed, or if the plaintiff fail in such action otherwise than upon the merits, and the time limited for the same shall have expired, the plaintiff, or, if he die and the cause of action survive, his representatives, may commence a new action within *one year* after the reversal or failure.

Sec. 5616. (4268.) **Effect of Payment or Acknowledgment.**—§§ 23(24). In any case founded on contract, when any part of the principal or interest shall have been paid, or an acknowledgment of an existing liability, debt, or claim, or any promise to pay the same, shall have been made, an action may be brought in such case within the period prescribed for the same, after such payment, acknowledgment, or promise; but such acknowledgment or promise must be in writing, signed by the party to be charged thereby.

Sec. 5617. (4269.) **Effect of Bar.**—§§ 24(25). When a right of action is barred by the provisions of any statute, it shall be unavailable either as a cause of action or ground of defense.

CHAPTER 38, ART. 5.

Sec. 3541. (2794.) **Action against Executors.**—§ 106. No executor or administrator, after having given notice of his appointment as provided in this act, shall be held to answer to the suit of any creditor of the deceased unless it be commenced within *three years* from the time of his giving bond.

CHAPTER 54, ART. 2.

Sec. 4069. (3244.) **Indian Lands.**—§ 7. Three years' quiet, undisturbed, actual possession of any such lands by any purchaser thereof, in good faith as aforesaid, under color of title, shall be a complete bar to any action for the recovery of said lands by the holder of any adverse title to the same, and such possession shall be deemed to vest in the possessor a full and complete title to the same in fee simple.

CHAPTER 116, ART. 22.

Sec. 9483. (7338.) **Action to Recover Land Sold for Taxes.**—§§ 270(141). Any suit or proceeding against the tax purchaser, his heirs or assigns, for the recovery of lands sold for taxes, or to defeat or avoid a sale or conveyance of lands for taxes, except in cases where the taxes have been paid or the land redeemed as provided by law, shall be commenced within *five years* from the time of recording the tax deed, and not thereafter.

KENTUCKY.

GENERAL STATUTES, 1909. (CARROLL, 4TH ED.) CHAP. 80(71.)

LIMITATION OF ACTIONS.

ART. I.—*Actions for the Recovery of Real Estate.*

Sec. 2505. **Limitation of Fifteen Years.**—An action for the recovery of real property can only be brought within *fifteen years* after the right to institute it first accrued to the plaintiff, or to the person through whom he claims.

Sec. 2508. **Thirty Years Utmost Limit.**—The period within which an action for the recovery of real property may be brought shall not in any case be extended beyond thirty years from the time at which the right to bring the action first accrued to the plaintiff, or the person through whom he claims, by reason of any death or the existence or continuance of any disability whatever.

Sec. 2509. **Claim does not Preserve Right.**—No continual claim upon or near real property shall preserve a right to bring an action.

ART. II.—*Possession of Seven Years, with Title.*

Sec. 2513. **Occupancy for Seven Years with Record Title.**—No action at law or in equity shall be brought under or by virtue of an adverse, interfering entry, survey, or patent, to recover the title or possession of land from an occupant where he, or the person under whom he claims, has a connected title thereto in law or equity, deducible of record from the Commonwealth, and has or shall have had an actual occupancy of the same by settlement thereon, under such title, for seven years before the commencement of the action; and such possession of land shall bar and toll the right of entry into such land by any person, under an adverse title or claim, and such possession as will bar the right to recover the same shall vest the title in the occupant, or his vendee. This limitation shall not apply to a person who is an infant, a married woman, of unsound mind, or out of the United States in the employment of the United States or of this State, at the time the cause of action accrued, nor until seven years after the removal of such disability; but the disability of one of several claimants shall save only his own right, and not that of another.

ART. III.—*Actions other than for Real Estate.*

Sec. 2514. **Limitation to Actions other than for Real Estate; when fifteen years.**—Civil actions, other than those for the recovery of real property, shall be commenced within the following periods after the cause of action has accrued, and not after: An action upon a judgment or decree of any court of this State or of the United States, or of any State or Territory thereof, the period to be computed from the date of the last execution thereon; an action or suit upon a recognizance, bond, or written contract; an action upon the official bond of a sheriff, marshal, sergeant, clerk, constable, or any other public officer, or any commissioner, receiver, curator, personal representative, guardian, committee, or trustee appointed by a court or authority of law; an action upon an appeal bond, or bond given on a supersedeas, attachment, injunction, order of arrest, or for the delivery of property, or for the forthcoming of property, or to obey or perform an order or judgment of court in an action, or upon a bond for costs, or any other bond taken by a court or judge, or by an officer pursuant to the directions of a court or judge, in an action, or after judgment or decree, or upon a replevin, sale, or delivery bond taken under an execution, decree, or warrant of distress, upon an indemnifying bond taken under a statute, or upon a bond to suspend a proceeding or sale under execution, distress warrant, order, or decree, or other judicial proceeding, or upon a bond or obligation for the payment of money or property, or for the performance of any undertaking—shall be commenced within *fifteen years* after the cause of action first accrued.

Sec. 2515. **When Five Years.**—An action upon a contract not in writing, signed by the party, express or implied; an action upon a liability created by statute, when no other time is fixed by the statute creating the liability; an action for a penalty or forfeiture when no time is fixed by the statute or law prescribing the same; an action for trespass on real or personal property; an action for the profits of or damages for withholding real or personal property; actions for the taking, detaining, or injuring personal property, including actions for the specific recovery thereof; an action for the injury to the rights of the plaintiff, not arising on contract, and not hereinafter enumerated; an action upon a bill of exchange, check, draft, or order, or any indorsement thereof, or upon a promissory note, placed upon the footing of a bill of exchange; an action to enforce the liability of a steamboat or other vessel; an action upon an account concerning the trade of merchandise between merchant and merchant, or their agents; an action for relief on the ground of fraud or mistake, and an action to enforce the liability of bail, shall be commenced within *five years* next after the cause of action accrued. (See also Sec. 2519.)

Sec. 2516. **When One Year.**—An action for an injury to the person of the plaintiff, or of his wife, child, ward, apprentice, or servant, or for injuries to person, cattle, or stock by railroads, or by any company or corporation; an action for a malicious prosecution, conspiracy, arrest, seduction, criminal conversation, or breach of promise of marriage; an action for libel or slander; an action for the escape of a prisoner arrested or imprisoned on civil process, shall be cemmenced within *one year* next after the cause of action accrued, and not thereafter.

Sec. 2517. **Usury, One Year.**—And no action shall be prosecuted in any of the courts of this Commonwealth, for the recovery of usury theretofore paid, for the loan or forbearance of money, or other thing against the loanor or forbearer, or assignee, or either, unless the same shall have been instituted within *one year* next after the payment thereof; and this limitation shall apply to all payments made on all demands, whether evidenced by writing or existing in parol.

Sec. 2518. **Merchants' Accounts.—Two Years.**

Sec. 2519. **Fraud or Mistake—Limit Ten Years.**—In actions for relief for fraud or mistake, or damages for either, the cause of action shall not be deemed to have accrued until the discovery of the fraud or mistake; but no such action shall be brought *ten years* after the time of making the contract or the perpetration of the fraud.

Sec. 2520. **Account between Merchant and Merchant.**—In an action to recover a balance due upon a mutual open and current account, concerning the trade of merchandise between merchant and merchant, or their agents, where there have been reciprocal demands between the parties, the cause of action is deemed to have accrued from the time of the last item proved in the account claimed, or proved to be chargeable on the adverse side. (See also Sec. 2518.)

Sec. 2521. **Rights of Infants against Fiduciaries.**

Sec. 2522. **Actions not otherwise provided for.**—An action for relief, not provided for in this or some other chapter, can only be commenced within ten years next after the cause of action accrued.

Sec. 2523. **State.**—The limitations prescribed in this chapter shall apply to actions brought by or in the name of the Commonwealth, in the same manner as to actions by private persons, except where a different time is prescribed by some other chapter in this revision.

ART. IV.—*General Provisions.*

Sec. 2524. **When Action is deemed to have been commenced.**—An action shall be deemed to have been commenced at the date of the first summons or process issued in good faith from the court or tribunal having jurisdiction of the cause of action.

Sec. 2529. **Personal Representative exempt from Suit after Seven Years, when.**—No action against a personal representative, who has settled his accounts, and made distribution of the whole assets in his hands, on any judgment or decree against such testator or intestate, or on any contract made by him, shall be brought after the expiration of *seven years* after the qualification of such representative.

Sec. 2530. **Action accruing against a Decedent in his Lifetime barred as against his Heir, etc., when.**—No action upon a cause which accrued against a deceased person in his lifetime shall, when his estate has been distributed and divided, be brought against his heirs or devisees, jointly with his personal representative, after the expiration of seven years from his death.

Sec. 2534. **Effect of War.**—Where the plaintiff is an alien, and a subject or citizen of a country at war with the United States, the time of the continuance of the war is not to be computed as part of the period limited for the commencement of the action.

Sec. 2535. **Injunction.**—When the collection of a judgment or the commencement of an action is stayed by injunction, the time of the continuance of the injunction is not part of the period limited for the collection of the judgment or the commencement of the action.

Sec. 2539. **Mortgagee of Real Property in Adverse Possession for Fifteen Years, protected.**—After a mortgagee of real property, or any person claiming under him, has had fifteen years' continued adverse possession, no action shall be brought by the mortgagor, or any one claiming under him, to redeem it.

Sec. 2540. **If of Personal Property, then Five Years.**—The provision of the last section shall apply in cases of a mortgage of personal property, with the difference that the period within which the action to redeem may be brought shall be *five years*.

Sec. 2541. **Foreign Judgment barred at Home, barred here, except.**—When, by the laws of any other State or country, an action upon a judgment or decree rendered in such State or country cannot be maintained there by reason of the lapse of time, and such judgment or decree is incapable of being otherwise enforced there, an action upon the same cannot be maintained in this State, except in favor of a resident thereof, who has had the cause of action from the time it accrued.

Sec. 2542. **Cause of Action barred in State where it originated.**—When a cause of action has arisen in another State or country, between residents of such State or country, or between them and residents of another State or country, and by the laws of the State or country where the cause of action accrued an action cannot be maintained thereon by reason of the lapse of time, no action can be maintained thereon in this State.

Sec. 2543. **Trusts and Suits by Vendee in Possession to Obtain a Title.**—The provisions of this chapter shall not apply in the case of a continuing and subsisting trust, nor to an action by a vendee of real property in the possession thereof, to obtain a conveyance.

Sec. 2544. **Injunction or other Restraint.**—In all cases where the doing of an act necessary to save any right or benefit is restrained or suspended by injunction or other lawful restraint, vacancy in office, absence of an officer, or his refusal to act, the time covered by the injunction, restraint, vacancy, absence, or refusal to act shall not be estimated in the application of any statute of limitations.

Sec. 2545. **Dismissal of Action.**—When an action has been or shall be commenced in due time, and in good faith, in any court of this Commonwealth, and the defendants, or either of them, have or shall make defense, and it shall be adjudged that such court had or has no jurisdiction of the action, the plaintiff or his representative may, within three months from the time of such judgment, commence a new action in the proper court, and the time between the commencement of the first and last action shall not be counted in applying the limitation.

LOUISIANA.

MERRICK'S REVISED CIVIL CODE, 1912, 2D ED.

BOOK III, TITLE XXIII, CHAP. 3.—*Of Prescription.*

SEC. 3. OF THE PRESCRIPTION WHICH OPERATES A RELEASE FROM DEBT.

Art. 3528. (3494.) **Liberative Prescription.**—The prescription which operates a release from debts, discharges the debtor by the mere silence of the creditor during the time fixed by law, from all actions, real or personal, which might be brought against him.

Art. 3529. (3495.) **As to Real Rights.**—This prescription has also the effect of releasing the owner of an estate from every species of real rights, to which the property may have been subject, if the person in possession of the right has not exercised it during the time required by law.

Art. 3530. (3496.) **Right of Debtor to Claim.**—To enable the debtor to claim the benefit of this prescription, it is not necessary that he should produce any title, or hold in good faith; the neglect of the creditor operates the prescription in this case.

Art. 3531. (3497.) **Term.**—The time necessary to acquire this prescription is longer or shorter, according to the different species of debts or of real rights, of which it produces the discharge or extinction.

Art. 3532. **Prescription on Foreign Contracts or Judgments.**—Whenever any contract or obligation has been entered into, or judgment rendered, between persons who reside out of the State of Louisiana, and to be paid or performed out of this State, and such contract, obligation or judgment is barred by prescription or the statute of limitations of the place where the contract or obligation is to be performed or judgment executed, the same shall be considered and held as barred by prescription in Louisiana, upon the debtor who is thus discharged subsequently coming into this State.

Art. 3533. (3498.) **Special Prescription.**—Besides the different prescriptions of actions, which are mentioned in other parts of this Code, others exist which are the subject of the following paragraphs:

SEC. I. OF THE PRESCRIPTION OF ONE YEAR.

Art. 3534. (3499.) **One Year's Prescription.**—The following actions are prescribed by one year:

Justices, Notaries and Constables.—That of justices of the peace and notaries, and persons performing their duties, as well as that of constables, for the fees and emoluments which are due to them in their official capacity.

Teachers by the Month.—That of masters and instructors in the arts and sciences, for lessons which they give by the month.

Innkeepers, etc.—That of innkeepers and such others, on account of lodging and board which they furnish.

Retail Liquor Dealers.—That of retailers of liquors, who sell ardent spirits in less quantities than one quart.

Laborers and Servants.—That of workmen, laborers and servants, for the payment of their wages.

Ship Freight; Officers and Crew.—That for the payment of the freight of ships and other vessels, the wages of the officers, sailors and others of the crew.

Materials and Provisions for Ships.—That for the supply of wood and other things necessary for the construction, equipment and provisioning of ships and other vessels.

Art. 3535. (3500.) **Continuous Accounts; Interruption; Voyage.**—In the cases mentioned in the preceding article, the prescription takes place, although there may have been a regular continuance of supplies, or of labor or other service.

It only ceases from the time when there has been an account acknowledged, a note or bond given, or a suit instituted. However, with respect to the wages of officers, sailors and others of the crew of a ship, this prescription runs only from the day when the voyage is completed.

Art. 3536. (3501.) **Torts; Claims by and against Vessels; Possessory Actions.**—The following actions are also prescribed by one year:—

That for injurious words, whether verbal or written, and that for damages caused by animals, or resulting from offenses or quasi-offenses.

That which a possessor may institute, to have himself maintained or restored to his possession, when he has been disturbed or evicted.

That for the delivery of merchandise or other effects, shipped on board any kind of vessel.

That for damage sustained by merchandise on board ships, or which may have happened by ships running foul of each other.

Art. 3537. (3502.) **Commencement of Prescription.**—The prescription mentioned in the preceding article runs:

With respect to the merchandise injured and not delivered, from the day of the arrival of the vessel, or that on which she ought to have arrived.

And in other cases from that on which the injurious words, disturbance or damage were sustained.

And where land, timber or property has been injured, cut, damaged or destroyed, from the date knowledge of such damage is received by the owner thereof.

SEC. II. OF THE PRESCRIPTION OF THREE YEARS.

Art. 3538. (3503.) **Three Years' Prescription.**—The following actions are prescribed by three years:

Rent, Annuities, Alimony.—That for arrearages of rent charge, annuities and alimony, or of the hire of movables and immovables.

Money Lent.—That for the payment of money lent.

Overseers, Clerks, Teachers by the Year or Quarter.—That for the salaries of overseers, clerks, secretaries, and of teachers of the sciences, who give lessons by the year or quarter.

Physicians, Apothecaries, etc.—That of physicians, surgeons and apothecaries, for visits, operations and medicines.

Recorders, Clerks, Sheriffs, Attorneys.—That of parish recorders, sheriffs, clerks, and attorneys, for their fees and emoluments.

Merchants' Accounts.—That on the accounts of merchants, whether selling for wholesale or retail.

Retailers of Provisions or Liquors.—That on the accounts of retailers of provisions, and that of retailers of liquors, who do not sell ardent spirits in less quantities than a quart.

Open Accounts.—That on all other open accounts.

This prescription only ceases from the time there has been an account acknowledged, in writing, a note or bond given or an action commenced.

Art. 3539. (3504.) **Against Attorneys for Return of Papers.**—The action of parties against their attorneys for the return of papers delivered to them for the interest of their suits, is prescribed also by *three years*, reckoning from the day when judgment was rendered in the suit, or from the revocation of the powers of the attorneys.

SEC. III. OF THE PRESCRIPTION OF FIVE YEARS.

Art. 3540. (3505.) **Bills and Notes.**—Action on bills of exchange, notes payable to order or bearer, except bank notes, those on all effects negotiable or transferable by indorsement or delivery, and those on all promissory notes, whether negotiable or otherwise, are prescribed by *five years*' reckoning from the day when the engagements were payable.

Art. 3541. (3506.) **Minors and Interdicts.**—The prescription mentioned in the preceding article, and those described above in paragraphs I. and II., run against minors and interdicted persons, reserving, however, to them their recourse against their tutors or curators.

They run also against persons residing out of the State.

Art. 3452. (3507.) The following actions are prescribed by *five years:*

Nullity or Rescission.—That for the nullity or rescission of contracts, testaments or other acts.

Reduction of Donations.—That for the reduction of excessive donations.

Rescission of Partitions.—That for the rescission of partitions and guaratee of the portions.

Minors.—This prescription only commences against minors after their majority.

Art. 3543. **Informalities in Public Sales.**—All informalities connected with or growing out of any public sale, made by any person authorized to sell at public auction, shall be prescribed against by those claiming under such sale, after the lapse of *five years* from the time of making it, whether against minors, married women, or interdicted persons.

SEC. IV. OF THE PRESCRIPTION OF TEN YEARS.

Art. 3544. (3508.) **Ten Years.**—In general, all personal actions, except those before enumerated, are prescribed by *ten years*.

Art. 3545. (3509.) **Architect or Builder in Brick or Stone.**—The action against an undertaker or architect, for defect of construction of buildings of brick or stone, is prescribed by *ten years.*

Art. 3546. (3511.) **Usufruct, Use, Servitudes.**—The rights of usufruct, use and habitation and servitudes are lost by non-use for *ten years.*

Art. 3547. **Judgments; Revival of.**—All judgments for money, whether rendered within or without the State, shall be prescribed by the lapse of *ten years* from the rendition of such judgments: *Provided, however,* that any party interested in any judgment may have the same revived at any time before it is prescribed by having a citation issued according to law, to the defendant or his representative, from the court which rendered the judgment, unless the defendant or his representative show good cause why the judgment should not be revived, and if such defendant be absent and not represented, the court may appoint a curator *ad hoc* to represent him in the proceedings, upon which curator *ad hoc* the citation shall be served.

Any judgment, revived as above provided, shall continue in full force for *ten years* from the date of the order of court reviving the same, and any judgment may be revived as often as the party interested may desire.

SEC. V. OF THE PRESCRIPTION OF THIRTY YEARS.

Art. 3548. (3512.) **Actions for Immovables and Entire Estates.**—All actions for immovable property, or for an entire estate, as a succession, are prescribed by *thirty years.*

Sec. 2810 (of Rev. Laws of 1897). **Absentees and Non-residents placed upon the same Footing as Residents.**—The laws of prescription now existing, whereby absentees and non-residents of the State are entitled to longer periods than persons present or residents in the State, before prescription can be acquired against them, are abolished; and hereafter absentees or non-residents of the State are to stand on the same footing, in relation to the laws of prescription, as persons present or residents of the State: *Provided,* that this section shall not apply to any prescription of one year or less. (*Acts of* 1848, *p.* 60.)

MAINE.

REVISED STATUTES, 1903. TITLE IX., CHAP. 83.

LIMITATION OF PERSONAL ACTIONS.

Sec. 85. (82.) **Actions barred in Six Years.**—*First.* Actions of debt, founded upon a contract or liability not under seal, except such as are brought upon a judgment or decree of some court of record of the United States, or of a State, or of some municipal or police court, trial justice, or justice of the peace in this State.

Second. Actions upon judgments of any court, not a court of record, except municipal and police courts, trial justices, and justices of the peace in this State.

Third. Actions for arrears of rent.

Fourth. Actions of assumpsit, or upon the case, founded on any contract or liability, express or implied.

Fifth. Actions for waste, of trespass on land, and of trespass, except those for assault and battery and false imprisonment.

Sixth. Actions of replevin, and other actions for taking, detaining, or injuring goods or chattels.

Seventh. All other actions on the case, except for slanderous words and for libel.

Sec. 86. (83.) **Actions against Sheriff.**—Actions for escape of prisoners committed on execution shall be actions on the case, and be commenced within one year after the cause of action accrues; but actions against a sheriff, for negligence or misconduct of himself or his deputies, shall be commenced within four years after the cause of action accrues.

Sec. 87. (84.) **Assault. Libel. False Imprisonment**—Actions of assault and battery, and for false imprisonment, slander, and libel, shall be commenced within two years after the cause of action accrues.

Sec. 88. (85.) **Scire Facias.**—No *scire facias* shall be served on bail unless within one year after judgment was rendered against the principal; nor on sureties in recognizances in criminal cases unless within one year after the default of the principal; nor against any person adjudged trustee, unless within one year from the expiration of the first execution against the principal and his goods, effects, and credits in the hands of the trustee.

Sec. 89. (86.) **Witnessed Notes and Bank-bills.**—The foregoing limitations do not apply to actions on promissory notes, signed in the presence of an attesting witness, or on the bills, notes, or other evidences of debt issued by a bank; nor to any case or suit limited to be commenced within a different time.

Sec. 90. (87.) **Mutual and Open Accounts Current.**—In actions of debt or assumpsit to recover the balance due, where there have been mutual dealings between the parties, the items of which are unsettled, whether kept or proved by one party or both, the cause of action shall be deemed to accrue at the time of the last item proved in such account.

Sec. 93. (90.) **General Limitation of Twenty Years.**—Personal actions on any contract, not otherwise limited, shall be brought within twenty years after the cause of action accrues.

Sec. 97. (94.) **Suits for Penalties.**—Actions and suits for any penalty or forfeiture on a penal statute, brought by a person to whom the penalty or forfeiture is given in whole or in part, shall be commenced within one year after the commission of the offense; and if no person so prosecutes, it may be recovered by suit, indictment, or information, in the name and for the use of the State, at any time within two years after the commission of the offense, and not afterwards.

Sec. 99. (96.) **Limitation in Cases of Fraud.**—If a person liable to any action mentioned herein, fraudulently conceals the cause thereof from the person entitled thereto, or if a fraud is committed which entitles any person to an action, the action may be commenced at any time within six years after the person entitled thereto shall discover that he has just cause of action.

Sec. 104. (101.) **Presumption of Payment.**—Every judgment and decree of any court of record of the United States, or any State, or of a trial justice or justice of the peace in this State, shall be presumed to be paid and satisfied at the end of twenty years after any duty or obligation accrued by virtue of such judgment or decree.

Sec. 105. (102.) **Set-offs.**—All the provisions hereof respecting limitations shall apply to any debt or contract filed in set-off by the defendant; and the time of such limitation of such debt or contract shall be computed, as if an action had been commenced therefor at the time when the plaintiff's action was commenced, unless the defendant is deprived of the benefit of the set-off by the nonsuit or other act of the plaintiff; and when he is thus defeated of a judgment on the merits of such debt or contract, he may commence an action thereon within six months after the final determination of the suit aforesaid.

Sec. 106. (103.) **Absence of Defendant from the State.**—If a person is out of the State when a cause of action accrues against him, the action may be commenced within the time limited therefor after he comes into the State; and if a person is absent from and resides out of the State after a cause of action has accrued against him, the time of his absence shall not be taken as a part of the time limited for the commencement of the action; or, if a person is adjudged an insolvent debtor after a cause of action has accrued against him, and such cause of action is one provable in insolvency, the time of the pending of his insolvency proceedings shall not be taken as a part of the time limited for the commencement of the action. But no action shall be brought by any person whose cause of action has been barred by the laws of any State, Territory, or country while all the parties have resided therein. (*As amended by Acts of* 1885, *chap.* 376; *Acts of* 1887, *chap.* 118.)

CHAP. 107.

LIMITATION OF REAL ACTIONS, AND RIGHTS OF ENTRY.

Sec. 1. **Rights of Entry and Action barred in Twenty Years.**—No person shall commence any real or mixed action for the recovery of lands, or make an entry thereon, unless within *twenty years* after the right to do so first accrued; or unless within *twenty years* after he, or those under whom he claims, were seized or possessed of the premises; except as hereinafter provided.

Sec. 2. **From what Time Right begins to run.**—If such right or title first accrued to an ancestor, predecessor, or other person under whom the demandant claims, said twenty years shall be computed from the time when the right or title first accrued to such ancestor, predecessor, or other person.

Sec. 3. **When such Right Shall be deemed to accrue.**

Sec. 4. **Entry for Condition broken.**—The preceding clause shall not prevent any person from entering when so entitled by reason of any forfeiture or breach of condition; but if he claims under such a title, his right accrues when the forfeiture was incurred or the condition broken.

Sec. 5. **Cases not specially provided for.**—In all cases not otherwise provided for, the right of entry accrues when the claimant, or the person under whom he claims, first became entitled to the possession of the premises under the title on which the entry or action is founded.

Sec. 10. **What constitutes a Disseisin.**—To constitute a disseisin, or such exclusive and adverse possession of lands as to bar or limit the right of the true owner thereof to recover them, such lands need not be surrounded with fences or rendered inaccessible by water; but it shall be sufficient, if the possession, occupation, and improvement are open, notorious, and comporting with the ordinary management of a farm; although that part of the same, which composes the woodland belonging to such farm and used therewith as a wood lot, is not so enclosed.

[Sec. 11, limiting to twenty years Real or Mixed Actions by the State was repealed by Chap. 368 of the Acts of 1885.]

Secs. 12, 13, 14. (13, 14.) **Right of Way, or other Easement, acquired by Adverse Use, twenty years.**

REAL ACTIONS.

Sec. 16. (15.) **Actions for the Recovery of Land barred in Forty Years.**—No real of mixed action, for the recovery of any lands, shall be commenced or maintained against any person in possession thereof, when such person or those under whom he claims have been in actual possession for more than forty years, claiming to hold them by adverse, open, peaceable, notorious, and exclusive possession, in their own right.

[Chap. 229 of the Acts of 1897, adds to this chapter: Secs. 13 (16), by which a right of way or other easement is not extinguished by adverse obstruction unless continued for twenty years and notice given. And Secs. 14 (17) provides how such notice is to be given.]

MARYLAND.

ANNOTATED CIVIL CODE, 1911 (BAGBY).

ART. 57. LIMITATION OF ACTIONS.

Sec. 1. **Within what Times Actions must be commenced.**—All actions of account, actions of assumpsit, or on the case, actions of debt on simple contract, detinue, or replevin, all actions for trespass, for injuries to real personal property, all actions for illegal arrest, false imprisonment, or violation of the twenty-third, twenty-sixth, thirty-first, and thirty-second articles of the Declaration of Rights, or any of them, or of any provisions of the code touching the writ of *habeas corpus*, or proceedings thereunder, and all actions, whether of debt, ejectment, or of any other description whatsoever, brought to recover rent in arrear, reserved under any form of lease, whether for ninety-nine years, renewable forever, or for a greater or lesser period, and all distraints issued to recover such rent, shall be commenced, sued, or issued within three years from the time the cause of action accrued; and all actions on the case for words, and all actions for assault, battery, and wounding, or any of them, within one year from the time the cause of action accrued. This section not to apply to such accounts as concern the trade of merchandise between merchant and merchant, their factors and servants, who are not residents within this State.

Sec. 2. **Within what Time after Disabilities removed.**—If any person entitled to any of the actions mentioned in the preceding section shall be at the time such cause of action accrues within the age of one and twenty years, or *non compos*, he or she shall be at liberty to bring the said action within the respective times so limited, after the disability is removed, as other persons having no such disability might or should have done. (*As amended by Laws of* 1890, *chap.* 548, *and of* 1894, *chap.* 661.)

Sec. 3. **Actions on Sealed Instrument or Specialty.**—No bill, testamentary, administration, or other bond (except sheriff's and constables' bonds), judgment, recognizance, statute merchant, or of the staple, or other specialty whatsoever, except such as shall be taken for the use of the State, shall be good and pleadable, or admitted in evidence against any person in this State after the principal debtor and creditor have been both dead twelve years, or the debt or thing in action is above twelve years' standing, provided, however, that every payment of interest upon any single bill or other specialty shall suspend the operation of this section as to such bill or specialty for three years after the date of such payment; saving to all persons who shall be under the aforementioned impediments of infancy, or insanity of mind, the full benefit of all such bills, bonds, judgments, recognizances, statute merchant, or of the staple or other specialties, for the period of six years after the removal of such disability. (*As amended by Laws of* 1890, *chap.* 548, *and of* 1894, *chap.* 661.)

Sec. 4. **Persons absenting or Absconding.**—No person absenting himself from this State, or who shall remove from county to county after any debt contracted, whereby the creditor may be at an uncertainty of finding out such person or his effects, shall have any benefit of any limitation herein contained; but nothing contained in this section shall debar any person from removing himself or family from one county to another for his convenience, or shall deprive any person leaving this State for the time herein limited, of the benefit thereof, he leaving effects sufficient and known for the payment of his just debts in the hands of some person who will assume the payment thereof to his creditors.

Sec. 5. **Person absent when Cause arises.**—If any person liable to any action shall be absent out of the State at the time when the cause of action may arise or accrue against him, he shall have no benefit of the limitation herein contained, if the person who has the cause of action shall commence the same after the presence in this State of the person liable thereto within the terms herein limited.

Sec. 6. **Actions on Sheriffs', Coroners', and Constables' Bonds.**—All actions on sheriffs', coroners' and constables' bonds shall be brought within *five years* after the date of such bonds, and not afterwards; but the State may sue on said bonds for her own use, at any time; and if any person entitled to suit on a sheriff's, coroner's, or constable's bond, shall be at the time of the accruing of any cause of action on such bond under the age of twenty-one years, or *non compos mentis,* he shall be at liberty to bring his or her action within *five years* after the removal of such disability. (*As amended by Laws of* 1894, *chap.* 661.)

Sec. 7. (6A.). The period within which any suit or action may be brought under any statute of limitations in force in this State, shall not be extended because the plaintiff, in such suit or action was, is or shall be a *feme covert,* imprisoned, or beyond the seas, or out of the jurisdiction of this State at the time of the accrual of the right, title or cause of action. (*Added by the Laws of* 1894, *chap.* 661.)

Sec. 14. (13.) **When Right to bring Suit Accrues.**—In all actions to be hereafter brought, when a party has a cause of action of which he has been kept in ignorance by the fraud of the adverse party, the right to bring suit shall be deemed to have first accrued at the time at which such fraud shall, or with usual and ordinary diligence might, have been known or discovered.

MASSACHUSETTS.

PUBLIC STATUTES 1902, PART III, TITLE V., CHAP. 202.

OF THE LIMITATION OF ACTIONS.

CHAP. 202.—*Limitation of Personal Actions.*

Sec. 1. (6, 7.) The following actions shall be commenced only within *twenty years* next after the cause of action accrues:

First. Actions upon contracts under seal.

Second. Actions upon bills, notes or other evidences of indebtedness issued by a bank.

Third. Actions upon promissory notes which have been signed in the presence of an attesting witness, if brought by the original payee, or by his executor or administrator.

Fourth. Actions upon contracts which are not limited by the provisions of the following section or by any other provision of law:

Sec. 2. (1.) The following actions shall, except as otherwise provided, be commenced only within *six years* next after the cause of action accrues:

First. Actions of contract founded upon contracts or liabilities, express or implied, except actions limited by the provisions of the preceding section or actions upon judgments or decrees of courts of record of the United States or of this or some other of the United States.

Second. Actions of tort.

Third. Actions of replevin.

Sec. 3. (2.) Actions against sheriffs for the misconduct or negligence of their deputies shall be commenced only within *four years* next after the cause of action accrues.

Sec. 4. (3.) Actions for assault and battery, for false imprisonment, for slander or libel, and actions against executors, administrators, guardians, trustees, sheriffs, deputy-sheriffs, constables, or assignees in insolvency, for the taking or conversion of personal property, shall be commenced only within *two years* next after the cause of action accrues.

Sec. 5. (4.) (5.) Actions for penalties or forfeitures under penal statutes, if brought by a person to whom the penalty or forfeiture is given in whole or in part, shall be commenced only within *one year* next after the offense is committed.

But if the penalty or forfeiture is given in whole or in part to the Commonwealth, an action therefor by or in behalf of the Commonwealth may be commenced at any time woithin *two years* after the offense is committed.

Sec. 6. (8.) In an action of contract brought to recover the balance due upon a mutual and open account current, the cause of action shall be held to have accrued at the time of the last item proved in the account.

Sec. 11. (14.) If a person who is liable to a personal action fraudulently conceals the cause of such action from the knowledge of the person who is entitled to bring it, the period prior to the discovery of his cause of action by the person who is so entitled shall be excluded in determining the time limited for the commencement of the action.

Sec. 17. (21.) The limitation of the preceding sections of this chapter, and of section 31 so far as it applies to personal actions, shall apply to actions brought by the Commonwealth or for its benefit.

Sec. 18. (22.) If a special provision is otherwise made relative to the limitation of any action, the provisions of this chapter which are inconsistent therewith shall not apply.

Sec. 19. (23.) A judgment or decree of a court of record of the United States, or of this or any other State of the United States, shall be presumed to be paid and satisfied at the expiration of twenty years after it was rendered.

Limitation of Real Actions and Right of Entry.

Sec. 20. (1.) An action for the recovery of land shall be commenced, or an entry made thereon, only within twenty years after the right of action or of entry first accrued, or within twenty years after the demandant or person who makes the entry or those under whom they claim, have been seised or possessed of the premises, except as hereinafter provided.

Sec. 21. (2.) If such right or title first accrued to an ancestor or predecessor of the person who brings the action or makes the entry, or to any other person under whom he claims, the twenty years shall be computed from the time when the right or title so first accrued.

Sec. 22. (3.) In the construction of sections twenty to thirty, inclusive, the right of entry or action to recover land shall be held to have first accrued at the times, respectively, hereinafter mentioned:

First. If a person has been disseised.

Second. If he claims as heir or devisee of a person who at his death was seized, at the time of such death; but if a tenancy by the curtesy or other estate intervened after the death of such ancestor or devisor, at the time when such intermediate estate expired, or would have expired by its own limitation.

Third. If there has been such intermediate estate, or if a person claims under a remainder or reversion, so far as his right is affected by the limitation herein prescribed, at the time when the intermediate or precedent estate would have expired by its own limitation, notwithstanding any forfeiture thereof for which he might have entered at an earlier time.

The provisions of this clause shall not prevent a person from entering if entitled to do so by reason of any forfeiture or breach of condition; but in such case, his right shall be held to have accrued when the forfeiture was incurred or the condition was broken.

Fourth. In all cases in which no other express provision is made, at the time when the claimant or the person under whom he claims first became entitled to the possession of the premises under the title upon which the entry or the action is founded.

Sec. 27. (8.) No person shall be held to have been in possession of lands within the meaning of this chapter merely by reason of having made an entry thereon, unless he has continued in open and peaceable possession thereof for *one year* next after such entry or unless an action is commenced upon such entry and seisin within one year after he is ousted or dispossessed.

SUPPLEMENTAL ACTS.

CHAP. 106, SEC. 75.

Sec. 75. (3.) **Action for Personal Injuries to an Employee.**—* * * No action for the recovery of damages for injury or death under the provisions of sections seventy-one to seventy-four inclusive, shall be maintained, unless notice of the time, place, and cause of the injury is given to the employer within sixty days, and the action is commenced within *one year* after the accident which causes the death or injury, etc.

CHAP. 51, SEC. 20.

Sec. 20. (1.) **Action for Injury from defective Highway, Two Years.**

Chap. 111, Sec. 267 (Act of 1887, Chap. 140), limits to one year an action against a railroad or street railway company for loss of life by negligence.

Chap. 182, Sec. 11. By Acts of 1889, Chap. 442, The Validity of incumbrances upon titles of real estate, imposed more than thirty years before the proceeding, may be determined on petition to the supreme court, and the decree thereupon made will exclude the respondent's claim.

MICHIGAN.

HOWELL'S ANNOTATED STATUTES, 1913, TITLE XXXIV, CHAP. 383.

LIMITATION OF ACTIONS RELATING TO REAL PROPERTY.

§ 14119. (9714.) Sec. 1. **Actions for the Recovery of Land, when to be brought.**—After the thirty-first day of December, in the year of our Lord eighteen hundred and sixty-three, no person shall bring or maintain any action for the recovery of any lands, or the possession thereof, or make any entry thereupon, unless such action is commenced, or entry made, within the time herein limited therefor, after the right to make such entry or to bring such action shall have first accrued to the plaintiff, or to some person through whom he claims, to wit:

First. Within *five years,* where the defendant claims title to the land in question by or through some deed made upon a sale thereof by an executor, administrator, or guardian, or by a sheriff or other proper ministerial officer, under the order, judgment, decree, or process of a court or legal tribunal of competent jurisdiction within this State; or by a sheriff upon a mortgage foreclosure sale; or through a devise in any will which shall have been probated in this State for fifteen years, during which period no suit in chancery has been brought to test the validity of such devise: *Provided,* that in cases where such fifteen-year period has already elapsed such rights of entry or action shall be barred after *two years* from the passage hereof, or in case such right has not accrued, then after *two years* from the accruing thereof.

Second. Within *ten years,* where the defendant claims title under a deed made by some officer of this State, or of the United States, authorized to make deeds upon the sale of lands for taxes assessed and levied within this State.

Third. Within *fifteen years* in all other cases.

§ 14120. (9715.) Sec. 2. **Computation of Time when Right accrued to Ancestor, etc.**—If such right or title first accrued to an ancestor, predecessor, or grantor of the person who brings the action or makes the entry, or to any other person from or under whom he claims, the said above periods of limitation shall be computed from the time when the right or title so first accrued to such ancestor, predecessor, grantor, or other person.

§ 14121. (9716.) Sec. 3. **When right deemed to have accrued.**

§ 14122. (9717.) Sec. 4. **Who presumed to have Possession.**—In every action for the recovery of real estate, or the possession thereof, the person establishing the legal title to the premises shall be presumed to have been possessed thereof, within the time limited by law for bringing such action, unless it shall appear that the same have been possessed adversely to such legal title by the defendant, or by those from or under whom he claims.

§ 14126. (9721.) Sec. 8. **Entry on Land, when effectual.**—No person shall be deemed to have been in possession of any lands, within the meaning of this chapter, merely by reason of having made an entry thereon, unless he shall have continued in open and peaceable possession of the premises for at least *one year* next after such entry, or unless an action shall be commenced upon such entry and seizin within *one year* after he shall be ousted or dispossessed of the premises.

§ 14129. (9724.) Sec. 11. **Suits by the People of this State.**—No suit for the recovery of any lands shall be commenced by or in behalf of the people of this State, unless within *twenty years* after the right or title of the people of the State therein first accrued, or within *twenty years* after the said people, or those from or through whom they claim, shall have been seised or possessed of the premises, or shall have received the rents and profits of the same, or some part thereof.

CHAP. 384.

LIMITATION OF PERSONAL ACTIONS.

§ 14135. (9728.) Sec. 1. **Certain Actions to be brought within Six Years.**—*First.* All actions of debt, founded upon any contract, or liability not under seal, except such as are brought upon the judgment or decree of some court of record of the United States, or of this or some other of the United States.

Second. All actions upon judgments rendered in any court, other than those above excepted.

Third. All actions for arrears of rent.

Fourth. All actions of assumpsit, or upon the case, founded upon any contract or liability, express or implied.

Fifth. All actions for waste.

Sixth. All actions of replevin and trover, and all other actions for taking, detaining, or injuring goods or chattels.

Seventh. All other actions on the case, except actions for slanderous words or for libels.

§ 14136. (9729.) Sec. 2. **Certain Actions to be brought within Two Years.**—All actions for trespass upon land, or for assault and battery, or for false imprisonment, and all actions for slanderous words, and all actions against physicians, surgeons and dentists for malpractice. And all actions for libels shall be commenced within *one year.*

§ 14137. (9730.) Sec. 3. **Actions against Sheriffs, etc.**—All actions against sheriffs, for the misconduct or neglect of their deputies, shall be commenced within *four years.*

§ 14138. (9731.) Sec. 4. **Exceptions.**—None of the provisions of this chapter shall apply to any action brought upon any bills, notes, or other evidences of debt issued by any bank.

§ 14139. (9732.) Sec. 5. **Cases of Accounts Current.**—In all actions of debt or assumpsit brought to recover the balance due upon a mutual and open account current, the cause of action shall be deemed to have accrued at the time of the last item proved in such account.

§ 14141. (9734.) Sec. 7. **General Limitation.**—All personal actions on any contract, not limited by the foregoing sections or by any law of this State, within *ten years.*

§ 14146. (9739.) Sec. 12. **Fraudulent Concealment by Defendant.**—If any person who is liable to any of the actions mentioned in this chapter shall fraudulently conceal the cause of such action from the knowledge of the person entitled thereto, the action may be commenced at any time within *two years* after the person who is entitled to bring the same shall discover that he has such cause of action, although such action would be otherwise barred by the provisions of this chapter.

§ 14153. (9746.) Sec. 19. **Limitation of Demands alleged as Set-offs.**—All the provisions of this chapter shall apply to the case of any debt or contract alleged by way of set-off on the part of a defendant; and the time of the limitation of such debt shall be computed in like manner as if an action had been commenced therefor at the time when the plaintiff's action was commenced, provided such debt or contract would have been barred according to law before the accruing of the claim or demand upon which such defendant is sued.

§ 14154. (9747.) Sec. 20. **Limitation of Suits by the People, etc.**—The limitations heretofore prescribed for the commencement of actions shall apply to the same actions when brought in the name of the people of this State, or in the name of any officer or otherwise, for the benefit of the State, in the same manner as to actions brought by individuals.

§ 14155. (9748.) Sec. 21. **Limitation of Suits for Penalties.**—All actions and suits for any penalty or forfeiture on any penal statute, brought in the name of the people of this State, within *two years.*

§ 14156. (9749.) Sec. 22. **Of Suits limited by other Statutes.**—The preceding section shall not apply to any suit which is or shall be limited by any statute, to be brought within a shorter or longer time than is prescribed in said section; but such suit shall be brought within the time that may be limited by such statute.

§ 14158. (9751.) Sec. 24. **When action upon Judgment shall be brought.**—Every action upon a judgment or decree heretofore rendered, or hereafter to be rendered, in a court of record of the United States, or of this State, or of any other State of the United States, shall be brought within *ten years* after the entry of the judgment or decree, and not afterwards: *Provided,* that in all cases of judgments, or decrees entered nine years or more before this act shall take effect, one year from the time when this act shall take effect shall be allowed for the commencement of an action or proceeding upon each judgment or decree, to revive the same: *Provided, further,* that no judgment or decree shall be revived, an action to recover or enforce which is now legally barred.

§ 14159. (9752.) Sec. 25. **Actions barred and Rights accrued under Former Statutes.**—No personal action shall be maintained, which, at the time when this chapter shall take effect as law, shall have been barred by the statute of limitation in force at the time when the cause of action accrued; and when any right of action shall have accrued before the time when this chapter shall take effect, it shall not be affected by this chapter, but all such causes of action shall be governed and determined according to the law under which the right of action accrued, in respect to the limitation of such actions.

§ 14160. (9754.) **Time Suit pending in Chancery not to be computed under Limitation Laws.**—The time during which any case in chancery, commenced by any debtor, has or may be pending and undetermined, shall not be computed as constituting any part of the period limited or prescribed by any statute of limitation in force at the time of the commencement of such case in chancery, prescribing the time within which an action in relation to the debtor or subject-matter in dispute, as set forth in the proceedings in such case in chancery, should or might be commenced.

§ 14163. **Actions to recover damages for personal injuries, three years.**

MINNESOTA.

GENERAL STATUTES, PART 3, CHAP. 77, TITLE II.

Tiffany's Compilation, 1913.

Sec. 7694. (5133.) **Limitations of Actions.**— Actions can only be commenced within the periods prescribed in this chapter, after the cause of action accrues, except where in special cases a different limitation is prescribed by statute.

Sec. 7696. (5134.) **Actions to recover Real Property.**—No action for the recovery of real estate, or the possession thereof, shall be maintained, unless it appears that the plaintiff, his ancestor, predecessor, or grantor, was seized or possessed of the premises in question within *fifteen years* before the beginning of the action: *Provided,* however, such limitation shall not be a bar to an action for the recovery of real estate assessed as tracts or parcels separate from other real estate, unless it appears that the party claiming title by adverse possession or his ancestor, predecessor, or grantor, or all of them together, shall have paid taxes on the real estate in question at least five (5) consecutive years of the time during which he claims said lands to have been occupied adversely.

Providing, further, that the provisions of the foregoing proviso shall not apply to actions relating to the boundary line of lands, which boundary lines are established by adverse possession, or to actions concerning lands included between the government or plotted line and the line established by such adverse possession, or to lands not assessed for taxes. (*R. L.*, § 4073, *amended* 1913 *c.* 239, § 1.)

Sec. 7700. (5135.) **Actions upon Judgments or Decrees.**—Within *ten years*:

An action upon a judgment or decree of a court of the United States, or of any State or Territory of the United States.

Sec. 7701. (5136.) **Actions upon Contracts, etc., within Six Years.**—Within *six years:*

1. An action upon a contract or other obligation, express or implied, as to which no other limitation is expressly prescribed.

2. An action upon a liability created by statute, other than those arising upon a penalty or forfeiture.

3. An action for a trespass upon real estate.

4. An action for taking, detaining, or injuring personal property, including actions for the specific recovery thereof.

5. An action for criminal conversation or for any other injury to the person or rights of another, not arising on contract, and not hereinafter enumerated.

6. An action for relief, on the ground of fraud; in which case the cause of action shall not to be deemed to have accrued until the discovery by the aggrieved party of the facts constituting the fraud.

7. Actions to enforce a trust or compel a trustee to account, where he has neglected to discharge his trust, or claims to have fully performed it, or has repudiated the trust relation.

Sec. 7702. (5137.) **Actions against Certain Officers, or for a Penalty.**—Within *three years:*

1. An action against a sheriff, coroner, or constable, for any act done in his official capacity, and in virtue of his office, or for any omission of an official duty, including the non-payment of money collected or received upon a judgment or execution.

2. An action upon a statute for a penalty or forfeiture to the party aggrieved.

Sec. 7703. (5138.) **Action for Libel, etc., within Two Years.**—Within *two years:*

1. An action for libel, slander, assault, battery, false imprisonment or other tort resulting in personal injury.

2. An action upon a statute for a forfeiture or penalty to the State.

3. For damages caused by a mill dam; but, as against one holding under the pre-emption or homestead laws, such limitation shall not begin to run until a patent has been issued for the land so damaged.

4. Against a master for a breach of an indenture of apprenticeship; the limitation, in such case, to run from the expiration of the term of service.

Sec. 7705. (5139.) **Action upon Mutual and Current Account** accrues, when.—If the action be to recover a balance due upon a mutual, open, and current account, and there have been reciprocal demands between the parties, the limitation shall begin to run from the date of the last item proved on either side.

Sec. 7698. (5141.) **Action to foreclose Mortgage.**—No action or proceeding to foreclose a real estate mortgage, whether by action or advertisement, or otherwise, shall be maintained unless commenced within fifteen years from the maturity of the whole of the debt secured by said mortgage, and this limitation shall not be extended by the nonresidence of any plaintiff or defendant or of any party interested in the land upon which said mortgage is a lien in any action commenced to foreclose such mortgage, nor by reason of any payment made after such maturity, nor by reason of any extension of the time of payment of said mortgage or the debt or obligation thereby secured or any portion thereof, unless such extension shall be in writing and shall have been recorded in the same office in which the original mortgage is recorded, within the limitation period herein provided, or prior to the expiration of any previously recorded extension of such mortgage or debt, nor by reason of any disability of any party interested in said mortgage.

MISSISSIPPI.

REVISED CODE, 1906. CHAP. 87.

LIMITATION OF ACTIONS.

Sec. 3090. (2730.) (2664.) **Actions concerning Land.**—A person may not make an entry, or commence an action to recover land, but within ten years next after the time at which the right to make the entry or to bring the action shall have first accrued to some person through whom he claims; or if the right shall not have accrued to any person through whom he claims, then within ten years next after the time at which the right to make the entry or to bring the action have first accrued to the person making or bringing the same. But if, at the time at which the right of any person to make an entry, or to bring an action to recover land, shall have first accrued, such person shall have been under the disability of infancy, or unsoundness of mind, then such person or the person claiming through him, may, notwithstanding the period of ten years hereinbefore limited shall have expired, make an entry, or bring an action to recover the land, at any time within ten years next after the time at which the person to whom the right shall have first accrued shall have ceased to be under either disability, or shall have died, whichever shall have first happened; but when any person, who shall be under either of the disabilities mentioned, at the time at which his right shall have first accrued, shall depart this life, without having ceased to be under such disability, no time to make an entry, or to bring an action to recover the land, beyond the period of ten years next after the time at which such person shall have died, shall be allowed, by reason of the disability of any other person.

Sec. 3091. (2731.) (2665.) **Same Limitation as to Suits in Equity.**—A person claiming land in equity may not bring suit to recover the same, but within the period during which, by virtue of the provisions hereinbefore contained, he might have made an entry, or brought an action to recover the same, if he had been entitled at law to such estate, interest, or right in or to the same, as he shall claim therein in equity; but in every case of a concealed fraud, the right of any person to bring suit in equity for the recovery of land, of which he or any person through whom he claims may have been deprived by such fraud, shall be deemed to have first accrued at and not before the time at which the fraud shall, or, with reasonable diligence might, have been first known or discovered.

Sec. 3094. (2734.) (2668.) **Ten Years' Adverse Possession gives Title.**—Ten years' actual adverse possession by any person claiming to be the owner for that time of any land, uninterruptedly continued for ten years by occupancy, descent, conveyance, or otherwise, in whatever way such occupancy may have been commenced or continued, shall vest in every actual occupant or possessor of such land a full and complete title, saving to persons under the disability of minority or unsoundness of mind the right to sue within ten years after the removal of such disability, as provided in the first section of this chapter, but the saving in favor of persons under disability of unsoundness of mind shall never extend longer than thirty-one years.

Sec. 3095. (2735.) (539.) **Three Years' Actual Possession under a Tax-title Bars Suit.**

Sec. 3096. (2736.) **Suits against the State or Municipalities.**—Statutes of limitation in civil cases shall not run against the State, or any subdivision or municipal corporation thereof; but all such statutes shall run in favor of the State, the counties, and the municipal corporations therein; and the statutes of limitation shall begin to run in favor of the State, the counties, and municipal corporations at the time when the plaintiff first had the right to demand payment of the officer or board authorized to allow or disallow the claim sued upon.

Sec. 3097. (2737.) (2669.) **Actions to be brought in Six Years.**—All actions for which no other period of limitation is prescribed shall be commenced within *six years* next after the cause of such action accrued, and not after.

Sec. 3099. (2739.) (2670.) **Actions to be brought in Three Years.**—Actions on an open account or stated account, not acknowledged in writing, signed by the debtor, and on any unwritten contract, express or implied.

Sec. 3100. (2740.) (2671.) **When Statute commences to run on Open Accounts.**—In all actions brought to recover the balance due upon a mutual and open current account, where both parties are merchants or traders, the cause of action shall be deemed to have accrued at the time of the true date of the last item proved in such account; and in all other actions upon open accounts, the period of limitations shall commence to run against the several items thereof, from the dates at which the same respectively became due and payable.

Sec. 3101. (2741.) (2672.) **Action for Penalty commenced in One Year.**—All actions and suits for any penalty or forfeiture on any penal statute, brought by any person to whom the penalty or forfeiture is given, in whole or in part, shall be commenced within one year next after the offense committed, and not after.

Sec. 3102. (2742.) (2673.) **Other Actions commenced in One Year.**—All actions for assault, battery, maiming, false imprisonment, malicious arrest or menace, and all actions for slanderous words concerning the person or title, and for libels, shall be commenced within *one year*. (See Sec. 3107 [2747], enacted in 1888.)

Sec. 3103. (2743.) (2674.) **Actions on Domestic Judgments.**—All actions founded on any judgment or decree rendered by any court of record in this State, shall be brought within *seven years* next after the rendition of such judgment or decree, and not after; and an execution shall not issue on any judgment or decree after seven years from the date of the judgment or decree.

Sec. 3104. (2744.) (2675.) **Actions on Foreign Judgments.**—All actions founded on any judgment or decree, rendered by any court of record without this State, shall be brought within *seven years* after the rendition of such judgment or decree, and not after. But if the person against whom such judgment or decree was or shall be rendered, was or shall be at the time of the institution of the action a resident of this State, such action, founded on such judgment or decree, shall be commenced within *three years* next after the rendition thereof, and not after.

Sec. 3107. (2747.) **Saving in Favor of Convicts.**—If any person entitled to bring an action for assault, assault and battery, or maiming, shall at the time the cause of such action accrued, have been in custody as a convict, such person may bring such action within one year after his release.

Sec. 3109. (2749. (2679.) **Concealed Fraud.**—If any person liable to any personal action shall fraudulently conceal the cause of action from the knowledge of the person entitled thereto, the cause of such action shall be deemed to have first accrued at, and not before, the time at which such fraud shall be, or with reasonable diligence might have been, first known or discovered. (See Sec. 2731.)

Sec. 3117. (2756a.) (2687.) **Limitation of Set-off.**—All the provisions of this chapter shall apply to the case of any debt or demand on contract, alleged by way of set-off on the part of a defendant; and the time of limitation of such debt or demand shall be computed in like manner as if an action had been commenced therefor at the time when the plaintiff's action was commenced; and the fact that a set-off is barred shall not preclude the defendant from using it as such if he held it against the debt sued on before it was barred.

Sec. 3120. (2758a.) (2691.) **Statute not to run when Person prohibited to Sue.**—When any person shall be prohibited by law, or restrained or enjoined by the order, decree, or process of any court in this State, from commencing or prosecuting any action or remedy, the time during which such person shall be so prohibited, enjoined, or restrained shall not be computed as any part of the period of time limited by this chapter for the commencement of such action.

Sec. 3121. (2759.) (2692.) **When the Limitation to commence.**—The several periods of limitation prescribed by this chapter shall commence from the date when it shall take effect; but the same shall not apply to any actions commenced, nor to any cases where the right of action or of entry shall have accrued, before that time, but the same shall be subject to the laws now in force; but this law may be pleaded in any case where a bar has accrued under the provisions thereof.

Sec. 3123. (2761.) (2694.) **Trustee barred, Beneficiaries barred.**—When the legal title to property or a right in action is in an executor, administrator, guardian, or other trustee, the time during which any statute of limitations runs against such trustee shall be computed against the person beneficially interested in such property or right in action, although such person may be under disability, and within the saving of any statute of limitations; and may be availed of in any suit or action by such person.

Sec. 3124. (2762.) (2695.) **Suits in Equity.**—Whenever there be a concurrent jurisdiction in the courts of common law and in the courts of equity of any cause of action, the provisions of this chapter, limiting a time for the commencement of a suit for such cause of action in a court of common law, shall apply to all suits to be brought for the same cause in a court of chancery. (See Sec. 3091 [2731.])

Sec. 3125. (2763.) (2696.) **Limitation of Express Trusts.**—Bills for relief, in case of the existence of a trust not cognizable by the courts of common law and in all other cases not herein provided for, shall be filed within ten years after the cause thereof shall accrue, and not after; saving, however, to all persons under disability of infancy, or unsoundness of mind, the like period of time after such disability shall be removed; but the saving in favor of persons under disability of unsoundness of mind shall never extend longer than thirty-one years.

MISSOURI.

LIMITATIONS OF ACTIONS.

ART. VIII.—*Limitations—Real Actions.*

Sec. 1879. (4262.) **Actions for Recovery of Lands to be commenced, when.**—No action for the recovery of any lands, tenements, or hereditaments, or for the recovery of the possession thereof, shall be commenced, had, or maintained by any person, whether citizen, denizen, alien, resident, or non-resident of this State, unless it appear that the plaintiff, his ancestor, predecessor, grantor, or other person under whom he claims was seized or possessed of the premises in question, within ten years before the commencement of such action.

Sec. 1882. (4266.) **Possession of Part, when Possession of the Whole Tract.**—The possession, under color of title, of a part of a tract or lot of land, in the name of the whole tract claimed, and exercising, during the time of such possession, the usual acts of ownership over the whole tract so claimed, shall be deemed a possession of the whole of such tract.

Sec. 1884. (4268.) **Limitation in Case of Certain Equitable Titles.**—Whenever any real estate, the equitable title to which shall have emanated from the government more than ten years, shall thereafter, on any date, be in the lawful possession of any person, and which shall or might be claimed by another, and which shall not at such date have been in possession of the said person claiming or who might claim the same, or of any one under whom he claims or might claim, for thirty consecutive years, and on which neither the said person claiming or who might claim the same, nor those under whom he claims or might claim has paid any taxes for all that period of time, the said person claiming or who might claim such real estate shall, within one year from said date, bring his action to recover the same, and in default thereof he shall be forever barred, and his right and title shall, *ipso facto*, vest in such possessor: *Provided, however*, that in all cases such action may be brought at any time within one year from the date at which this article takes effect and goes into force. (Sec. 2095 prescribes the procedure.)

Sec. 1885. (4269.) **When Legal Title has not emanated from the United States.**—In all cases in which the legal title has not yet emanated from the government of the United States, but in which there has been an equitable right or title for more than twenty years, under which a claimant has had a right of action by the statutes of this State, and in which the land has been in the possession of any person for twenty years, claiming the same in fee, any person claiming against the possessor shall bring his action under the legal title within one year after it issues from the government; and in default thereof he shall be forever barred, and his right and title shall, *ipso facto*, vest in such possessor.

Sec. 1886. (4270.) **Statutes not to extend to Certain Lands.**—Nothing contained in any statute of limitation shall extend to any lands given, granted, sequestered, or appropriated to any public, pious, or charitable use, or to any lands belonging to this State.

ART. IX.—*Personal Actions and General Provisions.*

Sec. 1887. (4271.) **Period of Limitation prescribed.**—Civil actions, other than those for the recovery of real property, can only be commenced within the periods prescribed in the following sections, after the causes of actions shall have accrued.

Sec. 1888. (4272.) **What Action shall be commenced within Ten Years.**—Within *ten years:*

First. An action upon any writing, whether sealed or unsealed, for the payment of money or property.

Second. Actions brought on any covenant of warranty contained in any deed of conveyance of land shall be brought within *ten years* next after there shall have been a final decision against the title of the covenantor in such deed, and actions on any covenant of seizin contained in any such deed shall be brought within *ten years* after the cause of such action shall accrue.

Third. Actions for relief, not herein otherwise provided for.

Sec. 1889. (4273.) **What within Five Years.**—Within *five years:*—

First. All actions upon contracts, obligations, or liabilities, express or implied, except those mentioned in section one thousand eight hundred and eighty-eight, and except upon judgments or decrees of a court of record, and except where a different time is herein limited.

Second. An action upon a liability created by a statute other than for a penalty or forfeiture.

Third. An action for trespass on real estate.

Fourth. An action for taking, detaining, or injuring any goods or chattels, including actions for the recovery of specific personal property, or for any other injury to the person or rights of another, not arising on contract, and not herein otherwise enumerated.

Fifth. An action for relief on the ground of fraud, the cause of action in such case to be deemed not to have accrued until the discovery by the aggrieved party, at any time within ten years, of the facts constituting the fraud.

Sec. 1890. (4274.) **What within Three Years.**—Within *three years*:—

First. An action against a sheriff, coroner, or other officer, upon a liability incurred by the doing of an act in his official capacity and in virtue of his office, or by the omission of an official duty, including the non-payment of money collected upon an execution or otherwise.

Second. An action upon a statute for a penalty or forfeiture, where the action is given to the party aggrieved, or to such party and the State.

Sec. 1891. (4275.) **What within Two Years.**—Within *two years*: An action for libel, slander, assault, battery, false imprisonment, or criminal conversation.

Sec. 1892. (4276.) **No Action to Foreclose Mortgage after Note Barred.**—No suit, action or proceeding under a power of sale to foreclose any mortgage or deed of trust, executed hereafter to secure any obligation to pay money or property, shall be had or maintained after such obligation has been barred by the statutes of limitations of this State. (Laws 1891, p. 184.)

Sec. 1893. (4278.) **In Account Current, when Cause of Action Accrued.**—In an action brought to recover a balance due on a mutual, open, and current account, where there have been reciprocal demands between the parties, the cause of action shall be deemed to have accrued from the time of the last item in the account on the adverse side.

Sec. 1895. (4280.) **Limitation on Actions Originating in other States.**—Whenever a cause of action has been fully barred by the laws of the State, Territory or country in which it originated, said bar shall be a complete defense to any action thereon, brought in any of the courts of this State. (*Added by Act of May* 24, 1899.)

Sec. 1912. (4297.) **Judgments presumed to be paid, when—Presumption, how repelled.**—Every judgment, order or decree of any court of record of the United States, or of this or any other State, Territory, or country, shall be presumed to be paid and satisfied after the expiration of *ten years* from the date of the original rendition thereof, or if the same has been revived upon personal service duly had upon the defendant or defendants therein, then after *ten years* from and after such revival, or in case a payment has been made on such judgment, order or decree, and duly entered upon the record thereof, after the expiration of ten years from the last payment so made, and after the expiration of ten years from the date of the original rendition or revival upon personal service, or from the date of the last payment, such judgment shall be conclusively presumed to be paid, and no execution, order or process shall issue thereon, nor shall any suit be brought, had or maintained thereon for any purpose whatever.

Sec. 1914. (4299.) **To apply to the State as well as to Private Parties.**—The limitations prescribed in this chapter shall apply to actions brought in the name of this State, or for its benefit, in the same manner as to actions by private parties.

Sec. 1915. (4300.) **Set-off, etc.**—When a defendant in action has interposed an answer, as a defense, set-off, or counterclaim, upon which he would be entitled to rely in such action, the remedy upon which, at the time of the commencement of such action, was not barred by law, and such complaint is dismissed, or the action is discontinued, the time which intervened between the commencement and the termination of such action shall not be deemed a part of the time limited for the commencement of an action by the defendant to recover for the cause of action so interposed as a defense, set-off, or counterclaim.

MONTANA.

CODE OF CIVIL PROCEDURE (1907).

TITLE II, CHAP. 1.—THE TIME OF COMMENCING ACTIONS IN GENERAL.

Sec. 6828. (470.) **Commencement of Civil Actions.**—Civil actions can only be commenced within the periods prescribed in this title, after the cause of action shall have accrued, except where, in special cases, a different limitation is prescribed by statute.

CHAP. 2.—THE TIME FOR COMMENCING ACTIONS FOR THE RECOVERY OF REAL PROPERTY.

Sec. 6432. (483.) **Actions to recover Real Property, Dower.**—No action for the recovery of real property, or for the possession thereof, can be maintained, unless it appear that the plaintiff, his ancestor, predecessor, or grantor, was seized or possessed of the property in question within *ten years* before the commencement of the action. No action for the recovery of dower can be maintained by a widow unless the action is commenced within *ten years* after the death of her husband.

Sec. 6433. (484.) **Same.**—No cause of action or defense to an action, arising out of the title to real property, or to rents or profits out of the same, can be effectual unless it appear that the person prosecuting the action or making the defense, or under whose title the action is prosecuted or the defense is made, or the ancestor, predecessor, or grantor of such person, was seized or possessed of the premises in question within *ten years* before the commencement of the act in respect to which such action is prosecuted or defense made.

Sec. 6434. (485.) **After Entry.**—No entry upon real estate is deemed sufficient or valid as a claim, unless an action be commenced thereupon within *one year* after making such entry, and within *ten years* from the time when the right to make it descended or accrued.

Sec. 6435. (486.) **Presumption from Legal Title.**—In every action for the recovery of real property, or the possession thereof, the person establishing a legal title to the property is presumed to have been possessed thereof, within the time required by law, and the occupation of the property by any other person is deemed to have been under and in subordination to the legal title, unless it appear that the property has been held and possessed adversely to such legal title, for *ten years* before the commencement of the action.

Sec. 6436. (487.) **Entry and Posssesion under Written Title.**—When it appears that the occupant, or those under whom he claims, entered into the possession of the property under claim of title, exclusive of other right, founding such claim upon a written instrument as being a conveyance of the property in question, or upon the decree or judgment of a competent court, and that there has been a continued occupation and possession of the property included in such instrument, decree, or judgment, or of some part of the property under such claim, for *ten years*, the property so included is deemed to have been held adversely, except that, when it consists of a tract divided into lots, the possession of one lot is not deemed a possession of any other lot of the same tract.

Sec. 6437. (488.) **Adverse Possession under Written Instrument, etc.**

Sec. 6438. (489.) **Adverse Possession under Claim of Title not in Writing.**

CHAP. 3.—THE TIME OF COMMENCING ACTIONS OTHER THAN FOR THE RECOVERY OF REAL PROPERTY.

Sec. 6444. (511.) **Personal Actions upon Contracts.**—Actions other than those for the recovery of real property, as follows: *Within ten years:* 1. An action upon a judgment or decree of any court of record of the United States, or of any State within the United States; 2. An action for mesne profits of real property.

Sec. 6445. (512.) **Within Eight Years.**—An action upon any contract, obligation, or liability, founded upon an instrument in writing.

Sec. 6446. (513.) **Within Five Years.**—1. An action upon a contract, account, promise, not founded on an instrument in writing; 2. An action to establish a will where the will has been lost, concealed, or destroyed. The cause of action is not deemed to have accrued until the discovery, by the plaintiff, or the person under whom he claims, of the facts upon which its validity depends; 3. An action upon a judgment or decree rendered in a cause not of record. The cause of action, in such case, is deemed to have accrued when the final judgment was rendered. (*As amended by the Act of March* 9, 1903.)

Sec. 6447. (514.) **Within Three Years.**—1. An action against a sheriff, coroner, or constable, upon a liability incurred by the doing of an act in his official capacity, and in virtue of his office, or by the omission of an official duty, including the non-payment of money collected upon an execution. But the subdivision does not apply to an action for an escape; 2. An action to recover damages for the death of one caused by the wrongful act or neglect of another; 3. An action upon an obligation or liability, not founded upon an instrument in writing, other than a contract, account or promise. (*As amended by the Act of* 1903 *above.*)

Sec. 6448. (515.) **Within Two Years.**—1. An action upon a statute for a penalty or forfeiture, when the action is given to an individual, or to an individual and the State, except where the statute imposing it prescribes a different limitation; 2. An action upon a statute, or upon an undertaking in a criminal action, for a forfeiture or penalty to the State; 3. An action for libel, slander, assault, battery, false imprisonment, or seduction.

Sec. 6450. (516.) **Within One Year.**—1. An action against a sheriff, or other officer, for an escape of a prisoner, arrested or imprisoned on civil process; 2. An action against a municipal corporation for damages or injuries to property caused by a mob or riot; or by a municipal corporation for the violation of any city or town ordinance; 3. An action against an officer, or officer *de facto*, to recover any goods, wares, merchandise, or other property, seized by any such officer in his official capacity as tax collector, to recover the price or value of any goods, wares, merchandise, or other personal property so seized, or for damages for the seizure, detention, sale of, or injury, to any goods, wares, merchandise, or other personal property seized, or for damages done to any person or property in making any such seizure.

Sec. 6450a. (517.) **Within Six Months.**—1. To recover stock sold for a delinquent assessment; 2. Actions on claims against a county, which have been rejected by the county commissioners, must be commenced within *six* months after the first rejection thereof by such board. (*Approved Feb.* 20, 1899.)

Sec. 6451. (518.) **Other Actions.**—An action for relief not otherwise hereinbefore provided, must be commenced within *five years* after the cause of action shall have accrued.

Sec. 6452. (519.) **Mutual and Open Accounts.**—In an action brought to recover a balance due upon a mutual, open, and current account, where there have been reciprocal demands between the parties, the cause of action is deemed to have accrued from the time of the last item proved in the account on either side.

Sec. 6456. (523.) **Deposits with Bankers.**—To actions brought to recover money or other property deposited with any bank, banker, trust company, or savings and loan corporation, association or society, there is no limitations; *provided*, however, that any action to obtain, set aside or question in any manner any stated or settled account, between any bank, banker, trust company or savings or loan corporation, association or society, and any depositor or depositors with such bank, banker, trust company or savings or loan corporation, association or society, must be commenced within five years from the date of the statement of such account. Any action based upon or arising from the payment of any bank, banker, company, corporation, association or society, of a forged, raised, or otherwise altered check, order or promissory note, out of the deposit, money or property of the plaintiff, shall be brought within three years from the day on which the plaintiff, his agent, assignee, or personal representatives shall have been notified of such payment, or on which he or they shall have received such check, order or note marked "paid." (*Act approved March* 3, 1905.)

Sec. 6457. (524.) An action for waste or trespass on real property, provided that when the trespass is committed by reason of underground works upon any mining claim, the cause of action shall not be deemed to have accrued until the discovery by the aggrieved party of the facts constituting such waste or trespass; 2. An action for a liability created by statute, other than a penalty or forfeiture; 3. An action for taking, detaining or injuring any goods or chattels, including actions for the specific recovery of personal property; 4. An action for relief on the ground of fraud or mistake (the cause of action in such case not to be deemed to have accrued until the discovery by the aggrieved party of the facts constituting fraud or mistake), shall be commenced within two years. (*Act approved, March* 9, 1893.)

NEBRASKA.

REVISED STATUTES, 1913, PART III, CIVIL CODE, CHAP. 2.

7563. Sec. 4. (5595. Sec. 5.) **Limitation.**—Civil actions can only be commenced within the time prescribed in this chapter, after the cause of action shall have accrued.

7564. Sec. 5 (5596. Sec. 6.) **Recovery of Real Property—Mortgages.**—An action for the recovery of the title or possession of lands, tenements, or hereditaments, can only be brought within *ten years* after the cause of action shall have accrued. This section shall be construed to apply also to mortgages. *Provided*, no limitation shall apply to the time within which any county, city, town or village or other municipal corporation may begin an action for the recovery of the title or possession of any public road, street, alley or other public grounds or city or town lots.

7575. Sec. 16. (5597. Sec. 7.) **Persons under Disability.**—Any person entitled to commence any action for the recovery of the title or possession of any lands, tenements, or hereditaments, who may be under any legal disability when the cause of action accrues, may bring such action within *ten years* after the disability is removed, and at no time thereafter.

7565. Sec. 6. (5598. Sec. 8.) **Forcible Entry and Detainer.**—An action for the forcible entry and detainer, or forcible detainer only, of real property, can only be brought within *one year* after the cause of such action shall have accrued.

7566. Sec. 7. (5599. Sec. 9.) **Other Civil Actions.**—Civil actions, other than for the recovery of real property, can only be brought within the following periods after the cause of action shall have accrued:

7567. Sec. 8. (5600. Sec. 10.) **Written Instruments—Foreign Judgment.**—Within *five years:* An action upon a specialty, or any agreement, contract, or promise in writing, or foreign judgment.

7568. Sec. 9. (5601. Sec. 11.) **Parol Contract.**—Within *four years*: An action upon a contract, not in writing, expressed or implied; an action upon a liability created by statute, other than a forfeiture or penalty.

7569. Sec. 10. (5602. Sec. 12.) **Trespass to Realty—Personalty—Replevin—Torts—Fraud.**—Within *four years*: An action for trespass upon real property; an action for taking, detaining, or injuring personal property, including actions for the specific recovery of personal property; an action for an injury to the rights of the plaintiff, not arising on contract, and not hereinafter enumerated; an action for relief on the ground of fraud, but the cause of action in such case shall not be deemed to have accrued until the discovery of the fraud.

7570. Sec. 11. (5603. Sec. 13.) **Injury to Character—Assault—Malicious Prosecution—False Imprisonment—Penalty.**—Within *one year*: An action for libel, slander, assault and battery, malicious prosecution or false imprisonment; an action upon a statute for a penalty or forfeiture, but where the statute giving such action prescribes a different limitation, the action may be brought within the period so limited.

1571. Sec. 12. (5604. Sec. 14.) **Official Bond — Undertaking.**— An action upon the official bond or undertaking of an executor, administrator, guardian, sheriff, or any other officer, or upon the bond or undertaking given in attachment, injunction, or in any case whatever required by statute, can only be brought within *ten years.*

7573. Sec. 14. (5605. Sec. 15.) **Contract—Failure of Consideration.**— Actions brought for damages growing out of the failure or want of consideration of contracts, express or implied, or for the recovery of money paid upon contracts, express or implied, the consideration of which has wholly or in part failed, shall be brought within *four years.*

7574. Sec 15. (5606. Sec. 16.) **Other Relief.**—An action for relief not hereinbefore provided for, can only be brought within *four years* after the cause of action shall have accrued.

7578. Sec. 19. (5608. Sec. 18.) **Actions Barred by Laws of Other States.**—All actions, or causes of action, which are barred by the laws of any other State, Territory or country, shall be deemed barred by the laws of this State; but no action shall be barred by laws of any other State, Territory or country unless the same would have been barred by the provisions of this chapter had the defendant been a resident of this State for the period herein provided.

7579. Sec. 20. **Part Payment or Acknowledgment of Debt.**—In any cause founded on contract, where any part of the principal or interest shall have been voluntarily paid, or an acknowledgment of an existing liability, debt, or claim, or any promise to pay the same shall have been made in writing an action may be brought in such case within the period prescribed for the same, after such payment, acknowledgment, or promise.

7581. Sec. 22. **Claims by and against State—When Barred.**—Every claim and demand against the State shall be forever barred, unless action be brought thereon within two years after the claim arose. Every claim and demand in behalf of the State, except for revenue, or upon official bonds, or for loans or moneys belonging to the school funds, or loans of school or other trust funds, or to lands or interest in lands thereto belonging, shall be barred by the same lapse of time as is provided by the law in case of like demands between private parties.

NEVADA.

REVISED LAWS, 1912, VOL. 2, PART III.

CHAP. 3.—LIMITATIONS—REAL PROPERTY.

4951. Sec. 9. (3706. Sec. 4.) **Action for Recovery of Mining Claims.**—No action for the recovery of mining claims, or for the recovery of possession thereof, shall be maintained, unless it appear that the plaintiff, or those through or from whom he claims, were seized or possessed of such mining claim, or were the owners thereof, according to the laws and customs of the district embracing the same, within *two years* before the commencement of such action. Occupation and adverse possession of a mining claim shall consist in holding and working the same in the usual and customary mode of holding and working similar claims in the vicinity thereof. All the provisions of this act which apply to other real estate, so far as applicable, shall be deemed to include and apply to mining claims: *Provided*, that in such application "two years" shall be held to be the period intended whenever the term "five years" is used; *And provided, further*, that when the terms "legal title" or "title" are used, they shall be held to include title acquired by location or occupation, according to the usages, laws, and customs of the district embracing the claim.

4952. Sec. 10. (3707. Sec. 5.) **Recovery of Real Property.**—No cause of action or defense to an action, founded upon the title to real property, or to rents, or to services out of the same, shall be effectual, unless it appear that the person prosecuting the action or making the defense, or under whose title the action is prosecuted, or the defense is made, or the ancestor, predecessor, or grantor of such person, was seized or possessed of the premises in question within *five years* before the committing of the act in respect to which such action is prosecuted or defense made.

4954. Sec. 12. (3708. Sec. 6.) **Peaceable Entry not Valid as Claim.**—No peaceable entry upon real estate shall be deemed sufficient and valid as a claim, unless an action be commenced by the plaintiff for possession within *one year* from the making of such entry, or within *five years* from the time when the right to bring such action accrued.

4955. Sec. 13. (3709. Sec. 7.) **Establishing Legal Title—Adverse Possession.**—In every action for the recovery of real property, or the possession thereof, the person establishing a legal title to the premises shall be presumed to have been possessed thereof within the time prescribed by law; and the occupation of such premises by any other person shall be deemed to have been under and in subordination to the legal title, unless it appear: (1) That it has been protected by a substantial enclosure; or, (2), That it has been cultivated or improved in accordance with the usual and ordinary methods of husbandry.

4956. Sec. 14. (3710. Sec. 8.) **Claim under Conveyance.**—Whenever it shall appear that the occupant, or those under whom he claims, entered into the possession of premises under claim of title, exclusive of any other right, founding such claim upon a written instrument, as being a conveyance of the premises in question, or upon the decree or judgment of a competent court, and that there has been a continued occupation and possession of the premises included in such instrument, decree, or judgment, or of some part of such premises, under such claim, for *five years*, the premises so included shall be deemed to have been held adversely, except that where the premises so included consist of a tract divided into lots, the possession of one lot shall not be deemed a possession of any other lot of this same tract.

4957-4959. Secs. 15, 16, 17. (3711-3713. Secs. 9-11.) **Adverse Possession Defined.**

4967. Sec. 25. (3718. Sec. 16. [1.]) **Actions other than for Recovery of Real Property.**—Actions other than those for the recovery of real property can only be commenced as follows:

Within six years: 1. An action upon a judgment or decree of any court of the United States, or of any State or Territory within the United States; 2. An action upon contract, obligation, or liability, founded upon an instrument in writing, except those mentioned in the preceding sections.

Within four years: 1. An action on an open account for goods, wares, and merchandise sold and delivered; 2. An action for any article charged in a store account; 3. An action upon a contract, obligation, or liability, not founded upon an instrument of writing.

Within three years: 1. An action upon a liability created by statute, other than a penalty or forfeiture; 2. An action for trespass upon real property; *provided,* that when the waste or trespass is committed by means of underground works upon any mining claim, the cause of action shall not be deemed to have accrued until the discovery by the aggrieved party of the facts constituting such waste or trespass; 3. An action for taking, detaining, or injuring personal property, including actions for the specific recovery thereof; *provided,* that in all cases where the subject of the action is a domestic animal usually included in the term "live stock," having upon it at the time of its loss a recorded mark or brand, and when such animal was strayed or stolen from the true owner without his fault, the statute shall not begin to run against an action for the recovery of such animal until the owner has actual knowledge of such facts as would put a reasonable man upon inquiry as to the possession thereof by the defendant; 4. An action for relief, on the ground of fraud, or mistake; the cause of action in such case not to be deemed to have accrued until the discovery by the aggrieved party of the facts constituting the fraud or mistake.

Within two years: 1. An action against a sheriff, coroner, or constable, upon the liability incurred by the doing of an act in his official capacity and in virtue of his office, or by the omission of an official duty, including the nonpayment of money collected upon an execution; 2. An action upon a statute for a penalty or forfeiture, where the action is given to an individual, or an individual and the State, except where the statute imposing it prescribes a different limitation; 3. An action for libel, slander, assault, battery, false imprisonment or seduction; 4. An action against a sheriff, or other officer, for the escape of a prisoner arrested or imprisoned on civil process; 5. An action to recover damages for the death of one caused by the wrongful act or neglect of another.

4970. Sec. 28. (3722. Sec. 18.) **Other Actions for Relief.**—An action for relief, not hereinbefore provided for, must be commenced within *four years* after the cause of action shall have accrued.

Within one year: 1. An action against an officer, or officers *de facto;* (a) To recover any goods, wares, merchandise or other property seized by any such officer in his official capacity, as tax collector, or to recover the price or value of any goods, wares, merchandise, or other personal property so seized, or for damages for the seizure, detention, sale of, or injury to any goods, wares, merchandise, or other personal property seized, or for damages done to any person or property in making any such seizure. (b) For money paid to any such officer under protest, or seized by such officer in his official capacity, as a collector of taxes, and which it is claimed, ought to be refunded.

2. Actions or claims against a county, incorporated city or town, which have been rejected by the board of county commissioners, city council, or board of trustees, as the case may be; after the first rejection thereof by such board, city council, or board of trustees.

4947. Sec. 5. (3736. Sec. 33.) **When Action Barred Abroad.**—When the cause of action has arisen in any other State, or in a foreign country, and by the laws thereof an action there cannot be maintained against a person by reason of the lapse of time, no action thereon shall be maintained against him in this State, except in favor of a citizen thereof who has held the cause of action from the time it accrued.

4953. Sec. 11. (3738. Sec. 1.) **Actions for Real Property.**—No action for the recovery of real property, or for the recovery of the possession thereof, other than mining claims, shall be maintained, unless it appear that the plaintiff, his ancestor, predecessor, or grantor was seized or possessed of the premises in question, within *five years* before the commencement thereof. (*Approved Feb.* 27, 1869.)

NEW HAMPSHIRE.

PUBLIC STATUTES, 1900, CHAP. 217.

LIMITATION OF ACTIONS.

Sec. 1. **Real Actions.**—No action for the recovery of real estate shall be brought after *twenty years* from the time the right to recover first accrued to the party claiming it, or to some person under whom he claims.

Sec. 2. **After Disability.**—If the person first entitled to bring such action is an infant, or insane person, at the time the right accrues, the action may be brought within *five years* after such disability is removed.

Sec. 3. **Personal.**—Actions of trespass to the person and actions for defamatory words may be brought within *two years*, and all other personal actions within *six years* after the cause of action accrued, and not afterward.

Sec. 4. **Debt on Judgments, etc.**—Actions of debt upon judgments, recognizances, and contracts under seal may be brought within *twenty years* after the cause of action accrued, and not afterward.

Sec. 5. **On Mortgage Notes.**—Actions upon notes secured by mortgage of real estate may be brought so long as the plaintiff is entitled to bring an action upon the mortgage.

Sec. 6. **Writs of Error.**—Writs of error may be sued out within *three years* after judgment, and not afterward, unless allowed by the court for sufficient cause, upon petition and notice.

Sec. 7. **Disability.**—Any infant or insane person may bring a personal action within *two years* after such disability is removed.

Sec. 8. **Absence.**—If the defendant in a personal action was absent from and residing out of the State at the time when the cause of action accrued, or afterward, the time of such absence shall be excluded in computing the time limited for bringing the action.

Sec. 9. **When Judgment against Plaintiff.**—If judgment is rendered against the plaintiff in an action brought within the time limited therefor, or upon a writ of error thereon, and the right of action is not barred by the judgment, a new action may be brought thereon in *one year* after the judgment.

Sec. 10. **Not when Different Time.**—The provisions of this chapter shall not apply to cases in which a different time is limited by statute.

By Chap. 244, Sec. 7, an **Action for Wilful Trespass** in cutting trees, timber, etc., must be brought within *two years.*

NEW JERSEY.

COMPILED STATUTE, VOL. 3 (1911), 3162.

1.—LIMITATION OF ACTIONS.

Sec. 1. **Actions within Six Years.**—All actions of trespass *quare clausum fregit,* all actions of trespass, detinue, trover, and replevin for taking away of goods and chattels, all actions of debt, founded upon any lending or contract without specialty, or for arrearages of rent due on a parol demise, and all actions of account and upon the case, except actions for slander, and except, also, such actions as concern the trade or merchandise between merchant and merchant, their factors, agents, and servants.

Sec. 2. **Within Four Years.**—All actions of trespass for assault, menace, battery, wounding, and imprisonment, or any of them, shall be commenced and sued within *four years* next after the cause of such action shall have accrued and not after.

Sec. 3. **Within Two Years.**—Every action upon the case for words shall be commenced and sued within *two years* next after the words spoken, and not after, and all actions hereafter accruing for injuries to persons caused by the wrongful act, neglect, or default of any person or persons, firm or firms, individual or individuals, corporation or corporations, within this State, shall be commenced and instituted within *two years* next after the cause of such action shall have accrued and not after. (*As amended by the Act of March* 24, 1896.)

Sec. 4. **Against whom not to run.**—If any person or persons who is, are, or shall be entitled to any of the actions specified in the three preceding sections of this act, is, are, or shall be, at the time of any such cause of action accruing, within the age of twenty-one years, or insane, that then such person or persons shall be at liberty to bring the said action so as he, she, or they institute or take the same within such time as is before limited, after his, her, or their coming to or being of full age, or of sane memory, as by other person or persons having no such impediment might be done.

Sec. 5. (*As amended P. L.* 1883, *p.* 33.) **Nine Years; Sheriffs', Constables' and Collectors' Bonds.**

Sec. 6. **Sealed Instruments.**—Every action of debt or covenant for rent or arrearages of rent, founded upon any lease under seal, whether indented or poll, and every action of debt upon any single or penal bill for the payment of money only, or upon any obligation with condition for the payment of money only, or upon any award under the hands and seals of arbitrators for the payment of money only, shall be commenced and sued within *sixteen years* next after the cause of such action shall have accrued, and not after; but if any payment shall have been made on any such lease, specialty, or award, within or after the said period of sixteen years, then an action instituted on such lease, specialty, or award, within sixteen years after such payment, shall be good and effectual in law, and not after: *Provided always,* the time during which the person who is or shall be entitled to any of the actions specified in this section shall have been within the age of twenty-one years, or insane, shall not be taken or computed as part of the said limited period of sixteen years.

Sec. 7. **Judgments.**—Judgments in any court of record of this State may be revived by *scire facias,* or an action of debt may be brought thereon within *twenty years* next after the date of such judgment, and not after: *Provided,* that the time during which the person who is or shall be entitled to the benefit of such judgment shall have been under the age of twenty-one years, or insane, shall not be taken or computed as part of the said limited period of twenty years.

Sec. 12. **Set-off.**—That this act shall be deemed and taken to apply to the case of any debt on simple contract alleged by way of set-off on the part of the defendant.

Sec. 16. **Right of Entry, Barred in Twenty Years.**

Sec. 17. **Actions for Lands.**—Every real, possessory, ancestral, mixed or other action, for any lands, tenements, or hereditaments, shall be brought or instituted within *twenty years* next after the right or title thereto, or cause of such action, shall accrue, and not after: *Provided always,* that the time during which the person who hath or shall have such right or title, or cause of action, shall have been under the age of twenty-one years, or insane, shall not be taken or computed as part of the said limited period of twenty years.

Sec. 18. **Equity of Redemption.**—If a mortgagee, and those under him, be in possession of the lands, tenements, and hereditaments contained in the mortgage, or any part thereof, for *twenty years* after default of payment by the mortgagor, then the right or equity of redemption therein shall be forever barred.

Sec. 20. **Actions by State, Twenty Years.**

Sec. 21. **Actions on Penal Statutes.**—Two years, where forfeiture is limited to the State; one year, where benefit is given to any person who shall prosecute.

Sec. 23. **Actions against Sheriffs or other Officers to Enforce Claims to Personal Property attached, etc.**, two months from the time of making the claim.

II.—TITLE TO LAND BY ADVERSE POSSESSION.

Sec. 28. **Sixty Years' Possession.**—Sixty years' actual possession of real estate, uninterruptedly continued, vests a full and complete right and title in every actual possessor or occupier of said land.

Sec. 29. **Thirty Years' Possession.**—Thirty years' actual possession, uninterruptedly continued, vests an absolute right and title in the actual possessor and occupier, wherever such possession commenced, or is founded upon a proprietary right duly laid thereon, and duly recorded, or wherever such possession was obtained by a fair *bona fide* purchaser of said right.

NEW MEXICO.

COMPILED LAWS, 1997, TITLE 33, CHAP. 8.

TIME OF COMMENCING ACTIONS.

Sec. 2913. (1860.) The following suits or actions may be brought within the time hereinafter limited, respectively, after their causes accrue, and not afterwards, except when otherwise specially provided:

Sec. 2914. (1861.) **On Judgments of Courts of Record, Fifteen Years.**—Actions upon any judgment of any court of New Mexico, or of any court of record of any other State or Territory of the United States, or the federal courts of the United States.

Sec. 2915. (1862.) **Bonds, Notes, etc., Six Years.**—Those founded upon any bond, promissory note, bill of exchange, or other contract in writing, or upon any judgment of any court not of record.

Sec. 2916. (1863.) **Accounts, etc., Four Years.**—Those founded upon accounts and unwritten contracts, those brought for injuries to property, or for the conversion of personal property, or for relief upon the ground of fraud, and all other actions not herein otherwise provided for and specified.

Sec. 2917. (1864.) **Sureties on Official Bonds, Two Years.**—Those against sureties upon official bonds, and those brought against sheriffs and other public officers for or on account of any liability incurred by the doing of any act in an official capacity, or by the omission of any official duty, and for injuries to the person or reputation.

Sec. 2918. (1865.) **Fraud.**—In actions for relief on the ground of fraud or mistake, and in actions for injuries to or conversion of property, the cause of action shall not be deemed to have accrued until the fraud, mistake, injury, or conversion complained of shall have been discovered by the party aggrieved.

Sec. 2919. (1866.) **Account, at last Item.**—When there is an open current account the cause of action shall be deemed to have accrued upon the date of the last item therein, as proven on the trial.

Sec. 2927. (1874.) **Set-off.**—A set-off or counterclaim may be pleaded as a defense to any cause of action, notwithstanding such set-off or counterclaim may be barred by the provisions of this act, if such set-off or counterclaim so pleaded was the property or right of the party pleading the same at the time it became barred and at the time of the commencement of the action, and the same was not barred at the time the cause of action sued for accrued or originated; but no judgment for any excess of such set-off or counterclaim over the demand of the plaintiff as proven shall be rendered in favor of the defendant.

Sec. 2931. (1878.) **Accounts.**—Accounts duly verified by the oath of the party claiming the same, or his agent, and promissory notes and other instruments in writing, not barred by the provisions of this act, shall be sufficient evidence in any suit to enable the plaintiff to recover judgment for the amount thereof, unless the defendant or his agent shall deny the same under oath.

Sec. 2937. (1880.) **Ten Years' Possession gives Title.**—Where any person or persons, their children, heirs, or assigns, shall, at the passing of this act or at any time after, have had possession for ten years of any lands, tenements, or hereditaments, which have been granted by the government of Spain, Mexico, or the United States, or by whatsoever authority empowered by said governments to make grants to lands, holding or claiming the same by virtue of a deed or deeds of conveyance, devise, grant, or other assurance purporting to convey an estate in fee-simple, and no claim by suit in law or equity effectually prosecuted shall have been set up or made to the said lands, tenements, or hereditaments, within the aforesaid time of ten years, etc.

Sec. 2938. (1881.) **Ten Years after Accrual, etc.**—No person or persons, or their children, heirs, or assigns, shall have or maintain any action or suit, either in law or equity, for any lands, tenements, or hereditaments but within ten years next after his, her, or their right to commence, have, or maintain such suit shall have come, fallen, or accrued, and that all suits either in law or equity for the recovery of any lands, tenements, or hereditaments shall be had and sued within *ten years* next after the title or cause of action or suits accrued or fallen, and at no time after the ten years shall have passed: *Provided,* etc.

By the Acts of 1897, chap. 73, sec. 66, a party is not to be deprived of the defense of the statute of limitations, when pleaded by him, because of his not denying the facts set forth in the adverse pleadings.

NEW YORK.

CODE OF CIVIL PROCEDURE.

CHAP. IV.—LIMITATION OF THE TIME OF ENFORCING A CIVIL REMEDY.

TITLE I.—ACTIONS FOR THE RECOVERY OF REAL PROPERTY.
TITLE II.—ACTIONS OTHER THAN FOR THE RECOVERY OF REAL PROPERTY.
TITLE III.—GENERAL PROVISIONS.

TITLE I.—*Actions for the Recovery of Real Property.*

Sec. 362. **When the People will not sue.**—The people of the State will not sue a person for or with respect to real property, or the issue or profits thereof, by reason of the right or title of the people to the same, unless either,

1. The cause of action accrued within *forty years* before the action is commenced; or,

2. The people, or those from whom they claim, have received the rents and profits of the real property, or of some part thereof, within the same period of time.

Sec. 365. **Seizin within Twenty Years, when necessary, etc.**—An action to recover real property, or the possession thereof cannot be maintained by a party, other than the people, unless the plaintiff, his ancestor, predecessor, or grantor, was seized or possessed of the premises in question, within *twenty years* before the commencement of the action.

Sec. 366. **The Same.**—A defence or counterclaim, founded upon the title to real property, or to rents or services out of the same, is not effectual, unless the person making it, or under whose title it is made, or his ancestor, predecessor, or grantor, was seized or possessed of the premises in question, within *twenty years* before the committing of the act, with respect to which it is made.

Sec. 367. **Action after Entry.**—An entry upon real property is not sufficient or valid as a claim, unless an action is commenced thereupon, within *one year* after the making thereof, and within *twenty years* after the time when the right to make it descended or accrued.

Secs. 368-372. **Possession, when presumed—Adverse Possession.**

TITLE II.—*Actions other than for the Recovery of Real Property.*[1]

Sec. 376. [**Amended, 1877, ch. 416; 1894, ch. 307.**] **When Satisfaction of Judgment presumed.**—A final judgment or decree for a sum of money, or directing the payment of a sum of money, heretofore rendered in a surrogate's court of the State, or heretofore or hereafter rendered, in a court of record

---

[1] An action for negligence against a city having 50,000 inhabitants must be brought within one year after the injury. L. 1886, chap. 572.

An action on a constable's bond must be brought within two years after expiration of the year for which he is elected.

within the United States, or elsewhere, or hereafter docketed pursuant to the provisions of Sec. 3017 of this Act, is presumed to be paid and satisfied, after the expiration of *twenty years* from the time when the party recovering it was first entitled to a mandate to enforce it. This presumption is conclusive, except as against a person, who, within *twenty years* from that time, makes a payment or acknowledges an indebtedness of some part of the amount recovered by the judgment or decree, or his heir or personal representatives, or a person whom he otherwise represents. Such an acknowledgment must be in writing, and signed by the person to be charged thereby.

Sec. 377. **Effect of Return of Execution.**—If the proof of payment, under the last section, consists of the return of an execution partly satisfied, the adverse party may show, in full avoidance of the effect thereof, that the alleged partial satisfaction did not proceed from a payment made, or a sale of property claimed, by him, or by a person whom he represents.

Sec. 378. **How presumption raised.**—A person may avail himself of the presumption created by the last section but one, under an allegation that the action was not commenced, or that the proceeding was not taken, within the time therein limited.

Sec. 379. **Limitation of Action to Redeem from a Mortgage.**—An action to redeem real property from a mortgage, with or without an account of rents and profits, may be maintained by the mortgagor, or those claiming under him, against the mortgagee in possession, or those claiming under him, unless he or they have continuously maintained an adverse possession of the mortgaged premises, for *twenty years* after the breach of a condition of the mortgage, or the non-fulfilment of a covenant therein contained.

Sec. 380. **Other Periods of Limitation.**—The following actions must be commencer within the following periods, after the cause of action has accrued.

Sec. 381. **[Amended, 1877, ch. 416.] Within Twenty Years.**—An action upon a sealed instrument.

But where the action is brought for breach of a covenant of seizin, or against incumbrances, the cause of action is, for the purposes of this section only, deemed to have accrued upon an eviction, and not before.

Sec. 382. **[Amended 1877, chs. 416, 422; 1894, ch. 307.] Within Six Years.**—1. An action upon a contract obligation or liability, express or implied; except a judgment or sealed instrument.

2. An action to recover upon a liability created by statute; except a penalty or forfeiture.

3. An action to recover damages for an injury to property, or a personal injury; except in a case where a different period is expressly prescribed in this chapter.

An action for damages from mobs must be brought within three months after the loss or injury.

An action to recover excessive fare, etc., must be brought within one year from the taking.

An action to recover for usury must be brought within one year after the payment.

4. An action to recover a chattel.

5. An action to procure a judgment, other than for a sum of money, on the ground of fraud, in a case which, on December 31, 1846, was cognizable by the Court of Chancery. The cause of action, in such a case, is not deemed to have accrued until the discovery by the plaintiff, or the person under whom he claims, of the facts constituting the fraud.

6. An action to establish a will. Where the will has been lost, concealed, or destroyed, the cause of action is not deemed to have accrued, until the discovery, by the plaintiff or the person under whom he claims, of the facts upon which its validity depends.

7. An action upon a judgment or decree, rendered in a court not of record, except where a transcript shall be filed, pursuant to Sec. 3017 of this Act, and, also, except a decree heretofore rendered in a surrogate's court of the State. The cause of action, in such a case, is deemed to have accrued when final judgment was rendered.

Sec. 383. **[Amended, 1877, ch. 416; 1886, ch. 572; 1889, ch. 440; 1902, ch. 600, § 2.] Within Three Years.**—1. An action against a sheriff, coroner, constable, or other officer, for the non-payment of money collected upon an execution.

2. An action against a constable, upon any other liability incurred by him, by doing an act in his official capacity, or by the omission of an official duty; except an escape.

3. An action upon a statute, for a penalty or forfeiture, where the action is given to the person aggrieved, or to that person and the people of the State; except where the statute imposing it prescribes a different limitation.

4. An action against an executor, administrator, or receiver, or against the trustee of an insolvent debtor, appointed, as prescribed by law, in a special proceeding instituted in a court or before a judge, brought to recover a chattel, or damages for taking, detaining, or injuring personal property by the defendant, or the person whom he represents.

5. An action to recover damages for a personal injury, resulting from negligence.

Sec. 384. **Within Two Years. [Amended 1896, ch. 335; 1900, ch. 117.]**—1. An action to recover damages for libel, slander, assault, battery, seduction, criminal conversation, or false imprisonment, malicious prosecution or malpractice.

2. An action upon a statute, for a forfeiture or penalty to the people of the State.

Sec. 385. **Within One Year.**—1. An action against a sheriff or coroner, upon a liability incurred by him, by doing an act in his official capacity, or by the omission of an official duty; except the non-payment of money collected upon an execution.

2. An action against any other officer, for the escape of a prisoner, arrested or imprisoned by virtue of a civil mandate.

Sec. 386. **When Cause of Action Accrues on a Current Account.**—In an action brought to recover a balance due upon a mutual, open, and current account, where there have been reciprocal demands between the parties, the cause of action is deemed to have accrued from the time of the last item proved in the account on either side.

Sec. 387. **Action for Penalty, etc., by any Person who will sue.**—An action upon a statute for a penalty or forfeiture, given wholly or partly to any person who will prosecute for the same, must be commenced within *one year* after the commission of the offense; and if the action is not commenced within the year by a private person, it may be commenced within two years thereafter, in behalf of the people of the State, by the attorney-general, or the district attorney of the county where the offense was committed.

Sec. 388. **Actions not provided for.**—An action, the limitation of which is not specially prescribed in this or the last title, must be commenced within *ten years* after the cause of action accrues.

Sec. 389. **Actions by the People subject to the same Limitations.**—The limitations prescribed in this title apply alike to actions brought in the name of the people of the State, or for their benefit, and to actions by private persons.

Sec. 390. **Action against a Non-resident, upon a Demand Barred by the Law of his Residence.**—Where a cause of action, which does not involve the title to or possesion of real property within this State, accrues against a person, who is not then a resident of the State, an action cannot be brought thereon in a court of the State, against him or his personal representative, after the expiration of the time limited, by the laws of his residence, for bringing a like action, except by a resident of the State, and in one of the following cases:

1. Where the cause of action originally accrued in favor of a resident of the State.

2. Where, before the expiration of the time so limited, the person in whose favor it originally accrued, was or became a resident of the State; or the cause of action was assigned to, and thereafter continuously owned by, a resident of the State.

Sec. 390a. **[Added ch. 193, 1902.] Cause of Action Arising in Another State.**

Sec. 391. **[Amended, 1877, ch. 416.] When Person Liable, etc., Dies without the State.**—If a person against whom a cause of action exists dies without the State, the time which elapses between his death and the expiration of eighteen months after the issuing, within the State, of letters testamentary or letters of administration, is not a part of the time limited for the commencement of an action therefor, against his executor or administrator.

Sec. 392. **[Amended, 1877, ch. 416.] Cause of Action accruing between the Death of a Testator or Intestate, and the Grant of Letters.**—For the purpose of computing the time within which an action must be commenced in a court of the State, by an executor or administrator, to recover personal property, taken after the death of a testator or intestate, and before the issuing of letters testamentary or letters of administration; or to recover damages for taking, detaining, or injuring personal property within the same period; the letters are deemed to have been issued within six years after the death of the testator or intestate. But where an action is barred by this section, any of the next of kin, legatees, or creditors, who, at the time of the transaction upon which it might have been founded, was within the age of twenty-one years, or insane, or imprisoned on a criminal charge, may, within five years after the cessation of such a disability, maintain an action to recover damages by reason thereof; in which he may recover such sum, or the value of such property, as he would have received upon the final distribution of the estate, if an action had been seasonably commenced by the executor or administrator.

Sec. 393. **No Limitation of Action on Bank-notes, etc.**—This chapter does not affect an action to enforce the payment of a bill, note, or other evidence of debt, issued by a moneyed corporation, or issued or put in circulation as money.

Sec. 394. **[Amended, 1877, ch. 416; 1897, ch. 281.] Action against Directors, etc., of Banks.**—This chapter does not affect an action against a director or stockholder of a moneyed corporation or banking association, to recover a penalty or forfeiture imposed, or to enforce a liability created by the common law or by statute; but such an action must be brought within three years after the cause of action has accrued.

Sec. 395. **Acknowledgment or New Promise must be in Writing.**—An acknowledgment or promise contained in a writing, signed by the party to be charged thereby, is the only competent evidence of a new or continuing contract, whereby to take a case out of the operation of this title. But this section does not alter the effect of a payment of principal or interest.

Sec. 396. **Exceptions as to Persons under Disabilities.**

Sec. 397. **Defence or Counterclaim.**—A cause of action, upon which an action cannot be maintained, as prescribed in this title, cannot be effectually interposed as a defence or counterclaim.

TITLE III.—*General Provisions.*

Sec. 398. **[Amended, 1877.] When Action deemed to be commenced.**—An action is commenced against a defendant, within the meaning of any provision of this act, which limits the time for commencing an action, when the summons is served on him; or on a co-defendant who is a joint contractor, or otherwise united in interest with him.

Sec. 399. **Attempt to commence Action in a Court of Record.**

Sec. 400. **Attempt to commence Action in a Court not of Record.**

Sec. 401. **[Amended, 1888, ch. 498; 1896, ch. 665.] Exception, when Defendant is without the State, or concealed therein.**—If, when the cause of action accrues against a person, he is without the State, the action may be commenced within the time limited therefor, after his return into the State. If, after a cause of action has accrued against a person, he departs from the State and remains continuously absent therefrom for the space of *one year* or more, or if, without the knowledge of the person entitled to maintain the action, he resides within the State under a false name, the time of his absence or of such residence within the State under such false name is not a part of the time limited for the commencement of the action. But this section does not apply while a designation made as prescribed in section 430, or in subdivision second of section 432 of this act remains in force.

Sec. 402. **Exception, when a Person entitled, etc., Dies before Limitation expires.**—If a person entitled to maintain an action, dies before the expiration of the time limited for the commencement thereof, and the cause of action survives, an action may be commenced by his representative, after the expiration of that time, and within one year after his death.

Sec. 403. **[See Amendment, 1891, ch. 70; 1896, ch. 897.] Exception, when a Person Liable, etc., Dies within the State.**—The term of eighteen months after the death, within this State, of a person against whom a cause of action exists, or of a person who shall have died within sixty days after an attempt shall have been made to commence an action against him pursuant to the provision of section three hundred and ninety-nine of this act, is not a part of the time limited for the commencement of an action against his executor or administrator. If letters testamentary or letters of administration upon his estate are not issued, within the State, at least six months before the expiration of the time to bring the action, as extended by the foregoing provision of this section, the term of one year after such letters are issued is not a part of the time limited for the commencement of such an action. * * *

Sec. 404. **In Suits by Aliens, Time of Disability in Case of War to be deducted.**

Sec. 406. **Stay by Injunction, etc., to be deducted.**—Where the commencement of an action has been stayed by injunction, or other order of a court or judge, or by statutory prohibition, the time of the continuance of the stay is not a part of the time limited for the commencement of the action.

Sec. 410. **Provision when the Action cannot be maintained without a Demand.**—Where a right exists, but a demand is necessary to entitle a person to maintain an action, the time, within which the action must be commenced, must be computed from the time when the right to make the demand is complete; except in one of the following cases:

1. Where the right grows out of the receipt or detention of money or property, by an agent, trustee, attorney, or other person acting in a fiduciary capacity, the time must be computed from the time when the person, having the right to make the demand has actual knowledge of the facts, upon which that right depends.

2. Where there was a deposit of money, not to be repaid at a fixed time, but only upon a special demand, or a delivery of personal property, not to be returned, specifically or in kind, at a fixed time or upon a fixed contingency, the time must be computed from the demand.

Sec. 411. **Provision in Case of Submission to Arbitration.**

Sec. 412. **Provision when Action is discontinued, etc., after Answer.**

Sec. 413. **How Objection taken, under this Chapter.**—The objection, that the action was not commenced within the time limited, can be taken only by answer. The corresponding objection to a defence or counterclaim can be taken only by reply, except where a reply is not required, in order to enable the plaintiff to raise an issue of fact upon an allegation contained in the answer.

Sec. 414. **Cases to which this Chapter applies.**—The provisions of this chapter apply, and constitute the only rules of limitation applicable, to a civil action or special proceeding, except in one of the following cases:

1. A case where a different limitation is specially prescribed by law, or a shorter limitation is prescribed by the written contract of the parties.

2. A cause of action or a defence which accrued before the first day of July, 1848. The statutes then in force govern with respect to such a cause of action or defence.

3. A case, not included in the last subdivision, in which a person is entitled, when this act takes effect, to commence an action, or to institute a special proceeding, or to take any proceeding therein, or to pursue a remedy upon a judgment, where he commences, institutes, or otherwise resorts to the same, before the expiration of two years after this act takes effect; in either of which cases the provisions of law applicable thereto, immediately before this act takes effect, continues to be so applicable, notwithstanding the repeal thereof.

4. A case where the time to commence an action has expired, when this act takes effect.

The word "action," contained in this chapter, is to be construed, when it is necessary so to do, as including a special proceeding, or any proceeding therein, or in an action.

Sec. 415. **Mode of computing Periods of Limitation.**—The periods of limitation prescribed by this chapter, except as otherwise specially prescribed therein, must be computed from the time of the accruing of the right to relief by action, special proceeding, defence, or otherwise, as the case requires, to the time when the claim to that relief is actually interposed by the party, as a plaintiff or a defendant, in the particular action or special proceeding.

NORTH CAROLINA.

CODE OF CIVIL PROCEDURE, 1908.

(*Pell's Revisal*, 1908.)

CHAP. 1, TITLE 3.

CHAP. 12.—ACTIONS IN GENERAL.[1]

III.—LIMITATIONS—GENERAL PROVISIONS.

Sec. 359. (161.) **When Action deemed commenced.**—An action is commenced as to each defendant when the summons is issued against him.

Sec. 366. (162.) **Action on Judgment when Defendant is out of State.**—If, when the cause of action accrue or judgment be rendered or docketed against any person, he shall be out of the State, action may be commenced or judgment enforced within the times herein respectively limited after the re-

---

[1] Sections 136 and 137 (as to time from May 20, 1861, etc.) were repealed by Laws of 1891, chap. 113.

turn of such person into this State; and if, after such cause of action shall have accrued or judgment rendered or docketed, such person shall depart from and reside out of this State, or remain continuously absent therefrom for the space of one year or more, the time of his absence shall not be deemed or taken as any part of the time limited for the commencement of such action or the enforcement of such judgment.

This section shall apply to all actions that have accrued and judgments rendered or transferred or docketed since August 24, 1868.

The Acts of 1891, Chaps. 92 and 356, making it the duty of *Personal Representatives* to plead the bar of the statute of limitations as a defense to all actions against them in their representative capacity, were repealed by the Act of 1893, Chap. 7.

Sec. 360. (138.) **Benefit of Limitation; must be taken by Answer.**—Civil actions can only be commenced within the periods prescribed in this chapter 366, next page, after the cause of action shall have accrued, except where, in special cases, a different limitation is prescribed by statute. But the objection that the action was not commenced within the time limited, can only be taken by answer.

IV.—LIMITATIONS—REAL PROPERTY.

Sec. 382. (141.) **When Persons having Title must sue.**—When the person in possession of any real property, or those under whom he claims, shall have been possessed of the same, under known and visible lines and boundaries, and under colorable title for *seven years,* no entry shall be made or action sustained against such possessor by any person having any right or title to the same, except during the seven years next after his right or title shall have descended or accrued, who, in default of suing within the time aforesaid, shall be excluded from any claim thereafter to be made; and such possession, so held, shall be a perpetual bar against all persons not under disability.

Sec. 383. (143.) **Seizin within Twenty Years, when necessary.**—No action for the recovery of real property, or the possession thereof, shall be maintained, unless it appear that the plaintiff or those under whom he claims, was seized or possessed of the premises in question within twenty years before the commencement of such action; unless he was under the disabilities prescribed by law.

Sec. 384. (144.) **Adverse Possession, Twenty Years.**

Sec. 385. (145.) **Action after Entry.**—No entry upon real estate shall be deemed sufficient or valid, as a claim, unless an action be commenced thereupon within *one year* after the making of such entry, and within the time prescribed in this title.

Sec. 388. (150.) **Railroads, etc., not Barred.**—No railroad, plank-road, turnpike, or canal company shall be barred of, or presumed to have conveyed, any real estate, right of way, easement, leasehold, or other interest in the soil which may have been condemned, or otherwise obtained for its use, as a right of way, depot, station-house, or place of landing, by any statute of limitation or by occupation of the same by any person whatever.

Sec. 389. (150a.) [By the Act of 1891, chap. 224, cities and towns are never barred as to their public ways, squares, etc.]

V.—LIMITATIONS OTHER THAN REAL PROPERTY.

Sec. 390. (151.) **Periods of Limitation prescribed.**—The periods prescribed for the commencement of actions, other than for the recovery of real property, shall be as set forth in this sub-chapter:

Sec. 391. (152.) **Within Ten Years.**—1. An action upon a judgment or decree of this State, or any court of the United States, or of any State or Territory thereof.

2. An action upon a sealed instrument against the principals thereto.

3. An action for the foreclosure of a mortgage, or deed in trust for creditors with a power of sale, of real property, where the mortgagor or grantor has been in possession of the property, within ten years after the forfeiture of the mortgage, or after the power of sale became absolute, or within ten years after the last payment on the same.

4. An action for the redemption of a mortgage, where the mortgagor has been in possession, or for a residuary interest under a deed in trust for creditors, where the trustee, or those holding under him, shall have been in possession, within ten years after the right of action accrued.

Sec. 392. (153.) **Within Seven Years.**—1. An action on a judgment rendered by a justice of the peace, from the date thereof.

2. By any creditor of a deceased person against his personal or real representative, within *seven years* next after the qualification of the executor or administrator and his making the advertisement required by law, for creditors of the deceased to present their claims, where no personal service of such notice in writing is made upon the creditor; and a creditor thus barred of a recovery against the representative of any principal debtor shall also be barred of a recovery against any surety to such debt.

Sec. 393. (154.) **Within Six Years.**—1. An action upon the official bond of any public officer.

2. An action against any executor, administrator, collector, or guardian on his official bond, within *six years* after the auditing of his final account by the proper officer, and the filing of such audited account as required by law.

3. An action for injury to any incorporeal hereditament.

Sec. 394. **Five Years.**—Within five years:

1. No suit, action or proceeding shall be brought or maintained against any railroad company owning or operating a railroad for damages or compensation for right of way or use or occupancy of any lands by said company for use of its railroad unless such suit, action or proceeding shall be commenced within five years after said lands shall have been entered upon for the purpose of constructing said road, or within two years after said road shall be in operation.

2. No suit, action or proceeding shall be brought or maintained against any railroad company by any person for damages caused by the construction of

said road, or the repairs thereto, unless such suit, action or proceeding shall be commenced within five years after the cause of action accrues, and the jury shall assess the entire amount of damages which the party aggrieved is entitled to recover by reason of the trespass on his property.

Sec. 395. (155.) **Within Three Years.**—1. An action upon a contract, obligation, or liability, arising out of a contract, express or implied, except those mentioned in the preceding sections.

2. An action upon a liability created by statute, other than a penalty or forfeiture, unless some other time be mentioned in the statute creating it.

3. An action for trespass upon real property; when the trespass is a continuing one, such action shall be commenced within three years from the original trespass, and not thereafter.

4. An action for taking, detaining, converting, or injuring any goods or chattels, including action for their specific recovery.

5. An action for criminal conversation, or for any other injury to the person or rights of another, not arising on contract and not hereinafter enumerated.

6. An action against the sureties of any executor, administrator, collector, or guardian, on the official bond of their principal, within three years after the breach thereof complained of.

7. An action against bail, within three years after judgment against their principal, but bail may discharge themselves by a surrender of their principal, at any time before final judgment against them.

8. Fees due to any clerk, sheriff, or other officer, by the judgment of a court, within three years from the time of the judgment rendered, or of the issuing of the last execution therefor.

9. An action for relief on the ground of fraud or mistake; the cause of action shall not be deemed to have accrued until the discovery by the aggrieved party of the facts constituting such fraud or mistake. (*As amended by Chap.* 269 *of the Acts of* 1889.)

10. An action for the recovery of real property sold for taxes within three years after the execution of the sheriff's deed.

Sec. 396. **Two Years.**—Within two years:

1. All claims against the several counties, cities and towns of this State, whether by bond or otherwise, shall be presented to the chairman of the board of county commissioners or to the chief officers of said cities and towns, as the case may be, within two years after the maturity of such claims, or the holders of such claims shall be forever barred from a recovery thereof.

Sec. 397. (156.) **Within One Year.**—1. An action against a sheriff, coroner, or constable, or other public officer, for a trespass under color of his office.

2. An action upon a statute for a penalty or forfeiture, where the action is given to the State alone, or in whole or in part to the party aggrieved, or to a common informer, except where the statute imposing it prescribes a different limitation.

3. An action for libel, assault, battery or false imprisonment.

4. An action against a sheriff, or other officer, for the escape of a prisoner arrested or imprisoned on civil process.

5. An application for a widow's year's provision.

Sec. 398. (157.) **Within Six Months.**—An action for slander.

Sec. 399. (158.) **Action for other Relief.**—An action for relief not herein provided for, *within ten years.*

Sec. 376. (160.) **Action upon an Account Current.**—In an action brought to recover a balance due upon a mutual, open, and current account, where there have been reciprocal demands between the parties, the cause of action shall be deemed to have accrued from the time of the latest item proved in the account, on either side.

NORTH DAKOTA.

CODE OF CIVIL PROCEDURE 1913.

CHAP. IV.—TIME OF COMMENCING ACTIONS. ART. 1. IN GENERAL.

Sec. 7358. (5184.) **Limitations.**—Civil actions can only be commenced within the periods prescribed in this code, after the cause of action shall have accrued, except where, in special cases, a different limitation is prescribed by statute. But the objection that the action was not commenced within the time limited can only be taken by answer.

ART. 2. *Time of commencing Actions for the Recovery of Real Property.*

Sec. 7359. (5185.) **By the State.**—The State of North Dakota will not sue any person for or in respect to any real property, or the issues or profits thereof, by reason of the right or title of the State to the same, unless:

1. Such right or title shall have accrued within *forty years* before any action or other proceeding for the same shall be commenced; or

2. The State, or those from whom it claims shall have received the rents and profits of such real property or of some part thereof within the space of *forty years.*

Sec. 7360. (5186.) **Persons claiming under.**—No action shall be brought for, or in respect to, real property, by any person claiming by virtue of grants from the State, unless the same might have been commenced, as herein specified, in case such grant has not been issued or made.

Sec. 7361. (4836.) **Extension of same.**—When grants of real property shall have been issued or made by the State, and the same shall be declared void by the determination of a competent court, rendered upon an allegation of a fraudulent suggestion, or concealment, or forfeiture, or mistake, or ignorance of a material fact, or wrongful detaining, or defective title, in such case an action for the recovery of the premises so conveyed may be brought either by the State, or by any subsequent grantee of the same premises, his heirs or assigns, within *twenty years* after such determination was made, but not after that period.

Sec. 7362. (5188.) **Seizin within Twenty Years.**—No action for the recovery of real property, or for the recovery of the possession thereof, shall be maintained, unless it appears that the plaintiff, his ancestor, predecessor, or grantor, was seized or possessed of the premises in question within *twenty years* before the commencement of such action.

Sec. 7363. (5189.) *Same.*—No cause of action, or defense or counterclaim to an action, founded upon the title to real property, or to rents or services out of the same, shall be effectual, unless it appears that the person prosecuting the action or interposing the defense or counterclaim, or under whose title the action is prosecuted or the defense or counterclaim is made, or the ancestor, predecessor, or grantor of such person, was seized or possessed of the premises in question within *twenty years* before the committing of the act in respect to which such action is prosecuted or defense or counterclaim made.

Sec. 7364. (5190.) **One Year after Entry.**—No entry upon real estate shall be deemed sufficient or valid as a claim, unless an action is commenced thereon within *one year* after the making of such entry, and within *twenty years* from the time when the right to make such entry descended or accrued.

Sec. 7365. (5191.) **Possession presumed.**—In every action for the recovery of real property, or the possession thereof, the person establishing a legal title to the premises shall be presumed to have been possessed thereof within the time required by law; and the occupation of such premises by any other person shall be deemed to have been under and in subordination to the legal title, unless it appear that such premises have been held and possessed adversely to such legal title for *twenty years* before the commencement of such action.

Sec. 7366. (5192.) **Occupation under Written Instrument.**

7367-7370. (Secs. 5193-5196.) **Adverse Possession.**

ART. 3. *Time of commencing other Actions.*

Sec. 7373. (5199.) **Other Periods.**—The following actions must be commenced within the periods set forth in the following five sections after the cause of action has accrued.

Sec. 7374. (5200.) **Ten Years.**—1. An action upon a judgment or decree of any court of the United States, or of any State or Territory within the United States.

2. An action upon a contract contained in any conveyance or mortgage of or instrument affecting the title to real property, except a covenant of warranty, an action upon which must be commenced within *ten years* after the final decision against the title of the covenantor.

3. A proceeding by advertisement or otherwise for the foreclosure of a mortgage upon said estate.

Sec. 7375. (5201.) **Six Years.**—1. An action upon a contract, obligation or liability, express or implied, excepting those mentioned in section 6762 (mortgages of personal property).

2. An action upon a liability created by statute, other than a penalty or forfeiture, when not otherwise expressly provided.

3. An action for trespass upon real property.

4. An action for taking, detaining, or injuring any goods or chattels, including actions for the specific recovery of personal property.

5. An action for criminal conversation, or for any other injury to the person or rights of another, not arising on contract, and not hereinafter enumerated.

6. An action for relief on the ground of fraud, in cases which heretofore were solely cognizable by the Court of Chancery, the cause of action in such case not to be deemed to have accrued until the discovery by the aggrieved party of the facts constituting the fraud.

7. An action for the foreclosure of a mechanic's lien; provided, that this subdivision shall not apply to any mechanic's lien filed prior to July 1, 1903.

Sec. 7376. (5202.) **Three Years.**—1. An action against a sheriff, coroner or constable, upon a liability incurred by the doing of an act in his official capacity and by virtue of his office, or by the omission of an official duty, including the nonpayment of money collected upon an execution. But this section shall not apply to an action for an escape.

2. An action upon a statute for a penalty or forfeiture, where the action is given to the party aggrieved, or to such party and the State, except when the statute imposing it prescribes a different limitation.

Sec. 7377. (5203.) **Two Years.**—1. An action for libel, slander, assault, battery, or false imprisonment.

2. An action upon a statute for a forfeiture or penalty, to the State.

3. An action for the recovery of damages resulting from malpractice.

4. An action for injuries done to the person of another, when death ensues from such injuries; and the cause of action shall be deemed to have accrued at the time of the death of the party injured.

Sec. 7378. (5204.) **One Year.**—An action against a sheriff or other officer for the escape of a prisoner arrested or imprisoned on civil process.

Sec. 7379. (5205.) **Open Account.**—In an action brought to recover a balance due upon a mutual, open, and current account, when there have been reciprocal demands between the parties, the cause of action shall be deemed to have accrued from the time of the last item proved in the account on either side.

Sec. 7380. (5206.) **Forfeiture by Person—State.**—An action upon a statute for a penalty or forfeiture given in whole or in part to any person who will prosecute for the same must be commenced within *one year* after the commission of the offense; and if the action is not commenced within the year by a private party, it may be commenced within *two years* thereafter in behalf of the State by the attorney-general, or by the State's attorney of the county where the offense was committed.

Sec. 7381. (5207.) **Other Relief, Ten Years.**—An action for relief not hereinbefore provided for must be commenced within *ten years* after the cause of action shall have accrued.

Sec. 7382. (5208.) **Same to Public and Persons.**—The limitations prescribed in this chapter shall apply to actions brought in the name of the State, or for its benefit, in the same manner as to actions by private parties.

ART. 4. *General Provisions as to the Time of commencing Actions.*

Sec. 7384. (5210.) **Exception—Absence.**—If, when the cause of action shall accrue against any person, he shall be out of the State, such action may be commenced within the terms herein respectively limited after the return of such person into this State, and if after such cause of action shall have accrued, such person shall depart from and reside out of this State or remain continuously absent therefrom for the space of one year or more, the time of his absence shall not be deemed or taken as any part of the time limited for the commencement of such action; provided, however, that the provisions of this section shall not apply to the foreclosure of real estate mortgages by action or otherwise; provided, further, that action against trustees acting under the town site laws of the United States and this State must be commenced within two years of the date when the cause of action accrued; provided, further, that as to causes of action now existing, this section shall be effective January 1, 1912.

Sec. 7389. (5215.) **Injunction, etc.**—When the commencement of an action is stayed by injunction or other order of a court or judge, or by statutory prohibition, the time of the continuance of the stay is not part of the time limited for the commencement of the action.

Sec. 7392. (5218.) **Bank Notes.**—This chapter does not affect actions to enforce the payment of bills, notes or other evidence of debt, issued by moneyed corporations, or issued or put in circulation as money.

OHIO.

ANNOTATED GENERAL CODE (PAGE & ADAMS, 1910).

PART III, TITLE 4, DIVISION 1, CHAP. 2.

LIMITATION OF ACTIONS.

General Limitations.

Sec. 11218 (4976, 4979.) **Lapse of time a bar.**—A civil action, unless a different limitation is prescribed by statute, can be commenced only within the period prescribed in this chapter. When interposed by proper plea by a party to an action mentioned in this chapter, lapse of time shall be a bar thereto as herein provided.

Real Property.

Sec. 11219 (4977, 4978.) **To recover real estate.**—An action to recover the title to or possession of real property, shall be brought within twenty-one years after the cause thereof accrued, but if a person entitled to bring such action at the time the cause thereof accrues, is within the age of minority, of unsound mind, or imprisoned, such person after the expiration of twenty-one years from the time the cause of action accrues, may bring such action within ten years after such disability is removed.

Sec. 11220. (4977.) **Real Estate Dedicated to Public Use.**—Twenty-one years' adverse possession and occupancy extinguishes public easement in any street or alley laid out and shown on the recorded plat of any city or village.

Contracts.

Sec. 11221. (4980.) **Contract in writing.**—An action upon a specialty or an agreement, contract or promise in writing shall be brought within fifteen years after the cause thereof accrued.

Sec. 11222. (4981.) **Contract not in writing.**—An action upon a contract not in writing, express or implied, or upon a liability created by statute other than a forfeiture or penalty, shall be brought within six years after the cause thereof accrued.

Certain Torts.

Sec. 11224. (4982.) **Four years.**—An action for either of the following causes shall be brought within four years after the cause thereof accrued:

1. For trespassing upon real property;
2. For the recovery of personal property, or for taking, detaining, or injuring it;
3. For relief on the ground of fraud;
4. For an injury to the rights of the plaintiff not arising on contract nor hereinafter enumerated.

If the action be for trespassing underground or injury to mines, or for the wrongful taking of personal property the cause thereof shall not accrue until the wrongdoer is discovered; nor, if it be for fraud, until the fraud is discovered.

Sec. 11225. (4983.) **One Year.**—An action for libel, slander, assault, battery, malicious prosecution, false imprisonment or malpractice, or upon a statute for a penalty or forfeiture, shall be brought within one year after the cause thereof accrues.

Sec. 11225-1. **When Bank Liable on Forged or Raised Check.**—No bank which has paid and charged to the account of a depositor any money on a forged or raised check issued in the name of said depositor shall be liable to said depositor for the amount paid thereon unless either, (1) within one year after actual written notice to said depositor that the vouchers representing payments charged to the account of said depositor for the period during which such payment was made are ready for delivery, or (2) in case no such notice has been given, within one year after the return to said depositor of the voucher representing such payment, said depositor shall notify the bank that the check so paid is forged or raised.

Other Cases.

Sec. 11226. (4976, 4984.) **On Official Bond.**—An action upon the official bond or undertaking of an officer, assignee, trustee, executor, administrator or guardian, or upon a bond or undertaking given in pursuance of a statute, can only be brought within *ten years* after the cause of action accrues; but this section shall be subject to the qualification in sec. 4976.

Sec. 11227. (4985.) **For other Relief.**—An action for relief not hereinbefore provided for can only be brought within ten years after the cause of action accrues. This section does not apply to an action on a judgment rendered in another State or territory.

Saving Clause—Disabilities.

Sec. 11229. (4986.) Disabilities.— Unless otherwise specially provided therein, if a person entitled to bring any action mentioned in this subdivision, except for a penalty or forfeiture, is, at the time the cause of action accrues, within the age of minority, of unsound mind, or imprisoned, such person may bring such action within the respective times limited by this subdivision, after such disability is removed. When the interests of two or more parties are joint and inseparable, the disability of one shall inure to the benefit of all.

When Action Begins.

Sec. 11230. (4987.) **When commenced.**

Sec. 11231. (4988.) **When Action deemed commenced.**—Within the meaning of this chapter, an attempt to commence an action shall be deemed equivalent to its commencement, when the party diligently endeavors to procure a service, if such attempt be followed by service within sixty days.

Bar of Foreign Law and Other Matters.

Sec. 11234. (4990.) **Action, Time for Bringing.**—If the laws of any State or country where the cause of action arose limits the time for the commencement of the action to a less number of years than do the statutes of this State in like causes of action then said cause of action shall be barred in this State at the expiration of said lesser number of years.

TITLE II., CHAP. 13.

Sec. 10448. (6599.) **Forceable Entry and Detainer—Jurisdiction of Justice—Limitation.**—* * * Such action can only be brought within two years after the cause thereof shall have accrued.

OKLAHOMA.

REVISED LAWS, CIVIL PROCEDURE, 1910.

VOL. 2, CHAP. 60, ART. 2.

Limitation of Actions.

4655. (3888. § 16.) Actions for the recovery of real property, or for the determination of any adverse right or interest therein, can only be brought within the periods hereinafter prescribed, after the cause of action shall have accrued, and at no time thereafter:

First. An action for the recovery of real property sold on execution, brought by the execution debtor, his heirs or any person claiming under him, by title acquired, after the date of the judgment, within *five years* after the date of the recording of the deed made in pursuance of the sale.

Second. An action for the recovery of real property sold by executors, administrators or guardians, upon an order or judgment of a court directing such sale, brought by the heirs or devisees of the deceased person; or the ward or his guardian, or any person claiming under any or either of them, by title acquired after the date of the judgment or order, within *five years* after the date of the recording of the deed made in pursuance of the sale.

Third. An action for the recovery of real property sold for taxes, within two years after the date of the recording of the tax deed.

Fourth. An action for the recovery of real property not hereinbefore provided for, within *fifteen years.*

Fifth. An action for the forcible entry and detention, or forcible detention only, of real property, within *two years.*

4656. (3889. § 17.) Any person entitled to bring an action for the recovery of real property, who may be under any legal disability when the cause of action accrues, may bring his action within *two years* after the disability is removed.

4657. (3890. § 18.) (*As amended by the Act of* 1895, *ch.* 39.)—Civil actions, other than for the recovery of real property, can only be brought within the following periods, after the cause of action shall have accrued, and not afterwards:

First. Within *five years:* An action upon any contract, agreement or promise in writing.

Second. Within *three years:* An action upon a contract, express or implied, not in writing; an action upon a liability created by statute other than a forfeiture or penalty.

Third. Within *two years:* An action for trespass upon real property; an action for taking, detaining or injuring personal property, including actions for the specific recovery of personal property; an action for injury to the rights of another, not arising on contract, and not hereinafter enumerated; an action for relief on the ground of fraud—the cause of action in such case shall not be deemed to have accrued until the discovery of the fraud.

Fourth. Within *one year:* An action on a foreign judgment; an action for libel, slander, assault, battery, malicious prosecution, or false imprisonment; an action upon a statute for penalty or forfeiture, except where the statute imposing it prescribes a different limitation.

Fifth. An action upon the official bond or undertaking of an executor, administrator, guardian, sheriff, or any other officer, or upon the bond or undertaking given in attachment, injunction, arrest, or in any case whatever required by the statute, can only be brought within *five years* after the cause of action shall have accrued.

Sixth. An action for relief, not hereinbefore provided for, can only be brought within *five years* after the cause of action shall have accrued.

4664. (3897. § **25.**) When a right of action is barred by the provisions of any statute, it shall be unavailable either as a cause of action or ground of defense, except as otherwise provided with reference to a counterclaim or set-off.

OREGON.

LORD'S OREGON LAWS, 1910. CODE CIVIL PROCEDURE, TITLE 1, CHAP. II.

CHAP. II.—LIMITATIONS OF ACTIONS.

Section 3. **Time of commencing Actions.**—Actions at law shall only be commenced within the periods prescribed in this title, after the cause of action shall have accrued; except where, in special cases, a different limitation is prescribed by statute. But the objection that the action was not commenced within the time limited shall only be taken by answer, except as otherwise provided in Section 67.

Sec. 4. **Real Property.**—The periods prescribed in the preceding section for the commencement of actions shall be as follows:

Within ten years, actions for the recovery of real property, or for the recovery of the possession thereof; and no action shall be maintained for such recovery, unless it appear that the plaintiff, his ancestor, predecessor, or grantor, was seized or possessed of the premises in question within *ten years* before the commencement of said action: *Provided,* that in all cases where a cause of action has already accrued, and the period prescribed by this section within which an action may be brought has expired, or will expire within one year from the approval of this act, an action may be brought on such cause of action within *one year* from the date of the approval of this act.

Sec. 5. **Within Ten Years.**—1. An action upon a judgment or decree of any court of the United States, or of any State or Territory within the United States.

2. An action upon a sealed instrument.

Sec. 6. **Within Six Years.**—1. An action upon a contract or liability, express or implied, excepting those mentioned in section 5.

2. An action upon a liability created by statute, other than a penalty or forfeiture.

3. An action for waste or trespass upon real property.

4. An action for taking, detaining, or injuring personal property, including an action for the specific recovery thereof.

Sec. 7. **Within Three Years.**—1. An action against a sheriff, coroner, or constable, upon a liability incurred by the doing of an act in his official capacity, and in virtue of his office; or by the omission of an official duty; including the non-payment of money collected upon an execution. But this section shall not apply to an action for an escape.

2. An action upon a statute for penalty or forfeiture, where the action is given to the party aggrieved, or to such party and the State, except where the statute imposing it prescribes a different limitation.

Sec. 8. **Within Two Years.**—1. An action for assault, battery, false imprisonment, for criminal conversation, or for any injury to the person or rights of another, not arising on contract, and not herein especially enumerated.

2. An action upon a statute for a forfeiture or penalty to the State, or county.

Sec. 9. **Within One Year.**—1. An action against a sheriff or other officer, for the escape of a prisoner arrested or imprisoned on civil process.

2. Actions for libel and slander.

Sec. 10. **Actions for Penalties.**—An action upon a statute for a penalty given in the whole or in part to the person who will prosecute for the same, shall be commenced within *one year* after the commission of the offense; and, if the action be not commenced within one year by a private party, it may be commenced within *two years* thereafter, in behalf of the State, by the district attorney of the county when the offense was committed, or is triable.

Sec. 11. **Other Actions.**—An action for any cause not hereinbefore provided for shall be commenced within *ten years* after the cause of action shall have accrued.

Sec. 12. **Accounts.**—In an action brought to recover a balance due upon a mutual, open, and current account, where there have been reciprocal demands between the parties, the cause of action shall be deemed to have accrued from the time of the last item proved in the account on either side; but whenever a period of more than *one year* shall elapse, between any of a series of items or demands, they are not to be deemed such an account.

Sec. 13. **Action by the State.**—The limitations prescribed in this title shall not apply to actions brought in the name of the State, or any county or other public corporation therein, or for its benefit, but causes of action that have heretofore become barred by virtue of any statutory provision are not intended to be revived thereby.

Sec. 16. **When Defendant is Absent or Concealed.**—If, when the cause of action shall accrue against any person, who shall be out of the State or concealed therein, such action may be commenced within the terms herein respectively limited, after the return of such person into the State, or the time of his concealment; and if, after such cause of action shall have accrued, such person shall depart from and reside out of this State, or conceal himself, the time of his absence or concealment shall not be deemed or taken as any part of the time limited for the commencement of such action.

Sec. 26. **Cause of Action Barred.**—When the cause of action has arisen in another State, Territory, or country, between non-residents of this State, and by the laws of the State, Territory, or country where the cause of action arose, an action cannot be maintained thereon by reason of lapse of time, no action shall be maintained thereon in this State.

TITLE VI., CHAP. I.

SUITS IN EQUITY.

Sec. 391. (382.) **Real Actions, ten years.**

TITLE II., CHAP. XIII.

Sec. 2178. **Mining Claims.**—One year's adverse possession of a mining claim, immediately preceding the commencement of an action therefor, by the defendant or those under whom he holds, if pleaded, is a bar to the action for the possession thereof.

SUPPLEMENTAL ACTS.

By the Act of Feb. 20, 1893, a person entitled to contest a will, if under legal disability, has *one year* after its removal to institute such contest.

By the Act of Feb. 23, 1895, the statute of limitations does not apply so as to cause the loss of title to public streets, country roads, or other public property, to cities and towns.

PENNSYLVANIA.

STEWARD'S PURDON'S DIGEST, 1910, VOL. 2, PAGE 2266.

LIMITATION OF ACTIONS.

[Note. As these statutes are lengthy and ancient, only their purport is here indicated.]

I.—*Actions for the Recovery of Real Estate.*

Secs. 1, 2. **Seven Years' Quiet Possession.**—Seven years' quiet possession of lands within this province, which were first entered on, upon an equitable right, shall forever give an unquestionable title to the same against all, during the estate whereof they are or shall be possessed, except in cases of infants, married women, lunatics, and persons not residing within this province or territories, etc.[1]

Secs. 3, 4. **Entry Barred in Twenty-one Years.**

Sec. 7. **Six Years' Possession to Validate Prior Sheriff's Deeds.** (As amended by the Acts of 1885, No. 196.)

Sec. 8. **All Persons to be Barred after Forty Years.**

Sec. 10. **Thirty Years' Possession to be Evidence of Title out of Commonwealth—Twenty-one Years, when.**

Sec. 11. **Limitation of Claim for Ground-rent.**

Sec. 12. **Limitation of Claim for Apportionment of Ground-rent.**

Sec. 13. **Persons under Disabilities to bring Suits within Thirty Years.**

[1] This act is declared in 9 Wheat. 319, to have been repealed by the act of 1785, sec. 2, of this act.

Sec. 16. (14.) **Specific Performance: Damages for Non-performance. Equity of Redemption. Implied or Resulting Trust.**

Sec. 17. (15.) **Not to Run in Favor of an Attorney-at-Law.**

Sec. 14. (16.) **Suits to be Brought within One Year after Entry.**—No entry upon lands shall arrest the running of the statute of limitations, unless an action of ejectment be commenced therefor within *one year* thereafter; nor shall such entry and action, without a recovery therein, arrest the running of said statute in respect to another ejectment, unless it be brought within a year after the first shall have been nonsuited, arrested, or decided against the plaintiff therein.

Sec. 15. (17.) **Statute to Run against Remaindermen, etc., unless.**

III.—*Personal Actions.*

Sec. 28. (18.) **Personal Actions.**—All actions of trespass *quaere clausum fregit*, all actions of detinue, trover, and replevin for taking away goods and cattle, all actions upon account, and upon the case, other than such accounts as concern the trade of merchandise between merchant and merchant, their factors or servants, all actions of debt, grounded upon any lending or contract, without specialty, all actions of debt for arrearages of rent, except the proprietaries' quit-rent, and all actions of trespass, of assault, menace, battery, wounding, and imprisonment, or any of them, which shall be sued or brought at any time after April 25, 1713, shall be commenced and sued within the time and limitation hereafter expressed, and not after; that is to say, the said actions upon the case, other than for slander, and the said actions for account, and the said actions for trespass, debt, detinue and replevin for goods or cattle, and the said actions of trespass *quaere clausum fregit*, within *six years* next after the cause of such action or suit, and not after. And the said actions of trespass, of assault, menace, battery, wounding, imprisonment, or any of them, within *two years* next after the cause of such action or suit, and not after. And the said actions upon the case for words, within *one year* next after the words spoken, and not after.

Sec. 29. (19.) **Libel.**—Extends to all cases of slander and libel, whether spoken, written, or printed.

Sec. 28. **Suits for Negligence against Passenger Railway Companies.**—No suit against any passenger railway company (whose route is wholly within the county of Philadelphia) for damages for injuries or death, shall be brought, unless the same shall be within six months from the time the right of action shall accrue.

IV.—*Action on Official Bonds.*

Sec. 45. (33.) **Bonds of Public Officers—Seven Years.**—Persons entering into bonds or recognizances, as sureties for any public officers, should be exonerated from their responsibility within a reasonable term after such officers respectively shall die, resign or be removed from office: *Therefore*, it shall not be lawful for any person or persons whomsoever to commence and maintain any suit or suits on any bonds or recognizances which shall hereafter be given and entered into by any person or persons, as sureties for any public officer, from and after the expiration of the term of seven years, to be computed from the time at which the cause of action shall have accrued; and if any such suit or suits shall be commenced contrary to the intent and meaning of this act, the defendant or defendants respectively shall and may plead the general issue, and give this fact and the special matter in evidence; and if the plaintiff or plaintiffs be nonsuited, or if a verdict or judgment pass against him or them respectively, the defendant or defendants shall respectively recover double costs.

V.—*Miscellaneous Provisions.*

Sec. 49. **Suspension of Limitation during Non-residence.**—In all civil suits and actions in which the cause of action shall have arisen within this State the defendant or defendants in such suit or action, who shall have become non-resident of the State after said cause of action shall have arisen, shall not have the benefit of any statute of this State for the limitation of actions during the period of such residence without the State.

RHODE ISLAND.

General Laws, 1909, chap. 284.

Of the Limitation of Actions.

Section 1. **Actions of Slander—Injuries to the Person.**—Actions for words spoken shall be commenced and sued within *one year* next after the words spoken, and not after. Actions for injuries to the person shall be commenced and sued within *two years* next after the cause of action shall accrue, and not after.

Sec. 2. **Trespass.**—Actions of trespass, except for injuries to the person, shall be commenced and sued within *four years* next after the cause of action shall accrue, and not after.

Sec. 3. **Of Account, Case and Debt, except, etc., and of Detinue and Replevin.**—All actions of account, except on such accounts as concern trade or merchandise between merchant and merchant, their factors and servants, all actions of the case, except for words spoken and injuries to the person, all actions of debt founded upon any contract without specialty or brought for arrearages of rents, and all actions of detinue and replevin, shall be commenced and sued within *six years* next after the cause of such action shall accrue, and not after.

Sec. 4. **Of Debt on Specialty and Covenant.**—All actions of debt other than those in the preceding section specified, and all actions of covenant, shall be commenced and sued within *twenty years* next after the cause of action shall accrue, and not after.

Sec. 5. **Saving in Favor of Residents, against Absent Defendants.**—If any person, against whom there is or shall be cause for any action hereinbefore enumerated in favor of a resident of this State, shall, at the time such cause accrue, be without the limits thereof, or being within the State at the time such cause accrues, shall go out of the State before said action shall be barred by the provisions of this chapter, and shall not have or leave property or estate therein that can be attached by process of law, then the person entitled to such action may commence the same within the time before limited, after such person shall return into the State, in such manner that an action may, with reasonable diligence, be commenced against him by the person entitled to the same.

Sec. 6. **General Savings.**—If any person at the time any such action shall accrue to him shall be within the age of twenty-one years, or of unsound mind, or imprisoned, or beyond the limits of the United States, such person may bring the same, within such time as is hereinbefore limited, after such impediment is removed.

Sec. 7. If any person liable to an action by another, shall fraudulently, by actual misrepresentation, conceal from him the existence of the cause of such action, said cause of action shall be deemed to accrue against said person so liable therefor, at the time when the person entitled to sue thereon shall first discover its existence.

Sec. 8. **Time extended by Death of Parties, when.**—If any person, for or against whom any of such actions shall accrue, shall die before the time limited for bringing action, or within sixty days after the expiration of said time, and the cause of such action shall survive, such action may be commenced by or against the executor or administrator of the deceased person, as the case may be, at any time within *one year* after the decease of the person so dying, and not afterwards, if barred by the provisions of this chapter.

Sec. 9. **Abatement of Action or Arrest of Judgment.**—If any action duly commenced within the time limited and allowed therefor in and by this chapter, shall be abated or otherwise avoided or defeated by the death of any party thereto, or for any matter, or if, after verdict for the plaintiff, the judgment shall be arrested, the plaintiff may commence a new action for the same cause, at any time within *one year* after the abatement or other determination of the original suit as aforesaid; and if the cause of action does by law survive, his executor or administrator may, in case of his death, commence said new action within the said *one year.*

Sec. 10. **Special Limitations Saved.**—The provisions of this chapter shall not apply to any case in which by special provision a different time is limited.

SOUTH CAROLINA.

CODE OF LAWS, 1912.

CODE OF CIVIL PROCEDURE. PART II., TITLE II.

TIME OF COMMENCING CIVIL ACTIONS.

CHAP. II.—FOR THE RECOVERY OF REAL PROPERTY.

Sec. 120. (98.) **When State Will Not Sue.**—The State will not sue any person for or in respect of any real property, or the issues or profits thereof, by reason of the right or title of the State to the same unless:

1. Such right or title shall have accrued within *twenty years* before any action or other proceeding for the same shall be commenced; or unless

2. The State, or those from whom it claims, shall have received the rents and profits of such real property, or of some part thereof, within the space of *twenty years*.

Sec. 122. (100.) **When Action by State or their Grantees to be Brought within Ten Years.**

Sec. 123. (101.) (98.) **Seizin within Ten Years, when necessary.**—1. No action for the recovery of real property, or for the recovery of the possession thereof, shall be maintained, unless it appear that the plaintiff, his ancestor, predecessor, or grantor, was seized or possessed of the premises in question within *ten years* before the commencement of such action.

2. **Person Limited to Two Actions for Realty.**—The plaintiff in all actions for the recovery of realty is hereby limited to two actions for the same, and no more: *Provided*, that the costs of the first action be first paid, and the second action be brought within two years from the rendition of the verdict or judgment in the first action, or from the granting of a nonsuit or discontinuance therein.

Sec. 124. (102.) (99.) **Seizin within Ten Years, when necessary.**—No cause of action, or defense to an action, founded upon the title to real property, or to rents or services out of the same, shall be effectual, unless it appear that the person prosecuting the action or making the defense, or under whose title the action is prosecuted or the defense is made, or the ancestor, predecessor, or grantor of such person, was seized or possessed of the premises in question within *ten years* before the committing of the act in respect to which such action is prosecuted or defense made.

Sec. 125. (103.) (100.) **Action after Entry.**—No entry upon real estate shall be deemed sufficient or valid, as a claim, unless an action be commenced thereupon within *one year* after the making of such entry, and within ten years from the time when the right to make such entry descended or accrued.

Sec. 126. (104.) (101.) **Possession presumed.**

Secs. 127-131. (105-109.) (102-106.) **Adverse Possession defined.**

Sec. 134. (109.) No action shall be commenced in any case for the recovery of real property, or for any interest therein, against a person in possession under claim of title by virtue of a written instrument, unless the person claiming, his ancestor or grantor, was actually in the possession of the same or a part thereof within *forty years* from the commencement of such action. And the possession of a defendant, sole or connected, pursuant to the provisions of this section, shall be deemed valid against the world after the lapse of said period.

CHAP. III.—TIME OF COMMENCING ACTIONS OTHER THAN FOR THE RECOVERY OF REAL PROPERTY.

Sec. 135. (112.) (110.) **Period of Limitation prescribed.**—The periods prescribed in section 119 for the commencement of actions other than for the recovery of real property shall be as follows:

Sec. 136. (113.) (111.) **Within Twenty Years.**—1. An action upon a judgment or decree of any court of the United States, or of any State or Territory within the United States.

2. An action upon a bond, or other contract in writing, secured by a mortgage of real property; an action upon a sealed instrument other than a sealed note and personal bond for the payment of money only, whereof the period of limitation shall be the same as prescribed in the following section.

Sec. 137. (114.) (112.) **Within Six Years.**—1. An action upon a contract, obligation, or liability, express or implied, excepting those mentioned in section 136.

2. An action upon a liability created by statute, other than a penalty or forfeiture.

3. An action for trespass upon or damage to real property.

4. An action for taking, detaining, or injuring any goods or chattels, including action for the specific recovery of personal property.

5. An action for criminal conversation, or for any other injury to the person or rights of another, not arising on contract, and not hereinafter eunmerated.

6. An action for relief on the ground of fraud, in cases which, heretofore, were solely cognizable by the Court of Chancery, the cause of action in such case not to be deemed to have accrued until the discovery by the aggrieved party of the facts constituting the fraud.

7. Actions may be brought in any of the courts of this State properly having jurisdiction thereof on any policies of insurance, either fire or life, whereby any person or property, resident or situate in this State, may be or may have been insured, or for or on account of any loss arising thereunder, within six years from the date of such loss, or from the accrual of the cause of action under said policy, any clause or condition in the said policies or limitations therein contained to the contrary notwithstanding.

Sec. 138. (115.) (113.) **Within Three Years.**—1. An action against a sheriff, coroner or constable, upon a liability incurred by the doing of an act in his official capacity, and in virtue of his office, or by the omission of an official duty, including the nonpayment of money collected upon an execution. But this section shall not apply to an action for an escape.

2. action upon a statute, for a penalty or forfeiture, where the action is given to the party aggrieved, or to such party and the State, except where the statute imposing it prescribes a different limitation.

Sec. 139. (116.) (114.) **Within Two Years.**—1. An action for libel, slander, assault, battery, or false imprisonment.

2. An action upon a statute for a forfeiture or penalty to the State.

Sec. 140. (117.) (115.) **Within One Year.**—An action against a sheriff or other officer for the escape of a prisoner arrested or imprisoned on civil process.

Sec. 141. (118.) (116.) **Action upon an Account Current.**—In an action brought to recover a balance due upon a mutual, open, and current account, where there have been reciprocal demands between the parties, the cause of action shall be deemed to have accrued from the time of the last item proved in the account on either side.

Sec. 142. (119.) (117.) **Action for Penalties, etc.**—An action upon a statute for a penalty or forfeiture given, in whole or in part, to any person who will prosecute for the same must be commenced within *one year* after the commission of the offense; and if the action be not commenced within the year by a private party, it may be commenced within two years thereafter, in behalf of the State, by the attorney-general or the solicitor of the circuit where the offense was committed, unless a different limitation be prescribed in the statute under which the action is brought.

Sec. 143. (120.) (118.) **Actions for other Relief.**—An action for relief not hereinbefore provided for must be commenced within *ten years* after cause of action shall have accrued.

Sec. 145. (121.) (119.) **Actions by the State.**—The limitations prescribed by this chapter shall apply to actions brought in the name of the State, or for its benefit, in the same manner as to actions by private parties.

CHAP. IV.—GENERAL PROVISIONS AS TO THE TIME OF COMMENCING ACTIONS.

Sec. 155. (131.) (129.) **Bills, Notes, etc.**—This title shall not affect actions to enforce the payment of bills, notes, or other evidences of debt, issued by moneyed corporations, or issued or put in circulation as money.

CIVIL CODE, PART III, TITLE III, CHAP. XCVI, ART. 1.

Sec. 4072. (2298.) **Forcible Entry and Detainer.**—They which keep their possessions with force in any lands and tenements whereof they or their ancestors, or they whose estate they have in such lands and tenements, have continued their possessions in the same by three years or more, shall not be endangered by force of this chapter.

SOUTH DAKOTA.

COMPILED LAWS—CODE OF CIVIL PROCEDURE, 1910.

(See NORTH DAKOTA, *ante*, p. 763, both states following the original Dakota statutes, except as follows):

Sec. 58. **Within Twenty Years.**—1. An action upon a judgment or decree of any court of this State.

2. An action upon a sealed instrument.

Sec. 62. This contains only the first two subdivisions of section 7377 (5203) of North Dakota.

Sec. 69. **Absence.**—This is the same as section 7384 (5210) of North Dakota, except that it omits the words "or remain continuously absent therefrom for the space of one year or more."

Sec. 74. **Injunction.**—This is the same as section 7389 (5215) of North Dakota, except that it omits the words "or other order of a court or judge, or by."

TENNESSEE.

CODE (1896, BY SHANNON), PART III, CHAP. 2.

ART. II.—LIMITATION OF REAL ACTIONS.

Sec. 4456. **Seven Years' Vested Estate, when.**—Any person having had, by himself or those through whom he claims, *seven years'* adverse possession of any lands, tenements, or hereditaments granted by this State or the State of North Carolina, holding by conveyance, devise, grant, or other assurance of title purporting to convey an estate in fee, without any claim by action at law or in equity commenced within that time and effectually prosecuted against him, is vested with a good and indefeasible title in fee to the land described in his assurance of title. But no title shall be vested by virtue of such adverse possession, unless such conveyance, devise, grant, or other assurance of title shall have been recorded in the register's office for the county or counties in which the land lies during the full term of said seven years' adverse possession.

Sec. 4457. **Seven Years' Neglect Bars Action.**—And, on the other hand, any person, and those claiming under him, neglecting for the said term of *seven years* to avail themselves of the benefit of any title, legal or equitable, by action at law or in equity, effectually prosecuted against the person in possession, under recorded assurance of title, as in the foregoing section, are forever barred.

Sec. 4458. **Suit Must be Brought within Seven Years.**—No person, or any one claiming under him, shall have any action, either at law or in equity, for any lands, tenements, or hereditaments, but within *seven years* after the right of action has accrued.

Sec. 4459. **School Lands.**—The provisions of the foregoing sections do not apply to lands, tenements, or hereditaments reserved for the use of schools.

Sec. 4460. **Twenty Years' Adverse Possession Bars Husband and Wife, when.**

Sec. 4461. **What Possession is not Adverse.**—Possession is not adverse, within the meaning of this article, as to any person claiming a right or interest in the land, when taken and continued under a title bond, mortgage or other instrument acknowledging that right or interest, or when taken and continued in subordination to the right or interest of another.

Secs. 4464, 4465. **Leins on Realty Barred after Ten Years—Exceptions.**

ART. III.—LIMITATION OF ACTIONS OTHER THAN REAL.

Sec. 4466. **Actions to be commenced within the Time limited.**—All civil actions, other than those for causes embraced in the foregoing article, shall be commenced after the cause of action has accrued, within the periods prescribed in this chapter, unless otherwise expressly provided.

Sec. 4467. **Property lost at Gaming.**— Within *ninety days.*

Sec. 4468. **Slander.**—Actions for slanderous words spoken shall be commenced within *six months* after the words are uttered.

Sec. 4469. **Libel, Personal Injuries, etc.**—Actions for libel, for injuries to the person, false imprisonment, malicious prosecution, criminal conversation, seduction, breach of marriage promise, and statute penalties, within *one year* after cause of action accrued.

Sec. 4470. **Injuries to Property, etc.**—Actions for injuries to personal or real property; actions for the detention or conversion of personal property, within *three years* from the accruing of the cause of action.

Sec. 4471. **Against Sureties of Collecting Officer, when Process returned satisfied.**—Actions against sureties of any collecting officer, for failing to pay over money collected, when he has made return of an execution or other process that the money is made or the process satisfied, within *three years* from the return of the process.

Sec. 4472. **Use and Occupation, Rent, Surety for Official Delinquencies, etc.**—Actions for the use and occupation of land and for rent; actions against the sureties of guardians, executors, and administrators, sheriffs, clerks, and other public officers, for nonfeasance, misfeasance, and malfeasance in office; actions on contracts not otherwise expressly provided for, within *six years* after the cause of action accrued.

Sec. 4473. **Guardians, Executors, Administrators, Public Officers, on Judgments, etc.**—Actions against guardians, executors, administrators, sheriffs, clerks, and other public officers on their bonds, actions on judgments and decrees of courts of record of this or any other State or government, and all other cases not expressly provided for, within ten years after the cause of action accrued.

Sec. 4474. **Exception in Favor of Merchants' Accounts.**—The limitations herein provided do not apply to such actions as concern the trade of merchandise between merchant and merchant, their agents and factors, while the accounts between them are current.

Sec. 4475. **Mutual Accounts between Individuals.**—When there are mutual accounts between persons who are not merchants, the time is computed from the true date of the last item, unless the account is liquidated and a balance struck.

Sec. 4476. **Note Issued as Money.**—The provisions of this chapter do not apply to actions to enforce payment of bills, notes, or other evidences of debt issued or put in circulation as money.

Sec. 4477. **Time runs from Accrual of Right, not Demand.**—When a right exists but a demand is necessary to entitle the party to an action, the limitation commences from the time the plaintiff's right to make the demand was completed, and not from the date of the demand.

Sec. 4480. **Action Barred in another State.**—When the statute of limitations of another State or government has created a bar to an action upon a cause accruing therein, whilst the party to be charged was a resident in such State or under such government, the bar is equally effectual in this State.

Sec. 4481. **Against Personal Representative by Resident, Two Years, and by Non-resident, Three Years.**

Sec. 4482. **Delay upon such Representative's Special Request not Counted.**

Sec. 4483. **Seven Years' Bar in Favor of Decedent's Estates.**—But all actions against the personal representatives of a decedent for demands against such decedent shall be brought within *seven years* after his death, notwithstanding any disability existing; otherwise they will be forever barred.

Sec. 4012. **Suits against Decedent's Estates.**—The creditors of deceased persons, if they reside within this State, shall within *two years*, and if without, shall, within *three years*, from the qualification of the executor or administrator, exhibit to them their accounts, debts and claims, and make demand, and bring suit for the recovery thereof, or be forever barred in law and equity.

Sec. 4013. **Suspension through Request of Executor.**—But if any creditor, after making demand of his debt or claim, delay to bring suit for a definite time, at the special request of the executor or administrator, the time of such delay shall not be counted in said periods of limitation.

Sec. 5096. **Forcible Entry and Detainer.**—The uninterrupted occupation or quiet possession of the premises in controversy by the defendant, for the space of three entire years together, immediately preceding the commencement of the action, is, if the estate of the defendant has not determined within that time, a bar to any proceeding under this article.

TEXAS.

M'EACHIN'S CIVIL STATUTES ANNOTATED, 1913, VOL. 3.

TITLE 87. LIMITATIONS.

CHAP. 1.—*Limitation of Actions for Land.*

Art. 5672. (3340.) **Three Years' Possession, when a Bar.**—Every suit to be instituted to recover real estate, as against any person in peaceable and adverse possession thereof under title or color of title, shall be instituted within *three years* next after the cause of action shall have accrued, and not afterwards.

Art. 5673. (3341.) **"Title" and "Color of Title" defined.**

Art. 5674. ((3342.) **Five Years' Possession, when a Bar.**—Every suit to be instituted to recover real estate as against any person having peaceable and adverse possession thereof, cultivating, using, or enjoying the same and paying taxes thereon, if any, and claiming under a deed or deeds duly registered, shall be instituted within *five years* next after the cause of action shall have accrued, and not afterward: *Provided*, that this article shall not apply to any one in possession of land, who, in the absence of this article, would deraign title through a forged deed: *Provided, further*, that no one claiming under a forged deed, or deed executed under a forged power of attorney, shall be allowed the benefits of this article.

Art. 5675. (3343.) **Ten Years' Possession, when a Bar**—Any person who has a right of action for the recovery of any lands, tenements, or hereditaments against another having peaceable and adverse possession thereof, cultivating, using, or enjoying the same, shall institute his suit therefor within *ten years* next after his cause of action shall have accrued, and not afterward.

Arts. 5676-5678, 5681. (3344-3346, 3349.) **Adverse Possession defined.**

Art. 5679. (3347.) **Possession gives Full Title, when.**—Whenever in any case the action of a person for the recovery of real estate is barred by any of the provisions of this chapter, the person having such peaceable and adverse possession shall be held to have full title, precluding all claims.

Art. 5682. (3350.) **Possession may be held by Different Persons.**—Peaceable and adverse possession need not be continued in the same person, but when held by different persons successively there must be a privity of estate between them.

Art. 5683. (3351.) **Limitation not to Run against State nor Favor Adverse Holder of Road.** [As amended 1887.]—As to university and asylum lands, see Acts of 1899, chap. 150.

Art. 5684. (3352.) **Does not Run against Infants, Married Women, etc.**—If a person entitled to commence suit for the recovery of real property, or to make any defense founded on the title thereto, be, at the time such title shall first descend or the adverse possession commence,

1. Under the age of twenty-one years; or,
2. If unsound mind; or,
3. A person imprisoned,

the time during which such disability shall continue shall not be deemed any portion of the time limited for the commencement of such suit, or the making of such defense; and such person shall have the same time after the removal of his disability that is allowed to others by the provisions of this chapter: *Provided*, that limitation shall not begin to run against married women until they arrive at the age of twenty-one years; and, further, that their disability shall continue one year from and after July 29, 1895, and that they shall have thereafter the same time allowed others by the provisions hereof; and, further, that this article shall in no way affect suits then pending, and all such suits shall be tried and disposed of under the law then in force.

CHAP. 2. *Limitation of Personal Actions.*

Art. 5685. (3353.) *Actions to be commenced in One Year.*—1. Actions for malicious prosecution or for injuries done to the character or reputation of another by libel or slander.

2. Actions for damages for seduction, or breach of promise of marriage.

Art. 5686. (3353a.) **Survival of such Cause of Action.**

Art. 5687. (3354.) **Actions to be commenced in Two Years.**—1. Actions of trespass for injury done to the estate or the property of another.

2. Actions for detaining the personal property of another, and for converting such personal property to one's own use.

3. Actions for taking or carrying away the goods and chattels of another.

4. Actions for debt where the indebtedness is not evidenced by a contract in writing.

5. Actions upon stated or open accounts, other than such mutual and current accounts as concern the trade of merchandise between merchant and merchant, their factors or agents. In all accounts, except those between merchant and merchant as aforesaid, their factors and agents, the respective times or dates of the delivery of the several articles charged shall be particularly specified, and limitation shall run against each item from the date of such delivery, unless otherwise specially contracted.

6. Actions for injuries done to the person of another.

7. Actions for injuries done to the person of another where death ensued from such injuries; and the cause of action shall be considered as having accrued at the death of the party injured.

Art. 5688. (3356.) **What Actions Barred in Four Years.**—1. Actions for debt where the indebtedness is evidenced by or founded upon any contract in writing.

2. Actions for the penalty or for damages on the penal clause of a bond to convey real estate.

3. Actions by one partner against his copartner for a settlement of the partnership accounts, or upon mutual and current accounts concerning the trade of merchandise between merchant and merchant, their factors or agents; and the cause of action shall be considered as having accrued on a cessation of the dealings in which they were interested together.

Art. 5689. (3357.) **On Bond of Executor, Administrator, or Guardian.**—All suits on the bond of any executor, administrator or guardian shall be commenced and prosecuted within *four years* next after the death, resignation, removal, or discharge of such executor, administrator, or guardian, and not thereafter.

Art. 5690. (3358.) **All other Actions.**—Every action other than for the recovery of real estate, for which no limitation is otherwise prescribed, shall be brought within *four years* next after the right to bring the same shall have accrued, and not afterward.

Art. 5691. (3359.) **Actions on Foreign Judgments.**—Every action upon a judgment or decree rendered in any other State or Territory of the United States, in the District of Columbia, or in any foreign country, shall be barred, if by the laws of such State or country such action would there be barred, and the judgment or decree be incapable of being otherwise enforced there; and whether so barred or not, no action against a person who shall have resided in this State during the ten years next preceding such action shall be brought upon any such judgment or decree rendered more than *ten years* before the commencement of such action.

Art. 5692. (3360.) **Actions for Specific Performance.**—Any action for the specific performance of a contract for the conveyance of real estate shall be commenced within *ten years* next after the cause of action shall have accrued, and not afterward.

Art. 5698. (3363.) **On the Action of Forcible Entry, etc.**—No action of forcible entry or forcible detainer, as provided for by law, shall be prosecuted at any time after two years from the commencement of the forcible entry or detainer.

Art. 5699. (3364.) On Actions to Contest a Will.—Within *four years.*

CHAP. 3.—*General Provisions.*

Art. 5706. (3371.) Limitation Must be Pleaded, etc.—The laws of limitation of this State shall not be made available to any person in any suit in any of the courts of this State, unless it be specially set forth as a defense in this answer.

Art. 7440. (5257.) Action of Trespass to try Title.—In actions of trespass to try title, the defense of limitation must be specially pleaded.

UTAH.

COMPLIED LAWS, 1907.

TITLE 88. CODE OF CIVIL PROCEDURE.

CHAP. 2.—LIMITATIONS—IN GENERAL.

2855. (3129.) (Sec. 175.) **When Time commences to Run.**—Civil actions can be commenced only within the period prescribed in the three succeeding chapters, after the cause of action shall have accrued, except where in special cases a different limitation is prescribed by statute.

CHAP. 3. LIMITATIONS—REAL PROPERTY.

Sec. 2859. *Suits for Real Property.*—No action for the recovery of real property, or for the possession thereof, shall be maintained, unless it appear that the plaintiff, his ancestor, grantor, or predecessor, was seized or possessed of the property in question within *seven years* before the commencement of the action.

Sec. 2860. **Suits for Rights Growing out of Real Property.**—No cause of action, or defense or counterclaim to an action, founded upon the title to real property or to rents or profits out of the same, shall be effectual, unless it appears that the person prosecuting the action, or interposing the defense or counterclaim, or under whose title the action is prosecuted or defense or counterclaim is made, or the ancestor, predecessor, or grantor of such person, was seized or possessed of the property in question within *seven years* before the committing of the act, in respect to which such action is prosecuted or defense or counterclaim made.

Sec. 2861. **Presumption of Possession.**—In every action for the recovery of real property, or the possession thereof, the person establishing a legal title to the property shall be presumed to have been possessed thereof within the time required by law, and the occupation of the property by any other person shall be deemed to have been under and in subordination to the legal title, unless it appear that the property has been held and possessed adversely to such legal title for *seven years* before the commencement of the action.

Sec. 2862. **Effect of Color of Title.**—Whenever it shall appear that the occupant, or those under whom he claims, entered into possession of the property, under claim of title exclusive of other right, founding such claim upon a written instrument, as being a conveyance of the property in question, or upon the decree or judgment of a competent court, and that there has been a continued occupation and possession of the property included in such instrument, decree, or judgment, or of some part of the property under such claim, for *seven years*, the property so included shall be deemed to have been held adversely, except that where the property so included consists of a tract divided into lots, the possession of one lot shall not be deemed a possession of any other lot of the same tract.

Secs. 2863-2866. **Adverse Possession defined.**

CHAP. 4.—LIMITATIONS OTHER THAN REAL PROPERTY.

Sec. 2874. **Eight Years.**—An action upon a judgment or decree of any court of the United States, or of any State or Territory within the United States.

Sec. 2875. **Six Years.**—1. An action for the mesne profits of real property.

2. An action upon any contract, obligation, or liability, founded upon an instrument of writing, except those mentioned in the preceding section.

Sec. 2876. **Contract not in Writing, Four Years.**—An action upon a contract, obligation, or liability not founded upon an instrument of writing; also on an open account for goods, wares, and merchandise, and for any article charged in a store account: *Provided*, that action in said cases may be commenced at any time within four years after the last charge is made, or the last payment is received.

Sec. 2877. **Three Years—Fraud, etc.**—1. An action for a liability created by statute of a foreign State or by the statute of this State, other than a penalty or forfeiture under the laws of this State.

2. An action for waste or trespass of real property; *provided*, that when the waste or trespass is committed by means of underground works upon any mining claim, the cause of action shall not be deemed to have accrued until the discovery by the aggrieved party of the facts constituting such waste or trespass.

3. An action for taking, detaining, or injuring personal property, including actions for the specific recovery thereof; *provided*, that in all cases where the subject of the action is a domestic animal usually included in the term "live stock," having upon it at the time of its loss a recorded mark or brand, and when such animal was strayed or stolen from the true owner without his fault, the statute shall not begin to run against an action for the recovery of such animal until the owner has actual knowledge of such facts as would put a reasonable man upon inquiry as to the possession thereof by the defendant.

4. An action for relief on the ground of fraud or mistake; the cause of action in such case not to be deemed to have accrued until the discovery by the aggrieved party of the facts constituting the fraud or mistake.

Sec. 2878. **Two Years.**—1. An action against a marshal, sheriff, constable, or other officer upon a liability incurred by the doing of an act in his official capacity, and in virtue of his office, or by the omission of an official duty, including the nonpayment of money collected upon an execution. But this section shall not apply to an action for an escape.

2. An action to recover damages for the death of one caused by the wrongful act or neglect of another.

Sec. 2879. **One Year.**—1. An action upon a statute for a penalty or forfeiture where the action is given to an individual, or to an individual and the State, except when the statute imposing it prescribes a different limitation.

2. An action upon a statute, or upon an undertaking in a criminal action, for a forfeiture or penalty to the State.

3. An action for libel, slander, assault, battery, false imprisonment, or seduction.

4. An action against a sheriff, or other officer, for the escape of a prisoner arrested or imprisoned upon either civil or criminal process.

5. An action against a municipal corporation for damages or injuries to property caused by a mob or riot.

Sec. 2880. **Six Months.**—An action against an officer, or officers *de facto*:—

1. To recover any goods, wares, merchandise, or other property, seized by any such officer in his official capacity, as tax collector, or to recover the price or value of any goods, wares, merchandise, or other personal property so seized, or for damages for the seizure, detention, sale of, or injury to any goods, wares, merchandise, or other personal property seized, or for damages done to any person or property in making any such seizure.

2. For money paid to any such officer under protest, or seized by such officer in his official capacity, as a collector of taxes, and which, it is claimed, ought to be refunded.

Sec. 2881. **On Claim against County or City, One Year.**—Actions on claims against a county, incorporated city or town, which have been rejected by the board of county commissioners, city council, or board of trustees, as the case may be, must be commenced within *one year* after the first rejection thereof by such board, city council, or board of trustees.

Sec. 2882. **Open Account.**—In an action brought to recover a balance due upon a mutual, open, and current account, where there have been reciprocal demands between the parties, the cause of action shall be deemed to have accrued from the time of the last item proved in the account on either side.

Sec. 2883. **Excepted Cases.**—An action for relief not hereinbefore provided for must be commenced within *four years* after the cause of action shall have accrued.

Sec. 2887. **Bank Deposits.**—To actions brought to recover money or other property deposited with any bank, banker, trust company, or savings or loan corporation, association, or society, there is no limitation.

CHAP. 5.—LIMITATIONS—MISCELLANEOUS.

Sec. 2899. **Limitation Laws of other States.**—When a cause of action has arisen in another State or Territory, or in a foreign country, and by the laws thereof an action thereon cannot there be maintained against a person by reason of the lapse of time, an action thereon shall not be maintained against him in this State, except in favor of one who has been a citizen of this State, and who has held the cause of action from the time it accrued.

VERMONT.

PUBLIC STATUTES 1906, TITLE 12, PART 1.

CHAP. 78.—LIMITATION OF TIME WITHIN WHICH ACTIONS CAN BE COMMENCED.

Sec. 1544. (1193.) **Actions to Recover Lands.**—No action for the recovery of lands, or the possession thereof, shall be maintained, unless commenced within *fifteen years* after the cause of action first accrues to the plaintiff, or those under whom he claims.

Sec. 1545. (1194.) **Entry into Houses or Lands.**—No person having right or title of entry into houses or lands, shall enter after *fifteen years* after such right of entry accrues.

Sec. 1546. (1195.) **Actions on a Covenant of Seisin.**—Actions of covenant, brought on a covenant of seisin in a deed of conveyance of land, shall be brought within *fifteen years* after the cause of action accrues, and not after.

Sec. 1547. (1196.) **On Judgments and Specialties.**—Actions of debt or *scire facias* on judgment shall be brought within *eight years* next after the rendition of such judgment, and actions of debt on specialties within *eight years* after the cause of action accrues, and not after.

Sec. 1548. (1197.) **On Covenants, unless of Warranty or Seisin.**—Actions of covenant, other than the covenants of warranty and seisin, contained in deeds of lands, shall be brought within *eight years* after the cause of action accrues, and not after.

Sec. 1549. (1198.) **On a Covenant of Warranty.**—Actions of covenant, brought on a covenant of warranty in a deed of land, shall be brought within *eight years* after a final decision against the title of the covenantor in such deed.

Sec. 1550. (1199.) **On Simple Contracts, Foreign Judgments, and on the Case.**—The following actions shall be commenced within *six years* after the cause of action accrues, and not after:

Actions of debt founded upon a contract, obligation, or liability, not under seal, or npon the judgment of a court, excepting such as are brought upon the judgment or decree of a court of record of the United States, or of this or some other State.

Actions of debt for rent.

Actions of account, assumpsit, or on the case, founded on contract or liability, express or implied.

Actions of trespass upon land.

Actions of replevin, and other actions for taking, detaining or injuring goods or chattels.

Other actions on the case, except actions for slanderous words and for libels.

Sec. 1552. (1201.) **On Witnessed Notes.**—The foregoing provisions shall not apply to an action brought on a promissory note signed in the presence of an attesting witness; but such action shall be commenced within *fourteen years* after the cause of action accrues, and not after.

Sec. 1554. (1202.) **On Evidences of Debt Issued by Moneyed Corporations.** —The provisions of this chapter shall not apply to suits brought to enforce payment on bills, notes, or other evidences of debt issued by moneyed corporations.

Sec. 1555. (1203.) **Demands Alleged in Set-off.**—The provisions of this chapter shall apply to debts and contracts alleged by way of set-off, and the time of limitation of such debts or contracts shall be computed as if an action had been commenced thereon at the time of the commencement of the plaintiff's action.

Sec. 1556. (1204.) **Action against Sheriffs for Deputies' Misfeasance.**—Actions against sheriffs, for the misconduct or negligence of their deputies, shall be commenced within *four years* after the cause of action accrues, and not after.

Sec. 1557. (1205.) **Assault and Battery—False Imprisonment.**—Actions for assault and battery, and for false imprisonment, shall be commenced within *three years* after the cause of action accrues, and not after.

Sec. 1558. (1206.) **Slanderous Words and Libels.**—Actions for slanderous words, and for libels, shall be commenced within *two years* after the cause of action accrues, and not after.

Sec. 1559. (1207.) **Actions to recover money paid, under protest, for taxes**, shall be commenced within *one year* after the cause of action accrues, and not after.

By section 2840 (2452) an action by the personal representative to **Recover for Death** resulting from a wrongful act, neglect, or default of a person or corporation, etc., must be commenced within *two years* from the decease.

SUPPLEMENTAL ACTS.

By the Act of 1896, chap. 30, the above chapter is not to apply to actions against school districts during a vacancy in the office of clerk and prudential committee.

Sec. 1553. The Act of 1900, chap. 34, prescribes the time for enforcing the liability of stockholders in foreign corporations.

VIRGINIA.

POLLARD'S ANNOTATED CODE, 1904, TITLE 42, CHAP. 139.

LIMITATION OF SUITS.

Sec. 2915. **Limitation of Entry.**—No person shall make an entry on, or bring an action to recover, any land lying east of the Alleghany Mountains, but within *fifteen years*, or any land lying west of the Alleghany Mountains, but within *ten years*, next after the time at which the right to make such entry or bring such action shall have first accrued to himself or to some person through whom he claims. For the purposes of this section, the county of

Carroll shall be held and considered as lying wholly west of the Alleghany Mountains.

Sec. 2916. **Right not Saved by Claim.**—No continual or other claim upon or near any land shall preserve any right of making an entry or of bringing an action.

Sec. 2919. **Period of Civil War excluded.** (*Amended by the Act of* 1888, *chap.* 295.)

Sec. 2920. **Limitation of Personal Actions generally.**—Every action to recover money which is founded upon an award, or on any contract other than a judgment or recognizance, shall be brought within the following number of years next after the right to bring the same shall have first accrued, that is to say: if the case be upon an indemnifying bond taken under any statute, or upon a bond of an executor, administrator, guardian, curator, committee, sheriff or sergeant, deputy sheriff or sergeant, clerk or deputy clerk, or any other fiduciary or public officer, or upon any other contract by writing under seal, within *ten years;* if it be upon an award, or be upon a contract by writing, signed by the party to be charged thereby, or by his agent, but not under seal, within five years; if it be upon any oral contract, express or implied, for articles charged in a store account, although such articles be sold on a written order, within two years; and if it be upon any other contract, within three years, unless it be an action by one partner against his copartner for a settlement of the partnership accounts, or upon accounts concerning the trade of merchandise between merchant and merchant, their factors or servants, where the action of account would lie, in either of which cases the action may be brought until the expiration of five years from a cessation of the dealings in which they are interested together, but not after; *provided,* that the right of action against the estate of any person hereafter dying, on any such award or contract, which shall have accrued at the time of his death, or the right to prove any such claim against his estate in any suit or proceeding, shall not in any case continue longer than *five years* from the qualification of his personal representative, or if the right of action shall not have accrued at the time of the decedent's death, it shall not continue longer than five years after the same shall have so accrued.

Sec. 2923. **Effect of Promise of Personal Representative or Joint Contractor.**—No acknowledgment or promise by any personal representative of a decedent, or by one of two or more joint contractors, shall charge the estate of such decedent, or charge any other of such contractors, in any case in which but for such acknowledgment or promise the decedent's estate or another contractor could have been protected under section 2920.

Sec. 2924. **Effect on Right of Action of Devise for Payment of Debts.**—No provision in the will of any testator devising his real estate, or any part thereof, subject to the payment of his debts, or charging the same therewith, shall prevent this chapter from operating against such debts, unless it plainly appear to be the testator's intent that it shall not so operate.

Sec. 2925. **Limitation of Actions, etc., on Recognizances, Ten Years.**

Sec. 2927. **Of Actions not before Specified.**—Every personal action for which no limitation is otherwise prescribed shall be brought within *five years* next after the right to bring the same shall have accrued, if it be for a matter of such nature that in case a party die it can be brought by or against his representative; and if it be for a matter not of such nature, shall be brought within one year next after the right to bring the same shall have accrued.

Sec. 2928. **Actions on Judgments, etc., of another State.**—Every action upon a judgment or decree rendered in any other state or country shall be barred, if by the laws of such State or country such action would there be barred, and the judgment or decree be incapable of being otherwise enforced there; and, whether so barred or not, no action against a person who shall have resided in this State during the ten years next preceding such action shall be brought upon any such judgment or decree, rendered more than ten years before the commencement of such action.

Sec. 2929. **Suits to Avoid Voluntary Deeds, etc., and to Repeal Grants, Five Years.**

Sec. 2933. **Saving to Plaintiff where Suing was Prevented by Defendant.** (*Amended by the Act of* 1898, *chap.* 404.)

Sec. 2934. **Further Time given when Suit Abates.** (*Amended by the Act of* 1898, *chap.* 226.)

Sec. 2935. **Mortgages, etc., by Natural Person.** (*Amended by the Act of* 1898, *chap.* 487.)

Chap. 123, Sec. 2716, limits an **Action for Forcible Entry and Detainer** within three years after such forcible or unlawful entry, or such unlawful detainer.

Chap. 127, Sec. 2790, limits a **Distress for Rent** within five years from the time it becomes due, and not afterwards, whether the lease be ended or not.

WASHINGTON.

CODES AND STATUTES (BY REMINGTON & BALLINGER, 1910).

CODES OF PROCEDURE, TITLE II, CHAP. III—LIMITATION OF ACTIONS.

Sec. 155. (4796.) *Limitations prescribed.*—Actions can only be commenced within the period herein prescribed after the cause of action shall have accrued, except when in special cases a different limitation is prescribed by statute; but the objection that the action was not commenced within the time limited can only be taken by answer or demurrer.

Sec. 156. (4797.) **Within Ten Years.**—Actions for the recovery of real property, or for the recovery of the possession thereof; and no action shall be maintained for such recovery unless it appear that the plaintiff, his ancestor, predecessor, or grantor, was seized or possessed of the premises in question within *ten years* before the commencement of the action.

Sec. 157. (4798.) **Within Six Years.**—1. An action upon a judgment or decree of any court of the United States, or of any State or Territory within the United States.

2. An action upon a contract in writing, or liability express or implied arising out of a written agreement.

3. An action for the rents and profits or for the use and occupation of real estate.

Sec. 158. (4799.) **Within Five Years.**—No action for the recovery of any real estate sold by an executor or administrator under the laws of this State, or the laws of the Territory of Washington, shall be maintained by any heir or other person claiming under the deceased, unless it is commenced within *five years* next after the sale, and no action for any estate sold by a guardian shall be maintained by the ward, or by any person claiming under him, unless commenced within *five years* next after the termination of the guardianship, except that minors and other persons under legal disability to sue at the time when the right of action first accrued may commence such action at any time within *three years* after the removal of the disability.

Sec. 159. (4800.) **Within Three Years.**—1. An action for waste or trespass upon real property.

2. An action for taking, detaining, or injuring personal property, including an action for the specific recovery thereof, or for any other injury to the person or rights of another not hereinafter enumerated;

3. An action upon a contract or liability, express or implied, which is not in writing, and does not arise out of any written instrument;

4. An action for relief upon the ground of fraud, the cause of action in such case not to be deemed to have accrued until the discovery by the aggrieved party of the facts constituting the fraud;

5. An action against a sheriff, coroner, or constable upon a liability incurred by the doing of an act in his official capacity and by virtue of his office, or by the omission of an official duty, including the nonpayment of money collected upon an execution; but this subdivision shall not apply to action for an escape;

6. An action upon a statute for penalty or forfeiture, where an action is given to the party aggrieved, or to such party and the State, except when the statute imposing it prescribed a different penalty [limitation];

7. An action for seduction and breach of promise of marriage.

Sec. 160. (4801.) **Within Two Years.**—1. An action for libel, slander, assault, assault and battery, and false imprisonment.

2. An action upon a statute for a forfeiture or penalty to the State.

Sec. 161. (4802.) **Within One Year.**—1. An action against a sheriff or other officer for the escape of a prisoner arrested or imprisoned on civil process;

2. An action by an heir, legatee, creditor, or other party interested, against an executor or administrator, for alleged misfeasance, malfeasance, or mismanagement of the estate within *one year* from the time of final settlement, or the time such alleged misconduct was discovered.

Sec. 163. (4803.) **Special Provisions for Action on Penalty.**—An action upon a statute for a penalty given in whole or in part to the person who may prosecute for the same shall be commenced within *three years* [*one year*] after the commission of the offense; and if the action be not commenced within *one year* by a private party, it may be commenced within *two years* after the commission of the offense in behalf of the State by the prosecuting attorney of the county where said offense was committed.

Sec. 164. (4804.) **Within Three Months.**—1. An appeal from an order of a board of county commissioners, or upon a claim registered by said board;

2. Upon claims against an estate, rejected by an executor or administrator within *three months* after the rejection.

Sec. 165. (4805.) **Actions not before Specified.**—An action for relief not hereinbefore provided for shall be commenced within *two years* after the cause of action shall have accrued.

Sec. 166. (4806.) **Actions on Mutual Open Accounts.**—In an action brought to recover a balance due upon a mutual, open, and current account, where there have been reciprocal demands between the parties, the cause of action shall be deemed to have accrued from the time of the last item proved in the account on either side; but whenever a period of more than one year shall have elapsed between any of a series of items or demands, they are not to be deemed such an account.

Sec. 178. (4818.) **Foreign Statutes, How Applied.**—Where the cause of action has arisen in another State, Territory, or country between nonresidents of this State, and by the laws of the State, Territory, or country where the action arose, an action cannot be maintained thereon by reason of the lapse of time, no action shall be maintained thereon in this State.

SUPPLEMENTAL ACTS.

Sec. 459. (5148.) The Act of 1897, chap. 39, limits **Judgment liens** to *six years.*

WEST VIRGINIA.

HOGG'S CODE, 1913, CHAP. 104.

Limitation of Suits.

Sec. 4414. (1.) **Entry on or Action for land.**—No person shall make an entry on, or bring an action to recover, any land, but within *ten years* next after the time at which the right to make such entry or to bring such action shall have first accrued to himself or to some person through whom he claims.

Sec. 4415. (2.) **Continual Claim.**—No continual or other claim, upon or near any land, shall preserve any right of making an entry or bringing an action.

Sec. 4419. (6.) **Personal Actions—Limitation of Personal Actions.**—Every action to recover money, which is founded upon an award, or in any contract other than a judgment or recognizance, shall be brought within the following number of years next after the right to bring the same shall have accrued, that is to say: If the case be upon an indemnifying bond taken under any statute, or upon a bond of an executor, administrator, guardian, curator, committee, sheriff or deputy sheriff, clerk or deputy clerk, or any other fiduciary or public officer, within *ten years;* if it be upon any other contract by writing under seal, executed before the first day of April, 1869, within *twenty years;* but if executed on or after that day, within *ten years;* if it be upon an award, or upon a contract by writing, signed by the party to be charged thereby, or by his agent, but not under seal, within *ten years;* and if it be upon any other contract, within *five years,* unless it be an action by one partner against his copartner for a settlement of the partnership accounts, or upon accounts concerning the trade or merchandise between merchant and merchant, their factors or servants, where the action of account would lie, in either of which cases the action may be brought until the expiration of *five years* from a cessation of the dealings in which they are interested together, but not after. (*As amended by the Act of* 1895, *ch.* 2.)

Sec. 4420. (7.) Bonds of Fiduciaries.

Sec. 4424. (11.) Recognizances.—Every action or *scire facias* upon a recognizance shall, if it be not a recognizance of bail, be commenced within *ten years* next after the right to bring the same shall have first accrued, and if it be a recognizance of bail, within *three years* after the right to bring the same shall have first accrued.

Sec. 4425. (12.) **Other Actions.**—Every personal action for which no limitation is otherwise prescribed, shall be brought within *five years* next after the right to bring the same shall have accrued, if it be for a matter of such nature that, in case a party die, it can be brought by or against his representative; and if it be for a matter not of such nature, shall be brought within *one year* next after the right to bring the same shall have accrued.

Sec. 4426. (13.) **Foreign Judgment.**—Every action or suit upon a judgment or decree, rendered in any other State or country, shall be barred, if by the laws of such State or country such action would there be barred, and the judgment or decree be incapable of being otherwise enforced there. And whether so barred or not, no action against a person who shall have resided in this State, during the ten years next preceding such action, shall be brought upon any such judgment or decree, rendered more than ten years before the commencement of such action.

Sec. 4427. (14.) **Suits to Avoid Gifts.**—No gift, conveyance, assignment, transfer, or charge, which is not on consideration deemed valuable in law, shall be avoided, either in whole or in part, for that cause only, unless, within *five years* after it is made, suit be brought for that purpose, or the subject thereof, or some part of it, be distrained or levied upon by or at the suit of a creditor, as to whom such gift, conveyance, assignment, transfer, or charge is declared to be void by the second section of the seventy-fourth chapter of this Code.

Sec. 4428. (15.) **Repeal of Grants.**—A bill in equity to repeal, in whole or in part, any grant of land by this State or of the State of Virginia, shall be brought within ten years next after the date of such grant, and not after.

Sec. 4431. (18.) **Prosecution prevented—Lex Loci.**—Where any such right as is mentioned in this chapter shall accrue against a person who had before resided in this State, if such person shall, by departing without the same, or by absconding or concealing himself, or by any other indirect ways or means, obstruct the prosecution of such right, or if such right has been or shall be hereafter obstructed by war, insurrection, or rebellion, the time that such obstruction may have continued shall not be computed as any part of the time within which the said right might or ought to have been prosecuted. But if another person be jointly or severally liable with the person so obstructing the prosecution of such right, and no such obstruction exists as to him, the exception contained in this section as to the person so absconding shall not apply to him in any action or suit brought against him to enforce such liability. And upon a contract which was made and was to be performed in another State or country, by a person who then resided therein, no action shall be maintained, after the right of action thereon is barred by the laws of said State or country.

1513, Chap. 37, Sec. (5), limits a Suit against the State to *five years* from the time the claim might have been presented or asserted; but in cases of legal disability, to *two years* after the removal thereof.

2765, Chap. 50, Sec. (211), limits an Action for Forcible Entry and Detainer to *two years* after the cause of action accrues.

4136, Chap. 93, Sec. (10), limits a Distress for Rent "within *one year* after the time it becomes due, whether the lease be ended or not."

By Acts of 1872-3, Chap. 61, Sec. 1 (Comp. 1891, p. 1045), an action to recover possession of lease of Oil and Mineral Lands or the profits, against a lessee in continuous possession, expending in good faith, etc., is limited to *three years.*

WISCONSIN.

STATUTES, 1913. CHAP. 177 (NASH AND BELITZ, REVISERS).

OF LIMITATIONS OF TIME FOR COMMENCEMENT OF ACTIONS AND PROCEEDINGS.

Sec. 4207. **Relating to Real Property.**—No action for the recovery of real property, or the possession thereof, shall be maintained, unless it appear that the plaintiff, his ancestor, predecessor or grantor, was seized or possessed of the premises in question within *twenty years* before the commencement of such action.

Sec. 4208. **Defence not to be made unless seisin within Twenty Years.**—No defense or counterclaim, founded upon the title to real property, or to rents or services out of the same, shall be effectual, unless the person making it, or under whose title it is made, or his ancestor, predecessor or grantor, was seized or possessed of the premises in question within *twenty years* before the committing of the act with respect to which it is made.

Sec. 4209.—**Entry not valid, unless.**—No entry upon real estate shall be deemed sufficient or valid, as a claim, unless an action be commenced thereupon within one year after the making of such entry and within *twenty years* from the time when the right to make such entry descended or accrued; and when held adversely under the provisions of section 4212, within *ten years* from the time when such adverse possession began.

Sec. 4210. **Possession presumed, when.**—In every action to recover real property, or the possession thereof, the person establishing a legal title to the premises shall be presumed to have been possessed thereof within the time required by law; and the occupation of such premises by another person shall be deemed to have been under and in subordination to the legal title, unless it appear that such premises have been held and possessed adversely to such legal title for *ten years* under the provisions of the next section, or *twenty years* under the provisions of section 4213, before the commencement of such action.

Sec. 4211-4215. **Adverse Possession.**

Sec. 4219. The following actions must be commenced within the periods respectively hereinafter prescribed, after the cause of action has accrued:

Sec. 4220. **Within Twenty Years.**—1. An action upon a judgment or decree of any court of record of this State or of the United States sitting within this State.

2. An action upon a sealed instrument when the cause of action accrues within this State, except those mentioned in sections 984, 3968, and 4222.

Sec. 4221. **Within Ten Years.**—1. An action upon a judgment or decree of any court of record of any other State or Territory of the United States or of any court of the United States sitting without this State.

2. An action upon a sealed instrument when the cause of action accrued without this State, except those mentioned in the next section.

3. An action for the recovery of damages for flowing lands, when such lands have been flowed by reason of the construction or maintenance of any mill-dam.

4. An action which, on and before February 28, 1857, was cognizable by the Court of Chancery, when no other limitation is prescribed in this chapter.

5. An action for the recovery of damages for flowing lands when such lands shall have been flowed by reason of the construction or maintenance of any flooding dam or other dams constructed, used, or maintained for the purpose of facilitating the driving or handling of saw logs on the Chippewa, Menomonee, or Eau Claire rivers or any tributary of either of them, provided that in cases where the ten years have already expired, the parties shall have six months from and after the passage and publication hereof within which an action may be brought.

Sec. 4222. **Within Six Years.**—1. An action upon a judgment of a court not of record.

2. An action upon any bond, coupon, interest-warrant, or other contract for the payment of money, whether sealed or otherwise, made or issued by any town, county, city, village, or school district in this State.

3. An action upon any other contract, obligation, or liability, express or implied, except those mentioned in the last two preceding sections.

4. An action upon a liability created by statute, other than a penalty or forfeiture, when a different limitation is not prescribed by law.

5. An action to recover damages for an injury to property, real or personal,

or for an injury to the person, character or rights of another, not arising on contract, except in case where a different period is expressly prescribed (also as to foreign limitation, and notice within two years of the injury).

6. An action to recover personal property or damages for the wrongful taking or detention thereof.

7. An action for relief on the ground of fraud, in a case which was, on and before February 28, 1857, solely cognizable by the Court of Chancery. The cause of action in such case is not deemed to have accrued until the discovery by the aggrieved party of the facts constituting the fraud.

Sec. 4223. **Within Three Years.**—An action against a sheriff, coroner, town clerk or constable upon a liability incurred by the doing of an act in his official capacity and in virtue of his office or by the omission of an official duty, including the non-payment of money collected upon execution. But this section shall not apply to an action for an escape.

Sec. 4224.—**Within Two Years.**—1. An action upon a statute penalty or forfeiture when the action is given to the party prosecuting therefor and the State, or to the State alone, except when the statute imposing it provides a different limitation.

2. An action to recover damages for libel, slander, assault, battery, or false imprisonment.

3. An action brought by the personal representatives of a deceased person to recover damages, when the death of such person was caused by the wrongful act, neglect, or default of another.

4. An action to recover a forfeiture or penalty imposed by any by-law, ordinance or regulation of any town, county, city or village or of any corporation organized under the laws of this State, when no other limitation is prescribed by law.

Sec. 4225. **Within One Year.**—An acttion against a sheriff or other officer, for the escape of a prisoner arrested or imprisoned on civil process.

Sec. 4226. **Accounts.**—In actions brought to recover the balance due upon a mutual and open account current the cause of action shall be deemed to have accrued at the time of the last item proved in such account.

Sec. 4227. **Other Personal Actions, within Ten Years.**—All personal actions on any contract not limited by this chapter, or any other law of this State, shall be brought within *ten years* after the accruing of the cause of action.

Sec. 4228. **Statute applied to Defences, etc.**—A cause of action upon which an action cannot be maintained, as prescribed in this chapter, cannot be effectually interposed as a defense, counterclaim, or set-off.

Sec. 4250. **Where Answer or Counterclaim is interposed and Suit is dismissed or discontinued.**—When a defendant in an action has interposed an answer, as a defense, set-off or counterclaim upon which he would be entitled to rely in such action, the remedy upon which, at the time of the commencement of such action, was not barred by law, and such complaint is dismissed or the action is discontinued, the time which intervened between the commencement and the termination of such action shall not be deemed a part of the time limited for the commencement of an action by the defendant to recover for the cause of action so interposed as a defense, set-off or counterclaim.

Sec. 4251. **Time extended when.**—There being no person in existence who is authorized to bring an action thereon at the time a cause of action accrues, shall not extend the time within which, according to the provisions of this chapter, an action can be commenced upon such cause of action, to more than double the period otherwise prescribed by law.

WYOMING.

COMPILED STATUTES, 1910 (MULLEN). CIVIL PROCEDURE CODE.

CHAP. 290. *Time of commencing Actions.*

ART. 1. *Actions in General—Abatement.*

Sec. 4290. (3447.) **Causes of Action that survive.**—In addition to the causes of action which survive at common law, causes of action for mesne profits or for an injury to real or personal estate, or for any deceit or fraud, shall also survive; and the action may be brought notwithstanding the death of the person entitled or liable to the same.

Sec. 4291. (3448.) **Actions for causing Death which survive.**—Whenever the death of a person shall be caused by wrongful act, neglect or default, and the act, neglect or default is such as would (if death had not ensued) have entitled the party injured to maintain an action to recover damages in respect thereof; then, and in every such case, the person who, or the corporation which, would have been liable if death had not ensued, shall be liable to an action for damages, notwithstanding the death of the person injured, and although the death shall have been caused under such circumstances as amount in law to murder in the first or second degree, or manslaughter.

ART. 2. *Actions concerning Real Property.*

Sec. 4295. (3451.) **Recovery of Lands, etc., Ten Years.**—An action for the recovery of the title or possession of lands, tenements or hereditaments, can only be brought within *ten years* after the cause of such action accrues.

Sec. 4296. (3452.) **Saving to Persons under Disability.**—Any person entitled to bring an action for the recovery of real property, who may be under any legal disability when the cause of action accrues, may bring his action within ten years after the disability is removed.

ART. 3. *Other Actions.*

Sec. 4297. (3453.) **Civil Actions.**—Civil actions other than for the recovery of real property can only be brought within the following periods, after the cause of action accrues.

Sec. 4298. (3454.) **Five Years.**—An action upon a specialty or any agreement, contract or promise in writing, and on all foreign claims, judgments or contracts, express or implied, contracted or incurred before the debtor becomes a resident of this State, action shall be commenced within *two years* after the debtor shall have established his residence in this State.

Sec. 4299. (3455.) **Eight Years.**—An action upon a contract not in writing, either express or implied; an action upon a liability created by statute other than a forfeiture or penalty.

Sec. 4300. (3456.) **Four Years.**—An action for trespass upon real property; an action for the recovery of personal property, or for taking, detaining or injuring the same, but in an action for the wrongful taking of personal property the cause of action shall not be deemed to have accrued until the wrongdoer is discovered; an action for an injury to the rights of the plaintiff not arising on contract, and not hereinafter enumerated; an action for relief on the ground of fraud; but the cause of action in such case shall not be deemed to have accrued until the discovery of the fraud.

Sec. 4301. (3457.) **One Year.**—An action for liable, slander, assault, battery, malicious prosecution or false imprisonment; an action upon a statute for a penalty or forfeiture; but where a different limitation is prescribed in the statute, by which the remedy is given, the action may be brought within the period so limited.

Sec. 4302. (3458.) **Ten Years.**—An action upon the official bond or undertaning of an officer, assignee, trustee, executor, administrator, or guardian, or upon a bond or undertaking given in pursuance of a statute can only be brought within *ten years* after the cause of action accrues; but this section shall be subject to the qualification in section 4294 (3450).

Sec. 4303. (3459.) **General Provision.**—An action for relief, not hereinbefore provided for, can only be brought within *ten years* after the cause of action accrues.

Sec. 4308. (3464.) **Lex Loci.**—If by the laws of the State or country where the cause of action arose the action is barred, it is also barred in this State.

ENGLISH STATUTES OF LIMITATION.

(Vol. 6 of Chitty's Statutes, Lely's edition (1895), with notes of decisions, should be consulted on these statutes.)

The Act **31 Eliz.**, ch. **5**, limited suits upon penal statutes to *two years* for actions by the crown, and *one year* by other parties.

THE LIMITATION ACT, 1623 (21 James I., ch. 16.)

Sec. 3. All actions of trespass *quare clausum fregit*, all actions of trespass, detinue, action, *sur trover*, and replevin for taking away of goods and cattle, all actions of account, and upon the case, other than such accounts as concern the trade of merchandise between merchant and merchant, their factors or servants, all actions of debt grounded upon any lending or contract without specialty; all actions of debt for arrearages of rent, and all actions of assault, menace, battery, wounding, and imprisonment, or any of them, which shall be sued or brought at any time after the end of this present session of Parliament, shall be commenced and sued within the time and limitation hereafter expressed, and not after; (that is to say) (2) the said actions upon the case (other than for slander), and the said actions for account, and the said actions for trespass, debt, detinue, and replevin for goods or cattle, and the said action of trespass *quare clausum fregit*, within three years next after the end of this present session of Parliament, or within six years next after the cause of such actions or suit, and not after; (3) and the said actions of trespass, of assault, battery, wounding, imprisonment, or any of them, within one year next after the end of this present session of Parliament, or within four years next after the cause of such actions or suit, and not after; (4) and the said action upon the case for words, within one year after the end of this present session of Parliament, or within two years next after the words spoken, and not after.

4 Anne, c. 16 (Seamen's **Wages**) §§ 17, 18, *and* 19 (*A. D.* 1705).

17. All suits and actions in the Court of Admiralty for seamen's wages, which shall become due after the said first day of Trinity term, shall be commenced and sued within six years next after the cause of such suits or actions shall accrue, and not afterwards.

18. Provided, nevertheless, and be it enacted, that if any person or persons who is, or shall be, entitled to any such suit or action for seamen's wages be, or shall be, at the time of any such cause of suit of action, accrued, fallen, or come within the age of twenty-one years, *feme covert, non compos mentis*, imprisoned, or beyond the seas, that then such person or persons shall be set at liberty to bring the same actions, so as they take the same within six years next after their coming to, or being of full age, discovert, of sane memory, at large, and returned from beyond the seas.

19. If any person or persons against whom there is or shall be any such cause of suit or action for seamen's wages, or against whom there shall be any cause of action of trespass, detinue, actions for trover or replevin, for taking away goods or cattle, or of action of account, or upon the case, or of debt grounded upon any lending or contract without specialty, of debt for arrearages of rent, or assault, menace, battery, wounding, and imprisonment, or any of them, be, or shall be, at the time of any such cause of suit or action given or accrued, fallen, or come beyond the seas, that then such person or persons, who is, or shall be entitled to any such suit or action, shall be at liberty to bring the said actions against such person and persons after their return from beyond the seas, so as they take the same after their return from beyond the seas within such times as are respectively limited for the bringing of the said actions before by this act, and by the said other act made in the one-and-twentieth year of the reign of King James the First.

9 Geo. III., *c.* 16[1] ("*Nullum Tempus Act,*" *A. D.* 1768).

By the first section of this act the crown is disabled to sue or implead any person for any manors, lands, tenements, rents, tithes, or hereditaments where the right had not, or shall not first accrue and grow within sixty years next before commencing suit, unless the same shall have been duly in charge, or stood *insuper* of record, or been answered to the crown. The second section provides for cases where the rent and profits of such hereditaments shall be duly in charge to the crown. The third and fourth sections provide for and exempt from the operation of the act reversions in the crown and grantees of the crown. The fifth and sixth sections provide for payment of certain services to the crown, and contain a general reservation of the rights of others than the crown. The seventh section secures to the crown such fee farm or other rents as had been paid within a limited time. The eighth and ninth sections contain temporary provisions. The tenth section declares what shall and shall not be deemed a putting in charge, standing *insuper* or taking or answering by or to the crown within the meaning of the first section.

9 Geo. IV., c. 14 ("*Lord Tenterden's Act*"), §§ 1, 2, 3, 4, *and* 8[2] (*May* 9, 1828).

1. Whereas by an act passed in England in the twenty-first year of the reign of King James the First, it was among other things enacted that all actions of account and upon the case other than such accounts as concern the trade of merchandise between merchant and merchant, their factors or servants, all actions of debt grounded upon any lending or contract without specialty, and all actions of debt for arrearages of rent, should be commenced within three years after the then present session of Parliament, or within six years next after the cause of such action or suit and not after; and whereas, a similar enactment is contained in an act passed in Ireland in the tenth year of the reign of King Charles the First; and whereas, various questions have arisen in actions founded on simple contract as to the proof and effect of acknowledgments and promises offered in evidence for the purpose of taking cases out of the operation of the said enactment; and it is expedient to prevent such questions and to make provision for giving effect to the said enactments and to the intention thereof: Be it therefore enacted, by the King's most excellent Majesty, by and with the advice and consent of the lords spiritual and temporal and commons in the present Parliament assembled, and by the authority of the same, that in actions of debt or upon the case grounded upon any simple contract, no acknowledgment or promise by words only shall be deemed sufficient evidence of a new or continuing contract whereby to take any case out of the operation of the said enactments or either them, or to deprive any party of the benefit thereof unless such acknowledgment or promise shall be made, or contained by or in some writing to be signed by the party charge-

[1] Extended to the Duchy of Cornwall by 23 & 24 Vict. c. 53, *infra*, p. 650; and see 24 & 25 Vict. c. 62, *infra*, p. 650.

[2] See 19 & 20 Vict. c. 97, § 13, *infra*, p. 649.

able thereby; and that where there shall be two or more joint contractors or executors, or administrators of any contractor, no such joint contractor, executor, or administrator shall lose the benefit of the said enactments or either of them, so as to be chargeable in respect or by reason only of any written acknowledgment or promise made and signed by any other or others of them: Provided always, that nothing herein contained shall alter or take away or lessen the effect of any payment of any principal or interest made by any person whatsoever: Provided also, that in actions to be commenced against two or more such joint contractors or executors or administrators, if it shall appear at the trial or otherwise that the plaintiff, though barred by either of the said recited acts or this act, as to one or more of such joint contractors or executors or administrators, shall nevertheless be entitled to recover against any other or others of the defendants by virtue of a new acknowledgment or promise, or otherwise judgment may be given and costs allowed for the plaintiff as to such defendant or defendants against whom he shall recover, and for the other defendant or defendants against the plaintiff.

2. If any defendant or defendants, in any action on any simple contract, shall plead any matter in abatement to the effect that any other person or persons ought to be jointly sued and issue be joined on such plea, and it shall appear at the trial that the action could not by reason of the said recited acts, or this act, or either of them, be maintained against the other person or persons named in such plea or any of them, the issue joined on such plea shall be found against the party pleading the same.

3. No indorsement or memorandum of any payment written or made, after the time appointed for this act to take effect, upon any promissory note, bill of exchange or other writing, by or on the behalf of the party to whom such payment shall be made, shall be deemed sufficient proof of such payment so as to take the case out of the operation of either of the said statutes.

4. The said recited acts and this act shall be deemed and taken to apply to the case of any debt or simple contract alleged by way of set-off on the part of any defendant either by plea, notice, or otherwise.

8. No memorandum or other writing made necessary by this act shall be deemed to be an agreement within the meaning of any statute relating to the duties of stamps.

9. Nothing in this act contained shall extend to Scotland.

3 & 4 Wm. IV., c. 27[1] (*"Real Property, Limitation Act,* 1833").

This Act, which is lengthy and important chiefly in England, may be thus outlined:

Sec. 1. Interpretation.
Sec. 2. (Repealed by 37 and 38 Vict., c. 57 §§ 1, 9.)
Sec. 3. When right of action for rent, etc., accrues.
Sec. 4. Remaindermen.
Sec. 5. (Repealed by 37 and 38 Vict., c. 57, §§ 2, 9.)
Sec. 6. Administrator.

[1] See 37 & 38 Vict. c. 57, §§ 1, 9, *infra*, p. ——.

Sec. 7. Tenant at will.
Sec. 8. Tenant from year to year.
Sec. 9. Tenant by lease in writing.
Sec. 10. Mere entry is not possession.
Sec. 11. No right by continual claim.
Sec. 12. Coparceners.
Sec. 13. Brother, etc., of heir.
Sec. 14. Written acknowledgment equivalent to possession.
Sec. 15. (Spent.)
Secs. 16, 17. (Repealed by Real Property Limitation Act, 1874, §§ 3-5, 9.)
Sec. 18. Succession of disabilities.
Sec. 19. (What is deemed "beyond seas.")
Secs. 20-22. Future estates and tenancies in tail.
Sec. 23. (Repealed by Real Property Limitation Act, 1874, §§ 6, 9.)
Sec. 24. Suits in equity.
Sec. 25. Express trusts.
Secs. 26, 27. Concealed fraud to prevent time from running.
Sec. 28. (Repealed by Real Property Limitation Act, 1874, §§ 7, 9.)
Sec. 29. Limit of action for land, etc., by ecclesiastical corporation sale, two incumbencies and six years, or sixty years.
Sec. 30. For advowson, three incumbencies, or sixty years.
Secs. 31, 32. Incumbencies and advowsons.
Sec. 33. For advowsons, one hundred years.
Sec. 34. Extinction of right at end of period for action.
Sec. 35. Receipt of rent deemed receipt of profits.
Sec. 36. (Abolition of real and mixed actions, except ejectment.)
Secs. 37, 38. (Repealed by Stat. Law Rev. Act, 1874, § 1.
Sec. 39. No descent cast, discontinuance, or warranty which may happen or be made (after Dec. 31, 1833), shall toll or defeat any right of entry or action for the recovery of land.
Sec. 40. (Repealed by Real Property Limitation Act, 1874, §§ 8, 9.)
Sec. 41. Limit of actions for arrears of dower, six years.
Sec. 42. For arrears of rent, or legacy, six years.
Sec. 44. This Act does not extend to Scotland.

3 & 4 Wm. IV., c. 42[1] (*Specialties*), §§ 3-7 (*August* 14, 1833).

This Act, which was extended to Ireland by 6 and 7 Vict., c. 54, may be Thus outlined:

Sec. 3. Limit for action for rent, on covenant, or on bond or other specialty, twenty years; on award, where submission is not by penalty, or for fine or copyright, six years; for action on statute by party aggrieved, two years.
Sec. 4. Party under disability.
Sec. 5. Acknowledgment in writing or part payment.
Sec. 6. Judgment reversed.

[1] Extended to Ireland by 6 & 7 Vict. c. 54.

7. **Wm.** IV. & **1** Vict., c. **28** (*Mortgages, July* 3, 1837).

It shall and may be lawful for any person entitled to, or claiming under any mortgage of land within the definition contained in the first section of the said act (3 and 4 **Wm.** IV., c. 27), to make an entry, or bring an action at law or suit in equity to recover such land at any time within twenty years next after the last payment of any part of principal money or interest secured by such mortgage, although more than twenty years may have elapsed since the time at which the right to make such entry, or bring such action or suit in equity, shall have first accrued, anything in the said act notwithstanding.

See **16** & **17** Vict., c. **113** (*C. L. P. Amendment Act, Ireland*), §§ 20-27.

Mercantile Law Amendment Act (19 & 20 Vict., c. 97), §§ 9-16 (*July* 29, 1856).

Sec. 9. Limits actions on merchants' accounts to *six years*.
Sec. 10. Absence beyond seas is not a disability.
Sec. 11. Joint debtors.
Sec. 12. What is "beyond seas."
Sec. 13. Acknowledgment by agent.
Sec. 14. Joint contractors.

23 & **24** Vict., c. **38** (*Intestate's Estate*), § 13 (*July* 23, 1860).

13. This section, after reciting the 3 and 4 **Wm.** IV., c. 27, § 40, enacts that after the thirty-first day of December, 1860, no suit or other proceedings shall be brought to recover the personal estate of any person dying intestate, but within twenty years next after a present right to receive the same shall have accrued to some person capable of giving a discharge for or release of the same, unless in the meantime some part of such estate or share, or some interest in respect thereof, shall have been accounted for or paid, or some acknowledgment of the right thereto shall have been given in writing, signed by the person accountable for the same, or his agent, to the person entitled thereto, or his agent; and in such case no such action or suit shall be brought but within twenty years after such accounting, payment, or acknowledgment, or the last of such accountings, payments, or acknowledgments, if more than one was made or given.

23 & **24** Vict., c. **53** (*Duchy of Cornwall Act*), §§ 1 *and* 2.

By section 1 of this Act all the provisions of the Act 9 Geo. III., c. 16, as to limitation of actions and suits, are extended to the Duke of Cornwall, subject to the provisions of certain previous Acts affecting the duchy.

24 & **25** Vict., c. **62** (*The Crown Act,* 1861).

By section 1 of this Act the crown is not to sue after sixty years by reason of the lands having been in charge or stood insuper of record.

By section 2 a similar provision is made as to the rights of the crown in respect of the Duchy of Cornwall.

By the third section provision is made as to the effect of answering of rents to the crown.

The fourth section contains a reservation of reversionary interests in the crown and Duke of Cornwall.

36 & 37 Vict., c. 66 (*Supreme Court of Judicature Act*, 1873).

25. No claim of a *cestui que trust* against his trustee for any property held on an express trust, or in respect to any breach of such trust, shall be held to be barred by any statute of limitations.

37 & 38 Vict., c. 57 ("*The Real Property Limitation Act*, 1874").

This Act may be thus outlined:

Secs. 1, 2. Limit for action for land or rent, twelve years; or where the person entitled to a particular estate is out of possession, six years.

Sec. 3. Allows an extension of six years in case of infancy, coverture, or lunacy.

Sec. 4. No time allowed for absence beyond seas.

Sec. 5. Utmost allowance for infancy, etc., thirty years.

Sec. 6. Tenancy in tail.

Sec. 7. Limit for action to redeem mortgage, twelve years.

Sec. 8. Limit for action for money charged on land or legacy, twelve years.

Sec. 9. Repeals part of 3 and 4 Wm. IV., c. 27, and this Act is to be read as one with the residue.

Sec. 10. The time for recovering charges is not to be enlarged by express trusts.

38 & 39 Vict., c. 77 (*The Supreme Court of Judicature Act*, 1875), *Order VIII*, § 1.

1. No original writ of summons shall be in force for more than twelve months from the day of the date thereof, including the day of such date, etc.

See 39 & 40 Vict., c. 37 (*Nullum Tempus, (Ireland) Act*, 1876).

51 & 52 Vict., c. 59 ("*The Trustee Act*, 1888").

Sec. 1. "Trustee" includes executor.

Secs. 1, 8. Pleading of statutes of limitations by trustees.

56 & 57 Vict., c. 61 ("*Public Authorities Protection Act*, 1893").

Sec. 1. Limitation of action against persons acting under statute, etc.

INDEX.

[The references are to sections.]

A.

B.

C.

D.

G.

L.

M.

N.

O.

P.

Vol. 1 ends with § 140. Vol. 2 begins with § 141.

Vol. 1 ends with § 140. Vol. 2 begins with § 141.

T.

Vol. 1 ends with § 140. Vol. 2 begins with § 141.

(Total number of pages 2032)

Lightning Source UK Ltd.
Milton Keynes UK
UKHW010049280219
338009UK00005B/180/P